West

Massachusetts Criminal Law and Procedure 2011

Constitutional Provisions

Statutes

Rules of Criminal Procedure

Rules of Appellate Procedure

Combined Index

WEST®

A Thomson Reuters business

Mat #40949992

ISBN 978–0–314–92224–3

PREFACE

Designed for use in the office or courtroom, this pamphlet brings together in one convenient publication the constitutional provisions, statutes, and rules of court relating to Massachusetts criminal law and procedure.

Constitutional provisions, including relevant portions of the Declaration of Rights, appear as amended to April 1, 2011. Statutory provisions are current through Chapter 8 of the 2011 First Annual Session of the General Court, approved April 8, 2011. The rules provisions include amendments received through April 1, 2011.

For research assistance, historical-derivation credits and official comments have been included. However, for complete annotative material supplementing the criminal law and procedure texts, the researcher should always consult West's Massachusetts General Laws Annotated set.

An analysis preceding each of the texts and a combined index at the end of the pamphlet assure quick access to the laws and rules.

ADDITIONAL INFORMATION OR RESEARCH ASSISTANCE

For additional information or research assistance call the West reference attorneys at 1–800–REF–ATTY (1–800–733–2889). Contact West's editorial department directly with your questions and suggestions by e-mail at west.editor@thomson.com. Visit West's home page at west.thomson.com.

THE PUBLISHER

May, 2011

*

*

TABLE OF CONTENTS

TABLE OF CONTENTS

MASSACHUSETTS
CRIMINAL LAW AND PROCEDURE

CONSTITUTION
OR
FORM OF GOVERNMENT
FOR THE
COMMONWEALTH OF MASSACHUSETTS

PART 1. A DECLARATION OF THE RIGHTS OF THE INHABITANTS OF THE COMMONWEALTH OF MASSACHUSETTS

PART 2. THE FRAME OF GOVERNMENT

A combined index to the provisions of the Constitution, Massachusetts General Laws and Rules of Court contained in this pamphlet appears following the court rules text.

PART THE FIRST

A DECLARATION OF THE RIGHTS OF THE INHABITANTS OF THE COMMONWEALTH OF MASSACHUSETTS

Art. XI. Remedy by recourse to the laws; obtaining of right and justice freely, completely and promptly

ART. XI. Every subject of the commonwealth ought to find a certain remedy, by having recourse to the laws, for all injuries or wrongs which he may receive in his person, property, or character. He ought to obtain right and justice freely, and without being obliged to purchase it; completely, and without any denial; promptly, and without delay; conformably to the laws.

Art. XII. Regulation of prosecutions; right of trial by jury in criminal cases

ART. XII. No subject shall be held to answer for any crimes or offence, until the same is fully and plainly, substantially and formally, described to him; or be compelled to accuse, or furnish evidence against himself. And every subject shall have a right to produce all proofs, that may be favorable to him; to meet the witnesses against him face to face, and to be fully heard in his defence by himself, or his council, at his election. And no subject shall be arrested, imprisoned, despoiled, or deprived of his property, immunities, or privileges, put out of the protection of the law, exiled, or deprived of his life, liberty, or estate, but by the judgment of his peers, or the law of the land. And the legislature shall not make any law, that shall subject any person to a capital or infamous punishment, excepting for the government of the army and navy, without trial by jury.

Art. XIII. Criminal prosecutions, verification of facts in vicinity

ART. XIII. In criminal prosecutions, the verification of facts in the vicinity where they happen, is one of the greatest securities of the life, liberty, and property of the citizen.

Art. XIV. Freedom from unreasonable searches and seizures; warrants

ART. XIV. Every subject has a right to be secure from all unreasonable searches, and seizures, of his person, his houses, his papers, and all his possessions. All warrants, therefore, are contrary to this right, if the cause or foundation of them be not previously supported by oath or affirmation; and if the order in the warrant to a civil officer, to make search in suspected places, or to arrest one or more suspected persons, or to seize their property, be not accompanied with a special designation of the persons or objects of search, arrest, or seizure: and no warrant ought to be issued but in cases, and with the formalities prescribed by the laws.

Art. XVI. Liberty of the press; free speech

ART. XVI. The liberty of the press is essential to the security of freedom in a state: it ought not, therefore, to be restrained in this commonwealth. The right of free speech shall not be abridged.

Amended by Amend. Art. LXXVII, 1948.

Art. XXIV. Ex post facto laws

ART. XXIV. Laws made to punish for actions done before the existence of such laws, and which have not been declared crimes by preceding laws, are unjust, oppressive, and inconsistent with the fundamental principles of a free government.

Art. XXV. Conviction of treason or felony by legislature

ART. XXV. No subject ought, in any case, or in any time, to be declared guilty of treason or felony by the legislature.

Art. XXVI. Excessive bail or fines; cruel or unusual punishments

ART. XXVI. No magistrate or court of law, shall demand excessive bail or sureties, impose excessive fines, or inflict cruel or unusual punishments. No provision of the Constitution, however, shall be construed as prohibiting the imposition of the punishment of death. The general court may, for the purpose of protecting the general welfare of the citizens, authorize the imposition of the punishment of death by the courts of law having jurisdiction of crimes subject to the punishment of death.

Amended by Amend. Art. CXVI, 1982.

PART THE SECOND

THE FRAME OF GOVERNMENT

CHAPTER II

EXECUTIVE POWER

SECTION I

GOVERNOR

Art. VIII. Pardons

ART. VIII. The power of pardoning offences, except such as persons may be convicted of before the senate by an impeachment of the house, shall be in the governor, by and with the advice of council, provided, that if the offence is a felony the general court shall have power to prescribe the terms and conditions upon which a pardon may be granted; but no charter of pardon, granted by the governor, with advice of the council before conviction, shall avail the party pleading the same, notwithstanding any general or particular expressions contained therein, descriptive of the offence or offences intended to be pardoned.

Amended by Amend. Art. LXXIII, 1944.

CHAPTER VI

OATHS AND SUBSCRIPTIONS; INCOMPATIBILITY OF AND EXCLUSION FROM OFFICES; PECUNIARY QUALIFICATIONS; COMMISSIONS; WRITS; CONFIRMATION OF LAWS; HABEAS CORPUS; THE ENACTING STYLE; CONTINUANCE OF OFFICERS; PROVISION FOR A FUTURE REVISAL OF THE CONSTITUTION, ETC.

Art. VII. Habeas corpus

ART. VII. The privilege and benefit of the writ of habeas corpus shall be enjoyed in this commonwealth in the most free, easy, cheap, expeditious and ample manner; and shall not be suspended by the legislature, except upon the most urgent and pressing occasions, and for a limited time not exceeding twelve months.

PART I

ADMINISTRATION OF THE GOVERNMENT

TITLE XIV

PUBLIC WAYS AND WORKS

CHAPTER 90

MOTOR VEHICLES AND AIRCRAFT

Selected Sections

The section headings for the General Laws in this pamphlet have been editorially supplied.

§ 21. Arrest without warrant

Any officer authorized to make arrests may arrest without a warrant and keep in custody for not more than twenty-four hours, unless a Saturday, Sunday or a legal holiday intervenes, any person who, while operating a motor vehicle on any way, as defined in section one, violates the provisions of the first paragraph of section ten of chapter ninety. Any arrest made pursuant to this paragraph shall be deemed an arrest for the criminal offense or offenses involved and not for any civil motor vehicle infraction arising out of the same incident.

Any officer authorized to make arrests, provided such officer is in uniform or conspicuously displaying his badge of office, may arrest without a warrant and keep in custody for not more than twenty-four hours, unless Saturday, Sunday or legal holiday intervenes, any person, regardless of whether or not such person has in his possession a license to operate motor vehicles issued by the registrar, if such person upon any way or in any place to which the public has the right of access, or upon any way or in any place to which members of the public have access as invitees, operates a motor vehicle after his license or right to operate motor vehicles in this state has been suspended or revoked by the registrar, or whoever upon any way or place to which the public has the right of access, or upon any way or in any place to which members of the public have access as invitees, or who the officer has probable cause to believe has operated or is operating a motor vehicle while under the influence of intoxicating liquor, marihuana or narcotic drugs, or depressant or stimulant substances, all as defined in section one of chapter ninety-four C, or under the influence of the vapors of glue, carbon tetrachloride, acetone, ethylene, dichloride, toluene, chloroform, xylene or any combination thereof, or whoever uses a motor vehicle without authority knowing that such use is unauthorized, or any person who, while operating or in charge of a motor vehicle, violates the provisions of section twenty-five of chapter ninety, or whoever operates a motor vehicle upon any way or in any place to which members of the public have a right of access as invitees or licensees and without stopping and making known his name, residence and the register number of his motor vehicle goes away after knowingly colliding with or otherwise causing injury to any person, or whoever operates a motor vehicle recklessly or negligently so that the lives or safety of the public might be endangered in violation of paragraph (a) of subdivision (2) of section 24 and by such operation causes another person serious bodily injury as defined in section 24L, or whoever commits motor vehicle homicide in violation of subsection (a) or (b) of section 24G.

Any person who is arrested pursuant to this section shall, at or before the expiration of the time period prescribed, be brought before the appropriate district court and proceeded against according to the law in criminal or juvenile cases, as the case may be, provided, however, that any violation otherwise cognizable as a civil infraction shall retain its character as, and be treated as, a civil infraction notwithstanding that the violator is arrested pursuant to this section for a criminal offense in conjunction with said civil infraction.

An investigator or examiner appointed under section twenty-nine may arrest without a warrant, keep in custody for a like period, bring before a magistrate and proceed against in like manner, any person operating a motor vehicle while under the influence of intoxicating liquor or marihuana, narcotic drugs, depressants or stimulant substances, all as defined in section one of chapter ninety-four C, irrespective of his possession of a license to operate motor vehicles issued by the registrar.

Amended by St.1936, c. 406; St.1954, c. 669; St.1961, c. 422, § 1; St.1962, c. 254; St.1962, c. 394, § 1; St.1963, c. 332; St.1963, c. 369, § 1; St.1968, c. 362; St.1971, c. 1071, § 3; St.1972, c. 806, § 32; St.1973, c. 461, § 1; St.1985, c. 794, § 1; St.1987, c. 83, § 2; St.2010, c. 296, eff. Nov. 8, 2010.

Historical and Statutory Notes

St.1907, c. 494.
St.1909, c. 534, §§ 19, 31.
St.1921, c. 349.
St.1931, c. 426, § 202.

§ 22F. Habitual traffic offender; revocation of license; reinstatement

A person shall be deemed an habitual traffic offender when records maintained by the registrar show that such person has accumulated the following convictions within a five-year period; provided, however, that when a person who has no prior record of an automobile law violation, as defined in section one of chapter ninety C, is convicted of more than one of the violations referred to in this section, if such offenses all occurred within a six-hour period, such convictions shall for the purposes of this section be treated as a single conviction:—(1) three or more convictions, singularly or in combination, of operating a motor vehicle while under the influence of intoxicating liquor or narcotic drugs in violation of paragraph (a) of subdivision (1) of section twenty-four; operating a motor vehicle recklessly or negligently so that the lives and safety of the public might be endangered; making a false statement in an application for a learner's permit or motor vehicle operator's license or in an application for registration of a motor vehicle; going away without making known his name, residence and the registration number of his vehicle after knowingly colliding with or otherwise causing injury to any person, other vehicle or property, all in violation of paragraph (a) of subdivision (2) of section twenty-four; operating a motor vehicle after suspension or revocation of the person's motor vehicle operator's license or his right to operate motor vehicles in violation of section twenty-three; operating a motor vehicle without a license in violation of section ten; or the commission of any felony in the commission of which a motor vehicle is used; or twelve or more convictions of offenses which are required by any provision of law to be reported to the registrar and for which the registrar is authorized or required to suspend or revoke the person's license or right to operate motor vehicles for a period of thirty days or more, including convictions of the offenses listed above.

When the records of the registrar on any person contain reports of such convictions as will constitute such person an habitual traffic offender, the registrar shall hold a hearing within six months from such third conviction, and shall give notice to such person that such hearing will be held to show cause why such person should not be designated as an habitual traffic offender. Such notice shall be sent not less than twenty-one days prior to the date for such hearing, shall contain a list of the person's convictions, and shall otherwise be in such form as the registrar shall prescribe. If the person named in such notice is a nonresident, such notice shall be sent to his last known address of which the registrar has a record; or, if none, to the motor vehicle department of any state in which such person resides or which has issued a motor vehicle operator's license or permit to such person. If such person denies he was convicted of any offense necessary for a determination that he is an habitual offender, and if the registrar cannot, on the evidence available to him, make such determination, the registrar may refer the decision of such issue to the court in which such conviction was made. The said court shall forthwith conduct a hearing to determine such issue and send a certified copy of its final order determining such issue to the registrar.

If the registrar finds that such person is not the same person named in the records of conviction, or that he is otherwise not an habitual offender under this section, no action shall be taken; but if the registrar finds that such person is the same person named in the record of conviction and that such person is an habitual offender, the registrar shall immediately revoke such person's license or right to operate. The registrar, after having revoked the license or right to operate of any person under this section, shall not issue a new license or reinstate the right to operate to such person for a period of four years from the date of revocation, nor until such person has satisfactorily completed a driver improvement course approved by the registrar and has passed such examination as to his competence to operate motor vehicles as the registrar may require; provided, however, that such person may, after the expiration of one year, apply for and shall be granted a hearing before the registrar for the purpose of requesting the issuance of a new license on a limited basis on the sole grounds of hardship, and the registrar may, in his discretion, issue such a license under such terms and conditions as he deems appropriate and necessary. An appeal to the superior court may be had, in accordance with the provisions of chapter thirty A, from any order of the registrar of motor vehicles made under the provisions of this section.

Added by St.1971, c. 1033, § 1. Amended by St.1974, c. 145; St.1977, c. 560.

§ 23. Operation of motor vehicle after suspension or revocation of license; concealment of identity of motor vehicle

Any person convicted of operating a motor vehicle after his license to operate has been suspended or revoked, or after notice of the suspension or revocation of his right to operate a motor vehicle without a license has been issued by the registrar and received by such person or by his agent or employer, and prior to the restoration of such license or right to operate or to the issuance to him of a new license to operate, and any person convicted of operating or causing or permitting any other person to operate a motor vehicle after the certificate of registration for such vehicle has been suspended or revoked and prior to the restoration of such registration or to the issuance of a new certificate of registration for such vehicle, or whoever exhibits to an officer authorized to make arrests, when requested by said officer to show his license, a license issued to another person with intent to conceal his identity, shall, except as provided by section twenty-eight of chapter two hundred and sixty-six, be punished for a first offence by a fine of not less than five hundred nor more than one thousand dollars or by imprisonment for not more than ten days, or both, and for any subsequent offence by imprisonment for not less than sixty days nor more than one year, and any person who attaches or permits to be attached to a motor vehicle or trailer a number plate assigned to another motor vehicle or trailer, or who obscures or permits to be obscured the figures on any number plate attached to any motor vehicle or trailer, or who fails to display on a motor vehicle or trailer the number plate and the register number duly issued therefor, with intent to conceal the identity of such motor vehicle or trailer, shall be punished by a fine of not more than one hundred dollars or by imprisonment for not more than ten days, or both. Any person convicted of operating a motor vehicle after his license to operate has been revoked by reason of his having been found to be an habitual traffic offender, as provided in section twenty-two F, or after notice of such revocation of his right to operate a motor vehicle without a license has been issued by the registrar and received by such person or by his agent or employer, and prior to the restoration of such license or right to operate or the issuance to him of a new license to operate shall be punished by a fine of not less than five hundred nor more than five thousand dollars or by imprisonment for not more than two years, or both. In no case shall a person be prosecuted for operating after suspension or revocation of a license upon a failure to pay an administrative reinstatement fee without a prior written notice from the registrar mandating payment thereof.

Notwithstanding the preceding paragraph or any other general or special law to the contrary, whoever has not been previously found responsible for or convicted of, or against whom a finding of delinquency or a finding of sufficient facts to support a conviction has not been rendered on, a complaint charging a violation of operating a motor vehicle after his license to operate has been suspended or revoked, or after notice of the suspension or revocation of his right to operate a motor vehicle without a license has been issued by the registrar and received by such person or by his agent or employer, and prior to the restoration of such license or right to operate or to the issuance to him of a new license to operate shall be punished by a fine of not more than $500. This paragraph shall not apply to any person who is charged with operating a motor vehicle after his license to operate has been suspended or revoked pursuant to a violation of paragraph (a) of subdivision (1) of section 24, or section 24D, 24E, 24G, 24L or 24N of this chapter, subsection (a) of section 8 or section 8A or 8B of chapter 90B, section 8, 9 or 11 of chapter 90F or after notice of such suspension or revocation of his right to operate a motor vehicle without a license has been issued and received by such person or by his agent or employer, and prior to the restoration of such license or right to operate or the issuance to him of a new license or right to operate because of any such violation.

Any person convicted of operating a motor vehicle after his license to operate has been suspended or revoked pursuant to a violation of paragraph (a) of subdivision (1) of section twenty-four, or pursuant to section twenty-four D, twenty-four E, twenty-four G, twenty-four L, or twenty-four N of this chapter, or pursuant to subsection (a) of section eight, or pursuant to a violation of section eight A or section eight B of chapter ninety B, or pursuant to a violation of section 8, 9 or 11 of chapter ninety F, or after notice of such suspension or revocation of his right to operate a motor vehicle without a license has been issued and received by such person or by his agent or employer, and prior to the restoration of such license or right to operate or the issuance to him of a new license to operate shall be punished by a fine of not less than one thousand nor more than ten thousand dollars and by imprisonment in a house of correction for not less than sixty days and not more than two and one-half years; provided, however, that the sentence of imprisonment imposed upon such person shall not be reduced to less than sixty days, nor suspended, nor shall any such person be eligible for probation, parole, or furlough or receive any deduction from his sentence for good conduct until he shall have served sixty days of such sentence; provided, further, that the commissioner of correction may, on the recommendation of the warden, superintendent or other person in charge of a correctional institution, or of the administrator of a county correctional institution, grant to an offender committed under this paragraph a temporary release in the custody of an officer of such institution for the following purposes only: to attend the funeral of a relative; to visit a critically ill relative; to obtain emergency medical or psychiatric services unavailable at said institution; or to engage in employment pursuant to a work release program. The provisions of section eighty-seven of chapter two hundred and seventy-six shall not apply to any person charged with a violation of this paragraph. Prosecutions commenced under this paragraph shall not be placed on file or continued without a finding.

Whoever operates a motor vehicle in violation of paragraph (a) of subdivision (1) of section 24, sections 24G or 24L, subsection (a) of section 8 of chapter 90B, sections 8A or 8B of chapter 90B or section 13½ of chapter 265, while his license or right to operate has been suspended or revoked, or after notice of such suspension or revocation of his right to operate a motor vehicle has been issued and received by such person or by his agent or employer, and prior to the restoration of such license or right to operate or the issuance to him of a new license or right to operate, pursuant to paragraph (a) of subdivision (1) of section 24, sections 24G or 24L, subsection (a) of section 8 of chapter 90B, sections 8A or 8B of chapter 90B or section 13½ of chapter 265 shall be punished by a fine of not less than $2,500 nor more than $10,000 and by imprisonment in a house of correction for a mandatory period of not less than 1 year and not more than 2½ years, with said sentence to be served consecutively to and not concurrent with any other sentence or penalty. Such sentence shall not be suspended, nor shall any such person be eligible for probation, parole, or furlough or receive any deduction from his sentence for good conduct until he shall have served said 1 year of such sentence; provided, however, that the commissioner of correction may, on the recommendation of the warden, superintendent or other person in charge of a correctional institution, or of the administrator of a county correctional institution, grant to an offender committed under this paragraph a temporary release in the custody of an officer of such institution only to obtain emergency medical or psychiatric services unavailable at said institution or to engage in employment pursuant to a work release program. Section 87 of chapter 276 shall not apply to any person charged with a violation of this paragraph. Prosecutions commenced under this paragraph shall not be placed on file or continued without a finding.

A certificate of the registrar or his authorized agent that a license or right to operate motor vehicles or a certificate of registration of a motor vehicle has not been restored or that the registrar has not issued a new license so to operate to the defendant or a new certificate of registration for a motor vehicle the registration whereof has been revoked, shall be admissible as evidence in any court of the commonwealth to prove the facts certified to therein, in any prosecution hereunder wherein such facts are material. A certificate of a clerk of court that a person's license or right to operate a motor vehicle was suspended for a specified period shall be admissible as prima facie evidence in any court of the commonwealth to prove the facts certified to therein in any prosecution commenced under this section.

Upon a conviction of operating after suspension or revocation of license or right to operate under the first paragraph, the registrar shall extend said suspension or revocation for an additional sixty days. Upon a conviction of operating after suspension or revocation of license or right to operate under the second paragraph, the registrar shall extend said suspension or revocation for an additional year.

If a person operating a motor vehicle after suspension or revocation of a license to operate or the right to operate a motor vehicle under the first or second paragraphs of this section, is found by the registrar to have operated a vehicle registered to another in violation of said suspension or revocation, the registrar shall, after hearing, revoke the certificate of registration of said motor vehicle for up to thirty days. Pursuant to said hearing, the certificate of registration and the number plates shall be immediately surrendered to the registrar.

Amended by St.1933, c. 69; St.1954, c. 74; St.1963, c. 331; St.1970, c. 186; St.1971, c. 1033, § 2; St.1982, c. 373, § 1; St.1986, c. 620, §§ 3, 4; St.1990, c. 256, §§ 2 to 4; St.1992, c. 286, § 159; St.1994, c. 25, §§ 1, 2; St.1994, c. 318, § 2; St.2005, c. 122, § 2, eff. Oct. 28, 2005; St.2006, c. 119, § 1, eff. June 21, 2006; St.2009, c. 27, § 67, eff. July 1, 2009.

Historical and Statutory Notes

St.1903, c. 473, § 9.
St.1905, c. 311, § 5.
St.1906, c. 412, § 3.
St.1908, c. 648, § 6.
St.1909, c. 534, §§ 21, 31.
St.1915, c. 16, §§ 6, 7.
St.1915, c. 19.
St.1921, c. 304.
St.1925, c. 201, § 2.
St.1926, c. 267, § 2.
St.1926, c. 296.

§ 24. Driving while under influence of intoxicating liquor, etc.; second and subsequent offenses; punishment; treatment programs; reckless and unauthorized driving; failure to stop after collision

(1) (a) (1) Whoever, upon any way or in any place to which the public has a right of access, or upon any way or in any place to which members of the public have access as invitees or licensees, operates a motor vehicle with a percentage, by weight, of alcohol in their blood of eight one-hundredths or greater, or while under the influence of intoxicating liquor, or of marijuana, narcotic drugs, depressants or stimulant substances, all as defined in section one of chapter ninety-four C, or the vapors of glue shall be punished by a fine of not less than five hundred nor more than five thousand dollars or by imprisonment for not more than two and one-half years, or both such fine and imprisonment.

There shall be an assessment of $250 against a person who is convicted of, is placed on probation for, or is granted a continuance without a finding for or otherwise pleads guilty to or admits to a finding of sufficient facts of operating a motor vehicle while under the influence of intoxicating liquor, marijuana, narcotic drugs, depressants or stimulant substances under this section; provided, however, that but $150 of the amount collected under this assessment shall be deposited monthly by the court with the state treasurer for who shall deposit it into the Head Injury Treatment Services Trust Fund, and the remaining amount of the assessment shall be credited to the General Fund. The assessment shall not be subject to reduction or waiver by the court for any reason.

There shall be an assessment of $50 against a person who is convicted, placed on probation or granted a continuance without a finding or who otherwise pleads guilty to or admits to a finding of sufficient facts for operating a motor vehicle while under the influence of intoxicating liquor or under the influence of marihuana, narcotic drugs, depressants or stimulant substances, all as defined by section 1 of chapter 94C, pursuant to this section or section 24D or 24E or subsection (a) or (b) of section 24G or section 24L. The assessment shall not be subject to waiver by the court for any reason. If a person against whom a fine is assessed is sentenced to a correctional facility and the assessment has not been paid, the court shall note the assessment on the mittimus. The monies collected pursuant to the fees established by this paragraph shall be transmitted monthly by the courts to the state treasurer who shall then deposit, invest and transfer the monies, from time to time, into the Victims of Drunk Driving Trust Fund established in section 66 of chapter 10. The monies shall then be administered, pursuant to said section 66 of said chapter 10, by the victim and witness assistance board for the purposes set forth in said section 66. Fees paid by an individual into the Victims of Drunk Driving Trust Fund pursuant to this section shall be in addition to, and not in lieu of, any other fee imposed by the court pursuant to this chapter or any other chapter. The administrative office of the trial court shall file a report detailing the amount of funds imposed and collected pursuant to this section to the house and senate committees on ways and means and to the victim and witness assistance board not later than August 15 of each calendar year.

If the defendant has been previously convicted or assigned to an alcohol or controlled substance education, treatment, or rehabilitation program by a court of the commonwealth or any other jurisdiction because of a like violation preceding the date of the commission of the offense for which he has been convicted, the defendant shall be punished by a fine of not less than six hundred nor more than ten thousand dollars and by imprisonment for not less than sixty days nor more than two and one-half years; provided, however, that the sentence imposed upon such person shall not be reduced to less than thirty days, nor suspended, nor shall any such person be eligible for probation, parole, or furlough or receive any deduction from his sentence for good conduct until such person has served thirty days of such sentence; provided, further, that the commissioner of correction may, on the recommendation of the warden, superintendent, or other person in charge of a correctional institution, or the administrator of a county correctional institution, grant to an offender committed under this subdivision a temporary release in the custody of an officer of such institution for the following purposes only: to attend the funeral of a relative; to visit a critically ill relative; to obtain emergency medical or psychiatric services unavailable at said institution; to engage in employment pursuant to a work release program; or for the purposes of an aftercare program designed to support the recovery of an offender who has completed an alcohol or controlled substance education, treatment or rehabilitation program operated by the department of correction; and provided, further, that the defendant may serve all or part of such thirty day sentence to the extent such resources are available in a correctional facility specifically designated by the department of correction for the incarceration and rehabilitation of drinking drivers.

If the defendant has been previously convicted or assigned to an alcohol or controlled substance education, treatment, or rehabilitation program by a court of the commonwealth, or any other jurisdiction because of a like offense two times preceding the date of the commission of the offense for which he has been convicted, the defendant shall be punished by a fine of not less than one thousand nor more than fifteen thousand dollars and by imprisonment for not less than one hundred and eighty days nor more than two and one-half years or by a fine of not less than one thousand nor more than fifteen thousand dollars and by imprisonment in the state prison for not less than two and one-half years nor more than five years; provided, however, that the sentence imposed upon such person shall not be reduced to less than one hundred and fifty days, nor suspended, nor shall any such person be eligible for probation, parole, or furlough or receive any deduction from his sentence for good conduct until he shall have served one hundred and fifty days of such sentence; provided, further, that the commissioner of correction may, on the recommendation of the warden, superintendent, or other person in charge of a correctional institution, or the administrator of a county correctional institution, grant to an offender committed under this subdivision a temporary release in the custody of an officer of such institution for the following purposes only: to attend the funeral of a relative, to visit a critically ill relative; to obtain emergency medical or psychiatric services unavailable at said institution; to engage in employment pursuant to a work release program; or for the purposes of an aftercare program designed to support the recovery of an offender who has completed an alcohol or controlled substance education, treatment or rehabilitation program operated by the department of correction; and provided, further, that the defendant may serve all or part of such one hundred and fifty days sentence to the extent such resources are available in a correctional facility specifically designated by the department of correction for the incarceration and rehabilitation of drinking drivers.

If the defendant has been previously convicted or assigned to an alcohol or controlled substance education, treatment, or rehabilitation program by a court of the commonwealth or any other jurisdiction because of a like offense three times preceding the date of the commission of the offense for which he has been convicted the defendant shall be punished by a fine of not less than one thousand five hundred nor more than twenty-five thousand dollars and by imprisonment for not less than two years nor more than two and one-half years, or by a fine of not less than one thousand five hundred nor more than twenty-five thousand dollars and by imprisonment in the state prison for not less than two and one-half years nor more than five years; provided, however, that the sentence imposed upon such person shall not be reduced to less than twelve months, nor suspended, nor shall any such person be eligible for probation, parole, or furlough or receive any deduction from his sentence for good conduct until such person has served twelve months of such sentence; provided, further, that the commissioner of correction may, on the recommendation of the warden, superintendent, or other person in charge of a correctional institution, or the administrator of a county correctional institution, grant to an offender committed under this subdivision a temporary release in the custody of an officer of such institution for the following purposes only: to attend the funeral of a relative; to visit a critically ill relative; to obtain emergency medical or psychiatric services unavailable at said institution; to engage in employment pursuant to a work release program; or for the purposes of an aftercare program designed to support the recovery of an offender who has completed an alcohol or controlled substance education, treatment or rehabilitation program operated by the department of correction; and provided, further, that the defendant may serve all or part of such twelve months sentence to the extent that resources are available in a correctional facility specifically designated by the department of correction for the incarceration and rehabilitation of drinking drivers.

If the defendant has been previously convicted or assigned to an alcohol or controlled substance education, treatment or rehabilitation program by a court of the commonwealth or any other jurisdiction because of a like offense four or more times preceding the date of the commission of the offense for which he has been convicted, the defendant shall be punished by a fine of not less than two thousand nor more than fifty thousand dollars and by imprisonment for not less than two and one-half years or by a fine of not less than two thousand nor more than fifty thousand dollars and by imprisonment in the state prison for not less than two and one-half years nor more than five years; provided, however, that the sentence imposed upon such person shall not be reduced to less than twenty-four months, nor suspended, nor shall any such person be eligible for probation, parole, or furlough or receive any deduction from his sentence for good conduct until he shall have served twenty-four months of such sentence; provided, further, that the commissioner of correction may, on the recommendation of the warden, superintendent, or other person in charge of a correctional institution, or the administrator of a county correctional institution, grant to an offender committed under this subdivision a temporary release in the custody of an officer of such institution for the following purposes only: to attend the funeral of a relative; to visit a critically ill relative; to obtain emergency medical or psychiatric services unavailable at said institution; to engage in employment pursuant to a work release program; or for the purposes of an aftercare program designed to support the recovery of an offender who has completed an alcohol or controlled substance education, treatment or rehabilitation program operated by the department of correction; and provided, further, that the defendant may serve all or part of such twenty-four months sentence to the extent that resources are available in a correctional facility specifically designated by the department of correction for the incarceration and rehabilitation of drinking drivers.

A prosecution commenced under the provisions of this subparagraph shall not be placed on file or continued without a finding except for dispositions under section twenty-four D. No trial shall be commenced on a complaint alleging a violation of this subparagraph, nor shall any plea be accepted on such complaint, nor shall the prosecution on such complaint be transferred to another division of the district court or to a jury-of-six session, until the court receives a report from the commissioner of probation pertaining to the defendant's record, if any, of prior convictions of such violations or of assignment to an alcohol or controlled substance education, treatment, or rehabilitation program because of a like offense; provided, however, that the provisions of this paragraph shall not justify the postponement of any such trial or of the acceptance of any such plea for more than five working days after the date of the defendant's arraignment. The commissioner of probation shall give priority to requests for such records.

At any time before the commencement of a trial or acceptance of a plea on a complaint alleging a violation of this subparagraph, the prosecutor may apply for the issuance of a new complaint pursuant to section thirty-five A of chapter two hundred and eighteen alleging a violation of this subparagraph and one or more prior like violations. If such application is made, upon motion of the prosecutor, the court shall stay further proceedings on the original complaint pending the determination of the application for the new complaint. If a new complaint is issued, the court shall dismiss the original complaint and order that further proceedings on the new complaint be postponed until the defendant has had sufficient time to prepare a defense.

If a defendant waives right to a jury trial pursuant to section twenty-six A of chapter two hundred and eighteen on a complaint under this subdivision he shall be deemed to have waived his right to a jury trial on all elements of said complaint.

(2) Except as provided in subparagraph (4) the provisions of section eighty-seven of chapter two hundred and seventy-six shall not apply to any person charged with a violation of subparagraph (1) and if said person has been convicted of or assigned to an alcohol or controlled substance education, treatment or rehabilitation program because of a like offense by a court of the commonwealth or any other jurisdiction preceding the commission of the offense with which he is charged.

(3) Notwithstanding the provisions of section six A of chapter two hundred and seventy-nine, the court may order that a defendant convicted of a violation of subparagraph (1) be imprisoned only on designated weekends, evenings or holidays; provided, however, that the provisions of this subparagraph shall apply only to a defendant who has not been convicted previously of such violation or assigned to an alcohol or controlled substance education, treatment or rehabilitation program preceding the date of the commission of the offense for which he has been convicted.

(4) Notwithstanding the provisions of subparagraphs (1) and (2), a judge, before imposing a sentence on a defendant who pleads guilty to or is found guilty of a violation of subparagraph (1) and who has not been convicted or assigned to an alcohol or controlled substance education, treatment or rehabilitation program by a court of the commonwealth or any other jurisdiction because of a like offense two or more times of the date of the commission of the offense for which he has been convicted, shall receive a report from the probation department of a copy of the defendant's driving record, the criminal record of the defendant, if any, and such information as may be available as to the defendant's use of alcohol and may, upon a written finding that appropriate and adequate treatment is available to the defendant and the defendant would benefit from such treatment and that the safety of the public would not be endangered, with the defendant's consent place a defendant on probation for two years; provided, however, that a condition for such probation shall be that the defendant be confined for no less than fourteen days in a residential alcohol treatment program and to participate in an out patient counseling program designed for such offenders as provided or sanctioned by the division of alcoholism, pursuant to regulations to be promulgated by said division in consultation with the department of correction and with the approval of the secretary of health and human

services or at any other facility so sanctioned or regulated as may be established by the commonwealth or any political subdivision thereof for the purpose of alcohol or drug treatment or rehabilitation, and comply with all conditions of said residential alcohol treatment program. Such condition of probation shall specify a date before which such residential alcohol treatment program shall be attended and completed.

Failure of the defendant to comply with said conditions and any other terms of probation as imposed under this section shall be reported forthwith to the court and proceedings under the provisions of section three of chapter two hundred and seventy-nine shall be commenced. In such proceedings, such defendant shall be taken before the court and if the court finds that he has failed to attend or complete the residential alcohol treatment program before the date specified in the conditions of probation, the court shall forthwith specify a second date before which such defendant shall attend or complete such program, and unless such defendant shows extraordinary and compelling reasons for such failure, shall forthwith sentence him to imprisonment for not less than two days; provided, however, that such sentence shall not be reduced to less than two days, nor suspended, nor shall such person be eligible for furlough or receive any reduction from his sentence for good conduct until such person has served two days of such sentence; and provided, further, that the commissioner of correction may, on the recommendation of the warden, superintendent, or other person in charge of a correctional institution, or of the administrator of a county correctional institution, grant to an offender committed under this subdivision a temporary release in the custody of an officer of such institution for the following purposes only: to attend the funeral of a relative; to visit a critically ill relative; to obtain emergency medical or psychiatric services unavailable at said institution; or to engage in employment pursuant to a work release program. If such defendant fails to attend or complete the residential alcohol treatment program before the second date specified by the court, further proceedings pursuant to said section three of said chapter two hundred and seventy-nine shall be commenced, and the court shall forthwith sentence the defendant to imprisonment for not less than thirty days as provided in subparagraph (1) for such a defendant.

The defendant shall pay for the cost of the services provided by the residential alcohol treatment program; provided, however, that no person shall be excluded from said programs for inability to pay; and provided, further, that such person files with the court, an affidavit of indigency or inability to pay and that investigation by the probation officer confirms such indigency or establishes that payment of such fee would cause a grave and serious hardship to such individual or to the family of such individual, and that the court enters a written finding thereof. In lieu of waiver of the entire amount of said fee, the court may direct such individual to make partial or installment payments of the cost of said program.

(b) A conviction of a violation of subparagraph (1) of paragraph (a) shall revoke the license or right to operate of the person so convicted unless such person has not been convicted of or assigned to an alcohol or controlled substance education, treatment or rehabilitation program because of a like offense by a court of the commonwealth or any other jurisdiction preceding the date of the commission of the offense for which he has been convicted, and said person qualifies for disposition under section twenty-four D and has consented to probation as provided for in said section twenty-four D; provided, however, that no appeal, motion for new trial or exceptions shall operate to stay the revocation of the license or the right to operate. Such revoked license shall immediately be surrendered to the prosecuting officer who shall forward the same to the registrar. The court shall report immediately any revocation, under this section, of a license or right to operate to the registrar and to the police department of the municipality in which the defendant is domiciled. Notwithstanding the provisions of section twenty-two, the revocation, reinstatement or issuance of a license or right to operate by reason of a violation of paragraph (a) shall be controlled by the provisions of this section and sections twenty-four D and twenty-four E.

(c) (1) Where the license or right to operate has been revoked under section twenty-four D or twenty-four E, or revoked under paragraph (b) and such person has not been convicted of a like offense or has not been assigned to an alcohol or controlled substance education, treatment or rehabilitation program because of a like offense by a court of the commonwealth or any other jurisdiction preceding the date of the commission of the offense for which he has been convicted, the registrar shall not restore the license or reinstate the right to operate to such person unless the prosecution of such person has been terminated in favor of the defendant, until one year after the date of conviction; provided, however, that such person may, after the expiration of three months from the date of conviction, apply for and shall be granted a hearing before the registrar for the purpose of requesting the issuance of a new license for employment or educational purposes, which license shall be effective for not more than an identical twelve hour period every day on the grounds of hardship and a showing by the person that the causes of the present and past violations have been dealt with or brought under control, and the registrar may, in his discretion, issue such license under such terms and conditions as he deems appropriate and necessary; and provided, further, that such person may, after the expiration of six months from the date of conviction, apply for and shall be granted a hearing before the registrar for the purpose of requesting the issuance of a new license on a limited basis on the grounds of hardship and a showing by the person that the causes of the present and past violations have been dealt with or brought under control and the registrar may, in his discretion, issue such a license under such terms and conditions as he deems appropriate and necessary.

(2) Where the license or the right to operate of a person has been revoked under paragraph (b) and such person has been previously convicted of or assigned to an alcohol or controlled substance education, treatment or rehabilitation program by a court of the commonwealth or any other jurisdiction because of a like violation preceding the date of the commission of the offense for which such person has been convicted, the registrar shall not restore the license or reinstate the right to operate of such person unless the prosecution of such person has been terminated in favor of the defendant, until two years after the date of the conviction; provided, however, that such person may, after the expiration of 1 year from the date of conviction, apply for and shall be granted a hearing before the registrar for the purpose of requesting the issuance of a new license for employment or education purposes, which license shall be effective for not more than an identical twelve hour period every day on the grounds of hardship and a showing by the person that the causes of the present and past violations have been dealt with or brought under control and that such person shall have successfully completed the residential treatment program in subparagraph (4) of paragraph (a) of subdivision (1), or such treatment program mandated by section twenty-four D, and the registrar may, in his discretion, issue such license under such terms and conditions as he deems appropriate and necessary; and provided, further, that such person may, after the expiration of 18 months from the date of conviction, apply for and shall be granted a hearing before the registrar for the purpose of requesting the issuance of a new license on a limited basis on the grounds of hardship and a showing by the person that the causes of the present and past violations have been dealt with or brought under control and the registrar may, in his discretion, issue such a license under such terms and conditions as he deems appropriate and necessary. A mandatory restriction on a hardship license granted by the registrar under this subparagraph shall be that such person have an ignition interlock device installed on each vehicle owned, each vehicle leased and each vehicle operated by the licensee for the duration of the hardship license.

(3) Where the license or right to operate of any person has been revoked under paragraph (b) and such person has been previously convicted or assigned to an alcohol or controlled substance education, treatment or rehabilitation program because of a like offense by a court of the commonwealth or any other jurisdiction two times preceding the date of the commission of the crime for which he has been convicted or where the license or right to operate has been revoked pursuant to section twenty-three due to a violation of said section due to a prior revocation under paragraph (b) or under section twenty-four D or twenty-four E, the registrar shall not restore the license or reinstate the right to operate to such person, unless the prosecution of such person has terminated in favor of the defendant, until eight years after the date of conviction; provided however, that such person may, after the expiration of two years from the date of the conviction, apply for and shall be granted a hearing before the registrar for the purpose of requesting the issuance of a new license for employment or education purposes, which license shall be effective for not more than an identical twelve hour period every day, on the grounds of hardship and a showing by the person that the causes of the present and past violations have been dealt with or brought under control and the registrar may, in his discretion, issue such license under such terms and conditions as he deems appropriate and necessary; and provided, further, that such person may, after the expiration of four years from the date of conviction, apply for and shall be granted a hearing before the registrar for the purpose of requesting the issuance of a new license on a limited basis on the grounds of hardship and a showing by the person that the causes of the present and past violations have been dealt with or brought under control and the registrar may, in his discretion, issue such a license under such terms and conditions as he deems appropriate and necessary. A mandatory restriction on a hardship license granted by the registrar under this subparagraph shall be that such person have an ignition interlock device installed on each vehicle owned, each vehicle leased and each vehicle operated by the licensee for the duration of the hardship license.

(3½) Where the license or the right to operate of a person has been revoked under paragraph (b) and such person has been previously convicted of or assigned to an alcohol or controlled substance education, treatment or rehabilitation program by a court of the commonwealth or any other jurisdiction because of a like violation three times preceding the date of the commission of the offense for which such person has been convicted, the registrar shall not restore the license or reinstate the right to operate of such person unless the prosecution of such person has been terminated in favor of the defendant, until ten years after the date of the conviction; provided, however, that such person may, after the expiration of five years from the date of the conviction, apply for and shall be granted a hearing before the registrar for the purpose of requesting the issuance of a new license for employment or education purposes which license shall be effective for an identical twelve hour period every day on the grounds of hardship and a showing by the person that the causes of the present and past violations have been dealt with or brought under control and the registrar may, in his discretion, issue such license under such terms and conditions as he deems appropriate and necessary; and provided, further, that such person may, after the expiration of eight years from the date of conviction, apply for and shall be granted a hearing before the registrar for the purpose of requesting the issuance of a new license on a limited basis on the grounds of hardship and a showing by the person that the causes of the present and past violations have been dealt with or brought under control and the registrar may, in his discretion, issue such a license under the terms and conditions as he deems appropriate and necessary. A mandatory restriction on a hardship license granted by the registrar under this subparagraph shall be that such person have an ignition interlock device installed on each vehicle owned, each vehicle leased and each vehicle operated by the licensee for the duration of the hardship license.

(3¾) Where the license or the right to operate of a person has been revoked under paragraph (b) and such person has been previously convicted of or assigned to an alcohol or controlled substance education, treatment or rehabilitation program by a court of the commonwealth or any other jurisdiction because of a like violation four or more times preceding the date of the commission of the offense for which such person has been convicted, such person's license or right to operate a motor vehicle shall be revoked for the life of such person, and such person shall not be granted a hearing before the registrar for the purpose of requesting the issuance of a new license on a limited basis on the grounds of hardship; provided, however, that such license shall be restored or such right to operate shall be reinstated if the prosecution of such person has been terminated in favor of such person. An aggrieved party may appeal, in accordance with the provisions of chapter thirty A, from any order of the registrar of motor vehicles under the provisions of this section.

(4) In any prosecution commenced pursuant to this section, introduction into evidence of a prior conviction or a prior finding of sufficient facts by either certified attested copies of original court papers, or certified attested copies of the defendant's biographical and informational data from records of the department of probation, any jail or house of corrections, the department of correction, or the registry, shall be prima facie evidence that the defendant before the court had been convicted previously or assigned to an alcohol or controlled substance education, treatment, or rehabilitation program by a court of the commonwealth or any other jurisdiction. Such documentation shall be self-authenticating and admissible, after the commonwealth has established the defendant's guilt on the primary offense, as evidence in any court of the commonwealth to prove the defendant's commission of any prior convictions described therein. The commonwealth shall not be required to introduce any additional corrobating[1] evidence, nor live witness testimony to establish the validity of such prior convictions.

(d) For the purposes of subdivision (1) of this section, a person shall be deemed to have been convicted if he pleaded guilty or nolo contendere or was found or adjudged guilty by a court of competent jurisdiction, whether or not he was placed on probation without sentence or under a suspended sentence or the case was placed on file, and a license may be revoked under paragraph (b) hereof notwithstanding the pendency of a prosecution upon appeal or otherwise after such a conviction. Where there has been more than one conviction in the same prosecution, the date of the first conviction shall be deemed to be the date of conviction under paragraph (c) hereof.

(e) In any prosecution for a violation of paragraph (a), evidence of the percentage, by weight, of alcohol in the defendant's blood at the time of the alleged offense, as shown by chemical test or analysis of his blood or as indicated by a chemical test or analysis of his breath, shall be admissible and deemed relevant to the determination of the question of whether such defendant was at such time under the influence of intoxicating liquor; provided, however, that if such test or analysis was made by or at the direction of a police officer, it was made with the consent of the defendant, the results thereof were made available to him upon his request and the defendant was afforded a reasonable opportunity, at his request and at his expense, to have another such test or analysis made by a person or physician selected by him; and provided, further, that blood shall not be withdrawn from any party for the purpose of such test or analysis except by a physician, registered nurse or certified medical technician. Evidence that the defendant failed or refused to consent to such test or analysis shall not be admissible against him in a civil or criminal proceeding, but shall be admissible in any action by the registrar under paragraph (f) or in any proceedings provided for in section twenty-four N. If such evidence is that such percentage was five one-hundredths or less, there shall be a permissible inference that such defendant was not under the influence of intoxicating liquor, and he shall be released from custody forthwith, but the officer who placed him under arrest shall not be liable for false arrest if such police officer had reasonable grounds to believe that the person arrested had been operating a motor vehicle upon any such way or place while under the influence of intoxicating liquor; provided, however, that in an instance where a defendant is under the age of twenty-one and such evidence is that the percentage, by weight, of alcohol in the defendant's blood is two one-hundredths or greater, the officer who placed him under arrest shall, in accordance with subparagraph (2) of paragraph (f), suspend such defendant's license or permit and take all other actions directed therein, if such evidence is that such percentage was more than five one-hundredths but less than eight one-hundredths there shall be no permissible inference. A certificate, signed and sworn to, by a chemist of the department of the state police or by a chemist of a laboratory certified by the department of public health, which contains the results of an analysis made by such chemist of the percentage of alcohol in such blood shall be prima facie evidence of the percentage of alcohol in such blood.

(f) (1) Whoever operates a motor vehicle upon any way or in any place to which the public has right to access, or upon any way or in any place to which the public has access as invitees or licensees, shall be deemed to have consented to submit to a chemical test or analysis of his breath or blood in the event that he is arrested for operating a motor vehicle while under the influence of intoxicating liquor; provided, however, that no such person shall be deemed to have consented to a blood test unless such person has been brought for treatment to a medical facility licensed under the provisions of section 51 of chapter 111; and provided, further, that no person who is afflicted with hemophilia, diabetes or any other condition requiring the use of anticoagulants shall be deemed to have consented to a withdrawal of blood. Such test shall be administered at the direction of a police officer, as defined in section 1 of chapter 90C, having reasonable grounds to believe that the person arrested has been operating a motor vehicle upon such way or place while under the influence of intoxicating liquor. If the person arrested refuses to submit to such test or analysis, after having been informed that his license or permit to operate motor vehicles or right to operate motor vehicles in the commonwealth shall be suspended for a period of at least 180 days and up to a lifetime loss, for such refusal, no such test or analysis shall be made and he shall have his license or right to operate suspended in accordance with this paragraph for a period of 180 days; provided, however, that any person who is under the age of 21 years or who has been previously convicted of a violation under this section, subsection (a) of section 24G, operating a motor vehicle with a percentage by weight of blood alcohol of eight one-hundredths or greater, or while under the influence of intoxicating liquor in violation of subsection (b) of said section 24G, section 24L or subsection (a) of section 8 of chapter 90B, section 8A or 8B of said chapter 90B, or section 13½ of chapter 265 or a like violation by a court of any other jurisdiction shall have his license or right to operate suspended forthwith for a period of 3 years for such refusal; provided, further, that any person previously convicted of 2 such violations shall have his license or right to operate suspended forthwith for a period of 5 years for such refusal; and provided, further, that a person previously convicted of 3 or more such violations shall have his license or right to operate suspended forthwith for life based upon such refusal. If a person refuses to submit to any such test or analysis after having been convicted of a violation of section 24L, the restistrar[2] shall suspend his license or right to operate for 10 years. If a person refuses to submit to any such test or analysis after having been convicted of a violation of subsection (a) of section 24G, operating a motor vehicle with a percentage by weight of blood alcohol of eight one-hundredths or greater, or while under the influence of intoxicating liquor in violation of subsection (b) of said section 24G, or section 13½ of chapter 265, the registrar shall revoke his license or right to operate for life. If a person refuses to take a test under this paragraph, the police officer shall:

(i) immediately, on behalf of the registrar, take custody of such person's license or right to operate issued by the commonwealth;

(ii) provide to each person who refuses such test, on behalf of the registrar, a written notification of suspension in a format approved by the registrar; and

(iii) impound the vehicle being driven by the operator and arrange for the vehicle to be impounded for a period of 12 hours after the operator's refusal, with the costs for the towing, storage and maintenance of the vehicle to be borne by the operator.

The police officer before whom such refusal was made shall, within 24 hours, prepare a report of such refusal. Each report shall be made in a format approved by the registrar and shall be made under the penalties of perjury by the police officer before whom such refusal was made. Each report shall set forth the grounds for the officer's belief that the person arrested had been operating a motor vehicle on a way or place while under the influence of intoxicating liquor, and shall state that such person had refused to submit to a chemical test or analysis when requested by the officer to do so, such refusal having been witnessed by another person other than the defendant. Each report shall identify the police officer who requested the chemical test or analysis and the other person witnessing the refusal. Each report shall be sent forthwith to the registrar along with a copy of the notice of intent to suspend in a form, including electronic or otherwise, that the registrar deems appropriate. A license or right to operate which has been confiscated pursuant to this subparagraph shall be forwarded to the registrar forthwith. The report shall constitute prima facie evidence of the facts set forth therein at any administrative hearing regarding the suspension specified in this section.

The suspension of a license or right to operate shall become effective immediately upon receipt of the notification of suspension from the police officer. A suspension for a refusal of either a chemical test or analysis of breath or blood shall run consecutively and not concurrently, both as to any additional suspension periods arising from the same incident, and as to each other.

No license or right to operate shall be restored under any circumstances and no restricted or hardship permits shall be issued during the suspension period imposed by this paragraph; provided, however, that the defendant may immediately, upon the entry of a not guilty finding or dismissal of all charges under this section, section 24G, section 24L, or section 13½ of chapter 265, and in the absence of any other alcohol related charges pending against said defendant, apply for and be immediately granted a hearing before the court which took final action on the charges for the purpose of requesting the restoration of said license. At said hearing, there shall be a rebuttable presumption that said license be restored, unless the commonwealth shall establish, by a fair preponderance of the evidence, that restoration of said license would likely endanger the public safety. In all such instances, the court shall issue written findings of fact with its decision.

(2) If a person's blood alcohol percentage is not less than eight one-hundredths or the person is under twenty-one years of age and his blood alcohol percentage is not less than two one-hundredths, such police officer shall do the following:

(i) immediately and on behalf of the registrar take custody of such person's drivers license or permit issued by the commonwealth;

(ii) provide to each person who refuses the test, on behalf of the registrar, a written notification of suspension, in a format approved by the registrar; and

(iii) immediately report action taken under this paragraph to the registrar. Each report shall be made in a format approved by the registrar and shall be made under the penalties of perjury by the police officer. Each report shall set forth the grounds for the officer's belief that the person arrested has been operating a motor vehicle on any way or place while under the influence of intoxicating liquor and that the person's blood alcohol percentage was not less than .08 or that the person was under 21 years of age at the time of the arrest and whose blood alcohol percentage was not less than .02. The report shall indicate that the person was administered a test or analysis, that the operator administering the test or analysis was trained and certified in the administration of the test or analysis, that the test was performed in accordance with the regulations and standards promulgated by the secretary of public safety, that the equipment used for the test was regularly serviced and maintained and that the person administering the test had every reason to believe the equipment was functioning properly at the time the test was administered. Each report shall be sent forthwith to the registrar along with a copy of the notice of intent to suspend, in a form, including electronic or otherwise, that the registrar deems appropriate. A license or right to operate confiscated under this clause shall be forwarded to the registrar forthwith.

The license suspension shall become effective immediately upon receipt by the offender of the notice of intent to suspend from a police officer. The license to operate a motor vehicle shall remain suspended until the disposition of the offense for which the person is being prosecuted, but in no event shall such suspension pursuant to this subparagraph exceed 30 days.

In any instance where a defendant is under the age of twenty-one years and such evidence is that the percentage, by weight, of alcohol in the defendant's blood is two one-hundredths or greater and upon the failure of any police officer pursuant to this subparagraph, to suspend or take custody of the driver's license or permit issued by the commonwealth, and, in the absence of a complaint alleging a violation of paragraph (a) of subdivision (1) or a violation of section twenty-four G or twenty-four L, the registrar shall administratively suspend the defendant's license or right to operate a motor vehicle upon receipt of a report from the police officer who administered such chemical test or analysis of the defendant's blood pursuant to subparagraph (1). Each such report shall be made on a form approved by the registrar and shall be sworn to under the penalties of perjury by such police officer. Each such report shall set forth the grounds for the officer's belief that the person arrested had been operating a motor vehicle on a way or place while under the influence of intoxicating liquor and that such person was under twenty-one years of age at the time of the arrest and whose blood alcohol percentage was two one-hundredths or greater. Such report shall also state that the person was administered such a test or analysis, that the operator administering the test or analysis was trained and certified in the administration of such test, that the test was performed in accordance with the regulations and standards promulgated by the secretary of public safety, that the equipment used for such test was regularly serviced and maintained, and that the person administering the test had every reason to believe that the equipment was functioning properly at the time the test was administered. Each such report shall be endorsed by the police chief as defined in section one of chapter ninety C, or by the person authorized by him, and shall be sent to the registrar along with the confiscated license or permit not later than ten days from the date that such chemical test or analysis of the defendant's blood was administered. The license to operate a motor vehicle shall thereupon be suspended in accordance with section twenty-four P.

(g) Any person whose license, permit or right to operate has been suspended under subparagraph (1) of paragraph (f) shall, within fifteen days of suspension, be entitled to a hearing before the registrar which shall be limited to the following issues: (i) did the police officer have reasonable grounds to believe that such person had been operating a motor vehicle while under the influence of intoxicating liquor upon any way or in any place to which members of the public have a right of access or upon any way to which members of the public have a right of access as invitees or licensees, (ii) was such person placed under arrest, and (iii) did such person refuse to submit to such test or analysis. If, after such hearing, the registrar finds on any one of the said issues in the negative, the registrar shall forthwith reinstate such license, permit or right to operate. The registrar shall create and preserve a record at said hearing for judicial review. Within thirty days of the issuance of the final determination by the registrar following a hearing under this paragraph, a person aggrieved by the determination shall have the right to file a petition in the district court for the judicial district in which the offense occurred for judicial review. The filing of a petition for judicial review shall not stay the revocation or suspension. The filing of a petition for judicial review shall be had as soon as possible following the submission of said request, but not later than thirty days following the submission thereof. Review by the court shall be on the record established at the hearing before the registrar. If the court finds that the department exceeded its constitutional or statutory authority, made an erroneous interpretation of the law, acted in an arbitrary and capricious manner, or made a determination which is unsupported by the evidence in the record, the court may reverse the registrar's determination.

Any person whose license or right to operate has been suspended pursuant to subparagraph (2) of paragraph (f) on the basis of chemical analysis of his breath may within ten days of such suspension request a hearing and upon such request shall be entitled to a hearing before the court in which the underlying charges are pending or if the individual is under the age of twenty-one and there are no pending charges, in the district court having jurisdiction where the arrest occurred, which hearing shall be limited to the following issue; whether a blood test administered pursuant to paragraph (e) within a reasonable period of time after such chemical analysis of his breath, shows that the percentage, by weight, of alcohol in such person's blood was less than eight one-hundredths or, relative to such person under the age of twenty-one was less than two one-hundredths. If the court finds that such a blood test shows that such percentage was less than eight one-hundredths or, relative to such person under the age of twenty-one, that such percentage was less than two one-hundredths, the court shall restore such person's license, permit or right to operate and shall direct the prosecuting officer to forthwith notify the department of criminal justice information services and the registrar of such restoration.

(h) Any person convicted of a violation of subparagraph (1) of paragraph (a) that involves operating a motor vehicle while under the influence of marihuana, narcotic drugs, depressants or stimulant substances, all as defined in section one of chapter ninety-four C, or the vapors of glue, may, as part of the disposition in the case, be ordered to participate in a driver education program or a drug treatment or drug rehabilitation program, or any combination of said programs. The court shall set such financial and other terms for the participation of the defendant as it deems appropriate.

(2) (a) Whoever upon any way or in any place to which the public has a right of access, or any place to which members of the public have access as invitees or licensees, operates a motor vehicle recklessly, or operates such a vehicle negligently so that the lives or safety of the public might be endangered, or upon a bet or wager or in a race, or whoever operates a motor vehicle for the purpose of making a record and thereby violates any provision of section seventeen or any regulation under section eighteen, or whoever without stopping and making known his name, residence and the register number of his motor vehicle goes away after knowingly colliding with or otherwise causing injury to any other vehicle or property, or whoever loans or knowingly permits his license or learner's permit to operate motor vehicles to be used by any person, or whoever makes false statements in an application for such a license or learner's permit, or whoever knowingly makes any false statement in an application for registration of a motor vehicle or whoever while operating a motor vehicle in violation of section 8M, 12A or 13B, such violation proved beyond a reasonable doubt, is the proximate cause of injury to any other person, vehicle or property by operating said motor vehicle negligently so that the lives or safety of the public might be endangered, shall be punished by a fine of not less than twenty dollars nor more than two hundred dollars or by imprisonment for not less than two weeks nor more than two years, or both; and whoever uses a motor vehicle without authority knowing that such use is unauthorized shall, for the first offense be punished by a fine of not less than fifty dollars nor more than five hundred dollars or by imprisonment for not less than thirty days nor more than two years, or both, and for a second offense by imprisonment in the state prison for not more than five years or in a house of correction for not less than thirty days nor more than two and one half years, or by a fine of not more than one thousand dollars, or by both such fine and imprisonment; and whoever is found guilty of a third or subsequent offense of such use without authority committed within five years of the earliest of his two most recent prior offenses shall be punished by a fine of not less than two hundred dollars nor more than one thousand dollars or by imprisonment for not less than six months nor more than two and one half years in a house of correction or for not less than two and one half years nor more than five years in the state prison or by both fine and imprisonment. A summons may be issued instead of a warrant for arrest upon a complaint for a violation of any provision of this paragraph if in the judgment of the court or justice receiving the complaint there is reason to believe that the defendant will appear upon a summons.

There shall be an assessment of $250 against a person who, by a court of the commonwealth, is convicted of, is placed on probation for or is granted a continuance without a finding for or otherwise pleads guilty to or admits to a finding of sufficient facts of operating a motor vehicle negligently so that the lives or safety of the public might be endangered under this section, but $150 of the $250 collected under this assessment shall be deposited monthly by the court with the state treasurer, who shall deposit it in the Head Injury Treatment Services Trust Fund, and the remaining amount of the assessment shall be credited to the General Fund. The assessment shall not be subject to reduction or waiver by the court for any reason.

(a½) (1) Whoever operates a motor vehicle upon any way or in any place to which the public has right of access, or upon any way or in any place to which members of the public shall have access as invitees or licensees, and without stopping and making known his name, residence and the registration number of his motor vehicle, goes away after knowingly colliding with or otherwise causing injury to any person not resulting in the death of any person, shall be punished by imprisonment for not less than six months nor more than two years and by a fine of not less than five hundred dollars nor more than one thousand dollars.

(2) Whoever operates a motor vehicle upon any way or in any place to which the public has a right of access or upon any way or in any place to which members of the public shall have access as invitees or licensees and without stopping and making known his name, residence and the registration number of his motor vehicle, goes away to avoid prosecution or evade apprehension after knowingly colliding with or otherwise causing injury to any person shall, if the injuries result in the death of a person, be punished by imprisonment in the state prison for not less than two and one-half years nor more than ten years and by a fine of not less than one thousand dollars nor more than five thousand dollars or by imprisonment in a jail or house of correction for not less than one year nor more than two and one-half years and by a fine of not less than one thousand dollars nor more than five thousand dollars. The sentence imposed upon such person shall not be reduced to less than one year, nor suspended, nor shall any person convicted under this paragraph be eligible for probation, parole, or furlough or receive any deduction from his sentence until such person has served at least one year of such sentence; provided, however, that the commissioner of correction may on the recommendation of the warden, superintendent or other person in charge of a correctional institution, or the administrator of a county correctional institution, grant to an offender committed under this paragraph, a temporary release in the custody of an officer of such institution for the following purposes only: to attend the funeral of a relative; to visit a critically ill relative; to obtain emergency medical or psychiatric services unavailable at said institution or to engage in employment pursuant to a work release program.

(3) Prosecutions commenced under subparagraph (1) or (2) shall not be continued without a finding nor placed on file.

(b) A conviction of a violation of paragraph (a) or paragraph (a½) of subdivision (2) of this section shall be reported forthwith by the court or magistrate to the registrar, who may in any event, and shall unless the court or magistrate recommends otherwise, revoke immediately the license or right to operate of the person so convicted, and no appeal, motion for new trial or exceptions shall operate to stay the revocation of the license or right to operate. If it appears by the records of the registrar that the person so convicted is the owner of a motor vehicle or has exclusive control of any motor vehicle as a manufacturer or dealer or otherwise, the registrar may revoke the certificate of registration of any or all motor vehicles so owned or exclusively controlled.

(c) The registrar, after having revoked the license or right to operate of any person under paragraph (b), in his discretion may issue a new license or reinstate the right to operate to him, if the prosecution has terminated in favor of the defendant. In addition, the registrar may, after an investigation or upon hearing, issue a new license or reinstate the right to operate to a person convicted in any court for a violation of any provision of paragraph (a) or (a½) of subdivision (2); provided, however, that no new license or right to operate shall be issued by the registrar to: (i) any person convicted of a violation of subparagraph (1) of paragraph (a½) until one year after the date of revocation following his conviction if for a first offense, or until two years after the date of revocation following any subsequent conviction; (ii) any person convicted of a violation of subparagraph (2) of paragraph (a½) until three years after the date of revocation following his conviction if for a first offense or until ten years after the date of revocation following any subsequent conviction; (iii) any person convicted, under paragraph (a) of using a motor vehicle knowing that such use is unauthorized, until one year after the date of revocation following his conviction if for a first offense or until three years after the date of revocation following any subsequent conviction; and (iv) any person convicted of any other provision of paragraph (a) until sixty days after the date of his original conviction if for a first offense or one year after the date of revocation following any subsequent conviction within a period of three years. Notwithstanding the forgoing, a person holding a junior operator's license who is convicted of operating a motor vehicle recklessly or negligently under paragraph (a) shall not be eligible for license reinstatement until 180 days after the date of his original conviction for a first offense or 1 year after the date of revocation following a subsequent conviction within a period of 3 years. The registrar, after investigation, may at any time rescind the revocation of a license or right to operate revoked because of a conviction of operating a motor vehicle upon any way or in any place to which the public has a right of access or any place to which members of the public have access as invitees or licensees negligently so that the lives or safety of the public might be endangered. The provisions of this paragraph shall apply in the same manner to juveniles adjudicated under the provisions of section fifty-eight B of chapter one hundred and nineteen.

(3) The prosecution of any person for the violation of any provision of this section, if a subsequent offence, shall not, unless the interests of justice require such disposition, be placed on file or otherwise disposed of except by trial, judgment and sentence according to the regular course of criminal proceedings; and such a prosecution shall be otherwise disposed of only on motion in writing stating specifically the reasons therefor and verified by affidavits if facts are relied upon. If the court or magistrate certifies in writing that he is satisfied that the reasons relied upon are sufficient and that the interests of justice require the allowance of the motion, the motion shall be allowed and the certificate shall be filed in the case. A copy of the motion and certificate shall be sent by the court or magistrate forthwith to the registrar.

(4) In any prosecution commenced pursuant to this section, introduction into evidence of a prior conviction or prior finding of sufficient facts by either original court papers or certified attested copy of original court papers, accompanied by a certified attested copy of the biographical and informational data from official probation office records, shall be prima facie evidence that a defendant has been convicted previously or assigned to an alcohol or controlled substance education, treatment, or rehabilitation program because of a like offense by a court of the commonwealth one or more times preceding the date of commission of the offense for which said defendant is being prosecuted.

Amended by St.1932, c. 26, § 1; St.1935, c. 360; St.1936, c. 182, §§ 1, 2; St.1936, c. 434, § 1; St.1937, c. 117; St.1937, c. 230, § 1; St.1938, c. 145; St.1939, c. 82; St.1955, c. 198, §§ 1 to 3; St.1961, c. 340; St.1961, c. 347; St.1961, c. 422, § 2; St.1962, c. 394, § 2; St.1963, c. 369, § 2; St.1964, c. 200, §§ 1 to 5; St.1966, c. 191, § 1; St.1966, c. 316; St.1967, c. 773; St.1968, c. 259; St.1969, c. 7; St.1969, c. 163; St.1969, c. 202; St.1970, c. 253; St.1971, c. 1007, § 1; St.1971, c. 1071, § 4; St.1972, c. 111; St.1972, c. 376; St.1972, c. 488, §§ 1, 2; St.1973, c. 227; St.1973, c. 243; St.1974, c. 206, § 2; St.1974, c. 418; St.1974, c. 425; St.1974, c. 647, § 2; St.1975, c. 156, § 1; St.1980, c. 383, §§ 1, 2; St.1982, c. 373, §§ 2 to 5; St.1984, c. 189, § 65; St.1986, c. 620, §§ 5 to 13; St.1986, c. 677, § 1; St.1991, c. 138, § 287; St.1991, c. 460, §§ 1 to 4; St.1992, c. 133, §§ 447, 587; St.1992, c. 379, §§ 1B, 1C; St.1993, c. 12, § 1; St.1994, c. 25, §§ 3 to 6; St.1994, c. 60, §§ 101 to 109; St.1995, c. 38, §§ 110 to 116; St.1996, c. 151, § 236; St.1996, c. 450, §§ 137, 138; St.1997, c. 43, §§ 79, 80; St.1998, c. 161, § 317; St.1999, c. 127, §§ 108, 109; St.2002, c. 52, § 2; St.2002, c. 302, §§ 1 to 4; St.2003, c. 26, §§ 228, 229, eff. July 1, 2003; St.2003, c. 28, §§1 to 7, eff. June 30, 2003; St.2005, c. 122, §§ 3 to 5, 6A and 9 to 12, eff. Oct. 28, 2005; St.2005, c. 122, §§ 6, 7 and 8, eff. Jan. 1, 2006; St.2006, c. 428, § 13, eff. Jan. 3, 2007; St.2008, c. 182, § 45, eff. July 1, 2008; St.2008, c. 302, §§ 14, 15, eff. July 1, 2008; St.2010, c. 155, § 11, eff. Sept. 30, 2010; St.2010, c. 256, § 63, eff. Nov. 4, 2010.

[1] So in enrolled bill; probably should read "corroborating".
[2] So in enrolled bill; probably should read "registrar".

Historical and Statutory Notes

St.1906, c. 412, § 4.
St.1908, c. 648, § 7.
St.1909, c. 534, §§ 22, 31.
St.1913, c. 123.
St.1916, c. 290.
St.1924, c. 183.
St.1925, c. 201, § 3.
St.1925, c. 297, § 1.
St.1926, c. 253.
St.1926, c. 296.
St.1928, c. 213, § 1.
St.1928, c. 281, § 1.
St.1929, c. 274.

§ 24½. Ignition interlock device license restriction; revocation of license for failure to install or maintain device; revocation of license for attempt to operate motor vehicle with elevated blood alcohol level

No person whose license has been suspended in the commonwealth or any other jurisdiction by reason of: an assignment to an alcohol or controlled substance education, treatment or rehabilitation program; or a conviction for violating paragraph (a) of subdivision (1) of section 24, subsection (a) of section 24G, operating a motor vehicle with a percentage by weight of blood alcohol of eight one-hundredths or greater, or while under the influence of intoxicating liquor in violation of subsection (b) of said section 24G, section 24L, section 13½ of chapter 265, subsection (a) of section 8 of chapter 90B, section 8A or 8B of chapter 90B or, in the case of another jurisdiction, for any like offense, shall be issued a new license or right to operate or have his license or right to operate restored if he has previously been so assigned or convicted, unless a certified ignition interlock device has been installed on each vehicle owned, each vehicle leased and each vehicle operated by that person as a precondition to the issuance of a new license or right to operate or the restoration of such person's license or right to operate. A certified ignition interlock device shall be installed on all vehicles owned, leased and operated by the licensee for a period of 2 years and person restricted by a certified ignition interlock device shall have such device inspected, maintained and monitored in accordance with such regulations as the registrar shall promulgate. The registrar may, after hearing, revoke for an extended period or for life, the license of whoever removes such device or fails to have it inspected, maintained or monitored on at least 2 occasions during the period of the restricted license or right to operate if the licensee has operated or attempted to operate a vehicle with a blood alcohol level that caused the certified ignition interlock device to prohibit a vehicle from starting on at least 2 occasions or that recorded a blood alcohol level in excess of .02 on at least 2 occasions. A person aggrieved by a decision of the registrar pursuant to this section may file an appeal in the superior court of the trial court department. If the court determines that the registrar abused his discretion, the court may vacate the suspension or revocation of a license or right to operate or reduce the period of suspension or revocation as ordered by the registrar.

Added by St.2005, c. 122, § 13, eff. Jan. 1, 2006.

§ 24A. Use of motor vehicles in commission of felony, larceny or other crimes

If a motor vehicle is used in connection with the commission of a felony, of any larceny, or of any offence punishable under any provision of sections twenty-two, one hundred and thirteen to one hundred and seventeen, inclusive, and one hundred and twenty of chapter two hundred and sixty-six, or section thirteen of chapter two hundred and sixty-nine, of which a person is convicted, the material facts relative to such use, including the registration number of the vehicle, so far as disclosed in the proceedings, shall be reported forthwith to the registrar by the clerk of the court in which the conviction occurs.

Amended by St.1970, c. 321.

Historical and Statutory Notes

St.1926, c. 361, § 1.

§ 24B. Stealing, forging or other falsification of learner's permit, operator's license, disability placard certificate of registration or inspection sticker; use or possession; penalties; suspension and reinstatement of license or right to operate motor vehicle

Whoever falsely makes, steals, alters, forges or counterfeits or procures or assists another to falsely make, steal, alter, forge or counterfeit a learner's permit, a license to operate motor vehicles, an identification card issued under section eight E, a special parking identification disability placard, a certificate of registration of a motor vehicle or trailer, or an inspection sticker, or whoever forges or without authority uses the signature, facsimile of the signature, or validating signature stamp of the registrar or deputy registrar upon a genuine, stolen or falsely made, altered, forged or counterfeited learner's permit, license to operate motor vehicles, certificate of registration of a motor vehicle or trailer or inspection sticker, or whoever has in his possession, or utters, publishes as true or in any way makes use of a falsely made, stolen, altered, forged or counterfeited learner's permit, license to operate motor vehicles, an identification card issued under section eight E, a special parking identification disability placard, certificate of registration of a motor vehicle or trailer or inspection sticker, and whoever has in his possession, or utters, publishes as true, or in any way makes use of a falsely made, stolen, altered, forged or counterfeited learner's permit, license to operate motor vehicles, certificate of registration of a motor vehicle or trailer or inspection sticker, and whoever has in his possession, or utters, publishes as true, or in any way makes use of a falsely made, stolen, altered, forged or counterfeited signature, facsimile of the signature or validating signature stamp of the registrar or deputy registrar, shall be punished by a fine of not more than five hundred dollars or by imprisonment in the state prison for not more than five years or in jail or house of correction for not more than two years.

Whoever falsely impersonates the person named in an application for a license or learner's permit to operate motor vehicles, or procures or assists another to falsely impersonate the person named in such an application whether of himself or another, or uses a name other than his own to falsely obtain such a license or whoever has in his possession, or utters, publishes as true, or in any way makes use of a license or learner's permit to operate motor vehicles that was obtained in such a manner shall be punished by a fine of not more than five hundred dollars or by imprisonment in the state prison for not more than five years or in a jail or house of correction for not more than two years.

A conviction of a violation of this section shall be reported forthwith by the court or magistrate to the registrar who shall suspend immediately the license or right to operate of the person so convicted, and no appeal, motion for new trial or exceptions shall operate to stay the suspension of the license or right to operate. The registrar after having suspended the license or right to operate in accordance with this paragraph shall not terminate such suspension nor reinstate the right to operate to such person until one year after the date of suspension following said conviction; provided, however, that if the prosecution against such person has terminated in his favor, the registrar shall forthwith reinstate his license or right to operate.

Added by St.1960, c. 249. Amended by St.1962, c. 23; St.1965, c. 224; St.1967, c. 151; St.1971, c. 176; St.1973, c. 212; St.1974, c. 206, § 1; St.1975, c. 156, § 2; St.1977, c. 666, § 2; St.2008, c. 226, eff. Oct. 29, 2008.

§ 24D. Probation of persons convicted of driving under the influence; driver alcohol education program; alcohol treatment and rehabilitation programs; fees; indigents; gifts and grants; report

Any person convicted of or charged with operating a motor vehicle with a percentage, by weight, of alcohol in their blood of eight one-hundredths or greater, or while under the influence of intoxicating liquor, controlled substance or the vapors of glue, may if such person consents, be placed on probation for not more than two years and shall, as a condition of probation, be assigned to a driver alcohol education program as provided herein and, if deemed necessary by the court, to an alcohol or controlled substance abuse treatment or rehabilitation program or to both, and such person's license or right to operate shall be suspended for a period of no less than forty-five nor more than ninety days; provided, however, that if such person was under the age of twenty-one when the offense was committed, the person's license or right to operate shall be suspended for two hundred and ten days, and such person shall be assigned to a program specifically designed by the department of public health for the education and treatment of drivers who operates[1] a motor vehicle after or while consuming alcohol, controlled substances or the vapors of glue, except for a person aged 17 to 21, inclusive, whose blood alcohol percentage, by weight, was not less than .20, in which case such person shall be assigned to a driver alcohol treatment and rehabilitation program known as the "14–day second offender in-home program". Such order of probation shall be in addition to any penalties imposed as provided in subparagraph (1) of paragraph (a) of subdivision (1) of section twenty-four and shall be in addition to any requirements imposed as a condition for any suspension of sentence. Said person shall cooperate in an investigation conducted by the probation staff of the court for supervision of cases of operating under the influence and operating with a blood alcohol percentage of eight one-hundredths or greater, or in such manner as the commissioner of probation shall determine. A defendant not otherwise prohibited by this section, upon conviction after a trial on the merits, shall be presumed to be an appropriate candidate for the above mentioned programs; provided, however, that a judge who deems that the defendant is not a suitable candidate for said programs shall make such findings in writing.

This section shall apply to any person who has never been convicted of operating a motor vehicle while under the influence of intoxicating liquor or assigned to an alcohol or controlled substance education, treatment or rehabilitation program because of a like offense by a court of the commonwealth or any other jurisdiction. This section shall also apply to any person convicted of or charged with operating a motor vehicle while under the influence of intoxicating liquor who has been convicted of such offense or assigned to an alcohol or controlled substance education, treatment or rehabilitation program because of a single like offense by a court of the commonwealth or any other jurisdiction 10 years or more before the date of the commission of the offense for which he is to be sentenced, once in his lifetime. If, after receiving a sentence for a second disposition pursuant to this paragraph, a person is convicted of an additional operating under the influence of intoxicating liquor all prior convictions or assignments to an alcohol or controlled substances program by a court of the commonwealth or any other jurisdiction shall be counted for purposes of sentencing under subdivision (1) of section 24.

This section shall not apply to any person who caused serious personal injury to or the death of another person during the events that gave rise to the complaint or indictment for operating under the influence of alcohol.

Upon each disposition under this section, the defendant will surrender any Massachusetts drivers license or permit in his possession to the probation department of that court. The probation department will dispose of the license, and the court shall report the disposition in the case in a manner as determined by the registrar. Notwithstanding the provisions of subparagraph (1) of paragraph (c) of subdivision (2) of section 24, subparagraph (1) of paragraph (f) of subdivision (1) of section 24, and section 24P, a defendant may immediately upon entering a program pursuant to this section apply to the registrar for consideration of a limited license for hardship purposes. The registrar, at his discretion, may issue such license under such terms and conditions as he may prescribe. Any such license shall be valid for an identical 12 hour period, 7 days a week. This provision shall also apply to any other suspensions due to the same incident that may be in effect pursuant to said subparagraph (1) of paragraph (c) of subdivision (2) of section 24, said subparagraph (1) of paragraph (f) of subdivision (1) of said section 24 and section 24P of this chapter. Nothing in this section shall be construed to authorize hardship eligibility if the person is suspended or revoked, or to be suspended or revoked, under any other statute not referenced in this section, or due to any other incident. Failure of the operator to complete his obligations to the program, or remain in compliance with court probation, shall be cause for immediate revocation of the hardship license. In these and all cases where a hardship license is sought by an operator, the probation office for the court where the offender is on probation will, upon request, furnish the registry with documentation verifying the person's status with probation.

Driver alcohol education programs utilized under the provisions of this section shall be established and administered by the department of public health in consultation with the registrar and the secretary of public safety. The department of public health may adopt rules and regulations to carry out its powers and duties to establish and administer driver alcohol education programs in the commonwealth. Any person who is qualified for a disposition under this section, and who at the time of disposition is legally domiciled out-of-state, or is a full-time student residing out-of-state, may at the discretion of the court, be assigned to an out-of-state driver alcohol education program. The out-of-state program must be licensed by the appropriate state authority in the jurisdiction where the person is legally domiciled or is a full-time student. If the out-of-state driver alcohol education program contains fewer treatment service hours than is required by the department of public health, additional service treatment hours must be obtained to achieve equivalence with the driver alcohol education program requirement of the commonwealth.

Alcohol or controlled substance abuse treatment, rehabilitation program or alcohol or controlled substance abuse treatment and rehabilitation programs utilized under the provisions of this section shall include any public or private out-patient clinic, hospital, employer or union-sponsored program, self-help group, or any other organization, facility, service or program which the department of public health has accepted as appropriate for the purposes of this section. The department of public health shall prepare and publish annually a list of all such accepted alcohol treatment, rehabilitation programs and alcohol treatment and rehabilitation programs in the commonwealth, shall make this list available upon request to members of the public, and shall from time to time furnish each court in the commonwealth, the registrar, and the secretary of public safety with a current copy of such list. The list shall also include the single state authority contacts for other states that operate driver alcohol education programs.

Each person placed in a program of driver alcohol or controlled substance abuse education and, if deemed necessary by the court, a program of alcohol or controlled substance abuse treatment, rehabilitation, or alcohol or controlled substance abuse treatment and rehabilitation pursuant to this section shall pay directly to such program a fee in an amount to be determined by the department of public health. The department of public health shall establish and may from time to time revise a schedule of uniform fees to be charged by such programs which shall not exceed the actual cost per client of running said programs after notice and a public hearing, provided that until such time as the department of public health establishes a schedule of such fees pursuant to this section the fee for such programs shall be two hundred dollars. The department of public health shall promulgate regulations relative to the methodology of setting such fees. No person may be excluded from said program for inability to pay the stated fee, provided that such person files an affidavit of indigency or inability to pay with the court within ten days of the date of disposition, that investigation by the probation officer confirms such indigency or establishes that the payment of such fee would cause a grave and serious hardship to such individual or to the family of such individual, and that the court enters a written finding thereof. In lieu of waiver of the entire amount of said fee, the court may direct such individual to make partial or installment payments of such fee when appropriate. Subject to appropriation, the department of public health shall reimburse each program for the costs of services provided to persons for whom payment of a fee has been waived on the grounds of indigency.

The state treasurer may accept for the commonwealth for the purpose of driver alcohol or controlled substance abuse education, treatment, or rehabilitation any gift or bequest of money or property and any grant, loan, service, payment of property from a governmental authority. Any such money received shall be deposited in the state treasury for expenditure by the department of public health subject to appropriation for the support of said driver alcohol or controlled substance abuse treatment or rehabilitation programs in accordance with the conditions of the gift, grant, or loan. Any federal legislation generating funds for driver alcohol or controlled substance abuse education or treatment or rehabilitation shall be used by the department of public health to the extent possible to support the purposes of this section.

An additional fee of two hundred and fifty dollars shall be paid to the chief probation officer of each court by each person placed in a program of driver alcohol or controlled substance abuse education pursuant to this section and all such fees shall be deposited with the state treasurer, subject to appropriation, for the support of programs operated by the secretary of public safety, the alcohol beverage control commission, and the department of public health for the investigation, enforcement, treatment and rehabilitation of those persons convicted of or charged with driving under the influence of intoxicating liquor or drugs.

No such fee shall be collected from any person who, after the filing of an affidavit of indigency or inability to pay with the court within ten days of disposition and investigation by the probation officer confirming such indigency or establishing that the payment of such fee would cause a grave and serious hardship to such individual or to the family thereof, is determined by the court to be indigent, provided that the court enters a written finding thereof. In lieu of waiver of the entire amount of said fee, the court may direct such individual to make partial or installment payments of such fee when appropriate. Failure to pay the fees required under this section shall, unless excused, constitute sufficient basis for a finding by the court at a hearing held pursuant to section twenty-four E that the person has failed to satisfactorily comply with the program.

The commissioner of probation shall report in writing at least once annually to the department of public health on the total number of persons who have received disposition hereunder and on the number of such persons who have been determined by the court to require alcohol or controlled substance abuse treatment or rehabilitation, or both. Said commissioner and the chief justices of the district courts and the Boston municipal court shall make further written report at least once annually to said department of public health on the resources available for alcohol or controlled substance abuse treatment or rehabilitation, or alcohol or controlled substance abuse treatment and rehabilitation, of alcohol-impaired or controlled substance abuse-impaired drivers, which report shall evaluate the existing resources and shall make recommendation as to additional necessary resources. Said department of public health shall take such reports into consideration in the development, implementation, and review of the state's alcoholism or controlled substance abuse plan and in the preparation of the division's annual budget in a manner consistent with the Alcoholism Treatment and Rehabilitation Law.[2]

When imposing a sentence pursuant to subparagraph (1) of paragraph (a) of section twenty-four or this section, the court may consider requiring the defendant, as a condition of probation, to serve a minimum of thirty hours in public service or in a community work project.

Added by St.1974, c. 647, § 1. Amended by St.1975, c. 505, § 1; St.1975, c. 758, § 4; St.1982, c. 373, § 6; St.1986, c. 620, § 14; St.1989, c. 653, § 61; St.1994, c. 25, §§ 7, 8; St.2002, c. 302, § 5; St.2003, c. 28, §§ 8 to 19, eff. June 30, 2003; St.2005, c. 122, § 14, eff. Jan. 1, 2006; St.2005, c. 122, §§ 15, 15A, eff. Oct. 28, 2005.

1 So in enrolled bill.

2 M.G.L.A. c. 111B, § 1 et seq.

§ 24E. Dismissal of charges upon compliance with terms of probation; records; reports

The provisions of this section shall apply to any person convicted of or charged with operating a motor vehicle with a percentage, by weight, of alcohol in their blood of eight one-hundredths or greater, or while under the influence of intoxicating liquor provided said person is qualified for a disposition under section twenty-four D. The provisions of this section shall not apply where notice from the registrar of intention to suspend or revoke a person's license or right to operate is pending prior to the date of complaint on the offense before the court.

In order to qualify for a disposition under this section such person shall, in the judgment of the court, have cooperated fully with the investigation as described in section twenty-four D and shall be and have been in full compliance with such order as the court may have made for a one year term of probation as provided therein, including participation in such driver alcohol education programs, alcohol treatment or alcohol treatment and rehabilitation programs as the court may have ordered.

Nothing in this section shall be construed to prevent the exercise by a court of its authority under law to make any other disposition of a case of operating under the influence of intoxicating liquor.

Where a person has been charged with operating a motor vehicle under the influence of intoxicating liquor, and where the case has been continued without a finding and such person has been placed on probation with his consent and where such person is qualified for disposition under this section, a hearing shall be held by the court at any time after sixty days but not later than ninety days from the date where the case has been continued without a finding to review such person's compliance with the program ordered as a condition of probation and to determine whether dismissal of the charge is warranted.

At said hearing the probation officer shall submit to the courts a written report which shall include but shall not be limited to a written statement by the supervisor of any program of alcohol education and of any program of alcohol education [1] and of any program of alcohol treatment, rehabilitation, or alcohol treatment and rehabilitation to which the court has assigned such person. Such statement shall consider such person's participation and attendance in each such court ordered program. The registrar shall submit a written report to the judge at said hearing regarding any entries made on said person's driving record in the period following placement in the program. If the court finds sufficient basis to conclude that said person has not satisfactorily completed or is not satisfactorily complying with such program, the court may notify the registrar and the registrar shall revoke the person's license or right to operate forthwith. If the judge finds that the person is satisfactorily complying with the conditions of probation, the judge may enter a dismissal of the charges and issue appropriate orders relative to said person's participation in a program or relative to a later hearing, subject to the duration of the term of probation. The court shall cause to be entered and to be maintained upon the probation record of said person notice of a dismissal of charges under this section. The probation officer supervising a person pursuant to the provisions of this section shall make a written report to the court if at any time such person has failed to satisfactorily comply with a court ordered program or if such person's operation of a motor vehicle constitutes a threat to the public safety. Upon receipt of such report the court shall forthwith hold a hearing on the matter. If at such hearing the court determines that said person has failed to satisfactorily comply with such program or that the said operation of a motor vehicle constitutes such a threat, the court may notify the registrar and the registrar shall without further hearing revoke said person's license or right to operate. Such revocation shall be for the remainder of the period from the date of conviction provided in subparagraph (1) of paragraph (c) of subdivision (1) of section twenty-four. Said person shall thereafter be subject to the same conditions for issuance of a new license or right to operate as any person applying for a new license or right to operate following revocation as provided in subparagraph (1) of paragraph (c) of said subdivision (1).

Where an order of probation has been revoked by the court, the court shall forthwith so notify the registrar in writing and the registrar shall forthwith revoke said person's operator's license or right to operate which was restored under this section and without further hearing.

Added by St.1974, c. 647, § 1. Amended by St.1975, c. 505, § 2; St.1982, c. 373, §§ 7, 8; St.2003, c. 28, § 20, eff. June 30, 2003.

1 So in enrolled bill.

§ 24G. Homicide by motor vehicle; punishment

(a) Whoever, upon any way or in any place to which the public has a right of access, or upon any way or in any place to which members of the public have access as invitees or licensees, operates a motor vehicle with a percentage, by weight, of alcohol in their blood of eight one-hundredths or greater, or while under the influence of intoxicating liquor, or of marihuana, narcotic drugs, depressants, or stimulant substances, all as defined in section one of chapter ninety-four C, or the vapors of glue, and so operates a motor vehicle recklessly or negligently so that the lives or safety of the public might be endangered, and by any such operation so described causes the death of another person, shall be guilty of homicide by a motor vehicle while under the influence of an intoxicating substance, and shall be punished by imprisonment in the state prison for not less than two and one-half years or more than fifteen years and a fine of not more than five thousand dollars, or by imprisonment in a jail or house of correction for not less than one year nor more than two and one-half years and a fine of not more than five thousand dollars. The sentence imposed upon such person shall not be reduced to less than one year, nor suspended, nor shall any person convicted under this subsection be eligible for probation, parole, or furlough or receive any deduction from his sentence until such person has served at least one year of such sentence; provided, however, that the commissioner of correction may, on the recommendation of the warden, superintendent, or other person in charge of a correctional institution, or the administrator of a county correctional institution, grant to an offender committed under this subsection a temporary release in the custody of an officer of such institution for the following purposes only: to attend the funeral of a relative; to visit a critically ill relative; to obtain emergency medical or psychiatric services unavailable at said institution; or to engage in employment pursuant to a work release program. Prosecutions commenced under this section shall neither be continued without a finding nor placed on file.

The provisions of section eighty-seven of chapter two hundred and seventy-six, shall not apply to any person charged with a violation of this subsection.

(b) Whoever, upon any way or in any place to which the public has a right of access or upon any way or in any place to which members of the public have access as invitees or licensees, operates a motor vehicle with a percentage, by weight, of alcohol in their blood of eight one-hundredths or greater, or while under the influence of intoxicating liquor, or of marihuana, narcotic drugs, depressants or stimulant substances, all as defined in section one of chapter ninety-four C, or the vapors of glue, or whoever operates a motor vehicle recklessly or negligently so that the lives or safety of the public might be endangered and by any such operation causes the death of another person, shall be guilty of homicide by a motor vehicle and shall be punished by imprisonment in a jail or house of correction for not less than thirty days nor more than two and one-half years, or by a fine of not less than three hundred nor more than three thousand dollars, or both.

(c) The registrar shall revoke the license or right to operate of a person convicted of a violation of subsection (a) or (b) for a period of 15 years after the date of conviction for a first offense. The registrar shall revoke the license or right to operate of a person convicted for a subsequent violation of this section for the life of such person. No appeal, motion for a new trial or exceptions shall operate to stay the revocation of the license or of the right to operate; provided, however, such license shall be restored or such right to operate shall be reinstated if the prosecution of such person ultimately terminates in favor of the defendant.

Added by St.1976, c. 227. Amended by St.1982, c. 373, § 9; St.1982, c. 376, §§ 1, 2; St.1986, c. 620, §§ 15, 16; St.2003, c. 28, §§ 21, 22, eff. June 30, 2003; St.2005, c. 122, § 16, eff. Oct. 28, 2005.

§ 24H. Removal of abandoned or stolen vehicles from public places; towing vehicles; machines that crush, mutilate or destroy vehicles; salvage or junk yard owners or agents

No person shall remove an abandoned or stolen motor vehicle on a public way or any place to which the public has right of access without the express consent of the owner of such vehicle or without the written permission of the police department. The owner or operator of a motor vehicle that is designed to carry or tow another vehicle shall be licensed for that specific purpose or as a towing service.

The owner of any machine that is designed to crush, mutilate or destroy a motor vehicle, whether the machine be mobile or affixed permanently, shall have that machine listed with the registry of motor vehicles.

If the owner or agent of a salvage or junk yard transports crushed or mutilated vehicles without the commonwealth for purposes of resale, the operator of the transporting vehicle shall carry a list of the vehicles being transported, and a copy of such list shall be forwarded to said registrar.

Any person convicted of violation of any provision of this section shall forfeit any license issued which is related to such violation and shall be punished by a fine of not less than one thousand dollars or by imprisonment for not less than two years, or both.

Added by St.1976, c. 266, § 5. Renumbered by St.1977, c. 829, § 9. Amended by St.1988, c. 273, §§ 4 to 7.

§ 24*I*. Possession of alcoholic beverages in motor vehicles

(a) As used in this section, the following words shall have the following meanings:

"Open container," a bottle, can or other receptacle used to contain a liquid that has been opened or has a broken seal or the contents of which have been partially removed or consumed; provided, however, that a bottle resealed pursuant to section 12 of chapter 138 shall not be considered an open container; provided further, that a resealed bottle shall not be transported in the passenger area.

"Passenger area," the area designed to seat the driver and passengers while the motor vehicle is in operation and any area that is readily accessible to the driver or a passenger while in a seated position including, but not limited to, the glove compartment; provided, however, that the passenger area shall not include a motor vehicle's trunk or a locked glove compartment or, if a motor vehicle is not equipped with a trunk, the area behind the last upright seat or an area not normally occupied by the driver or passenger.

(b) Whoever, upon any way or in any place to which the public has a right of access, or upon any way or in any place to which members of the public have access as invitees or licensees, possesses an open container of alcoholic beverage in the passenger area of any motor vehicle shall be punished by a fine of not less than $100 nor more than $500.

(c) This section shall not apply to (1) the passengers of a motor vehicle designed, maintained and used for the transportation of persons for compensation, or (2) the living quarters of a house coach or house trailer.

(d) Notwithstanding this section, the driver of any motor vehicle, including but not limited to a house coach or house trailer, shall not possess an open container of alcoholic beverage.

Added by St.1982, c. 373, § 10. Amended by St.2000, c. 294, § 1; St.2001, c. 91; St.2006, c. 33, § 1, eff. Feb. 15, 2006; St.2008, c. 303, § 18, eff. Aug. 8, 2008.

§ 24J. Inquiry of defendant convicted of driving under influence of intoxicating liquors as to establishment serving alcohol

In every case of a conviction of or a plea of guilty to a violation of subdivision (1) of section twenty-four involving operating a motor vehicle with a percentage, by weight, of alcohol in their blood of eight one-hundredths or greater, or under the influence of intoxicating liquor or a disposition under section twenty-four D, the court shall inquire of the defendant, before sentencing, regarding whether he was served alcohol prior to his violation of said section at an establishment licensed to serve alcohol on the premises and the name and location of said establishment.

Any information so acquired by the court shall be transmitted by the clerk's office to the alcohol beverage control commission, the office of the attorney general, the office of the district attorney for the district in which the establishment is located, and such establishment.

Added by St.1982, c. 373, § 10. Amended by St.1985, c. 223, § 14; St.1994, c. 25, § 9; St. 2003, c. 28, § 23, eff. June 30, 2003.

§ 24K. Chemical breath analysis; validity; testing procedures; report forms

Chemical analysis of the breath of a person charged with a violation of this chapter shall not be considered valid under the provisions of this chapter, unless such analysis has been performed by a certified operator, using infrared breath-testing devices according to methods approved by the secretary of public safety. The secretary of public safety shall promulgate rules and regulations regarding satisfactory methods, techniques and criteria for the conduct of such tests, and shall establish a statewide training and certification program for all operators of such devices and a periodic certification program for such breath testing devices; provided, however, that the secretary may terminate or revoke such certification at his discretion.

Said regulations shall include, but shall not be limited to the following: (a) that the chemical analysis of the breath of a person charged be performed by a certified operator using a certified infrared breath-testing device in the following sequence: (1) one adequate breath sample analysis; (2) one calibration standard analysis; (3) a second adequate breath sample analysis; (b) that no person shall perform such a test unless certified by the secretary of public safety; (c) that no breath testing device, mouthpiece or tube shall be cleaned with any substance containing alcohol.

The secretary of public safety shall prescribe a uniform form for reports of such chemical analysis to be used by law enforcement officers and others acting in accordance with the provisions of this chapter. Such forms shall be sequentially numbered. Each chief of police or other officer or official having charge or control of a law enforcement agency shall be responsible for the furnishing and proper disposition of such uniform forms. Each party so responsible shall prepare or cause to be prepared such records and reports relating to such uniform forms and their disposition in such manner and at such times as the secretary of public safety shall prescribe.

Added by St.1986, c. 620, § 17.

§ 24L. Serious bodily injury by motor vehicle while under influence of intoxicating substance; penalties

(1) Whoever, upon any way or in any place to which the public has a right of access, or upon any way or in any place to which members of the public have access as invitees or licensees, operates a motor vehicle with a percentage, by weight, of alcohol in their blood of eight one-hundredths or greater, or while under the influence of intoxicating liquor, or marihuana, narcotic drugs, depressants, or stimulant substances, all as defined in section one of chapter ninety-four C, or the vapors of glue, and so operates a motor vehicle recklessly or negligently so that the lives or safety of the public might be endangered, and by any such operation so described causes serious bodily injury, shall be punished by imprisonment in the state prison for not less

than two and one-half years nor more than ten years and by a fine of not more than five thousand dollars, or by imprisonment in a jail or house of correction for not less than six months nor more than two and one-half years and by a fine of not more than five thousand dollars.

The sentence imposed upon such person shall not be reduced to less than six months, nor suspended, nor shall any person convicted under this subsection be eligible for probation, parole, or furlough or receive any deduction from his sentence until such person has served at least six months of such sentence; provided, however, that the commissioner of correction may, on the recommendation of the warden, superintendent, or other person in charge of a correctional institution, or of the administrator of a county correctional institution, grant to an offender committed under this subsection a temporary release in the custody of an officer of such institution for the following purposes only: to attend the funeral of a relative; to visit a critically ill relative; to obtain emergency medical or psychiatric services unavailable at said institution; or to engage in employment pursuant to a work release program. Prosecutions commenced under this subdivision shall neither be continued without a finding nor placed on file.

The provisions of section eighty-seven of chapter two hundred and seventy-six shall not apply to any person charged with a violation of this subdivision.

(2) Whoever, upon any way or in any place to which the public has a right of access or upon any way or in any place to which members of the public have access as invitees or licensees, operates a motor vehicle with a percentage, by weight, of alcohol in their blood of eight one-hundredths or greater, or while under the influence of intoxicating liquor, or of marihuana, narcotic drugs, depressants or stimulant substances, all as defined in section one of chapter ninety-four C, or vapors of glue, and by any such operation causes serious bodily injury, shall be punished by imprisonment in a jail or house of correction for not more than two and one-half years, or by a fine of not less than three thousand dollars, or both.

(3) For the purposes of this section "serious bodily injury" shall mean bodily injury which creates a substantial risk of death or which involves either total disability or the loss or substantial impairment of some bodily function for a substantial period of time.

(4) The registrar shall revoke the license or right to operate of a person convicted of a violation of subdivision (1) or (2) for a period of two years after the date of conviction. No appeal, motion for new trial or exception shall operate to stay the revocation of the license or the right to operate; provided, however, such license shall be restored or such right to operate shall be reinstated if the prosecution of such person ultimately terminates in favor of the defendant.

Added by St.1986, c. 620, § 17. Amended by St.2003, c. 28, §§ 24, 25.

§ 24M. Training for law enforcement personnel regarding alcohol-related offenses; alcohol sensitive selective traffic enforcement program

The officials and agencies designated in this section are hereby directed to perform the duties specified in this section and any other action within their authority in order to ensure effective enforcement of sections twenty-four to twenty-four *O*, inclusive.

(1) The municipal police training committee established in section one hundred and sixteen of chapter six shall provide training, including but not limited to alcohol education and education concerning the aforesaid sections, to all law enforcement personnel throughout the commonwealth.

(2) The chief administrative justice of the trial court department shall provide training, including but not limited to alcohol education and education concerning the aforesaid sections, to all appropriate court personnel throughout the commonwealth, including, but not limited to, judges, district attorneys and probation officers.

(3) The courts of the commonwealth shall give priority to the speedy and effective disposition of all matters arising under the aforesaid sections.

(4) The executive office of public safety shall establish and implement an alcohol sensitive selective traffic enforcement program.

Added by St.1986, c. 620, § 17. Amended by St.1986, c. 677, § 2; St.2002, c. 196, § 21.

§ 24N. Suspension of operator's license upon issuance of complaint; hearing

Upon the issuance of a complaint alleging a violation of paragraph (a) of subdivision (1) of section twenty-four or a violation of section twenty-four G or twenty-four L of this chapter, or a violation of paragraph (1) of subsection (a) of section eight, or a violation of section eight A or section eight B of chapter ninety B, the judge, in addition to any other terms of bail or recognizance, shall, upon the failure of any police officer to suspend or take custody of the drivers license or permit issued by the commonwealth of any such defendant under paragraph (f) of subdivision (1) of section twenty-four, immediately suspend the defendant's license or right to operate a motor vehicle or vessel in the following instances: (i) if the prosecutor makes a prima facie showing at the arraignment that said defendant was operating a motor vehicle while the percentage, by weight, of alcohol in his blood was eight one-hundredths or more, or, relative to any defendant under the age of twenty-one, while the percentage by weight, of alcohol in his blood was two one-hundredths or more, as shown by chemical test or analysis of his blood or breath, and presents written certification of oral testimony from the person administering to the defendant such chemical test or analysis of his blood or breath that the defendant was administered such a test or analysis, that the operator administering the test or analysis of his blood or breath was trained and certified in the administration of such tests, that the test was performed in accordance with regulations and standards promulgated by the secretary of public safety, that the equipment used for such test was regularly serviced and maintained, and that the person administering the test had every reason to believe the equipment was functioning properly at the time the test was administered. Such certification shall be prima facie evidence of the facts so certified. Upon such a showing and presentation, the judge shall take immediate physical possession of such defendant's license or permit issued by the commonwealth to operate a motor vehicle, and shall direct the prosecuting officer to forthwith notify the department of criminal justice information services and the registrar of such suspension by the most expeditious means available. The defendant's license or permit to operate a motor vehicle shall remain suspended until the disposition of the offense for which said defendant is being prosecuted, but in no event shall such suspension pursuant to this section exceed 30 days; or (ii) if the prosecutor makes a prima facie showing at arraignment that said defendant was arrested on the charge of driving a motor vehicle on any such way or place while under the influence of intoxicating liquor, and said defendant refused to submit to a chemical test or analysis of his breath or blood. Upon such a showing and presentation, the judge shall take immediate physical possession of such defendant's license or permit issued by the commonwealth to operate a motor vehicle, and shall direct the prosecuting officer to forthwith notify the department of criminal justice information services and the registrar of such suspension by the most expeditious means available. The defendant's license or permit to operate a motor vehicle shall remain suspended for a period of 180 days; provided, however, that any person who is under the age of 21 or who has been previously convicted of a violation under section 24 or a like violation by a court of any other jurisdiction shall have his license or right to operate suspended forthwith for a period of 1 year for such refusal; provided, further, that any person previously convicted 2 or more times of a violation under section 24 of a like violation by a court of any other jurisdiction shall have his license or right to operate suspended forthwith for a period of 18 months for such refusal. No license shall be restored under any circumstances and no restricted or hardship permits shall be issued during the suspension period imposed by this paragraph; provided, however, that the defendant may immediately, upon entry of a not guilty finding or dismissal of all charges under section twenty-four, sections twenty-four G and twenty-four L, and in the absence of any other alcohol related charges pending against said defendant, apply for and be granted a hearing forthwith before the court which shall have entered said finding for the purpose of requesting the restoration of said license. At said hearing, there shall be a rebuttable presumption that said license be restored, unless the commonwealth shall establish, by a fair preponderance of the evidence that restoration of said license would likely endanger the public safety. In all such instances, the court shall issue written findings of fact with its decision.

Any person whose license or right to operate has been suspended pursuant to this section on the basis of chemical analysis of his breath may within ten days of such suspension request a hearing and upon such request shall be entitled to a hearing before the court in which the underlying charge is pending, which hearing shall be limited to the following issue: whether a blood test administered pursuant to paragraph (e) of subdivision (1) of section twenty-four, within a reasonable period of time after such chemical analysis of his breath, shows that the percentage, by weight, of alcohol in such person's blood was less than eight one-hundredths, or, relative to such person under the age of twenty-one was less than two one-hundredths. If the court finds that such a blood test shows that such percentage was less than eight one-hundredths, or, relative to such person under the age of twenty-one, that such percentage was less than two one-hundredths, the court shall restore such person's license or right to operate and shall direct the prosecuting officer to forthwith notify the department of criminal justice information services and the registrar of such restoration.

Any person whose right to operate has been suspended pursuant to this section on the basis of the failure of such person to submit to a chemical test or analysis of his breath or blood may within ten days of his suspension request a hearing and upon such request shall be entitled to a hearing before the court in which the underlying charges are pending, which hearing shall be limited to the following issues: (1) did the police officer have reasonable grounds to believe that such person had been operating a motor vehicle while under the influence of intoxicating liquor upon any way or in any place to which members of the public have a right of access or upon any way to which members of the public have a right of access as invitees or licensees, (2) was such person placed under arrest, and (3) did such person refuse to submit to such test or analysis. If, after such hearing, the court finds on any one of the said issues in the negative, the court shall restore such person's license or right to operate and shall direct the prosecuting officer to forthwith notify the criminal history systems board and the registrar of such restoration.

Added by St.1986, c. 620, § 17. Amended by St.1986, c. 677, § 3; St.1994, c. 25, § 10; St.1994, c. 60, § 110; St.1994, c. 318, §§ 3, 4; St.2003, c. 28, §§ 26, 27, eff. June 30, 2003; St.2010, c. 256, § 64, eff. Nov. 4, 2010.

§ 24O. Statement to defendant regarding further violations

Upon conviction of any violation of the provisions of this chapter, the defendant shall be provided by the probation office in the court in which said conviction was entered a statement in writing prepared by the secretary of public safety of the statutory provisions that apply to any further violation of this chapter.

Added by St.1986, c. 620, § 17. Amended by St.1994, c. 25, § 11.

§ 24P. Minors; further violations; education and treatment programs

(a) Upon evidence that a person under the age of 21, after having been arrested for or charged with a violation under section 24, 24G or 24L, had a blood alcohol percentage of two one-hundredths or greater or upon evidence that such person refused to submit to a chemical test or analysis of his breath or blood under section 24, notwithstanding the finding upon any such charge, such person shall have his license or permit to operate a motor vehicle suspended by the registrar for a period of 180 days; provided, however, that any such person who is less than 18 years of age at the time of such violation shall have his license suspended by the registrar for one year. Such suspension by the registrar shall be imposed in addition to any penalty, license suspension or revocation imposed upon such person by the court as required by said section 24, 24G or 24L.

If a person has not been previously arrested for or charged with a violation under said section 24, 24G or 24L, such person shall, if he consents, be assigned to a program specifically designed by the department of public health for the treatment of underage drinking drivers; provided, however, that such assignment shall not be precluded by a finding or disposition upon a charge against such person under said section 24, 24G or 24L. Upon entry into such program, as authorized by this section or as otherwise required under any disposition pursuant to section 24D, the suspension of a license or permit to operate as required by this section shall be waived by the registrar for a person under 21 years of age but over 18 years of age; provided, however, that such suspension shall be for a period of 180 days for such person who was under the age of 18 at the time of such violation. Upon the failure of a person under the age of 21 to successfully complete such program, the registrar shall forthwith suspend such license or permit to operate for 180 days; provided, however, that upon such failure to successfully complete such program by a person who was under the age of 18 at the time of such violation, the registrar shall forthwith suspend the license or permit to operate for one year.

(b) The license or permit to operate of a person convicted of any violation under section 24, 24G, 24*I* or 24L who was under the age of 18 at the time of such violation and whose license or permit to operate was not suspended under subsection (a) for such violation shall have such license or permit suspended for a period of 180 days for a first offense and for a period of one year for a second or subsequent offense.

Added by St.1994, c. 25, § 11. Amended by St.1994, c. 60, §§ 111, 112; St.1998, c. 220, § 7.

§ 24Q. Alcohol or drug assessment as condition for certain sentences imposed under chapter

A mandatory condition of any sentence imposed for: (1) a conviction or an assignment to an alcohol or controlled substance education, treatment or rehabilitation program if evidence in the prosecution of a violation of this chapter or chapter 90B was that a person's blood alcohol percentage, by weight, was not less .20 or (2) an assignment to an alcohol or controlled substance education, treatment or rehabilitation program or a conviction for violating paragraph (a) of subdivision (1) of section 24, subsection (a) of section 24G, operating a motor vehicle with a percentage by weight of blood alcohol of eight one-hundredths or greater, or while under the influence of intoxicating liquor in violation of subsection (b) of said section 24G, section 24L, subsection (a) of section 8 of chapter 90B, section 8A or 8B of chapter 90B, or section 13½ of chapter 265 or, in the case of any other jurisdiction, for any like offense, if the person being sentenced has previously been so assigned or convicted of a like offense, shall be that such person complete an alcohol or drug assessment conducted by the department of public health or other court-approved program. The assessment shall include, but not be limited to, an assessment of the level of the offender's addiction to alcohol or drugs, and the department's recommended course of treatment. Such assessment and recommended course of treatment shall be reported to the offender's probation or parole officer. No person shall be excluded from an assessment for inability to pay if the offender files an affidavit of indigency or inability to pay with the court and an investigation by the probation or parole officer confirms such indigency or establishes that such payment would cause a grave and serious hardship to the offender or his family, and the court enters written findings relative thereto. The commissioner of public health may make such rules and regulations as are necessary or proper to carry out this section.

Added by St.2005, c. 122, § 17, eff. Oct. 28, 2005.

§ 24R. Revocation for life of license or right to operate

(a) Notwithstanding section 24 or section 24D, the registrar shall revoke for life the license or right to operate of a person assigned to an alcohol or controlled substance education, treatment, or rehabilitation program or convicted of a violation of subsection (a) of section 24G, operating a motor vehicle with a percentage by weight of blood alcohol of eight one-hundredths or greater, or while under the influence of intoxicating liquor in violation of subsection (b) of said section 24G, section 24L, section 8A or 8B of chapter 90B, or section 13½ of chapter 265 who has previously been convicted of a violation of subdivision (a) of section 24 or a like violation in another jurisdiction.

(b) Notwithstanding section 24, the registrar shall revoke for life the license or right to operate of any person convicted of a violation of subdivision (a) of section 24G who has previously been assigned to an alcohol or controlled substance education, treatment, or rehabilitation program by a court of the commonwealth, or convicted of violation of paragraph (a) of subdivision (1) of section 24, subsection (a) of section 24G, operating a motor vehicle with a percentage by weight of blood alcohol of eight one-hundredths or greater, or while under the influence of intoxicating liquor in violation of subsection (b) of said section 24G, section 24L, subsection (a) of section 8 of chapter 90B, or section 8A or 8B of chapter 90B, section 13½ of chapter 265 or a like violation in another jurisdiction.

Added by St.2005, c. 122, § 17, eff. Oct. 28, 2005.

§ 24S. Operation of motor vehicle on public way in violation of ignition interlock device license restriction; penalties

(a) Whoever, upon any way or place to which the public has a right of access, or upon any way or place to which members of the public have access as invitees or licensees, operates a motor vehicle that is not equipped with a certified functioning ignition interlock device while his license or right to operate has been restricted to operating only motor vehicles equipped with such device shall be punished by fine of not less than $1,000 nor more than $15,000 and by imprisonment for not less than 180 days nor more than 2½ years or by a fine of not less than $1,000 nor more than $15,000 and by imprisonment in the state prison for not less than 2½ years nor more than 5 years. The sentence imposed upon such person shall not be reduced to less than 150 days, nor suspended, nor shall any such person be eligible for probation, parole or furlough or receive any deduction from his sentence for good conduct until he shall have served 150 days of such sentence. The commissioner of correction may, on the recommendation of the warden, superintendent, or other person in charge of a correctional institution, or the administrator of a county correctional institution, grant to an offender committed under this subsection a temporary release in the custody of an officer of such institution for the following purposes only: to attend the funeral of a relative; to visit a critically ill relative; to obtain emergency medical or psychiatric services unavailable at that institution; to engage in employment pursuant to a work release program; or for the purposes of an aftercare program designed to support the recovery of an offender who has completed an alcohol or controlled substance education, treatment or rehabilitation program operated by the department of correction. The defendant may serve all or part of such 150–day sentence, to the extent such resources are available, in a correctional facility specifically designated by the department of correction for the incarceration and rehabilitation of drinking drivers.

(b) For the purposes of this section the term "certified ignition interlock device" shall mean an alcohol breath screening device that prevents a vehicle from starting if it detects a blood alcohol concentration over a preset limit of .02 or 20 mg of alcohol per 100 ml of blood.

Added by St.2005, c. 122, § 17, eff. Jan. 1, 2006.

§ 24T. Tampering with ignition interlock device; penalties

(a) Whoever interferes with or tampers with a certified ignition interlock device, with the intent to disable such device, shall be punished by imprisonment in the house of correction for not less than 6 months nor more than 2½ years or by imprisonment in the state prison for not less than 3 years nor more than 5 years.

(b) For the purposes of this section the term "certified ignition interlock device" shall mean an alcohol breath screening device that prevents a vehicle from starting if it detects a blood alcohol concentration over a preset limit of .02 or 20 mg of alcohol per 100 ml of blood.

Added by St.2005, c. 122, § 17, eff. Jan. 1, 2006.

§ 24U. Starting motor vehicle equipped with ignition interlock device for another person under a restricted license

(a)(1) Whoever knowingly breathes into a certified ignition interlock device as defined in section 24T or starts a motor vehicle equipped with such a device for the purpose of providing an operable motor vehicle to a person whose license or right to operate a vehicle is restricted to the operation of vehicles equipped with a certified ignition interlock device shall be punished by a fine not less than $1,000 nor more than $5,000 or imprisonment in a house of correction for not less than 6 months nor more than 2½ years in the house of correction and, for a second or subsequent conviction, by imprisonment in a state prison for not less than 3 nor more than 5 years.

(2) A certified copy of an acknowledgement of the existence and terms of certified ignition interlock device restriction, executed by a person alleged to have violated this section shall be admissible as evidence to prove the existence of such knowledge by the person who executed the document.

[There is no subsection (b).]

Added by St.2005, c. 122, § 17, eff. Jan. 1, 2006.

§ 24V. Child endangerment while operating a motor vehicle or vessel under the influence; penalties; suspension of license

(a) Whoever violates paragraph (a) of subdivision (1) of section 24, subsection (a) of section 24G, operating a motor vehicle with a percentage by weight of blood alcohol of eight one-hundredths or greater, or while under the influence of intoxicating liquor in violation of subsection (b) of said section 24G, section 24L, subsection (a) of section 8 of chapter 90B, or section 8A or 8B of chapter 90B, or section 13½ of chapter 265 with a child 14 years of age or younger in the motor vehicle or vessel shall also be guilty of child endangerment while operating a motor vehicle or vessel under the influence and shall be punished by an enhanced penalty of a fine of not less than $1,000 nor more than $5,000 and by imprisonment in the house of correction for not less than 90 days nor more than 2½ years. If a defendant has previously violated this subsection or a like offense in another jurisdiction preceding the date of the commission of the offense for which he has been convicted, he shall be punished by a fine of not less than $5,000 nor more than $10,000 and by imprisonment in the house of correction for not less than 6 months nor more than 2½ years or by imprisonment in state prison for not less than 3 years but not more than 5 years. The sentence of imprisonment imposed upon such person shall not be reduced to less than 6 months, nor suspended, nor shall any such person be eligible for probation, parole, or furlough or receive any deduction from his sentence for good conduct until he shall have served at least 6 months of such sentence but the commissioner of correction may, on the recommendation of the warden, superintendent or other person in charge of a correctional institution, or of the administrator of a county correctional institution, grant to an offender committed under this subsection a temporary release in the custody of an officer of such institution for the following purposes only: to attend the funeral of a relative; to visit a critically ill relative; to obtain emergency medical or psychiatric services unavailable at the institution; or to engage in employment pursuant to a work release program. A sentence imposed under this subsection shall be served consecutively to and not concurrently with the predicate violation of said paragraph (a) of subdivision (1) of section 24, subsection (a) of section 24G, subsection (b) of section 24G, section 24L, subsection (a) of section 8 of chapter 90B, or section 8A or 8B of chapter 90B, section 13½ of chapter 265. Section 87 of chapter 276 and sections 1 to 9, inclusive, of chapter 276A shall not apply to a person charged with a violation of this subsection. Prosecutions commenced under this subsection shall not be placed on file or continued without a finding.

(b) The registrar shall suspend the license or right to operate of person who violates this section for a period of 1 year for a first offense, and for a period of 3 years for a second or subsequent violation.

Added by St.2005, c. 122, § 17, eff. Oct. 28, 2005.

§ 24W. Forfeiture of motor vehicle owned by certain drunk driving offenders; procedure; Operating Under the Influence Deterrent Trust Fund

(a) A motor vehicle or vessel owned by a person who has been assigned to an alcohol or controlled substance education, treatment or rehabilitation program or who was convicted of a violation of paragraph (a) of subdivision (1) of section 24, subsection (a) of section 24G, operating a motor vehicle with a percentage by weight of blood alcohol of eight one-hundredths or greater, or while under the influence of intoxicating liquor in violation of subsection (b) of said section 24G, section 24L, subsection (a) of section 8 of chapter 90B, section 8A or 8B of chapter 90B, or section 13½ of chapter 265 or, in the case of another jurisdiction, for any like offense, if owned by such operator, may be forfeited to the commonwealth if such person has been so assigned or so convicted previously at least 3 times.

(b) A district attorney or the attorney general may petition the superior or district court in the name of the commonwealth in the nature of a proceeding in rem to order forfeiture of such motor vehicle or vessel. The petition shall be filed in the court having jurisdiction over the criminal proceeding brought under this section. The proceeding shall be deemed a civil suit in equity. In all such actions where the motor vehicle or vessel is jointly owned before the date of the second or subsequent operating under the influence offense committed by the defendant by either a parent, spouse, child, grandparent, brother, sister, or parent of the spouse living in the defendant's household, the commonwealth shall have the burden of proving to the court the existence of probable cause to institute the action, and the claimant shall have the burden of proving to the court's satisfaction that the property is not forfeitable because the claimant is dependent on the motor vehicle or vessel for his livelihood or the maintenance of his family. The court shall order the commonwealth to give notice by certified or registered mail to the owners of the motor vehicle or vessel and to such other persons or entities who appear to have an interest therein, and the court shall promptly, but not less than 2 weeks after notice, hold a hearing on the petition. Upon the motion of an owner of the motor vehicle or vessel, the court may continue the hearing on the petition pending the outcome of a criminal trial related to a charge of operating under the influence in violation of this chapter or chapter 90B. During the pendency of the proceedings, the court may issue at the request of the commonwealth ex parte any preliminary order or process as is necessary to seize or secure the property for which forfeiture is sought and to provide for its custody. Process for seizure of the property shall issue only upon a showing of probable cause, and the application therefore and the issuance, execution and return thereof shall be subject to chapter 276, as applicable.

(c) At a hearing under this section, the court shall hear evidence and make findings of fact and conclusions of law, and shall thereon issue a final order from which the parties shall have such right of appeal as from a decree in equity. No forfeiture under this section shall extinguish a perfected security interest held by a creditor in the property at the time of the filing of the forfeiture action. In all actions where a final order results in forfeiture, the final order shall provide for disposition of the property by the commonwealth or any subdivision thereof in any manner not prohibited by law, including official use by an authorized law enforcement or other agency, or at sale at public auction or by competitive bidding, with such sale being conducted by the office of the district attorney or the attorney general that obtained the final order of forfeiture.

(d) The final order of the court shall provide that the proceeds of any such sale shall be used to pay the reasonable expenses of the forfeiture proceedings, seizure, storage, maintenance of custody, advertising and notice, and the balance of any such sale shall be distributed equally among the prosecuting district attorney or attorney general, the city, town or state police department involved in the forfeiture and the Victims of Drunk Driving Trust Fund established in section 66 of chapter 10. If more than 1 department was substantially involved in the seizure, the court having jurisdiction over the forfeiture proceeding shall distribute the portion for law enforcement equitably among the departments.

(e) There shall be established within the office of the state treasurer a separate Operating Under the Influence Deterrent Trust Fund for each district attorney and for the attorney general. All monies and proceeds received by a prosecuting district attorney or attorney general pursuant to this section shall be deposited in the fund and shall be expended without further appropriation to defray the costs of investigations, to provide additional technical equipment or expertise, to provide matching funds to obtain federal grants, or for such other law enforcement purposes as the district attorney or attorney general deems appropriate. Any program seeking to be an eligible recipient of the funds shall file an annual audit report with the local district attorney and attorney general. Such report shall include, but not be limited to, a listing of the assets, liabilities, itemized expenditures and board of directors of the program. Within 90 days of the close of the fiscal year, each district attorney and the attorney general shall file an annual report with the house and senate committees on ways and means on the use of the monies in the trust fund for the purposes of deterring operating under the influence programs.

(f) All moneys and proceeds received by a police department shall be deposited into the fund and shall be expended without further appropriation to defray the costs of investigations, to provide additional technical equipment or expertise, to provide matching funds to obtain federal grants, or to accomplish such other law enforcement purposes as the chief of police of such city or town, or the colonel of state police deem appropriate, but such funds shall not be considered a source of revenue to meet the operating needs of such department.

Added by St.2005, c. 122, § 17, eff. Oct. 28, 2005.

§ 24X. Cancellation of registration for motor vehicles owned by certain drunk driving offenders

The registration of a motor vehicle owned by a person who is assigned to an alcohol or controlled substance education, treatment or rehabilitation program or who is convicted of a violation of paragraph (a) of subdivision (1) of section 24, subsection (a) of section 24G, operating a motor vehicle with a percentage by weight of blood alcohol of eight one-hundredths or greater, or while under the influence of intoxicating liquor in violation of subsection (b) of section 24G, section 24L, subsection (a) of section 8 of chapter 90B, section 13½ of chapter 265, or section 8A or 8B of chapter 90B, or, in the case of another jurisdiction, for any like offense, may be cancelled and the registration plates for such vehicle seized for the period of the suspension or revocation of the license or right to operate due to such assignment or conviction, if the person has been so assigned or so convicted previously at least 2 times. No new registration shall be issued to such person during the period of the suspension or revocation of the license or right to operate.

Added by St.2005, c. 122, § 17, eff. Oct. 28, 2005.

TITLE XV

REGULATION OF TRADE

CHAPTER 94C

CONTROLLED SUBSTANCES ACT

Chapter 94C of the General Laws was added by St.1971, c. 1071, § 1.

The section headings for the General Laws in this pamphlet have been editorially supplied.

§ 1. Definitions

As used in this chapter, the following words shall, unless the context clearly requires otherwise, have the following meanings:

"Administer", the direct application of a controlled substance whether by injection, inhalation, ingestion, or any other means to the body of a patient or research subject by—

(a) a practitioner, or

(b) a nurse at the direction of a practitioner in the course of his professional practice, or

(c) an ultimate user or research subject at the direction of a practitioner in the course of his professional practice.

"Agent", an authorized person who acts on behalf of or at the direction of a manufacturer, distributor, or dispenser; except that such term does not include a common or contract carrier, public warehouseman, or employee of the carrier or warehouseman, when acting in the usual and lawful course of the carrier's or warehouseman's business.

"Bureau", the Bureau of Narcotics and Dangerous Drugs, United States Department of Justice, or its successor agency.

"Class", the lists of controlled substances for the purpose of determining the severity of criminal offenses under this chapter.

"Commissioner", the commissioner of public health.

"Controlled substance", a drug, substance, or immediate precursor in any schedule or class referred to in this chapter.

"Counterfeit substance", a substance which is represented to be a particular controlled drug or substance, but which is in fact not that drug or substance.

"Deliver", to transfer, whether by actual or constructive transfer, a controlled substance from one person to another, whether or not there is an agency relationship.

"Department", the department of public health.

"Depressant or stimulant substance",

(a) a drug which contains any quantity of barbituric acid or any of the salts of barbituric acid; or any derivative of barbituric acid which the United States Secretary of Health, Education, and Welfare has by regulation designated as habit forming; or

(b) a drug which contains any quantity of amphetamine or any of its optical isomers; any salt of amphetamine or any salt of an optical isomer of amphetamine; or any substance which the United States Attorney General has by regulation designated as habit forming because of its stimulant effect on the central nervous system; or

(c) lysergic acid diethylamide; or

(d) any drug except marihuana which contains any quantity of a substance which the United States Attorney General has by regulation designated as having a potential for abuse because of its depressant or stimulant effect on the central nervous system or its hallucinogenic effect.

"Dispense", to deliver a controlled substance to an ultimate user or research subject or to the agent of an ultimate user or research subject by a practitioner or pursuant to the order of a practitioner, including the prescribing and administering of a controlled substance and the packaging, labeling, or compounding necessary for such delivery.

"Distribute", to deliver other than by administering or dispensing a controlled substance.

"Drug",

(a) substances recognized as drugs in the official United States Pharmacopoeia, official Homeopathic Pharmacopoeia of the United States, or official National Formulary, or any supplement to any of them;

(b) substances intended for use in the diagnosis, cure, mitigation, treatment, or prevention of disease in man or animals;

(c) substances, other than food, intended to affect the structure, or any function of the body of man and animals; or

(d) substances intended for use as a component of any article specified in clauses (a), (b) or (c), exclusive of devices or their components, parts or accessories.

"Drug paraphernalia", all equipment, products, devices and materials of any kind which are primarily intended or designed for use in planting, propagating, cultivating, growing, harvesting, manufacturing, compounding, converting, producing, processing, preparing, testing, analyzing, packaging, repackaging, storing, containing, concealing, ingesting, inhaling or otherwise introducing into the human body a controlled substance in violation of this chapter. It includes, but is not limited to:

(1) kits used, primarily intended for use or designed for use in planting, propagating, cultivating, growing or harvesting of any species of plant which is a controlled substance or from which a controlled substance can be derived;

(2) kits used, primarily intended for use or designed for use in manufacturing, compounding, converting, producing, processing or preparing controlled substances;

(3) isomerization devices used, primarily intended for use or designed for use in increasing the potency of any species of plant which is a controlled substance;

(4) testing equipment used, primarily intended for use or designed for use in identifying or in analyzing the strength, effectiveness or purity of controlled substances;

(5) scales and balances used, primarily intended for use or designed for use in weighing or measuring controlled substances;

(6) diluents and adulterants, such as quinine hydrochloride, mannitol, mannite, dextrose and lactose, used, primarily intended for use or designed for use in cutting controlled substances;

(7) separation gins and sifters used, primarily intended for use or designed for use in removing twigs and seeds from or in otherwise cleaning or refining marihuana;

(8) blenders, bowls, containers, spoons and mixing devices used, primarily intended for use or designed for use in compounding controlled substances;

(9) capsules, balloons, envelopes and other containers used, primarily intended for use or designed for use in packaging small quantities of controlled substances;

(10) containers and other objects used, primarily intended for use or designed for use in storing or concealing controlled substances;

[There is no clause (11).]

(12) objects used, primarily intended for use or designed for use in ingesting, inhaling, or otherwise introducing marihuana, cocaine, hashish or hashish oil into the human body, such as:

(a) metal, wooden, acrylic, glass, stone, plastic or ceramic pipes, which pipes may or may not have screens, permanent screens, hashish heads or punctured metal bowls;

(b) water pipes;

(c) carburetion tubes and devices;

(d) smoking and carburetion masks;

(e) roach clips; meaning objects used to hold burning material, such as a marihuana cigarette that has become too small or too short to be held in the hand;

(f) miniature cocaine spoons and cocaine vials;

(g) chamber pipes;

(h) carburetor pipes;

(i) electric pipes;

(j) air-driven pipes;

(k) chillums;

(*l*) bongs;

(m) ice pipes or chillers;

(n) wired cigarette papers;

(*o*) cocaine freebase kits.

In determining whether an object is drug paraphernalia, a court or other authority should consider, in addition to all other logically relevant factors, the following:

(a) the proximity of the object, in time and space, to a direct violation of this chapter;

(b) the proximity of the object to controlled substances;

(c) the existence of any residue of controlled substances on the object;

(d) instructions, oral or written, provided with the object concerning its use;

(e) descriptive materials accompanying the object which explain or depict its use;

(f) national and local advertising concerning its use;

(g) the manner in which the object is displayed for sale;

(h) whether the owner, or anyone in control of the object, is a supplier of like or related items to the community, such as a licensed distributor or dealer of tobacco products;

(i) direct or circumstantial evidence of the ratio of sales of the object to the total sales of the business enterprise;

(j) the existence and scope of legitimate uses for the object in the community;

(k) expert testimony concerning its use.

For purposes of this definition, the phrase "primarily intended for use" shall mean the likely use which may be ascribed to an item by a reasonable person. For purposes of this definition, the phrase "designed for use" shall mean the use a reasonable person would ascribe to an item based on the design and features of said item.

"Immediate precursor", a substance which the commissioner has found to be and by rule designates as being a principal compound commonly used or produced primarily for use, and which is an immediate chemical intermediary used or likely to be used in the manufacture of a controlled substance, the control of which is necessary to prevent, curtail, or limit manufacture.

"Isomer", the optical isomer, except that wherever appropriate it shall mean the optical, position or geometric isomer.

"Manufacture", the production, preparation, propagation, compounding, conversion or processing of a controlled substance, either directly or indirectly by extraction from substances of natural origin, or independently by means of chemical synthesis, including any packaging or repackaging of the substance or labeling or relabeling of its container except that this term does not include the preparation or compounding of a controlled substance by an individual for his own use or the preparation, compounding, packaging, or labeling of a controlled substance:

(a) by a practitioner as an incident to his administering a controlled substance in the course of his professional practice, or

(b) by a practitioner, or by his authorized agent under his supervision, for the purpose of, or as an incident to, research, teaching or chemical analysis and not for sale, or

(c) by a pharmacist in the course of his professional practice.

"Marihuana", all parts of the plant Cannabis sativa L., whether growing or not; the seeds thereof; and resin extracted from any part of the plant; and every compound, manufacture, salt, derivative, mixture, or preparation of the plant, its seeds or resin. It does not include the mature stalks of the plant, fiber produced from the stalks, oil, or cake made from the seeds of the plant, any other compound, manufacture, salt, derivative, mixture, or preparation of the mature stalks, except the resin extracted therefrom, fiber, oil, or cake or the sterilized seed of the plant which is incapable of germination.

"Narcotic drug", any of the following, whether produced directly or indirectly by extraction from substances of vegetable origin, or independently by means of chemical synthesis, or by a combination of extraction and chemical synthesis:

(a) Opium and opiate, and any salt, compound, derivative, or preparation of opium or opiate;

(b) Any salt, compound, isomer, derivative, or preparation thereof which is chemically equivalent or identical with any of the substances referred to in clause (a), but not including the isoquinoline alkaloids of opium;

(c) Opium poppy and poppy straw;

(d) Coca leaves and any salt, compound, derivative, or preparation of coca leaves, and any salt, compound, isomer, derivative, or preparation thereof which is chemically equivalent or identical with any of these substances, but not including decocainized coca leaves or extractions of coca leaves which do not contain cocaine or ecgonine.

"Nuclear pharmacy", a facility under the direction or supervision of a registered pharmacist which is authorized by the board of registration in pharmacy to dispense radiopharmaceutical drugs.

"Nurse", a nurse registered or licensed pursuant to the provisions of section seventy-four or seventy-four A of chapter one hundred and twelve, a graduate nurse as specified in section eighty-one of said chapter one hundred and twelve or a student nurse enrolled in a school approved by the board of registration in nursing.

"Nurse anesthetist", a nurse with advanced training authorized to practice by the board of registration in nursing as a nurse anesthetist in an advanced practice nursing role as provided in section 80B of chapter 112.

"Nurse practitioner", a nurse with advanced training who is authorized to practice by the board of registration in nursing as a nurse practitioner, as provided for in section eighty B of chapter one hundred and twelve.

"Opiate", any substance having an addiction-forming or addiction-sustaining liability similar to morphine or being capable of conversion into a drug having addiction-forming or addiction-sustaining liability. It does not include, unless specifically designated as controlled under section two, the dextrorotatory isomer of 3-methoxy-n-methyl-morphinan and its salts, dextromethorphan. It does include its racemic and levorotatory forms.

"Opium poppy", the plant of the species Papaver somniferum L., except its seeds.

"Oral prescription", an oral order for medication which is dispensed to or for an ultimate user, but not including an order for medication which is dispensed for immediate administration to the ultimate user by a practitioner, registered nurse, or practical nurse.

"Person", individual, corporation, government, or governmental subdivision or agency, business trust, estate, trust, partnership or association, or any other legal entity.

"Pharmacist", any pharmacist registered in the commonwealth to dispense controlled substances, and including any other person authorized to dispense controlled substances under the supervision of a pharmacist registered in the commonwealth.

"Pharmacy", a facility under the direction or supervision of a registered pharmacist which is authorized to dispense controlled substances, including but not limited to "retail drug business" as defined below.

"Physician assistant", a person who is a graduate of an approved program for the training of physician assistants who is supervised by a registered physician in accordance with sections nine C to nine H, inclusive, of chapter one hundred and twelve.

"Poppy straw", all parts, except the seeds of the opium poppy, after mowing.

"Practitioner",

(a) A physician, dentist, veterinarian, podiatrist, scientific investigator, or other person registered to distribute, dispense, conduct research with respect to, or use in teaching or chemical analysis, a controlled substance in the course of professional practice or research in the commonwealth;

(b) A pharmacy, hospital, or other institution registered to distribute, dispense, conduct research with respect to or to administer a controlled substance in the course of professional practice or research in the commonwealth.

(c) An optometrist authorized by sections 66 and 66B of chapter 112 and registered pursuant to paragraph (h) of section 7 to utilize and prescribe therapeutic pharmaceutical agents in the course of professional practice in the commonwealth.

"Prescription drug", any and all drugs upon which the manufacturer or distributor has, in compliance with federal law and regulations, placed the following: "Caution, Federal law prohibits dispensing without prescription".

"Production", includes the manufacture, planting, cultivation, growing, or harvesting of a controlled substance.

"Radiopharmaceutical drug", any drug which is radioactive as defined in the Federal Food, Drug and Cosmetic Act.

"Registrant", a person who is registered pursuant to any provision of this chapter.

"Registration", unless the context specifically indicates otherwise, such registration as is required and permitted only pursuant to the provisions of this chapter.

"Registration number", such registration number or numbers, either federal or state, that are required with respect to practitioners by appropriate administrative agencies.

"Retail drug business", a store for the transaction of "drug business" as defined in section thirty-seven of chapter one hundred and twelve.

"Schedule", the list of controlled substances established by the commissioner pursuant to the provisions of section two for purposes of administration and regulation.

"State", when applied to a part of the United States other than Massachusetts includes any state, district, commonwealth, territory, insular possession thereof, and any area subject to the legal authority of the United States of America.

"Tetrahydrocannabinol", tetrahydrocannabinol or preparations containing tetrahydrocannabinol excluding marihuana except when it has been established that the concentration of delta-9 tetrahydrocannabinol in said marihuana exceeds two and one-half per cent.

"Ultimate user", a person who lawfully possesses a controlled substance for his own use or for the use of a member of his household or for the use of a patient in a facility licensed by the department or for administering to an animal owned by him or by a member of his household.

"Written prescription", a lawful order from a practitioner for a drug or device for a specific patient that is communicated directly to a pharmacist in a licensed pharmacy; provided, however, that "written prescription" shall not include an order for medication which is dispensed for immediate administration to the ultimate user by a practitioner, registered nurse or licensed practical nurse.

Added by St.1971, c. 1071, § 1. Amended by St.1972, c. 806, §§ 1 to 6; St.1973, c. 1190, §§ 1 to 6; St.1981, c. 669, § 1; St.1983, c. 565, §§ 1, 2; St.1986, c. 97, §§ 1, 2; St.1997, c. 55, § 1; St.1998, c. 50, § 1; St.1998, c. 104, § 1; St.2006, c. 172, §§ 1, 2, eff. July 13, 2006; St.2010, c. 191, § 1, eff. Oct. 27, 2010.

§ 2. Establishment of schedules of drugs or other controlled substances

(a) For the purpose of administration and regulation of the manufacture, distribution, dispensing, and possession of controlled substances by persons authorized under this chapter, the commissioner shall establish by regulations pursuant to the provisions of chapter thirty A five schedules incorporating the five schedules of controlled substances under the "Comprehensive Drug Abuse, Prevention and Control Act of 1970" [1] or any amendment thereof. In addition thereto the commissioner shall by regulation as aforesaid establish a sixth schedule which shall include all prescription drugs not included in the first five schedules.

(a½) The commissioner may, pursuant to the provisions of chapter thirty-A, delete or reschedule all substances enumerated in the schedules established pursuant to the provisions of subsection (a), except that if any substance which has not been scheduled pursuant to the provisions of this section is designated a controlled substance under the Federal Comprehensive Drug Abuse Prevention and Control Act of 1970 [1] or any amendment thereof, or if any substance which has been scheduled pursuant to the provisions of this section is designated a controlled substance of greater abuse liability under the Federal Comprehensive Drug Abuse Prevention and Control Act of 1970 or any amendment thereof, the commissioner, pursuant to the provisions of chapter thirty A, shall, not more than thirty days after publication of final notice in the federal register or not more than thirty days after the effective date of any federal statute affecting the scheduling of controlled substances under said federal act or any amendment thereof, issue a regulation controlling the substance in a schedule corresponding to the federal schedules.

(b) In making any finding under subsection (a) of this section or under subsection (a) of section three, the commissioner shall consider the following factors with respect to each drug or other substance proposed to be controlled or removed from the schedules:

(1) Its actual or relative potential for abuse.

(2) Scientific evidence of its pharmacological effect, if known.

(3) The state of current scientific knowledge regarding the drug or other substance.

(4) Its history and current pattern of abuse.

(5) The scope, duration and significance of abuse.

(6) What, if any, risk there is to the public health.

(7) Its psychological or physiological dependence liability.

(8) Whether the substance is an immediate precursor of a substance already controlled under this chapter.

(c) The commissioner acting jointly with the board of registration in pharmacy shall by regulation pursuant to the provisions of chapter thirty A exclude any nonnarcotic substance from a schedule if such substance may, under the Federal "Comprehensive Drug Abuse Prevention and Control Act of 1970"[2] and the Food, Drug, and Cosmetic Act,[3] be lawfully sold over the counter without a prescription.

(d) Authority to control under this section shall not extend to distilled spirits, wine, malt beverages, or tobacco, as those terms are defined or used in subtitle E of the Internal Revenue Code of 1954.[4]

Added by St.1971, c. 1071, § 1. Amended by St.1972, c. 806, § 7.

[1] 21 U.S.C.A. § 812.

[2] 21 U.S.C.A. § 801 et seq.

[3] 21 U.S.C.A. § 301 et seq.

[4] 26 U.S.C.A. § 5001 et seq.

§ 3. Findings required for placement in schedules

Except in the case of an immediate precursor, a drug or other substance may not be placed in any schedule unless such drug or substance has been scheduled pursuant to the provisions of the Federal Comprehensive Drug Abuse, Prevention and Control Act of 1970, or any amendment thereof,[1] or unless the findings required for such schedule are made with respect to such drug or other substance. The findings required for each of the schedules are as follows:

(1) SCHEDULE I.—

(A) The drug or other substance has a high potential for abuse.

(B) The drug or other substance has no currently accepted medical use in treatment in the United States.

(C) There is a lack of accepted safety for use of the drug or other substance under medical supervision.

(2) SCHEDULE II.—

(A) The drug or other substance has a high potential for abuse.

(B) The drug or other substance has a currently accepted medical use in treatment in the United States or a currently accepted medical use with severe restrictions.

(C) Abuse of the drug or other substances may lead to severe psychological or physical dependence.

(3) SCHEDULE III.—

(A) The drug or other substance has a potential for abuse less than the drugs or other substances in schedules I and II.

(B) The drug or other substance has a currently accepted medical use in treatment in the United States.

(C) Abuse of the drug or other substance may lead to moderate or low physical dependence or high psychological dependence.

(4) SCHEDULE IV.—

(A) The drug or other substance has a low potential for abuse relative to the drugs or other substances in schedule III.

(B) The drug or other substance has a currently accepted medical use in treatment in the United States.

(C) Abuse of the drug or other substance may lead to limited physical dependence or psychological dependence relative to the drugs or other substances in schedule III.

(5) SCHEDULE V.—

(A) The drug or other substance has a low potential for abuse relative to the drugs or other substances in schedule IV.

(B) The drug or other substance has a currently accepted medical use in treatment in the United States.

(C) Abuse of the drug or other substance may lead to limited physical dependence or psychological dependence relative to the drugs or other substances in schedule IV.

(6) SCHEDULE VI.—

(A) The substance is a prescription drug; and

(B) Said prescription drug has not been included in Schedules I through V.

Added by St.1971, c. 1071, § 1. Amended by St.1972, c. 806, § 8.

[1] 21 U.S.C.A. § 812.

§ 4. Exceptions from schedules

The commissioner acting jointly with the board of registration in pharmacy may by regulation pursuant to the provisions of chapter thirty A except any compound, mixture or preparation containing any substances in paragraph (a) or (b) of Schedule III or in Schedule IV, V or VI established pursuant to the provisions of section two from the application of all or any part of this chapter if

(1) the compound, mixture, or preparation contains one or more active medicinal ingredients not having a depressant or stimulant effect on the central nervous system, and

(2) such ingredients are included therein in such combinations, quantity, proportion, or concentration as to vitiate the potential for abuse of the substances which do have a depressant or stimulant effect on the central nervous system, and

(3) the compound, mixture, or preparation has been similarly excepted under the provisions of the Federal "Comprehensive Drug Abuse, Prevention and Control Act of 1970", or any amendment thereof.[1]

Such regulation shall state the weight of the controlled substance per fluid ounce, or if a solid or semisolid preparation the weight in the avoirdupois amounts, and if the metric system is used, the weight in grams per hundred cubic centimeters in the case of a fluid, or the weight per gram in the case of a solid or semi-solid preparation.

The commissioner shall by regulation modify, rescind or revoke an exception whenever it has been modified, rescinded or revoked under the provisions of the Federal Comprehensive Drug Abuse, Prevention and Control Act of 1970 or any amendment thereof.[1]

Added by St.1971, c. 1071, § 1. Amended by St.1972, c. 806, § 9.

[1] 21 U.S.C.A. § 801 et seq.

§ 5. Dispensing controlled substances excepted under Sec. 4

Controlled substances which are excepted pursuant to section four may be dispensed, or sold at retail, except that the exception authorized by this section shall be subject to the following conditions:

(1) that such preparation shall be dispensed, or sold in good faith as a medicine, and not for the purpose of evading the provisions of the controlled substances law; (2) that the purchaser of such preparation identify himself to the satisfaction of the pharmacist; and (3) that of such preparation not more than four ounces are dispensed, or sold to a person during any 48 hour period.

The pharmacist dispensing such excepted substances shall keep an accurate record book including the name and address of the purchaser, the name of the preparation, the strength per dosage unit, the quantity dispensed and the date.

Added by St.1971, c. 1071, § 1.

§ 6. Rules and regulations

The board of registration in pharmacy in the case of a retail drug business or wholesale druggist and the commissioner in all other cases may promulgate rules and regulations relative to registration and control of the manufacture, distribution, dispensing and possession of controlled substances within the commonwealth.

Added by St.1971, c. 1071, § 1.

§ 7. Registration of persons who manufacture, distribute, dispense or possess controlled substances

(a) Except in the case of a pharmacy or wholesale druggist, every person who manufactures, distributes or dispenses, or possesses with intent to manufacture, distribute or dispense any controlled substance within the commonwealth shall upon payment of a fee, the amount of which shall be determined annually by the commissioner of administration under the provision of section three B of chapter seven, register with the commissioner of public health, in accordance with his regulations, said registration to be effective for one year from the date of issuance. Every wholesale druggist shall register with the board of registration in pharmacy in accordance with its regulations. Such registration shall be effective until July first, nineteen hundred and seventy-four, if such registration is issued prior to July first, nineteen hundred and seventy-four. Such registration shall be effective until January first, nineteen hundred and seventy-six, if such registration is issued between July first, nineteen hundred and seventy-four, and January first, nineteen hundred and seventy-six. Such registration shall be effective until the end of the calendar year in which said registration is issued if registration is issued subsequent to December thirty-first, nineteen hundred and seventy-five; provided, that such wholesale druggist shall pay a registration fee of twenty-five dollars for any initial registration issued prior to July first, nineteen hundred and seventy-four, and shall pay any registration fee of thirty-seven dollars and fifty cents for a registration which is issued between July first, nineteen hundred and seventy-four, and January first, nineteen hundred and seventy-six. Such wholesale druggist shall, commencing January first, nineteen hundred and seventy-six, pay an annual registration fee, the amount of which shall be determined by the commissioner of administration, for each year or any part thereof. For the purposes of this section, "wholesale druggist" shall mean any person who distributes controlled substances at wholesale. Every pharmacy shall register with the said board in accordance with its regulations. Such registration shall be effective until July first, nineteen hundred and seventy-four, if any registration is issued prior to July first, nineteen hundred and seventy-four. Such registration shall be effective until January first, nineteen hundred and seventy-six, if such registration is issued between July first, nineteen hundred and seventy-four, and January first, nineteen hundred and seventy-six. Such registration shall be effective until the end of the first uneven numbered year following the date of issuance of such registration if such registration is issued subsequent to December thirty-first, nineteen hundred and seventy-five; provided, that such pharmacy shall pay a registration fee of twenty-five dollars for an initial registration issued prior to midnight of July first, nineteen hundred and seventy-four, and shall pay a registration fee of thirty-seven dollars and fifty cents for any registration issued between July first, nineteen hundred and seventy-four, and January first, nineteen hundred and seventy-six, and shall, commencing January first, nineteen hundred and seventy-six, pay a biennial registration fee, the amount of which shall be determined by the commissioner of administration, for every two years, or any part thereof.

(b) Every person who is engaged in the qualitative or quantitative analysis of controlled substances within a scientific laboratory shall, upon payment of a fee, as determined annually by the commissioner of administration under the provision of section three B of chapter seven obtain a registration issued by the commissioner in accordance with his rules, said registration to be effective for one year from date of issuance.

(c) A person registered under this chapter to manufacture, distribute, dispense, or possess controlled substances may possess, manufacture, distribute, or dispense those substances to the extent authorized by his registration and in conformity with the other provisions of this chapter.

(d) The following persons shall not require registration and may lawfully possess and distribute controlled substances:

(1) an agent or employee of any manufacturer, distributor, or dispenser registered under this chapter, if he is acting in the usual course of his business or employment, except that a salesman, detail man or other field representative of a registered manufacturer, wholesaler, jobber or dealer in controlled substances may not possess any controlled substance in schedule I, II, III, IV, or V of section three for the purpose of demonstrating, displaying, selling, or distributing as samples said controlled substances to a practitioner;

(2) a common or contract carrier or warehouseman, or an employee thereof, whose possession of any controlled substance is in the usual course of business or employment;

(3) any public official or law enforcement officer acting in the regular performance of his official duties.

(4) a registered nurse or licensed practical nurse or a licensed dental hygienist under the supervision of a practitioner as defined in section 1 for the purposes of administering local anesthesia agents only when acting under the supervision of a practitioner;

(5) a graduate of a school for nurses or practical nurses which has been approved in accordance with the provisions of chapter one hundred and twelve, whenever said person is acting under the supervision of a practitioner and is engaged in professional practice during the period from such person's graduation from said school until the announcement of the results of the first licensing examination for registered nurses or licensed practical nurses, as the case may be, thereafter held in accordance with the provisions of said chapter one hundred and twelve;

(6) any person duly licensed to practice nursing within any other jurisdiction, whenever such person is acting under the supervision of a practitioner and is discharging official duties as an employee of the federal government;

(7) any person covered by clauses (1), (2), (3) and (5) of section eighty B of chapter one hundred and twelve when any such person is acting under the supervision of a practitioner;

(8) any therapist, technician, or medical student when performing under the supervision of a practitioner those services which are defined to be functions of their respective callings;

(9) any person who belongs to a class of persons which is authorized by regulation of the commissioner to provide services for the purpose of diagnosis, care, treatment, or research.

(10) a duly licensed optometrist who utilizes diagnostic pharmaceutical agents, as defined in section sixty-six A of chapter one hundred and twelve, and who qualifies to utilize such agents for the purpose of conducting an examination of the eye as provided in sections sixty-six A and sixty-eight A of chapter one hundred and twelve; provided, however, that a wholesale distributor or pharmacist may dispense such diagnostic pharmaceutical agents to a licensed optometrist for subsequent administration to optometry patients only if such optometrist provides the wholesale distributor or pharmacist with the number of the optometrist's certification of qualification to administer such diagnostic pharmaceutical agents.

(e) An ultimate user or research subject may lawfully possess or administer a controlled substance at the direction of a practitioner in the course of his professional practice.

(f) Notwithstanding any other provision of this section, the commissioner shall, upon receipt of the fee as hereinbefore provided, automatically issue to any physician, dentist, podiatrist or veterinarian who is duly authorized to practice his profession in the commonwealth a registration to dispense, other than for research pursuant to section eight, unless the registration of such physician, dentist, podiatrist, or veterinarian has been suspended or revoked pursuant to the provisions of sections thirteen or fourteen or unless said registration is denied for cause by the commissioner pursuant to the provisions of chapter thirty A. Such registration shall continue in full force and effect unless it is suspended or revoked, or unless it is recalled and a new registration issued in accordance with the rules and regulations of the commissioner.

(g) The commissioner may by regulation authorize the registration for a specific activity or activities requiring registration under this section of such persons as he determines to be qualified for such registration.

The commissioner shall promulgate regulations which provide for the registration of nurse practitioners and for psychiatric nurse mental health clinical specialists, as defined in section eighty B of chapter one hundred and twelve, to issue written prescriptions for patients pursuant to guidelines mutually developed and agreed upon by the nurse and supervising physician under regulations approved by the board of registration in nursing and the board of registration in medicine. Prior to promulgating such regulations, the commissioner shall consult with the board of registration in nursing, the board of registration in medicine and the board of registration in pharmacy with regard to those schedules of controlled substances for which nurse practitioners and psychiatric nurse mental health clinical specialists may be registered.

The commissioner shall promulgate regulations which provide for the registration of certified nurse-midwives, as provided in section eighty C of chapter one hundred and twelve, to issue written prescriptions for patients pursuant to guidelines mutually developed and agreed upon by the certified nurse-midwife and the supervising physician in accordance with regulations approved by the board of registration in medicine and the board of registration in nursing. Prior to promulgating such regulations, the commissioner shall consult with the board of registration in nursing, the board of registration in medicine and the board of registration in pharmacy with regard to those schedules of controlled substances for which certified nurse-midwives may be registered.

The commissioner shall promulgate regulations which provide for the registration of physicians assistants to issue written prescriptions for patients pursuant to guidelines mutually developed and agreed upon by the supervising physician and the physician assistant. Prior to promulgating such regulations, the commissioner shall consult with the board of registration of physician assistants, the board of registration in medicine and the board of registration in pharmacy with regard to those schedules of controlled substances for which physician assistants may be registered to issue written prescriptions therefor; provided, however, that a physician assistant who has not successfully passed the national certification examination for physician assistants or who does not meet all of the current requirements for obtaining an initial physician assistant's registration as listed in section nine *I* of chapter one hundred and twelve may not be authorized to write prescriptions under any circumstances.

The commissioner shall issue regulations authorizing pharmacists, who have been duly registered in accordance with section 24½ of chapter 112, to engage in collaborative drug therapy management and to issue written prescriptions in accordance with the provisions of said section 24½ of said chapter 112 and guidelines mutually developed and agreed upon by the supervising physician and the pharmacist in a collaborative practice agreement, as defined in section 24½ of said chapter 112, established in accordance with regulations of the board of registration in medicine and board of registration in pharmacy. Prior to issuing such regulations, the commissioner shall consult with the board of registration in medicine and the board of registration in pharmacy with regard to the schedules of controlled substances for which a pharmacist may be authorized to prescribe within the scope of his collaborative practice.

The commissioner may gather patient outcome and cost-savings data if available from objective sources and review community retail drug business-based collaborative drug therapy management. If the commissioner finds that sufficient data and funding sources exist to conduct a valid study, he shall conduct a study within 2 years after that finding. The study shall include representatives of the board of registration in medicine and the board of registration in pharmacy. In conducting the study, the commissioner shall hold at least 1 public hearing to receive testimony from the public, including representatives of pharmacy and medicine and other concerned parties.

The commissioner shall promulgate regulations which provide for the registration of nurse anesthetists in an advanced practice nursing role, as defined in section 80B of chapter 112, to issue written prescriptions for patients under section 80H of chapter 112 and under guidelines mutually-developed and agreed upon by the nurse and supervising physician in accordance with said section 80H and regulations approved by the board of registration in nursing and the board of registration in medicine. Prior to promulgating the regulations, the commissioner shall consult with the board of registration in nursing, board of registration in medicine and the board of registration in pharmacy with regard to those schedules of controlled substances for which nurse anesthetists may be registered.

(h) The commissioner shall promulgate regulations which provide for the automatic registration of optometrists, upon the receipt of the fee as herein provided, to issue written prescriptions in accordance with the provisions of sections 66 and 66B of chapter 112, unless the registration of such optometrist has been suspended or revoked pursuant to the provisions of section 13 or section 14 or unless such registration is denied for cause by the commissioner pursuant to the provisions of chapter 30A. Prior to promulgating such regulations, the commissioner shall consult with the board of registration in optometry.

Added by St.1971, c. 1071, § 1. Amended by St.1972, c. 684, §§ 13 to 15; St.1973, c. 1190, §§ 7 to 9; St.1973, c. 1220; St.1974, c. 770; St.1980, c. 572, §§ 81, 82; St.1983, c. 565, § 3; St.1984, c. 403, § 1; St.1985, c. 654, § 2; St.1990, c. 515, § 1; St.1991, c. 445, § 1; St.1992, c. 10, §§ 1, 2; St.1997, c. 55, § 2; St.2004, c. 368, § 1, eff. Jan. 5, 2005; St.2008, c. 528, § 1, eff. April 15, 2009; St.2010, c. 191, § 2, eff. Oct. 27, 2010.

§ 8. Research projects and studies

(a) No person shall carry out any research project or study involving any narcotic drug in Schedule II or the investigational use on human beings of any new drug as defined in section two hundred and one (p) of the Federal Food, Drug and Cosmetic Act, as amended,[1] unless he supplies the commissioner with satisfactory evidence of compliance with any applicable federal law, and, if the commissioner so requires, with a protocol describing the research project or study to be undertaken.

(b) The commissioner shall pursuant to the provisions of chapter thirty A promulgate rules and regulations establishing standards for such protocol and requiring, among such other conditions relating to the protection of the public health that the commissioner may prescribe, the establishment and maintenance of records and the making of reports to the commissioner of data, including but not limited to analytical reports by investigators, obtained as the result of the investigational use of the drug. The commissioner may waive any or all such conditions with respect to a particular research project or study described in this section if he deems it consistent with the public interest.

(c) The commissioner shall, after due notice and opportunity for hearing pursuant to the provisions of chapter thirty A, issue an order that such research project or study be terminated if the commissioner finds (1) that the drug under investigation is unsafe under the conditions of use; or (2) that the investigators lack the necessary training and experience to conduct such research project or study; or (3) that the research protocol contains any untrue statement of a material fact, provided, that if the commissioner finds that there is an imminent hazard to health he shall order that the research project or study be discontinued upon notice and afford those persons who are undertaking the research the opportunity for an expedited hearing. The commissioner may also, after due notice and opportunity for a hearing pursuant to the provisions of chapter thirty A order that a research project or study be discontinued if the commissioner finds (1) that the persons who are undertaking the research have failed to establish a system for maintaining required records, or have repeatedly or deliberately failed to maintain such records or to make reports which are required by the commissioner or the persons undertaking the research project or study have refused to permit access to or copying or verification of such records; or (2) the methods used in, or the facilities and controls used for the research project or study are inadequate to safeguard against unlawful diversion of the drug under investigation.

(d) Every person who is required pursuant to the provisions of this section to maintain records, and every person in charge or custody thereof, shall, upon request of an officer or employee designated by the commissioner permit such officer or employee at all reasonable times to have access to and copy and verify such records.

(e) No person who undertakes research pursuant to the provisions of this section shall use as a subject for such research any human being unless such subject or his legal representative has given in writing his informed consent based upon information about the nature, duration and purpose of the investigation; the method and means by which it is to be conducted; all inconveniences and hazards reasonably to be expected; and the effects upon the subject's health or person which may reasonably be expected to come from his participation.

(f) A person who is conducting research pursuant to the provisions of this section may to the extent authorized by the commissioner and in conformity with the provisions of this section dispense any drug for investigational use without an oral or written prescription.

(g) Notwithstanding any other provision of this section, the administering or dispensing directly or prescribing of narcotic drugs listed in any schedule to a narcotic drug dependent person for the purpose of continuing his dependence upon such drugs in the course of conducting an authorized clinical investigation pursuant to a narcotic addict rehabilitation program shall be deemed to be within the meaning of the term "in the course of professional practice" as used in this chapter, provided, that federal approval, if such approval is required by federal law, is obtained prior to the initiation of such a program, and satisfactory evidence of such approval is submitted to the commissioner.

(h) Notwithstanding the provisions of paragraphs (a) to (g), inclusive, this section shall not apply to any drug recognized as safe and which has been exempted by section one hundred and seven of the Federal Drug Amendments Act of 1962[2] from the operation of sections two hundred and one (p) and five hundred and five of the Federal Food, Drug and Cosmetic Act, as amended.[3]

(i) Whoever knowingly or intentionally violates any provision of this section shall be punished for each offense by imprisonment in a jail or house of correction for not more than one year or by a fine of not more than one thousand dollars, or both.

Added by St.1971, c. 1071, § 1. Amended by St.1972, c. 806, §§ 10, 11; St.1974, c. 359; St.1989, c. 468.

1 21 U.S.C.A. § 321.

2 21 U.S.C.A. § 321 note.

3 21 U.S.C.A. §§ 321, 355.

§ 9. Administering and dispensing of controlled substances in course of professional practice; records, inspection

(a) A physician, dentist, podiatrist, optometrist as limited by sections 66 and 66B of chapter 112 and subsection (h) of section 7, nurse practitioner and psychiatric nurse mental health clinical specialist as limited by subsection (g) of said section 7 and section 80E of said chapter 112, physician assistant as limited by said subsection (g) of said section 7 and section 9E of said chapter 112, certified nurse midwife as provided in section 80C of said chapter 112, nurse anesthetist, as limited by subsection (g) of said section 7 and section 80H of said chapter 112, pharmacist as limited by said subsection (g) of said section 7 and section 24B½ of said chapter 112, or veterinarian when registered under said section 7, may, when acting in accordance with applicable federal law and any provision of this chapter which is consistent with federal law and in good faith and in the course of a professional practice for the alleviation of pain and suffering or for the treatment or alleviation of disease, possess controlled substances as may reasonably be required for the purpose of patient treatment and may administer controlled substances or may cause the same to be administered under his direction by a nurse.

A practitioner may cause controlled substances to be administered under his direction by a licensed dental hygienist for the purposes of local anesthesia only.

(b) Notwithstanding section 17, a physician, physician assistant, dentist, podiatrist, optometrist, certified nurse midwife, nurse practitioner, psychiatric nurse mental health clinical specialist, nurse anesthetist, pharmacist as limited by said subsection (g) of said section 7 and section 24B½ of said chapter 112, or veterinarian registered under said section 7, may, when acting in good faith and in the practice of medicine, dentistry, podiatry, optometry, nurse-midwifery, pharmacy or veterinary medicine or as a nurse, as the case may be, and when authorized by a physician, dentist, podiatrist, optometrist, nurse practitioner, physician assistant, certified nurse midwife, psychiatric nurse mental health clinical specialist, nurse anesthetist, or veterinarian in the course of such nurse's professional practice, dispense by delivering to an ultimate user a controlled substance in a single dose or in a quantity that is, in the opinion of such physician, dentist, podiatrist, optometrist, nurse practitioner, physician assistant, certified midwife, psychiatric nurse mental health clinical specialist, nurse anesthetist, pharmacist or veterinarian, essential for the treatment of a patient. The amount or quantity of any controlled substance dispensed under this subsection shall not exceed the quantity of a controlled substance necessary for the immediate and proper treatment of the patient until it is possible for the patient to have a prescription filled by a pharmacy. All controlled substances required by the patient as part of the patient's treatment shall be dispensed by prescription to the ultimate user in accordance with this chapter.

This section shall not prohibit or limit the dispensing of a prescription medication that is classified by the department as schedule VI and that is provided by the manufacturer as part of an indigent patient program or for use as samples if the prescription medication is: (i) dispensed to the patient by a professional authorized to dispense controlled substances pursuant to this section; (ii) dispensed in the package provided by the manufacturer; and (iii) provided at no charge to the patient. The department shall promulgate rules and regulations governing the dispensing of medication pursuant to this section. These rules and regulations shall include, but not be limited to, the types and amounts of medications that may be dispensed and the appropriate safeguards for the labeling and dispensing of such medications.

This section shall not be construed to prohibit a physician or an optometrist from the in-office dispensing and sale of therapeutic contact lenses as long as the medication contained in such lenses is within the profession's designated scope of practice.

For the purposes of this section, "therapeutic contact lenses" shall mean contact lenses which contain 1 or more medications and which deliver such medication to the eye.

(c) A nurse who has obtained from a physician, dentist, physician assistant, podiatrist, certified nurse midwife, nurse practitioner, psychiatric nurse mental health clinical specialist, nurse anesthetist, pharmacist or veterinarian a controlled substance for dispensing to an ultimate user pursuant to subsection (b) or for administration to a patient pursuant to subsection (a) during the absence of the physician, physician assistant, dentist, podiatrist, certified nurse midwife, nurse practitioner, psychiatric nurse mental health clinical specialist, nurse anesthetist, pharmacist or veterinarian, shall return to the physician, physician assistant, dentist, podiatrist, certified nurse midwife, nurse practitioner, psychiatric nurse mental health clinical specialist, nurse anesthetist, pharmacist or veterinarian any unused portion of the controlled substance which is no longer required by the patient.

A licensed dental hygienist who has obtained a controlled substance from a practitioner for dispensing to an ultimate user pursuant to subsection (a) shall return to such practitioner any unused portion of the substance which is no longer required by the patient.

(d) Every physician, physician assistant, dentist, podiatrist, certified nurse midwife, nurse practitioner, psychiatric nurse mental health clinical specialist, nurse anesthetist, pharmacist or veterinarian shall, in the course of a professional practice, keep and maintain records, open to inspection by the commissioner during reasonable business hours, which shall include the following: the names and quantities of any controlled substances in schedules I, II or III received by the practitioner; the name and address of each patient to whom such controlled substance is administered or dispensed; the name, dosage and strength per dosage unit of each such controlled substance; and the date of such administration or dispensing.

(e) Notwithstanding subsection (b), a physician, nurse practitioner, physician assistant, pharmacist as limited by subsection (g) of section 7 and section 24B½ of said chapter 112 or certified nurse midwife, when acting in good faith and providing care under a program funded in whole or in part by 42 U.S.C. section 300, or in a clinic licensed by the department to provide comparable medical services or a registered nurse, registered under section 74 of said chapter 112 and authorized by such physician, nurse practitioner, physician assistant, pharmacist as limited by said subsection (g) of said section 7 and section 24B½ of said chapter 112, certified nurse midwife may lawfully dispense controlled substances pursuant to schedule VI to recipients of such services in such quantity as needed for treatment and shall be exempt from the requirement that such dispensing be in a single dose or as necessary for immediate and proper treatment under subsection (b). A registered nurse shall dispense under this subsection only as provided in section 17. The department may establish rules and regulations controlling the dispensing of these medications, including, but not limited to, the types and amounts of medications dispensed and appropriate safeguards for dispensing.

Added by St.1971, c. 1071, § 1. Amended by St.1973, c. 1190, §§ 10 to 13; St.1983, c. 565, § 4; St.1985, c. 364; St.1986, c. 82, §§ 1, 2; St.1990, c. 515, § 2; St.1991, c. 445, § 2; St.1991, c. 545; St.1992, c. 10, §§ 3 to 7; St.1993, c. 47, § 1; St.1997, c. 55, § 3; St.2004, c. 368, §§ 2, 3, eff. Jan. 5, 2005; St.2008, c. 528, § 2, eff. April 15, 2009; St.2010, c. 191, § 3, eff. Oct. 27, 2010; St.2010, c. 288, § 6, eff. Aug. 10, 2010.

§ 10. Separate registration

A separate registration shall be required at each principal place of business or professional practice where the registrant manufactures, distributes, or dispenses controlled substances.

Added by St.1971, c. 1071, § 1. Amended by St.1973, c. 1190, § 14.

§ 11. Inspection of establishments of registrants or applicants

The board of registration in pharmacy in the case of a pharmacy and the commissioner in any case may inspect in accordance with his or its rules and regulations the establishment of a registrant or applicant for registration pursuant to the provisions of this chapter.

Added by St.1971, c. 1071, § 1.

§ 12. Issuance of registration to manufacture or distribute controlled substances

(a) The board of registration in pharmacy in the case of a retail drug business or wholesale druggist and the commissioner in all other cases shall register an applicant to manufacture or distribute controlled substances included in the schedules established pursuant to section two unless he determines that the issuance of that registration would be inconsistent with the public interest. In determining the public interest, the board of registration in pharmacy in the case of a retail drug store or a wholesale druggist and the commissioner in all other cases shall consider the following factors:

(1) maintenance of effective controls against diversion of controlled substances into other than legitimate medical, scientific, or industrial channels;

(2) compliance with applicable federal, state and local law;

(3) any conviction of the applicant under any federal and state law relating to any controlled substance;

(4) past experience in the manufacture or distribution of controlled substances, and the existence in the applicant's establishment of effective controls against diversion;

(5) furnishing by the applicant of false or fraudulent material in any application filed under the provisions of this chapter;

(6) suspension or revocation of the applicant's federal registration to manufacture, distribute or dispense controlled substances as authorized by federal law; and

(7) any other factors relevant to and consistent with the public health and safety.

(b) Registration under subsection (a) of this section shall not entitle a registrant to manufacture or distribute controlled substances in Schedules I or II established pursuant to the provisions of section two except to the extent specified in the registration.

Added by St.1971, c. 1071, § 1.

§ 13. Suspension or revocation of registration; report of criminal violations; controlled substances affected placed under embargo; forfeiture; notice to bureau

(a) The board of registration in pharmacy in the case of a retail drug business or wholesale druggist and the commissioner in all other cases may suspend or revoke a registration to manufacture, distribute, dispense or possess a controlled substance, after a hearing pursuant to the provisions of chapter thirty A upon a finding that the registrant:

(1) has furnished false or fraudulent material information in any application filed under the provisions of this chapter;

(2) has been convicted under any state or federal law of any criminal violation relating to his fitness to be registered under this chapter;

(3) has had his federal registration suspended or revoked to manufacture, distribute, dispense, administer or possess controlled substances; or

(4) is, upon good cause, found to be unfit or unqualified to manufacture, distribute, dispense, or possess any controlled substance.

(b) The board of registration in pharmacy in the case of a retail drug business or wholesale druggist and the commissioner in all other cases may pursuant to the provisions of this section or section fourteen suspend or revoke any registration issued by him or it for violation of any provision of this chapter.

(c) Whenever the commissioner, the board of registration in pharmacy, or the commissioner of mental health has substantial reason to believe that a registrant has committed a criminal violation of any provision of this chapter, he or it shall promptly report all pertinent facts to the district attorney in the county where the violation is believed to have occurred, or to the attorney general.

(d) The board of registration in pharmacy in the case of a retail drug business or wholesale druggist and the commissioner in all other cases may limit revocation or suspension of a registration to the particular controlled substance with respect to which grounds for revocation or suspension exists.

(e) If the board of registration in pharmacy in the case of a retail drug business or wholesale druggist or the commissioner in all other cases suspends or revokes a registration, all controlled substances which are affected by such suspension or revocation order at the time of suspension or the effective date of the revocation order shall be placed under embargo pursuant to the procedures prescribed in sections one hundred and eighty-nine and one hundred and eighty-nine A of chapter ninety-four. No disposition may be made of substances under such embargo until the time for taking an appeal has elapsed or until all appeals have been concluded unless a court, upon application therefor, orders the sale of perishable substances and the deposit of the proceeds of the sale with the court. Upon a revocation order becoming final, all controlled substances may be forfeited to the commonwealth under the provisions of section forty-seven.

(f) The board of registration in pharmacy in the case of a retail drug business or wholesale druggist and the commissioner in all other cases shall promptly notify the bureau of all orders suspending or revoking a registration and all forfeitures of controlled substances.

Added by St.1971, c. 1071, § 1. Amended by St.1972, c. 806, §§ 12, 13.

§ 14. Suspension of or refusal to renew registration pending proceedings in cases of imminent danger to public

The board of registration in pharmacy in the case of a retail drug business or wholesale druggist or the commissioner in all other cases may without hearing suspend or refuse to renew any registration if he finds that there is an imminent danger to the public health or safety which warrants this action, provided he promptly affords the registrant an opportunity for a hearing under chapter thirty A. The suspension shall continue in effect until the conclusion of the proceedings including judicial review thereof, unless sooner dissolved by a court of competent jurisdiction, or withdrawn by the board of registration in pharmacy in the case of a retail drug business or wholesale druggist, or withdrawn by the commissioner in any other case.

Added by St.1971, c. 1071, § 1.

§ 15. Record-keeping and inventory requirements

Persons registered to manufacture, distribute, dispense, or possess controlled substances shall keep records and maintain inventories in conformance with the record-keeping and inventory requirements of the Federal "Comprehensive Drug Prevention and Control Act of 1970" or any amendment thereof,[1] and the Federal Food, Drug and Cosmetic Act,[2] and with any additional rules or regulations promulgated by the board of registration in pharmacy in the case of a retail drug business or wholesale druggist or by the commissioner in all other cases.

Added by St.1971, c. 1071, § 1.

1 21 U.S.C.A. § 827.

2 21 U.S.C.A. § 301 et seq.

§ 16. Distribution between registrants; order form

Controlled substances in Schedules I and II shall be distributed by a registrant to another registrant only pursuant to such order form as may be required by the Federal "Comprehensive Drug Abuse Prevention and Control Act of 1970" or any amendment thereof[1] and the Federal Food, Drug, and Cosmetic Act.[2]

Added by St.1971, c. 1071, § 1.

[1] 21 U.S.C.A. § 828.
[2] 21 U.S.C.A. § 301 et seq.

§ 17. Necessity of prescription for dispensing controlled substances

(a) No controlled substance in Schedule II may be dispensed without the written prescription of a practitioner, except that—

(b) In emergency situations, as defined by rule or regulation of the commissioner acting jointly with the board of registration in pharmacy, drugs in said Schedule II may be dispensed upon oral prescription of a practitioner, reduced promptly to writing and filed by the pharmacy, pursuant to the provisions of subsection (a) of section twenty.

(c) A controlled substance included in Schedule III, IV, V or VI shall not be dispensed without a written or oral prescription of a practitioner.

Added by St.1971, c. 1071, § 1.

§ 18. Issuance of prescription by practitioner or physician

(a) A prescription for a controlled substance may be issued only by a practitioner who is:

(1) authorized to prescribe controlled substances; and

(2) registered pursuant to the provisions of this chapter.

(b) An oral prescription issued by a practitioner may be communicated to a pharmacist by an expressly authorized employee or agent of the practitioner.

(c) A prescription for a controlled substance contained in schedules III to VI, inclusive, as defined in section three may also be issued by an authorized practitioner who is duly licensed to practice medicine and duly registered in the state wherein he resides, if required, and duly registered under federal law to write prescriptions. It is the duty of the registered pharmacist who is filling a prescription under this paragraph to determine, in accordance with professional standards and personal judgment, that such prescription is authentic and valid; provided, however, that if the substance is in schedules III to V, inclusive, the registered pharmacist shall verify the prescription by telephone or other means. A pharmacist shall not fill a prescription for which said verification cannot be obtained. The pharmacist shall not be held liable for refusing to fill a prescription for which said verification cannot be obtained, provided that documented good faith efforts were made to determine the authenticity and validity of the prescription. This paragraph shall be valid only for the purpose of authorizing the filling of prescriptions, issued within the preceding thirty days, and shall not authorize said physician to process, administer or dispense controlled substances as provided in section nine or to practice medicine within the commonwealth. In the case of any oral prescription for a schedule III through V substance, the pharmacist shall record that he has requested that the practitioner deliver or mail to the dispensing pharmacy a written prescription for the controlled substance within seven days or such shorter period required by Federal law. Any prescription issued under this paragraph shall be issued in the manner prescribed in section twenty-two and all relevant provisions of this chapter shall apply to such physician and prescription. Nothing contained in this section shall be deemed to authorize any mail order pharmacies.

(d) A prescription for a controlled substance contained in Schedule II of section three may also be issued by a physician who is licensed to practice medicine and registered in another state where he resides or practices, if required, and registered under federal law to write prescriptions. A registered pharmacist filling a prescription under the provisions of this paragraph shall determine, in accordance with professional standards and personal judgment, that such prescription is authentic and valid; and shall verify such prescription by telephone or other means. A pharmacist shall not fill a prescription for which said verification cannot be obtained. A pharmacist shall not be held liable for refusing to fill such prescription for which said verification cannot be obtained; provided, however, that documented good faith efforts were made to determine the authenticity and validity of such prescription. This paragraph is only for the purpose of authorizing the filling of prescriptions within the commonwealth, issued within the preceding five days, and shall not authorize such practitioner to possess, administer or dispense controlled substances as provided in section nine, or to practice medicine within the commonwealth. Any prescription issued under the provisions of this paragraph shall be issued in the manner prescribed in section twenty-two and all relevant provisions of this chapter shall apply to such practitioner and prescription. In the case of any prescription for a Schedule II substance filled under the provisions of this paragraph, a pharmacist filling such prescription shall within thirty days after the filling of such prescription deliver to the department a copy of each such Schedule II prescription; provided, however, that such copy shall not include the name and address of the patient for whom the prescription is issued and that such copy and the information contained thereon shall not be deemed to be public record within the meaning of section seven of chapter four and shall be subject to the restrictions set forth in section two of chapter sixty-six A. Nothing contained in this section shall be deemed to authorize any mail order pharmacies.

(e) Practitioners who prescribe controlled substances, except veterinarians, shall be required, as a prerequisite to obtaining or renewing their professional license, to complete appropriate training relative to: (i) effective pain management; (ii) identification of patients at high risk for substance abuse; and (iii) counseling patients about the side effects, addictive nature and proper storage and disposal of prescription medications. The boards of registration for each professional license that requires such training shall develop the standards for appropriate training programs.

Added by St.1971, c. 1071, § 1. Amended by St.1972, c. 806, § 14; St.1976, c. 498; St.1987, c. 347; St.1989, c. 278; St.1998, c. 104, § 2; St.2010, c. 283, § 2, eff. Nov. 7, 2010.

§ 19. Prescription; restrictions on issuance

(a) A prescription for a controlled substance to be valid shall be issued for a legitimate medical purpose by a practitioner acting in the usual course of his professional practice. The responsibility for the proper prescribing and dispensing of controlled substances shall be upon the prescribing practitioner, but a corresponding responsibility shall rest with the pharmacist who fills the prescription. An order purporting to be a prescription issued not in the usual course of professional treatment or in legitimate and authorized research is not a prescription within the meaning and intent of section one and the person knowingly filling such a purported prescription, as well as the person issuing it, shall be subject to the penalties provided by sections thirty-two, thirty-two A, thirty-two B, thirty-two C, thirty-two D, thirty-two E, thirty-two F, thirty-two G, and thirty-two H, as applicable.

(b) No prescription shall be issued in order for a practitioner to obtain controlled substances for supplying the practitioner for the purpose of general dispensing to patients.

(c) Unless permitted by federal law, a prescription shall not be issued for the dispensing of drugs or controlled substances as defined in section thirty-eight of chapter one hundred and twenty-three, listed in any schedule to a drug dependent person for the purpose of continuing his dependence upon such drugs, in the course of conducting an authorized clinical investigation pursuant to an addict rehabilitation program.

Added by St.1971, c. 1071, § 1. Amended by St.1972, c. 806, § 15; St.1982, c. 650, § 1.

§ 19A. Emergency contraception

(a) As used in this section "emergency contraception" shall, unless the context clearly requires otherwise, mean any drug approved by the federal Food and Drug Administration as a contraceptive method for use after sexual intercourse.

(b) Notwithstanding any other law, a licensed pharmacist may dispense emergency contraception in accordance with written, standardized procedures or protocols developed by an actively practicing physician registered with the commissioner to distribute or dispense a controlled substance in the course of professional practice pursuant to section 7 if such procedures or protocols are filed at the pharmacist's place of practice and with the board of registration in pharmacy before implementation.

(c) Before dispensing emergency contraception authorized under this section, a pharmacist shall complete a training program approved by the commissioner on emergency contraception, which training shall include but not be limited to proper documentation, quality assurance, and referral to additional services, including appropriate recommendation that the patient follow-up with a medical practitioner.

(d) A pharmacist dispensing emergency contraception under this section shall annually provide to the department of public health the number of times such emergency contraception is dispensed. Reports made pursuant to this section shall not identify any individual patient, shall be confidential and shall not be public records as defined by clause twenty-sixth of section 7 of chapter 4.

(e) The department of public health, board of registration in medicine, and board of registration in pharmacy shall adopt regulations to implement this section.

Added by St.2005, c. 91, § 2, eff. Dec. 14, 2005.

§ 20. Oral prescriptions

(a) Upon receiving an oral prescription for a controlled substance or instrument described in section twenty-seven from an authorized practitioner, the pharmacist shall immediately reduce the prescription to writing on a prescription form and shall record the name, address and registration number of the practitioner and the name of any expressly authorized representative, the date of the prescription, the name, dosage and strength per dosage unit of the controlled substance, the serial number assigned to the prescription by the dispensing pharmacy, the name of said pharmacy, the name and address of the patient unless it is a veterinary prescription, the directions for use and any cautionary statements required, and a statement indicating the number of times to be refilled.

(b) If the prescribing practitioner is not known to the pharmacist, he shall make a reasonable effort to determine that the oral authorization came from a registered practitioner.

(c) Whenever a practitioner dispenses a controlled substance by oral prescription, such practitioner shall, within a period of not more than seven days or such shorter period that is required by federal law cause a written prescription for the prescribed controlled substance to be delivered to the dispensing pharmacy. The prescription may be delivered to the pharmacy in person or by mail, but if delivered by mail the envelope shall be postmarked within the seven-day period or such shorter period that is required by federal law. Upon receipt, the dispensing pharmacy shall attach said prescription to the oral prescription which the pharmacy has reduced to writing. Persons charged with the enforcement of this chapter shall report violations of this subsection to the board of registration in medicine, the board of registration in dentistry, the board of registration in podiatry or the board of registration in veterinary medicine, whichever is applicable, and to the commissioner or board of registration in pharmacy, whichever is applicable. The requirements of this subsection shall not apply to controlled substances in Schedule VI of section 3.

Added by St.1971, c. 1071, § 1. Amended by St.1993, c. 224, § 1; St.1998, c. 104, § 3.

§ 20A. Radiopharmaceutical drugs

Notwithstanding any other provisions of this chapter, a prescription for a radiopharmaceutical drug shall be dispensed only to an individual authorized by the nuclear regulatory commission to possess and administer such drug.

Upon receiving an oral prescription for a radiopharmaceutical drug from an authorized practitioner, the nuclear pharmacist shall immediately reduce the prescription to writing and shall record the name, address and registration number of the practitioner and the name of any expressly authorized representative, the date of the prescription, the name and the dose of the radiopharmaceutical drug, the serial number assigned to the prescription by the dispensing nuclear pharmacy, the name of said nuclear pharmacy, the name and address of the patient and any specific instructions required. If the radiopharmaceutical drug is not administered, it shall be returned to the nuclear pharmacy to be disposed of in accordance with requirements established by the nuclear regulatory commission and any applicable law and the nuclear pharmacist shall note on the prescription form the amount of the radiopharmaceutical drug that has been returned and disposed of as required.

Added by St.1986, c. 97, § 3.

§ 21. Packaging and labeling by pharmacist filling prescription

The pharmacist filling a written or oral prescription for a controlled substance shall package the controlled substance in a container, affixing to the container a label showing the date of filling, the pharmacy name and address, the filling pharmacist's initials, the serial number of the prescription, the name of the patient, unless it is a veterinary prescription, the name of the prescribing practitioner, the name of the controlled substance, directions for use and cautionary statements, if any, contained in such prescription or required by law, and if the controlled substance is dispensed as tablets or capsules the number of same in such container.

Upon the request of an elderly person, as defined in section fourteen of chapter nineteen A or a person visually impaired, directions on the label affixed by the pharmacist to a container of a prescription drug shall be typed in a print size allowing no more than ten characters per inch.

Added by St.1971, c. 1071, § 1. Amended by St.1976, c. 110; St.1983, c. 282, § 1; St.1988, c. 277.

§ 21A. Prescriptions; prospective drug review and counseling by pharmacist

A pharmacist shall conduct a prospective drug review before each new prescription is dispensed or delivered to a patient or a person acting on behalf of such patient. Such review may include, but not be limited to, screening for potential drug therapy problems due to therapeutic duplication, drug disease contraindication, drug interactions, including serious interactions with nonprescription or over-the-counter drugs, incorrect drug dosage, duration of drug treatment, drug allergy interactions and clinical abuse or misuse.

A pharmacist shall offer to counsel any person who presents a new prescription for filling. Such offer shall be made either by face to face communication between the pharmacist or the pharmacist's designee and the patient, or by telephone, except when the patient's needs or availability require an alternative method of counseling.

If a person elects delivery of a prescription drug at a location other than a pharmacy, the requirements of this section may be satisfied by providing such person with access to a toll-free telephone service to facilitate communication between such person and the pharmacist at such pharmacy. The number of such toll-free telephone service shall be printed on a label affixed to each container of a prescription drug dispensed by a pharmacy to a patient.

For the purposes of medical assistance and other third party reimbursements or payment programs, any of the above methods, or a combination thereof, shall constitute an acceptable offer to provide counseling.

If an offer to provide counseling is accepted, the pharmacist shall counsel the person presenting the prescription to the extent the pharmacist deems appropriate. Such counseling may include, but not be limited to, the following:

(1) the name and description of the medication;

(2) the dosage form, dosage, route of administration and duration of drug therapy;

(3) special instructions and precautions for preparation, administration and use by the patient;

(4) common adverse or severe side effects or interactions and therapeutic contraindications that may be encountered, including their avoidance and the action required if they occur;

(5) techniques for self-monitoring drug therapy;

(6) proper storage;

(7) prescription refill information; and

(8) action to be taken in the event of a missed dose.

Nothing in this section shall be construed to require a pharmacist to provide counseling if the person presenting the prescription declines to accept such offer for counseling.

The pharmacist or his designee shall make reasonable efforts to obtain, record and maintain the following patient information generated at an individual pharmacy:

(1) the name, address, telephone number, date of birth or age, and gender;

(2) individual history where significant, including known allergies and drug reactions, and a comprehensive list of medications and relevant devices; and

(3) any additional comments relevant to the patient's drug use, including any failure to accept the pharmacist's offer to counsel.

Such information may be recorded in the patient's manual or electronic profile or in the prescription signature log, or in any other system of records and may be considered by the pharmacist in the exercise of his professional judgement concerning both the offer to counsel and the content of counseling. The absence of any record of a failure to accept the pharmacist's offer to counsel shall create a presumption that such counseling was provided.

The provisions of this section shall not apply to any drug dispensed to an inpatient at a hospital or nursing home, except to the extent required by regulations promulgated by the Federal Health Care Financing Administration pursuant to the provisions of 42 USC 1396r-8.

Added by St.1992, c. 176, § 1.

§ 22. Contents of prescription written by practitioner

(a) A practitioner who dispenses a controlled substance by issuing a written prescription shall state on the prescription the name, address and registration number of the practitioner, the date of delivery of the prescription, the name, dosage and strength per dosage unit of the controlled substance, the name and address of the patient unless it is a veterinary prescription, the directions for use and any cautionary statements required, and a statement indicating the number of times to be refilled.

(b) A practitioner who dispenses by delivering to an ultimate user a controlled substance which is not for immediate administration shall package the controlled substance in a container, affixing to the container a label bearing the practitioner's name and address, the date of dispensing, the name of the patient unless it is a veterinary prescription, the name, dosage and strength per dosage unit, of the controlled substance, directions for use and any necessary cautionary statements.

Added by St.1971, c. 1071, § 1. Amended by St.1972, c. 806, § 16.

§ 23. Written prescriptions; requirements and restrictions

(a) A written prescription for a controlled substance in Schedule II shall become invalid 30 days after the date of issuance.

(b) A written prescription for a controlled substance in Schedule II shall not be refilled and shall be kept in a separate file.

(c) The pharmacist filling a written prescription for a controlled substance in Schedule II shall endorse his own signature on the face thereof.

(d) In regard to a controlled substance in Schedule II or III, no prescription shall be filled for more than a thirty-day supply of such substance upon any single filling; provided, however, that with regard to dextro amphetamine sulphate and methyl phenidate hydrochloride, a prescription may be filled for up to a sixty-day supply of such substance upon any single filling if said substance is being used for the treatment of minimal brain dysfunction or narcolepsy; provided further, that subject to regulations of the department and the board of pharmacy, prescriptions for implantable infusion pumps consisting of Schedule II or Schedule III controlled substances may be filled for a maximum of 90 days.

(e) All prescriptions for controlled substances shall be kept for two years by the pharmacy and shall be subject to inspection pursuant to the provisions of this chapter.

(f) No prescription for a controlled substance shall be refilled unless the original prescription provides for such refilling and unless the number of refills has been specified in said prescription.

(g) Unless otherwise prohibited by law, a prescription shall be: (1) written in ink, indelible pencil or by other means; or (2) transmitted electronically; and (3) signed by the prescriber. A prescription may be transmitted electronically with the electronic signature and electronic instructions of the prescriber, and shall be transmitted directly from the prescriber to the pharmacy designated by the patient without alteration of the prescription information, except that third-party intermediaries may act as conduits to route the prescription from the prescriber to the pharmacy.

(h) Clinic pharmacies operated by a health maintenance organization licensed under chapter one hundred and seventy-six G and licensed pursuant to section fifty-one of chapter one hundred and eleven may refill prescriptions which have been previously dispensed by another health maintenance organization clinic pharmacy, provided that prior to dispensing a refill, the pharmacy refilling the prescription verifies the appropriateness of the refill through a centralized database.

Added by St.1971, c. 1071, § 1. Amended by St.1972, c. 806, § 17; St.1974, c. 264; St.1992, c. 133, § 454; St.1996, c. 450, §§ 143, 144; St.1998, c. 104, §§ 4 to 6; St.2003, c. 133, § 2, eff. Feb. 24, 2004.

§ 24. Dispensing by practitioner for narcotic drug research or treatment of drug dependent persons

(a) If the commissioner determines that a research subject or patient is receiving a controlled substance from more than one source and in quantities which he determines to be harmful to the health of such research subject or patient, said commissioner shall so notify the practitioners who have dispensed the controlled substance.

(b) In order to prevent the dispensing of controlled substances to the same individual from multiple sources or the unlawful diversion of controlled substances, the commissioner shall, pursuant to the provisions of chapter 30A, adopt rules and regulations for carrying out the provisions of this section.

Added by St.1971, c. 1071, § 1. Amended by St.1972, c. 806, §§ 18, 19; St.1973, c. 469; St.1986, c. 434, § 1; St.1998, c. 104, § 7.

§ 24A. Electronic monitoring of the prescribing and dispensing of controlled substances and certain additional drugs

(a)(1) The department shall establish and maintain an electronic system to monitor the prescribing and dispensing of all schedule II to V, inclusive, controlled substances and certain additional drugs by all professionals licensed to prescribe or dispense such substances. For the purposes of this section, "additional drugs" shall mean substances determined by the department to carry a bona fide potential for abuse.

(2) The department shall enter into reciprocal agreements with other states that have compatible prescription drug monitoring programs to share prescription drug monitoring information among the states.

(b) The requirements of this section shall not apply to the dispensing of controlled substances to inpatients in a hospital.

(c) For the purposes of monitoring the prescribing and dispensing of all schedule II to V, inclusive, controlled substances and additional drugs, as authorized in subsection (a), the department shall promulgate regulations including, but not limited to, (1) a requirement that each pharmacy that delivers a schedule II to V, inclusive, controlled substance or a substance classified as an additional drug by the department to the ultimate user shall submit to the department, by electronic means, information regarding each prescription dispensed for a drug included under subsection (a); and (2) a requirement that each pharmacy collects and reports, for each prescription dispensed for a drug under subsection (a), a customer identification number and other information associated with the customer identification number, as specified by the department. Each pharmacy shall submit the information in accordance with transmission methods and frequency requirements promulgated by the department; provided, however, that the information shall be submitted at least once every 7 days. The department may issue a waiver to a pharmacy that is unable to submit prescription information by electronic means. The waiver shall permit the pharmacy to submit prescription information by other means promulgated by the department; provided, however, that all information required in this section is submitted in this alternative format.

(d) Prescription information submitted to the department under this section shall be confidential and exempt from disclosure under clause Twenty-sixth of section 7 of chapter 4 and chapter 66. The department shall maintain procedures to ensure that the privacy and confidentiality of patients and patient information collected, recorded, transmitted and maintained is not disclosed to persons except as provided for in this chapter.

(e) The department shall review the prescription and dispensing monitoring information. If there is reasonable cause to believe a violation of law or breach of professional standards may have occurred, the department shall notify the appropriate law enforcement or professional licensing, certification or regulatory agency or entity and provide prescription information required for an investigation.

(f) The department shall, upon request, provide data from the prescription monitoring program to the following:—

(1) persons authorized to prescribe or dispense controlled substances, for the purpose of providing medical or pharmaceutical care for their patients;

(2) individuals who request their own prescription monitoring information in accordance with procedures established under chapter 66A;

(3) persons authorized to act on behalf of state boards and regulatory agencies that supervise or regulate a profession that may prescribe controlled substances; provided, however, that the data request is in connection with a bona fide specific controlled substance or additional drug-related investigation;

(4) local, state and federal law enforcement or prosecutorial officials working with the executive office of public safety engaged in the administration, investigation or enforcement of the laws governing prescription drugs; provided, however, that the data request is in connection with a bona fide specific controlled substance or additional drug-related investigation;

(5) personnel of the executive office of health and human services regarding Medicaid program recipients;

provided, however that the data request is in connection with a bona fide specific controlled substance or additional drug-related investigation; or

(6) personnel of the United States attorney, office of the attorney general or a district attorney; provided, however, that the data request is in connection with a bona fide specific controlled substance or additional drug related investigation.

(g) The department may, at its initiative, provide data from the prescription monitoring program to practitioners in accordance with section 24.

(h) The department may provide de-identified, aggregate information to a public or private entity for statistical research or educational purposes.

(i) The department may contract with another agency or with a private vendor, as necessary, to ensure the effective operation of the prescription monitoring program. A contractor shall be bound to comply with the provisions regarding confidentiality of prescription information in this section.

(j) The department shall promulgate rules and regulations setting forth the procedures and methods for implementing this section.

(k) The department shall submit an annual report on the effectiveness of the prescription monitoring program with the clerks of the house and senate, the chairs of the joint committee on public health, the chairs of the joint committee on health care financing and the chairs of the joint committee on public safety and homeland security.

Added by St.2010, c. 283, § 3, eff. Jan. 1, 2011.

§ 25. Restrictions

No person—

(1) who is subject to the requirements of sections six and seven and twelve to seventeen, inclusive, shall dispense a controlled substance in violation of said section seventeen;

(2) shall distribute or dispense a controlled substance not authorized by his registration to another registrant or other authorized person or manufacturer a controlled substance not authorized by his registration;

(3) who is a registrant shall distribute a controlled substance in violation of section sixteen;

(4) shall remove, alter, or obliterate a symbol or label required by federal law and the laws of the commonwealth;

(5) shall refuse or fail to make, keep, or furnish any record, report, notification, declaration, order or order form, statement, invoice, or information required under this chapter;

(6) shall refuse any entry into any premises or inspection authorized by this chapter;

(7) shall remove, break, injure, or deface a seal placed upon controlled substances pursuant to this chapter, or remove or dispose of substances so placed under seal;

(8) shall use, to his own advantage, or reveal, other than to duly authorized officers or employees of the United States or of the commonwealth or to the courts when relevant in any judicial proceeding under this chapter, any information acquired in the course of an inspection authorized by this chapter concerning any method or process which is a trade secret.

No person who is a registrant shall manufacture a controlled substance in Schedule I or II which is not expressly authorized by his registration.

Added by St.1971, c. 1071, § 1.

§ 26. Distribution in course of business in violation of Sec. 16 or furnishing false information in application, etc., prohibited

No person who is a registrant shall knowingly or intentionally;

(1) distribute a controlled substance classified in Schedule I or II in the course of his legitimate business, except pursuant to an order or an order form as required by section sixteen; or

(2) furnish false or fraudulent material information in, or omit any material information from, any application, report, record, or other document required to be made, kept, or filed pursuant to the provisions of this chapter.

Added by St.1971, c. 1071, § 1.

§ 27. Sale of hypodermic syringes or hypodermic needles

Hypodermic syringes or hypodermic needles for the administration of controlled substances by injection may be sold in the commonwealth, but only to persons who have attained the age of 18 years and only by a pharmacist or wholesale druggist licensed under the provisions of chapter 112, a manufacturer of or dealer in surgical supplies or a manufacturer of or dealer in embalming supplies. When selling hypodermic syringes or hypodermic needles without a prescription, a pharmacist or wholesale druggist must require proof of identification that validates the individual's age.

Added by St.1971, c. 1071, § 1. Amended by St.1972, c. 806, § 20; St.1973, c. 1190, §§ 15 to 17; St.1980, c. 572, §§ 83, 84; St.1982, c. 554, §§ 1, 2; St.1993, c. 110, § 142; St.1993, c. 224, § 2; St.2006, c. 172, § 3, eff. Sept. 18, 2006.

§ 27A. Collection and disposal of spent non-commercially generated hypodermic needles and lancets

(a) Notwithstanding any general or special law to the contrary, the department of environmental protection and the department of public health, in conjunction with other relevant state and local agencies and government departments, shall design, establish and implement, or cause to be implemented a program for the collection and disposal of spent non-commercially generated hypodermic needles and lancets. The program shall be designed to protect the public health and the environment by providing for the safe, secure and accessible collection and disposal of hypodermic needles and lancets. The departments may collaborate with private companies as well as not-for-profit agencies when designing, establishing and implementing this program.

(b) (1) Sharps disposal programs may include, but are not limited to the following:-

(i) a program for safe, secure home sharp disposal;

(ii) establishing sharps collection centers in medical facilities and pharmacies;

(iii) establishing sharps collection centers in municipal facilities, including, but not limited to, fire stations, police stations and public health offices; provided that sharps collection centers may be located at senior centers only for the purpose of disposing of medically necessary hypodermic needles; and

(iv) medical waste mail-back programs approved by the United States Postal Service.

(2) Medical facilities, pharmacies and participating municipal facilities may work with the department of public health and the department of environmental protection to determine the proper program for sharps disposal implementation within each community.

(c) For the purposes of this section, a "sharps collection center" shall be an identified site within a community which:

(1) uses only collection containers that meet the requirements of the federal Occupational Safety and Health Administration and the federal Department of Transportation and is marked with the international biohazard symbol;

(2) provides secure and accessible collection containers on site;

(3) accepts sharps from sharps users that are in leak-proof, rigid, puncture-resistant and shatterproof containers;

(4) provides appropriate transfer containers for sharps users who fail to bring their sharps in suitable containers for placement in the collection container;

(5) has a written agreement with a medical waste transporter providing for regularly scheduled waste pickups; and

(6) stores, handles, transports and treats the collected waste in accordance with department of public health regulations.

(d) The program shall be designed to protect the public health and the environment by providing for the safe, secure and accessible collection and disposal of hypodermic needles and lancets. The department of public health, in consultation with the department of environmental protection, shall adopt regulations to ensure the safe, secure and accessible collection and disposal of hypodermic needles and lancets, and shall provide recommendations for legislative action to the joint committee on public health, the senate and house committees on ways and means and the clerks of the senate and house of representatives. Included in the recommendations for legislative action shall be recommended punishments and fines for the inappropriate, unsafe or unlawful disposal of the hypodermic needles and lancets.

Added by St.2006, c. 172, § 3, eff. July 13, 2006.

§ 28. Jurisdiction of superior court

Upon petition of the board of registration in pharmacy or the commissioner in the case of a pharmacy, or upon petition of the commissioner in any case, the superior court shall have jurisdiction to restrain or enjoin a violation of this chapter.

Added by St.1971, c. 1071, § 1.

§ 29. Educational programs for prevention of abuse of controlled substances

(a) The commissioner in cooperation with the commissioner of mental health and the commissioner of education shall carry out educational programs designed to prevent and deter misuse and abuse of controlled substances. In connection with these programs he shall:

(1) promote better recognition of the problem of misuse and abuse of controlled substances within the regulated industry and among interested groups and organizations;

(2) assist the regulated industry and interested groups and organizations in contributing to the reduction of misuse and abuse of controlled substances;

(3) consult with interested groups and organizations to aid them in solving administrative and organizational problems;

(4) evaluate procedures, projects, techniques and controls conducted or proposed as part of educational programs on misuse and abuse of controlled substances;

(5) disseminate the results of research on misuse and abuse of controlled substances to promote a better public understanding of what problems exist and what can be done to combat them; and

(6) assist the attorney general in the education and training of state and local law enforcement officials in their efforts to control misuse and abuse of controlled substances.

(b) The commissioner shall encourage research on misuse and abuse of controlled substances. In connection with the research, and in furtherance of the enforcement of this chapter, he shall:

(1) establish methods to assess accurately the effects of controlled substances and identify and characterize those with potential for abuse;

(2) make studies and undertake programs of research to:

(i) develop new or improved approaches, techniques, systems, equipment and devices to strengthen the enforcement of this chapter;

(ii) determine patterns of misuse and abuse of controlled substances and the social effects thereof; and

(iii) improve methods for preventing, predicting, understanding and dealing with the misuse and abuse of controlled substances; and

(3) enter into contracts with public agencies, institutions of higher education and private organizations or individuals for the purpose of conducting research, demonstrations or special projects which bear directly on misuse and abuse of controlled substances.

(c) The commissioner and the commissioner of mental health may enter into contracts for educational and research activities.

Added by St.1971, c. 1071, § 1. Amended by St.1986, c. 434, § 2.

§ 30. Administrative inspection of controlled premises

(a) Administrative inspection warrants shall issue for the inspection of controlled premises in accordance with the provisions of this section. As used in this section "administrative inspection warrants" are warrants for the purpose of inspecting, copying and verifying the correctness of records, reports or other documents required to be kept by a registrant on controlled premises and for the seizure of property appropriate to such inspection. For the purposes of this section "controlled premises" means any place or area, including but not limited to any building, conveyance, warehouse, factory, or establishment, in which persons registered under the provisions of this chapter or required thereunder to keep records, are permitted to hold, manufacture, compound, process, distribute, deliver, dispense, or administer any controlled substance or in which such persons make or maintain records pertaining thereto.

(b) A district court or justice or superior court justice may, upon proper oath or affirmation by the commissioner or his designee except in the case of a pharmacy, by the commissioner or his designee or by the designee of the board of registration in pharmacy, or by a police officer showing probable cause, issue warrants for the purpose of conducting administrative inspections authorized by this chapter or rules hereunder, and seizures of property if appropriate to the inspections. For the purposes of the issuance of administrative inspection warrants, probable cause exists upon a showing of a reasonable and valid public interest in the effective enforcement of this chapter or rules or regulations hereunder under a general plan sufficient to justify administrative inspection of an area, premises, buildings or conveyances in the circumstances specified in the application or such warrant.

(c) An administrative inspection warrant shall issue only upon affidavit sworn to before the court, or justice establishing the grounds for issuing the warrant. If the court or justice is satisfied that grounds for the issuance of such warrant exists or that there is probable cause to believe they exist, he shall issue such warrant identifying the area, premises, buildings or conveyances to be inspected, the purpose of the inspection, and, if appropriate, the type of property to be inspected, if any. Such warrant shall:

(1) be directed to the commissioner or his designee, except in the case of a pharmacy to the commissioner or to the designee of the board of registration in pharmacy, or to a police officer;

(2) command the person to whom it is directed to inspect the area, premises, buildings or conveyances identified for the purpose specified and, if appropriate, direct the seizure of the property specified;

(3) describe the item or types of property to be inspected or seized, if any;

(4) direct that it be served during normal business hours.

(d) An administrative inspection warrant issued and executed pursuant to the provisions of this section shall be returned to the issuing court, except if said warrant is issued by the superior court it shall be returned to any court named in such warrant, within ten days of the date of issuance thereof unless, upon a showing of a need for additional time, the court or justice orders otherwise. If property is seized pursuant to such warrant, a copy of the inventory shall be given to the person from whom or from whose premises the property is taken, together with a receipt for the property taken. The inventory shall be made in the presence of the person executing such warrant and of the person from whose possession or premises the property was taken, if present. A copy of the inventory shall be delivered to the person from whom or from whose premises the property was taken and to the applicant for such warrant at the time it is returned to a court.

(e) When authorized by an administrative inspection warrant issued pursuant to this section a person designated by the commissioner, except in the case of a pharmacy by the commissioner or by the board of registration in pharmacy, upon showing such warrant to the owner, operator, or agent in charge, may enter controlled premises for the purpose of conducting an administrative inspection.

(f) A person executing an administrative inspection warrant may:

(1) use reasonable force and means to execute the warrant;

(2) inspect and copy records required by this chapter to be kept;

(3) inspect, within reasonable limits and in a reasonable manner, controlled premises and all pertinent equipment, finished and unfinished material, containers and labeling found therein, and except as provided in subsection (h), all other things therein, including records, files, papers, processes, controls, and facilities bearing on violation of this chapter; and

(4) inventory any stock of any controlled substance therein and obtain samples thereof.

(g) This section shall not prevent entries and administrative inspections, including seizures of property, without a warrant:

(1) if the owner, operator, or agent in charge of the controlled premises consents;

(2) in situations presenting imminent danger to health or safety;

(3) in situations involving inspection of conveyances if there is reasonable cause to believe that the mobility of the conveyance makes it impracticable to obtain a warrant;

(4) in any other exceptional or emergency circumstance where time or opportunity to apply for a warrant is lacking; or

(5) in all other situations in which a warrant is not required by the laws and constitution of the commonwealth or of the United States.

(h) An inspection authorized by this section shall not extend to financial data, sales data, other than shipment data, or pricing data unless the owner, operator, or agent in charge of the controlled premises consents in writing.

Added by St.1971, c. 1071, § 1. Amended by St.1972, c. 806, § 21.

§ 31. Classes of controlled substances; establishment of criminal penalties for violations of this chapter

For the purposes of establishing criminal penalties for violation of a provision of this chapter, there are established the following five classes of controlled substances:

CLASS A

(a) Unless specifically excepted or unless listed in another schedule, any of the following opiates, including their isomers, esters, ethers, salts, and salts of isomers, esters and ethers, whenever the existence of such isomers, esters, ethers and salts is possible within the specific chemical designation:

(1) Acetylmethadol

(2) Allylprodine

(3) Alphacetylmethadol

(4) Alphameprodine

(5) Alphamethadol

(6) Benzethidine

(7) Betacetylmethadol

(8) Betameprodine

(9) Betamethadol

(10) Betaprodine

(11) Clonitazene

(12) Dextromoramide

(13) Dextrorphan

(14) Diampromide

(15) Diethylthiambutene

(16) Dimenoxadol

(17) Dimepheptanol

(18) Dimethylthiambutene

(19) Dioxaphetylbutyrate

(20) Dipipanone

(21) Ethylmethylthiambutene

(22) Etonitazene

(23) Etoxeridine

(24) Furethidine

(25) Hydroxypethidine

(26) Ketobemidone

(27) Levomoramide

(28) Levophenacylmorphan

(29) Morpheridine

(30) Noracymethadol

(31) Norlevorphanol

(32) Normethadone

(33) Norpipanone

(34) Phenadoxone

(35) Phenampromide

(36) Phenomorphan

(37) Phenoperidine

(38) Piritramide

(39) Proheptazine

(40) Properidine

(41) Racemoramide

(42) Trimeperidine

(b) Unless specifically excepted or unless listed in another schedule, any of the following opium derivatives, their salts, isomers, and salts of isomers whenever the existence of such salts, isomers, and salts of isomers is possible within the specific chemical designation:

(1) Acetorphine

(2) Acetyldihydrocodeine

(3) Benzylmorphine

(4) Codeine methylbromide

(5) Codeine–N–Oxide

(6) Cyprenorphine

(7) Desomorphine

(8) Dihydromorphine

(9) Etorphine

(10) Heroin

(11) Hydromorphinol

(12) Methyldesorphine

(13) Methylhydromorphine

(14) Morphine methylbromide

(15) Morphine methylsulfonate

(16) Morphine–N–Oxide

(17) Myrophine

(18) Nicocodeine

(19) Nicomorphine

(20) Normorphine

(21) Pholcodine

(22) Thebacon

(c) Unless specifically excepted or unless listed in another schedule, any material, compound, mixture or preparation that contains any quantity of the following substances including its salts, isomers and salts of isomers whenever the existence of such salts, isomers and salts of isomers is possible within the specific chemical designations:

(1) Flunitrazepam

(2) Gamma Hydroxy Butyric Acid

(3) Ketamine.

CLASS B

(a) Unless specifically excepted or unless listed in another schedule, any of the following substances whether produced directly or indirectly by extraction from substances of vegetable origin, or independently by means of chemical synthesis, or by a combination of extraction and chemical synthesis:

(1) Opium and opiate, and any salt, compound, derivative, or preparation of opium or opiate

(2) Any salt, compound, derivative, or preparation thereof which is chemically equivalent or identical with any of the substances referred to in paragraph (1) except that these substances shall not include the isoquinoline alkaloids of opium

(3) Opium poppy and poppy straw

(4) Coca leaves and any salt, compound, derivative, or preparation of coca leaves, and any salt, compound, derivative, or preparation thereof which is chemically equivalent or identical with any of these substances, except that the substances shall not include decocainized coca leaves or extraction of coca leaves, which extractions do not contain cocaine or ecgonine.

(5) Phenyl–2–Propanone (P2P)

(6) Phenylcyclohexylamine (PCH)

(7) Piperidinocyclohexanecarbonitrile (PCC)

(8) 3,4–methylenedioxy methamphetamine (MDMA).

(b) Unless specifically excepted or unless listed in another schedule, any of the following opiates, including isomers, esters, ethers, salts, and salts of isomer, esters, and ethers, whenever the existence of such isomers, esters, ethers and salts is possible within the specific chemical designation:

(1) Alphaprodine

(2) Anileridine

(3) Bezitramide

(4) Dihydrocodeine

(5) Diphenoxylate

(6) Fentanyl

(7) Isomethadone

(8) Levomethorphan

(9) Levorphanol

(10) Metazocine

(11) Methadone

(12) Methadone–Intermediate, 4–cyano–2–dimethylamino–4, 4–diphenyl butane

(13) Moramide–Intermediate, 2–methyl–3 morpholine–1, 1–diphenyl-propane carboxylic acid

(14) Pethidine

(15) Pethidine–Intermediate–A, 4–cyano–1–methyl–4–phenylpiperidine

(16) Pethidine–Intermediate–B, ethyl–4–phenylpiperidine–4–carboxylate

(17) Pethidine–Intermediate–C, 1–methyl–4–phenylpiperidine–4–carboxylic acid

(18) Phenazocine

(19) Piminodine

(20) Racemethorphan

(21) Racemorphan

(c) Unless specifically excepted or unless listed in another schedule, any material, compound, mixture, or preparation which contains any quantity of the following substances having a stimulant effect on the central nervous system:

(1) Amphetamine, its salts, optical isomers and salts of its optical isomers.

(2) Any substance which contains any quantity of methamphetamine, including its salts, isomers and salts of isomers.

(3) Phenmetrazine and its salts.

(4) Methylphenidate.

(d) Unless specifically excepted or unless listed in another schedule, any material, compound, mixture or preparation which contains any quantity of the following substances having a depressant effect on the central nervous system:

(1) Any substance which contains any quantity of a derivative of barbituric acid, or any salt of a derivative of barbituric acid.

(2) Any substance which contains any quantity of methaqualone, or any salt or derivative of methaqualone.

(e) Unless specifically excepted or listed in another schedule, any material, compound, mixture, or preparation, which contains any quantity of the following hallucinogenic substances or which contains any of their salts, isomers, and salts of isomers whenever the existence of such salts, isomers, and salts of isomers is possible within the specific chemical designation:

(1) Lysergic acid

(2) Lysergic acid amide

(3) Lysergic acid diethylamide

(4) Phencyclidine.

CLASS C

(a) Unless specifically excepted or unless listed in another schedule, any material, compound, mixture, or preparation which contains any quantity of the following substances having a depressant effect on the central nervous system:

(1) Chlordiazepoxide

(2) Chlorhexadol

(3) Clonazepam

(4) Clorazepate

(5) Diazepam

(6) Flurazepam

(7) Glutethimide

(8) Lorazepam

(9) Methyprylon

(10) Oxazepam

(11) Prazepam

(12) Sulfondiethylmethane

(13) Sulfonethylmethane

(14) Sulfonmethane

(15) Temazepam.

(b) Nalorphine

(c) Unless specifically excepted or unless listed in another schedule, any material, compound, mixture, or preparation containing limited quantities of any of the following narcotic drugs, or any salts thereof:

(1) Not more than 1.8 grams of codeine per 100 milliliters or not more than 90 milligrams per dosage unit with an equal or greater quantity of an isoquinoline alkaloid of opium.

(2) Not more than 1.8 grams of codeine per 100 milliliters or not more than 90 milligrams per dosage unit, with one or more active, nonnarcotic ingredients in recognized therapeutic amounts.

(3) Not more than 300 milligrams of dihydrocodeinone per 100 milliliters or not more than 15 milligrams per dosage unit, with a fourfold or greater quantity of an isoquinoline alkaloid of opium.

(4) Not more than 300 milligrams of dihydrocodeinone per 100 milliliters or not more than 15 milligrams per dosage unit, with one or more active nonnarcotic ingredients in recognized therapeutic amounts.

(5) Not more than 1.8 grams of dihydrocodeine per 100 milliliters or not more than 90 milligrams per dosage unit, with one or more active nonnarcotic ingredients in recognized therapeutic amounts.

(6) Not more than 300 milligrams of ethylmorphine per 100 milliliters or not more than 15 milligrams per dosage unit with one or more active nonnarcotic ingredients in recognized therapeutic amounts.

(7) Not more than 500 milligrams of opium per 100 milliliters or per 100 grams, or not more than 25 milligrams per dosage unit, with one or more active, nonnarcotic ingredients in recognized therapeutic amounts.

(8) Not more than 50 milligrams of morphine per 100 milliliters or per 100 grams with one or more active nonnarcotic ingredients in recognized therapeutic amounts.

[There is no paragraph (d).]

(e) Unless specifically excepted or listed in another schedule, any material, compound, mixture, or preparation, which contains any quantity of the following hallucinogenic substances, or which contains any of their salts, isomers, and salts of isomers whenever the existence of such salts, isomers, and salts of isomers is possible within the specific chemical designation:

(1) 3, 4–methylenedioxy amphetamine

(2) 5–methoxy–3, 4–methylenedioxy amphetamine

(3) 3, 4, 5–trimethoxy amphetamine

(4) Bufotenine

(5) Diethyltryptamine

(6) Dimethyltryptamine

(7) 4–methyl–2, 5–dimethoxyamphetamine

(8) Ibogaine

(9) Mescaline

(10) Peyote

(11) N–ethyl–3–piperidyl benzilate

(12) N–methyl–3–piperidyl benzilate

(13) Psilocybin

(14) Psilocyn

(15) Tetrahydrocannabinols

(16) 4–Bromo–2, 5–Dimethoxy-amphetamine.

CLASS D

(a)

(1) Barbital

(2) Chloral betaine

(3) Chloral hydrate

(4) Ethchlorvynol

(5) Ethinamate

(6) Methohexital

(7) Meprobamate

(8) Methylphenobarbital

(9) Paraldehyde

(10) Petrichloral

(11) Phenobarbital

(b) Unless specifically excepted or unless listed in another schedule, any material, compound, mixture, or preparation, which contains any quantity of the following substances, or which contains any of their salts, isomers, and salts of isomers whenever the existence of such salts, isomers, and salts of isomers is possible within the specific chemical designation:

(1) Marihuana

(2) Butyl Nitrite

(3) Isobutyl Nitrite

(4) 1–Nitrosoxy–Methyl–Propane.

CLASS E

(a) Any compound, mixture, or preparation containing any of the following limited quantities of narcotic drugs, which shall include one or more nonnarcotic active medicinal ingredients in sufficient proportion to confer upon the compound, mixture, or preparation valuable medicinal qualities other than those possessed by the narcotic drug alone:

(1) Not more than 200 milligrams of codeine per 100 milliliters or per 100 grams

(2) Not more than 100 milligrams of dihydrocodeine per 100 milliliters or per 100 grams

(3) Not more than 100 milligrams of ethylmorphine per 100 milliliters or per 100 grams

(4) Not more than 2.5 milligrams of diphenoxylate and not less than 25 micrograms of atropine sulfate per dosage unit

(5) Not more than 100 milligrams of opium per 100 milliliters or per 100 grams

(b) Prescription drugs other than those included in Classes A, B, C, D, and subsection (a) of this Class.

Added by St.1971, c. 1071, § 1. Amended by St.1972, c. 806, § 22; St.1973, c. 459, § 1; St.1977, c. 824; St.1979, c. 379; St.1980, c. 241, §§ 1, 2; St.1980, c. 436, §§ 1 to 3; St.1982, c. 650, §§ 2 to 5; St.1991, c. 341; St.1998, c. 232, § 1; St.2010, c. 346, eff. Sept. 30, 2010.

§ 32. Class A controlled substances; unlawful manufacture, distribution, dispensing or possession with intent to manufacture, etc.; eligibility for parole

(a) Any person who knowingly or intentionally manufactures, distributes, dispenses, or possesses with intent to manufacture, distribute or dispense a controlled substance in Class A of section thirty-one shall be punished by imprisonment in the state prison for not more than ten years or in a jail or house of correction for not more than two and one-half years or by a fine of not less than one thousand nor more than ten thousand dollars, or by both such fine and imprisonment.

(b) Any person convicted of violating this section after one or more prior convictions of manufacturing, distributing, dispensing or possessing with the intent to manufacture, distribute, or dispense a controlled substance as defined by section thirty-one of this chapter under this or any prior law of this jurisdiction or of any offense of any other jurisdiction, federal, state, or territorial, which is the same as or necessarily includes the elements of said offense shall be punished by a term of imprisonment in the state prison for not less than five nor more than fifteen years. No sentence imposed under the provisions of this section shall be for less than a mandatory minimum term of imprisonment of five years and a fine of not less than two thousand and five hundred nor more than twenty-five thousand dollars may be imposed but not in lieu of the mandatory minimum five year term of imprisonment, as established herein.

(c) Any person serving a mandatory minimum sentence for violating any provision of this section shall be eligible for parole after serving one-half of the maximum term of the sentence if the sentence is to the house of correction, except that such person shall not be eligible for parole upon a finding of any 1 of the following aggravating circumstances:

(i) the defendant used violence or threats of violence or possessed a firearm, rifle, shotgun, machine gun or a weapon described in paragraph (b) of section 10 of chapter 269, or induced another participant to do so, during the commission of the offense;

(ii) the defendant engaged in a course of conduct whereby he directed the activities of another who committed any felony in violation of chapter 94C; or

(iii) the offense was committed during the commission or attempted commission of a violation of section 32F or section 32K of chapter 94C.

A condition of such parole may be enhanced supervision; provided, however, that such enhanced supervision may, at the discretion of the parole board, include, but shall not be limited to, the wearing of a global positioning satellite tracking device or any comparable device, which shall be administered by the board at all times for the length of the parole.

Added by St.1980, c. 436, § 4. Amended by St.1982, c. 458; St.1982, c. 650, § 6; St.1983, c. 571, § 1; St.2010, c. 256, § 67, eff. Nov. 4, 2010.

§ 32A. Class B controlled substances; unlawful manufacture, distribution, dispensing or possession with intent to manufacture, etc.; eligibility for parole

(a) Any person who knowingly or intentionally manufactures, distributes, dispenses, or possesses with intent to manufacture, distribute or dispense a controlled substance in Class B of section thirty-one shall be punished by imprisonment in the state prison for not more than ten years, or in a jail or house of correction for not more than two and one-half years, or by a fine of not less than one thousand nor more than ten thousand dollars, or both such fine and imprisonment.

(b) Any person convicted of violating this section after one or more prior convictions of manufacturing, distributing, dispensing, or possessing with the intent to manufacture, distribute or dispense a controlled substance as defined by section thirty-one of this chapter under this or any other prior law of this jurisdiction or of any offense of any other jurisdiction, federal, state, or territorial, which is the same as or necessarily includes the elements of said offense shall be punished by a term of imprisonment in the state prison for not less than three nor more than ten years. No sentence imposed under the provisions of this section shall be for less than a mandatory minimum term of imprisonment of three years and a fine of not less than two thousand and five hundred nor more than twenty-five thousand dollars may be imposed but not in lieu of the mandatory minimum term of imprisonment, as established herein.

(c) Any person who knowingly or intentionally manufactures, distributes, dispenses or possesses with intent to manufacture, distribute or dispense phencyclidine or a controlled substance defined in clause (4) of paragraph (a) or in clause (2) of paragraph (c) of class B of section thirty-one shall be punished by a term of imprisonment in the state prison for not less than two and one-half nor more than ten years or by imprisonment in a jail or house of correction for not less than one nor more than two and one-half years. No sentence imposed under the provisions of this section shall be for less than a mandatory minimum term of imprisonment of one year and a fine of not less than one thousand nor more than ten thousand dollars may be imposed but not in lieu of the mandatory minimum one year term of imprisonment, as established herein.

(d) Any person convicted of violating the provisions of subsection (c) after one or more prior convictions of manufacturing, distributing, dispensing or possessing with the intent to manufacture, distribute, or dispense a controlled substance, as defined in section thirty-one or of any offense of any other jurisdiction, either federal, state or territorial, which is the same as or necessarily includes, the elements of said offense, shall be punished by a term of imprisonment in the state prison for not less than five nor more than fifteen years and a fine of not less than two thousand five hundred nor more than twenty-five thousand dollars may be imposed but not in lieu of the mandatory minimum term of imprisonment, as established herein.

(e) Any person serving a mandatory minimum sentence for violating this section shall be eligible for parole after serving one-half of the maximum term of the sentence if the sentence is to the house of correction, provided that said person shall not be eligible for parole upon a finding of any one of the following aggravating circumstances:

(i) the defendant used violence or threats of violence or possessed a firearm, rifle, shotgun, machine gun or a weapon described in paragraph (b) of section 10 of chapter 269, or induced another participant to do so, during the commission of the offense;

(ii) the defendant engaged in a course of conduct whereby he directed the activities of another who committed any felony in violation of chapter 94C; or

(iii) the offense was committed during the commission or attempted commission of a violation of section 32F or section 32K of chapter 94C.

A condition of such parole may be enhanced supervision; provided, however, that such enhanced supervision may, at the discretion of the parole board, include, but shall not be limited to, the wearing of a global positioning satellite tracking device or any comparable device, which shall be administered by the board at all times for the length of the parole.

Added by St.1980, c. 436, § 4. Amended by St.1981, c. 522; St.1982, c. 650, § 7; St.1983, c. 571, § 2; St.1988, c. 125, §§ 1, 2; St.1991, c. 391; St.2010, c. 256, § 68, eff. Nov. 4, 2010.

§ 32B. Class C controlled substances; unlawful manufacturer, distribution, dispensing or possession with intent to manufacture, etc.; eligibility for parole

(a) Any person who knowingly or intentionally manufactures, distributes, dispenses, or possesses with intent to manufacture, distribute, or dispense a controlled substance in Class C of section thirty-one shall be imprisoned in state prison for not more than five years or in a jail or house of correction for not more than two and one-half years, or by a fine of not less than five hundred nor more than five thousand dollars, or both such fine and imprisonment.

(b) Any person convicted of violating this section after one or more prior convictions of manufacturing, distributing, dispensing or possessing with the intent to manufacture, distribute or dispense a controlled substance as defined by section thirty-one under this or any prior law of this jurisdiction or of any offense of any other jurisdiction, federal, state, or territorial, which is the same as or necessarily includes the elements of said offense shall be punished by a term of imprisonment in the state prison for not less than two and one-half nor more than ten years, or by imprisonment in a jail or house of correction for not less than two nor more than two and one-half years. No sentence imposed under the provisions of this section shall be for less than a mandatory minimum term of imprisonment of two years and a fine of not less than one thousand nor more than ten thousand dollars may be imposed, but not in lieu of the mandatory minimum term of imprisonment, as established herein.

(c) Any person serving a mandatory minimum sentence for violating this section shall be eligible for parole after serving one-half of the maximum term of the sentence if the sentence is to the house of correction, except that such person shall not be eligible for parole upon a finding of any 1 of the following aggravating circumstances:

(i) the defendant used violence or threats of violence or possessed a firearm, rifle, shotgun, machine gun or a weapon described in paragraph (b) of section 10 of chapter 269, or induced another participant to do so, during the commission of the offense;

(ii) the defendant engaged in a course of conduct whereby he directed the activities of another who committed any felony in violation of chapter 94C; or

(iii) the offense was committed during the commission or attempted commission of a violation of section 32F or section 32K of chapter 94C.

A condition of such parole may be enhanced supervision; provided, however, that such enhanced supervision may, at the discretion of the parole board, include, but shall not be limited to, the wearing of a global positioning satellite tracking device or any comparable device, which shall be administered by the board at all times for the length of the parole.

Added by St.1980, c. 436, § 4. Amended by St.1982, c. 650, § 8; St.2010, c. 256, § 69, eff. Nov. 4, 2010.

§ 32C. Class D controlled substances; unlawful manufacture, distribution, dispensing, cultivation or possession with intent to manufacture, etc.

(a) Any person who knowingly or intentionally manufactures, distributes, dispenses or cultivates, or possesses with intent to manufacture, distribute, dispense or cultivate a controlled substance in Class D of section thirty-one shall be imprisoned in a jail or house of correction for not more than two years or by a fine of not less than five hundred nor more than five thousand dollars, or both such fine and imprisonment.

(b) Any person convicted of violating this section after one or more prior convictions of manufacturing, distributing, dispensing, cultivating or possessing with intent to manufacture, distribute, dispense or cultivate a controlled substance as defined by section thirty-one under this or any prior law of this jurisdiction or of any offense of any other jurisdiction, federal, state, or territorial, which is the same as or necessarily includes the elements of said offense shall be punished by a term of imprisonment in a jail or house of correction for not less than one nor more than two and one-half years, or by a fine of not less than one thousand nor more than ten thousand dollars, or both such fine and imprisonment.

Added by St.1980, c. 436, § 4. Amended by St.1982, c. 650, § 9.

§ 32D. Class E controlled substances; unlawful manufacture, distribution, dispensing, or possession with intent to manufacture, etc.

(a) Any person who knowingly or intentionally manufactures, distributes, dispenses or possesses with intent to manufacture, distribute, or dispense a controlled substance in Class E of section thirty-one shall be imprisoned in a jail or house of correction for not more than nine months, or by a fine of not less than two hundred and fifty nor more than two thousand and five hundred dollars, or both such fine and imprisonment.

(b) Any person convicted of violating this section after one or more prior convictions of manufacturing, distributing, dispensing or possessing with the intent to manufacture, distribute or dispense a controlled substance as defined by section thirty-one under this or any prior law of this jurisdiction or of any offense of any other jurisdiction, federal, state, or territorial which is the same as or necessarily includes the elements of said offense shall be punished by a term of imprisonment in a jail or house of correction for not more than one and one-half years, or by a fine of not less than five hundred nor more than five thousand dollars, or both such fine and imprisonment.

Added by St.1980, c. 436, § 4. Amended by St.1982, c. 650, § 10.

§ 32E. Trafficking in marihuana, cocaine, heroin, morphine, opium, etc.; eligibility for parole

(a) Any person who trafficks in marihuana by knowingly or intentionally manufacturing, distributing, dispensing, or cultivating or possessing with intent to manufacture, distribute, dispense, or cultivate, or by bringing into the commonwealth a net weight of fifty pounds or more of marihuana or a net weight of fifty pounds or more of any mixture containing marihuana shall, if the net weight of marihuana or any mixture thereof is:

(1) Fifty pounds or more, but less than one hundred pounds, be punished by a term of imprisonment in the state prison for not less than two and one-half nor more than fifteen years or by imprisonment in a jail or house of correction for not less than one nor more than two and one-half years. No sentence imposed under the provisions of this section shall be for less than a mandatory minimum term of imprisonment of one year and a fine of not less than five hundred nor more than ten thousand dollars may be imposed but not in lieu of the mandatory minimum one year term of imprisonment, as established herein.

(2) One hundred pounds or more, but less than two thousand pounds, be punished by a term of imprisonment in the state prison for not less than three nor more than fifteen years. No sentence imposed under the provisions of this section shall be for less than a mandatory minimum term of imprisonment of three years and a fine of not less than two thousand and five hundred nor more than twenty-five thousand dollars may be imposed but not in lieu of the mandatory minimum term of imprisonment, as established herein.

(3) Two thousand pounds or more, but less than ten thousand pounds, be punished by a term of imprisonment in the state prison for not less than five nor more than fifteen years. No sentence imposed under the provisions of this section shall be for less than a mandatory minimum term of imprisonment of five years and a fine of not less than five thousand nor more than fifty thousand dollars may be imposed but not in lieu of the mandatory minimum term of imprisonment, as established herein.

(4) Ten thousand pounds or more, be punished by a term of imprisonment in the state prison for not less than ten nor more than fifteen years. No sentence imposed under the provisions of this section shall be for less than a mandatory minimum term of imprisonment of ten years and a fine of not less than twenty thousand nor more than two hundred thousand dollars may be imposed but not in lieu of the mandatory minimum term of imprisonment, as established herein.

(b) Any person who trafficks in a controlled substance defined in clause (4) of paragraph (a) or in clause (3) of paragraph (c) of Class B of section thirty-one by knowingly or intentionally manufacturing, distributing or dispensing or possessing with intent to manufacture, distribute or dispense or by bringing into the commonwealth a net weight of fourteen grams or more of a controlled substance as so defined, or a net weight of fourteen grams or more of any mixture containing a controlled substance as so defined shall, if the net weight of a controlled substance as so defined, or any mixture thereof is:

(1) Fourteen grams or more but less than twenty-eight grams, be punished by a term of imprisonment in the state prison for not less than three nor more than fifteen years. No sentence imposed under the provisions of this clause shall be for less than a minimum term of imprisonment of three years, and a fine of not less than two thousand five hundred nor more than twenty-five thousand dollars may be imposed but not in lieu of the mandatory minimum term of imprisonment, as established herein.

(2) Twenty-eight grams or more, but less than one hundred grams, be punished by a term of imprisonment in the state prison for not less than five nor more than twenty years. No sentence imposed under the provisions of this clause shall be for less than a mandatory minimum term of imprisonment of five years, and a fine of not less than five thousand nor more than fifty thousand dollars may be imposed but not in lieu of the mandatory minimum term of imprisonment, as established herein.

(3) One hundred grams or more, but less than two hundred grams, be punished by a term of imprisonment in the state prison for not less than ten nor more than twenty years. No sentence imposed under the provisions of this clause shall be for less than a mandatory minimum term of imprisonment of ten years and a fine of not less than ten thousand nor more than one hundred thousand dollars may be imposed but not in lieu of the mandatory minimum term of imprisonment, as established herein.

(4) Two hundred grams or more, be punished by a term of imprisonment in the state prison for not less than fifteen nor more than twenty years. No sentence imposed under the provisions of this clause shall be for less than a mandatory minimum term of imprisonment of fifteen years and a fine of not less than fifty thousand nor more than five hundred thousand dollars may be imposed but not in lieu of the mandatory minimum term of imprisonment, as established herein.

(c) Any person who trafficks in heroin or any salt thereof, morphine or any salt thereof, opium or any derivative thereof by knowingly or intentionally manufacturing, distributing or dispensing or possessing with intent to manufacture, distribute, or dispense or by bringing into the commonwealth a net weight of fourteen grams or more of heroin or any salt thereof, morphine or any salt thereof, opium or any derivative thereof or a net weight of fourteen grams or more of any mixture containing heroin or any salt thereof, morphine or any salt thereof, opium or any derivative thereof shall, if the net weight of heroin or any salt thereof, morphine or any salt thereof, opium or any derivative thereof or any mixture thereof is:—

(1) Fourteen grams or more but less than twenty-eight grams, be punished by a term of imprisonment in the state prison for not less than five nor more than twenty years. No sentence imposed under the provisions of this clause shall be for less than a mandatory minimum term of imprisonment of five years and a fine of not less than five thousand nor more than fifty thousand dollars may be imposed but not in lieu of the mandatory minimum term of imprisonment, as established herein.

(2) Twenty-eight grams or more but less than one hundred grams, be punished by a term of imprisonment in the state prison for not less than seven nor more than twenty years. No sentence imposed under the provisions of this clause shall be for less than a mandatory minimum term of imprisonment of seven years and a fine of not less than five thousand nor more than fifty thousand dollars may be imposed, but not in lieu of the mandatory minimum term of imprisonment, as established herein.

(3) One hundred grams or more but less than two hundred grams, be punished by a term of imprisonment in the state prison for not less than ten nor more than twenty years. No sentence imposed under the provisions of this clause shall be for less than the mandatory minimum term of imprisonment of ten years, and a fine of not less than ten thousand nor more than one hundred thousand dollars may be imposed but not in lieu of the mandatory minimum term of imprisonment, as established therein.

(4) Two hundred grams or more, be punished by a term of imprisonment in the state prison for not less than fifteen nor more than twenty years. No sentence imposed under the provisions of this clause shall be for less than a mandatory minimum term of imprisonment of fifteen years and a fine of not less than fifty thousand nor more than five hundred thousand dollars may be imposed but not in lieu of the mandatory minimum term of imprisonment, as established therein.

(d) Any person serving a mandatory minimum sentence for violating this section shall be eligible for parole after serving one-half of the maximum term of the sentence if the sentence is to the house of correction, except that such person shall not be eligible for parole upon a finding of any 1 of the following aggravating circumstances:

(i) the defendant used violence or threats of violence or possessed a firearm, rifle, shotgun, machine gun or a weapon described in paragraph (b) of section 10 of chapter 269, or induced another participant to do so, during the commission of the offense;

(ii) the defendant engaged in a course of conduct whereby he directed the activities of another others who committed any felony in violation of chapter 94C; or

(iii) the offense was committed during the commission or attempted commission of a violation of section 32F or section 32K of chapter 94C.

A condition of such parole may be enhanced supervision; provided, however, that such enhanced supervision may, at the discretion of the parole board, include, but shall not be limited to, the wearing of a global positioning satellite tracking device or any comparable device, which shall be administered by the board at all times for the length of the parole.

Added by St.1980, c. 436, § 4. Amended by St.1982, c. 650, § 11; St.1983, c. 571, § 3; St.1988, c. 124; St.1991, c. 395; St.1992, c. 396, §§ 1 to 3; St.2010, c. 256, § 70, eff. Nov. 4, 2010.

§ 32F. Unlawful manufacture, distribution, dispensing or possession with intent to manufacture, etc. of controlled substances in Classes A to C to minors

(a) Any person who knowingly or intentionally manufactures, distributes, dispenses, or possesses with intent to manufacture, distribute, or dispense a controlled substance in Class A of section thirty-one to a person under the age of eighteen years shall be punished by a term of imprisonment in the state prison for not less than five nor more than fifteen years. No sentence imposed under the provisions of this section shall be for less than a mandatory minimum term of imprisonment of five years and a fine of not less than one thousand nor more than twenty-five thousand dollars may be imposed but not in lieu of the mandatory minimum term of imprisonment, as established herein.

(b) Any person who knowingly or intentionally manufactures, distributes, dispenses, or possesses with intent to manufacture, distribute, or dispense a controlled substance in Class B of section thirty-one to a person under the age of eighteen years shall be punished by a term of imprisonment in the state prison for not less than three nor more than fifteen years. No sentence imposed under the provisions of this section shall be for less than a mandatory minimum term of imprisonment of three years and a fine of not less than one thousand nor more than twenty-five thousand dollars may be imposed but not in lieu of the mandatory minimum term of imprisonment, as established herein.

(c) Any person who knowingly or intentionally manufactures, distributes, dispenses, or possesses with intent to manufacture, distribute, or dispense a controlled substance in Class C of section thirty-one to a person under the age of eighteen years shall be punished by a term of imprisonment in the state prison for not less than two and one-half nor more than fifteen years or in a jail or house of correction for not less than two nor more than two and one-half years. No sentence imposed under the provisions of this section shall be for less than a mandatory minimum term of imprisonment of two years and a fine of not less than one thousand nor more than twenty-five thousand dollars may be imposed but not in lieu of the mandatory minimum two year term of imprisonment, as established herein.

(d) Any person who knowingly or intentionally manufactures, distributes, dispenses, or possesses with intent to manufacture, distribute or dispense a controlled substance as defined in clause (4) of paragraph (a) of class B of section thirty-one, to a person under the age of eighteen years shall be punished by a term of imprisonment in the state prison for not less than five nor more than fifteen years. No sentence imposed under the provisions of this section shall be for less than a minimum term of imprisonment of five years, and a fine of not less than one thousand nor more than twenty-five thousand dollars may be imposed but not in lieu of the mandatory minimum term of imprisonment, as established herein.

Added by St.1980, c. 436, § 4. Amended by St.1982, c. 650, § 12; St.1983, c. 571, § 4; St.1988, c. 125, § 3.

§ 32G. Counterfeit substances; unlawful creation, distribution, dispensing or possession with intent to distribute or dispense

Any person who knowingly or intentionally creates, distributes, dispenses or possesses with intent to distribute or dispense a counterfeit substance shall be punished by imprisonment in a jail or house of correction for not more than one year or by a fine of not less than two hundred and fifty nor more than two thousand and five hundred dollars, or both such fine and imprisonment.

Added by St.1980, c. 436, § 4. Amended by St.1982, c. 650, § 13.

§ 32H. Prosecutions not to be continued or placed on file; suspension or reduction of sentence; eligibility for parole, etc.

A prosecution commenced under paragraph (b) of section thirty-two, paragraphs (b), (c) and (d) of section thirty-two A, paragraph (b) of section thirty-two B, sections thirty-two E thirty-two F and thirty-two J shall not be placed on file or continued without a finding, and the sentence imposed upon a person convicted of violating any provision of said sections shall not be reduced to less than the mandatory minimum term of imprisonment as established in said section, nor shall any sentence of imprisonment imposed upon any person be suspended or reduced until such person shall have served said mandatory minimum term of imprisonment.

A person convicted of violating said sections shall not, until he shall have served the mandatory minimum term of imprisonment established in said sections, be eligible for probation, furlough, work release or receive any deduction from his sentence for good conduct under sections 129C and 129D of chapter 127, nor shall he be eligible for parole except as authorized pursuant to subsection (c) of Section 32, subsection (e) of section 32A, subsection (c) of section 32B, subsection (d) of section 32E, or section 32J; provided, however, that the commissioner of correction, on the recommendation of the warden, superintendent or other person in charge of the correctional institution, or a sheriff, on the recommendation of the administrator of a county correctional institution, may grant to said offender a temporary release, subject to the rules and regulations of the institution and under the direction, control and supervision of the officers thereof, for the following purposes: (1) to attend the funeral of a relative, to visit a critically ill relative, to obtain emergency medical or psychiatric services unavailable at said institution; (2) to participate in education, training, or employment programs established under section 48 of chapter 127; or (3) to participate in a program to provide services under section 49B or 49C of chapter 127. Section 87 of chapter 276 shall not apply to any person, 17 years of age or older, charged with a violation of said sections, or to any child between age 14 and 17, so charged by indictment under section 54 of chapter 119.

Added by St.1980, c. 436, § 4. Amended by St.1982, c. 650, § 14; St.1988, c. 125, § 4; St.1989, c. 227, § 1; St.1989, c. 415; St.2010, c. 256, § 71, eff. Nov. 4, 2010.

§ 32*I*. Drug paraphernalia; sale, possession or manufacture with intent to sell; penalty; sale of tobacco rolling papers

(a) No person shall sell, possess or purchase with intent to sell, or manufacture with intent to sell drug paraphernalia, knowing, or under circumstances where one reasonably should know, that it will be used to plant, propagate, cultivate, grow, harvest, manufacture, compound, convert, produce, process, prepare, test, analyze, pack, repack, store, contain, conceal, ingest, inhale, or otherwise introduce into the human body a controlled substance in violation of this chapter. Whoever violates any provision of this paragraph shall be punished by imprisonment in jail or house of correction for not less than one nor more than two years, or by a fine of not less than five hundred nor more than five thousand dollars, or both.

(b) Any person who violates the foregoing provision by selling drug paraphernalia to a person under eighteen years of age shall be imprisoned in the state prison for not less than three nor more than five years, or by a fine of not less than one thousand nor more than five thousand dollars, or both.

(c) On any premises where tobacco rolling papers are sold, the person in control of such premises shall cause to be displayed in a prominent place therein a printed warning that such papers shall not be used in conjunction with the possession of a controlled substance the possession of which is punishable by a fine or imprisonment. Whoever violates the provisions of this subsection shall be punished by a fine of not less than fifty nor more than two hundred dollars.

(d) This section shall not apply to the sale of hypodermic syringes or hypodermic needles to persons over the age of 18 pursuant to section 27.

Added by St.1981, c. 669, § 2. Amended by St.1987, c. 211; St.2006, c. 172, §§ 4 to 6, eff. July 13, 2006.

§ 32J. Controlled substances violations in, on, or near school property; eligibility for parole

Any person who violates the provisions of section thirty-two, thirty-two A, thirty-two B, thirty-two C, thirty-two D, thirty-two E, thirty-two F or thirty-two *I* while in or on, or within one thousand feet of the real property comprising a public or private accredited preschool, accredited headstart facility, elementary, vocational, or secondary school whether or not in session, or within one hundred feet of a public park or playground shall be punished by a term of imprisonment in the state prison for not less than two and one-half nor more than fifteen years or by imprisonment in a jail or house of correction for not less than two nor more than two and one-half years. No sentence imposed under the provisions of this section shall be for less than a mandatory minimum term of imprisonment of two years. A fine of not less than one thousand nor more than ten thousand dollars may be imposed but not in lieu of the mandatory minimum two year term of imprisonment as established herein. In accordance with the provisions of section eight A of chapter two hundred and seventy-nine such sentence shall begin from and after the expiration of the sentence for violation of section thirty-two, thirty-two A, thirty-two B, thirty-two C, thirty-two D, thirty-two E, thirty-two F or thirty-two *I*.

Lack of knowledge of school boundaries shall not be a defense to any person who violates the provisions of this section.

Any person serving a mandatory minimum sentence for violating this section shall be eligible for parole after serving one-half of the maximum term of the sentence if the sentence is to a house of correction, except that such person shall not be eligible for parole upon a finding of any 1 of the following aggravating circumstances:

(i) the defendant used violence or threats of violence or possessed a firearm, rifle, shotgun, machine gun or a weapon described in paragraph (b) of section 10 of chapter 269, or induced another participant to do so, during the commission of the offense;

(ii) the defendant engaged in a course of conduct whereby he directed the activities of another who committed any felony in violation of chapter 94C.

(iii) the offense was committed during the commission or attempted commission of the a violation of section 32F or section 32K of chapter 94C.

A condition of such parole may be enhanced supervision; provided, however, that such enhanced supervision may, at the discretion of the parole board, include, but shall not be limited to, the wearing of a global positioning satellite tracking device or any comparable device, which shall be administered by the board at all times for the length of the parole.

Added by St.1989, c. 227, § 2. Amended by St.1993, c. 335; St.1998, c. 194, § 146; St.2010, c. 256, § 72, eff. Nov. 4, 2010.

§ 32K. Inducing or abetting minor to distribute or sell controlled substances

Any person who knowingly causes, induces or abets a person under the age of eighteen to distribute, dispense or possess with the intent to distribute or dispense any controlled substance as defined herein, or to accept, deliver or possess money used or intended for use in the procurement, manufacture, compounding, processing, delivery, distribution or sale of any such controlled substance shall be punished by imprisonment in the state prison for not less than five years nor more than fifteen years. No sentence imposed under the provisions of this section shall be for less than a mandatory minimum term of imprisonment of five years and a fine of not less than one thousand nor more than one hundred thousand dollars may be imposed but not in lieu of the mandatory minimum five year term of imprisonment established herein.

Added by St.1990, c. 198.

§ 32L. Possession of one ounce or less of marihuana; civil penalty and forfeiture; other sanctions or disqualifications prohibited

Notwithstanding any general or special law to the contrary, possession of one ounce or less of marihuana shall only be a civil offense, subjecting an offender who is eighteen years of age or older to a civil penalty of one hundred dollars and forfeiture of the marihuana, but not to any other form of criminal or civil punishment or disqualification. An offender under the age of eighteen shall be subject to the same forfeiture and civil penalty provisions, provided he or she completes a drug awareness program which meets the criteria set forth in Section 32M of this Chapter. The parents or legal guardian of any offender under the age of eighteen shall be notified in accordance with Section 32N of this Chapter of the offense and the availability of a drug awareness program and community service option. If an offender under the age of eighteen fails within one year of the offense to complete both a drug awareness program and the required community service, the civil penalty may be increased pursuant to

Section 32N of this Chapter to one thousand dollars and the offender and his or her parents shall be jointly and severally liable to pay that amount.

Except as specifically provided in "An Act Establishing A Sensible State Marihuana Policy," neither the Commonwealth nor any of its political subdivisions or their respective agencies, authorities or instrumentalities may impose any form of penalty, sanction or disqualification on an offender for possessing an ounce or less of marihuana. By way of illustration rather than limitation, possession of one ounce or less of marihuana shall not provide a basis to deny an offender student financial aid, public housing or any form of public financial assistance including unemployment benefits, to deny the right to operate a motor vehicle or to disqualify an offender from serving as a foster parent or adoptive parent. Information concerning the offense of possession of one ounce or less of marihuana shall not be deemed "criminal offender record information," "evaluative information," or "intelligence information" as those terms are defined in Section 167 of Chapter 6 of the General Laws and shall not be recorded in the Criminal Offender Record Information system.

As used herein, "possession of one ounce or less of marihuana" includes possession of one ounce or less of marihuana or tetrahydrocannabinol and having cannabinoids or cannibinoid metabolites in the urine, blood, saliva, sweat, hair, fingernails, toe nails or other tissue or fluid of the human body. Nothing contained herein shall be construed to repeal or modify existing laws, ordinances or bylaws, regulations, personnel practices or policies concerning the operation of motor vehicles or other actions taken while under the influence of marihuana or tetrahydrocannabinol, laws concerning the unlawful possession of prescription forms of marihuana or tetrahydrocannabinol such as Marinol, possession of more than one ounce of marihuana or tetrahydrocannabinol, or selling, manufacturing or trafficking in marihuana or tetrahydrocannabinol. Nothing contained herein shall prohibit a political subdivision of the Commonwealth from enacting ordinances or bylaws regulating or prohibiting the consumption of marihuana or tetrahydrocannabinol in public places and providing for additional penalties for the public use of marihuana or tetrahydrocannabinol.

Added by St.2008, c. 387, § 2, eff. Dec. 4, 2008.

§ 32M. Possession of one ounce or less of marihuana; drug awareness program

An offender under the age of eighteen is required to complete a drug awareness program within one year of the offense for possession of one ounce or less of marihuana. In addition to the civil penalties authorized by Section 32L and 32N of this Chapter, the failure of such an offender to complete such a program may be a basis for delinquency proceedings for persons under the age of seventeen at the time of their offense. The drug awareness program must provide at least four hours of classroom instruction or group discussion and ten hours of community service. In addition to the programs and curricula it must establish and maintain pursuant to Section 7 of Chapter 18A of the General Laws, the bureau of educational services within the department of youth services or any successor to said bureau shall develop the drug awareness programs. The subject matter of such drug awareness programs shall be specific to the use and abuse of marihuana and other controlled substances with particular emphasis on early detection and prevention of abuse of substances.

Added by St.2008, c. 387, § 3, eff. Dec. 4, 2008.

§ 32N. Possession of one ounce or less of marihuana; enforcement consistent with non-criminal disposition provisions of Sec. 21D of Chapter 40; duty of police department; notice; failure to file certificate of completion of drug awareness program

The police department serving each political subdivision of the Commonwealth shall enforce Section 32L in a manner consistent with the non-criminal disposition provisions of Section 21D of Chapter 40 of the General Laws, as modified in this Section.

The person in charge of each such department shall direct the department's public safety officer or another appropriate member of the department to function as a liaison between the department and persons providing drug awareness programs pursuant to Section 32M of this Chapter and the Clerk–Magistrate's office of the District Court serving the political subdivision. The person in charge shall also issue books of non-criminal citation forms to the department's officers which conform with the provisions of this Section and Section 21D of Chapter 40 of the General Laws.

In addition to the notice requirements set forth in Section 21D of Chapter 40 of the General Laws, a second copy of the notice delivered to an offender under the age of eighteen shall be mailed or delivered to at least one of that offender's parents having custody of the offender, or, where there is no such person, to that offender's legal guardian at said parent or legal guardian's last known address. If an offender under the age of eighteen, a parent or legal guardian fails to file with the Clerk of the appropriate Court a certificate that the offender has completed a drug awareness program in accordance with Section 32M within one year of the relevant offense, the Clerk shall notify the offender, parent or guardian and the enforcing person who issued the original notice to the offender of a hearing to show cause why the civil penalty should not be increased to one thousand dollars. Factors to be considered in weighing cause shall be limited to financial capacity to pay any increase, the offender's ability to participate in a compliant drug awareness program and the availability of a suitable drug awareness program. Any civil penalties imposed under the provisions of "An Act Establishing A Sensible State Marihuana Policy" shall inure to the city or town where the offense occurred.

Added by St.2008, c. 387, § 4, eff. Dec. 4, 2008.

§ 33. Unlawful use of registration numbers in manufacture or distribution, or fraudulently obtaining possession, of controlled substances; criminal penalties

(a) No person shall knowingly or intentionally use in the course of the manufacture or distribution of a controlled substance a registration number which is fictitious, revoked, suspended, or issued to another person.

(b) No person shall utter a false prescription for a controlled substance, nor knowingly or intentionally acquire or obtain possession of a controlled substance by means of forgery, fraud, deception or subterfuge, including but not limited to the forgery or falsification of a prescription or the nondisclosure of a material fact in order to obtain a controlled substance from a practitioner.

(c) Whoever violates any provision of this section shall be punished by imprisonment in the state prison for not more than four years or in a house of correction for not more than two and one half years or by a fine of not more than twenty thousand dollars, or by both such fine and imprisonment. Whoever violates any provision of this section after one or more prior convictions of a violation of this section, or of a felony under any other provision of this chapter, or under a provision of prior law relative to the sale or manufacture of a narcotic drug or a harmful drug as defined in said earlier law shall be punished by imprisonment in the state prison for not more than eight years or in a jail or house of correction for not more than two and one half years, or by a fine of not more than thirty thousand dollars or by both such fine and imprisonment.

Added by St.1971, c. 1071, § 1. Amended by St.1974, c. 102.

§ 34. Unlawful possession of particular controlled substances, including heroin and marihuana

No person knowingly or intentionally shall possess a controlled substance unless such substance was obtained directly, or pursuant to a valid prescription or order, from a practitioner while acting in the course of his professional practice, or except as otherwise authorized by the provisions of this chapter. Except as provided in Section 32L of this Chapter or as hereinafter provided, any person who violates this section shall be punished by imprisonment for not more than one year or by a fine of not more than one thousand dollars, or by both such fine and imprisonment. Any person who violates this section by possessing heroin shall for the first offense be punished by imprisonment in a house of correction for not more than two years or by a fine of not more than two thousand dollars, or both, and for a second or subsequent offense shall be punished by imprisonment in the state prison for not less than two and one-half years nor more than five years or by a fine of not more than five thousand dollars and imprisonment in a jail or house of correction for not more than two and one-half years. Any person who violates this section by possession of more than one ounce of marihuana or a controlled substance in Class E of section thirty-one shall be punished by imprisonment in a house of correction for not more than six months or a fine of five hundred dollars, or both. Except for an offense involving a controlled substance in Class E of section thirty-one, whoever violates the provisions of this section after one or more convictions of a violation of this section or of a felony under any other provisions of this chapter, or of a corresponding provision of earlier law relating to the sale or manufacture of a narcotic drug as defined in said earlier law, shall be punished by imprisonment in a house of correction for not more than two years or by a fine of not more than two thousand dollars, or both.

If any person who is charged with a violation of this section has not previously been convicted of a violation of any provision of this chapter or other provision of prior law relative to narcotic drugs or harmful drugs as defined in said prior law, or of a felony under the laws of any state or of the United States relating to such drugs, has had his case continued without a finding to a certain date, or has been convicted and placed on probation, and if, during the period of said continuance or of said probation, such person does not violate any of the conditions of said continuance or said probation, then upon the expiration of such period the court may dismiss the proceedings against him, and may order sealed all official records relating to his arrest, indictment, conviction, probation, continuance or discharge pursuant to this section; provided, however, that departmental records which are not public records, maintained by police and other law enforcement agencies, shall not be sealed; and provided further, that such a record shall be maintained in a separate file by the department of probation solely for the purpose of use by the courts in determining whether or not in subsequent proceedings such person qualifies under this section. The record maintained by the department of probation shall contain only identifying information concerning the person and a statement that he has had his record sealed pursuant to the provisions of this section. Any conviction, the record of which has been sealed under this section, shall not be deemed a conviction for purposes of any disqualification or for any other purpose. No person as to whom such sealing has been ordered shall be held thereafter under any provision of any law to be guilty of perjury or otherwise giving a false statement by reason of his failure to recite or acknowledge such arrest, indictment, conviction, dismissal, continuance, sealing, or any other related court proceeding, in response to any inquiry made of him for any purpose.

Notwithstanding any other penalty provision of this section, any person who is convicted for the first time under this section for the possession of marihuana or a controlled substance in Class E and who has not previously been convicted of any offense pursuant to the provisions of this chapter, or any provision of prior law relating to narcotic drugs or harmful drugs as defined in said prior law shall be placed on probation unless such person does not consent thereto, or unless the court files a written memorandum stating the reasons for not so doing. Upon successful completion of said probation, the case shall be dismissed and records shall be sealed.

It shall be a prima facie defense to a charge of possession of marihuana under this section that the defendant is a patient certified to participate in a therapeutic research program described in chapter ninety-four D, and possessed the marihuana for personal use pursuant to such program.

Added by St.1971, c. 1071, § 1. Amended by St.1972, c. 806, §§ 23, 24; St.1974, c. 207; St.1974, c. 440; St.1975, c. 369; St.1996, c. 271, § 1; St.2008, c. 387, § 5, eff. Dec. 4, 2008.

§ 35. Unlawful presence at a place where heroin is kept or being in company of person in possession thereof

Any person who is knowingly present at a place where heroin is kept or deposited in violation of the provisions of this chapter, or any person who is in the company of a person, knowing that said person is in possession of heroin in violation of the provisions of this chapter, shall be punished by imprisonment for not more than one year or by a fine of not more than one thousand dollars, or both; provided, however, that the provisions of the third paragraph of section thirty-four relative to probation sealing of the records and repeated violations shall apply to him.

Added by St.1971, c. 1071, § 1. Amended by St.1972, c. 806, § 25.

§ 36. Protective custody of children found present where controlled substances are unlawfully kept or possessed

Notwithstanding the provisions of section thirty-five, if a police officer finds a child present where said officer finds a substance which he reasonably believes to be a controlled substance listed in Class A, B, or C of section thirty-one kept or possessed in violation of any provision of this chapter, and if the police officer reasonably believes that the child has not reached his seventeenth birthday and that the child knew of the presence of such controlled substance, the police officer may lawfully take such child into protective custody for a period not to exceed four hours. Persons having custody of a child under this section shall make reasonable efforts to notify the child's parent or guardian or other person having lawful custody. Such persons shall be considered to be acting in the conduct of their official duties and shall not be held criminally or civilly liable for such acts. A child detained pursuant to the provisions of this section shall not be considered to have been arrested or to have a criminal record for any purpose; however, only a departmental record of custody shall be made by the officer indicating the circumstances of custody. The procedures and processes provided by this section for the care, protection, and custody of children are not exclusive but are in addition to all others provided by law.

Added by St.1971, c. 1071, § 1. Amended by St.1972, c. 806, § 26.

§ 37. Theft of controlled substances from persons authorized to dispense or possess

Whoever steals a controlled substance from a registered manufacturer, wholesale druggist, pharmacy or other person authorized to dispense or possess any controlled substance shall be punished by imprisonment in the state prison for not more than ten years or in a jail or house of correction for not more than two and one-half years or by a fine of not more than five hundred dollars.

Added by St.1971, c. 1071, § 1.

§ 38. Violation of Secs. 24(a), 25, 26 or 27

Any person who knowingly violates any provision of subsection (a) of section twenty-four, or of section twenty-five, twenty-six or twenty-seven shall be punished by imprisonment for not more than one year or by a fine of not more than one thousand dollars, or both. Whoever violates any of the provisions of any of said sections after one or more prior convictions of a violation of any provision of this chapter or of a provision of prior law relating to the sale or manufacture of narcotic drugs or harmful drugs as defined in said prior law shall be punished by imprisonment for not more than two years or by a fine of not more than two thousand dollars, or both.

Added by St.1971, c. 1071, § 1. Amended by St.1972, c. 806, § 27.

§ 39. Violation of Secs. 21 or 22

Any person who knowingly violates any provision of sections twenty-one or twenty-two shall be punished by imprisonment for not more than six months or by a fine of not more that fifteen hundred dollars, or by both. Whoever violates any of the provisions of said sections after one or more prior convictions of a violation of any provision of this chapter, or of a provision of prior law relating to narcotic drugs or harmful drugs as defined in said prior law shall be punished by imprisonment for not more than two years or by a fine of not more than two thousand dollars, or both.

Added by St.1971, c. 1071, § 1. Amended by St.1972, c. 806, § 28.

§ 40. Conspiracy

Whoever conspires with another person to violate any provision of this chapter shall be punished by imprisonment or fine, or both, which punishment shall not exceed the maximum punishment prescribed for the offense, the commission of which was the object of the conspiracy.

Added by St.1971, c. 1071, § 1.

§ 41. Arrest without warrant

A police officer shall have the authority to arrest without a warrant:

(a) any person committing in his presence any offense set forth in this chapter;

(b) any person who he has probable cause to believe has committed or is committing a felony set forth under the provisions of this chapter; or

(c) any person who he has probable cause to believe has committed or is committing a violation of the provisions of sections twenty-seven, thirty-two, thirty-two A, thirty-two B, thirty-two C, thirty-two D, thirty-two E, thirty-two F, thirty-three, thirty-four, thirty-five, thirty-seven and forty.

Added by St.1971, c. 1071, § 1. Amended by St.1972, c. 806, § 29; St.1982, c. 650, § 15.

§ 42. Cooperation with federal and other state agencies

The commissioner and the attorney general shall cooperate with federal and other state agencies in discharging their responsibilities concerning traffic in controlled substances and in suppressing the abuse of controlled substances. To this end they may:

(1) Arrange for the exchange of information among governmental officials concerning the use and abuse of controlled substances;

(2) Coordinate and cooperate in training programs concerning the enforcement of laws governing controlled substances at local and state levels;

(3) Cooperate with the bureau by establishing a centralized unit to accept, catalog, file and collect statistics including statistics regarding drug dependent persons and controlled substance law offenders within the commonwealth and make the information available for federal, state and local law enforcement purposes, provided that they shall not furnish the name or identity of a patient or research subject; and

(4) Conduct programs of eradication aimed at destroying wild or illicit growth of plant species from which controlled substances may be extracted.

Added by St.1971, c. 1071, § 1.

§ 43. Conformity with federal acts

Notwithstanding any other provisions of this chapter, no practitioner shall dispense, distribute, administer, or possess any controlled substance except in conformity with the provisions of the Federal "Comprehensive Drug Abuse Prevention and Control Act of 1970" [1] or any amendment thereof and the Federal Food, Drug and Cosmetic Act.[2]

Added by St.1971, c. 1071, § 1.

[1] 21 U.S.C.A. § 801 et seq.

[2] 21 U.S.C.A. § 301 et seq.

§ 44. Violations of Sec. 34; acquittal, dismissal or indictment nol prossed; sealing of records

If any person is found not guilty of the violation of any provision of section thirty-four or if a complaint against him is dismissed or an indictment nol prossed for a violation of said section, the court shall order all official records relating to his arrest, indictment, conviction, continuance or discharge to be sealed; provided, however, that departmental records maintained by police and other law enforcement agencies which are not public records shall not be sealed.

No person as to whom such sealing has been ordered shall be held thereafter under any provision of any law to be guilty of perjury or otherwise making a false statement by reason of his failure to recite or acknowledge such arrest, indictment, disposition, sealing or any other related court proceeding, in response to any inquiry made of him for any purpose.

Added by St.1971, c. 1071, § 1. Amended by St.1973, c. 533, § 1.

§ 45. Photographing and fingerprinting of persons charged with felony

Any person arrested for or charged with the criminal violation of any provision of this chapter which constitutes a felony may at the time of arrest or as soon thereafter as is practicable be photographed and fingerprinted according to the system of the state bureau of identification, and upon conviction any such fingerprints and photographs shall be made a part of permanent records of the police department of the municipality where the arrest took place, and without delay two copies of the fingerprints and photographs shall be forwarded, with such other description as may be required and a written history of the offense, to the state bureau of identification.

Added by St.1971, c. 1071, § 1.

§ 46. Repealed, 1978, 508, Sec. 1

§ 47. Forfeiture of property

(a) The following property shall be subject to forfeiture to the commonwealth and all property rights therein shall be in the commonwealth:

(1) All controlled substances which have been manufactured, delivered, distributed, dispensed or acquired in violation of this chapter.

(2) All materials, products, and equipment of any kind which are used, or intended for use, in manufacturing, compounding, processing, delivering, dispensing, distributing, importing, or exporting any controlled substance in violation of this chapter.

(3) All conveyances, including aircraft, vehicles or vessels used, or intended for use, to transport, conceal, or otherwise facilitate the manufacture, dispensing, distribution of or possession with intent to manufacture, dispense or distribute, a controlled substance in violation of any provision of section thirty-two, thirty-two A, thirty-two B, thirty-two C, thirty-two D, thirty-two E, thirty-two F, thirty-two G, thirty-two *I*, thirty-two J, or forty.

(4) All books, records, and research, including formulas, microfilm, tapes and data which are used, or intended for use, in violation of this chapter.

(5) All moneys, negotiable instruments, securities or other things of value furnished or intended to be furnished by any person in exchange for a controlled substance in violation of this chapter, all proceeds traceable to such an exchange, including real estate and any other thing of value, and all moneys, negotiable instruments, and securities used or intended to be used to facilitate any violation of any provision of section thirty-two, thirty-two A, thirty-two B, thirty-two C, thirty-two D, thirty-two E, thirty-two F, thirty-two G, thirty-two *I*, thirty-two J, or forty.

(6) All drug paraphernalia.

(7) All real property, including any right, title, and interest in the whole of any lot or tract of land and any appurtenances or improvements thereto, which is used in any manner or part, to commit or to facilitate the commission of a violation of any provision of section thirty-two, thirty-two A, thirty-two B, thirty-two C, thirty-two D, thirty-two E, thirty-two F, thirty-two G, thirty-two *I*, thirty-two J or forty.

(8) All property which is used, or intended for use, as a container for property described in subparagraph (1) or (2).

(9) No forfeiture under this section shall extinguish a perfected security interest held by a creditor in a conveyance or in any real property at the time of the filing of the forfeiture action.

(b) Property subject to forfeiture under subparagraphs (1), (2), (4), (5), (6), (7) and (8) of subsection (a) shall, upon motion of the attorney general or district attorney, be declared forfeit by any court having jurisdiction over said property or having final jurisdiction over any related criminal proceeding brought under any provision of this chapter. Property subject to forfeiture under subparagraph (1) of subsection (a) shall be destroyed, regardless of the final disposition of such related criminal proceeding, if any, unless the court for good cause shown orders otherwise.

(c) The court shall order forfeiture of all conveyances subject to the provisions of subparagraph (3) and of all real property subject to the provisions of subparagraph (7) of subsection (a) of this section, except as follows:

(1) No conveyance used by any person as a common carrier in the transaction of business as a common carrier shall be forfeited unless it shall appear that the owner or other person in charge of such conveyance was a consenting party of privy to a violation of this chapter.

(2) No conveyance shall be forfeited by reason of any act or omission established by the owner thereof to have been committed or omitted by any person other than such owner while such conveyance was unlawfully in the possession of a person other than the owner in violation of the criminal laws of the United States, or of the commonwealth, or of any state.

(3) No conveyance or real property shall be subject to forfeiture unless the owner thereof knew or should have known that such conveyance or real property was used in and for the business of unlawfully manufacturing, dispensing, or distributing controlled substances. Proof that the conveyance or real property was used to facilitate the unlawful dispensing, manufacturing, or distribution of, or possession with intent unlawfully to manufacture, dispense or distribute, controlled substances on three or more different dates shall be prima facie evidence that the conveyance or real property was used in and for the business of unlawfully manufacturing, dispensing, or distributing controlled substances.

(4) No conveyance or real property used to facilitate the unlawful manufacturing, dispensing, or distribution of, or the possession with intent unlawfully to manufacture, dispense, or distribute marihuana or a substance, not itself a controlled substance, containing any marihuana shall be forfeited if the net weight of the substance so manufactured, dispensed, or distributed or possessed with intent to manufacture, dispense or distribute, is less than ten pounds in the aggregate.

(d) A district attorney or the attorney general may petition the superior court in the name of the commonwealth in the nature of a proceeding in rem to order forfeiture of a conveyance, real property, moneys or other things of value subject to forfeiture under the provisions of subparagraphs (3), (5), and (7) of subsection (a). Such petition shall be filed in the court having jurisdiction over said conveyance, real property, monies or other things of value or having final jurisdiction over any related criminal proceeding brought under any provision of this chapter. In all such suits where the property is claimed by any person, other than the commonwealth, the commonwealth shall have the burden of proving to the court the existence of probable cause to institute the action, and any such claimant shall then have the burden of proving that the property is not forfeitable pursuant to subparagraph (3), (5), or (7) of said subsection (a). The owner of said conveyance or real property, or other person claiming thereunder shall have the burden of proof as to all exceptions set forth in subsections (c) and (i). The court shall order the commonwealth to give notice by certified or registered mail to the owner of said conveyance, real property, moneys or other things of value and to such other persons as appear to have an interest therein, and the court shall promptly, but not less than two weeks after notice, hold a hearing on the petition. Upon the motion of the owner of said conveyance, real property, moneys or other things of value, the court may continue the hearing on the petition pending the outcome of any criminal trial related to the violation of this chapter. At such hearing the court shall hear evidence and make conclusions of law, and shall thereupon issue a final order, from which the parties shall have a right of appeal. In all such suits where a final order results in a forfeiture, said final order shall provide for disposition of said conveyance, real property, moneys or any other thing of value by the commonwealth or any subdivision thereof in any manner not prohibited by law, including official use by an authorized law enforcement or other public agency, or sale at public auction or by competitive bidding. The proceeds of any such sale shall be used to pay the reasonable expenses of the forfeiture proceedings, seizure, storage, maintenance of custody, advertising, and notice, and the balance thereof shall be distributed as further provided in this section.

The final order of the court shall provide that said moneys and the proceeds of any such sale shall be distributed equally between the prosecuting district attorney or attorney general and the city, town or state police department involved in the seizure. If more than one department was substantially involved in the seizure, the court having jurisdiction over the forfeiture proceeding shall distribute the fifty percent equitably among these departments.

There shall be established within the office of the state treasurer separate special law enforcement trust funds for each district attorney and for the attorney general. All such monies and proceeds received by any prosecuting district attorney or attorney general shall be deposited in such a trust fund and shall then be expended without further appropriation to defray the costs of protracted investigations, to provide additional technical equipment or expertise, to provide matching funds to obtain federal grants, or such other law enforcement purposes as the district attorney or attorney general deems appropriate. The district attorney or attorney general may expend up to ten percent of the monies and proceeds for drug rehabilitation, drug education and other anti-drug or neighborhood crime watch programs which further law enforcement purposes. Any program seeking to be an eligible recipient of said funds shall file an annual audit report with the local district attorney and attorney general. Such report shall include, but not be limited to, a listing of the assets, liabilities, itemized expenditures, and board of directors of such program. Within ninety days of the close of the fiscal year, each district attorney and the attorney general shall file an annual report with the house and senate committees on ways and means on the use of the monies in the trust fund for the purposes of drug rehabilitation, drug education, and other anti-drug or neighborhood crime watch programs.

All such moneys and proceeds received by any police department shall be deposited in a special law enforcement trust fund and shall be expended without further appropriation to defray the costs of protracted investigations, to provide additional technical equipment or expertise, to provide matching funds to obtain federal grants, or to accomplish such other law enforcement purposes as the chief of police of such city or town, or the colonel of state policc deems appropriate, but such funds shall not be considered a source of revenue to meet the operating needs of such department.

(e) Any officer, department, or agency having custody of any property subject to forfeiture under this chapter or having disposed of said property shall keep and maintain full and complete records showing from whom it received said property, under what authority it held or received or disposed of said property, to whom it delivered said property, the date and manner of destruction or disposition of said property, and the exact kinds, quantities and forms of said property. Said records shall be open to inspection by all federal and state officers charged with enforcement of federal and state drug control laws. Persons making final disposition or destruction of said property under court order shall report, under oath, to the court the exact circumstances of said disposition or destruction.

(f) (1) During the pendency of the proceedings the court may issue at the request of the commonwealth *ex parte* any preliminary order or process as is necessary to seize or secure the property for which forfeiture is sought and to provide for its custody, including but not limited to an order that the commonwealth remove the property if possible, and safeguard it in a secure location in a reasonable fashion; that monies be deposited in an interest-bearing escrow account; and, that a substitute custodian be appointed to manage such property or a business enterprise. Property taken or detained under this section shall not be repleviable, but once seized shall be deemed to be lawfully in the custody of the commonwealth pending forfeiture, subject only to the orders and decrees of the court having jurisdiction thereof. Process for seizure of said property shall issue only upon a showing of probable cause, and the application therefor and the issuance, execution, and return thereof shall be subject to the provisions of chapter two hundred and seventy-six, so far as applicable.

(2) There shall be created within the division of capital asset management and maintenance an office of seized property management to which a district attor-

ney or the attorney general may refer any real property, and any furnishings, equipment and related personal property located therein, for which seizure is sought. The office of seized property management shall be authorized to preserve and manage such property in a reasonable fashion and to dispose of such property upon a judgment ordering forfeiture issued pursuant to the provisions of subsection (d), and to enter into contracts to preserve, manage and dispose of such property. The office of seized property management may receive initial funding from the special law enforcement trust funds of the attorney general and each district attorney established pursuant to subsection (d) and shall subsequently be funded by a portion of the proceeds of each sale of such managed property to the extent provided as payment of reasonable expenses in subsection (d).

(g) Species of plants from which controlled substances in Schedules I and II may be derived which have been planted or cultivated in violation of this chapter, or of which the owners or cultivators are unknown, or which are wild growths may be seized by any police officer and summarily forfeited to the commonwealth.

(h) The failure, upon demand by a police officer of the person in occupancy or in control of land or premises upon which the species of plants are growing to produce an appropriate registration, or proof that he is a holder thereof, constitutes authority for the seizure and forfeiture of the plants.

(i) The owner of any real property which is the principal domicile of the immediate family of the owner and which is subject to forfeiture under this section may file a petition for homestead exemption with the court having jurisdiction over such forfeiture. The court may, in its discretion, allow the petition exempting from forfeiture an amount allowed under section one of chapter one hundred and eighty-eight. The value of the balance of said principal domicile, if any, shall be forfeited as provided in this section. Such homestead exemption may be acquired on only one principal domicile for the benefit of the immediate family of the owner.

(j) A forfeiture proceeding affecting the title to real property or the use and occupation thereof or the buildings thereon shall not have any effect except against the parties thereto and persons having actual notice thereof, until a memorandum containing the names of the parties to such proceeding, the name of the town where the affected real property lies, and a description of such real property sufficiently accurate for identification is recorded in the registry of deeds for the county or district where the real property lies. At any time after a judgment on the merits, or after the discontinuance, dismissal or other final disposition is recorded by the court having jurisdiction over such matter, the clerk of such court shall issue a certificate of the fact of such judgment, discontinuance, dismissal or other final disposition, and such certificate shall be recorded in the registry in which the original memorandum recorded pursuant to this section was filed.

Added by St.1971, c. 1071, § 1. Amended by St.1972, c. 806, §§ 30, 31; St.1977, c. 556, §§ 1 to 3; St.1981, c. 669, § 3; St.1982, c. 132; St.1982, c. 650, §§ 16, 17; St.1984, c. 486, §§ 1, 2; St.1989, c. 162; St.1989, c. 653, §§ 73 to 80; St.1991, c. 412, §§ 66A, 67; St.1992, c. 133, §§ 455 to 459; St.1992, c. 289, §§ 6, 7; St.1996, c. 450, § 145; St.1998, c. 194, § 147.

§ 47A. Seized controlled substances and narcotic drugs; custodian; mailing for chemical analysis; destruction or disposal upon completion of trial

The police commissioner, chief superintendent or other officer or board at the head of each police department in the commonwealth shall appoint a police officer to act as custodian of all controlled substances and narcotic drugs seized in the course of any arrest or investigation. Such custodian shall be designated as the "evidence officer".

Notwithstanding the provisions of any general or special law or rule or regulation to the contrary, controlled substances or narcotic drugs seized in cases under the provisions of this chapter where the violation is a misdemeanor and requiring chemical analyses which are to be performed at a laboratory operated by the department of public health or the department of state police or the University of Massachusetts medical center may be mailed to or from the place of such analyses by using the registered mail service of the United States Postal Service, and testimony from a law enforcement officer that he mailed or received such substances or narcotic drugs by registered mail together with the return receipts accompanying such mailing shall be prima facie evidence that said substances or drugs are the substances or drugs so seized.

At any time after the seizure of a controlled substance or narcotic drug, a district attorney or the attorney general may petition the superior court in the name of the commonwealth to order the destruction of said controlled substance or narcotic drug seized in the course of any arrest or investigation. The court shall order the commonwealth to give notice by certified or registered mail to the known defendant and his attorney and shall promptly, but not less than two weeks after notice, hold a hearing on the petition. At such hearing, the court shall hear evidence from the parties on the issue of destruction, the extent of the proposed destruction, the preservation of samples, the inspection, examination and testing of the controlled substance or narcotic drugs. The court, after such hearing, shall have the power to order the forfeiture and destruction of such controlled substance or narcotic drug as it so determines, under procedures and to the extent as so determined by the court, with the remainder to be kept under the provisions of this section and shall thereupon issue a final order in writing.

Such final order shall provide for the analysis of representative and fair samples of such forfeited controlled substances or narcotic drugs by a chemist of the department of state police or by a chemist at the University of Massachusetts medical school or by an analyst of the department of public health who shall issue a signed certificate, on oath, of the results of such analysis. Such certificate shall be sworn to before a justice of the peace or a notary public and shall be prima facie evidence of the composition and quality of such controlled substances or narcotic drugs when introduced as evidence before a grand jury or any court proceeding in the commonwealth. Upon completion of such analysis, such order shall direct the evidence officer to deliver such controlled substances or narcotic drugs ordered destroyed to the department for such destruction or disposition in any way not prohibited by law; provided, however, that the evidence officer shall make proper provisions for maintaining and securing such samples as may be directed by the court.

The court having jurisdiction shall, upon completion of a trial or other disposition by the trial court and after the expiration of the period for an appeal from that trial or disposition, in writing, order such forfeited controlled substances or narcotic drugs not destroyed prior thereto to be caused to be delivered forthwith by the evidence officer to the department for destruction or disposition in any way not prohibited by law. In the event of an appeal as prescribed by law, the evidence officer shall retain possession of such controlled substances or narcotic drugs until final disposition of the case, at which time, the district attorney or attorney general may petition the superior court for summary destruction of such controlled substances or narcotic drugs.

The department shall keep a record of the place where such controlled substances or narcotic drugs were seized, of the kinds and quantities of drugs received, by whose order the controlled substance or narcotic drugs were received, by whom the controlled substance or narcotic drugs were delivered and received, the date and manner of destruction or disposition of such controlled substances or narcotic drugs, and a report under oath of such destruction or disposition shall be made to the court, which record shall be open to inspection by attorneys of record in the case and by all federal and state officers charged with enforcement of federal and state narcotic laws.

The department may at its discretion upon an official written order, deliver to any hospital within the state, not operated for private gain, any narcotic drugs, except heroin and its salts and derivatives, for medicinal purposes.

The department shall keep a complete record of all drugs received and of all drugs disposed of, showing the exact kinds, quantities and forms of such drugs; the persons from whom received and the dates of receipt, disposal or destruction, which record shall be open to inspection by all federal and state officers charged with enforcement of federal and state narcotic laws.

Added by St.1974, c. 318. Amended by St.1977, c. 798; St.1983, c. 184, § 1; St.1984, c. 69; St.1996, c. 151, § 250.

§ 48. Severability

If any provision of this chapter or the application thereof to any person or circumstance is held invalid, the invalidity does not affect other provisions or applications of the chapter which can be given effect without the invalid provisions or application, and to this end the provisions of this chapter are severable.

Added by St.1971, c. 1071, § 1.

§ 49. Enforcement of Sec. 24A

The department of public health shall enforce section 24A in accordance with rules and regulations promulgated by the department.

Added by St.2010, c. 283, § 5, eff. Nov. 7, 2010.

TITLE XVII

PUBLIC WELFARE

Chapter

CHAPTER 119

PROTECTION AND CARE OF CHILDREN, AND PROCEEDINGS AGAINST THEM

Section

The section headings for the General Laws in this pamphlet have been editorially supplied.

§ 1. Declaration of policy; purpose

It is hereby declared to be the policy of this commonwealth to direct its efforts, first, to the strengthening and encouragement of family life for the care and protection of children; to assist and encourage the use by any family of all available resources to this end; and to provide substitute care of children only when the family itself or the resources available to the family are unable to provide the necessary care and protection to insure the rights of any child to sound health and normal physical, mental, spiritual and moral development.

The purpose of this chapter is to insure that the children of the commonwealth are protected against the harmful effects resulting from the absence, inability, inadequacy or destructive behavior of parents or parent substitutes, and to assure good substitute parental care in the event of the absence, temporary or permanent inability or unfitness of parents to provide care and protection for their children.

The health and safety of the child shall be of paramount concern and shall include the long-term well-being of the child.

In all matters and decisions by the department of children and families, the policy of the department, as applied to children in its care and protection or children who receive its services, shall be to define best interests of the child as that which shall include, but not be limited to, considerations of precipitating factors and previous conditions leading to any decisions made in proceedings related to the past, current and future status of the child, the current state of the factors and conditions together with an assessment of the likelihood of their amelioration or elimination; the child's fitness, readiness, abilities and developmental levels; the particulars of the service plan designed to meet the needs of the child within the child's current placement whether with the child's family or in a substitute care placement and whether such service plan is used by the department or presented to the courts with written documentation; and the effectiveness, suitability and adequacy of the services provided and of placement decisions, including the progress of the child or children therein. The department's considerations of appropriate services and placement decisions shall be made in a timely manner in order to facilitate permanency planning for the child.

In all department proceedings that affect the child's past, current and future placements and status, when determining the best interests of the child, there shall be a presumption of competency that a child who has attained the age of 12 is able to offer statements on the child's own behalf and shall be provided with timely opportunities and access to offer such statements, which shall be considered by the department if the child is capable and willing. In all matters relative to the care and protection of a child, the ability, fitness and capacity of the child shall be considered in all department proceedings.

For purposes of this section, the words "all department proceedings" shall include departmental hearings and proceedings but shall not include a court proceeding even when the department is a party.

Added by St.1954, c. 646, § 1. Amended by St.1972, c. 785, § 5; St.1999, c. 3, § 4; St.2008, c. 176, § 82, eff. July 8, 2008.

§§ 2 to 20. Repealed, 1972, 785, Sec. 6

§ 21. Definitions applicable to Secs. 21 to 51H

As used in sections 21 to 51H, inclusive, the following words shall have the following meanings, unless the context clearly otherwise requires:—

"51A report", a report filed with the department under section 51A that details suspected child abuse or neglect.

"Child", a person under the age of 18.

"Child advocate", the child advocate appointed under chapter 18C.

"Child in need of services", a child between the ages of 6 and 17 who: (a) repeatedly runs away from the home of a parent or legal guardian; (b) repeatedly fails to obey the lawful and reasonable commands of a parent or legal guardian, thereby interfering with the parent's or legal guardian's ability to adequately care for and protect the child; (c) repeatedly fails to obey lawful and reasonable school regulations; or (d) when not otherwise excused from attendance in accordance with lawful and reasonable school regulations, willfully fails to attend school for more than 8 school days in a quarter.

"Commissioner", the commissioner of children and families.

"Custody", the power to: (1) determine a child's place of abode, medical care and education; (2) control visits to a child; and (3) consent to enlistments, marriages and other contracts otherwise requiring parental consent. If a parent or guardian objects to the carrying out of any power conferred by this paragraph, that parent or guardian may take application to the committing court and the court shall review and make an order on the matter.

"Department", the department of children and families.

"Mandated reporter", a person who is: (i) a physician, medical intern, hospital personnel engaged in the examination, care or treatment of persons, medical examiner, psychologist, emergency medical technician, dentist, nurse, chiropractor, podiatrist, optometrist, osteopath, allied mental health and human services professional licensed under section 165 of chapter 112, drug and alcoholism counselor, psychiatrist or clinical social worker; (ii) a public or private school teacher, educational administrator, guidance or family counselor, child care worker, person paid to care for or work with a child in any public or private facility, or home or program funded by the commonwealth or licensed under chapter 15D that provides child care or residential services to children or that provides the services of child care resource and referral agencies, voucher management agencies or family child care systems or child care food programs, licensor of the department of early education and care or school attendance officer; (iii) a probation officer, clerk-magistrate of a district court, parole officer, social worker, foster parent, firefighter, police officer; (iv) a priest, rabbi, clergy member, ordained or licensed minister, leader of any church or religious body, accredited Christian Science practitioner, person performing official duties on behalf of a church or religious body that are recognized as the duties of a priest, rabbi, clergy, ordained or licensed minister, leader of any church or religious body, accredited Christian Science practitioner, or person employed by a church or religious body to supervise, educate, coach, train or counsel a child on a regular basis; (v) in charge of a medical or other public or private institution, school or facility or that person's designated agent; or (vi) the child advocate.

"Parent", a mother or father, unless another relative has been designated as a parent as defined in section 1 of chapter 118 for the purposes of receiving benefits from the department of transitional assistance.

"Relative", the father or mother of a child; a stepfather, stepmother, stepbrother, stepsister, or any blood relative of a child, including those of the half blood, except cousins who are more distantly related than first cousins; any adoptive relative of equal propinquity to the foregoing; or a spouse of any such persons.

"Serious bodily injury", bodily injury which involves a substantial risk of death, extreme physical pain, protracted and obvious disfigurement or protracted loss or impairment of the function of a bodily member, organ or mental faculty.

"Young adult", a person between the ages of 18 and 22.

Added by St.1972, c. 785, § 7. Amended by St.1973, c. 1073, § 3; St.1973, c. 1076, § 1A; St.1978, c. 552, § 28; St.1996, c. 151, § 276; St.2008, c. 176, § 83, eff. July 8, 2008; St.2008, c. 215, §§ 63, 64A, eff. July 8, 2008; St.2008, c. 215, §§ 64, 64½, eff. July 31, 2008; St.2010, c. 359, § 18, eff. Jan. 3, 2011.

§ 21A. Admissibility of evidence; qualified experts

Evidence in proceedings under sections 21 to 51H, inclusive, shall be admissible according to the rules of the common law and the General Laws and may include reports to the court by any person who has made an investigation of the facts relating to the welfare of the child and is qualified as an expert according to the rules of the common law or by statute or is an agent of the department or of an approved charitable corporation or agency substantially engaged in the foster care or protection of children. Such person may file with the court in a proceeding under said sections 21 to 51H, inclusive, a full report of all facts obtained as a result of such investigation. The person reporting may be called as a witness by any party for examination as to the statements made in the report. Such examination shall be conducted as though it were on cross-examination. Evidence may include testimony of foster parents or pre-adoptive parents concerning the welfare of a child if such child has been in the care of the foster or pre-adoptive parents for 6 months or more, and may include the testimony of the child if the court determines that the child is competent and willing, after consultation with counsel, if any, to testify.

Added by St.2008, c. 176, § 83, eff. July 8, 2008. Amended by St.2008, c. 215, § 64B, eff. July 8, 2008.

§ 22. Visitation of family foster homes; removal of child; discharge of child to parent or legal guardian

An agent of the department shall visit each family foster home, not supervised and approved by a licensed placement agency, at least once a year and may be authorized by the department to remove a child to its care if, in its judgment, the welfare of the child or its protection from neglect or abuse so require. An agent who is refused entry or hindered in the removal of such child may make complaint, on oath, to a justice of the court having jurisdiction, who may thereupon issue a warrant authorizing the agent to obtain sufficient aid and, at any reasonable time, enter the building designated, and any part thereof, to investigate the treatment and condition of a child found there and to remove the child as herein provided. The department shall take the child temporarily into its care, immediately notify the child's parent or legal guardian and, upon request, discharge the child to a parent or legal guardian. If the parent or legal guardian is unable or refuses to make suitable provisions for the child, the department shall make lawful provisions for the child's care under section 23 or 24.

Added by St.1972, c. 785, § 8. Amended by St.2008, c. 176, § 83, eff. July 8, 2008.

§ 23. Responsibility of department to provide foster care for children; placement with relatives; funeral expenses; child profile form; extension of support of child until 22 years of age; assignment of support rights; assistance to foster care families

(a) The department shall have the responsibility, including financial responsibility, for providing foster care for children through its own resources or by use of appropriate voluntary agencies, according to the rules and regulations of the department, in the following instances:—

(1) If a child, parent, guardian, or any person acting on behalf of a child, applies for foster care, the department may accept a child who, in the judgment of the department, is in need of foster care. Such acceptance shall entail no abrogation of parental rights or responsibilities, but the department may accept from parents a temporary delegation of certain rights and responsibilities necessary to provide the foster care for a period of time under conditions agreed upon by both and terminable by either. If the department determines that continued placement beyond 6 months is required for reasons unrelated to parental unfitness and the parent consents to continued placement, the department may file a petition for care and responsibility in the probate court on behalf of a child accepted into foster care. At the initial hearing on the petition, the court shall determine whether continued placement with the department is in the child's best interests and shall issue its determination, including its rationale, in written form. The allowance of the petition shall not abrogate a parent's right to make decisions on behalf of the child, but the department may accept from the parent a temporary delegation of certain rights and responsibilities necessary to continue to provide foster care for the child under conditions agreed upon by both and terminable by either. Notwithstanding any general or special law to the contrary, a permanency hearing shall be held within 60 days of the transfer of responsibility by order of the probate court or within 12 months of initial placement into foster care with the department, whichever date is later. The hearing shall be conducted as provided in section 29B.

(2) If a parent or parents apply for voluntary surrender of custody of a child for purposes of giving consent to adoption, the department may accept the child following the procedure described in clause (1).

(3) If a child is without proper guardianship due to death, unavailability, incapacity or unfitness of a parent or guardian or with the consent of a parent or parents, the department may seek, and shall accept, an order of the probate court granting responsibility for the child to the department. Such responsibility shall include the right to: (i) determine the child's abode, medical care and education; (ii) control visits to the child; (iii) consent to enlistments, marriages and other contracts requiring parental consent; and (iv) consent to adoption only when it is expressly included in an order of the court. In making an order, the probate court shall consider section 29C and shall make the written certification and determinations required by said section 29C. If a child is in the care of the department of mental health or the department of developmental services, the responsibility for the child as described in this section and all rights therein contained shall continue in the department. If a person with mental retardation who has been declared mentally incompetent was the responsibility of the department prior to reaching the age of 18, the department shall continue to exercise responsibility for that person until that person is declared to be no longer legally incompetent.

(4) The department shall accept on commitment from the juvenile court any child declared in need of foster care under section 26 or declared to be a child in need of services under section 39G.

(5) Any child who is left in any place and who is seemingly without a parent or legal guardian available shall be immediately reported to the department, which shall proceed to arrange care for that child temporarily and shall forthwith cause search to be made for that child's parent or guardian. If a parent or guardian cannot be located or is unable or refuses to make suitable provision for the child, the department shall make such lawful provision it deems in the best interest of that child as provided under this chapter.

(6) If the department has in its care a child whose parent or parents have consented to the child's adoption and the department has been unable to place that child in an adoptive home within 60 days of receipt of the consent, the department shall so notify all children's foster care agencies in the commonwealth licensed to place children for adoption. The notice shall request that each such agency attempt to find an adoptive home for such child. If 1 of the agencies locates an adoptive home for this child, the department shall cooperate with the agency in the placement of the child in this home and in the supervision of the placement during the 1 year waiting period. Any person in whose home a child has been placed by the department shall also be informed by the department if the child has become eligible for adoption, and this person may request consideration as a prospective adoptive parent.

(7) A temporary shelter care facility program or a group care facility, licensed under chapter 15D, may provide temporary shelter for a 72–hour period to a child without parental consent, if the child's welfare would be endangered if such shelter were not immediately provided. At the expiration of the 72–hour period, the licensee shall: (i) secure the consent of a parent or guardian to continued custody and care; (ii) refer the child to the department for custody and care; or (iii) refuse to provide continued care and custody to the child.

(b) The department shall develop guidelines and standards for the placement of children in foster care. The guidelines and standards shall be reviewed by the executive office of health and human services and the child advocate.

(c) Whenever the department places a child in foster care, the department shall immediately commence a search to locate any relative of the child or other adult person who has played a significant positive role in that child's life in order to determine whether the child may appropriately be placed with that relative or person if, in the judgment of the department, that placement would be in the best interest of the child.

The department shall also seek to identify any minor sibling or half-sibling of the child and attempt to place these children in the same foster family if, in the judgment of the department, that placement would be in the best interests of the children.

(d) The department may pay to a funeral establishment a sum not to exceed $1,100 for the funeral and final disposition of a child in its care if there are insufficient resources to pay for the cost of such funeral and final disposition. The commonwealth shall have the right of reimbursement from whatever resources may exist in the estate of the child.

(e) If a child is placed in or transferred to a foster home, a completed child profile form shall precede or accompany the child to the foster home. In the case of an emergency placement, the department, the department of youth services, the department of mental health, other departments of the commonwealth responsible for the placement of foster children, or a placement agency shall immediately provide a brief verbal or written statement describing the child's outstanding problem behaviors and mental and emotional problems and shall provide the child profile form within 10 days to the foster parents.

The department shall develop a child profile form to be used by all other departments of the commonwealth or placement agencies that shall contain the child profile and any other relevant information necessary to the care, well-being, protection and parenting of the child by the foster parents, including, but not be limited to: (i) a history of the child's previous placements and reasons for placement changes; (ii) a history of the child's problem behaviors and mental and emotional problems; (iii) educational status and school related problem behaviors; and (iv) any other necessary psychological, educational, medical or health information.

The child profile form shall immediately be prepared by the department of the commonwealth which is granted care and custody of the child at the time such care and custody is granted.

(f) The department shall offer to continue its responsibility to any young adult who is under the custody, care, or responsibility of the department including, but not limited to, those persons who meet any of the criteria set forth in 42 USC § 675(8)(B)(iv): (i) for the purposes of specific educational or rehabilitative programs, or (ii) to promote and support that person in fully developing and fulfilling that person's potential to be a participating citizen of the commonwealth under conditions agreed upon by both the department and that person. The department's continued responsibility for such persons is contingent upon the express written consent of the person or their guardian unless: (i) before reaching the age of 18, the person had an intellectual disability and was declared mentally incompetent under clause (3) of subsection (a) while under the responsibility of the department; or (ii) the person is under the responsibility of the department pursuant to section 5–305 of chapter 190B. The purposes and conditions of such responsibility may be reviewed and revised or terminated by either the person or the department; provided, however, that within 90 days before the termination of such responsibility, the department shall provide the person with assistance and support in developing a transition plan which fulfills the requirements of 42 USC § 675(5)(H). If after termination the person requests that the department renew its responsibility therefor, the department shall make every reasonable attempt to provide a program of support which is acceptable to the person and which permits the department to renew its responsibility; provided, however, that the department may require the person to meet 1 of the criteria set forth in 42 USC § 675(8)(B)(iv). If the department renews its responsibility, all other provisions of this subsection shall apply. The department shall report annually to the child advocate, the senate and house chairs of the joint committee on children, families and persons with disabilities and the chairs of the senate and house committees on ways and means on the number of persons it serves and declines to serve under this subsection.

(g) The department shall obtain and provide to the IV–D agency, as set forth in chapter 119A, an assignment of support rights on behalf of each child receiving foster care maintenance payments under Title IV, Part E, of the Social Security Act. The department shall be subrogated to the rights of each such child and shall obtain and provide to the IV–D agency information that may be reasonably necessary to enforce the department's right including, but not limited to, the following information: the child's name, date of birth, place of birth, Social Security number, address and benefit level and, if known, each parent's name, date of birth, place of birth, Social Security number, most recent address and most recent employer. The department shall immediately notify the IV–D agency when a child whose rights to support are subrogated no longer receives foster care maintenance payments under said Title IV, Part E, of the Social Security Act.

(h) The department shall, subject to appropriation, provide assistance to foster care families which includes maintenance payments at the daily rate recommended and periodically adjusted by the United States Department of Agriculture. The department shall periodically review the level of assistance including maintenance payments provided to adoptive and guardianship families and may, subject to appropriation, and consistent with federal law and policy, adjust such assistance as warranted by the financial circumstances of the family, the needs of the child or the rate of inflation.

The department shall report annually on September 1, to the senate and house committees on ways and means and the joint committee on children, families and persons with disabilities on the amounts expended to provide to foster care, adoptive and guardianship families financial and other assistance including, but not limited to, payments to provide for the care of children.

(i) The department, in consultation with the executive office of public safety and security, shall work with the department of state police and municipal police departments to ensure that adequate efforts are being made to identify and to provide for the immediate protection, care and custody of the minor children of a person arrested or placed in custody by police officers in the performance of their official duties.

Added by St.1954, c. 646, § 1. Amended by St.1960, c. 325; St.1962, c. 535; St.1969, c. 859, § 7; St.1970, c. 825; St.1970, c. 888, § 5; St.1972, c. 731, § 7; St.1973, c. 433; St.1973, c. 925, § 40; St.1973, c. 1073, § 4; St.1974, c. 682, § 4; St.1975, c. 276, §§ 1, 2; St.1980, c. 478; St.1983, c. 633, § 7; St.1986, c. 310, § 10; St.1986, c. 557, § 113; St.1986, c. 599, § 36; St.1988, c. 128; St.1989, c. 341, § 72; St.1991, c. 492; St.1992, c. 379, § 7; St.1993, c. 486, §§ 1, 2; St.1997, c. 43, § 98; St.1999, c. 3, § 5; St.2002, c. 371, § 1; St.2005, c. 163, § 40, eff. Dec. 8, 2005; St.2008, c. 176, § 83, eff. July 8, 2008; St.2008, c. 451, § 82, eff. June 30, 2009; St.2010, c. 131, § 86, eff. July 1, 2010; St.2010, c. 359, § 19, eff. Jan. 3, 2011.

§ 23A. Children born to inmates of correctional institutions or jails; care and custody

Any child born to an inmate of the Massachusetts Correctional Institution, Framingham, or of the Industrial School for Girls at Lancaster, or of a jail or a house of correction, shall be accepted by the department, and any child whose mother is committed to the Massachusetts Correctional Institution, Framingham, to a jail or a house of correction, or to the custody of the youth service board, may be accepted by the department. Thereupon the department in consultation with the commissioner of correction or the chairman of the youth service board shall make such provision at said place of commitment or elsewhere for the care of said child as may seem to be for the best interests of said child.

Added by St.1958, c. 588, § 2. Amended by St.1966, c. 473.

§ 23B. Services to unwed mothers

The department may, through its own resources or the resources of other appropriate agencies, provide services to mothers bearing children out of wedlock.

Added by St.1966, c. 495.

§ 24. Procedure to commit child to custody or other disposition; notice and summons; emergency order transferring custody; investigation; abandoned children

A person may petition under oath the juvenile court alleging on behalf of a child within its jurisdiction that the child: (a) is without necessary and proper physical or educational care and discipline; (b) is growing up under conditions or circumstances damaging to the child's sound character development; (c) lacks proper attention of the parent, guardian with care and custody or custodian; or (d) has a parent, guardian or custodian who is unwilling, incompetent or unavailable to provide any such care, discipline or attention.

The court may issue a precept to bring the child before the court, and shall issue a notice to the department and summonses to both parents of the child to show cause why the child should not be committed to the custody of the department or why any other appropriate order should not be made. A petition under this section may be brought in the judicial district where the child is located or where the parent, guardian with care and custody or custodian is domiciled. The summonses shall include notice that the court may dispense with the right of the parents to notice of or consent to the adoption, custody or guardianship or any other disposition of the child named therein if it finds that the child is in need of care and protection and that the best interests of the child would be served by any such disposition. Notice shall be by personal service upon the parent. If the identity or whereabouts of a parent is unknown, the petitioner shall cause notice in a form prescribed by the court to be served upon such parent by publication once in each of 3 successive weeks in any newspaper as the court may order. If no parent can be found after reasonable search, a summons shall be issued to the child's legal guardian, if any, known to reside within the commonwealth and, if none, to the person with whom such child last resided, if known.

If the court is satisfied after the petitioner testifies under oath that there is reasonable cause to believe that: (i) the child is suffering from serious abuse or neglect or is in immediate danger of serious abuse or neglect; and (ii) that immediate removal of the child is necessary to protect the child from serious abuse or neglect, the court may issue an emergency order transferring custody of the child for up to 72 hours to the department or to a licensed child care agency or individual described in subclause (ii) of clause (2) of subsection (b) of section 26.

Upon entry of the order, notice to appear before the court shall be given to either parents, both parents, a guardian with care and custody or another custodian. At that time, the court shall determine whether temporary custody shall continue beyond 72 hours until a hearing on the merits of the petition for care and protection is concluded before the court. The court shall also consider the provisions of section 29C and shall make the written certification and determinations required by said section 29C.

Upon the issuance of the precept and order of notice, the court shall appoint a person qualified under section 21A to investigate the conditions affecting the child and to make a report under oath to the court, which shall be attached to the petition and be a part of the record.

If the child is alleged to be abandoned, as defined in section 3 of chapter 210, hearings on the petition under section 26 shall be expedited. If the parents or guardians consent, a child may be committed to the department under this section without a hearing or notice.

Added by St.1954, c. 646, § 1. Amended by St.1969, c. 859, § 8; St.1972, c. 731, § 8; St.1973, c. 1076, § 2; St.1974, c. 260, § 19; St.1975, c. 276, § 3; St.1977, c. 799; St.1978, c. 478, §§ 49, 50; St.1980, c. 181; St.1983, c. 182; St.1984, c. 197, § 2; St.1992, c. 303, § 1; St.1992, c. 379, § 8; St.1996, c. 450, § 159; St.1999, c. 3, § 6; St.2008, c. 176, § 84, eff. July 8, 2008; St.2008, c. 215, § 64C, eff. July 8, 2008.

§ 25. Hearing; custody of child

The petition under section 24 may be heard on the merits when a child is taken into custody and brought before the court or may be continued to a time fixed for hearing. Pending the hearing on the merits, the court may allow the child to be placed in the care of some suitable person or licensed agency providing foster care for children or may commit the child to the custody of the department. If the court commits a child to the custody of the department, the court shall consider the provisions of section 29C and shall make the written certification and determinations required by said section 29C.

Added by St.1954, c. 646, § 1. Amended by St.1999, c. 3, § 7; St.2008, c. 176, § 84, eff. July 8, 2008.

§ 26. Procedure at hearing; order of commitment; petition to dispense with parental consent to adoption; reimbursement of commonwealth; petition for review

(a) If the child is identified by the court and it appears that the precept and summonses have been duly and legally served, that notice has been issued to the department and the report of the person qualified under section 21A is received, the court may excuse the child from the hearing and shall proceed to hear the evidence.

(b) If the court finds the allegations in the petition proved within the meaning of this chapter, it may adjudge that the child is in need of care and protection. In making such adjudication, the health and safety of the child shall be of paramount concern. If the child is adjudged to be in need of care and protection, the court may commit the child to the custody of the department until he becomes an adult or until, in the opinion of the department, the object of his commitment has been accomplished, whichever occurs first; and the court shall consider the provisions of section 29C and shall make the written certification and determinations required by said section 29C. The court also may make any other appropriate order, including conditions and limitations, about the care and custody of the child as may be in the child's best interest including, but not limited to, any 1 or more of the following:

(1) It may permit the child to remain with a parent, guardian or other custodian, and may require supervision as directed by the court for the care and protection of the child.

(2) It may transfer temporary or permanent legal custody to:

(i) any person, including the child's parent, who, after study by a probation officer or other person or agency designated by the court, is found by the court to be qualified to give care to the child;

(ii) any agency or other private organization licensed or otherwise authorized by law to receive and provide care for the child; or

(iii) the department of children and families.

(3) It may order appropriate physical care including medical or dental care.

(4) It may dispense with the need for consent of any person named in section 2 of chapter 210 to the adoption, custody, guardianship or other disposition of the child named therein.

In determining whether such an order should be made, the standards set forth in section 3 of said chapter 210 concerning an order to dispense with the need for consent to adoption of a child shall be applied. If the child who is the subject of the petition is under the age of 12, and if the court adjudicates the child to be in need of care and protection under this section, the court shall enter an order dispensing with the need for consent to adoption upon finding that the best interests of the child, as defined in paragraph (c) of said section 3 of said chapter 210, will be served thereby. The entry of such an order shall have the effect of terminating the rights of a person named therein to receive notice of or to consent to any legal proceeding affecting the custody, guardianship, adoption or other disposition of the child named therein.

The department shall file a petition or a motion to amend a petition to dispense with parental consent to adoption, custody, guardianship or other disposition of the child if: (i) the child has been abandoned; (ii) the parent has been convicted by a court of competent jurisdiction of the murder or voluntary manslaughter of another child of such parent, of aiding, abetting, attempting, conspiring or soliciting to commit such murder or voluntary manslaughter or of an assault constituting a felony which resulted in serious bodily injury to the child or to another child of such parent; or (iii) the child has been in foster care in the custody of the state for 15 of the immediately preceding 22 months. Under this paragraph, a child shall be considered to have entered foster care on the earlier of: (a) the date of the first judicial finding, under section 24 or this section, that the child has been subjected to abuse or neglect; or (b) the date that is 60 days after the date on which the child is removed from the home. The department shall concurrently identify, recruit, process and approve a qualified family for adoption.

The department need not file such a motion or petition to dispense with parental consent to the adoption, custody, guardianship or other disposition of the child if the child is being cared for by a relative or the department has documented in the case plan a compelling reason for determining that such a petition would not be in the best interests of the child or that the family of the child has not been provided, consistent with the time period in the case plan, such services as the department deems necessary for the safe return of the child to the child's home if reasonable efforts as set forth in section 29C are required to be made with respect to the child.

Notwithstanding the foregoing, the following circumstances shall constitute grounds for dispensing with the need for consent to adoption, custody, guardianship or other disposition of the child: (i) the child has been abandoned; or (ii) the parent has been convicted by a court of competent jurisdiction of the murder or voluntary manslaughter of another child of such parent, of aiding, abetting, attempting, conspiring or soliciting to commit such murder or voluntary manslaughter or of an assault constituting a felony which resulted in serious bodily injury to the child or to another child of the parent.

(5) The court may order the parents or parent of said child to reimburse the commonwealth or other agency for care in appropriate cases.

(c) On any petition filed in any court under this section, the department or the parents, person having legal custody, probation officer or guardian of a child or the counsel or guardian ad litem for a child may petition the court not more than once every 6 months for a review and redetermination of the current needs of such child whose case has come before the court, except that any person against whom a decree to dispense with consent to adoption has been entered under clause (4) of subsection (b) shall not have such right of petition for review and redetermination. Unless the court enters written findings setting forth specific extraordinary circumstances that require continued intervention by the court, the court shall enter a final order of adjudication and permanent disposition, not later than 15 months after the date the case was first filed in court. The date by which a final order of adjudication and permanent disposition shall be entered may be extended once for a period not to exceed 3 months and only if the court makes a written finding that the parent has made consistent and goal-oriented progress likely to lead to the child's return to the parent's care and custody. Findings in support of such final order of adjudication and permanent disposition shall be made in writing within a reasonable time of the court's order. The court shall not lose jurisdiction over the petition by reason of its failure to enter a final order and the findings in support thereof within the time set forth in this paragraph.

Added by St.1954, c. 646, § 1. Amended by St.1973, c. 925, § 41; St.1973, c. 1076, § 3; St.1978, c. 552, § 29; St.1983, c. 117; St.1992, c. 303, §§ 2, 3; St.1993, c. 486, § 3; St.1997, c. 43, § 99; St.1998, c. 14, § 1; St.1999, c. 3, §§ 8, 9; St.1999, c. 6, § 1; St.2008, c. 176, § 84, eff. July 8, 2008; St.2008, c. 215, § 64D, eff. July 8, 2008.

§ 26A. Registration of interest for foster care placement; criminal record review

When deciding whether to approve or reject a registration of interest for foster care placement, the department shall conduct a review of any misdemeanor offense discovered through a criminal offender record information search conducted under section 172B of chapter 6 in order to assist the department in accurately evaluating whether the mere existence of the offense has a substantial effect on the applicant's current or future ability to assume and carry out the responsibilities of a foster parent in such a manner that the rights of the child to sound health and normal physical, mental, spiritual and moral development are insured. The review shall include, but not be limited to, a review of the following: (i) the time that has elapsed between the date of the offense and the filing of the registration of interest; (ii) the seriousness and specific circumstances of the offense; (iii) the number and nature of other offenses; (iv) the age of the offender at the time of the offense; (v) the findings and recommendations of the family resource worker assigned by the department to discuss the facts surrounding the misdemeanor with the applicant; (vi) the recommendations given to the family resource worker by personal or employment references chosen by the applicant or received otherwise; (vii) the current and future needs of the child to be placed and the probable effect that the misdemeanor would have on the applicant's ability to fulfill those needs; (viii) any reports or recommendations received by the department from the applicant's parole or probation officer if 1 was assigned; (ix) a copy of the police report pertaining to the offense in question if obtainable within a reasonable period of time or discussions with a police officer familiar with the facts surrounding the offense; and (x) discussions with the child to be placed regarding his current and past relationship with the applicant, unless these discussions are inappropriate. Nothing in this section shall affect the discretion of the department to approve or reject the registration of interest for foster care placement.

Added by St.1999, c. 3, § 10. Amended by St.2008, c. 176, § 84, eff. July 8, 2008.

§ 26B. Grandparent visitation; sibling visitation; appeal of decision to deny visitation

(a) Whenever a child is placed in family foster care, the court and the department shall ensure that a grandparent of a child who is in the department's care or is the subject of a petition under this chapter shall, upon that grandparent's request, have access to reasonable visitation and that the department establish a schedule for that visitation, unless it is determined by the court or the department that grandparent visitation is not in the child's best interests. In determining the best interests of the child, the court or the department shall consider the goal of the service plan and the relationship between the grandparent and the child's parents or legal guardian. Upon recommendation by the department or on its own accord, the court may establish reasonable conditions governing grandparent visitation, including requiring that the grandparent be restrained from revealing the whereabouts of the child's placement.

A grandparent of a child who is placed with the department voluntarily under clause (1) of subsection (a) of section 23 or placed in the custody of the department under an adoption surrender under section 2 of chapter 210, who is denied grandparent visitation by the department, may appeal through the department's fair hearing process. A grandparent may appeal the decision reached through the department's fair hearing process by filing a petition in the probate and family court for grandparent visitation. That grandparent shall have the right to court review by trial de novo.

A grandparent of a child who is the subject of a petition under this chapter and placed in the custody of the department may file a petition for visitation in the court which has committed the child to the custody of the department.

(b) The court or the department shall, whenever reasonable and practical and based upon a determination of the best interests of the child, ensure that children placed in foster care shall have access to and visitation with siblings in other foster or pre-adoptive homes or in the homes of parents or extended family members throughout the period of placement in the care and custody of the department, or after such placements, if the children or their siblings are separated through adoption or long-term or short-term placements in foster care.

The court or the department shall determine, at the time of the initial placements wherein children and their siblings are separated through placements in foster, pre-adoptive or adoptive care, that sibling visitation rights be implemented through a schedule of visitations or supervised visitations, to be arranged and monitored through the appropriate public or private agency, and with the participation of the foster, pre-adoptive or adoptive parents, or extended family members, and the child, if reasonable, and other parties who are relevant to the preservation of sibling relationships and visitation rights.

A child in foster care or sibling of a child placed voluntarily under clause (1) of subsection (a) of section 23 or under an adoption surrender under section 2 of chapter 210, who are denied visitation rights by the department, may appeal through the department's fair hearing process. The child or sibling may appeal the decision reached through the department's fair hearing process by filing a petition in the probate and family court for visitation. That child or sibling shall have the right to court review by trial de novo.

For children in the custody of the department pursuant to petition under this chapter, a child, sibling, parent, legal guardian or the department may file a petition for sibling visitation in the court committing the child to the custody of the department.

Periodic reviews shall evaluate the effectiveness and appropriateness of sibling visitations.

Any child over 12 years of age may request visitation with siblings who have been separated and placed in care or have been adopted in a foster or adoptive home other than where the child resides.

(c) A parent: (i) against whom a decree to dispense with consent to adoption has been entered under clause 4 of subsection (b) of section 26 or section 3 of chapter 210 or (ii) who has signed a voluntary adoption surrender under section 2 of chapter 210 shall not have the rights provided under this section as to the child who is the subject of that decree or surrender.

(d) A child, parent, guardian, grandparent or the department may appeal a decision or order of the trial court to the appeals court under this section if such person or the department is a party thereto. The claim of appeal shall be filed in the office of the clerk or register of the trial court within 30 days following the court's decision or order. Thereafter, the appeal shall be governed by the Massachusetts Rules of Appellate Procedure.

Added by St.2008, c. 176, § 84, eff. July 8, 2008.

§ 26C. Summary of foster care providers' employment

The department shall provide all children's foster care agencies acting as agents of the department and that employ foster care providers, a summary of the record of any such foster care provider's employment as a foster care provider as compiled by the department. Said summary shall include names and contacts of all other agencies that employed such person as a foster care provider, the tenure of each such employment as a foster care provider, the reasons for ending each such employment, and any other information the department deems relevant and necessary to determine the employee's fitness to continue to be employed as a foster care provider. The department shall require any foster care agency that employs foster care providers and with which it contracts to supply the information included in such summary to the department and maintain this information in a database. The department shall consult the department of early education and care if necessary to facilitate the collection of this information.

Added by St.2008, c. 176, § 84, eff. July 8, 2008.

§ 27. Appeals; procedure; notice of right of appeal; time limits

A child, parent, guardian or person appearing in behalf of such child, or the department, may appeal from the adjudication of the court and from any order of commitment made as a result of the adjudication under the provisions of section twenty-six to the appeals court. The trial justice entering the adjudication or order of commitment shall, prior to said adjudication, or within ten days thereafter, file detailed findings of fact and conclusions of law. Pending the appeal, the child may be committed to the custody of the department or placed in the care of some suitable person or licensed children's foster care agency. The district court or juvenile court where the order of adjudication was entered shall retain jurisdiction to and may enter any order for the needs of the child. The court shall notify the child, parent, guardian or person appearing in behalf of such child of the right of appeal at the time of adjudication and also at the time of commitment.

The claim of appeal under this section shall be filed in the office of the clerk of the said division of the district court department or the division of the juvenile court department within 30 days of the entry of the adjudication or order of commitment by the court. The completion of said appeal shall be governed by the Massachusetts rules of appellate procedure.

Added by St.1954, c. 646, § 1. Amended by St.1973, c. 1005; St.1978, c. 478, § 51; St.1981, c. 715, § 1; St.1983, c. 314; St.1990, c. 141; St.1992, c. 379, § 9; St.1999, c. 3, § 11.

§ 28. Orders for payment of support; who may bring action; expiration of order or judgment

(a) During the pendency of an action brought under section 24, temporary orders providing for the support of a child may be entered. The court may thereafter enter a judgment against the party chargeable with support. When the court makes an order of support on behalf of a party, and that party is not covered by a private group health insurance plan, the court shall determine whether the person chargeable with support has private health insurance or a group plan available to him through an employer or organization that may be extended to cover the party for whom support is ordered. When the court has determined that the person chargeable with support has this insurance, such court shall include in the order or judgment a provision relating to the insurance. Any such order of support shall conform to and be enforced under section 12 of chapter 119A.

(b) Actions under this section to establish support of a child may be commenced by a parent, whether a minor or not; by the child; by the child's guardian, next of kin or other person standing in a parental relationship to the child; by the authorized agent of the department of children and families or any agency licensed under chapter 15D if the child is in its custody or is or was a recipient of any type of public assistance by the IV–D agency as set forth in chapter 119A on behalf of the department of transitional assistance, the department of children and families, the division of medical assistance, or any other public assistance program of the commonwealth. In the event that someone other than the IV–D agency commences the action, if the parent or child is or was a recipient of any type of public assistance, the court shall notify the IV–

D agency of the pendency of the action and the IV–D agency shall be permitted to intervene in the action.

(c) An order, or judgment of support under this section, may be entered notwithstanding the default of the person chargeable with support or his failure to appear personally.

(d) In determining the amount of current support to be paid, the court shall apply the child support guidelines established by the chief administrative justice of the trial court, or, in the absence of such standards, shall consider the factors set forth in section 32 of chapter 209.

(e) The person chargeable with support shall comply with this order, or judgment until it is dismissed or expires. When an action brought under section 24 is dismissed or a final order of commitment is entered, the order or judgment of support shall expire 6 months after the judgment of dismissal or final order of commitment. At the time of the dismissal or final order of commitment, the court shall notify the parties and the IV–D agency, as set forth in chapter 119A, of the expiration date of the support order or judgment.

Added by St.1954, c. 646, § 1. Amended by St.1986, c. 310, § 10A; St.1995, c. 5, § 55; St.1997, c. 19, § 52; St.1998, c. 64, §§ 60 to 62; St.2008, c. 176, § 85, eff. July 8, 2008.

§ 29. Right to counsel; notice of right; court appointed counsel

The following persons shall have and shall be informed of the right to counsel, and the court shall appoint counsel for all such persons if the person is not able to retain counsel: (i) an adult who is under the responsibility of the department under clause (1) of subsection (a) of section 23; (ii) a child who is before the court under clauses (1) and (3) of said subsection (a) of said section 23, sections 24 to 27, inclusive, or section 29B; (iii) a child in a custody proceeding where the department or a licensed placement agency is a party; and (iv) any young adult to whom subsection (f) of section 23 applies.

Whenever the department or a licensed child placement agency is a party to child custody proceedings, the parent, guardian or custodian of the child, or a parent or guardian of an adult who is the responsibility of the department under clause (3) of subsection (a) of section 23: (i) shall have and be informed of the right to counsel at all such hearings, including proceedings under sections 5–201, 5–204 or 5–206 of chapter 190B, and that the court shall appoint counsel if the parent, guardian or custodian is financially unable to retain counsel; and (ii) shall have and be informed of the right to a service plan or case plan for the child and the child's family, or an adult who is the responsibility of the department under clause (3) of subsection (a) of section 23, which complies with applicable state and federal laws and regulations for these plans. Any young adult to whom subsection (f) of section 23 applies is also entitled to such service plan or case plan. The probate and family court and the juvenile court departments of the trial court shall establish procedures for: (i) notifying the parent, guardian or custodian of these rights; and (ii) appointing counsel for an indigent parent, guardian or custodian within 14 days of a licensed child placement agency filing or appearing as a party in any such action. The department or agency shall provide a copy of the service or case plan to the parent, guardian or custodian of the child or of an adult who is the responsibility of the department under clause (3) of subsection (a) of section 23, or to an adult who is the responsibility of the department under clause (3) of subsection (a) of section 23 or section 5–305 of chapter 190B, or any young adult to whom subsection (f) of section 23 applies and to the attorneys for all parties appearing in the proceeding within 45 days of the department or agency filing an appearance in such proceeding. Thereafter, any party may have the original or changed plan introduced as evidence, and with the consent of all parties the plan shall be filed with the court. Notwithstanding this section, the court may make such temporary orders as may be necessary to protect the adult who is under the responsibility of the department under clause (3) of subsection (a) of section 23 or the child and society.

The department, upon its request, shall be represented by the district attorney for the district in which the case is being heard.

Added by St.1954, c. 646, § 1. Amended by St.1973, c. 1076, § 4; St.1978, c. 501; St.1983, c. 517; St.1984, c. 197, § 3; St.2008, c. 176, § 85, eff. July 8, 2008; St.2010, c. 239, § 38, eff. Nov. 2, 2010; St.2010, c. 359, § 20, eff. Jan. 3, 2011.

§ 29A. Legal fees of minors in criminal proceedings; liability of parents

The parents of an unemancipated minor shall be liable for such reasonable legal fees and expenses of an attorney representing the minor in criminal proceedings. Except where the parent is the alleged victim, the court shall determine whether the parent or guardian of an unemancipated minor is indigent. If the parent or guardian is not determined to be indigent, the court shall assess a $300 fee against the parent or guardian to pay for the cost of any attorney that is supplied by the committee for public counsel services or assigned to represent the minor by the court and paid out of public funds in the criminal proceedings. If the parent is determined to be indigent but is still able to contribute toward the payment of some of the costs, the court shall order the parent to pay a reasonable amount toward the cost of appointed counsel. This section shall not apply to a parent who, as a result of a decree of a court of competent jurisdiction, does not have custody of the minor.

Added by St.1970, c. 386. Amended by St.2000, c. 313, § 36; St.2003, c. 26, § 168, eff. July 1, 2003.

§ 29B. Determination of future status of committed children; orders; permanency hearings; appeals

[Text of section applicable as provided by 2010, 359, Sec. 133.]

(a) Except as provided in subsection (d), within 12 months of the original commitment, grant of custody or transfer of responsibility of a child to the department by a court of competent jurisdiction and not less than every 12 months thereafter while the child remains in the care of the department, the committing court shall conduct a permanency hearing, in accordance with rules established by the chief justice for administration and management, to determine and periodically review thereafter the permanency plan for the child. The plan shall address whether and, if applicable, when: (i) the child will be returned to the parent; (ii) the child will be placed for adoption and the steps the department will take to free the child for adoption; (iii) the child will be referred for legal guardianship; (iv) the child will be placed in permanent care with relatives; or (v) the child will be placed in another permanent planned living arrangement. The department shall file a permanency plan prior to a permanency hearing that shall address the above placement alternatives. The court shall consult with the child in an age-appropriate manner about the permanency plan developed for the child.

(b) The committing court shall continue to hold annual permanency hearings as described in subsection (a) for young adults to whom subsection (f) of section 23 applies. The young adult shall be entitled to counsel under section 29.

(c) If a child or a young adult is not to be returned to the child or young adult's parents, the permanency plan shall consider in-state and out-of-state placement options. In the case of a child placed in foster care outside the state in which the home of the parents of the child is located or a young adult in an out-of-state placement, the permanency plan shall also address whether the out-of-state placement continues to be appropriate and in the best interests of the child or young adult. In the case of a child who has attained age 16 or any young adult, the permanency plan shall also address the services needed to assist the child or young adult in making the transition from foster care to independent living; provided, however, that the court shall consult with the child or young adult in an age-appropriate manner about the permanency plan. If a person in the custody of or under the responsibility of the department has attained the age of 17 years and 9 months, the permanency plan shall also address the status of and the topics of the transition plan required under 42 USC § 675(5)(H); provided, however, that the court shall retain jurisdiction until it finds, after a hearing at which the person is present unless the person chooses otherwise, that a satisfactory transition plan has been provided for the person.

(d) In conducting a permanency hearing, the court may make any appropriate order as may be in the child or the young adult's best interests including, but not limited to, orders with respect to care or custody. At the same time, the court shall consider the provisions of section 29C, and shall make the written certification and determinations required by said section 29C. The health and safety of the child or young adult shall be of paramount, but not exclusive, concern.

The permanency hearing for a child or young adult shall be held within 30 days of a hearing at which a court determines that reasonable efforts to preserve and reunify families are not required pursuant to section 29C. The court may, however, make such determination at the time of the permanency hearing.

If continuation of reasonable efforts to return a child or young adult safely to the child or young adult's parent or guardian are found to be inconsistent with the permanency plan for the child or young adult or if reasonable efforts are not required pursuant to section 29C, or in the case of any young adult to whom subsection (f) of section 23 applies, the department shall make reasonable efforts to place the child or young adult in a timely manner in accordance with the permanency plan including, if appropriate, through an interstate placement, and to complete whatever steps are necessary to finalize the permanent placement of the child or young adult. In subsequent permanency hearings held on behalf of the child or young adult, the court shall determine whether the department has made such efforts in accordance with section 29C.

(e) A child, parent of a child, guardian, young adult, or the department may appeal to the appeals court from the determination or order of the trial court. The claim of appeal shall be filed in the office of the clerk or register of the trial court within 30 days following the court's determination or order. Thereafter, the appeal shall be governed by the Massachusetts Rules of Appellate Procedure. The scope of appellate review shall be limited to abuse of judicial discretion.

Added by St.1984, c. 197, § 4. Amended by St.1989, c. 663; St.1992, c. 69, § 5; St.1999, c. 3, § 12; St.1999, c. 6, § 2; St.2008, c. 4, §§ 1, 2, eff. Jan. 11, 2008; St.2008, c. 176, § 86, eff. July 8, 2008; St.2010, c. 359, § 21, eff. Jan. 3, 2011.

§ 29C. Judicial certification of need to remove child from home

If a court of competent jurisdiction commits, grants custody or transfers responsibility for a child to the department or its agent, the court shall certify that the continuation of the child in his home is contrary to his best interests and shall determine whether the department or its agent, as appropriate, has made reasonable efforts prior to the placement of a child with the department to prevent or eliminate the need for removal from the home; but, if a child has been placed voluntarily with the department by the parent under clause (1) of subsection (a) of section 23 and the parent consents to continued placement under a petition filed under said clause (1) or clause (2) of said subsection (a) of said section 23, the court shall determine at an initial hearing only whether continued placement is in the child's best interests. Except as provided herein, if a court has previously committed, granted custody or transferred responsibility for a child to the department or its agent, the court shall determine not less than annually whether the department or its agent has made reasonable efforts to make it possible for the child to return safely to his parent or guardian. In making any determination, the health and safety of the child shall be of paramount concern.

[Second paragraph applicable as provided by 2010, 359, Sec. 133.]

If a young adult continues under the responsibility of the department pursuant to subsection (f) of section 23, the committing court shall continue to annually determine whether the department or the department's agent has made reasonable efforts to achieve the permanent plan approved by the court under section 29B.

Reasonable efforts by the department prior to removal of a child from the home or to return the child to a parent or guardian shall not be required if the court finds that: (i) the child has been abandoned as defined in section 3 of chapter 210; (ii) the parent's consent to adoption of a sibling of the child was dispensed with under section 26 or under said section 3 of said chapter 210, or the parent's rights were involuntarily terminated in a case involving a sibling of the child; (iii) the parent has been convicted of 1 of the following crimes by a court of competent jurisdiction: (a) murder or voluntary manslaughter of another child of the parent or aiding, abetting, attempting, conspiring or soliciting to commit such a murder or voluntary manslaughter; or (b) an assault constituting a felony which resulted in serious bodily injury to the child or another child of the parent; or (iv) a parent has subjected the child to aggravated circumstances consisting of murder of another parent of the child in the presence of the child or by subjecting the child or other children in the home to sexual abuse or exploitation or severe or repetitive conduct of a physically or emotionally abusive nature. For the purposes of this section, conduct of an "emotionally abusive nature" shall mean any conduct causing an impairment to or disorder of the intellectual or psychological capacity of a child as evidenced by observable and substantial reduction in the child's ability to function within a normal range of performance and behavior.

If a court has determined at a permanency hearing convened under section 29B, that reasonable efforts to safely return the child to his parent or guardian are inconsistent with the permanency plan for the child or if a court has determined that reasonable efforts are not required as set forth herein, the court shall determine at least annually thereafter whether the department has made reasonable efforts to place the child in a timely manner in accordance with the permanency plan determined and reviewed under section 29B.

The court shall make the certification and determinations required under this section in written form, which shall include the basis for the certification and determinations. A determination by the court that reasonable efforts were not made shall not preclude the court from making any appropriate order conducive to the child's best interest.

Added by St.1984, c. 197, § 5. Amended by St.1992, c. 69, § 6; St.1999, c. 3, § 12; St.2002, c. 371, § 2; St.2008, c. 176, § 87, eff. July 8, 2008; St.2010, c. 359, § 22, eff. Jan. 3, 2011.

§ 29D. Notice of hearing

The department shall provide notice of hearings held under sections 26, 29B and 39G to a foster parent, pre-adoptive parent or relative providing care for the child who is the subject of the petition and shall inform the foster parent, pre-adoptive parent or relative of his right to attend the hearing and to be heard. Nothing in this provision shall be construed to provide that such foster parent, pre-adoptive parent or relative shall be made a party to the proceeding.

Added by St.1999, c. 3, § 12.

§§ 30, 31. Repealed, 1961, 396, Sec. 5

§ 32. Placement of children in private families; early and periodic screening, diagnostic and treatment standards; individualized health care plan

Children in the care or custody of the department shall be placed in private families; provided, that any child who upon examination is found to be in need of special care, treatment or education may, if it is found by the department to be in the best interest of the child, be placed in a public or private institution or school, the primary purpose of which is the special care, treatment or education of children. The reasons for the placement of any such child shall be entered in the records of the department.

The department shall insure that every foster child upon entry into the foster care system shall be screened and evaluated under the early and periodic screening, diagnostic and treatment standards established by Title XIX of the Social Security Act, unless the child has been screened and evaluated within 30 days prior to his entry into the system.

A medically needy child who is in foster care, whether specialized or other type of care as provided by the department or its agents, may not be placed in another foster home or other placement without an individualized health care plan that is unique to the child's health care needs; provided, however, that in an emergency due to abuse or neglect, the child may be removed without a plan. The plan shall include, but not be limited to: a description of the specific health care needs of the child and specific treatment and services necessary to meet those needs; identification of health care agencies or personnel or other professionals who may conduct transitional training on the child's health care needs for the subsequent foster parents or other placement or the family to whom the child will return. The department shall also provide to the subsequent foster parents or other placement or to the family to whom the child will return information on health care resources available and health care and other personnel whose services are required by the child.

Added by St.1954, c. 646, § 1. Amended by St.1999, c. 3, § 13; St.2008, c. 176, § 88, eff. July 8, 2008.

§ 33. Placement of children in family home care

In placing a child in family home care, the department, or any private charitable or child-care agency, shall consider all factors relevant to the child's physical, mental and moral health.

Added by St.1954, c. 646, § 1. Amended by St.1970, c. 404, § 1.

§ 33A. [There is no 119:33A.]

§ 33B. Placement in family home care of juvenile who has or may have committed a sexual offense or arson

At the time of placing a child in family home care, but in any event no later that five working days following such placement, the department or any other child-care agency shall determine whether the child has been adjudicated delinquent for a sexual offense or the commission of arson, or has admitted to such behavior, or is the subject of a documented or substantiated report of such behavior. If the department or other agency determines that the child has been so adjudicated, admitted, or found to have engaged in such behavior, it shall immediately refer the child to a qualified diagnostician for evaluation and assessment, including a risk management assessment of the child and a recommendation as to the type of appropriate and safe placement for the child. Such evaluation and assessment shall be completed within not more than ten working days from referral by the department or agency. No delay beyond the time periods in this section by the department shall in itself give rise to any claim of negligence or any other claim for damages. For the purposes of this section, a qualified diagnostician shall mean an individual who possesses specialized training and experience in the evaluation and treatment of sexually abusive youth or arsonists, as appropriate. Pending completion of such evaluation, the department or agency may place the child in an interim setting that is able to provide appropriate safety and security in light of the known risks posed by the child. Such risks shall be disclosed to the caretaker, including an interim safety plan to be implemented by the caretaker.

If the diagnostician recommends that the placement, including situations in which the child remains at home, should have adequate sex offender or arson specific risk management procedures, the department or agency responsible for placing the child shall prepare and implement a plan to address the safety of the child and other children in the home or residence, and to address the safety of the children in the immediate neighborhood. Such plan must include notification to all adults responsible for supervising the child in the home or residence of the child's behavioral history, including adjudications, if any, and education of all persons living in the home or residence about the known risks attendant to the child's behavior and methods of preventing such behavior, and provision for appropriate treatment for the child who is being placed. Where the department or agency makes a referral of such child to a foster home, residential facility, other agencies or organizations, or individuals for the purpose of receiving custodial services, the department or agency shall disclose the child's behavioral history, including adjudications, if any, to the designated recipient of the referral, prior to placement or at referral.

Added by St.1996, c. 151, § 277. Amended by St.1997, c. 43, § 100.

§ 34. Transportation of children in patrol wagons

A child involved in any proceeding shall not be transported in a patrol wagon from his home or from any other place to any court or institution, but if a conveyance is necessary shall convey him in such other suitable vehicle as shall be provided or designated by the department. Violation of this section shall be punished by a fine of not less than twenty-five nor more than fifty dollars or by imprisonment for not more than three months.

Added by St.1954, c. 646, § 1. Amended by St.1967, c. 658, § 74.

§ 35. Furnishing parent or guardian information as to child; permission to visit; notice; parents convicted of first degree murder

If the parent or guardian of a child placed in charge of any person, association or public or private institution by any state department, town board, or by any public or private corporation or body of persons authorized by law to so place children, or if one of the next of kin of an orphan so placed in charge and without guardian, is not, upon request, informed by such department, board, corporation or body of persons where the child is, the probate court for the county where such child has his legal residence may, upon petition of such parent, guardian or next of kin, and upon notice, if in its opinion the welfare of the child and the public interest will not be injured thereby, require such department, board, corporation or body of persons to give the information and permit the parent, guardian or next of kin to visit the child at such times and under such conditions as the court orders; and the court may revise its order or make new orders or decrees as the welfare of the child and the public interest may require. No court shall make an order providing visitation rights to a parent who has been convicted of murder in the first degree of the other parent of the child who is the subject of the order, unless such child is of suitable age to signify his assent and assents to such order; provided, further, that until such order is issued, no person shall visit, with the child present, a parent who has been convicted of murder in the first degree of the other parent of the child without the consent of the child's custodian or legal guardian.

Added by St.1954, c. 646, § 1. Amended by St.1997, c. 77, § 1.

§ 36. Bringing child into commonwealth with view to adoption, guardianship, custody or care; permit; application; bond

No person or institution shall bring or cause to be brought into the commonwealth, or receive therein, from any other state, province or country, any child for the purpose of placing or boarding, or of procuring the placing or boarding of such child, in a family or home within the commonwealth, with a view to adoption, guardianship, custody or care by any person other than one related to him by blood or marriage, without first obtaining a permit therefor from the department. Such a permit shall not issue until a written application therefor has been filed with the department on forms by it prepared, containing such information relative to such child as the department may require, accompanied by an individual or blanket bond running to the commonwealth in such penal sum and with such surety or sureties as the department may approve, conditioned on the following:—(1) that all statements contained in such an application are true in substantial particulars; (2) that any such child becoming a public charge during his minority shall be removed from the state not later than thirty days after notice from the department; (3) that such child shall be removed from the state immediately upon his release from any penal or reformatory institution or training school to which he has been committed, within three years of his arrival within the state, for juvenile delinquency or crime; (4) that such child shall be placed or boarded under such agreement as will secure to him a proper home and surroundings, and as will render his custodian responsible for his proper care, education and training, under adequate supervision and subject to annual visitation by an agent; and (5) that such reports relative to the child shall be made to the department as it may require. In case of a breach of any condition of such a bond, the attorney general, upon request of the department, shall put the bond in suit, and the commonwealth or any city or town thereof shall be reimbursed from the proceeds for any expense incurred by reason of a breach of any such condition. Violation of this section shall be punished by a fine of not more than one hundred dollars or by imprisonment for not more than six months, or both.

Added by St.1954, c. 646, § 1.

§ 37. Rules and regulations of department

The department shall make rules and regulations concerning the administration of its duties.

Added by St.1954, c. 646, § 1. Amended by St.1967, c. 658, § 75.

§ 38. Closed hearings; publication of names

All hearings under sections 1 to 38A, inclusive, except those related to court orders to not resuscitate or to withdraw life-sustaining medical treatment for children in the custody of the department under a care and protection order, shall be closed to the general public. It shall be unlawful to publish the names of persons before the court in any closed hearing.

Added by St.1954, c. 646, § 1. Amended by St.2008, c. 176, § 89, eff. July 8, 2008.

§ 38A. Petitions for order to not resuscitate or to withdraw life-sustaining medical treatment; required recommendations; appeals

In any proceedings related to court orders to not resuscitate or to withdraw life-sustaining medical treatment, the department or the party petitioning for the order shall require: (i) a written opinion from the child's treating physician, (ii) a written recommendation from the ethics committee of the hospital at which the child is a patient, and (iii) a written second opinion from a physician who is certified in the same medical specialty as the child's treating physician and who is not affiliated with the hospital at which the child is a patient. The department or the party petitioning for the order shall submit these documents to the court. The commissioner shall determine and make the department's recommendation to the court. The court shall also seek a recommendation from the child's parent or guardian. The court shall appoint a guardian ad litem to make a recommendation to the court on behalf of the child. Any appeal made under this section shall be an interlocutory appeal.

Added by St.2008, c. 176, § 89, eff. July 8, 2008.

§ 39. Abandonment of infant under age of ten

Whoever abandons an infant under the age of ten within or without any building, or, being its parent, or being under a legal duty to care for it, and having made a contract for its board or maintenance, absconds or fails to perform such contract, and for four weeks after such absconding or breach of his contract, if of sufficient physical and mental ability, neglects to visit or remove such infant or notify the department of his inability to support such infant, shall be punished by imprisonment in a jail or house of correction for not more than two years; or, if the infant dies by reason of such abandonment, by imprisonment in a jail or house of correction for not more than two and one half years or in the state prison for not more than five years. Added by St.1954, c. 646, § 1. Amended by St.1967, c. 658, § 76.

§ 39½. Placement of a newborn into foster care

Subject to appropriation, the department shall accept for placement into foster care any newborn infant 7 days of age or less that is voluntarily placed with a hospital, police department or manned fire station, hereinafter "designated facility" by a parent of said newborn infant. Such a voluntary placement under this section shall not constitute, in an of itself, an automatic termination of parental rights or an abrogation of the parental rights or responsibilities but shall, for purposes of authorizing the department to initiate a petition to terminate parental rights under chapter 210, be presumed to be an abandonment of the newborn infant that has been so placed.

Voluntary abandonment of a newborn infant 7 days of age or younger to an appropriate person at a hospital, police department or manned fire station shall not by itself constitute either a finding of abuse or neglect or a violation of any criminal statue [1] for child abuse or neglect or for abandonment. If child abuse or neglect, that is not based solely on the newborn infant having been left in the hospital, police department or manned fire station is suspected, hospital, police or fire department personnel who are mandated reporters under section 51A shall report the abuse or neglect.

The designated facility receiving a newborn infant shall immediately notify the department of the placement of the newborn infant at the facility. Upon receipt of such notice, the department shall take immediate custody of the newborn infant and shall initiate all actions authorized by law to achieve the safety and permanent placement of the newborn infant in a manner that is consistent with the best interests of the child.

The person accepting a newborn infant at a designated facility shall make every effort to solicit the following information from the parent placing the newborn infant: (1) the name of the newborn infant; (2) the name and address of the parent placing the newborn infant; (3) the location of the newborn infant's birthplace; (4) information relative to the newborn infant's medical history and his or her biological family's medical history, if available; and (5) and any other information that might reasonably assist the department or the court in current or future determinations of the best interests of the child, including whether the parent or guardian plans on returning to seek future custody of the child. The person receiving the newborn infant shall encourage the parent to provide the information but the parent shall not be required to provide such information.

The department shall develop and implement a public information program to inform the general public of the provisions of this section, teen pregnancy prevention programs and adoption information. The department shall also work in conjunction with other departments and agencies of the commonwealth and the Massachusetts Hospital Association relative to development of the program. The program may include, but not be limited to, educational and informational materials in print, audio video, electronic and other media, public service announcements and advertisements and the establishment of a toll-free hotline.

For purposes of this section only, the following term shall be defined in the following manner unless the context shall clearly indicate a different meaning or intent:— "hospital", a hospital that is licensed under section 51 of chapter 111, or operated by the teaching hospital of the University of Massachusetts Medical School.

The department shall explore the possibility of expending funds received from the United States Department of Health and Human Services pursuant to the Promoting Safe and Stable Families Program, as most recently amended by the Promoting Safe and Stable Families of 2001, in order to implement the public information program required by this section and to alleviate the burden said information program may have on the department's appropriation from the commonwealth. When implementing its public information program, the department shall prioritize those areas of the commonwealth that have been identified by the department of public health as having the highest teen pregnancy rates.

The department, in conjunction with a designee of the juvenile court, the probate and family court, the center for adoption research at the University of Massachusetts, Massachusetts Families for Kids, Massachusetts Children's Trust Fund, Massachusetts Society for the Prevention of Cruelty to Children, Alliance on Teen Pregnancy and the department of early care and education, shall report every 2 years on the overall effectiveness of the program of voluntary placement of newborn infants established pursuant to this section. The report shall include, but not be limited to, the following: (1) an analysis of this section's effectiveness in decreasing the number of newborns that are abandoned in an unsafe manner in the commonwealth; (2) the department's success or failure in permanently placing in the adoption process any newborn placed with a designated facility pursuant to this section; (3) the average length of time that newborns remain in foster care after being so placed; (4) any issues arising from the termination of parental rights following the placement of a newborn pursuant to this section; (5) the success or failure of any public information campaign implemented by the department pursuant to this section; (6) any increased administrative burdens that may be placed upon any department or agency of the commonwealth as a result of this section; (7) issues with regard to the eligibility of any newborn infant placed pursuant to this section for federal entitlements such as foster care or adoption subsidies under Title IV–E of the United States Social Security Act or any other applicable federal law; and (8) the frequency or infrequency with which a parent placing a newborn at a designated facility supplies the facility with the information sought by the facility pursuant to the fourth paragraph of this section and any negative effects the lack of medical or background information on the child or parents may have had on facilitating the temporary or permanent placement of the child through the foster care or adoption process. The report, including any legislative recommendations, shall be submitted to the joint committee on children, families and persons with disabilities and the house and senate committees on ways and means on or before December 1, 2008 and not later than December 1 of each even numbered year thereafter.

Added by St.2004, c. 227, § 1, eff. Oct. 28, 2004. Amended by St.2007, c. 86, § 1, eff. Nov. 4, 2007; St.2008, c. 176, §§ 90, 91, eff. July 8, 2008.

1 So in original; probably should read "statute."

§§ 39A to 39C. Repealed, 1973, 1076, Sec. 6

§ 39D. Visitation rights to certain grandparents of unmarried minor children; place to file petition

If the parents of an unmarried minor child are divorced, married but living apart, under a temporary order or judgment of separate support, or if either or both parents are deceased, or if said unmarried minor child was born out of wedlock whose paternity has been adjudicated by a court of competent jurisdiction or whose father has signed an acknowledgement of paternity, and the parents do not reside together, the grandparents of such minor child may be granted reasonable visitation rights to the minor child during his minority by the probate and family court department of the trial court upon a written finding that such visitation rights would be in the best interest of the said minor child; provided, however, that such adjudication of paternity or acknowledgment of paternity shall not be required in order to proceed under this section where maternal grandparents are seeking such visitation rights. No such visitation rights shall be granted if said minor child has been adopted by a person other than a stepparent of such child and any visitation rights granted pursuant to this section prior to such adoption of the said minor child shall be terminated upon such adoption without any further action of the court.

A petition for grandparents visitation authorized under this section shall, where applicable, be filed in the county within the commonwealth in which the divorce or separate support complaint or the complaint to establish paternity was filed. If the divorce, separate support or paternity judgment was entered without the commonwealth but the child presently resides within the commonwealth, said petition may be filed in the county where the child resides.

Added by St.1972, c. 631. Amended by St.1982, c. 514; St.1991, c. 292; St.1994, c. 358; St.1998, c. 65.

§ 39E. Petitions seeking determination that child is in need of services; jurisdiction; standing

The divisions of the juvenile court department may receive and hear petitions seeking a determination that a child is in need of services as defined in section twenty-one, in accordance with the provisions of this section and of sections thirty-nine F to thirty-nine *I*, inclusive. Proceedings pursuant to sections thirty-nine E to thirty-nine *I*, inclusive, shall not be deemed criminal proceedings. The jurisdiction of the Boston juvenile court for the subject matter of this section shall extend to the territorial limits of Suffolk county.

A parent or legal guardian of a child having custody of such child, or a police officer may apply for a petition in one of said courts alleging that said child persistently runs away from the home of said parent or guardian or persistently refuses to obey the lawful and reasonable commands of said parent or guardian resulting in said parent's or guardian's inability to adequately care for and protect said child.

Any supervisor of attendance, duly appointed pursuant to section nineteen of chapter seventy-six may apply for a petition in said court alleging that said child persistently and wilfully fails to attend school or persistently violates the lawful and reasonable regulations of his school.

If the child is not brought into court on arrest, the clerk shall set a date for a hearing to determine whether a petition should issue, shall notify the child of such hearing and shall request the chief probation officer or his designee to conduct a preliminary inquiry to determine whether in his opinion the best interests of the child require that a petition be issued. The court shall hold a hearing in which it shall receive the recommendation of the probation officer and shall either (i) decline to issue the petition because there is no probable cause to believe that the child is in need of services; (ii) decline to issue the petition because it finds that the interests of the child would best be served by informal assistance without a trial on the merits, in which case the court shall, with the consent of the child and his parents or guardian, refer the child to a probation officer for assistance; or (iii) issue the petition and schedule a trial on the merits. If the child is brought in on arrest, the petition shall issue if it has not already issued, and the court shall immediately request the probation officer promptly to make like inquiry and thereafter report to the court his recommendation as to whether the interests of the child can best be served by informal assistance without a trial on the merits. Upon receiving such recommendation, the court may hold a hearing and shall decide whether to proceed with a trial on the merits or to refer the child to the care of a probation officer for assistance.

Whenever a child is referred to a probation officer for assistance, such officer shall have the authority to refer the child to an appropriate public or private organization or person for psychiatric, psychological, educational, occupational, medical, dental or social services and shall have the authority to conduct conferences with the child and the child's family for the purpose of effecting adjustments or agreements which are calculated to resolve the situation which formed the basis of the application or petition and which will eliminate the need for a judicial trial on the merits. During the pendency of such referrals or conferences, neither the child nor his parents may be compelled to appear at any conferences, produce any papers, or visit any place. However, if the child or his parents fail to participate in good faith in the referrals or conferences arranged by the probation officer, the probation officer shall so certify in writing, and the clerk shall issue a petition, if one has not already been issued, and shall set a date for a trial on the merits. The judge who conducted the hearing on the issuance of a petition shall not preside at any subsequent hearing on the merits. If the child is being detained in any facility pending the determination as to whether a petition shall issue, or pending a trial on the merits, and a determination is made either not to issue the petition or to refer the child to the probation officer, the person in charge of the facility wherein the child is detained shall be notified immediately and the child shall be immediately released. Conferences and referrals arranged under this section may extend for a period not to exceed six months from the date that the application was initially made for the petition, unless the parent and child voluntarily agree in writing to a continuation of such conferences or referrals for an additional period not to exceed six months from the expiration of the original period. Upon the expiration of the initial six-month period, or of such additional six-month period, the petition, if any, shall be dismissed and the child and his parents discharged from any further obligation to participate in such conferences and referrals, or a petition shall, if not already issued, be issued and a date set for a trial on the merits. No statements made by a child or by any other person during the period of inquiries, conferences, or referrals may be used against the child at any subsequent hearing for the purpose of adjudicating him a child in need of services, but such statements may be received by the court after adjudication for the purpose of disposition.

Upon the filing of a petition under this section, the court may issue a summons, to which a copy of the petition shall be attached, requiring the child named in such petition to appear before said court at the time named therein. If such child fails to obey the summons, said court may issue a warrant reciting the substance of the petition and requiring the officer to whom it is directed forthwith to take and bring such child before said court. Notice of the hearing shall be given to the department of youth services and to the department of children and families.

Where the court summons such child, the court shall in addition issue a summons to both parents of the child, if both parents are known to reside in the commonwealth, or to one parent if only one is known to reside within the commonwealth, or, if there is no parent residing in the commonwealth, then to the parent having custody or to the lawful guardian of such child. Said summons shall require the person served to appear at a time and place stated therein at a hearing to determine whether or not such child is in need of services.

Unless service of the summons required by this section is waived in writing, such summons shall be served by the constable or police officer, either by delivering it personally to the person to whom addressed, or by leaving it with a person of proper age to receive the same, at the place of residence or business of such person, and said constable or police officer shall immediately make return to the court of the time and manner of service.

The hearing of a petition filed under section thirty-nine E in a division of the district court department or of the juvenile court department shall be by a jury of six, unless the child files a written waiver and consent to the petition being heard without a jury, subject to his right of appeal therefrom for trial by a jury of six pursuant to section thirty-nine *I*. Such waiver shall not be received unless the child is represented by counsel or has filed, through his parent or guardian, a written waiver of counsel. Such trials by jury in the first instance shall be in jury sessions designated for their respective departments by the administrative justices of the district and juvenile courts for the hearing of appeals claimed pursuant to section thirty-nine *I*. All provisions of law and rules of court relative to the hearing and trial of such appeals shall apply also to jury trials in the first instance.

Added by St.1973, c. 1073, § 5. Amended by St.1976, c. 412, § 1; St.1978, c. 478, §§ 52 to 53; St.1978, c. 552, § 30; St.1986, c. 557, § 114; St.1992, c. 379, § 10; St.2008, c. 176, § 92, eff. July 8, 2008.

§ 39F. Right to counsel; determination of indigency; assessment of costs

When a child alleged to be in need of services is brought before a juvenile court or a juvenile session of a district court pursuant to section thirty-nine E, said child shall be informed that he has a right to counsel at all hearings, and if said child is not able to retain counsel, the court shall appoint counsel for said child. The court shall determine whether the parent or guardian of a child alleged to be in need of services is indigent. If the court determines that the parent or guardian is not indigent, the court shall assess a $300 fee against the parent or guardian to pay for the cost of appointed counsel. If the parent is determined to be indigent but is still able to contribute toward the payment of some of said costs, the court shall order the parent to pay a reasonable amount toward the cost of appointed counsel.

Added by St.1973, c. 1073, § 5. Amended by St.2003, c. 26, § 169, eff. July 1, 2003.

§ 39G. Hearing; determination of child in need of services

At any hearing to determine whether a child is in need of services, said child and his attorney shall be present. If the court finds the allegations in the petition have been proved at the hearing beyond a reasonable doubt, it may adjudge the child named in such petition to be in need of services. Upon making such adjudication the court, taking into consideration the physical and emotional welfare of the child, may make any of the following orders of disposition:

(a) subject to any conditions and limitations the court may prescribe, including provision for medical, psychological, psychiatric, educational, occupational and social services, and for supervision by a court clinic or by any public or private organization providing counseling or guidance services, permit the child to remain with his parents;

(b) subject to such conditions and limitations as the court may prescribe, including, but not limited to provisions for those services described in clause (a), place the child in the care of any of the following:

(1) a relative, probation officer, or other adult individual who, after inquiry by the probation officer or other person or agency designated by the court, is found to be qualified to receive and care for the child; (2) a private charitable or childcare agency or other private organization, licensed or otherwise authorized by law to receive and provide care for such children; or (3) a private organization which, after inquiry by the probation officer or other person or agency designated by the court, is found to be qualified to receive and care for the child; or

(c) subject to the provisions of sections 32 and 33 and with such conditions and limitations as the court may recommend, commit the child to the department of children and families. At the same time, the court shall consider the provisions of section 29C and shall make the written certification and determinations required by said section 29C. The department shall give due consideration to the recommendations of the court. The department may not refuse out-of-home placement of a child if the placement is recommended by the court provided that the court has made the written certification and determinations required by said section 29C. The department shall direct the type and length of such out-of-home placement. The department shall give due consideration to the requests of the child that the child be placed outside the home of a parent or guardian where there is a history of abuse and neglect in the home by the parent or guardian.

A child found to be in need of services shall not be committed to any county training school. A child found to be in need of services shall not be committed to an institution designated or operated for juveniles adjudicated delinquent. However, such child may be committed to a facility which operates as a group home to provide therapeutic care for juveniles regardless of whether juveniles adjudicated delinquent are also provided care in such facility and may, in addition, be referred to the department of youth services for placement in individual foster care.

Any order of disposition pursuant to this section shall continue in force for not more than six months; provided, however, that the court which entered the order may, after a hearing, extend its duration for additional periods, each such period not to exceed six months if the court finds that the purposes of the order have not been accomplished and that such extension would be reasonably likely to further those purposes.

No order shall continue in effect after the eighteenth birthday of a child named in a petition authorized to be filed by a parent or a legal guardian having custody, or a police officer, under the provisions of the second paragraph of section thirty-nine E, or after the sixteenth birthday of a child named in a petition authorized to be filed by a supervisor of attendance under the provisions of the third paragraph of said section thirty-nine E.

Added by St.1973, c. 1073, § 5. Amended by St.1976, c. 412, § 2; St.1978, c. 552, § 31; St.1979, c. 334; St.1988, c. 170; St.1995, c. 38, § 138; St.1999, c. 3, § 14; St.2008, c. 176, § 93, eff. July 8, 2008.

§ 39H. Arrest of child; notification and placement; bail; detention; right of appeal

A child may be arrested for committing the behavior described in the definition of child in need of services in section twenty-one, only if such child has failed to obey a summons issued pursuant to section thirty-nine E, or if the arresting law enforcement officer has probable cause to believe that such child has run away from the home of his parents or guardian and will not respond to a summons.

Whenever such child is arrested and the court with jurisdiction over the case is not in session, the law enforcement officer in charge of the police station or town lockup to which the child has been taken, or his designee, shall immediately notify (1) the probation officer of the division of the juvenile court department within whose district such child was arrested or resides, or such other probation officer who may have knowledge of the child and (2) a representative of the department of children and families, if the law enforcement officer has reason to believe that the child is or has been in the care or custody of such department, and shall inquire into the case.

The law enforcement officer, in consultation with the probation officer, shall then immediately make all reasonable diversion efforts so that such child is delivered to the following types of placements, and in the following order of preference:

(i) to one of the child's parents, or to the child's guardian or other responsible person known to the child, or to the child's legal custodian including the department of children and families or the child's foster home;

(ii) to a temporary shelter facility licensed or approved by the department of early education and care, a shelter home approved by a temporary shelter facility licensed or approved by said department of early education and care, or a family foster care home approved by a placement agency licensed or approved by said department of early education and care; provided, however, that such a placement is available and, in the view of the probation officer, appropriate for the child; provided, further, that such a placement furnish said law enforcement officer with a written statement that it will make reasonable efforts to secure the child's appearance at the next available court session and that such placement will furnish the necessary transportation to such placement and to the court, unless the law enforcement officer chooses to furnish said transportation, provided, further, that such child may not be securely detained in a police station or town lockup.

Notwithstanding the foregoing requirements for placement, any such child who is arrested shall, if necessary, be taken to a medical facility for treatment or observation.

If the court finds that a child alleged to be a child in need of services by reason of persistently refusing to obey the lawful and reasonable commands of his parents or legal guardian is likely not to appear at the preliminary inquiry or at the hearing on the merits, the court shall order the child to be admitted to such bail or to be released upon such terms and conditions as it determines to be reasonable. A child who does not post bail and is not otherwise released may be detained under such terms and conditions as the court may impose in a facility operated by or under contract with the department for the care of juveniles, provided that no such child is so detained for more than fifteen days without being brought again before the court for a hearing on whether such detention should be continued for another fifteen day period. If the court decides to so continue said detention, it shall note in writing the detailed reasons for its decision. Any child aggrieved by such decision shall have an immediate right to appeal to the superior court under the procedures set forth in section fifty-eight of chapter two hundred and seventy-six; provided further, however, that in no event shall any child be detained under this section for more than forty-five days. If a child fails without good cause to respond to a summons, the court may similarly admit the child to bail, or release the child upon conditions set by the court, or, if the child fails to post bail, and is not otherwise released, detain the child subject to the above limitations. Whenever bail is imposed under this section, the provisions of section fifty-eight of chapter two hundred and seventy-six shall be applicable.

Added by St.1973, c. 1073, § 5. Amended by St.1977, c. 543; St.1991, c. 519, § 1; St.1992, c. 379, § 11; St.2008, c. 176, § 94, eff. July 8, 2008; St.2008, c. 215, § 65, eff. July 31, 2008.

§ 39*I*. Appeal; trial de novo, with or without jury; rights and procedures

Any child who is adjudicated a child in need of services may appeal for a trial de novo in a jury-of-six session of the juvenile court department for the county where the hearing is held, as designated by the chief justice of the juvenile court department. Such appeal shall be made by filing a written notice of same by the end of the next business day after the entry of judgment or adjudication, or within such further time as the court may allow.

The child may waive his claim to jury trial and have the appeal heard by a judge without jury. When an appeal is claimed, the clerk of the court in which said claim is filed shall forward forthwith all papers in the case to the clerk of the court designated to hear such appeals. The verdict of the jury shall be unanimous and the court shall enter and record its findings upon the verdict of the jury.

All the rights and procedures provided in sections thirty-nine E to thirty-nine H, inclusive, shall apply at the trial of the appeal. The justice presiding at said trial shall have all the powers and duties of a justice sitting in a juvenile court under this chapter. No justice shall preside over a trial on appeal in a case in which he presided at the initial trial. The trial on appeal in a district court jury session shall be heard in a session set apart from the other business of the district court and devoted exclusively to juvenile cases. This shall be known as the juvenile appeals session and shall have a separate trial list and docket.

An appeal shall not stay the order, judgment or decree appealed from, but the district court or juvenile court may otherwise order, on application and hearing consistent with this chapter, if suitable provision is made for the care and custody of the child.

Review may be had in the appeals court in the same manner as is provided for trials of civil cases held in the superior court department.

Added by St.1973, c. 1073, § 5. Amended by St.1978, c. 478, § 54; St.1985, c. 314, § 2; St.1992, c. 379, §§ 12, 13.

§ 39J. Payment of expenses for services by counties under Secs. 39E to 39*I*

Expenses for services provided children alleged or adjudicated to be children in need of services shall be paid by the county in which the court sits upon written certification thereof by the court. The clerk of court shall collect and transmit to the county treasurer, or, in Suffolk county, to the auditor of Boston, hereinafter included in the term "county treasurer", together with an attested copy of the court's order, all bills and vouchers for the costs of any services authorized by the court under the provisions of sections thirty-nine E to thirty-nine *I*, inclusive. The county treasurer shall keep a record of all payments made for said services, including therein the name of the child, the name or names and addresses of any public or private organization or persons to whom payment is made, the services for which payment is made, and the date upon which payment was made. Periodically, according to a schedule established by the treasurer and receiver-general of the commonwealth, the several county treasurers shall requisition funds from the commonwealth to cover such payments made by the counties during the preceding period. The state treasurer shall pay said requisitions from such sums as may have been appropriated or are otherwise available therefor, and he may require any documentation that he deems appropriate before making payment. Any state agency, department or secretariat which provides, operates, maintains, supervises or funds a program under which any of the services authorized in sections thirty-nine E to thirty-nine *I*, inclusive, are available may, to the extent consistent with the purposes of such program, provide such services or release funds to the state treasurer for reimbursement by him to the counties for services provided by others which are within the scope of the services authorized in said sections thirty-nine E to thirty-nine *I*, inclusive.

The state treasurer shall on or before December first of each year render a written report to the general court containing statistics showing the purpose and amounts of expenditures for said services by the various counties for which the commonwealth has made reimbursement, and making such recommendations for change in the law as he shall see fit.

Added by St.1973, c. 1073, § 5.

§§ 40 to 51. Repealed, 1954, 646, Sec. 1

§ 51A. Reporting of suspected abuse or neglect; mandated reporters; collection of physical evidence; penalties; content of reports; liability; privileged communication

(a) A mandated reporter who, in his professional capacity, has reasonable cause to believe that a child is suffering physical or emotional injury resulting from: (i) abuse inflicted upon him which causes harm or substantial risk of harm to the child's health or welfare, including sexual abuse; (ii) neglect, including malnutrition; or (iii) physical dependence upon an addictive drug at birth, shall immediately communicate with the department orally and, within 48 hours, shall file a written report with the department detailing the suspected abuse or neglect.

If a mandated reporter is a member of the staff of a medical or other public or private institution, school or facility, the mandated reporter may instead notify the person or designated agent in charge of such institution, school or facility who shall become responsible for notifying the department in the manner required by this section.

A mandated reporter may, in addition to filing a report under this section, contact local law enforcement authorities or the child advocate about the suspected abuse or neglect.

(b) For the purpose of reporting under this section, hospital personnel may have photographs taken of the areas of trauma visible on the child without the consent of the child's parents or guardians. These photographs or copies thereof shall be sent to the department with the report.

If hospital personnel collect physical evidence of abuse or neglect of the child, the local district attorney, local law enforcement authorities, and the department shall be immediately notified. The physical evidence shall be processed immediately so that the department may make an informed determination within the time limits in section 51B. If there is a delay in processing, the department shall seek a waiver under subsection (d) of section 51B.

(c) Notwithstanding subsection (g), whoever violates this section shall be punished by a fine of not more than $1,000. Whoever knowingly and willfully files a frivolous report of child abuse or neglect under this section shall be punished by: (i) a fine of not more than $2,000 for the first offense; (ii) imprisonment in a house of correction for not more than 6 months and a fine of not more than $2,000 for the second offense; and (iii) imprisonment in a house of correction for not more than 2½ years and a fine of not more than $2,000 for the third and subsequent offenses.

Any mandated reporter who has knowledge of child abuse or neglect that resulted in serious bodily injury to or death of a child and willfully fails to report such abuse or neglect shall be punished by a fine of up to $5,000 or imprisonment in the house of correction for not more than 2½ years or by both such fine and imprisonment; and, upon a guilty finding or a continuance without a finding, the court shall notify any appropriate professional licensing authority of the mandated reporter's violation of this paragraph.

(d) A report filed under this section shall contain: (i) the names and addresses of the child and the child's parents or other person responsible for the child's care, if known; (ii) the child's age; (iii) the child's sex; (iv) the nature and extent of the child's injuries, abuse, maltreatment or neglect, including any evidence of prior injuries, abuse, maltreatment or neglect; (v) the circumstances under which the person required to report first became aware of the child's injuries, abuse, maltreatment or neglect; (vi) whatever action, if any, was taken to treat, shelter or otherwise assist the child; (vii) the name of the person or persons making the report; (viii) any other information that the person reporting believes might be helpful in establishing the cause of the injuries; (ix) the identity of the person or persons responsible for the neglect or injuries; and (x) other information required by the department.

(e) A mandated reporter who has reasonable cause to believe that a child has died as a result of any of the conditions listed in subsection (a) shall report the death to the district attorney for the county in which the death occurred and the office of the chief medical examiner as required by clause (16) of section 3 of chapter 38. Any person who fails to file a report under this subsection shall be punished by a fine of not more than $1,000.

(f) Any person may file a report under this section if that person has reasonable cause to believe that a child is suffering from or has died as a result of abuse or neglect.

(g) No mandated reporter shall be liable in any civil or criminal action for filing a report under this section or for contacting local law enforcement authorities or the child advocate, if the report or contact was made in good faith, was not frivolous, and the reporter did not cause the abuse or neglect. No other person filing a report under this section shall be liable in any civil or criminal action by reason of the report if it was made in good faith and if that person did not perpetrate or inflict the reported abuse or cause the reported neglect. Any person filing a report under this section may be liable in a civil or criminal action if the department or a district attorney determines that the person filing the report may have perpetrated or inflicted the abuse or caused the neglect.

(h) No employer shall discharge, discriminate or retaliate against a mandated reporter who, in good faith, files a report under this section, testifies or is about to testify in any proceeding involving child abuse or neglect. Any employer who discharges, discriminates or retaliates against that mandated reporter shall be liable to the mandated reporter for treble damages, costs and attorney's fees.

(i) Within 30 days of receiving a report from a mandated reporter, the department shall notify the mandated reporter, in writing, of its determination of the nature, extent and cause or causes of the injuries to the child and the services that the department intends to provide to the child or the child's family.

(j) Any privilege relating to confidential communications, established by sections 135 to 135B, inclusive, of chapter 112 or by sections 20A and 20B of chapter 233, shall not prohibit the filing of a report under this section or a care and protection petition under section 24, except that a priest, rabbi, clergy member, ordained or licensed minister, leader of a church or religious body or accredited Christian Science practitioner need not report information solely gained in a confession or similarly confidential communication in other religious faiths. Nothing in the general laws shall modify or limit the duty of a priest, rabbi, clergy member, ordained or licensed minister, leader of a church or religious body or accredited Christian Science practitioner to report suspected child abuse or neglect under this section when the priest, rabbi, clergy member, ordained or licensed minister, leader of a church or religious body or accredited Christian Science practitioner is acting in some other capacity that would otherwise make him a mandated reporter.

(k) A mandated reporter who is professionally licensed by the commonwealth shall complete training to recognize and report suspected child abuse or neglect.

Added by St.1973, c. 1076, § 5. Amended by St.1975, c. 276, § 4; St.1977, c. 501; St.1977, c. 942; St.1978, c. 215, § 1; St.1979, c. 312, § 1; St.1980, c. 434; St.1981, c. 91, § 2; St.1982, c. 102; St.1983, c. 222; St.1984, c. 83, §§ 1, 2; St.1985, c. 209; St.1986, c. 230, §§ 1, 2; St.1989, c. 219; St.1989, c. 535, § 5; St.1990, c. 474, § 1; St.1991, c. 280; St.1992, c. 115, § 1; St.1993, c. 50, § 23; St.1997, c. 197; St.2002, c. 107, §§ 1 to 4; St.2008, c. 176, § 95, eff. July 8, 2008; St.2008, c. 176, § 96, eff. July 1, 2010; St.2008, c. 176, § 97, eff. Jan. 1, 2010.

§ 51B. Investigation of report of abuse filed under Sec. 51A; removal of child; transmission and filing of written reports; notice to district attorney; disclosure of information by mandated reporter

(a) Upon receipt of a report filed under section 51A, the department shall investigate the suspected child abuse or neglect, provide a written evaluation of the household of the child, including the parents and home environment and make a written determination relative to the safety of and risk posed to the child and whether the suspected child abuse or neglect is substantiated.

(b) The investigation shall include: (i) a home visit at which the child is viewed, if appropriate; (ii) a determination of the nature, extent and cause or causes of the injuries; (iii) the identity of the person or persons responsible therefore; (iv) the name, age and condition of other children in the same household; (v) an evaluation of the parents and the home environment; and (vi) all other pertinent facts or matters. The department shall coordinate with other agencies to make all reasonable efforts to minimize the number of interviews of any potential victim of child abuse or neglect. Upon completion of the investigation and evaluation, the department shall make a written determination relative to: (i) the safety of the child and risk of physical or emotional injury to that child and the safety of and risk thereto of any other children in the household; and (ii) whether the suspected child abuse or neglect is substantiated.

(c) If the department has reasonable cause to believe a child's health or safety is in immediate danger from abuse or neglect, the department shall take a child into immediate temporary custody if it has reasonable cause to believe that the removal is necessary to protect the child from abuse or neglect. The investigation and evaluation shall commence within 2 hours of initial contact and an interim report with an initial determination regarding the child's safety and custody shall be completed as soon as possible but not more than 24 hours after initial contact. The final report required under this section shall be complete within 5 business days of initial contact. If a child is taken into immediate temporary custody, the department shall make a written report stating the reasons for such removal and shall file a care and protection petition under section 24 on the next court day.

(d) If the department does not have reasonable cause to believe that a child's health or safety is in immediate danger from abuse or neglect, the investigation and evaluation shall commence within 2 business days of initial contact and a determination shall be made within 15 business days, unless a waiver has been approved by the area director or requested by law enforcement.

(e) Notwithstanding subsection (c), whenever the department has reasonable cause to believe that removal is necessary to protect a child from abuse or neglect, it shall take the child into immediate temporary custody. If a child is taken into immediate temporary custody, the department shall make a written report stating the reasons for such removal and shall file a care and protection petition under section 24 on the next court day.

(f) If a child named in a report filed under section 51A is in an out-of-home placement and the suspected child abuse or neglect is substantiated, the department shall notify his parents that such report was filed and has been substantiated by the department. If the child died or suffered serious bodily injury, the department shall notify the parents, including the biological parents, if the department determines that such notification is in the best interest of the child or of another child in the same placement. The department shall consult with these parents in decisions about removal or further placement. These notifications and consultations shall not be required if the commissioner determines that such notifications or consultations are not appropriate or in the best interests of a child.

(g) The department shall offer appropriate services to the family of any child which it has reasonable cause to believe is suffering from any of the conditions described in the report to prevent further injury to the child, to safeguard his welfare, and to preserve and stabilize family life whenever possible. If the family declines or is unable to accept or to participate in the offered services, the department or any person may file a care and protection petition under section 24.

(h) The department shall file in the central registry, established under section 51F, a written report containing information sufficient to identify each child whose name is reported under this section or section 51A. A notation shall be sent to the central registry whenever further reports on each such child are filed with the department. If the department determines during the initial screening period of an investigation that a report filed under section 51A is frivolous, or other absolute determination that abuse or neglect has not taken place, such report shall be declared as "allegation invalid". If a report is declared "allegation invalid", the name of the child, or identifying characteristics relating to the child, or the names of his parents or guardian or any other person relevant to the report, shall not be placed in the central registry or in any other computerized program utilized in the department.

(i) The department may purchase and utilize such protective services of private and voluntary agencies as it determines necessary.

(j) The department shall adopt regulations to implement the sections 51A to 51F, inclusive.

(k) The department shall notify and shall transmit copies of substantiated 51A reports and its written evaluations and written determinations under subsection (a) or (b) to the district attorney for the county in which the child resides and for the county in which the suspected abuse or neglect occurred, and to the local law enforcement authorities in the city or town in which the child resides and in the city or town in which the suspected abuse or neglect occurred when the department has reasonable cause to believe that 1 of the conditions listed below resulted from abuse or neglect.

The department shall immediately report to the district attorney and local law enforcement authorities listed above when early evidence indicates there is reasonable cause to believe that 1 of the conditions listed below resulted from abuse or neglect:

(1) a child has died or has suffered brain damage, loss or substantial impairment of a bodily function or organ, substantial disfigurement, or serious physical injury including, but not limited to, a fracture of any bone, a severe burn, an impairment of any organ or an injury requiring the child to be placed on life-support systems;

(2) a child has been sexually assaulted, which shall include a violation of section 13B, 13B½, 13B¾, 13H, 22, 22A, 22B, 22C, 23, 23A, 23B, 24 or 24B of chapter 265.

(3) a child has been sexually exploited, which shall include a violation of section 4A, 4B or 29A of said chapter 272; or

(4) any other disclosure of physical abuse involving physical evidence which may be destroyed, any current

disclosure by a child of sexual assault, or the presence of physical evidence of sexual assault.

Within 45 days of the notification under the first paragraph, the department shall further notify the district attorney of a service plan, if any, developed for such child and his family.

No provision of chapter 66A, sections 135 to 135B, inclusive, of chapter 112, or sections 51E and 51F of this chapter relating to confidential data or confidential communications shall prohibit the department from making such notifications or from providing to the district attorney or local law enforcement authorities any information obtained under this section. No person providing notification or information to a district attorney or local law enforcement authorities under this section shall be liable in any civil or criminal action by reason of such action. Nothing herein shall be construed to prevent the department from notifying a district attorney relative to any incident reported to the department under section 51A or to limit the prosecutorial power of a district attorney.

(*l*) If the department substantiates a report alleging that abuse or neglect occurred at a facility approved, owned, operated or funded, in whole or in part, by the department of elementary and secondary education, the department of early education and care, the department of mental health, the department of developmental services, the department of public health or the department of youth services, the department shall notify the office of the child advocate and the affected department, in writing, by transmitting a copy of the report filed under section 51A and the department's written evaluation and written determination.

If the department is aware of a licensing violation in any such facility, the department shall immediately notify the affected department.

No provision of chapter 66A, sections 135 to 135B, inclusive, of chapter 112, or sections 51E and 51F, or any other provision of law shall prohibit: (i) the department from transmitting copies of reports filed under section 51A or its written evaluations and written determinations to the office of the child advocate or the affected departments; (ii) the department, the office of the child advocate and the affected departments from coordinating activities and sharing information for the purposes of this section or for investigating a licensing violation; or (iii) the department's employees from testifying at administrative hearings held by the affected department in connection with a licensing violation.

(m) Notwithstanding any privilege created by statute or common law relating to confidential communications or any statute prohibiting the disclosure of information but subject to subsection (j) of section 51A, a mandated reporter shall answer questions and provide information posed by the department relating to an investigation conducted under this section, whether or not that person filed the 51A report being investigated. A statutory or common law privilege shall not preclude the admission of any such information in any civil proceeding concerning abuse or neglect of a child, placement or custody of a child.

(n) No person required to provide such information under this section or permitted to disclose information under section 5A of chapter 119A shall be liable in any civil or criminal action for providing such information.

(*o*) No employer shall discharge, discriminate or retaliate against a mandated reporter who, in good faith, provides such information, testifies or is about to testify in any proceeding involving child abuse or neglect unless such person perpetrated or inflicted such abuse or neglect. Any employer who discharges, discriminates or retaliates against such a person shall be liable to such person for treble damages, costs and attorney's fees.

(p) If the department determines that a 51A report is not substantiated, the department shall notify in writing any and all sources or recipients of information in connection with the investigation that the report of abuse or neglect has not been substantiated, unless the target of the investigation requests that such notification not occur.

(q) The department and the private agencies under contract with it, shall conduct periodic and regular training and education to caseworkers, screeners of 51A reports, and administrators of the department and the agencies regarding their duties and obligations under section 51A and 51B.

(r) There shall be a review by a regional clinical review team when 3 or more 51A reports involving separate incidents have been filed on any child in a family within 3 months and a review by an area clinical review team when 3 or more 51A reports involving separate incidents have been filed on any child in a family within 1 year.

Added by St.1973, c. 1076, § 5. Amended by St.1978, c. 131; St.1983, c. 288, § 2; St.1984, c. 87; St.1985, c. 343; St.1985, c. 776, § 2; St.1986, c. 478; St.1986, c. 599, § 37; St.1989, c. 396; St.1989, c. 560; St.1990, c. 474, § 2; St.1992, c. 115, § 2; St.1993, c. 303; St.1996, c. 151, § 278; St.1996, c. 215; St.1996, c. 450, §§ 160, 161; St.1998, c. 64, § 63; St.2008, c. 176, § 98, eff. July 8, 2008; St.2008, c. 451, § 83, eff. June 30, 2009; St.2010, c. 267, § 13, eff. Nov. 5, 2010.

§ 51C. Custody of injured child pending transfer to department or pending hearing

If a parent or other person requests the release from a hospital of a child reported pursuant to section fifty-one A, the presiding judge of the juvenile court of the judicial district in which such hospital is located may, if he believes such release would be detrimental to the child's health or safety, authorize the hospital and the attending physician, by any means of communication, to keep such a child in the hospital until custody is transferred to the department or until a hearing may be held relative to the care and custody of such child.

Any other physician treating a child reported pursuant to section fifty-one A may be so authorized by the court to keep such child in his custody until such time as the custody of the child has been transferred to the department or until a hearing may be held relative to the care and custody of such child.

Added by St.1973, c. 1076, § 5. Amended by St.1992, c. 379, § 14.

§ 51D. Powers and duties of area directors; multidisciplinary service teams

Each area director of the department shall be responsible for implementing subsection (k) of section 51B.

Each area director shall, in cooperation with the appropriate district attorney, establish 1 or more multidisciplinary service teams to review the provision of services to the children and families who are the subject of 51A reports that meet the conditions of subsection (k).

Each team shall consist of the department's caseworker for the particular case, 1 representative of the appropriate district attorney, and at least 1 other member appointed by the area director who is not an employee of either office. The additional member shall have training and experience in the fields of child welfare or criminal justice and, as far as practicable, be involved with the provision of services to these families. No members of a team shall receive any compensation, or in the case of a state employee, any additional compensation, for service on the team.

The team shall review and monitor the service plan developed by the department under subsection (g) of section 51B. The team shall evaluate the effectiveness of the service plan in protecting the child from further abuse or neglect. The team shall make recommendations regarding amendments to the service plan, the advisability of prosecuting members of the family, and the possibility of utilizing diversionary alternatives. If the team finds that services required under such plan are not provided to the family, the case shall be referred to the commissioner.

The team shall have full access to the service plan and any personal data known to the department which is directly related to the implementation of the plan, notwithstanding sections 51E and 51F, chapter 66A, and section 135 of chapter 112. The members of the team shall be considered to be employees of the department for purposes of protecting the confidentiality of the data and the data shall be utilized solely to carry out the provisions of this section; provided, however, that the team may report to the district attorney if the family has failed to participate in the plan.

Each area director shall file a monthly report with the commissioner regarding the activities in the area which have occurred in the previous month pursuant to this section. The report shall be written on a form prescribed by the commissioner and shall include, but not be limited to, the number of cases reported under said subsection (k) of said section 51B, the activities of the teams, the availability of services described in the service plans, and the number of family members that are subject of the reports that have been prosecuted. The commissioner, after deleting all personal identifying information, shall combine these area reports into a monthly report that shall be filed with the secretary of health and human services, each district attorney, the joint committee on children, families and persons with disabilities, and the house and senate committees on ways and means.

Added by St.1973, c. 1076, § 5. Amended by St.1978, c. 552, § 32; St.1983, c. 288, § 3; St.1992, c. 3, § 9; St.1998, c. 161, § 449; St.2008, c. 176, § 99, eff. July 8, 2008.

§ 51E. Reports of injured children; files; confidentiality; penalties

The department shall maintain a file of the written reports prepared under this section and sections 51A to 51D, inclusive. These written reports shall be confidential. Upon request and with the approval of the commissioner, copies of written reports of initial investigations may be provided to: (i) the child's parent, guardian, or counsel, (ii) the reporting person or agency, (iii) the appropriate review board, (iv) a child welfare agency of another state for the purpose of assisting that agency in determining whether to approve a prospective foster or adoptive parent, or (v) a social worker assigned to the case. No such report shall be made available to any persons other than those specified in this section without the written and informed consent of the child's parent or guardian, the written approval of the commissioner, or an order of a court of competent jurisdiction. Pursuant to chapter 18C, the child advocate shall have access to these reports.

A child welfare agency of another state may, upon request, and upon the approval of the commissioner, receive a copy of the written report of the initial investigation if the agency has a need for such information in order to carry out its responsibilities under law to protect children from abuse and neglect.

The name and all other identifying information relating to any child, or to his parents or guardian, shall be removed from said reports 1 year after the department determines that the allegation of serious physical or emotional injury resulting from abuse or neglect cannot be substantiated, or, if said allegations are substantiated, when the child reaches the age of 18, or 1 year after the date of termination of services to the child or his family, whichever date occurs last; provided, however, that the department may retain information on unsubstantiated reports to assist in future risk and safety assessments of children and families and may release said information to the child welfare agencies of other states upon request of said child welfare agency for the purpose of assisting said child welfare agency in determining whether to approve a prospective foster or adoptive parent.

Any person who permits any information in the files to be released to persons other than those specified in this section shall be punished by a fine of not more than $1,000 or by imprisonment for not more than 2½ years, or both.

Added by St.1973, c. 1076, § 5. Amended by St.1975, c. 528, § 1; St.1983, c. 391, § 1; St.2008, c. 3, §§ 1, 2, eff. Jan. 11, 2008; St.2008, c. 176, § 100, eff. July 8, 2008.

§ 51F. Central registry of information; confidentiality; penalties

The department shall maintain a central registry of information sufficient to identify children whose names are reported under sections 51A to 51B. Data and information relating to individual cases in the central registry shall be confidential and shall be made available only with the approval of the commissioner or upon court order; provided, however, that the department, upon request, may release this data and information to a child welfare agency of another state for the purpose of assisting that agency in determining whether to approve a prospective foster or adoptive parent. The commissioner shall establish rules and regulations governing the availability of such data and information. Pursuant to chapter 18C, the child advocate shall have access to the information in the registry.

A child welfare agency of another state may, upon request, and upon the approval of the commissioner, receive information from the central registry if the agency has a need for such information in order to carry out its responsibilities under law to protect children from abuse and neglect.

The name and all other identifying characteristics relating to any child which is contained in the central registry, or to his parents or guardian, shall be removed 1 year after the department determines, after investigation, that the allegation of serious physical or emotional injury resulting from abuse or neglect cannot be substantiated or, if said allegations are substantiated, when the child reaches the age of 18, or 1 year after the date of termination of services to the child or his family, whichever date occurs last. If the department determines during the initial screening period of an investigation that said report under section 51A is frivolous, or other absolute determination that abuse or neglect has not taken place, then said report shall be declared as "allegation invalid". If such reports are declared "allegation invalid", the name of the child, or identifying characteristics relating to the child, or the names of his parents or guardian or any other person relevant to the report, shall not be placed in the central registry, nor under any other computerized program utilized in the department. Nothing in this section shall prevent the department from keeping information on unsubstantiated reports to assist in future risk and safety assessments of children and families.

Any person employed in the central registry who permits the data and information stored in the registry to be released without authorization to persons other than those specified in the rules and regulations shall be punished by a fine of not more than $1,000 or by imprisonment for not more than 2½ years, or both.

Added by St.1973, c. 1076, § 5. Amended by St.1975, c. 528, § 2; St.1983, c. 391, § 2; St.1992, c. 115, § 3; St.2000, c. 247, § 5; St.2008, c. 3, § 3, eff. Jan. 11, 2008; St.2008, c. 176, § 100, eff. July 8, 2008.

§ 51G. Severability of Secs. 51A to 51F

Sections fifty-one A to fifty-one F, inclusive, are severable and the invalidity of any of said sections shall not affect the continuing validity of any other of said sections.

Added by St.1973, c. 1076, § 5.

§ 51H. Protective alerts; transport of child to another state or country

Notwithstanding any general or special law to the contrary, the department may send to, or receive from, any other state or country a protective alert containing any information about a child related to a substantiated report of child abuse or neglect if the department reasonably believes that the child has been or will be transported to another state or country.

Added by St.2008, c. 176, § 101, eff. July 8, 2008.

§ 52. Definitions

The following words as used in the following sections shall, except as otherwise specifically provided, have the following meanings:

"Court", a division of the juvenile court department.

"Delinquent child", a child between seven and seventeen who violates any city ordinance or town by-law or who commits any offence against a law of the commonwealth.

"Probation officer", a probation officer or assistant probation officer of the court having jurisdiction of the pending case.

"Punishment as is provided by law", any sentence which may be imposed upon an adult by a justice of the district court or superior court.

"Youthful offender", a person who is subject to an adult or juvenile sentence for having committed, while between the ages of fourteen and seventeen, an offense against a law of the commonwealth which, if he were an adult, would be punishable by imprisonment in the state prison, and (a) has previously been committed to the department of youth services, or (b) has committed an offense which involves the infliction or threat of serious bodily harm in violation of law, or (c) has committed a violation of paragraph (a), (c) or (d) of section ten or section ten E of chapter two hundred and sixty-nine; provided that, nothing in this clause shall allow for less than the imposition of the mandatory commitment periods provided in section fifty-eight of chapter one hundred and nineteen.

Amended by St.1948, c. 310, § 3; St.1960, c. 353, § 1; St.1965, c. 659, § 2; St.1969, c. 859, § 9; St.1972, c. 731, § 9; St.1973, c. 1073, § 6; St.1978, c. 478, § 55; St.1986, c. 557, § 115; St.1992, c. 379, § 15; St.1996, c. 200, § 1.

Historical and Statutory Notes

St.1906, c. 413, § 1.
St.1906, c. 486, § 4.
St.1917, c. 326, § 2.

§ 53. Liberal construction; nature of proceedings

Sections fifty-two to sixty-three, inclusive, shall be liberally construed so that the care, custody and discipline of the children brought before the court shall approximate as nearly as possible that which they should receive from their parents, and that, as far as practicable, they shall be treated, not as criminals, but as children in need of aid, encouragement and guidance. Proceedings against children under said sections shall not be deemed criminal proceedings.

Historical and Statutory Notes

St.1906, c. 413, § 2.

§ 54. Complaint; indictment; examination of complainant; summons; warrant

If complaint is made to any court that a child between seven and seventeen years of age is a delinquent child, said court shall examine, on oath, the complainant and the witnesses, if any, produced by him, and shall reduce the complaint to writing, and cause it to be subscribed by the complainant.

If said child is under twelve years of age, said court shall first issue a summons requiring him to appear before it at the time and place named therein, and such summons shall be issued in all other cases, instead of a warrant, unless the court has reason to believe that he will not appear upon summons, in which case, or if such a child has been summoned and did not appear, said court may issue a warrant reciting the substance of the complaint, and requiring the officer to whom it is directed forthwith to take such child and bring him before said court, to be dealt with according to law, and to summon the witnesses named therein to appear and give evidence at the examination.

The commonwealth may proceed by complaint in juvenile court or in a juvenile session of a district court, as the case may be, or by indictment as provided by chapter two hundred and seventy-seven, if a person is alleged to have committed an offense against a law of the commonwealth while between the ages of fourteen and seventeen which, if he were an adult, would be punishable by imprisonment in the state prison, and the person has previously been committed to the department of youth services, or the offense involves the infliction or threat of serious bodily harm in violation of law or the person has committed a violation of paragraph (a), (c) or (d) of section ten or section ten E of chapter two hundred and sixty-nine. The court shall proceed on the complaint or the indictment, as the case may be, in accordance with sections fifty-five to seventy-two, inclusive. Complaints and indictments brought against persons for such offenses, and for other criminal offenses properly joined under Massachusetts Rules of Criminal Procedure 9 (a) (1), shall be brought in accordance with the usual course and manner of criminal proceedings.

Amended by St.1966, c. 374; St.1973, c. 1073, § 7; St.1996, c. 200, § 2.

Historical and Statutory Notes

St.1882, c. 127, §§ 3, 4.
R.L.1902, c. 86, § 15.
St.1906, c. 413, § 3.

§ 55. Summoning of parent or guardian

If a child has been summoned to appear or is brought before such court upon a warrant, as provided in section fifty-four, a summons shall be issued to at least one of its parents, if either of them is known to reside within the commonwealth, and, if there is no such parent, then to its lawful guardian, if there is one known to be so resident, and if not, then to the person with whom such child resides, if known. Said summons shall require the person served to appear at a time and place stated therein, and show cause why such child should not be adjudged a delinquent child and why it is not in such child's best interest that he be removed from his home and whether reasonable efforts were made to prevent or eliminate the need for removal from his home. If there is no such parent, guardian or person who can be summoned as aforesaid, the court may appoint a suitable person to act for such child. A parent, guardian or person with whom such child resides who is summoned to appear before the court to show cause why such child shall not be adjudged a delinquent child by reason of having committed the offense of wilful or malicious destruction or wanton destruction of property, in violation of the provisions of section one hundred and twenty-seven or one hundred and twenty-seven A of chapter two hundred and sixty-six, and who wilfully fails to so appear shall be punished by a fine of not less than two hundred nor more than three hundred dollars.

If such child is summoned, the time for appearance fixed in the summons to a parent, guardian or other person, as herein provided, shall, when practicable, be that fixed for the appearance of said child.

A summons required by this and said section fifty-four, unless service thereof is waived in writing, shall be served by a constable or police officer, by delivering it personally to the person to whom addressed, or by leaving it with a person of proper age to receive the same, at the place of residence or business of such person; and said constable or officer shall immediately make return to the court of the time and manner of the service.

If the court shall be of the opinion that the interests of the child require the attendance at any proceedings of an agent of the department of youth services and shall request such attendance by reasonable notice to the commissioner of youth services, such agent shall attend to protect the interests of said child.

Amended by St.1949, c. 593, § 6; St.1952, c. 605, § 3; St.1969, c. 838, § 14; St.1973, c. 1073, § 8; St.1986, c. 96; St.1993, c. 110, § 158.

Historical and Statutory Notes

St.1855, c. 442, §§ 4, 5.
St.1859, c. 286, § 1.
G.S.1860, c. 75, §§ 6, 8; c. 76, §§ 17, 20.
St.1863, c. 139, § 3.
St.1870, c. 359, § 8.
P.S.1882, c. 89, §§ 20, 32.
St.1883, c. 110.
St.1886, c. 101, § 4.
St.1898, c. 433, § 24.
R.L.1902, c. 86, §§ 17, 30.
St.1906, c. 413, § 4.
St.1919, c. 350, § 87.
St.1931, c. 207.

§ 55A. Jury trials; discovery orders; jury-waived trials; appointment of stenographer

Trial of a child complained of as a delinquent child or indicted as a youthful offender in a division of the juvenile court department shall be by a jury, unless the child files a written waiver and consent to be tried by the court without a jury. Such waiver shall not be received unless the child is represented by counsel or has filed, through his parent or guardian, a written waiver of counsel. No decision on such waiver shall be received until after the completion of a pretrial conference and a hearing on the results of such conference and until after the disposition of any pretrial discovery motions and compliance with any order of the court pursuant to said motions. Such waiver shall be filed in accordance with the provisions of section six of chapter two hundred and sixty-three; provided, however, that defense counsel shall execute a certificate signed by said counsel indicating that he has made all the necessary explanations and determinations regarding such waiver. The form of such certificates shall be prescribed by the chief justice for the juvenile court department.

In the juvenile court department upon the motion of a child consistent with criminal procedure, or upon the court's own motion, the judge shall issue an order of discovery requiring the prosecutor to provide in writing any information to which the child is entitled and also requiring that the child be permitted to discover, inspect, and copy any material and relevant evidence, documents, statements or persons, or reports of physical or mental examinations of any person or of scientific tests or experiments, within the possession, custody, or control of the prosecutor or persons under his direction and control. Upon motion of the child the judge shall order the production by the commonwealth of the names and addresses of the prospective witnesses and the production by the probation department of the record of prior convictions of any such witnesses. The commonwealth shall be entitled to reciprocal discovery as set forth in Rule 14 (a) (1) (3) of the Massachusetts Rules of Criminal Procedure.

Trial by jury in the juvenile court department shall be in those jury sessions designated in accordance with section fifty-six. Where the child has properly filed a waiver and consented to be tried without a jury, as hereinbefore provided, trial shall proceed in accordance with the provisions of law applicable to jury-waived trials in the superior court; provided, however, that at the option of the child, the trial may be before a judge who has not rejected an agreed upon recommendation or disposition request made by the child pursuant to the provisions of section fifty-five B. Review in such cases may be had directly by the appeals court, by appeal, report or otherwise in the same manner provided for trials of criminal cases in the superior court.

The justice presiding over such jury-waived trial in the juvenile court department shall have and exercise all of the powers which a justice sitting in the superior court department has and may exercise in the trial and disposition of criminal cases including the power to report questions of law to the appeals court.

The justice presiding at such jury-waived session in the juvenile court department shall, upon the request of the child, appoint a stenographer; provided, however, that where the child claims indigence, such appointment is determined to be reasonably necessary in accordance with the provisions of sections twenty-seven A to twenty-seven G, inclusive, of chapter two hundred and sixty-one. Such stenographer shall be sworn, and shall take stenographic notes of all the testimony given at the trial, and shall provide the parties thereto with a transcript of his notes or any part thereof taken at the trial or hearing for which he shall be paid by the party requesting it at the rate fixed by the chief justice of the juvenile court department; provided, however, that such rate shall not exceed the rate provided pursuant to section eighty-eight of chapter two hundred and twenty-one. Said chief justice may make regulations not inconsistent with law relative to the assignments, duties and services of stenographers appointed for sessions in his department and any other matter relative to stenographers. The compensation and expenses of a stenographer shall be paid by the commonwealth.

The request for the appointment of a stenographer to preserve the testimony at a trial in the juvenile court department shall be given to the clerk of the court by the child in writing no later than forty-eight hours prior to the proceeding for which the stenographer has been requested. The child shall file with such request an affidavit of indigence and request for payment by the commonwealth of the cost of the transcript and the court shall hold a hearing on such request prior to appointing a stenographer, in those cases where the child alleges that he will be unable to pay said cost. Said hearing shall be governed by the provisions of sections twenty-seven A to twenty-seven G, inclusive, of chapter two hundred and sixty-one, and the cost of such transcript shall be considered an extra cost as provided therein. If the court is unable, for any reason, to provide a stenographer, the proceedings may be recorded by electronic means. The original recording of proceedings in the juvenile court department made with a recording device under the exclusive control of the court shall be the official record of such proceedings. Said record or a copy of all or a part thereof, certified by the presiding justice or his designee, to be an accurate electronic reproduction of said record or part thereof, or a typewritten transcript of all or part of said record or copy thereof, certified to be accurate by the court or by the preparer of said transcript, or stipulated to by the parties, shall be admissible in any court as evidence of testimony given wherever proof of such testimony is otherwise competent. The child may request payment by the commonwealth of the cost of said transcript subject to the same provisions regarding a transcript of a stenographer as provided hereinbefore.

Added by St.1978, c. 478, § 56. Amended by St.1992, c. 379, § 16; St.1996, c. 200, § 3.

§ 55B. Plea; disposition request; pretrial motions

A child who is before the juvenile court on a delinquency complaint or an indictment within the court's jurisdiction shall plead not delinquent, or that he should not be adjudged as a youthful offender, as the case may be. Such plea shall be submitted by the child and acted upon by the court; provided, however, that a child with whom the commonwealth cannot reach agreement for a recommended disposition shall be allowed to tender a plea together with a request for a specific disposition. Such request may include any disposition or dispositional terms within the court's jurisdiction, including, unless otherwise prohibited by law, a disposition request that a finding not be entered, but rather the case be continued without a finding to a specific date thereupon to be dismissed, such continuance conditioned upon compliance with specific terms and conditions or that the child be placed on probation pursuant to the provisions of section 57; provided, however, that a complaint alleging a child to be a delinquent child by reason of having violated the provisions of section 13B, 13B½, 13B¾, section 22A, 22B, 22C or section 23, 23A, 23B of chapter 265 shall not be placed on file or continued without a finding. If a plea, with an agreed upon recommendation or with a disposition request by the child, is tendered, the court shall inform the child that it will not impose a disposition that exceeds the terms of the agreed upon recommendation or the disposition request by the child, whichever is applicable, without giving the child the right to withdraw the plea.

Notwithstanding the foregoing requirements, if a child attempts to enter a plea or statement consisting of an admission of facts sufficient for a finding of delinquency or adjudication as a youthful offender, or some similar statement, such admission shall be deemed a tender of plea for purposes of the procedures set forth in this section.

Any pretrial motion filed in a delinquency case or case in which the commonwealth has proceeded by indictment pending in the juvenile court and decided before entry of the child's decision on waiver of the right to jury trial shall not be refiled or reheard thereafter, except in the discretion of the court as substantial justice requires. Any such pretrial motion not filed or filed but not decided prior to entry of the child's decision on waiver of the right to jury trial may be filed thereafter but not later than twenty-one days after entry of said decision on waiver of the right to jury trial, except for good cause shown.

Added by St.1996, c. 200, § 3. Amended by St.1998, c. 194, § 176; St.2010, c. 267, §§ 14 to 16, eff. Nov. 5, 2010.

§ 56. Adjournments; jury sessions; appointment of stenographer

Hearings upon cases arising under sections fifty-two to eighty-four, inclusive, may be adjourned from time to time; provided however, that no adjournment shall exceed fifteen days at any one time against the objection of the child. Section thirty-five of chapter two hundred and seventy-six relative to recognizance in cases continued shall apply to cases arising under sections fifty-two to eighty-four, inclusive.

(a) Every division of the juvenile court department shall be authorized to hold jury sessions for the purpose of conducting jury trials of cases commenced in the several courts of offenses over which the juvenile courts have original jurisdiction.

(b) The chief justice for the juvenile court department shall designate at least one division in each county or an adjoining county for the purpose of conducting jury trials.

The chief justice of the juvenile court department may also designate one or more divisions in each county for the purpose of conducting jury-waived trials of cases commenced in any court of said county consistent with the requirements of the proper administration of justice.

(c) A child in any division of the juvenile court who waives his right to jury trial as provided in section fifty-five A shall be provided a jury-waived trial in the same division.

A child in any division of the juvenile court who does not waive his right to jury trial as provided in section fifty-five A shall be provided a jury trial in a jury session in the same division if such session has been established in said division. If such session has not been so established, the child shall be provided a jury trial in a jury session in an adjoining county as designated by the clerk in the division where the case is pending. In cases where the child declines to waive the right to jury trial, the clerk shall forthwith transfer the case for trial in the appropriate jury session. Such transfer shall be governed by procedures to be established by the chief justice for the juvenile court department.

(d) The justice presiding over a jury session shall have and exercise all the powers and duties which a justice sitting in the superior court department has and may exercise in the trial and disposition of criminal cases including the power to report questions of law to the appeals court. No justice so sitting shall act in a case in which he has sat or held an inquest or otherwise taken part in any proceeding therein.

(e) Trials by jury shall proceed in accordance with the provisions of law applicable to trials by jury in the superior court. The commonwealth shall be entitled to as many challenges as equal the whole number to which all the children in the case are entitled. Trial by jury shall be by juries of six persons, except that in cases where the commonwealth has proceeded by indictment, said child shall be entitled to a jury of twelve.

(f) For the jury sessions, jurors shall be provided by the office of the jury commissioner in accordance with the provisions of chapter two hundred and thirty-four A.

(g) The district attorney for the district in which the alleged offense or offenses occurred shall appear for the commonwealth in the trial of all cases in which the right to jury trial has not been waived and may appear in any other case. The chief justice for the juvenile court department shall arrange for the sittings of the jury sessions and shall assign justices thereto, to the end that speedy trials may be provided. Review may be had directly by the appeals court, by appeal, report or otherwise in the same manner provided for trials of criminal cases in the superior court. A claim of trial by jury under this section may be withdrawn before trial, in which event trial and disposition of the case shall be by a justice in a jury session sitting without a jury.

(h) The justice presiding at such session in the juvenile court department shall, upon request of the child, appoint a stenographer in accordance with section fifty-five A herein.

The request for the appointment of a stenographer to preserve the testimony at a trial in the juvenile court department shall be given to the clerk of the court by the child in writing no later than forty-eight hours prior to the proceeding for which the stenographer has been requested. The child shall file with such request an affidavit of indigence and request for payment by the commonwealth of the cost of the transcript and the court shall hold a hearing on such request prior to appointing a stenographer, in those cases where the child alleges that he will be unable to pay said cost. Said hearing shall be governed by the provisions of sections twenty-seven A to twenty-seven G, inclusive, of chapter two hundred and sixty-one, and the cost of such transcript shall be considered an extra cost as provided therein. If the court is unable, for any reason, to provide a stenographer, the proceedings may be recorded by electronic means. The original recording of proceedings in the juvenile court department made with a recording device under the exclusive control of the court shall be the official record of such proceedings. Said record or a copy of all or a part thereof, certified by the presiding justice or his designee, to be an accurate electronic reproduction of said record or part thereof, or a typewritten transcript of all or part of said record or copy thereof, certified to be accurate by the court or by the preparer of said transcript, or stipulated to by the parties, shall be admissible in any court as evidence of testimony given wherever proof of such testimony is otherwise competent. The child may request payment by the commonwealth of the cost of said transcript subject to the same provisions regarding a transcript of a stenographer as provided hereinbefore.

Amended by St.1943, c. 244, § 1; St.1964, c. 308, § 1; St.1971, c. 336; St.1973, c. 1073, §§ 9 to 11; St.1975, c. 813; St.1977, c. 431, § 2; St.1978, c. 478, § 57; St.1979, c. 344, § 1; St.1989, c. 341, § 73; St.1992, c. 379, §§ 17 to 19; St.1996, c. 200, § 4.

Historical and Statutory Notes

St.1906, c. 413, § 5.
St.1916, c. 243, § 1.
St.1927, c. 181, § 1.

§ 57. Investigation by probation officer; record of performance; reports

Every case of a delinquent child shall be investigated by the probation officer, who shall make a report regarding the character of such child, his school record, home surroundings and the previous complaints against him, if any. In every case involving a child attending a special class authorized by law, he shall secure from the bureau of special education a record of performance of said child. He shall be present in court at the trial of the case, and furnish the court with such information and assistance as shall be required. At the end of the probation period of a child who has been placed on probation, the officer in whose care he has been shall make a report as to his conduct during such period.

Amended by St.1966, c. 147; St.1973, c. 1073, § 12.

Historical and Statutory Notes

St.1906, c. 413, § 7.

§ 58. Adjudication as delinquent child or youthful offender

At the hearing of a complaint against a child the court shall hear the testimony of any witnesses who appear and take such evidence relative to the case as shall be produced. If the allegations against a child are proved beyond a reasonable doubt, he may be adjudged a delinquent child, or in lieu thereof, the court may continue the case without a finding and, with the consent of the child and at least one of the child's parents or guardians, place said child on probation; provided, however, that any such probation may be imposed until such child reaches age eighteen or age nineteen in the case of a child whose case is disposed of after he has attained his eighteenth birthday; provided further, that a complaint alleging a child to be a delinquent child by reason of having violated the provisions of section 13B, 13B½, 13B¾, section 22A, 22B, 22C, 23, 23A or 23B of chapter 265 shall not be placed on file or continued without a finding. Said probation may include a requirement, subject to agreement by the child and at least one of the child's parents or guardians, that the child do work or participate in activities of a type and for a period of time deemed appropriate by the court.

If a child is adjudicated a delinquent child on a complaint, the court may place the case on file or may place the child in the care of a probation officer for such time and on such conditions as it deems appropriate or may commit him to the custody of the department of youth services, but the probationary or commitment period shall not be for a period longer than until such child attains the age of eighteen, or nineteen in the case of a child whose case is disposed of after he has attained his eighteenth birthday.

If a child is adjudicated a youthful offender on an indictment, the court may sentence him to such punishment as is provided by law for the offense. The court shall make a written finding, stating its reasons therefor, that the present and long-term public safety would be best protected by:

(a) a sentence provided by law; or

(b) a combination sentence which shall be a commitment to the department of youth services until he reaches the age of twenty-one, and an adult sentence to a house of correction or to the state prison as is provided by law for the offense. The adult sentence shall be suspended pending successful completion of a term of probation, which shall include, but not be limited to, the successful completion of the aforementioned commitment to the department of youth services. Any juvenile receiving a combination sentence shall be under the sole custody and control of the department of youth services unless or until discharged by the department or until the age of twenty-one, whichever occurs first, and thereafter under the supervision of the juvenile court probation department until the age of twenty-one and thereafter by the adult probation department; provided, however, that in no event shall the aggregate sentence imposed on the combination sentence exceed the maximum adult sentence provided by law; or

(c) a commitment to the department of youth services until he reaches the age of twenty-one.

In making such determination the court shall conduct a sentencing recommendation hearing to determine the sentence by which the present and long-term public safety would be best protected. At such hearing, the court shall consider, but not be limited to, the following factors: the nature, circumstances and seriousness of the offense; victim impact statement; a report by a probation officer concerning the history of the youthful offender; the youthful offender's court and delinquency records; the success or lack of success of any past treatment or delinquency dispositions regarding the youthful offender; the nature of services available through the juvenile justice system; the youthful offender's age and maturity; and the likelihood of avoiding future criminal conduct. In addition, the court may consider any other factors it deems relevant to disposition. No such sentence shall be imposed until a pre-sentence investigation report has been filed by the probation department and made available to the parties no less than seven days prior to sentencing.

A youthful offender who is sentenced as is provided by law either to a state prison or to a house of correction but who has not yet reached his seventeenth birthday shall be held in a youthful offender unit separate from the general population of adult prisoners; provided, however, that such youthful offender shall be classified at a facility other than the reception and diagnostic center at the Massachusetts Correctional Institution, Concord, and shall not be held at the Massachusetts Correctional Institution, Cedar Junction, prior to his seventeenth birthday.

If it is alleged in the complaint upon which the child is so adjudged that a penal law of the commonwealth, a city ordinance or a town by-law has been violated, the court may commit such child to the custody of the commissioner of youth services and authorize him to place such child in the charge of any person, and, if at any time thereafter the child proves unmanageable, to transfer such child to that facility which in the opinion of said commissioner, after study, will best serve the needs of the child. The department of youth services shall provide for the maintenance, in whole or part, of any child so placed in the charge of any person.

Notwithstanding any other provisions of this chapter, a person adjudicated a delinquent child by reason of a violation of paragraph (a), (c) or (d) of section ten or section ten E of chapter two hundred and sixty-nine, shall be committed to the custody of the commissioner of youth services who shall place such child in the custody of a facility supported by the commonwealth for the care, custody and training of such delinquent children for a period of at least one hundred and eighty days or until such child attains his eighteenth birthday, whichever first occurs, provided, however, that said period of time shall not be reduced or suspended.

Upon the second or subsequent violation of said paragraph (a), (c) or (d) of said section ten or ten E of said chapter two hundred and sixty-nine, the commissioner of youth services shall place such child in the custody of a facility supported by the commonwealth for the care, custody and training of such delinquent child for not less than one year; provided, however, that said period of time shall not be reduced or suspended.

The court may make an order for payment by the child's parents or guardian from the child's property, or by any other person responsible for the care and support of said child, to the institution, department, division, organization or person furnishing care and support at times to be stated in an order by the court of sums not exceeding the cost of said support after ability to pay has been determined by the court; provided, however, that no order for the payment of money shall be entered until the person by whom payments are to be made shall have been summoned before the court and given an opportunity to be heard. The court may from time to time, upon petition by, or notice to the person ordered to pay such sums of money, revise or alter such order or make a new order, as the circumstances may require.

The court may commit such delinquent child to the department of youth services, but it shall not commit such child to any institution supported by the commonwealth for the custody, care and training of delinquent children or juvenile offenders.

Except in cases in which the child has attained the age of majority, whenever a court of competent jurisdiction adjudicates a child as delinquent and commits the child to the department of youth services, the court, in order to comply with the requirements contained in the federal Adoption Assistance and Child Welfare Act of 1980 and any amendments thereto, shall receive evidence in order to determine whether continuation of the child in his home is contrary to his best interest, and whether reasonable efforts were made prior to the commitment of the child to the department, to prevent or eliminate the need for removal from his home; or whether an emergency situation existed making such efforts impossible. No such determination shall be made unless the parent or guardian of the delinquent shall have been summoned before the court and, if present, given an opportunity to be heard. The court, in its discretion, may make its determinations concerning said best interest and reasonable efforts in written form, but in the absence of a written determination to the contrary, it shall be presumed that the court did find that continuation of the child in his home was contrary to his best interest and that reasonable efforts to prevent or eliminate the need for removal of the child from his home did occur. Nothing in this section shall diminish the department's responsibility to prevent delinquent acts and to protect the public safety.

Amended by St.1941, c. 264, § 1; St.1948, c. 310, § 4; St.1948, c. 385; St.1969, c. 838, § 15; St.1969, c. 859, § 10; St.1972, c. 731, § 10; St.1973, c. 925, § 42; St.1973, c. 1073, §§ 13 to 15; St.1976, c. 533; St.1978, c. 478, § 58; St.1986, c. 557, § 116; St.1990, c. 267, §§ 1, 2; St.1992, c. 379, § 20; St.1992, c. 398, § 1; St.1993, c. 110, § 159; St.1995, c. 278, § 1; St.1996, c. 200, § 5; St.1998, c. 194, § 177; St.2010, c. 267, §§ 17 to 19, eff. Nov. 5, 2010.

Historical and Statutory Notes

St.1870, c. 359, §§ 11, 12.
P.S.1882, c. 89, §§ 28, 29.
R.L.1902, c. 86, § 27.
St.1906, c. 413, § 8.
St.1916, c. 243, § 3.

§ 58A. Repealed, 1948, 310, Sec. 5

§ 58B. Motor vehicle violations; disposition; admissibility of adjudication and disposition as evidence in other proceedings

If, under the provisions of section fifty-eight, a child is adjudged a delinquent child by reason of having violated any statute, by-law, ordinance or regulation relating to the operation of motor vehicles, the court may place the case on file, or may place the child in the care of a probation officer, or may commit him to the custody of the department of youth services, as provided in section fifty-eight, and may require restitution as provided in section sixty-two; and in addition to or in lieu of such disposition, the court may impose upon such child a fine not exceeding the amount of the fine authorized for the violation of such statute, by-law, ordinance or regulation. Any fine imposed under the authority of this section shall be collected, recovered and paid over in the manner provided by chapters two hundred and seventy-nine and two hundred and eighty; provided, however, that if any child shall neglect, fail or refuse to pay a fine imposed under this section, he may be arrested upon order of the court and brought before the court, which may thereupon place him in the care of a probation officer or commit him to the custody of the department of youth services; but no such child shall be committed to any jail, house of correction, or correctional institution of the commonwealth. The provisions of sections sixty and sixty A shall apply to any case disposed of under this section; provided, however, that the court shall provide the registrar of motor vehicles with an abstract of every such adjudication and disposition, in the manner provided by section twenty-seven of chapter ninety; and provided, further, that such adjudication and disposition shall be admissible as evidence in any proceeding for the revocation or restoration of the child's license or right to operate a motor vehicle and for the cancellation of a motor vehicle insurance policy covering the vehicle operated by such child, and in any action of tort arising out of the negligent operation of a motor vehicle by said child, to the same extent that such evidence would be admissible if said child were an adult.

Added by St.1957, c. 194, § 1. Amended by St.1969, c. 838, § 16; St.1980, c. 95.

§ 59. Violation of terms of probation

If a child has been placed in care of a probation officer, said officer, at any time before the final disposition of the case, may arrest such child without a warrant and take him before the court, or the court may issue a warrant for his arrest. When such child is before the court, it may make any disposition of the case which it might have made before said child was placed on probation, or may continue or extend the period of probation.

Amended by St.1941, c. 648, § 1.

Historical and Statutory Notes

St.1906, c. 413, § 9.

§ 60. Admissibility of adjudication in subsequent proceeding; disqualification for public service

An adjudication of any child as a delinquent child under sections fifty-two to fifty-nine, inclusive, or any disposition thereunder of any child so adjudicated, or any evidence given in any case arising against any child under said sections fifty-two to fifty-nine, or any records in cases arising against any child under said sections fifty-two to fifty-nine shall not be received in evidence or used against such child for any purpose in any proceedings in any court except in subsequent delinquency or criminal proceedings against the same person; nor shall such adjudication or disposition or evidence operate to disqualify a child in any future examination, appointment, or application for public service under the government either of the commonwealth or of any political subdivision thereof; provided, however, that adjudication of delinquency by reason of the child having committed an offense against the commonwealth may be used for impeachment purposes in subsequent delinquency or criminal proceedings in the same manner and to the same extent as prior criminal convictions.

Amended by St.1938, c. 174, § 1; St.1948, c. 310, § 6; St.1973, c. 1073, § 16; St.1986, c. 199; St.1991, c. 488, § 1; St.1992, c. 398, § 2.

Historical and Statutory Notes

St.1906, c. 413, § 10.

§ 60A. Inspection of records in youthful offender and delinquency cases

The records of a youthful offender proceeding conducted pursuant to an indictment shall be open to public inspection in the same manner and to the same extent as adult criminal court records. All other records of the court in cases of delinquency arising under sections fifty-two to fifty-nine, inclusive, shall be withheld from public inspection except with the consent of a justice of such court; provided, however, that such records shall be open, at all reasonable times, to inspection by the child proceeded against, his parents, guardian or attorney; provided further, that nothing herein shall be construed to provide access to privileged or confidential communications and information; and provided further, that said protections shall be construed to include information and communications entered at the indictment.

Notwithstanding the provisions of this section, the name of a child shall be made available to the public by the probation officer without such consent if the child is: alleged to have committed an offense while between his fourteenth and seventeenth birthdays; and has previously been adjudicated delinquent on at least two occasions for acts which would have been punishable by imprisonment in the state prison if such child had been age seventeen or older; and is charged with delinquency by reason of an act which would be punishable by imprisonment in the state prison if such child were age seventeen or older.

Added by St.1938, c. 174, § 1. Amended by St.1973, c. 1073, § 17; St.1978, c. 478, § 59; St.1985, c. 425; St.1996, c. 200, § 6.

§ 61. Repealed, 1996, 200, Sec. 7

§ 62. Restitution or reparation by child to injured person

If, in adjudging a person a delinquent child, the court finds, as an element of such delinquency, that he has committed an act involving liability in a civil action, and such delinquent child is placed on probation, the court may require, as a condition thereof, that he shall make restitution or reparation to the injured person to such an extent and in such sum as the court determines. If the payment is not made at once, it shall be made to the probation officer, who shall give a receipt therefor, keep a record of the payment, pay the money to said injured person, and keep on file his receipt therefor.

Historical and Statutory Notes

St.1906, c. 413, § 12.

§ 63. Inducing or abetting delinquency of child

Any person who shall be found to have caused, induced, abetted, or encouraged or contributed toward the delinquency of a child, or to have acted in any way tending to cause or induce such delinquency, may be punished by a fine of not more than five hundred dollars or by imprisonment of not more than one year, or both. The court may release on probation under section eighty-seven of chapter two hundred and seventy-six, subject to such orders as it may make as to future conduct tending to cause, induce or contribute to such delinquency, or it may suspend sentence under section one of chapter two hundred and seventy-nine, or before trial, with the defendant's consent, it may allow the defendant to enter into a recognizance, in such penal sum as the court may fix, conditioned to comply with such terms as the court may order for the promotion of the future welfare of the child, and the said case may then be placed on file. The provisions for recognizance in section fifty-six shall be applicable to cases arising hereunder. The divisions of the juvenile court department shall, within their respective territorial limits, have exclusive jurisdiction over complaints alleging violations of this section.

Amended by St.1932, c. 95, § 1; St.1965, c. 348; St.1965, c. 659, § 3; St.1969, c. 859, § 11; St.1972, c. 731, § 11; St.1973, c. 1073, §§ 18, 19; St.1978, c. 478, § 60; St.1992, c. 379, § 21; St.1996, c. 200, § 8; St.1996, c. 450, § 162.

Historical and Statutory Notes

St.1906, c. 413, § 13.
St.1916, c. 243, § 4.

§ 64. Powers of commissioner of probation; annual report

The commissioner of probation may supervise the probation work for delinquent children, and make necessary inquiries in regard to the same, and in his annual report may make such recommendations as he considers advisable for the improvement of methods of dealing with such children.

Amended by St.1956, c. 731, § 2; St.1996, c. 450, § 163.

Historical and Statutory Notes

St.1906, c. 413, § 14.
St.1912, c. 187.
St.1929, c. 179, § 3.

§ 65. Juvenile sessions; presence of minors; exclusion of public

Courts shall designate suitable times for the hearing of cases of children under seventeen years of age, which shall be called the juvenile session, for which a separate docket and record shall be kept. Said session shall be separate from that for the trial of criminal cases, shall not, except as otherwise expressly provided, be held in conjunction with other business of the court, and shall be held in rooms not used for criminal trials; and in places where no separate juvenile courtroom is provided, hearings, so far as possible, shall be held in chambers. The court shall exclude the general public from juvenile sessions admitting only such persons as may have a direct interest in the case, except in cases where the commonwealth has proceeded by indictment. A complaint under section sixty-three may be heard in such juvenile session.

Amended by St.1932, c. 95, § 2; St.1990, c. 267, § 4; St.1996, c. 200, § 9.

Historical and Statutory Notes

St.1874, c. 258, § 3.
St.1877, c. 210, § 5.
P.S.1882, c. 89, § 19.
R.L.1902, c. 86, § 16.
St.1906, c. 413, § 6.
St.1906, c. 489, § 5.
St.1916, c. 243, § 2.
St.1931, c. 217.

§ 66. Detention of child in police station; commitment to jail, house of correction or state farm

Except as otherwise provided in section sixty-seven and in section twelve of chapter one hundred and twenty, no child under seventeen years of age shall be detained by the police in a lockup, police station or house of detention pending arraignment, examination or trial by the court. No child under seventeen years of age shall be committed by the court to a jail or house of correction or to the state farm, pending further examination or trial by the court or pending any continuance of his case or, except as otherwise provided in sections fifty-two through eighty-four upon adjudication as a youthful offender.

Amended by St.1941, c. 648, § 2; St.1943, c. 244, § 2; St.1960, c. 353, § 2; St.1978, c. 478, § 61; St.1996, c. 200, § 10.

Historical and Statutory Notes

R.S.1836, c. 143, § 18.
St.1859, c. 286, § 3.
G.S.1860, c. 174, § 15.
St.1865, c. 208, § 1.
P.S.1882, c. 215, § 18.
St.1882, c. 127, § 1.
St.1890, c. 440, § 3.
St.1896, c. 536, § 9.
R.L.1902, c. 86, § 20.
St.1902, c. 314.
St.1906, c. 413, § 3.

§ 67. Notice of arrest of child to probation officer and parent or guardian; detention

Except for children in need of service arrested pursuant to section thirty-nine H, whenever a child between seven and seventeen years of age is arrested with or without a warrant, as provided by law, the officer in charge of the police station or town lockup to which the child has been taken shall immediately notify the probation officer of the district court, or of the juvenile court, if there is one, within whose judicial district such child was arrested and at least one of the child's parents, or, if there is no parent, the guardian or person with whom it is stated that such child resides, and shall inquire into the case. Pending such notice and inquiry, such child shall be detained. Upon the acceptance by the officer in charge of said police station or town lockup of the written promise of said parent, guardian or any other reputable person to be responsible for the presence of such child in court at the time and place when such child is to appear or upon the receipt of such officer in charge from said probation officer of a request for the release of such child to him, such child shall be released to said person giving such promise or to said probation officer making such request; provided, that, if the arresting officer requests in writing that a child between fourteen and seventeen years of age be detained, and if the court issuing a warrant for the arrest of a child between fourteen and seventeen years of age directs in the warrant that such child shall be held in safekeeping pending his appearance in court, or, if the probation officer shall so direct, such child shall be detained in a police station or town lockup, or place of temporary custody commonly referred to as a detention home of the department of youth services, or any other home approved by the department of youth services pending his appearance in court. In the event any such child is so detained, the officer in charge at the police station or town lockup shall notify the probation officer and parent or parents, guardian, or person with whom it is stated that such child resides of the detention of such child. Nothing contained in this section shall prevent the admitting of such child to bail in accordance with law. Said probation officer or officer in charge at the police station or town lockup shall notify such child and his parent or parents or guardian or person with whom it is stated that such child resides of the time and place of the hearing of his case. No child between fourteen and seventeen years of age shall be detained in a police station or town lockup unless the detention facilities for children at such police station or town lockup have received the approval in writing of the commissioner of youth services. The department of youth services shall make inspection at least annually of police stations or town lockups wherein children are detained. If no such approved detention facilities exist in any city or town, such city or town may contract with an adjacent city or town for the use of approved detention facilities in order to prevent children who are detained from coming in contact with adult prisoners. Nothing in this section shall permit a child between fourteen and seventeen years of age being detained in a jail or house of correction. A separate and distinct place shall be provided in police stations, town lockups or places of detention for such children.

Amended by St.1941, c. 648, § 3; St.1943, c. 244, § 2; St.1955, c. 609, § 1; St.1969, c. 838, § 17; St.1978, c. 478, § 62; St.1991, c. 519, § 2.

Historical and Statutory Notes

St.1870, c. 359, § 9.
P.S.1882, c. 89, § 21.
St.1882, c. 127, §§ 1, 2.
R.L.1902, c. 86, §§ 18, 19.
St.1906, c. 413, § 5.
St.1916, c. 243, § 1.
St.1919, c. 350, § 87.
St.1927, c. 221.
St.1931, c. 216.
St.1931, c. 284, § 1.

§ 68. Commitment of children held for examination or trial

A child who has attained the age of seven but not yet attained the age of seventeen held by the court for further examination, trial or continuance, or for indictment and trial, if unable to furnish bail, shall be committed by the court to the care of the department of youth services or to a probation officer, a parent, guardian, or other responsible person who shall provide for his safekeeping; provided, however, that the appearance of the child at such examination or trial, shall be the responsibility of the court for which he is being held in safekeeping.

The court may recommend that a child who has attained the age of fourteen and who is committed to the care of the department shall be held in a secure detention facility if the court further determines that the child (a) is a fugitive from another jurisdiction on a delinquency petition; or (b) is charged with an offense for which the commonwealth may proceed by indictment in accordance with the provisions of section fifty-four; provided, however, that such child is already detained or on conditional release in conjunction with another delinquency proceeding, or has demonstrated a recent record of willful failure to appear at juvenile court proceedings, or has demonstrated a recent record of violent conduct resulting in physical injury to others.

The court shall forward such recommendation and the reasons therefor, in writing, to the department. Such recommendation shall not be binding upon the department, but if the department chooses not to comply with such recommendation, the department shall inform the court within two business days.

The department may provide special foster homes, and places of temporary custody commonly referred to as detention homes of the department of youth services for the care, maintenance and safekeeping of such children who may be committed by the court to said department under this section; provided, however, that no more than five such children shall be detained in any such special foster home at any one time.

A child between seven and seventeen years of age so committed by the court to the department to await further examination or trial by the court, shall be returned thereto within fifteen days after the date of the order of such commitment, and final disposition of the case shall thereupon be made by adjudication or otherwise, unless, in the opinion of the court, the interest of the child and the public otherwise require.

The provisions of section twenty-four of chapter two hundred and twelve, relative to the precedence of cases of persons actually confined in prison and awaiting trial, shall apply to children held in detention facilities of the department of youth services under this section.

Said probation officer shall have the same authority, rights and powers in relation to a child committed to his care under this section, and in relation to a child released to him as provided in section sixty-seven, as he would have if he were surety on the recognizance of such child.

A person who at the time of the offense had attained the age of fourteen but had not attained the age of seventeen, and who is charged with murder in the first or second degree and is held by the superior court for trial or continuance, or for indictment and trial, if unable to furnish bail, shall be committed by the court to the custody of the sheriff of the county in which the court is situated; provided, however, that the appearance of the person at such examination or trial shall be the responsibility of the court for which he is being held in safekeeping.

Amended by St.1943, c. 244, § 2; St.1948, c. 310, § 8; St.1955, c. 609, § 2; St.1956, c. 269; St.1969, c. 838, § 18; St.1969, c. 859, § 12; St.1972, c. 731, § 12; St.1978, c. 478, § 63; St.1985, c. 334; St.1996, c. 200, § 11.

Historical and Statutory Notes

St.1906, c. 489, § 8.
St.1918, c. 257, § 419.
St.1919, c. 5.
St.1920, c. 2.

§ 68A. Diagnostic study by department of youth services; report and recommendations

A child between seven and seventeen years of age, held by the court for further examination, trial or continuance, or for indictment and trial, may at the discretion of the court be referred to the department of youth services, any court clinic, or the department of mental health, with its consent, and with the consent of the parents or guardian, for diagnostic study on an inpatient or outpatient basis; and, upon completion of such study, the department of youth services, court clinic or department of mental health, as the case may be, shall forward a report and recommendations to the court. In default of bail, any such child may be committed by the court to the department of youth services for a period not to exceed thirty days while undergoing diagnostic study. At the expiration of such period, such child shall be returned to the court, together with the report and recommendations to the department of youth services.

Added by St.1955, c. 609, § 3. Amended by St.1969, c. 838, § 19; St.1978, c. 478, § 64; St.1996, c. 200, § 12.

§ 68B. Special foster homes; detention homes; alternate placements of child

The department of youth services may use or provide special foster homes and places of temporary custody commonly referred to as detention homes, at various places in the commonwealth which shall be completely separate from any police station, town lockup or jail, and which shall be used solely for the temporary care, custody and study of children committed to the care of the department of youth services. Nothing in this section shall prevent the department from using or providing alternative placements and employing alternative measures which, in its discretion, will reasonably assure the appearance of the children before the court.

Added by St.1955, c. 609, § 3. Amended by St.1969, c. 838, § 20; St.2009, c. 166, § 29A, eff. Nov. 24, 2009.

§ 68C. Diagnostic services by department of youth services

The department of youth services shall maintain and provide diagnostic services for the purpose of providing the diagnostic studies and making the reports and recommendations provided for under section sixty-eight A, and the department may provide offices and facilities for such diagnostic services, at such places in the commonwealth as will best serve the needs of the several courts.

Added by St.1955, c. 609, § 3. Amended by St.1969, c. 838, § 21.

§ 69. Information and reports of superintendents of schools and teachers

The superintendent of the public schools in any town, any teacher therein, and any person in charge of a private school, or any teacher therein, shall furnish to any court from time to time any information and reports requested by any justice thereof relating to the attendance, conduct and standing of any pupil enrolled in such school, if said pupil is at the time awaiting examination or trial by the court or is under the supervision of the court.

Amended by St.1943, c. 244, § 2.

Historical and Statutory Notes

St.1906, c. 489, § 7.
St.1908, c. 286.
St.1918, c. 257, § 419.
St.1919, c. 5.
St.1920, c. 2.

§ 69A. Information of probation officers, police and school authorities

When a person has been committed to the department of youth services, the court, the probation officers, and other public and police authorities, the school authorities, and other public officials shall make available to said department all pertinent information in their possession in respect to the case.

Added by St.1948, c. 310, § 9. Amended by St.1969, c. 838, § 22.

§ 70. Summoning of parent or guardian during case

At any time during the pendency of any case before a court or trial justice against a child under seventeen years of age, whether pending adjudication or during continuances or probation or after the case has been taken from the files, the court or trial justice may summon any parent or guardian of said child, or any person with whom the child resides, in the manner provided in section fifty-five.

Historical and Statutory Notes

St.1907, c. 195, § 1.

§ 71. Failure to appear on summons; capias

If any person to whom a summons is issued under the preceding section or section forty-two or fifty-five fails to appear in response to such summons, the court issuing the summons may issue a capias to compel the attendance of such person, and such capias shall be issued and served in the same manner as a capias to compel the attendance of witnesses who have failed to appear on a subpoena issued in behalf of the commonwealth in a criminal case.

Historical and Statutory Notes

St.1907, c. 195, § 2.

§ 72. Continuance of jurisdiction of courts in juvenile sessions

(a) The divisions of the juvenile court department shall continue to have jurisdiction over children who attain their eighteenth birthday pending final adjudication of their cases, including all remands and retrials following appeals from their cases, or during continuances or probation, or after their cases have been placed on file, or for any other proceeding arising out of their cases. Except as provided in subsection (b), nothing herein shall authorize the commitment of a person to the department of youth services after he has attained his nineteenth birthday.

If a child commits an offense prior to his seventeenth birthday, and is not apprehended until between his seventeenth and eighteenth birthday, the court shall deal with such child in the same manner as if he has not attained his seventeenth birthday, and all provisions and rights applicable to a child under seventeen shall apply to such child.

(b) If the commonwealth has proceeded by indictment, the divisions of the juvenile court department shall continue to have jurisdiction over such persons who attain their eighteenth birthday pending the final adjudication of their cases, including all remands and retrials following appeals from their cases, or pending the determination allowed under section 58, or during continuances or probation, or after their cases have been placed on file, or for any other proceeding arising out of their cases. Nothing herein shall authorize the commitment of a youthful offender to the department of youth services after he has attained his twenty-first birthday.

Amended by St.1947, c. 235; St.1948, c. 310, § 10; St.1949, c. 595; St.1964, c. 308, § 3; St.1969, c. 838, § 23; St.1978, c. 478, § 65; St.1990, c. 267, § 5; St.1991, c. 488, § 7; St.1992, c. 379, § 22; St.1992, c. 398, §§ 4, 5; St.1996, c. 200, § 13; St.1998, c. 98, §§ 1, 2.

Historical and Statutory Notes

St.1907, c. 411.
St.1918, c. 257, § 418.
St.1919, c. 5.
St.1920, c. 2.

§ 72A. Proceedings upon apprehension after eighteenth birthday

If a person commits an offense or violation prior to his seventeenth birthday, and is not apprehended until after his eighteenth birthday, the court, after a hearing, shall determine whether there is probable cause to believe that said person committed the offense charged, and shall, in its discretion, either order that the person be discharged, if satisfied that such discharge is consistent with the protection of the public; or, if the court is of the opinion that the interests of the public require that such person be tried for such offense or violation instead of being discharged, the court shall dismiss the delinquency complaint and cause a criminal complaint to be issued. The case shall thereafter proceed according to the usual course of criminal proceedings and in accordance with the provisions of section thirty of chapter two hundred and eighteen and section eighteen of chapter two hundred and seventy-eight. Said hearing shall be held prior to, and separate from, any trial on the merits of the charges alleged.

Added by St.1964, c. 308, § 4. Amended by St.1975, c. 840, § 2; St.1996, c. 200, § 13A.

§ 72B. Persons between the ages of fourteen and seventeen convicted of murder; penalties

If a person is found guilty of murder in the first degree committed on or after his fourteenth birthday and before his seventeenth birthday under the provisions of section one of chapter two hundred and sixty-five, the superior court shall commit the person to such punishment as is provided by law for the offense.

If a person is found guilty of murder in the second degree committed on or after his fourteenth birthday and before his seventeenth birthday under the provisions of section one of chapter two hundred and sixty-five, the superior court shall commit the person to such punishment as is provided by law. Said person shall be eligible for parole under section one hundred and thirty-three A of chapter one hundred and twenty-seven when such person has served fifteen years of said confinement. Thereafter said person shall be subject to the provisions of law governing the granting of parole permits by the parole board.

The superior court shall not suspend the commitment of a person found guilty of murder in the first or second degree, nor shall the provisions of section one hundred and twenty-nine C or one hundred and twenty-nine D of chapter one hundred and twenty-seven apply to such commitment. In all cases where a person is alleged to have violated section one of chapter two hundred and sixty-five, the person shall have the right to an indictment proceeding under section four of chapter two hundred and sixty-three.

A person who is found guilty of murder and is sentenced to a state prison but who has not yet reached his seventeenth birthday shall be held in a youthful offender unit separate from the general population of adult prisoners; provided, however, that such person shall be classified at a facility other than the reception and diagnostic center at the Massachusetts Correctional Institution, Concord, and shall not be held at the Massachusetts Correctional Institution, Cedar Junction, prior to his seventeenth birthday.

If a defendant is not found guilty of murder in the first or second degree, but is found guilty of a lesser included offense or a criminal offense properly joined under Massachusetts Rules of Criminal Procedure 9 (a) (1), then the superior court shall make its disposition in accordance with section fifty-eight.

Added by St.1996, c. 200, § 14.

§ 73. Repealed, 1964, 308, Sec. 5

§ 74. Limitations on criminal proceedings against children

Except as hereinafter provided and as provided in sections fifty-two to eighty-four, inclusive, no criminal proceeding shall be begun against any person who prior to his seventeenth birthday commits an offense against the laws of the commonwealth or who violates any city ordinance or town by-law, provided, however, that a criminal complaint alleging violation of any city ordinance or town by-law regulating the operation of motor vehicles, which is not capable of being judicially heard and determined as a civil motor vehicle infraction pursuant to the provisions of chapter ninety C may issue against a child between sixteen and seventeen years of age without first proceeding against him as a delinquent child.

The juvenile court shall not have jurisdiction over a person who had at the time of the offense attained the age of fourteen but not yet attained the age of seventeen who is charged with committing murder in the first or second degree. Complaints and indictments brought against persons for such offenses, and for other criminal offenses properly joined under Massachusetts Rules of Criminal Procedure 9 (a) (1), shall be brought in accordance with the usual course and manner of criminal proceedings.

Amended by St.1933, c. 196, § 1; St.1948, c. 310, § 12; St.1960, c. 353, § 3; St.1964, c. 308, § 6; St.1967, c. 787; St.1985, c. 794, § 5; St.1996, c. 200, § 15.

Historical and Statutory Notes

St.1906, c. 413, § 11.

§ 75. Repealed, 1975, 840, Sec. 2A

§§ 76 to 82. Repealed, 1964, 308, Sec. 5

§ 83. Repealed, 1996, 200, Sec. 16

§ 84. Warrant of commitment to department of youth services

Whenever a person is committed to the department of youth services by a court under section fifty-six, fifty-eight or eighty-three, a warrant of commitment shall be issued in substance as follows:

THE COMMONWEALTH OF MASSACHUSETTS

(COUNTY) ss.

To the Sheriff of the County of ________ or his Deputy, or any Constable or Police Officer in said County, and to the Department of Youth Services at

GREETING:

Whereas, (name of person committed) of ________ in the county of ________, a boy (or girl) between seven and seventeen (or eighteen) years of age, has this day been brought before the ________ court of ________ by virtue of a summons (or warrant) issued to (against) him (or her) on the complaint of ________ of ________ in the county of ________ who therein, upon oath, says that said defendant, at ________ in the county of ________ on the ________ day of ________ in the year one thousand nine hundred and ________ was guilty of ________ as is more fully alleged in said complaint.

And after hearing all matters and things concerning the same, and all persons entitled thereto having been summoned and notified of the pendency of said complaint, as required by law, it is adjudged by said court that said defendant is delinquent and that he (or she) is of the age of ________ years and ________ months, and is a suitable subject for commitment to the custody of the department of youth services, and that his (or her) moral welfare and best interest and the good of society require that he (or she) should be sent thereto for diagnosis, treatment and training, and said court shall also find that reasonable efforts were made to prevent or eliminate the need for the defendant's removal from his home or that an emergency situation made such efforts impossible and it is thereupon ordered by said court that said defendant stand committed to the custody of the department of youth services during his (or her) minority, or until he (or she) be discharged according to law.

You are therefore hereby required, in the name of the Commonwealth of Massachusetts, to take said defendant and him (or her) carry to the department of youth services and him (or her) deliver to the (designated officer) thereof, together with an attested copy thereof, and thereafterward forthwith to return this warrant with your doings thereon into said court.

And you, the department of youth services, are alike required to receive said defendant into your custody, and him (or her) safely keep for diagnosis, treatment, instruction and training until the expiration of said term of his (or her) minority, or he (or she) be discharged according to law.

Witness, _________ at said _________ this _________ day of _________ in the year one thousand nine hundred and _________.

Clerk.

A true copy. (*Constable of*_____________)
Attest: (*Sheriff of*_____________)

No variance from said form shall be considered material if it sufficiently appears upon the face thereof that the person is committed by the court in the exercise of the powers conferred by this chapter. The warrant may be executed by any officer qualified to serve civil or criminal process in the county where the case is heard. Accompanying the warrant, the court or magistrate shall transmit to the designated officer of the department of youth services, by the officer serving it, a statement of the substance of the complaint and testimony given in the case, and such other particulars relative to the person committed as can be ascertained.

Added by St.1964, c. 308, § 9. Amended by St.1969, c. 838, § 25; St.1993, c. 110, §§ 160, 160A; St.1993, c. 151, § 111; St.1996, c. 450, § 164.

§ 85. Department employees reporting animal cruelty, abuse or neglect; immunity from liability

(a) During any investigation or evaluation reported under section 51A, any employee of the department or person employed pursuant to a contract with the department, when acting in his professional capacity or within the scope of his or her employment, who has knowledge of or observes an animal whom he knows or reasonably suspects has been the victim of animal cruelty, abuse or neglect, may report the known or suspected animal cruelty, abuse or neglect to the entities that investigate reports of animal cruelty, abuse or neglect, as described in section 57 of chapter 22C, or any local animal control authority.

(b) The report may be made within 2 working days of receiving the information concerning the animal, by facsimile transmission or a written report or by telephone. In cases where an immediate response may be necessary in order to protect the health and safety of the animal, the report should be made by telephone as soon as possible.

(c) When 2 or more employees of the department are present and jointly have knowledge of known or reasonably suspected animal cruelty, abuse or neglect, and where there is agreement among them, a report may be made by 1 person by mutual agreement. Any reporter who has knowledge that the person designated to report has failed to do so may thereafter make the report.

(d) No person making such report shall be liable in any civil or criminal action by reason of such report if it was made in good faith. Any privilege established by sections 135A and 135B of chapter 112 or by section 20B of chapter 233, relating to confidential communications, shall not prohibit the filing of a report pursuant to this section.

(e) Nothing in this section shall impose a duty on the department to investigate known or reasonably suspected animal cruelty, abuse or neglect.

(f) Nothing in this section shall prevent the department, area office or subdivision from entering into an agreement, contract or memorandum of understanding with the entities that investigate reports of animal cruelty, abuse or neglect as described in section 57 of chapter 22C, to require such reports or to engage in training in identification and reporting of animal abuse, cruelty and neglect.

Added by St.2004, c. 319, § 1, eff. Nov. 17, 2004.

CHAPTER 123

MENTAL HEALTH

Selected sections

The section headings for the General Laws in this pamphlet have been editorially supplied.

§ 15. Competence to stand trial or criminal responsibility; examination; period of observation; reports; hearing; commitment; delinquents

(a) Whenever a court of competent jurisdiction doubts whether a defendant in a criminal case is competent to stand trial or is criminally responsible by reason of mental illness or mental defect, it may at any stage of the proceedings after the return of an indictment or the issuance of a criminal complaint against the defendant, order an examination of such defendant to be conducted by one or more qualified physicians or one or more qualified psychologists. Whenever practicable, examinations shall be conducted at the court house or place of detention where the person is being held. When an examination is ordered, the court shall instruct the examining physician or psychologist in the law for determining mental competence to stand trial and criminal responsibility.

(b) After the examination described in paragraph (a), the court may order that the person be hospitalized at a facility or, if such person is a male and appears to require strict security, at the Bridgewater state hospital, for a period not to exceed twenty days for observation and further examination, if the court has reason to believe that such observation and further examination are necessary in order to determine whether mental illness or mental defect have so affected a person that he is not competent to stand trial or not criminally responsible for the crime or crimes with which he has been charged. Copies of the complaints or indictments and the physician's or psychologist's report under paragraph (a) shall be delivered to the facility or said hospital with the person. If, before the expiration of such twenty day period, an examining qualified physician or an examining qualified psychologist believes that observation for more than twenty days is necessary, he shall so notify the court and shall request in writing an extension of the twenty day period, specifying the reason or reasons for which such further observation is necessary. Upon the receipt of such request, the court may extend said observation period, but in no event shall the period exceed forty days from the date of the initial court order of hospitalization; provided, however, if the person requests continued care and treatment during the pendency of the criminal proceedings against him and the superintendent or medical director agrees to provide such care and treatment, the court may order the further hospitalization of such person at the facility or the Bridgewater state hospital.

(c) At the conclusion of the examination or the observation period, the examining physician or psychologist shall forthwith give to the court written signed reports of their findings, including the clinical findings bearing on the issue of competence to stand trial or criminal responsibility. Such reports shall also contain an opinion, supported by clinical findings, as to whether the defendant is in need of treatment and care offered by the department.

(d) If on the basis of such reports the court is satisfied that the defendant is competent to stand trial, the case shall continue according to the usual course of criminal proceedings; otherwise the court shall hold a hearing on whether the defendant is competent to stand trial; provided that at any time before trial any party to the case may request a hearing on whether the defendant is competent to stand trial. A finding of incompetency shall require a preponderance of the evidence. If the defendant is found incompetent to stand trial, trial of the case shall be stayed until such time as the defendant becomes competent to stand trial, unless the case is dismissed.

(e) After a finding of guilty on a criminal charge, and prior to sentencing, the court may order a psychiatric or other clinical examination and, after such examination, it may also order a period of observation in a facility, or at the Bridgewater state hospital if the court determines that strict security is required and if such person is male. The purpose of such observation or examination shall be to aid the court in sentencing. Such period of observation or examination shall not exceed forty days. During such period of observation, the superintendent or medical director may petition the court for commitment of such person. The court, after imposing sentence on said person, may hear the petition as provided in section eighteen, and if the court makes necessary findings as set forth in section eight, it may in its discretion commit the person to a facility or the Bridgewater state hospital. Such order of commitment shall be valid for a period of six months. All subsequent proceedings for commitment shall take place under the provisions of said section eighteen in the district court which has jurisdiction of the facility or hospital. A person committed to a facility or Bridgewater state hospital pursuant to this section shall have said time credited against the sentence imposed as provided in paragraph (c) of said section eighteen.

(f) In like manner to the proceedings under paragraphs (a), (b), (c), and (e) of this section, a court may order a psychiatric or psychological examination or a period of observation for an alleged delinquent in a facility to aid the court in its disposition. Such period shall not exceed forty days.

Added by St.1986, c. 599, § 38. Amended by St.1987, c. 465, § 25; St.1996, c. 266; St.2000, c. 357.

§ 16. Hospitalization of persons incompetent to stand trial or not guilty by reason of mental illness; examination period; commitment; hearing; restrictions; dismissal of criminal charges

(a) The court having jurisdiction over the criminal proceedings may order that a person who has been found incompetent to stand trial or not guilty by reason of mental illness or mental defect in such proceedings be hospitalized at a facility for a period of forty days for observation and examination; provided that, if the defendant is a male and if the court determines that the failure to retain him in strict security would create a likelihood of serious harm by reason of mental illness, or other mental defect, it may order such hospitalization at the Bridgewater state hospital; and provided, further, that the combined periods of hospitalization under the provisions of this section and paragraph (b) of section fifteen shall not exceed fifty days.

(b) During the period of observation of a person believed to be incompetent to stand trial or within sixty days after a person is found to be incompetent to stand trial or not guilty of any crime by reason of mental illness or other mental defect, the district attorney, the superintendent of a facility or the medical director of the Bridgewater state hospital may petition the court having jurisdiction of the criminal case for the commitment of the person to a facility or to the Bridgewater state hospital. However, the petition for the commitment of an untried defendant shall be heard only if the defendant is found incompetent to stand trial, or if the criminal charges are dismissed after commitment. If the court makes the findings required by paragraph (a) of section eight it shall order the person committed to a facility; if the court makes the findings required by paragraph (b) of section eight, it shall order the commitment of the person to the Bridgewater state hospital; otherwise the petition shall be dismissed and the person discharged. An order of commitment under the provisions of this paragraph shall be valid for six months. In the event a period of hospitalization under the provisions of paragraph (a) has expired, or in the event no such period of examination has been ordered, the court may order the temporary detention of such person in a jail, house of correction, facility or the Bridgewater state hospital until such time as the findings required by this paragraph are made or a determination is made that such findings cannot be made.

(c) After the expiration of a commitment under paragraph (b) of this section, a person may be committed for additional one year periods under the provisions of sections seven and eight of this chapter, but no untried defendant shall be so committed unless in addition to the findings required by sections seven and eight the court also finds said defendant is incompetent to stand trial. If the person is not found incompetent, the court shall notify the court with jurisdiction of the criminal charges, which court shall thereupon order the defendant returned to its custody for the resumption of criminal proceedings. All subsequent proceedings for the further commitment of a person committed under this section shall be in the court which has jurisdiction of the facility or hospital.

(d) The district attorney for the district within which the alleged crime or crimes occurred shall be notified of any hearing conducted for a person under the provisions of this section or any subsequent hearing for such person conducted under the provisions of this chapter relative to the commitment of the mentally ill and shall have the right to be heard at such hearings.

(e) Any person committed to a facility under the provisions of this section may be restricted in his movements to the buildings and grounds of the facility at which he is committed by the court which ordered the commitment. If such restrictions are ordered, they shall not be removed except with the approval of the court. In the event the superintendent communicates his intention to remove or modify such restriction in writing to the court and within fourteen days the court does not make written objection thereto, such restrictions shall be removed by the superintendent. If the superintendent or medical director of the Bridgewater state hospital intends to discharge a person committed under this section or at the end of a period of commitment intends not to petition for his further commitment, he shall notify the court and district attorney which have or had jurisdiction of the criminal case. Within thirty days of the receipt of such notice, the district attorney may petition for commitment under the provisions of paragraph (c). During such thirty day period, the person shall be held at the facility or hospital. This paragraph shall not apply to persons originally committed after a finding of incompetence to stand trial whose criminal charges have been dismissed.

(f) If a person is found incompetent to stand trial, the court shall send notice to the department of correction which shall compute the date of the expiration of the period of time equal to the time of imprisonment which the person would have had to serve prior to becoming eligible for parole if he had been convicted of the most serious crime with which he was charged in court and sentenced to the maximum sentence he could have received, if so convicted. For purposes of the computation of parole eligibility, the minimum sentence shall be regarded as one half of the maximum sentence potential sentence. Where applicable, the provisions of sections one hundred and twenty-nine, one hundred and twenty-nine A, one hundred and twenty-nine B, and one hundred and twenty-nine C of chapter one hundred and twenty-seven shall be applied to reduce such period of time. On the final date of such period, the court shall dismiss the criminal charges against such person, or the court in the interest of justice may dismiss the criminal charges against such person prior to the expiration of such period.

Added by St.1986, c. 599, § 38. Amended by St.1992, c. 286, § 190.

§ 17. Periodic review of incompetence to stand trial; petition; hearing; continued treatment; defense to charges; release

(a) The periodic review of a person found incompetent to stand trial shall include a clinical opinion with regard to the person's competence to stand trial, which opinion shall be noted in writing on the patient's record. If any person found incompetent to stand trial is determined by the superintendent of the facility or the medical director of the Bridgewater state hospital to be no longer incompetent, the superintendent or medical director shall notify the court, which shall without delay hold a hearing on the person's competency to stand trial. Any person found incompetent to stand trial may at any time petition the court for a hearing on his competency. Whenever a hearing is held and the court finds that the person is competent to stand trial, his commitment, if any, to a facility or to the Bridgewater state hospital shall be terminated and he shall be returned to the custody of the court for trial. However, if the person requests continued care and treatment during the pendency of the criminal proceedings against him and the superintendent or medical director agrees to provide such care and treatment, the court may order the further hospitalization of such person at the facility or the Bridgewater state hospital.

(b) If either a person or counsel of a person who has been found to be incompetent to stand trial believes that he can establish a defense of not guilty to the charges pending against the person other than the defense of not guilty by reason of mental illness or mental defect, he may request an opportunity to offer a defense thereto on the merits before the court which has criminal jurisdiction. The court may require counsel for the defendant to support the request by affidavit or other evidence. If the court in its discretion grants such a request, the evidence of the defendant and of the commonwealth shall be heard by the court sitting without a jury. If after hearing such petition the court finds a lack of substantial evidence to support a conviction it shall dismiss the indictment or other charges or find them defective or insufficient and order the release of the defendant from criminal custody.

(c) Notwithstanding any finding of incompetence to stand trial under the provisions of this chapter, the court having jurisdiction may, at any appropriate stage of the criminal proceedings, allow a defendant to be released with or without bail.

Added by St.1986, c. 599, § 38.

§ 18. Hospitalization of mentally ill prisoners; examination; reports; hearing; commitment; voluntary admission; reduction of sentence; discharge

(a) If the person in charge of any place of detention within the commonwealth has reason to believe that a person confined therein is in need of hospitalization by reason of mental illness at a facility of the department or at the Bridgewater state hospital, he shall cause such prisoner to be examined at such place of detention by a physician or psychologist, designated by the department as qualified to perform such examination. Said physician or psychologist shall report the results of the examination to the district court which has jurisdiction over the place of detention or, if the prisoner is awaiting trial, to the court which has jurisdiction of the criminal case. Such report shall include an opinion, with reasons therefore, as to whether such hospitalization is actually required. The court which receives such report may order the prisoner to be taken to a facility or, if a male, to the Bridgewater state hospital to be received for examination and observation for a period not to exceed thirty days. After completion of such examination and observation, a written report shall be sent to such court and to the person in charge of the place of detention. Such report shall be signed by the physician or psychologist conducting such examination, and shall contain an evaluation, supported by clinical findings, of whether the prisoner is in need of further treatment and care at a facility or, if a male, the Bridgewater state hospital by reason of mental illness. The person in charge of the place of detention shall have the same right as a superintendent of a facility and the medical director of the Bridgewater state hospital to file a petition with the court which received the results of the examination for the commitment of the person to a facility or to the Bridgewater state hospital; provided, however, that, notwithstanding the court's failure, after an initial hearing or after any subsequent hearing, to make a finding required for commitment to the Bridgewater state hospital, the prisoner shall be confined at said hospital if the findings required for commitment to a facility are made and if the commissioner of correction certifies to the court that confinement of the prisoner at said hospital is necessary to insure his continued retention in custody. An initial court order of commitment issued subject to the provisions of this section shall be valid for a six-month period, and all subsequent commitments during the term of the sentence shall take place under the provisions of sections seven and eight and shall be valid for one year.

(b) Notwithstanding any contrary provision of general or special law, a prisoner who is retained in any place of detention within the commonwealth and who is in need of care and treatment in a facility may, with the approval of the person in charge of such place of detention apply for voluntary admission under the provisions of paragraph (a) of section ten.

(c) At the commencement of hospitalization under the provisions of paragraph (a) or paragraph (b) the department of correction shall enter in the patient record of such prisoner the date of the expiration of the sentence of the prisoner. Where applicable, the provisions of sections one hundred and twenty-nine, one hundred and twenty-nine A, one hundred and twenty-nine B and one hundred and twenty-nine C of chapter one hundred and twenty-seven may be applied to reduce such sentence, and on such date the prisoner shall be discharged; provided, however, that if the superintendent or other head of a facility or the medical director of the Bridgewater state hospital determines that the discharge of the prisoner committed subject to the provisions of paragraph (a) would create a likelihood of serious harm by reason of mental illness, he shall petition the district court having jurisdiction over the facility prior to the date of expiration to order the commitment of such person to a facility or to the Bridgewater state hospital under the provisions of this chapter other than paragraph (a); and provided, further, that any prisoner resident in a facility subject to the provisions of paragraph (b) shall be free to leave such facility subject to the provisions of section eleven.

(d) In the event the provisions of this chapter require the release of a prisoner from a facility or from the Bridgewater state hospital prior to the date of expiration of his sentence calculated under the provisions of paragraph (c), such prisoner shall be forthwith returned to the place of detention from which he was transferred to such facility or to said hospital.

Added by St.1986, c. 599, § 38. Amended by St.1990, c. 272.

§ 18A. Facility residents; contribution towards cost of counsel

A person who is a resident in a facility of the department of mental health or in the Bridgewater state hospital and who has funds held in trust for him by the department of mental health or the department of correction, shall contribute toward the cost of any counsel appointed pursuant to chapter two hundred and eleven D to provide representation in proceedings under this chapter, in an amount not exceeding five hundred dollars unless a larger contribution has been ordered by a court pursuant to sections two and five of chapter two hundred and eleven D. Whenever the department of correction or the department of mental health holds funds in trust for such a person, the department shall turn over such funds, but not exceeding five hundred dollars, to the treasurer to be credited toward the cost of providing such counsel.

Added by St.1991, c. 138, § 275.

§ 19. Parties or witnesses; determination of mental condition

In order to determine the mental condition of any party or witness before any court of the commonwealth, the presiding judge may, in his discretion, request the department to assign a qualified physician or psychologist, who, if assigned shall make such examinations as the judge may deem necessary.

Added by St.1986, c. 599, § 38.

§ 20. Extradition of mental institution escapees

(a) The governor may upon demand deliver to the executive of any other state any person who has escaped from an institution for the mentally ill to which he has been committed under the laws of such state, and who may be dangerous to the safety of the public, or may upon application appoint an agent to demand of the executive authority of any other state any person who has escaped from an institution in this commonwealth. Such demand or application shall be accompanied by an attested copy of the commitment and sworn evidence of the superintendent or manager of the institution stating that the person demanded has escaped from such institution, and by such further evidence as the governor requires.

(b) If the governor is satisfied that the demand made upon him under the preceding paragraph conforms to law and ought to be complied with, he shall issue his warrant under the seal of the commonwealth to an officer authorized to serve warrants in criminal cases, directing him at the expense of the agent who makes the demand, and at a time designated in the warrant, to deliver custody of such person to such agent.

(c) A person arrested upon such a warrant shall not be delivered to the agent of another state until he has been notified of the demand for his surrender and has had an opportunity to apply for a writ of habeas corpus, if he claims such right of the officer making the arrest. If said writ is applied for, notice thereof and of the time and place of hearing shall be given to the attorney general or to the district attorney for the district where the arrest is made. An officer who delivers such person in his custody upon such warrant to such agent for rendition without having complied with this section shall forfeit not more than one thousand dollars. Pending the determination of the court upon an application for said writ, the person shall be detained in custody in a suitable facility.

Added by St.1986, c. 599, § 38.

§ 33. Expenses of apprehension, examination, hearing, commitment or delivery; certification; audit; payment; fees

All necessary expenses attending the apprehension, examination, hearing, commitment or delivery of a mentally ill person, or an alleged alcoholic shall be allowed and certified by the judge if said person is committed pursuant to this chapter, and presented as often as once a year to the comptroller, who shall examine and audit the same. Necessary expenses attending the apprehension, examination or hearing of any person sought to be committed pursuant to this chapter but not so committed shall be so presented, examined and audited if they have been allowed in the discretion of the judge and certified by him. All expenses certified, examined and audited as provided in this section shall be paid by the commonwealth. If application is made for the commitment of a person whose expenses and support are not to be paid by the commonwealth, said expenses shall be paid by the applicant or by a person in his behalf. The compensation of the physicians and officers taking part in the commitment or admission of persons to facilities in accordance with this chapter shall be as follows: The fee for each physician making an authorized mental examination and for making a written report thereon to the court, or for making a medical certificate, shall be twenty-five dollars, and twenty cents for each mile traveled one way or such other rates as may be set by the division of health care finance and policy. Any physician required to appear before a judge or justice in any commitment proceedings, in which such physician has made an examination, shall receive a fee of twenty-five dollars, and twenty cents for each mile traveled one way for such appearance before the court, or such other rate as may be set by the division of health care finance and policy. The fees for officers servicing process shall be the same as are allowed by law in like cases.

Added by St.1986, c. 599, § 38. Amended by St.1987, c. 465, § 26; St.1998, c. 161, § 473.

§ 35. Commitment of alcoholics or substance abusers

For the purposes of this section, "alcoholic" shall mean a person who chronically or habitually consumes alcoholic beverages to the extent that (1) such use substantially injures his health or substantially interferes with his social or economic functioning, or (2) he has lost the power of self-control over the use of such beverages.

For the purposes of this section, "substance abuser" shall mean a person who chronically or habitually consumes or ingests controlled substances or who intentionally inhales toxic vapors to the extent that: (i) such use substantially injures his health or substantially interferes with his social or economic functioning; or (ii) he has lost the power of self-control over the use of such controlled substances or toxic vapors.

Any police officer, physician, spouse, blood relative, guardian or court official may petition in writing any district court or any division of the juvenile court department for an order of commitment of a person whom he has reason to believe is an alcoholic or substance abuser. Upon receipt of a petition for an order of commitment of a person and any sworn statements the court may request from the petitioner, the court shall immediately schedule a hearing on the petition and shall cause a summons and a copy of the application to be served upon the person in the manner provided by section twenty-five of chapter two hundred and seventy-six. In the event of the person's failure to appear at the time summoned, the court may issue a warrant for the person's arrest. Upon presentation of such a petition, if there are reasonable grounds to believe that such person will not appear and that any further delay in the proceedings would present an immediate danger to the physical well-being of the respondent, said court may issue a warrant for the apprehension and appearance of such person before it. No arrest shall be made on such warrant unless the person may be presented immediately before a judge of the district court. The person shall have the right to be represented by legal counsel and may present independent expert or other testimony. If the court finds the person indigent, it shall immediately appoint counsel. The court shall order examination by a qualified physician or a qualified psychologist.

If, after a hearing, the court based upon competent medical testimony finds that said person is an alcoholic or substance abuser and there is a likelihood of serious harm as a result of his alcoholism or substance abuse, it may order such person to be committed for a period not to exceed thirty days. Such commitment shall be for the purpose of inpatient care in public or private facilities approved by the department of public health under the provisions of chapter one hundred and eleven B for the care and treatment of alcoholism or substance abuse. The person may be committed to the Massachusetts correctional institution at Bridgewater, if a male, or at Framingham, if a female, provided that there are not suitable facilities available under chapter one hundred and eleven B; and provided, further, that the person so committed shall be housed and treated separately from convicted criminals. A person so committed may be released prior to the expiration of the period of commitment upon determination by the superintendent that release of said person will not result in a likelihood of serious harm. Said person shall be encouraged to consent to further treatment and shall be allowed voluntarily to remain in the facility for such purposes. The department of mental health, in conjunction with the department of public health, shall maintain a roster of public and private facilities available, together with the number of beds currently available, for the care and treatment of alcoholism or substance abuse and shall make it available to the district courts of the commonwealth on a monthly basis.

Nothing in this section shall preclude any public or private facility for the care and treatment of alcoholism or substance abuse, including the separated facilities at the Massachusetts correctional institutions at Bridgewater and Framingham, from treating persons on a voluntary basis.

Added by St.1986, c. 599, § 38. Amended by St.1987, c. 465, § 27; St.1987, c. 500; St.1989, c. 352; St.1992, c. 379, § 30; St.2010, c. 292, eff. Nov. 8, 2010.

CHAPTER 123A

CARE, TREATMENT AND REHABILITATION OF SEXUALLY DANGEROUS PERSONS

The section headings for the General Laws in this pamphlet have been editorially supplied.

§ 1. Definitions

As used in this chapter the following words shall, except as otherwise provided, have the following meanings:—

"Agency with jurisdiction", the agency with the authority to direct the release of a person presently incarcerated, confined or committed to the department of youth services, regardless of the reason for such incarceration, confinement or commitment, including, but not limited to a sheriff, keeper, master or superintendent of a jail, house of correction or prison, the director of a custodial facility in the department of youth services, the parole board and, where a person has been found incompetent to stand trial, a district attorney.

"Community access board", a board consisting of five members appointed by the commissioner of correction, whose function shall be to consider a person's placement within a community access program and conduct an annual review of a person's sexual dangerousness.

"Community Access Program", a program established pursuant to section six A that provides for a person's reintegration into the community.

"Conviction", a conviction of or adjudication as a delinquent juvenile or a youthful offender by reason of sexual offense, regardless of the date of offense or date of conviction or adjudication.

"Mental abnormality", a congenital or acquired condition of a person that affects the emotional or volitional capacity of the person in a manner that predisposes that person to the commission of criminal sexual acts to a degree that makes the person a menace to the health and safety of other persons.

"Personality disorder", a congenital or acquired physical or mental condition that results in a general lack of power to control sexual impulses.

"Qualified examiner", a physician who is licensed pursuant to section two of chapter one hundred and twelve who is either certified in psychiatry by the American Board of Psychiatry and Neurology or eligible to be so certified, or a psychologist who is licensed pursuant to sections one hundred and eighteen to one hundred and twenty-nine, inclusive, of chapter one hundred and twelve; provided, however, that the examiner has had two years of experience with diagnosis or treatment of sexually aggressive offenders and is designated by the commissioner of correction. A "qualified examiner" need not be an employee of the department of correction or of any facility or institution of the department.

"Sexual offense", includes any of the following crimes: indecent assault and battery on a child under fourteen under the provisions of section thirteen B of chapter two hundred and sixty-five; aggravated indecent assault and battery on a child under the age of 14 under section 13B½ of chapter 265; a repeat offense under section 13B¾ of chapter 265; indecent assault and battery on a mentally retarded person under the provisions of section thirteen F of chapter two hundred and sixty-five; indecent assault and battery on a person who has obtained the age of fourteen under the provisions of section thirteen H of chapter two hundred and sixty-five; rape under the provisions of section twenty-two of chapter two hundred and sixty-five; rape of a child under sixteen with force under the provisions of section twenty-two A of chapter two hundred and sixty-five; aggravated rape of a child under 16 with force under section 22B of chapter 265; a repeat offense under section 22C of chapter 265; rape and abuse of a child under sixteen under the provisions of section twenty-three of chapter two hundred and sixty-five;

aggravated rape and abuse of a child under section 23A of chapter 265; a repeat offense under section 23B of chapter 265; assault with intent to commit rape under the provisions of section twenty-four of chapter two hundred and sixty-five; assault on a child with intent to commit rape under section 24B of chapter 265; kidnapping under section 26 of said chapter 265 with intent to commit a violation of section 13B, 13B½, 13B¾, 13F, 13H, 22, 22A, 22B, 22C, 23, 23A, 23B, 24 or 24B of said chapter 265; enticing away a person for prostitution or sexual intercourse under section 2 of chapter 272; drugging persons for sexual intercourse under section 3 of chapter 272; inducing a person under 18 into prostitution under section 4A of said chapter 272; living off or sharing earnings of a minor prostitute under section 4B of said chapter 272; open and gross lewdness and lascivious behavior under section 16 of said chapter 272; incestuous intercourse under section 17 of said chapter 272 involving a person under the age of 21; dissemination or possession with the intent to disseminate to a minor matter harmful to a minor under section 28 of said chapter 272; posing or exhibiting a child in a state of nudity under section 29A of said chapter 272; dissemination of visual material of a child in a state of nudity or sexual conduct under section 29B of said chapter 272; purchase or possession of visual material of a child depicted in sexual conduct under section 29C of said chapter 272; dissemination of visual material of a child in the state of nudity or in sexual conduct under section 30D of chapter 272; unnatural and lascivious acts with a child under the age of sixteen under the provisions of section thirty-five A of chapter two hundred and seventy-two; accosting or annoying persons of the opposite sex and lewd, wanton and lascivious speech or behavior under section 53 of said chapter 272; and any attempt to commit any of the above listed crimes under the provisions of section six of chapter two hundred and seventy-four or a like violation of the laws of another state, the United States or a military, territorial or Indian tribal authority; and any other offense, the facts of which, under the totality of the circumstances, manifest a sexual motivation or pattern of conduct or series of acts of sexually-motivated offenses.

"Sexually dangerous person", any person who has been (i) convicted of or adjudicated as a delinquent juvenile or youthful offender by reason of a sexual offense and who suffers from a mental abnormality or personality disorder which makes the person likely to engage in sexual offenses if not confined to a secure facility; (ii) charged with a sexual offense and was determined to be incompetent to stand trial and who suffers from a mental abnormality or personality disorder which makes such person likely to engage in sexual offenses if not confined to a secure facility; or (iii) previously adjudicated as such by a court of the commonwealth and whose misconduct in sexual matters indicates a general lack of power to control his sexual impulses, as evidenced by repetitive or compulsive sexual misconduct by either violence against any victim, or aggression against any victim under the age of 16 years, and who, as a result, is likely to attack or otherwise inflict injury on such victims because of his uncontrolled or uncontrollable desires.

Added by St.1985, c. 752, § 1. Amended by St.1993, c. 489, § 1; St.1999, c. 74, §§ 3 to 6; St.2002, 492; St.2004, c. 66, §§ 1 to 6, eff. April 7, 2004; St.2008, c. 451, § 84, eff. Jan. 5, 2009; St.2010, c. 267, §§ 23 to 28, eff. Nov. 1, 2010.

§ 2. Nemansket Correctional Center; treatment and rehabilitation personnel

The commissioner of correction shall maintain subject to the jurisdiction of the department of correction a treatment program or branch thereof at a correctional institution for the care, custody, treatment and rehabilitation of persons adjudicated as being sexually dangerous. Said facility shall be known as the "Nemansket Correctional Center". The commissioner of correction shall appoint a chief administrative officer who shall have responsibility for providing personnel with respect to the treatment and rehabilitation of the sexually dangerous persons, consistent with public safety. The commissioner of correction shall have the authority to promulgate regulations consistent with the provisions of this chapter.

Added by St.1985, c. 752, § 1. Amended by St.1993, c. 489, § 2; St.1997, c. 19, § 57.

§ 2A. Transfer to a correctional institution; provision of voluntary treatment services

An individual committed as sexually dangerous and who has also been sentenced for a criminal offense and said sentence has not expired may be transferred from the treatment center to another correctional institution designated by the commissioner of correction. In determining whether a transfer to a correctional institution is appropriate the commissioner of correction may consider the following factors:

(1) the person's unamenability to treatment;

(2) the person's unwillingness or failure to follow treatment recommendations;

(3) the person's lack of progress in treatment at the center or branch thereof;

(4) the danger posed by the person to other residents or staff at the Treatment Center or branch thereof;

(5) the degree of security necessary to protect the public.

The department of correction shall promulgate regulations establishing a transfer board and procedures governing transfer, including notification of hearing, opportunity to be heard, written decision notification of decision, opportunity for appeal, and periodic review of placement.

The commissioner of correction shall make available to the remanded individuals a program of voluntary treatment services. An annual review shall be conducted of the current sexual dangerousness of each transferred individual and a report prepared which shall be admissible in a hearing under section nine of this chapter. Upon completion of said person's criminal sentence, he shall be returned to the treatment center and considered for participation in the community access program. Existing civil commitments to the treatment center shall not be vacated by the transfer to a correctional institution.

Added by St.1993, c. 489, § 3.

§§ 3 to 6. Repealed, 1990, 150, Sec. 304

§ 6A. Most appropriate level of security; participation in community access program; notice required

Any person committed as a sexually dangerous person to the treatment center or a branch thereof under the provisions of this chapter shall be held in the most appropriate level of security required to ensure protection of the public, correctional staff, himself and others. Any juvenile who is committed as a sexually dangerous person to the treatment center or a branch thereof under the provisions of this chapter shall be segregated from any adults held at such facility.

Only a person whose criminal sentence has expired or upon whom a criminal sentence was never imposed shall be entitled to apply for participation in a community access program once in every twelve months. Said program shall be administered pursuant to the rules and regulations promulgated by the department of correction. As part of its program of community access the department of correction shall establish a board known as the community access board which board shall consist of five members appointed by the commissioner of correction, consistent with the rules and regulations of the department. Membership shall include three department of correction employees and two persons who are not department of correction employees, but who may be independent contractors or consultants. The non-employee members shall consist of psychiatrists or psychologists licensed by the commonwealth. The board shall evaluate residents for participation in the community access program and establish conditions to ensure the safety of the general community. The board shall have access to all records of the person being evaluated and shall give a report of its findings including dissenting views, to the chief administrative officer of the center. Such report shall be admissible in any hearing under section nine of this chapter. The board shall also conduct annual reviews of and prepare reports on the current sexual dangerousness of all persons at the treatment center, including those whose criminal sentences have not expired. The reports shall be admissible in a hearing under section nine of this chapter.

Any person participating in a community access program under this section shall continue to reside within the secure confines of MCI–Bridgewater and be under daily evaluation by treatment center personnel to determine if he presents a danger to the community. Upon approval of a person for participation in a community access program, notice shall be given to the colonel of state police, to the attorney general, to the district attorney in the district from which the person's criminal commitment originated, to the police department of the city or town from which the commitment originated, the police department of the town of Bridgewater, the police department where such person's participation in the community access program will occur the employer of persons participating in the access program, and any victim of the sexual offense from which the commitment originated. If such victim is deceased at the time of such program participation, notice of the person's participation in a community access program shall be given to the parent, spouse or other member of the immediate family of such deceased victim.

Added by St.1985, c. 752, § 1. Amended by St.1993, c. 489, § 4; St.1996, c. 151, § 281; St.1999, c. 74, § 7.

§ 7. Repealed, 1990, 150, Sec. 304

§ 8. Repealed, 1993, 489, Sec. 5

§ 9. Petitions for examination and discharge

Any person committed to the treatment center shall be entitled to file a petition for examination and discharge once in every twelve months. Such petition may be filed by either the committed person, his parents, spouse, issue, next of kin or any friend. The department of correction may file a petition at any time if it believes a person is no longer a sexually dangerous person. A copy of any petition filed under this subsection shall be sent within fourteen days after the filing thereof to the department of the attorney general and to the district attorney for the district where the original proceedings were commenced. Said petition shall be filed in the district of the superior court department in which said person was committed. The petitioner shall have a right to a speedy hearing on a date set by the administrative justice of the superior court department. Upon the motion of the person or upon its own motion, the court shall appoint counsel for the person. The hearing may be held in any court or any place designated for such purpose by the administrative justice of the superior court department. In any hearing held pursuant to the provisions of this section, either the petitioner or the commonwealth may demand that the issue be tried by a jury. If a jury trial is demanded, the matter shall proceed according to the practice of trial in civil cases in the superior court.

The court shall issue whatever process is necessary to assure the presence in court of the committed person.

The court shall order the petitioner to be examined by two qualified examiners, who shall conduct examinations, including personal interviews, of the person on whose behalf such petition is filed and file with the court written reports of their examinations and diagnoses, and their recommendations for the disposition of such person. Said reports shall be admissible in a hearing pursuant to this section. If such person refuses, without good cause, to be personally interviewed by a qualified examiner appointed pursuant to this section, such person shall be deemed to have waived his right to a hearing on the petition and the petition shall be dismissed upon motion filed by the commonwealth. The qualified examiners shall have access to all records of the person being examined. Evidence of the person's juvenile and adult court and probation records, psychiatric and psychological records, the department of correction's updated annual progress report of the petition, including all relevant materials prepared in connection with the section six A process, and any other evidence that tends to indicate that he is a sexually dangerous person shall be admissible in a hearing under this section. The chief administrative officer of the treatment center or his designee may testify at the hearing regarding the annual report and his recommendations for the disposition of the petition. Unless the trier of fact finds that such person remains a sexually dangerous person, it shall order such person to be discharged from the treatment center. Upon such discharge, notice shall be given to the chief administrative officer, to the commissioner of correction and the colonel of state police, to the attorney general, to the district attorney in the district from which the commitment originated, to the police department of the city or town from which the commitment originated, the police department of the town of Bridgewater, the police department where such person is anticipated to take up residency, any employer of the resident, the department of criminal justice information services, and any victim of the sexual offense from which the commitment originated; provided, however, that said victim has requested notification pursuant to section three of chapter two hundred and fifty-eight B. If such victim is deceased at the time of such discharge, notice of such discharge shall be given to the parent, spouse or other member of the immediate family of such deceased victim.

Added by St.1985, c. 752, § 1. Amended by St.1987, c. 116; St.1989, c. 555; St.1993, c. 489, § 7; St.1996, c. 151, § 282; St.2010, c. 256, § 76, eff. Nov. 4, 2010.

§§ 9A, 9B. Repealed, 1993, 489, Sec. 5

§§ 10, 11. Repealed, 1993, 489, Sec. 6

§ 12. Notification of persons adjudicated as delinquent juvenile or youthful offender by reason of a sexual offense; petitions for classification as sexually dangerous person; hearings

(a) Any agency with jurisdiction of a person who has ever been convicted of or adjudicated as a delinquent juvenile or a youthful offender by reason of a sexual offense as defined in section 1, regardless of the reason for the current incarceration, confinement or commitment, or who has been charged with such offense but has been found incompetent to stand trial, or who has been charged with any offense, is currently incompetent to stand trial and has previously been convicted of or adjudicated as a delinquent juvenile or a youthful offender by reason of a sexual offense, shall notify in writing the district attorney of the county where the offense occurred and the attorney general six months prior to the release of such person, except that in the case of a person who is returned to prison for no more than six months as a result of a revocation of parole or who is committed for no more than six months, such notice shall be given as soon as practicable following such person's admission to prison. In such notice, the agency with jurisdiction shall also identify those prisoners or youths who have a particularly high likelihood of meeting the criteria for a sexually dangerous person.

(b) When the district attorney or the attorney general determines that the prisoner or youth in the custody of the department of youth services is likely to be a sexually dangerous person as defined in section 1, the district attorney or the attorney general at the request of the district attorney may file a petition alleging that the prisoner or youth is a sexually dangerous person and stating sufficient facts to support such allegation in the superior court where the prisoner or youth is committed or in the superior court of the county where the sexual offense occurred.

(c) Upon the filing of a petition under this section, the court in which the petition was filed shall determine whether probable cause exists to believe that the person named in the petition is a sexually dangerous person. Such person shall be provided with notice of, and an opportunity to appear in person at, a hearing to contest probable cause.

(d) At the probable cause hearing, the person named in the petition shall have the following rights:

(1) to be represented by counsel;

(2) to present evidence on such person's behalf;

(3) to cross-examine witnesses who testify against such person; and

(4) to view and copy all petitions and reports in the court file.

(e) If the person named in the petition is scheduled to be released from jail, house of correction, prison or a facility of the department of youth services at any time prior to the court's probable cause determination, the court, upon a sufficient showing based on the evidence before the court at that time, may temporarily commit such person to the treatment center pending disposition of the petition. The person named in the petition may move the court for relief from such temporary commitment at any time prior to the probable cause determination.

Added by St.1999, c. 74, § 8. Amended by St.2004, c. 66, §§ 7 to 9, eff. April 7, 2004.

§ 13. Temporary commitment of prisoner or youth to treatment center; right to counsel; psychological examination

(a) If the court is satisfied that probable cause exists to believe that the person named in the petition is a sexually dangerous person, the prisoner or youth shall be committed to the treatment center for a period not exceeding 60 days for the purpose of examination and diagnosis under the supervision of two qualified examiners who shall, no later than 15 days prior to the expiration of said period, file with the court a written report of the examination and diagnosis and their recommendation of the disposition of the person named in the petition.

(b) The court shall supply to the qualified examiners copies of any juvenile and adult court records which shall contain, if available, a history of previous juvenile and adult offenses, previous psychiatric and psychological examinations and such other information as may be pertinent or helpful to the examiners in making the diagnosis and recommendation. The district attorney or the attorney general shall provide a narrative or police reports for each sexual offense conviction or adjudication as well as any psychiatric, psychological, medical or social worker records of the person named in the petition in the district attorney's or the attorney general's possession. The agency with jurisdiction over the person named in the petition shall provide such examiners with copies of any incident reports arising out of the person's incarceration or custody.

(c) The person named in the petition shall be entitled to counsel and, if indigent, the court shall appoint an attorney. All written documentation submitted to the two qualified examiners shall also be provided to counsel for the person named in the petition and to the district attorney and attorney general.

(d) Any person subject to an examination pursuant to the provisions of this section may retain a psychologist or psychiatrist who meets the requirements of a qualified examiner, as defined in section 1, to perform an examination on his behalf. If the person named in the petition is indigent, the court shall provide for such qualified examiner.

Added by St.1999, c. 74, § 8.

§ 14. Trial by jury; right to counsel; admissibility of evidence; commitment to treatment; temporary commitments pending disposition of petitions

(a) The district attorney, or the attorney general at the request of the district attorney, may petition the court for a trial. In any trial held pursuant to this section, either the person named in the petition or the petitioning party may demand, in writing, that the case be tried to a jury and, upon such demand, the case shall be tried to a jury. Such petition shall be made within 14 days of the filing of the report of the two qualified examiners. If such petition is timely filed within the allowed time, the court shall notify the person named in the petition and his attorney, the district attorney and the attorney general that a trial by jury will be held within 60 days to determine whether such person is a sexually dangerous person. The trial may be continued upon motion of either party for good cause shown or by the court on its own motion if the interests of justice so require, unless the person named in the petition will be substantially prejudiced thereby. The person named in the petition shall be confined to a secure facility for the duration of the trial.

(b) The person named in the petition shall be entitled to the assistance of counsel and shall be entitled to have counsel appointed if he is indigent in accordance with section 2 of chapter 211D. In addition, the person named in the petition may retain experts or professional persons to perform an examination on his behalf. Such experts or professional persons shall be permitted to have reasonable access to such person for the purpose of the examination as well as to all relevant medical and psychological records and reports of the person named in the petition. If the person named in the petition is indigent under said section 2 of said chapter 211D, the court shall, upon such person's request, determine whether the expert or professional services are necessary and shall determine reasonable compensation for such services. If the court so determines, the court shall assist the person named in the petition in obtaining an expert or professional person to perform an examination and participate in the trial on such person's behalf. The court shall approve payment for such services upon the filing of a certified claim for compensation supported by a written statement specifying the time expended, services rendered, expenses incurred and compensation received in the same case or for the same services from any other source. The court shall inform the person named in the petition of his rights under this section before the trial commences. The person named in the petition shall be entitled to have process issued from the court to compel the attendance of witnesses on his behalf. If such person intends to rely upon the testimony or report of his qualified examiner, the report must be filed with the court and a copy must be provided to the district attorney and attorney general no later than ten days prior to the scheduled trial.

(c) Juvenile and adult court probation records, psychiatric and psychological records and reports of the person named in the petition, including the report of any qualified examiner, as defined in section 1, and filed under this chapter, police reports relating to such person's prior sexual offenses, incident reports arising out of such person's incarceration or custody, oral or written statements prepared for and to be offered at the trial by the victims of the person who is the subject of the petition and any other evidence tending to show that such person is or is not a sexually dangerous person shall be admissible at the trial if such written information has been provided to opposing counsel reasonably in advance of trial.

(d) If after the trial, the jury finds unanimously and beyond a reasonable doubt that the person named in the petition is a sexually dangerous person, such person shall be committed to the treatment center or, if such person is a youth who has been adjudicated as a delinquent, to the department of youth services until he reaches his twenty-first birthday, and then to the treatment center for an indeterminate period of a minimum of one day and a maximum of such person's natural life until discharged pursuant to the provisions of section 9. The order of commitment, which shall be forwarded to the treatment center and to the appropriate agency with jurisdiction, shall become effective on the date of such person's parole or in all other cases, including persons sentenced to community parole supervision for life pursuant to section 133C of chapter 127, on the date of discharge from jail, the house of correction, prison or facility of the department of youth services.

(e) If the person named in the petition is scheduled to be released from jail, house of correction, prison or a facility of the department of youth services at any time prior to the final judgment, the court may temporarily commit such person to the treatment center pending disposition of the petition.

Added by St.1999, c. 74, § 8. Amended by St.2010, c. 256, § 77, eff. Nov. 4, 2010.

§ 15. Competence to stand trial; hearing

If a person who has been charged with a sexual offense has been found incompetent to stand trial and his commitment is sought and probable cause has been determined to exist pursuant to section 12, the court, without a jury, shall hear evidence and determine whether the person did commit the act or acts charged. The hearing on the issue of whether the person did commit the act or acts charged shall comply with all procedures specified in section 14, except with respect to trial by jury. The rules of evidence applicable in criminal cases shall apply and all rights available to criminal defendants at criminal trials, other than the right not to be tried while incompetent, shall apply. After hearing evidence the court shall make specific findings relative to whether the person did commit the act or acts charged; the extent to which the cause of the person's incompetence to stand trial affected the outcome of the hearing, including its effect on the person's ability to consult with and assist counsel and to testify on his own behalf; the extent to which the evidence could be reconstructed without the assistance of the person; and the strength of the prosecution's case. If the court finds, beyond a reasonable doubt, that the person did commit the act or acts charged, the court shall enter a final order, subject to appeal by the person named in the petition and the court may proceed to consider whether the person is a sexually dangerous person according to the procedures set forth in sections 13 and 14. Any determination made under this section shall not be admissible in any subsequent criminal proceeding.

Added by St.1999, c. 74, § 8.

§ 16. Annual reports describing treatments offered

The department of correction and the department of youth services shall annually prepare reports describing the treatment offered to each person who has been committed to the treatment center or the department of youth services as a sexually dangerous person and, without disclosing the identity of such persons, describe the treatment provided. The annual reports shall be submitted, on or before January 1, 2000 and every November 1 thereafter, to the clerk of the house of representatives and the clerk of the senate, who shall forward the same to the house and senate committees on ways and means and to the joint committee on criminal justice. The treatment center shall submit on or before December 12, 1999 its plan for the administration and management of the treatment center to the clerk of the house of representatives and the clerk of the senate, who shall forward the same to the house and senate committees on ways and means and to the joint committee on criminal justice. The treatment center shall promptly notify said committees of any modifications to said plan.

Added by St.1999, c. 74, § 8.

TITLE XX

PUBLIC SAFETY AND GOOD ORDER

CHAPTER 138

ALCOHOLIC LIQUORS

Selected sections

The section headings for the General Laws in this pamphlet have been editorially supplied.

§ 34. Sale, delivery or furnishing alcoholic beverages to persons under twenty-one years of age; employment of persons under eighteen years of age

No person shall receive a license or permit under this chapter who is under 21 years of age. Whoever makes a sale or delivery of any alcoholic beverage or alcohol to any person under 21 years of age, either for his own use or for the use of his parent or any other person, or whoever, being a patron of an establishment licensed under section 12 or 15, delivers or procures to be delivered in any public room or area of such establishment if licensed under section 12, 15, 19B, 19C or 19D or in any area of such establishment if licensed under said section 15, 19B, 19C or 19D any such beverages or alcohol to or for use by a person who he knows or has reason to believe is under 21 years of age or whoever procures any such beverage or alcohol for a person under 21 years of age in any establishment licensed under section 12 or procures any such beverage or alcohol for a person under 21 years of age who is not his child, ward or spouse in any establishment licensed under said section 15, 19B, 19C or 19D or whoever furnishes any such beverage or alcohol for a person under 21 years of age shall be punished by a fine of not more than $2,000 or by imprisonment for not more than one year or both. For the purpose of this section the word "furnish" shall mean to knowingly or intentionally supply, give, or provide to or allow a person under 21 years of age except for the children and grandchildren of the person being charged to possess alcoholic beverages on premises or property owned or controlled by the person charged. Nothing in this section shall be construed to prohibit any person licensed under this chapter from employing any person 18 years of age or older for the direct handling or selling of alcoholic beverages or alcohol.

Notwithstanding the provisions of clause (14) of section 62 of chapter 149, a licensee under this chapter may employ a person under the age of 18 who does not directly handle, sell, mix or serve alcohol or alcoholic beverages.

Added by St.1933, Ex.Sess., c. 376, § 2. Amended by St.1935, c. 440, § 34; St.1936, c. 171; St.1937, c. 424, § 5; St.1943, c. 542, § 15; St.1962, c. 354; St.1972, c. 155, § 2; St.1977, c. 929, § 14; St.1979, c. 15, § 6; St.1980, c. 193; St.1982, c. 97; St.1982, c. 627, § 13; St.1984, c. 312, § 5; St.1988, c. 149; St.1998, c. 113, § 9; St.2000, c. 175.

§ 34A. Persons under twenty-one years; purchase or attempt to purchase alcoholic beverages

Any person under twenty-one years of age who purchases or attempts to purchase alcoholic beverages or alcohol, or makes arrangements with any person to purchase or in any way procure such beverages, or who willfully misrepresents his age, or in any way alters, defaces or otherwise falsifies his identification offered as proof of age, with the intent of purchasing alcoholic beverages, either for his own use or for the use of any other person shall be punished by a fine of three hundred dollars and whoever knowingly makes a false statement as to the age of a person who is under twenty-one years of age in order to procure a sale or delivery of such beverages or alcohol to such person under twenty-one years of age, either for the use of the person under twenty-one years of age or for the use of some other person, and whoever induces a person under twenty-one years of age to make a false statement as to his age in order to procure a sale or delivery of such beverages or alcohol to such person under twenty-one years of age, shall be punished by a fine of three hundred dollars. A conviction of a violation of this section shall be reported forthwith to the registrar of motor vehicles by the court. Upon receipt of such notice the registrar shall thereupon suspend for 180 days the defendant's license or right to operate a motor vehicle.

The commission shall prepare and distribute to business establishments which sell, serve or otherwise dispense alcohol or alcoholic beverages to the general public, posters to be displayed therein in a conspicuous place. Said posters shall contain a summary and explanation of this section.

Added by St.1935, c. 146. Amended by St.1935, c. 440, § 35; St.1977, c. 859; St.1979, c. 15, § 7; St.1984, c. 312, § 6; St.1988, c. 85; St.1994, c. 25, § 12; St.1998, c. 220, § 8.

§ 34B. Liquor purchase identification cards

Any person who shall have attained age twenty-one and does not hold a valid operator's license issued by the registry of motor vehicles, pursuant to section eight of chapter ninety, may apply for a liquor purchase identification card. Such cards shall be valid for five years and shall be issued by the registry of motor vehicles pursuant to regulations prescribed by the registrar with the advice of the commission and shall bear the name, signature, date of birth, address and photograph of such person. The registry of motor vehicles shall require payment of a twenty-five dollar fee for any card issued pursuant to this section.

Any licensee, or agent or employee thereof, under this chapter who reasonably relies on such a liquor purchase identification card or motor vehicle license issued pursuant to section eight of chapter ninety, or on a valid passport issued by the United States government, or by the government, recognized by the United States government, of a foreign country, or a valid United States issued military identification card, for proof of a person's identity and age shall not suffer any modification, suspension, revocation or cancellation of such license, nor shall he suffer any criminal liability, for delivering or selling alcohol or alcoholic beverages to a person under twenty-one years of age. Any licensee, or agent or employee thereof, under this chapter, who reasonably relies on such a liquor purchase identification card or motor vehicle license issued pursuant to said section eight, for proof of a person's identity and age shall be presumed to have exercised due care in making such delivery or sale of alcohol or alcoholic beverages to a person under twenty-one years of age. Such presumption shall be rebuttable; provided, however, that nothing contained herein shall affect the applicability of section sixty-nine.

Any person in a licensed premises shall, upon request of an agent of the commission or the local licensing authorities, state his name, age, and address. Whoever, upon such request, refuses to state his name, age or address, or states a false name, age, or address, including a name or address which is not his name or address in ordinary use, shall be guilty of a misdemeanor and shall be punished by a fine of not more than five hundred dollars.

Any person who transfers, alters or defaces any such card or license, or who makes, uses, carries, sells or distributes a false identification card or license, or uses the identification card or motor vehicle license of another, or furnishes false information in obtaining such card or license, shall be guilty of a misdemeanor and shall be punished by a fine of not more than two hundred dollars or by imprisonment for not more than three months.

Any person who is discovered by a police officer or special police officer in the act of violating the provisions of this section may be arrested without a warrant by such police officer or special police officer and held in custody, in jail or otherwise, until a complaint is made against him for such offense, which complaint shall be made as soon as practicable and in any case within twenty-four hours, Sundays and legal holidays excepted.

Added by St.1964, c. 735. Amended by St.1967, c. 556; St.1972, c. 155, § 3; St.1979, c. 15, § 8; St.1984, c. 312, § 7; St.1985, c. 340; St.1986, c. 629, § 3; St.1989, c. 322, § 2; St.1989, c. 674; St.1992, c. 133, § 493; St.1994, c. 48, §§ 1, 2.

§ 34C. Minors; operation of motor vehicle containing alcoholic beverage; suspension of driver's license

Whoever, being under twenty-one years of age and not accompanied by a parent or legal guardian, knowingly possesses, transports or carries on his person, any alcohol or alcoholic beverages, shall be punished by a fine of not more than fifty dollars for the first offense and not more than one hundred and fifty dollars for a second or subsequent offense; provided, however, that this section shall not apply to a person between the ages of eighteen and twenty-one who knowingly possesses, transports or carries on his person, alcohol or alcoholic beverages in the course of his employment. A police officer may arrest without a warrant any person who violates this section. A conviction of a violation of this section shall be reported forthwith to the registrar of motor vehicles by the court, and said registrar shall thereupon suspend for a period of ninety days the license of such person to operate a motor vehicle.

Added by St.1966, c. 317, § 2. Amended by St.1967, c. 377; St.1979, c. 15, § 9; St.1984, c. 312, § 8; St.1992, c. 110; St.1994, c. 25, § 13.

TITLE XXII

CORPORATIONS

CHAPTER 175H

FALSE HEALTH CARE CLAIMS

Chapter 175H of the General Laws was added by St.1988, c. 295.

The section headings for the General Laws in this pamphlet have been editorially supplied.

§ 1. Definitions

As used in this chapter the following words shall have the following meanings, unless the context otherwise requires:—

"False", wholly or partially false, fictitious, fraudulent, untrue or deceptive.

"Health care benefit", a payment for health care services or the right under a contract or a certificate or policy of insurance to have a payment made by a health care corporation or health care insurer for a specified health care service.

"Health care corporation", a nonprofit hospital service corporation organized pursuant to chapter one hundred and seventy-six A, a nonprofit medical service corporation organized pursuant to chapter one hundred and seventy-six B, a medical service corporation organized pursuant to chapter one hundred and seventy-six C, a dental service corporation organized pursuant to chapter one hundred and seventy-six E, an optometric service plan organized pursuant to chapter one hundred and seventy-six F, and a health maintenance organization organized pursuant to chapter one hundred and seventy-six G.

"Health care insurer", any insurance company authorized to provide health insurance in this state or any legal entity which is self-insured and providing health care benefits to its employees.

"Person", an individual, corporation, partnership, association, or any other legal entity.

Added by St.1988, c. 295.

§ 2. False statements on applications for coverage and claims; failure to disclose

Any person who (1) knowingly and willfully makes or causes to be made any false statement or representation of a material fact in any application for a payment of a health care benefit; or (2) knowingly and willfully presents or causes to be presented an application for a health care benefit containing any false statement or representation of a material fact; or (3) knowingly and willfully makes or causes to be made any false statement or representation of a material fact for use in determining rights to a health care benefit, including whether goods or services were medically necessary in accordance with professionally accepted standards; or (4) having knowledge of the occurrence of any event affecting his initial or continued right to any health care benefit, conceals or fails to disclose such an event with an intent to fraudulently secure such benefit either in a greater amount than is due or when no such benefit is due; or (5) having knowledge of the occurrence of any event affecting the health care benefit of any other individual in whose behalf he has made or presented an application for such benefit, or in whose behalf he is receiving any health care benefit, conceals or fails to disclose such an event with an intent to fraudulently secure such benefit either in a greater amount than is due or when no such benefit is due, shall be punished by a fine of not more than ten thousand dollars, or by imprisonment in a jail or house of correction for not more than two and one-half years or in the state prison for not more than five years, or by both such fine and imprisonment, and may be held liable in a civil action under section seven. Notwithstanding the foregoing, a person who is not a provider of services for which a health care benefit may be paid shall not be subject to prosecution hereunder for any statement or representation which such person makes without fraudulent intent.

Added by St.1988, c. 295.

§ 3. Solicitation, improper inducement to use goods, facilities, services, or products covered by insurance

Any person who solicits or receives any remuneration, directly or indirectly, overtly or covertly, in cash or in kind in return for purchasing, leasing, ordering or arranging for or recommending purchasing, leasing, or ordering of any good, facility, service, or item for which payment is or may be made in whole or in part by a health care insurer, or any person who offers or pays any remuneration, including any bribe or rebate, directly or indirectly, overtly or covertly, in cash or in kind to induce any person to purchase, lease, order or arrange for or recommend purchasing, leasing or ordering of any good, facility, service, or item for which payment is or may be made in whole or in part by a health care insurer, shall be punished by a fine of not more than ten thousand dollars, or by imprisonment in a jail or house of correction for not more than two and one-half years or in the state prison for not more than five years, or by both such fine and imprisonment, and may be held liable in a civil action under section seven.

Added by St.1988, c. 295.

§ 4. Criminal proceedings

Any criminal proceeding brought under this chapter may be filed in the district, municipal or superior courts of Suffolk county.

Added by St.1988, c. 295.

§ 5. Investigation and proceedings by attorney general

The attorney general may conduct an investigation of an alleged violation of this chapter and may commence a proceeding pursuant to section four.

Added by St.1988, c. 295.

§ 6. Liability for false claims; civil proceedings

A person who receives a health care benefit or payment from a health care corporation or health care insurer which such person knows that he or she is not entitled to receive or be paid, or a person who knowingly presents or causes to be presented with fraudulent intent a claim which contains a false statement, shall be liable to the health care corporation or health care insurer for the full amount of the benefit or payment made, and for reasonable attorneys fees and costs, inclusive of costs of investigation.

A health care corporation or health care insurer may bring a civil action under this chapter in the superior court department of the trial court.

Added by St.1988, c. 295.

§ 7. Restitution; attorneys fees, costs

Any person convicted of a violation of sections two or three, in addition to any fines or sentences imposed, including any order of probation, shall be ordered to make restitution to a health care corporation or health care insurer for the full amount of the benefit or payment made, and for reasonable attorneys fees and costs, inclusive of costs of investigation.

Added by St.1988, c. 295.

§ 8. Remedies

The remedies provided for in this chapter are in addition to any other remedies provided by law.

Added by St.1988, c. 295.

PART II

REAL AND PERSONAL PROPERTY AND DOMESTIC RELATIONS

TITLE III

DOMESTIC RELATIONS

CHAPTER 209A

ABUSE PREVENTION

Chapter 209A of the General Laws was added by St.1978, c. 447, § 2.

The section headings for the General Laws in this pamphlet have been editorially supplied.

§ 1. Definitions

As used in this chapter the following words shall have the following meanings:

"Abuse", the occurrence of one or more of the following acts between family or household members:

(a) attempting to cause or causing physical harm;

(b) placing another in fear of imminent serious physical harm;

(c) causing another to engage involuntarily in sexual relations by force, threat or duress.

"Court", the superior, probate and family, district or Boston municipal court departments of the trial court, except when the petitioner is in a dating relationship when "Court" shall mean district, probate, or Boston municipal courts.

"Family or household members", persons who:

(a) are or were married to one another;

(b) are or were residing together in the same household;

(c) are or were related by blood or marriage;

(d) having a child in common regardless of whether they have ever married or lived together; or

(e) are or have been in a substantive dating or engagement relationship, which shall be adjudged by district, probate or Boston municipal courts consideration of the following factors:

(1) the length of time of the relationship; (2) the type of relationship; (3) the frequency of interaction between the parties; and (4) if the relationship has been terminated by either person, the length of time elapsed since the termination of the relationship.

"Law officer", any officer authorized to serve criminal process.

"Protection order issued by another jurisdiction", any injunction or other order issued by a court of another state, territory or possession of the United States, the Commonwealth of Puerto Rico, or the District of Columbia, or tribal court that is issued for the purpose of preventing violent or threatening acts or harassment against, or contact or communication with or physical proximity to another person, including temporary and final orders issued by civil and criminal courts filed by or on behalf of a person seeking protection.

"Vacate order", court order to leave and remain away from a premises and surrendering forthwith any keys to said premises to the plaintiff. The defendant shall not damage any of the plaintiff's belongings or those of any other occupant and shall not shut off or cause to be shut off any utilities or mail delivery to the plaintiff. In the case where the premises designated in the vacate order is a residence, so long as the plaintiff is living at said residence, the defendant shall not interfere in any way with the plaintiff's right to possess such residence, except by order or judgment of a court of competent jurisdiction pursuant to appropriate civil eviction proceedings, a petition to partition real estate, or a proceeding to divide marital property. A vacate order may include in its scope a household, a multiple family dwelling and the plaintiff's workplace. When issuing an order to vacate the plaintiff's workplace, the presiding justice must consider whether the plaintiff and defendant work in the same location or for the same employer.

Added by St.1978, c. 447, § 2. Amended by St.1983, c. 678, § 2; St.1986, c. 310, § 15; St.1990, c. 403, § 2; St.1996, c. 298, § 1; St.1996, c. 450, § 232.

§ 2. Venue

Proceedings under this chapter shall be filed, heard and determined in the superior court department or the Boston municipal court department or respective divisions of the probate and family or district court departments having venue over the plaintiff's residence. If the plaintiff has left a residence or household to avoid abuse, such plaintiff shall have the option of commencing an action in the court having venue over such prior residence or household, or in the court having venue over the present residence or household.

Added by St.1978, c. 447, § 2. Amended by St.1983, c. 678, § 3.

§ 3. Remedies; period of relief

A person suffering from abuse from an adult or minor family or household member may file a complaint in the court requesting protection from such abuse, including, but not limited to, the following orders:

(a) ordering the defendant to refrain from abusing the plaintiff, whether the defendant is an adult or minor;

(b) ordering the defendant to refrain from contacting the plaintiff, unless authorized by the court, whether the defendant is an adult or minor;

(c) ordering the defendant to vacate forthwith and remain away from the household, multiple family dwelling, and workplace. Notwithstanding the provisions of section thirty-four B of chapter two hundred and eight, an order to vacate shall be for a fixed period of time, not to exceed one year, at the expiration of which time the court may extend any such order upon motion of the plaintiff, with notice to the defendant, for such additional time as it deems necessary to protect the plaintiff from abuse;

(d) awarding the plaintiff temporary custody of a minor child; provided, however, that in any case brought in the probate and family court a finding by such court by a preponderance of the evidence that a pattern or serious incident of abuse, as defined in section 31A of chapter 208, toward a parent or child has occurred shall create a rebuttable presumption that it is not in the best interests of the child to be placed in sole custody, shared legal custody or shared physical custody with the abusive parent. Such presumption may be rebutted by a preponderance of the evidence that such custody award is in the best interests of the child. For the purposes of this section, an "abusive parent" shall mean a parent who has committed a pattern of abuse or a serious incident of abuse;

For the purposes of this section, the issuance of an order or orders under chapter 209A shall not in and of itself constitute a pattern or serious incident of abuse; nor shall an order or orders entered ex parte under said chapter 209A be admissible to show whether a pattern or serious incident of abuse has in fact occurred; provided, however, that an order or orders entered ex parte under said chapter 209A may be admissible for other purposes as the court may determine, other than showing whether a pattern or serious incident of abuse has in fact occurred; provided further, that the underlying facts upon which an order or orders under said chapter 209A was based may also form the basis for a finding by the probate and family court that a pattern or serious incident of abuse has occurred.

If the court finds that a pattern or serious incident of abuse has occurred and issues a temporary or permanent custody order, the court shall within 90 days enter written findings of fact as to the effects of the abuse on the child, which findings demonstrate that such order is in the furtherance of the child's best interests and provides for the safety and well-being of the child.

If ordering visitation to the abusive parent, the court shall provide for the safety and well-being of the child and the safety of the abused parent. The court may consider:

(a) ordering an exchange of the child to occur in a protected setting or in the presence of an appropriate third party;

(b) ordering visitation supervised by an appropriate third party, visitation center or agency;

(c) ordering the abusive parent to attend and complete, to the satisfaction of the court, a certified batterer's treatment program as a condition of visitation;

(d) ordering the abusive parent to abstain from possession or consumption of alcohol or controlled substances during the visitation and for 24 hours preceding visitation;

(e) ordering the abusive parent to pay the costs of supervised visitation;

(f) prohibiting overnight visitation;

(g) requiring a bond from the abusive parent for the return and safety of the child;

(h) ordering an investigation or appointment of a guardian ad litem or attorney for the child; and

(i) imposing any other condition that is deemed necessary to provide for the safety and well-being of the child and the safety of the abused parent.

Nothing in this section shall be construed to affect the right of the parties to a hearing under the rules of domestic relations procedure or to affect the discretion of the probate and family court in the conduct of such hearing.

(e) ordering the defendant to pay temporary support for the plaintiff or any child in the plaintiff's custody or both, when the defendant has a legal obligation to support such a person. In determining the amount to be paid, the court shall apply the standards established in the child support guidelines. Each judgment or order of support which is issued, reviewed or modified pursuant to this chapter shall conform to and shall be enforced in accordance with the provisions of section 12 of chapter 119A;

(f) ordering the defendant to pay the person abused monetary compensation for the losses suffered as a direct result of such abuse. Compensatory losses shall include, but not be limited to, loss of earnings or support, costs for restoring utilities, out-of-pocket losses for injuries sustained, replacement costs for locks or personal property removed or destroyed, medical and moving expenses and reasonable attorney's fees;

(g) ordering information in the case record to be impounded in accordance with court rule;

(h) ordering the defendant to refrain from abusing or contacting the plaintiff's child, or child in plaintiff's care or custody, unless authorized by the court;

(i) the judge may recommend to the defendant that the defendant attend a batterer's intervention program that is certified by the department of public health.

No filing fee shall be charged for the filing of the complaint. Neither the plaintiff nor the plaintiff's attorney shall be charged for certified copies of any orders entered by the court, or any copies of the file reasonably required for future court action or as a result of the loss or destruction of plaintiff's copies.

Any relief granted by the court shall be for a fixed period of time not to exceed one year. Every order shall on its face state the time and date the order is to expire and shall include the date and time that the matter will again be heard. If the plaintiff appears at the court at the date and time the order is to expire, the court shall determine whether or not to extend the order for any additional time reasonably necessary to protect the plaintiff or to enter a permanent order. When the expiration date stated on the order is on a weekend day or holiday, or a date when the court is closed to business, the order shall not expire until the next date that the court is open to business. The plaintiff may appear on such next court business day at the time designated by the order to request that the order be extended. The court may also extend the order upon motion of the plaintiff, for such additional time as it deems necessary to protect from abuse the plaintiff or any child in the plaintiff's care or custody. The fact that abuse has not occurred during the pendency of an order shall not, in itself, constitute sufficient ground for denying or failing to extend the order, of allowing an order to expire or be vacated, or for refusing to issue a new order.

The court may modify its order at any subsequent time upon motion by either party. When the plaintiff's address is inaccessible to the defendant as provided in section 8 of this chapter and the defendant has filed a motion to modify the court's order, the court shall be responsible for notifying the plaintiff. In no event shall the court disclose any such inaccessible address.

No order under this chapter shall in any manner affect title to real property.

No court shall compel parties to mediate any aspect of their case. Although the court may refer the case to the family service office of the probation department or victim/witness advocates for information gathering purposes, the court shall not compel the parties to meet together in such information gathering sessions.

A court shall not deny any complaint filed under this chapter solely because it was not filed within a particular time period after the last alleged incident of abuse.

A court may issue a mutual restraining order or mutual no-contact order pursuant to any abuse prevention action only if the court has made specific written findings of fact. The court shall then provide a detailed order, sufficiently specific to apprise any law officer as to which party has violated the order, if the parties are in or appear to be in violation of the order.

Any action commenced under the provisions of this chapter shall not preclude any other civil or criminal remedies. A party filing a complaint under this chapter shall be required to disclose any prior or pending actions involving the parties for divorce, annulment, paternity, custody or support, guardianship, separate support or legal separation, or abuse prevention.

If there is a prior or pending custody support order from the probate and family court department of the trial court, an order issued in the superior, district or Boston municipal court departments of the trial court pursuant to this chapter may include any relief available pursuant to this chapter except orders for custody or support.

If the parties to a proceeding under this chapter are parties in a subsequent proceeding in the probate and family court department for divorce, annulment, paternity, custody or support, guardianship or separate support, any custody or support order or judgment issued in the subsequent proceeding shall supersede any prior custody or support order under this chapter.

Added by St.1978, c. 447, § 2. Amended by St.1983, c. 678, § 4; St.1990, c. 403, § 3; St.1998, c. 64, § 204; St.1998, c. 179, § 5; St.1999, c. 127, § 155; St.2000, c. 236, §§ 22, 23; St.2002, c. 184, § 113.

§ 3A. Nature of proceedings and availability of other criminal proceedings; information required to be given to complainant upon filing

Upon the filing of a complaint under this chapter, a complainant shall be informed that the proceedings hereunder are civil in nature and that violations of orders issued hereunder are criminal in nature. Further, a complainant shall be given information prepared by the appropriate district attorney's office that other criminal proceedings may be available and such complainant shall be instructed by such district attorney's office relative to the procedures required to initiate criminal proceedings including, but not limited to, a complaint for a violation of section forty-three of chapter two hundred and sixty-five. Whenever possible, a complainant shall be provided with such information in the complainant's native language.

Added by St.1992, c. 188, § 3.

§ 3B. Order for suspension and surrender of firearms license; surrender of firearms; petition for review; hearing

Upon issuance of a temporary or emergency order under section four or five of this chapter, the court shall, if the plaintiff demonstrates a substantial likelihood of immediate danger of abuse, order the immediate suspension and surrender of any license to carry firearms and or firearms identification card which the defendant may hold and order the defendant to surrender all firearms, rifles, shotguns, machine guns and ammunition which he then controls, owns or possesses in accordance with the provisions of this chapter and any license to carry firearms or firearms identification cards which the defendant may hold shall be surrendered to the appropriate law enforcement officials in accordance with the provisions of this chapter and, said law enforcement official may store, transfer or otherwise dispose of any such weapon in accordance with the provisions of section 129D of chapter 140; provided however, that nothing herein shall authorize the transfer of any weapons surrendered by the defendant to anyone other than a licensed dealer. Notice of such suspension and ordered surrender shall be appended to the copy of abuse prevention order served on the defendant pursuant to section seven. Law enforcement officials, upon the service of said orders, shall immediately take possession of all firearms, rifles, shotguns, machine guns, ammunition, any license to carry firearms and any firearms identification cards in the control, ownership, or possession of said defendant. Any violation of such orders shall be punishable by a fine of not more than five thousand dollars, or by imprisonment for not more than two and one-half years in a house of correction, or by both such fine and imprisonment.

Any defendant aggrieved by an order of surrender or suspension as described in the first sentence of this section may petition the court which issued such suspension or surrender order for a review of such action and such petition shall be heard no later than ten court business days after the receipt of the notice of the petition by the court. If said license to carry firearms or firearms identification card has been suspended upon the issuance of an order issued pursuant to section four or five, said petition may be heard contemporaneously with the hearing specified in the second sentence of the second paragraph of section four. Upon the filing of an affidavit by the defendant that a firearm, rifle, shotgun, machine gun or ammunition is required in the performance of the defendant's employment, and upon a request for an expedited hearing, the court shall order said hearing within two business days of receipt of such affidavit and request but only on the issue of surrender and suspension pursuant to this section.

Added by St.1994, c. 24, § 6. Amended by St.1996, c. 298, § 2; St.1998, c. 180, § 48.

§ 3C. Continuation or modification of order for surrender or suspension

Upon the continuation or modification of an order issued pursuant to section 4 or upon petition for review as described in section 3B, the court shall also order or continue to order the immediate suspension and surrender of a defendant's license to carry firearms, including a Class A or Class B license, and firearms identification card and the surrender of all firearms, rifles, shotguns, machine guns or ammunition which such defendant then controls, owns or possesses if the court makes a determination that the return of such license to carry firearms, including a Class A or Class B license, and firearm identification card or firearms, rifles, shotguns, machine guns or ammunition presents a likelihood of abuse to the plaintiff. A suspension and surrender order issued pursuant to this section shall continue so long as the restraining order to which it relates is in effect; and, any law enforcement official to whom such weapon is surrendered may store, transfer or otherwise dispose of any such weapon in accordance with the provisions of section 129D of chapter 140; provided, however, that nothing herein shall authorize the transfer of any weapons surrendered by the defendant to anyone other than a licensed dealer. Any violation of such order shall be punishable by a fine of not more than $5,000 or by imprisonment for not more than two and one-half years in a house of correction or by both such fine and imprisonment.

Added by St.1994, c. 24, § 6. Amended by St.1996, c. 450, § 233; St.1998, c. 180, § 49.

§ 4. Temporary orders; notice; hearing

Upon the filing of a complaint under this chapter, the court may enter such temporary orders as it deems necessary to protect a plaintiff from abuse, including relief as provided in section three. Such relief shall not be contingent upon the filing of a complaint for divorce, separate support, or paternity action.

If the plaintiff demonstrates a substantial likelihood of immediate danger of abuse, the court may enter such temporary relief orders without notice as it deems necessary to protect the plaintiff from abuse and shall immediately thereafter notify the defendant that the temporary orders have been issued. The court shall give the defendant an opportunity to be heard on the question of continuing the temporary order and of granting other relief as requested by the plaintiff no later than ten court business days after such orders are entered.

Notice shall be made by the appropriate law enforcement agency as provided in section seven.

If the defendant does not appear at such subsequent hearing, the temporary orders shall continue in effect without further order of the court.

Added by St.1978, c. 447, § 2. Amended by St.1983, c. 678, § 4; St.1984, c. 189, § 152; St.1990, c. 403, § 4.

§ 5. Granting of relief when court closed; certification

When the court is closed for business or the plaintiff is unable to appear in court because of severe hardship due to the plaintiff's physical condition, any justice of the superior, probate and family, district or Boston municipal court departments may grant relief to the plaintiff as provided under section four if the plaintiff demonstrates a substantial likelihood of immediate danger of abuse. In the discretion of the justice, such relief may be granted and communicated by telephone to an officer or employee of an appropriate law enforcement agency, who shall record such order on a form of order promulgated for such use by the chief administrative justice and shall deliver a copy of such order on the next court day to the clerk-magistrate of the court having venue and jurisdiction over the matter. If relief has been granted without the filing of a complaint pursuant to this section of this chapter, then the plaintiff shall appear in court on the next available business day to file said complaint. If the plaintiff in such a case is unable to appear in court without severe hardship due to the plaintiff's physical condition, then a representative may appear in court on the plaintiff's behalf and file the requisite complaint with an affidavit setting forth the circumstances preventing the plaintiff from appearing personally. Notice to the plaintiff and defendant and an opportunity for the defendant to be heard shall be given as provided in said section four.

Any order issued under this section and any documentation in support thereof shall be certified on the next court day by the clerk-magistrate or register of the court issuing such order to the court having venue and jurisdiction over the matter. Such certification to the court shall have the effect of commencing proceedings under this chapter and invoking the other provisions of this chapter but shall not be deemed necessary for an emergency order issued under this section to take effect.

Added by St.1978, c. 447, § 2. Amended by St.1983, c. 678, § 4; St.1990, c. 403, §§ 5, 6; St.1996, c. 298, §§ 3, 4.

§ 5A. Protection order issued by another jurisdiction; enforcement; filing; presumption of validity

Any protection order issued by another jurisdiction, as defined in section one, shall be given full faith and credit throughout the commonwealth and enforced as if it were issued in the commonwealth for as long as the order is in effect in the issuing jurisdiction.

A person entitled to protection under a protection order issued by another jurisdiction may file such order in the superior court department or the Boston municipal court department or any division of the probate and family or district court departments by filing with the court a certified copy of such order which shall be entered into the statewide domestic violence record keeping system established pursuant to the provisions of section seven of chapter one hundred and eighty-eight of the acts of nineteen hundred and ninety-two and maintained by the office of the commissioner of probation. Such person shall swear under oath in an affidavit, to the best of such person's knowledge, that such order is presently in effect as written. Upon request by a law enforcement agency, the register or clerk of such court shall provide a certified copy of the protection order issued by the other jurisdiction.

A law enforcement officer may presume the validity of, and enforce in accordance with section six, a copy of a protection order issued by another jurisdiction which has been provided to the law enforcement officer by any source; provided, however, that the officer is also provided with a statement by the person protected by the order that such order remains in effect. Law enforcement officers may rely on such statement by the person protected by such order.

Added by St.1996, c. 298, § 5.

§ 6. Powers of police

Whenever any law officer has reason to believe that a family or household member has been abused or is in danger of being abused, such officer shall use all reasonable means to prevent further abuse. The officer shall take, but not be limited to the following action:

(1) remain on the scene of where said abuse occurred or was in danger of occurring as long as the officer has reason to believe that at least one of the parties involved would be in immediate physical danger

without the presence of a law officer. This shall include, but not be limited to remaining in the dwelling for a reasonable period of time;

(2) assist the abused person in obtaining medical treatment necessitated by an assault, which may include driving the victim to the emergency room of the nearest hospital, or arranging for appropriate transportation to a health care facility, notwithstanding any law to the contrary;

(3) assist the abused person in locating and getting to a safe place; including but not limited to a designated meeting place for a shelter or a family member's or friend's residence. The officer shall consider the victim's preference in this regard and what is reasonable under all the circumstances;

(4) give such person immediate and adequate notice of his or her rights. Such notice shall consist of handing said person a copy of the statement which follows below and reading the same to said person. Where said person's native language is not English, the statement shall be then provided in said person's native language whenever possible.

"You have the right to appear at the Superior, Probate and Family, District or Boston Municipal Court, if you reside within the appropriate jurisdiction, and file a complaint requesting any of the following applicable orders: (a) an order restraining your attacker from abusing you; (b) an order directing your attacker to leave your household, building or workplace; (c) an order awarding you custody of a minor child; (d) an order directing your attacker to pay support for you or any minor child in your custody, if the attacker has a legal obligation of support; and (e) an order directing your attacker to pay you for losses suffered as a result of abuse, including medical and moving expenses, loss of earnings or support, costs for restoring utilities and replacing locks, reasonable attorney's fees and other out-of-pocket losses for injuries and property damage sustained.

For an emergency on weekends, holidays, or weeknights the police will refer you to a justice of the superior, probate and family, district, or Boston municipal court departments.

You have the right to go to the appropriate district court or the Boston municipal court and seek a criminal complaint for threats, assault and battery, assault with a deadly weapon, assault with intent to kill or other related offenses.

If you are in need of medical treatment, you have the right to request that an officer present drive you to the nearest hospital or otherwise assist you in obtaining medical treatment.

If you believe that police protection is needed for your physical safety, you have the right to request that the officer present remain at the scene until you and your children can leave or until your safety is otherwise ensured. You may also request that the officer assist you in locating and taking you to a safe place, including but not limited to a designated meeting place for a shelter or a family member's or a friend's residence, or a similar place of safety.

You may request a copy of the police incident report at no cost from the police department."

The officer shall leave a copy of the foregoing statement with such person before leaving the scene or premises.

(5) assist such person by activating the emergency judicial system when the court is closed for business;

(6) inform the victim that the abuser will be eligible for bail and may be promptly released; and

(7) arrest any person a law officer witnesses or has probable cause to believe has violated a temporary or permanent vacate, restraining, or no-contact order or judgment issued pursuant to section eighteen, thirty-four B or thirty-four C of chapter two hundred and eight, section thirty-two of chapter two hundred and nine, section three, three B, three C, four or five of this chapter, or sections fifteen or twenty of chapter two hundred and nine C or similar protection order issued by another jurisdiction. When there are no vacate, restraining, or no-contact orders or judgments in effect, arrest shall be the preferred response whenever an officer witnesses or has probable cause to believe that a person:

(a) has committed a felony;

(b) has committed a misdemeanor involving abuse as defined in section one of this chapter;

(c) has committed an assault and battery in violation of section thirteen A of chapter two hundred and sixty-five.

The safety of the victim and any involved children shall be paramount in any decision to arrest. Any officer arresting both parties must submit a detailed, written report in addition to an incident report, setting forth the grounds for dual arrest.

No law officer investigating an incident of domestic violence shall threaten, suggest, or otherwise indicate the arrest of all parties for the purpose of discouraging requests for law enforcement intervention by any party.

No law officer shall be held liable in any civil action regarding personal injury or injury to property brought by any party to a domestic violence incident for an arrest based on probable cause when such officer acted reasonably and in good faith and in compliance with this chapter and the statewide policy as established by the secretary of public safety.

Whenever any law officer investigates an incident of domestic violence, the officer shall immediately file a written incident report in accordance with the standards of the officer's law enforcement agency and, wherever possible, in the form of the National Incident–Based Reporting System, as defined by the Federal Bureau of Investigation. The latter information may be submitted voluntarily by the local police on a monthly basis to the crime reporting unit of the department of criminal justice information services.

The victim shall be provided a copy of the full incident report at no cost upon request to the appropriate law enforcement department.

When a judge or other person authorized to take bail bails any person arrested under the provisions of this chapter, he shall make reasonable efforts to inform the victim of such release prior to or at the time of said release.

When any person charged with or arrested for a crime involving abuse under this chapter is released from custody, the court or the emergency response judge shall issue, upon the request of the victim, a written no-contact order prohibiting the person charged or arrested from having any contact with the victim and shall use all reasonable means to notify the victim immediately of release from custody. The victim shall be given at no cost a certified copy of the no-contact order.

Added by St.1978, c. 447, § 2. Amended by St.1983, c. 678, § 4; St.1987, c. 761; St.1990, c. 403, § 7; St.1996, c. 298, §§ 6, 7; St.2010, c. 256, § 103, eff. Nov. 4, 2010.

§ 7. Abuse prevention orders; domestic violence record search; service of order; enforcement; violations

When considering a complaint filed under this chapter, a judge shall cause a search to be made of the records contained within the statewide domestic violence record keeping system maintained by the office of the commissioner of probation and shall review the resulting data to determine whether the named defendant has a civil or criminal record involving domestic or other violence. Upon receipt of information that an outstanding warrant exists against the named defendant, a judge shall order that the appropriate law enforcement officials be notified and shall order that any information regarding the defendant's most recent whereabouts shall be forwarded to such officials. In all instances where an outstanding warrant exists, a judge shall make a finding, based upon all of the circumstances, as to whether an imminent threat of bodily injury exists to the petitioner. In all instances where such an imminent threat of bodily injury is found to exist, the judge shall notify the appropriate law enforcement officials of such finding and such officials shall take all necessary actions to execute any such outstanding warrant as soon as is practicable.

Whenever the court orders under sections eighteen, thirty-four B, and thirty-four C of chapter two hundred and eight, section thirty-two of chapter two hundred and nine, sections three, four and five of this chapter, or sections fifteen and twenty of chapter two hundred and nine C, the defendant to vacate, refrain from abusing the plaintiff or to have no contact with the plaintiff or the plaintiff's minor child, the register or clerk-magistrate shall transmit two certified copies of each such order and one copy of the complaint and summons forthwith to the appropriate law enforcement agency which, unless otherwise ordered by the court, shall serve one copy of each order upon the defendant, together with a copy of the complaint, order and summons and notice of any suspension or surrender ordered pursuant to section three B of this chapter. The law enforcement agency shall promptly make its return of service to the court.

Law enforcement officers shall use every reasonable means to enforce such abuse prevention orders. Law enforcement agencies shall establish procedures adequate to insure that an officer on the scene of an alleged violation of such order may be informed of the existence and terms of such order. The court shall notify the appropriate law enforcement agency in writing whenever any such order is vacated and shall direct the agency to destroy all record of such vacated order and such agency shall comply with that directive.

Each abuse prevention order issued shall contain the following statement: VIOLATION OF THIS ORDER IS A CRIMINAL OFFENSE.

Any violation of such order or a protection order issued by another jurisdiction shall be punishable by a fine of not more than five thousand dollars, or by imprisonment for not more than two and one-half years in a house of correction, or by both such fine and imprisonment. In addition to, but not in lieu of, the forgoing penalties and any other sentence, fee or assessment, including the victim witness assessment in section 8 of chapter 258B, the court shall order persons convicted of a crime under this statute to pay a fine of $25 that shall be transmitted to the treasurer for deposit into the General Fund. For any violation of such order, the court shall order the defendant to complete a certified batterer's intervention program unless, upon good cause shown, the court issues specific written findings describing the reasons that batterer's intervention should not be ordered or unless the batterer's intervention program determines that the defendant is not suitable for intervention. The court shall not order substance abuse or anger management treatment or any other form of treatment as a substitute for certified batterer's intervention. If a defendant ordered to undergo treatment has received a suspended sentence, the original sentence shall be reimposed if the defendant fails to participate in said program as required by the terms of his probation. If the court determines that the violation was in retaliation for the defendant being reported by the plaintiff to the department of revenue for failure to pay child support payments or for the establishment of paternity, the defendant shall be punished by a fine of not less than one thousand dollars and not more than ten thousand dollars and by imprisonment for not less than sixty days; provided, however, that the sentence shall not be suspended, nor shall any such person be eligible for probation, parole, or furlough or receive any deduction from his sentence for good conduct until he shall have served sixty days of such sentence.

When a defendant has been ordered to participate in a treatment program pursuant to this section, the defendant shall be required to regularly attend a certified or provisionally certified batterer's treatment program. To the extent permitted by professional requirements of confidentiality, said program shall communicate with local battered women's programs for the purpose of protecting the victim's safety. Additionally, it shall specify the defendant's attendance requirements and keep the probation department informed of whether the defendant is in compliance.

In addition to, but not in lieu of, such orders for treatment, if the defendant has a substance abuse problem, the court may order appropriate treatment for such problem. All ordered treatment shall last until the end of the probationary period or until the treatment program decides to discharge the defendant, whichever comes first. When the defendant is not in compliance with the terms of probation, the court shall hold a revocation of probation hearing. To the extent possible, the defendant shall be responsible for paying all costs for court ordered treatment.

Where a defendant has been found in violation of an abuse prevention order under this chapter or a protection order issued by another jurisdiction, the court may, in addition to the penalties provided for in this section after conviction, as an alternative to incarceration and, as a condition of probation, prohibit contact with the victim through the establishment of court defined geographic exclusion zones including, but not limited to, the areas in and around the complainant's residence, place of employment, and the complainant's child's school, and order that the defendant to wear a global positioning satellite tracking device designed to transmit and record the defendant's location data. If the defendant enters a court defined exclusion zone, the defendant's location data shall be immediately transmitted to the complainant, and to the police, through an appropriate means including, but not limited to, the telephone, an electronic beeper or a paging device. The global positioning satellite device and its tracking shall be administered by the department of probation. If a court finds that the defendant has entered a geographic exclusion zone, it shall revoke his probation and the defendant shall be fined, imprisoned or both as provided in this section. Based on the defendant's ability to pay, the court may also order him to pay the monthly costs or portion thereof for monitoring through the global positioning satellite tracking system.

In each instance where there is a violation of an abuse prevention order or a protection order issued by another jurisdiction, the court may order the defendant to pay the plaintiff for all damages including, but not limited to, cost for shelter or emergency housing, loss of earnings or support, out-of-pocket losses for injuries sustained or property damaged, medical expenses, moving expenses, cost for obtaining an unlisted telephone number, and reasonable attorney's fees.

Any such violation may be enforced in the superior, the district or Boston municipal court departments. Criminal remedies provided herein are not exclusive and do not preclude any other available civil or criminal remedies. The superior, probate and family, district and Boston municipal court departments may each enforce by civil contempt procedure a violation of its own court order.

The provisions of section eight of chapter one hundred and thirty-six shall not apply to any order, complaint or summons issued pursuant to this section.

Added by St.1983, c. 678, § 5. Amended by St.1987, c. 213; St.1990, c. 403, § 8; St.1992, c. 188, § 4; St.1994, c. 24, § 7; St.1995, c. 5, § 81; St.1996, c. 298, § 8; St.2002, c. 184, § 114; St.2003, c. 26, § 448, eff. July 1, 2003; St.2006, c. 418, § 1, eff. April 3, 2007.

§ 8. Confidentiality of records

The records of cases arising out of an action brought under the provisions of this chapter where the plaintiff or defendant is a minor shall be withheld from public inspection except by order of the court; provided, that such records shall be open, at all reasonable times, to the inspection of the minor, said minor's parent, guardian, attorney, and to the plaintiff and the plaintiff's attorney, or any of them.

The plaintiff's residential address, residential telephone number and workplace name, address and telephone number, contained within the court records of cases arising out of an action brought by a plaintiff under the provisions of this chapter, shall be confidential and withheld from public inspection, except by order of the court, except that the plaintiff's residential address and workplace address shall appear on the court order and accessible to the defendant and the defendant's attorney unless the plaintiff specifically requests that this information be withheld from the order. All confidential portions of the records shall be accessible at all reasonable times to the plaintiff and plaintiff's attorney, to others specifically authorized by the plaintiff to obtain such information, and to prosecutors, victim-witness advocates as defined in section 1 of chapter 258B, domestic violence victim's counselors as defined in section 20K of chapter 233, sexual assault counselors as defined in section 20J of chapter 233, and law enforcement officers, if such access is necessary in the performance of their duties. The provisions of this paragraph shall apply to any protection order issued by another jurisdiction, as defined in section 1, that is filed with a court of the commonwealth pursuant to section 5A. Such confidential portions of the court records shall not be deemed to be public records under the provisions of clause twenty-sixth of section 7 of chapter 4.

Added by St.1983, c. 678, § 5. Amended by St.1996, c. 298, § 9; St.1999, c. 127, § 156; St.2000, c. 236, § 24.

§ 9. Form of complaint; promulgation

The administrative justices of the superior court, probate and family court, district court, and the Boston municipal court departments shall jointly promulgate a form of complaint for use under this chapter which shall be in such form and language to permit a plaintiff to prepare and file such complaint *pro se*.

Added by St.1983, c. 678, § 5.

§ 10. Assessments against persons referred to certified batterers' treatment program as condition of probation

The court shall impose an assessment of three hundred and fifty dollars against any person who has been referred to a certified batterers' treatment program as a condition of probation. Said assessment shall be in addition to the cost of the treatment program. In the discretion of the court, said assessment may be reduced or waived when the court finds that the person is indigent or that payment of the assessment would cause the person, or the dependents of such person, severe financial hardship. Assessments made pursuant to this section shall be in addition to any other fines, assessments, or restitution imposed in any disposition. All funds collected by the court pursuant to this section shall be transmitted monthly to the state treasurer, who shall deposit said funds in the General Fund.

Added by St.1993, c. 110, § 217. Amended by St.1993, c. 151, § 49; St.1996, c. 151, § 466.

PART III

COURTS, JUDICIAL OFFICERS AND PROCEEDINGS IN CIVIL CASES

TITLE I

COURTS AND JUDICIAL OFFICERS

CHAPTER 211D

COMMITTEE FOR PUBLIC COUNSEL SERVICES

Chapter 211D of the General Laws was added by St.1983, c. 673, § 1.

The section headings for the General Laws in this pamphlet have been editorially supplied.

§ 1. Committee for public counsel services; establishment

There shall be a committee for public counsel services, hereinafter referred to as the committee, to plan, oversee, and coordinate the delivery of criminal and certain noncriminal legal services by all salaried public counsel, bar advocate and other assigned counsel programs, and private attorneys serving on a per case basis. The committee shall consist of fifteen persons to be appointed for a term of three years by the justices of the supreme judicial court. Said court shall request and give appropriate consideration to nominees for the fifteen positions from the Massachusetts Bar Association, county bar associations, the Boston Bar Association, and other appropriate bar groups including, but not limited to, the Massachusetts Black Lawyers' Association, Women's Bar Association, and the Massachusetts Association of Women Lawyers. Each member of the committee shall serve until his successor in office has been appointed and qualified. Vacancies shall be filled by the justices of the supreme judicial court by appointment to an unexpired term. Members of the committee may be removed by the justices of the supreme judicial court. No member of the committee shall receive any compensation for his services, but each member shall be reimbursed for actual expenses incurred in attending the committee meetings.

The provisions of chapter two hundred and sixty-eight A shall apply to all members, officers and employees of the committee, except that the committee may provide representation or enter into a contract pursuant to the provisions of sections three or six although a member of the committee may have an interest or involvement in any such matter; provided, however, that such interest and involvement is disclosed in advance to the other members of the committee and recorded in the minutes of the committee; and provided, further, that no member having an interest or involvement in any contract under section three may participate in any particular matter, as defined in section one of chapter two hundred and sixty-eight A, relating to such contract.

Added by St.1983, c. 673, § 1.

§ 2. Indigency; definition, standards and procedures for determination

The committee for public counsel shall establish a definition of "indigency" for the purposes of this chapter and uniform standards and procedures for the determination by the courts of the commonwealth that (1) a person is indigent and is unable to obtain counsel or (2) said indigent person has the ability to pay a reduced fee for the appointment of counsel. Said definition and standards, and any amendments thereto, shall be subject to the approval of the supreme judicial court and shall be used by the courts of the commonwealth in determining assignment of cases to the committee pursuant to section five. In the formulation of said definition, standards, and procedures, the committee shall consider the reporting system operated by the commissioner of revenue for the purpose of verifying financial eligibility of participants in state or federally funded programs, and its potential applicability to the provision of legal services for indigent defendants. Payment of any reduced fee by an indigent person for the appointment of counsel shall be made to the probation department of the appointing court, and shall be forwarded to the state treasurer who shall deposit such in the general fund.

Added by St.1983, c. 673, § 1.

§ 2½. Affidavit of indigency; waiver authorizing access to verifying information; quarterly reports on implemented procedures

(a) Notwithstanding any general or special law to the contrary, a person claiming indigency under the provisions of section 2 must execute a waiver authorizing the court's chief probation officer or his designee, to obtain the person's wage and tax information from the department of revenue and any other information from the registry of motor vehicles that the court may find useful in verifying the person's claim of indigency. The waiver shall authorize the chief probation officer, or his designee, to conduct any further re-assessment required by this section.

(b) It shall be the responsibility of the chief probation officer assigned to each court to ensure that a person claiming to be indigent meets the definition of indigency under section 2. A person seeking the appointment of counsel shall be interviewed by the chief probation officer or his designee before the appointment of counsel. The person conducting the interview shall explain to the person seeking appointment of counsel (1) the definition of indigency, (2) the process used to verify his information with other state agencies, and (3) the consequences of misrepresenting his financial information in applying for the appointment of counsel. The person conducting the interview shall prepare a written indigency intake report that shall record the results of the interview and his recommendation on whether or not the person seeking appointment of counsel is indigent. The person seeking appointment of counsel and the person conducting the interview shall sign the indigency intake report. In signing the report, the person seeking appointment of counsel shall certify under the pains and penalties of perjury that the information contained therein is true and that he has not concealed any information relevant to his financial status. All statements contained in the report shall be deemed material statements. The completed report shall be presented to a judge who may adopt or reject the recommendations in the report, either in whole or in part.

(c) Any appointment of counsel by the court is at all times subject to verification of indigency by the chief probation officer assigned to each court. Not later than 60 days after the appointment of counsel, the chief probation officer or his designee shall complete a re-assessment of the financial circumstances of the person for whom counsel was appointed to ensure that such person continues to meet the definition of indigency. In preparing his re-assessment, the chief probation officer or his designee may access wage and tax information in the possession of the department of revenue and such other information relevant to the verification of indigency in the possession of the registry of motor vehicles. Said departments shall provide such information to the chief probation officer or his designee upon request. Upon completion of his re-assessment, the chief probation officer shall prepare a written report of his findings. The chief probation officer shall sign the report, certifying that the person for whom counsel was appointed either continues to meet or does not continue to meet the definition of indigency. The report shall be filed with the case papers and shall be presented to the judge presiding at the person's next court appearance. If, upon receipt of the report, a judge finds that the person for whom counsel was appointed no longer meets the definition of indigency, he shall revoke the appointment of counsel and allow such person a reasonable continuance to obtain new counsel. Not later than 6 months after the appointment of counsel, and every 6 months thereafter, the chief probation officer or his designee shall conduct a further re-assessment of the financial circumstances of the person for whom counsel was appointed to ensure that he continues to meet the definition of indigency and shall prepare, sign and file a written report certifying that the person either continues to meet, or does not continue to meet, the definition of indigency.

(d) If a criminal defendant is charged with a second or further offense while continuing to be represented by court-appointed counsel for a previously charged offense, the court in its discretion shall determine whether any further determination of indigency, other than the 60–day and bi-annual re-assessments required by the defendant's representation for the first offense, need be undertaken. Upon completion of a re-assessment, the chief probation officer shall prepare a written report of his findings. The chief probation officer shall sign the report, certifying that the defendant either continues to meet or does not continue to meet the definition of indigency. The report shall be filed with the case papers and shall be presented to the judge presiding at the defendant's next court appearance. If, upon receipt of the report, a judge finds that the defendant no longer meets the definition of indigency, he shall revoke the appointment of counsel and allow the defendant a reasonable continuance to obtain new counsel.

(e) If the court finds that a person has materially misrepresented or omitted information concerning his property or assets for purposes of determining indigency, and that such person does not meet the definition of indigency, the court shall immediately terminate any assignment or appointment of counsel made under chapter 211D and shall assess costs of not less than $500 against such person.

(f) A person provided counsel under this chapter shall be assessed a counsel fee of $150, which the court may waive only upon determining that the person is unable to pay such $150 within 180 days. If, upon reviewing the chief probation officer's report on the 60–day re-assessment of the person's indigency, the court concludes that the person is able to pay the $150 counsel fee of which he obtained a waiver, the court shall invalidate the waiver and re-impose the $150 counsel fee.

(g) The court may authorize a person for whom counsel was appointed to perform community service in lieu of payment of the counsel fee. A person seeking to work off his counsel fee in community service shall perform 10 hours of community service for each $100 he owes in legal counsel fees. Notwithstanding any general or special law, rule or regulation to the contrary, a court proceeding shall not be terminated and the person shall not be discharged if he owes any portion of the legal counsel fee imposed by this section. The clerk shall not release any bail posted on such court proceeding until the legal counsel fee is satisfied in accordance with this chapter.

(h) The clerk of the court shall, within 60 days of appointment after counsel, report to the department of revenue and the registry of motor vehicles the amount of any legal counsel fee owed by the person for whom counsel was appointed under this chapter. The department of revenue shall intercept the fee from tax refunds due to persons who have not paid it. The registrar of motor vehicles shall place a lien in the amount of any portion of the legal counsel fee owed by the person for whom counsel was appointed upon the title of any motor vehicle owned in whole or in part by him. If the person for whom counsel was appointed does not own a motor vehicle the registry of motor vehicles shall not issue or renew such persons' driver's license or motor vehicle registration for any vehicle subsequently purchased by such person. The registry of motor vehicles shall not release the lien or issue or renew the license or motor vehicle registration until it receives notification from the clerk of the court that the fee has been collected or worked off in community service.

(i) The office of the commissioner of probation shall submit quarterly reports to the house and senate committees on ways and means detailing the effectiveness of any procedures implemented pursuant to this section to verify an individual's claim of indigency. The report shall include, but not limited to, the number of individuals determined to be indigent, number of individuals determined not to be indigent, number of individuals found to have concealed or otherwise misrepresented information relevant to his financial status, number of individuals found to no longer qualify for appointment of counsel upon any re-assessment of indigency required by this section, revenue generated through collection of indigent client fees, the average indigent client fee that each court division collects per case, recommendations to improve the procedures for verifying eligibility for counsel and other pertinent information to ascertain the effectiveness of verification procedures. The information within such report shall be delineated by court division.

Added by St.2003, c. 26, § 452, eff. July 1, 2003. Amended by St.2004, c. 149, § 195, eff. July 1, 2004; St.2005, c. 54, § 1, eff. July 29, 2005.

§ 2A. Legal counsel for criminal defendant charged with misdemeanor or municipal ordinance violation; fee assessment

Notwithstanding any other provision of law, a criminal defendant charged with a misdemeanor or a violation of a municipal ordinance or bylaw, on motion of the commonwealth, the defendant, or on the court's own motion, shall not be appointed counsel if the judge, at arraignment, informs such defendant on the record that, if the defendant is convicted of such offense, his sentence will not include any period of incarceration. For good cause, that judge or another judge of the same court may later revoke such determination on the record and appoint counsel, and on the request such counsel shall be entitled to a continuance to conduct any necessary discovery and to prepare adequately for trial. Any such determination or revocation by a judge shall be endorsed upon the docket of the case.

Any person provided counsel under the provisions of this chapter shall be assessed a counsel fee of $150, which may be waived at the discretion of the court. Said fee shall be in addition to any reduced fee required pursuant to section two and shall be collected in accordance with said section.

The department of revenue shall be authorized to intercept said fee from tax refunds due to persons who have not paid said fee.

The department of public welfare shall be authorized to deduct said fee in weekly or monthly increments from persons who have not paid said fee.

Added by St.1990, c. 150, § 330. Amended by St.1991, c. 138, § 205; St.1992, c. 133, § 555; St.1994, c. 60, § 153; St.2002, c. 184, § 116; St.2005, c. 54, § 1A, eff. July 29, 2005.

§ 3. Accepting of gifts, grants or contributions; contracts

Said committee may accept gifts, grants or contributions from any source, whether public or private, and may enter into contracts to provide or receive services with any federal, state, county or municipal entity, with any group or individual, whether profit or nonprofit, or with any nonprofit or voluntary charitable group, corporation, association or organization, including any bar association or bar advocate group.

Added by St.1983, c. 673, § 2.

§ 4. Rules and regulations; annual report; training; rotating appointment mechanism

Said committee shall adopt such rules and regulations as may be necessary for the conduct of its affairs and may from time to time amend or revise the same. The committee shall prepare an annual report which shall be a public document. The committee shall establish standards and guidelines for the training, qualification and removal of counsel in the public and private counsel divisions who accept its appointments, and shall provide pre-service and in-service training for both private counsel who accept assignments and salaried public counsel. The committee may establish a rotating appointment mechanism that will encourage open access among attorneys participating within the private counsel division.

Added by St.1983, c. 673, § 2.

§ 5. Appointment or assignment of counsel

Said committee shall establish, supervise and maintain a system for the appointment or assignment of counsel at any stage of a proceeding, either criminal or noncriminal in nature, provided, however, that the laws of the commonwealth or the rules of the supreme judicial court require that a person in such proceeding be represented by counsel; and, provided further, that such person is unable to obtain counsel by reason of his indigency. The committee may also establish a system for the provision of counsel in any pre-arraignment procedure. A justice or associate justice shall assign a case to the committee, as hereafter provided, after receiving from the probation officer a written report containing the probation officer's opinion as to the defendant's ability to pay for counsel, based on the standards and procedures provided for in section two.

Added by St.1983, c. 673, § 2.

§ 6. Public defender and private counsel divisions; duties

In carrying out its duties as prescribed in section five, the committee shall:

(a) Utilize its staff of attorneys, which shall be known hereafter as the "public defender division". Said division shall include a unit to be known as the Roxbury defenders unit, which shall represent clients as assigned pursuant to this chapter in the Roxbury division of the district court department. Said division shall also include a unit to be known as the youth advocacy project. Said division shall be assigned to represent indigent defendants in all criminal cases, except that:

(i) said division shall not be assigned to represent more than one defendant in any matter before any court on the same case or arising out of the same incident;

(ii) said division shall not be assigned to represent a defendant in any case in which there is a conflict of interest with any of its clients;

(iii) said division shall not be assigned to a case where a person is before the probate and family court department or the housing court department for criminal contempt or in such other proceeding in said departments in which such person is entitled to be represented by counsel;

(iv) said division shall not be assigned to represent any child alleged to be delinquent, except in such cases which may result in exposure to adult incarceration or commitment to the department of youth services until the age of twenty-one, and except in cases charging delinquency by conduct which would be punishable by imprisonment in the state prison if committed by an adult and except in the Boston and Bristol county divisions of the juvenile court department or in the Roxbury division of the district court department. Private counsel who have been certified to accept assignments in such cases shall also be eligible to provide representation to persons thus charged;

(v) said division shall not be assigned to represent any person charged with a misdemeanor unless said misdemeanor is in conjunction with a felony charge for which said division has been assigned;

(vi) notwithstanding any special or general law to the contrary, the division shall be assigned in any civil or criminal matter described in paragraph (b) where the chief counsel determines in writing that insufficient numbers of qualified attorneys are available for assignment by the private counsel division in courts located in Hampden, Hampshire, Franklin or Berkshire counties.

(b) Establish, supervise, and maintain a system for the appointment of private counsel, hereafter called the private counsel division which shall include a children and family law program and a mental health unit. The committee shall enter into contractual agreements with any state, county or local bar association or voluntary charitable group, corporation or association, including bar advocate groups, for the purpose of providing such counsel. Said committee may also contract with such other organized groups of attorneys as may be formed to afford representation to indigent defendants and may appoint and compensate private attorneys, on a case-by-case basis, as counsel for indigents entitled to representation. Neither individuals nor members nor participants in any group, corporation or association with whom the committee may contract under this paragraph shall be considered to be or have any rights as state employees.

(i) Said division shall be assigned for all persons accused of crimes entitled to counsel who, through their inability to pay for counsel, must have counsel appointed to them, but who, pursuant to the provisions of subparagraph (a) of this section are not to be represented by the public counsel division.

(ii) Said division shall be assigned to represent a person who is before the probate and family court department or the housing court department in a criminal contempt proceeding or in such other proceeding in said departments in which a person is entitled to be represented by counsel.

(iii) Said division shall also be assigned to represent persons in such other proceedings as the chief counsel shall determine to be necessary.

Added by St.1983, c. 673, § 2. Amended by St.1990, c. 150, § 331; St.1995, c. 38, § 178; St.1996, c. 200, §§ 30, 31; St.1998, c. 194, § 213; St.2004, c. 149, § 193, eff. July 1, 2004.

§ 6A. Utilization of attorney staff within private counsel division; establishment of children and family law program

In carrying out its duties as prescribed in sections 5 and 6, the committee shall, subject to appropriation, utilize its attorney staff within the private counsel division. The committee shall establish a children and family law program in the counties of Essex and Hampden which shall, upon the court's appointment, provide representation to indigent persons in children and family law cases. Nothing herein shall be construed to limit the system as established in sections 5 and 6 of this chapter, whereby the court appoints certified private counsel to represent children and parents in the majority of children and family law cases.

Added by St.1998, c. 194, § 213A.

§ 6B. Payment of counsel

Not more than 1 counsel assigned or appointed under section 5, 6 or 6A shall be paid for representation of a party in civil proceedings pending in any trial court under paragraph C of section 23, section 24 or 29B or sections 39E to 39*I*, inclusive, of chapter 119 or section 3 of chapter 210. The chief counsel of the committee for public counsel services may permit an exception to this provision in extraordinary circumstances, such as the pendency of separate actions in distant counties on behalf of a client.

Added by St.2004, c. 149, § 194, eff. July 1, 2004.

§ 7. Division assignments

Said divisions shall be assigned to represent persons charged in the district court department with concurrent felonies under section twenty-six of chapter two hundred and eighteen as further defined by the committee.

Added by St.1983, c. 673, § 2.

§ 8. Assignment of case of indigent accused of murder

Upon a determination by a court that a person accused of murder in the first or second degree is indigent, the chief counsel or his designee may assign the case to either the public defender division or the private counsel division, subject to the approval of the justice making the determination of indigency.

Added by St.1983, c. 673, § 2. Amended by St.1995, c. 38, § 179.

§ 9. Division standards

The committee shall establish standards for the public defender division and the private counsel division which shall include but not be limited to:

(a) vertical or continuous representation at the pretrial and trial stages by the attorney either assigned or appointed, whenever possible;

(b) required participation by each attorney in an approved course of training in the fundamentals of criminal trial practice, unless the attorney has a level of ability which makes such participation unnecessary;

(c) specified caseload limitation levels;

(d) investigative services;

(e) a method for the provision of social services or social service referrals;

(f) availability of expert witnesses to participating counsel;

(g) clerical assistance, interview facilities, and the availability of a law library and model forms to participating counsel; and

(h) adequate supervision provided by experienced attorneys who shall be available to less experienced attorneys.

(i) qualifications for vendors for the services provided in clauses (d), (e) and (f) and a range of rates payable for said services, taking into consideration the rates, qualifications and history of performance; provided, however, that such ranges may be exceeded with approval of the court. Payment of such costs and fees shall be in accordance with the provisions of section twenty-seven A to G, inclusive, of chapter two hundred and sixty-one.

Added by St.1983, c. 673, § 2. Amended by St.1995, c. 38, § 180; St.1996, c. 151, § 474.

§ 10. Committee monitoring of standards compliance; review of client complaints

The committee shall monitor and evaluate compliance with the standards and the performance of counsel in its divisions in order to insure competent representation of defendants in all courts of the commonwealth and shall establish a procedure for the review and disposition of client complaints. The committee shall also establish procedures whereby comments on the standard of performance of counsel in its divisions may be submitted by the justice hearing a particular matter.

Added by St.1983, c. 673, § 2. Amended by St.1990, c. 150, § 332.

§ 11. Compensation rates; review at public hearings; notice; limitation on appointments

The rates of compensation payable to all counsel, who are appointed or assigned to represent indigents within the private counsel division of the committee in accordance with the provisions of paragraph (b) of section 6, shall, subject to appropriation, be as follows: for homicide cases the rate of compensation shall be $100 per hour; for superior court non-homicide cases, including sexually dangerous person cases, the rate of compensation shall be $60; for district court cases and children in need of services cases the rate of compensation shall be $50 per hour; for children and family law cases, care and protection cases, sex offender registry cases and mental health cases the rate of compensation shall be $50 per hour. These rates of compensation shall be reviewed periodically at public hearings held by the committee at appropriate locations throughout the state, and notice shall be given to all state, county and local bar associations and other interested groups, of such hearings by letter and publication in advance of such hearings. This periodic review shall take place not less than once every 3 years.

Any counsel who is appointed or assigned to represent indigents within the private counsel division, except any counsel appointed or assigned to represent indigents within the private counsel division in a homicide case, shall be prohibited from accepting any new appointment or assignment to represent indigents after he has billed 1400 billable hours during any fiscal year.

Added by St.1983, c. 673, § 2. Amended by St.2005, c. 54, § 2, eff. July 1, 2005; St.2008, c. 182, § 69, eff. July 1, 2008.

§ 12. Private counsel compensation; audit and oversight department; invoices

The committee shall establish policies and procedures to provide fair compensation to private counsel, which shall include a remedy for an attorney aggrieved by the amount of payment. The committee shall also establish an audit and oversight department to monitor billing and private attorney compensation. All invoices shall be processed for payment within 30 days of receipt by the chief counsel. Bills shall be submitted to the committee within 60 days of the conclusion of a case or, if the case is pending at the end of the fiscal year, within 30 days after the end of such fiscal year. The amount of payment for invoices received by the chief counsel more than 60 days but less than 90 days after the final disposition of the case or more than 30 days but less than 90 days after the end of the fiscal year shall be reduced by 10 per cent. Bills submitted after such date need not be processed for payment within 30 days. For all bills not submitted to the committee within 90 days after the conclusion of a case or, if the case is pending at the end of the fiscal year, within 90 days after the end of the fiscal year, those bills so submitted after such date shall not be processed for payment; provided, however, that the chief counsel may authorize the payment of such bills either in whole or in part upon a determination that the delay was due to extraordinary circumstances beyond the control of the attorney. The committee may further prescribe such policies and procedures for payment as it deems appropriate; provided, however, that the committee may impose interest and penalties, where appropriate, upon overpayment of the private attorney bills recovered from private attorneys.

Added by St.1983, c. 673, § 2. Amended by St.1992, c. 133, § 556; St.1993, c. 110, § 221; St.1996, c. 151, § 475; St.1996, c. 204, § 41; St.2002, c. 184, § 117; St.2009, c. 27, § 88, eff. July 1, 2009.

§ 13. Chief counsel; deputies; staff; compensation

The committee shall appoint a chief counsel, whose responsibilities and duties shall be defined by the committee and shall include, but not be limited to, the overall supervision of the workings of the various divisions of the committee. The committee shall further appoint two deputy chief counsel, with duties defined by the committee, one of whom shall supervise the public defender division, and the other shall supervise the private counsel division. The committee shall also prescribe the procedures for the appointment of all legal and nonlegal staff of the public defender division and for the procurement of office space as may be required. The chief counsel shall authorize the certification of all payments under section twenty-seven G of chapter two hundred and sixty-one and section twenty of chapter twenty-nine. All legal and nonlegal staff of the public counsel division shall be full time and shall devote their entire time during ordinary business hours to their duties and shall neither directly or indirectly engage in the private practice of law. The chief counsel and deputy chief counsels shall likewise devote full time to their duties. The chief counsel, deputy chief counsels and all legal and non-legal staff of the committee, including staff attorneys hired under subparagraphs (a) and (b) of section 6 but not including persons described in the fourth sentence of said subparagraph (b) of said section 6, shall be considered public employees for purposes of chapter 258. The chief counsel shall be paid a salary comparable to the salary paid to a district attorney. The salaries of the deputy chief counsels shall be established by the committee. All other legal staff of the public defender division shall be paid at salaries comparable to the salary paid to an attorney employed in a district attorney's office.

The counsel and other employees appointed by the committee shall not be subject to the provisions of chapter thirty-one.

Added by St.1983, c. 673, § 2. Amended by St.1995, c. 38, § 181; St.1997, c. 19, § 116; St.1998, c. 194, § 214.

§ 14. Appeals and post-conviction remedies; indigent representation

The public counsel division, except in cases of conflict of interest, shall represent indigent defendants in all appeals and related post-conviction remedies. In the case of a conflict of interest, the assignment shall be to the private counsel division.

Added by St.1983, c. 673, § 2.

§ 15. Community advisory board; Roxbury community; consultation

The committee shall consult regularly with a community advisory board appointed by the committee to represent the greater Roxbury community. Members of the community advisory board shall not receive compensation or reimbursement for expenses.

Added by St.1983, c. 673, § 2.

§ 16. Appointment of counsel; sex offender registry classification system

The committee shall establish, supervise and maintain a system for the appointment of counsel for the provision of legal services for indigents subject to the sex offender registry classification system and resulting appeals pursuant to sections 178C to 178P, inclusive, of chapter 6.

Added by St.1999, c. 74, § 10.

CHAPTER 211E

MASSACHUSETTS SENTENCING COMMISSION

Chapter 211E of the General Laws was added by St.1996, c. 12, § 9.

The section headings for the General Laws in this pamphlet have been editorially supplied.

§ 1. Massachusetts sentencing commission; members; powers and duties

(a) There is established, as an independent commission in the judicial branch of the commonwealth, a Massachusetts sentencing commission which shall consist of nine voting members and six non-voting members. The governor shall appoint the voting members of the commission, and shall designate one member as chairman. Three of the voting members shall be present district court, Boston municipal court or superior court department judges, selected from a list of seven judges recommended by the chief justice for administration and management, and at least one district court judge or Boston municipal court and one superior court judge shall be appointed. Two of the voting members shall be assistant district attorneys, selected from a list of seven assistant district attorneys recommended by the Massachusetts District Attorneys' Association. One of the voting members shall be an assistant attorney general, selected from a list of three assistant attorneys general recommended by the attorney general. Two of the voting members shall be members of the Massachusetts Association of Criminal Defense Attorneys, selected from a list of five such members recommended by the Massachusetts Association of Criminal Defense Attorneys. One voting member shall be a public defender, selected from a list of three public defenders recommended by the committee for public counsel services. The non-voting members shall be the commissioner of corrections, or his designee; the commissioner of probation, or his designee; and the secretary of public safety, or his designee; the chairman of the Massachusetts parole board, or his designee; the president of the Massachusetts Sheriffs Association or his designee; a victim witness advocate selected by the victim witness board.

The chairman and the members of the commission shall be subject to removal from the commission by the governor only for neglect of duty or malfeasance in office or for a showing of other good cause.

(b) (1) The voting members of the commission shall be appointed for six-year terms; provided, however, that the initial terms of the first members of the commission shall be staggered so that four members, including the chairman, serve terms of six years; three members serve terms of four years; and two members serve terms of two years. Terms of those members appointed because of their public office or position shall end when the member leaves such public office or position, and a successor shall be appointed in the prescribed manner.

(2) No voting member may serve more than two full terms. A voting member appointed to fill a vacancy that occurs before the expiration of the term for which his predecessor was appointed shall be appointed only for the remainder of such term.

(3) Members of the commission shall serve without compensation, but each member shall be reimbursed by the commonwealth for all reasonable expenses incurred in the performance of official duties.

(4) Judges who serve on the commission and shall not be required to resign their judicial appointments.

(c) The commission shall have the power to perform such functions as may be necessary to carry out the purposes of this chapter, and may delegate to any member or designated person such powers as may be appropriate to the accomplishment of the duties of the commission as set forth below. In particular, the commission shall:

(1) appoint and fix the salary and duties of a director and other personnel, who shall serve at the discretion of the commission;

(2) submit appropriations requests to the secretary of administration and finance;

(3) utilize, with their consent, the services, equipment, personnel, information, and facilities of federal, state, local, and private agencies and instrumentalities with or without reimbursement therefor;

(4) enter into and perform such contracts, leases, cooperative agreements, and other transactions as may be necessary in the conduct of the functions of the commission, with any public agency, or with any person, firm, association, corporation, educational institution, or nonprofit organization;

(5) accept and employ, in carrying out the provisions of this chapter, voluntary and uncompensated services;

(6) request such information, data, and reports from any Massachusetts agency or judicial officer as the commission may from time to time require and as may be produced consistent with other law;

(7) serve as a clearinghouse for the collection, preparation, and dissemination of information on sentencing practices and assist courts, departments, and agencies in the development, maintenance, and coordination of sound sentencing practices;

(8) make recommendations to the legislature concerning modification or enactment of laws relating to crimes, sentencing, and correctional matters, as well as recommendations concerning programmatic, budgetary and capital matters that the commission finds to be necessary and advisable to carry out the purposes of this chapter;

(9) hold hearings and call witnesses to assist the commission in the exercise of its powers or duties.

(d) Except as hereinafter provided, the commission shall act by affirmative vote of at least five of its voting members.

(e) Upon the request of the commission, each agency and department of the commonwealth is hereby authorized and directed to make its services, equipment, personnel, facilities and information available to the greatest practicable extent to the commission in the execution of its functions. The commission shall, to the extent practicable, utilize existing resources of the administrative office of the trial court for the purpose of avoiding unnecessary duplication.

(f) Except as otherwise provided by law, the commission shall maintain and make available for public inspection a record of the final vote of each member on any action taken by it.

(g) The director shall supervise the activities of persons employed by the commission and perform other duties assigned to the director by the commission. The director shall, subject to the approval of the commission, appoint such officers and employees as are necessary in the execution of the functions of the commission.

Added by St.1996, c. 12, § 9.

§ 2. Purpose of sentencing commission

The purposes of the Massachusetts sentencing commission shall be to recommend sentencing policies and practices for the commonwealth which:

(1) punish the offender justly;

(2) secure the public safety of the commonwealth by providing a swift and sure response to the commission of crime;

(3) meet the purposes of sentencing, which are:

(A) to reflect the seriousness of the offense;

(B) to promote respect for the law;

(C) to provide just punishment for the offense;

(D) to afford adequate deterrence to criminal conduct;

(E) to protect the public from further crimes of the defendant; and

(F) to provide the defendant with educational or vocational training;

(4) provide certainty and fairness in sentencing, avoiding unwarranted sentencing disparities among defendants with similar criminal records who have been found guilty of similar criminal conduct, while maintaining judicial discretion and sufficient flexibility to permit individualized sentences warranted by mitigating or aggravating factors;

(5) promote truth in sentencing, in order that all parties involved in the criminal justice process, including the prosecution, the defendant, the court, the victim and the public, are aware of the nature and length of the sentence and its basis;

(6) ration correctional capacity and other criminal justice resources to sentences imposed, making said rationing explicit, rational and coherent, in order to:

(A) afford sufficient correctional capacity to incarcerate violent offenders consistent with paragraph one;

(B) evaluate, on a yearly basis, the performance of said rationing, making appropriate remedial recommendations consistent with subparagraph (8) of paragraph (c) of section one;

(C) prevent the prison population in the commonwealth from exceeding the capacity of the prisons, and to prevent premature release for any other reason, and to serve the ends of truth in sentencing by taking into account, in establishing sentencing policies and practices for the commonwealth, the nature and capacity of correctional facilities and community sanctions available in the commonwealth consistent with protecting public safety;

(7) encourage the development and implementation of intermediate sanctions in appropriate cases as a sentencing option, consistent with protecting public safety;

(8) enhance the value of criminal sanctions and ensure that the criminal penalties imposed are the most appropriate ones by encouraging the development of a wider array of criminal sanctions;

(9) make offenders accountable to the community for their criminal behavior, through community service, restitution, and a range of intermediate sanctions;

(10) evaluate the impact, if any, on correctional facility capacity of the discontinuation of sentence reductions for good conduct;

(11) nothing contained in this section shall be construed as creating any right of action.

Added by St.1996, c. 12, § 9.

§ 3. Recommended sentencing guidelines

(a) (1) The commission, by affirmative vote of at least six members of the commission and consistent with all pertinent provisions of this chapter and existing law, shall recommend sentencing guidelines, which shall take effect only if enacted into law.

(2) The sentencing guidelines shall be used by the district and superior courts of the commonwealth, and the Boston municipal court, in imposing a sentence in every criminal case. Said sentence shall not be suspended in whole or in part. The sentencing judge shall impose a sentence within a range prescribed by the sentencing guidelines for every offense, unless the sentencing judge sets forth in writing reasons for departing from that range, on a sentencing statement as set forth in paragraph (h), based on a finding that there exists one or more aggravating or mitigating circumstances that should result in a sentence different from the one otherwise prescribed by the guidelines. The commission shall establish non-exclusive aggravating and mitigating circumstances to guide the sentencing judge, as set forth in paragraph (d). In the absence of an applicable sentencing guideline the court shall impose an appropriate sentence, having due regard for the purposes set forth in section two.

(3) The sentencing guidelines shall be based on reasonable offense characteristics, taking into account the nature and seriousness of each offense, and reasonable offender characteristics taking into account the offender's character, background, amenability to correction, and criminal history and the availability of the commonwealth's criminal justice and public safety resources.

For every criminal offense under the laws of the commonwealth, the guidelines shall establish:

(A) The circumstances, if any, under which the imposition of intermediate sanctions may be proper, and the circumstances under which imprisonment may be proper.

(B) Appropriate intermediate sanctions for offenders for whom imprisonment may not be necessary or appropriate. In establishing such intermediate sanctions, the commission shall make specific reference to non-institutional sanctions, including but not limited to: standard probation, intensive supervision probation, community service, home confinement, weekend jail sentences, day reporting, residential programming, substance abuse treatment, restitution, means-based fines, continuing education, including but not limited to the "Changing Lives Through Literature" program administered by the trial court and the University of Massachusetts at Dartmouth, vocational training, special education, and psychological counseling; provided, however, that in no event shall a state employee be replaced by an offender serving an intermediate sanction.

(C) A target sentence for offenders for whom an intermediate sanction may not be appropriate based on a combination of reasonable offense and offender characteristics for each offense, and the adequacy of the commonwealth's criminal justice and public safety resources. The guidelines shall provide that, for each target sentence, the sentencing judge may impose a maximum sentence within a range to be established by the commission for each offense, and a minimum sentence of two-thirds of the maximum sentence; provided, however, that for target sentences of two years or greater the range may not be greater than twenty percent greater or less than the target sentence; and provided, further, that for target sentences of less than two years, the sentencing judge may impose an intermediate sanction. Within that range, the sentencing court may impose any sentence without stating its reasons therefor.

The commission shall act consistent with the need for flexibility, expeditious administration, case-flow management and resources of the trial court departments in sentencing guidelines.

(D) The circumstances, which shall not be considered exclusive, under which a sentencing judge may depart upward or downward from the range otherwise prescribed by the guidelines.

(E) The circumstances, if any, under which substance abuse treatment may be mandated, and the circumstances under which substance abuse treatment may be offered to an offender for voluntary participation.

(b) The commission shall adopt, in conjunction with the sentencing guidelines, general policy statements, which shall be used in interpreting the guidelines.

(c) In its development of the sentencing guidelines, the commission shall not be bound by any existing mandatory maximum or minimum term prescribed by statute and may recommend target sentences that exceed existing mandatory maximum terms or that fall below existing mandatory minimum terms. The commission shall conduct an empirical study in order to ascertain, to the extent practical, a survey of those individuals appearing before the commonwealth's criminal courts, and those committed to probation, prison and jail. It should also include the average sentences imposed for all offenses prior to the promulgation by the commission of the sentencing guidelines, and the length of prison terms actually served in such cases. The commission shall not be bound by such average sentences, and shall independently develop a sentencing range that is consistent with the purposes of sentencing described in section two; provided, however, that the commission shall assure that the target sentences established for each offense shall not be higher than the averages determined herein solely because of the discontinuation of sentence reductions for good conduct. The commission shall promulgate guidelines regarding participation in work release, education, training, employment or treatment programs outside correctional facilities. The commission shall utilize this data and develop any other data it deems necessary in order to assess the impact of the sentencing guidelines and carry out the purposes set forth in said section two.

(d) In establishing non-exclusive aggravating and mitigating circumstances pursuant to subparagraph (2) of paragraph (a), the commission shall determine whether the following kinds of factors, among others, are relevant, and shall take such factors into account only to the extent that it deems to be relevant:

(1) factors that describe the nature and circumstances of the offense;

(2) factors that describe the offender's mental state at the time of the offense;

(3) factors that describe the relationship, if any, between the offender and victim;

(4) factors that describe the nature and degree of the harm caused by the offense;

(5) the community view of the gravity of the offense;

(6) the public concern generated by the offense;

(7) the deterrent effect a particular sentence may have on the commission of the offense by others;

(8) the current incidence of the offense in the community and in the commonwealth as a whole;

(9) the role in the offense of each offender in cases involving multiple offenders;

(10) the age of the offender;

(11) the mental and emotional condition of the offender, to the extent that such condition mitigates the defendant's culpability or to the extent that such condition is otherwise plainly relevant;

(12) the offender's physical condition, including drug dependence;

(13) the offender's family ties and responsibilities;

(14) the offender's community ties;

(15) the offender's degree of dependence upon criminal activity for a livelihood;

(16) the offender's character and personal history; and

(17) the offender's amenability to correction, treatment, or supervision.

(e) Except for the crimes set forth in section one of chapter two hundred and sixty-five, the sentencing judge may depart from the range established by the sentencing guidelines and impose a sentence below any mandatory minimum term prescribed by statute, if the judge sets forth in writing reasons for departing from that range on a sentencing statement as set forth in paragraph (h) of this section, based on a finding that there exists one or more mitigating circumstances that should result in a sentence different from the one otherwise prescribed by the guidelines and below any applicable mandatory minimum term.

The commission shall assure that the guidelines are neutral as to the race, sex, national origin, creed, religion and socio-economic status of offenders.

(f) The commission periodically shall assess the impact of the sentencing guidelines in order to determine the type and amount of correctional resources needed. In particular, the commission shall examine the impact of said guidelines on intermediate sanctions and correctional institutions and may consult with all appropriate authorities for this purpose. Beginning in the year after the sentencing guidelines become law, but no later than May first, the following persons shall submit comments and recommendations to the commission regarding the implementation and impact of the sentencing guidelines: The governor's chief legal counsel, the commissioner of probation; the chairman of the parole board; every district attorney; the chief counsel of the committee for public counsel services; the commissioner of corrections; the chief justices of the superior court, district court, and Boston municipal court; the attorney general; and the Massachusetts Association of Criminal Defense Attorneys.

(g) Beginning in the calendar year following the effective date of the sentencing guidelines, the commission, at or after the beginning of a regular session of the legislature, but not later than the first day of October, may submit to the legislature proposed amendments to the sentencing guidelines. Such amendments shall be accompanied by a report stating the reasons therefor. The amendments to the guidelines shall take effect only if enacted into law.

(h) The chief justice for administration and management, in consultation with the sentencing commission, shall promulgate the form of a sentencing statement, conforming to the sentencing guidelines, which shall be used by the sentencing judge in the application of the guidelines when imposing a sentence. The sentencing judge shall complete the statement for every sentence imposed. If the sentencing judge imposes a sentence that departs from the range established by the guidelines, he shall, in the sentencing statement, give the facts, circumstances, evidence, opinions and any other matters considered by him to support the mitigating circumstances justifying the imposition of a sentence different from the one otherwise prescribed by the guidelines or below any applicable mandatory minimum term. One copy of the sentencing statement shall be forwarded by the court to the commission, which shall be used by the commission to submit to the legislature, at least annually, an analysis of sentencing patterns under the guidelines.

(i) Any inmate sentenced to a state or county correctional facility prior to the effective date of any sentencing guidelines enacted into law shall be subject to the law, regulation and rules governing the issuance of parole and the supervision of parole at the time the offense was committed.

(j) A person sentenced to a term of imprisonment as prescribed by any sentencing guidelines enacted into law may be eligible for parole after serving the minimum sentence imposed, less credit for deductions for good conduct earned under section one hundred and twenty-nine D of chapter one hundred and twenty-seven.

(k) The commission shall provide a public hearing and opportunity for public comment on its sentencing guidelines prior to submitting said guidelines to the legislature.

Added by St.1996, c. 12, § 9.

§ 4. Review of sentence

(a) A defendant may file a notice of appeal for review of an otherwise final sentence if:

(1) the sentence was imposed in violation of law; or

(2) the sentence was imposed as a result of an incorrect application of the sentencing guidelines; or

(3) the departure upward from the applicable guideline range was an abuse of discretion; or

(4) the sentence was imposed for an offense for which there is no sentencing guideline and is plainly unreasonable.

(b) The commonwealth, with the personal approval of the attorney general or a district attorney, may appeal an otherwise final sentence if:

(1) the sentence was imposed in violation of law;

(2) the sentence was imposed as a result of an incorrect application of the sentencing guidelines;

(3) the departure downward from the applicable guideline range was an abuse of discretion; or

(4) the sentence was imposed for an offense for which there is no sentencing guideline and is plainly unreasonable.

(c) In the case of a plea agreement entered into pursuant to Rule twelve of the Massachusetts rules of criminal procedure:

(1) a defendant may not appeal a sentence unless the sentence imposed is greater than the sentence prescribed by the sentencing guidelines; and

(2) the commonwealth may not appeal a sentence unless the sentence imposed is less than the sentence prescribed by the sentencing guidelines.

(3) a sentence imposed by the court in accordance with the recommendation of either the defendant or the commonwealth may not be appealed by the party which made the recommendation; and a sentence imposed in accordance with a jointly-agreed recommendation may not be appealed by either the defendant or the commonwealth.

(d) Appeals from sentences imposed under the sentencing guidelines shall be conducted in accordance with the Massachusetts rules of appellate procedure.

(e) If imprisonment is imposed, the entry of an appeal under the provisions of this section shall not stay the execution of the sentence unless the judge imposing it, upon a showing of a reasonable likelihood of success, finds that execution of the sentence should be stayed pending final determination of the appeal.

Added by St.1996, c. 12, § 9.

CHAPTER 218

DISTRICT COURTS

Selected sections

The section headings for the General Laws in this pamphlet have been editorially supplied.

§ 26. General provisions

The district courts and divisions of the Boston municipal court department shall have original jurisdiction, concurrent with the superior court, of the following offenses, complaint of which shall be brought in the court of the district court department, or in the Boston municipal court department, as the case may be, within which judicial district the offense was allegedly committed or is otherwise made punishable:— all violations of by-laws, orders, ordinances, rules and regulations, made by cities, towns and public officers, all misdemeanors, except libels, all felonies punishable by imprisonment in the state prison for not more than five-years, the crimes listed in paragraph (1) of subsection (a) of section eight of chapter ninety B, subparagraph (1) of paragraph (a) of subdivision (1) of section twenty-four, paragraph (a) of section twenty-four G and paragraph (1) of section twenty-four L of chapter ninety, paragraph (a) of section thirty-two and paragraph (a) of section thirty-two A of chapter ninety-four C, and section thirty-two J of chapter ninety-four C, section 38B of chapter 127, section one hundred and thirty-one E of chapter one hundred and forty, sections thirteen K, fifteen A and twenty-one A of chapter two hundred and sixty-five and sections sixteen, seventeen, eighteen, nineteen, twenty-eight, thirty, forty-nine and one hundred and twenty-seven of chapter two hundred and sixty-six, and sections one, fifteen and fifteen A of chapter two hundred and seventy-three, and the crimes of malicious destruction of personal property under section one hundred and twenty-seven of chapter two hundred and sixty-six, indecent assault and battery on a child under fourteen years of age, intimidation of a witness or juror under section thirteen B of chapter two hundred and sixty-eight, escape or attempt to escape from any penal institution, forgery of a promissory note, or of an order for money or other property, and of uttering as true such a forged note or order, knowing the same to be forged. They shall have jurisdiction of proceedings referred to them under the provisions of section four A of chapter two hundred and eleven.

Amended by St.1937, c. 301, § 1; St.1938, c. 365, § 1; St.1958, c. 138; St.1962, c. 722, § 8; St.1964, c. 140; St.1969, c. 496; St.1973, c. 585; St.1976, c. 235; St.1978, c. 478, § 187; St.1980, c. 122; St.1981, c. 470; St.1982, c. 175; St.1982, c. 229, § 1; St.1982, c. 373, § 19; St.1983, c. 636, § 27; St.1986, c. 677, § 4; St.1987, c. 266; St.1989, c. 227, § 3; St.1992, c. 379, § 138; St.1994, c. 24, § 5; St.1994, c. 318, § 23; St.1995, c. 5, § 90; St.1995, c. 297, §§ 2, 3; St.1996, c. 393, § 1; St.1996, c. 450, § 244; St.1997, c. 19, § 117; St.2003, c. 26, § 469, eff. July 1, 2003; St.2010, c. 74, § 1A, eff. July 11, 2010.

Historical and Statutory Notes

St.1692–3, c. 18, § 6.
St.1783, c. 51, § 1.
St.1794, c. 26, § 2.
St.1801, c. 62.
St.1821, c. 109.
R.S.1836, c. 15, § 13; c. 85, § 24; c. 87, §§ 3, 32; c. 126, § 23.
St.1846, c. 52.
St.1848, c. 331, § 4.
St.1849, c. 211, § 7.
St.1853, c. 196, § 1.
St.1854, c. 277, § 2.
St.1855, c. 135, § 2.
St.1855, c. 448, §§ 1, 2.
St.1857, c. 80.
St.1857, c. 157, § 1.
St.1858, c. 45, § 1.
G.S.1860, c. 116, §§ 12 to 14; c. 120, §§ 38, 40; c. 161, § 85.
St.1866, c. 279, § 8.
St.1874, c. 271, § 5.
St.1876, c. 174.
St.1876, c. 227, § 1.
St.1881, c. 189.
P.S.1882, c. 154, §§ 11, 17 to 20, 50; c. 155, §§ 46, 48; c. 203, § 103.
St.1885, c. 149.
St.1885, c. 322.
St.1887, c. 293.
St.1893, c. 396, §§ 24, 34, 36, 40.
St.1894, c. 431.

St.1897, c. 180.
St.1897, c. 349.
R.L.1902, c. 160, §§ 24, 26 to 31.
St.1904, c. 282, § 3.
St.1909, c. 442.
St.1911, c. 176, § 1.
St.1916, c. 174, § 2.

§ 26A. Trial by jury; discovery; jury-waived trial; record of proceedings; probation

Trial of criminal offenses in the Boston municipal court department and in the district court department shall be by a jury of six persons, unless the defendant files a written waiver and consent to be tried by the court without a jury. Such waiver shall not be received unless the defendant is represented by counsel or has filed a written waiver of counsel. No decision on such waiver shall be received until after the completion of a pretrial conference and a hearing on the results of such conference and until after the disposition of any pretrial discovery motions and compliance with any order of the court pursuant to said motions. Such waiver shall be filed in accordance with the provisions of section six of chapter two hundred and sixty-three; provided, however, that defense counsel shall execute a certificate signed by said counsel indicating that he has made all the necessary explanations and determinations regarding such waiver. The form of such certificate shall be prescribed by the chief justice for the district court department.

In the Boston municipal court department and the district court department upon the motion of a defendant consistent with criminal procedure, or upon the court's own motion, the judge shall issue an order of discovery requiring any information to which the defendant is entitled and also requiring that the defendant be permitted to discover, inspect, and copy any material and relevant evidence, documents, statements of persons, or reports of physical or mental examinations of any person or of scientific tests or experiments, within the possession, custody, or control of the prosecutor or persons under his direction and control. Upon motion of the defendant the judge shall order the production by the commonwealth of the names and addresses of the prospective witnesses and the production by the probation department of the record of prior convictions of any such witness.

Trial by jury in the Boston municipal court department and the district court department shall be in those jury sessions designated in accordance with section twenty-seven A. Where the defendant has properly filed a waiver and consented to be tried without a jury, as hereinbefore provided, trial shall proceed in accordance with the provisions of law applicable to jury-waived trials in the superior court; provided, however, that at the option of the defendant, the trial may be before a judge who has not rejected an agreed recommendation or dispositional request made by the defendant pursuant to the provisions of section eighteen of chapter two hundred and seventy-eight. Review in such cases may be had directly by the appeals court, by appeal, report or otherwise in the same manner provided for trials of criminal cases in the superior court.

The justice presiding over such jury-waived trial in the Boston municipal court department or the district court department shall have and exercise all of the powers and duties which a justice sitting in the superior court department has and may exercise in the trial and disposition of criminal cases including the power to report questions of law to the appeals court, but in no case may he impose a sentence to the state prison.

The justice presiding at such jury-waived session in the Boston municipal court department or the district court department shall, upon the request of the defendant, appoint a stenographer; provided, however, that where the defendant claims indigency, such appointment is determined to be reasonably necessary in accordance with the provisions of sections twenty-seven A to twenty-seven G, inclusive, of chapter two hundred and sixty-one. Such stenographer shall be sworn, and shall take stenographic notes of all the testimony given at the trial, and shall provide the parties thereto with a transcript of his notes or any part thereof taken at the trial or hearing for which he shall be paid by the party requesting it at the rate fixed by the chief justice of the Boston municipal court department or for the district court department as the case may be; and provided, further, that such rate shall not exceed the rate provided by section eighty-eight of chapter two hundred and twenty-one. Said chief justice may make regulations not inconsistent with law relative to the assignments, duties and services of stenographers appointed for sessions in his department and any other matter relative to stenographers. The compensation and expenses of a stenographer shall be paid by the commonwealth.

The request for the appointment of a stenographer to preserve the testimony at a trial in the Boston municipal court department or district court department shall be given to the clerk of the court by the defendant in writing no later than forty-eight hours prior to the proceeding for which the stenographer has been requested. The defendant shall file with such request an affidavit of indigency and request for payment by the commonwealth of the cost of the transcript and the court shall hold a hearing on such request prior to appointing a stenographer, in those cases where the defendant alleges that he will be unable to pay said cost. Said hearing shall be governed by the provisions of sections twenty-seven A to twenty-seven G, inclusive, of chapter two hundred and sixty-one, and the cost of such transcript shall be considered an extra cost as provided therein. If the court is unable, for any reason, to provide a stenographer, the proceedings may be recorded by electronic means. The original recording of proceedings in the Boston municipal court department or of a division of the district court department made with a recording device under the exclusive control of the court shall be the official record of such proceedings. Said record or a copy of all or a part thereof, certified by the chief justice for the Boston municipal court department or a district court department, or his designee, to be an accurate electronic reproduction of said record or part thereof, or a typewritten transcript of all or a part of said record or copy thereof, certified to be accurate by the court or by the preparer of said transcript, or stipulated to by the parties, shall be admissible in any court as evidence of testimony given whenever proof of such testimony is otherwise competent. The defendant may request payment by the commonwealth of the cost of said transcript subject to the same provisions regarding a transcript of a stenographer as provided hereinbefore.

In any case heard in a jury waived session in the Boston municipal court department or a district court department where a defendant is placed on probation or placed under probation supervision, he shall thereafter be supervised by the probation officer of the court in which the case originated, unless the trial justice shall order otherwise and unless the regulations of the commissioner of probation provide otherwise.

Added by St.1978, c. 478, § 188. Amended by St.1992, c. 379, § 139.

§ 27. Imposition of penalties

The district court may impose the same penalties as the superior court for all crimes of which they have jurisdiction, except that they may not impose a sentence to the state prison; provided, however, that the divisions of the juvenile court department shall have the authority to hear cases and impose penalties in accordance with the provisions of sections fifty-two through eighty-four of chapter one hundred and nineteen, and section one through nineteen of chapter one hundred and twenty.

Amended by St.1991, c. 488, § 9; St.1992, c. 379, § 140; St.1993, c. 12, § 6; St.1996, c. 200, § 32.

Historical and Statutory Notes

St.1692–3, c. 18, § 6.
St.1783, c. 51, § 1.
St.1794, c. 26, § 2.
St.1821, c. 109.
R.S.1836, c. 85, § 24; c. 87, §§ 3, 32; c. 126, § 23.
St.1853, c. 196, § 1.
St.1854, c. 277, § 2.
St.1854, c. 328.
St.1855, c. 135, § 2.
St.1855, c. 448, §§ 1, 2.
St.1857, c. 80.
St.1857, c. 157, § 1.
G.S.1860, c. 116, §§ 12 to 14; c. 120, § 38.
St.1871, c. 115.
St.1874, c. 271, § 5.
St.1876, c. 174.
St.1881, c. 189.
P.S.1882, c. 154, §§ 11, 18, 19, 50; c. 155, § 46.
St.1885, c. 149.
St.1885, c. 322.
St.1887, c. 293, § 2.
St.1887, c. 349.
St.1893, c. 396, §§ 34, 36 to 39.
St.1894, c. 431.
St.1894, c. 432.
St.1897, c. 180.
R.L.1902, c. 160, §§ 24, 26 to 30.
St.1909, c. 442.
St.1911, c. 176, § 1.
St.1918, c. 257, § 420.
St.1919, c. 5.
St.1920, c. 2.
St.1924, c. 149.

§ 27A. Jury sessions

(a) Every division of the district court department is authorized to hold jury sessions for the purpose of conducting jury trials of cases commenced in the several courts of criminal offenses over which the district courts have original jurisdiction under the provisions of section twenty-six. The Boston municipal court department shall also be authorized for the purpose of conducting jury trials in cases commenced in said department and for the purpose of conducting jury trials of cases commenced in the divisions of the district court department in Suffolk county.

(b) The chief justice for the district court department shall designate at least one division in each county or an adjoining county for the purpose of conducting jury trials; provided, however, that jury trials in cases commenced in the courts within Suffolk county shall be held in the Boston municipal court department or district courts in Suffolk county or with the approval of the chief justice, may be held in such divisions of the district court department the judicial districts of which adjoin Suffolk county as are designated by said chief justice; and jury trials in cases commenced in the divisions for Dukes county and Nantucket county may be held in Barnstable county or Bristol county; and provided further that, with the approval of the chief justice for the superior court department, facilities of said superior court may be designated by the chief justice for administration and management of the trial court for jury trials in cases commenced in the district court department or in the Boston municipal court department. Jurors shall be drawn from the county in which trial is held.

The chief justice of the district court department may also designate one or more divisions in each county for the purpose of conducting jury-waived trials of cases commenced in any court of said county consistent with the requirements of the proper administration of justice.

(c) A defendant in any division of the district court who waives his right to jury trial as provided in section twenty-six A shall be provided a jury-waived trial in the same division.

A defendant in any division of the district court who does not waive his right to jury trial as provided in section twenty-six A shall be provided a jury trial in a jury session in the same division if such has been established in said division. If such session has not been so established, the defendant shall be provided a jury trial in a jury session as hereinbefore designated. In cases where the defendant declines to waive the right to jury trial, the clerk shall forthwith transfer the case for trial in the appropriate jury session. Such transfer shall be governed by procedures to be established by the chief justice for the district court department.

(d) The justice presiding over a jury session shall have and exercise all the powers and duties which a justice sitting in the superior court department has and may exercise in the trial and disposition of criminal cases including the power to report questions of law to the appeals court, but in no case may he impose a sentence to the state prison. No justice so sitting shall act in a case in which he has sat or held an inquest or otherwise taken part in any proceeding therein.

(e) Trials by juries of six persons shall proceed in accordance with the provisions of law applicable to trials by jury in the superior court except that the number of peremptory challenges shall be limited to two to each defendant. The commonwealth shall be entitled to as many challenges as equal the whole number to which all the defendants in the case entitled.[1]

(f) For the jury sessions, jurors shall be provided by the office of the jury commissioner in accordance with the provisions of chapter two hundred and thirty-four A.

(g) The district attorney for the district in which the alleged offense or offenses occurred shall appear for the commonwealth in the trial of all cases in which the right to jury trial has not been waived and may appear in any other case. The chief justices for the district court department and the Boston municipal court department shall arrange for the sittings of the jury sessions of their respective departments and shall assign justices thereto, to the end that speedy trials may be provided. Review may be had directly by the appeals court, by appeals, report or otherwise in the same manner provided for trials of criminal cases in the superior court.

(h) The justice presiding at such jury session in the Boston municipal court department or district court department shall, upon the request of the defendant, appoint a stenographer; provided, however, that where the defendant claims indigency, such appointment is determined to be reasonably necessary in accordance with the provisions of chapter two hundred and sixty-one. Such stenographer shall be sworn, and shall take stenographic notes of all the testimony given at the trial, and shall provide the parties thereto with a transcript of his notes or any part thereof taken at the trial or hearing for which he shall be paid by the party requesting it at the rate fixed by the chief justice for the department where the case is tried; and provided, further, that such rate shall not exceed the rate provided by section eighty-eight of chapter two hundred and twenty-one. Said chief justice may make regulations not inconsistent with law relative to the assignments, duties and services of stenographers appointed for sessions in his department and any other matter relative to stenographers. The compensation and expenses of a stenographer shall be paid by the commonwealth.

The request for the appointment of a stenographer to preserve the testimony at a trial shall be given to the clerk of the court by the defendant in writing no later than forty-eight hours prior to the proceeding for which the stenographer has been requested. In the Boston municipal court department or the district court department, the defendant shall file with such request an affidavit of indigency and request for payment by the commonwealth of the cost of the transcript and the court shall hold a hearing on such request prior to appointing a stenographer, in those cases where the defendant alleges that he will be unable to pay said cost. Said hearing shall be governed by the provisions of sections twenty-seven A to twenty-seven G, inclusive, of chapter two hundred and sixty-one, and the cost of such transcript shall be considered an extra cost as provided therein. If the court is unable, for any reason, to provide a stenographer, the proceedings may be recorded by electronic means. The original recording of proceedings in the Boston municipal court department or the district court department made with a recording device under the exclusive control of the court shall be the official record of such proceedings. Said record or a copy of all or a part thereof, certified by the chief justices for the Boston municipal court department or the district court department, or his designee, to be an accurate electronic reproduction of said record or part thereof, or a typewritten transcript of all or a part of said record or copy thereof, certified to be accurate by the court or by the preparer of said transcript, or stipulated to by the parties, shall be admissible in any court as evidence of testimony given whenever proof of such testimony is otherwise competent. The defendant may request payment by the commonwealth of the cost of said transcript subject to the same provisions regarding a transcript of a stenographer as provided hereinbefore.

(i) In any case heard in a jury session where a defendant is found guilty and placed on probation, he shall thereafter be supervised by the probation officer of the court in which the case originated, unless the trial justice shall order otherwise and unless the regulations of the commissioner of probation provide otherwise.

Added by St.1972, c. 620, § 1. Amended by St.1978, c. 478, § 189; St.1979, c. 344, §§ 3, 4; St.1984, c. 371; St.1992, c. 133, § 557; St.1992, c. 379, § 141; St.1993, c. 151, § 50.

[1] So in enrolled bill.

§ 28. Recognizances to keep peace

District courts may require persons found guilty of any crime within their final jurisdiction, except a violation of by-laws, orders, ordinances, rules and regulations, made by cities, towns and public officers, or of the laws and regulations relative to the public health or relative to defective highways, in addition to the punishment prescribed by law, to recognize with sureties, in a reasonable sum, to keep the peace or be of good behavior, or both, for not more than one year, and to stand committed until they so recognize. Sections thirteen, sixteen and seventeen of chapter two hundred and seventy-five shall apply to recognizances so taken.

Historical and Statutory Notes

R.S.1836, c. 85, § 25.
G.S.1860, c. 120, § 39.
P.S.1882, c. 154, § 11; c. 155, § 47.
St.1893, c. 396, § 41.
St.1894, c. 431.
R.L.1902, c. 160, § 32.

§ 29. Repealed, 1964, 308, Sec. 10

§ 30. Binding over to superior court

They shall commit or bind over for trial in the superior court persons brought before them who appear to be guilty of crimes not within their final jurisdiction, and may so commit or bind over persons brought before them who appear to be guilty of crimes within their final jurisdiction. If such a person is committed for failure to recognize as ordered, the superior court shall thereupon have jurisdiction of the case against such person for the purpose of revising the amount of bail theretofore fixed.

Amended by St.1941, c. 194, § 19; St.1970, c. 888, § 25; St.1979, c. 344, § 5.

Historical and Statutory Notes

St.1853, c. 196, § 2.
St.1855, c. 448, § 2.
St.1857, c. 157, § 2.
G.S.1860, c. 116, § 15.
P.S.1882, c. 154, § 21.
St.1893, c. 396, § 42.
R.L.1902, c. 160, §§ 33, 34.
St.1918, c. 257, § 411.
St.1919, c. 5.
St.1920, c. 2.
St.1929, c. 216, § 1.

§ 31. Repealed, 1992, 379, Sec. 142

§ 32. Complaints and warrants

District courts may receive complaints and issue warrants and other processes for the apprehension of persons charged with crime and found within their county, or who after committing crime therein escape therefrom, returnable before a court of the county having jurisdiction of the trial or examination of the person charged with the crime.

Amended by St.1958, c. 48, § 1.

Historical and Statutory Notes

R.S.1836, c. 87, § 33.
St.1858, c. 138, § 3.
G.S.1860, c. 120, §§ 32, 36.
St.1877, c. 211, § 4.
P.S.1882, c. 154, § 11; c. 155, §§ 43, 44.
St.1893, c. 396, § 42.
St.1894, c. 431.
R.L.1902, c. 160, § 33.
St.1918, c. 257, § 411.
St.1919, c. 5.
St.1920, c. 2.

§ 33. Warrants and process; power of clerks to issue

A clerk, assistant clerk, temporary clerk or temporary assistant clerk, may receive complaints, administer to complainants the oath required thereto, and issue warrants, search warrants and summonses, returnable as required when such process are issued by said courts. No other person, except a judge, shall be authorized to issue warrants, search warrants or summonses.

Amended by St.1978, c. 478, § 191.

Historical and Statutory Notes

St.1858, c. 138, § 1.
G.S.1860, c. 120, § 36.
St.1877, c. 211, § 1.
P.S.1882, c. 155, § 6.
St.1893, c. 396, § 44.
St.1894, c. 431.
R.L.1902, c. 160, § 36.

§ 34. Arrest without warrant; endorsement of complaint by arresting officer

Said courts may dispense with the issuing of a warrant if the person charged with a crime has been arrested without a warrant and brought before the court or admitted to bail; but in such case the officer making the arrest shall endorse upon the complaint a statement of his doings.

Historical and Statutory Notes

St.1893, c. 396, § 45.
St.1894, c. 431.
R.L.1902, c. 160, § 37.

§ 35. Complaints, warrants and process; power to issue; disqualification to hear case; destruction of applications for complaints

A justice or special justice of a district court, or a justice of the peace who is also a clerk or assistant clerk of such a court, may at any time receive complaints and issue warrants and summonses, under his own hand and seal, and such justice or special justice may likewise issue search warrants, returnable before a court or trial justice having jurisdiction of the trial or examination of the person charged with the crime. If, after a hearing on the issuance of a complaint or a request for a search warrant, by a justice or special justice of a district court he issues such complaint or warrant, he shall be disqualified from presiding over a trial on the merits of any matter brought to trial because of such complaint or warrant if the defendant objects to his sitting before any evidence is taken.

If such an application for the issuance of a complaint is denied, the clerk of the district court wherein such application was made shall destroy such application one year after the date such application was filed, unless a justice of such court or the chief justice of the district courts shall for good cause order that such application be retained on file for a further period of time. The clerk shall enter on the face of any application so denied a conspicuous notation to that effect, and such applications shall be maintained separately from other records of such court. The provisions of this paragraph relating to the destruction of such applications shall not apply to applications filed pursuant to section twenty C of chapter ninety.

Amended by St.1964, c. 201; St.1975, c. 552; St.1978, c. 478, § 192; St.1992, c. 379, § 143.

Historical and Statutory Notes

St.1852, c. 94, § 25.
St.1855, c. 312, § 5.
St.1858, c. 138, § 1.
G.S.1860, c. 116, § 16; c. 120, § 36.
St.1877, c. 211, § 1.
P.S.1882, c. 154, § 22; c. 155, § 2.
St.1893, c. 396, § 43.
R.L.1902, c. 160, § 35; c. 161, § 5.

§ 35A. Process; issuance on complaints for misdemeanors; consideration of criminal records and domestic violence records; right to hearing

If a complaint is received by a district court, or by a justice, associate justice or special justice thereof, or by a clerk, assistant clerk, temporary clerk or temporary assistant clerk thereof under section 32, 33 or 35, as the case may be, the person against whom such complaint is made, if not under arrest for the offense for which the complaint is made, shall, in the case of a complaint for a misdemeanor or a complaint for a felony received from a law enforcement officer who so requests, and may, in the discretion of any said officers in the case of a complaint for a felony which is not received from a law enforcement officer, be given an opportunity to be heard personally or by counsel in opposition to the issuance of any process based on such complaint unless there is an imminent threat of bodily injury, of the commission of a crime, or of flight from the commonwealth by the person against whom such complaint is made. The court or said officers referred to above shall consider the named defendant's criminal record and the records contained within the statewide domestic violence record keeping system maintained by the office of the commissioner of probation in determining whether an imminent threat of bodily injury exists. Unless a citation as defined in section 1 of chapter 90C has been issued, notice shall also be given of the manner in which he may be heard in opposition as provided herein.

The court, or said officer thereof, may upon consideration of the evidence, obtained by hearing or otherwise, cause process to be issued unless there is no probable cause to believe that the person who is the object of the complaint has committed the offense charged.

The term district court as used in this section shall include the Boston municipal court department and the juvenile court department.

Added by St.1943, c. 349, § 1. Amended by St.1945, c. 293; St.1978, c. 478, § 193; St.1992, c. 188, § 6; St.2004, c. 149, § 200, eff. July 1, 2004.

§ 36. Justice of peace; taking bail

The governor, with the advice and consent of the council, may from time to time, upon the petition of the aldermen or the selectmen of any town within the judicial district of a district court, except a town in which the clerk of such court resides, designate and commission a justice of the peace residing in such town to take bail in criminal cases arising within said judicial district.

Amended by St.1967, c. 350, § 1.

Historical and Statutory Notes

St.1879, c. 254.
P.S.1882, c. 155, § 4.
St.1884, c. 286.
St.1897, c. 461.
St.1898, c. 381.
R.L.1902, c. 161, §§ 3, 4.
St.1924, c. 58.

§ 37. Process for witnesses and defendants in criminal and juvenile cases; direction and service

District courts, justices, special justices, clerks, assistant clerks, temporary clerks and temporary assistant clerks thereof may issue summonses and other processes for witnesses in criminal cases, and at all hearings upon applications for complaints wherein a person may be charged with the commission of a crime, and such processes and likewise warrants and other processes in such cases, issued by said courts or persons, may be directed to a court officer or probation officer of the court issuing the process, or either specifically or in general terms to any person in the commonwealth qualified to serve criminal process, and any such process may be served and executed in any part of the commonwealth by the person to whom it is delivered for that purpose. This section shall apply to summonses, warrants and other processes for parties and witnesses in cases of wayward, delinquent or neglected children.

Amended by St.1945, c. 250, § 1; St.1958, c. 48, § 2; St.1967, c. 225.

Historical and Statutory Notes

St.1838, c. 147, § 1.
G.S.1860, c. 116, § 24.
St.1876, c. 94.
P.S.1882, c. 154, §§ 28, 31.
St.1885, c. 141.
St.1886, c. 247.
St.1893, c. 396, § 46.
St.1894, c. 431.
R.L.1902, c. 160, § 38.
St.1918, c. 257, §§ 412, 413.
St.1919, c. 5.
St.1920, c. 2.

CHAPTER 221

CLERKS, ATTORNEYS AND OTHER OFFICERS OF JUDICIAL COURTS

Selected section

The section headings for the General Laws in this pamphlet have been editorially supplied.

§ 40. Removal; grounds; expenses

An attorney may be removed by the supreme judicial or superior court for deceit, malpractice or other gross misconduct, and shall also be liable in damages to the person injured thereby, and to such other punishment as may be provided by law. Whenever a petition is filed for the removal of an attorney, the proceedings thereafter shall be conducted by an attorney to be designated by the court. The expenses of the inquiry and proceedings in either court shall be paid as in criminal prosecutions in the superior court.

Historical and Statutory Notes

R.S.1836, c. 88, § 25.
G.S.1860, c. 121, § 34.
P.S.1882, c. 159, § 39.
R.L.1902, c. 165, § 44.
St.1919, c. 260.
St.1924, c. 134.

TITLE II

ACTIONS AND PROCEEDINGS THEREIN

CHAPTER 231

PLEADING AND PRACTICE

Selected sections

The section headings for the General Laws in this pamphlet have been editorially supplied.

§ 94B. False arrest; shoplifting; defrauding innkeepers; defenses

In an action for false arrest or false imprisonment brought by any person by reason of having been detained for questioning on or in the immediate vicinity of the premises of a merchant or an innkeeper, if such person was detained in a reasonable manner and for not more than a reasonable length of time by a person authorized to make arrests or by the merchant or innkeeper or his agent or servant authorized for such purpose and if there were reasonable grounds to believe that the person so detained was committing or attempting to commit a violation of section thirty A of chapter two hundred and sixty-six, or section twelve of chapter one hundred and forty, or was committing or attempting to commit larceny of goods for sale on such premises or larceny of the personal property of employees or customers or others present on such premises, it shall be a defense to such action.

Added by St.1958, c. 337. Amended by St.1971, c. 447; St.1981, c. 618, §§ 1, 2; St.1985, c. 348, § 2.

§ 94C. False arrest; theft of public records; defenses

In an action for false arrest or false imprisonment brought by any person by reason of having been detained for questioning on or in the immediate vicinity of the custodian of the record, it shall be a defense to such action if such person was detained in a reasonable manner and for not more than a reasonable length of time by a person authorized to make arrests or by the custodian or his agent authorized for such purpose and if reasonable grounds existed at the time of such detention to believe that such person so detained was committing or attempting to commit a violation of section one hundred and forty-five of chapter two hundred and sixty-six.

Added by St.1986, c. 196, § 1.

CHAPTER 233

WITNESSES AND EVIDENCE

Selected sections

The section headings for the General Laws in this pamphlet have been editorially supplied.

§ 1. Issuance of summonses for witnesses

A clerk of a court of record, a notary public or a justice of the peace may issue summonses for witnesses in all cases pending before courts, magistrates, auditors, referees, arbitrators or other persons authorized to examine witnesses, and at all hearings upon applications for complaints wherein a person may be charged with the commission of a crime; but a notary public or a justice of the peace shall not issue summonses for witnesses in criminal cases except upon request of the attorney general, district attorney or other person who acts in the case in behalf of the commonwealth or of the defendant. If the summons is issued at the request of the defendant that fact shall be stated therein. The summons shall be in the form heretofore adopted and commonly used, but may be altered from time to time like other writs.

Amended by St.1945, c. 250, § 2.

Historical and Statutory Notes

St.1701–2, c. 5, § 4.
St.1743–4, c. 24, § 1.
St.1783, c. 42, § 5; c. 51, § 2.
St.1784, c. 28, §§ 5, 6.
St.1791, c. 53, § 6.
R.S.1836, c. 85, § 38; c. 94, § 1; c. 96, § 28.
G.S.1860, c. 131, § 1.
P.S.1882, c. 169, § 1.
St.1884, c. 247.
St.1885, c. 141.
St.1889, c. 197.
St.1896, c. 476.
R.L.1902, c. 175, § 1.

St.1923, c. 263.
St.1931, c. 394, § 190.

§ 2. Service of summons

Such summons may be served in any county by an officer qualified to serve civil process or by a disinterested person by exhibiting and reading it to the witness, by giving him a copy thereof or by leaving such copy at his place of abode.

Historical and Statutory Notes

St.1826, c. 86, § 5.
R.S.1836, c. 94, § 2.
G.S.1860, c. 131, § 2.
St.1863, c. 157, § 3.
P.S.1882, c. 169, § 2.
R.L.1902, c. 175, § 2.

§ 3. Witness fees; payment or tender

No person shall be required to attend as a witness in a civil case or for the defendant in a criminal case except a person summonsed to attend as a witness for an indigent defendant in a criminal case, unless the legal fees for one day's attendance and for travel to and from the place where he is required to attend are paid or tendered to him.
Amended by St.1979, c. 344, § 7.

Historical and Statutory Notes

C.L. c. 159, § 3.
St.1701–2, c. 5, § 5.
St.1743–4, c. 24, § 1.
St.1784, c. 28, § 6.
R.S.1836, c. 94, § 3.
G.S.1860, c. 131, § 3.
P.S.1882, c. 169, § 3.
St.1885, c. 141.
R.L.1902, c. 175, § 3.

§ 3A. Representation of commissioner of banks

If the commissioner of banks is summoned as a witness in any proceeding involving his official acts, unless the court or tribunal shall otherwise order, it shall be a sufficient compliance if he causes an employee or other assistant in his department having knowledge in the premises to appear.
Added by St.1933, c. 262.

§ 4. Liability for nonattendance

If a person who has been duly summoned and required to attend as a witness under the preceding sections or section thirty-seven of chapter two hundred and eighteen fails, without a sufficient excuse, to attend, he shall be liable to the aggrieved party in tort for all damages caused by such failure.

Historical and Statutory Notes

St.1701–2, c. 5, § 5.
St.1743–4, c. 24, § 1.
St.1784, c. 28, § 6.
R.S.1836, c. 94, § 4.
G.S.1860, c. 131, § 4.
P.S.1882, c. 169, § 4.
R.L.1902, c. 175, § 4.
St.1918, c. 257, § 435.
St.1918, c. 285.
St.1919, c. 5.
St.1920, c. 2.

§ 5. Penalty for nonattendance; contempt

Such failure to attend as a witness before a court, justice of the peace, master in chancery, master or auditor appointed by a court, or the county commissioners, shall also be a contempt of the court, and may be punished, in case of such failure to attend as a witness in a criminal prosecution, by a fine of not more than two hundred dollars or by imprisonment for not more than one month or both, or, in case of any other such failure to attend as aforesaid, by a fine of not more than twenty dollars.

Historical and Statutory Notes

St.1701–2, c. 5, § 5.
St.1743–4, c. 24, § 1.
St.1784, c. 28, § 6.
R.S.1836, c. 94, § 5.
St.1838, c. 42.
St.1856, c. 284, § 9.
St.1858, c. 93, §§ 2, 3.
G.S.1860, c. 131, § 5.
P.S.1882, c. 169, § 5.
R.L.1902, c. 175, § 5.
St.1926, c. 230.
St.1926, c. 296.

§ 6. Warrant for nonattending witness

The court, justice, master in chancery, master, auditor or county commissioners may in such case issue a warrant to bring such witness before them to answer for the contempt, and also to testify in the case in which he was summoned.

Historical and Statutory Notes

St.1784, c. 28, § 6.
R.S.1836, c. 94, § 6.
G.S.1860, c. 131, § 6.
P.S.1882, c. 169, § 6.
R.L.1902, c. 175, § 6.

§ 7. Witnesses before executive council

Witnesses may be summoned to attend and testify at a hearing before the executive council, or a committee thereof, as to matters within its authority. They shall be summoned in the same manner, be paid the same fees and in the same manner, and be subject to the same penalties for default, as witnesses before the general court.

Historical and Statutory Notes

St.1861, c. 166.
P.S.1882, c. 169, § 9.
R.L.1902, c. 175, § 7.

§ 8. Bodies authorized to summon witnesses; oath

Witnesses may be summoned to attend and testify and to produce books and papers at a hearing before a city council, or either branch thereof, or before a joint or special committee of the same or of either branch thereof, or before a board of selectmen, a board of police commissioners, a fire commissioner or a board of fire commissioners, a commissioner of public safety, a school board, the alcoholic beverages control commission established by section forty-three of chapter six, a licensing board or licensing authorities, as defined in section one of chapter one hundred and thirty-eight, a board of registrars of voters, the police commissioner or election commissioners of Boston, the Massachusetts Water Resources Authority, the state racing commission, the parole board or a board of appeals designated or appointed under section thirty of chapter forty, as to matters within their authority; and such witnesses shall be summoned in the same manner, be paid the same fees and be subject to the same penalties for default, as witnesses in civil cases before the courts. The presiding officer of such council, or of either branch thereof, or a member of any such committee, board or commission, or any such commissioner, may administer oaths to witnesses who appear before such council, branch thereof, committee, board, commission or commissioner, respectively.

Amended by St.1933, c. 269, § 3; St.1933, Ex.Sess., c. 376, § 3; St.1949, c. 292; St.1975, c. 466; St.1984, c. 372, § 58; St. 2003, c. 26, § 493, eff. July 1, 2003.

Historical and Statutory Notes

St.1863, c. 158, § 1.
P.S.1882, c. 169, § 7.
St.1882, c. 267, § 1.
St.1885, c. 323, § 2.
St.1900, c. 267, § 1.
R.L.1902, c. 175, § 8.
St.1906, c. 291.
St.1907, c. 328.
St.1913, c. 85.
St.1916, c. 31.
St.1919, c. 350, § 123.
St.1930, c. 62.

§ 9. Warrant for witness failing to attend before nonjudicial tribunal

If a witness who has been so summoned and paid or tendered the proper fees fails to attend in pursuance thereof, the presiding officer of such city council, or of either branch thereof, or the chairman of such committee, board or commission, or any such commissioner, may issue a warrant to bring such witness before them, to testify in the case in which he was summoned.

Historical and Statutory Notes

St.1863, c. 158, § 2.
P.S.1882, c. 169, § 8.
St.1882, c. 267, § 2.
St.1900, c. 267, § 2.
R.L.1902, c. 175, § 9.

§ 10. Enforcing attendance before nonjudicial tribunal

A justice of the supreme judicial or the superior court, upon application of a tribunal authorized to summon but not to compel the attendance of witnesses and the giving of testimony before it, may, in his discretion, compel the attendance of such witnesses and the giving of testimony before any such tribunal, in the same manner and to the same extent as before said courts.

Historical and Statutory Notes

St.1879, c. 155.
P.S.1882, c. 112, § 25.
St.1883, c. 195.
St.1891, c. 140.
St.1901, c. 286.
R.L.1902, c. 175, § 10.

§ 11. Requiring testimony

A justice of the supreme judicial or the superior court, upon the application of a magistrate or tribunal authorized to summon and compel the attendance of witnesses may, in his discretion, compel the giving of testimony by them before such magistrate or tribunal, in the same manner and to the same extent as before said courts.

Historical and Statutory Notes

St.1879, c. 155.
P.S.1882, c. 112, § 25.
St.1898, c. 374.
St.1901, c. 286.
R.L.1902, c. 175, § 11.

§ 12. Summons for attendance at criminal trial outside state

A justice of the peace, upon receipt of a certificate of the clerk of a court of record in the state of Maine or in a state adjoining this commonwealth that a criminal prosecution is pending in such court, and that a resident of the commonwealth is supposed to be a material witness therein, shall issue a summons requiring such witness to appear and testify at the court in which such case is pending.

Historical and Statutory Notes

St.1777–8, c. 5, § 1.
St.1873, c. 319, § 1.
St.1874, c. 150.
P.S.1882, c. 169, § 10.
R.L.1902, c. 175, § 12.

§ 13. Penalty for nonattendance outside state

If the person on whom such summons is served is paid or tendered double the fees allowed by law for travel and attendance of witnesses in the supreme judicial court, and double traveling expenses for the whole distance out and home by the ordinary traveled route, he shall, if he neglects without good cause to attend as a witness at the court named in such summons, forfeit not more than three hundred dollars.

Historical and Statutory Notes

St.1873, c. 319, § 2.
P.S.1882, c. 169, § 11.
R.L.1902, c. 175, § 13.

§ 13A. Attendance of witnesses outside state; hearing and summons; failure to attend

If a certificate wherein a judge of a court of record in any state which by its laws has made provision for commanding persons within its borders to attend and testify in criminal actions, prosecutions and other criminal proceedings pending, or grand jury investigations and other proceedings commenced or about to commence, in this commonwealth certifies under the seal of such court that there is a criminal proceeding pending in such court, or that a grand jury investigation or proceeding has commenced or is about to commence within the jurisdiction of such court, that a person being within this commonwealth is a material witness in such proceeding or investigation and that his presence will be required for a specified number of days, is presented to a justice of the superior court sitting in and for the county, or the justice or a special justice of the district court in the judicial district, in which such person is, such justice or special justice shall make an order directing such person to appear at a time and place certain for a hearing upon the question of compelling his attendance at such proceeding or investigation.

If at the hearing the justice or special justice determines that the witness is material and necessary, that it will not cause undue hardship to the witness to be compelled to attend and testify in the proceeding or investigation in such other state, and that the laws of such other state and of any other state through which the witness may be required to pass by the ordinary traveled route will give to him protection from arrest and the service of process, civil or criminal, as provided in section thirteen C, he shall issue a summons, which term shall include a subpoena, order or other notice requiring the appearance of a witness in any state where such process is used in lieu of a summons, with a copy of such certificate attached, directing the witness to attend and testify in the court where the proceeding is pending, or before the grand jury before which the investigation or proceeding has commenced or is about to commence, at a time and place specified in the summons. At any such hearing such certificate shall be prima facie evidence of all the facts stated therein.

If in any such certificate it is recommended that the witness be taken into immediate custody and delivered to an officer of the requesting state to assure his attendance at such a proceeding or investigation therein, such justice or special justice may, in lieu of notification of the hearing, direct that such witness be forthwith brought before him for said hearing and the justice or special justice at the hearing, if satisfied of the desirability of such custody and delivery, for which determination such certificate shall be prima facie evidence of such desirability, may, in lieu of issuing a summons, order that said witness be taken into custody and delivered to an officer of the requesting state.

If a witness who is summoned as hereinbefore provided, after being paid or tendered by some properly authorized person the sum of ten cents a mile for each mile by the ordinary traveled route to and from the place where the proceeding is pending, or the grand jury investigation or proceeding has commenced or is about to commence, and five dollars for each day that he is required to travel and attend as a witness, fails without good cause to attend and testify as directed in the summons, he shall be punished in the manner provided for the punishment of a witness who disobeys a summons issued from a court of record of this commonwealth.

Added by St.1937, c. 210, § 1.

§ 13B. Attendance of witness from another state; fees; failure to attend

If a person in any state which by its laws has made provision for commanding persons within its borders to attend and testify in criminal proceedings pending, or grand jury investigations and proceedings commenced or about to commence, in this commonwealth is a material witness in a criminal proceeding pending in a court of record of this commonwealth, or in a grand jury investigation or proceeding which has commenced or is about to commence within the jurisdiction of such a court of record, a justice or special justice of such court may issue a certificate under the seal of the court, stating such facts and specifying the number of days the witness will be required, which certificate may be presented in accordance with the laws of such other state to a magistrate or officer thereof for appropriate action to secure the attendance of such witness in this commonwealth. Such certificate may include a recommendation that the witness be taken into immediate custody and delivered to an officer of this commonwealth to assure his attendance in this commonwealth.

If the witness is summoned to attend and testify in this commonwealth he shall be tendered the sum of ten cents a mile for each mile by the ordinary traveled route to and from the place where the criminal proceeding is pending, or the grand jury investigation or proceeding has commenced or is about to commence, and five dollars for each day that he is required to travel and attend as a witness. A witness who has appeared in accordance with the provisions of the summons shall not be required to remain within this commonwealth a longer period of time than the period mentioned in the certificate, unless otherwise ordered by the court having jurisdiction of the criminal proceeding or grand jury investigation or proceeding; and any court order that such witness remain after the time for which he was summoned shall be conditioned upon the immediate tender to him of five dollars for each day during which his further attendance as a witness is ordered. If such a witness, after coming into this commonwealth, fails without good cause to attend and testify as directed in the summons, he shall be punished in the manner provided for the punishment of a witness who disobeys a summons issued from a court of record of this commonwealth.

Added by St.1937, c. 210, § 1.

§ 13C. Exemption from arrest and process of witnesses from outside state

If a person comes into this commonwealth in obedience to a summons or order directing him to attend and testify in a criminal proceeding or grand jury investigation or proceeding in this commonwealth he shall not, while in this commonwealth pursuant to such summons or order, be subject to arrest or the service of process, civil or criminal, in connection with matters which arose before his entrance into this commonwealth under the summons or order.

If a person passes through this commonwealth while going to another state in obedience to a summons or order to attend and testify in a criminal proceeding or grand jury investigation or proceeding in that state, or while returning therefrom, he shall not, while so passing through this commonwealth, be subject to arrest or the service of process, civil or criminal, in connection with matters which arose before his entrance into this commonwealth under the summons or order.

Nothing in this section or either of the two preceding sections shall preclude action under sections twelve and thirteen or under similar reciprocal provisions of law in other states.

Added by St.1937, c. 210, § 1.

§ 13D. Short title; construction of law

Sections thirteen A to thirteen C, inclusive, may be cited as the uniform law to secure the attendance of witnesses from without a state in criminal proceedings, and shall be so interpreted and construed as to effectuate their general purpose to make uniform the law of the states which enact similar laws.

Added by St.1937, c. 210, § 1.

§ 14. Persons authorized to administer oaths

Arbitrators, referees, masters and auditors appointed according to law may administer oaths or affirmations to all persons offered as witnesses before them.

Historical and Statutory Notes

St.1852, c. 54.
G.S.1860, c. 131, § 7.
P.S.1882, c. 169, § 12.
R.L.1902, c. 175, § 14.

§ 15. Mode of administering oaths

The usual mode of administering oaths now practiced in the commonwealth, with the ceremony of holding up the hand, shall be observed in all cases in which an oath may be administered by law, except as provided in sections sixteen to nineteen, inclusive.

Historical and Statutory Notes

St.1701–2, c. 5, § 7.
St.1797, c. 35, § 10.
R.S.1836, c. 94, § 7.
G.S.1860, c. 131, § 8.
P.S.1882, c. 169, § 13.
R.L.1902, c. 175, § 15.

§ 16. Mode requested by affiant

If a person to be sworn declares that a different mode of taking the oath is in his opinion more solemn and obligatory than the upholding of the hand, the oath may be administered in such mode.

Historical and Statutory Notes

St.1797, c. 35, § 10.
R.S.1836, c. 94, § 8.
G.S.1860, c. 131, § 9.
St.1873, c. 212, § 1.
P.S.1882, c. 169, § 14.
R.L.1902, c. 175, § 16.

§ 17. Affirmation by Quakers

A Friend or Quaker when called on to take an oath may solemnly and sincerely affirm under the penalties of perjury.

Historical and Statutory Notes

St.1743–4, c. 20, §§ 1, 2.
St.1758–9, c. 18, §§ 1, 2.
St.1797, c. 35, §§ 9, 10.
St.1810, c. 127, § 1.
R.S.1836, c. 94, § 9.
G.S.1860, c. 131, § 10.
P.S.1882, c. 169, § 15.
R.L.1902, c. 175, § 17.

§ 18. Affirmation for reasons of conscience

A person who declares that he has conscientious scruples against taking an oath shall, when called upon for that purpose, be permitted to affirm in the manner prescribed for Quakers, if the court or magistrate on inquiry is satisfied of the truth of such declaration.

Historical and Statutory Notes

St.1824, c. 91, § 1.
R.S.1836, c. 94, § 10.
G.S.1860, c. 131, § 11.
P.S.1882, c. 169, § 16.
R.L.1902, c. 175, § 18.

§ 19. Oaths of non–Christians

A person believing in any other than the Christian religion may be sworn according to the appropriate ceremonies of his religion. A person not a believer in any religion shall be required to testify truly under the penalties of perjury, and evidence of his disbelief in the existence of God may not be received to affect his credibility as a witness.

Amended by St.1973, c. 964.

Historical and Statutory Notes

St.1797, c. 35, § 10.
R.S.1836, c. 94, § 11.
G.S.1860, c. 131, § 12.
P.S.1882, c. 169, § 17.
R.L.1902, c. 175, § 19.

§ 20. Competency of witnesses; husband and wife; criminal defendant; parent and child

Any person of sufficient understanding, although a party, may testify in any proceeding, civil or criminal, in court or before a person who has authority to receive evidence, except as follows:

First, Except in a proceeding arising out of or involving a contract made by a married woman with her husband, a proceeding under chapter two hundred and nine D and in a prosecution begun under sections one to ten, inclusive, of chapter two hundred and seventy-three, any criminal proceeding in which one spouse is a defendant alleged to have committed a crime against the other spouse or to have violated a temporary or permanent vacate, restraining, or no-contact order or judgment issued pursuant to section eighteen, thirty-four B or thirty-four C of chapter two hundred and eight, section thirty-two of chapter two hundred and nine, section three, three B, three C, four, or five of chapter two hundred and nine A, or sections fifteen or twenty of chapter two hundred and nine C, or a similar protection order issued by another jurisdiction, obtained by the other spouse, and except in a proceeding involving abuse of a person under the age of eighteen, including incest, neither husband nor wife shall testify as to private conversations with the other.

Second, Except as otherwise provided in section seven of chapter two hundred and seventy-three and except in any proceeding relating to child abuse, including incest, neither husband nor wife shall be compelled to testify in the trial of an indictment, complaint or other criminal proceeding against the other;

Third, The defendant in the trial of an indictment, complaint or other criminal proceeding shall, at his own request, but not otherwise, be allowed to testify; but his neglect or refusal to testify shall not create any presumption against him.

Fourth, An unemancipated, minor child, living with a parent, shall not testify before a grand jury, trial of an indictment, complaint or other criminal proceeding, against said parent, where the victim in such proceeding is not a member of said parent's family and who does not reside in the said parent's household. For the purposes of this clause the term "parent" shall mean the natural or adoptive mother or father of said child.

Amended by St.1951, c. 657, § 3; St.1963, c. 765, § 3; St.1983, c. 145; St.1986, c. 145; St.1995, c. 5, § 94; St.1996, c. 298, § 10.

Historical and Statutory Notes

St.1851, c. 233, § 97.
St.1851, c. 255, § 3.
St.1852, c. 312, § 60.
St.1856, c. 188.
St.1857, c. 305, § 1.
St.1859, c. 230.
G.S.1860, c. 131, §§ 13, 14, 16.
St.1864, c. 304, § 1.
St.1865, c. 207, § 2.
St.1866, c. 148, § 5.
St.1866, c. 260.
St.1870, c. 393, § 1.
P.S.1882, c. 169, § 18.
R.L.1902, c. 175, § 20.
St.1911, c. 456, § 7.

§ 20A. Privileged communications; communications with clergymen

A priest, rabbi or ordained or licensed minister of any church or an accredited Christian Science practitioner shall not, without the consent of the person making the confession, be allowed to disclose a confession made to him in his professional character, in the course of discipline enjoined by the rules or practice of the religious body to which he belongs; nor shall a priest, rabbi or ordained or licensed minister of any church or an accredited Christian Science practitioner testify as to any communication made to him by any person in seeking religious or spiritual advice or comfort, or as to his advice given thereon in the course of his professional duties or in his professional character, without the consent of such person.

Added by St.1962, c. 372.

§ 20B. Privileged communications; patients and psychotherapists; exceptions

The following words as used in this section shall have the following meanings:—

"Patient", a person who, during the course of diagnosis or treatment, communicates with a psychotherapist;

"Psychotherapist", a person licensed to practice medicine, who devotes a substantial portion of his time to the practice of psychiatry. "Psychotherapist" shall also include a person who is licensed as a psychologist by the board of registration of psychologists; a graduate of, or student enrolled in, a doctoral degree program in psychology at a recognized educational institution as that term is defined in section 118, who is working under the supervision of a licensed psychologist; or a person who is a registered nurse licensed by the board of registration in nursing whose certificate of registration has been endorsed authorizing the practice of professional nursing in an expanded role as a psychiatric nurse mental health clinical specialist, pursuant to the provisions of section eighty B of chapter one hundred and twelve.

"Communications" includes conversations, correspondence, actions and occurrences relating to diagnosis or treatment before, during or after institutionalization, regardless of the patient's awareness of such conversations, correspondence, actions and occurrences, and any records, memoranda or notes of the foregoing.

Except as hereinafter provided, in any court proceeding and in any proceeding preliminary thereto and in legislative and administrative proceedings, a patient shall have the privilege of refusing to disclose, and of preventing a witness from disclosing, any communication, wherever made, between said patient and a psychotherapist relative to the diagnosis or treatment of the patient's mental or emotional condition. This privilege shall apply to patients engaged with a psychotherapist in marital therapy, family therapy, or consultation in contemplation of such therapy.

If a patient is incompetent to exercise or waive such privilege, a guardian shall be appointed to act in his behalf under this section. A previously appointed guardian shall be authorized to so act.

Upon the exercise of the privilege granted by this section, the judge or presiding officer shall instruct the jury that no adverse inference may be drawn therefrom.

The privilege granted hereunder shall not apply to any of the following communications:—

(*a*) If a psychotherapist, in the course of his diagnosis or treatment of the patient, determines that the patient is in need of treatment in a hospital for mental or emotional illness or that there is a threat of imminently dangerous activity by the patient against himself or another person, and on the basis of such determination discloses such communication either for the purpose of placing or retaining the patient in such hospital, provided however that the provisions of this section shall continue in effect after the patient is in said hospital, or placing the patient under arrest or under the supervision of law enforcement authorities.

(*b*) If a judge finds that the patient, after having been informed that the communications would not be privileged, has made communications to a psychotherapist in the course of a psychiatric examination ordered by the court, provided that such communications shall be admissible only on issues involving the patient's mental or emotional condition but not as a confession or admission of guilt.

(*c*) In any proceeding, except one involving child custody, adoption or adoption consent, in which the patient introduces his mental or emotional condition as an element of his claim or defense, and the judge or presiding officer finds that it is more important to the interests of justice that the communication be disclosed than that the relationship between patient and psychotherapist be protected.

(*d*) In any proceeding after the death of a patient in which his mental or emotional condition is introduced by any party claiming or defending through or as a beneficiary of the patient as an element of the claim or defense, and the judge or presiding officer finds that it is more important to the interests of justice that the communication be disclosed than that the relationship between patient and psychotherapist be protected.

(*e*) In any case involving child custody, adoption or the dispensing with the need for consent to adoption in which, upon a hearing in chambers, the judge, in the exercise of his discretion, determines that the psychotherapist has evidence bearing significantly on the patient's ability to provide suitable care or custody, and that it is more important to the welfare of the child that the communication be disclosed than that the relationship between patient and psychotherapist be protected; provided, however, that in such cases of adoption or the dispensing with the need for consent to adoption, a judge shall determine that the patient has been informed that such communication would not be privileged.

(*f*) In any proceeding brought by the patient against the psychotherapist, and in any malpractice, criminal or license revocation proceeding, in which disclosure is necessary or relevant to the claim or defense of the psychotherapist.

The provision of information acquired by a psychotherapist relative to the diagnosis or treatment of a patient's emotional condition, to any insurance company, nonprofit hospital service corporation, medical service corporation, or health maintenance organization, or to a board established pursuant to section twelve of chapter one hundred and seventy-six B, pertaining to the administration or provision of benefits, including utilization review or peer review, for expenses arising from the out-patient diagnosis or treatment, or both, of mental or nervous conditions, shall not constitute a waiver or breach of any right to which said patient is otherwise entitled under this section and section thirty-six B of chapter one hundred and twenty-three.

Added by St.1968, c. 418. Amended by St.1974, c. 240; St.1977, c. 817; St.1985, c. 85; St.1986, c. 188, § 7; St.1986, c. 557, § 178; St.1986, c. 594; St.1987, c. 398, § 2; St.1989, c. 117, § 7; St.1989, c. 270, § 2; St.1989, c. 373; St.1990, c. 177, § 361; St.2000, c. 348, § 2.

§ 20C. Immunity from prosecution; privilege against self-incrimination

In any investigation or proceeding before a grand jury, or in a criminal proceeding in the supreme judicial court, appeals court or superior court involving any offense listed in section 20D, a witness shall not be excused from testifying or from producing books, papers or other evidence on the ground that the testimony or evidence required of him may tend to incriminate him or subject him to a penalty or forfeiture, if he has been granted immunity with respect to the transactions, matters or things concerning which he is compelled, after having claimed his privilege against self-incrimination, to testify or produce evidence by a justice of the supreme judicial court, appeals court or superior court, as provided in section 20E.

Added by St.1970, c. 408. Amended by St.1998, c. 188, § 1.

§ 20D. Crimes subject to immunity

A witness who is called or who may be called to testify before a grand jury or in a criminal proceeding in the supreme judicial court, appeals court or superior court may, in the manner provided in section twenty E, be granted immunity in any proceeding or investigation involving the following crimes: abortion, arson, assault and battery to collect a loan, assault and battery by means of a dangerous weapon, assault to murder, breaking and entering a dwelling house or a building, bribery, burning of a building or dwelling house or other property, burglary, counterfeiting, deceptive advertising, electronic eavesdropping, embezzlement, extortion, firearm violations, forgery, fraudulent personal injury and property damage claims, violation of the gaming laws, gun registration violations, intimidation of a witness or of a juror, insurance law violations, kidnapping, larceny, lending of money or thing of value in violation of the general laws, liquor law violations, mayhem, murder, violation of the narcotic or harmful drug laws, perjury, prostitution, violations of environmental control laws (pollution), violations of conflicts of interest laws, consumer protection laws, pure food and drug law violations, receiving stolen property, robbery, subornation of perjury, uttering, or any felony, being an accessory to any of the foregoing offenses and conspiracy or attempt or solicitation to commit any of the foregoing offenses.

Added by St.1970, c. 408. Amended by St.1998, c. 188, §§ 2, 3.

§ 20E. Application for witness immunity by attorney general or district attorney; hearing; representation of witness; notice or waiver; transcript

(a) A justice of the supreme judicial court, appeals court or superior court shall, at the request of the attorney general or a district attorney, and after a hearing, issue an order granting immunity to a witness, provided that such justice finds that the investigation or proceeding before the grand jury or the criminal proceeding in the supreme judicial court, appeals court or superior court involves an offense listed in section 20D and that the witness did validly refuse, or is likely to refuse, to answer questions or produce evidence on the grounds that such testimony or such evidence might tend to incriminate him. If such justice so finds, such justice shall order the witness to answer the questions or produce the evidence requested and, if he so orders, such order and the order granting immunity shall be in writing and shall become effective upon the refusal of the witness to answer any question or produce any evidence requested on the basis of his privilege against self-incrimination.

(b) The witness shall be entitled to representation by an attorney at the hearing, which shall not be open to the public. The court may appoint counsel for the witness.

(c) An application filed pursuant to this section shall, at the request of the attorney general or a district attorney, act to stay any criminal proceedings in the supreme judicial court, appeals court or superior court, but not grand jury proceedings, until such time as a justice acts upon such application; provided, however, that a justice shall conduct an expedited hearing when such application is brought after the impanelment of a jury in the superior court.

(d) When the attorney general or a district attorney brings such application, he shall, at least three days before the date fixed for hearing on his application, send by certified mail or deliver a copy of such application to the attorney general and to each other district attorney in the commonwealth. The attorney general and any of the district attorneys may waive, either orally or in writing, his right to be served with such application. The attorney general and any such district attorney may file an appearance and have the right to be heard at the hearing as herein provided.

(e) An affidavit of proof of service or, in the alternative, waiver of such service, upon each district attorney and the attorney general shall be filed with the court.

(f) A transcript shall be made of the proceedings at the hearing and a certified copy of said transcript shall be transmitted to the grand jury or the court, whichever is appropriate.

Added by St.1970, c. 408. Amended by St.1998, c. 188, § 4.

§ 20F. Repealed, 1998, 188, Sec. 5

§ 20G. Scope of immunity; copies of transcript of testimony compelled and documents furnished; availability to witness

A witness who has been granted immunity as provided in section 20E shall not be prosecuted or subjected to any penalty or forfeiture for or on account of any transaction matter, or thing concerning which he is so compelled, after having claimed his privilege against self-incrimination, to testify or produce evidence, nor shall testimony so compelled be used as evidence in any criminal or civil proceeding against him in any court of the commonwealth, except in a prosecution for perjury or contempt committed while giving testimony or producing evidence under compulsion, pursuant to section 20C or 20E.

A witness who has been granted immunity shall be given a certified copy of the transcript, if he so requests, of any testimony that he furnished in compliance with an order of the court to testify, and shall be given a copy of all documents he has furnished in compliance with such order.

A transcript of said testimony and copies of said documents shall be maintained by the supreme court, appeals court or superior court, and shall be available at the request of such witness in any subsequent proceeding involving the witness.

Added by St.1970, c. 408. Amended by St.1998, c. 188, §§ 6 to 8.

§ 20H. Contempt of court; punishment; appeal

If a witness has been granted immunity pursuant to the provisions of section twenty E by a justice of the supreme judicial court, appeals court or superior court and thereafter refuses to testify or produce evidence after being so ordered by such justice, the attorney general or district attorney shall institute contempt proceedings against such witness in the court where the alleged contempt occurred, and, after hearing or trial, if such witness is adjudged in contempt of court, he shall be punished by imprisonment in the house of correction for a term not to exceed one year or until he complies with the order of the court, whichever occurs first. The rules of practice and procedure relative to criminal appeals as provided by the Massachusetts Rules of Criminal Procedure and the Massachusetts Rules of Appellate Procedure shall apply to appeals under this section.

Added by St.1970, c. 408. Amended by St.1979, c. 344, § 8; St.1998, c. 188, §§ 9, 10.

§ 20*I*. Necessity of corroborating testimony of, or evidence produced by, person granted immunity

No defendant in any criminal proceeding shall be convicted solely on the testimony of, or the evidence produced by, a person granted immunity under the provisions of section twenty E.

Added by St.1970, c. 408.

§ 20J. Sexual assault; confidential communications with sexual assault counsellor; disclosure; discovery

As used in this section the following words, unless the context clearly requires otherwise, shall have the following meaning:—

"Rape crisis center", any office, institution or center offering assistance to victims of sexual assault and the families of such victims through crisis intervention, medical and legal counseling.

"Sexual assault counsellor", a person who is employed by or is a volunteer in a rape crisis center, has undergone thirty-five hours of training, who reports to and is under the direct control and supervision of a licensed social worker, nurse, psychiatrist, psychologist or psychotherapist and whose primary purpose is the rendering of advice, counseling or assistance to victims of sexual assault.

"Victim", a person who has suffered a sexual assault and who consults a sexual assault counsellor for the purpose of securing advice, counseling or assistance concerning a mental, physical or emotional condition caused by such sexual assault.

"Confidential communication", information transmitted in confidence by and between a victim of sexual assault and a sexual assault counsellor by a means which does not disclose the information to a person other than a person present for the benefit of the victim, or to those to whom disclosure of such information is reasonably necessary to the counseling and assisting of such victim. The term includes all information received by the sexual assault counsellor which arises out of and in the course of such counseling and assisting, including, but not limited to, reports, records, working papers or memoranda.

A sexual assault counsellor shall not disclose such confidential communication, without the prior written consent of the victim; provided, however, that nothing in this chapter shall be construed to limit the defendant's right of cross-examination of such counsellor in a civil or criminal proceeding if such counsellor testifies with such written consent.

Such confidential communications shall not be subject to discovery and shall be inadmissible in any criminal or civil proceeding without the prior written consent of the victim to whom the report, record, working paper or memorandum relates.

Added by St.1984, c. 207. Amended by St.1987, c. 477; St.1998, c. 463, § 180.

§ 20K. Domestic violence victims' counselors; confidential communications

As used in this section the following words shall unless the context clearly requires otherwise have the following meanings:—

"Abuse", causing or attempting to cause physical harm; placing another in fear of imminent physical harm; causing another to engage in sexual relations against his will by force, threat of force, or coercion.

"Confidential communication", information transmitted in confidence by and between a victim and a domestic violence victims' counselor by a means which does not disclose the information to a person other than a person present for the benefit of the victim, or to those to whom disclosure of such information is reasonably necessary to the counseling and assisting of such victim. The term includes all information received by the domestic violence victims' counselor which arises out of and in the course of such counseling and assisting, including, but not limited to, reports, records, working papers, or memoranda.

"Domestic violence victims' counselor", a person who is employed or volunteers in a domestic violence victims' program, who has undergone a minimum of twenty-five hours of training and who reports to and is under the direct control and supervision of a direct service supervisor of a domestic violence victims' program, and whose primary purpose is the rendering of advice, counseling or assistance to victims of abuse.

"Domestic violence victims' program", any refuge, shelter, office, safe home, institution or center established for the purpose of offering assistance to victims of abuse through crisis intervention, medical, legal or support counseling.

"Victim", a person who has suffered abuse and who consults a domestic violence victims' counselor for the purpose of securing advice, counseling or assistance concerning a mental, physical or emotional condition caused by such abuse.

A domestic violence victims' counselor shall not disclose such confidential communication without the prior written consent of the victim, except as hereinafter provided. Such confidential communication shall not be subject to discovery in any civil, legislative or administrative proceeding without the prior written consent of the victim to whom such confidential communication relates. In criminal actions such confidential communication shall be subject to discovery and shall be admissible as evidence but only to the extent of information contained therein which is exculpatory in relation to the defendant; provided, however, that the court shall first examine such confidential communication and shall determine whether or not such exculpatory information is therein contained before allowing such discovery or the introduction of such evidence.

Added by St.1986, c. 492.

§ 20L. Confidentiality of domestic violence victims' program and rape crisis center locations

The location and street address of all domestic violence victims' programs, as defined in section twenty K and rape crisis centers, as defined in section twenty J, shall be absolutely confidential and shall not be required to be revealed in any criminal or civil proceeding.

Added by St.1996, c. 177.

§ 21. Proof of conviction of crime to affect credibility

The conviction of a witness of a crime may be shown to affect his credibility, except as follows:

First, The record of his conviction of a misdemeanor shall not be shown for such purpose after five years from the date on which sentence on said conviction was imposed, unless he has subsequently been convicted of a crime within five years of the time of his testifying.

Second, The record of his conviction of a felony upon which no sentence was imposed or a sentence was imposed and the execution thereof suspended, or upon which a fine only was imposed, or a sentence to a reformatory prison, jail, or house of correction, shall not be shown for such purpose after ten years from the date of conviction, if no sentence was imposed, or from the date on which sentence on said conviction was imposed, whether the execution thereof was suspended or not, unless he has subsequently been convicted of a crime within ten years of the time of his testifying. For the purpose of this paragraph, a plea of guilty or a finding or verdict of guilty shall constitute a conviction within the meaning of this section.

Third, The record of his conviction of a felony upon which a state prison sentence was imposed shall not be shown for such purpose after ten years from the date of expiration of the minimum term of imprisonment imposed by the court, unless he has subsequently been convicted of a crime within ten years of the time of his testifying.

Fourth, the record of his conviction for a traffic violation upon which a fine only was imposed shall not be shown for such purpose unless he has been convicted of another crime or crimes within five years of the time of his testifying.

For the purpose of this section, any period during which the defendant was a fugitive from justice shall be excluded in determining time limitations under the provisions of this section.

[Paragraph added by 2010, 256, Sec. 105 effective May 4, 2012. See 2010, 256, Sec. 145 as amended by 2010, 359, Sec. 102.]

Upon order of the court, a party may obtain a witness's criminal offender record information from the department of criminal justice information services.

Amended by St.1950, c. 426; St.1974, c. 502; St.1982, c. 87; St.2010, c. 256, § 105, eff. May 4, 2012.

Historical and Statutory Notes

R.S.1836, c. 94, § 56.
St.1851, c. 233, § 97.
St.1852, c. 312, § 60.
G.S.1860, c. 131, § 13.
St.1870, c. 393, § 3.
P.S.1882, c. 169, § 19.
R.L.1902, c. 175, § 21.
St.1913, c. 81.
St.1914, c. 406.
St.1919, c. 268.
St.1920, c. 120.

§ 21A. Evidence of reputation

Evidence of the reputation of a person in a group with the members of which he has habitually associated in his work or business shall be admissible to the same extent and subject to the same limitations as is evidence of such reputation in a community in which he has resided.

Added by St.1947, c. 410, § 1.

§ 21B. Evidence of sex crime victim's sexual conduct; admission hearing; findings

Evidence of the reputation of a victim's sexual conduct shall not be admissible in any investigation or proceeding before a grand jury or any court of the commonwealth for a violation of sections thirteen B, 13B½, 13B¾, thirteen F, thirteen H, twenty-two, twenty-two A, 22B, 22C, twenty-three, 23A, 23B, twenty-four and twenty-four B of chapter two hundred and sixty-five or section five of chapter two hundred and seventy-two. Evidence of specific instances of a victim's sexual conduct in such an investigation or proceeding shall not be admissible except evidence of the victim's sexual conduct with the defendant or evidence of recent conduct of the victim alleged to be the cause of any physical feature, characteristic, or condition of the victim; provided, however, that such evidence shall be admissible only after an in camera hearing on a written motion for admission of same and an offer of proof. If, after said hearing, the court finds that the weight and relevancy of said evidence is sufficient to outweigh its prejudicial effect to the victim, the evidence shall be admitted; otherwise not. If the proceeding is a trial with jury, said hearing shall be held in the absence of the jury. The finding of the court shall be in writing and filed but shall not be made available to the jury.

Added by St.1977, c. 110. Amended by St.1983, c. 367; St.2010, c. 267, §§ 46 to 48, eff. Nov. 5, 2010.

§ 22. Cross-examination of adverse party; corporation's agent as adverse party

A party who calls the adverse party as a witness shall be allowed to cross-examine him. In case the adverse party is a corporation, an officer or agent thereof, so called as a witness, shall be deemed such an adverse party for the purposes of this section.

Amended by St.1932, c. 97, § 1.

Historical and Statutory Notes

St.1870, c. 393, § 4.
P.S.1882, c. 169, § 20.
R.L.1902, c. 175, § 22.

§ 23. Impeachment of party's own witness

The party who produces a witness shall not impeach his credit by evidence of bad character, but may contradict him by other evidence, and may also prove that he has made at other times statements inconsistent with his present testimony; but before proof of such inconsistent statements is given, the circumstances thereof sufficient to designate the particular occasion shall be mentioned to the witness, and he shall be asked if he has made such statements, and, if so, shall be allowed to explain them.

Historical and Statutory Notes

St.1869, c. 425.
P.S.1882, c. 169, § 22.
R.L.1902, c. 175, § 24.

§ 23A. Admissibility of written or recorded statements of party to personal injury action

In any action to recover damages for personal injuries or consequential damages, so called, resulting therefrom, no statement in writing signed by any party to the action or statement taken on a recording instrument, concerning the facts out of which the cause of action arose, given by such party, or a person in his behalf, to any other party to the action, or to his agent or attorney, or to the insurer of such other party, or to the agent or attorney of such insurer, shall be admissible in evidence in, or referred to at, the trial of such action or in any proceeding connected therewith unless a copy of such statement or verbatim written transcription of such recorded statement is furnished to the party making the same or to his attorney within ten days after written request therefor made by such party or attorney to the adverse party or his attorney, or within such further time as the court may allow on motion and notice.

Added by St.1945, c. 424, § 1. Amended by St.1953, c. 242; St.1964, c. 537.

§ 23B. Accused; statements made while undergoing psychiatric examination; admissibility

In the trial of an indictment or complaint for any crime, no statement made by a defendant therein subjected to psychiatric examination pursuant to sections fifteen or sixteen of chapter one hundred and twenty-three for the purposes of such examination or treatment shall be admissible in evidence against him on any issue other than that of his mental condition, nor shall it be admissible in evidence against him on that issue if such statement constitutes a confession of guilt of the crime charged.

Added by St.1958, c. 256. Amended by St.1970, c. 888, § 27.

§ 23C. Work product of mediator confidential; confidential communications; exception; mediator defined

All memoranda, and other work product prepared by a mediator and a mediator's case files shall be confidential and not subject to disclosure in any judicial or administrative proceeding involving any of the parties to any mediation to which such materials apply. Any communication made in the course of and relating to the subject matter of any mediation and which is made in the presence of such mediator by any participant, mediator or other person shall be a confidential communication and not subject to disclosure in any judicial or administrative proceeding; provided, however, that the provisions of this section shall not apply to the mediation of labor disputes.

For the purposes of this section a "mediator" shall mean a person not a party to a dispute who enters into a written agreement with the parties to assist them in resolving their disputes and has completed at least thirty hours of training in mediation and who either has four years of professional experience as a mediator or is accountable to a dispute resolution organization which has been in existence for at least three years or one who has been appointed to mediate by a judicial or governmental body.

Added by St.1985, c. 325.

§ 23D. Admissibility of benevolent statements, writings or gestures relating to accident victims

As used in this section the following words shall, unless the context clearly requires otherwise, have the following meanings:

"Accident", an occurrence resulting in injury or death to one or more persons which is not the result of willful action by a party.

"Benevolent gestures", actions which convey a sense of compassion or commiseration emanating from humane impulses.

"Family", the spouse, parent, grandparent, stepmother, stepfather, child, grandchild, brother, sister, half brother, half sister, adopted children of parent, or spouse's parents of an injured party.

Statements, writings or benevolent gestures expressing sympathy or a general sense of benevolence relating to the pain, suffering or death of a person involved in an accident and made to such person or to the family of such person shall be inadmissible as evidence of an admission of liability in a civil action.

Added by St.1986, c. 652.

§ 23E. Alternative procedure for determining competency of witnesses with an intellectual disability

(a) For the purposes of this section, the following words shall have the following meanings, unless the context clearly requires otherwise:—

"Witnesses with an intellectual disability", a witness in a proceeding whom the presiding justice has found after hearing, as provided in paragraph (1) of subsection (b), to have an intellectual disability.

"Intellectual disability", substantial limitations in present functioning manifesting before age eighteen and characterized by significantly subaverage intellectual functioning, existing concurrently with related limitations in two or more of the following applicable skill areas: communication, self-care, home living, social skills, community use, self-direction, health and safety, functional academics, leisure and work.

(b)(1) In any judicial proceeding in which a witness with an intellectual disability will testify, the court, on its own motion or on motion of the proponent of the witness with an intellectual disability and after hearing on the witness's competency to testify, may order the use of alternative procedures for taking testimony of the witness with an intellectual disability; provided, however, that the court finds at the time of the order, by clear and convincing evidence in the case of a criminal proceeding, and by a preponderance of the evidence in the case of a noncriminal proceeding, that the witness with an intellectual disability is likely, as a result of submitting to usual procedures for determining competency or as a result of testifying in open court, as the case may be, (i) to suffer severe psychological or emotional trauma; or (ii) to suffer a temporary loss of or regression in cognitive or behavioral functioning or communicative abilities, such that his ability to testify will be significantly impaired. If the court so finds, the court may order the use of alternative procedures for determining competency to testify or for taking testimony of the witness with an intellectual disability including, but not limited to, the following:

(i) permitting a person familiar to the witness, such as a family member, clinician, counselor, social worker or friend, to sit near or next to such witness;

(ii) permitting the witness with mental retardation to testify in court but off the witness stand; provided, however, that if the proceeding is a bench proceeding, testimony may be taken at another location within the courthouse but outside the courtroom; and, provided further, that if the proceeding is a jury trial, testimony may be taken on videotape out of the presence of the jury or in a location chosen by the court or by agreement of the parties; or

(iii) combining alternative procedures provided in clauses (i) and (ii).

(c) When the proceedings are not criminal or juvenile delinquency related, testimony taken by videotape pursuant to an order under paragraph (1) of subsection (b) shall be taken in the presence of the judge, counsel for all parties and such other persons as the court may allow. Counsel shall be given the opportunity to examine or cross-examine the witness with mental retardation to the same extent as he would be permitted if ordinary procedures had been followed.

(d) When the proceedings are criminal or juvenile delinquency related, the defendant shall have the right to be present during the taking of the testimony, to have an unobstructed view of the witness with an intellectual disability, and to have the witness's view of the defendant be unobstructed.

(e) If the court orders that the testimony of the witness with an intellectual disability be videotaped out of the presence of the jury, the videotape shall be shown in court to the jury in the presence of the judge, the parties and the parties' counsel. The videotape shall be marked as an exhibit and retained by the court as part of the record of the case.

(f) Testimony taken by alternative procedures authorized by this section shall be admissible as substantive evidence to the same extent as and in lieu of live testimony by the witness in any proceeding in which such testimony is taken.

(g) The witness requesting that testimony be taken by videotape shall bear the responsibility of producing an acceptable videotape of the testimony. The commonwealth shall reimburse such witness for reasonable costs of producing such videotape. Each party shall be afforded an opportunity to view the recording before it is shown in the courtroom.

(h) The fact that the witness with an intellectual disability has been found in a court proceeding to be incompetent to make informed decisions of a personal, medical or financial nature or that he is under a guardianship or conservatorship shall not preclude such witness from testifying if he is found to be competent to testify and shall not preclude a determination of competency to testify.

(i) A witness shall not be denied the benefit of appropriate alternative procedures provided by this section and the court shall allow such additional time or continuances to permit application of such procedures.

(j) A person with expertise in persons with an intellectual disability may be called by the proponent of the witness to testify in all relevant matters, including the competency determination of such witness.

(k) Nothing in this section shall be construed to prohibit a court from using other appropriate means consistent with this section and any other general or special law and with the defendant's rights to accomplish the purposes of this section.

Added by St.1994, c. 352, § 1. Amended by St.2010, c. 239, §§ 68 to 70, eff. Nov. 2, 2010.

§ 23F. Admissibility of past physical, sexual or psychological abuse of defendant

In the trial of criminal cases charging the use of force against another where the issue of defense of self or another, defense of duress or coercion, or accidental harm is asserted, a defendant shall be permitted to introduce either or both of the following in establishing the reasonableness of the defendant's apprehension that death or serious bodily injury was imminent, the reasonableness of the defendant's belief that he had availed himself of all available means to avoid physical combat or the reasonableness of a defendant's perception of the amount of force necessary to deal with the perceived threat:

(a) evidence that the defendant is or has been the victim of acts of physical, sexual or psychological harm or abuse;

(b) evidence by expert testimony regarding the common pattern in abusive relationships; the nature and effects of physical, sexual or psychological abuse and typical responses thereto, including how those effects relate to the perception of the imminent nature of the threat of death or serious bodily harm; the relevant facts and circumstances which form the basis for such opinion; and evidence whether the defendant displayed characteristics common to victims of abuse.

Nothing in this section shall be interpreted to preclude the introduction of evidence or expert testimony as described in clause (a) or (b) in any civil or criminal action where such evidence or expert testimony is otherwise now admissible.

Added by St.1996, c. 450, § 248.

§ 81. Criminal proceedings; out-of-court statements describing sexual contact; admissibility

(a) An out-of-court statement of a child under the age of ten describing an act of sexual contact performed on or with the child, the circumstances under which it occurred, or which identifies the perpetrator shall be admissible as substantive evidence in any criminal proceeding; provided, however, that the statement is offered as evidence of a material fact and is more probative on the point for which it is offered than any other evidence which the proponent can procure through reasonable efforts; the person to whom the statement was made or who heard the child make the statement testifies; the judge finds pursuant to subsection (b) that the child is unavailable as a witness; and the judge finds pursuant to subsection (c) that the statement is reliable.

(b) The proponent of such statement shall demonstrate a diligent and good faith effort to produce the child and shall bear the burden of showing unavailability. A finding of unavailability shall be supported by specific findings on the record, describing facts with particularity, demonstrating that:

(1) the child is unable to be present or to testify because of death or physical or mental illness or infirmity; or

(2) by a ruling of the court, the child is exempt on the ground of privilege from testifying concerning the subject matter of such statement; or

(3) the child testifies to a lack of memory of the subject matter of such statement; or

(4) the child is absent from the hearing and the proponent of such statement has been unable to procure the attendance of the child by process or by other reasonable means; or

(5) the court finds, based upon expert testimony from a treating psychiatrist, psychologist, or clinician, that testifying would be likely to cause severe psychological or emotional trauma to the child; or

(6) the child is not competent to testify.

(c) If a finding of unavailability is made, the out-of-court statement shall be admitted if the judge further finds: (1) after holding a separate hearing, that such statement was made under oath, that it was accurately recorded and preserved, and there was sufficient opportunity to cross-examine; or (2) after holding a separate hearing and, where practicable and where not inconsistent with the best interests of the child, meeting with the child, that such statement was made under circumstances inherently demonstrating a special guarantee of reliability.

For the purposes of finding circumstances demonstrating reliability pursuant to clause (2) of subsection (c), a judge may consider whether the relator documented the child witness's statement, and shall consider the following factors:

(i) the clarity of the statement, meaning, the child's capacity to observe, remember, and give expression to that which such child has seen, heard, or experienced; provided, however, that a finding under this clause shall be supported by expert testimony from a treating psychiatrist, psychologist, or clinician;

(ii) the time, content and circumstances of the statement;

(iii) the child's sincerity and ability to appreciate the consequences of such statement.

(d) An out-of-court statement which is admissible by common law or by statute shall remain admissible notwithstanding the provisions of this section.

Added by St.1990, c. 339.

TITLE IV

CERTAIN WRITS AND PROCEEDINGS IN SPECIAL CASES

CHAPTER 258B

RIGHTS OF VICTIMS AND WITNESSES OF CRIME

Chapter 258B of the General Laws was added by St.1983, c. 694, § 2.

The section headings for the General Laws in this pamphlet have been editorially supplied.

§ 1. Definitions

As used in this chapter, the following words shall have the following meanings, unless the context otherwise requires:—

"Board", the victim and witness assistance board as established in section four.

"Court", a forum established under the General Laws for the adjudication of criminal and delinquency complaints, indictments and civil motor vehicle infractions.

"Crime", an act committed in the commonwealth which would constitute a crime if committed by a competent adult including any act which may result in an adjudication of delinquency.

"Disposition", the sentencing or determination of penalty or punishment to be imposed upon a person convicted of a crime or found delinquent or against whom a finding of sufficient facts for conviction or finding of delinquency is made.

"Family member", a spouse, child, stepchild, sibling, parent, stepparent, dependent, as defined in section one of chapter two hundred and fifty-eight C, or legal guardian of a victim, unless such family member has been charged in relation to the crime against the victim.

"Prosecutor", the attorney general, assistant attorneys general, district attorney, assistant district attorneys, police prosecutors, other attorneys specially appointed to aid in the prosecution of a case, law students approved for practice pursuant to and acting as authorized by the rules of the supreme judicial court, or any other person acting on behalf of the commonwealth, including victim-witness advocates.

"Restitution", money or services which a court orders a defendant to pay or render to a victim as part of the disposition.

"Victim", any natural person who suffers direct or threatened physical, emotional, or financial harm as the result of the commission or attempted commission of a crime or delinquency offense, as demonstrated by the issuance of a complaint or indictment, the family members of such person if the person is a minor, incompetent or deceased, and, for relevant provisions of this chapter, a person who is the subject of a case reported to a prosecutor pursuant to section eighteen of chapter nineteen A, sections five and nine of chapter nineteen C, and section fifty-one B of chapter one hundred and nineteen, and the family members of such person if the person is a minor, incompetent or deceased.

"Victim-witness advocate", an individual employed by a prosecutor, the board, or other criminal justice agency to provide necessary and essential services in carrying out policies and procedures under this chapter.

"Witness", any person who has been or is expected to be summoned to testify for the prosecution whether or not any action or proceeding has yet been commenced.

Added by St.1983, c. 694, § 2. Amended by St.1985, c. 794, § 8; St.1995, c. 24, §§ 2 to 4; St.1996, c. 450, § 251.

§ 2. Eligibility of victim for services

Prosecutors shall not be precluded from providing, subject to appropriation, services under this chapter to any natural person or family member of such natural person who suffers direct or threatened physical, emotional or financial harm as the result of the commission or attempted commission of a crime or delinquency offense in which complaints or indictments have not been issued.

Added by St.1983, c. 694, § 2. Amended by St.1995, c. 24, § 5.

§ 3. Rights afforded victims, witnesses or family members

To provide victims a meaningful role in the criminal justice system, victims and witnesses of crime, or in the event the victim is deceased, the family members of the victim, shall be afforded the following basic and fundamental rights, to the greatest extent possible and subject to appropriation and to available resources, with priority for services to be provided to victims of crimes against the person and crimes where physical injury to a person results:

(a) for victims, to be informed by the prosecutor about the victim's rights in the criminal process, including but not limited to the rights provided under this chapter. At the beginning of the criminal justice process, the prosecutor shall provide an explanation to the victim of how a case progresses through the criminal justice system, what the victim's role is in the process, what the system may expect from the victim, why the system requires this, and, if the victim requests, the prosecutor shall periodically apprise the victim of significant developments in the case;

(b) for victims and family members, to be present at all court proceedings related to the offense committed against the victim, unless the victim or family member is to testify and the court determines that the person's testimony would be materially affected by hearing other testimony at trial and orders the person to be excluded from the courtroom during certain other testimony;

(c) for victims and witnesses, to be notified by the prosecutor, in a timely manner, when a court proceeding to which they have been summoned will not go on as scheduled, provided that such changes are known in advance. In order to notify victims and witnesses, a form shall be provided to them by the prosecutor for the purpose of maintaining a current telephone number and address. The victim or witness shall thereafter maintain with the prosecutor a current telephone number and address;

(d) for victims and witnesses, to be provided with information by the prosecutor as to the level of protection available and to receive protection from the local law enforcement agencies from harm and threats of harm arising out of their cooperation with law enforcement and prosecution efforts;

(e) for victims, to be informed by the prosecutor of financial assistance and other social services available to victims, including information relative to applying for such assistance or services;

(f) for victims and witnesses, to a prompt disposition of the case in which they are involved as a victim or a witness;

(g) for victims, to confer with the prosecutor before the commencement of the trial, before any hearing on motions by the defense to obtain psychiatric or other confidential records, and before the filing of a nolle prosequi or other act by the commonwealth terminating the prosecution or before the submission of the commonwealth's proposed sentence recommendation to the court. The prosecutor shall inform the court of the victim's position, if known, regarding the prosecutor's sentence recommendation. The right of the victim to confer with the prosecutor does not include the authority to direct the prosecution of the case;

(h) for victims and witnesses, to be informed of the right to request confidentiality in the criminal justice system. Upon the court's approval of such request, no law enforcement agency, prosecutor, defense counsel, or parole, probation or corrections official may disclose or state in open court, except among themselves, the residential address, telephone number, or place of employment or school of the victim, a victim's family member, or a witness, except as otherwise ordered by the court. The court may enter such other orders or conditions to maintain limited disclosure of the information as it deems appropriate to protect the privacy and safety of victims, victims' family members and witnesses;

(i) for victims, family members and witnesses to be provided, by the court as provided in section 17 of chapter 211B, with a secure waiting area or room which is separate from the waiting area of the defendant or the defendant's family, friends, attorneys or witnesses and separate from the district attorney's office; provided, however, that the court shall designate a waiting area at each courthouse; and provided further, that designation of those areas shall be made in accordance with the implementation plan developed by the task force.

(j) for victims and witnesses, to be informed by the court and the prosecutor of procedures to be followed in order to apply for and receive any witness fee to which they are entitled;

(k) for victims and witnesses, to be provided, where appropriate, with employer and creditor intercession services by the prosecutor to seek employer cooperation in minimizing employees' loss of pay and other benefits resulting from their participation in the criminal justice process, and to seek consideration from creditors if the victim is unable, temporarily, to continue payments;

(*l*) for victims or witnesses who have received a subpoena to testify, to be free from discharge or penalty or threat of discharge or penalty by his employer by reason of his attendance as a witness at a criminal proceeding. A victim or witness who notifies his employer of his subpoena to appear as a witness prior to his attendance, shall not on account of his absence from employment by reason of such witness service be subject to discharge or penalty by his employer. Any employer or agent of said employer who discharges or disciplines or continues to threaten to discharge or discipline a victim or witness because that victim or witness is subpoenaed to attend court for the purpose of giving testimony may be subject to the sanctions stated in section fourteen A of chapter two hundred and sixty-eight;

(m) for victims and witnesses, to be informed of the right to submit to or decline an interview by defense counsel or anyone acting on the defendant's behalf, except when responding to lawful process, and, if the victim or witness decides to submit to an interview, the right to impose reasonable conditions on the conduct of the interview;

(n) for victims, to confer with the probation officer prior to the filing of the full presentence report. If the victim is not available or declines to confer, the probation officer shall record that information in the report. If the probation officer is not able to confer with the victim or the victim declines to confer, the probation officer shall note in the full presentence report the reason why the probation officer did not make contact with the victim;

(*o*) for victims, to request that restitution be an element of the final disposition of a case and to obtain assistance from the prosecutor in the documentation of the victim's losses. If restitution is ordered as part of a case disposition, the victim has the right to receive from the probation department a copy of the schedule of restitution payments and the name and telephone number of the probation officer or other official who is responsible for supervising the defendant's payments. If the offender seeks to modify the restitution order, the offender's supervising probation officer shall provide notice to the victim and the victim shall have the right to be heard at any hearing relative to the proposed modification.

(p) for victims, to be heard through an oral and written victim impact statement at sentencing or the disposition of the case against the defendant about the effects of the crime on the victim and as to a recommended sentence, pursuant to section four B of chapter two hundred and seventy-nine, and to be heard at any other time deemed appropriate by the court. The victim also has a right to submit the victim impact statement to the parole board for inclusion in its records regarding the perpetrator of the crime;

(q) for victims, to be informed by the prosecutor of the final disposition of the case, including, where applicable, an explanation of the type of sentence imposed by the court and a copy of the court order setting forth the conditions of probation or other supervised or unsupervised release within thirty days of establishing the conditions, with the name and telephone number of the probation officer, if any, assigned to the defendant;

(r) for victims, to have any personal property that was stolen or taken for evidentiary purposes, except contraband, property subject to evidentiary analysis, and property the ownership of which is disputed, returned by the court, the prosecutor or law enforcement agencies within ten days of its taking or recovery if it is not needed for law enforcement or prosecution purposes or as expeditiously as possible when said property is no longer needed for law enforcement or prosecution purposes;

(s) for victims, to be informed by the parole board of information regarding the defendant's parole eligibility and status in the criminal justice system;

(t) for victims, to be informed in advance by the appropriate custodial authority whenever the defendant receives a temporary, provisional or final release from custody, whenever a defendant is moved from a secure facility to a less-secure facility, and whenever the defendant escapes from custody. The victim shall be informed by the prosecutor about notification rights and the certification process required to access the criminal offender record information files. Persons requesting such notice must provide the appropriate authority with current information as to their address and telephone number;

(u) for victims, to be informed that the victim may have a right to pursue a civil action for damages relating to the crime, regardless of whether the court has ordered the defendant to make restitution to the victim.

(v) for one family member of a victim of a homicide, which the matter before the court is related, to possess in the courtroom a photograph, that is not of itself of an inflammatory nature, of the deceased victim that is not larger than eight by ten inches; provided, however, that at no time may the photograph be exposed or in anyway displayed in the presence of any member of the jury, or the jury pool from which a jury is to be selected in a particular matter; provided, further, that nothing in this section shall preclude the admission into evidence of a photograph that the court deems relevant and material.

There shall be conspicuously posted in all courthouses and police stations a summary of the rights afforded under this section. The victim and witness assistance board, pursuant to section 4, shall devise and provide posters to satisfy this requirement to court officials and police station personnel, and, upon request and at the discretion of the office and board, to any other institution or organization to post and maintain in space accessible to the general public. The board shall develop such posters in a variety of languages as determined by the Massachusetts office for victim assistance. Upon request, the board will respond, to the extent possible, to any requests for additional language translations of such posters.

Added by St.1983, c. 694, § 2. Amended by St.1986, c. 420; St.1989, c. 233, § 1; St.1995, c. 24, § 5; St.1996, c. 200, § 34; St.1998, c. 463, § 189; St.2010, c. 131, §§ 99, 100, eff. July 1, 2010.

§ 4. Victim and witness assistance board

There is hereby established a victim and witness assistance board, to consist of five members who shall serve without compensation. Notwithstanding any provision of section six of chapter two hundred and sixty-eight A to the contrary, the board shall consist of the attorney general or his designee who shall be chairman, two district attorneys who shall be appointed by the governor, and two members of the public who shall be appointed by the governor, of whom one shall be a victim. The members of the board first appointed shall serve as follows: of the district attorneys appointed by the governor, one shall serve for three years, and one shall serve for one year, of the members of the public appointed by the governor, one shall serve for three years and one shall serve for two years. The successor of each such member shall serve for a term of three years and until his successor is duly appointed and qualified, except that any person appointed to fill a vacancy shall serve only for the unexpired term. Any member of the board shall be eligible for reappointment.

The board shall by majority vote of its members, appoint an executive director who shall serve, subject to appropriation, at such rate of compensation as the board directs for a term of three years unless removed for cause by a vote of four members of the board. The executive director, subject to appropriation, shall have the power to hire such staff, subject to the approval of the board, as is needed to fulfill the powers and duties of the board. The executive director shall have such other powers and duties as the board may delegate to him.

The provisions of chapter thirty-one shall not apply to the executive director or any employee of the board.

The board shall review program plans, annual reports, and the implementation and operation of programs as described in this chapter. The board shall promulgate rules for the preparation and review of such program plans and annual reports.

In addition to the foregoing, the board shall:

(a) have printed and shall make available to social service agencies, medical facilities, and law enforcement agencies, cards, posters, brochures or other materials explaining the victim and witness rights and services established under this chapter;

(b) assist hospitals, clinics and other medical facilities, whether public or private, in disseminating information giving notice of the rights established under this chapter. This assistance may include providing informational materials including posters suitable to be displayed in emergency and waiting rooms;

(c) assist law enforcement agencies in familiarizing all of their officers and employees with the crime victims' rights as provided under this chapter. This assistance may include supplying informational literature on this subject to be utilized as part of the training curriculum for all trainee officers; and

(d) assist all local law enforcement agencies in establishing procedures whereby expedient notification is given to victims and witnesses, as defined under this chapter, of the rights provided under this chapter. In municipalities which do not have a local law enforcement agency, the board shall establish procedures whereby it, in cooperation with the state police, shall give notice to victims of crimes as provided in this section.

Added by St.1983, c. 694, § 2. Amended by St.1986, c. 557, § 186; St.1991, c. 138, § 274; St.1993, c. 478, § 4.

§ 5. Programs created and maintained by district attorneys; services

Each district attorney shall create and maintain, to the extent reasonably possible and subject to the available resources, a program to afford victims and witnesses of crimes the rights and services described in this chapter. Those services shall include but not be limited to the following:

(a) court appearance notification services, including cancellations of appearances;

(b) informational services relative to the availability and collection of witness fees, victim compensation and restitution;

(c) escort and other transportation services related to the investigation or prosecution of the case, if necessary;

(d) case process notification services;

(e) employer intercession services;

(f) expedited return of property services;

(g) protection services;

(h) family support services including child and other dependent care services;

(i) waiting facilities; and

(j) social service referrals.

Added by St.1983, c. 694, § 2.

§ 6. Program plan

Each district attorney shall submit annually on January fifteenth to the board, the secretary of administration and finance and the house and senate committees on ways and means, a program plan to be implemented within the district attorney's jurisdiction. The program plan shall include, but not be limited to: a description of the services to be provided to victims and witnesses in each judicial district within the district attorney's jurisdiction; the personnel or agencies responsible for providing individual services and related administrative programs; proposed staffing for the program; proposed education, training and experience requirements for program staff and, where appropriate, the staff of agencies providing individual services and related administrative services; and a proposed budget for implementing the program. The district attorney shall include in the annual program plan a detailed report on the operation of the program, as well as a detailed report of deposits and expenditures of all funds made available to said district attorney for the preceding fiscal year and the current fiscal year, and proposed for the upcoming fiscal year, pursuant to section nine.

Added by St.1983, c. 694, § 2. Amended by St.1991, c. 138, § 208; St.1993, c. 110, § 228; St.1994, c. 60, § 168.

§ 7. Interagency cooperation

The district attorney, local law enforcement agencies, local social service agencies, and court shall cooperate to afford victims and witnesses of crimes, the rights and services described in this chapter.

Added by St.1983, c. 694, § 2.

§ 8. Assessments imposed by court

The court shall impose an assessment of no less than $90 against any person who has attained the age of seventeen years and who is convicted of a felony or against whom a finding of sufficient facts for a conviction is made on a complaint charging a felony. The court shall impose an assessment of $50 against any person who has attained the age of seventeen and who is convicted of a misdemeanor or against whom a finding of sufficient facts for a conviction is made on a complaint charging a misdemeanor. The court shall impose an assessment of $45 against any person who has attained the age of fourteen years and who is adjudicated a delinquent child or against whom a finding of sufficient facts for a finding of delinquency is made. The court, including the clerk-magistrate, or the registrar of motor vehicles shall impose an assessment of $45 against any violator who fails to pay the scheduled civil assessment for a civil motor vehicle infraction or to request a noncriminal hearing within the twenty day period provided for in subsection (A) of section three of chapter ninety C, except where the person is required by law to exercise the right to pay before a justice. When multiple civil motor vehicle infractions arising from a single incident are charged, the total assessment shall not exceed $75; provided, however, that the total assessment against a person who has not attained seventeen years shall not exceed thirty dollars. In the discretion of the court or the clerk magistrate in the case of a civil motor vehicle infraction that has not been heard by or brought before a justice, a civil motor vehicle assessment imposed pursuant to this section which would cause the person against whom the assessment is imposed severe financial hardship, may be reduced or waived. An assessment other than for a civil motor vehicle infraction imposed pursuant to this section may be reduced or waived only upon a written finding of fact that such payment would cause the person against whom the assessment is imposed severe financial hardship. Such a finding shall be made independently of a finding of indigency for purposes of appointing counsel. If the person is sentenced to a correctional facility in the commonwealth and the assessment has not been paid, the court shall note the assessment on the mittimus.

All such assessments made shall be collected by the court or by the registrar, as the case may be, and shall be transmitted monthly to the state treasurer. If the person convicted is sentenced to a correctional facility in the commonwealth, the superintendent or sheriff of the facility shall deduct any part or all of the monies earned or received by any inmate and held by the correctional facility, to satisfy the victim and witness assessment, and shall transmit such monies to the court monthly. The assessment from any conviction or adjudication of delinquency which is subsequently overturned on appeal shall be refunded by the court to the person whose conviction or adjudication of delinquency is overturned. Said court shall deduct such funds from the assessments transmitted to the state treasurer. Assessments pursuant to this section shall be in addition to any other fines or restitution imposed in any disposition.

When a determination of the order of priority for payments required of a defendant must be made by the court or other criminal justice system personnel required to assess and collect such fines, assessments or other payments, the victim and witness assessment mandated by this section shall be the defendant's first obligation.

Added by St.1983, c. 694, § 2. Amended by St.1985, c. 794, § 9; St.1989, c. 362, § 1; St.1990, c. 150, § 341A; St.1991, c. 138, §§ 209, 210; St.1994, c. 60, §§ 169 to 171; St.1996, c. 151, §§ 485, 486; St.2002, c. 184, §§ 125 to 128.

§ 9. Deposit of assessments

Any assessment imposed pursuant to section eight shall be deposited in the Victim and Witness Assistance Fund, established by section forty-nine of chapter ten. In addition, the board may also apply for and accept on behalf of the commonwealth any private grants, bequests, gifts or contributions to further aid in financing programs or policies of the division. Such funds shall be received by the state treasurer on behalf of the commonwealth and deposited into said fund; provided, that said board shall submit to the house and senate committees on ways and means, as necessary, a report detailing all such amounts as deposited into said fund. All monies deposited into said fund that are unexpended at the end of the year shall not revert to the General Fund. The proceeds of the fund shall be made available, subject to appropriation, to the district attorney victim and witness programs, to the attorney general and the parole board for programs serving crime victims and witnesses.

Added by St.1983, c. 694, § 2. Amended by St.1989, c. 362, § 2; St.1991, c. 138, § 212; St.1993, c. 478, § 5; St.1994, c. 60, § 172.

§ 10. Construction

Nothing in this chapter shall be construed as creating an entitlement or a cause of action on behalf of any person against any public employee, public agency, the commonwealth or any agency responsible for the enforcement of rights and provision of services set forth in this chapter.

Added by St.1983, c. 694, § 2. Amended by St.1995, c. 24, § 6.

§ 11. Duration of rights and duties

The rights and duties established under this chapter shall continue to be enforceable until the final disposition of the charges, including acquittal or dismissal of charges, all post-conviction release proceedings, post-conviction relief proceedings, all appellate proceedings, and the discharge of all criminal proceedings relating to restitution. If a defendant's conviction or adjudication of delinquency is reversed and the case is returned to the trial court for further proceedings, the victim shall have the same rights that applied to the criminal or delinquency proceedings that led to the appeal or other post-conviction relief proceeding.

Added by St.1995, c. 24, § 6.

§ 12. Assurance of rights; assistance by criminal justice agencies

Law enforcement agencies, prosecutors, judges, probation officers, clerks and corrections officials shall assure that victims of crime are afforded the rights established in this chapter.

Unless specifically stated otherwise, the requirements to provide information to the victim may be satisfied by either written or oral communication with the victim. The person responsible for providing such information shall do so in a timely manner and shall advise the victim of any significant changes in such information.

The board shall assist the prosecutors in providing the rights set forth in this chapter by preparing for distribution to victims written materials explaining the rights and services to which they are entitled.

A victim or family member may request assistance from the board in obtaining the rights provided under this chapter by the court or by any criminal justice agency responsible for implementing such rights. In order to address the victim's concerns, the board may seek assistance from the district attorney governing the jurisdiction in which the crime against the victim is alleged to have been committed or from the attorney general.

A victim or family member may request assistance from the district attorney or the attorney general in obtaining the rights provided under this chapter by the court or by any criminal justice agency responsible for implementing such rights.

Added by St.1995, c. 24, § 6.

§ 13. Failure to provide rights, privileges, or notice to victim; no grounds for appeal of or objection to conviction

A defendant or person convicted of a criminal or delinquency offense against the victim shall have no standing to object to any failure to comply with this chapter, and the failure to provide a right, privilege or notice to a victim under this chapter shall not be grounds for the defendant or person convicted of a criminal or delinquency offense to seek to have the conviction or sentence set aside.

Added by St.1995, c. 24, § 6.

CHAPTER 258C

COMPENSATION OF VICTIMS OF VIOLENT CRIMES

Chapter 258C of the General Laws was added by St.1993, c. 478, § 6.

The section headings for the General Laws in this pamphlet have been editorially supplied.

§ 1. Definitions

As used in this chapter, the following words shall, unless the context clearly requires otherwise, have the following meanings:—

"Claim", an application for compensation under this chapter.

"Claimant", a person who files a claim for compensation under this chapter.

"Crime", an act committed by a person which, if committed by a mentally competent, criminally responsible adult who has no legal exemption or defense, would constitute a crime. Crime shall apply to an act occurring within the commonwealth, and to an act of terrorism, as defined in 18 USC section 2331, occurring outside the United States or territories against a resident of the commonwealth.

"Crime scene cleanup", the removal of, or the attempted removal of, blood or other stains that are the direct result of the commission of a crime or other dirt and debris caused by the processing of the crime scene; provided, however, that crime scene cleanup shall not include the replacement or repair of property damaged during the commission of the crime, in accordance with section 4.

"Department", the department of the attorney general.

"Dependent", mother, father, spouse, spouse's mother, spouse's father, child, grandchild, adopted child, child born out of wedlock, brother, sister, niece or nephew, or other person who is wholly or partially dependent for support upon the victim at the time of his injury or death due to a crime alleged in a claim made pursuant to this chapter.

"Division", the division of victim compensation and assistance within the department of the attorney general, established in section 11K of chapter 12.

"Family", the spouse, parent, grandparent, stepmother, stepfather, child, grandchild, brother, sister, half brother, half sister, adopted child of parents, or spouse's parents of the victim.

"Medical care", the medical, psychological, surgical, dental, optometric, chiropractic, podiatric and hospital care provided to a victim including, but not limited to, medicines, medical, dental and surgical supplies, crutches, artificial members and appliances and training in the use of artificial members and appliances.

"Offender", an adult or juvenile person who commits a crime as defined in this section for which a claimant seeks compensation.

"Out-of-pocket loss", unreimbursed or unreimbursable expenses for services eligible for compensation pursuant to this chapter.

"Security measures", the replacement, repair or installation of locks, windows or other security devices deemed to be reasonably necessary for the promotion of the victim's safety by the program director after taking into consideration the nature of the crime in accordance with section 4.

"State", a state of the United States, the district of Columbia, the commonwealth of Puerto Rico or any other possession or territory of the United States.

"Victim", a person who suffers personal physical or psychological injury or death:

(a) as a direct result of a crime as defined in this section;

(b) as a result of attempting to assist a person against whom a crime was attempted or committed; or

(c) as a result of efforts to prevent a crime or an attempted crime from occurring in his presence or to apprehend a person who had committed a crime in his presence.

Added by St.1993, c. 478, § 6. Amended by St.1997, c. 43, § 146; St.2002, c. 438, § 33; St.2010, c. 256, §§ 107, 108, eff. Nov. 4, 2010.

§ 2. Eligibility for compensation

(a) No compensation shall be paid under this chapter unless the division finds that a crime was committed and that such crime directly resulted in personal physical or psychological injury to, or death of, the victim.

(b) No compensation shall be paid under this chapter unless the claimant demonstrates that the crime was reported to the police or other law enforcement authorities or to an agency or entity obligated by law to report complaints of criminal misconduct to law enforcement authorities. Except in the case where the division finds such report to have been delayed for good cause, such report shall have been made within five days after the occurrence of such crime.

(c) A claimant shall be eligible for compensation only if such claimant cooperates with law enforcement authorities in the investigation and prosecution of the crime in which the victim was injured or killed unless the claimant demonstrates that he possesses or possessed a reasonable excuse for failing to cooperate.

(d) A claimant shall not be eligible for compensation if such compensation would unjustly benefit the offender; provided, however, that a claimant shall not, except pursuant to regulations enacted in accordance with section four to prevent unjust enrichment, be denied compensation because of such claimant's or victim's familial relationship with the offender or because of the sharing of a residence by the victim or claimant and the offender.

(e) An offender or an accomplice of an offender shall not be eligible to receive compensation with respect to a crime committed by an offender. To the extent that the victim's acts or conduct provoked or contributed to the injuries, the division shall reduce or deny an award to the claimant or claimants in accordance with regulations enacted pursuant to section four.

[There is no subsection (f).]

(g) The claimant may retain counsel under this chapter. Attorneys fees shall be deducted from, and not in addition to, the total award for compensation. No attorneys fees shall be paid unless the attorney submits an affidavit which sets forth the hours worked and the services rendered for representing the claimant in the claim for compensation. The division may include as part of its award, reasonable attorneys fees to be determined by the division in an amount not to exceed fifteen percent of the total award for compensation.

Added by St.1993, c. 478, § 6. Amended by St.2010, c. 256, § 109, eff. Nov. 4, 2010.

§ 3. Maximum award; compensable expenses

(a) The maximum award for compensation to a claimant under this chapter shall be twenty-five thousand dollars. If there are two or more claimants eligible for compensation arising out of a crime committed against one individual for the same crime, each claimant shall be entitled to receive compensation to the extent of out-of-pocket loss, in proportion to the out-of-pocket losses of every other claimant. The cumulative total of all awards based on such crime shall not exceed twenty-five thousand dollars.

(b) Except as otherwise provided in this chapter, the following expenses are compensable in accordance with this section:

(1)(A) The maximum award or compensation for funeral and burial expenses shall be $6,500. A legal guardian, dependent or other family member of the victim or a person who actually incurs funeral and burial expenses directly related to the death of a victim shall be eligible for compensation for such funeral and burial expenses.

(B) The maximum award or compensation for expenses other than funeral and burial expenses associated with the interment of a victim whose death is the direct result of a crime shall be $800. For purposes of this subsection compensable expenses shall include, but not be limited to, transportation of the victim to the location of interment, travel of a legal guardian or family member to accompany the victim to the location of interment, memorial markers at the location of interment or other associated expenses as determined by the program director in accordance with section 4.

(2) (A) Expenses incurred for hospital services as the direct result of injury to the victim shall be compensable in accordance with this chapter; provided, however, that when claiming compensation for hospital expenses, the claimant must demonstrate an out-of-pocket loss or a legal liability for payment of said expenses. No hospital expenses shall be paid where the expense is reimbursable by medicaid or where the services are covered by chapter 118G. Every claim for compensation for hospital services shall include a certification by the hospital that the services are not reimbursable by medicaid and that the services are not covered by chapter 118G. In no event shall the amounts awarded for hospital services exceed the rates for services established by the division of health care finance and policy if rates have been established for such services.

(B) Expenses incurred for physician, dental, ambulance, or other medically necessary services or prosthetic devices as the direct result of injury to the victim shall be compensable in accordance with this chapter; provided however, that when claiming compensation for such expenses, the claimant must demonstrate an out-of-pocket loss or legal liability for payment of such expenses. No physician, dental, ambulance or other necessary services or prosthetic device shall be paid where the services were reimbursable by medicaid. Every claim for compensation for physician, dental, ambulance or other medically necessary services or for prosthetic devices shall include a certification by the health care provider that the expense was not reimbursable by medicaid.

(C) A victim, parent or legal guardian of a victim who is a minor in accordance with section 4 or, where death results from the crime, the dependents and family members of the victim, shall be eligible for compensation for reasonable mental health counseling obtained as a result of the crime.

(D) If the victim was employed or had received a bona fide employment offer at the time of the crime, he shall be eligible for compensation for loss of actual earnings due to disability from work as the result of injuries caused by the crime. In order to be eligible for lost earnings, the victim must demonstrate medical disability and causal relationship to the crime. The amount of compensation shall be based on the victim's net earnings or expected net earnings as a result of an employment offer at the time of the crime. If the victim is a minor at the time of the crime, he shall be eligible for future lost earnings due to disability from future employment as a result of injuries caused by the crime.

(E) If the sole occupation of the victim at the time of the crime and for the preceding one year was limited to performing the duties and responsibilities of a homemaker, the victim or his dependents shall be eligible for reimbursement for the reasonable costs of maintaining such services. In order to be eligible for compensation for homemaker services in nonhomicide cases, the victim must demonstrate a medical disability which is causally related to the crime.

(F) In the case of the death of the victim as a direct result of the crime, a dependent of a victim shall be eligible for compensation for loss of the victim's support. No compensation for loss of support shall be paid unless the claimant demonstrates either that the dependent was living with the victim at the time of the crime or, in the case of minor children of a deceased victim who were not residing in the victim's household at the time of the crime, that the minor children received financial support directly from the victim prior to the crime or were legally entitled to receive such support, such entitlement having been established by a court order or a judicially enforceable agreement. An award for loss of support shall be based upon the victim's actual earnings and the life expectancy of the victim.

(G) Expenses incurred for professional crime scene cleanup services necessary as the direct result of the commission of a crime at a private residence or in a motor vehicle that is owned or leased by a victim, family member or other dependent shall be compensable in accordance with this chapter; provided, however, that the maximum amount of compensation shall not exceed $1,500.

(H) A victim shall be eligible for compensation for the reasonable replacement costs of clothing and bedding seized as evidence or rendered unusable as the result of a criminal investigation that is the direct result of a crime; provided, however, that the maximum compensable amount shall not exceed $250.

(I) A victim or a family member residing with the victim at the time a crime is committed, shall be eligible for compensation for the costs associated with the implementation of security measures; provided, however, that the maximum compensable amount shall not exceed $500.

Added by St.1993, c. 478, § 6. Amended by St.1998, c. 161, § 554; St.2010, c. 256, §§ 110 to 113, eff. Nov. 4, 2010.

§ 4. Division of victim compensation and assistance; program director; powers and duties

(a) The division of victim compensation and assistance shall administer the provisions of this chapter. Subject to appropriation, the attorney general shall designate a program director of said division. Said program director may appoint and remove, subject to the approval of the attorney general, such investigative, legal and clerical or other staff as the work of the division requires.

(b) The program director shall have the authority to promulgate rules and regulations pursuant to chapter thirty A as may be necessary to carry out the provisions of this chapter.

(c) The program director shall be authorized to apply for and receive sums which may be transmitted to the victim compensation fund maintained by the treasurer and for any other such funds as may become available to administer the requirements of this chapter.

Added by St.1993, c. 478, § 6.

§ 5. Filing and proof of claims; civil investigative demands

(a)(1) A claim for compensation under this chapter shall be filed within three years of the date of the crime.

(2) The claimant has the burden of proving by a preponderance of the evidence that he is eligible to receive compensation.

(3) A claim under this chapter shall be made on a claim form prescribed by the division. The claim shall be accompanied by copies of bills and other documentation supporting the claim, and shall be signed under the pains and penalties of perjury. Any claim for loss of support or other expenses incurred as the result of the death of a victim must be accompanied by proof of dependency of the claimant upon the victim. All claims must contain a release of information necessary to investigate the claim.

Law enforcement agencies, district attorneys, the department of children and families and the department of transitional assistance, hospitals, physicians and other service providers shall cooperate with the department in the investigation of claims filed under this chapter.

(b) Upon receipt of a claim hereunder, the division shall acknowledge receipt of same, in writing, to the claimant or counsel of record. The division shall, thereafter, conduct an investigation of the claim to verify the information contained on the application.

The division shall be authorized to issue a written civil investigative demand, issue interrogatories, under oath, and requests for production of documents, and take oral testimony, under oath, in order to obtain information necessary to verify a claim. All information collected by the division shall be kept in accordance with the provisions of chapters four, sixty-six and sixty-six A.

A civil investigative demand may be served by certified mail, return receipt requested, and first class mail and shall be returned within twenty days from the date of service. Failure to comply with this provision may result in dismissal of the claim for compensation.

Whenever a person fails to comply with a civil investigative demand served upon him pursuant to this section, the attorney general may petition the district court of any county in which such person resides, is found, or transacts business, to enter such orders as may be necessary to carry into effect the provisions of this section. A failure to comply with an order entered under this section shall be punished as a contempt of court.

Added by St.1993, c. 478, § 6. Amended by St.2008, c. 176, § 127, eff. July 8, 2008.

§ 6. Notification by claimant of change in address

The claimant shall have a continuing obligation to notify the division of a change in address. Failure to comply with this requirement may result in the dismissal of the claim for compensation or the termination of a proceeding set forth in this chapter.

Added by St.1993, c. 478, § 6.

§ 7. Notice to claimant; payment of compensation

(a) Within fifteen days of completion of the investigation, the program director shall mail notice to the claimant or the attorney of record stating the amount of compensation to be paid or denied, and the reasons therefor, and the payees, if any. The program director may direct that warrant for payment by the department of the attorney general be made jointly to the claimant and to a provider. The notice shall contain information regarding the right of the claimant to petition for judicial review of the decision of the program director.

(b) Upon receipt of the notice of assent by a claimant, the division shall present the notice to the department of the attorney general for payment. Subject to the availability of funds appropriated for this purpose, said department of the attorney general shall cause payment to be made in accordance with the division's award without further authorization.

Added by St.1993, c. 478, § 6. Amended by St.2000, c. 159, §§ 285 to 287.

§ 8. Request for reconsideration of award or denial

(a) Within 20 days of the date of mailing of the notice of award or denial, a claimant aggrieved by the program director's decision may request, in writing, a reconsideration of such decision. Said program director shall reconsider any order for which a request for reconsideration is received. Said program director may in his discretion reconsider a decision granting or denying an award or the amount of an award where there has been no request for reconsideration. After reconsideration of the award, said program director shall affirm the decision or issue an amended notice of award or denial.

(b) The program director shall notify the claimant by certified mail, return receipt required, and first class mail of the decision upon reconsideration within 30 days of the claimant's request for reconsideration. Such notice shall include information regarding the claimant's right to a petition for judicial review of the decision of the program director.

Added by St.1993, c. 478, § 6. Amended by St.2010, c. 256, §§ 114, 115, eff. Nov. 4, 2010.

§ 9. Judicial review

(a) Within thirty days of the date of mailing of the notice of award or denial by the program director, the claimant may petition for judicial review in the district court within the judicial district in which the claimant resides or, in the case of a nonresident claimant, in the Boston municipal court. Where the claimant requests reconsideration of the decision of the program director, the petition for judicial review shall be filed within 30 days from the date of mailing of the decision of reconsideration. If no petition is filed within the time specified, the decision of the program director shall be final.

(b) The program director shall, in response to the aforesaid, within thirty days, file in such court a copy of his official decision.

(c) The district court shall schedule the matter for hearing and shall notify the parties of the date and time thereof.

(d) The review shall be conducted by the district court without a jury.

(e) For the purpose of determining the amount of compensation payable pursuant to this chapter, the chief justice for administration and management shall formulate standards for the uniform application of this chapter. The court shall take into consideration the provisions of this chapter, the rates and amounts of compensation payable for injuries and death under other laws of the commonwealth and of the United States, excluding pain and suffering. All decisions of the court on claims heard under this chapter shall be in writing, setting forth the name of the claimant, the amount of compensation and the reasons for the decision. The clerk of the court shall immediately notify the claimant in writing of the decision and shall forward to the department of the attorney general a certified copy of the decision. the[1] department of the attorney general without further authorization shall, subject to appropriation, pay the claimant the amount determined by the court.

In determining the amount of compensation payable, the court shall determine whether because of his conduct the victim contributed to the infliction of his injury; and the court shall reduce the amount of the compensation or deny the claim altogether, in accordance with such determination; provided, however, that the court may disregard the responsibility of the victim for his own injury where such responsibility was attributable to efforts by the victim to aid a victim, or to prevent a crime or an attempted crime from occurring in his presence or to apprehend a person who had committed a crime in his presence or had in fact committed a felony.

(f) Judicial review of the finding and decisions of the program director shall be a de novo hearing of the claim.

Added by St.1993, c. 478, § 6. Amended by St.2000, c. 159, §§ 288, 289; St.2010, c. 256, § 116, eff. Nov. 4, 2010.

[1] So in original; probably should read "The".

§ 10. Amounts received by claimant from other sources; offset

No compensation shall be awarded or paid unless the out-of-pocket expenses or legal liability of the claimant for services rendered as the result of the crime exceeds any and all of the amounts received, applied for, or to be applied for as the result of the crime from any of the following or any combination of the following:

(a) insurance, including, but not limited to, homeowner's insurance, renter's insurance, automobile insurance, disability;

(b) workers' compensation, unemployment compensation, social security benefits, veteran's benefits, retirement benefits;

(c) medicaid, medicare, free care, any other forms of public assistance including aid to families with dependent children and assistance to the aged and disabled or any successor thereto;

(d) restitution in the criminal action;

(e) proceeds from a civil suit; or

(f) institutional gifts.

Added by St.1993, c. 478, § 6. Amended by St.2010, c. 256, § 117, eff. Nov. 4, 2010.

§ 11. Subrogation

Acceptance of any compensation under this chapter shall subrogate the commonwealth, to the extent of such compensation paid, to any right or right of action accruing to the claimant or to the victim to recover payments on account of losses resulting from the crime with respect to which the compensation has been paid, and the claimant has a continuing obligation to so notify the attorney general of such recovery. The attorney general may enforce the subrogation, and he shall bring suit to recover from any person to whom compensation is paid, to the extent of compensation actually paid under this chapter, any amount received by the claimant from any source exceeding the actual loss to the victim.

Added by St.1993, c. 478, § 6.

§ 12. Misrepresentations or concealment; fines and damages

Any person who: (a) submits a false or fraudulent application or claim for an award; (b) intentionally makes or causes to be made any false statement or representation of a material fact in relation to any claim pending before the division; or (c) intentionally conceals or fails to disclose information affecting the amount of or the initial or continued right to any such award shall be punished by a fine of not more than one thousand dollars or by imprisonment in a house of correction for not more than six months, or both.

The commonwealth shall, in addition, have a civil cause of action for relief against any person who violates the provisions of this chapter for the amount of damages which the commonwealth sustains by reason of such violation which shall include costs of the action and attorneys fees and, in addition, for punitive damages of not more than triple the amount of damages which the commonwealth sustains, and interest. The attorney general may bring any such action necessary to enforce this section.

Any amount reimbursed or any fine or damages paid pursuant to this section shall be paid to the victim compensation fund maintained by the treasurer.

Added by St.1993, c. 478, § 6.

§ 13. "Good Samaritans"; liability

No person who, in good faith, provides or obtains, or attempts to provide or obtain, assistance for a victim of a crime as defined in section one, shall be liable in a civil suit for damages as a result of any acts or omissions in providing or obtaining, or attempting to provide or obtain, such assistance unless such acts or omissions constitute willful, wanton or reckless conduct.

Added by St.1993, c. 478, § 6.

CHAPTER 258D

COMPENSATION FOR CERTAIN ERRONEOUS FELONY CONVICTIONS

Chapter 258D of the General Laws was added by St.2004, c. 444, § 1.

The section headings for the General Laws in this pamphlet have been editorially supplied.

§ 1. Erroneous felony conviction claims; class of eligible persons; burden of proof; definitions; right to jury trial

[Text of section applicable as provided by 2004, 444, Sec. 3.]

(A) A claim may be brought against the commonwealth for an erroneous felony conviction resulting in incarceration as provided in this chapter.

(B) The class of persons eligible to obtain relief under this chapter shall be limited to the following:—

(i) those that have been granted a full pardon pursuant to section 152 of chapter 127, if the governor expressly states in writing his belief in the individual's innocence, or

(ii) those who have been granted judicial relief by a state court of competent jurisdiction, on grounds which tend to establish the innocence of the individual as set forth in clause (vi) of subsection (C), and if (a) the judicial relief vacates or reverses the judgment of a felony conviction, and the felony indictment or complaint used to charge the individual with such felony has been dismissed, or if a new trial was ordered, the individual was not retried and the felony indictment or complaint was dismissed or a nolle prosequi was entered, or if a new trial was ordered the individual was found not guilty at the new trial; and (b) at the time of the filing of an action under this chapter no criminal proceeding is pending or can be brought against the individual by a district attorney or the attorney general for any act associated with such felony conviction.

(C) In order for an individual to prevail and recover damages against the commonwealth in a cause of action brought under this chapter, the individual must establish, by clear and convincing evidence, that:—

(i) he is a member of the class of persons defined in subsection (B);

(ii) he was convicted of an offense classified as a felony;

(iii) he did not plead guilty to the offense charged, or to any lesser included offense, unless such guilty plea was withdrawn, vacated or nullified by operation of law on a basis other than a claimed deficiency in the plea warnings required by section 29D of chapter 278;

(iv) he was sentenced to incarceration for not less than 1 year in state prison or a house of correction as a result of the conviction and has served all or any part of such sentence;

(v) he was incarcerated solely on the basis of the conviction for the offense that is the subject of the claim;

(vi) he did not commit the crimes or crime charged in the indictment or complaint or any other felony arising out of or reasonably connected to the facts supporting the indictment or complaint, or any lesser included felony; and

(vii) to the extent that he is guilty of conduct that would have justified a conviction of any lesser included misdemeanor arising out of or reasonably connected to facts supporting the indictment or complaint, that he has served the maximum sentence he would have received for such lesser included misdemeanor and not less than one additional year in a prison.

(D) The claimant shall attach to his claim certified copies of: the mittimus that shows the claimant's sentence to incarceration and; the warrants necessary to grant a pardon pursuant to section 152 of chapter 127 or; criminal case docket entries or documents related thereto in the case of judicial relief.

(E) For the purposes of this chapter "conviction" or "convicted" shall include an adjudication as a youthful offender, if such adjudication resulted in the youthful offender's incarceration in a house of correction or state prison.

(F) The commonwealth and any individual filing an action for compensation under this chapter shall have the right to a jury trial on any action so filed. In the interest of doing substantial justice, with regard to weight and admissibility of evidence submitted by the claimant or the commonwealth, the court presiding at a jury-waived trial shall exercise its discretion by giving due consideration to any difficulties of proof caused by the passage of time, the death or unavailability or witnesses, or other factors not caused by the claimant, or those acting on the claimant's or the commonwealth's behalf. At a jury trial, the court shall consider these same factors as part of the exercise of its discretion when determining the admissibility and weight of evidence, and the court shall instruct the jury that it may consider the same factors when it weighs the evidence presented at trial. No evidence proffered by any party shall be excluded on grounds that it was seized or obtained in violation of the Fourth, Fifth or Sixth amendments to the Constitution of the United States, or in violation of Articles 12 or 14 of Part the First of the Constitution of Massachusetts.

Added by St.2004, c. 444, § 1, eff. Dec. 30, 2004.

§ 2. Compensation for claimants

[Text of section applicable as provided by 2004, 444, Sec. 3.]

A claimant shall not be entitled to compensation from the commonwealth for any incarceration or portion thereof, which was or will be credited toward a sentence for, or during which the claimant was also serving a concurrent sentence for the conviction of another crime. In those cases in which only a pardon from the governor is used to support a pending action against the commonwealth brought under this chapter, the subsequent exercise of the governor's authority to revoke such pardon pursuant to section 152 of chapter 127 shall immediately negate the validity of any such pending action and the superior court shall immediately issue a summary judgment in favor of the commonwealth on such grounds.

Added by St.2004, c. 444, § 1, eff. Dec. 30, 2004.

§ 3. Jurisdiction

[Text of section applicable as provided by 2004, 444, Sec. 3.]

A civil action brought against the commonwealth under this chapter shall be brought in the county where the claimant was convicted or in Suffolk county. The superior court shall have exclusive jurisdiction of all such actions. All civil actions brought pursuant to this chapter shall in all manner proceed by and be governed by the rules of civil procedure except as otherwise expressly provided in this chapter.

Added by St.2004, c. 444, § 1, eff. Dec. 30, 2004.

§ 4. Service of process; notification; victim's right to testify; evidence; arbitration and settlements.

[Text of section applicable as provided by 2004, 444, Sec. 3.]

Service of process for a civil action brought pursuant to this chapter shall be made upon the attorney general for the commonwealth who shall defend the commonwealth against all such claims. The attorney general shall immediately notify the district attorney for the county that prosecuted the felony that forms the basis for the claim. Any district attorney so notified by the attorney general shall immediately notify any individual meeting the definition of "victim", as set forth in section 1 or chapter 258B, of the felony conviction that forms the basis of the claim. Any such victim shall be allowed, but may not be compelled, to testify or furnish other evidence. If such victim is unavailable to testify or decides not to testify, his prior recorded testimony, given under oath at a relevant proceeding, shall only be admissible after judicial review and determination that such testimony, or portion thereof, may be helpful to the factfinder. The attorney general shall consult with the appropriate district attorney relative to the merits of such action and, following consultation, shall have discretion to determine whether to proffer as evidence any documents, records, testimony or other information brought forward to the attorney general by such district attorney in defense of the commonwealth at a time deemed appropriate by the attorney general. The attorney general may arbitrate or settle any claim for damages filed under this chapter, but any award or settlement in excess of $80,000 shall be made only with the prior approval of the secretary of administration and finance. The acceptance by the claimant of any such award or settlement shall be in writing and shall, except when procured by fraud, be final and conclusive on the claimant, and shall constitute a complete release of any claim by the claimant against the commonwealth and a complete bar to any action by the claimant against the commonwealth by reason of the same subject matter.

Added by St.2004, c. 444, § 1, eff. Dec. 30, 2004.

§ 5. Damages

[Text of section applicable as provided by 2004, 444, Sec. 3.]

(A) Upon a finding or verdict that the claimant has met the requirements of section 1 by the requisite standard of proof and is not barred from compensation by section 2, the court or the jury shall determine the damages that shall be payable to the claimant. In making such determination, the court or jury shall consider, but not be limited to, the consideration of: the income the claimant would have earned, but for his incarceration; the particular circumstances of the claimant's trial and other proceedings; the length and conditions under which the claimant was incarcerated and; any other factors deemed appropriate under the circumstances in order to fairly and reasonably compensate the claimant. The court, in its discretion, may admit expert testimony on these or any factors. The court may include, as part of its judgment against the commonwealth, an order requiring the commonwealth to provide the claimant with services that are reasonable and necessary to address any deficiencies in the individual's physical and emotional condition that are shown to be directly related to the individual's erroneous felony conviction and resulting incarceration through documentary or oral evidence presented to the court or jury by the claimant as part of the claim if the claimant provided in his original claim for compensation under this chapter: (i) the nature of the services that he seeks; and (ii) the agencies, departments or commissions of the commonwealth from which he seeks to receive such services. Any such agency, department or commission so named in the claim shall be entitled to reasonable notice of the court proceedings pertaining to the possible ordering of such services and shall be given an opportunity to be heard on whether such agency is the appropriate entity to provide such services if so ordered. The court may also include in its judgment an order that entitles any claimant who wishes to apply for and receive educational services from any state or community college of the commonwealth including, but not limited to, the University of Massachusetts at Amherst and its satellite campuses, a 50 per cent reduction of the tuition and fees applicable to such services at said institutions. Once the damages have been determined, the court shall enter a judgment against the commonwealth for the claimant in an amount certain, payable in either a lump sum or in annuity installment payments set by the court; provided, however, that any such annuity installment payments shall have fixed limits on their annual amount and on the time period which they shall be paid to the claimant. A judgment against the commonwealth may not include punitive or exemplary damages. The total liability of the commonwealth for any judgment entered under this chapter shall not exceed $500,000. Notwithstanding any general or special law to the contrary, the clerk of court shall not add to the judgment and the commonwealth shall not be liable for paying, any prejudgment or post judgment interest on damages. Subject to section 4, relative to award or settlements, the rights and remedies afforded to certain individuals by this chapter are not intended to limit in any way any rights or remedies that such individuals or other individuals may be entitled to exercise and pursue under chapter 258.

(B) In awarding damages under this section, the court or jury shall not offset the award by any expenses incurred by the commonwealth or any political subdivision of the commonwealth including, but not limited to, expenses incurred to secure the claimant's custody, or to feed, clothe or provide medical services for the claimant nor shall the court offset against the award the value of any reduction in tuition or fees for educational services or the value of services to be provided to the claimant that may be awarded to the claimant pursuant to this section.

(C) The commonwealth shall not be liable to levy of execution on any real or personal property to satisfy a judgment ordered pursuant to this chapter. Any judgments ordered by the court pursuant to this chapter shall be paid from funds appropriated by the general court for such purpose. Payments by the commonwealth under this chapter are made to remedy the claimant's injury of unjust incarceration. Only those portions of a judgment that are paid or retained as compensation for services in bringing a claim under this chapter by an attorney representing the claimant pursuant to a signed agreement with the claimant or otherwise shall be subject to taxation by the commonwealth.

(D) The court shall give due consideration to the possible bifurcation of court proceedings to separate the consideration of issues to be resolved by the court, as required by sections 1 and 2, from the determination of reasonable damages and other relief as required by this section.

Added by St.2004, c. 444, § 5, eff. Dec. 30, 2004.

§ 6. Motion for costs; appeals

[Text of section applicable as provided by 2004, 444, Sec. 3.]

Any party to an action filed under this chapter is entitled to make a motion seeking costs, expenses and interest for wholly insubstantial, frivolous or bad faith claims or defenses advanced by the opposing party during proceedings under this chapter as set forth in section 6F of chapter 231 and is also entitled to the rights of appeal afforded parties in a civil action following a decision on such motions as set forth in section 6G of said chapter 231.

Added by St.2004, c. 444, § 1, eff. Dec. 30, 2004.

§ 7. Expungement or sealing of records; hearings

[Text of section applicable as provided by 2004, 444, Sec. 3.]

(A) Upon the entry of a judgment in favor of a claimant under this chapter and following a separate hearing on the matter, the court shall enter an order either directing the expungement or sealing of those records of the claimant maintained by the department of criminal justice information services, the probation department, and the sex offender registry that directly pertain to the claimant's erroneous felony conviction case, including documents and other materials and any samples obtained from the claimant. The commonwealth, as well as any other law enforcement agency that may be directly affected by such expungement or sealing of such records including, but not limited to, the district attorney that prosecuted the felony case against the claimant, shall be given reasonable notice and an opportunity to be heard on the issue of whether such records, documents and materials shall be so expunged or sealed. In making its determination as to whether such records, documents and materials shall be so expunged or sealed, the court shall consider the interests of privacy and justice pertaining to the claimant's erroneous felony conviction as well as the probable effect of such expungement or sealing on relevant law enforcement entities and their ability to appropriately investigate and prosecute other persons for the felony which forms the basis of the claim or other crimes that may relate to the information contained in such records, documents and materials.

(B) Following a separate hearing conducted by the court, the court may also order the expungement or sealing of those records that directly pertain to the claimant's erroneous felony conviction case that are currently in the care, custody and control of other state, municipal or local departments, agencies, commissions or committees, including law enforcement entities. Any such agency, commission, committee or entity shall be given reasonable notice and an opportunity to be heard on the issue of whether such records, documents and materials shall be expunged or sealed pursuant to this section. In making its determination as to whether such records, documents and materials shall be expunged or sealed, the court shall consider those factors required for consideration by the court in paragraph (A).

(C) Any order to expunge or seal entered by the court shall provide that, in any employment application, the claimant may answer "no record" as to any charges expunged or sealed pursuant to this section in response to an inquiry regarding prior felony arrests, court appearances or criminal convictions.

(D) The charges and convictions expunged or sealed shall not operate to disqualify the claimant in any examination, appointment or application for public employment in the service of the commonwealth or any other political subdivision thereof, nor shall such charges and convictions be used against the claimant in any way in any court proceedings or hearings before any court, board or commission to which the claimant is a party to the proceedings.

Added by St.2004, c. 444, § 1, eff. Dec. 30, 2004. Amended by St.2010, c. 256, § 118, eff. Nov. 4, 2010.

§ 8. Limitation on action

[Text of section applicable as provided by 2004, 444, Sec. 3.]

A claim for compensation brought under this chapter shall be commenced within 2 years after either the grant of a pardon or the grant of judicial relief and satisfaction of other conditions described in subsection (B) of section 1. Any action by the commonwealth challenging or appealing the grant of such judicial relief shall toll the 2 year period. Every action brought pursuant to this chapter that is not commenced within the time required by this section is forever barred from consideration by the courts of the commonwealth.

Added by St.2004, c. 444, § 1, eff. Dec. 30, 2004.

§ 9. Receipt of chapter

[Text of section applicable as provided by 2004, 444, Sec. 3.]

(A) A court granting judicial relief consistent with the criteria set forth in subclause (a) of clause (ii) of subsection (B) of section 1 shall provide a copy of this chapter to an individual seeking such relief at the time the criteria of said subclause (a) of said clause (ii) of said subsection (B) of said section 1 are satisfied. Such individual shall be required to acknowledge receipt of a copy of this chapter in writing on a form established by the chief justice for administration and management of the trial court. This acknowledgement shall be entered on the docket by the court and shall be admissible in any proceeding filed by a claimant under this chapter.

(B) The parole board, upon the issuance of a full pardon under section 152 of chapter 127, shall provide a copy of this chapter to an individual granted clemency at the time warrants necessary to grant the pardon are issued. Such individual shall be required to acknowledge receipt of a copy of this chapter in writing on a form established by the parole board, which shall be retained on file by the parole board as part of its official records and shall be admissible in any proceeding filed by a claimant under this chapter.

(C) If a claimant granted judicial relief or a full pardon shows he did not properly receive a copy of the information required by this section, he shall receive a 1 year extension on the 2 year time limit provided in section 8.

Added by St.2004, c. 444, § 1, eff. Dec. 30, 2004.

CHAPTER 258E

HARASSMENT PREVENTION ORDERS

Chapter 258E of the General Laws was added by St.2010, c. 23.

The section headings for the General Laws in this pamphlet have been editorially supplied.

§ 1. Definitions

As used in this chapter the following words shall, unless the context clearly requires otherwise, have the following meanings:-

"Abuse", attempting to cause or causing physical harm to another or placing another in fear of imminent serious physical harm.

"Harassment", (i) 3 or more acts of willful and malicious conduct aimed at a specific person committed with the intent to cause fear, intimidation, abuse or damage to property and that does in fact cause fear, intimidation, abuse or damage to property; or (ii) an act that: (A) by force, threat or duress causes another to involuntarily engage in sexual relations; or (B) constitutes a violation of section 13B, 13F, 13H, 22, 22A, 23, 24, 24B, 26C, 43 or 43A of chapter 265 or section 3 of chapter 272.

"Court", the district or Boston municipal court, the superior court or the juvenile court departments of the trial court.

"Law officer", any officer authorized to serve criminal process.

"Malicious", characterized by cruelty, hostility or revenge.

"Protection order issued by another jurisdiction", an injunction or other order issued by a court of another state, territory or possession of the United States, the Commonwealth of Puerto Rico, or the District of Columbia, or a tribal court that is issued for the purpose of preventing violent or threatening acts, abuse or harassment against, or contact or communication with or physical proximity to another person, including temporary and final orders issued by civil and criminal courts filed by or on behalf of a person seeking protection.

Added by St.2010, c. 23, eff. May 10, 2010.

§ 2. Jurisdiction

Proceedings under this chapter shall be filed, heard and determined in the superior court department or the respective divisions of the district court department or the Boston municipal court department having venue over the plaintiff's residence. The juvenile court department shall have exclusive jurisdiction of proceedings under this chapter in which the defendant is under the age of 17. Such proceedings shall be filed, heard and determined in the division of the juvenile court department having venue over the plaintiff's residence.

Added by St.2010, c. 23, eff. May 10, 2010. Amended by St.2010, c. 112, § 29, eff. May 22, 2010.

§ 3. Filing of complaint; impounding of case record information; filing fee; expiration of order; modification of order; time for filing; nonexclusivity of remedy

(a) A person suffering from harassment may file a complaint in the appropriate court requesting protection from such harassment. A person may petition the court under this chapter for an order that the defendant:

(i) refrain from abusing or harassing the plaintiff, whether the defendant is an adult or minor;

(ii) refrain from contacting the plaintiff, unless authorized by the court, whether the defendant is an adult or minor;

(iii) remain away from the plaintiff's household or workplace, whether the defendant is an adult or minor; and

(iv) pay the plaintiff monetary compensation for the losses suffered as a direct result of the harassment; provided, however, that compensatory damages shall include, but shall not be limited to, loss of earnings, out-of-pocket losses for injuries sustained or property damaged, cost of replacement of locks, medical expenses, cost for obtaining an unlisted phone number and reasonable attorney's fees.

(b) The court may order that information in the case record be impounded in accordance with court rule.

(c) No filing fee shall be charged for the filing of the complaint. The plaintiff shall not be charged for certified copies of any orders entered by the court, or any copies of the file reasonably required for future court action or as a result of the loss or destruction of plaintiff's copies.

(d) Any relief granted by the court shall not extend for a period exceeding 1 year. Every order shall, on its face, state the time and date the order is to expire and shall include the date and time that the matter will again be heard. If the plaintiff appears at the court at the date and time the order is to expire, the court shall determine whether or not to extend the order for any additional time reasonably necessary to protect the plaintiff or to enter a permanent order. When the expiration date stated on the order is on a date when the court is closed to business, the order shall not expire until the next date that the court is open to business. The plaintiff may appear on such next court business day at the time designated by the order to request that the order be extended. The court may also extend the order upon motion of the plaintiff, for such additional time as it deems necessary to protect the plaintiff from harassment. The fact that harassment has not occurred during the pendency of an order shall not, in itself, constitute sufficient ground for denying or failing to extend the order, or allowing an order to expire or be vacated or for refusing to issue a new order.

(e) The court may modify its order at any subsequent time upon motion by either party; provided, however, that the non-moving party shall receive sufficient notice and opportunity to be heard on said modification. When the plaintiff's address is inaccessible to the defendant as provided in section 10 and the defendant has filed a motion to modify the court's order, the court shall be responsible for notifying the plaintiff. In no event shall the court disclose any such inaccessible address.

(f) The court shall not deny any complaint filed under this chapter solely because it was not filed within a particular time period after the last alleged incident of harassment.

(g) An action commenced under this chapter shall not preclude any other civil or criminal remedies. A party filing a complaint under this chapter shall be required to disclose any prior or pending actions involving the parties; including, but not limited to, court actions, administrative proceedings and disciplinary proceedings.

Added by St.2010, c. 23, eff. May 10, 2010. Amended by St.2010, c. 112, § 30, eff. May 22, 2010.

§ 4. Notice of nature of proceedings and availability of other criminal proceedings

Upon the filing of a complaint under this chapter, a complainant shall be informed that the proceedings hereunder are civil in nature and that violations of orders issued hereunder are criminal in nature. Further, a complainant shall be given information prepared by the appropriate district attorney's office that other criminal proceedings may be available and such complainant shall be instructed by such district attorney's office relative to the procedures required to initiate criminal proceedings including, but not limited to, a complaint for a violation of section 13B, 13F, 13H, 22, 22A, 23, 24, 24B, 26C, 43 and 43A of chapter 265 or section 3 of chapter 272. Whenever possible, a complainant shall be provided with such information in the complainant's native language.

Added by St.2010, c. 23, eff. May 10, 2010.

§ 5. Temporary orders

Upon the filing of a complaint under this chapter, the court may enter such temporary orders as it deems necessary to protect a plaintiff from harassment, including relief as provided in section 3.

If the plaintiff demonstrates a substantial likelihood of immediate danger of harassment, the court may enter such temporary relief orders without notice as it deems necessary to protect the plaintiff from harassment and shall immediately thereafter notify the defendant that the temporary orders have been issued. The court shall give the defendant an opportunity to be heard on the question of continuing the temporary order and of granting other relief as requested by the plaintiff not later than 10 court business days after such orders are entered.

Notice shall be made by the appropriate law enforcement agency as provided in section 9.

If the defendant does not appear at such subsequent hearing, the temporary orders shall continue in effect without further order of the court.

Added by St.2010, c. 23, eff. May 10, 2010.

§ 6. Granting of relief without the filing of a complaint

When the court is closed for business or the plaintiff is unable to appear in court because of severe hardship due to the plaintiff's physical condition, the court may grant relief to the plaintiff as provided under section 5 if the plaintiff demonstrates a substantial likelihood of immediate danger of harassment. In the discretion of the justice, such relief may be granted and communicated by telephone to an officer or employee of an appropriate law enforcement agency, who shall record such order on a form of order promulgated for such use by the chief justice for administration and management and shall deliver a copy of such order on the next court day to the clerk or clerk-magistrate of the court having venue and jurisdiction over the matter. If relief has been granted without the filing of a complaint pursuant to this section, the plaintiff shall appear in court on the next available business day to file a complaint. If the plaintiff in such a case is unable to appear in court without severe hardship due to the plaintiff's physical condition, a representative may appear in court, on the plaintiff's behalf and file the requisite complaint with an affidavit setting forth the circumstances preventing the plaintiff from appearing personally. Notice to the plaintiff and defendant and an opportunity for the defendant to be heard shall be given as provided in said section 5.

Any order issued under this section and any documentation in support thereof shall be certified on the next court day by the clerk or clerk-magistrate of the court issuing such order to the court having venue and jurisdiction over the matter. Such certification to the court shall have the effect of commencing proceedings under this chapter and invoking the other provisions of this chapter but shall not be deemed necessary for an emergency order issued under this section to take effect.

Added by St.2010, c. 23, eff. May 10, 2010.

§ 7. Enforcement of protection order issued by another jurisdiction

Any protection order issued by another jurisdiction shall be given full faith and credit throughout the commonwealth and enforced as if it were issued in the commonwealth for as long as the order is in effect in the issuing jurisdiction.

A person entitled to protection under a protection order issued by another jurisdiction may file such order with the appropriate court by filing with the court a certified copy of such order. Such person shall swear under oath in an affidavit, to the best of such person's knowledge, that such order is presently in effect as written. Upon request by a law enforcement agency, the clerk or clerk-magistrate of such court shall provide a certified copy of the protection order issued by the other jurisdiction.

A law officer may presume the validity of, and enforce in accordance with section 8, a copy of a protection order issued by another jurisdiction which has been provided to the law officer by any source; provided, however, that the officer is also provided with a statement by the person protected by the order that such order remains in effect. Law officers may rely on such statement by the person protected by such order.

Added by St.2010, c. 23, eff. May 10, 2010.

§ 8. Law officer emergency response to prevent further abuse or harassment

Whenever a law officer has reason to believe that a person has been abused or harassed or is in danger of being abused or harassed, such officer shall use all reasonable means to prevent further abuse or harassment. Law officers shall make every reasonable effort to do the following as part of the emergency response:

(1) assess the immediate physical danger to the victim and provide assistance reasonably intended to mitigate the safety risk;

(2) if there is observable injury to the victim or if the victim is complaining of injury, encourage the victim to seek medical attention and arrange for medical assistance or request an ambulance for transport to a hospital;

(3) if a sexual assault has occurred, notify the victim that there are time-sensitive medical or forensic options that may be available, encourage the victim to seek medical attention and arrange for medical assistance or request an ambulance for transport to a hospital;

(4) provide the victim with referrals to local resources that may assist the victim in locating and getting to a safe place;

(5) provide adequate notice to the victim of the victim's rights including, but not limited to, obtaining a harassment prevention order; provided, however, that the notice shall consist of providing the victim with a copy of the following statement before the officer leaves the scene or premises and after reading the statement to the victim; provided further, that if the victim's native language is not English, the statement shall be then provided in the victim's native language whenever possible:

"You have the right to appear at the Superior, Juvenile (only if the attacker is under 17), District or Boston Municipal Court, if you reside within the appropriate jurisdiction, and file a complaint requesting any of the following applicable orders: (i) an order restraining your attacker from harassing or abusing you; (ii) an order directing your attacker to refrain from contacting you; (iii) an order directing your attacker to stay away from your home and your workplace; (iv) an order directing your attacker to pay you for losses suffered as a result of the harassment or abuse, including loss of earnings, out-of-pocket losses for injuries sustained or property damaged, costs of replacement of locks, medical expenses, cost for obtaining an unlisted phone number, and reasonable attorneys' fees.

For an emergency on weekends, holidays or weeknights, the police will assist you in activating the emergency response system so that you may file a complaint and request a harassment prevention order.

You have the right to go to the appropriate court and apply for a criminal complaint for sexual assault, threats, criminal stalking, criminal harassment, assault and battery, assault with a deadly weapon, assault with intent to kill or other related offenses.

If you are in need of medical treatment, you have the right to request that an officer present drive you to the nearest hospital or otherwise assist you in obtaining medical treatment.

If you believe that police protection is needed for your physical safety, you have the right to request that the officer present remain at the scene until you can leave or until your safety is otherwise ensured. You may also request that the officer assist you in locating and taking you to a safe place including, but not limited to, a designated meeting place for a shelter or a family member's or a friend's residence or a similar place of safety.

You may request and obtain a copy of the police incident report at no cost from the police department.";

(6) assist the victim by activating the emergency judicial system when the court is closed for business;

(7) inform the victim that the abuser will be eligible for bail and may be promptly released; and

(8) arrest any person that a law officer witnessed or has probable cause to believe violated a temporary or permanent vacate, restraining, stay-away or no-contact order or judgment issued under this chapter or similar protection order issued by another jurisdiction; provided, however, that if there are no vacate, restraining, stay-away or no-contact orders or judgments in effect, arresting the person shall be the preferred response if the law officer witnessed or has probable cause to believe that a person: (i) has committed a felony; (ii) has committed a misdemeanor involving harassment or abuse as defined in section 1; or (iii) has committed an assault and battery in violation of section 13A of chapter 265; provided further, that the safety of the victim shall be paramount in any decision to arrest; and provided further, that if a law officer arrests both parties, the law officer shall submit a detailed, written report in addition to an incident report, setting forth the grounds for arresting both parties.

No law officer shall be held liable in a civil action for personal injury or property damage brought by a party to an incident of abuse or for an arrest based on probable cause when such officer acted reasonably and in good faith and in compliance with this chapter.

Whenever a law officer investigates an incident of harassment, the officer shall immediately file a written incident report in accordance with the standards of the law officer's law enforcement agency and, wherever possible, in the form of the National Incident-Based Reporting System, as defined by the Federal Bureau of Investigation. The latter information may be submitted voluntarily by the local police on a monthly basis to the crime reporting unit of the state police crime reporting unit established in section 32 of chapter 22C.

The victim shall be provided with a copy of the full incident report at no cost upon request to the appropriate law enforcement department.

When a judge or other person authorized to take bail bails any person arrested under this chapter, reasonable efforts shall be made to inform the victim of such release prior to or at the time of the release. When any person charged with or arrested for a crime involving harassment under this chapter is released from custody, the court or the emergency response judge shall issue, upon the request of the victim, a written no-contact order or stay-away order prohibiting the person charged or arrested from having any contact with the victim and shall use all reasonable means to notify the victim immediately of release from custody. The victim shall be provided, at no cost, with a certified copy of the no-contact or stay-away order.

Added by St.2010, c. 23, eff. May 10, 2010. Amended by St.2010, c. 112, § 31, eff. May 22, 2010.

§ 9. Review and filing of records within court activity record information system and statewide domestic violence recordkeeping system; execution of outstanding warrants; service upon defendant; order for payment of damages

When considering a complaint filed under this chapter, the court shall order a review of the records contained within the court activity record information system and the statewide domestic violence recordkeeping system, as provided in chapter 188 of the acts of 1992 and maintained by the commissioner of probation, and shall review the resulting data to determine whether the named defendant has a civil or criminal record involving violent crimes or abuse. Upon receipt of information that an outstanding warrant exists against the named defendant, a judge shall order that the appropriate law enforcement officials be notified and shall order that any information regarding the defendant's most recent whereabouts shall be forwarded to such officials. In all instances in which an outstanding warrant exists, the court shall make a finding, based upon all of the circumstances, as to whether an imminent threat of bodily injury exists to the petitioner. In all instances in which such an imminent threat of bodily injury is found to exist, the judge shall notify the appropriate law enforcement officials of such finding and such officials shall take all necessary actions to execute any such outstanding warrant as soon as is practicable.

Whenever the court orders that the defendant refrain from harassing the plaintiff or have no contact with the plaintiff under section 3, 5 or 6, the clerk or clerk-magistrate shall transmit: (i) to the office of the commissioner of probation information for filing in the court activity record information system or the statewide domestic violence recordkeeping system as provided in said chapter 188 of the acts of 1992 or in a recordkeeping system created by the commissioner of probation to record the issuance of, or violation of, prevention orders issued pursuant to this chapter; and (ii) 2 certified copies of each such order and 1 copy of the complaint and summons forthwith to the appropriate law enforcement agency which, unless otherwise ordered by the court, shall serve 1 copy of each order upon the defendant, together with a copy of the complaint and order and summons. The law enforcement agency shall promptly make its return of service to the court. The commissioner of probation may develop and implement a statewide harassment prevention order recordkeeping system.

Law officers shall use every reasonable means to enforce such harassment prevention orders. Law enforcement agencies shall establish procedures adequate to ensure that an officer on the scene of an alleged violation of such order may be informed of the existence and terms of such order. The court shall notify the appropriate law enforcement agency in writing whenever any such order is vacated and shall direct the agency to destroy all record of such vacated order and such agency shall comply with that directive.

Each harassment prevention order issued shall contain the following statement:

VIOLATION OF THIS ORDER IS A CRIMINAL OFFENSE.

Any violation of such order or a protection order issued by another jurisdiction shall be punishable by a fine of not more than $5,000, or by imprisonment for not more than 2½ years in a house of correction, or both. In addition to, but not in lieu of, the foregoing penalties and any other sentence, fee or assessment, including the victim witness assessment in section 8 of chapter 258B, the court shall order persons convicted of a violation of such an order to pay a fine of $25 that shall be transmitted to the treasurer for deposit into the General Fund. For any violation of such order, the court may order the defendant to complete an appropriate treatment program based on the offense.

In each instance in which there is a violation of a harassment prevention order or a protection order issued by another jurisdiction, the court may order the defendant to pay the plaintiff for all damages including, but not limited to, loss of earnings, out-of-pocket losses for injuries sustained or property damaged, cost of replacement locks, medical expenses, cost for obtaining an unlisted telephone number and reasonable attorney's fees.

Any such violation may be enforced by the court. Criminal remedies provided herein are not exclusive and do not preclude any other available civil or criminal remedies. The court may enforce by civil contempt procedure a violation of its own court order.

Section 8 of chapter 136 shall not apply to any order, complaint or summons issued pursuant to this section.

Added by St.2010, c. 23, eff. May 10, 2010.

§ 10. Confidentiality of records

The records of cases arising out of an action brought under this chapter in which the plaintiff or defendant is a minor shall be withheld from public inspection except by order of the court; provided, however, that such records shall be open, at all reasonable times, to the inspection of the minor, such minor's parent, guardian and attorney and to the plaintiff and the plaintiff's attorney.

The plaintiff's residential address, residential telephone number and workplace name, address and telephone number, contained within the court records of cases arising out of an action brought by a plaintiff under this chapter, shall be confidential and withheld from public inspection, except by order of the court; provided, however, that the plaintiff's residential address and workplace address shall appear on the court order and be accessible to the defendant and the defendant's attorney unless the plaintiff specifically requests that this information be withheld from the order. All confidential portions of the records shall be accessible at all reasonable times to the plaintiff and plaintiff's attorney, to others specifically authorized by the plaintiff to obtain such information and to prosecutors, victim-witness advocates as defined in section 1 of chapter 258B, sexual assault counselors as defined in section 20J of chapter 233 and law officers, if such access is necessary in the performance of their duties. This paragraph shall apply to any protection order issued by another jurisdiction filed with a court of the commonwealth pursuant to section 7. Such confidential portions of the court records shall not be deemed to be public records under clause Twenty-sixth of section 7 of chapter 4.

Added by St.2010, c. 23, eff. May 10, 2010.

§ 11. Adoption of suitable form of complaint

The chief justice for administration and management shall adopt a form of complaint for use under this chapter which shall be in such form and language to permit a plaintiff to prepare and file such complaint pro se.

Added by St.2010, c. 23, eff. May 10, 2010.

§ 12. Assessment against persons referred to a treatment program as condition of probation

The court shall impose an assessment of $350 against any person who has been referred to a treatment program as a condition of probation. Such assessment shall be in addition to the cost of the treatment program. In the discretion of the court, such assessment may be reduced or waived if the court finds that such person is indigent or that payment of the assessment would cause the person, or the dependents of such person, severe financial hardship. Assessments made pursuant to this section shall be in addition to any other fines, assessments or restitution imposed in any disposition. All funds collected by the court pursuant to this section shall be transmitted monthly to the state treasurer, who shall deposit such funds into the General Fund.

Added by St.2010, c. 23, eff. May 10, 2010.

PART IV

CRIMES, PUNISHMENTS AND PROCEEDINGS IN CRIMINAL CASES

TITLE I

CRIMES AND PUNISHMENTS

CHAPTER 263

RIGHTS OF PERSONS ACCUSED OF CRIME

The section headings for the General Laws in this pamphlet have been editorially supplied.

§ 1. Nature of crime; right to be informed; penalty

Whoever is arrested by virtue of process, or whoever is taken into custody by an officer, has a right to know from the officer who arrests or claims to detain him the true ground on which the arrest is made; and an officer who refuses to answer a question relative to the reason for such arrest, or answers such question untruly, or assigns to the person arrested an untrue reason for the arrest, or neglects upon request to exhibit to the person arrested, or to any other person acting in his behalf, the precept by virtue of which such arrest has been made, shall be punished by a fine of not more than one thousand dollars or by imprisonment for not more than one year.

Historical and Statutory Notes

St.1852, c. 224, § 1.
G.S.1860, c. 158, § 1.
P.S.1882, c. 200, § 1.
R.L.1902, c. 205, § 1.

§ 1A. Fingerprinting and photographing

Whoever is arrested by virtue of process, or is taken into custody by an officer, and charged with the commission of a felony shall be fingerprinted, according to the system of the bureau of investigation and intelligence in the department of state police, and may be photographed. Two copies of such fingerprints and photographs shall be forwarded within a reasonable time to the colonel of state police by the person in charge of the police department taking such fingerprints and photographs.

Added by St.1964, c. 443. Amended by St.1972, c. 217; St.1991, c. 412, § 96.

§ 2. Arrest on false pretence; penalty

An officer who arrests or takes into or detains in custody a person, pretending to have a process if he has none, or pretending to have a different process from that which he has, shall be punished by a fine of not more than one thousand dollars or by imprisonment for not more than one year.

Historical and Statutory Notes

St.1852, c. 224, § 2.
G.S.1860, c. 158, § 2.
P.S.1882, c. 200, § 2.
R.L.1902, c. 205, § 2.

§ 3. False imprisonment; actions against officers

No action, except for use of excessive force, shall lie against any officer other than the arresting officer, by reason of the fact that, in good faith and in the performance of his duties, he participates in the arrest or imprisonment of any person believed to be guilty of a crime unless it can be shown that such other officer in the performance of his duties took an active part in the arrest or imprisonment as aforesaid, either by ordering or directing that said arrest or imprisonment take place or be made, or by actually initiating the making and carrying out of said arrest and imprisonment. No action, except for use of excessive force, shall lie against any bystander assisting an officer in making an arrest, at the request of the officer.

Historical and Statutory Notes

St.1914, c. 126.

§ 4. Prosecution of crimes; manner

No person shall be held to answer in any court for an alleged crime, except upon an indictment by a grand jury or upon a complaint before a district court, the housing court of the city of Boston, the western division of the housing court department, the northeastern division of the housing court department, the southeastern division of the housing court department, the housing court of the county of Worcester or in proceedings before a court-martial.

A defendant charged with an offense punishable by imprisonment in state prison shall have the right to be proceeded against by indictment except when the offense charged is within the concurrent jurisdiction of the district and superior courts and the district court retains jurisdiction.

No juvenile shall be sentenced to any punishment as is provided by law for the offense by a juvenile court or a juvenile session of a district court, as the case may be, unless he has been proceeded against by indictment or has waived indictment pursuant to section four A of chapter two hundred and sixty-three, except as otherwise provided in section seventy-two A of chapter one hundred and nineteen. The clerk of the superior court in which an indictment of such juvenile is returned shall promptly remit the indictment to the clerk of the juvenile court or the juvenile session of the district court, as the case may be, in which such indictment is to be tried.

Amended by St.1953, c. 319, § 28; St.1971, c. 843, § 20; St.1973, c. 591, § 19; St.1979, c. 344, § 17; St.1983, c. 575, § 11; St.1987, c. 755, § 14; St.1991, c. 488, § 10; St.1992, c. 379, § 180; St.1992, c. 398, § 7; St.1996, c. 200, § 35; St.2000, c. 159, § 292.

Historical and Statutory Notes

R.S.1836, c. 123, § 1.
G.S.1860, c. 158, § 3.
P.S.1882, c. 200, § 3.
R.L.1902, c. 205, § 3.

§ 4A. Waiver of indictment; procedure

A defendant charged in the district court with an offense as to which he has the right to be proceeded against by indictment shall have the right, except when the offense charged is a capital crime, to waive that right, whereupon the court shall have as full jurisdiction of the complaint as if an indictment had been found. If a defendant is so charged and requests a probable cause hearing in district court, that request shall constitute a waiver of the right to be proceeded against by indictment and the prosecution may proceed upon the complaint. If a defendant waives the right to be proceeded against by indictment, a probable cause hearing shall be held in the district court unless the defendant waives the probable cause hearing or unless the prosecutor elects to proceed by indictment pursuant to the Massachusetts Rules of Criminal Procedure.

If the district attorney desires to charge a defendant who waives indictment hereunder with an additional non-capital crime which is not charged in the complaint upon which the prosecution is proceeding and as to which there is the right to be proceeded against by indictment, the district attorney may prepare an additional complaint charging such additional crime and serve that complaint upon the defendant so as to give the defendant an opportunity to waive indictment upon such additional charge.

Added by St.1934, c. 358. Amended by St.1979, c. 344, § 18; St.1986, c. 557, § 189.

§ 5. Counsel; right of accused

A person accused of crime shall at his trial be allowed to be heard by counsel, to defend himself, to produce witnesses and proofs in his favor and to meet the witnesses produced against him face to face.

Historical and Statutory Notes

R.S.1836, c. 123, § 2.
G.S.1860, c. 158, § 4.
P.S.1882, c. 200, § 4.
R.L.1902, c. 205, § 4.

§ 5A. Driving while intoxicated; right to medical examination; notice

A person held in custody at a police station or other place of detention, charged with operating a motor vehicle while under the influence of intoxicating liquor, shall have the right, at his request and at his expense, to be examined immediately by a physician selected by him. The police official in charge of such station or place of detention, or his designee, shall inform him of such right immediately upon being booked, and shall afford him a reasonable opportunity to exercise it. Such person shall, immediately upon being booked, be given a copy of this section unless such a copy is posted in the police station or other place of detention in a conspicuous place to which such person has access.

Added by St.1958, c. 401. Amended by St.1960, c. 237; St.1983, c. 557.

§ 6. Conviction; manner; waiver of jury trial

A person indicted for a crime shall not be convicted thereof except by confessing his guilt in open court, by admitting the truth of the charge against him by his plea or demurrer or by the verdict of a jury accepted and recorded by the court or, in any criminal case other than a capital case, by the judgment of the court. Any defendant in a criminal case other than a capital case, whether begun by indictment or upon complaint, may, if he shall so elect, when called upon to plead, or later and before a jury has been impanelled to try him upon such indictment or complaint, waive his right to trial by jury by signing a written waiver thereof and filing the same with the clerk of the court. If the court consents to the waiver, he shall be tried by the court instead of by a jury, but not, however, unless all the defendants, if there are two or more charged with related offenses, whether prosecuted under the same or different indictments or complaints shall have exercised such election before a jury has been impanelled to try any of the defendants; and in every such case the court shall have jurisdiction to hear and try such cause and render judgment and sentence thereon. Except where there is more than one defendant involved as aforesaid, consent to said waiver shall not be denied in the district court or the Boston municipal court if the waiver is filed before the case is transferred for jury trial to the appropriate jury session, as provided in section twenty-seven A of chapter two hundred and eighteen.

Amended by St.1933, c. 246, § 1; St.1971, c. 843, § 21; St.1973, c. 591, § 20; St.1979, c. 344, § 19; St.1992, c. 379, § 181.

Historical and Statutory Notes

R.S.1836, c. 123, § 3.
G.S.1860, c. 158, § 5.
P.S.1882, c. 200, § 5.
R.L.1902, c. 205, § 5.
St.1929, c. 185, § 1.

§ 7. Acquittal; effect on subsequent charges

A person shall not be held to answer on a second indictment or complaint for a crime of which he has been acquitted upon the facts and merits; but he may plead such acquittal in bar of any subsequent prosecution for the same crime, notwithstanding any defect in the form or substance of the indictment or complaint on which he was acquitted.

Historical and Statutory Notes

R.S.1836, c. 123, § 4.
G.S.1860, c. 158, § 6.
P.S.1882, c. 200, § 6.
R.L.1902, c. 205, § 6.

§ 8. Acquittal on defective pleadings; subsequent indictment

If a person has been acquitted by reason of a variance between the indictment or complaint and the proof, or by reason of a defect of form or substance in the indictment or complaint, he may be again arraigned, tried and convicted for the same crime on a new indictment or complaint, notwithstanding such former acquittal.

Historical and Statutory Notes

R.S.1836, c. 123, § 5.
G.S.1860, c. 158, § 7.
P.S.1882, c. 200, § 7.
R.L.1902, c. 205, § 7.

§ 8A. Acquittal on merits in district court or housing courts of city of Boston and county of Worcester; effect

A person shall not be held to answer in a district court or the housing court of the city of Boston, the western division of the housing court department, the northeastern division of the housing court department, the southeastern division of the housing court department, or the housing court of the county of Worcester to a second complaint for an offense for which he has already been tried upon the merits in a district court or in the housing court of the city of Boston, the housing court of the county of Hampden, the northeastern division of the housing court department, the southeastern division of the housing court department, or the housing court of the county of Worcester.

Amended by St.1953, c. 319, § 29; St.1971, c. 843, § 22; St.1973, c. 591, § 21; St.1983, c. 575, § 12; St.1987, c. 755, § 15; St.2000, c. 159, § 293.

Historical and Statutory Notes

St.1922, c. 432.

§ 9. Punishment; conditions precedent

A person shall not be punished for a crime unless he has been legally convicted thereof by a court having competent jurisdiction of the cause and of the person.

Historical and Statutory Notes

R.S.1836, c. 123, § 6.
G.S.1860, c. 158, § 8.
P.S.1882, c. 200, § 8.
R.L.1902, c. 205, § 8.

CHAPTER 263A

WITNESS PROTECTION IN CRIMINAL MATTERS

Chapter 263A of the General Laws was added by St.2006, c. 48, § 1.

The section headings for the General Laws in this pamphlet have been editorially supplied.

§ 1. Definitions

For the purposes of this chapter, the following words shall have the following meanings:—

"Board", the witness protection board established in section 2.

"Prosecuting officer", the attorney general or a district attorney from each county.

"Critical witness", any person who is participating in a criminal investigation, or has received a subpoena or who is reasonably expected to give testimony that is, in the judgment of the prosecuting officer, essential to a criminal investigation or proceeding or such person's relatives, guardians, friends or associates who are reasonably endangered by such person's participation in the criminal investigation or proceeding.

Added by St.2006, c. 48, § 1, eff. Mar. 30, 2006.

§ 2. Witness protection board; composition; powers and duties

There is hereby established a witness protection board within the executive office of public safety consisting of the secretary of public safety, the attorney general, the auditor, a chief of police appointed by the Massachusetts Chiefs of Police Association, and a district attorney appointed by the Massachusetts District Attorney's Association, or any member's respective designees. The board shall oversee the commonwealth's witness protection program and coordinate the efforts of state, county and law enforcement agencies to protect the health, safety and welfare of witnesses including, but not limited to, the administration and approval of funding for witness protection services. The board shall promulgate rules and regulations for the administration of the commonwealth's witness protection program and establish procedures to maximize federal funds for witness protection services.

Added by St.2006, c. 48, § 1, eff. Mar. 30, 2006.

§ 3. Petition requesting witness protection services

In any criminal investigation or proceeding, the prosecuting officer with jurisdiction over the investigation or proceeding may file a petition with the board requesting witness protection services for a critical witness if the prosecuting officer certifies that such witness's participation in the investigation or proceeding places the witness at risk of harm including, but not limited to, intimidation or retaliatory violence. The petition shall include a proposed plan for protective services which shall include, but not be limited to, projected costs, method of protection and likely duration of services. The board shall review the petition as soon as possible and if, by a vote of 3 or more board members, finds that the petition and plan comply with the rules and regulations established by the board, the board shall assist the prosecuting officer to coordinate the efforts of state, county and local agencies to secure witness protection services. The board shall, subject to appropriation, reimburse the prosecuting officer for any witness protection related costs that comply with the regulations and guidelines established by the board.

Added by St.2006, c. 48, § 1, eff. Mar. 30, 2006.

§ 4. Temporary action based on exigent circumstances without prior approval by board

If a prosecuting officer determines that exigent circumstances exist regarding an imminent threat to the safety of a critical witness, he may take any appropriate temporary action he determines is necessary to protect the safety of the witness without prior approval of the board. The prosecuting officer shall inform the board of the action taken and the related costs within 48 hours. Any such costs, which would otherwise be in compliance with the rules and regulations established by the board pursuant to section 2, may be reimbursed to the prosecuting officer.

Added by St.2006, c. 48, § 1, eff. Mar. 30, 2006.

§ 5. Protective services provided to critical witnesses; notice to defense counsel

Protective services provided to a critical witness may include, but not be limited to:—

(a) any necessary armed protection or escort, marked or unmarked surveillance or periodic visits or contact by law enforcement officials prior, during or subsequent to a criminal proceeding;

(b) physical relocation to an alternate shelter, housing or residence;

(c) reasonable housing expenses;

(d) transportation or storage of personal possessions;

(e) basic living expenses; and

(f) petition for a protective order on any individual identified as a threat to a critical witness.

Any protective services provided to a critical witness shall be made known to defense counsel pursuant to Rule 14 of the Massachusetts Rules of Criminal Procedure.

Added by St.2006, c. 48, § 1, eff. Mar. 30, 2006.

§ 6. Written memorandum of understanding; persons required to sign; contents

Before providing witness protection services to any critical witness under this chapter, except where it is determined that temporary protective services are necessary pursuant to section 4, the prosecuting officer shall enter into a written memorandum of understanding with such witness. If temporary protective services have been provided pursuant to section 4, a written memorandum of understanding shall be entered into as soon as practicable. The written memorandum of understanding shall be signed by: the prosecuting officer or his designee; the witness to be afforded protective services; the witness' guardian if the witness is a minor; and the witness'; attorney if the witness is represented by counsel. Such written memorandum of understanding shall not be considered a grant of immunity. The written memorandum of understanding shall include:—

(a) The responsibilities agreed to by the witness while receiving protective services, shall include, but not limited to, an agreement to:—

(i) provide complete and truthful information to all relevant law enforcement officials related to all relevant investigations, and to testify completely and truthfully in all appropriate proceedings;

(ii) not commit any crime;

(iii) take all necessary precautions to avoid making known to others his participation in the witness protection program or the provision of protective services under such program;

(iv) comply with any legal obligations or civil judgments against the witness;

(v) cooperate with all reasonable requests of officers and employees of the commonwealth who are providing protective services under this chapter;

(vi) designate another person to act as an agent for the service of process. Under no circumstances shall the person so designated be an employee of the prosecuting officer or other law enforcement agency, or be a member of or perform duties on behalf of the witness protection board;

(vii) make a sworn statement of all outstanding legal obligations, including obligations concerning child custody and visitation, and child support;

(viii) disclose any probation or parole conditions, obligations, or responsibilities; and

(ix) regularly inform the prosecuting officer of the activities and current address of the witness.

(b) The responsibilities agreed to by the commonwealth while providing protective services shall include, but not be limited to:

(i) The names and telephone numbers of representatives of the prosecuting officer or law enforcement personnel to contact if the witness has questions or concerns related to the protective services or the witness' safety;

(ii) The protective services that the prosecuting officer has determined will be requested, and, if authorized, to be provided to the witness under this chapter; and

(iii) The procedures to be followed, if there is a determination by the prosecuting officer that there has occurred a material breach of the memorandum of understanding, as established by the prosecuting officer.

Added by St.2006, c. 48, § 1, eff. Mar. 30, 2006.

§ 7. Refusal of protective services; revocation of services upon violation of memorandum of understanding

If a witness, after being offered protective services under this chapter, at any time declines to receive such services, the prosecuting officer shall request that the witness make such refusal in writing, or, if the witness refuses to document such refusal of services in writing, the prosecuting officer shall document the refusal and inform the witness protection board forthwith that the witness has declined protective services. If a witness violates the terms of the memorandum of understanding set forth in section 6 or any other condition of receiving witness protection services under this chapter, the prosecuting officer may revoke and terminate all protective services, and shall so advise the witness in writing. The prosecuting officer shall notify the board forthwith of such revocation and grounds therefore.

Added by St.2006, c. 48, § 1, eff. Mar. 30, 2006.

§ 8. Relocation of critical witness within public housing system

Notwithstanding any general or special law to the contrary, or any regulation, rule or ordinance, if a petition and plan for witness protection, approved by the board, requires relocation of a critical witness within the public housing system, such relocation shall be effectuated without regard to any impediment including, but not limited to, any existing waiting list.

Added by St.2006, c. 48, § 1, eff. Mar. 30, 2006.

§ 9. Relocation of critical witness to another public school

Notwithstanding any general or special law to the contrary, or any regulation, rule or ordinance, if a petition and plan for witness protection, approved by the witness protection board, requires relocation of a critical witness to another public school within or without of the witness's current school system, such relocation shall be effectuated without regard to any impediment including, but not limited to, class capacity limits and jurisdictional boundaries of any given school district.

Added by St.2006, c. 48, § 1, eff. Mar. 30, 2006.

§ 10. Entitlement or private right of action not available; governmental immunity

Nothing in this section shall be construed as creating a right, entitlement or cause of action on behalf of any person against any public employee, public agency, the commonwealth, or any agency responsible for the provision of services set forth in this chapter. The commonwealth, its officers and employees, and law enforcement personnel shall have immunity from suit based on any decision, act or omission related to this chapter.

Added by St.2006, c. 48, § 1, eff. Mar. 30, 2006.

§ 11. Liaison with United States Marshal's office; pursuit of federal resources and funding

The board shall establish a liaison with the United States Marshal's office in order to facilitate the legal processes over which the federal government has sole authority. The liaison shall coordinate all requests for federal assistance relating to witness protection.

The board shall pursue all federal sources that may be available for implementing this chapter. For that purpose, the board shall establish a liaison with the United States Department of Justice.

The board shall, in conjunction with the executive office of administration and finance and the senate and house ways and means committees, establish procedures to maximize federal funding for witness protection services.

Added by St.2006, c. 48, § 1, eff. Mar. 30, 2006.

§ 12. Confidentiality of records

Records of the board and all records relating to petitions and filed with the board shall be confidential and shall not be public records. Section 11A and section 11A½ of chapter 30A shall not apply to meetings, discussions or deliberations of the board.

Added by St.2006, c. 48, § 1, eff. Mar. 30, 2006.

§ 13. Disclosure of identity or location of witness or other sensitive information; penalties

(a) A prosecuting officer may disclose or refuse to disclose the identity or location of a protected witness, or any other matter concerning a protected witness or the program, after balancing the danger such disclosure may pose to the protected witness, the detriment it may cause to the general effectiveness of the program, and the benefit it may afford to the public or the person seeking discovery, except that a prosecuting officer shall, upon the request of a federal, state or local law enforcement official, or pursuant to a court order, disclose to such official the identity, location and criminal records relating to the protected witness when the prosecuting officer knows, or the request from such official indicates, that the protected witness is under criminal investigation for, or has been arrested for, or charged with, a felony.

(b) Whoever, without the express written authorization of the prosecuting officer, knowingly discloses any information received from the prosecuting officer or generated in connection with witness protection services and which poses a risk of harm: to a program participant; of disclosure of any person's participation in such program; or of jeopardizing the objectives of the program shall be punished by imprisonment in the house of correction for not more than 2½ years or by a fine of not more than $5,000, or by both such fine and imprisonment. This section shall not apply to: any members of the board; members of the attorney general's office; members of the district attorneys' offices; law enforcement; or agents thereof, acting in the lawful discharge of their duties.

Added by St.2006, c. 48, § 1, eff. Mar. 30, 2006.

CHAPTER 264

CRIMES AGAINST GOVERNMENTS

The section headings for the General Laws in this pamphlet have been editorially supplied.

§ 1. Treason defined

Treason against the commonwealth shall consist only in levying war against it, or in adhering to the enemies thereof, giving them aid and comfort; it shall not be bailable.

Historical and Statutory Notes

C.L. c. 15, § 12; c. 263, § 2.
St.1696, c. 255, § 1.
St.1744–5, c. 6, § 1.
St.1776–7, c. 32, §§ 2, 3.
R.S.1836, c. 124, § 1.
St.1852, c. 259, § 4.
G.S.1860, c. 159, § 1; c. 170, § 54.
St.1871, c. 61.
P.S.1882, c. 201, § 1; c. 212, § 72.
R.L.1902, c. 206, § 1.

§ 2. Penalty for treason

Whoever commits treason against the commonwealth shall be punished by imprisonment in the state prison for life.

Historical and Statutory Notes

B.L. c. 94, § 12.
C.L. c. 263, § 2.
St.1696, c. 255, § 1.
St.1744–5, c. 6, § 1.
St.1776–7, c. 32, § 2.
R.S.1836, c. 124, § 2.
St.1852, c. 259, § 1.
G.S.1860, c. 159, § 2.
P.S.1882, c. 201, § 2.
R.L.1902, c. 206, § 2.

§ 3. Misprision of treason; penalty

Whoever, having knowledge of the commission of treason, conceals the same and does not as soon as may be disclose and make known such treason to the governor, or to a justice of the supreme judicial or superior court, shall be guilty of misprision of treason, and shall be punished by a fine of not more than one thousand dollars or by imprisonment in the state prison for not more than five years, or in jail for not more than two years.

Historical and Statutory Notes

St.1776–7, c. 32, §§ 4, 5.
R.S.1836, c. 124, § 3.
G.S.1860, c. 159, § 3.
P.S.1882, c. 201, § 3.
R.L.1902, c. 206, § 3.

§ 4. Treason; manner of conviction

No person shall be convicted of treason except by the testimony of two witnesses to the same overt act of treason whereof he stands indicted, unless he confesses the same in open court.

Historical and Statutory Notes

St.1776–7, c. 32, § 11.
R.S.1836, c. 124, § 4.
G.S.1860, c. 159, § 4.
P.S.1882, c. 201, § 4.
R.L.1902, c. 206, § 4.

§ 5. Flag; penalty for misuse

Whoever publicly burns or otherwise mutilates, tramples upon, defaces or treats contemptuously the flag of the United States or of Massachusetts, whether such flag is public or private property, or whoever displays such flag or any representation thereof upon which are words, figures, advertisements or designs, or whoever causes or permits such flag to be used in a parade as a receptacle for depositing or collecting money or any other article or thing, or whoever exposes to public view, manufactures, sells, exposes for sale, gives away or has in his possession for sale or to give away or for use for any purpose, any article or substance, being an article of merchandise or a receptacle of merchandise or articles upon which is attached, through a wrapping or otherwise, engraved or printed in any manner, a representation of the United States flag, or whoever uses any representation of the arms or the great seal of the commonwealth for any advertising or commercial purpose, shall be punished by a fine of not less than one hundred dollars or by imprisonment for not more than one year, or both. Words, figures, advertisements or designs attached to, or directly or indirectly connected with, such flag or any representation thereof in such manner that such flag or its representation is used to attract attention to or advertise such words, figures, advertisements or designs, shall for the purposes of this section be deemed to be upon such flag. Notwithstanding the foregoing, there may be attached to the staff bearing a flag of the United States or of Massachusetts belonging to an organization of veterans of the Civil War, to a camp of the United Spanish War Veterans, to a post or department of The American Legion, or to a post or department of the Veterans of Foreign Wars of the United States, or to a post or department of the Jewish War Veterans of the United States, or to a camp or department of the Sons of Union Veterans of the Civil War, or to a barracks or department of the Veterans of World War I of the U. S. A., or belonging to or used in the service of the United States or the commonwealth, a streamer having inscribed thereon the names of battles and the name and number of the organization to which such flag belongs. For the purposes of this section, a flag shall be deemed to continue to belong to any organization of veterans hereinbefore specified, although such organization has ceased to exist, during such time as it remains in the lawful ownership or custody of any other of the aforesaid organizations or of the commonwealth or of any political subdivision thereof, or of any patriotic or historical society incorporated under the laws of the commonwealth or determined by the adjutant general to be a proper custodian thereof. For the purposes of this section the term "flag of the United States" shall mean any flag which has been designated by Act or Resolution of the Congress of the United States as the national emblem, whether or not such designation is currently in force.

Amended by St.1932, c. 298; St.1933, c. 153, § 3; St.1934, c. 56; St.1941, c. 117, § 1; St.1959, c. 59, § 4; St.1971, c. 74; St.1971, c. 655.

Historical and Statutory Notes

St.1899, c. 254.
St.1901, c. 153.
R.L.1902, c. 206, § 5.
St.1903, c. 195.
St.1907, c. 232, § 2.
St.1913, c. 464.
St.1913, c. 604.
St.1914, c. 570.
St.1917, c. 265.
St.1918, c. 257, § 1.
St.1919, c. 5.
St.1920, c. 2.
St.1921, c. 278.
St.1922, c. 227.

§ 6. Flag; use in print in certain cases

The preceding section shall not apply to publications issued solely for the purpose of giving information in relation to the flag, or of promoting patriotism or of encouraging the study of American history, or to any newspaper, periodical, book, pamphlet, certificate, diploma, warrant, or commission of appointment to office, ornamental picture, article of jewelry, or stationery for use in correspondence, on which is printed, painted, or placed the flag of the United States not connected with any advertisement and not used for advertising purposes, or to any article of jewelry upon which is placed a representation of the arms or flag of the commonwealth not connected with any advertisement and not used for advertising purposes; but no words, figures, designs or other marks of any kind shall be placed upon the flag of the United States or of the commonwealth or representation thereof, or upon any representation of the arms of the commonwealth.

Historical and Statutory Notes

St.1916, c. 36.
St.1917, c. 289.
St.1928, c. 154.

§ 7. Foreign flags; misuse; penalty

Whoever publicly mutilates, tramples upon, defaces or treats contemptuously the flag or emblem of a foreign country at peace with the United States, whether such flag or emblem is public or private property, or whoever displays such flag or emblem or any representation thereof upon which are words, figures, advertisements or designs, shall be punished by a fine of not less than five nor more than fifty dollars.

Historical and Statutory Notes

St.1912, c. 197.

§ 8. Foreign flag; display; penalty; exception

Whoever displays the flag or emblem of a foreign country upon the outside of a state, county, city or town building or public schoolhouse shall be punished by a fine of not more than twenty dollars; but, except as to public schoolhouses, this section shall not apply when a citizen of such foreign country becomes the guest of the United States or of the commonwealth, or when a diplomatic representative of a foreign country is a guest at said public building and,[1] if the governor by proclamation authorizes the flag of the country of which such guest is a citizen to be displayed upon public buildings.

Amended by St.1998, c. 34.

[1] So in enrolled bill. Probably should read ", and".

Historical and Statutory Notes

St.1895, c. 115.
R.L.1902, c. 206, § 6.

§ 9. National anthem; manner of playing

Whoever plays, sings or renders the "Star Spangled Banner" in any public place, theatre, motion picture hall, restaurant or café, or at any public entertainment, other than as a whole and separate composition or number, without embellishment or addition in the way of national or other melodies, or whoever plays, sings or renders the "Star Spangled Banner", or any part thereof, as dance music, as an exit march or as a part of a medley of any kind, shall be punished by a fine of not more than one hundred dollars.

Historical and Statutory Notes

St.1917, c. 311, §§ 1, 2.

§ 10. Repealed, 1962, 285, Sec. 1

§ 10A. Uniforms; penalty for unlawful use

Whoever wears the uniform, or any distinctive part thereof, of the United States army, navy, marine corps, revenue cutter service, or coast guard, or of the national guard, or of any organization enumerated in section seventy of chapter two hundred and sixty-six, or wears a hat, cap or other apparel similar to or resembling the hat, cap or other distinctive part of any such uniform, while engaged, for personal profit, in soliciting alms, in selling merchandise or taking orders for the same, in seeking or receiving contributions in support of any cause, enterprise or undertaking or in soliciting or receiving subscriptions to any book, paper or magazine, shall be punished by a fine of not more than one hundred dollars, or by imprisonment for not more than three months; provided, that this section shall not apply to the sale of property or any other act or transaction conducted under authority of the government of the United States, and provided further, that no person shall be subject to prosecution hereunder for wearing the uniform, or any distinctive part thereof, while engaged as aforesaid, of any organization enumerated in said section seventy if he so acted under authority of such organization or any post, camp or other unit thereof.

Amended by St.1933, c. 276.

Historical and Statutory Notes

St.1924, c. 219.

§ 11. Promotion of anarchy; prohibition

Whoever by speech or by exhibition, distribution or promulgation of any written or printed document, paper or pictorial representation advocates, advises, counsels or incites assault upon any public official, or the killing of any person, or the unlawful destruction of real or personal property, or the overthrow by force or violence or other unlawful means of the government of the commonwealth or of the United States, shall be punished by imprisonment in the state prison for not more than three years, or in jail for not more than two and one half years, or by a fine of not more than one thousand dollars; provided, that this section shall not be construed as reducing the penalty now imposed for the violation of any law. It shall be unlawful for any person who shall have been convicted of a violation of this section, whether or not any sentence shall have been imposed, to perform the duties of a teacher or of an officer of administration in any public or private educational institution, and the superior court, in a suit by the commonwealth, shall have jurisdiction in equity to restrain and enjoin any such person from performing such duties thereafter; provided, that any such restraining order or injunction shall be forthwith vacated if such conviction shall be set aside.

Amended by St.1948, c. 160, § 1; St.1954, c. 584, § 1.

Historical and Statutory Notes

St.1919, c. 191, § 1.

§ 12. Repealed, 1954, 584, Sec. 2

§ 13. Repealed, 1951, 805, Sec. 1

§ 14. Repealed, 1986, 30

§ 14A. Educational activities; participation; exchange teachers; necessity of oath

Any city or town of the commonwealth may, through its school committee, participate in the educational activities under the United States Educational Program conducted by the department of state pursuant to Public Law 584, 79th Congress, and Public Law 402, 80th Congress, whereby there is an interchange of teaching positions between a teacher of such city or town and a teacher from abroad under an arrangement or agreement which provides that each teacher shall continue to receive his salary from his own school. The salary may be paid by such city or town notwithstanding that the teacher to whom it is paid is not actually rendering service within the schools thereof. The exchange teacher from abroad shall not be required to take or subscribe to any oaths or pledge of allegiance which is inconsistent with his citizenship in a foreign country.

Added by St.1954, c. 677.

§ 15. Repealed, 1986, 30

§ 16. Subversive organization defined

The term "subversive organization" as used in sections seventeen, eighteen, nineteen, twenty-one, twenty-two and twenty-three of this chapter shall mean any form of association of three or more persons, however named or characterized, and by whatever legal or non-legal entity or non-entity it be established, and whether incorporated or otherwise for the common purpose of advocating, advising, counseling or inciting the overthrow by force or violence, or by other unlawful means, of the government of the commonwealth or of the United States.

Added by St.1951, c. 805, § 3.

§ 16A. Communist Party

The Communist Party is hereby declared to be a subversive organization.

Added by St.1951, c. 805, § 3.

§ 17. Subversive organizations; prohibition

A subversive organization is hereby declared to be unlawful.

Added by St.1951, c. 805, § 3.

§ 18. Subversive organizations; actions to enjoin; duty of attorney general

The attorney general shall bring an action in the superior court by an information or petition in equity against any organization which he has reasonable cause to believe is a subversive organization. The fact that such information or petition has been or is to be filed shall not be made public until an order of notice, hereinafter referred to, is issued.

A justice of the superior court shall, upon a summary examination of the information or petition and such supporting depositions, other testimony or evidence as he may require, if he is of the opinion that there is reasonable cause to believe that such organization is subversive, issue an order of notice against such organization to show cause why there should not be an adjudication to that effect. Notice of such order of notice shall be sent by registered mail to such officers of such organization as are known to the court, and to any other persons, including members, as the court may order, at least fourteen days before the return day of said order of notice. Notice of such order shall also be given by publication once each week for two successive weeks in a daily newspaper published in the city of Boston. Any officer or member of any such organization or its attorney may appear and answer on its behalf on or before the return day or such later time as the court may allow. The respondent shall have the right to claim a trial by jury within the time allowed for filing its answer or within such further time as the court may allow within its discretion. If no person appears and answers the court may on its own motion or upon motion of the petitioner default the organization. If an appearance is entered and answer filed the case shall be set down for a speedy hearing.

Such hearing shall be conducted in accordance with the usual course of proceedings in equity, including all rights of exception and appeal. Upon such hearing or upon default the court may make an adjudication that the organization is a subversive organization and may enjoin such organization from acting further as such, may order the dissolution of the organization and shall cause the secretary of state to be notified of the finding of the court; provided, however, that the effectiveness of any such adjudication, injunction and order shall be stayed pending determination by the supreme judicial court of any exceptions or appeals; or the court may find that the organization is not a subversive organization. Upon any final determination that the organization is subversive notice thereof shall be published by the secretary of state once each week for two successive weeks in a daily newspaper published in the city of Boston and the court shall order any funds or property of such organization turned over to the treasurer of the commonwealth which shall then be considered escheated. The fact that proceedings have begun or findings or decision made under this section shall not be admissible in evidence in any action brought under the provisions of sections eleven, nineteen, twenty-one or twenty-three.

Added by St.1951, c. 805, § 3. Amended by St.1952, c. 380.

§ 19. Subversive organization; knowingly becoming or remaining member; penalty

Any person who becomes or remains a member of any organization knowing it to be a subversive organization shall be punished by imprisonment in the state prison for not more than three years or in jail for not more than two and one half years or by a fine of not more than one thousand dollars, provided that this section shall not be construed as reducing the penalty now imposed for the violation of any law.

Added by St.1951, c. 805, § 3. Amended by St.1954, c. 584, § 4.

§ 20. Public office; ineligibility of certain persons; removal of disability

No person who has been convicted of a violation of the provisions of section eleven, nineteen or twenty-three shall be eligible to election or appointment to any public office, or employment, nor as a teacher in any public or private educational institution, nor shall any person continue to hold any such office after final conviction. The superior court on petition of the attorney general shall have jurisdiction in equity to restrain and enjoin any such person from performing such duties thereafter and to prevent any such person's name being placed on any ballot for election to any office. The court may upon petition in its discretion after a lapse of five years from the date of final conviction under sections eleven, nineteen or twenty-three remove the disability if in its opinion such person can then be adjudged to be loyal to the government of the commonwealth and the United States.

Added by St.1951, c. 805, § 3.

§ 21. Subversive organizations; destruction or concealment of books; penalty

Whoever destroys or conceals books, records, files, membership lists or funds belonging to an organization which he knows to be a subversive organization shall be punished by imprisonment in the state prison for not more than three years or in jail for not more than two and one half years or by a fine of not more than one thousand dollars; provided, that this section shall not be construed as reducing the penalty now imposed for the violation of any law.

Added by St.1951, c. 805, § 3. Amended by St.1954, c. 584, § 3.

§ 22. Subversive organization; knowingly permitting to use building; penalty

Whoever being in charge of an auditorium, hall or other building shall knowingly permit it to be used by the Communist Party or by an organization which has been adjudicated a subversive organization under the provisions of section eighteen shall be punished by a fine of not more than one thousand dollars or by imprisonment for not more than one year, or both.

Added by St.1951, c. 805, § 3.

§ 23. Subversive organizations; contribution; penalty

Whoever contributes money or any other property having a value in money to an organization which he knows to be a subversive organization shall be punished by imprisonment in the state prison for not more than three years or in jail for not more than two and one half years or by a fine of not more than one thousand dollars.

Added by St.1951, c. 805, § 3. Amended by St.1954, c. 584, § 5.

CHAPTER 265

CRIMES AGAINST THE PERSON

The section headings for the General Laws in this pamphlet have been editorially supplied.

§ 1. Murder defined

Murder committed with deliberately premeditated malice aforethought, or with extreme atrocity or cruelty, or in the commission or attempted commission of a crime punishable with death or imprisonment for life, is murder in the first degree. Murder which does not appear to be in the first degree is murder in the second degree. Petit treason shall be prosecuted and punished as murder. The degree of murder shall be found by the jury.

Historical and Statutory Notes

St.1784, c. 69.
R.S.1836, c. 133, § 15.
St.1858, c. 154, §§ 1 to 3.
G.S.1860, c. 160, §§ 1 to 3, 7.
P.S.1882, c. 202, §§ 1 to 3, 7.
R.L.1902, c. 207, § 1.

§ 2. Punishment for murder; parole; executive clemency

Whoever is guilty of murder committed with deliberately premeditated malice aforethought or with extreme atrocity or cruelty, and who had attained the age of eighteen years at the time of the murder, may suffer the punishment of death pursuant to the procedures set forth in sections sixty-eight to seventy-one, inclusive, of chapter two hundred and seventy-nine. Any other person who is guilty of murder in the first degree shall be punished by imprisonment in the state prison for life. Whoever is guilty of murder in the second degree shall be punished by imprisonment in state prison for life. No person shall be eligible for parole under section one hundred and thirty-three A of chapter one hundred and twenty-seven while he is serving a life sentence for murder in the first degree, but if his sentence is commuted therefrom by the governor and council under the provisions of section one hundred and fifty-two of said chapter one hundred and twenty-seven he shall thereafter be subject to the provisions of law governing parole for persons sentenced for lesser offenses.

Amended by St.1951, c. 203; St.1955, c. 770, § 78; St.1956, c. 731, § 12; St.1979, c. 488, § 2; St.1982, c. 554, § 3.

The Massachusetts Supreme Judicial Court, in Com. v. Colon-Cruz, 470 N.E.2d 116, held the death penalty provisions of the punishment for murder law unconstitutional. The provisions of the law not related to the death penalty were held severable and valid.

Historical and Statutory Notes

B.L. c. 94, §§ 4 to 6.
C.L. c. 14, §§ 4, 5.
St.1697, c. 17.
St.1784, c. 44, § 1.
St.1804, c. 123, § 1.
R.S.1836, c. 125, § 1.
St.1858, c. 154, §§ 4, 5.
G.S.1860, c. 160, §§ 4, 5.
P.S.1882, c. 202, §§ 4, 5.
R.L.1902, c. 207, § 2.

§ 3. Duel; wound without and death within state; venue

An inhabitant or resident of this commonwealth who, by previous appointment or engagement made within the same, fights a duel outside its jurisdiction, and in so doing inflicts a mortal wound upon a person whereof he dies within the commonwealth shall be guilty of murder within this commonwealth, and may be indicted, tried and convicted in the county where the death occurs.

Historical and Statutory Notes

R.S.1836, c. 125, § 3.
G.S.1860, c. 160, § 9.
P.S.1882, c. 202, § 9.
R.L.1902, c. 207, § 3.

§ 4. Accessory in duel

An inhabitant or resident of this commonwealth who, by previous appointment or engagement made within the same, becomes the second of either party in such duel and is present as a second when a mortal wound is inflicted upon a person whereof he dies within this commonwealth shall be an accessory before the fact to murder in this commonwealth, and may be indicted, tried and convicted in the county where the death occurs.

Historical and Statutory Notes

R.S.1836, c. 125, § 4.
G.S.1860, c. 160, § 10.
P.S.1882, c. 202, § 10.
R.L.1902, c. 207, § 4.

§ 5. Duel; conviction or acquittal in foreign state; effect

A person indicted under either of the two preceding sections may plead a former conviction or acquittal of the same crime in any other state or country; and if his plea is admitted or established, it shall be a bar to all further proceedings against him for the same crime within this commonwealth.

Historical and Statutory Notes

R.S.1836, c. 125, § 5.
G.S.1860, c. 160, § 11.
P.S.1882, c. 202, § 11.
R.L.1902, c. 207, § 5.

§§ 6 to 8. Repealed, 1962, 285, Sec. 2

§ 9. Prize fighting; engaging

Whoever, except as provided in sections thirty-two to fifty, inclusive, of chapter one hundred and forty-seven, by previous appointment or arrangement, engages in a fight with another person shall be punished by imprisonment in the state prison for not more than ten years or by a fine of not more than five thousand dollars.

Historical and Statutory Notes

St.1849, c. 49, § 1.
G.S.1860, c. 160, § 15.
P.S.1882, c. 202, § 15.
R.L.1902, c. 207, § 9.

§ 10. Prize fight; aiding or promoting; penalty

Whoever, except as provided in sections thirty-two to fifty, inclusive, of chapter one hundred and forty-seven, is present at such fight as an aid, second or surgeon, or advises, encourages or promotes such fight, shall be punished by imprisonment in the state prison for not more than five years or by a fine of not more than one thousand dollars and by imprisonment in jail for not more than two and one half years.

Historical and Statutory Notes

St.1849, c. 49, § 2.
G.S.1860, c. 160, § 16.
P.S.1882, c. 202, § 16.
R.L.1902, c. 207, § 10.
St.1914, c. 635.
St.1918, c. 257, § 464.
St.1919, c. 5.
St.1920, c. 2.

§ 11. Prize fight; appointment within and fight without state; penalty

An inhabitant or resident of this commonwealth who, by previous appointment or engagement made in the same, leaves the same and engages in a fight with another person outside the limits thereof shall be punished by imprisonment in the state prison for not more than five years or by a fine of not more than five thousand dollars.

Historical and Statutory Notes

St.1849, c. 49, § 3.
G.S.1860, c. 160, § 17.
P.S.1882, c. 202, § 17.
R.L.1902, c. 207, § 11.

§ 12. Boxing, kickboxing, mixed martial arts or other unarmed combative sporting matches or sparring exhibitions; penalty

Whoever directly or indirectly, except as provided in sections 32 to 50A, inclusive, of chapter 147, gives, promotes or engages in a public boxing, kickboxing, mixed martial arts or other unarmed combative sporting match or sparring exhibition, or engages in a private boxing, kickboxing, mixed martial arts or other unarmed combative sporting event match or sparring exhibition, for which the contestants have received or have been promised any pecuniary reward, remuneration or consideration whatsoever shall be punished by imprisonment in the house of corrections for not more than 3 months or by a fine of not more than $5,000, or both such fine and imprisonment.

Amended by St.2009, c. 169, § 15, eff. Feb. 28, 2010.

Historical and Statutory Notes

St.1896, c. 422.
R.L.1902, c. 207, § 12.

§ 13. Manslaughter; punishment

Whoever commits manslaughter shall, except as hereinafter provided, be punished by imprisonment in the state prison for not more than twenty years or by a fine of not more than one thousand dollars and imprisonment in jail or a house of correction for not more than two and one half years. Whoever commits manslaughter while violating the provisions of sections 102 to 102C, inclusive, of chapter 266 shall be imprisoned in the state prison for life or for any term of years.

Amended by St.1971, c. 426; St.2010, c. 160, § 5, eff. July 15, 2010.

Historical and Statutory Notes

St.1784, c. 44, § 2.
St.1804, c. 123, § 3.
St.1818, c. 124, § 2.
R.S.1836, c. 125, § 9.
G.S.1860, c. 160, § 18.
P.S.1882, c. 202, § 18.
R.L.1902, c. 207, § 13.
St.1914, c. 635.
St.1918, c. 257, § 464.

St.1919, c. 5.
St.1920, c. 2.

§ 13½. Punishment for manslaughter while operating a motor vehicle

Whoever commits manslaughter while operating a motor vehicle in violation of paragraph (a) of subdivision (1) of section 24 of chapter 90 or section 8A of chapter 90B, shall be punished by imprisonment in the state prison for not less than 5 years and not more than 20 years, and by a fine of not more than $25,000. The sentence of imprisonment imposed upon such person shall not be reduced to less than 5 years, nor suspended, nor shall any such person be eligible for probation, parole or furlough or receive a deduction from his sentence for good conduct until he shall have served 5 years of such sentence. The commissioner of correction may, on the recommendation of the warden, superintendent or other person in charge of a correctional institution, or of the administrator of a county correctional institution, grant to an offender committed under this section a temporary release in the custody of an officer of such institution for the following purposes only: to attend the funeral of a relative; to visit a critically ill relative; to obtain emergency medical or psychiatric services unavailable at said institution; or to engage in employment pursuant to a work release program. Upon receipt of notice of a conviction under this section, the registrar may suspend the license or right to operate of such person for any extended period up to life, provided that such suspension be at least a 15 year period. A person aggrieved by a decision of the registrar pursuant to this section may file an appeal in the superior court of the trial court department. If the court determines that the registrar abused his discretion, the court may vacate the suspension or revocation of a license or right to operate and reduce the period of suspension or revocation as ordered by the registrar, but in no event may the reduced period of suspension be for less than 15 years.

Added by St.2005, c. 122, § 20, eff. Oct. 28, 2005.

§ 13A. Assault or assault and battery; punishment

(a) Whoever commits an assault or an assault and battery upon another shall be punished by imprisonment for not more than 2½ years in a house of correction or by a fine of not more than $1,000.

A summons may be issued instead of a warrant for the arrest of any person upon a complaint for a violation of any provision of this subsection if in the judgment of the court or justice receiving the complaint there is reason to believe that he will appear upon a summons.

(b) Whoever commits an assault or an assault and battery:

(i) upon another and by such assault and battery causes serious bodily injury;

(ii) upon another who is pregnant at the time of such assault and battery, knowing or having reason to know that the person is pregnant; or

(iii) upon another who he knows has an outstanding temporary or permanent vacate, restraining or no contact order or judgment issued pursuant to section 18, section 34B or 34C of chapter 208, section 32 of chapter 209, section 3, 4 or 5 of chapter 209A, or section 15 or 20 of chapter 209C, in effect against him at the time of such assault or assault and battery; shall be punished by imprisonment in the state prison for not more than 5 years or in the house of correction for not more than 2½ years, or by a fine of not more than $5,000, or by both such fine and imprisonment.

(c) For the purposes of this section, "serious bodily injury" shall mean bodily injury that results in a permanent disfigurement, loss or impairment of a bodily function, limb or organ, or a substantial risk of death.

Added by St.1943, c. 259, § 1. Amended by St.1945, c. 230; St.2002, c. 35, § 1.

§ 13B. Indecent assault and battery on child under age of 14; penalties

Whoever commits an indecent assault and battery on a child under the age of 14 shall be punished by imprisonment in the state prison for not more than 10 years, or by imprisonment in the house of correction for not more than 2½ years. A prosecution commenced under this section shall neither be continued without a finding nor placed on file.

In a prosecution under this section, a child under the age of 14 years shall be deemed incapable of consenting to any conduct of the defendant for which such defendant is being prosecuted.

Added by St.1953, c. 299; Amended by St.1958, c. 189; St.1980, c. 459, § 4; St.1986, c. 187; St.1998, c. 194, § 236; St.2008, c. 205, § 1, eff. Oct. 22, 2008.

§ 13B½. Commission of indecent assault and battery on a child under the age of 14 during commission of certain offenses or by mandated reporters; penalties

Whoever commits an indecent assault and battery on a child under the age of 14 and:

(a) the indecent assault and battery was committed during the commission or attempted commission of the following offenses:— (1) armed burglary as set forth in section 14 of chapter 266; (2) unarmed burglary as set forth in section 15 of said chapter 266; (3) breaking and entering as set forth in section 16 of said chapter 266; (4) entering without breaking as set forth in section 17 of said chapter 266; (5) breaking and entering into a dwelling house as set forth in section 18 of said chapter 266; (6) kidnapping as set forth in section 26 of chapter 265; (7) armed robbery as set forth in section 17 of said chapter 265; (8) unarmed robbery as set forth in section 19 of said chapter 265;

(9) assault and battery with a dangerous weapon or assault with a dangerous weapon, as set forth in sections 15A and 15B of said chapter 265; (10) home invasion as set forth in section 18C of said chapter 265; or (11) posing or exhibiting child in state of nudity or sexual conduct as set forth in section 29A of chapter 272; or

(b) at the time of commission of said indecent assault and battery, the defendant was a mandated reporter as is defined in section 21 of chapter 119, shall be punished by imprisonment in the state prison for life or for any term of years, but not less than 10 years. The sentence imposed on such person shall not be reduced to less than 10 years, or suspended, nor shall any person convicted under this section be eligible for probation, parole, work release, or furlough or receive any deduction from his sentence for good conduct until he shall have served 10 years of such sentence. Prosecutions commenced under this section shall neither be continued without a finding nor placed on file.

In a prosecution under this section, a child under the age of 14 years shall be deemed incapable of consenting to any conduct of the defendant for which such defendant is being prosecuted.

Added by St.2008, c. 205, § 1, eff. Oct. 22, 2008.

§ 13B¾. Commission of indecent assault and battery on a child under the age of 14 by certain previously convicted offenders; penalties

Whoever commits an indecent assault and battery on a child under the age of 14 and has been previously convicted of or adjudicated delinquent or as a youthful offender for: indecent assault and battery on a child under 14 as set forth in section 13B; aggravated indecent assault and battery on a child under 14 as set forth in section 13B½; indecent assault and battery on a person 14 or older as set forth in section 13H; assault of a child with intent to commit rape as set forth in section 24B; rape of a child with force as set forth in section 22A; aggravated rape of a child with force as set forth in section 22B; rape and abuse of a child as set forth in section 23; aggravated rape and abuse of a child as set forth in section 23A; rape as set forth in section 22 or; a like violation of the laws of another state, the United States or a military, territorial or Indian tribal authority, shall be punished by imprisonment in the state prison for life or for any term of years, but not less than 15 years. The sentence imposed on such person shall not be reduced to less than 15 years, or suspended, nor shall any person convicted under this section be eligible for probation, parole, work release or furlough or receive any deduction from his sentence for good conduct until he shall have served 15 years of such sentence. Prosecutions commenced under this section shall neither be continued without a finding nor placed on file.

In any prosecution commenced pursuant to this section, introduction into evidence of a prior adjudication or conviction or a prior finding of sufficient facts by either certified attested copies of original court papers, or certified attested copies of the defendant's biographical and informational data from records of the department of probation, any jail or house of correction or the department of correction shall be prima facie evidence that the defendant before the court had been convicted previously by a court of the commonwealth or any other jurisdiction. Such documentation shall be self-authenticating and admissible, after the commonwealth has established the defendant's guilt on the primary offense, as evidence in any court of the commonwealth to prove the defendant's commission of any prior conviction described therein. The commonwealth shall not be required to introduce any additional corroborating evidence or live witness testimony to establish the validity of such prior conviction.

Added by St.2008, c. 205, § 1, eff. Oct. 22, 2008.

§ 13C. Assault and battery to collect loan; penalty

Whoever commits an assault and battery upon another for the purpose of collecting a loan shall for the first offense be punished by imprisonment in the state prison for not less than three nor more than five years or by imprisonment for not more than two and one half years in a jail or house of correction; and for a second or subsequent offense, by imprisonment in the state prison for not less than five nor more than ten years. Except in the case of a conviction for the first offense for violation of this section, the imposition or execution of the sentence shall not be suspended and no probation or parole shall be granted until the minimum imprisonment herein provided for the offense shall have been served.

Added by St.1967, c. 226.

§ 13D. Assault and battery upon public employees; penalty

Whoever commits an assault and battery upon any public employee when such person is engaged in the performance of his duties at the time of such assault and battery, shall be punished by imprisonment for not less than ninety days nor more than two and one-half years in a house of correction or by a fine of not less than five hundred nor more than five thousand dollars.

Added by St.1969, c. 359. Amended by St.1973, c. 839; St.1975, c. 680; St.1983, c. 100; St.1985, c. 153; St.1985, c. 555; St.1988, c. 285; St.1990, c. 498.

§ 13D½. Firefighters, injuries resulting from criminal offenses; penalty

Whoever commits an offense set forth in section one, two, five or seven of chapter two hundred and sixty-six where said offense results in injury to a firefighter in the performance of his duty, shall be punished by imprisonment in the state prison for not more than ten years, or by a fine of not more than one thousand dollars and imprisonment in a jail or house of correction for not more than two and one-half years.

Added by St.1990, c. 300.

§ 13E. Repealed, 1971, 1011, Sec. 2

§ 13F. Indecent assault and battery on a person with an intellectual disability; assault and battery

Whoever commits an indecent assault and battery on a person with an intellectual disability knowing such person to have an intellectual disability shall for the first offense be punished by imprisonment in the state prison for not less than five years or not more than ten years; and for a second or subsequent offense, by imprisonment in the state prison for not less than ten years. Except in the case of a conviction for the first offense for violation of this section, the imposition or execution of the sentence shall not be suspended, and no probation or parole shall be granted until the minimum imprisonment herein provided for the offense shall have been served. This section shall not apply to the commission of an indecent assault and battery by a person with an intellectual disability upon another person with an intellectual disability.

Whoever commits an assault and battery on a person with an intellectual disability knowing such person to have an intellectual disability shall for the first offense be punished by imprisonment in a house of correction for not more than two and one-half years or by imprisonment in the state prison for not more than five years; and, for a second or subsequent offense, by imprisonment in the state prison for not more than ten years. This section shall not apply to the commission of an assault and battery by a mentally retarded person upon another mentally retarded person.

Added by St.1973, c. 468. Amended by St.1992, c. 374; St.2010, c. 239, § 71, 72, eff. Nov. 2, 2010.

§ 13G. Commission of a felony for hire; additional punishment

Whoever, for the payment of consideration or for the promise of the payment of such consideration, commits a felony, shall be punished by imprisonment in the state prison for not more than five years. The punishment imposed by this section shall be in addition to the punishment provided by law for the commission of a felony so committed.

Added by St.1973, c. 618. Renumbered by St.1974, c. 302.

§ 13H. Indecent assault and battery on person fourteen or older; penalties

Whoever commits an indecent assault and battery on a person who has attained age fourteen shall be punished by imprisonment in the state prison for not more than five years, or by imprisonment for not more than two and one-half years in a jail or house of correction.

Whoever commits an indecent assault and battery on an elder or person with a disability, as defined in section 13K, shall be punished by imprisonment in the state prison for not more than 10 years, or by imprisonment in the house of correction for not more than 2½ years, and whoever commits a second or subsequent such offense shall be punished by imprisonment in the state prison for not more than 20 years. A prosecution commenced under this paragraph shall not be placed on file nor continued without a finding.

Added by St.1980, c. 459, § 5. Amended by St.2004, c. 501, § 2, eff. April 11, 2005.

§ 13*I*. Assault or assault and battery on emergency medical technician, ambulance operator, ambulance attendant or health care provider

Whoever commits an assault or an assault and battery on an emergency medical technician, an ambulance operator, an ambulance attendant or a health care provider as defined in section 1 of chapter 111, while the technician, operator, attendant or provider is treating or transporting a person in the line of duty, shall be punished by imprisonment in the house of correction for not less than 90 days nor more than 2 and one-half years or by a fine of not less than $500 nor more than $5,000, or both.

Added by St.1985, c. 347. Amended by St.1989, c. 464; St.2010, c. 151, eff. July 2, 2010.

§ 13J. Assault and battery upon a child; penalties

(a) For the purposes of this section, the following words shall, unless the context indicates otherwise, have the following meanings:—

"Bodily injury", substantial impairment of the physical condition including any burn, fracture of any bone, subdural hematoma, injury to any internal organ, any injury which occurs as the result of repeated harm to any bodily function or organ including human skin or any physical condition which substantially imperils a child's health or welfare.

"Child", any person under fourteen years of age.

"Person having care and custody", a parent, guardian, employee of a home or institution or any other person with equivalent supervision or care of a child, whether the supervision is temporary or permanent.

"Substantial bodily injury", bodily injury which creates a permanent disfigurement, protracted loss or impairment of a function of a body member, limb or organ, or substantial risk of death.

(b) Whoever commits an assault and battery upon a child and by such assault and battery causes bodily injury shall be punished by imprisonment in the state prison for not more than five years or imprisonment in the house of correction for not more than two and one-half years.

Whoever commits an assault and battery upon a child and by such assault and battery causes substantial bodily injury shall be punished by imprisonment in the state prison for not more than fifteen years or imprisonment in the house of correction for not more than two and one-half years.

Whoever, having care and custody of a child, wantonly or recklessly permits bodily injury to such child or wantonly or recklessly permits another to commit an assault and battery upon such child, which assault and battery causes bodily injury, shall be punished by imprisonment for not more than two and one-half years in the house of correction.

Whoever, having care and custody of a child, wantonly or recklessly permits substantial bodily injury to such child or wantonly or recklessly permits another to commit an assault and battery upon such child, which assault and battery causes substantial bodily injury, shall be punished by imprisonment in the state prison for not more than five years, or by imprisonment in a jail or house of correction for not more than two and one-half years.

Added by St.1993, c. 340, § 2.

§ 13K. Assault and battery upon an elderly or disabled person; definitions; penalties

(a) For the purpose of this section the following words shall, unless the context requires otherwise, have the following meanings:—

"Abuse", physical contact which either harms or creates a substantial likelihood of harm.

"Bodily injury", substantial impairment of the physical condition, including, but not limited to, any burn, fracture of any bone, subdural hematoma, injury to any internal organ, or any injury which occurs as the result of repeated harm to any bodily function or organ, including human skin.

"Caretaker", a person with responsibility for the care of an elder or person with a disability, which responsibility may arise as the result of a family relationship, or by a fiduciary duty imposed by law, or by a voluntary or contractual duty undertaken on behalf of such elder or person with a disability. A person may be found to be a caretaker under this section only if a reasonable person would believe that such person's failure to fulfill such responsibility would adversely affect the physical health of such elder or person with a disability. Minor children and adults adjudicated incompetent by a court of law may not be deemed to be caretakers under this section.

(i) "Responsibility arising from a family relationship", it may be inferred that a husband, wife, son, daughter, brother, sister, or other relative of an elder or person with a disability is a caretaker if the person has provided primary and substantial assistance for the care of the elder or person with a disability as would lead a reasonable person to believe that failure to provide such care would adversely affect the physical health of the elder or person with a disability.

(ii) "Responsibility arising from a fiduciary duty imposed by law", it may be inferred that the following persons are caretakers of an elder or person with a disability to the extent that they are legally required to apply the assets of the estate of the elder or person with a disability to provide the necessities essential for the physical health of the elder or person with a disability: (i) a guardian of the person or assets of an elder or person with a disability; (ii) the conservator of an elder or person with a disability, appointed by the probate court pursuant to chapter two hundred and one; and (iii) an attorney-in-fact holding a power of attorney or durable power of attorney pursuant to chapter two hundred and one B.

(iii) "Responsibility arising from a contractual duty", it may be inferred that a person who receives monetary or personal benefit or gain as a result of a bargained-for agreement to be responsible for providing primary and substantial assistance for the care of an elder or person with a disability is a caretaker.

(iv) "Responsibility arising out of the voluntary assumption of the duties of caretaker", it may be inferred that a person who has voluntarily assumed responsibility for providing primary and substantial assistance for the care of an elder or person with a disability is a caretaker if the person's conduct would lead a reasonable person to believe that failure to provide such care would adversely affect the physical health of the elder or person with a disability, and at least one of the following criteria is met: (i) the person is living in the household of the elder or person with a disability, or present in the household on a regular basis; or (ii) the person would have reason to believe, as a result of the actions, statements or behavior of the elder or person with a disability, that he is being relied upon for providing primary and substantial assistance for physical care.

"Elder", a person sixty years of age or older.

"Mistreatment", the use of medications or treatments, isolation, or physical or chemical restraints which harms or creates a substantial likelihood of harm.

"Neglect", the failure to provide treatment or services necessary to maintain health and safety and which either harms or creates a substantial likelihood of harm.

"Person with disability", a person with a permanent or long-term physical or mental impairment that prevents or restricts the individual's ability to provide for his or her own care or protection.

"Serious bodily injury", bodily injury which results in a permanent disfigurement, protracted loss or impairment of a bodily function, limb or organ, or substantial risk of death.

(a½) Whoever commits an assault and battery upon an elder or person with a disability shall be punished by imprisonment in the state prison for not more than 3 years or by imprisonment in a house of correction for not more than 2½ years, or by a fine of not more than $1,000, or both such fine and imprisonment.

(b) Whoever commits an assault and battery upon an elder or person with a disability and by such assault and battery causes bodily injury shall be punished by imprisonment in the state prison for not more than five years or in the house of correction for not more than two and one-half years or by a fine of not more than one thousand dollars or by both such fine and imprisonment.

(c) Whoever commits an assault and battery upon an elder or person with a disability and by such assault and battery causes serious bodily injury shall be punished by imprisonment in the state prison for not more than ten years or in the house of correction for not more than two and one-half years or by a fine of not more than five thousand dollars or by both such fine and imprisonment.

(d) Whoever, being a caretaker of an elder or person with a disability, wantonly or recklessly permits bodily injury to such elder or person with a disability, or wantonly or recklessly permits another to commit an assault and battery upon such elder or person with a disability which assault and battery causes bodily injury, shall be punished by imprisonment in the state prison for not more than five years or in the house of correction for not more than two and one-half years or by a fine of not more than five thousand dollars or by both such fine and imprisonment.

(d½) Whoever, being a caretaker of an elder or person with a disability, wantonly or recklessly commits or permits another to commit abuse, neglect or mistreatment upon such elder or person with a disability, shall be punished by imprisonment in the state prison for not more than 3 years, or imprisonment in the house of correction for not more than 2½ years, or by a fine of not more than $5,000, or by both such fine and imprisonment.

(e) Whoever, being a caretaker of an elder or person with a disability, wantonly or recklessly permits serious bodily injury to such elder or person with a disability, or wantonly or recklessly permits another to commit an assault and battery upon such elder or person with a disability which assault and battery causes serious bodily injury, shall be punished by imprisonment in the state prison for not more than ten years or by imprisonment in the house of correction for not more than two and one-half years or by a fine of not more than ten thousand dollars or by both such fine and imprisonment.

(f) Conduct shall not be construed to be wanton or reckless conduct under this section if directed by a competent elder or person with a disability, or for the sole reason that, in lieu of medical treatment, an elder or person with a disability is being furnished or relies upon treatment by spiritual means through prayer if such treatment is in accordance with the tenets and practices of the established religious tradition of such elder or person with a disability, and is provided at the direction of such elder or person with a disability, who shall be competent, or pursuant to the direction of a person who is properly designated a health care proxy under chapter two hundred and one D.

Added by St.1995, c. 297, § 4. Amended by St.2004, c. 501, §§ 3 to 8, eff. April 11, 2005.

§ 13L. Wanton or reckless behavior creating a risk of serious bodily injury or sexual abuse to a child; duty to act; penalty

For the purposes of this section, the following words shall have the following meanings:—

"Child", any person under 18 years of age.

"Serious bodily injury", bodily injury which results in a permanent disfigurement, protracted loss or impairment of a bodily function, limb or organ, or substantial risk of death.

"Sexual abuse", an indecent assault and battery on a child under 14 under section 13B of chapter 265; aggravated indecent assault and battery on a child under 14 under section 13B½ of said chapter 265; a repeat offense under section 13B¾ of said chapter 265; indecent assault and battery on a person age 14 or over under section 13H of said chapter 265; rape under section 22 of said chapter 265; rape of a child under 16 with force under section 22A of said chapter 265; aggravated rape of a child under 16 with force under section 22B of said chapter 265; a repeat offense under section 22C of said chapter 265; rape and abuse of a child under section 23 of said chapter 265; aggravated rape and abuse of a child under section 23A of said chapter 265; a repeat offense under section 23B of said chapter 265; assault with intent to commit rape under section 24 of said chapter 265; and assault of a child with intent to commit rape under section 24B of said chapter 265.

Whoever wantonly or recklessly engages in conduct that creates a substantial risk of serious bodily injury or sexual abuse to a child or wantonly or recklessly fails to take reasonable steps to alleviate such risk where there is a duty to act shall be punished by imprisonment in the house of correction for not more than 2½ years.

For the purposes of this section, such wanton or reckless behavior occurs when a person is aware of and consciously disregards a substantial and unjustifiable risk that his acts, or omissions where there is a duty to act, would result in serious bodily injury or sexual abuse to a child. The risk must be of such nature and degree that disregard of the risk constitutes a gross deviation from the standard of conduct that a reasonable person would observe in the situation.

Added by St.2002, c. 322, § 2. Amended by St.2010, c. 267, §§ 52 to 54, eff. Nov. 5, 2010.

§ 13M. Assault and battery on a family or household member; second or subsequent offense; penalty

Whoever is convicted of a second or subsequent offense of assault or assault and battery on a family or household member shall be punished by imprisonment in the house of correction for not more than 2½ years or by imprisonment in the state prison for not more than 5 years. For the purposes of this section, "family or household member" shall be limited to persons who: (a) are married to each other or were married to each other within the 5 years preceding the date of the alleged offense; (b) are residing together in the same household or were residing together in the same household within the 5 years preceding the date of the alleged offense; (c) are related by blood; (d) have a child in common; or (e) are or have been in a substantive dating or engagement relationship within the 5 years preceding the date of the alleged offense; provided, however, that in determining that relationship, the court shall consider the following factors: (1) the length of time of the relationship; (2) the type of relationship; (3) the frequency of interaction between the parties; and (4) if the relationship has been terminated by either person, the length of time that has elapsed since the termination of the relationship.

Added by St.2008, c. 534, eff. Jan. 16, 2009.

§ 14. Mayhem; punishment

Whoever, with malicious intent to maim or disfigure, cuts out or maims the tongue, puts out or destroys an eye, cuts or tears off an ear, cuts, slits or mutilates the nose or lip, or cuts off or disables a limb or member, of another person, and whoever is privy to such intent, or is present and aids in the commission of such crime, or whoever, with intent to maim or disfigure, assaults another person with a dangerous weapon, substance or chemical, and by such assault disfigures, cripples or inflicts serious or permanent physical injury upon such person, and whoever is privy to such intent, or is present and aids in the commission of such crime, shall be punished by imprisonment in the state prison for not more than twenty years or by a fine of not more than one thousand dollars and imprisonment in jail for not more than two and one half years.

Historical and Statutory Notes

B.L. c. 87.
St.1804, c. 123, § 4.
R.S.1836, c. 125, § 10.
G.S.1860, c. 160, § 19.
P.S.1882, c. 202, § 19.
R.L.1902, c. 207, § 14.
St.1914, c. 635.
St.1918, c. 257, § 464.
St.1919, c. 5.
St.1920, c. 2.
St.1923, c. 280.

§ 15. Assault; intent to murder or maim; penalty

Whoever assaults another with intent to commit murder, or to maim or disfigure his person in any way described in the preceding section, shall be punished by imprisonment in the state prison for not more than ten years or by a fine of not more than one thousand dollars and imprisonment in jail for not more than two and one half years.

Historical and Statutory Notes

St.1784, c. 65, § 3.
St.1804, c. 123, § 5.
St.1818, c. 124, § 3.
R.S.1836, c. 125, § 11.
G.S.1860, c. 160, § 20.
P.S.1882, c. 202, § 20.
R.L.1902, c. 207, § 15.
St.1914, c. 635.
St.1918, c. 257, § 464.
St.1919, c. 5.
St.1920, c. 2.

§ 15A. Assault and battery with dangerous weapon; victim sixty or older; punishment; subsequent offenses

(a) Whoever commits assault and battery upon a person sixty years or older by means of a dangerous weapon shall be punished by imprisonment in the state prison for not more than ten years or by a fine of not more than one thousand dollars or imprisonment in jail for not more than two and one-half years.

Whoever, after having been convicted of the crime of assault and battery upon a person sixty years or older, by means of a dangerous weapon, commits a second or subsequent such crime, shall be punished by imprisonment for not less than two years. Said sentence shall not be reduced until two years of said sentence have been served nor shall the person convicted be eligible for probation, parole, furlough, work release or receive any deduction from his sentence for good conduct until he shall have served two years of such sentence; provided, however, that the commissioner of correction may, on the recommendation of the warden, superintendent, or other person in charge of a correctional institution, or the administrator of a county correctional institution, grant to said offender a temporary release in the custody of an officer of such institution for the following purposes only: to attend the funeral of next of kin or spouse; to visit a critically ill close relative or spouse; or to obtain emergency medical services unavailable at said institution. The provisions of section eighty-seven of chapter two hundred and seventy-six relating to the power of the court to place certain offenders on probation shall not apply to any person seventeen years of age or over charged with a violation of this subsection.

(b) Whoever commits an assault and battery upon another by means of a dangerous weapon shall be punished by imprisonment in the state prison for not more than 10 years or in the house of correction for not more than 2½ years, or by a fine of not more than $5,000, or by both such fine and imprisonment.

(c) Whoever:

(i) by means of a dangerous weapon, commits an assault and battery upon another and by such assault and battery causes serious bodily injury;

(ii) by means of a dangerous weapon, commits an assault and battery upon another who is pregnant at the time of such assault and battery, knowing or having reason to know that the person is pregnant;

(iii) by means of a dangerous weapon, commits an assault and battery upon another who he knows has an outstanding temporary or permanent vacate, restraining or no contact order or judgment issued pursuant to section 18, section 34B or section 34C of chapter 208, section 32 of chapter 209, section 3, 4 or 5 of chapter 209A, or section 15 or 20 of chapter 209C, in effect against him at the time of such assault and battery; or

(iv) is 17 years of age or older and, by means of a dangerous weapon, commits an assault and battery upon a child under the age of 14;

shall be punished by imprisonment in the state prison for not more than 15 years or in the house of correction for not more than 2½ years, or by a fine of not more than $10,000, or by both such fine and imprisonment.

(d) For the purposes of this section, "serious bodily injury" shall mean bodily injury which results in a permanent disfigurement, loss or impairment of a bodily function, limb or organ, or a substantial risk of death.

Amended by St.1981, c. 678, § 1; St.1995, c. 297, § 5; St.2002, c. 35, § 2.

Historical and Statutory Notes

St.1927, c. 187, § 1.

§ 15B. Assault with dangerous weapon; victim sixty or older; punishment; subsequent offenses

(a) Whoever, by means of a dangerous weapon, commits an assault upon a person sixty years or older, shall be punished by imprisonment in the state prison for not more than five years or by a fine of not more than one thousand dollars or imprisonment in jail for not more than two and one-half years.

Whoever, after having been convicted of the crime of assault upon a person sixty years or older, by means of a dangerous weapon, commits a second or subsequent such crime, shall be punished by imprisonment for not less than two years. Said sentence shall not be reduced until one year of said sentence has been served nor shall the person convicted be eligible for probation, parole, furlough, work release or receive any deduction from his sentence for good conduct until he shall have served one year of such sentence; provided, however, that the commissioner of correction may, on the recommendation of the warden, superintendent, or other person in charge of a correctional institution, or the administrator of a county correctional institution, grant to said offender a temporary release in the custody of an officer of such institution for the following purposes only: to attend the funeral of next of kin or spouse; to visit a critically ill close relative or spouse; or to obtain emergency medical services unavailable at said institution. The provisions of section eighty-seven of chapter two hundred and seventy-six relative to the power of the court to place certain offenders on probation shall not apply to any person seventeen years of age or over charged with a violation of this subsection.

For the purposes of prosecution, a conviction obtained under subsection (a) of section fifteen A or paragraph (a) of section 18 shall count as a prior criminal conviction for the purpose of prosecution and sentencing as a second or subsequent conviction.

(b) Whoever, by means of a dangerous weapon, commits an assault upon another shall be punished by imprisonment in the state prison for not more than five years or by a fine of not more than one thousand dollars or imprisonment in jail for not more than two and one-half years.

Added by St.1955, c. 112. Amended by St.1981, c. 678, § 2; St.1995, c. 297, § 6.

§ 15C. Assault by means of hypodermic syringe or needle; assault and battery by means of hypodermic syringe or needle

(a) Whoever commits an assault upon another, by means of a hypodermic syringe, hypodermic needle, or any instrument adapted for the administration of controlled or other substances by injection, shall be punished by imprisonment in the state prison for not more than 10 years or in the house of correction for not more than 2½ years, or by a fine of not more than $1,000, or by both such fine and imprisonment.

(b) Whoever commits an assault and battery upon another, by means of a hypodermic syringe, hypodermic needle, or any instrument adapted for the administration of controlled or other substances by injection, shall be punished by imprisonment in the state prison for not more than 15 years or in the house of correction for not more than 2½ years, or by a fine of not more than $5,000, or by both such fine and imprisonment.

Added by St.2006, c. 172, § 12, eff. July 13, 2006.

§ 16. Attempt to murder

Whoever attempts to commit murder by poisoning, drowning or strangling another person, or by any means not constituting an assault with intent to commit murder, shall be punished by imprisonment in the state prison for not more than twenty years or by a fine of not more than one thousand dollars and imprisonment in jail for not more than two and one half years.

Historical and Statutory Notes

St.1832, c. 62.
R.S.1836, c. 125, § 12.
G.S.1860, c. 160, § 21.
P.S.1882, c. 202, § 21.
R.L.1902, c. 207, § 16.
St.1914, c. 635.
St.1918, c. 257, § 464.
St.1919, c. 5.
St.1920, c. 2.

§ 17. Armed robbery; punishment

Whoever, being armed with a dangerous weapon, assaults another and robs, steals or takes from his person money or other property which may be the subject of larceny shall be punished by imprisonment in the state prison for life or for any term of years; provided, however, that any person who commits any offence described herein while masked or disguised or while having his features artificially distorted shall, for the first offence be sentenced to imprisonment for not less than five years and for any subsequent offence for not less than ten years. Whoever commits any offense described herein while armed with a firearm, shotgun, rifle, machine gun or assault weapon shall be punished by imprisonment in the state prison for not less than five years. Any person who commits a subsequent offense while armed with a firearm, shotgun, rifle, machine gun or assault weapon shall be punished by imprisonment in the state prison for not less than 15 years.

Amended by St.1943, c. 250, § 1; St.1952, c. 406, § 1; St.1998, c. 180, § 50.

Historical and Statutory Notes

St.1818, c. 124, § 1.
R.S.1836, c. 125, § 13.
St.1839, c. 127.
G.S.1860, c. 160, § 22.
P.S.1882, c. 202, § 22.
R.L.1902, c. 207, § 17.
St.1911, c. 84.

§ 18. Assault with intent to rob or murder; weapons; punishment; victim sixty years or older; minimum sentence for repeat offenders

(a) Whoever, being armed with a dangerous weapon, assaults a person sixty years or older with intent to rob or murder shall be punished by imprisonment in the state prison for not more than twenty years. Whoever commits any offense described herein while armed with a firearm, shotgun, rifle, machine gun or assault weapon shall be punished by imprisonment in the state prison for not less than ten years.

Whoever, after having been convicted of the crime of assault upon a person sixty years or older with intent to rob or murder while being armed with a dangerous weapon, commits a second or subsequent such crime, shall be punished by imprisonment for not less than two years. Said sentence shall not be reduced until two years of said sentence have been served nor shall the person convicted be eligible for probation, parole, furlough, work release or receive any deduction from his sentence for good conduct until he shall have served two years of such sentence; provided, however, that the commissioner of correction may, on the recommendation of the warden, superintendent, or other person in charge of a correctional institution, or the administrator of a county correctional institution, grant to said offender a temporary release in the custody of an officer of such institution for the following purposes only: to attend the funeral of next of kin or spouse; to visit a critically ill close relative or spouse; or to obtain emergency medical services unavailable at said institution. The provisions of section eighty-seven of chapter two hundred and seventy-six relating to the power of the court to place certain offenders on probation shall not apply to any person seventeen years of age or over charged with a violation of this subsection. Whoever, after having been convicted of the crime of assault upon a person 60 years or older with intent to rob or murder while armed with a firearm, shotgun, rifle, machine gun or assault weapon commits a second or subsequent such crime shall be punished by imprisonment in the state prison for not less than 20 years.

(b) Whoever, being armed with a dangerous weapon, assaults another with intent to rob or murder shall be punished by imprisonment in the state prison for not more than twenty years. Whoever, being armed with a firearm, shotgun, rifle, machine gun or assault weapon assaults another with intent to rob or murder shall be punished by imprisonment in state prison for not less than five years and not more than 20 years.

Amended by St.1981, c. 678, § 3; St.1995, c. 297, § 7; St.1998, c. 180, §§ 51 to 53.

Historical and Statutory Notes

St.1761–2, c. 21, § 1.
St.1784, c. 52, § 2.
St.1804, c. 143, § 9.
St.1818, c. 124, § 3.
R.S.1836, c. 125, § 14.
G.S.1860, c. 160, § 23.
P.S.1882, c. 202, § 23.
R.L.1902, c. 207, § 18.

§ 18A. Dangerous weapon; assault in dwelling house; punishment

Whoever, being armed with a dangerous weapon, enters a dwelling house and while therein assaults another with intent to commit a felony shall be punished by imprisonment in the state prison for life, or for a term of not less than ten years. No person imprisoned under this paragraph shall be eligible for parole in less than five years.

Whoever, being armed with a dangerous weapon defined as a firearm, shotgun, rifle or assault weapon, enters a dwelling house and while therein assaults another with intent to commit a felony shall be punished by imprisonment in the state prison for a term of not less than ten years. Such person shall not be eligible for parole prior to the expiration of ten years.

Added by St.1956, c. 408. Amended by St.1969, c. 473; St.1998, c. 180, §§ 54, 55.

§ 18B. Use of firearms while committing a felony; second or subsequent offenses; punishment

Whoever, while in the commission of or the attempted commission of an offense which may be punished by imprisonment in the state prison, has in his possession or under his control a firearm, rifle or shotgun shall, in addition to the penalty for such offense, be punished by imprisonment in the state prison for not less than five years; provided, however, that if such firearm, rifle or shotgun is a large capacity weapon, as defined in section 121 of chapter 140, or if such person, while in the commission or attempted commission of such offense, has in his possession or under his control a machine gun, as defined in said section 121, such person shall be punished by imprisonment in the state prison for not less than ten years. Whoever has committed an offense which may be punished by imprisonment in the state prison and had in his possession or under his control a firearm, rifle or shotgun including, but not limited to, a large capacity weapon or machine gun and who thereafter, while in the commission or the attempted commission of a second or subsequent offense which may be punished by imprisonment in the state prison, has in his possession or under his control a firearm, rifle or shotgun shall, in addition to the penalty for such offense, be punished by imprisonment in the state prison for not less than 20 years; provided, however, that if such firearm, rifle or shotgun is a large capacity semiautomatic weapon or if such person, while in the commission or attempted commission of such offense, has in his possession or under his control a machine gun, such person shall be punished by imprisonment in the state prison for not less than 25 years.

A sentence imposed under this section for a second or subsequent offense shall not be reduced nor suspended, nor shall any person convicted under this section be eligible for probation, parole, furlough or work release or receive any deduction from his sentence for good conduct until he shall have served the minimum term of such additional sentence; provided, however, that the commissioner of correction may, on the recommendation of the warden, superintendent or other person in charge of a correctional institution or the administrator of a county correctional institution, grant to such offender a temporary release in the custody of an officer of such institution for the following purposes only: (i) to attend the funeral of a spouse or next of kin; (ii) to visit a critically ill close relative or spouse; or (iii) to obtain emergency medical services unavailable at such institution. Prosecutions commenced under this section shall neither be continued without a finding nor placed on file. The provisions of section 87 of chapter 276 relative to the power of the court to place certain offenders on probation shall not apply to any person 17 years of age or over charged with a violation of this section.

Added by St.1974, c. 830. Amended by St.1984, c. 189, § 162; St.1998, c. 180, § 56.

§ 18C. Entry of dwelling place; persons present within; weapons; punishment

Whoever knowingly enters the dwelling place of another knowing or having reason to know that one or more persons are present within or knowingly enters the dwelling place of another and remains in such dwelling place knowing or having reason to know that one or more persons are present within while armed with a dangerous weapon, uses force or threatens the imminent use of force upon any person within such dwelling place whether or not injury occurs, or intentionally causes any injury to any person within such dwelling place shall be punished by imprisonment in the state prison for life or for any term of not less than twenty years.

Added by St.1993, c. 333. Amended by St.1998, c. 180, § 57; St.2004, c. 150, § 17, eff. Sept. 13, 2004.

§ 19. Robbery by unarmed person; punishment; victim sixty or older; minimum sentence for repeat offenders

(a) Whoever, not being armed with a dangerous weapon, by force and violence, or by assault and putting in fear, robs, steals or takes from the person of a person sixty years or older, or from his immediate control, money or other property which may be the subject of larceny, shall be punished by imprisonment in the state prison for life or for any term of years.

Whoever, after having been convicted of said crime, commits a second or subsequent such crime, shall be punished by imprisonment for not less than two years. Said sentence shall not be reduced until two years of said sentence have been served nor shall the person convicted be eligible for probation, parole, furlough, work release or receive any deduction from his sentence for good conduct until he shall have served two years of such sentence; provided, however, that the commissioner of correction may, on the recommendation of the warden, superintendent, or other person in charge of a correctional institution, or the administrator of a county correctional institution, grant to said offender a temporary release in the custody of an officer of such institution for the following purposes only: to attend the funeral of next of kin or spouse; to visit a critically ill close relative or spouse; or to obtain emergency medical services unavailable at said institution. The provisions of section eighty-seven of chapter two hundred and seventy-six relative to the power of the court to place certain offenders on probation shall not apply to any person seventeen years of age or over charged with a violation of this subsection.

(b) Whoever, not being armed with a dangerous weapon, by force and violence, or by assault and putting in fear, robs, steals or takes from the person of another, or from his immediate control, money or other property which may be the subject of larceny, shall be punished by imprisonment in the state prison for life or for any term of years.

Amended by St.1981, c. 678, § 4; St.1995, c. 297, § 8.

Historical and Statutory Notes

C.L. c. 12, § 4.
St.1692–3, c. 18, § 4.
St.1711–12, c. 2, § 1.
St.1761–2, c. 21, § 1.
St.1784, c. 52, § 2.
St.1804, c. 143, § 7.
R.S.1836, c. 125, § 15.
G.S.1860, c. 160, § 24.
P.S.1882, c. 202, § 24.
R.L.1902, c. 207, § 19.

§ 20. Simple assault; intent to rob or steal; punishment

Whoever, not being armed with a dangerous weapon, assaults another with force and violence and with intent to rob or steal shall be punished by imprisonment in the state prison for not more than ten years.

Historical and Statutory Notes

St.1804, c. 143, § 9.
R.S.1836, c. 125, § 16.
G.S.1860, c. 160, § 25.
P.S.1882, c. 202, § 25.
R.L.1902, c. 207, § 20.

§ 21. Stealing by confining or putting in fear

Whoever, with intent to commit larceny or any felony, confines, maims, injures or wounds, or attempts or threatens to kill, confine, maim, injure or wound, or puts any person in fear, for the purpose of stealing from a building, bank, safe, vault or other depository of money, bonds or other valuables, or by intimidation, force or threats compels or attempts to compel any person to disclose or surrender the means of opening any building, bank, safe, vault or other depository of money, bonds, or other valuables, shall whether he succeeds or fails in the perpetration of such larceny or felony, be punished by imprisonment in the state prison for life or for any term of years.

Amended by St.1974, c. 462, § 1.

Historical and Statutory Notes

St.1876, c. 202.
P.S.1882, c. 202, § 26.
R.L.1902, c. 207, § 21.
St.1918, c. 257, § 446.
St.1919, c. 5.
St.1920, c. 2.

§ 21A. Assault, confinement, etc. of person for purpose of stealing motor vehicle; weapons; punishment

Whoever, with intent to steal a motor vehicle, assaults, confines, maims or puts any person in fear for the purpose of stealing a motor vehicle shall, whether he succeeds or fails in the perpetration of stealing the motor vehicle be punished by imprisonment in the state prison for not more than fifteen years or in a jail or house of correction for not more than two and one-half years and a fine of not less than one thousand nor more than fifteen thousand dollars; provided, however, that any person who commits any offense described herein while being armed with a dangerous weapon shall be punished by imprisonment in the state prison for not more than twenty years or in a jail or house of correction for not less than one year nor more than two and one-half years and a fine of not less than five nor more than fifteen thousand dollars. Whoever commits any offense described in this section while being armed with a firearm, rifle, shotgun, machine gun or assault weapon, shall be punished by imprisonment in the state prison for not less than five years in state prison.

Added by St.1992, c. 412, § 2. Amended by St.1998, c. 180, § 58.

§ 22. Rape, generally; weapons; punishment; eligibility for furlough, education, training or employment programs

(a) Whoever has sexual intercourse or unnatural sexual intercourse with a person, and compels such person to submit by force and against his will, or compels such person to submit by threat of bodily injury and if either such sexual intercourse or unnatural sexual intercourse results in or is committed with acts resulting in serious bodily injury, or is committed by a joint enterprise, or is committed during the commission or attempted commission of an offense defined in section fifteen A, fifteen B, seventeen, nineteen or twenty-six of this chapter, section fourteen, fifteen, sixteen, seventeen or eighteen of chapter two hundred and sixty-six or section ten of chapter two hundred and sixty-nine shall be punished by imprisonment in the state prison for life or for any term of years.

No person serving a sentence for a second or subsequent such offense shall be eligible for furlough, temporary release, or education, training or employment programs established outside a correctional facility until such person shall have served two-thirds of such minimum sentence or if such person has two or more sentences to be served otherwise than concurrently, two-thirds of the aggregate of the minimum terms of such several sentences.

(b) Whoever has sexual intercourse or unnatural sexual intercourse with a person and compels such person to submit by force and against his will, or compels such person to submit by threat of bodily injury, shall be punished by imprisonment in the state prison for not more than twenty years; and whoever commits a second or subsequent such offense shall be punished by imprisonment in the state prison for life or for any term or years.

Whoever commits any offense described in this section while being armed with a firearm, rifle, shotgun, machine-gun or assault weapon, shall be punished by imprisonment in the state prison for not less than ten years. Whoever commits a second or subsequent such offense shall be punished by imprisonment in the state prison for life or for any term of years, but not less than 15 years.

No person serving a sentence for a second or subsequent such offense shall be eligible for furlough, temporary release, or education, training or employment programs established outside a correctional facility until such person shall have served two-thirds of such minimum sentence or if such person has two or more sentences to be served otherwise than concurrently, two-thirds of the aggregate of the minimum terms of such several sentences.

For the purposes of prosecution, the offense described in subsection (b) shall be a lesser included offense to that described in subsection (a).

Amended by St.1974, c. 474, § 1; St.1980, c. 459, § 6; St.1998, c. 180, § 59.

Historical and Statutory Notes

C.L. c. 15, § 15.
St.1697, c. 18.
St.1784, c. 68.
St.1805, c. 97, § 1.
R.S.1836, c. 125, § 18.
St.1852, c. 259, § 2.
G.S.1860, c. 160, § 26.
St.1871, c. 55.
P.S.1882, c. 202, § 27.
St.1886, c. 305.
St.1888, c. 391.
St.1893, c. 466, § 1.
R.L.1902, c. 207, § 22.

§ 22A. Rape of child; punishment

Whoever has sexual intercourse or unnatural sexual intercourse with a child under 16, and compels such child to submit by force and against his will or compels such child to submit by threat of bodily injury, shall be punished by imprisonment in the state prison for life or for any term of years. A prosecution commenced under this section shall neither be continued without a finding nor placed on file.

Added by St.1955, c. 763, § 2. Amended by St.1973, c. 925, § 77; St.1974, c. 474, § 2; St.1998, c. 180, § 60; St.1998, c. 194, § 237; St.2008, c. 205, § 2, eff. Oct. 22, 2008.

§ 22B. Rape of a child during commission of certain offenses or by use of force; penalties

Whoever has sexual intercourse or unnatural sexual intercourse with a child under 16, and compels such child to submit by force and against his will or compels such child to submit by threat of bodily injury and:

(a) the sexual intercourse or unnatural sexual intercourse is committed during the commission or attempted commission of any of the following offenses: (1) armed burglary as set forth in section 14 of chapter 266; (2) unarmed burglary as set forth in section 15 of said chapter 266; (3) breaking and entering as set forth in section 16 of said chapter 266; (4) entering without breaking as set forth in section 17 of said chapter 266; (5) breaking and entering into a dwelling house as set forth in section 18 of said chapter 266; (6) kidnapping as set forth in section 26 of chapter 265; (7) armed robbery as set forth in section 17 of said chapter 265; (8) unarmed robbery as set forth in section 19 of said chapter 265; (9) assault and battery with a dangerous weapon or assault with a dangerous weapon as set forth in sections 15A and 15B of said chapter 265; (10) home invasion as set forth in section 18C of said chapter 265; or (11) posing or exhibiting child in state of nudity or sexual conduct as set forth in section 29A of chapter 272;

(b) the sexual intercourse or unnatural sexual intercourse results in, or is committed by means of an act or acts resulting in, substantial bodily injury as defined in section 13J;

(c) the sexual intercourse or unnatural sexual intercourse is committed while the victim is tied, bound or gagged;

(d) the sexual intercourse or unnatural sexual intercourse is committed after the defendant administered, or caused to be administered, alcohol or a controlled substance by injection, inhalation, ingestion, or any other means to the victim without the victim's consent;

(e) the sexual intercourse or unnatural sexual intercourse is committed by a joint enterprise; or

(f) the sexual intercourse or unnatural sexual intercourse was committed in a manner in which the victim could contract a sexually transmitted disease or infection of which the defendant knew or should have known he was a carrier, shall be punished by imprisonment in the state prison for life or for any term of years, but not less than 15 years. The sentence imposed on such person shall not be reduced to less than 15 years, or suspended, nor shall any person convicted under this section be eligible for probation, parole, work release or furlough or receive any deduction from his sentence for good conduct until he shall have served 15 years of such sentence. Prosecutions commenced under this section shall neither be continued without a finding nor placed on file.

Added by St.2008, c. 205, § 2, eff. Oct. 22, 2008.

§ 22C. Rape of a child through use of force by certain previously convicted offenders; penalties

Whoever has sexual intercourse or unnatural sexual intercourse with a child under 16, and compels such child to submit by force and against his will or compels such child to submit by threat of bodily injury, and has been previously convicted of or adjudicated delinquent or as a youthful offender for: indecent assault and battery on a child under 14 as set forth in section 13B; aggravated indecent assault and battery on a child under 14 as set forth in section 13B½; indecent assault and battery on a person 14 or older as set forth in section 13H; assault of a child with intent to commit rape as set forth in section 24B; rape of a child with force as set forth in section 22A; aggravated rape of a child with force as set forth in section 22B; rape and abuse of a child as set forth in section 23; aggravated rape and abuse of a child as set forth in section 23A; rape as set forth in section 22; or a like violation of the laws of another state, the United States or a military, territorial or Indian tribal authority, shall be punished by imprisonment in the state prison for life or for any term of years, but not less than 20 years. The sentence imposed on such person shall not be reduced to less than 20 years, or suspended, nor shall any person convicted under this section be eligible for probation, parole, work release or furlough or receive any deduction from his sentence for good conduct until he shall have served 20 years of such sentence. Prosecutions commenced under this section shall neither be continued without a finding nor placed on file.

In any prosecution commenced pursuant to this section, introduction into evidence of a prior adjudication or conviction or a prior finding of sufficient facts by either certified attested copies of original court papers, or certified attested copies of the defendant's biographical and informational data from records of the department of probation, any jail or house of correction or the department of correction, shall be prima facie evidence that the defendant before the court has been convicted previously by a court of the commonwealth or any other jurisdiction. Such documentation shall be self-authenticating and admissible, after the commonwealth has established the defendant's guilt on the primary offense, as evidence in any court of the commonwealth to prove the defendant's commission of any prior conviction described therein. The commonwealth shall not be required to introduce any additional corroborating evidence or live witness testimony to establish the validity of such prior conviction.

Added by St.2008, c. 205, § 2, eff. Oct. 22, 2008.

§ 23. Rape and abuse of child

Whoever unlawfully has sexual intercourse or unnatural sexual intercourse, and abuses a child under 16 years of age, shall be punished by imprisonment in the state prison for life or for any term of years or, except as otherwise provided, for any term in a jail or house of correction. A prosecution commenced under this section shall neither be continued without a finding nor placed on file.

Amended by St.1966, c. 291; St.1974, c. 474, § 3; St.1998, c. 194, § 238; St.2008, c. 205, § 2, eff. Oct. 22, 2008.

Historical and Statutory Notes

C.L. c. 15, § 17.
St.1697, c. 18.
St.1784, c. 68.
St.1805, c. 97, § 1.
R.S.1836, c. 125, § 18.
St.1852, c. 259, § 2.
G.S.1860, c. 160, § 26.
St.1871, c. 55.
P.S.1882, c. 202, § 27.
St.1886, c. 305.
St.1888, c. 391.
St.1893, c. 466, § 2.
R.L.1902, c. 207, § 23.

§ 23A. Rape and abuse of child aggravated by age difference between defendant and victim or by when committed by mandated reporters; penalties

Whoever unlawfully has sexual intercourse or unnatural sexual intercourse, and abuses a child under 16 years of age and:

(a) there exists more than a 5 year age difference between the defendant and the victim and the victim is under 12 years of age;

(b) there exists more than a 10 year age difference between the defendant and the victim where the victim is between the age of 12 and 16 years of age; or

(c) at the time of such intercourse, was a mandated reporter as defined in section 21 of chapter 119, shall be punished by imprisonment in the state prison for life or for any term of years, but not less than 10 years. The sentence imposed on such person shall not be reduced to less than 10 years, or suspended, nor shall any person convicted under this section be eligible for probation, parole, work release, or furlough or receive any deduction from his sentence for good conduct until he shall have served 10 years of such sentence. Prosecutions commenced under this section shall neither be continued without a finding nor placed on file.

Added by St.2008, c. 205, § 2, eff. Oct. 22, 2008.

§ 23B. Rape and abuse of child by certain previously convicted offenders; penalties

Whoever unlawfully has sexual intercourse or unnatural sexual intercourse, and abuses a child under 16 years of age and has been previously convicted of or adjudicated delinquent or as a youthful offender for: indecent assault and battery on a child under 14 under section 13B; aggravated indecent assault and battery on a child under 14 under section 13B½; indecent assault and battery on a person 14 or older under section 13H; assault of a child with intent to commit rape under section 24B; rape of a child with force under section 22A; aggravated rape of a child with force under section 22B; rape and abuse of a child under section 23; aggravated rape and abuse of a child under section 23A; rape under section 22; or a like violation of the laws of another state, the United States or a military, territorial or Indian tribal authority, shall be punished by imprisonment in the state prison for life or for any term of years, but not less than 15 years. The sentence imposed on such person shall not be reduced to less than 15 years, or suspended, nor shall any person convicted under this section be eligible for probation, parole, work release, or furlough or receive any deduction from his sentence for good conduct until he shall have served 15 years of such sentence. Prosecutions commenced under this section shall neither be continued without a finding nor placed on file.

In any prosecution commenced pursuant to this section, introduction into evidence of a prior adjudication or conviction or a prior finding of sufficient facts by either certified attested copies of original court papers, or certified attested copies of the defendant's biographical and informational data from records of the department of probation, any jail or house of correction or the department of correction, shall be prima facie evidence that the defendant before the court has been convicted previously by a court of the commonwealth or any other jurisdiction. Such documentation shall be self-authenticating and admissible, after the commonwealth has established the defendant's guilt on the primary offense, as evidence in any court of the commonwealth to prove the defendant's commission of any prior conviction described therein. The commonwealth shall not be required to introduce any additional corroborating evidence or live witness testimony to establish the validity of such prior conviction.

Added by St.2008, c. 205, § 2, eff. Oct. 22, 2008.

§ 24. Assault with intent to commit rape; weapons; punishment; eligibility for furloughs, education, training or employment programs

Whoever assaults a person with intent to commit a rape shall be punished by imprisonment in the state prison for not more than twenty years or by imprisonment in a jail or house of correction for not more than two and one-half years; and whoever commits a second or subsequent such offense shall be punished by imprisonment in the state prison for life or for any term of years. Whoever commits any offense described in this section while armed with a firearm, rifle, shotgun, machine gun or assault weapon shall be punished by imprisonment in the state prison for not less than five years. Whoever commits a second or subsequent such offense shall be punished by imprisonment in the state prison for life or for any term of years, but not less than 20 years.

No person serving a sentence for a second or subsequent such offense shall be eligible for furlough, temporary release, or education, training or employment programs established outside a correctional facility until such person shall have served two-thirds of such minimum sentence or if such person has two or more sentences to be served otherwise than concurrently, two-thirds of the aggregate of the minimum terms of such several sentences.

Amended by St.1974, c. 474, § 4; St.1978, c. 379, § 1; St.1980, c. 459, § 7; St.1998, c. 180, § 61.

Historical and Statutory Notes

St.1784, c. 65, § 3.
St.1805, c. 97, § 3.
St.1815, c. 86.
R.S.1836, c. 125, § 19.
G.S.1860, c. 160, § 27.
P.S.1882, c. 202, § 28.
R.L.1902, c. 207, § 24.
St.1914, c. 635.
St.1918, c. 257, § 464.
St.1919, c. 5.
St.1920, c. 2.

§ 24A. Venue

If, in connection with the alleged commission of a crime described in section thirteen B, 13B½, 13B¾, thirteen F, thirteen H, twenty-two, twenty-two A, 22B, 22C, twenty-three, 23A, 23B, twenty-four or twenty-four B of this chapter or in section five of chapter two hundred and seventy-two, the person against whom said crime is alleged to have been committed has been conveyed from one county or judicial district into another, said crime may be alleged to have been committed, and may be prosecuted and punished, in the county or judicial district where committed or from which such person was so conveyed.

Amended by St.1974, c. 474, § 5; St.1983, c. 200; St.2010, c. 267, §§ 55 to 57, eff. Nov. 5, 2010.

Historical and Statutory Notes

St.1923, c. 339.

§ 24B. Assault of child; intent to commit rape; weapons; punishment

Whoever assaults a child under sixteen with intent to commit a rape, as defined in section thirty-nine of chapter two hundred and seventy-seven, shall be punished by imprisonment in the state prison for life or for any term of years; and whoever over the age of eighteen commits a subsequent such offense shall be punished by imprisonment in the state prison for life or for any term of years but not less than five years.

Whoever commits any offense described in this section while being armed with a firearm, rifle, shotgun, machine gun or assault weapon shall be punished by imprisonment in the state prison for life or for any term of years, but not less than ten years. Whoever over the age of 18 commits a second or subsequent such offense shall be punished by imprisonment in the state prison for life or for any term of years, but not less than 15 years.

Added by St.1955, c. 763, § 3. Amended by St.1973, c. 925, § 78; St.1974, c. 474, § 6; St.1978, c. 379, § 2; St.1998, c. 180, § 62.

§ 24C. Victim's name; confidentiality

That portion of the records of a court or any police department of the commonwealth or any of its political subdivisions, which contains the name of the victim in an arrest, investigation or complaint for rape or assault with intent to rape under section thirteen B, 13B½, 13B ¾, twenty-two, twenty-two A, 22B, 22C, twenty-three, 23A, 23B, twenty-four or twenty-four B, inclusive, of chapter two hundred and sixty-five, shall be withheld from public inspection, except with the consent of a justice of such court where the complaint or indictment is or would be prosecuted.

Said portion of such court record or police record shall not be deemed to be a public record under the provisions of section seven of chapter four.

Except as otherwise provided in this section, it shall be unlawful to publish, disseminate or otherwise disclose the name of any individual identified as an alleged victim of any of the offenses described in the first paragraph. A violation of this section shall be punishable by a fine of not less than two thousand five hundred dollars nor more than ten thousand dollars.

Added by St.1986, c. 234. Amended by St.1987, c. 177, §§ 1, 2; St.2010, c. 267, §§ 58 to 60, eff. Nov. 5, 2010.

§ 25. Attempted extortion; punishment

Whoever, verbally or by a written or printed communication, maliciously threatens to accuse another of a crime or offence, or by a verbal or written or printed communication maliciously threatens an injury to the person or property of another, or any police officer or person having the powers of a police officer, or any officer, or employee of any licensing authority who verbally or by written or printed communication maliciously and unlawfully uses or threatens to use against another the power or authority vested in him, with intent thereby to extort money or any pecuniary advantage, or with intent to compel any person to do any act against his will, shall be punished by imprisonment in the state prison for not more than fifteen years, or in the house of correction for not more than two and one half years, or by a fine of not more than five thousand dollars, or both.

Amended by St.1932, c. 211; St.1953, c. 294.

Historical and Statutory Notes

R.S.1836, c. 125, § 17.
St.1853, c. 412.
G.S.1860, c. 160, § 28.
P.S.1882, c. 202, § 29.
R.L.1902, c. 207, § 25.
St.1914, c. 635.
St.1918, c. 257, § 464.
St.1919, c. 5.
St.1920, c. 2.

§ 26. Kidnapping; weapons; child under age 16; punishment

Whoever, without lawful authority, forcibly or secretly confines or imprisons another person within this commonwealth against his will, or forcibly carries or sends such person out of this commonwealth, or forcibly seizes and confines or inveigles or kidnaps another person, with intent either to cause him to be secretly confined or imprisoned in this commonwealth against his will, or to cause him to be sent out of this commonwealth against his will or in any way held to service against his will, shall be punished by imprisonment in the state prison for not more than ten years or by a fine of not more than one thousand dollars and imprisonment in jail for not more than two years. Whoever commits any offence described in this section with the intent to extort money or other valuable thing thereby shall be punished by imprisonment in the state prison for life or for any term of years.

Whoever commits any offense described in this section while armed with a firearm, rifle, shotgun, machine gun or assault weapon shall be punished by imprisonment in the state prison for not less than ten years or in the house of correction for not more than two and one-half years. The provisions of the preceding sentence shall not apply to the parent of a child under 18 years of age who takes custody of such child. Whoever commits such offense described in this section while being armed with a firearm, rifle, shotgun, machine gun or assault weapon with the intent to extort money or other valuable thing thereby shall be punished by imprisonment in the state prison for life or for any term of years but not less than 20 years.

Whoever commits any offense described in this section while armed with a dangerous weapon and inflicts serious bodily injury thereby upon another person or who sexually assaults such person shall be punished by imprisonment in the state prison for not less than 25 years. For purposes of this paragraph the term "serious bodily injury" shall mean bodily injury which results in a permanent disfigurement, protracted loss or impairment of a bodily function, limb or organ or substantial risk of death. For purposes of this paragraph, the term "sexual assault" shall mean the commission of any act set forth in sections 13B, 13B½, 13B¾, 13F, 13H, 22, 22A, 22B, 22C, 23, 23A, 23B, 24 or 24B.

Whoever, without lawful authority, forcibly or secretly confines or imprisons a child under the age of 16 within the commonwealth against his will or forcibly carries or sends such person out of the commonwealth or forcibly seizes and confines or inveigles or kidnaps a child under the age of 16 with the intent either to cause him to be secretly confined or imprisoned in the commonwealth against his will or to cause him to be sent out of the commonwealth against his will or in any way held to service against his will, shall be punished by imprisonment in the state prison for not more than 15 years. The provisions of the preceding sentence shall not apply to the parent of a child under 16 years of age who takes custody of such child.

Amended by St.1934, c. 1; St.1971, c. 900; St.1979, c. 465, § 1; St.1998, c. 180, § 63; St.1999, c. 74, §§ 11, 12; St.2010, c. 267, § 61, eff. Nov. 5, 2010.

Historical and Statutory Notes

B.L. c. 94, § 10.
C.L. c. 15, § 10.
St.1784, c. 72, § 10.
St.1787, c. 48, § 1.
R.S.1836, c. 125, § 20.
G.S.1860, c. 160, § 30.
P.S.1882, c. 202, § 30.
St.1901, c. 428.
R.L.1902, c. 207, § 26.
St.1931, c. 426, § 43.

§ 26A. Kidnapping of minor or incompetent by relative; punishment

Whoever, being a relative of a child less than eighteen years old, without lawful authority, holds or intends to hold such a child permanently or for a protracted period, or takes or entices such a child from his lawful custodian, or takes or entices from lawful custody any incompetent person or other person entrusted by authority of law to the custody of another person or institution shall be punished by imprisonment in the house of correction for not more than one year or by a fine of up to one thousand dollars, or both. Whoever commits any offense described in this section by taking or holding said child outside the commonwealth or under circumstances which expose the person taken or enticed from lawful custody to a risk which endangers his safety shall be punished by a fine of not more than five thousand dollars, or by imprisonment in the state prison for not more than five years, or by both such fine and imprisonment.

Added by St.1979, c. 465, § 2. Amended by St.1983, c. 175.

§ 26B. Drugging persons for kidnapping

Whoever applies, administers to or causes to be taken by a person any drug, matter or thing with intent to stupefy or overpower such person so as to, without lawful authority, forcibly or secretly confine or imprison another person within the commonwealth against his will or to forcibly carry or send such person out of the commonwealth, or to forcibly seize and confine or inveigle or kidnap such person with intent to cause him to be secretly confined or imprisoned in the commonwealth against his will, or to cause him to be sent out of the commonwealth against his will or in any way held to service against his will, shall be punished by imprisonment in the state prison for life or for any term of years not less than ten years. Whoever violates the provisions of this section with the intent to extort money or other valuable thing thereby shall be punished by imprisonment in the state prison for life or for any term of years not less than 15 years.

Added by St.1998, c. 232, § 2.

§ 26C. Definition of "entice"; enticement of child under age 16; punishment

(a) As used in this section, the term "entice" shall mean to lure, induce, persuade, tempt, incite, solicit, coax or invite.

(b) Any one who entices a child under the age of 16, or someone he believes to be a child under the age of 16, to enter, exit or remain within any vehicle, dwelling, building, or other outdoor space with the intent that he or another person will violate section 13B, 13B½, 13B¾, 13F, 13H, 22, 22A, 22B, 22C, 23, 23A, 23B, 24 or 24B of chapter 265, section 4A, 16, 28, 29, 29A, 29B, 29C, 35A, 53 or 53A of chapter 272, or any offense that has as an element the use or attempted use of force, shall be punished by imprisonment in the state prison for not more than 5 years, or in the house of correction for not more than 2½ years, or by both imprisonment and a fine of not more than $5,000.

Added by St.2002, c. 385, § 3. Amended by St.2010, c. 267, §§ 62 to 64, eff. Nov. 4, 2010.

§ 27. Kidnapping; venue

A crime described in section twenty-six may be tried in the county where committed or in any county in or to which the person so seized, inveigled or kidnapped is confined, held, carried or brought; and upon the trial of any such crime, the consent thereto of the person so seized, inveigled, kidnapped or confined shall not be a defence unless the jury finds that such consent was not obtained by fraud or extorted by duress or threats.

Amended by St.1979, c. 465, § 3.

Historical and Statutory Notes

R.S.1836, c. 125, § 21.
G.S.1860, c. 160, § 31.
P.S.1882, c. 202, § 31.
R.L.1902, c. 207, § 27.
St.1931, c. 426, § 44.

§ 27A. Kidnapping of minor or incompetent by relative; venue

A crime described in section twenty-six A may be tried in the county where committed or in a county in or to which the person so taken or enticed is held, carried to, or brought.

Added by St.1979, c. 465, § 4.

§ 28. Poison; use with intent to injure; punishment

Whoever mingles poison with food, drink or medicine with intent to kill or injure another person, or wilfully poisons any spring, well or reservoir of water with such intent, shall be punished by imprisonment in the state prison for life or for any term of years.

Historical and Statutory Notes

R.S.1836, c. 125, § 22.
G.S.1860, c. 160, § 32.
P.S.1882, c. 202, § 32.
R.L.1902, c. 207, § 28.

§ 29. Assault; intent to commit felony; punishment

Whoever assaults another with intent to commit a felony shall, if the punishment of such assault is not hereinbefore provided, be punished by imprisonment in the state prison for not more than ten years or by a fine of not more than one thousand dollars and imprisonment in jail for not more than two and one half years.

Historical and Statutory Notes

R.S.1836, c. 125, § 23.
G.S.1860, c. 160, § 33.
P.S.1882, c. 202, § 33.
R.L.1902, c. 207, § 29.
St.1914, c. 635.
St.1918, c. 257, § 464.
St.1919, c. 5.
St.1920, c. 2.

§ 30. Gross negligence; persons having care of common carrier; penalty

Whoever, having the management or control of or over a steamboat or other public conveyance used for the common carriage of persons, is guilty of gross negligence in or relative to the management or control of such steamboat or other public conveyance, while being so used for the common carriage of persons, shall be punished by a fine of not more than five thousand dollars or by imprisonment in jail for not more than two and one half years.

Historical and Statutory Notes

St.1853, c. 418.
G.S.1860, c. 160, § 35.
P.S.1882, c. 202, § 34.
R.L.1902, c. 207, § 30.
St.1914, c. 635.
St.1918, c. 257, § 464.
St.1919, c. 5.
St.1920, c. 2.

§ 31. Repealed, 1962, 285, Sec. 2

§ 32. Glass; throwing in public streets and beaches; penalty

Whoever throws or drops glass on a public way, or on or near a bathing beach, or on a public way, sidewalk or reservation in the immediate neighborhood of a bathing beach, shall be punished by a fine of not more than one hundred dollars or by imprisonment for not more than one month.

Amended by St.1975, c. 322.

Historical and Statutory Notes

St.1913, c. 214.
St.1914, c. 76.

§ 33. Repealed, 1962, 285, Sec. 2

§ 34. Tattooing body of person by other than qualified physician; punishment

Whoever, not being registered as a qualified physician under section two of chapter one hundred and twelve, or corresponding provisions of earlier laws, marks the body of any person by means of tattooing, shall be punished by a fine of not more than three hundred dollars or by imprisonment for not more than one year, or both.

Added by St.1957, c. 76. Amended by St.1962, c. 214.

§ 35. Throwing or dropping objects onto public way; punishment

Whoever willfully or negligently drops, throws or otherwise releases any object, missile or other article onto any way as defined in section one of chapter ninety, the turnpike as defined in clause *(b)* of section four of chapter three hundred and fifty-four of the acts of nineteen hundred and fifty-two or the tunnels as defined in clause *(d)* of section one of chapter five hundred and ninety-eight of the acts of nineteen hundred and fifty-eight so that the lives or safety of the public might be endangered shall be punished by a fine of not more than one hundred dollars, or by imprisonment for not more than one year, or both.

Added by St.1968, c. 139. Amended by St.1973, c. 432.

§ 36. Throwing or dropping objects at sporting events; punishment

Any person who willfully drops, throws or otherwise releases any object, missile or other article at any sporting event with the intent to injure any person at such event shall be punished by a fine of not more than five hundred dollars or by imprisonment in the house of correction for not more than one year, or both.

Added by St.1975, c. 435.

§ 37. Violations of constitutional rights; punishment

No person, whether or not acting under color of law, shall by force or threat of force, willfully injure, intimidate or interfere with, or attempt to injure, intimidate or interfere with, or oppress or threaten any other person in the free exercise or enjoyment of any right or privilege secured to him by the constitution or laws of the commonwealth or by the constitution or laws of the United States. Any person convicted of violating this provision shall be fined not more than one thousand dollars or imprisoned not more than one year or both; and if bodily injury results, shall be punished by a fine of not more than ten thousand dollars or by imprisonment for not more than ten years, or both.

Added by St.1979, c. 801, § 2.

§ 38. Repealed, 2004, 501, Sec. 9

§ 39. Assault or battery for purpose of intimidation; weapons; punishment

(a) Whoever commits an assault or a battery upon a person or damages the real or personal property of a person with the intent to intimidate such person because of such person's race, color, religion, national origin, sexual orientation, or disability shall be punished by a fine of not more than five thousand dollars or by imprisonment in a house of correction for not more than two and one-half years, or by both such fine and imprisonment. The court may also order restitution to the victim in any amount up to three times the value of property damage sustained by the owners of such property. For the purposes of this section, the term "disability" shall have the same meaning as "handicap" as defined in subsection 17 of section one of chapter one hundred and fifty-one B; provided, however, that for purposes of this section, the term "disability" shall not include any condition primarily resulting from the use of alcohol or a controlled substance as defined in section one of chapter ninety-four C.

(b) Whoever commits a battery in violation of this section and which results in bodily injury shall be punished by a fine of not more than ten thousand dollars or by imprisonment in the state prison for not more than five years, or by both such fine and imprisonment. Whoever commits any offense described in this subsection while armed with a firearm, rifle, shotgun, machine gun or assault weapon shall be punished by imprisonment in the state prison for not more than ten years or in the house of correction for not more than two and one-half years. For purposes of this section, "bodily injury" shall mean substantial impairment of the physical condition, including, but not limited to, any burn, fracture of any bone, subdural hematoma, injury to any internal organ, or any injury which occurs as the result of repeated harm to any bodily function or organ, including human skin.

There shall be a surcharge of one hundred dollars on a fine assessed against a defendant convicted of a violation of this section; provided, however, that moneys from such surcharge shall be delivered forthwith to the treasurer of the commonwealth and deposited in the Diversity Awareness Education Trust Fund established under the provisions of section thirty-nine Q of chapter ten. In the case of convictions for multiple offenses, said surcharge shall be assessed for each such conviction.

A person convicted under the provisions of this section shall complete a diversity awareness program designed by the secretary of the executive office of public safety in consultation with the Massachusetts commission against discrimination and approved by the chief justice for administration and management of the trial court. A person so convicted shall complete such program prior to release from incarceration or prior to completion of the terms of probation, whichever is applicable.

Added by St.1983, c. 165, § 1. Amended by St.1996, c. 163, § 2; St.1998, c. 180, § 64.

§ 40. Causing serious bodily injury to participants in physical exercise training programs; punishment

Whoever, having the direct management or direct control over the conduct of physical exercise as part of a course of study or training program at any public or private institution, agency or entity, willfully, wantonly and recklessly causes serious bodily injury to a person participating in a course of study or training program involving physical exercise, shall be punished by a fine of not more than five thousand dollars or by imprisonment in a jail or house of correction for not more than two and one-half years or both.

For the purposes of this section "serious bodily injury" shall mean bodily injury which creates a substantial risk of death or which involves either total disability or the loss or substantial impairment of some bodily function for a substantial period of time.

Added by St.1989, c. 244.

§ 41. Sentence not imposing imprisonment; specific reasons in record

In sentencing a person for a violation of any provision of this chapter, the penalty for which includes imprisonment, a judge sitting in superior court or in a jury of six session who does not impose such sentence of imprisonment shall include in the record of the case specific reasons for not imposing a sentence of imprisonment. Notwithstanding any general or special law to the contrary, the record of such reasons shall be a public record.

Added by St.1989, c. 363, § 1. Renumbered by St.1990, c. 177, § 367.

§ 42. Use of radios without earphones on public conveyances; punishment

Whoever uses a radio or boom box, so-called, or similar broadcasting equipment without the use of earphones or other apparatus on a public conveyance used for the common carriage of persons, shall be punished by a fine of not less than one hundred dollars nor more than five hundred dollars or by imprisonment for not more than one month. Evidence seized pursuant to this section shall be sold at public auction and the proceeds therefrom may be applied against outstanding fines and court costs.

Added by St.1991, c. 33, § 101.

§ 43. Stalking; punishment

(a) Whoever (1) willfully and maliciously engages in a knowing pattern of conduct or series of acts over a period of time directed at a specific person which seriously alarms or annoys that person and would cause a reasonable person to suffer substantial emotional distress, and (2) makes a threat with the intent to place the person in imminent fear of death or bodily injury, shall be guilty of the crime of stalking and shall be punished by imprisonment in the state prison for not more than 5 years or by a fine of not more than $1,000, or imprisonment in the house of correction for not more than 2½ years or by both such fine and imprisonment. The conduct, acts or threats described in this subsection shall include, but not be limited to, conduct, acts or threats conducted by mail or by use of a telephonic or telecommunication device or electronic communication device including, but not limited to, any device that transfers signs, signals, writing, images, sounds, data, or intelligence of any nature transmitted in whole or in part by a wire, radio, electromagnetic, photo-electronic or photo-optical system, including, but not limited to, electronic mail, internet communications, instant messages or facsimile communications.

(b) Whoever commits the crime of stalking in violation of a temporary or permanent vacate, restraining, or no-contact order or judgment issued pursuant to sections eighteen, thirty-four B, or thirty-four C of chapter two hundred and eight; or section thirty-two of chapter two hundred and nine; or sections three, four, or five of chapter two hundred and nine A; or sections fifteen or twenty of chapter two hundred and nine C or a protection order issued by another jurisdiction; or a temporary restraining order or preliminary or permanent injunction issued by the superior court, shall be punished by imprisonment in a jail or the state prison for not less than one year and not more than five years. No sentence imposed under the provisions of this subsection shall be less than a mandatory minimum term of imprisonment of one year.

A prosecution commenced hereunder shall not be placed on file or continued without a finding, and the sentence imposed upon a person convicted of violating any provision of this subsection shall not be reduced to less than the mandatory minimum term of imprisonment as established herein, nor shall said sentence of imprisonment imposed upon any person be suspended or reduced until such person shall have served said mandatory term of imprisonment.

A person convicted of violating any provision of this subsection shall not, until he shall have served the mandatory minimum term of imprisonment established herein, be eligible for probation, parole, furlough, work release or receive any deduction from his sentence for good conduct under sections one hundred and twenty-nine, one hundred and twenty-nine C and one hundred and twenty-nine D of chapter one hundred and twenty-seven; provided, however, that the commissioner of correction may, on the recommendation of the warden, superintendent, or other person in charge of a correctional institution, grant to said offender a temporary release in the custody of an officer of such institution for the following purposes only: to attend the funeral of next of kin or spouse; to visit a critically ill close relative or spouse; or to obtain emergency medical services unavailable at said institution. The provisions of section eighty-seven of chapter two hundred and seventy-six relating to the power of the court to place certain offenders on probation shall not apply to any person seventeen years of age or over charged with a violation of this subsection. The provisions of section thirty-one of chapter two hundred and seventy-nine shall not apply to any person convicted of violating any provision of this subsection.

(c) Whoever, after having been convicted of the crime of stalking, commits a second or subsequent such crime shall be punished by imprisonment in a jail or the state prison for not less than two years and not more than ten years. No sentence imposed under the provisions of this subsection shall be less than a mandatory minimum term of imprisonment of two years.

A prosecution commenced hereunder shall not be placed on file or continued without a finding, and the sentence imposed upon a person convicted of violating any provision of this subsection shall not be reduced to less than the mandatory minimum term of imprisonment as established herein, nor shall said sentence of imprisonment imposed upon any person be suspended or reduced until such person shall have served said mandatory term of imprisonment.

A person convicted of violating any provision of this subsection shall not, until he shall have served the mandatory minimum term of imprisonment established herein, be eligible for probation, parole, furlough, work release or receive any deduction from his sentence for good conduct under sections one hundred and twenty-nine, one hundred and twenty-nine C and one hundred and twenty-nine D of chapter one hundred and twenty-seven; provided, however, that the commissioner of correction may, on the recommendation of the warden, superintendent, or other person in charge of a correctional institution, grant to said offender a temporary release in the custody of an officer of such institution for the following purposes only: to attend the funeral of next of kin or spouse; to visit a critically ill close relative or spouse; or to obtain emergency medical services unavailable at said institution. The provisions of section eighty-seven of chapter two hundred and seventy-six relating to the power of the court to place certain offenders on probation shall not apply to any person seventeen years of age or over charged with a violation of this subsection. The provisions of section thirty-one of chapter two hundred and seventy-nine shall not apply to any person convicted of violating any provision of this section.

Added by St.1992, c. 31. Amended by St.1996, c. 298, §§ 11, 12; St.1997, c. 238, §§ 1, 2; St.2010, c. 92, § 9, eff. May 3, 2010.

§ 43A. Criminal harassment; punishment

(a) Whoever willfully and maliciously engages in a knowing pattern of conduct or series of acts over a period of time directed at a specific person, which seriously alarms that person and would cause a reasonable person to suffer substantial emotional distress, shall be guilty of the crime of criminal harassment and shall be punished by imprisonment in a house of correction for not more than 2½ years or by a fine of not more than $1,000, or by both such fine and imprisonment. The conduct or acts described in this paragraph shall include, but not be limited to, conduct or acts conducted by mail or by use of a telephonic or telecommunication device or electronic communication device including, but not limited to, any device that transfers signs, signals, writing, images, sounds, data or intelligence of any nature transmitted in whole or in part by a wire, radio, electromagnetic, photo-electronic or photo-optical system, including, but not limited to, electronic mail, internet communications, instant messages or facsimile communications.

(b) Whoever, after having been convicted of the crime of criminal harassment, commits a second or subsequent such crime, or whoever commits the crime of criminal harassment having previously been convicted of a violation of section 43, shall be punished by imprisonment in a house of correction for not more than two and one-half years or by imprisonment in the state prison for not more than ten years.

Added by St.2000, c. 164. Amended by St.2010, c. 92, § 10, eff. May 3, 2010.

§ 44. Coercion of child under eighteen into criminal conspiracy; penalties

Whoever commits an assault and battery on a child under the age of eighteen for the purpose of causing or coercing such child to join or participate in a criminal conspiracy in violation of section seven of chapter two hundred and seventy-four, including but not limited to a criminal street gang or other organization of three or more persons which has a common name, identifying sign or symbol and whose members individually or collectively engage in criminal activity, shall, for the first offense, be punished by imprisonment in the state prison for not less than three nor more than five years or by imprisonment in the house of correction for not more than two and one-half years; and for a second or subsequent offense by imprisonment in the state prison for not less than five nor more than ten years.

Added by St.1996, c. 200, § 36.

§ 45. Community parole supervision for life following imprisonment, probation or treatment center sentence; covered offenses

Any person who commits indecent assault and battery on a child under 14 under section 13B, indecent assault and battery on a mentally retarded person under the first paragraph of section 13F or indecent assault and battery on a person who has attained the age of 14 under section 13H may, in addition to the term of imprisonment authorized by such section, be punished by a term of community parole supervision for life to be served under the jurisdiction of the parole board, as set forth in section 133C of chapter 127. Any person who commits rape under section 22; rape of a child under 16 with force under section 22A; rape and abuse of a child under section 23; assault with intent to commit rape under section 24; assault of a child under 16 with intent to commit rape under section 24B; kidnapping a child under the age of 16 under section 26; drugging persons for sexual intercourse under section 3 of chapter 272; unnatural and lascivious acts with a child under 16 under section 35A of said chapter 272; or commits an attempt to violate any such section pursuant to section 6 of chapter 274, shall, except as provided for in section 18 of chapter 275, and in addition to the term of imprisonment authorized by such section, receive a sentence of community parole supervision for life to be served under the jurisdiction of the parole board, as set forth in section 133D of chapter 127. Any person convicted of violating section 13B, 13B½, 13B¾, 13F, 13H, 22, 22A, 22B, 22C, 23, 23A, 23B, 24, 24B or 26 of this chapter or of an attempt to violate any of such sections pursuant to section 6 of chapter 274, after one or more prior convictions of indecent assault and battery, rape, assault with intent to commit rape, unnatural and lascivious acts, drugging for sex, kidnap or of any offense which is the same as or necessarily includes the same elements of said offense shall, in addition to the term of imprisonment authorized by such section, be punished by a term of community parole supervision for life, to be served under the jurisdiction of the parole board, as set forth in said section 133D of said chapter 127. The sentence of community parole supervision for life shall commence immediately upon the expiration of the term of imprisonment imposed upon such person by the court or upon such person's release from probation supervision or upon discharge from commitment to the treatment center pursuant to section 9 of chapter 123A, whichever first occurs.

Added by St.1999, c. 74, § 13. Amended by St.2010, c. 267, § 65, eff. Nov. 5, 2010.

§ 46. Taking from deceased victim's estate prohibited

The court shall prohibit any person charged with the unlawful killing of the decedent from taking from the decedent's estate through its distribution and disposition, including property held between the person charged and the decedent in joint tenancy or by tenancy in the entirety. The court shall consider any person convicted of the unlawful killing of the decedent as predeceasing the decedent for the purpose of distribution and disposition of the decedent's estate including property held between the person charged and the decedent in joint tenancy or by tenancy in the entirety. The bar to succession shall apply only to murder in the first degree, murder in the second degree or manslaughter; it shall not include vehicular homicide or negligent manslaughter in the death of the decedent. No court shall distribute the accused's share of the decedent's assets until a verdict or finding on the charge has been rendered in open court. If the court determines the accused not guilty of the unlawful killing of the decedent, the accused may take by decent or distribution from the decedent's estate under law. The provisions of this section and any order of a court entered pursuant thereto, shall not have any effect on title to real property, except against the person charged with an offense to which this section applies, or that person's heirs and devisees, until a memorandum that recites the name of that person is recorded in the manner provided in section 15 of chapter 184, and no order so entered shall divest any person who has given fair consideration for any interest in such property before such recording.

Added by St.2002, c. 420, § 11.

§ 47. Global positioning system device to be worn by certain sex offender probationers

Any person who is placed on probation for any offense listed within the definition of "sex offense", a "sex offense involving a child" or a "sexually violent offense", as defined in section 178C of chapter 6, shall, as a requirement of any term of probation, wear a global positioning system device, or any comparable device, administered by the commissioner of probation, at all times for the length of his probation for any such offense. The commissioner of probation, in addition to any other conditions, shall establish defined geographic exclusion zones including, but not limited to, the areas in and around the victim's residence, place of employment and school and other areas defined to minimize the probationer's contact with children, if applicable. If the probationer enters an excluded zone, as defined by the terms of his probation, the probationer's location data shall be immediately transmitted to the police department in the municipality wherein the violation occurred and the commissioner of probation, by telephone, electronic beeper, paging device or other appropriate means. If the commissioner or the probationer's probation officer has probable cause to believe that the probationer has violated this term of his probation, the commissioner or the probationer's probation officer shall arrest the probationer pursuant to section 3 of chapter 279. Otherwise, the commissioner shall cause a notice of surrender to be issued to such probationer.

The fees incurred by installing, maintaining and operating the global positioning system device, or comparable device, shall be paid by the probationer. If an offender establishes his inability to pay such fees, the court may waive them.

Added by St.2006, c. 303, § 8, eff. Dec. 20, 2006.

§ 48. Ice cream truck vending by sex offender prohibited

[Text of section added by 2010, 256, Sec. 119 effective May 4, 2012. See 2010, 256, Sec. 145 as amended by 2010, 359, Sec. 102.]

A sex offender, as defined by section 178C of chapter 6, who engages in ice cream truck vending, as defined in section 25 of chapter 270, shall be punished by imprisonment in the house of correction for not more than 2½ years or by a fine of $1,000, or by both such fine and imprisonment. A police officer or officer authorized to serve criminal process may arrest, without a warrant, any person whom he has probable cause to believe has violated this section.

Added by St.2010, c. 256, § 119, eff. May 4, 2012.

CHAPTER 266

CRIMES AGAINST PROPERTY

The section headings for the General Laws in this pamphlet have been editorially supplied.

§ 1. Dwelling houses; burning or aiding in burning

Whoever wilfully and maliciously sets fire to, burns, or causes to be burned, or whoever aids, counsels or procures the burning of, a dwelling house, or a building adjoining or adjacent to a dwelling house, or a building by the burning whereof a dwelling house is burned, whether such dwelling house or other building is the property of himself or another and whether the same is occupied or unoccupied, shall be punished by imprisonment in the state prison for not more than twenty years, or by imprisonment in a jail or house of correction for not more than two and one half years, or by a fine of not more than ten thousand dollars, or by both such fine and imprisonment. The words "dwelling house", as used in this section, shall mean and include all buildings used as dwellings such as apartment houses, tenement houses, hotels, boarding houses, dormitories, hospitals, institutions, sanatoria, or other buildings where persons are domiciled.

Amended by St.1932, c. 192, § 1; St.1948, c. 43, § 1; St.1974, c. 281.

Historical and Statutory Notes

C.L. c. 52, § 1.
St.1705–6, c. 9.
St.1784, c. 58, §§ 1, 2.
St.1804, c. 131, §§ 1, 2.
St.1830, c. 72, § 1.
R.S.1836, c. 126, §§ 1, 2.
St.1852, c. 259, § 3.
G.S.1860, c. 161, § 1.
St.1871, c. 76.
P.S.1882, c. 203, § 1.
R.L.1902, c. 208, § 1.
St.1930, c. 382.

§ 2. Meeting house; burning or aiding in burning

Whoever wilfully and maliciously sets fire to, burns, or causes to be burned, or whoever aids, counsels or procures the burning of, a meeting house, church, court house, town house, college, academy, jail or other building which has been erected for public use, or a banking house, warehouse, store, manufactory, mill, barn, stable, shop, outhouse or other building, or an office building, lumber yard, ship, vessel, street car

or railway car, or a bridge, lock, dam, flume, tank, or any building or structure or contents thereof, not included or described in the preceding section, whether the same is the property of himself or of another and whether occupied, unoccupied or vacant, shall be punished by imprisonment in the state prison for not more than ten years, or by imprisonment in a jail or house of correction for not more than two and one half years.
Amended by St.1932, c. 192, § 2; St.1948, c. 43, § 2.

Historical and Statutory Notes

C.L. c. 52, § 1.
St.1705–6, c. 9.
St.1784, c. 58, § 2.
St.1804, c. 131, § 2.
R.S.1836, c. 126, § 3.
G.S.1860, c. 161, § 2.
St.1871, c. 76.
P.S.1882, c. 203, § 2.
R.L.1902, c. 208, § 2.

§§ 3, 4. Repealed, 1932, 192, Sec. 3

§ 5. Wood and other property; burning or aiding in burning

Whoever wilfully and maliciously sets fire to, or burns or otherwise destroys or injures by burning, or causes to be burned or otherwise so destroyed or injured, or whoever aids, counsels or procures the burning of, a pile or parcel of wood, boards, timber or other lumber, or any fence, bars or gate, or a stack of grain, hay or other vegetable product, or any vegetable product severed from the soil and not stacked, or any standing tree, grain, grass or other standing product of the soil, or the soil itself, or any personal property of whatsoever class or character exceeding a value of twenty-five dollars, of another, or any boat, motor vehicle as defined in section one of chapter ninety, or other conveyance, whether of himself or another, shall be punished by imprisonment in the state prison for not more than three years, or by a fine of not more than five hundred dollars and imprisonment in a jail or house of correction for not more than one year.
Amended by St.1932, c. 192, § 4.

Historical and Statutory Notes

C.L. c. 51, § 2; c. 52, § 1.
St.1705–6, c. 9.
St.1784, c. 58, §§ 3, 4.
St.1804, c. 131, § 4.
R.S.1836, c. 126, § 6.
G.S.1860, c. 161, § 5.
P.S.1882, c. 203, § 5.
R.L.1902, c. 208, § 5.

§ 5A. Attempts

Whoever wilfully and maliciously attempts to set fire to, or attempts to burn, or aids, counsels or assists in such an attempt to set fire to or burn, any of the buildings, structures or property mentioned in the foregoing sections, or whoever commits any act preliminary thereto or in furtherance thereof, shall be punished by imprisonment in the state prison for not more than ten years, or by imprisonment in a jail or house of correction for not more than two and one half years or by a fine of not more than one thousand dollars.

The placing or distributing of any flammable, explosive or combustible material or substance or any device in or against any building, structure or property mentioned in the foregoing sections in an arrangement or preparation with intent eventually to wilfully and maliciously set fire to or burn such building, structure or property, or to procure the setting fire to or burning of the same shall, for the purposes of this section, constitute an attempt to burn such building, structure or property.
Added by St.1932, c. 192, § 5. Amended by St.1977, c. 975.

§ 6. Repealed, 1932, 192, Sec. 3

§ 7. Woods; wanton or reckless injury or destruction by fire

Whoever by wantonly or recklessly setting fire to any material, or by increasing a fire already set, causes injury to, or the destruction of, any growing or standing wood of another shall be punished by a fine of not more than one thousand dollars or by imprisonment for not more than two years.
Amended by St.1958, c. 526, § 1.

Historical and Statutory Notes

St.1882, c. 163.
R.L.1902, c. 208, § 7.
St.1912, c. 419, § 1.

§ 8. Injury by fire; negligent use

Whoever, not being a tenant thereof, sets or increases a fire upon land of another whereby the property of another is injured, or whoever negligently or wilfully suffers any fire upon his own land to extend beyond the limits thereof whereby the woods or property of another are injured, shall be punished by a fine of not more than one thousand dollars or by imprisonment for not more than two years, and the town where such fire occurred may recover in an action of tort, brought within two years after the cause of action accrues, against any such person the expense of extinguishing such fire.
Amended by St.1932, c. 192, § 6; St.1948, c. 370, § 1; St.1958, c. 526, § 2.

Historical and Statutory Notes

St.1886, c. 296, § 1.
R.L.1902, c. 208, § 8.
St.1912, c. 419, § 2.

§ 9. Injury by fire; negligent use in town; damages

Whoever, in a town which accepts this section or has accepted corresponding provisions of earlier laws, sets a fire on land which is not owned or controlled by him and before leaving the same neglects to entirely extinguish such fire, or whoever wilfully or negligently sets a fire on land which is not owned or controlled by him whereby property is endangered or injured, or whoever wilfully or negligently suffers a fire upon his own land to escape beyond the limits thereof to the injury of another, shall be punished by a fine of not more than one hundred dollars or by imprisonment in jail for not more than one month, or both, and shall also be liable for all damages caused thereby. Such fine shall be equally divided between the complainant and the town. This section shall not apply to cities.

Historical and Statutory Notes

St.1897, c. 254, §§ 1, 9.
R.L.1902, c. 208, § 9.

§ 10. Insured property; burning with intent to defraud

Whoever, wilfully and with intent to defraud or injure the insurer, sets fire to, or attempts to set fire to, or whoever causes to be burned, or whoever aids, counsels or procures the burning of, a building, or any goods, wares, merchandise or other chattels, belonging to himself or another, and which are at the time insured against loss or damage by fire, shall be punished by imprisonment in the state prison for not more than five years or in a jail or house of correction for not more than two and one half years.

Amended by St.1932, c. 192, § 7.

Historical and Statutory Notes

R.S.1836, c. 126, § 8.
G.S.1860, c. 161, § 7.
P.S.1882, c. 203, § 7.
R.L.1902, c. 208, § 10.

§ 11. Fire alarm, engine or apparatus; injury before fire

Whoever, within twenty-four hours prior to the burning of a building or other property, wilfully, intentionally and without right cuts or removes a bell rope or a wire or conduit connected with a fire alarm signal system or injures or disables any fire alarm signal box or any part of such system in the vicinity of such building or property, or cuts, injures or destroys an engine, hose or other fire apparatus in said vicinity shall be punished by a fine of not more than five hundred dollars or by imprisonment for not more than two years.

Historical and Statutory Notes

St.1855, c. 446, § 1.
G.S.1860, c. 161, § 8.
P.S.1882, c. 203, § 8.
R.L.1902, c. 208, § 11.
St.1918, c. 257, § 447.
St.1919, c. 5.
St.1920, c. 2.

§ 12. Fire alarm, engine or apparatus; injury during fire to prevent alarm or extinction of fire

Whoever, during the burning of a building or other property, wilfully and maliciously cuts or removes a bell rope or a wire or conduit connected with a fire alarm signal system or injures or disables any fire alarm signal box or any part of such system in the vicinity of such building or property, or otherwise prevents an alarm being given, or whoever cuts, injures or destroys an engine, hose or other fire apparatus, in said vicinity, or otherwise wilfully and maliciously prevents or obstructs the extinction of a fire shall be punished by imprisonment in the state prison for not more than seven years or in jail for not more than two and one half years or by a fine of not more than one thousand dollars.

Historical and Statutory Notes

St.1855, c. 446, § 2.
G.S.1860, c. 161, § 9.
P.S.1882, c. 203, § 9.
R.L.1902, c. 208, § 12.
St.1918, c. 257, § 448.
St.1919, c. 5.
St.1920, c. 2.

§ 13. Fire engines; wanton or malicious injury

Whoever wantonly or maliciously injures a fire engine or other fire apparatus shall be punished by a fine of not more than five hundred dollars or by imprisonment for not more than two years, and shall be further ordered to recognize with sufficient surety or sureties for his good behavior during such term as the court shall order.

Historical and Statutory Notes

St.1801, c. 29.
R.S.1836, c. 18, § 23.
G.S.1860, c. 24, § 22.
P.S.1882, c. 35, § 26.
R.L.1902, c. 208, § 13.
St.1918, c. 257, § 449.
St.1919, c. 5.
St.1920, c. 2.

§ 13A. Duty of hotel manager to notify fire department and sound alarm; penalty

The manager of a hotel or family hotel or such other person as may be in charge of the premises in the absence of the manager, shall, as soon as he becomes aware that there is a fire therein, notify the fire department and, if such fire, or heat, smoke or gas therefrom, threatens to spread to rooms occupied by guests, sound the alarm system required by the state building code.

Whoever violates any provision of this section shall be punished by imprisonment in a jail or house of correction for not more than two and a half years or by a fine of not more than one thousand dollars.

Added by St.1963, c. 690, § 4. Amended by St.1972, c. 802, § 61; St.1981, c. 71.

§ 14. Burglary; armed; assault on occupants; weapons; punishment

Whoever breaks and enters a dwelling house in the night time, with intent to commit a felony, or whoever, after having entered with such intent, breaks such dwelling house in the night time, any person being then lawfully therein, and the offender being armed with a dangerous weapon at the time of such breaking or entry, or so arming himself in such house, or making an actual assault on a person lawfully therein, shall be punished by imprisonment in the state prison for life or for any term of not less than ten years.

Whoever commits any offense described in this section while armed with a firearm, rifle, shotgun, machine gun or assault weapon shall be punished by imprisonment in the state prison for life or for any term of years, but not less than 15 years. Whoever commits a subsequent such offense shall be punished by imprisonment in the state prison for life or for any term of years, but not less than 20 years. The sentence imposed upon a person who, after being convicted of any offence mentioned in this section, commits the like offence, or any other of the offences therein mentioned, shall not be suspended, nor shall he be placed on probation.

Amended by St.1966, c. 330; St.1998, c. 180, § 65.

Historical and Statutory Notes

C.L. c. 13, § 1.
St.1692–3, c. 18, § 4.
St.1715–16, c. 1.
St.1769–70, c. 16, § 2.
St.1784, c. 48.
St.1805, c. 101, § 1.
R.S.1836, c. 126, § 9.
St.1839, c. 127.
G.S.1860, c. 161, § 10.
St.1871, c. 76.
P.S.1882, c. 203, § 10.
St.1888, c. 135, § 1.
R.L.1902, c. 208, § 14.

§ 15. Burglary; unarmed

Whoever breaks and enters a dwelling house in the night time, with the intent mentioned in the preceding section, or, having entered with such intent, breaks such dwelling house in the night time, the offender not being armed, nor arming himself in such house, with a dangerous weapon, nor making an assault upon a person lawfully therein, shall be punished by imprisonment in the state prison for not more than twenty years and, if he shall have been previously convicted of any crime named in this or the preceding section, for not less than five years.

Historical and Statutory Notes

C.L. c. 13, § 1.
St.1692–3, c. 18, § 4.
St.1715–16, c. 1.
St.1769–70, c. 16, § 3.
St.1784, c. 48.
St.1805, c. 101, § 2.
St.1830, c. 72, § 2.
R.S.1836, c. 126, § 10.
G.S.1860, c. 161, § 11.
P.S.1882, c. 203, § 11.
St.1888, c. 135, § 2.
R.L.1902, c. 208, § 15.

§ 16. Breaking and entering at night

Whoever, in the night time, breaks and enters a building, ship, vessel or vehicle, with intent to commit a felony, or who attempts to or does break, burn, blow up or otherwise injures or destroys a safe, vault or other depository of money, bonds or other valuables in any building, vehicle or place, with intent to commit a larceny or felony, whether he succeeds or fails in the perpetration of such larceny or felony, shall be punished by imprisonment in the state prison for not more than twenty years or in a jail or house of correction for not more than two and one-half years.

Amended by St.1943, c. 343, § 1; St.1974, c. 462, § 2; St.1985, c. 312, § 1.

Historical and Statutory Notes

C.L. c. 204, § 3.
St.1692–3, c. 18, § 4.
St.1804, c. 143, § 4.
R.S.1836, c. 126, § 11.
St.1839, c. 31.
St.1851, c. 156, § 1.
G.S.1860, c. 161, § 12.
P.S.1882, c. 203, § 12.
R.L.1902, c. 208, § 16.

§ 16A. Building, vessel or vehicle; breaking and entering with intent to commit misdemeanor

Whoever in the nighttime or daytime breaks and enters a building, ship, vessel or vehicle with intent to commit a misdemeanor shall be punished by a fine of not more than two hundred dollars or by imprisonment for not more than six months, or both.

Added by St.1945, c. 229. Amended by St.1966, c. 408.

§ 17. Entering without breaking at night; breaking and entering in day time; weapons; punishment

Whoever, in the night time, enters without breaking, or breaks and enters in the day time, a building, ship, vessel, or vehicle, with intent to commit a felony, the owner or any other person lawfully therein being put in fear, shall be punished by imprisonment in the state prison for not more than ten years. Whoever commits any offense described in this section while armed with a firearm, rifle, shotgun, machine gun or assault weapon shall be punished by imprisonment in the state prison for not less than five years or in the house of correction for not more than two and one-half years.

Amended by St.1985, c. 312, § 2; St.1998, c. 180, § 66.

Historical and Statutory Notes

C.L. c. 204, § 3.
St.1692–3, c. 18, § 4.
St.1784, c. 66, § 8.

St.1804, c. 143, § 5.
R.S.1836, c. 126, § 12.
St.1851, c. 156, § 2.
G.S.1860, c. 161, § 13.
P.S.1882, c. 203, § 13.
R.L.1902, c. 208, § 17.

§ 18. Dwelling house; entry at night; breaking and entering in day time; weapons; punishment

Whoever, in the night time, enters a dwelling house without breaking, or breaks and enters in the day time a building, ship or motor vehicle or vessel, with intent to commit a felony, no person lawfully therein being put in fear, shall be punished by imprisonment in the state prison for not more than ten years or by a fine of not more than five hundred dollars and imprisonment in jail for not more than two years. Whoever commits any offense described in this section while armed with a firearm, rifle, shotgun, machine gun or assault weapon shall be punished by imprisonment in the state prison for not less than five years or by imprisonment in the house of correction for not more than two and one-half years.

Amended by St.1989, c. 490; St.1998, c. 180, § 67.

Historical and Statutory Notes

St.1784, c. 66, § 8.
St.1805, c. 101, § 4.
R.S.1836, c. 126, § 13.
St.1851, c. 156, § 3.
G.S.1860, c. 161, § 14.
St.1869, c. 386.
P.S.1882, c. 203, § 15.
R.L.1902, c. 208, § 18.

§ 18A. Entering dwelling house by false pretenses; intent to commit felony; larceny; punishment

Whoever enters a dwelling house by false pretenses, without breaking and with the intent to commit a felony, no person lawfully therein being put in fear, or whoever enters a dwelling house by false pretenses, without breaking and, after having entered, commits a larceny, as defined by section 30, no person lawfully therein being put in fear, shall be punished by imprisonment in the state prison for not more than ten years or by a fine of not more than $5,000 and imprisonment in a house of correction for not more than two years, or by both such fine and imprisonment.

Added by St.1998, c. 320.

§ 19. Railroad car; breaking and entering

Whoever breaks and enters, or enters in the night time without breaking, a railroad car, with intent to commit a felony, shall be punished by imprisonment in the state prison for not more than ten years or by a fine of not more than five hundred dollars and imprisonment in the house of correction for not more than two years.

Historical and Statutory Notes

St.1874, c. 70.
St.1874, c. 372, § 158.
P.S.1882, c. 203, § 14.
R.L.1902, c. 208, § 19.

§ 20. Stealing in building, ship or railroad car

Whoever steals in a building, ship, vessel or railroad car shall be punished by imprisonment in the state prison for not more than five years or by a fine of not more than five hundred dollars or by imprisonment in jail for not more than two years.

Historical and Statutory Notes

St.1804, c. 143, § 6.
St.1830, c. 72, § 3.
R.S.1836, c. 126, § 14.
St.1843, c. 1, § 1.
St.1845, c. 28.
St.1851, c. 156, § 4.
G.S.1860, c. 161, § 15.
P.S.1882, c. 203, § 16.
St.1896, c. 389.
R.L.1902, c. 208, § 20.

§ 20A. Breaking and entering of trucks, tractors, trailers or freight containers

Whoever breaks and enters, or enters without breaking, a truck, tractor/trailer unit, trailer, semi-trailer or freight container with intent to commit a felony, shall be punished by imprisonment in the state prison for not more than ten years or by a fine of not more than five hundred dollars and imprisonment in the house of correction for not more than two years.

Added by St.1976, c. 236.

§ 20B. Stealing in trucks, tractors, trailers or freight containers

Whoever steals in a truck, tractor/trailer unit, trailer, semi-trailer or freight container shall be punished by imprisonment in the state prison for not more than five years or by a fine of not more than five hundred dollars or by imprisonment in jail for not more than two years.

Added by St.1976, c. 236.

§ 21. Stolen property; refusal to surrender

Whoever, having been convicted, either as principal or accessory, of burglary or robbery, or of any of the crimes described in sections seventeen to twenty, inclusive, of chapter two hundred and sixty-five, or of breaking and entering or of entering a building with intent to commit robbery or larceny, has in his possession or control money, goods, bonds or bank notes, or any paper of value, or any property of another, which was obtained or taken by means of such crime, and, upon being requested by the lawful owner thereof to deliver the same to him, refuses or fails so to do while having power to deliver the same, shall be punished by imprisonment in the state prison for not more than five years or in jail or house of correction for not more than two years.

Historical and Statutory Notes

St.1879, c. 168.
P.S.1882, c. 203, § 17.
R.L.1902, c. 208, § 21.

§ 22. Poultry thieves; detention by owner; penalty

Whoever, with intent to commit larceny, breaks or enters or enters in the night without breaking any building or enclosure wherein is kept or confined any kind of live poultry, may be detained or kept in custody in a convenient place by the owner of the poultry, or by his agent or employee, for not more than twenty-four hours, Sunday excepted, until a complaint can be made against him for the offence and he be taken upon a warrant issued upon such complaint, and, upon conviction of such trespassing or breaking or entering shall be punished by imprisonment in the state prison for not more than three years, or by a fine of not more than five hundred dollars and imprisonment in the house of correction for not more than two years.

Amended by St.1935, c. 365; St.1950, c. 30.

Historical and Statutory Notes

St.1914, c. 594, §§ 1, 2.
St.1930, c. 185.

§ 23. Embezzlement of property at fire; effect

Whoever steals, conveys away or conceals any furniture, goods, chattels, merchandise or effects of persons whose houses or buildings are on fire or are endangered thereby, and does not, within two days thereafter, restore the same or give notice of his possession thereof to the owner, if known, or, if unknown, to the mayor or one of the aldermen, selectmen or firewards of the place, shall be guilty of larceny.

Historical and Statutory Notes

St.1711–12, c. 5, § 4.
St.1744–5, c. 30, § 4.
St.1796, c. 88, § 4.
R.S.1836, c. 18, § 8.
G.S.1860, c. 24, § 8.
P.S.1882, c. 35, § 8.
R.L.1902, c. 208, § 22.

§ 24. Stealing at a fire; punishment

Whoever steals in a building which is on fire, or steals property which has been removed in consequence of an alarm caused by fire, shall be punished by imprisonment in the state prison for not more than five years or by a fine of not more than five hundred dollars and imprisonment in jail for not more than two years.

Historical and Statutory Notes

R.S.1836, c. 126, § 15.
G.S.1860, c. 161, § 16.
P.S.1882, c. 203, § 18.
R.L.1902, c. 208, § 23.

§ 25. Larceny by stealing; punishment; victim sixty-five or older; minimum sentence for repeat offenders

(a) Whoever commits larceny by stealing from the person of a person sixty-five years or older shall be punished by imprisonment in the state prison for not more than five years or in jail for not more than two and one-half years.

Whoever, after having been convicted of said crime commits a second or subsequent such crime, shall be punished by imprisonment for not less than two years. Said sentence shall not be reduced until one year of said sentence has been served nor shall the person convicted be eligible for probation, parole, furlough, work release or receive any deduction from his sentence for good conduct until he shall have served one year of such sentence; provided, however, that the commissioner of correction may, on the recommendation of the warden, superintendent, or other person in charge of a correctional institution, or the administrator of a county correctional institution, grant to said offender a temporary release in the custody of an officer of such institution for the following purposes only: to attend the funeral of next of kin or spouse; to visit a critically ill close relative or spouse; or to obtain emergency medical services unavailable at said institution. The provisions of section eighty-seven of chapter two hundred and seventy-six relating to the power of the court to place certain offenders on probation shall not apply to any person seventeen years of age or over charged with a violation of this subsection.

(b) Whoever commits larceny by stealing from the person of another shall be punished by imprisonment in the state prison for not more than five years or in jail for not more than two and one-half years.

Amended by St.1943, c. 518, § 1; St.1981, c. 678, § 5.

Historical and Statutory Notes

St.1784, c. 66, § 2.
St.1804, c. 143, § 8.
R.S.1836, c. 126, § 16.
G.S.1860, c. 161, § 17.
P.S.1882, c. 203, § 19.
R.L.1902, c. 208, § 24.

§ 26. Repealed, 1945, 282, Sec. 1

§ 27. Tools of contractors, builders or mechanics; stealing; penalty

Whoever steals any tool belonging to any contractor, builder or mechanic from any building during the course of its construction, completion, alteration or repair, shall, for a first offence be punished by a fine of not more than one hundred dollars or by imprisonment for not more than six months, or both, and for a subsequent offence by a fine of one hundred dollars or by imprisonment for six months, or both.

Historical and Statutory Notes

St.1907, c. 500, § 1.

§ 27A. Motor vehicle or trailer; removal or concealment to defraud insurer

Whoever, with intent to defraud the insurer, removes or conceals a motor vehicle or trailer belonging to himself or another which is at the time insured against theft, or whoever, with intent as aforesaid, aids or abets in such removal or concealment, shall be punished by imprisonment in the state prison for not more than five years or by imprisonment in jail or house of correction for not less than one year nor more than two and one-half years, and a fine of not less than five hundred or more than five thousand dollars.

The court shall, after conviction, conduct an evidentiary hearing to ascertain the extent of the damages or financial loss suffered as a result of the defendant's crime. A person found guilty of violating this section shall, in all cases, upon conviction, in addition to any other punishment, be ordered to make restitution to the insurer for any financial loss sustained as a result of the commission of the crime; provided, however, that restitution shall not be ordered to a party whom the court determines to be aggrieved without that party's consent. Restitution shall be imposed in addition to incarceration or fine, and not in lieu thereof; provided, however, the court shall consider the defendant's present and future ability to pay in its determinations regarding a find; provided, further, that, whenever possible subject to the constraints of this paragraph and the preceding paragraph, the amount of a fine imposed for a violation of this section shall equal twice the amount of damages or financial loss suffered as a result of the defendant's crime.

In determining the amount, time and method of payment of restitution, the court shall consider the financial resources of the defendant and the burden restitution will impose on the defendant. Upon a real or impending change in financial circumstances, a defendant ordered to pay restitution may petition the court for a modification of the amount, time or method of payment of restitution. If the court finds that because of any such change the payment of restitution will impose an undue financial hardship on the defendant or his family, the court may modify the amount, time or method of payment, but may not grant complete remission from payment of restitution.

If a defendant who is required to make restitution defaults in any payment of restitution or installment thereof, the court shall hold him in contempt unless said defendant has made a good faith effort to pay such restitution. If said defendant has made a good faith effort to pay such restitution, the court may modify the amount, time or method of payment, but may not grant complete remission from payment of restitution.

A prosecution commenced under this section shall not be placed on file, or continued without a finding and the sentence imposed upon a person convicted of violating this section for a second or subsequent offense shall not be reduced to less than one year nor shall any sentence of imprisonment imposed upon any person be suspended or reduced until such person shall have served one year of such sentence if convicted of a second or subsequent offense.

A person convicted of a second or subsequent offense of violating the provisions of this section shall not be eligible for probation, parole, furlough or work release; provided, however that the commissioner of correction may, on the recommendation of the warden, superintendent, or other person in charge of a correctional institution, grant to said offender a temporary release in the custody of an officer of such institution for the following purposes: to attend the funeral of next of kin or spouse; to visit a critically ill close relative or spouse; or to obtain emergency medical services unavailable at said institutions.

Amended by St.1959, c. 160, § 1; St.1980, c. 463, § 3; St.1988, c. 273, §§ 56, 57; St.1989, c. 334.

Historical and Statutory Notes

St.1923, c. 347, § 1.

§ 28. Motor vehicle or trailer; theft or concealment; operation without owner's consent after revocation of license; penalty

(a) Whoever steals a motor vehicle or trailer, whoever maliciously damages a motor vehicle or trailer, whoever buys, receives, possesses, conceals, or obtains control of a motor vehicle or trailer, knowing or having reason to know the same to have been stolen, or whoever takes a motor vehicle without the authority of the owner and steals from it any of its parts or accessories, shall be punished by imprisonment in the state prison for not more than fifteen years or by imprisonment in a jail or house of correction for not more than two and one-half years or by a fine of not more than fifteen thousand dollars, or by both such fine and imprisonment.

Evidence that an identifying number or numbers of a motor vehicle or trailer or part thereof has been intentionally and maliciously removed, defaced, altered, changed, destroyed, obliterated, or mutilated, shall be prima facie evidence that the defendant knew or had reason to know that the motor vehicle, or trailer or part thereof had been stolen.

A prosecution commenced under this subdivision shall not be placed on file or continued without a finding and the sentence imposed upon a person convicted of violating this subdivision for a second or subsequent offense shall not be reduced to less than one year imprisonment, nor shall any sentence imposed upon any person be suspended, or reduced, until such person shall have served one year of such sentence if convicted of a second or subsequent such offense.

A person convicted of a second or subsequent offense of violating the provisions of this subdivision shall not be eligible for probation, parole, furlough or work release; provided, however that the commissioner of correction may, on the recommendation of warden, superintendent, or other person in charge of a correctional institution, or the administrator of a county correctional institution, grant to said offender a temporary release in the custody of an officer of such institution for the following purposes: to attend the funeral of next of kin or spouse; to visit a critically ill close relative or spouse; or to obtain emergency medical services unavailable at said institution.

(b) Whoever conceals any motor vehicle or trailer thief knowing him to be such, shall be punished by imprisonment for not more than ten years or by imprisonment in jail or house of correction for not more than two and one-half years or by a fine of not more than five thousand dollars, or both.

(c) A conviction of a violation of this section or any adjudication that a person is a delinquent child by reason thereof shall be reported forthwith by the court or magistrate to the registrar of motor vehicles who shall revoke immediately the license to operate motor vehicles or the right to operate motor vehicles of the person so convicted or adjudged, and no appeal, motion for new trial or exceptions shall operate to stay the revocation of such license or right to operate. The registrar of motor vehicles after having revoked the license or right to operate of any such person so convicted or adjudged shall issue a new license or reinstate such right to operate, if the prosecution of such person is finally terminated in his favor; otherwise, no new license shall be issued nor shall such right to operate be reinstated until one year after the date of revocation following his original conviction or adjudication if for a first offense, or until five years after the date of revocation following any subsequent conviction or adjudication.

Amended by St.1959, c. 160, § 2; St.1966, c. 191, § 2; St.1967, c. 662; St.1967, c. 849; St.1971, c. 123; St.1972, c. 78; St.1980, c. 463, § 4; St.1985, c. 380; St.1988, c. 273, § 58; St.1989, c. 341, § 101.

Historical and Statutory Notes

St.1919, c. 249, § 1.
St.1920, c. 322.
St.1926, c. 267, § 1.
St.1926, c. 296.

§ 29. Statement concerning theft; recovery of vehicles; restitution

Whenever a motor vehicle is stolen or misappropriated, the owner of record shall sign and submit to the appropriate police authority a statement under the penalties of perjury on a form containing such information relating to the theft or misappropriation of the vehicle as is prescribed by the registrar of motor vehicles.

Whenever a stolen or misappropriated motor vehicle is recovered by a police officer or other law enforcement officer, the police department shall notify the registry of motor vehicles, the owner of record and the storage facility if any, as soon as possible after the identity of the owner is determined. Such notification may be made by letter, telephone call or personal visit to the owner and shall include information as to the location of the recovered vehicle. In the event the vehicle is placed in a garage or other storage facility, the owner of said facility shall lose his lien for the reasonable charges for storage and towing unless he notifies the owner of record of the vehicle by certified mail and return receipt requested within five days of the date of said recovery or his actual knowledge of the identity of the owner of record. Said notice shall contain the information on the location of the vehicle and the amount of charge due on said vehicle.

The court shall, after a defendant is convicted of a violation of subsection (a) of section twenty-eight, conduct an evidentiary hearing to ascertain the extent of the damages or financial loss suffered as a result of the defendant's crime. A person found guilty of violating subsection (a) of section twenty-eight shall in all cases, upon conviction, in addition to any other punishment, be ordered to make restitution to the insurer for any financial loss sustained as a result of the commission of the crime; provided, however, that restitution shall not be ordered to a party whom the court determines to be aggrieved without that party's consent. Restitution shall be imposed in addition to incarceration or fine, and not in lieu thereof; provided, however, the court shall consider the defendant's present and future ability to pay in its determinations regarding a fine; provided, further, that, whenever possible subject to the constraints of this paragraph and the first paragraph of said subsection (a) of section twenty-eight, the amount of a fine imposed for a violation of said subsection (a) of section twenty-eight shall equal twice the amount of damages or financial loss suffered as a result of the defendant's crime.

In determining the amount, time and method of payment of restitution, the court shall consider the financial resources of the defendant and the burden restitution will impose on the defendant. Upon a real or impending change in financial circumstances, a defendant ordered to pay restitution may petition the court for a modification of the amount, time or method of payment of restitution. If the court finds that because of any such change the payment of restitution will impose an undue financial hardship on the defendant or his family, the court may modify the amount, time or method of payment, but may not grant complete remission from payment of restitution.

If a defendant who is required to make restitution defaults in any payment of restitution or installment thereof, the court shall hold him in contempt unless said defendant has made a good faith effort to pay such restitution. If said defendant has made a good faith effort to pay such restitution, the court may modify the amount, time or method of payment, but may not grant complete remission from payment of restitution.

Amended by St.1980, c. 463, § 4; St.1988, c. 273, § 59.

Historical and Statutory Notes

St.1919, c. 249, § 2.
St.1923, c. 347, § 2.

§ 29A. Repealed, 1980, 463, Sec. 4

Historical and Statutory Notes

See, now, M.G.L.A. c. 266, § 29.

§ 29B. Burning motor vehicle; owner's statement to fire department

Whenever a motor vehicle is burned, the owner of record of such vehicle shall submit to the appropriate fire department a statement signed under the penalties of perjury containing such information concerning the burning of such vehicle as the state fire marshall shall require.

Added by St.1987, c. 44, § 2.

§ 30. Larceny; general provisions and penalties

(1) Whoever steals, or with intent to defraud obtains by a false pretence, or whoever unlawfully, and with intent to steal or embezzle, converts, or secretes with intent to convert, the property of another as defined in this section, whether such property is or is not in his possession at the time of such conversion or secreting, shall be guilty of larceny, and shall, if the property stolen is a firearm, as defined in section one hundred and twenty-one of chapter one hundred and forty, or, if the value of the property stolen exceeds two hundred and fifty dollars, be punished by imprisonment in the state prison for not more than five years, or by a fine of not more than twenty-five thousand dollars and imprisonment in jail for not more than two years; or, if the value of the property stolen, other than a firearm as so defined, does not exceed two hundred and fifty dollars, shall be punished by imprisonment in jail for not more than one year or by a fine of not more than three hundred dollars; or, if the property was stolen from the conveyance of a common carrier or of a person carrying on an express business, shall be punished for the first offence by imprisonment for not less than six months nor more than two and one half years, or by a fine of not less than fifty nor more than six hundred dollars, or both, and for a subsequent offence, by imprisonment for not less than eighteen months nor more than two and one half years, or by a fine of not less than one hundred and fifty nor more than six hundred dollars, or both.

(2) The term "property", as used in the section, shall include money, personal chattels, a bank note, bond, promissory note, bill of exchange or other bill, order or certificate, a book of accounts for or concerning money or goods due or to become due or to be delivered, a deed or writing containing a conveyance of land, any valuable contract in force, a receipt, release or defeasance, a writ, process, certificate of title or duplicate certificate issued under chapter one hundred and eighty-five, a public record, anything which is of the realty or is annexed thereto, a security deposit received pursuant to section fifteen B of chapter one hundred and eighty-six, electronically processed or stored data, either tangible or intangible, data while in transit, telecommunications services, and any domesticated animal, including dogs, or a beast or bird which is ordinarily kept in confinement.

(3) The stealing of real property may be a larceny from one or more tenants, sole, joint or in common, in fee, for life or years, at will or sufferance, mortgagors or mortgagees, in possession of the same, or who may have an action of tort against the offender for trespass upon the property, but not from one having only the use or custody thereof. The larceny may be from a wife in possession, if she is authorized by law to hold such property as if sole, otherwise her occupation may be the possession of the husband. If such property which was of a person deceased is stolen, it may be a larceny from any one or more heirs, devisees, reversioners, remaindermen or others, who have a right upon such deceased to take possession, but not having entered, as it would be after entry. The larceny may be from a person whose name is unknown, if it would be such if the property stolen were personal, and may be committed by those who have only the use or custody of the property, but not by a person against whom no action of tort could be maintained for acts like those constituting the larceny.

(4) Whoever steals, or with intent to defraud obtains by a false pretense, or whoever unlawfully, and with intent to steal or embezzle, converts, secretes, unlawfully takes, carries away, conceals or copies with intent to convert any trade secret of another, regardless of value, whether such trade secret is or is not in his possession at the time of such conversion or secreting, shall be guilty of larceny, and shall be punished by imprisonment in the state prison for not more than five years, or by a fine of not more than twenty-five thousand dollars and imprisonment in jail for not more than two years. The term "trade secret" as used in this paragraph means and includes anything tangible or intangible or electronically kept or stored, which constitutes, represents, evidences or records a secret scientific, technical, merchandising, production or management information, design, process, procedure, formula, invention or improvement.

(5) Whoever steals or with intent to defraud obtains by a false pretense, or whoever unlawfully, and with intent to steal or embezzle, converts, or secretes with

intent to convert, the property of another, sixty years of age or older, or of a person with a disability as defined in section thirteen K of chapter two hundred and sixty-five, whether such property is or is not in his possession at the time of such conversion or secreting, shall be guilty of larceny, and shall, if the value of the property exceeds two hundred and fifty dollars, be punished by imprisonment in the state prison for not more than ten years or in the house of correction for not more than two and one-half years, or by a fine of not more than fifty thousand dollars or by both such fine and imprisonment; or if the value of the property does not exceed two hundred and fifty dollars, shall be punished by imprisonment in the house of correction for not more than two and one-half years or by a fine of not more than one thousand dollars or by both such fine and imprisonment. The court may order, regardless of the value of the property, restitution to be paid to the victim commensurate with the value of the property.

Amended by St.1945, c. 282, § 2; St.1966, c. 153, § 1; St.1967, c. 817, § 1; St.1968, c. 737, § 10; St.1977, c. 979, § 3; St.1983, c. 147, §§ 1, 2; St.1985, c. 306, §§ 1, 2; St.1987, c. 75; St.1987, c. 124, § 1; St.1987, c. 468, § 1; St.1995, c. 272, § 3; St.1995, c. 297, § 9.

Historical and Statutory Notes

C.L. c. 13, §§ 2, 3.
St.1692–3, c. 18, § 3.
St.1784, c. 66, § 1.
St.1804, c. 143, § 1.
St.1815, c. 136, § 1.
St.1834, c. 186, §§ 1, 3.
R.S.1836, c. 126, §§ 17, 29 to 32.
St.1857, c. 233.
G.S.1860, c. 161, §§ 18, 35, 38, 41, 53, 54.
P.S.1882, c. 203, §§ 20, 37, 40, 43, 58, 59.
St.1889, c. 458.
St.1899, c. 316, § 1.
R.L.1902, c. 208, § 26.
St.1906, c. 261.
St.1914, c. 635.
St.1918, c. 257, § 464.
St.1919, c. 5.
St.1920, c. 2.

§ 30A. Shoplifting; penalty; arrest without warrant

Any person who intentionally takes possession of, carries away, transfers or causes to be carried away or transferred, any merchandise displayed, held, stored or offered for sale by any store or other retail mercantile establishment with the intention of depriving the merchant of the possession, use of benefit of such merchandise or converting the same to the use of such person without paying to the merchant the value thereof; or

any person who intentionally conceals upon his person or otherwise any merchandise offered for sale by any store or other retail mercantile establishment with the intention of depriving the merchant of proceeds, use or benefit of such merchandise or converting the same to the use of such person without paying to the merchant the value thereof; or

any person who intentionally alters, transfers or removes any label, price tag or marking indicia of value or any other markings which aid in determining value affixed to any merchandise displayed, held, stored or offered for sale by any store or other retail mercantile establishment and to attempt to purchase such merchandise personally or in consort with another at less than the full retail value with the intention of depriving the merchant of all or some part of the retail value thereof; or

any person who intentionally transfers any merchandise displayed, held, stored or offered for sale by any store or other retail mercantile establishment from the container in or on which the same shall be displayed to any other container with intent to deprive the merchant of all or some part of the retail value thereof; or

any person who intentionally records a value for the merchandise which is less than the actual retail value with the intention of depriving the merchant of the full retail value thereof; or

any person who intentionally removes a shopping cart from the premises of a store or other retail mercantile establishment, without the consent of the merchant given at the time of such removal, with the intention of permanently depriving the merchant of the possession, use or benefit of such cart; and where the retail value of the goods obtained is less than one hundred dollars, shall be punished for a first offense by a fine not to exceed two hundred and fifty dollars, for a second offense by a fine of not less than one hundred nor more than five hundred dollars and for a third or subsequent offense by a fine of not more than five hundred dollars or imprisonment in a jail for not more than two years, or by both such fine and imprisonment. Where the retail value of the goods obtained equals or exceeds one hundred dollars, any violation of this section shall be punished by a fine of not more than one thousand dollars or by imprisonment in the house of correction for not more than two and one-half years, or by both such fine and imprisonment.

If the retail value of the goods obtained is less than one hundred dollars, this section shall apply to the exclusion of section thirty.

Law enforcement officers may arrest without warrant any person he has probable cause for believing has committed the offense of shoplifting as defined in this section. The statement of a merchant or his employee or agent that a person has violated a provision of this section shall constitute probable cause for arrest by any law enforcement officer authorized to make an arrest in such jurisdiction.

Added by St.1981, c. 618, § 3. Amended by St.1996, c. 430; St.1998, c. 295, § 43; St.1998, c. 463, § 190.

§ 31. Signature; obtaining under false pretences

Whoever by a false pretence, with intent to defraud, obtains the signature of a person to a written instrument, the false making whereof would be a forgery, shall be punished by imprisonment in the state prison for not more than ten years, or by a fine of not more than five hundred dollars and imprisonment in the jail for not more than two years.

Historical and Statutory Notes

R.S.1836, c. 126, § 32.
G.S.1860, c. 161, § 54.
P.S.1882, c. 203, § 59.
R.L.1902, c. 208, § 27.

§ 32. Fraudulent conversion of property by captain of vessel

Whoever, being a captain of a vessel, embezzles or fraudulently converts or appropriates money, goods or property, held or possessed by or delivered to him, which belong wholly or in part to the crew of such vessel, the owners of the vessel, or to those who have furnished supplies to the vessel, although he is a joint charterer or co-partner with the members of the crew or with the owners of the vessel, or with the person who furnished the supplies, shall be guilty of larceny.

Historical and Statutory Notes

St.1907, c. 389.

§ 33. Larceny; false pretences relating to contracts, banking transactions or credit

(1) Whoever, with intent to defraud, obtains by a false pretence the making, acceptance or endorsement of a bill of exchange or promissory note, the release or substitution of collateral or other security, an extension of time for the payment of an obligation, or the release or alteration of the obligation of a written contract, or (2) whoever, with intent to defraud, by a false statement in writing respecting the financial condition, or means or ability to pay, of himself or of any other person, obtains for himself or for any other person credit from any bank or trust company or any banking institution or any mortgage lender, as defined in section 1 of chapter 255E, or any retail seller of goods or services accustomed to give credit in any form whatsoever shall be guilty of larceny.

Amended by St.1945, c. 282, § 3; St.1967, c. 236; St.2010, c. 258, § 9, eff. Aug. 7, 2010.

Historical and Statutory Notes

St.1910, c. 378, § 1.

§ 33A. Obtaining computer services by fraud or misrepresentation; penalties

Whoever, with intent to defraud, obtains, or attempts to obtain, or aids or abets another in obtaining, any commercial computer service by false representation, false statement, unauthorized charging to the account of another, by installing or tampering with any facilities or equipment or by any other means, shall be punished by imprisonment in the house of correction for not more than two and one-half years or by a fine of not more than three thousand dollars, or both. As used in this section, the words "commercial computer service" shall mean the use of computers, computer systems, computer programs or computer networks, or the access to or copying of the data, where such use, access or copying is offered by the proprietor or operator of the computer, system, program, network or data to others on a subscription or other basis for monetary consideration.

Added by St.1994, c. 168, § 2.

§ 34. Larceny; inducement to part with property

Whoever, with intent to defraud and by a false pretence, induces another to part with property of any kind or with any of the benefits described in sections 33 and 33A shall be guilty of larceny.

Amended by St.2010, c. 258, § 10, eff. Aug. 7, 2010.

Historical and Statutory Notes

St.1910, c. 378, § 2.

§ 35. Non-applicability of Secs. 30, 31 and 34

Sections thirty, thirty-one and thirty-four shall not apply to a purchase of property by means of a false pretence relative to the purchaser's means or ability to pay, if, by the terms of the purchase, payment therefor is not to be made upon or before the delivery of the property purchased, unless such pretence is made in writing and is signed by the person to be charged.

Historical and Statutory Notes

St.1854, c. 12.
G.S.1860, c. 161, § 54.
P.S.1882, c. 203, § 59.
St.1899, c. 316, § 2.
R.L.1902, c. 208, § 28.
St.1919, c. 333, §§ 37, 38.
St.1920, c. 2.

§ 35A. False material statements or omissions during or in connection with mortgage lending process; penalties; mitigating factors with respect to sentencing

(a) As used in this section, the following words shall have the following meanings, unless the context clearly otherwise requires:—

"Funds", shall include, but not be limited to, a commission, fee, yield spread premium or compensation in any form.

"Material omission", the omission or concealment of a material fact necessary to prevent a statement from being misleading, in the light of the circumstances under which the statement is made.

"Mortgage lending process", the process through which a person seeks or obtains a residential mortgage loan including, but not limited to, solicitation, application, origination, negotiation of terms, third-party provider services, underwriting, signing and closing, and funding of the loan; provided, however, that documents involved in the mortgage lending process shall include, but not be limited to, uniform residential loan applications or other loan applications, appraisal reports, HUD–1 settlement statements, supporting personal documentation for loan applications such as W–2 forms, verification of income and employment, bank statements, tax returns and payroll stubs and any required disclosures.

"Pattern of residential mortgage fraud", violation of subsection (b) in connection with 3 or more residential properties.

"Person", a natural person, corporation, company, limited liability company, partnership, real estate trust, association or any other entity.

"Residential mortgage loan", a loan or agreement to extend credit made to a person, which loan is secured by a mortgage, security interest, deed to secure debt, deed of trust, or other document representing a security interest or lien upon any interest in a 1 to 4 family residential property located in the commonwealth, including the renewal or refinancing of any such loan.

(b) Whoever intentionally: (1) makes or causes to be made any material statement that is false or any statement that contains a material omission, knowing the same to be false or to contain a material omission, during or in connection with the mortgage lending process, with the intent that such statement be relied upon by a mortgage lender, borrower or any other party to the mortgage lending process; (2) uses, or facilitates the use of, any material statement that is false or any statement that contains a material omission, knowing the same to be false or to contain a material omission, during or in connection with the mortgage lending process, with the intent that such statement be relied upon by a mortgage lender, borrower or any other party to the mortgage lending process; (3) receives any proceeds or any other funds in connection with a residential mortgage closing, knowing such proceeds or funds were obtained in violation of clause (1) or (2); or (4) files or causes to be filed with a registrar of deeds any document that contains a material statement that is false or a material omission, knowing such document to contain a material statement that is false or a material omission, shall be punished by imprisonment in the state prison for not more than 5 years or by imprisonment in the house of correction for not more than 2 and one-half years or by a fine of not more than $10,000 in the case of a natural person or not more than $100,000 in the case of any other person, or by both such fine and imprisonment.

Any person who engages in a pattern of residential mortgage fraud shall be punished by imprisonment in the state prison for not more than 15 years or by a fine of not more than $50,000, in the case of a natural person, or not more than $500,000 in the case of any other person, or by both such fine and imprisonment.

(c) If a defendant is convicted of a violation of this section as a result of conduct or an omission by an employee or agent of the defendant the court may consider the following mitigating factors with respect to sentencing:

(1) that the defendant had instituted and maintained at the time of the violation, and continues to have, a written policy including:

(i) a prohibition against conduct that violates this section by employees and agents of the defendant;

(ii) penalties or discipline for violation of the policy;

(iii) a process for educating employees and agents concerning the policy and consequences of a violation thereof; and

(iv) with respect to a defendant authorized to conduct criminal history checks for the employee's or agent's position, a requirement for a criminal history check before employing an employee or engaging an agent and a requirement that the defendant will not employ or engage an individual who has been convicted of a crime involving fraud;

(2) a demonstration that the defendant enforces the policy described in clause (1); and

(3) prior to the violation of this section the defendant provided a copy of the policy described in clause (1), including a description of the consequences for violating the policy, to the employee or agent who committed the violation.

Added by St.2010, c. 258, § 11, eff. Aug. 7, 2010.

§ 36. Repealed, 1945, 282, Sec. 1

§ 37. Fraudulent checks, etc.; drawing or uttering

Whoever, with intent to defraud, makes, draws, utters or delivers any check, draft or order for the payment of money upon any bank or other depositary, with knowledge that the maker or drawer has not sufficient funds or credit at such bank or other depositary for the payment of such instrument, although no express representation is made in reference thereto, shall be guilty of attempted larceny, and if money or property or services are obtained thereby shall be guilty of larceny. As against the maker or drawer thereof, the making, drawing, uttering or delivery of such a check, draft or order, payment of which is refused by the drawee, shall be prima facie evidence of intent to defraud and of knowledge of insufficient funds in, or credit with, such bank or other depositary, unless the maker or drawer shall have paid the holder thereof the amount due thereon, together with all costs and protest fees, within two days after receiving notice that such check, draft or order has not been paid by the drawee. The word "credit", as used herein, shall be construed to mean an arrangement or understanding with the bank or depositary for the payment of such check, draft or order.

Amended by St.1937, c. 99; St.1955, c. 133.

Historical and Statutory Notes

St.1919, c. 141.

§ 37A. Misuse of credit cards; definitions

As used in sections thirty-seven A to thirty-seven C, inclusive, the following words shall have the following meanings, unless the context otherwise requires:

"Cardholder", the person named on the face of a credit card to whom or for whose benefit the credit card is issued by an issuer.

"Credit card", any instrument or device, whether known as a credit card, credit plate, or by any other name, issued with or without fee by an issuer for the use of the cardholder in obtaining money, goods, services or anything else of value on credit.

"Expired credit card", a credit card which is no longer valid because the term shown on its face has elapsed.

"Falsely embosses", completion of a credit card, without the authorization of the named issuer, by adding any of the matter, other than the signature of the cardholder, which an issuer requires to appear on the credit card before it can be used by a cardholder.

"Falsely makes", making or drawing, in whole or in part, a device or instrument which purports to be the credit card of a named issuer but which is not such a credit card because the issuer did not authorize the making or drawing, or altering a credit card which was validly issued.

"Incomplete credit card", a credit card that does not contain all of the matter that must be stamped, embossed, imprinted or written on said card other than the signature, as required by the issuer before it can be used by a cardholder.

"Issuer", the business organization or financial institution which issues a credit card or his duly authorized agent.

"Receives" or "receiving", acquiring possession or control or accepting as security for a loan.

"Revoked credit card", a credit card which is no longer valid because permission to use it has been suspended or terminated by the issuer.

Added by St.1960, c. 456. Amended by St.1969, c. 51; St.1969, c. 832.

§ 37B. Misuse of credit cards; penalties; multiple possession, presumption; arrest

Whoever, with intent to defraud, (a) makes or causes to be made, either directly or indirectly, any false statement as to a material fact in writing, knowing it to be false and with intent that it be relied on, respecting his identity or that of any other person, or his financial condition or that of any other person, for the purpose of procuring the issuance of a credit card, or (b) takes a credit card from the person, possession, custody or control of another without the cardholder's consent by any conduct which would constitute larceny, or who, with knowledge that it has been so taken, receives the credit card with intent to use it or to sell it, or to transfer it to a person other than the issuer or cardholder, or (c) receives a credit card that he knows to have been lost, mislaid, or delivered under a mistake as to the identity or address of the cardholder, and who retains possession with intent to use it or to sell it or to transfer it to a person other than the issuer or the cardholder, or (d) being a person other than the issuer or his authorized agent, sells a credit card, or buys a credit card from a person other than the issuer or his authorized agent, or (e) being a person other than the cardholder or a person authorized by him, signs a credit card, or (f) uses, for the purpose of obtaining money, goods, services or anything else of value, a credit card obtained or retained in violation of clauses (b) to (e), inclusive, or a credit card which he knows is forged, expired or revoked, where the value of money, goods or services obtained in violation of this section is not in excess of two hundred and fifty dollars, or (g) obtains money, goods, services or anything else of value by representing without the consent of the cardholder that he is said cardholder or by representing that he is the holder of a card and such card has not in fact been issued, where the value of money, goods or services obtained is not in excess of two hundred and fifty dollars, or (h) being a person authorized by an issuer to furnish money, goods, services or anything else of value upon presentation of a credit card by the cardholder, or any agent or employees of such person, furnishes money, goods, services or anything else of value upon presentation of a credit card which he knows was obtained or retained in violation of clauses (b) to (e), inclusive, or a credit card which he knows is forged, expired or revoked where the value of the goods or services obtained is not in excess of two hundred and fifty dollars, or (i) being a person who is authorized by an issuer to furnish money, goods, services or anything else of value upon presentation of a credit card by the cardholder, or any agent or employee of such person, fails to furnish money, goods, services or anything else of value which he represents in writing to the issuer that he has furnished, and the difference between the value of all money, goods, services and anything else of value actually furnished and the value represented to the issuer to have been furnished does not exceed two hundred and fifty dollars, or (j) receives money, goods, services or anything else of value obtained in violation of clauses (f) to (i), inclusive, or (k) makes a false statement in reporting a credit card to be lost or stolen, shall be punished by a fine of not more than five hundred dollars or by imprisonment in a jail or house of correction for not more than one year or both.

Whoever has in his possession or under his control stolen credit cards issued in the names of four or more other persons shall be presumed to have violated clause (b).

Whoever is discovered by a police officer in the act of violating this section, while such officer is lawfully at or within the place where such violation occurs, may be arrested without a warrant by such police officer.

Added by St.1969, c. 832. Amended by St.1971, c. 90, § 1; St.1984, c. 231, § 1; St.1987, c. 468, § 2.

§ 37C. Fraudulent use of credit cards to obtain money, goods or services; false embossment of credit cards, multiple possession, presumption; arrest

Whoever, with intent to defraud, (a) obtains control over a credit card as security for debt, or (b) receives a credit card which he knows was taken or retained under circumstances which constitute credit card theft or a violation of clauses (a) or (d) of section thirty-seven B or clause (a) of this section, or (c) falsely makes or falsely embosses a purported credit card or utters such a credit card, or (d) obtains money, goods, services or anything else of value by use of a credit card obtained or retained in violation of clauses (b) to (e), inclusive, of section thirty-seven B, or by use of a credit card which he knows is forged, expired or revoked, where the value of the money, goods or services obtained in violation of this section is in excess of two hundred and fifty dollars, or (e) obtains money, goods or services or anything else of value by representing without the consent of the cardholder that he is said cardholder or by representing that he is the holder of a card and such card has not in fact been issued, where the value of money, goods or services obtained in violation of this section is in excess of two hundred and fifty dollars, or (f) being a person authorized by an issuer to furnish money, goods, services or anything else of value upon presentation of a credit card which he knows was obtained in violation of subsections (b) to (e), inclusive, of section thirty-seven B, or a credit card which he knows is forged, expired or revoked, when the value of the money, goods or services obtained is in excess of two hundred and fifty dollars, or (g) being a person authorized by an issuer to furnish money, goods, services or anything else of value upon presentation of a credit card by the cardholder or any agent or employee of such person, fails to furnish money, goods or services or anything else of value which he represents in writing to the issuer that he has furnished, and the difference between the value of all money, goods, services and anything else of value actually furnished and the value represented to the issuer to have been furnished exceeds two hundred and fifty dollars, or (h) receives money, goods, services or anything else of value obtained in violation of subsections (f) or (g) of section thirty-seven B, or (i) possesses one or more incomplete credit cards, intending to complete them without the consent of the issuer, or (j) possesses, with knowledge of its character, machinery, plates or any other contrivance designed to reproduce instruments purporting to be the credit cards of an issuer who has not consented to the preparation of such credit cards, shall be punished by a fine of not more than two thousand dollars, or by imprisonment in a jail or house of correction for not more than two and one half years or in the state prison for not more than five years, or by both such fine and imprisonment.

Whoever has in his possession or under his control four or more credit cards which are falsely embossed shall be presumed to have violated clause (c).

Whoever is discovered by a police officer in the act of violating this section, while such officer is lawfully at or within the place where such violation occurs, may be arrested without a warrant by such police officer.

Added by St.1969, c. 832. Amended by St.1971, c. 90, § 2; St.1987, c. 468, § 3.

§ 37D. Publishing credit card numbering or coding systems

Whoever publishes or causes to be published the number or code of an existing, canceled, revoked, expired, or nonexistent credit card issued by a public utility company or the numbering or coding system which is employed in the issuance of such credit cards, or any method, scheme, instruction or information on how to fraudulently avoid payment for telecommunication services, with the intent that such number or coding system or information be used or with knowledge that such system or information are to be used to fraudulently avoid the payment of any lawful charges imposed by a public utility company shall be punished by a fine not exceeding two thousand dollars or by imprisonment for not more than twelve months, or both.

As used in this section, "publishes" means the communication of information to any one or more persons, either orally, in person, or by telephone, radio, or television, or in a writing of any kind, including a letter or memorandum, circular, poster, or handbill, newspaper or magazine article, or book with the intent that such information be used or employed in violation of this section.

Added by St.1973, c. 1156.

§ 37E. Use of personal identification of another; identity fraud; penalty; restitution

(a) For purposes of this section, the following words shall have the following meanings:—

"Harass", willfully and maliciously engage in an act directed at a specific person or persons, which act seriously alarms or annoys such person or persons and would cause a reasonable person to suffer substantial emotional distress.

"Personal identifying information", any name or number that may be used, alone or in conjunction with any other information, to assume the identity of an individual, including any name, address, telephone number, driver's license number, social security number, place of employment, employee identification number, mother's maiden name, demand deposit account number, savings account number, credit card number or computer password identification.

"Pose", to falsely represent oneself, directly or indirectly, as another person or persons.

"Victim", any person who has suffered financial loss or any entity that provided money, credit, goods, services or anything of value and has suffered financial loss as a direct result of the commission or attempted commission of a violation of this section.

(b) Whoever, with intent to defraud, poses as another person without the express authorization of that person and uses such person's personal identifying information to obtain or to attempt to obtain money, credit, goods, services, anything of value, any identification card or other evidence of such person's identity, or to harass another shall be guilty of identity fraud and shall be punished by a fine of not more than $5,000 or imprisonment in a house of correction for not more than two and one-half years, or by both such fine and imprisonment.

(c) Whoever, with intent to defraud, obtains personal identifying information about another person without the express authorization of such person, with the intent to pose as such person or who obtains personal identifying information about a person without the express authorization of such person in order to assist another to pose as such person in order to obtain money, credit, goods, services, anything of value, any identification card or other evidence of such person's identity, or to harass another shall be guilty of the crime of identity fraud and shall be punished by a fine of not more than $5,000 or imprisonment in a house of correction for not more than two and one-half years, or by both such fine and imprisonment.

(d) A person found guilty of violating any provisions of this section shall, in addition to any other punishment, be ordered to make restitution for financial loss sustained by a victim as a result of such violation. Financial loss may include any costs incurred by such victim in correcting the credit history of such victim or any costs incurred in connection with any civil or administrative proceeding to satisfy any debt or other obligation of such victim, including lost wages and attorney's fees.

(e) A law enforcement officer may arrest without warrant any person he has probable cause to believe has committed the offense of identity fraud as defined in this section.

(f) A law enforcement officer shall accept a police incident report from a victim and shall provide a copy to such victim, if requested, within 24 hours. Such police incident reports may be filed in any county where a victim resides, or in any county where the owner or license holder of personal information stores or maintains said personal information, the owner's or license holder's principal place of business or any county in which the breach of security occurred, in whole or in part.

Added by St.1998, c. 397, § 1. Amended by St.2000, c. 166, § 13; St.2007, c. 82, § 18, eff. Oct. 31, 2007.

§ 38. Larceny; wrongful detention of money by carriers

Whoever, being engaged in the business of transporting merchandise, parcels or other property for hire, accepts from a consignor or his agent or from a connecting carrier any merchandise, parcel or other property for delivery to a consignee upon payment by the consignee of an amount of money for said merchandise, parcel or other property, and embezzles or fraudulently converts to his own use, or with intent to use or embezzle, takes, secretes or otherwise disposes of, or fraudulently withholds, appropriates, lends, invests or otherwise uses or applies such money in whole or in part or any substitute therefor received by him from such consignee, contrary to the instructions or without the consent of the consignor, shall be deemed guilty of larceny. A member or employee of a copartnership, or an officer or employee of a corporation, engaged in said business of transporting merchandise, parcels or other property for hire who so disposes of such money in whole or in part or any substitute therefor for his own use or for the use of said copartnership or corporation, contrary to the instructions or without the consent of the consignor, shall be guilty of larceny.

Historical and Statutory Notes

St.1919, c. 188.

§ 38A. Construction loan; misapplication

Whoever obtains a building or construction loan, secured by a mortgage of real estate, for the payment for labor furnished or to be furnished and/or materials used and/or employed or to be used and/or employed in the construction, repair, removal or alteration of a building or other structure which is attached or is to be attached to such real estate, and, before payment in full for all labor furnished or to be furnished and/or materials used or to be used and/or employed or to be employed as aforesaid, applies the proceeds of such loan, or any part thereof, to any use other than payment for labor and/or materials as aforesaid, shall be punished by a fine of not more than five hundred dollars or by imprisonment in jail for not more than one year, or both.

Historical and Statutory Notes

St.1928, c. 351.

§ 39. Wills; destruction or concealment

Whoever steals or for any fraudulent purpose destroys, mutilates or conceals a will, codicil or other testamentary instrument shall be punished by imprisonment in the state prison for not more than five years or in the house of correction for not more than two years. An indictment for a violation of this section need not contain any allegation of value or ownership; and in the trial of such an indictment, no disclosure made by any person under section fourteen of chapter one hundred and ninety-one shall be used in evidence against him.

Historical and Statutory Notes

G.S.1860, c. 161, §§ 19, 20.
P.S.1882, c. 203, §§ 21, 22.
St.1890, c. 391.
R.L.1902, c. 208, § 29.

§ 40. Common and notorious thief

Whoever, having been convicted, upon indictment, of larceny or of being accessory to larceny before the fact, afterward commits a larceny or is accessory thereto before the fact, and is convicted thereof upon indictment, and whoever is convicted at the same sitting of the court, as principal or accessory before the fact, of three distinct larcenies, shall be adjudged a common and notorious thief, and shall be punished by imprisonment in the state prison for not more than twenty years or in jail for not more than two and one half years.

Historical and Statutory Notes

St.1784, c. 66, §§ 6, 7.
St.1804, c. 143, § 3.
R.S.1836, c. 126, § 19.
G.S.1860, c. 161, § 22.
P.S.1882, c. 203, § 24.
R.L.1902, c. 208, § 31.
St.1914, c. 635.
St.1918, c. 257, § 464.
St.1919, c. 5.
St.1920, c. 2.

§ 41. Larceny of bicycles; second conviction

Whoever is convicted of a second offence of the larceny of a bicycle shall, if the value of the bicycle stolen exceeds ten dollars, be punished by imprisonment in the state prison for not more than five years or by a fine of not more than two hundred dollars or by imprisonment in jail for not more than two years.

Historical and Statutory Notes

St.1897, c. 409.
R.L.1902, c. 208, § 32.

§ 42. Larceny of paper designated for bank bills

Whoever commits larceny of a printed piece of paper or blank designed for issue by any incorporated bank or banking company in the United States as a bank bill, certificate or promissory note, or printed by means of an engraved plate designed for printing such pieces of paper or blanks, with intent to injure or defraud either by uttering or passing the same, or causing or allowing the same to be uttered or passed as true, either with or without alteration or addition, shall be punished by imprisonment in the state prison for life or for any term of years.

Historical and Statutory Notes

St.1858, c. 67, § 1.
G.S.1860, c. 161, § 23.
P.S.1882, c. 203, § 25.
R.L.1902, c. 208, § 33.

§ 43. Paper designated for bank bills; retention by printer with intent to pass

Whoever, having been employed to print or having assisted in printing a printed piece of paper or blank described in the preceding section, or having been intrusted with the care or custody thereof, retains it in his possession without the knowledge and consent of the corporation for which it was printed, with intent to injure or defraud either by uttering or passing it or causing or allowing it to be uttered or passed as true, either with or without alteration or addition, shall be punished by imprisonment in the state prison for life or for any term of years.

Historical and Statutory Notes

St.1858, c. 67, § 2.
G.S.1860, c. 161, § 24.
P.S.1882, c. 203, § 26.
R.L.1902, c. 208, § 34.

§§ 44 to 46. Repealed, 1945, 282, Sec. 1

§ 47. Dogs; wrongful removal of collar; penalty

Whoever wrongfully removes the collar from a dog which is licensed and collared as provided in chapter one hundred and forty shall be punished by a fine of not more than one hundred dollars, or by six months' imprisonment, or both.

Amended by St.1945, c. 282, § 4; St.1966, c. 153, § 2; St.1987, c. 124, § 2.; St.2004, c. 319, § 2, eff. Nov. 17, 2004.

Historical and Statutory Notes

St.1858, c. 139, § 2.
St.1859, c. 225, §§ 4, 5.
G.S.1860, c. 88, § 57.
P.S.1882, c. 102, § 88.
R.L.1902, c. 208, § 38.
St.1913, c. 551.

§ 48. Stolen goods; duty of arresting officers to secure

An officer who arrests a person charged as principal or accessory in a robbery or larceny shall secure the property which is alleged to have been stolen, annex a schedule thereof to his return and be answerable for the same; and, upon conviction of the offender, it shall be restored to the owner.

Historical and Statutory Notes

St.1804, c. 143, § 15.
R.S.1836, c. 126, § 25.
G.S.1860, c. 161, § 31.
P.S.1882, c. 203, § 33.
R.L.1902, c. 208, § 39.

§ 49. Burglarious instruments; making; possession; use

Whoever makes or mends, or begins to make or mend, or knowingly has in his possession, an engine, machine, tool or implement adapted and designed for cutting through, forcing or breaking open a building, room, vault, safe or other depository, in order to steal therefrom money or other property, or to commit any other crime, knowing the same to be adapted and designed for the purpose aforesaid, with intent to use or employ or allow the same to be used or employed for such purpose, or whoever knowingly has in his possession a master key designed to fit more than one motor vehicle, with intent to use or employ the same to steal a motor vehicle or other property therefrom, shall be punished by imprisonment in the state prison for not more than ten years or by a fine of not more than one thousand dollars and imprisonment in jail for not more than two and one half years.

Amended by St.1966, c. 269, § 1.

Historical and Statutory Notes

St.1853, c. 194.
G.S.1860, c. 161, § 34.
P.S.1882, c. 203, § 36.
R.L.1902, c. 208, § 41.
St.1914, c. 635.
St.1918, c. 257, § 464.
St.1919, c. 5.
St.1920, c. 2.

§ 50. State treasury; fraud or embezzlement by employee

A person employed in the treasury of the commonwealth who commits a fraud or embezzlement therein shall be punished by a fine of not more than two thousand dollars or by imprisonment in the state prison for life or for any term of years.

Historical and Statutory Notes

St.1791, c. 59, § 5.
R.S.1836, c. 13, § 23; c. 126, § 28.
G.S.1860, c. 161, § 36.
P.S.1882, c. 203, § 38.
R.L.1902, c. 208, § 42.

§ 51. City, town or county officers; fraud or embezzlement

A county, city or town officer who embezzles or fraudulently converts, or who fraudulently takes or secretes with intent so to do, effects or property which belong to or are in possession of said county, city or town, shall be punished by imprisonment in the state prison for not more than ten years or by a fine of not more than one thousand dollars and imprisonment in jail for not more than two years.

Historical and Statutory Notes

St.1855, c. 487.
G.S.1860, c. 161, § 37.
P.S.1882, c. 203, § 39.
R.L.1902, c. 208, § 43.

§ 52. Bank officers and employees; fraud or embezzlement

An officer, director, trustee, agent or employee of a bank, as defined in section one of chapter one hundred and sixty-seven, who fraudulently converts, or fraudulently takes and secretes with intent so to do, any bullion, money, note, bill or other security for money which belongs to and is in possession of such bank, or which belongs to any person and is deposited therein, shall, whether intrusted with the custody thereof or not, be guilty of larceny from said bank. Any such officer, director, trustee, agent or employee so guilty of larceny and any person who knowingly aids, counsels or procures such larceny to be committed shall be punished by imprisonment in the state prison for not more than fifteen years, or by a fine of not more than two thousand dollars and imprisonment in jail for not more than two and one half years.

Amended by St.1934, c. 270, § 3.

Historical and Statutory Notes

St.1783, c. 53, § 1.
St.1824, c. 51.
St.1828, c. 96, § 26.
R.S.1836, c. 126, § 27.
St.1846, c. 171, § 1.
G.S.1860, c. 161, § 39.
P.S.1882, c. 203, § 41.
R.L.1902, c. 208, § 44.
St.1911, c. 216.
St.1914, c. 635.
St.1918, c. 257, § 464.
St.1919, c. 5.
St.1920, c. 2.
St.1922, c. 313, § 1.

§ 53. Bank officers or employees; prosecution for fraud or embezzlement; evidence

In prosecutions for such crimes, the fraudulent taking or receiving by any person of bullion, money, notes, bills or other security for money which belongs to such bank, by reason of an unlawful confederacy or agreement between him and an officer of said bank or any person in the employment thereof, with intent to defraud the same, shall be deemed to be a fraudulent taking by such officer or person in the employment of the bank to his own use, within the meaning of the preceding section; and it shall not be necessary, upon the trial, to identify the particular bullion, money, note, bill or security for money which is so taken or received. Upon the trial of the crime of embezzling, fraudulently converting or fraudulently taking and secreting, with intent so to embezzle or convert, the bullion, money, notes, bank notes, checks, drafts, bills of exchange, obligations or other securities for money of any person, bank, corporation, partnership, county, city or town by a cashier or other officer, clerk, agent or servant of such person, bank, corporation, partnership, county, city or town, evidence may be given of any such embezzlement, fraudulent conversion or taking with such intent committed within six months after the time stated in the indictment.

Historical and Statutory Notes

St.1834, c. 186, § 2.
R.S.1836, c. 133, § 10.
St.1845, c. 215.
St.1846, c. 171, §§ 2, 3.
G.S.1860, c. 161, §§ 40, 42.
St.1878, c. 186.
P.S.1882, c. 203, §§ 42, 44.
R.L.1902, c. 208, § 45.

§ 53A. Bank officers and employees; misconduct; penalty

An officer, director, trustee, agent or employee of a bank, as defined in section one of chapter one hundred and sixty-seven, who wilfully misapplies otherwise than as described in section fifty-two or fifty-three, any of the moneys, funds, credits or other property of such bank; or who, without authority from the directors or trustees of such bank, executes or issues a certificate of deposit, order or bill of exchange, or makes an acceptance, purporting to be executed, issued or made by such bank; or who, without such authority, assigns any note, bond, draft, bill of exchange, mortgage, judgment, decree or other property of such bank; or who loans the funds or credit of such bank to any individual, corporation, joint stock company, trust, association or partnership when the assets of such borrower are known by such officer, director, trustee, agent or employee to be less than all the liabilities of such borrower other than debts subordinated to such loan, unless such loan is adequately secured or is necessary for the protection of existing loans; or who knowingly receives or accepts for such bank any fictitious, valueless, inadequate or irresponsible obligation directly or as security or endorsement unless the consideration or security is otherwise sufficient, or unless it shall be necessary to prevent loss upon a debt previously contracted in good faith; or who certifies any check drawn upon such bank unless the drawer then has on deposit with the bank and entered to his credit on its books not less than the amount of money specified in the check; or who resorts to any fictitious or colorable loan, transfer or device to avoid any provision of law relating to such bank; or who knowingly makes or causes to be made any false entry in any book, report or statement of such bank; and any person who knowingly aids or abets any violation of this section shall be punished by a fine of not more than ten thousand dollars or by imprisonment in the state prison for not more than ten years, or in a jail or house of correction for not more than two and one half years, or by both such fine and imprisonment.

Amended by St.1956, c. 297.

Historical and Statutory Notes

St.1922, c. 313, § 2.

§ 54. Receipt of deposits by insolvent banks; penalty

Any officer or employee of a bank, as defined in section one of chapter one hundred and sixty-seven, who receives or permits the receipt of any deposit knowing that such bank is insolvent, shall be punished by imprisonment for not more than two and one half years or by a fine of not more than five thousand dollars, or both.

Amended by St.1958, c. 58.

Historical and Statutory Notes

St.1914, c. 567.
St.1914, c. 635.
St.1918, c. 257, § 464.
St.1919, c. 5.
St.1920, c. 2.

§ 55. Liquidating agent or receiver; embezzlement

An agent appointed by the commissioner of banks for the purposes of liquidating the affairs of a bank, as defined in section one of chapter one hundred and sixty-seven, or a person employed by said commissioner under section twenty-six of said chapter, or a receiver or other officer appointed by a court of record, who embezzles or fraudulently converts, or fraudulently takes and secretes with intent so to do, or wilfully misapplies, moneys, funds, credits or other property in his possession by virtue of his appointment or employment, shall be guilty of larceny and shall be punished by imprisonment in the state prison for not more than ten years, or by a fine of not more than one thousand dollars and imprisonment in a jail or house of correction for not more than two years.

Historical and Statutory Notes

St.1874, c. 79.
P.S.1882, c. 203, § 45.
R.L.1902, c. 208, § 46.
St.1922, c. 313, § 3.

§ 56. Brokers or agents; embezzlement

A broker, or officer, manager or agent of a corporation doing the business of brokers, who, having been intrusted, solely or jointly, with money, stock or security for the payment of money, with any direction in writing to invest, dispose of, apply, pay or deliver such money, stock or security, or any part thereof, or the proceeds or any part of the proceeds thereof, in any manner, for any purpose or to any person mentioned or specified in such direction, in violation of good faith and contrary to the terms of such direction, embezzles or fraudulently converts such money, stock or security, or any part thereof, or the proceeds or any part of the proceeds thereof, shall be punished by imprisonment in the state prison for not more than five years or in jail for not more than two and one half years or by a fine of not more than five hundred dollars.

Historical and Statutory Notes

St.1892, c. 138.
R.L.1902, c. 208, § 47.
St.1914, c. 635.
St.1918, c. 257, § 464.
St.1919, c. 5.
St.1920, c. 2.

§ 57. Fiduciaries; embezzlement

A trustee under an express trust created by a deed, will or other instrument in writing, or a guardian, conservator, executor or administrator, or any person upon or to whom such a trust has devolved or come, who embezzles or fraudulently converts or appropriates money, goods or property held or possessed by him for the use or benefit, either wholly or partially, of some other person or for a public or charitable purpose, to or for his own use or benefit or to or for the use or benefit of any person other than such person as aforesaid, or for any purpose other than such public or charitable purpose as aforesaid, or who otherwise fraudulently disposes of or destroys such property, shall be punished by imprisonment in the state prison for not more than ten years or by a fine of not more than two thousand dollars and imprisonment in jail for not more than two years.

Historical and Statutory Notes

St.1877, c. 231.
P.S.1882, c. 203, § 46.
R.L.1902, c. 208, § 48.
St.1915, c. 23.

§ 58. Larceny; embezzlement from voluntary association

Whoever, being an officer, agent, clerk or servant of a voluntary association or society, embezzles or fraudulently converts, or fraudulently takes or secretes with intent so to do, effects or property which belong to such association or society, or which have come to his possession or are under his care by virtue of his office or employment, shall be guilty of larceny.

Historical and Statutory Notes

St.1884, c. 174.
R.L.1902, c. 208, § 49.

§ 59. Simple larceny; embezzlement from voluntary association

Whoever embezzles or fraudulently converts, or secretes with intent to embezzle or fraudulently convert, money, goods or property or any part thereof which has been delivered to him, which may be the subject of larceny and which belong to any organization of the volunteer militia, post of the Grand Army of the Republic, or other voluntary association, shall be guilty of simple larceny, although he is a member of such organization or voluntary association and, as such, entitled to an interest in the property thereof. In a prosecution under this section, it shall be sufficient to describe such organization or association by the name by which it is generally known and as a voluntary association.

Historical and Statutory Notes

St.1886, c. 328.
R.L.1902, c. 208, § 50.

§ 60. Stolen goods; buying or receiving

Whoever buys, receives or aids in the concealment of stolen or embezzled property, knowing it to have been stolen or embezzled, or whoever with intent to defraud buys, receives or aids in the concealment of property, knowing it to have been obtained from a person by a false pretense of carrying on business and dealing in the ordinary course of trade, shall, if the value of such property does not exceed two hundred and fifty dollars, be punished for a first offense by imprisonment in jail or house of correction for not more than two and one half years, or by a fine of not more than two hundred and fifty dollars; or, if for a second or subsequent offense, or if the value of such property exceeds two hundred and fifty dollars, be punished by imprisonment in the state prison for not more than five years, or by imprisonment in a jail or house of correction for not more than two and one half years or by a fine of not more than five hundred dollars.

Amended by St.1971, c. 681; St.1973, c. 624; St.1987, c. 468, § 4.

Historical and Statutory Notes

St.1698, c. 8.
St.1723–4, c. 9.
St.1784, c. 66, § 9.
St.1804, c. 143, § 10.
R.S.1836, c. 126, § 20.
St.1853, c. 184, § 1.
G.S.1860, c. 161, §§ 43, 46.
St.1863, c. 248, § 3.
P.S.1882, c. 203, §§ 48, 51, 61.
R.L.1902, c. 208, § 51.

§ 60A. Stolen trade secrets; buying or selling

Whoever buys, receives, conceals, stores, barters, sells or disposes of any trade secret, or pledges or accepts as security for a loan any trade secret, regardless of value, knowing the same to have been stolen, unlawfully converted, or taken, shall be punished by imprisonment for not more than five years or by a fine of not more than five hundred dollars and imprisonment in jail for not more than two years. The term "trade secret" as used in this section shall have the same meaning as is set forth in section thirty.

Added by St.1967, c. 817, § 2.

§ 61. Stolen property; restitution; effect

If, upon a first conviction under the preceding section [1], it is shown that the act of stealing the property was a simple larceny, and if the person convicted makes restitution to the person injured to the full value of the property stolen and not restored, he shall not be imprisoned in the state prison.

[1] Section 60 of this chapter.

Historical and Statutory Notes

St.1804, c. 143, § 13.
R.S.1836, c. 126, § 21.
G.S.1860, c. 161, § 44.
P.S.1882, c. 203, § 49.
R.L.1902, c. 208, § 52.

§ 62. Stolen goods; common receiver

Whoever is convicted of buying, receiving or aiding in the concealment of stolen or embezzled property, knowing it to have been stolen or embezzled, having been before convicted of the like offence, and whoever is convicted at the same sitting of the court of three or more distinct acts of buying, receiving or aiding in the concealment of money, goods or property stolen or embezzled as aforesaid, shall be adjudged a common receiver of stolen or embezzled goods and shall be punished by imprisonment in the state prison for not more than ten years.

Historical and Statutory Notes

St.1804, c. 143, § 12.
R.S.1836, c. 126, § 22.
St.1853, c. 184, § 2.
G.S.1860, c. 161, § 47.
P.S.1882, c. 203, § 52.
R.L.1902, c. 208, § 53.

§ 63. Unlawful taking or use of transportation media

Whoever wilfully, mischievously and without right takes or uses a boat or vehicle, other than a motor vehicle, or takes, drives, rides or uses any draught animal which is the property of another, without the consent of the owner or other person who has the legal custody, care or control thereof, shall be punished by a fine of not more than three hundred dollars or by imprisonment for not more than six months; but this section shall not apply to the property of another taken with intent to steal it, or under a claim of right, or with the presumed consent of the owner or other person who has the legal control, care or custody thereof.

Historical and Statutory Notes

C.L. c. 19, § 5.
St.1854, c. 295.
St.1856, c. 39, § 1.
G.S.1860, c. 161, § 48.
P.S.1882, c. 203, § 53.
R.L.1902, c. 208, § 54.
St.1926, c. 203.
St.1926, c. 296.

§ 64. Fraudulent hiring of media of transportation

Whoever hires a horse, carriage or other vehicle, and, with intent to cheat or defraud the owner thereof, makes to him or to his agent at the time of such hiring a false statement of the distance which he proposes to travel with such horse, carriage or other vehicle, or whoever, with such intent, makes to the owner or his agent, after the use of a horse, carriage or other vehicle, a false statement of the distance which he has actually traveled with such horse, carriage or other vehicle, and whoever, with such intent, refuses to pay for the use of a horse, carriage or other vehicle the lawful fare established therefor by any town, shall be punished by a fine of not more than twenty dollars or by imprisonment for not more than two months, or both.

Historical and Statutory Notes

St.1882, c. 236.
R.L.1902, c. 208, § 55.
St.1910, c. 516.

§ 65. Stock; unauthorized issue

An officer, agent, clerk or servant of a corporation, or any other person, who issues or signs with intent to issue a certificate of stock in a corporation, or who issues, signs or endorses with intent to issue, a bond, note, bill or other obligation or security in the name of such corporation, beyond the amount authorized by law or limited by the legal votes of such corporation or its proper officers, or negotiates, transfers or disposes of such certificate with intent to defraud, shall be punished by imprisonment in the state prison for not more than ten years or in the house of correction for not more than one year.

Historical and Statutory Notes

St.1856, c. 123, § 1.
St.1858, c. 114.
G.S.1860, c. 161, § 49.
P.S.1882, c. 203, § 54.
R.L.1902, c. 208, § 56.

§ 66. Stock; fraudulent issue or transfer

An officer, agent, clerk or servant of a corporation, or any other person, who fraudulently issues or transfers a certificate of the stock of a corporation to a person who is not entitled thereto, or who fraudulently signs such certificate, in blank or otherwise, with the intent that it shall be so issued or transferred by himself or any other person, shall be punished by imprisonment in the state prison for not more than ten years or in the house of correction for not more than one year.

Historical and Statutory Notes

St.1856, c. 123, § 2.
G.S.1860, c. 161, § 50.
P.S.1882, c. 203, § 55.
R.L.1902, c. 208, § 57.

§ 67. Corporate books; false entries with intent to defraud

An officer of a corporation or an agent, clerk or servant of a person, firm or corporation who makes a false entry or omits to make a true entry in any book of such person, firm or corporation, with intent to defraud, and any person whose duty it is to make a record or entry of the transfer of stock, or of the issuing or cancelling of certificates thereof, or of the amount of stock issued by a corporation, in any book thereof, who, with intent to defraud, omits to make a true record or entry thereof, shall be punished by imprisonment in the state prison for not more than ten years or in the house of correction for not more than one year.

Historical and Statutory Notes

St.1856, c. 123, § 3.
G.S.1860, c. 161, § 51.
P.S.1882, c. 203, § 56.
St.1885, c. 223.
R.L.1902, c. 208, § 58.

§ 67A. Departments, agencies and public instrumentalities; false statements, etc. in procurement of supplies; penalty

Whoever, in any matter, relative to procurement of supplies, services or construction, as defined in section one of chapter twelve A, within the jurisdiction of any department, agency or public instrumentality of the commonwealth, or of any political subdivision thereof, intentionally:

(1) makes a material statement that is false;

(2) omits or conceals a material fact in a written statement;

(3) submits or invites reliance on a material writing or recording that is false, forged, altered, or otherwise lacking in authenticity;

(4) submits or invites reliance on a sample, specimen, map, photograph, boundary-mark, or other object that is misleading in a material respect; or

(5) uses any trick, scheme, or device that is misleading in a material respect;

shall be punished by a fine of not more than ten thousand dollars or by imprisonment in the state prison for not more than five years, or in the house of correction for not more than two and one-half years, or both.

Added by St.1980, c. 531, § 2. Amended by St.1982, c. 184.

§ 67B. Presentation of false claims

Whoever makes or presents to any employee, department, agency or public instrumentality of the commonwealth, or of any political subdivision thereof, any claim upon or against any department, agency, or public instrumentality of the commonwealth, or any political subdivision thereof, knowing such claim to be false, fictitious, or fraudulent, shall be punished by a fine of not more than ten thousand dollars or by imprisonment in the state prison for not more than five years, or in the house of correction for not more than two and one-half years, or both.

Added by St.1980, c. 531, § 2.

§ 67C. Capital facility construction projects, etc.; false entries in records; penalties

Any person who knowingly and wilfully, directly or indirectly makes, or knowingly and wilfully causes to be made, a false entry or omission of a true entry in any books, record or account subject to the provisions of section thirty-nine R of chapter thirty shall be punished by a fine of not more than five thousand dollars, or by imprisonment in the state prison for not more than five years, or in the house of correction for not more than two years, or both.

Added by St.1980, c. 579, § 67.

§ 68. Corporate books as evidence

Upon the trial of a person for a crime under the three preceding sections, the books of any person, firm or corporation to which he had access or the right of access shall be admissible in evidence.

Historical and Statutory Notes

St.1856, c. 123, § 4.
G.S.1860, c. 161, § 52.
P.S.1882, c. 203, § 57.
R.L.1902, c. 208, § 59.

§ 69. Insignia of societies; unlawful use

Whoever, not being a member of a society, association or labor union, for the purpose of representing that he is a member thereof, wilfully wears or uses the insignia, ribbon, badge, rosette, button or emblem thereof, if it has been registered in the office of the state secretary, shall be punished by a fine of not more than twenty dollars or by imprisonment for not more than one month, or both.

Historical and Statutory Notes

St.1902, c. 430.
St.1904, c. 335, §§ 2, 3.
St.1909, c. 514, §§ 32, 145.

§ 69A. Fraudulent use of labor union seal, trademark or insignia

Whoever knowingly and fraudulently displays or otherwise uses, in any manner whatsoever, the seal, trademark or insignia of any labor organization as defined by subsection (5) of section two of chapter one hundred and fifty A shall be punished by a fine of not more than one thousand dollars.

Added by St.1970, c. 128.

§ 70. Insignia of veteran organizations; unlawful use

Whoever, not being a member and without authority of the Military Order of the Loyal Legion of the United States, the Grand Army of the Republic, the Sons of Union Veterans of the Civil War, the Woman's Relief Corps, the American Gold Star Mothers, Inc., the Union Veterans' Union, the Union Veteran Legion, the Military and Naval Order of the Spanish–American War, the United Spanish War Veterans, the American Officers of the Great War, the Veterans of Foreign Wars of the United States, the Military Order of Foreign Wars of the United States, the Disabled American Veterans of the World War, the Yankee Division Veterans' Association, The American Legion, the Army and Navy Union, U.S.A., the American Veterans of World War II, AMVETS, the American Veterans' Committee, Inc., the Franco–American War Veterans, Inc., the Military Order of the Purple Heart, the Seabee Veterans of America, Inc.—Department of Massachusetts, the Italian American War Veterans of the United States, Incorporated, the PT Veterans Association, Inc., the Fleet Reserve Association, United States Navy, the American Portuguese War Veterans Association, Polish–American Veterans of Massachusetts, Inc., and its affiliated posts, the Navy Club of the United States of America, or the Marine Corps League or the Veterans of World War I of the U.S.A., wilfully wears or uses the insignia, distinctive ribbons or membership rosette or button thereof for the purpose of representing that he is a member thereof or displays on his property or permits to be displayed thereon any such insignia, distinctive ribbon, membership rosette or button, or any sign or statement for the purpose of falsely representing that such property is occupied by or is the quarters of any such veterans' organization, shall be punished by a fine of not more than twenty dollars or by imprisonment for not more than one month, or both.

Amended by St.1933, c. 245, § 4; St.1939, c. 144, § 2; St.1941, c. 217, § 3; St.1946, c. 209, § 3; St.1946, c. 409, § 4; St.1947, c. 468, § 4; St.1948, c. 445, § 2; St.1949, c. 118, § 4; St.1950, c. 27, § 3; St.1950, c. 240; St.1950, c. 354, § 3; St.1950, c. 492, § 3; St.1955, c. 271, § 2; St.1957, c. 117; St.1959, c. 59, § 5; St.1960, c. 626, § 5.

Historical and Statutory Notes

St.1887, c. 67.
St.1891, c. 15.
St.1894, c. 27.
St.1894, c. 117.
St.1901, c. 151.
R.L.1902, c. 208, § 60.
St.1907, c. 232, § 3.
St.1920, c. 367.

§ 71. Signature, money or membership; obtaining under false pretences

Whoever wilfully, by color or aid of any false token or writing, or other false pretence or false statement, verbal or written, or without authority of the grand or supreme governing lodge, council, union or other governing body hereinafter mentioned, obtains the signature of any person to any written application, or obtains any money or property for any alleged or pretended degree, or for any alleged or pretended membership in any fraternity, association, society, order, organization or union having a grand or supreme governing lodge, council, union or other governing body in the commonwealth, or in any subordinate lodge or body thereof, shall be punished by imprisonment for not more than one year or by a fine of not more than five hundred dollars, or both.

Historical and Statutory Notes

St.1908, c. 280, § 1.

§ 71A. Individuals and corporations; false use of names of benevolent organizations

No person, society, association or corporation shall knowingly assume, adopt or use the name of a benevolent, humane, fraternal, charitable or labor organization, whether incorporated or unincorporated, or a name so nearly resembling the name of such incorporated or unincorporated organization as to be a colorable imitation thereof or calculated to deceive persons not members with respect to such organizations. Whoever violates this section shall be punished by a fine of not more than two hundred dollars or by imprisonment for not more than one year or by both such fine and imprisonment. The superior court shall have jurisdiction in equity to enjoin any violation of this section.

Added by St.1950, c. 718.

§ 72. Fraternal names; use in publication

Whoever, in a newspaper or other publication, or in any written or printed letter, notice, matter or device, without authority of the grand or supreme governing lodge, council, union or other governing body, fraudulently uses or aids in any way in the use of the name, title or common designation of any fraternity, association, society, order, organization or union which has such a governing body, having priority in such use in the commonwealth, or any name, title or designation so nearly resembling the same as to be calculated or likely to deceive; and whoever, without such authority, fraudulently publishes, sells, circulates or distributes any written or printed letter, notice, matter or device, in any way soliciting members of such fraternity, association, society, order, organization or union, or for any alleged or pretended fraternity, association, society, order, organization or union, using any such name, title, designation, or near resemblance thereto; and whoever therein or thereby in any way, without such authority, fraudulently offers to sell, confer, communicate or give information where, of whom or by what means any degree or work, in whole or in part, of such fraternity, association, society, order, organization or union, or of any alleged or pretended fraternity, association, society, order, organization or union using any such name, title or designation or near resemblance thereto, can or may be obtained, conferred or communicated, shall be punished by imprisonment for not more than one year or by a fine of not more than five hundred dollars, or both.

Historical and Statutory Notes

St.1908, c. 280, § 2.

§ 73. Obtaining goods under false pretences

Whoever, with intent to defraud, by a false pretence of carrying on business and dealing in the ordinary course of trade, obtains from any person goods or chattels shall be punished by imprisonment in the state prison for not more than five years or by a fine of not more than five hundred dollars and imprisonment in jail for not more than two years.

Historical and Statutory Notes

St.1863, c. 248, § 2.
P.S.1882, c. 203, § 60.
R.L.1902, c. 208, § 61.
St.1902, c. 544, § 29.

§ 74. Corporate credit; fraudulent use

An officer, agent, clerk or servant of a corporation organized or doing business in the commonwealth, who wilfully uses the name of such corporation, or his own name as such officer, agent, clerk or servant, to obtain money upon the credit of such corporation for his own use or benefit, without authority from such corporation, or who fraudulently lends, invests or appropriates the money or disposes of the property of such corporation, or fraudulently converts it, shall be punished by imprisonment in the state prison for not more than ten years.

Historical and Statutory Notes

St.1878, c. 274.
P.S.1882, c. 203, § 62.
R.L.1902, c. 208, § 62.

§ 75. Obtaining property by trick

Whoever, by a game, device, sleight of hand, pretended fortune telling or by any trick or other means by the use of cards or other implements or instruments, fraudulently obtains from another person property of any description shall be punished as in the case of larceny of property of like value.

Historical and Statutory Notes

St.1855, c. 135, § 1.
G.S.1860, c. 161, § 57.
P.S.1882, c. 203, § 65.
R.L.1902, c. 208, § 63.

§ 75A. Gambling devices and vending machines; fraudulent use

Whoever operates or causes to be operated, or attempts to operate or to cause to be operated, any automatic vending machine, slot machine, turnstile, coin-box telephone or other receptacle designed to receive lawful coin of the United States or tokens provided by the person entitled to the coin-contents or token-contents of such receptacle in connection with the sale, use or enjoyment of property, transportation or other service, by means of a slug or any false, counterfeited, mutilated or sweated coin or token or by any means, method, trick or device whatsoever not lawfully authorized by the owner, lessee or licensee of such machine, turnstile, coin-box telephone or receptacle; or whoever takes, obtains or receives from or in connection with any automatic vending machine, slot machine, turnstile, coin-box telephone or other receptacle designed to receive lawful coin of the United States or tokens provided by the person entitled to the coin-contents or token-contents of such receptacle in connection with the sale, use of or enjoyment of property or service, any goods, wares, merchandise, transportation, gas, electric current, article of value, or the use or enjoyment of any transportation or any telephone or telegraph facilities or service, or of any musical instrument, phonograph or other property, without depositing in and surrendering to such machine, turnstile, coin-box telephone or other receptacle lawful coin or a token or tokens to the amount or value required therefor by the owner, lessee or licensee of such machine, turnstile, coin-box telephone or receptacle, shall be punished by a fine of not more than one hundred dollars or by imprisonment in the house of correction for not more than thirty days, or both. The word "person" as used in this section shall include any municipal corporation or political subdivision of the commonwealth.

Added by St.1932, c. 11. Amended by St.1954, c. 145.

§ 75B. Slugs; manufacture and sale

Whoever manufactures for sale, advertises for sale, sells, offers for sale, or gives away any slug, device or substance whatsoever, designed or calculated to be placed or deposited in any automatic vending machine, slot machine, turnstile, coin-box telephone or other such receptacle, depository or contrivance, designed to receive lawful coin of the United States or tokens provided by the person entitled to the coin-contents or token-contents of such receptacle, depository or contrivance in connection with the sale, use or enjoyment of property or service, with the intent that such slug, device or substance shall be used to cheat or defraud the person entitled to the contents of any such machine, turnstile, coin-box telephone or other such receptacle, depository or contrivance, shall be punished by a fine of not more than five hundred dollars, or by imprisonment in the house of correction for not more than one year, or both. The word "person" as used in this section shall include any municipal corporation or political subdivision of the commonwealth.

Added by St.1932, c. 11. Amended by St.1954, c. 145.

§ 75C. Gift certificates; expiration dates; failure to redeem

Whoever sells or offers to sell a gift certificate as defined in section 1 of chapter 255D, which imposes a time limit of less than 7 years within which such certificate may be redeemed, shall be punished by a fine of not more than $300. This section shall not apply when the purchaser of the gift certificate is not obligated to pay for it until the time of use. Whoever, after having sold a gift certificate refuses to redeem the certificate before it has reached the expiration date, shall be punished by a fine of not more than $300.

Added by St.1985, c. 511. Amended by St.2002, c. 510, § 7, eff. June 1, 2003.

§ 75D. Imposition of certain fees reducing total value amount of gift certificate; penalty

Whoever sells or offers to sell a gift certificate, as defined in section 1 of chapter 255D, which imposes dormancy fees, latency fees, administrative fees, periodic fees, service fees or other fees that have the effect of reducing the total value amount for which the holder may redeem such gift certificate, shall be punished by a fine of not more than $300 per violation.

Added by St.2008, c. 58, § 3, eff. June 9, 2008.

§ 75E. Printed notice required for certain fees associated with gift certificates; penalty for violation

Whoever sells or offers to sell a gift certificate, as defined in section 1 of chapter 255D, which imposes any fees or charges including, but not limited to, purchase fees, activation fees, renewal fees or cancellation fees, shall provide to consumers notice of any such fees, in writing, on the gift certificate, on the packaging of the gift certificate, or on both. Failure to print such notice shall be punished by a fine of not more than $300 per violation.

Added by St.2008, c. 58, § 3, eff. June 9, 2008.

§ 75F. Deduction of gratuity from gift certificate without consent; penalty

Whoever redeems a gift certificate, as defined in section 1 of chapter 255D and deducts a gratuity therefrom without the consent of the holder of the gift certificate, shall be punished by a fine of not more than $300 per violation.

Added by St.2008, c. 58, § 3, eff. June 9, 2008.

§ 76. Gross fraud or cheat at common law; punishment

Whoever is convicted of any gross fraud or cheat at common law shall be punished by imprisonment in the state prison for not more than ten years or in jail for not more than two years or by a fine of not more than four hundred dollars.

Historical and Statutory Notes

St.1785, c. 21, § 4.
St.1815, c. 136, § 2.
R.S.1836, c. 126, § 33.
G.S.1860, c. 161, § 58.
P.S. 1882, c. 203, § 66.
R.L.1902, c. 208, § 64.

§ 77. Sterling and coin silver; contents; sale; penalty

Whoever makes or sells, or offers to sell or dispose of, or has in his possession with intent so to do, any article of merchandise marked, stamped or branded with the words "sterling", "sterling silver", "coin" or "coin silver", or encased or enclosed in any box, package, cover or wrapper or other thing in or by which the said article is packed, enclosed or otherwise prepared for sale or disposition, having thereon any engraving or printed label, stamp, imprint, mark or trade mark, indicating or denoting by such marking, stamping, branding, engraving or printing, that such article is silver, sterling silver, solid silver, coin or coin silver, shall, unless nine hundred and twenty-five one-thousandths of the component parts of the metal of which the said article so marked, stamped or branded with the words "sterling" or "sterling silver" is manufactured are pure silver, or unless nine hundred one-thousandths of the component parts of the metal of which the article so marked, stamped or branded with the words "coin" or "coin silver" is manufactured, are pure silver, be punished by a fine of not more than one hundred dollars.

Historical and Statutory Notes

St.1894, c. 292.
R.L.1902, c. 208, § 65.

§ 78. Articles made of gold; false marking; prohibition

Whoever makes or sells, or offers for sale or disposes of, or has in his possession with intent so to do, any article constructed in whole or in part of gold or alloy of gold, or of any metal resembling gold, having marked thereon or upon any tag or label attached thereto, or upon any package, cover or wrapper in which such article is enclosed or wrapped, any word or mark indicating or designed or intended to indicate that the gold or alloy of gold in said article, or in the plating, surface or any other part of said article is of a greater degree or carat of fineness by more than one carat than the actual quality or fineness of such gold or alloy of gold, or any so-called gold filled, rolled gold plated or electro gold plated article having marked thereon, or upon any tag or label attached thereto, or upon any package, cover or wrapper in which such article is enclosed or wrapped, any word or mark indicating or designed or intended to indicate that the gold or alloy of gold upon such article is of a greater percentage of weight of the article by more than one per cent than the actual percentage of gold or alloy of gold, shall be punished by a fine of not more than five hundred dollars. The word or mark upon the article or upon the tag or label attached thereto, or upon the package, cover or wrapper in which such article is enclosed, shall be held to apply to the whole article, all the gold, alloys, solder and base metals being assayed as one piece, unless the word or mark plainly indicates that it applies to the plating, surface or other particular part of such article.

Historical and Statutory Notes

St.1907, c. 460, §§ 1 to 3.

§ 79. Imitation of furs; false representation; prohibition

Whoever, himself, or by his agent or servant, or as the agent or servant of another person, sells or exchanges, or has in his custody or possession with intent so to do, or exposes for sale or exchange, any manufactured imitations of furs of fur-bearing animals, representing the same to be the genuine fur of certain animals, shall be punished by a fine of not less than two hundred nor more than five hundred dollars.

Historical and Statutory Notes

St.1919, c. 134.

§ 80. Encumbered land; conveyance without notice

Whoever conveys land, knowing that an encumbrance exists thereon, without informing the grantee, before the consideration is paid, of the existence and nature of such encumbrance, so far as he has knowledge thereof, shall be punished by imprisonment for not more than one year or by a fine of not more than one thousand dollars.

Historical and Statutory Notes

St.1855, c. 177, § 2.
G.S.1860, c. 161, § 59.
P.S.1882, c. 203, § 67.
R.L.1902, c. 208, § 66.

§ 81. Attached land; conveyance without notice

Whoever, knowing that his land is attached on mesne process, sells and conveys it without giving notice of the attachment to the grantee, and with intent to defraud, shall be punished by imprisonment in the state prison for not more than three years or in jail for not more than one year.

Historical and Statutory Notes

R.S.1836, c. 126, § 34.
G.S.1860, c. 161, § 60.
P.S.1882, c. 203, § 68.
R.L.1902, c. 208, § 67.

§ 82. Concealment of mortgaged personalty; use of rented personalty for illegal sale of liquor

Whoever, with a fraudulent intent to place personal property which is subject to a mortgage beyond the control of the mortgagee, removes or conceals or aids or abets in removing or concealing the same, and a mortgagor of such property who assents to such removal or concealment, or whoever shall use rented, leased or mortgaged personal property as a container or implement of sale of intoxicating liquor contrary to law, shall be punished by a fine of not more than one thousand dollars or by imprisonment for not more than one year.

Historical and Statutory Notes

St.1859, c. 246.
G.S.1860, c. 161, § 61.
P.S.1882, c. 203, § 69.
R.L.1902, c. 208, § 68.
St.1929, c. 329, § 3.

§ 83. Personalty; sale by mortgagor without consent

A mortgagor of personal property who sells or conveys the same or any part thereof without the written consent of the mortgagee, and without informing the vendee or grantee that the same is mortgaged, shall be punished by a fine of not more than one hundred dollars or by imprisonment for not more than one year.

Historical and Statutory Notes

St.1850, c. 284.
G.S.1860, c. 161, § 62.
P.S.1882, c. 203, § 70.
R.L.1902, c. 208, § 69.

§ 84. Personalty; sale by hirer without consent

A hirer or lessee of personal property who sells or conveys the same or any part thereof without the written consent of the owner or lessor, and without informing the vendee or grantee that it is so hired or leased, shall be punished by a fine of not more than one hundred dollars or by imprisonment for not more than one year.

Historical and Statutory Notes

St.1857, c. 156.
G.S.1860, c. 161, § 63.
P.S.1882, c. 203, § 71.
R.L.1902, c. 208, § 70.

§ 85. Collateral security; sale before debt due

Whoever, holding collateral security deposited with him for the payment of a debt which may be due to him, sells, pledges, lends or in any way disposes of the same before such debt becomes due and payable, without the authority of the depositor thereof, shall be punished by a fine of not more than five hundred dollars or by imprisonment in jail for not more than two years.

Historical and Statutory Notes

St.1855, c. 213.
G.S.1860, c. 161, § 64.
P.S.1882, c. 203, § 72.
R.L.1902, c. 208, § 71.

§ 86. Hired property; buying or receiving with intent to defraud

Whoever, with intent to defraud, buys, receives or aids in concealing personal property, knowing it to be hired or leased or held as collateral security, shall be punished by a fine of not more than one hundred dollars or by imprisonment for not more than one year.

Historical and Statutory Notes

St.1865, c. 127, § 1.
P.S.1882, c. 203, § 73.
R.L.1902, c. 208, § 72.

§ 87. Larceny of leased or rented property

Any person leasing or renting personal property who, with the intent to place such property beyond the control of the owner, conceals or aids or abets the concealment of such property or any part thereof, or fails or refuses to return such property to the owner within ten days after expiration of the lease or rental agreement, or sells, conveys or pledges such property or any part thereof without the written consent of the owner, shall be guilty of larceny of leased or rented personal property.

Any person convicted of larceny of leased or rented personal property shall be punished by a fine of not more than one thousand dollars or imprisonment of not more than one year, or both. A person found guilty of violating this section shall, in all cases upon conviction in addition to any other punishment, be ordered to make restitution to the owner for any financial loss.

It shall be prima facie evidence of intent to place such property beyond the control of the owner when a person in obtaining such property presents identification or information which is materially false, fictitious, misleading or not current with respect to such person's name, address, place of employment or any other material matter or fails to return such property to the owner or his representative within ten days after proper notice to return such property. For purposes of this section proper notice shall be actual notice or a written demand sent by certified or registered mail to such person at the address given at the time of making the lease or rental agreement.

It shall be a defense to prosecution for conversion of leased or rented property that the defendant was unaware the property belonged to another or that he had a right to acquire or dispose of the property as he did.

Amended by St.1971, c. 210; St.1975, c. 540; St.1982, c. 259.

Historical and Statutory Notes

St.1870, c. 261.
P.S.1882, c. 203, § 74.
R.L.1902, c. 208, § 73.

§ 87A. Stolen leased or rented motor vehicles; report; dissemination of information by police

The owner or lessee of a leased or rented motor vehicle which has been stolen or placed beyond his control shall report the loss of the same to the police department of the city or town wherein said vehicle was leased or rented or stolen.

Notwithstanding any provision of law to the contrary, a police department receiving a report of said stolen vehicle shall list the same as stolen and shall, by the use of radio, teletype, computer or other communication, disseminate the information concerning said stolen vehicle using the same standards as applicable to other stolen motor vehicles.

Added by St.1983, c. 430. Amended by St.1986, c. 81.

§ 88. Consignee or factor; fraudulent deposit or pledge of property

A consignee or factor who, in violation of good faith and with intent to defraud the owners thereof, deposits or pledges, as security for money borrowed by him, a negotiable instrument received by him, merchandise consigned or intrusted to him, or a bill of lading, certificate or order for the delivery of merchandise; or who, in like violation and with like intent, disposes of or applies such property or evidence of property to his own use; or who, in like violation and with like intent, disposes of or applies to his own use money which has been raised or a negotiable instrument which has been acquired by the sale or other disposition of such property or evidence of property, shall be punished by a fine of not more than five thousand dollars and imprisonment for not more than five years.

Historical and Statutory Notes

St.1849, c. 216, § 6.
G.S.1860, c. 161, § 65.
P.S.1882, c. 203, § 75.
R.L.1902, c. 208, § 74.

§ 89. Degrees; pretending to hold or conferring without authority; use of designation "university" or "college"

Whoever, in a book, pamphlet, circular, advertisement or advertising sign, or by a pretended written certificate or diploma, or otherwise in writing, knowingly and falsely pretends to have been an officer or teacher, or to be a graduate or to hold any degree, of a college or other educational institution of this commonwealth or elsewhere, which is authorized to confer degrees, or of a public school of this commonwealth, and whoever, without having lawful authority to confer degrees, offers or confers degrees as a school, college or as a private individual, alone or associated with others, shall be punished by a fine of not more than one thousand dollars or by imprisonment for not more than one year, or both. Any individual, school, association, corporation or institution of learning, not having lawful authority to confer degrees, using the designation of "university" or "college" shall be punished by a fine of one thousand dollars; but this shall not apply to any educational institution whose name on July ninth, nineteen hundred and nineteen, included the word "university" or "college".

Amended by St.1943, c. 549, § 7.

Historical and Statutory Notes

St.1893, c. 355, § 1.
R.L.1902, c. 208, § 75.
St.1919, c. 293, § 4.

§ 90. Endorsement or approval; penalty for false claim

Whoever, in a book, pamphlet, circular, advertisement or advertising sign, or otherwise in writing, makes any false and fraudulent statement or assertion of endorsement, authority, approval or sanction of an incorporated college, university or professional school in this commonwealth or elsewhere, or of officers or instructors thereof, as a commendation or advertisement of a person or of his services, or of goods, wares, commodities, processes or treatment, shall be punished by a fine of not more than one thousand dollars or by imprisonment for not more than one year, or both.

Historical and Statutory Notes

St.1893, c. 355, § 2.
R.L.1902, c. 208, § 76.

§ 91. Untrue and misleading advertisements; prohibitions

Any person who, with intent to sell or in any way dispose of merchandise, securities, service, or anything offered by such person, directly or indirectly, to the public for sale or distribution, or who, with intent to increase the consumption of or demand for such merchandise, securities, service or other thing, or to induce the public in any manner to enter into any obligation relating thereto, or to acquire title thereto, or an interest therein, makes, publishes, disseminates, circulates or places before the public, or causes, directly or indirectly, to be made, published, disseminated, circulated or placed before the public within the commonwealth, in a newspaper or other publication, or in the form of a book, notice, handbill, poster, bill, circular, pamphlet or letter, or in any other way, an advertisement of any sort regarding merchandise, securities, service or anything so offered to the public, which advertisement contains any assertion, representation or statement of fact which is untrue, deceptive or misleading, and which such person knew, or might on reasonable investigation have ascertained to be untrue, deceptive or misleading, shall be punished by a fine of not less than one thousand nor more than two thousand dollars; provided, that this section shall not apply to any owner, publisher, printer, agent or employee of a newspaper or other publication, periodical or circular, or to any agent of the advertiser who in good faith and without knowledge of the falsity or deceptive character thereof publishes, causes to be published, or participates in the publication of such advertisement.

Whoever violates the provisions of this section may be enjoined therefrom by a petition in equity brought by the attorney general or any aggrieved party.

Amended by St.1958, c. 217, § 1; St.1963, c. 222; St.1993, c. 439.

Historical and Statutory Notes

St.1902, c. 397.
St.1912, c. 489.
St.1914, c. 288.
St.1916, c. 149.

§ 91A. Merchandise, commodities and service; advertisement; penalty

Any person who offers for sale merchandise, commodities or service by making, publishing, disseminating, circulating or placing before the public within the commonwealth, in a newspaper or other publication, or in the form of a book, notice, handbill, poster, bill, circular, pamphlet or letter, or in any other way, an advertisement describing the said merchandise, commodities or service, as part of a plan or scheme with the intent not to sell said merchandise, commodities or service so advertised at the price stated therein, or with intent not to sell said merchandise, commodities or service so advertised, shall be punished by a fine of not less than five hundred nor more than one thousand dollars or by imprisonment for not more than one year.

Added by St.1953, c. 250. Amended by St.1958, c. 217, § 2.

§ 91B. Deceptive advertising of merchandise for sale; injunction

Any person offering for sale merchandise, commodities or service by making, publishing, disseminating, circulating or placing before the public within the commonwealth in any manner an advertisement of merchandise, commodities, or service, with the intent, design or purpose not to sell the merchandise, commodities, or service so advertised at the price stated therein or otherwise communicated, or with the intent not to sell the merchandise, commodities, or service so advertised, may be enjoined from such advertising by a bill in equity in the superior court brought by the attorney general or any aggrieved party; provided, however, that the provisions of this section shall not apply to any medium for the printing, publishing, or disseminating of advertising, or any owner, agent or employee thereof, nor to any advertising agency or owner, agent or employee thereof, nor to any radio or television station, or owner, agent, or employee thereof, for printing, publishing, or disseminating or causing to be printed, published, or disseminated such advertisement in good faith and without knowledge of the deceptive character thereof.

Added by St.1958, c. 217, § 3.

§ 92. False or exaggerated statements; making or publishing; prohibition

Whoever wilfully and with intent to defraud makes or publishes, or causes or permits to be made or published in any way whatever, any book, prospectus, notice, report, statement, exhibit, advertisement or other publication of or concerning the affairs, financial condition, property or assets of any corporation, joint stock association, partnership or individual, which said book, prospectus, notice, report, statement, exhibit, advertisement or other publication contains any statement which is false or wilfully exaggerated and which shall have a tendency to give a less or greater apparent value to the shares, bonds, property or assets of such corporation, joint stock association, partnership or individual, or any part of said shares, bonds, property or assets, than said shares, bonds, property or assets or any part thereof shall really and in fact possess, shall be punished by a fine of not more than five thousand dollars or by imprisonment for not more than ten years, or both.

Historical and Statutory Notes

St.1907, c. 383.
St.1911, c. 428.

§ 92A. Motor vehicles; sale in certain condition; written disclosure on bill of sale; penalty

Whoever sells a motor vehicle knowing that its engine or electrical parts have been submerged in water, or knowing that it has been used as a police car, a taxicab, a rental vehicle by a motor vehicle rental agency, or a leased vehicle which has been leased to any corporation, individual or entity, other than a motor vehicle rental company, without indicating such fact in writing on the bill of sale, and whoever, other than the commonwealth or any political subdivision thereof, sells any such police car to an ultimate user for other than police purposes without first having obliterated all evidence of distinctive police insignias or markings thereon, and painting the exterior of every marked state police vehicle thereof one solid color, shall be punished by a fine of not less than ten nor more than five hundred dollars.

Added by St.1956, c. 216. Amended by St.1957, c. 261; St.1959, c. 235; St.1968, c. 40; St.1973, c. 141; St.1975, c. 324; St.1979, c. 184.

§ 93. Animals; obtaining or giving false pedigree

Whoever, by a false pretence, obtains from any club, association, society or company for improving the breed of cattle, horses, sheep, swine or other domestic animals, the registration, or a certificate thereof, of any animal in the herd register, or any other register of such club, association, society or company, or a transfer of such registration, or whoever knowingly makes, exhibits or gives a false pedigree in writing of any animal, shall be punished by imprisonment for not more than two years or by a fine of not more than five hundred dollars, or both.

Historical and Statutory Notes

St.1887, c. 143.
St.1890, c. 334, § 2.
R.L.1902, c. 208, § 77.

§ 94. Boundary monuments and miscellaneous markers; malicious destruction

Whoever wilfully, intentionally and without right breaks down, injures, removes or destroys a monument erected for the purpose of designating the boundaries of a town or of a tract or lot of land, or a tree which has been marked for that purpose, or so breaks down, injures, removes or destroys a milestone, mileboard or guideboard erected upon a public way or railroad, or wilfully, intentionally and without right defaces or alters the inscription on any such stone or board, or wilfully, intentionally and without right mars or defaces a building or signboard, or extinguishes a light or breaks, destroys or removes a lamp, lamp post, railing or post erected on a bridge, sidewalk, public way, court or passage, or wilfully, intentionally and without right defaces or otherwise injures, removes, interferes with or destroys any traffic regulating sign, light, signal, marking or device lawfully erected or placed under public authority on any public way, shall be punished by imprisonment for not more than six months or by a fine of not more than two hundred dollars. Any person convicted under the provisions of this section shall, in addition to any imprisonment or fine, make restitution.

Amended by St.1939, c. 451, § 65; St.1987, c. 416.

Historical and Statutory Notes

St.1785, c. 28, § 2.
St.1823, c. 113, § 1.
R.S.1836, c. 126, § 43.
G.S.1860, c. 161, § 66.
P.S.1882, c. 203, § 76.
St.1901, c. 268, § 2.
R.L.1902, c. 208, § 78.

§ 95. Historical monuments; malicious destruction or injury

Whoever wilfully or maliciously removes, displaces, destroys, defaces, mars or injures any monument, tablet or other device erected to mark an historic place or to commemorate an historic event shall be punished by a fine of not more than one thousand dollars or by imprisonment for not more than two years. Any person convicted under the provisions of this section shall, in addition to any fine assessed, reimburse the commonwealth for the total amount of damage incurred.

Amended by St.1975, c. 722.

Historical and Statutory Notes

St.1899, c. 358.
R.L.1902, c. 208, § 79.

§ 96. State building; defacement or injury

Whoever wilfully, intentionally and without right defaces, mars or injures the walls, wainscoting or any other part of any building belonging to the commonwealth, or the appurtenances thereof, by cutting, writing or otherwise, shall be punished by a fine of not less than one hundred nor more than one thousand dollars or by imprisonment for not more than two years. Any person convicted under the provisions of this section shall, in addition to any fine assessed, reimburse the commonwealth for the total amount of damages incurred.

Amended by St.1975, c. 722.

Historical and Statutory Notes

St.1833, c. 178.
R.S.1836, c. 11, § 8.
G.S.1860, c. 5, § 14.
P.S.1882, c. 203, § 77.
St.1901, c. 268, § 3.
R.L.1902, c. 208, § 80.

§ 97. County buildings; defacement

Whoever wilfully mars or injures the walls, wainscoting or any other part of a court house, jail or house of correction, or of any other building or room used for county business, or the appurtenances thereof, by cutting, writing or otherwise, shall be punished by imprisonment for not more than two years or by a fine of not less than one hundred nor more than one thousand dollars. Any person convicted under the provisions of this section shall, in addition to any fine assessed, reimburse the county for the total amount of damage incurred.

Amended by St.1975, c. 722.

Historical and Statutory Notes

St.1899, c. 196, § 1.
R.L.1902, c. 208, § 81.

§ 98. Schoolhouse or church; defacement or injury

Whoever wilfully, intentionally and without right, or wantonly and without cause, destroys, defaces, mars or injures a schoolhouse, church or other building erected or used for purposes of education or religious instruction, or for the general diffusion of knowledge, or an outbuilding, fence, well or appurtenance of such schoolhouse, church or other building, or furniture, apparatus or other property belonging thereto or connected therewith, shall be punished by a fine of not more than one thousand dollars, or by imprisonment for not more than two years, or both.

Amended by St.1960, c. 169.

Historical and Statutory Notes

St.1857, c. 222.
G.S.1860, c. 161, § 67.
P.S.1882, c. 203, § 78.
St.1901, c. 268, § 4.
R.L.1902, c. 208, § 82.

§ 98A. Public park or playground equipment; destruction, defacement or injury

Whoever wilfully, intentionally and without right, or wantonly and without cause destroys, defaces, mars or injures any playground apparatus or equipment located in a public park or playground shall be punished by a fine of not more than one thousand dollars.

Added by St.1966, c. 280. Amended by St.1991, c. 350.

§ 99. Libraries; definitions

As used in sections ninety-nine A and one hundred, the following words shall have the following meanings:—

"Library materials and property", any book, plate, picture, portrait, photograph, broadside, engraving, painting, drawing, map, specimen, print, lithograph, chart, musical score, catalog card, catalog record, statue, coin, medal, computer software, film, periodical, newspaper, magazine, pamphlet, document, manuscript, letter, archival material, public record, microform, sound recording, audio-visual material in any format, magnetic or other tape, tape recorder, film projector or other machinery or equipment, electronic data-processing record, artifact or other documentary written or printed material regardless of the physical form or characteristics which is a constituent element of a library's collection or any part thereof, belonging to, on loan to or otherwise in the custody of any library. Library materials and property shall also include the walls, wainscotting or any part of the library, or any other building or room used for library business or the appurtenances thereof, including furnishings.

"Library premises", the interior of the building, structure or other enclosure in which a library is located, bookmobiles and kiosks, the exterior appurtenances to such building, structure or enclosure is located.

Amended by St.1975, c. 374; St.1990, c. 61.

Historical and Statutory Notes

St.1867, c. 69.
St.1872, c. 42.
P.S.1882, c. 203, § 79.
St.1883, c. 81.
St.1901, c. 268, § 4.
R.L.1902, c. 208, § 83.

§ 99A. Libraries; theft of materials or property; destruction of records

Whoever willfully conceals on his person or among his belongings any library materials or property and removes said library materials or property, if the value of the property stolen exceeds two hundred and fifty dollars, shall be punished by imprisonment in the state prison for not more than five years, or by a fine of not less than one thousand nor more than twenty-five thousand dollars, or both; or, if the value of the property stolen does not exceed two hundred and fifty dollars, shall be punished by imprisonment in jail for not more than one year or by a fine of not less than one hundred nor more than one thousand dollars, or both, and ordered to pay the replacement value of such library materials or property, including all reasonable processing costs, as determined by the governing board of said library.

Any person who has properly charged out any library materials or property, and who, upon neglect to return the same within the time required and specified in the by-laws, rules or regulations of the library owning the property, after receiving notice from the librarian or other proper custodian of the property that the same is overdue, shall willfully fail to return the same within thirty days from the date of such notice shall pay a fine of not less than one hundred nor more than five hundred dollars and shall pay the replacement value of such library materials or property, including all reasonable processing costs, as determined by said governing board. Each piece of library property shall be considered a separate offense.

The giving of a false identification or fictitious name, address or place of employment with the intent to deceive, or borrowing or attempting to borrow any library material or property by: the use of a library card issued to another without the other's consent; the use of a library card knowing that it is revoked, canceled or expired; or, the use of a library card knowing that it is falsely made, counterfeit or materially altered shall be punished by a fine of not less than one hundred dollars nor more than one thousand dollars.

The willful alteration or destruction of library ownership records, electronic or catalog records retained apart from or applied directly to the library materials or property shall be punished by imprisonment in the state prison for not more than five years or by a fine of not less than one thousand nor more than twenty-five thousand dollars, or both, and shall pay the replacement value of such library materials or property, including all reasonable processing costs, as determined by the governing board having jurisdiction.

Added by St.1990, c. 61.

§ 100. Libraries; mutilation or destruction of materials or property

Whoever willfully, maliciously or wantonly writes upon, injures, defaces, tears, cuts, mutilates or destroys any library material or property, shall make restitution in full replacement value of the library materials or property, and, in addition, shall be punished by imprisonment in a house of correction for not more than two years or by a fine of not less than one hundred nor more than one thousand dollars, or both.

A law enforcement officer may arrest without warrant any person he has probable cause to believe has violated the provisions of section ninety-nine A and this section. The statement of an employee or agent of the library, eighteen years of age or older, that a person has violated the provisions of said section ninety-nine A and this section shall constitute probable cause for arrest by a law enforcement officer authorized to make an arrest in such jurisdiction. The activation of an electronic anti-theft device shall constitute probable cause for believing that a person has violated the provisions of this section.

A library shall prepare posters to be displayed therein in a conspicuous place. Said posters shall contain a summary and explanation of said section ninety-nine A and this section.

Amended by St.1961, c. 316; St.1976, c. 206; St.1990, c. 61.

Historical and Statutory Notes

St.1883, c. 77.
St.1901, c. 268, § 4.
R.L.1902, c. 208, § 84.

§ 101. Definitions applicable to Secs. 101 to 102D

For the purposes of sections 101 to 102D, inclusive, the following terms shall have the following meanings, unless otherwise clearly required:—

"Ammunition", cartridges or cartridge cases, primers (igniter), bullets or propellant powder designed for use in any weapon utilizing a propellant including, but not limited to, ammunition produced by or for the military for national defense and security.

"Biological weapon", any microorganism, virus, infectious substance or biological product that may be engineered as a result of biotechnology, or any naturally occurring or bioengineered component of any such microorganism, virus, infectious substance or biological product, except if intended for a purpose not prohibited under this chapter or chapter 265, specifically prepared in a manner to cause death, disease or other biological malfunction in a human, animal, plant or another living organism, deterioration of food, water, equipment supplies or material of any kind, or deleterious alteration of the environment.

"Black powder", a compound or mixture of sulfur, charcoal and an alkali nitrate including, but not limited to, potassium or sodium nitrate.

"Chemical weapon", (i) a toxic chemical or substance, including the precursors to any toxic chemical or substance; and (ii) ammunition or a device designed to cause death or bodily harm by means of the release of a toxic chemical or substance.

"Delivery system", any equipment designed or adapted for use in connection with the deployment of chemical, biological or nuclear weapons.

"Denial of access", contamination to an area, including any structures thereon, which poses a health risk to humans, animals or plants and which precludes the safe use of such area until the contaminant becomes inactive, decays or is removed.

"Destructive or incendiary device or substance", an explosive, article or device designed or adapted to cause physical harm to persons or property by means of fire, explosion, deflagration or detonation and consisting of substance capable of being ignited, whether or not contrived to ignite or explode automatically.

"Element", a substance that is made entirely from 1 type of atom.

"Explosive", any element, compound or mixture that is manufactured, designed or used to produce an explosion and that contains an oxidizer, fuel or other ingredient, in such proportion, quantity or packing that an ignition by fire, friction, concussion, percussion or detonation of the element or of any part of the compound or mixture may cause such a sudden generation of highly heated gases that the resultant gaseous pressures, release of heat or fragmentation is capable of producing destructive effects on contiguous objects or of destroying life or causing bodily harm including, but not limited to, all material which is classified as division 1.1, 1.2, 1.3, 1.4, 1.5 or 1.6 explosives by the United States Department of Transportation or listed pursuant to 18 USC 841(d) and 27 CFR 555.23. Explosive shall not include a pyrotechnic, small arms ammunition, small arms ammunition primers, smokeless powder weighing less than 50 pounds and black powder weighing less than 5 pounds, unless possessed or used for an illegal purpose.

"Hoax explosive", "hoax destructive or incendiary device or substance" or "hoax chemical, biological or nuclear weapon", any device, article or substance that would cause a person to reasonably believe that such device, article or substance is: (i) an explosive; (ii) a destructive or incendiary device or substance; or (iii) a chemical, biological or nuclear weapon, harmful radioactive substance or poison capable of causing bodily injury which is actually an inoperable facsimile.

"Nuclear weapon", a device designed for the purpose of causing bodily injury, death or denial of access through the release of radiation or radiological material either by propagation of nuclear fission or by means of any other energy source.

"Oxidizer", a substance that yields oxygen readily to stimulate the combustion of organic matter or other fuel.

"Pyrotechnic", any commercially manufactured combustible or explosive composition or manufactured article designed and prepared for the purpose of producing an audible effect or a visible display and regulated by chapter 148 including, but not limited to: (i) fireworks, firecrackers; (ii) flares, fuses and torpedoes, so-called, and similar signaling devices.

"Small arms ammunition", any shotgun, rifle, pistol, or revolver cartridge, and cartridges for propellant-actuated power devices and industrial guns.

"Smokeless powder", a rapid-burning solid material containing nitrocellulose used as a propellant.

Added St.2010, c. 160, § 6, eff. July 15, 2010.

§ 102. Possession or control of incendiary device or material; possession of hoax device or material; penalty

(a) Whoever, without lawful authority, has in his possession or under his control:

(i) any substance, material, article, explosive or ingredient which, alone or in combination, could be used to make a destructive or incendiary device or substance and who intends to make a destructive or incendiary device or substance; or

(ii) any substance, material, article, explosive or ingredient which, alone or in combination, could be used to make a chemical, biological or nuclear weapon and who intends to make a chemical, biological or nuclear weapon, shall be punished by imprisonment in the house of correction for not more than 2 and one-half years or in state prison for not less than 5 years nor more than 10 years or by a fine of not more than $25,000, or by both such fine and imprisonment. It shall not be a defense to a violation of this subsection that the defendant did not possess or have under his control every substance, material, article, explosive or ingredient, or combination thereof, required to make a complete and functional destructive or incendiary device or substance or chemical, biological or nuclear weapon.

(b) Whoever, without lawful authority, has in his possession or uses or places, or causes another to knowingly or unknowingly possess, use or place, any hoax explosive, hoax destructive or incendiary device or substance or any hoax chemical, biological or nuclear weapon, with the intent that such hoax explosive, device or substance or weapon be used to cause anxiety, unrest, fear or personal discomfort to any person or group of persons, shall be punished by imprisonment in the house of correction for not more than 2 and one-half years or by imprisonment in the state prison for not more than 5 years or by a fine of not more than $10,000, or by both such fine and imprisonment.

(c) Whoever, without lawful authority, has in his possession or under his control any explosive or any destructive or incendiary device or substance shall be punished by imprisonment for not more than 2 and one-half years in the house of correction or for not less than 10 years nor more than 20 years in the state prison or by a fine of not more than $25,000, or by both such fine and imprisonment.

Added by St.2010, c. 160, § 6, eff. July 15, 2010.

§ 102A. Throwing, secreting, launching or placing of incendiary device; intent; punishment

Whoever, without lawful authority, secretes, throws, launches or otherwise places an explosive or a destructive or incendiary device or substance with the intent: (i) to cause fear, panic or apprehension in any person; or (ii) to ignite, explode or discharge such explosive or such destructive or incendiary device or substance; or (iii) to release or discharge any chemical, biological or nuclear weapon, shall be punished by imprisonment for not more than 2 and one-half years in the house of correction or for not less than 10 years nor more than 25 years in the state prison or by a fine of not more than $25,000, or by both such fine and imprisonment.

Added by St.2010, c. 160, § 6, eff. July 15, 2010.

§ 102A½. Repealed, 2010, 160, Sec. 6

§ 102B. Malicious explosion

Whoever, without lawful authority, willfully discharges, ignites or explodes any destructive or incendiary device or substance shall be punished by imprisonment in the state prison by not less than 15 years nor more than 25 years or by a fine of $50,000 or by both such fine and imprisonment.

Added by St.2010, c. 160, § 6, eff. July 15, 2010.

§ 102C. Biological, chemical, or nuclear weapon or delivery system; possession; punishment

Whoever, without lawful authority, knowingly develops, produces, stockpiles, acquires, transports, possesses, controls, places, secretes or uses any biological, chemical or nuclear weapon or delivery system, with the intent to cause death, bodily injury or property damage, shall be punished by imprisonment in the house of correction for not more than 2 and one-half years or by imprisonment in the state prison for not more than 25 years or by a fine of not more than $50,000, or by both such fine and imprisonment.

Added by St.2010, c. 160, § 6, eff. July 15, 2010. Amended by St.2010, c. 359, § 33, eff. Oct. 15, 2010.

§ 102D. Notice of seizure of explosive or incendiary device resulting from a violation of Secs. 102 to 102C; restitution

(a) Notice of the seizure of an explosive, destructive or incendiary device or substance, any weapon or the component parts thereof, in violation of any provision of section 102 to 102C, inclusive, shall be sent forthwith to the state fire marshal by the officer who made such seizure. The marshal may, in his sole discretion, render safe or direct any other official to assist him in rendering safe any item so seized, if such item cannot be safely kept pending trial. Upon final conviction of such person, such explosive, device, substance or weapon, or component parts thereof, shall be adjudged forfeited to the commonwealth and be disposed of by the marshal or his authorized representative.

(b) Upon conviction for a violation of sections 102 to 102C, inclusive, the court shall conduct a hearing to ascertain the extent of costs incurred, damages and financial loss suffered by local, county or state public safety agencies and the amount of property damage caused as a result of the violation of this section, if any. A person found guilty of violating sections 102 to 102C, inclusive, shall, in all cases, in addition to any other punishment, be ordered to make restitution to the local, county or state government for any costs incurred, damages and financial loss sustained as a result of the commission of such offense. Restitution shall be imposed in addition to incarceration or fine; provided, however, that the court shall consider the defendant's present and future ability to pay in its determinations regarding a fine. In determining the amount, time and method of payment of restitution, the court shall consider the financial resources of the defendant and the burden restitution will impose on the defendant.

Added by St.2010, c. 160, § 6, eff. July 15, 2010.

§ 103. Oil of vitriol, or other substances; throwing into building or vessel

Whoever wilfully, intentionally and without right throws into, against or upon a dwelling house, office, shop or other building, or vessel, or puts or places therein or thereon oil of vitriol, coal tar or other noxious or filthy substance, with intent unlawfully to injure, deface or defile such dwelling house, office, shop, building or vessel, or any property therein, shall be punished by imprisonment in the state prison for not more than five years or in jail for not more than two and one half years or by a fine of not more than three hundred dollars.

Historical and Statutory Notes

St.1851, c. 129, § 3.
G.S.1860, c. 161, § 70.
P.S.1882, c. 203, § 82.
St.1901, c. 268, § 4.
R.L.1902, c. 208, § 87.
St.1918, c. 257, § 464.
St.1919, c. 5.
St.1920, c. 2.

§ 104. Buildings; destruction or injury

Whoever wilfully, intentionally and without right destroys, injures, defaces or mars a dwelling house or other building, whether upon the inside or outside, shall be punished by imprisonment for not more than two months or by a fine of not more than fifty dollars.

Historical and Statutory Notes

St.1862, c. 160.
P.S.1882, c. 203, § 83.
St.1901, c. 268, § 5.
R.L.1902, c. 208, § 88.

§ 104A. Goal posts; penalty for destruction

Whoever wilfully and without right destroys, injures or removes a goal post on a football field shall be punished by a fine of not less than fifty nor more than two hundred dollars.

Added by St.1960, c. 610.

§ 104B. Research animals; unauthorized removal

Whoever enters any premises in which animals are being housed or used in research by a research institution and, without authority, injures, damages, commits any trespass upon, removes or carries away any data, equipment, facility or property or injures, damages, removes, carries away, interferes with or releases any animal shall, if such injury, damage, trespass, removal, carrying away, interference or release is malicious and wilful, be punished by imprisonment in the state prison for not more than ten years or by a fine of not more than twenty-five thousand dollars and imprisonment in a jail or house of correction for not more than two and one-half years; or if such injury, damage, trespass, removal, carrying away, interference or release is wilful but not malicious, be punished by imprisonment in the state prison for not more than five years or by a fine of not more than ten thousand dollars and imprisonment in a jail or house of correction for not more than two and one-half years.

Added by St.1988, c. 224.

§ 105. Stone walls or fences; unauthorized removal

Whoever wilfully and without right pulls down or removes any portion of a stone wall or fence which is erected or maintained for the purpose of enclosing land shall be punished by a fine of not more than ten dollars. Natural resource officers and deputy natural resource officers of the office of the secretary of the executive office of environmental affairs, may arrest without a warrant any person found violating this section.

Amended by St.1975, c. 706, § 300.

Historical and Statutory Notes

St.1901, c. 298.
R.L.1902, c. 208, § 91.
St.1911, c. 173.
St.1919, c. 350, § 40.

§ 106. Ice ponds; injury

Whoever wilfully, intentionally and without right or license, cuts, injures, mars or otherwise damages or destroys ice upon waters from which ice is or may be taken as an article of merchandise, whereby the taking thereof is hindered or the value thereof diminished for that purpose, shall be punished by a fine of not more than one hundred dollars.

Historical and Statutory Notes

St.1850, c. 114.
G.S.1860, c. 161, § 73.
P.S.1882, c. 203, § 86.
St.1901, c. 268, § 6.
R.L.1902, c. 208, § 92.

§ 107. Bridge or canal; injury

Whoever wilfully, intentionally and without right breaks down, injures, removes or destroys a public bridge, or a lock, culvert or embankment of a canal, or wilfully, intentionally and without right makes an aperture or breach in such embankment with intent to destroy or injure the same, shall be punished by imprisonment in the state prison for not more than five years or by a fine of not more than five hundred dollars and imprisonment in jail for not more than two years.

Historical and Statutory Notes

R.S.1836, c. 126, § 41.
G.S.1860, c. 161, § 74.
P.S.1882, c. 203, § 87.
St.1901, c. 268, § 1.
R.L.1902, c. 208, § 93.

§ 108. Vessel; destruction to injure or defraud owner or insurer; punishment; restitution

Whoever casts away, burns, sinks or otherwise destroys a ship or vessel, with intent to injure or defraud an owner thereof, or of any property laden on board the same, or an insurer of such ship, vessel or property, or of any part thereof, shall be punished by imprisonment in the state prison for not more than ten years or imprisonment in a jail for not more than two and one-half years.

A person found guilty of violating this section shall, in addition to any other punishment, be ordered to make restitution to the insurer or owner for any financial loss sustained as a result of the commission of the crime except as hereinafter provided. Restitution shall be imposed in addition to incarceration or fine. In the case of an indigent defendant, the court may determine that the interests of the victim and of justice would not be served by ordering such restitution. In such case, the court shall make specific written findings of the evidence presented which militated against the imposition of restitution.

The court shall, after conviction, conduct an evidentiary hearing to ascertain the extent of the damages or financial loss suffered as a result of the defendant's crime and may then determine the amount and method of restitution. In so determining, the court shall consider the financial resources of the defendant and the burden restitution will impose on the defendant. The defendant's present and future ability to make such restitution shall be considered.

A defendant ordered to make restitution may petition the court for remission from any payment of restitution or from any unpaid portion thereof. If the court finds that the payment of restitution due will impose an undue financial hardship on the defendant or his family, the court may grant remission from any payment of restitution or modify the time and method of payment.

If a defendant who is required to make restitution defaults in any payment of restitution or installment thereof, the court may hold him in contempt unless said defendant has made a good faith effort to make restitution. If the defendant has made such good faith effort, the court may, upon motion of the defendant, modify the order requiring restitution by:

(a) providing for additional time to make any payment in restitution;

(b) reducing the amount of any payment in restitution or installment thereof;

(c) granting a remission from any payment of restitution or part thereof.

Restitution shall not be authorized to a party whom the court determines to be aggrieved, without such party's consent.

Amended by St.1985, c. 659, §§ 1, 2.

Historical and Statutory Notes

St.1802, c. 136, § 1.
St.1824, c. 137, § 1.
R.S.1836, c. 126, § 35.
G.S.1860, c. 161, § 76.
P.S.1882, c. 203, § 89.
R.L.1902, c. 208, § 94.

§ 109. Vessel; fitting out with intent to destroy

Whoever lades, equips or fits out, or assists in lading, equipping or fitting out, a ship or vessel, with intent that it shall be wilfully cast away, burnt, sunk or otherwise destroyed, and with intent to injure or defraud an owner or insurer of such ship or vessel, or of any property laden on board the same, shall be punished by imprisonment in the state prison for not more than twenty years or by a fine of not more than five thousand dollars and imprisonment in jail for not more than two and one half years.

Historical and Statutory Notes

St.1802, c. 136, § 2.
St.1824, c. 137, § 2.
R.S.1836, c. 126, § 36.
G.S.1860, c. 161, § 77.
P.S.1882, c. 203, § 90.
R.L.1902, c. 208, § 95.
St.1914, c. 635.
St.1918, c. 257, § 464.
St.1919, c. 5.
St.1920, c. 2.

§ 110. False invoice of cargo; intent to defraud insurer

An owner of a ship or vessel, or of property laden or pretended to be laden on board the same, or any other person concerned in the lading or fitting out of a ship or vessel, who makes out or exhibits, or causes to be made out or exhibited, a false or fraudulent invoice, bill of lading, bill or parcels or other false estimates of any goods or property laden or pretended to be laden on board such ship or vessel, with intent to injure or defraud an insurer of such ship, vessel or property or of any part thereof, shall be punished by imprisonment in the state prison for not more than ten years or by a fine of not more than five thousand dollars and imprisonment in jail for not more than two years.

Historical and Statutory Notes

St.1802, c. 136, § 3.
R.S.1836, c. 126, § 37.
G.S.1860, c. 161, § 78.
P.S.1882, c. 203, § 91.
R.L.1902, c. 208, § 96.

§ 111. False affidavit or protest; penalty

A master, officer or mariner of a ship or vessel who makes or causes to be made or swears to a false affidavit or protest, or an owner of or other person concerned in such ship or vessel, or the owner of or the person concerned in the goods or property laden on board the same, who procures such false affidavit or protest to be made, or exhibits the same, with intent to injure, deceive or defraud an insurer of such ship or vessel, or of any goods or property laden on board the same, shall be punished by imprisonment in the state prison for not more than ten years or by a fine of not more than five thousand dollars and imprisonment in jail for not more than two years.

Historical and Statutory Notes

St.1802, c. 136, § 4.
R.S.1836, c. 126, § 38.
G.S.1860, c. 161, § 79.
P.S.1882, c. 203, § 92.
R.L.1902, c. 208, § 97.

§ 111A. Insurance policies; penalty for fraudulent claims

Whoever, in connection with or in support of any claim under any policy of insurance issued by any company, as defined in section one of chapter one hundred and seventy-five, and with intent to injure, defraud or deceive such company, presents to it, or aids or abets in or procures the presentation to it of, any notice, statement, proof of loss, bill of lading, bill of parcels, invoice, schedule, account or other written document, whether or not the same is under oath or is required or authorized by law or by the terms of such policy, knowing that such notice, statement, proof of loss, bill of lading, bill of parcels, invoice, schedule, account or other written document contains any false or fraudulent statement or representation of any fact or thing material to such claim, or whoever with intent as aforesaid makes, prepares or subscribes, or aids or abets in or procures the making, preparation or subscription of, any such notice, statement, proof of loss, bill of lading, bill of parcels, invoice, schedule, account or other written document intended to be presented to any such company in connection with or in support of any claim under any such policy issued by it knowing that such notice, statement, proof of loss, bill of lading, bill of parcels, invoice, schedule, account or other written document contains any false or fraudulent statement or representation as aforesaid, shall, except as provided in section one hundred and ten or one hundred and eleven, be punished by imprisonment in the state prison for not more than five years or by imprisonment in jail for not less than six months nor more than two and one half years or by a fine of not less than $500 nor more than $10,000, or by both such fine and imprisonment in jail.

Amended by St.1982, c. 150; St.2002, c. 138, § 1.

Historical and Statutory Notes

St.1926, c. 198.

§ 111B. Motor vehicle insurance policies; penalty for fraudulent claims

Whoever, in connection with or in support of any application for or claim under any motor vehicle, theft or comprehensive insurance policy issued by an insurer, and with intent to injure, defraud or deceive such insurer knowingly presents to it, or aids or abets in or procures the presentation to it of, any notice, statement, or proof of loss, whether or not the same is under oath or is required or authorized by law or the terms of such policy, knowing that such notice, statement or proof of loss contains any false or fraudulent statement or representation of any fact or thing material to such application or claim, shall be punished by imprisonment in the state prison for not more than 5 years or by imprisonment in the house of correction for not less than 6 months nor more than 2½ years or by a fine of not less than $1,000 nor more than $10,000, or by both such fine and imprisonment.

A person licensed as a motor vehicle damage appraiser pursuant to section eight G of chapter twenty-six or registered as a motor vehicle repair shop pursuant to chapter one hundred A who violates this section, by fraudulently inflating an appraisal of damage to a motor vehicle or the charges for repairing a damaged motor vehicle or otherwise, shall be punished by the additional penalty of revocation of such license or registration for a period not to exceed two years.

The court shall, after conviction, conduct an evidentiary hearing to ascertain the extent of the damages or financial loss suffered as a result of the defendant's crime. A person found guilty of violating this section shall, in all cases, upon conviction, in addition to any other punishment, be ordered to make restitution to the insurer for any financial loss sustained as a result of the commission of the crime; provided, however, that restitution shall not be ordered to a party whom the court determines to be aggrieved without that party's consent. Restitution shall be imposed in addition to incarceration or fine, and not in lieu thereof; provided, however, the court shall consider the defendant's present and future ability to pay in its determinations regarding a fine; provided, further, that, whenever possible subject to the constraints of this paragraph and the first paragraph of this section, the amount of a fine imposed for a violation of this section shall equal twice the amount of damages or financial loss suffered as a result of the defendant's crime.

In determining the amount, time and method of payment of restitution, the court shall consider the financial resources of the defendant and the burden restitution will impose on the defendant. Upon a real or impending change in financial circumstances, a defendant ordered to pay restitution may petition the court for a modification of the amount, time or method of payment of restitution. If the court finds that because of any such change the payment of restitution will impose an undue financial hardship on the defendant or his family, the court may modify the amount, time or method of payment, but may not grant complete remission from payment of restitution.

If a defendant who is required to make restitution defaults in any payment of restitution or installment thereof, the court shall hold him in contempt unless said defendant has made a good faith effort to pay such restitution. If said defendant has made a good faith effort to pay such restitution, the court may modify the amount, time or method of payment, but may not grant complete remission from payment of restitution.

Added by St.1980, c. 463, § 5. Amended by St.1988, c. 273, § 60; St.2002, c. 138, § 2.

§ 111C. Fraudulently obtaining benefits under insurance contract; runners; punishment

(a) As used in this section, the following words shall have the following meanings:—

"Provider", an attorney, a health care professional licensed pursuant to chapter 112, an owner or operator of a health care practice or facility, any person who creates the impression that he or his practice or facility can provide legal or health care services, or any person employed or acting on behalf of any of the aforementioned persons.

"Public media", telephone directories, professional directories, newspapers and other periodicals, radio and television, billboards and mailed or electronically transmitted written communications that do not involve in-person contact with a specific prospective client, patient or customer.

"Runner", a person who, for a pecuniary benefit, procures or attempts to procure a client, patient or customer at the direction of, request of, or in cooperation with a provider whose purpose is to seek to fraudulently obtain benefits under a contract of insurance or fraudulently assert a claim against an insured or an insurance carrier for providing services to the client, patient or customer. "Runner" shall not include a person who procures or attempts to procure clients, patients or customers for a provider through public media or a person who refers clients, patients or customers to a provider as otherwise authorized by law.

(b) Whoever knowingly acts as a runner or uses, solicits, directs, hires or employs another to act as a runner for the purpose of defrauding an insured or an insurance carrier shall be punished by imprisonment in the state prison for not more than 5 years, by imprisonment in a jail or house of correction for not less than 6 months nor more than 2½ years or by a fine of not less than $1,000 nor more than $4,000.

Added by St.2004, c. 464, § 7, eff. Jan. 3, 2005.

§ 112. Domestic animals; malicious killing or injury

Whoever wilfully and maliciously kills, maims or disfigures any horse, cattle or other animal of another person, or wilfully and maliciously administers or exposes poison with intent that it shall be taken or swallowed by any such animal, shall be punished by imprisonment in the state prison for not more than five years or by imprisonment in the house of correction for not more than 2½ years or by a fine of not more than $2,500, or by both such fine and imprisonment.

Amended by St.1986, c. 157; St.2004, c. 319, § 3, eff. Nov. 17, 2004.

Historical and Statutory Notes

St.1804, c. 131, § 4.
R.S.1836, c. 126, § 39.
G.S.1860, c. 161, § 80.
P.S.1882, c. 203, § 93.
R.L.1902, c. 208, § 98.

§ 113. Timber, wood and shrubs; wilful cutting and destruction on land of another

Whoever wilfully cuts down or destroys timber or wood standing or growing on the land of another, or carries away any kind of timber or wood cut down or lying on such land, or digs up or carries away stone, ore, gravel, clay, sand, turf or mould from such land, or roots, nuts, berries, grapes or fruit of any kind or any plant there being, or cuts down or carries away sedge, grass, hay or any kind of corn, standing, growing or being on such land, or cuts or takes therefrom any ferns, flowers or shrubs, or carries away from a wharf or landing place any goods in which he has no interest or property, without the license of the owner thereof, shall be punished by imprisonment for not more than six months or by a fine of not more than five hundred dollars; and if the offence is committed on Sunday, or in disguise, or secretly in the night time, the imprisonment shall not be for less than five days nor the fine less than five dollars.

Historical and Statutory Notes

St.1698, c. 7, §§ 1, 2.
St.1723–4, c. 10, §§ 1, 2.
St.1726–7, c. 3, §§ 1, 2.
St.1727, c. 8.
St.1785, c. 28, § 1.
St.1818, c. 3, §§ 2, 4.
R.S.1836, c. 126, §§ 44, 45.
G.S.1860, c. 161, §§ 81, 84.
St.1868, c. 321.
P.S.1882, c. 203, §§ 94, 97.
R.L.1902, c. 208, § 99.
St.1904, c. 444, § 1.

§ 114. Trees and fences; malicious injury

Whoever wilfully and maliciously or wantonly breaks glass in a building which is not his own, or whoever wilfully and maliciously breaks down, injures, mars or defaces a fence belonging to or enclosing land which is not his own, or wilfully and maliciously throws down or opens a gate, bars or fence, and leaves the same down or open, or maliciously and injuriously severs from the freehold of another any produce thereof or anything attached thereto, shall be punished by imprisonment for not more than six months or by a fine of not more than five hundred dollars.

Historical and Statutory Notes

St.1698, c. 7, § 1.
St.1785, c. 28, § 1.
St.1829, c. 63.
R.S.1836, c. 126, § 42.
G.S.1860, c. 161, § 82.
St.1868, c. 321.
P.S.1882, c. 203, § 95.
R.L.1902, c. 208, § 100.
St.1902, c. 544, § 30.

§ 115. Trespass in orchards and gardens

Whoever wilfully and maliciously enters an orchard, nursery, garden or cranberry meadow, and takes away, mutilates or destroys a tree, shrub or vine, or steals, takes and carries away any fruit or flower, without the consent of the owner thereof, shall be punished by a fine of not more than five hundred dollars or by imprisonment for not more than six months.

Historical and Statutory Notes

C.L. c. 13, § 1.
St.1698, c. 7, § 1.
St.1855, c. 457.
G.S.1860, c. 161, § 83.
St.1868, c. 321.
P.S.1882, c. 203, § 96.
R.L.1902, c. 208, § 105.

§ 116. Repealed, 1962, 172

§ 116A. Protection of certain flowers

No person shall pull up or dig up the plant of a wild azalea, wild orchid or cardinal flower (lobelia cardinalis), or any part thereof, or injure any such plant or any part thereof except in so far as is reasonably necessary in procuring the flower therefrom, within the limits of any state highway or any other public way or place, or upon the land of another person without written authority from him, and no person shall buy or sell, or offer or expose for sale, any such flower, or the whole or any part of the plant thereof, knowing, or having reasonable cause to believe, that in procuring such flower or plant the foregoing provisions have been violated. Violation of any provision of this section shall be punished by a fine of not more than five dollars.

Added by St.1935, c. 116.

§ 117. Orchards and gardens; entry with intent to injure or destroy

Whoever wilfully, intentionally and without right enters upon the orchard, garden or other improved land of another, with intent to cut, take, carry away, destroy or injure the trees, grain, grass, hay, fruit or vegetables there growing or being, shall be punished by imprisonment for not more than six months or by a fine of not more than five hundred dollars; and if the offence is committed on Sunday, or in disguise, or secretly in the night time, the imprisonment shall not be for less than five days nor the fine less than five dollars.

Historical and Statutory Notes

R.S.1836, c. 126, § 45.
G.S.1860, c. 161, § 84.
St.1868, c. 321.
P.S.1882, c. 203, § 97.
R.L.1902, c. 208, § 106.
St.1902, c. 544, § 33.

§ 118. Domestic animals; trespass on land

Whoever, having the charge or custody of sheep, goats, cattle, horses, swine or fowl, wilfully suffers or permits them to enter or remain on or pass over any orchard, garden, mowing land or other improved or enclosed land of another, after being forbidden so to do in writing or by notice posted thereon by the owner or occupant thereof, or by the authorized agent of such owner or occupant, shall be punished by a fine of not more than ten dollars.

Historical and Statutory Notes

St.1878, c. 168.
St.1879, c. 70.
P.S.1882, c. 203, § 98.
R.L.1902, c. 208, § 107.

§ 119. Pests; bringing into state; penalty; exception

Whoever knowingly brings into the commonwealth, or transports from one town to another therein, any pest referred to in section eleven or twenty-five of chapter one hundred and thirty-two, or the eggs, nests, larvae or pupae thereof, except when engaged in research work for the commonwealth or for the United States department of agriculture, and for the purpose of suppressing such pests, or whoever knowingly evades the requirements of a quarantine regulation duly established under any provision of said chapter one hundred and thirty-two, shall be punished by fine of not more than two hundred dollars, or imprisonment for not more than two months, or both.

Amended by St.1948, c. 660, § 25; St.1949, c. 761, § 14.

Historical and Statutory Notes

St.1890, c. 95, § 7.
St.1891, c. 210, § 7.
St.1898, c. 544, § 3.
R.L.1902, c. 208, § 108.

§ 120. Entry upon private property after being forbidden as trespass; prima facie evidence; penalties; arrest; tenants or occupants excepted

Whoever, without right enters or remains in or upon the dwelling house, buildings, boats or improved or enclosed land, wharf, or pier of another, or enters or remains in a school bus, as defined in section 1 of chapter 90, after having been forbidden so to do by the person who has lawful control of said premises, whether directly or by notice posted thereon, or in violation of a court order pursuant to section thirty-four B of chapter two hundred and eight or section three or four of chapter two hundred and nine A, shall be punished by a fine of not more than one hundred dollars or by imprisonment for not more than thirty days or both such fine and imprisonment. Proof that a court has given notice of such a court order to the alleged offender shall be prima facie evidence that the notice requirement of this section has been met. A person who is found committing such trespass may be arrested by a sheriff, deputy sheriff, constable or police officer and kept in custody in a convenient place, not more than twenty-four hours, Sunday excepted, until a complaint can be made against him for the offence, and he be taken upon a warrant issued upon such complaint.

This section shall not apply to tenants or occupants of residential premises who, having rightfully entered said premises at the commencement of the tenancy or occupancy, remain therein after such tenancy or occupancy has been or is alleged to have been terminated. The owner or landlord of said premises may recover possession thereof only through appropriate civil proceedings.

Amended by St.1969, c. 463, § 2; St.1974, c. 109; St.1978, c. 447, § 3; St.1983, c. 678, § 6; St.1999, c. 102.

Historical and Statutory Notes

St.1862, c. 89.
St.1876, c. 181.
P.S.1882, c. 203, §§ 99, 100.
St.1890, c. 410.
R.L.1902, c. 208, § 109.
St.1929, c. 109.
St.1931, c. 426, § 45.

§ 120A. Motor vehicle; parking on private way; prosecution; evidence

In any prosecution for committing the crime of trespass by parking a motor vehicle upon a private way or upon improved or enclosed land, proof that the defendant named in the complaint was at the time of such parking the registered owner of such vehicle shall be prima facie evidence that the defendant was the person who parked such vehicle upon such way or land at such time.

Added by St.1955, c. 269.

§ 120B. Entry on land by abutting property owners not constituting trespass

Whoever, being the owner of land abutting that of another, the building or buildings on which are so close to the land of such other person as to require an entry on said abutting land for the purpose of maintaining or repairing said building or buildings in order to prevent waste, shall not be deemed guilty of trespass or liable civilly for damages, provided that such entry is made expeditiously and in the exercise of due care and that no damage is caused by such entry to the land or buildings of said abutting owner. Before such entry said owner shall notify the chief or other officer in charge of the police department of the city or town in which the land is located that he has requested permission to enter on adjoining land from the owner or occupants thereof for the purpose of maintaining or repairing a building or buildings and that such permission has been refused, and that he intends to enter under the provisions of this section. Before entering on said land, said owner shall post bond with the chief of police in the amount of one thousand dollars to protect the adjoining land owner from damage caused by said entry. No person so entering on land of another shall store material or tools thereon for more than eight hours in any one day nor shall he continue to enter thereon for more than thirty days in the aggregate in any calendar year. After said entry, said owner shall in all respects restore said adjoining land to the condition in which it was prior to said entry.

Added by St.1971, c. 1039.

§ 120C. Entry upon adjoining lands by surveyors not constituting trespass

Whenever a land surveyor registered under chapter one hundred and twelve deems it reasonably necessary to enter upon adjoining lands to make surveys of any description included under "Practice of land surveying", as defined in section eighty-one D of said chapter one hundred and twelve, for any private person, excluding any public authority, public utility or railroad, the land surveyor or his authorized agents or employees may, after reasonable notice, enter upon lands, waters and premises, not including buildings, in the commonwealth, within a reasonable distance from the property line of the land being surveyed, and such entry shall not be deemed a trespass. Nothing in this act shall relieve a land surveyor of liability for damage caused by entry to adjoining property, by himself or his agents or employees.

Added by St.1972, c. 158.

§ 120D. Removal of motor vehicles from private ways or property; penalties; liability for removal and storage charges; release of vehicle

No person shall remove a motor vehicle which is parked or standing on a private way or upon improved or enclosed property unless the operator of such vehicle has been forbidden so to park or stand, either directly or by posted notice, by the person who has lawful control of such way or property. No vehicle shall be removed from such way or property without the consent of the owner of such vehicle unless the person who has lawful control of such way or property shall have notified the chief of police or his designee in a city or town, or, in the city of Boston the police commissioner, or a person from time to time designated by said police commissioner, that such vehicle is to be removed. Such notification shall be made before any such vehicle shall be removed, and shall be in writing unless otherwise specified by such chief of police or police commissioner and shall include the address from which the vehicle is to be removed, the address to which the vehicle is to be removed, the registration number of the vehicle, the name of the person in lawful control of the way or property from which such vehicle is being removed, and the name of the person or company or other business entity removing the vehicle. Vehicles so removed shall be stored in a convenient location. Neither the city or town, nor its chief of police or police commissioner or his designee, shall be liable for any damages incurred during the removal or storage of any such vehicle removed under this section. Any person who, without notifying the chief of police or his designee, or the police commissioner or his designee, or without obtaining the consent of the owner, removes a vehicle from a private way or from improved or enclosed property as aforesaid, shall, in addition to any other penalty of law, be punished by a fine of not more than one hundred dollars. The employer of such person if any, shall also be punished by a fine of not more than one hundred dollars.

Any person who purports to authorize the removal of a vehicle from a way or property as aforesaid without having fully complied with the provision of this section shall be punished by a fine of not more than one hundred dollars.

In addition to any other penalty provided by law, the registered owner of a vehicle illegally parked or standing on a private way or upon improved or enclosed property shall be liable for charges for the removal and storage of such vehicle; provided, however, that the liability so imposed shall not exceed the following, and provided, further, that the vehicle has been removed after compliance with the provisions of this section:

(1) the maximum amount for towing or transportation of motor vehicles established by the department of telecommunications and energy for motor vehicles towed away when such towing is ordered by the police or other public authority under the provisions of section six B of chapter one hundred and fifty-nine B; and

(2) the maximum charge for storage of non-commercial passenger motor vehicles with a maximum capacity of nine persons, shall be not more than the maximum storage charge allowed under the provisions of said section six B of said chapter one hundred and fifty-nine B.

A person lawfully holding a vehicle removed under the provisions of this section may hold such vehicle until the registered owner pays the removal and storage charges.

Any person who is called to remove by towing a vehicle illegally parked or standing on a private way or upon improved or enclosed property may, at his discretion, if the owner appears to remove said vehicle before the towing is completed, charge said owner one half of the fee usually charged for such towing.

Any person who removes a vehicle illegally parked or standing on a private way or upon improved or enclosed property, or holds such a vehicle after its removal, and who has not complied in full with the provisions of this section, shall release such vehicle to its owner without assessing any charges for its removal or storage.

Added by St.1974, c. 537, § 1. Amended by St.1982, c. 333, § 2; St.1990, c. 169; St.1997, c. 164, § 288.

§ 120E. Obstructing entry to or departure from medical facilities; penalties; injunctive relief

As used in this section, the following words shall have the following meanings:—

"Medical facility", any medical office, medical clinic, medical laboratory, or hospital.

"Notice", (i) receipt of or awareness of the contents of a court order prohibiting blocking of a medical facility; (ii) oral request by an authorized representative of a medical facility, or law enforcement official to refrain from obstructing access to a medical facility; or (iii) written posted notice outside the entrance to a medical facility to refrain from obstructing access to a medical facility.

Whoever knowingly obstructs entry to or departure from any medical facility or who enters or remains in any medical facility so as to impede the provision of medical services, after notice to refrain from such obstruction or interference, shall be punished for the first offense by a fine of not more than one thousand dollars or not more than six months in jail or a house of correction or both, and for each subsequent violation of this section by a fine of not less than five hundred dollars and not more than five thousand dollars or not more than two and one-half years in jail or a house of correction or both. These penalties shall be in addition to any penalties imposed for violation of a court order.

A person who knowingly obstructs entry to or departure from such medical facility or who enters or remains in such facility so as to impede the provision of medical services after notice to refrain from such obstruction or interference, may be arrested by a sheriff, deputy sheriff, constable, or police officer.

Any medical facility whose rights to provide services under the provisions of this section have been violated or which has reason to believe that any person or entity is about to engage in conduct proscribed herein may commence a civil action for injunctive and other equitable relief, including the award of compensatory and exemplary damages. Said civil action shall be instituted either in superior court for the county in which the conduct complained of occurred, or in the superior court for the county in which any person or entity complained of resides or has a principal place of business. An aggrieved facility which prevails in an action authorized by this paragraph, in addition to other damages, shall be entitled to an award of the costs of the litigation and reasonable attorney's fees in an amount to be fixed by the court.

Nothing herein shall be construed to interfere with any rights provided by chapter one hundred and fifty A or by the federal Labor–Management Act of 1947 or other rights to engage in peaceful picketing which does not obstruct entry or departure.

Added by St.1993, c. 218.

§ 120E½. Reproductive health care facilities

(a) For the purposes of this section, "reproductive health care facility" means a place, other than within or upon the grounds of a hospital, where abortions are offered or performed.

(b) No person shall knowingly enter or remain on a public way or sidewalk adjacent to a reproductive health care facility within a radius of 35 feet of any portion of an entrance, exit or driveway of a reproductive health care facility or within the area within a rectangle created by extending the outside boundaries of any entrance, exit or driveway of a reproductive health care facility in straight lines to the point where such lines intersect the sideline of the street in front of such entrance, exit or driveway. This subsection shall not apply to the following:—

(1) persons entering or leaving such facility;

(2) employees or agents of such facility acting within the scope of their employment;

(3) law enforcement, ambulance, firefighting, construction, utilities, public works and other municipal agents acting within the scope of their employment; and

(4) persons using the public sidewalk or street right-of-way adjacent to such facility solely for the purpose of reaching a destination other than such facility.

(c) The provisions of subsection (b) shall only take effect during a facility's business hours and if the area contained within the radius and rectangle described in said subsection (b) is clearly marked and posted.

(d) Whoever knowingly violates this section shall be punished, for the first offense, by a fine of not more than $500 or not more than three months in a jail or house of correction, or by both such fine and imprisonment, and for each subsequent offense, by a fine of not less than $500 and not more than $5,000 or not more than two and one-half years in a jail or house of correction, or both such fine and imprisonment. A person who knowingly violates this section may be arrested without a warrant by a sheriff, deputy sheriff or police officer if that sheriff, deputy sheriff, or police officer observes that person violating this section.

(e) Any person who knowingly obstructs, detains, hinders, impedes or blocks another person's entry to or exit from a reproductive health care facility shall be punished, for the first offense, by a fine of not more than $500 or not more than three months in a jail or house of correction, or by both such fine and imprisonment, and for each subsequent offense, by a fine of not less than $500 nor more than $5,000 or not more than two and one-half years in a jail or house of correction, or by both such fine and imprisonment. A person who knowingly violates this provision may be arrested without a warrant by a sheriff, deputy sheriff or police officer.

(f) A reproductive health care facility or a person whose rights to provide or obtain reproductive health care services have been violated or interfered with by a violation of this section or any person whose rights to express their views, assemble or pray near a reproductive health care facility have been violated or interfered with may commence a civil action for equitable relief. The civil action shall be commenced either in the superior court for the county in which the conduct complained of occurred, or in the superior court for the county in which any person or entity complained of resides or has a principal place of business.

Added by St.2000, c. 217, § 2. Amended by St.2007, c. 155, §§ 1, 2, eff. Nov. 13, 2007.

§ 120F. Unauthorized access to computer system; penalties

Whoever, without authorization, knowingly accesses a computer system by any means, or after gaining access to a computer system by any means knows that such access is not authorized and fails to terminate such access, shall be punished by imprisonment in the house of correction for not more than thirty days or by a fine of not more than one thousand dollars, or both.

The requirement of a password or other authentication to gain access shall constitute notice that access is limited to authorized users.

Added by St.1994, c. 168, § 3.

§ 121. Entry on land with firearms

Whoever, without right, enters upon the land of another with firearms, with intent to fire or discharge them thereon, and, having been requested by the owner or occupant of such land or by his agent to leave such land, remains thereon, shall be punished by a fine of not more than two hundred dollars or by imprisonment for not more than two months, or both.

Historical and Statutory Notes

St.1890, c. 403, § 1.
R.L.1902, c. 208, § 110.

§ 121A. Trespasses involving motor vehicles and other powered devices

Whoever, without right, enters upon the private land of another, whether or not such land be posted against trespass, and in so entering makes use of or has in his immediate possession or control any vehicle, machine, or device which includes an internal combustion engine or other source of mechanical power, shall be punished by a fine of not more than $500.

The provisions of this section shall not apply to such an entry at the junction of a public way with a paved private roadway, unless said private roadway is distinguished from the public way by a sign, gatepost, or the display of a street number or the name of the occupant of the premises, or by the improvement of adjacent land, the type of construction of the roadway, or other distinguishing feature, or unless such entry has been forbidden by the person having lawful control of said private roadway.

Nothing herein shall in any way restrict the operation of power boats on waterways not otherwise restricted.

Added by St.1973, c. 573. Amended by St.1974, c. 171; St.2010, c. 202, § 20, eff. Oct. 29, 2010.

§ 122. Notice against trespassers; defacement; penalty

Whoever wilfully tears down, removes or defaces any notice posted on land, or other property described in section one hundred and twenty, by the owner, lessee or custodian thereof, warning persons not to trespass thereon, shall be punished by a fine of not more than twenty-five dollars.

Historical and Statutory Notes

St.1890, c. 403, § 2.
R.L.1902, c. 208, § 111.
St.1931, c. 426, § 307.

§ 123. State land; public institutions; trespass; penalty

Whoever willfully trespasses upon land or premises belonging to the commonwealth, or to any authority established by the general court for purposes incidental to higher education, appurtenant to a public institution of higher education, any correctional institution of the commonwealth, Tewksbury hospital, Soldiers' Home in Massachusetts, Soldiers' Home in Holyoke, any public institution for the care of mentally ill and developmentally disabled persons, any Massachusetts training school or state charitable institution, or upon land or premises belonging to any county and appurtenant to a jail, house of correction or courthouse, or whoever, after notice from an officer of any of said institutions to leave said land, remains thereon, shall be punished by a fine of not more than fifty dollars or by imprisonment for not more than three months.

Amended by St.1941, c. 344, § 27; St.1958, c. 613, § 8E; St.1959, c. 213; St.1960, c. 315; St.1969, c. 362; St.1987, c. 522, § 21; St.1993, c. 326.

Historical and Statutory Notes

St.1885, c. 303.
R.L.1902, c. 208, § 112.
St.1905, c. 434.
St.1906, c. 243.
St.1911, c. 104.
St.1911, c. 181.
St.1911, c. 194.
St.1913, c. 404.
St.1914, c. 358.
St.1918, c. 257, § 307.
St.1919, c. 5.
St.1920, c. 2.
St.1931, c. 426, § 308.

§ 124. Legal notice; penalty for malicious injury

Whoever wilfully and maliciously, or wantonly and without cause, tears down, removes or defaces a warrant for a town meeting, list of jurors or other notice or paper which has been posted in compliance with law shall, except as otherwise provided, be punished by a fine of not more than ten dollars.

Historical and Statutory Notes

St.1883, c. 156.
R.L.1902, c. 208, § 113.

§ 125. Show bill or advertisement; penalty for malicious injury

Whoever wilfully and maliciously removes, destroys or mutilates a show bill, placard, program or other advertisement posted upon a wall, fence, billboard or structure not lawfully under his control, of an exhibition, show or amusement licensed under section one hundred and eighty-one of chapter one hundred and forty, before such exhibition, show or amusement has taken place, shall be punished by a fine of not more than ten dollars.

Historical and Statutory Notes

St.1870, c. 259.
P.S.1882, c. 203, § 101.
R.L.1902, c. 208, § 114.

§ 126. Natural scenery; penalty for defacement

Whoever paints, or puts upon, or in any manner affixes to, any fence, structure, pole, rock or other object which is public property or the property of another, whether within or without the limits of the highway, any words, device, trade mark, advertisement or notice which is not required by law to be posted thereon, without first obtaining the written consent of the municipal or public officer in charge thereof or the owner or tenant of such property, shall, upon complaint of such municipal or public officer, or of such owner or tenant, be punished by a fine of not less than ten nor more than one hundred dollars, and in addition shall forfeit to the use of the public or private owner of such property or the tenant thereof the cost of removing or obliterating such defacement to be recovered in an action of tort. Any word, device, trade mark, advertisement or notice which has been painted, put up or affixed within the limits of a highway in violation of this section shall be considered a public nuisance, and may be forthwith removed or obliterated and abated by any person.

Amended by St.1965, c. 482.

Historical and Statutory Notes

St.1873, c. 349.
P.S.1882, c. 203, § 102.
St.1898, c. 500.
R.L.1902, c. 208, § 115.

§ 126A. Defacement of real or personal property; penalties; suspension of driver's license

Whoever intentionally, willfully and maliciously or wantonly, paints, marks, scratches, etches or otherwise marks, injures, mars, defaces or destroys the real or personal property of another including but not limited to a wall, fence, building, sign, rock, monument, gravestone or tablet, shall be punished by imprisonment in a state prison for a term of not more than three years or by imprisonment in a house of correction for not more than two years or by a fine of not more than fifteen hundred dollars or not more than three times the value of the property so marked, injured, marred, defaced or destroyed, whichever is greater, or both imprisonment and fine, and shall also be required to pay for the removal or obliteration of such painting, marking, scratching or etching, or to remove or obliterate such painting, marking, scratching or etching; provided, however, that when a fine is levied pursuant to the value of the property marked, injured, marred, defaced or destroyed or when the cost of removal or obliteration is assessed, the court shall, after conviction, conduct an evidentiary hearing to ascertain the value of the property so marked, injured, marred, defaced or destroyed or to ascertain the cost of the removal or obliteration; and provided, however, that if the property marked, injured, marred, defaced or destroyed is a war or veterans' memorial, monument or gravestone, the fine under this section shall be doubled and the person convicted shall be ordered to perform not less than 500 hours of court-approved community service. A police officer may arrest any person for commission of the offenses prohibited by this section without a warrant if said police officer has probable cause to believe that said person has committed the offenses prohibited by this section.

Upon conviction for said offense the individual's driver's license shall be suspended for one year. If the individual convicted of defacing or vandalizing the real or personal property of another is under the age of sixteen then one year shall be added to the minimum age eligibility for driving.

Added by St.1994, c. 60, § 174. Amended by St.2010, c. 131, § 101, eff. July 1, 2010.

§ 126B. Tagging; penalties; suspension of driver's license

Whoever sprays or applies paint or places a sticker upon a building, wall, fence, sign, tablet, gravestone, monument or other object or thing on a public way or adjoined to it, or in public view, or on private property, such person known or commonly known as "taggers" and such conduct or activity known or commonly known as "tagging", or other words or phrases associated to such persons, conduct or activity, and either as an individual or in a group, joins together with said group, with the intent to deface, mar, damage, mark or destroy such property, shall be punished by imprisonment in a house of correction for not more than two years or by a fine of not less than fifteen hundred dollars or not more than three times the value of such damage to the property so defaced, marked, marred, damaged or destroyed, whichever is greater, or both fine and imprisonment and shall also be required to pay for the removal or obliteration of such "tagging" or to obliterate such "tagging"; provided, however that when a fine is levied pursuant to the value of the property marred, defaced, marked, damaged or destroyed or where the cost of removal or obliteration is assessed the court shall, after conviction, conduct an evidentiary hearing to ascertain the value of the property so defaced, marked, marred, damaged or destroyed or to ascertain the cost of the removal or obliteration. A police officer may arrest any person for commission of the offenses prohibited by this section without a warrant if said police officer has probable cause to believe that said person has committed the offenses prohibited by this section.

Upon conviction for said offense the individual's drivers license shall be suspended for one year. If the individual convicted of defacing or vandalizing the real or personal property of another is under the age of sixteen then one year shall be added to the minimum age eligibility for driving.

Added by St.1994, c. 60, § 174.

§ 127. Personal property; malicious or wanton injuries

Whoever destroys or injures the personal property, dwelling house or building of another in any manner or by any means not particularly described or mentioned in this chapter shall, if such destruction or injury is wilful and malicious, be punished by imprisonment in the state prison for not more than ten years or by a fine of three thousand dollars or three times the value of the property so destroyed or injured, whichever is greater and imprisonment in jail for not more than two and one-half years; or if such destruction or injury is wanton, shall be punished by a fine of fifteen hundred dollars or three times the value of the property so destroyed or injured, whichever is greater, or by imprisonment for not more than two and one-half years; if the value of the property so destroyed or injured is not alleged to exceed two hundred and fifty dollars, the punishment shall be by a fine of three times the value of the damage or injury to such property or by imprisonment for not more than two and one-half months; provided, however, that where a fine is levied pursuant to the value of the property destroyed or injured, the court shall, after conviction, conduct an evidentiary hearing to ascertain the value of the property so destroyed or injured. The words "personal property", as used in this section, shall also include electronically processed or stored data, either tangible or intangible, and data while in transit.

Amended by St.1978, c. 544; St.1982, c. 229, § 2; St.1987, c. 468, § 5; St.1994, c. 168, § 4.

Historical and Statutory Notes

R.S.1836, c. 126, § 39.
St.1846, c. 52, § 1.
G.S.1860, c. 161, § 85.
P.S.1882, c. 203, § 103.
R.L.1902, c. 208, § 116.
St.1904, c. 305.

§ 127A. Destruction of place of worship, etc.; threats; punishment

Whoever willfully, intentionally and without right, or wantonly and without cause, destroys, defaces, mars, or injures a church, synagogue or other building, structure or place used for the purpose of burial or memorializing the dead, or a school, educational facility or community center or the grounds adjacent to and owned or leased by any of the foregoing or any personal property contained in any of the foregoing shall be punished by a fine of not more than two thousand dollars or not more than three times the value of the property so destroyed, defaced, marred or injured, whichever is greater, or by imprisonment in a house of correction for not more than two and one-half years, or both; provided, however, that if the damage to or loss of such property exceeds five thousand dollars, such person shall be punished by a fine of not more than three times the value of the property so destroyed, defaced, marred or injured or by imprisonment in a state prison for not more than five years, or both.

Whoever threatens to burn, deface, mar, injure, or in any way destroy a church, synagogue or other building, structure, or place of worship, shall be punished by a fine of not more than one thousand five hundred dollars, or by imprisonment in a jail or house of correction for not more than one year, or both.

Added by St.1983, c. 165, § 2. Amended by St.1989, c. 121, §§ 1, 2.

§ 127B. Actions for civil rights violations; liability

Any person incurring injury to his person or damage or loss to his property as a result of conduct in violation of section one hundred and twenty-seven A or of section thirty-nine of chapter two hundred and sixty-five shall have a civil action to secure injunctive relief, special and general damages, reasonable attorney fees and costs against the person whose conduct has violated said section one hundred and twenty-seven A of this chapter or of section thirty-nine of chapter two hundred and sixty-five. In any such action the burden of proof shall be the same as in other civil actions for similar relief.

Notwithstanding any other provision of law to the contrary, the parent or legal guardian of an unemancipated minor child shall be liable for any judgment rendered against such minor under the provisions of this section.

Added by St.1983, c. 165, § 2.

§ 128. Milk cans; defacement

Whoever, without the consent of the owner thereof, knowingly and wilfully effaces, alters or covers over, or procures to be effaced, altered or covered over, the name, initial or device of any dealer in milk, marked or stamped upon a milk can, or whoever, with intent to defraud and without such consent, detains or uses in his business any such can having the name, initial or device of any dealer in milk so marked or stamped thereon, shall be punished by a fine of not more than ten dollars.

Historical and Statutory Notes

St.1885, c. 133.
R.L.1902, c. 208, § 117.

§ 129. Correctional institutions; injury to property

An inmate of a correctional institution of the commonwealth who wilfully and maliciously destroys or injures the property of the commonwealth at such correctional institution, or the property of any person who furnishes materials for the employment of the prisoners, may be sentenced to the state prison for not more than three years.

Amended by St.1955, c. 770, § 79.

Historical and Statutory Notes

St.1891, c. 295.
St.1896, c. 344.
R.L.1902, c. 208, § 119.
St.1931, c. 426, § 309.

§ 130. Penal institutions; injury to property

Whoever, being a prisoner at a jail or house of correction, wilfully and maliciously injures or destroys any public property or any materials furnished for the employment of prisoners in such jail or house of correction may be punished by imprisonment for not less than six months nor more than two and one half years.

Amended by St.1955, c. 770, § 80.

Historical and Statutory Notes

St.1896, c. 344.
R.L.1902, c. 208, § 120.
St.1905, c. 241.
St.1906, c. 243.
St.1911, c. 181.
St.1914, c. 635.
St.1918, c. 257, § 464.
St.1919, c. 5.
St.1920, c. 2.

§ 131. Sunday trespassers; arrest and detention without warrant

Whoever is discovered in the act of wilfully injuring a fruit or forest tree or of committing any kind of malicious mischief on Sunday may be arrested without a warrant by a sheriff, deputy sheriff, constable, police officer or other person, and detained in jail or otherwise until a complaint can be made against him for the offence, and he be taken upon a warrant issued upon such complaint; but such detention without warrant shall not continue beyond the following day.

Historical and Statutory Notes

St.1851, c. 246.
St.1852, c. 245.
G.S.1860, c. 161, § 86.
P.S.1882, c. 203, § 104.
R.L.1902, c. 208, § 121.
St.1931, c. 426, § 46.

§ 132. Pigeons; killing or frightening

Whoever wilfully kills pigeons upon, or frightens them from, beds which have been made for the purpose of taking them in nets, by any method, within one hundred rods of the same, except on land lawfully occupied by himself, shall be punished by imprisonment for not more than one month or by a fine of not more than twenty dollars, and shall also be liable for the actual damages to the owner or occupant of such beds.

Historical and Statutory Notes

St.1848, c. 85.
St.1849, c. 29.
G.S.1860, c. 161, § 87.
P.S.1882, c. 203, § 105.
R.L.1902, c. 208, § 122.

§ 133. Humane society; injury to property

Whoever unlawfully enters a house, boat house or hut which is the property of the Humane Society of the Commonwealth of Massachusetts and wilfully injures, removes or carries away any property belonging to said society, or wilfully injures or unlawfully uses or commits any trespass upon the property of said society which is intended or kept for the purpose of saving or preserving human life, or commits any trespass upon such house, hut or boat house, shall be punished by a fine of not more than two hundred dollars or by imprisonment for not more than six months; but the penalties of this section shall not apply to persons for whose use said boats, houses and other property are intended and kept. Pilots, sheriffs and their deputies, and constables shall make complaint against all persons guilty of a violation of this section. One half of any fine paid hereunder shall be paid to the person who gives information upon which a conviction is obtained.

Historical and Statutory Notes

St.1854, c. 358.
G.S.1860, c. 161, § 88.
P.S.1882, c. 203, § 106.
St.1889, c. 399.
R.L.1902, c. 208, § 123.

§ 134. Repealed, 1962, 285, Sec. 3

§ 135. Vessels; mooring the buoy, beacon or floating guide; penalty

Whoever moors or in any manner makes fast a vessel, scow, boat or raft to a buoy, beacon or floating guide placed by the government of the United States in the navigable waters of the commonwealth shall be punished by a fine of not more than fifty dollars; and whoever wilfully destroys, injures or removes any such beacon or guide shall be punished by a fine of not more than one hundred dollars or by imprisonment for not more than three months. One third of all fines which accrue under this section shall be paid to the complainant and two-thirds to the commonwealth.

Amended by St.1978, c. 478, § 278.

Historical and Statutory Notes

St.1860, c. 53, §§ 1, 2.
P.S.1882, c. 203, §§ 110, 111.
R.L.1902, c. 208, § 125.

§ 136. Repealed, 1962, 285, Sec. 3

§ 137. Injury to mill by raising water

Whoever, by erecting or maintaining a dam, either within or without the commonwealth, knowingly causes the water of a river or stream so to be raised as to flow upon or injure a mill lawfully existing in the commonwealth and belonging to a citizen thereof, without right as against the owner of such mill, shall be punished by a fine of not more than one thousand dollars or by imprisonment for not more than six months; but this section shall not apply to cases in which the courts of the commonwealth have jurisdiction to abate a dam so raised or maintained.

Historical and Statutory Notes

St.1849, c. 98.
G.S.1860, c. 161, § 71.
P.S.1882, c. 203, § 84.
R.L.1902, c. 208, § 89.

§ 138. Dams or reservoirs; malicious injury

Whoever wilfully, intentionally and without right breaks down, injures, removes or destroys a dam, reservoir, canal or trench, or a gate, flume, flashboards or other appurtenances thereof, or a wheel, or mill gear, or machinery of a water mill or steam mill, or wilfully or wantonly, without color of right, draws off the water contained in a mill pond, reservoir, canal or trench, or obstructs such water from flowing out of the same, shall be punished by imprisonment in the state prison for not more than five years or by a fine of not more than five hundred dollars and imprisonment in jail for not more than two years.

Historical and Statutory Notes

St.1727–8, c. 3.
St.1829, c. 98.
R.S.1836, c. 126, § 40.
St.1857, c. 160.
G.S.1860, c. 161, § 72.
St.1875, c. 101.
P.S.1882, c. 203, § 85.
St.1901, c. 268, § 4.
R.L.1902, c. 208, § 90.

§ 138A. Irrigation equipment; malicious injury

Whoever wilfully, intentionally and without right damages or renders unusable machinery or equipment used in the transmission of water for agricultural purposes shall be punished by imprisonment in state prison for not more than five years or by a fine of not more than five hundred dollars and imprisonment in jail for not more than two years.

Added by St.1969, c. 56. Amended by St.1971, c. 30.

§ 139. Motor vehicles or trailers; defacement, etc., of identifying numbers; penalties; arrests

(a) Whoever intentionally and maliciously removes, defaces, alters, changes, destroys, obliterates or mutilates or causes to be removed or destroyed or in any way defaced, altered, changed, obliterated or mutilated, the identifying number or numbers of a motor vehicle or trailer shall be punished by a fine of not more than one thousand dollars or by imprisonment in the state prison for not more than three years, or both. The possession of any motor vehicle or trailer by a person who knows, should know, or has reason to know that the identifying number or numbers of such vehicle has been removed, defaced, altered, changed, destroyed, obliterated or mutilated shall be a prima facie evidence of a violation of this paragraph.

(b) Whoever sells, transfers, distributes, dispenses or otherwise disposes of or attempts to sell, transfer, distribute, dispense or otherwise dispose of any motor vehicle or trailer or motor vehicle part knowing or having reason to believe that the identifying number or numbers to said motor vehicle, trailer, or vehicle part have been so removed, defaced, altered, changed, destroyed, obliterated, or mutilated, unless authorized by law to do so, shall be punished by a fine of not more than one thousand dollars or by imprisonment in the state prison for not more than three years, or both.

(c) Whoever buys, receives, possesses, or obtains control of a motor vehicle, trailer, or motor vehicle part knowing or having reason to believe that an identifying number to said vehicle, trailer, or vehicle part has been removed, obliterated, tampered with, or altered, unless authorized by law to do so, shall be punished by a fine of not more than five hundred dollars or by imprisonment in a house of correction for not more than two years, or both.

The phrase "identifying number or numbers", as used in this section, shall mean the manufacturer's number or numbers identifying the motor vehicle, trailer or motor vehicle part as required to be contained in an application for registration by section two of chapter ninety, including the identifying number or numbers as restored or substituted under authority of section thirty-two A of said chapter ninety or similar law of another state.

An officer authorized to make arrests may arrest without warrant any person who he has probable cause to believe has committed or is committing a violation of the provisions of this section.

A conviction of a violation of this section or any adjudication that a person is a delinquent child by reason thereof shall be reported forthwith by the court or magistrate to the registrar of motor vehicles who shall revoke immediately the license to operate motor vehicles or the right to operate motor vehicles of the person so convicted or adjudged, and no appeal, motion for new trial or exceptions shall operate to stay the revocation of such license or right to operate. The registrar of motor vehicles after having revoked the license or right to operate of any such person so convicted or adjudged shall issue a new license or reinstate such right to operate, if the prosecution of such person is finally terminated in his favor; otherwise, no new license shall be issued nor shall such right to operate be reinstated until sixty days after the date of revocation following his original conviction or adjudication if for a first offense, or until one year after the date of revocation following any subsequent conviction or adjudication.

Whoever takes and carries away the registration plate that is attached to the vehicle of another or is assigned by the registry of motor vehicles to another shall be punished by a fine of not less than $500 nor more than $1,000 or imprisonment in the house of correction for not more than 2½ years, or both.

Amended by St.1961, c. 73, § 4; St.1979, c. 792; St.1981, c. 264, §§ 1 to 3; St.1985, c. 386; St.2005, c. 122, § 18, eff. Oct. 28, 2005.

Historical and Statutory Notes

St.1925, c. 237, § 2.
St.1930, c. 353, § 2.

§ 139A. Machines, electrical or mechanical devices; alteration or obliteration of identifying numbers; possession; sale; punishment

Whoever removes, defaces, alters, changes, destroys, obliterates or mutilates or causes to be removed or destroyed or in any way defaced, altered, changed, obliterated or mutilated, the identifying number or numbers of any machine or any electrical or mechanical device, with intent thereby to conceal its identity, to defraud the manufacturer, seller, or purchaser, to hinder competition in the areas of sales and servicing, or to prevent the detection of a crime shall be punished by a fine of not more than five hundred dollars or by imprisonment in a jail or house of correction for not more than one year or by both such fine and imprisonment. Possession of any machine or electrical or mechanical device the identifying number or numbers of which have been so removed, defaced, altered, changed, destroyed, obliterated or mutilated shall be prima facie evidence of a violation of the foregoing provision.

Whoever sells or otherwise disposes of or attempts to sell or otherwise dispose of a machine or an electrical or a mechanical device, knowing or having reason to believe that the identifying number or numbers of the same have been so removed, defaced, altered, changed, destroyed, obliterated or mutilated, shall be punished by a fine of not more than five hundred dollars or by imprisonment for not more than one year in a jail or house of correction or by both such fine and imprisonment.

Added by St.1974, c. 434.

§ 140. Sale or offer for sale of master keys; penalty

Whoever sells or offers to sell or solicits offers to purchase a master key designed to fit more than one motor vehicle knowing, or having reasonable cause to believe, that said key will be used for an illegal purpose shall be punished by a fine of not more than five hundred dollars or by imprisonment for not more than one year, or both.

Added by St.1966, c. 269, § 2. Amended by St.1968, c. 90.

§ 141. Tampering with odometer of motor vehicle; intent to defraud; civil remedy; treble damages; costs and fees; unfair competition; repair or replacement excepted

Whoever advertises for sale, sells, uses, installs or has installed any device which causes an odometer to register any mileage other than the true mileage driven, or whoever resets, or alters the odometer of any motor vehicle with the intent to change the number of miles indicated thereon, or whoever, with the intent to defraud, operates a motor vehicle on any street or highway knowing that the odometer of such vehicle is disconnected to nonfunctional,[1] shall be liable in a civil action of tort or contract in an amount equal to the sum of three times the amount of actual damages sustained or one thousand five hundred dollars, whichever is the greater, plus the costs of the action together with reasonable attorney fees as determined by the court.

A violation of the provisions of this section shall constitute an unfair method of competition under chapter ninety-three A.

For the purposes of this section, the true mileage driven shall be that mileage traveled by the motor vehicle as registered by the odometer within the manufacturer's designed tolerance.

The term "odometer", as used in this section and in section one hundred and forty-one A, shall mean an instrument for measuring and recording the actual distance a motor vehicle travels while in operation; but shall not include any auxiliary odometer designed to be reset by the operator of the motor vehicle for the purpose of recording mileage on trips.

Nothing in this section and section one hundred and forty-one A shall prevent the service, repair or replacement of an odometer, provided the mileage indicated thereon remains the same as before the service, repair or replacement. Where the odometer is incapable of registering the same mileage as before such service, repair or replacement, the odometer shall be adjusted to read zero and a notice in writing shall be attached to the left door frame of the vehicle by the owner or his agent specifying the mileage prior to repair or replacement of the odometer and the date on which it was repaired or replaced.

Added by St.1973, c. 456.

[1] So in original.

§ 141A. Misrepresentation of mileage of motor vehicle by turning back or readjusting speedometer or odometer; criminal penalty

Whoever, with the intent to misrepresent to a prospective or eventual purchaser the number of miles traveled by a motor vehicle, turns back or readjusts the speedometer or odometer thereof shall be punished by a fine of not less than five hundred nor more than one thousand dollars, or by imprisonment in a jail or house of correction for not less than thirty days nor more than two years, or both. In a prosecution under this section, evidence that a dealer, as defined in section one of chapter ninety, or a person required to be licensed under the provisions of section fifty-nine of chapter one hundred and forty, by himself or by another turned back or readjusted the speedometer or odometer shall constitute prima facie evidence of such intent to misrepresent.

Added by St.1966, c. 468. Renumbered and amended by St.1973, c. 456. Amended by St.1985, c. 155.

§ 142. Record of purchases by dealers in scrap copper wire; inspection; penalty

Whoever is in the business of purchasing copper line wire or scrap copper wire shall enter in a book kept for that purpose a description of the same, the quantity purchased, the purchase price and a name and address of the seller. Said book shall at all times be open to the inspection of the chief of police of a city or town or any other officer having similar duties or any officer authorized by either of them, or a state police officer. Whoever violates any provision of this section shall be punished by a fine of not more than fifty dollars.

Added by St.1971, c. 36.

§ 142A. Gold, silver and platinum dealers; records; penalty

Whoever is in the business of purchasing gold, silver or platinum shall enter in a book kept for that purpose a description of the item, quantity purchased, the purchase price and the name and address of the seller; provided that the purchase price of such item is at least fifty dollars. Any person who sells gold, silver or platinum shall be required to show to the buyer prior to said sale identification which includes a photograph of said seller. Said book shall at all times be open to the inspection of the chief of police of a city or town or of any other officer having similar duties or any officer authorized by either of them, or a state police officer. Whoever violates any provision of this section shall be punished by a fine of not more than one thousand dollars or imprisonment of not more than one year, or both such fine and imprisonment.

Added by St.1980, c. 400.

§ 143. Definitions applicable to Secs. 143A to 143H

As used in sections 143A to 143H, inclusive, the following words shall have the following meanings:

"Article" or "recorded device", the tangible medium upon which sounds or images are recorded or otherwise stored, and shall include any original phonograph record, disc, wire, tape, audio or video cassette, film or other medium now known or later developed on which sounds or images may be recorded or otherwise stored, or any copy or reproduction which duplicates, in whole or in part, the original.

"Audiovisual recording function", the capability to record or transmit visual images or soundtrack, including any portion thereof, from a motion picture.

"Motion picture theater", movie theater, screening room, or other venue if used primarily for the exhibition of motion pictures.

"Owner", the person or other entity who owns a master phonograph record, master disc, master tape, master film or other device used for reproducing recorded visual images or sounds on a phonograph record, disc, tape, film, video cassette or other article on which visual images or sound is recorded, and from which the transferred recorded images or sounds are directly or indirectly derived.

Added by St.1973, c. 979, § 1. Amended by St.1990, c. 163; St.2004, c. 395, § 1, eff. Feb. 14, 2005.

§ 143A. Unauthorized reproduction and transfer of sound recordings

Whoever directly or indirectly by any means, knowingly transfers or causes to be transferred any sound recorded on a phonograph record, disc, wire, tape, film, videocassette or other article on which such sound is recorded, with intent to sell, rent or transport, or cause to be sold, rented or transported, or to use or cause to be used for profit through public performance such article on which such sound is so transferred, without the consent of the owner, or whoever sells any such article with the knowledge that the sound thereon has been so transferred without the consent of the owner, shall be punished as provided in section 143E.

Added by St.1990, c. 163. Amended by St.2004, c. 395, § 2, eff. Feb. 14, 2005.

§ 143B. Unauthorized reproduction and sale of live performances

Whoever for commercial advantage or private financial gain records or causes to be recorded a live performance with knowledge that such recording is without the consent of the owner, or advertises, sells, rents, transports or causes to be advertised, sold, rented or transported, or possesses for any of such purposes, a recording of a live performance with the knowledge that the live performance was recorded without the consent of the owner, shall be punished as provided in section 143E.

Added by St.1990, c. 163. Amended by St.2004, c. 395, § 3, eff. Feb. 14, 2005.

§ 143C. Manufacture, rental, or sale of recorded devices in packaging not bearing reproducer's name and address

Whoever for commercial advantage or private financial gain knowingly manufactures, rents, sells, transports, or causes to be manufactured, rented, sold or transported, or possesses for purposes of sale, rental or transport, any recorded device the outside packaging of which does not clearly and conspicuously bear the true name and address of the transferor of the sounds or images contained thereon shall be punished as provided in section 143E.

Added by St.1990, c. 163. Amended by St.2004, c. 395, § 4, eff. Feb. 14, 2005.

§ 143D. Application of Secs. 143 to 143C; exceptions

(a) Nothing in sections 143A to 143C, inclusive, shall be construed to apply to any person lawfully entitled to use or who causes to be used such sound or images for profit through public performance, or who transfers or causes to be transferred any such sound or images as part of a radio or television broadcast or for archival preservation.

(b) Nothing in section 143A to 143C, inclusive, shall be construed to apply to local, state or federal law enforcement officers employing an audiovisual recording function during the lawful exercise of law enforcement duties.

Added by St.1990, c. 163. Amended by St.2004, c. 395, § 5, eff. Feb. 14, 2005.

§ 143E. Violations of Secs. 143A to 143C; punishment

Whoever violates any provision of section 143A to section 143C, inclusive, shall be punished:

(i) by imprisonment for not more than 1 year in the house of correction or by a fine of not more than $25,000, or by both such fine and imprisonment;

(ii) by imprisonment in the house of correction for not more than 2 years or by a fine of not more than $100,000, or by both such fine and imprisonment if the offense involves less than 1,000 but not less than 100 unlawful sound recordings or less the 65 but not less than 7 unlawful audio visual recordings; or

(iii) by imprisonment in state prison for not more than 5 years or by a fine of not more than $250,000, or by both such fine and imprisonment if the offense involves not less than 1,000 unlawful sound recordings or not less than 65 unlawful audio visual recordings.

Added by St.1990, c. 163. Amended by St.2004, c. 395, § 5, eff. Feb. 14, 2005.

§ 143F. Unlawful recording of motion picture in motion picture theater; punishment

(a) Any person, in a motion picture theater while a motion picture is being exhibited, who knowingly operates an audiovisual recording function, with the intent to unlawfully record the motion picture and without the consent of the owner or lessee of the motion picture theater, shall be punished for a first offense by imprisonment in the house of correction for not more than 2 years or by a fine of not more than $100,000, or by both such fine and imprisonment and for a second or subsequent conviction, by imprisonment in the state prison for not more than 5 years or by a fine of not more than $250,000, or by both such fine and imprisonment.

(b) Nothing in subsection (a) shall be construed to apply to local, state or federal law enforcement officers employing an audiovisual recording function during the lawful exercise of law enforcement duties.

Added by St.2004, c. 395, § 5, eff. Feb. 14, 2005.

§ 143G. Persons detained for possible violation of Sec. 143F; defense to false imprisonment or false arrest action

In an action for false arrest or false imprisonment brought by any person, by reason of having been detained for questioning or awaiting the arrival of law enforcement, on or in the immediate vicinity of a motion picture theater, if such person was detained in a reasonable manner and for not more than a reasonable length of time by a person authorized to make arrests or by the owner or his agent or servant authorized for such purpose and if there were reasonable grounds to believe that the person so detained was committing or attempting to commit any violation of section 143F, it shall be a defense to such action.

Added by St.2004, c. 395, § 5, eff. Feb. 14, 2005.

§ 143H. Forfeiture of recordings upon conviction for violation of Secs. 143A to 143C or Sec. 143F

Upon conviction of a person for a violation of sections 143A to 143C, inclusive, or section 143F, the court may order the forfeiture, destruction or other disposition of all recordings on which the conviction is based and all implements, devices and equipment used or intended to be used in the manufacture of the recordings on which the conviction is based. Such order shall be stayed pending any appeal.

Added by St.2004, c. 395, § 5, eff. Feb. 14, 2005.

§ 144. Carrying away or conversion of certain milk containers without permission of owners

Whoever, without permission of the owner, carries away or converts to his own use a plastic or wire milk case or a plastic or wire container for milk products which has been indelibly stamped with the name of a milk dealer or association of milk dealers shall be punished by a fine of not less than ten and not more than one hundred dollars.

Added by St.1975, c. 538.

§ 145. Theft of public records

Any person who intentionally conceals upon his person or otherwise any record of the commonwealth or a political subdivision thereof, as defined in section three of chapter sixty-six, with the intention of permanently depriving said commonwealth or said political subdivision of its use shall be punished by a fine of not more than five hundred dollars.

A custodian of such records or his agent who has probable cause to believe that a person has violated the provisions of this section may detain such person in a reasonable manner and for a reasonable time.

A law enforcement officer may arrest without warrant any person he has probable cause to believe has violated the provisions of this section. The statement of a custodian of such records or his agent that a person has violated the provisions of this section shall constitute probable cause for arrest by a law enforcement officer authorized to make an arrest in such jurisdiction.

Added by St.1986, c. 196, § 2.

§ 146. Disposal of solid waste in commercial disposal container of another without consent of owner; penalties

For purposes of this section "solid waste" shall mean garbage, refuse, trash, rubbish, sludge, residue or by-products of processing or treatment of discarded material, and any other solid, semi-solid or liquid discarded material resulting from domestic, commercial, mining, industrial, agricultural, municipal, or other sources or activities, but shall not include solid or dissolved material in domestic sewage.

Whoever willfully and without right deposits solid waste in a commercial disposal container of another without the consent of the owner or other person who has legal custody, care or control thereof shall be punished by a fine of not less than one hundred dollars, nor more than one thousand dollars.

Added by St.1992, c. 64.

§ 147. Items or services bearing or identified by counterfeit mark; sales; penalties

(a) For purposes of this section, the following words shall have the following meanings:—

"Counterfeit mark", any unauthorized reproduction or copy of intellectual property, or intellectual property affixed to any item knowingly sold, offered for sale, manufactured or distributed, or identifying services offered or rendered, without the authority of the owner of the intellectual property.

"Intellectual property", any trademark, service mark, trade name, label, term, device, design or word that is (1) adopted or used by a person to identify such person's goods or services, and (2) registered, filed or recorded under the laws of the commonwealth or of any other state, or registered in the principal register of the United States Patent and Trademark Office.

"Retail value", the counterfeiter's regular selling price for the item or service bearing or identified by the counterfeit mark; provided, however, that in the case of items bearing a counterfeit mark which are components of a finished product, the retail value shall be the counterfeiter's regular selling price of the finished product on or in which the component would be utilized.

(b) Whoever willfully manufactures, uses, displays, advertises, distributes, offers for sale, sells or possesses with intent to sell or distribute any item or services bearing or identified by a counterfeit mark shall be punished as follows:

(1) if the violation involves 100 or fewer items bearing a counterfeit mark or the total retail value of all items bearing or of services identified by a counterfeit mark is $1,000 or less and is a first offense, by imprisonment in a jail or house of correction for not more than two and one-half years;

(2) if the violation involves more than 100 but fewer than 1,000 items bearing a counterfeit mark or the total retail value of all items bearing or of services identified by a counterfeit mark is more than $1,000 but less than $10,000 or is a second offense, by imprisonment in the state prison for not more than five years;

(3) if the violation involves 1,000 or more items bearing a counterfeit mark or the total retail value of all items bearing or of services identified by a counterfeit mark is $10,000 or more or if the violation involves the manufacture or production of items bearing counterfeit marks or if the violation involves the manufacture or production of items that pose a threat to the public health or safety or it is a third or subsequent offense, by imprisonment in the state prison for not more than ten years.

(c) For the purposes of this section, the quantity or retail value of items or services shall include the aggregate quantity or retail value of all items bearing or of services identified by every counterfeit mark the defendant manufactures, uses, displays, advertises, distributes, offers for sale, sells or possesses.

(d) A person having possession, custody or control of more than 25 items bearing a counterfeit mark shall be presumed to possess said items with the intent to sell or distribute. Any state or federal certificate of registration of any intellectual property shall be prima facie evidence of the facts stated therein.

(e) Any person convicted under this section shall, in addition to any penalty imposed pursuant to subsection (b), be punished by a fine in an amount not to exceed three times the retail value of the items bearing or of services identified by a counterfeit mark, unless extenuating circumstances are shown by the defendant.

(f) Any person convicted under this section shall, in addition to any penalty imposed pursuant to subsections (b) and (e), be punished by a fine in an amount equal to 75 per cent of the retail value of the items bearing or of services identified by a counterfeit mark, when the items involved pose a threat to public health or safety.

(g) Any items bearing a counterfeit mark and all personal property including, but not limited to, any items, objects, tools, machines, equipment, instrumentalities or vehicles of any kind, employed or used in connection with a violation of this section shall be seized by any law enforcement office; provided, however, that all such seized personal property shall be forfeited in accordance with the provisions of chapter 257. Upon the request of the intellectual property owner, all seized items bearing a counterfeit mark shall be released to the intellectual property owner for destruction or disposition; provided, however, that if the intellectual property owner does not request release of seized items bearing a counterfeit mark, such items shall be destroyed unless the intellectual property owner consents to another disposition.

Added by St.1998, c. 115.

CHAPTER 267

FORGERY AND CRIMES AGAINST THE CURRENCY

The section headings for the General Laws in this pamphlet have been editorially supplied.

§ 1. False or forged records, certificates, returns, attestations and other writings

Whoever, with intent to injure or defraud, falsely makes, alters, forges or counterfeits a public record, or a certificate, return or attestation of a clerk or register of a court, public register, notary public, justice of the peace, town clerk or any other public officer, in relation to a matter wherein such certificate, return or attestation may be received as legal proof; or a charter, deed, will, testament, bond or writing obligatory, power of attorney, policy of insurance, bill of lading, bill of exchange or promissory note; or an order, acquittance or discharge for money or other property or a credit card or an instrument described as a United States Dollar Traveller's Check or Cheque, purchased from a bank or other financially responsible institution, the purpose of which is a source of ready money on cashing the instrument without identification other than the signature of the purchaser; or an acceptance of a bill of exchange, or an endorsement or assignment of a bill of exchange or promissory note for the payment of money; or an accountable receipt for money, goods or other property; or a stock certificate, or any evidence or muniment of title to property; or a certificate of title, duplicate certificate of title, certificate issued in place of a duplicate certificate, the registration book, entry book, or any indexes provided for by chapter one hundred and eighty-five, or the docket of the recorder; shall be punished by imprisonment in the state prison for not more than ten years or in jail for not more than two years.

Amended by St.1974, c. 369, § 1; St.1984, c. 231, § 2; St.1986, c. 557, § 190.

Historical and Statutory Notes

C.L. c. 54, § 3.
St.1692–3, c. 18, § 8.
St.1784, c. 67.
St.1785, c. 21, § 3.
St.1804, c. 120, § 1.
St.1805, c. 88, § 1.
R.S.1836, c. 127, § 1.
G.S.1860, c. 162, § 1.
St.1874, c. 78.
P.S.1882, c. 204, § 1.
St.1898, c. 562, § 113.
St.1901, c. 371, § 1.
R.L.1902, c. 209, § 1.
St.1909, c. 155, § 1.
St.1931, c. 394, § 202.

§ 2. Railroad or admission tickets, passes or badges

Whoever, with intent to injure or defraud, falsely makes, alters, forges or counterfeits a railroad ticket, railroad mileage book or railroad pass, or a ticket, badge, pass or any written or printed license purporting to entitle the holder or owner thereof to admission to any exhibition, entertainment, performance, match or contest of any kind, shall be punished by imprisonment in the state prison for not more than three years or in jail for not more than two years, or by a fine of not more than five hundred dollars.

Historical and Statutory Notes

St.1901, c. 371, § 1.
R.L.1902, c. 209, § 1.
St.1909, c. 155, § 1.

§ 3. Seal of land court; stamping documents without authority

Whoever forges, procures to be forged or assists in forging, the seal of the land court, or, without lawful authority, stamps or procures to be stamped, or assists in stamping, any document with such forged seal or with the genuine seal of said court, shall be punished by imprisonment in the state prison for not more than ten years or in jail for not more than two years.

Historical and Statutory Notes

St.1898, c. 562, § 114.
R.L.1902, c. 209, § 2.
St.1904, c. 448, § 1.

§ 4. Railroad company stamp; forging or using without authority

Whoever forges, procures to be forged or assists in forging, the stamp of any railroad company or of any railroad ticket agent, or, without lawful authority, stamps or procures to be stamped, or assists in stamping, any railroad ticket or railroad mileage book with such forged stamp, or with a genuine stamp of any railroad company or railroad ticket agent, shall be punished by imprisonment in the state prison for not more than three years or in jail for not more than two years, or by a fine of not more than five hundred dollars.

Historical and Statutory Notes

St.1901, c. 371, § 3.
R.L.1902, c. 209, § 2.

§ 5. Uttering false or forged records, deeds or other writings

Whoever, with intent to injure or defraud, utters and publishes as true a false, forged or altered record, deed, instrument or other writing mentioned in the four preceding sections, knowing the same to be false, forged or altered, shall be punished by imprisonment in the state prison for not more than ten years or in jail for not more than two years.

Historical and Statutory Notes

St.1692–3, c. 18, § 8.
St.1784, c. 67.
St.1785, c. 21, § 3.
St.1804, c. 120, § 1.
St.1805, c. 88, § 1.
R.S.1836, c. 127, § 2.
G.S.1860, c. 162, § 2.
P.S.1882, c. 204, § 2.
St.1901, c. 371, § 2.
R.L.1902, c. 209, § 3.
St.1909, c. 155, § 2.

§ 6. Uttering a forged railroad or admission ticket, pass or badge

Whoever, with intent to injure or defraud, utters and publishes as true a false, forged or altered railroad ticket, railroad mileage book or railroad pass, or a ticket, badge, pass or any written or printed license purporting to entitle the holder or owner thereof to admission to any exhibition, entertainment, performance, match or contest of any kind mentioned in section two, knowing the same to be false, altered or forged, shall be punished by imprisonment in the state prison for not more than three years or in jail for not more than two years, or by a fine of not more than five hundred dollars.

Historical and Statutory Notes

St.1901, c. 371, § 2.
R.L.1902, c. 209, § 3.
St.1909, c. 155, § 2.

§ 7. False or forged note, certificate or other bill of credit issued for debt of commonwealth

Whoever, with intent to injure or defraud, falsely makes, alters, forges or counterfeits a note, certificate or other bill of credit issued by the state treasurer, or by any commissioner or other officer authorized to issue the same for a debt of this commonwealth, shall be punished by imprisonment in the state prison for life or for any term of years.

Historical and Statutory Notes

St.1804, c. 120, § 2.
R.S.1836, c. 127, § 3.
G.S.1860, c. 162, § 3.
P.S.1882, c. 204, § 3.
R.L.1902, c. 209, § 4.

§ 8. False, forged or counterfeited bank bill, note or traveller's check

Whoever, with intent to injure or defraud, falsely makes, alters, forges or counterfeits a bank bill or promissory note payable to the bearer thereof or to the order of any person, issued by any incorporated banking company or an instrument described as a United States Dollar Traveller's Check or Cheque, purchased from a bank or other financially responsible institution, the purpose of which is a source of ready money on cashing the instrument without identification other than the signature of the purchaser, shall be punished by imprisonment in the state prison for life or for any term of years.

Amended by St.1974, c. 369, § 2.

Historical and Statutory Notes

St.1781, c. 34.

St.1783, c. 53, § 2.
St.1785, c. 21, § 5.
St.1804, c. 120, § 2.
R.S.1836, c. 127, § 4.
G.S.1860, c. 162, § 4.
P.S.1882, c. 204, § 4.
R.L.1902, c. 209, § 5.

§ 9. Possession of ten or more of false, forged or counterfeited notes or bills

Whoever has in his possession at the same time ten or more similar false, altered, forged or counterfeit notes, bills of credit, bank bills or notes, such as are mentioned in any of the preceding sections, payable to the bearer thereof or to the order of any person, knowing the same to be false, altered, forged or counterfeit, with intent to utter or pass the same as true, and thereby to injure or defraud, shall be punished by imprisonment in the state prison for life or for any term of years.

Historical and Statutory Notes

St.1804, c. 120, § 2.
R.S.1836, c. 127, § 5.
G.S.1860, c. 162, § 5.
P.S.1882, c. 204, § 5.
R.L.1902, c. 209, § 6.

§ 10. Uttering, passing or tendering false, forged or counterfeited note, certificate, bill or traveller's check

Whoever utters or passes or tenders in payment as true any such false, altered, forged or counterfeit note, certificate or bill of credit for any debt of the commonwealth, or a bank bill or promissory note payable to the bearer thereof or to the order of any person, issued as aforesaid, or an instrument described as a United States Dollar Traveller's Check or Cheque, purchased from a bank or other financially responsible institution, the purpose of which is a source of ready money on cashing the instrument without identification other than the signature of the purchaser, knowing the same to be false, altered, forged or counterfeit, with intent to injure or defraud, shall be punished by imprisonment in the state prison for not more than five years, or by a fine of not more than one thousand dollars and imprisonment in jail for not more than one year.
Amended by St.1974, c. 369, § 3.

Historical and Statutory Notes

St.1704–5, c. 8, § 1.
St.1720–1, c. 10.
St.1735–6, c. 18.
St.1736–7, c. 9, § 1.
St.1775–6, c. 18, §§ 1, 3.
St.1776–7, c. 44, § 2.
St.1778–9, c. 25, §§ 1, 2.
St.1781, c. 34.
St.1783, c. 53, § 3.
St.1785, c. 21, § 5.
St.1804, c. 120, § 3.
R.S.1836, c. 127, § 6.
G.S.1860, c. 162, § 6.
P.S.1882, c. 204, § 6.
R.L.1902, c. 209, § 7.

§ 11. Common utterers of counterfeit bills

Whoever, having been convicted of the crime mentioned in the preceding section, is again convicted of the like crime committed after the former conviction, and whoever is at the same sitting of the court convicted upon three distinct charges of such crime, shall be adjudged a common utterer of counterfeit bills, and be punished by imprisonment in the state prison for not more than ten years.

Historical and Statutory Notes

St.1714, c. 6.
St.1804, c. 120, § 3.
R.S.1836, c. 127, § 7.
G.S.1860, c. 162, § 7.
P.S.1882, c. 204, § 7.
R.L.1902, c. 209, § 8.

§ 12. Possession of false, forged or counterfeit bills, notes or traveller's checks

Whoever brings into this commonwealth or has in his possession a false, forged or counterfeit bill or note, in the similitude of the bills or notes, payable to the bearer thereof or to the order of any person, issued by or for any bank or banking company, or an instrument described as a United States Dollar Traveller's Check or Cheque, purchased from a bank or other financially responsible institution, the purpose of which is a source of ready money on cashing the instrument without identification other than the signature of the purchaser, with intent to utter or pass the same or to render the same current as true, knowing the same to be false, forged or counterfeit, shall be punished by imprisonment in the state prison for not more than five years, or by a fine of not more than one thousand dollars and imprisonment in jail for not more than one year.
Amended by St.1974, c. 369, § 4.

Historical and Statutory Notes

St.1804, c. 120, § 4.
St.1833, c. 222, § 1.
R.S.1836, c. 127, § 8.
St.1836, c. 4, §§ 15, 16.
G.S.1860, c. 162, § 8.
P.S.1882, c. 204, § 8.
R.L.1902, c. 209, § 9.

§ 13. Tools or material for making false, forged or counterfeited notes, certificates, bills or traveller's checks

Whoever engraves, makes or mends, or begins to engrave, make or mend, a plate, block, press or other tool, instrument or implement, or makes or provides paper or other material adapted to and designed for the forging or making of a false and counterfeit note, certificate or other bill of credit, purporting to be issued by lawful authority for a debt of the commonwealth, or a false and counterfeit note or bill in the similitude of the notes or bills issued by any bank or banking company, or an instrument described as a United States Dollar Traveller's Check or Cheque, purchased from a bank or other financially responsible institution, the purpose of which is a source of ready money on cashing the instrument without identification other than the signature of the purchaser, and whoever has in his possession such a plate or block engraved in any part, or a press or other tool, instrument or implement, or paper or other material, adapted and designed as aforesaid, with intent to use the same or to cause or permit the same to be used in forging or making such false and counterfeit certificates, bills or notes, shall be punished by imprisonment in the state prison for not more than ten years, or by a fine of not more than one thousand dollars and imprisonment in jail for not more than two years.

Amended by St.1974, c. 369, § 5.

Historical and Statutory Notes

St.1704–5, c. 8, § 1.
St.1720–1, c. 10.
St.1735–6, c. 18.
St.1775–6, c. 18, § 1.
St.1776–7, c. 44, § 1.
St.1783, c. 53, § 4.
St.1804, c. 120, § 5.
St.1833, c. 222, § 2.
R.S.1836, c. 127, § 9.
G.S.1860, c. 162, § 9.
P.S.1882, c. 204, § 9.
R.L.1902, c. 209, § 10.

§ 14. Evidence relative to forged or counterfeited bank or institution bills or notes

In prosecutions for forging or counterfeiting notes or bills of the banks or institutions before mentioned, or for uttering, publishing or tendering in payment as true forged or counterfeit bank bills or notes, or for being possessed thereof with intent to utter and pass the same as true, the testimony of the president and cashier of any such bank may be dispensed with, if their place of residence is out of the commonwealth or more than forty miles from the place of trial; and the testimony of any person acquainted with the signature of such president or cashier, or who has knowledge of the difference in the appearance of the true and the counterfeit bills or notes of such banks, may be admitted to prove that such bills or notes are counterfeit.

Amended by St.1974, c. 369, § 6.

Historical and Statutory Notes

St.1818, c. 110.
St.1833, c. 222, § 3.
R.S.1836, c. 127, § 10.
G.S.1860, c. 162, § 10.
P.S.1882, c. 204, § 10.
R.L.1902, c. 209, § 11.

§ 15. Certificates of certain officials of the United States, a state or territory, as evidence

In prosecutions for forging or counterfeiting a note, certificate, bill of credit or other security issued on behalf of the United States, or on behalf of any state or territory, or for uttering, publishing or tendering in payment as true such forged or counterfeit note, certificate, bill of credit or security, or for being possessed thereof with intent to utter or pass the same as true, the certificate under oath of the secretary of the treasury, or of the treasurer of the United States, or of the secretary or treasurer of any state or territory, on whose behalf such note, certificate, bill of credit or security purports to have been issued, shall be admitted as evidence for the purpose of proving the same to be forged or counterfeit.

Historical and Statutory Notes

St.1791, c. 61.
R.S.1836, c. 127, § 11.
G.S.1860, c. 162, § 11.
P.S.1882, c. 204, § 11.
R.L.1902, c. 209, § 12.

§ 16. Fictitious signatures of corporate officers or agents

If a fictitious or pretended signature, purporting to be the signature of an officer or agent of a corporation, is fraudulently affixed to an instrument or writing purporting to be a note, draft or other evidence of debt issued by such corporation, with intent to pass the same as true, it shall be a forgery, although no such person may ever have been an officer or agent of such corporation, or ever have existed.

Historical and Statutory Notes

R.S.1836, c. 127, § 13.
G.S.1860, c. 162, § 12.
P.S.1882, c. 204, § 12.
R.L.1902, c. 209, § 13.

§ 17. Counterfeiting coin; possession of ten or more pieces of false money

Whoever counterfeits any gold or silver coin current by law or usage within the commonwealth, or has in his possession at the same time ten or more pieces of false money, or coin counterfeited in the similitude of any gold or silver coin current as aforesaid, knowing the same to be false and counterfeit, and with intent to utter or pass the same as true, shall be punished by imprisonment in the state prison for life or for any term of years.

Historical and Statutory Notes

St.1702–3, c. 2, §§ 1, 2.
St.1749–50, c. 22, § 1.
St.1753–4, c. 20.
St.1804, c. 120, § 6.
R.S.1836, c. 127, § 15.
G.S.1860, c. 162, § 14.

P.S.1882, c. 204, § 14.
R.L.1902, c. 209, § 14.

§ 18. Possession of less than ten pieces of counterfeit coin; uttering, passing or tendering in payment

Whoever has in his possession less than ten pieces of the counterfeit coin mentioned in the preceding section, knowing the same to be counterfeit, with intent to utter or pass the same as true, or utters, passes or tenders in payment as true any such counterfeit coin, knowing the same to be false and counterfeit, shall be punished by imprisonment in the state prison for not more than ten years or by a fine of not more than one thousand dollars and imprisonment in jail for not more than two years.

Historical and Statutory Notes

St.1804, c. 120, § 7.
R.S.1836, c. 127, § 16.
G.S.1860, c. 162, § 15.
P.S.1882, c. 204, § 15.
R.L.1902, c. 209, § 15.

§ 19. Common utterers of counterfeit coin

Whoever, having been convicted of any of the crimes mentioned in the preceding section, is again convicted of the same crimes committed after the former conviction, and whoever is at the same sitting of the court convicted upon three distinct charges of said crimes, shall be adjudged a common utterer of counterfeit coin, and punished by imprisonment in the state prison for not more than twenty years.

Historical and Statutory Notes

St.1804, c. 120, § 7.
R.S.1836, c. 127, § 17.
G.S.1860, c. 162, § 16.
P.S.1882, c. 204, § 16.
R.L.1902, c. 209, § 16.

§ 20. Tools for making counterfeit coin

Whoever casts, stamps, engraves, makes or mends, or knowingly has in his possession a mould, pattern, die, puncheon, engine, press or other tool or instrument, adapted to and designed for coining or making counterfeit coin, in the similitude of any gold or silver coin current by law or usage in the commonwealth, with intent to use or employ the same or to cause or permit the same to be used or employed in coining or making any such false and counterfeit coin as aforesaid, shall be punished by imprisonment in the state prison for not more than ten years or by a fine of not more than one thousand dollars and imprisonment in jail for not more than two years.

Historical and Statutory Notes

St.1804, c. 120, § 8.
R.S.1836, c. 127, § 18.
G.S.1860, c. 162, § 17.
P.S.1882, c. 204, § 17.
R.L.1902, c. 209, § 17.

§ 21. Notes, bills, orders or checks as currency

Whoever issues or passes a note, bill, order or check, other than foreign bills of exchange, the notes or bills of a bank incorporated by the laws of this commonwealth, of the United States, of some one of the United States or of any of the British provinces of North America, with the intent that the same shall be circulated as currency, shall be punished by a fine of fifty dollars.

Historical and Statutory Notes

St.1833, c. 206.
R.S.1836, c. 36, § 70.
G.S.1860, c. 162, § 18.
P.S.1882, c. 204, § 18.
R.L.1902, c. 209, § 18.

§ 22. Notes, bills, orders or checks for less than five dollars, as currency

Whoever issues or passes a note, bill, order or check, other than the notes or bills of a bank incorporated under the authority of this commonwealth, of the United States or of some one of the United States, for an amount less than five dollars, or whereon a less amount than five dollars is due at the time of such issuing or passing thereof, with intent that the same shall be circulated as currency, shall be punished by a fine of fifty dollars.

Historical and Statutory Notes

St.1804, c. 58, §§ 1, 2; c. 136, § 1.
R.S.1836, c. 33, § 7.
G.S.1860, c. 162, § 19.
P.S.1882, c. 204, § 19.
R.L.1902, c. 209, § 19.

§ 23. Bank notes or bills for a fraction of a dollar

Whoever receives or puts in circulation as currency a bank note or bill which is, or a part of which is, for any fractional part of a dollar shall be punished by a fine of twenty-five dollars.

Historical and Statutory Notes

St.1853, c. 392, § 2.
G.S.1860, c. 162, § 20.
P.S.1882, c. 204, § 20.
R.L.1902, c. 209, § 20.

§ 24. Connecting parts of instruments

Whoever fraudulently connects different parts of several bank notes or other genuine instruments in such manner as to produce one additional note or instrument, with intent to pass all of them as genuine, shall be guilty of forgery, in like manner as if each of them had been falsely made or forged.

Historical and Statutory Notes

R.S.1836, c. 127, § 12.
G.S.1860, c. 162, § 21.
P.S.1882, c. 204, § 21.
R.L.1902, c. 209, § 21.

§ 25. Damaging or impairing bank bills or notes

Whoever wilfully and maliciously tears, cuts or in any manner damages and impairs the usefulness for circulation of a bank bill or note of a bank in this commonwealth shall be punished by a fine of not more than ten dollars; but the possession or uttering of a bill so injured shall not be evidence against a party charged, unless connected with other circumstances tending to prove that the bill or note was injured by him.

Historical and Statutory Notes

St.1852, c. 64.
G.S.1860, c. 162, § 22.
P.S.1882, c. 204, § 22.
R.L.1902, c. 209, § 22.

§ 26. Gathering or retaining bank bills or notes

Whoever maliciously gathers up or retains or maliciously aids in gathering up or retaining bills or notes of a bank or banking company, current by law or usage in the commonwealth, for the purpose of injuring or impeding the circulation or business of such bank or banking company, or of compelling it to do any act out of the usual course of its business, shall be punished by a fine of not more than five hundred dollars or by imprisonment for not more than two years; and in the prosecution of any such crime it shall not be necessary to set out and describe each bill, but it shall be sufficient to aver and prove any amount of the bills of any bank which have been so gathered up or retained.

Historical and Statutory Notes

St.1859, c. 116, §§ 3, 4.
G.S.1860, c. 162, § 23.
P.S.1882, c. 204, § 23.
R.L.1902, c. 209, § 23.

§ 27. Possession of worthless bank bills or notes

Whoever has in his possession at the same time five or more bank bills or notes not current which are worthless as bank bills or notes, knowing the same to be worthless as aforesaid, or has papers not bank bills or notes, but made in the similitude thereof, or papers purporting to be the bills or notes of a bank which has never existed, knowing the character of such papers, with intent to pass, utter or circulate the same, or to procure any other person so to do, for the purpose of injuring or defrauding, shall be punished by imprisonment in the state prison for not more than five years, or by a fine of not more than five hundred dollars and imprisonment in the house of correction for not more than two and one half years.

Historical and Statutory Notes

St.1857, c. 231, § 1.
G.S.1860, c. 162, § 24.
P.S.1882, c. 204, § 24.
R.L.1902, c. 209, § 24.
St.1914, c. 635.
St.1918, c. 257, § 464.
St.1919, c. 5.
St.1920, c. 2.

§ 28. Uttering, passing or tendering worthless bank bills or notes

Whoever utters or passes or tenders in payment as true any such worthless bank bill or note not current, or any paper not a bank bill or note but made in the similitude thereof, or any paper purporting to be the bill or note of a bank which has never existed, knowing the same to be worthless and not current, as aforesaid, with intent to injure and defraud, shall be punished by imprisonment in the state prison for not more than five years, or by a fine of not more than five hundred dollars and imprisonment in the house of correction for not more than two and one half years.

Historical and Statutory Notes

St.1857, c. 231, § 2.
G.S.1860, c. 162, § 25.
P.S.1882, c. 204, § 25.
R.L.1902, c. 209, § 25.
St.1914, c. 635.
St.1918, c. 257, § 464.
St.1919, c. 5.
St.1920, c. 2.

§ 29. Shop bills or advertisements similar to bank bills or treasury notes or other United States Securities

Whoever engraves, prints, issues, utters or circulates a shop bill or advertisement, in similitude, form and appearance like a bank bill, on paper similar to paper used for bank bills, and with vignettes, figures or decorations used on bank bills, or having the general appearance of a bank bill, or in similitude, form and appearance, like a treasury note, note, certificate, bill of credit or other security issued by or on behalf of the United States, on paper similar to paper used for the same, respectively, and with vignettes, figures or decorations used thereon, or having the general appearance of a treasury note, note, certificate, bill of credit or other security issued by or on behalf of the United States, shall be punished by a fine of not more than fifty dollars or by imprisonment in jail for not more than three months.

Historical and Statutory Notes

St.1849, c. 5.
G.S.1860, c. 162, § 26.
St.1862, c. 63.
P.S.1882, c. 204, § 26.
R.L.1902, c. 209, § 26.

§ 30. Seizure of false, forged or counterfeit bills, notes or bonds or counterfeiter's tools; destruction; return

When false, forged or counterfeit bank bills or notes, or forged or counterfeit notes or bonds of any state or corporation, or plates, dies or other tools, instruments or implements used by counterfeiters, or designed for the forging or making of false or counterfeit notes, coin or bills, or worthless bank bills or notes not current described in sections twenty-seven and twenty-eight, come to the knowledge of a sheriff, constable, police officer or other officer of justice, he shall immediately seize and take possession of and deliver them into the custody of the superior court, which shall cause them to be destroyed by an officer of the court, who shall make return to the court of his doings in the premises.

Historical and Statutory Notes

St.1855, c. 168, § 1.
St.1857, c. 231, § 3.
G.S.1860, c. 162, § 27.
St.1875, c. 40.
P.S.1882, c. 204, § 27.
R.L.1902, c. 209, § 27.

§ 31. Compensation to prosecutors and officers

Upon a conviction of any crime mentioned in sections seven, eight, seventeen, eighteen, twenty or twenty-eight or upon forfeiture by persons prosecuted for any such crime of any recognizance for their appearance to answer to the same, the superior court may order compensation to the prosecutor and to the officer who has secured and kept the evidence of the crime, not exceeding their actual expenses, with a reasonable allowance for their time and trouble, which shall be paid by the county.

Historical and Statutory Notes

St.1713–14, c. 11, § 1.
St.1715–16, c. 15.
St.1749–50, c. 22, § 5.
St.1804, c. 120, § 9.
St.1814, c. 95.
R.S.1836, c. 127, § 19.
St.1845, c. 153.
St.1845, c. 248.
St.1846, c. 142.
G.S.1860, c. 162, § 28.
St.1860, c. 191, § 10.
P.S.1882, c. 204, § 28.
R.L.1902, c. 209, § 28.

CHAPTER 268

CRIMES AGAINST PUBLIC JUSTICE

The section headings for the General Laws in this pamphlet have been editorially supplied.

§ 1. Perjury

Whoever, being lawfully required to depose the truth in a judicial proceeding or in a proceeding in a course of justice, wilfully swears or affirms falsely in a matter material to the issue or point in question, or whoever, being required by law to take an oath or affirmation, wilfully swears or affirms falsely in a matter relative to which such oath or affirmation is required, shall be guilty of perjury. Whoever commits perjury on the trial of an indictment for a capital crime shall be punished by imprisonment in the state prison for life or for any term of years, and whoever commits perjury in any other case shall be punished by imprisonment in the state prison for not more than twenty years or by a fine of not more than one thousand dollars or by imprisonment in jail for not more than two and one half years, or by both such fine and imprisonment in jail.

An indictment or complaint for violation of this section alleging that, in any proceedings before or ancillary to any court or grand jury proceedings relating to an indictment or complaint for the commission of a violent crime, as defined in section 121 of chapter 140, the defendant under oath has knowingly made 2 or more declarations, which are inconsistent to the degree that 1 of them is necessarily false, need not specify which declaration is false if: (1) each declaration was material to the point in question and (2) each declaration was made within the period of the statue [1] of limitations for the offense charged under this section. In any prosecution under this section, the falsity of a declaration set forth in the indictment or complaint shall be established sufficient for conviction by proof that the defendant, while under oath, made irreconcilably contradictory declarations material to the point in question. If, in the same continuous court or grand jury proceeding in which a declaration is made, the person making the declaration admits to such declaration to be false, such admission shall bar prosecution under this section if, at the time the admission is made, the declaration has not substantially affected the proceeding, or it has not become manifest that such falsity has been or will be exposed. It shall be a defense to an indictment or complaint made pursuant to this section that the defendant, at the time he made each declaration, believed each such declaration to be true or its falsity was the result of a good faith mistake or error.

Amended by St.2006, c. 48, § 2, eff. Mar. 30, 2006.

1 So in original; probably should read "statute".

Historical and Statutory Notes

R.L. c. 94, § 11.
C.L. c. 15, § 11.
St.1692–3, c. 18, § 9.
St.1784, c. 51, § 1.
St.1797, c. 35, § 10.
St.1812, c. 144, § 1.
St.1824, c. 91, § 2.
St.1829, c. 56.
R.S.1836, c. 94, § 12; c. 128, §§ 1, 2.
G.S.1860, c. 163, §§ 1, 2.
P.S.1882, c. 205, §§ 1, 2.
St.1892, c. 123.
St.1898, c. 562, § 112.
R.L.1902, c. 210, § 1.
St.1912, c. 719, § 9.
St.1914, c. 635.
St.1917, c. 165, § 2.
St.1918, c. 257, § 464.
St.1919, c. 5.
St.1920, c. 2.

§ 1A. Statements containing declaration relative to penalties of perjury; verification; false statements

No written statement required by law shall be required to be verified by oath or affirmation before a magistrate if it contains or is verified by a written declaration that it is made under the penalties of perjury. Whoever signs and issues such a written statement containing or verified by such a written declaration shall be guilty of perjury and subject to the penalties thereof if such statement is wilfully false in a material matter.

Amended by St.1947, c. 106.

Historical and Statutory Notes

St.1926, c. 187, § 1.

§ 2. Subornation of perjury

Whoever is guilty of subornation of perjury, by procuring another person to commit perjury, shall be punished as for perjury.

Historical and Statutory Notes

St.1692–3, c. 18, § 9.
St.1784, c. 51, § 2.
St.1812, c. 144, § 2.
R.S.1836, c. 128, § 3.
G.S.1860, c. 163, § 3.
P.S.1882, c. 205, § 3.
R.L.1902, c. 210, § 2.

§ 3. Attempt to procure another to commit perjury

Whoever attempts to incite or procure another person to commit perjury, although no perjury is committed, shall be punished by imprisonment in the state prison for not more than five years or in jail for not more than one year.

Historical and Statutory Notes

St.1784, c. 51, § 3.
St.1812, c. 144, § 3.
R.S.1836, c. 128, § 4.
G.S.1860, c. 163, § 4.
P.S.1882, c. 205, § 4.
R.L.1902, c. 210, § 3.

§ 4. Testimony creating presumption of perjury; commitment; recognizance; witnesses bound over; notice

If it appears to a court of record that a party or a witness who has been legally sworn and examined, or has made an affidavit, in any proceeding in a court or course of justice has so testified as to create a reasonable presumption that he has committed perjury therein, the court may forthwith commit him or may require him to recognize with sureties for his appearance to answer to an indictment for perjury; and thereupon the witnesses to establish such perjury may, if present, be bound over to the superior court, and notice of the proceedings shall forthwith be given to the district attorney.

Historical and Statutory Notes

R.S.1836, c. 128, § 6.
G.S.1860, c. 163, § 5.
P.S.1882, c. 205, § 7.
R.L.1902, c. 210, § 4.

§ 5. Presumption of perjury; papers, books and documents detained for prosecution

If perjury is reasonably presumed, as aforesaid, papers, books or documents which have been produced and are considered necessary to be used on a prosecution for such perjury may by order of the court be detained from the person who produces them so long as may be necessary for their use in such prosecution.

Historical and Statutory Notes

R.S.1836, c. 128, § 7.
G.S.1860, c. 163, § 6.
P.S.1882, c. 205, § 8.
R.L.1902, c. 210, § 5.

§ 6. False reports or testimony before state departments, board or commissioner; false entries in company books or statements; aiders or abettors

Except as provided in sections forty-eight and forty-nine of chapter one hundred and fifty-five, whoever shall wilfully make false report to the department of public utilities, the department of telecommunications and cable, the department of highways, the department of banking and insurance, the department of environmental protection, the board of registration of waste cleanup professionals, or the commissioner of revenue, or who before any such department, board or commissioner, shall testify or affirm falsely to any material fact in any matter wherein an oath or affirmation is required or authorized, or who shall make any false entry or memorandum upon any book, report, paper or statement of any company making report to any of the said departments or board or said commissioner, with intent to deceive the department or board or commissioner, or any agent appointed to examine the affairs of any such company, or to deceive the stockholders or any officer of any such company, or to injure or defraud any such company, and any persons who with like intent aids or abets another in any violation of this section shall be punished by a fine of not more than one thousand dollars or by imprisonment for not more than one year, or both such fine and imprisonment.

Amended by St.1978, c. 514, § 232; St.1991, c. 552, § 132; St.1993, c. 495, § 58; St.1997, c. 164, § 289; St.2008, c. 522, § 44, eff. April 15, 2009.

Historical and Statutory Notes

St.1911, c. 184.
St.1914, c. 742, §§ 149, 199.
St.1931, c. 426, § 310.

§ 6A. False written reports by public officers or employees

Whoever, being an officer or employee of the commonwealth or of any political subdivision thereof or of any authority created by the general court, in the course of his official duties executes, files or publishes any false written report, minutes or statement, knowing the same to be false in a material matter, shall be punished by a fine of not more than one thousand dollars or by imprisonment for not more than one year, or by both such fine and imprisonment.

Added by St.1964, c. 444.

§ 6B. Process servers; false statements; penalty

Any process server who returns to the court a writ or other official instrument of process on which he has willfully falsified either the fact that service has been made, or the fact that a particular kind of service has been made, shall be punished by a fine of not more than five hundred dollars or by imprisonment for not more than one year.

Added by St.1969, c. 293.

§§ 7 to 8A. Repealed, 1962, 779, Sec. 3

Historical and Statutory Notes

See, now, M.G.L.A. c. 268A, §§ 2 to 4.

§ 8B. Compulsion or coercion to refuse appointment or promotion

Any appointing authority or appointing officer, both as defined in chapter thirty-one, who, by himself or by some other person acting on his behalf, compels, or induces by the use of threats or other form of coercion, any person on an eligible list, as defined in chapter thirty-one, to refuse an appointment or promotion by such authority or officer to any position in the classified civil service shall be punished by a fine of not less than fifty nor more than two hundred dollars or by imprisonment in a jail or house of correction for not more than two months, or by both such fine and imprisonment.

Added by St.1961, c. 342.

§ 9. Repealed, 1962, 779, Sec. 3

Historical and Statutory Notes

See, now, M.G.L.A. c. 268A, § 1 et seq.

§ 9A. Public officers or employees; solicitations regarding testimonial dinners

No person shall sell, offer for sale, or accept payment for, tickets or admissions to, nor solicit or accept contributions for, a testimonial dinner or function, or any affair, by whatever name it may be called, having a purpose similar to that of a testimonial dinner or function, for any person, other than a person holding elective public office, whose office or employment is in any law enforcement, regulatory or investigatory body or agency of the commonwealth or any political subdivision thereof.

Whoever violates any provision of this section shall be punished by a fine of not more than five hundred dollars.

Added by St.1962, c. 633.

§§ 10 to 12. Repealed, 1962, 779, Sec. 3

Historical and Statutory Notes

See, now, M.G.L.A. c. 268A, § 1 et seq.

§ 13. Corrupting or attempting to corrupt masters, auditors, jurors, arbitrators, umpires or referees

Whoever corrupts or attempts to corrupt a master in chancery, master, auditor, juror, arbitrator, umpire or referee by giving, offering or promising any gift or gratuity whatever, with intent to influence his opinion or decision, relative to a cause or matter pending in a court, or before an inquest, or for the decision of which he has been chosen or appointed, shall be punished by imprisonment in the state prison for not more than five years or by a fine of not more than one thousand dollars and imprisonment in jail for not more than one year.

Historical and Statutory Notes

R.S.1836, c. 128, § 10.
G.S.1860, c. 163, § 9.
P.S.1882, c. 205, § 14.
R.L.1902, c. 210, § 12.

§ 13A. Picketing court, judge, juror, witness or court officer

Whoever, with the intent of interfering with, obstructing, or impeding the administration of justice, or with the intent of influencing any judge, juror, witness, or court officer, in the discharge of his duty, pickets or parades in or near a building housing a court of the commonwealth, or in or near a building or residence occupied or used by such judge, juror, witness, or court officer, shall be punished by a fine of not more than five thousand dollars or by imprisonment for not more than one year, or both.

Nothing in this section shall interfere with or prevent the exercise by any court of the commonwealth of its power to punish for contempt.

Added by St.1950, c. 109.

§ 13B. Intimidation of witnesses, jurors and persons furnishing information in connection with criminal proceedings

(1) Whoever, directly or indirectly, willfully

(a) threatens, or attempts or causes physical injury, emotional injury, economic injury or property damage to;

(b) conveys a gift, offer or promise of anything of value to; or

(c) misleads, intimidates or harasses another person who is:

(i) a witness or potential witness at any stage of a criminal investigation, grand jury proceeding, trial or other criminal proceeding of any type;

(ii) a person who is or was aware of information, records, documents or objects that relate to a violation of a criminal statute, or a violation of conditions of probation, parole or bail;

(iii) a judge, juror, grand juror, prosecutor, police officer, federal agent, investigator, defense attorney, clerk, court officer, probation officer or parole officer;

(iv) a person who is furthering a civil or criminal proceeding, including criminal investigation, grand jury proceeding, trial, other criminal proceeding of any type, probate and family proceeding, juvenile proceeding, housing proceeding, land proceeding, clerk's hearing, court ordered mediation, any other civil proceeding of any type; or

(v) a person who is or was attending or had made known his intention to attend a civil or criminal proceeding, including criminal investigation, grand jury proceeding, trial, other criminal proceeding of any type, probate and family proceeding, juvenile proceeding, housing proceeding, land proceeding, clerk's hearing, court-ordered mediation, any other civil proceeding of any type with the intent to impede, obstruct, delay, harm, punish or otherwise interfere thereby, or do so with reckless disregard, with such a proceeding shall be punished by imprisonment in a jail or house of correction for not more than 2 and one-half years or by imprisonment in a state prison for not more than 10 years, or by a fine of not less than $1,000 nor more than $5,000, or by both such fine and imprisonment.

(2) As used in this section, "investigator" shall mean an individual or group of individuals lawfully authorized by a department or agency of the federal government, or any political subdivision thereof, or a department or agency of the commonwealth, or any political subdivision thereof, to conduct or engage in an investigation of, prosecution for, or defense of a violation of the laws of the United States or of the commonwealth in the course of his official duties.

(3) As used in this section, "harass" shall mean to engage in any act directed at a specific person or persons, which act seriously alarms or annoys such person or persons and would cause a reasonable person to suffer substantial emotional distress. Such act shall include, but not be limited to, an act conducted by mail or by use of a telephonic or telecommunication device or electronic communication device including but not limited to any device that transfers signs, signals, writing, images, sounds, data, or intelligence of any nature transmitted in whole or in part by a wire, radio, electromagnetic, photo-electronic or photo-optical system, including, but not limited to, electronic mail, internet communications, instant messages or facsimile communications.

(4) A prosecution under this section may be brought in the county in which the criminal investigation, grand jury proceeding, trial or other criminal proceeding is being conducted or took place, or in the county in

which the alleged conduct constituting an offense occurred.

Added by St.1969, c. 460. Amended by St.1970, c. 177; St.1990, c. 369; St.1996, c. 393, §§ 2 to 4; St.2006, c. 48, § 3, eff. Mar. 30, 2006; St.2010, c. 92, § 11, eff. May 3, 2010; St.2010, c. 256, § 120, eff. Nov. 4, 2010.

§ 13C. Disruption of court proceedings

Whoever causes or actively participates in the willful disruption of proceedings of any court of the commonwealth may be punished by a fine of not more than one thousand dollars or by imprisonment in a jail or house of correction for not more than one year, or both. Nothing in this section shall interfere with or prevent the exercise by any court of the commonwealth of its power of contempt.

Added by St.1971, c. 524.

§ 13D. Distributing transcript or description of grand jury testimony with intent to interfere with criminal proceedings

(a) Whoever knowingly distributes or possesses with intent to distribute any transcript of grand jury testimony or any substantially verbatim description of grand jury testimony with the intent to impede, obstruct, delay or otherwise interfere with any criminal proceeding, or the participation of any victim, witness or juror in any stage of a trial, grand jury, or other criminal proceeding, or the continued participation of any person furnishing information to a criminal proceeding, or the continued participation of any person furnishing information to a criminal investigator relating to a violation of any criminal statue, [1] shall be punished by imprisonment in a house of correction for not more than 2½ years or in the state prison for not more than 5 years, or by a fine of not more than $5,000, or both. Nothing in this subsection shall abridge any right protected by the First Amendment to the United States Constitution.

(b) Nothing in this section shall be construed so as to prohibit any person performing an official function in relation to the grand jury from disclosing a grand jury transcript or description thereof pursuant to Massachusetts Rules of Procedure or Federal Rule of Criminal Procedure 6.

(c) Any attorney representing a defendant in a criminal proceeding, including court appointed counsel, who receives a grand jury transcript or a description thereof related to such proceeding from a prosecutor, may provide the transcript or description to his client or any investigator employed by such attorney or another attorney employed by, or appointed by the court to represent, his client, unless such transfer would be in violation of a protective order from a court of competent jurisdiction. Such attorney may further disclose a grand jury transcript or description thereof related to such proceeding to assist in the legal defense of another defendant in a criminal proceeding, unless such transfer would be in violation of a protective order from a court of competent jurisdiction.

(d) Upon motion of the commonwealth and after hearing, a court may issue a protective order prohibiting defense counsel from distributing grand jury transcripts to a criminal defendant, if the commonwealth demonstrates that the defendant is accused of a violent crime, as defined in section 121 of chapter 140, and that there is a reason to believe, based on specific and articulable facts including, but not limited to, the defendant's past history of violence and the nature of the charges against the defendant, that the defendant poses a threat to a witness or victim. The defendant shall have a right to cross examine any commonwealth witness. In making a determination relative to the issuance of a protective order under this section, the court shall consider whether the defendant has an exceptional need to receive such grand jury transcripts.

(e) Any grand jury transcript or document citing or describing grand jury testimony filed with any court shall be filed and maintained under seal, unless the paper is filed in a criminal prosecution for perjury before a grand jury.

Added by St.2006, c. 48, § 4, eff. Mar. 30, 2006.

[1] So in enrolled bill; probably should read "statute".

§ 13E. Tampering with record, document or other object for use in an official proceeding

(a) As used in this section the following word shall, unless the context clearly requires otherwise, have the following meaning:—

"Official proceeding", a proceeding before a court or grand jury, or a proceeding before a state agency or commission, which proceeding is authorized by law and relates to an alleged violation of a criminal statute or the laws and regulations enforced by the state ethics commission, the state secretary, the office of the inspector general, or the office of campaign and political finance, or an alleged violation for which the attorney general may issue a civil investigative demand.

(b) Whoever alters, destroys, mutilates, or conceals a record, document, or other object, or attempts to do so, with the intent to impair the record, document or object's integrity or availability for use in an official proceeding, whether or not the proceeding is pending at that time, shall be punished, by (i) a fine of not more than $10,000, or by imprisonment in the state prison for not more than 5 years, or in a jail or house of correction for not more than 2½ years, or both, or (ii) if the official proceeding involves a violation of a criminal statute, by a fine of not more than $25,000, or by imprisonment in the state prison for not more than 10 years, or in a jail or house of correction for not more than 2½ years, or both.

(c) The record, document, or other object need not be admissible in evidence or free of a claim of privilege.

(d) A prosecution under this section may be brought in the county where the official proceeding was or would have been convened or where the alleged conduct constituting an offense occurred.

Added by St.2009, c. 28, § 60, eff. Sept. 29, 2009.

§ 14. Receipt of gift by juror, arbitrator, umpire, referee, master or auditor

Whoever, being summoned as a juror or chosen or appointed as an arbitrator, umpire or referee, or, being a master in chancery, master or auditor, corruptly takes anything to give his verdict, award or report, or corruptly receives any gift or gratuity from a party to a suit, cause or proceeding for the trial or decision of which such juror has been summoned, or for the hearing or determination of which such master in chancery, master, auditor, arbitrator, umpire or referee has been chosen or appointed, shall be punished by imprisonment in the state prison for not more than five years or by a fine of not more than one thousand dollars and imprisonment in jail for not more than one year.

Historical and Statutory Notes

R.S.1836, c. 128, § 11.
G.S.1860, c. 163, § 10.
P.S.1882, c. 205, § 15.
R.L.1902, c. 210, § 13.

§ 14A. Juror discharged from employment

No person shall be discharged from or deprived of his employment because of his attendance or service as a grand or traverse juror in any court. Violation of this section by an employer shall be a contempt of the court upon which such person is or has been in attendance or in which he is or has been serving as a grand or traverse juror, and such employer may be prosecuted upon complaint verified upon oath and be punished for such contempt.

Added by St.1936, c. 168.

§ 14B. Witnesses in criminal actions; discharge, etc. from employment

Any person who is a victim of a crime upon which an accusatory instrument is based, or is subpoenaed to attend a criminal action as a witness and who notifies his employer of such subpoena prior to the day of his attendance, shall not be subject to discharge or penalty by said employer on account of his absence from employment by reason of such witness service. An employer shall not subject an employee to discharge or penalty or the threat of discharge or penalty on account of the absence of such employee from employment by reason of his attendance as a witness at a criminal action. An employer who violates the provisions of this section shall be punished by a fine of not more than two hundred dollars or by imprisonment for not more than one month, or both such fine and imprisonment.

Added by St.1989, c. 233, § 2.

§ 15. Aiding escape from a correctional institution or jail; rescue

Whoever conveys into a correctional institution of the commonwealth or into a jail, house of correction, house of reformation or like place of confinement, a disguise, instrument, tool, weapon or other thing which is adapted or useful to aid a prisoner in making his escape, with intent to aid the escape of a prisoner, or whoever, by any means, aids or assists such prisoner in endeavoring to escape therefrom, whether such escape is effected or attempted or not, and whoever forcibly or fraudulently rescues or attempts to rescue a prisoner held in custody upon a conviction or charge of crime, shall, if the person whose escape or rescue was effected or intended is a convict under sentence to the state prison or is charged with a felony, be punished by a fine of not more than five hundred dollars or by imprisonment in the state prison for not more than ten years; but if he is a convict under sentence to any other of said institutions, by imprisonment in the state prison for not more than seven years; and if he is charged with a misdemeanor, then by a fine of not more than five hundred dollars or by imprisonment in jail for not more than two years.

Amended by St.1955, c. 770, § 81.

Historical and Statutory Notes

C.L. c. 127, § 4.
St.1700–1, c. 2, §§ 3, 4.
St.1784, c. 41, § 2.
St.1805, c. 113, §§ 6, 8.
St.1811, c. 32, § 8.
St.1827, c. 118, § 24.
R.S.1836, c. 128, § 12; c. 144, § 41.
G.S.1860, c. 163, § 11; c. 179, § 57.
P.S.1882, c. 205, § 16; c. 221, § 40.
R.L.1902, c. 210, § 14.

§ 15A. Escapes from jail

Whoever, after lawfully being placed in custody in a jail of a city or town, escapes from any such jail shall be punished by imprisonment in a jail or house of correction for not more than two and one-half years, or by a fine of not more than five hundred dollars, or both.

Added by St.1989, c. 431.

§ 16. Escape or attempt to escape, or failure to return from temporary release or furlough

A prisoner of any penal institution including a prisoner who is held in custody for a court appearance or a person committed under the provisions of section five or six of chapter one hundred and twenty-three A to a treatment center or branch thereof described in sections two and four of said chapter one hundred and twenty-three A, or a prisoner committed to any jail or correctional institution under a lawful order of a court, who escapes or attempts to escape from any such institution or from land appurtenant thereto, or from any courthouse or from land appurtenant thereto or from the custody of any officer thereof while being conveyed to or from said institution, center or branch, or who knowingly disables or attempts to disable or defeat electronic monitoring of the prisoner, or fails to return from any temporary release from said institution under the provisions of section ninety A of chapter one hundred and twenty-seven, or fails to return from any temporary release from said institution, center or branch, may be pursued and recaptured and shall be punished by imprisonment in the state prison for not more than ten years or by imprisonment in a jail or house of correction for not more than two and one-half years.

Amended by St.1934, c. 344; St.1941, c. 344, § 28; St.1943, c. 19, § 1; St.1955, c. 770, § 82; St.1973, c. 1062, § 1; St.1985, c. 241; St.1989, c. 313, § 2; St.1993, c. 376; St.2010, c. 256, § 121, eff. Nov. 4, 2010.

Historical and Statutory Notes

St.1805, c. 113, §§ 9, 10.
St.1811, c. 32, §§ 9, 10.
St.1818, c. 123, § 7.
St.1827, c. 118, §§ 11, 12.
St.1834, c. 151, § 14.
R.S.1836, c. 143, §§ 49 to 51; c. 144, §§ 37, 38.
St.1851, c. 93.
G.S.1860, c. 178, § 46; c. 179, §§ 53, 54.
St.1866, c. 198, § 5.
St.1870, c. 288, § 3.
St.1873, c. 73, § 1.
St.1880, c. 257, § 8.
P.S.1882, c. 88, § 8; c. 220, § 50; c. 221, §§ 36, 37.
St.1882, c. 198.
St.1885, c. 94, §§ 2, 3.
R.L.1902, c. 85, § 33; c. 210, §§ 15 to 18.
St.1903, c. 188.
St.1904, c. 243, § 2.
St.1905, c. 355, § 3.
St.1916, c. 187.
St.1918, c. 257, § 464.
St.1919, c. 5.
St.1920, c. 2.
St.1920, c. 380.
St.1925, c. 53.

§ 16A. Repealed, 1973, 1062, Sec. 2

§ 17. Aiding escape from officer or person having custody

Whoever aids or assists a prisoner in escaping or attempting to escape from an officer or person who has the lawful custody of such prisoner shall be punished by a fine of not more than five hundred dollars or by imprisonment for not more than two years.

Historical and Statutory Notes

St.1811, c. 32, § 8.
St.1827, c. 118, § 24.
R.S.1836, c. 128, § 13.
G.S.1860, c. 163, § 12.
P.S.1882, c. 205, § 17.
R.L.1902, c. 210, § 21.

§ 18. Jailer or officer suffering prisoner to escape

A jailer or officer who, except as provided in the following section, voluntarily suffers a prisoner in his custody upon conviction or upon a charge of crime to escape shall suffer the punishment and penalties to which the prisoner whom he suffered to escape was sentenced or would be liable to suffer upon conviction of the crime wherewith he stood charged.

Historical and Statutory Notes

St.1700–1, c. 2, § 6.
St.1784, c. 41, § 3.
R.S.1836, c. 128, § 14.
G.S.1860, c. 163, § 13.
P.S.1882, c. 205, § 18.
R.L.1902, c. 210, § 25.

§ 19. Suffering or consenting to an escape from a penal institution

An officer or other person, who, being employed in any penal institution, voluntarily suffers a convict confined therein to escape, or in any way consents to such escape, shall be punished by imprisonment in the state prison for not more than twenty years.

Historical and Statutory Notes

St.1805, c. 113, § 6.
St.1827, c. 118, § 22.
R.S.1836, c. 144, § 39.
G.S.1860, c. 179, § 55.
P.S.1882, c. 221, § 38.
R.L.1902, c. 210, § 26.
St.1929, c. 170, § 3.

§ 20. Negligently suffering prisoner to escape; refusal to receive prisoner

A jailer or officer who, through negligence, suffers a prisoner in his custody upon conviction or upon a charge of crime to escape, or wilfully refuses to receive into his custody a prisoner lawfully directed to be committed thereto upon conviction, upon a charge of crime, or upon a lawful process, shall be punished by a fine of not more than five hundred dollars or by imprisonment for not more than two years.

Historical and Statutory Notes

C.L. c. 128, § 2.
St.1700–1, c. 2, § 7.
St.1784, c. 41, § 3.
R.S.1836, c. 128, § 15.
G.S.1860, c. 163, § 14.
P.S.1882, c. 205, § 19.
R.L.1902, c. 210, § 27.

§ 21. Suffering convict to be at large, visited, relieved or comforted

An officer or person who, being employed in the state prison, suffers a convict under sentence of solitary imprisonment to be at large or out of the cell assigned to him, or suffers any convict confined in the prison to be at large out of the prison, or to be visited, conversed with or in any way relieved or comforted, contrary to the regulations of the prison, shall be punished by a fine of not more than five hundred dollars.

Historical and Statutory Notes

St.1805, c. 113, § 7.
St.1811, c. 32, § 7.
St.1827, c. 118, § 23.
G.S.1860, c. 179, § 56.
P.S.1882, c. 221, § 39.
R.L.1902, c. 210, § 28.

§ 21A. Officer or other employee of penal or correctional institution; sexual relations with inmate; punishment

An officer or other person who is employed by or contracts with any penal or correctional institution in the commonwealth, and who, in the course of such employment or contract or as a result thereof, engages in sexual relations with an inmate confined therein, within or outside of such institution, or an inmate who is otherwise under the direct custodial supervision and control of such officer or other person, shall be punished by imprisonment for not more than five years in a state prison or by a fine of $10,000 or both. In a prosecution commenced under this section, an inmate shall be deemed incapable of consent to sexual relations with such person. For purposes of this section, sexual relations shall include intentional, inappropriate contact of a sexual nature, including, but not limited to conduct prohibited by section 22 or 24 of chapter 265 or section 2, 3, 35 or 53A of chapter 272.

Added by St.1999, c. 127, § 183.

§ 22. Delay of service of warrants

An officer who wilfully delays service of a warrant of arrest or a search warrant committed to him for service shall be punished by a fine of not more than fifty dollars.

Historical and Statutory Notes

St.1899, c. 389.
R.L.1902, c. 210, § 29.

§ 23. Refusal or delay to execute process resulting in escape

An officer who, being authorized to serve process, wilfully and corruptly refuses to execute a lawful process directed to him and requiring him to apprehend or confine a person convicted of or charged with crime, or wilfully and corruptly omits or delays to execute such process, whereby such person escapes, shall be punished by a fine of not more than five hundred dollars or by imprisonment for not more than one year.

Historical and Statutory Notes

R.S.1836, c. 128, § 16.
G.S.1860, c. 163, § 15.
P.S.1882, c. 205, § 20.
R.L.1902, c. 210, § 30.

§ 24. Neglect or refusal to assist officer or watchman

Whoever, being required in the name of the commonwealth by a sheriff, deputy sheriff, constable, police officer or watchman, neglects or refuses to assist him in the execution of his office in a criminal case, in the preservation of the peace or in the apprehension or securing of a person for a breach of the peace, or in a case of escape or rescue of persons arrested upon civil process, shall be punished by a fine of not more than fifty dollars or by imprisonment for not more than one month.

Historical and Statutory Notes

St.1795, c. 68, § 1.
R.S.1836, c. 128, § 17.
St.1855, c. 45.
G.S.1860, c. 163, § 16.
P.S.1882, c. 205, § 21.
R.L.1902, c. 210, § 31.

§ 25. Refusal or neglect to obey order of justice of the peace to apprehend offender

Whoever, being required by a justice of the peace, upon view of a breach of the peace or of any other offence proper for his cognizance, to apprehend the offender, refuses or neglects to obey such justice, shall be punished as provided in the preceding section; and no person to whom such justice is known or declares himself to be a justice of the peace shall plead any excuse on pretence of ignorance of his office.

Historical and Statutory Notes

St.1795, c. 68, § 3.
R.S.1836, c. 128, § 18.
G.S.1860, c. 163, § 17.
P.S.1882, c. 205, § 22.
R.L.1902, c. 210, § 32.

§ 26. Delivering alcoholic beverages to prisoners; possession

Whoever gives, sells or delivers alcoholic beverages, as defined in section one of chapter one hundred and thirty-eight, to a person confined in any correctional institution or other place of confinement, or to a person in the custody of a sheriff, constable, police officer, superintendent of a correctional institution, or other superintendent or keeper of a place of confinement, or has in his possession, within the precincts of any prison or other place of confinement, any such beverages, with intent to convey or deliver them to any person confined therein, except under the direction of the physician appointed to attend such prisoner, shall be punished by a fine of not more than fifty dollars or by imprisonment for not more than two months.

Amended by St.1934, c. 328, § 24; St.1955, c. 770, § 84; St.1957, c. 777, § 33; St.1979, c. 485, § 41.

Historical and Statutory Notes

St.1834, c. 151, § 21.
R.S.1836, c. 143, § 37.
St.1854, c. 93.
G.S.1860, c. 178, § 43.
P.S.1882, c. 222, § 2.
R.L.1902, c. 210, § 19.

§ 27. Delivering alcoholic beverages to patients of public institutions; possession

Whoever gives, sells or delivers any alcoholic beverages, as defined in section one of chapter one hundred and thirty-eight, to any patient or inmate of any public institution, or to any patient or inmate under the control of any such institution, except under the direction of a physician authorized so to do, and whoever has in his possession within the precincts of any such institution any such beverages with intent to consume the same or to convey, give, sell or deliver the same to any patient or inmate thereof, except under direction as aforesaid, shall be punished by a fine of not more than fifty dollars or by imprisonment for not more than two months.

Amended by St.1934, c. 328, § 25.

Historical and Statutory Notes

St.1903, c. 410.
St.1909, c. 504, § 94.
St.1918, c. 63.

§ 28. Delivering drugs or articles to prisoners in correctional institutions or jails; possession

Whoever gives or delivers to a prisoner in any correctional institution, or in any jail or house of correction, any drug or article whatever, or has in his possession within the precincts of any prison herein named with intent to give or deliver to any prisoner any such drug or article without the permission of the superintendent or keeper, shall be punished by imprisonment in the state prison for not more than five years, or in a jail or house of correction for not more than two years, or by a fine of not more than one thousand dollars.

Amended by St.1955, c. 770, § 85; St.1957, c. 777, § 34; St.1965, c. 407; St.1979, c. 485, § 42.

Historical and Statutory Notes

St.1905, c. 258.
St.1906, c. 243, § 1.

§ 29. Delivery, or permission of delivery, by officers, of alcoholic beverages, to prisoners; keeping together prisoners of different sexes or classes

A sheriff, jailer, superintendent of a house of correction or officer of a correctional institution who, under any pretence, gives, sells or delivers or knowingly permits to be given, sold or delivered to a prisoner in his custody any alcoholic beverages, as defined in section one of chapter one hundred and thirty-eight, or cider, unless the physician of the penal institution certifies in writing that the health of the prisoner requires the same; or such sheriff, jailer, superintendent of a house of correction or officer of a correctional institution who willingly or negligently suffers such prisoner to have or drink any alcoholic beverages, as so defined, or who places or keeps together prisoners in his custody of different sexes or classes, contrary to section twenty-two of chapter one hundred and twenty-seven, shall forfeit twenty-five dollars for the first offence and fifty dollars for any offence committed subsequent to the first conviction, and, upon such second conviction, shall be removed from office, and be ineligible to hold the office of sheriff, deputy sheriff, jailer, superintendent or keeper of any correctional institution for five years thereafter. If the physician certifies that the health of the prisoner requires such liquor, the prisoner shall be allowed the quantity prescribed and no more.

Amended by St.1934, c. 328, § 26; St.1955, c. 770, § 86; St.1979, c. 485, § 43.

Historical and Statutory Notes

St.1817, c. 149, §§ 3, 4.
St.1823, c. 148, §§ 2, 4.
St.1834, c. 151, §§ 20, 21.
R.S.1836, c. 143, §§ 36, 37.
G.S.1860, c. 178, §§ 42, 44.
P.S.1882, c. 220, §§ 47, 48.
R.L.1902, c. 210, § 20.

§ 30. Disturbing correctional institutions or jail; attracting attention of, or communicating with, inmates

Whoever wilfully disturbs any correctional institution of the commonwealth, the Lyman school, industrial school for boys, industrial school for girls, or a jail or house of correction, or in any manner seeks to attract the attention of, or without the permission of the officer in charge has communication with, an inmate thereof, shall be punished by a fine of not more than fifty dollars or by imprisonment for not more than three months.

Amended by St.1955, c. 770, § 87.

Historical and Statutory Notes

St.1885, c. 303.
R.L.1902, c. 210, § 22.
St.1909, c. 255.
St.1911, c. 181.
St.1918, c. 257, § 307.
St.1919, c. 5.
St.1920, c. 2.
St.1931, c. 426, § 311.

§ 31. Delivery or receipt of articles to or from inmates

Whoever delivers or procures to be delivered, or has in his possession with intent to deliver, to an inmate confined in any penal institution, or whoever deposits or conceals in or about the institution, or the dependencies thereof, or upon any land appurtenant thereto, or in any boat or vehicle going into the premises belonging to the institution, any article, with intent that an inmate shall obtain or receive it, and whoever receives from an inmate any article with intent to convey it out of the institution, contrary to the rules and regulations thereof, and without the knowledge and permission of the commissioner of correction or of the superintendent, keeper, sheriff or other officer in charge thereof shall be punished by a fine of not more than five hundred dollars or by imprisonment in the state prison for not more than three years or in jail for not more than two and one half years.

Any inmate of a correctional institution who, upon returning from a furlough or a work program, brings or attempts to bring into said institution an illegal drug, gun, knife or other similar weapon as defined in section ten of chapter two hundred and sixty-nine of the General Laws, shall be punished by an additional sentence of not less than seven nor more than ten years in state prison.

Amended by St.1955, c. 770, § 88; St.1957, c. 777, § 35; St.1962, c. 747; St.1979, c. 485, § 44; St.1987, c. 411.

Historical and Statutory Notes

St.1805, c. 113, § 8.
St.1825, c. 84, § 4.
R.S.1836, c. 144, § 42.
St.1838, c. 152, § 1.
G.S.1860, c. 179, § 58.
St.1878, c. 133.
St.1879, c. 294, § 34.
P.S.1882, c. 221, § 41.
St.1887, c. 339.
R.L.1902, c. 210, § 23.
St.1911, c. 181.
St.1914, c. 635.
St.1918, c. 257, § 464.
St.1919, c. 5; 350, § 83.
St.1920, c. 2.
St.1929, c. 170, § 4.

§ 32. Interference or tampering with police or fire signal systems, or motorist highway emergency aid call boxes; false alarms or calls

Whoever opens a signal box connected with a police signal system for the purpose of giving, or causing to be given, a false alarm, or interferes in any way with such box by breaking, cutting, injuring or defacing the same; or whoever, without authority, opens, tampers or meddles with such box, or with any part or parts thereof, or with the police signal wires, or with anything connected therewith, or with such purpose, wantonly and without cause tampers or meddles with a signal box connected with a fire signal system or with any part or thing connected therewith, shall be subject to immediate arrest and shall be punished by a fine of not less than five hundred nor more than one thousand dollars, or by imprisonment for not more than two years, or both.

Whoever opens a motorist highway emergency aid call box on any state highway connected with a highway emergency signal system for the purpose of giving or causing to be given a false call for aid, or interferes in any way with such box by breaking, cutting, injuring or defacing the same; or, without authority, opens, tampers or meddles with such box, or with any part or parts thereof, or with anything connected therewith, or, with such purpose, wantonly and without cause tampers or meddles with a motorist highway emergency aid call box or with any part or thing connected therewith, shall be punished by a fine of not less than one hundred dollars nor more than five hundred dollars.

Amended by St.1970, c. 278; St.1979, c. 205; St.1989, c. 513.

Historical and Statutory Notes

St.1888, c. 291.
St.1901, c. 527.
R.L.1902, c. 210, § 24.

§ 32A. Interference with fire fighting operations

Whoever willfully obstructs, interferes with or hinders a fire fighter in the lawful performance of his duty, or whoever willfully obstructs, interferes with or hinders a fire fighting force in the lawful performance of its duty, shall be punished by a fine of not less than one hundred nor more than one thousand dollars or by imprisonment in a jail or house of correction for not less than thirty days nor more than two and one half years or by imprisonment in the state prison for not more than five years, or by both such fine and imprisonment in a jail or house of correction.

Added by St.1966, c. 289. Amended by St.1968, c. 82.

§ 32B. Resisting arrest

(a) A person commits the crime of resisting arrest if he knowingly prevents or attempts to prevent a police officer, acting under color of his official authority, from effecting an arrest of the actor or another, by:

(1) using or threatening to use physical force or violence against the police officer or another; or

(2) using any other means which creates a substantial risk of causing bodily injury to such police officer or another.

(b) It shall not be a defense to a prosecution under this section that the police officer was attempting to make an arrest which was unlawful, if he was acting under color of his official authority, and in attempting to make the arrest he was not resorting to unreasonable or excessive force giving rise to the right of self-defense. A police officer acts under the color of his official authority when, in the regular course of assigned duties, he is called upon to make, and does make, a judgment in good faith based upon surrounding facts and circumstances that an arrest should be made by him.

(c) The term "police officer" as used in this section shall mean a police officer in uniform or, if out of uniform, one who has identified himself by exhibiting his credentials as such police officer while attempting such arrest.

(d) Whoever violates this section shall be punished by imprisonment in a jail or house of correction for not more than two and one-half years or a fine of not more than five hundred dollars, or both.

Added by St.1995, c. 276.

§ 33. Falsely assuming to be justice of the peace or other officers

Whoever falsely assumes or pretends to be a justice of the peace, notary public, sheriff, deputy sheriff, medical examiner, associate medical examiner, constable, police officer, probation officer, or examiner, investigator or other officer appointed by the registrar of motor vehicles, or inspector, investigator or examiner of the department of public utilities or the department of telecommunications and cable, or investigator or other officer of the alcoholic beverages control commission, or investigator or other official of the bureau of special investigations, or examiner, investigator or other officer of the department of revenue, and acts as such or requires a person to aid or assist him in a matter pertaining to the duty of such officer, shall be punished by a fine of not more than four hundred dollars or by imprisonment for not more than one year.

Amended by St.1935, c. 440, § 44; St.1941, c. 71; St.1945, c. 400, § 7; St.1971, c. 150; St.1983, c. 233, § 82; St.1984, c. 110; St.1997, c. 164, § 290; St.2008, c. 522, § 45, eff. April 15, 2009.

Historical and Statutory Notes

St.1795, c. 68, § 2.
R.S.1836, c. 128, § 19.
G.S.1860, c. 163, § 18.
St.1877, c. 200, § 24.
P.S.1882, c. 205, § 23.
St.1898, c. 318.
St.1899, c. 178, § 7.
R.L.1902, c. 210, § 33.
St.1922, c. 52.
St.1930, c. 21.
St.1931, c. 426, § 312.

§ 33A. Engaging in lead paint inspection without a license

Whoever engages in or conducts a lead paint inspection without being licensed to do so, or holds himself out to the public as a licensed lead paint inspector and is not so licensed, shall be punished by a fine of not more than five thousand dollars or imprisonment in jail for not more than one year, or both.

Added by St.1993, c. 482, § 21.

§ 34. Disguises to obstruct execution of law, performance of duties, or exercise of rights

Whoever disguises himself with intent to obstruct the due execution of the law, or to intimidate, hinder or interrupt an officer or other person in the lawful performance of his duty, or in the exercise of his rights under the constitution or laws of the commonwealth, whether such intent is effected or not, shall be punished by a fine of not more than five hundred dollars or by imprisonment for not more than one year and may if imprisoned also be bound to good behavior for one year after the expiration of such imprisonment.

Historical and Statutory Notes

St.1809, c. 123, § 2.
R.S.1836, c. 128, § 20.
G.S.1860, c. 163, § 19.
P.S.1882, c. 205, § 25.
R.L.1902, c. 210, § 35.

§ 34A. Furnishing false name or Social Security number to law enforcement officer or official; penalty; restitution

Whoever knowingly and willfully furnishes a false name or Social Security number to a law enforcement officer or law enforcement official following an arrest shall be punished by a fine of not more than $1,000 or by imprisonment in a house of correction for not more than one year or by both such fine and imprisonment. Such sentence shall run from and after any sentence imposed as a result of the underlying offense. The court may order that restitution be paid to persons whose identity has been assumed and who have suffered monetary losses as a result of a violation of this section.

Added by St.1998, c. 397, § 2.

§ 35. Unauthorized use of town seal; making or possessing badge of town officer

Whoever, without being duly authorized thereto, prints, stamps, engraves or affixes, or causes to be printed, stamped, engraved or affixed to any paper or other article a representation of the seal of a town in the commonwealth, with intent to give to such paper or article an official character which it does not possess, or, without being duly authorized thereto, and with intent to assume an official character which he does not possess, casts, stamps, engraves, makes or has in his possession a badge or thing in the likeness of an official badge of a police officer, member of a fire department, or other officer appointed by a town in the commonwealth, or by any department of such town, shall be punished by a fine of not more than fifty dollars.

Historical and Statutory Notes

St.1881, c. 9.
P.S.1882, c. 205, § 26.
R.L.1902, c. 210, § 36.

§ 36. Compounding or concealing felonies

Whoever, having knowledge of the commission of a felony, takes money, or a gratuity or reward, or an engagement therefor, upon an agreement or understanding, express or implied, to compound or conceal such felony, or not to prosecute therefor, or not to give evidence thereof, shall, if such crime is punishable with death or imprisonment in the state prison for life, be punished by imprisonment in the state prison for not more than five years or in jail for not more than one year; and if such crime is punishable in any other manner, by a fine of not more than five hundred dollars or by imprisonment in jail for not more than two years.

Historical and Statutory Notes

R.S.1836, c. 128, § 21.
G.S.1860, c. 163, § 20.
P.S.1882, c. 205, § 27.
R.L.1902, c. 210, § 37.

§§ 37, 38. Repealed, 1962, 779, Sec. 3

Historical and Statutory Notes

See, now, M.G.L.A. c. 268A, § 1 et seq.

§ 39. Perjury; statements alleging motor vehicle theft; penalty; subsequent offenses

Whoever knowingly makes a false written statement on a form bearing notice that false statements made therein are punishable under the penalty of perjury, to a police officer, police department or the registry of motor vehicles alleging the theft or conversion of a motor vehicle, shall be punished by imprisonment for a first offense not less than five months, nor more than two years, or a fine of not less than two hundred and fifty dollars and not more than two thousand five hundred dollars, or both. A person found guilty of violating this section for a second or subsequent offense shall be punished by imprisonment not less than one, nor more than five years, or a fine of not less than five hundred dollars and not more than five thousand dollars, or both.

The sentence imposed upon a person convicted of violating this section for a second or subsequent offense shall not be reduced to less than one year.

A person convicted of a second or subsequent offense of violating the provisions of this section shall not be eligible for probation, parole, furlough or work release; provided, however that the commissioner of correction may, on the recommendation of warden, superintendent, or other person in charge of a correctional institution, or the administrator of a county correctional institution, grant to said offender a temporary release in the custody of an officer of such institution for the following purposes: to attend the funeral of next of kin or spouse; to visit a critically ill close relative or spouse; or to obtain emergency medical services unavailable at said institutions. A prosecution commenced under this section shall neither be continued without a finding nor placed on file.

Added by St.1980, c. 463, § 6. Renumbered by St.1981, c. 795, § 13.

§ 40. Reports of crimes to law enforcement officials

Whoever knows that another person is a victim of aggravated rape, rape, murder, manslaughter or armed robbery and is at the scene of said crime shall, to the extent that said person can do so without danger or peril to himself or others, report said crime to an appropriate law enforcement official as soon as reasonably practicable. Any person who violates this section shall be punished by a fine of not less than five hundred nor more than two thousand and five hundred dollars.

Added by St.1983, c. 597, § 2.

CHAPTER 268A

CONDUCT OF PUBLIC OFFICIALS AND EMPLOYEES

The section headings for the General Laws in this pamphlet have been editorially supplied.

§ 1. Definitions

In this chapter the following words, unless a different meaning is required by the context or is specifically prescribed, shall have the following meanings:—

(a) "Compensation", any money, thing of value or economic benefit conferred on or received by any person in return for services rendered or to be rendered by himself or another.

(b) "Competitive bidding", all bidding, where the same may be prescribed by applicable sections of the General Laws or otherwise, given and tendered to a state, county or municipal agency in response to an open solicitation of bids from the general public by public announcement or public advertising, where the contract is awarded to the lowest responsible bidder.

(c) "County agency", any department or office of county government and any division, board, bureau, commission, institution, tribunal or other instrumentality thereof or thereunder.

(d) "County employee", a person performing services for or holding an office, position, employment, or membership in a county agency, whether by election, appointment, contract of hire or engagement, whether serving with or without compensation, on a full, regular, part-time, intermittent, or consultant basis.

(e) "Immediate family", the employee and his spouse, and their parents, children, brothers and sisters.

(f) "Municipal agency", any department or office of a city or town government and any council, division, board, bureau, commission, institution, tribunal or other instrumentality thereof or thereunder.

(g) "Municipal employee," a person performing services for or holding an office, position, employment or membership in a municipal agency, whether by election, appointment, contract of hire or engagement, whether serving with or without compensation, on a full, regular, part-time, intermittent, or consultant basis, but excluding (1) elected members of a town meeting and (2) members of a charter commission established under Article LXXXIX of the Amendments to the Constitution.

(h) "Official act", any decision or action in a particular matter or in the enactment of legislation.

(i) "Official responsibility", the direct administrative or operating authority, whether intermediate or final, and either exercisable alone or with others, and whether personal or through subordinates, to approve, disapprove or otherwise direct agency action.

(j) "Participate", participate in agency action or in a particular matter personally and substantially as a state, county or municipal employee, through approval, disapproval, decision, recommendation, the rendering of advice, investigation or otherwise.

(k) "Particular matter", any judicial or other proceeding, application, submission, request for a ruling or other determination, contract, claim, controversy, charge, accusation, arrest, decision, determination, finding, but excluding enactment of general legislation by the general court and petitions of cities, towns, counties and districts for special laws related to their governmental organizations, powers, duties, finances and property.

(*l*) "Person who has been selected", any person who has been nominated or appointed to be a state, county or municipal employee or has been officially informed that he will be so nominated or appointed.

(m) "Special county employee", a county employee who is performing services or holding an office, position, employment or membership for which no compensation is provided; or who is not an elected official and (1) occupies a position which, by its classification in the county agency involved or by the terms of the contract or conditions of employment, permits personal or private employment during normal working hours, provided that disclosure of such classification or permission is filed in writing with the State Ethics Commission and the office of the county commissioners prior to the commencement of any personal or private employment, or (2) in fact does not earn compensation as a county employee for an aggregate of more than eight hundred hours during the preceding three hundred and sixty-five days. For this purpose compensation by the day shall be considered as equivalent to compensation for seven hours per day. A special county employee shall be in such a status on days for which he is not compensated as well as on days on which he earns compensation.

(n) "Special municipal employee", a municipal employee who is not a mayor, a member of the board of aldermen, a member of the city council, or a selectman in a town with a population in excess of ten thousand persons and whose position has been expressly classified by the city council, or board of aldermen if there is no city council, or board of selectmen, as that of a special employee under the terms and provisions of this chapter; provided, however, that a selectman in a town with a population of ten thousand or fewer persons shall be a special municipal employee without being expressly so classified. All employees who hold equivalent offices, positions, employment or membership in the same municipal agency shall have the same classification; provided, however, no municipal employee shall be classified as a "special municipal employee" unless he occupies a position for which no compensation is provided or which, by its classification in the municipal agency involved or by the terms of the contract or conditions of employment, permits personal or private employment during normal working hours, or unless he in fact does not earn compensation as a municipal employee for an aggregate of more than eight hundred hours during the preceding three hundred and sixty-five days. For this purpose compensation by the day shall be considered as equivalent to compensation for seven hours per day. A special municipal employee shall be in such status on days for which he is not compensated as well as on days on which he earns compensation. All employees of any city or town wherein no such classification has been made shall be deemed to be "municipal employees" and shall be subject to all the provisions of this chapter with respect thereto without exception.

(*o*) "Special state employee", a state employee:

(1) Who is performing services or holding an office, position, employment or membership for which no compensation is provided, or

(2) Who is not an elected official and

(a) occupies a position which, by its classification in the state agency involved or by the terms of the contract or conditions of employment, permits personal or private employment during normal working hours, provided that disclosure of such classification or permission is filed in writing with the state ethics commission prior to the commencement of any personal or private employment, or

(b) in fact does not earn compensation as a state employee for an aggregate of more than eight hundred hours during the preceding three hundred and sixty-five days. For this purpose compensation by the day shall be considered as equivalent to compensation for seven hours per day. A special state employee shall be in such a status on days for which he is not compensated as well as on days on which he earns compensation.

(p) "State agency", any department of state government including the executive, legislative or judicial, and all councils thereof and thereunder, and any division, board, bureau, commission, institution, tribunal or other instrumentality within such department, and any independent state authority, district, commission, instrumentality or agency, but not an agency of a county, city or town.

(q) "State employee", a person performing services for or holding an office, position, employment, or membership in a state agency, whether by election, appointment, contract of hire or engagement, whether serving with or without compensation, on a full, regular, part-time, intermittent or consultant basis, including members of the general court and executive council. No construction contractor nor any of their personnel shall be deemed to be a state employee or special state employee under the provisions of paragraph (*o*) or this paragraph as a result of participation in the engineering and environmental analysis for major construction projects either as a consultant or part of a consultant group for the commonwealth. Such contractors or personnel may be awarded construction contracts by the commonwealth and may continue with outstanding construction contracts with the commonwealth during the period of such participation; provided, that no such contractor or personnel shall directly or indirectly bid on or be awarded a contract for any construction project if they have participated in the engineering or environmental analysis thereof.

Added by St.1962, c. 779, § 1. Amended by St.1965, c. 351; St.1966, Ex.Sess., c. 734, § 2; St.1969, c. 350, §§ 1, 2; St.1977, c. 245; St.1981, c. 430; St.1982, c. 612, §§ 1 to 4; St.1989, c. 289; St.1990, c. 192.

§ 2. Corrupt gifts, offers or promises to influence official acts; corruption of witnesses

(a) Whoever, directly or indirectly, corruptly gives, offers or promises anything of value to any state, county or municipal employee, or to any person who has been selected to be such an employee, or to any member of the judiciary, or who offers or promises any such employee or any member of the judiciary, or any person who has been selected to be such an employee or member of the judiciary, to give anything of value to any other person or entity, with intent

(1) to influence any official act or any act within the official responsibility of such employee or member of the judiciary or person who has been selected to be such employee or member of the judiciary, or

(2) to influence such an employee or member of the judiciary or person who has been selected to be such an employee or member of the judiciary, to commit or aid in committing, or collude in, or allow, any fraud, or make opportunity for the commission of any fraud on the commonwealth or a state, county or municipal agency, or

(3) to induce such an employee or member of the judiciary or person who has been selected to be such an employee or member of the judiciary to do or omit to do any act in violation of his lawful duty; or

(b) Whoever, being a state, county or municipal employee or a member of the judiciary or a person selected to be such an employee or member of the judiciary, directly or indirectly, corruptly asks, demands, exacts, solicits, seeks, accepts, receives or agrees to receive anything of value for himself or for any other person or entity, in return for

(1) being influenced in his performance of any official act or any act within his official responsibility, or

(2) being influenced to commit or aid in committing, or to collude in, or allow any fraud, or make opportunity for the commission of any fraud, on the commonwealth or on a state, county or municipal agency, or

(3) being induced to do or omit to do any acts in violation of his official duty; or

(c) Whoever, directly or indirectly, corruptly gives, offers or promises anything of value to any person, or offers or promises such person to give anything of value to any other person or entity, with intent to influence the testimony under oath or affirmation of such first-mentioned person or any other person as a witness upon a trial, or other proceeding, before any court, any committee of either house or both houses of the general court, or any agency, commission or officer authorized by the laws of the commonwealth to hear evidence or take testimony, or with intent to influence such witness to absent himself therefrom; or

(d) Whoever, directly or indirectly, corruptly asks, demands, exacts, solicits, seeks, accepts, receives or agrees to receive anything of value for himself or for any other person or entity in return for influence upon the testimony under oath or affirmation of himself or any other person as a witness upon any such trial, hearing or other proceeding or in return for the absence of himself or any other person therefrom;—shall be punished by a fine of not more than $100,000, or by imprisonment in the state prison for not more than 10 years, or in a jail or house of correction for not more than 2½ years, or both; and in the event of final conviction shall be incapable of holding any office of honor, trust or profit under the commonwealth or under any state, county or municipal agency.

Clauses (c) and (d) shall not be construed to prohibit the payment or receipt of witness fees provided by law or the payment by the party upon whose behalf a witness is called and receipt by a witness of the reasonable cost of travel and subsistence incurred and the reasonable value of time lost in attendance at any such trial, hearing or proceeding, or, in the case of expert witnesses, involving a technical or professional opinion, a reasonable fee for time spent in the preparation of such opinion, in appearing or testifying.

Added by St.1962, c. 779, § 1. Amended by St.1964, c. 287; St.2009, c. 28, § 61, eff. Sept. 29, 2009.

§ 3. Gifts, offers or promises for acts performed or to be performed; corruption of witnesses; solicitation of gifts; witness fees; regulations

(a) Whoever knowingly, otherwise than as provided by law for the proper discharge of official duty, directly or indirectly, gives, offers or promises anything of substantial value to any present or former state, county or municipal employee or to any member of the judiciary, or to any person selected to be such an employee or member of the judiciary: (i) for or because of any official act performed or to be performed by such an employee or member of the judiciary or person selected to be such an employee or member of the judiciary; or (ii) to influence, or attempt to influence, an official action of the state, county or municipal employee or to any member of the judiciary; or

(b) Whoever knowingly, being a present or former state, county or municipal employee or member of the judiciary, or person selected to be such an employee or member of the judiciary, otherwise than as provided by law for the proper discharge of official duty, directly or indirectly, asks, demands, exacts, solicits, seeks, accepts, receives or agrees to receive anything of substantial value: (i) for himself for or because of any official act or act within his official responsibility performed or to be performed by him; or (ii) to influence, or attempt to influence, him in an official act taken; or

(c) Whoever knowingly, directly or indirectly, gives, offers or promises anything of substantial value to any person, for or because of testimony under oath or affirmation given or to be given by such person or any other person as a witness upon a trial, hearing or other proceeding, before any court, any committee of either house or both houses of the general court, or any agency, commission or officer authorized by the laws of the commonwealth to hear evidence or take testimony or for or because of his absence therefrom; or

(d) Whoever knowingly, directly or indirectly, asks, demands, exacts, solicits, seeks, accepts, receives or agrees to receive anything of substantial value for himself for or because of the testimony under oath or affirmation given or to be given by him or any other person as a witness upon any such trial, hearing or other proceeding, or for or because of his absence therefrom; shall be punished by a fine of not more than $50,000, or by imprisonment in the state prison for not more than 5 years, or in a jail or house of correction for not more than 2 ½ years, or both.

(e) Clauses (c) and (d) shall not prohibit the payment or receipt of witness fees provided by law or the payment by the party upon whose behalf a witness is called and receipt by a witness of the reasonable cost of travel and subsistence incurred and the reasonable value of time lost in attendance at any such trial, hearing or proceeding, or, in the case of expert witnesses, involving a technical or professional opinion, a reasonable fee for time spent in the preparation of such opinion, in appearing or testifying.

(f) The state ethics commission shall adopt regulations: (i) defining "substantial value," ; provided, however, that "substantial value" shall not be less than $50; (ii) establishing exclusions for ceremonial gifts; (iii) establishing exclusions for gifts given solely because of family or friendship; and (iv) establishing additional exclusions for other situations that do not present a genuine risk of a conflict or the appearance of a conflict of interest.

Added by St.1962, c. 779, § 1. Amended by St.2009, c. 28, § 62, eff. Sept. 29, 2009.

§ 4. Other compensation; offer, gift, receipt or request; acting as agent or attorney for other than state; legislators; special state employees

(a) No state employee shall otherwise than as provided by law for the proper discharge of official duties, directly or indirectly receive or request compensation from anyone other than the commonwealth or a state agency, in relation to any particular matter in which the commonwealth or a state agency is a party or has a direct and substantial interest.

(b) No person shall knowingly, otherwise than as provided by law for the proper discharge of official duties, directly or indirectly give, promise or offer such compensation.

(c) No state employee shall, otherwise than in the proper discharge of his official duties, act as agent or attorney for anyone other than the commonwealth or a state agency for prosecuting any claim against the commonwealth or a state agency, or as agent or attorney for anyone in connection with any particular matter in which the commonwealth or a state agency is a party or has a direct and substantial interest.

Whoever violates any provision of this section shall be punished by a fine of not more than $10,000, or by imprisonment in the state prison for not more than 5 years, or in a jail or house of correction for not more than 2½ years, or both.

Neither a member of the general court nor a member of the executive council shall be subject to paragraphs (a) or (c). However, no member of the general court or executive council shall personally appear for any compensation other than his legislative or executive council salary before any state agency, unless:

(1) the particular matter before the state agency is ministerial in nature; or

(2) the appearance is before a court of the commonwealth; or

(3) the appearance is in a quasi-judicial proceeding.

For the purposes of this paragraph, ministerial functions include, but are not limited to, the filing or amendment of: tax returns, applications for permits or licenses, incorporation papers, or other documents. For the purposes of this paragraph, a proceeding shall be considered quasi-judicial if:

(1) the action of the state agency is adjudicatory in nature; and

(2) the action of the state agency in appealable to the courts; and

(3) both sides are entitled to representation by counsel and such counsel is neither the attorney general nor the counsel for the state agency conducting the proceeding.

A special state employee shall be subject to paragraphs (a) and (c) only in relation to a particular matter (a) in which he has at any time participated as a state employee, or (b) which is or within one year has been a subject of his official responsibility, or (c) which is pending in the state agency in which he is serving. Clause (c) of the preceding sentence shall not apply in the case of a special state employee who serves on no more than sixty days during any period of three hundred and sixty-five consecutive days.

This section shall not prevent a state employee from taking uncompensated action, not inconsistent with the faithful performance of his duties, to aid or assist any person who is the subject of disciplinary or other personnel administration proceedings with respect to those proceedings.

This section shall not prevent a state employee, including a special employee, from acting, with or without compensation, as agent or attorney for or otherwise aiding or assisting members of his immediate family or any person for whom he is serving as guardian, executor, administrator, trustee or other personal fiduciary except in those matters in which he has participated or which are the subject of his official responsibility; provided, that the state official responsible for appointment to his position approves.

This section shall not prevent a present or former special state employee from aiding or assisting another person for compensation in the performance of work under a contract with or for the benefit of the commonwealth; provided, that the head of the special state employee's department or agency has certified in writing that the interest of the commonwealth requires such aid or assistance and the certification has been filed with the state ethics commission.

This section shall not prevent a state employee from giving testimony under oath or making statements required to be made under penalty for perjury or contempt.

This section shall not prohibit a state employee from holding an elective or appointive office in a city, town or district, nor in any way prohibit such an employee from performing the duties of or receiving the compensation provided for such office. No such elected or appointed official may vote or act on any matter which is within the purview of the agency by which he is employed or over which such employee has official responsibility.

This section shall not prevent a state employee, other than an employee in the department of revenue, from requesting or receiving compensation from anyone other than the commonwealth in relation to the filing or amending of state tax returns.

Added by St.1962, c. 779, § 1. Amended by St.1978, c. 210, §§ 4, 5; St.1980, c. 10, § 1; St.1982, c. 143; St.2007, c. 204, §§ 1 to 3, eff. Feb. 27, 2008; St.2009, c. 28, § 63, eff. Sept. 29, 2009.

§ 5. Former state employees; acting as agent or attorney or receiving compensation; partners of state employees or legislators

(a) A former state employee who knowingly acts as agent or attorney for, or receives compensation directly or indirectly from anyone other than the commonwealth or a state agency, in connection with any particular matter in which the commonwealth or a state agency is a party or has a direct and substantial interest and in which he participated as a state employee while so employed, or

(b) a former state employee who, within one year after his last employment has ceased, appears personally before any court or agency of the commonwealth as agent or attorney for anyone other than the commonwealth in connection with any particular matter in which the commonwealth or a state agency is a party or has a direct and substantial interest and which was under his official responsibility as a state employee at any time within a period of two years prior to the termination of his employment, or

(c) a partner of a former state employee who knowingly engages, during a period of one year following the termination of the latter's employment by the commonwealth, in any activity in which the former state employee is himself prohibited from engaging in by clause (a), or

(d) a partner of a state employee who knowingly acts as agent or attorney for anyone other than the commonwealth in connection with any particular matter in which the commonwealth or a state agency is a party or has a direct and substantial interest and in which the state employee participates or has participated as a state employee or which is the subject of his official responsibility, or

(e) a former state employee or elected official, including a former member of the general court, who acts as legislative or executive agent, as defined in section thirty-nine of chapter three, for anyone other than the commonwealth or a state agency before the governmental body, as determined by the state ethics commission with which he has been associated, within one year after he leaves that body or

(f) a former state employee whose salary was not less than that in step one of job group M–VII in the management salary schedule in section forty-six C of chapter thirty, and who becomes an officer or employee of a business organization which is or was a party to any privatization contract as defined in section fifty-three of chapter seven in which contract he participated as such state employee, if he becomes such officer or employee while the business organization is such a party or within one year after he terminates his state employment, unless before the termination of his state employment the governor determines, in a writing filed with the state ethics commission, that such participation did not significantly affect the terms or implementation of such contract, shall be punished by a fine of not more than $10,000, or by imprisonment in the state prison for not more than 5 years, or in a jail or house of correction for not more than 2 ½ years, or both.

If a partner of a member of the general court or of a special state employee or of a former state employee is also a member of another partnership in which the member of the general court or special or former employee has no interest, the activities of the latter partnership in which the member of the general court or special or former employee takes no part shall not thereby be subject to clause (c) or (d).

This section shall not prevent a present or former special state employee from aiding or assisting another person for compensation in the performance of work under a contract with or for the benefit of the commonwealth; provided, that the head of the special state employee's department or agency has certified in writing that the interest of the commonwealth requires such aid or assistance and the certification has been filed with the state ethics commission.

Added by St.1962, c. 779, § 1. Amended by St.1978, c. 210, §§ 6 to 8; St.1986, c. 557, § 191; St.1993, c. 296, § 2; St.2009, c. 28, §§ 64 to 66, eff. Sept. 29, 2009.

§ 6. Financial interest of state employee, relative or associates; disclosure

(a) Except as permitted by this section, any state employee who participates as such employee in a particular matter in which to his knowledge he, his immediate family or partner, a business organization in which he is serving as officer, director, trustee, partner or employee, or any person or organization with whom he is negotiating or has any arrangement concerning prospective employment, has a financial interest, shall be punished by a fine of not more than $10,000, or by imprisonment in the state prison for not more than 5 years, or in a jail or house of correction for not more than 2½ years, or both.

Any state employee whose duties would otherwise require him to participate in such a particular matter shall advise the official responsible for appointment to his position and the state ethics commission of the nature and circumstances of the particular matter and make full disclosure of such financial interest, and the appointing official shall thereupon either

(1) assign the particular matter to another employee; or

(2) assume responsibility for the particular matter; or

(3) make a written determination that the interest is not so substantial as to be deemed likely to affect the integrity of the services which the commonwealth may expect from the employee, in which case it shall not be a violation for the employee to participate in the particular matter. Copies of such written determination shall be forwarded to the state employee and filed with the state ethics commission by the person who made the determination. Such copy shall be retained by the commission for a period of six years.

[There is no subsection (b).]

Added by St.1962, c. 779, § 1. Amended by St.1978, c. 210, § 9; St.2009, c. 28, § 67, eff. Sept. 29, 2009.

§ 6A. Conflict of interest of public official; reporting requirement

Any public official, as defined by section one of chapter two hundred and sixty-eight B, who in the discharge of his official duties would be required knowingly to take an action which would substantially affect such official's financial interests, unless the effect on such an official is no greater than the effect on the general public, shall file a written description of the required action and the potential conflict of interest with the state ethics commission established by said chapter two hundred and sixty-eight B.

Added by St.1978, c. 210, § 10. Amended by St.1984, c. 189, § 163.

§ 7. Financial interest in contracts of state agency; application of section

A state employee who has a financial interest, directly or indirectly, in a contract made by a state agency, in which the commonwealth or a state agency is an interested party, of which interest he has knowledge or has reason to know, shall be punished by a fine of not more than $10,000, or by imprisonment in the state prison for not more than 5 years, or in a jail or house of correction for not more than 2½ years, or both.

This section shall not apply if such financial interest consists of the ownership of less than one per cent of the stock of a corporation.

This section shall not apply (a) to a state employee who in good faith and within thirty days after he learns of an actual or prospective violation of this section makes full disclosure of his financial interest to the contracting agency and terminates or disposes of the interest, or (b) to a state employee other than a member of the general court who is not employed by the contracting agency or an agency which regulates the activities of the contracting agency and who does not participate in or have official responsibility for any of the activities of the contracting agency, if the contract is made after public notice or where applicable, through competitive bidding, and if the state employee files with the state ethics commission a statement making full disclosure of his interest and the interests of his immediate family in the contract, and if in the case of a contract for personal services (1) the services will be provided outside the normal working hours of the state employee, (2) the services are not required as part of the state employee's regular duties, the employee is compensated for not more than five hundred hours during a calendar year, and (3) the head of the contracting agency makes and files with the state ethics commission a written certification that no employee of that agency is available to perform those services as a part of their regular duties, or (c) to the interest of a member of the general court in a contract made by an agency other than the general court or either branch thereof, if his direct and indirect interests and those of his immediate family in the corporation or other commercial entity with which the contract is made do not in the aggregate amount to ten per cent of the total proprietary interests therein, and the contract is made through competitive bidding and he files with the state ethics commission a statement making full disclosure of his interest and the interests of his immediate family or (d) to a special state employee who does not participate in or have official responsibility for any of the activities of the contracting agency and who files with the state ethics commission a statement making full disclosure of his interest and the interests of his immediate family in the contract, or (e) to a special state employee who files with the state ethics commission a statement making full disclosure of his interest and the interests of his immediate family in the contract, if the governor with the advice and consent of the executive council exempts him.

This section shall not apply to a state employee who provides services or furnishes supplies, goods and materials to a recipient of public assistance, provided that such services or such supplies, goods and materials are provided in accordance with a schedule of charges promulgated by the department of transitional assistance or the division of health care policy and finance and provided, further, that such recipient has the right under law to choose and in fact does choose the person or firm that will provide such services or furnish such supplies, goods and materials.

This section shall not prohibit a state employee from teaching or performing other related duties in an educational institution of the commonwealth; provided, that such employee does not participate in, or have official responsibility for, the financial management of such educational institution; and provided, further, that such employee is so employed on a part-time basis. Such employee may be compensated for such services, notwithstanding the provisions of section twenty-one of chapter thirty.

This section shall not prohibit a state employee from being employed on a part-time basis by a facility operated or designed for the care of mentally ill or mentally retarded persons, public health, correctional facility or any other facility principally funded by the state which provides similar services and which operates on an uninterrupted and continuous basis; provided that such employee does not participate in, or have official responsibility for, the financial management of such facility, that he is compensated for such part-time employment for not more than four hours in any day in which he is otherwise compensated by the commonwealth, and at a rate which does not exceed that of a state employee classified in step one of job group XX of the general salary schedule contained in section forty-six of chapter thirty, and that the head of the facility makes and files with the state ethics commission a written certification that there is a critical need for the services of the employee. Such employee may be compensated for such services, notwithstanding the provisions of section twenty-one of chapter thirty.

This section shall not preclude an officer or employee of the Massachusetts Port Authority from eligibility for any residential sound insulation program or the bayswater environmental program provided that the officer or employee has no responsibility for the administration for that program from which he is to receive the benefit.

Added by St.1962, c. 779, § 1. Amended by St.1968, c. 446; St.1978, c. 210, § 11; St.1980, c. 303; St.1982, c. 612, §§ 5 to 7; St.1986, c. 599, § 53; St.1990, c. 487, § 1; St.1993, c. 301, § 1; St.1998, c. 161, § 556; St.2009, c. 28, § 68, eff. Sept. 29, 2009; St.2010, c. 264, § 1, eff. Nov. 5, 2010.

§ 8. Public building or construction contracts

No state, county or municipal employee and no person acting or purporting to act on behalf of such employee, or any state, county or municipal agency, shall with respect to any public building or construction contract which is about to be or which has been competitively bid, require the bidder to make application to or furnish financial data to, or to obtain, or procure, any of the surety bonds or insurance specified in connection with such contract or specified by any law from any particular insurance or surety company, agent, or broker. This section shall not prevent the exercise by such employee on behalf of a state, county, or municipal agency of its right to approve the form, sufficiency, or manner of execution of the surety bonds and insurance furnished by the insurance or surety company selected by the bidder to underwrite said insurance and bonds. Any provisions in any invitation for bids, or in any of the contract documents, in conflict with this section are hereby declared to be contrary to the public policy of this commonwealth.

Whoever violates any provision of this section shall be punished by a fine of not more than $10,000, or by imprisonment in the state prison for not more than 5 years, or in a jail or house of correction for not more than 2½ years, or both.

Added by St.1962, c. 779, § 1. Amended by St.2009, c. 28, § 69, eff. Sept. 29, 2009.

§ 8A. Members of state commissions or boards; prohibited appointments to other positions

No member of a state commission or board shall be eligible for appointment or election by the members of such commission or board to any office or position under the supervision of such commission or board. No former member of such commission or board shall be so eligible until the expiration of thirty days from the termination of his service as a member of such commission or board.

Added by St.1964, c. 314.

§ 8B. Members of commonwealth utilities commission; prohibited lobbying activities

No member of the commonwealth utilities commission, appointed pursuant to section 2 of chapter 25, or the commissioner of telecommunications and cable shall, within one year after his service has ceased or terminated on said commission, be employed by, or lobby said commission on behalf of, any company or regulated industry over which said commission had jurisdiction during the tenure of such member of the commission.

Added by St.1997, c. 164, § 291. Amended by St.2008, c. 522, §§ 46, 47, eff. April 15, 2009.

§ 9. Avoiding, rescinding or canceling state agency actions resulting from violations of chapter; restitution and damages

(a) In addition to any other remedies provided by law, any violation of sections 2 to 8, inclusive, or section 23 which has substantially influenced the action taken by any state agency in any particular matter, shall be grounds for avoiding, rescinding or canceling the action on such terms as the interests of the commonwealth and innocent third persons shall require.

(b) In addition to the remedies set forth in subsection (a), the state ethics commission upon a finding pursuant to an adjudicatory proceeding that a person has acted to his economic advantage in violation of sections 2 to 8, inclusive, or section 23, may issue an order: (1) requiring the violator to pay the commission on behalf of the commonwealth damages in the amount of the economic advantage or $500, whichever is greater; and (2) requiring the violator to make restitution to an injured third party. If there has been no final criminal judgment of conviction or acquittal of the same violation, upon receipt of the written approval of the attorney general, the commission may order payment of additional damages in an amount not exceeding twice the amount of the economic advantage or $500, and payment of such additional damages shall bar any criminal prosecution for the same violation.

The maximum damages that the commission may order a violator to pay under this section shall be $25,000. If the commission determines that the damages authorized by this section exceed $25,000, it may bring a civil action against the violator to recover such damages.

(c) The remedies authorized by this section shall be in addition to any civil penalty imposed by the state ethics commission in accordance with clause (3) of subsection (j) of section 4 of chapter 268B.

Added by St.1962, c. 779, § 1. Amended by St.1978, c. 210, § 12; St.2009, c. 28, § 70, eff. Sept. 29, 2009.

§ 10. Opinions of state ethics commission

The state ethics commission shall issue opinions interpreting the requirements of this chapter in accordance with clause (g) of section three of chapter two hundred and sixty-eight B.

Added by St.1962, c. 779, § 1. Amended by St.1978, c. 210, § 13; St.1984, c. 189, § 164.

§ 11. County employees; receiving or requesting compensation from, or acting as agent or attorney for other than county agency

(a) No county employee shall, otherwise than as provided for the proper discharge of official duties, directly or indirectly receive or request compensation from anyone other than a county or a county agency in relation to any particular matter in which a county agency is a party or has a direct and substantial interest.

(b) No person shall knowingly, otherwise than as provided by law for the proper discharge of official duties, directly or indirectly give, promise or offer such compensation.

(c) No county employee shall, otherwise than as provided by law for the proper discharge of official duties, act as agent or attorney for anyone other than a county or a county agency in prosecuting any claim against a county or county agency, or as agent or attorney for anyone in connection with any particular matter in which a county or county agency is a party or has a direct and substantial interest.

Whoever violates any provision of this section shall be punished by a fine of not more than $10,000, or by imprisonment in the state prison for not more than 5 years, or in a jail or house of correction for not more than 2½ years, or both.

A county employee shall be subject to paragraphs (a) and (c) only in relation to the county of which he is an employee. A special county employee shall be subject to said paragraphs (a) and (c) only in relation to a particular matter (a) in which he has at any time participated as a county employee, or (b) which is or within one year has been a subject of his official responsibility, or (c) which is pending in the county agency in which he is serving. Clause (c) of the preceding sentence shall not apply in the case of a county employee who serves on no more than sixty days during any period of three hundred and sixty-five consecutive days.

This section shall not prevent a county employee from taking uncompensated action, not inconsistent with the faithful performance of his duties, to aid or assist any person who is the subject of disciplinary or other personnel administration proceedings with respect to those proceedings.

This section shall not prevent a county employee, including a special employee, from acting, with or without compensation, as agent or attorney for or otherwise aiding or assisting members of his immediate family or any person for whom he is serving as guardian, executor, administrator, trustee or other personal fiduciary except in those matters in which he has participated or which are the subject of his official responsibility; provided, that the state or county official responsible for appointment to his position approves.

This section shall not prevent a present or former special county employee from aiding or assisting another person for compensation in the performance of work under a contract with or for the benefit of the county; provided, that the head of the special county employee's department or agency has certified in writing that the interest of the county requires such aid or assistance and the certification has been filed with the state ethics commission. The certification shall be open to public inspection.

This section shall not prevent a county employee from giving testimony under oath or making statements required to be made under penalty for perjury or contempt.

This section shall not prohibit a county employee from holding an elective or appointive office in a city, town or district nor in any way prohibit such an employee from performing the duties or receiving the compensation provided for such office. No such elected or appointed official may vote or act on any matter which is within the purview of the agency by which he is employed or over which such employee has official responsibility.

Added by St.1962, c. 779, § 1. Amended by St.1978, c. 210, § 14; St.1980, c. 10, § 2; St.1982, c. 612, § 8; St.2009, c. 28, § 71, eff. Sept. 29, 2009.

§ 12. Former county employees; acting as attorney or receiving compensation from other than county; partners of employees or former employees or legislators

(a) A former county employee who knowingly acts as agent or attorney for or receives compensation directly or indirectly from anyone other than a county or a county agency in connection with any particular matter in which the county or a county agency of the same county is a party or has a direct and substantial interest and in which he participated as a county employee while so employed, or

(b) A former county employee who, within one year after his last employment has ceased, appears personally before any agency of the county as agent or attorney for anyone other than the county in connection with any particular matter in which the county or a county agency of the same county is a party or has a direct and substantial interest and which was under his official responsibility as a county employee at any time within a period of two years prior to the termination of his employment, or

(c) A partner of a former county employee who knowingly engages, during a period of one year following the termination of the latter's employment by the county, in any activity in which the former county employee is himself prohibited from engaging by clause (a), or

(d) A partner of a county employee who knowingly acts as agent or attorney for anyone other than the county in connection with any particular matter in which the county or a county agency of the same county is a party or has a direct and substantial interest and in which the county employee participates or has participated as a county employee or which is the subject of his official responsibility, shall be punished by a fine of not more than $10,000, or by imprisonment in the state prison for not more than 5 years, or in a jail or house of correction for not more than 2½ years, or both.

If a partner of a special county employee or of a former county employee is also a member of another partnership in which the special or former employee has no interest, activities of the latter partnership in which the special or former employee takes no part shall not thereby be subject to clause (c) or (d).

This section shall not prevent a present or former special county employee from aiding or assisting another person for compensation in the performance of work under a contract with or for the benefit of the county; provided, that the head of the special county employee's department or agency has certified in writing that the interest of the county requires such aid or assistance and the certification has been filed with the state ethics commission. The certification shall be open to public inspection.

Added by St.1962, c. 779, § 1. Amended by St.1978, c. 210, § 15; St.1982, c. 612, § 9; St.2009, c. 28, § 72, eff. Sept. 29, 2009.

§ 13. Financial interest of county employee, relatives or associates; disclosure

(a) Except as permitted by paragraph (b), a county employee who participates as such an employee in a particular matter in which to his knowledge he, his immediate family or partner, a business organization which he is serving as officer, director, trustee, partner or employee, or any person or organization with whom he is negotiating or has any arrangement concerning prospective employment, has a financial interest, shall be punished by a fine of not more than $10,000, or by imprisonment in the state prison for not more than 5 years, or in a jail or house of correction for not more than 2½ years, or both.

(b) Any county employee whose duties would otherwise require him to participate in such a particular matter shall advise the official responsible for appointment to his position and the state ethics commission of the nature and circumstances of the particular matter and make full disclosure of such financial interest, and the appointing official shall thereupon either

(1) assign the particular matter to another employee; or

(2) assume responsibility for the particular matter; or

(3) make a written determination that the interest is not so substantial as to be deemed likely to affect the integrity of the services which the county may expect from the employee, in which case it shall not be a violation for the employee to participate in the particular matter. Copies of such written determination shall be forwarded to the county employee and filed with the state ethics commission by the person who made the determination. Such copy shall be retained by the commission for a period of six years.

Added by St.1962, c. 779, § 1. Amended by St.1978, c. 210, § 16; St.2009, c. 28, § 73, eff. Sept. 29, 2009.

§ 14. County employees; financial interest in contracts of county agency

A county employee who has a financial interest, directly or indirectly, in a contract made by a county agency of the same county, in which the county or a county agency is an interested party of which financial interest he has knowledge or has reason to know, shall be punished by a fine of not more than $10,000, or by imprisonment in the state prison for not more than 5 years, or in a jail or house of correction for not more than 2½ years, or both.

This section shall not apply if such financial interest consists of the ownership of less than one per cent of the stock of a corporation.

This section shall not apply (a) to a county employee who in good faith and within thirty days after he learns of an actual or prospective violation of this section makes full disclosure of his financial interest to the contracting agency and terminates or disposes of the interest, or (b) to a county employee who does not participate in or have official responsibility for any of the activities of the contracting agency, if the contract is made through competitive bidding and his direct and indirect interests and those of his immediate family in the corporation or other commercial entity with which the contract is made do not in the aggregate amount to ten per cent of the total proprietary interests therein, or (c) to a special county employee who does not participate in or have official responsibility for any of the activities of the contracting agency and who files with the state ethics commission a statement making full disclosure of his interest and the interests of his immediate family in the contract, if the county commissioners approve the exemption of his interest from this section.

Added by St.1962, c. 779, § 1. Amended by St.1978, c. 210, § 17; St.1982, c. 612, § 10; St.2009, c. 28, § 74, eff. Sept. 29, 2009.

§ 15. Avoiding, rescinding or canceling county agency actions resulting from violations of chapter; restitution and damages

(a) In addition to any other remedies provided by law, a violation of section 2, 3, 8, or sections 11 to 14, inclusive, or section 23 which has substantially influenced the action taken by any county agency in any particular matter, shall be grounds for avoiding, rescinding, or canceling the action on such terms as the interests of the county and innocent third persons shall require.

(b) In addition to the remedies set forth in subsection (a), the commission may, upon a finding pursuant to an adjudicatory proceeding that a person has acted to his economic advantage in violation of section 2, 3, 8, sections 11 to 14, inclusive, or section 23, issue an order (1) requiring the violator to pay the commission on behalf of the county damages in the amount of the economic advantage or $500, whichever is greater; and (2) requiring the violator to make restitution to an injured third party. If there has been no final criminal judgment of conviction or acquittal of the same violation, upon receipt of the written approval of the attorney general and the district attorney, the commission may order payment of additional damages in an amount not exceeding twice the amount of the economic advantage or $500, and payment of such additional damages shall bar any criminal prosecution for the same violation.

The maximum damages that the commission may order a violator to pay under this section shall be $25,000. If the commission determines that the damages authorized by this section exceed $25,000, it may bring a civil action against the violator to recover such damages.

(c) The remedies authorized by this section shall be in addition to any civil penalty imposed by the commission in accordance with clause (3) of subsection (j) of section 4 of chapter 268B.

Added by St.1962, c. 779, § 1. Amended by St.1978, c. 210, § 18; St.2009, c. 28, § 75, eff. Sept. 29, 2009.

§ 15A. Members of county commission or board; restrictions on appointments to certain positions

No member of a county commission or board shall be eligible for appointment or election by the members of such commission or board to any office or position under the supervision of such commission or board. No former member of such commission or board shall be so eligible until the expiration of thirty days from the termination of his service as a member of such commission or board.

Added by St.1967, c. 887, § 1.

§ 16. Repealed, 1978, 210, Sec. 19

Historical and Statutory Notes

See, now, M.G.L.A. c. 268B, § 3(g).

§ 17. Municipal employees; gift or receipt of compensation from other than municipality; acting as agent or attorney

(a) No municipal employee shall, otherwise than as provided by law for the proper discharge of official duties, directly or indirectly receive or request compensation from anyone other than the city or town or municipal agency in relation to any particular matter in which the same city or town is a party or has a direct and substantial interest.

(b) No person shall knowingly, otherwise than as provided by law for the proper discharge of official duties, directly or indirectly give, promise or offer such compensation.

(c) No municipal employee shall, otherwise than in the proper discharge of his official duties, act as agent or attorney for anyone other than the city or town or municipal agency in prosecuting any claim against the same city or town, or as agent or attorney for anyone in connection with any particular matter in which the same city or town is a party or has a direct and substantial interest.

Whoever violates any provision of this section shall be punished by a fine of not more than $10,000, or by imprisonment in the state prison for not more than 5 years, or in a jail or house of correction for not more than 2½years, or both.

A special municipal employee shall be subject to paragraphs (a) and (c) only in relation to a particular matter (a) in which he has at any time participated as a municipal employee, or (b) which is or within one year has been a subject of his official responsibility, or (c) which is pending in the municipal agency in which he is serving. Clause (c) of the preceding sentence shall not apply in the case of a special municipal employee who serves on no more than sixty days during any period of three hundred and sixty-five consecutive days.

This section shall not prevent a municipal employee from taking uncompensated action, not inconsistent with the faithful performance of his duties, to aid or assist any person who is the subject of disciplinary or other personnel administration proceedings with respect to those proceedings.

This section shall not prevent a municipal employee, including a special employee, from acting, with or without compensation, as agent or attorney for or otherwise aiding or assisting members of his immediate family or any person for whom he is serving as guardian, executor, administrator, trustee or other personal fiduciary except in those matters in which he has participated or which are the subject of his official responsibility; provided, that the official responsible for appointment to his position approves.

This section shall not prevent a present or former special municipal employee from aiding or assisting another person for compensation in the performance of work under a contract with or for the benefit of the city or town; provided, that the head of the special municipal employee's department or agency has certified in writing that the interest of the city or town requires such aid or assistance and the certification has been filed with the clerk of the city or town. The certification shall be open to public inspection.

This section shall not prevent a municipal employee from giving testimony under oath or making statements required to be made under penalty for perjury or contempt.

This section shall not prevent a municipal employee from applying on behalf of anyone for a building, electrical, wiring, plumbing, gas fitting or septic system permit, nor from receiving compensation in relation to any such permit, unless such employee is employed by or provides services to the permit-granting agency or an agency that regulates the activities of the permit-granting agency.

Added by St.1962, c. 779, § 1. Amended by St.1998, c. 100; St.2009, c. 28, § 76, eff. Sept. 29, 2009.

§ 18. Former municipal employee; acting as attorney or receiving compensation; from other than municipality; partners

(a) A former municipal employee who knowingly acts as agent or attorney for or receives compensation, directly or indirectly from anyone other than the same city or town in connection with any particular matter in which the city or town is a party or has a direct and substantial interest and in which he participated as a municipal employee while so employed, or (b) a former municipal employee who, within one year after his last employment has ceased, appears personally before any agency of the city or town as agent or attorney for anyone other than the city or town in connection with any particular matter in which the same city or town is a party or has a direct and substantial interest and which was under his official responsibility as a municipal employee at any time within a period of two years prior to the termination of his employment, or (c) a partner of a former municipal employee who knowingly engages, during a period of one year following the termination of the latter's employment by the city or town, in any activity in which the former municipal employee is himself prohibited from engaging by clause (a), or (d) a partner of a municipal employee who knowingly acts as agent or attorney for anyone other than the city or town in connection with any particular matter in which the same city or town is a party or has a direct and substantial interest and in which the municipal employee participates or has participated as a municipal employee or which is the subject of his official responsibility, shall be punished by a fine of not more than $10,000, or by imprisonment in the state prison for not more than 5 years, or in a jail or house of correction for not more than 2½ years, or both.

If a partner of a former municipal employee or of a special municipal employee is also a member of another partnership in which the former or special employee has no interest, the activities of the latter partnership in which the former or special employee takes no part shall not thereby be subject to clause (c) or (d).

Notwithstanding the provisions of clause (b), a former town counsel who acted in such capacity on a salary or retainer of less than two thousand dollars per year shall be prohibited from appearing personally before any agency of the city or town as agent or attorney for anyone other than the city or town only in connection with any particular matter in which the same city or town is a party or has a direct and substantial interest and in which he participated while so employed.

This section shall not prevent a present or former special municipal employee from aiding or assisting another person for compensation in the performance of work under a contract with or for the benefit of the city or town; provided, that the head of the special municipal employee's department or agency has certified in writing that the interest of the city or town requires such aid or assistance and the certification has been filed with the clerk of the city or town. The certification shall be open to public inspection.

Added by St.1962, c. 779, § 1. Amended by St.2009, c. 28, § 77, eff. Sept. 29, 2009.

§ 19. Municipal employees, relatives or associates; financial interest in particular matter

(a) Except as permitted by paragraph (b), a municipal employee who participates as such an employee in a particular matter in which to his knowledge he, his immediate family or partner, a business organization in which he is serving as officer, director, trustee, partner or employee, or any person or organization with whom he is negotiating or has any arrangement concerning prospective employment, has a financial interest, shall be punished by a fine of not more than $10,000, or by imprisonment in the state prison for not more than 5 years, or in a jail or house of correction for not more than 2½ years, or both.

(b) It shall not be a violation of this section (1) if the municipal employee first advises the official responsible for appointment to his position of the nature and circumstances of the particular matter and makes full disclosure of such financial interest, and receives in advance a written determination made by that official that the interest is not so substantial as to be deemed likely to affect the integrity of the services which the municipality may expect from the employee, or (2) if, in the case of an elected municipal official making demand bank deposits of municipal funds, said official first files, with the clerk of the city or town, a statement making full disclosure of such financial interest, or (3) if the particular matter involves a determination of general policy and the interest of the municipal employee or members of his immediate family is shared with a substantial segment of the population of the municipality.

Added by St.1962, c. 779, § 1. Amended by St.1965, c. 395; St.1982, c. 612, § 11; St.2009, c. 28, § 78, eff. Sept. 29, 2009.

§ 20. Municipal employees; financial interest in contracts; holding one or more elected positions

(a) A municipal employee who has a financial interest, directly or indirectly, in a contract made by a municipal agency of the same city or town, in which the city or town is an interested party of which financial interest he has knowledge or has reason to know, shall be punished by a fine of not more than $10,000, or by imprisonment in the state prison for not more than 5 years, or in a jail or house of correction for not more than 2½ years, or both.

This section shall not apply if such financial interest consists of the ownership of less than one per cent of the stock of a corporation.

This section shall not apply (a) to a municipal employee who in good faith and within thirty days after he learns of an actual or prospective violation of this section makes full disclosure of his financial interest to the contracting agency and terminates or disposes of the interest, or (b) to a municipal employee who is not employed by the contracting agency or an agency which regulates the activities of the contracting agency and who does not participate in or have official responsibility for any of the activities of the contracting agency, if the contract is made after public notice or where applicable, through competitive bidding, and if the municipal employee files with the clerk of the city or town a statement making full disclosure of his interest and the interest of his immediate family, and if in the case of a contract for personal services (1) the services will be provided outside the normal working hours of the municipal employee, (2) the services are not required as part of the municipal employee's regular duties, the employee is compensated for not more than five hundred hours during a calendar year, (3) the head of the contracting agency makes and files with the clerk of the city or town a written certification that no employee of that agency is available to perform those services as part of their regular duties, and (4) the city council, board of selectmen or board of aldermen approve the exemption of his interest from this section, or (c) to a special municipal employee who does not participate in or have official responsibility for any of the activities of the contracting agency and who files with the clerk of the city or town a statement making full disclosure of his interest and the interests of his immediate family in the contract, or (d) to a special municipal employee who files with the clerk of the city, town or district a statement making full disclosure of his interest and the interests of his immediate family in the contract, if the city council or board of aldermen, if there is no city council, board of selectmen or the district prudential committee, approve the exemption of his interest from this section, or (e) to a municipal employee who receives benefits from programs funded by the United States or any other source in connection with the rental, improvement, or rehabilitation of his residence to the extent permitted by the funding agency, or (f) to a municipal employee if the contract is for personal services in a part time, call or volunteer capacity with the police, fire, rescue or ambulance department of a fire district, town or any city with a population of less than thirty-five thousand inhabitants; provided, however, that the head of the contracting agency makes and files with the clerk of the city, district or town a written certification that no employee of said agency is available to perform such services as part of his regular duties, and the city council, board of selectmen, board of aldermen or district prudential committee approve the exemption of his interest from this section or (g) to a municipal employee who has applied in the usual course and is otherwise eligible for a housing subsidy program administered by a local housing authority, unless the employee is employed by the local housing authority in a capacity in which he has responsibility for the administration of such subsidy programs or (h) to a municipal employee who is the owner of residential rental property and rents such property to a tenant receiving a rental subsidy administered by a local housing authority, unless such employee is employed by such local housing authority in a capacity in which he has responsibility for the administration of such subsidy programs.

This section shall not prohibit an employee or an official of a town from holding the position of selectman in such town nor in any way prohibit such employee from performing the duties of or receiving the compensation provided for such office; provided, however, that such selectman shall not, except as hereinafter provided, receive compensation for more than one office or position held in a town, but shall have the right to choose which compensation he shall receive; provided, further, that no such selectman may vote or act on any matter which is within the purview of the agency by which he is employed or over which he has official responsibility; and, provided further, that no such selectman shall be eligible for appointment to any such additional position while he is still a member of the board of selectmen or for six months thereafter. Any violation of the provisions of this paragraph which has substantially influenced the action taken by any municipal agency in any matter shall be grounds for avoiding, rescinding or cancelling the action on such terms as the interest of the municipality and innocent third parties may require.

This section shall not prohibit any elected official in a town, whether compensated or uncompensated for such elected position, from holding one or more additional elected positions, in such town, whether such additional elected positions are compensated or uncompensated.

This section shall not prohibit an employee of a municipality with a city or town council form of government from holding the elected office of councillor in such municipality, nor in any way prohibit such an employee from performing the duties of or receiving the compensation provided for such office; provided, however, that no such councillor may vote or act on any matter which is within the purview of the agency by which he is employed or over which he has official responsibility; and provided, further, that no councillor shall be eligible for appointment to such additional position while a member of said council or for six months thereafter. Any violation of the provisions of this paragraph which has substantially influenced the action taken by a municipal agency in any matter shall be grounds for avoiding, rescinding or cancelling such action on such terms as the interest of the municipality and innocent third parties require. No such elected councillor shall receive compensation for more than one office or position held in a municipality, but shall have the right to choose which compensation he shall receive.

This section shall not prohibit an employee of a housing authority in a municipality from holding any elective office, other than the office of mayor, in such municipality nor in any way prohibit such employee from performing the duties of or receiving the compensation provided for such office; provided, however, that such elected officer shall not, except as otherwise expressly provided, receive compensation for more than one office or position held in a municipality, but shall have the right to choose which compensation he shall receive; provided further that no such elected official may vote or act on any matter which is within the purview of the housing authority by which he is employed; and provided further that no such elected official shall be eligible for appointment to any such additional position while he is still serving in such elective office or for six months thereafter. Any violation of the provisions of this paragraph which has substantially influenced the action taken by the housing authority in any matter shall be grounds for avoiding, rescinding, or cancelling the action on such terms as the interest of the municipality and innocent third parties may require.

This section shall not prohibit an employee in a town having a population of less than three thousand five hundred persons from holding more than one appointed position with said town, provided that the board of selectmen approves the exemption of his interest from this section.

[There is no subsection (b).]

Added by St.1962, c. 779, § 1. Amended by St.1979, c. 135; St.1982, c. 107; St.1982, c. 612, § 12; St.1983, c. 481; St.1984, c. 459; St.1985, c. 98; St.1985, c. 252, §§ 3, 4; St.1985, c. 415; St.1987, c. 374, § 2; St.1987, c. 497; St.1989, c. 262, §§ 2, 3; St.1999, c. 7, § 3; St.2009, c. 28, § 79, eff. Sept. 29, 2009.

§ 21. Avoiding, rescinding or canceling municipal action resulting from violations of chapter; restitution and damages

(a) In addition to any other remedies provided by law, a finding by the commission pursuant to an adjudicatory proceeding that there has been any violation of sections 2, 3, 8, 17 to 20, inclusive, or section 23, which has substantially influenced the action taken by any municipal agency in any particular matter, shall be grounds for avoiding, rescinding or canceling the action of said municipal agency upon request by said municipal agency on such terms as the interests of the municipality and innocent third persons require.

(b) In addition to the remedies set forth in subsection (a), the commission may, upon a finding pursuant to an adjudicatory proceeding that a person has acted to his economic advantage in violation of sections 2, 3, 8, 17 to 20, inclusive, or section 23, may issue an order (1) requiring the violator to pay the commission on behalf of the municipality damages in the amount of the economic advantage or $500, whichever is greater; and (2) requiring the violator to make restitution to an injured third party. If there has been no final criminal judgment of conviction or acquittal of the same violation, upon receipt of the written approval of the district attorney, the commission may order payment of additional damages in an amount not exceeding twice the amount of the economic advantage or $500, and payment of such additional damages shall bar any criminal prosecution for the same violation. The maximum damages that the commission may order a violator to pay under this section shall be $25,000. If the commission determines that the damages authorized by this section exceed $25,000, it may bring a civil action against the violator to recover such damages.

(c) The remedies authorized by this section shall be in addition to any civil penalty imposed by the commission in accordance with clause (3) of subsection (j) of section 4 of chapter 268B.

Added by St.1962, c. 779, § 1. Amended by St.1982, c. 612, § 13; St.2009, c. 28, § 80, eff. Sept. 29, 2009.

§ 21A. Members of municipal commission or board; restrictions on appointments to certain positions

Except as hereinafter provided, no member of a municipal commission or board shall be eligible for appointment or election by the members of such commission or board to any office or position under the supervision of such commission or board. No former member of such commission or board shall be so eligible until the expiration of thirty days from the termination of his service as a member of such commission or board.

The provisions of this section shall not apply to a member of a town commission or board, if such appointment or election has first been approved at an annual town meeting of the town.

Added by St.1967, c. 887, § 2.

§ 21B. Prospective municipal appointees; demanding undated resignations prohibited

No mayor, city manager, or town manager shall require a prospective appointee to a board, commission or position under his jurisdiction to submit as a condition precedent to said appointment an undated resignation from said board, commission or position. Whoever violates the provisions of this section shall be punished by a fine of not more than five hundred dollars.

Added by St.1973, c. 810.

§ 22. Opinions of corporation counsel, city solicitor or town counsel

Any municipal employee shall be entitled to the opinion of the corporation counsel, city solicitor or town counsel upon any question arising under this chapter relating to the duties, responsibilities and interests of such employee. All requests for such opinions by a subordinate municipal employee shall be made in confidence directly to the chief officer of the municipal agency in which he is employed, who shall in turn request in confidence such opinion of the corporation counsel, city solicitor or town counsel on behalf of such subordinate municipal employee, and all constitutional officers and chief officers or heads of municipal agencies may make direct confidential requests for such opinions on their own account. The town counsel or city solicitor shall file such opinion in writing with the city or town clerk and such opinion shall be a matter of public record; however, no opinion will be rendered by the town counsel or city solicitor except upon the submission of detailed existing facts which raise a question of actual or prospective violation of any provision of this chapter.

Added by St.1962, c. 779, § 1. Amended by St.1964, c. 408.

§ 23. Supplemental provisions; standards of conduct

(a) In addition to the other provisions of this chapter, and in supplement thereto, standards of conduct, as hereinafter set forth, are hereby established for all state, county, and municipal employees.

(b) No current officer or employee of a state, county or municipal agency shall knowingly, or with reason to know:

(1) accept other employment involving compensation of substantial value, the responsibilities of which are inherently incompatible with the responsibilities of his public office;

(2) (i) solicit or receive anything of substantial value for such officer or employee, which is not otherwise authorized by statute or regulation, for or because of the officer or employee's official position; or (ii) use or attempt to use such official position to secure for such officer, employee or others unwarranted privileges or exemptions which are of substantial value and which are not properly available to similarly situated individuals;

(3) act in a manner which would cause a reasonable person, having knowledge of the relevant circumstances, to conclude that any person can improperly influence or unduly enjoy his favor in the performance of his official duties, or that he is likely to act or fail to act as a result of kinship, rank, position or undue influence of any party or person. It shall be unreasonable to so conclude if such officer or employee has disclosed in writing to his appointing authority or, if no appointing authority exists, discloses in a manner which is public in nature, the facts which would otherwise lead to such a conclusion; or

(4) present a false or fraudulent claim to his employer for any payment or benefit of substantial value.

(c) No current or former officer or employee of a state, county or municipal agency shall knowingly, or with reason to know:

(1) accept employment or engage in any business or professional activity which will require him to disclose confidential information which he has gained by reason of his official position or authority;

(2) improperly disclose materials or data within the exemptions to the definition of public records as defined by section seven of chapter four, and were acquired by him in the course of his official duties nor use such information to further his personal interest.

(d) Any activity specifically exempted from any of the prohibitions in any other section of this chapter shall also be exempt from the provisions of this section. The state ethics commission, established by chapter two hundred and sixty-eight B, shall not enforce the provisions of this section with respect to any such exempted activity.

(e) Where a current employee is found to have violated the provisions of this section, appropriate administrative action as is warranted may also be taken by the appropriate constitutional officer, by the head of a state, county or municipal agency. Nothing in this section shall preclude any such constitutional officer or head of such agency from establishing and enforcing additional standards of conduct.

(f) The state ethics commission shall adopt regulations: (i) defining substantial value; provided, however, that substantial value shall not be less than $50; (ii) establishing exclusions for ceremonial privileges and exemptions; (iii) establishing exclusions for privileges and exemptions given solely because of family or friendship; and (iv) establishing additional exclusions for other situations that do not present a genuine risk of a conflict or the appearance of a conflict of interest.

Added by St.1962, c. 779, § 1. Amended by St.1975, c. 508; St.1982, c. 612, § 14; St.1983, c. 409; St.1986, c. 12, § 2; St.2009, c. 28, §§ 81 to 83, eff. Sept. 29, 2009.

§ 23A. Trustees of public institutions of higher learning; prohibited positions

No trustee of any public institution of higher education operated by the commonwealth shall be eligible to be appointed to or hold any other office or position with said institution for a period of three years next after the termination of his services as such trustee, or in the case of an elected student trustee at said institution, for a period of one year next after the termination of his services as such trustee; provided, however, that any such elected student trustee may accept and hold part-time employment at said institution while a student thereat, and provided further, that a trustee may be appointed to or hold an unpaid office or position with said institution after his services as such trustee.

Added by St.1964, c. 389. Amended by St.1973, c. 775; St.1974, c. 330.

§ 24. Disclosures and certifications; form; public inspection

All disclosures and certifications provided for in this chapter and made in accordance with its provisions shall be made in writing and, unless otherwise specifically provided in this chapter, shall be kept open to inspection by the public by the official with whom such disclosure has been filed.

Added by St.1962, c. 779, § 1.

§ 25. Suspension of persons under indictment for misconduct in office; notice; compensation and fringe benefits; temporary replacements; reinstatement

An officer or employee of a county, city, town or district, howsoever formed, including, but not limited to, regional school districts and regional planning districts, or of any department, board, commission or agency thereof may, during any period such officer or employee is under indictment for misconduct in such office or employment or for misconduct in any elective or appointive public office, trust or employment at any time held by him, be suspended by the appointing authority, whether or not such appointment was subject to approval in any manner. Notice of said suspension shall be given in writing and delivered in hand to said person or his attorney, or sent by registered mail to said person at his residence, his place of business, or the office or place of employment from which he is being suspended. Such notice so given and delivered or sent shall automatically suspend the authority of such person to perform the duties of his office or employment until he is notified in like manner that his suspension is removed. A copy of any such notice together with an affidavit of service shall be filed as follows: in the case of a county, with the clerk of the superior court of the county in which the officer or employee is employed; in the case of a city, with the city clerk; in the case of a town, with the town clerk; in the case of a regional school district, with the secretary of the regional school district; and in the case of all other districts, with the clerk of the district.

Any person so suspended shall not receive any compensation or salary during the period of suspension, nor shall the period of his suspension be counted in computing his sick leave or vacation benefits or seniority rights, nor shall any person who retires from service while under such suspension be entitled to any pension or retirement benefits, notwithstanding any contrary provisions of law, but all contributions paid by him into a retirement fund, if any, shall be returned to him, subject to section 15 of chapter 32. The employer of a person so suspended shall immediately notify the retirement system of which the person is a member of the suspension and shall notify the retirement board of the outcome of any charges brought against the individual.

A suspension under this section shall not, in any way, be used to prejudice the rights of the suspended person either civilly or criminally. During the period of any such suspension, the appointing authority may fill the position of the suspended officer or employee on a temporary basis, and the temporary officer or employee shall have all the powers and duties of the officer or employee suspended.

Any such temporary officer or employee who is appointed as a member of a board, commission or agency may be designated as chairman.

If the criminal proceedings against the person suspended are terminated without a finding or verdict of guilty on any of the charges on which he was indicted, his suspension shall be forthwith removed, and he shall receive all compensation or salary due him for the period of his suspension, and the time of his suspension shall count in determining sick leave, vacation, seniority and other rights, and shall be counted as creditable service for purposes of retirement.

Added by St.1972, c. 257. Amended by St.2004, c. 149, § 210, eff. July 1, 2004.

§ 26. Penalty for violations of clause (b)(2) or (b)(4) of Sec. 23

(a) Any person who, directly or through another, with fraudulent intent, violates clause (2) or (4) of subsection (b) of section 23, or any person who, with fraudulent intent, causes any other person to violate said clauses (2) or (4) of said subsection (b) of said section 23 or with fraudulent intent offers or gives any privileges or exemptions of substantial value in violation of said clause (2) or (4) of said subsection (b) of said section 23, shall be punished by a fine of not more than $10,000, or by imprisonment in the state prison for not more than 5 years, or in a jail or house of correction for not more than 2½ years, or both, if the unwarranted privileges or exemptions have a fair market value in the aggregate of more than $1,000 in any 12 month period.

[There is no subsection (b).]

Added by St.2009, c. 28, § 84, eff. Sept. 29, 2009.

§ 27. Publication of summaries of Chapter 268A; filing of acknowledgment by employees

The commission shall prepare, and update as necessary, summaries of this chapter for state, county, and municipal employees, respectively, which the commission shall publish on its official website. Every state, county and municipal employee shall, within 30 days of becoming such an employee, and on an annual basis thereafter, be furnished with a summary of this chapter prepared by the commission and sign a written acknowledgment that he has been provided with such a summary. Municipal employees shall be furnished with the summary by, and file an acknowledgment with, the city or town clerk. Appointed state and county employees shall be furnished with the summary by, and file an acknowledgment with, the employee's appointing authority or his designee. Elected state and county employees shall be furnished with the summary by, and file an acknowledgment with, the commission. The commission shall establish procedures for implementing this section and ensuring compliance.

Added by St.2009, c. 28, § 84, eff. Sept. 29, 2009.

§ 28. Online training programs

The state ethics commission shall prepare and update from time to time the following online training programs, which the commission shall publish on its official website: (1) a program which shall provide a general introduction to the requirements of this chapter; and (2) a program which shall provide information on the requirements of this chapter applicable to former state, county, and municipal employees. Every state, county, and municipal employee shall, within 30 days after becoming such an employee, and every 2 years thereafter, complete the online training program. Upon completion of the online training program, the employee shall provide notice of such completion to be retained for 6 years by the appropriate employer.

The commission shall establish procedures for implementing this section and ensuring compliance.

Added by St.2009, c. 28, § 84, eff. Sept. 29, 2009.

§ 29. Municipal liaisons to state ethics commission

Each municipality, acting through its city council, board of selectmen, or board of aldermen, shall designate a senior level employee of the municipality as its liaison to the state ethics commission. The municipality shall notify the commission in writing of any change to such designation within 30 days of such change. The commission shall disseminate information to the designated liaisons and conduct educational seminars for designated liaisons on a regular basis on a schedule to be determined by the commission in consultation with the municipalities.

Added by St.2009, c. 28, § 84, eff. Sept. 29, 2009.

CHAPTER 268B

FINANCIAL DISCLOSURE BY CERTAIN PUBLIC OFFICIALS AND EMPLOYEES

Chapter 268B of the General Laws was added by St.1978, c. 210, § 20.

The section headings for the General Laws in this pamphlet have been editorially supplied.

§ 1. Definitions

Definitions.

As used in this chapter, the following words shall, unless the context clearly requires otherwise have the following meanings:

"Amount", a category of value, rather than an exact dollar figure, as follows: greater than $1,000 but not more than $5,000; greater than $5,000 but not more than $10,000; greater than $10,000 but not more than $20,000; greater than $20,000 but not more than $40,000; greater than $40,000 but not more than $60,000; greater than $60,000 but not more than $100,000; greater than $100,000.

"Business", any corporation, partnership, sole proprietorship, firm, franchise, association, organization, holding company, joint stock company, receivership, business or real estate trust or any other legal entity organized for profit or charitable purposes.

"Business with which he is associated", any business in which the reporting person or a member of his immediate family is a general partner, proprietor, officer or other employee, including one who is self-employed or serves as a director, trustee or in any similar managerial capacity and any business more than 1 per cent of any class of the outstanding equity of which is beneficially owned in the aggregate by the reporting person and members of his immediate family.

"Candidate for public office", any individual who seeks nomination or election to public office; provided, however, that, an individual shall be deemed to be seeking nomination or election to public office if he has: (1) received a political contribution or made an expenditure, or has given his consent for any other person or committee to receive a political contribution or make an expenditure, for the purpose of influencing his nomination or election to such office, whether or not the specific public office for which he will seek nomination or election is known at the time the political contribution is received or the expenditure is made; or (2) taken the action necessary under the laws of the commonwealth to qualify himself for nomination or election to such office.

"Commission", the state ethics commission established by section 2;

"Equity", any stock or similar ownership interest in a business.

"Executive agent", an executive agent as defined in section 39 of chapter 3.

"Gift", a payment, entertainment, subscription, advance, services or anything of value, unless consideration of equal or greater value is received; provided, however, that "gift" shall not include a political contribution reported as required by law, a commercially reasonable loan made in the ordinary course of business, anything of value received by inheritance or a gift received from a member of the reporting immediate family or from a relative within the third degree of consanguinity of the reporting person or of the reporting person's spouse or from the spouse of any such relative.

"Governmental body", a state or county agency, authority, board, bureau, commission, council, department, division or other entity, including the general court and the courts of the commonwealth.

"Immediate family", a spouse and any dependent children residing in the reporting person's household.

"Income", income from whatever source derived, whether in the form of a fee, salary, allowance, forebearance, forgiveness, interest, dividend, royalty, rent, capital gain or any other form of recompense or any combination thereof; provided, however, that interest from savings accounts or from government obligations other than those of the commonwealth or any political subdivision thereof or any public agency or authority created by the general court, alimony and support payments, proceeds from a life insurance policy, retirement or disability benefits and social security payments shall not be considered income for the purposes of this chapter.

"Legislative agent", a legislative agent as defined in section 39 of chapter 3.

"Major policymaking position", the executive or administrative head of a governmental body, all members of the judiciary, any person whose salary equals or exceeds that of a state employee classified in step 1 of job group XXV of the general salary schedule contained in section 46 of chapter 30 and who reports directly to said executive or administrative head, the head of each division, bureau or other major administrative unit within such governmental body and persons exercising similar authority.

"Person", a business, individual, corporation, union, association, firm, partnership, committee or other organization or group of persons.

"Political contribution", a contribution of money or anything of value to an individual, candidate, political committee or person acting on behalf of an individual, candidate or political committee, for the purpose of influencing the nomination or election of the individual or candidate or for the purpose of promoting or opposing a charter change, referendum question, constitutional amendment or other question submitted to the voters and shall include any: (1) gift, subscription, loan, advance, deposit of money, or thing of value, except a loan of money to a candidate by a national or state bank made in accordance with the applicable banking laws and regulations and in the ordinary course of business; (2) transfer of money or anything of value between political committees; (3) payment, by any person other than a candidate or political committee, or compensation for the personal services of another person which are rendered to such candidate or committee; (4) purchase from an individual, candidate or political committee, or person acting on behalf of an individual, candidate or political committee, whether through the device of tickets, advertisements, or otherwise, for fund-raising activities, including testimonials, held on behalf of said individual, candidate or political committee, to the extent that the purchase price exceeds the actual cost of the goods sold or services rendered; (5) discount or rebate not available to other candidates for the same office and to the general public; and (6) forgiveness of indebtedness or payment of indebtedness by another person; provided, however, that political contribution shall not include the rendering of services by speakers, editors, writers, poll watchers, poll checkers or others, or the payment by those rendering such services of such personal expenses as may be incidental thereto, or the exercise of ordinary hospitality.

"Public employee", a person who holds a major policymaking position in a governmental body; provided, however, that a person who receives no compensation other than reimbursements for expenses, or any person serving on a governmental body that has no authority to expend public funds other than to approve reimbursements for expenses shall not be considered a public employee for the purposes of this chapter; provided, further, that the members of the board of bar examiners shall not be considered public employees for the purposes of this chapter.

"Public office", a position for which one is nominated at a state primary or chosen at a state election, excluding the positions of senator and representative in congress and the office of regional district school committee member elected district-wide.

"Public official", a person who holds a public office.

"Reporting person", a person required to file a statement of financial interest pursuant to section 5.

Added by St.1978, c. 210, § 20. Amended by St.1980, c. 256, § 2; St.1986, c. 557, § 192; St.1986, c. 693, § 1; St.1988, c. 10, § 11; St.1992, c. 286, § 264; St.2009, c. 28, § 85, eff. Sept. 29, 2009; St.2009, c. 105, § 1, eff. Oct. 2, 2009.

§ 2. State ethics commission

State ethics commission.

(a) There is established a state ethics commission composed of five members. At no time shall more than three members be from the same political party.

(b) Three members of the commission shall be appointed by the governor, one of whom shall be designated as chairman, and one member shall be appointed by the state secretary and one member shall be appointed by the attorney general. At no time shall more than two of the members to be appointed by the governor be from the same political party.

(c) Members of the commission shall serve for terms of five years.

(d) No person shall be appointed to more than one full five year term on the commission.

(e) Not less than thirty days prior to making any appointment to the commission, the appointing official shall give public notice that a vacancy on the commission exists.

(f) No member or employee of the commission shall:

(1) hold or be a candidate for any other public office while a member or employee or for one year thereafter;

(2) hold office in any political party or political committee;

(3) participate in or contribute to the political campaign of any candidate for public office.

(g) Members of the commission may be removed by a majority vote of the governor, state secretary, and attorney general, for substantial neglect of duty, inability to discharge the powers and duties of office, violation of subsection (f) of this section, gross misconduct, or conviction of a felony.

(h) Any vacancy occurring on the commission shall be filled within ninety days by the original appointing authority. A person appointed to fill a vacancy occurring other than by expiration of a term of office shall be appointed for the unexpired term of the member he succeeds, and shall be eligible for appointment to one full five year term.

(i) The commission shall elect a vice chairman. The vice chairman shall act as chairman in the absence of the chairman or in the event of a vacancy in that position.

(j) Three members of the commission shall constitute a quorum and three affirmative votes shall be required for any action or recommendation of the commission; the chairman or any three members of the commission may call a meeting; advance notice of all meetings shall be given to each member of the commission and to any other person who requests such notice;

(k) Members of the commission shall be compensated for work performed for the commission at such rate as the secretary of administration and finance shall determine, and shall be reimbursed for their expenses.

(*l*) The commission shall annually report to the general court and the governor concerning the action it has taken; the names and salaries and duties of all individuals in its employ and the money it has disbursed; and shall make such further reports on matters within its jurisdiction as may appear necessary;

(m) The commission shall employ an executive director, a general counsel, and, subject to appropriation, such other staff, including but not limited to clerks, accountants, and investigators, as are necessary to carry out its duties pursuant to this chapter and chapter two hundred and sixty-eight A. The staff shall serve at the pleasure of the commission and shall not be subject to the provisions of chapter thirty-one or section nine A of chapter thirty. The executive director shall be responsible for the administrative operation of the commission and shall perform such other tasks as the commission shall determine. The general counsel shall be the chief legal officer of the commission. The commission may employ, subject to appropriation, the services of experts and consultants necessary to carry out its duties. The colonel of state police, the state auditor, the comptroller, the attorney general, and the director of the office of campaign and political finance may make available to the commission personnel and other assistance as the commission may request.

Added by St.1978, c. 210, § 20. Amended by St.1986, c. 557, § 193; St.1991, c. 412, § 97.

§ 3. Powers and duties of the commission

Powers and duties of the commission.

The commission shall:

(a) prescribe and publish, pursuant to chapter 30A, rules and regulations: (1) to carry out this chapter, including rules governing the conduct of proceedings hereunder; and (2) to carry out chapter 268A; provided, however, that the rules and regulations shall be limited to providing exemptions from the provisions of sections 3 to 7, inclusive, sections 11 to 14, inclusive, sections 17 to 20, inclusive, and section 23 of said chapter 268A;

(b) prepare and publish, after giving the public an opportunity to comment, forms for the statements and reports required to be filed by this chapter and make such forms available to any and all persons required to file statements and reports pursuant to the provisions of this chapter;

(c) prepare and publish, pursuant to the provisions of chapter thirty A, methods of accounting and reporting to be used by persons required to file statements and reports by this chapter;

(d) make statements and reports filed with the commission available for public inspection and copying during regular office hours upon the written request of any individual who provides identification acceptable to the commission, including his affiliation, if any, at a charge not to exceed the actual administrative and material costs required in reproducing said statements and reports; provided, however, that the commission shall be authorized, in its discretion, to exempt from public disclosure those portions of a statement of financial interest filed pursuant to section five which contain the home address of the filer; and provided, further, that the commission shall forward a copy of said request to the person whose statement has been examined;

(e) compile and maintain an index of all reports and statements filed with the commission to facilitate public access to such reports and statements;

(f) inspect all statements of financial interests filed with the commission in order to ascertain whether any reporting person has failed to file such a statement or has filed a deficient statement. If, upon inspection, it is ascertained that a reporting person has failed to file a statement of financial interests, or if it is ascertained that any such statement filed with the commission fails to conform with the requirements of section five of this chapter, then the commission shall, in writing, notify the delinquent; such notice shall state in detail the deficiency and the penalties for failure to file a statement of financial interests;

(g) upon written request from a person who is or may be subject to the provisions of this chapter or chapter two hundred and sixty-eight A, render advisory opinions on the requirements of said chapters. An opinion rendered by the commission, until and unless amended or revoked, shall be a defense in a criminal action brought under chapter two hundred and sixty-eight A and shall be binding on the commission in any subsequent proceedings concerning the person who requested the opinion and who acted in good faith, unless material facts were omitted or misstated by the person in the request for an opinion. Such requests shall be confidential; provided, however, that the commission may publish such opinions, but the name of the requesting person and any other identifying information shall not be included in such publication unless the requesting person consents to such inclusion;

(h) preserve all statements and reports filed with the commission for a period of six years from the date of receipt;

(i) act as the primary civil enforcement agency for violations of all sections of chapter two hundred and sixty-eight A and of this chapter.

(j) on or before February first of each year the executive director of the commission shall request a list of all major policymaking positions for the governmental bodies below from the persons listed below:

(1) the house of representatives, the speaker of the house;

(2) the senate, the president of the senate;

(3) the state secretary's office, the state secretary;

(4) the attorney general's office, the attorney general;

(5) the state auditor's office, the state auditor;

(6) the treasurer and receiver general's office, the state treasurer;

(7) for each court of the commonwealth, the chief judge of such court;

(8) for each executive office in the commonwealth and all governmental bodies within such executive office, the secretary for such executive office;

(9) the governor's office, the governor;

(10) the lieutenant governor's office, the lieutenant governor;

(11) for each county, the chairman of the county commissioners;

(12) for each authority or other governmental body not covered by clauses one through eleven above, the executive or administrative head of such authority or governmental body; and such persons shall furnish such lists within sixty days. The executive director may add any position that he determines to be a major policymaking position in such governmental body to such list. Any person aggrieved by such action of the executive director may appeal such action to the commission.

Added by St.1978, c. 210, § 20. Amended by St.1986, c. 12, §§ 3, 4; St.1986, c. 557, § 194; St.1987, c. 9, § 1; St.1996, c. 39, § 2; St.2004, c. 399, § 1, eff. Feb. 16, 2005.

§ 4. Investigations by the commission

Investigations by the commission.

(a) Upon receipt of a sworn complaint signed under the penalties of perjury, or upon receipt of evidence which is deemed sufficient by the commission, the commission shall initiate a preliminary inquiry into any alleged violation of chapter 268A or 268B. At the commencement of a preliminary inquiry into any such alleged violation, the general counsel shall notify the attorney general in order to avoid overlapping civil and criminal investigations. All commission proceedings and records relating to a preliminary inquiry or initial staff review used to determine whether to initiate an inquiry shall be confidential, except that the general counsel may turn over to the attorney general, the United States Attorney or a district attorney of competent jurisdiction evidence which may be used in a criminal proceeding. The general counsel shall notify any person who is the subject of the preliminary inquiry of the existence of such inquiry and the general nature of the alleged violation within 30 days of the commencement of the inquiry.

(b) If a preliminary inquiry fails to indicate reasonable cause for belief that this chapter or said chapter two hundred and sixty-eight A has been violated, the commission shall immediately terminate the inquiry and so notify, in writing, the complainant, if any, and the person who had been the subject of the inquiry. All commission records and proceedings from any such preliminary inquiry, or from any initial staff review to determine whether to initiate an inquiry, shall be confidential.

(c) If a preliminary inquiry indicates reasonable cause for belief that this chapter or said chapter two hundred and sixty-eight A has been violated, the commission may, upon a majority vote, initiate an adjudicatory proceeding to determine whether there has been such a violation. The commission shall initiate such an adjudicatory proceeding within 5 years from the date the commission learns of the alleged violation, but not more than 6 years from the date of the last conduct relating to the alleged violation.

(d) The commission may require by summons the attendance and testimony of witnesses and the production of books, papers and other records relating to any matter being investigated by it pursuant to this chapter or said chapter two hundred and sixty-eight A. Such summons may be issued by the commission only upon a majority vote of the commission and shall be served in the same manner as summonses for witnesses in civil cases, and all provisions of law relative to summonses issued in such cases, including the compensation of witnesses, shall apply to summonses issued by the commission. Such summonses shall have the same force, and be obeyed in the same manner, and under the same penalties in case of default, as if issued by order of a justice of the superior court and may be quashed only upon motion of the summonsed party and by order of a justice of the superior court.

(e) Any member of the commission may administer oaths and any member of the commission may hear testimony or receive other evidence in any proceeding before the commission.

(f) All testimony in a commission adjudicatory proceeding shall be under oath. All parties shall have the right to call and examine witnesses, to introduce exhibits, to cross-examine witnesses who testify, to submit evidence, and to be represented by counsel. Before testifying, all witnesses shall be given a copy of the regulations governing commission proceedings. All witnesses shall be entitled to be represented by counsel.

(g) Any person whose name is mentioned during an adjudicatory proceeding of the commission and who may be adversely affected thereby may appear personally before the commission on his own behalf, with or without an attorney, to give a statement in opposition to such adverse mention or file a written statement of such opposition for incorporation into the record of the proceeding.

(h) All adjudicatory proceedings of the commission carried out pursuant to the provisions of this section shall be public, unless the members vote to go into executive session.

(i) Within thirty days after the end of an adjudicatory proceeding pursuant to the provisions of this section, the commission shall meet in executive session for the purpose of reviewing the evidence before it. Within thirty days after completion of deliberations, the commission shall publish a written report of its findings and conclusions.

(j) The commission, upon a finding pursuant to an adjudicatory proceeding that there has been a violation of said chapter two hundred and sixty-eight A or a violation of this chapter, may issue an order requiring the violator to:

(1) cease and desist such violation of said chapter two hundred and sixty-eight A or this chapter;

(2) file any report, statement or other information as required by said chapter two hundred and sixty-eight A or this chapter; or

(3) pay a civil penalty of not more than $10,000 for each violation of this chapter or chapter 268A, with the exception of a violation of section 2 of chapter 268A, which shall be subject to a civil penalty of not more than $25,000.

The commission may file a civil action in superior court to enforce such order and any order issued by the commission in accordance with chapter 268A.

(k) Any final action by the commission made pursuant to chapter 268A or 268B shall be subject to review in superior court upon petition of any party in interest filed within thirty days after the action for which review is sought. The court shall enter a judgment enforcing, modifying or setting aside the order of the commission or it may remand the proceedings to the commission for such further action as the court may direct. If the court modifies or sets aside the commission order or remands the proceedings to the commission, the court shall determine whether such modification, set aside or remand is substantial. If the court does find such modification, set aside or remand to be substantial, the employee shall be entitled to be reimbursed from the treasury of the commonwealth for reasonable attorneys' fees and all court costs incurred by him in the defense of the charges contained in said proceedings. The amount of such reimbursement shall be awarded by the court, but shall not exceed $30,000 per person, per case. Reimbursement of such costs shall be applicable to state, county or municipal employees whose conduct is so regulated by the provisions of chapter two hundred and sixty-eight A and this chapter.

(*l*) The superior court shall have concurrent jurisdiction to issue orders under paragraph (j) in a civil action brought by the attorney general. In any such action, an advisory opinion of the commission under clause (g) of section 3 shall be binding to the same extent as it is against the commission under that clause.

Added by St.1978, c. 210, § 20. Amended by St.1982, c. 612, §§ 15, 16; St.1986, c. 12, § 5; St.1990, c. 150, § 349A; St.1990, c. 487, § 2; St.2009, c. 28, §§ 86 to 93, eff. Sept. 29, 2009.

§ 5. Statements of financial interests

Statements of financial interests.

(a) Every candidate for public office shall file a statement of financial interest for the preceding calendar year with the commission on or before the date on which a certificate of nomination or nomination papers for such candidate are submitted to the state secretary. Every candidate for public office who has not filed nomination papers with the state secretary, but on whose behalf a statement of organization of a political committee has been filed with the director of campaign and political finance under section five of chapter fifty-five, and who is seeking public office by the so-called "write in" or "sticker" method, shall within three days after such filing file a statement of financial interest with the commission.

(b) Every public official shall file a statement of financial interest for the preceding calendar year with the commission on or before the last Tuesday in May of the year in which such public official first enters such public office and of each year that such public official holds such office, and on or before May first of the year after such public official leaves such office; provided, however, that no public official shall be required to file a statement of financial interests for the year in which he ceased to be a public official if he served for less than thirty days in such year.

(c) Every public employee shall file a statement of financial interests for the preceding calendar year with the commission within thirty days after becoming a public employee, on or before May first of each year thereafter that such person is a public employee and on or before May first of the year after such person ceases to be a public employee; provided, however, that no public employee shall be required to file a statement of financial interests for the year in which he ceased to be a public employee if he served less than thirty days in such year.

(d) The commission shall, upon receipt of a statement of financial interests pursuant to the provisions of this section, issue to the person filing such statement a receipt verifying the fact that a statement of financial interests has been filed and a receipted copy of such statement.

(e) No public employee shall be allowed to continue in his duties or to receive compensation from public funds unless he has filed a statement of financial interests with the commission as required by this chapter.

(f) The statement of financial interests filed pursuant to the provisions of this section shall be on a form prescribed by the commission and shall be signed under penalty of perjury by the reporting person.

(g) Reporting persons shall disclose, to the best of their knowledge, the following information for the preceding calendar year, or as of the last day of said year with respect to the information required by clauses (2), (3) and (6) below; such persons shall also disclose the same information with respect to their immediate family provided, however, that no amount need be given for such information with regard to the reporting person's immediate family:

(1) the name and address of, the nature of association with, the share of equity in, if applicable, and the amount of income if greater than one thousand dollars derived from each business with which he is associated;

(2) the identity of all securities and other investments with a fair market value of greater than one thousand dollars which were beneficially owned, not otherwise reportable hereunder; and the amount of income if over one thousand dollars from any such security which is issued by the commonwealth or any political subdivision thereof or any public agency or authority created by the general court;

(3) the name and address of each creditor to whom more than one thousand dollars was owed and the original amount, the amount outstanding, the terms of repayment, and the general nature of the security pledged for each such obligation except that the original amount and the amount outstanding need not be reported for a mortgage on the reporting person's primary residence; provided, however, that obligations arising out of retail installment transactions, educational loans, medical and dental expenses, debts incurred in the ordinary course of business, and any obligation to make alimony or support payments, shall not be reported; and provided, further, that such information need not be reported if the creditor is a relative of the reporting person within the third degree of consanguinity or affinity;

(4) the name and address of the source, and the cash value of any reimbursement for expenses aggregating more than one hundred dollars in the calendar year if the source of such reimbursement is a legislative or executive agent; or if the recipient is a public official and the source of such reimbursement is a person having a direct interest in legislation, legislative action, or a matter before a governmental body; or if the recipient is a public employee and the source of such reimbursement is person having a direct interest in a matter before the governmental body by which the recipient is employed;

(5) the name and address of the donor, and the fair market value, if determinable, of any gifts aggregating more than one hundred dollars in the calendar year, if the recipient is a public official and the source of such gift(s) is a person having a direct interest in legislation, legislative action, or a matter before a governmental body; or if the recipient is a public employee and the source of such gift(s) is a person having a direct interest in a matter before the governmental body by which the recipient is employed;

(6) the description, as appearing on the most recent tax bill, and the amount of assessed value of all real property located within the commonwealth, in which a direct or indirect financial interest was held, which has an assessed value greater than one thousand dollars; and, if the property was transferred during the year, the name and address of the person furnishing consideration to the reporting person or receiving it from him in respect to such transfer;

(7) the name and address of the source, and the fair market value, of any honoraria aggregating more than one hundred dollars if the source of such honoraria is a legislative agent; or if the recipient is a public official and the source of such honoraria is a person having a direct interest in legislation, legislative action, or a matter before a governmental body; or if the recipient is a public employee and the source of such honoraria is a person having a direct interest in a matter before the governmental body by which the recipient is employed;

(8) the name and address of any creditor who has forgiven an indebtedness of over one thousand dollars, and the amount forgiven; provided, however, that no such information need be reported if the creditor is a relative within the third degree of consanguinity or affinity of the reporting person, or the spouse of such a relative;

(9) the name and address of any business from which the reporting person is taking a leave of absence;

(10) the identity of any equity in a business with which the reporting person is associated which has been transferred to a member of the reporting person's immediate family; provided, however, that a member of the reporting person's family need not report any such transfer to the reporting person.

Nothing in this section shall be construed to require the disclosure of information which is privileged by law.

Failure of a reporting person to file a statement of financial interests within ten days after receiving notice as provided in clause (f) of section three of this chapter, or the filing of an incomplete statement of financial interests after receipt of such a notice, is a violation of this chapter and the commission may initiate appropriate proceedings pursuant to the provisions of section four.

Added by St.1978, c. 210, § 20. Amended by St.1981, c. 386, § 14; St.1986, c. 557, §§ 195, 196; St.1986, c. 693, § 2; St.1992, c. 286, § 265; St.2009, c. 28, § 94, eff. Sept. 29, 2009.

§ 6. Gifts from executive or legislative agents; exclusions to be established by state ethics commission

No executive or legislative agent shall knowingly and willfully offer or give to any public official or public employee or a member of such person's immediate family, and no public official or public employee or member of such person's immediate family shall knowingly and willfully solicit or accept from any executive or legislative agent, any gift of any kind or nature; provided, however, that the state ethics commission shall promulgate regulations: (i) establishing exclusions for ceremonial gifts; (ii) establishing exclusions for gifts given solely because of family or friendship; and (iii) establishing additional exclusions for other situations that do not present a genuine risk of a conflict or the appearance of a conflict of interest.

Added by St.1978, c. 210, § 20. Amended by St.2009, c. 28, § 95, eff. Sept. 29, 2009.

§ 7. Penalties for violation of confidentiality and for perjury

Penalties for violation of confidentiality and for perjury.

Any person who violates the confidentiality of a commission inquiry under the provisions of paragraph (a) of section four of this chapter shall be punished by a fine of not more than one thousand dollars or by imprisonment for not more than one year, or both.

Any person who willfully affirms or swears falsely in regard to any material matter before a commission proceeding under paragraph (c) of section four of this chapter, or who willfully files a materially false statement of financial interests under section five of this chapter shall be punished by a fine of not more than $10,000, or by imprisonment in the state prison for not more than 5 years, or in a jail or house of correction for not more than 2½ years, or both.

Added by St.1978, c. 210, § 20. Amended by St.1985, c. 118; St.1986, c. 557, § 197; St.2009, c. 28, §§ 96, 97, eff. Sept. 29, 2009.

§ 8. Retribution for engaging in commission proceedings

No officer or employee of the commonwealth or of any county, city or town shall discharge an officer or employee, or change his official rank, grade or compensation, or deny him a promotion, or threaten so to do, for filing a complaint with or providing information to the commission or testifying in any commission proceeding.

Added by St.1982, c. 612, § 17.

CHAPTER 269

CRIMES AGAINST PUBLIC PEACE

The section headings for the General Laws in this pamphlet have been editorially supplied.

§ 1. Dispensing and suppressing unlawful assembly; arresting persons

If five or more persons, being armed with clubs or other dangerous weapons, or if ten or more persons, whether armed or not, are unlawfully, riotously or tumultuously assembled in a city or town, the mayor and each of the aldermen of such city, each of the selectmen of such town, every justice of the peace living in any such city or town, any member of the city, town, or state police and the sheriff of the county and his deputies shall go among the persons so assembled, or as near to them as may be with safety, and in the name of the commonwealth command all persons so assembled immediately and peaceably to disperse; and if they do not thereupon immediately and peaceably disperse, each of said magistrates and officers shall command the assistance of all persons there present in suppressing such riot or unlawful assembly and arresting such persons. For the purposes of this section, the University of Massachusetts at Amherst shall be considered to be a town.

Amended by St.1965, c. 647, § 1; St.1966, c. 158; St.1991, c. 412, § 98; St.2004, c. 348, § 1, eff. Dec. 15, 2004.

Historical and Statutory Notes

St.1750–1, c. 17, § 1.
St.1786, c. 38, § 1.
St.1835, c. 140, § 1.
R.S.1836, c. 129, § 1.
G.S.1860, c. 164, § 1.
P.S.1882, c. 206, § 1.
R.L.1902, c. 211, § 1.

§ 2. Refusing or neglecting to depart or to assist in suppressing assembly or in arresting persons

Whoever, being present and being so commanded to assist in arresting such rioters or persons so unlawfully assembled, or in suppressing such riot or unlawful assembly, refuses or neglects to obey such command, or, if required by such magistrate or officer to depart from the place, refuses or neglects so to do, shall be considered one of the rioters or persons unlawfully assembled, and shall be punished by imprisonment for not more than one year or by a fine of not less than one hundred dollars or more than five hundred dollars, or both.

Amended by St.1965, c. 647, § 1A.

Historical and Statutory Notes

St.1786, c. 38, § 2.
St.1835, c. 140, § 1.
R.S.1836, c. 129, § 2.
G.S.1860, c. 164, § 2.
P.S.1882, c. 206, § 2.
R.L.1902, c. 211, § 2.

§ 3. Neglect or refusal to exercise authority to suppress assembly

A mayor, alderman, selectman, justice of the peace, sheriff or deputy sheriff who, having notice of any such riotous or tumultuous and unlawful assembly in the city or town where he lives, neglects or refuses immediately to proceed to the place of such assembly, or as near thereto as he can with safety, or omits or neglects to exercise the authority conferred upon him by this chapter for suppressing such assembly and for arresting the offenders, shall be punished by a fine of not more than three hundred dollars.

Historical and Statutory Notes

St.1835, c. 140, § 2.
R.S.1836, c. 129, § 3.
G.S.1860, c. 164, § 3.
P.S.1882, c. 206, § 3.
R.L.1902, c. 211, § 3.

§ 4. Requiring aid; dispersing and suppressing assembly; seizure of persons

If any persons who are so riotously or unlawfully assembled, and who have been commanded to disperse, as before provided, refuse or neglect to disperse without unnecessary delay, any two of the magistrates or officers before mentioned may require the aid of a sufficient number of persons, in arms or otherwise as may be necessary, and shall proceed, in such manner as they deem expedient, forthwith to disperse and suppress such assembly, and seize and secure the persons composing the same, so that they may be proceeded with according to law.

Historical and Statutory Notes

St.1750–1, c. 17, § 2.
St.1786, c. 38, § 3.
St.1835, c. 140, § 3.
R.S.1836, c. 129, § 4.
G.S.1860, c. 164, § 4.
P.S.1882, c. 206, § 4.
R.L.1902, c. 211, § 4.

§ 5. Armed forces obeying orders for suppressing riot and dispersing and arresting persons

When an armed force, called out under chapter thirty-three to suppress a tumult or riot, or to disperse a body of men acting together by force and with intent to commit a felony, or to offer violence to persons or property, or with intent by force or violence to resist or oppose the execution of the laws of the commonwealth, arrives at the place of such unlawful, riotous or tumultuous assembly, its members shall obey such orders for suppressing the riot or tumult, and for dispersing and arresting all persons who are committing any of said offences, as they have received from the governor, or a judge of a court of record, or the sheriff of the county, and also such orders as they there receive from any two of the magistrates or officers before mentioned.

Historical and Statutory Notes

R.S.1836, c. 129, § 5.
G.S.1860, c. 164, § 5.
P.S.1882, c. 206, § 5.
R.L.1902, c. 211, § 5.

§ 6. Person killed or wounded as result of an assembly; guilt and responsibility

If, by reason of the efforts made by any two or more of said magistrates or officers or by their direction to disperse such assembly, or to seize and secure the persons composing the same who have refused to disperse, though the number remaining may be less than five, any such person or any other person then present is killed or wounded, the magistrates and officers, and all persons acting by their order or under their direction, and all persons acting under the two preceding sections, shall be held guiltless, and fully justified in law; and if any of said magistrates or officers, or any person acting under or by the direction of any of the officers before mentioned, is killed or wounded, all persons so assembled, and all other persons who, when commanded or required, refused to aid and assist said magistrates or officers, shall be held answerable therefor.

Amended by St.1965, c. 647, § 2.

Historical and Statutory Notes

St.1750–1, c. 17, § 1.
St.1786, c. 38, § 1.
St.1835, c. 140, § 3.
R.S.1836, c. 129, § 6.
St.1839, c. 54, § 1.
G.S.1860, c. 164, § 6.
P.S.1882, c. 206, § 6.
R.L.1902, c. 211, § 6.

§ 7. Injury to building or vessel by persons unlawfully assembled

If any of the persons so unlawfully assembled demolishes, pulls down or destroys, or begins to demolish, pull down or destroy, a dwelling house or other building, or a ship or vessel, he shall be punished by imprisonment in the state prison for not more than five years or by a fine of not more than one thousand dollars and imprisonment in jail for not more than two years, and shall also be liable in tort to any person for all damages sustained by him thereby.

Historical and Statutory Notes

St.1750–1, c. 17, § 3.
St.1786, c. 38, § 3.
R.S.1836, c. 129, § 7.
G.S.1860, c. 164, § 7.
P.S.1882, c. 206, § 7.
R.L.1902, c. 211, § 7.

§ 8. Destruction of or damage to property by persons riotously assembled; liability of town

If property of the value of fifty dollars or more is destroyed or if property is damaged to that amount or to a value in excess thereof by fifteen or more persons who are riotously or tumultuously assembled and provided that the activities of such riotous or tumultuous group are observed and reported to the police during the period that such activities are occurring, the town within which the property was situated shall, if the owner of such property uses all reasonable diligence to prevent said destruction or damage and to procure the conviction of the offenders, be liable to indemnify the owner thereof in tort to the amount of three-fourth's of the value of the property destroyed or of the amount of such damage thereto, and may recover the same against any or all of the persons who so destroyed or damaged such property.

Amended by St.1965, c. 647, § 3; St.1982, c. 476.

Historical and Statutory Notes

St.1839, c. 54, §§ 2, 3.
G.S.1860, c. 164, §§ 8, 9.
P.S.1882, c. 206, §§ 8, 9.
R.L.1902, c. 211, § 8.

§ 9. Repealed, 1923, 248, Sec. 2

§ 10. Carrying dangerous weapons; possession of machine gun or sawed-off shotguns; possession of large capacity weapon or large capacity feeding device; punishment

(a) Whoever, except as provided or exempted by statute, knowingly has in his possession; or knowingly has under his control in a vehicle; a firearm, loaded or unloaded, as defined in section one hundred and twenty-one of chapter one hundred and forty without either:

(1) being present in or on his residence or place of business; or

(2) having in effect a license to carry firearms issued under section one hundred and thirty-one of chapter one hundred and forty; or

(3) having in effect a license to carry firearms issued under section one hundred and thirty-one F of chapter one hundred and forty; or

(4) having complied with the provisions of sections one hundred and twenty-nine C and one hundred and thirty-one G of chapter one hundred and forty; or

(5) having complied as to possession of an air rifle or BB gun with the requirements imposed by section twelve B; and whoever knowingly has in his possession; or knowingly has under control in a vehicle; a rifle or shotgun, loaded or unloaded, without either:

(1) being present in or on his residence or place of business; or

(2) having in effect a license to carry firearms issued under section one hundred and thirty-one of chapter one hundred and forty; or

(3) having in effect a license to carry firearms issued under section one hundred and thirty-one F of chapter one hundred and forty; or

(4) having in effect a firearms identification card issued under section one hundred and twenty-nine B of chapter one hundred and forty; or

(5) having complied with the requirements imposed by section one hundred and twenty-nine C of chapter one hundred and forty upon ownership or possession of rifles and shotguns; or

(6) having complied as to possession of an air rifle or BB gun with the requirements imposed by section twelve B; shall be punished by imprisonment in the state prison for not less than two and one-half years nor more than five years, or for not less than 18 months nor more than two and one-half years in a jail or house of correction. The sentence imposed on such person shall not be reduced to less than 18 months, nor suspended, nor shall any person convicted under this subsection be eligible for probation, parole, work release, or furlough or receive any deduction from his sentence for good conduct until he shall have served 18 months of such sentence; provided, however, that the commissioner of correction may on the recommendation of the warden, superintendent, or other person in charge of a correctional institution, grant to an offender committed under this subsection a temporary release in the custody of an officer of such institution for the following purposes only: to attend the funeral of a relative; to visit a critically ill relative; or to obtain emergency medical or psychiatric service unavailable at said institution. Prosecutions commenced under this subsection shall neither be continued without a finding nor placed on file.

No person having in effect a license to carry firearms for any purpose, issued under section one hundred and thirty-one or section one hundred and thirty-one F of chapter one hundred and forty shall be deemed to be in violation of this section.

The provisions of section eighty-seven of chapter two hundred and seventy-six shall not apply to any person seventeen years of age or older, charged with a violation of this subsection, or to any child between ages fourteen and seventeen so charged, if the court is of the opinion that the interests of the public require that he should be tried as an adult for such offense instead of being dealt with as a child.

The provisions of this subsection shall not affect the licensing requirements of section one hundred and twenty-nine C of chapter one hundred and forty which require every person not otherwise duly licensed or exempted to have been issued a firearms identification card in order to possess a firearm, rifle or shotgun in his residence or place of business.

(b) Whoever, except as provided by law, carries on his person, or carries on his person or under his control in a vehicle, any stiletto, dagger or a device or case which enables a knife with a locking blade to be drawn at a locked position, any ballistic knife, or any knife with a detachable blade capable of being propelled by any mechanism, dirk knife, any knife having a double-edged blade, or a switch knife, or any knife having an automatic spring release device by which the blade is released from the handle, having a blade of over one and one-half inches, or a slung shot, blowgun, blackjack, metallic knuckles or knuckles of any substance which could be put to the same use with the same or similar effect as metallic knuckles, nunchaku, zoobow, also known as klackers or kung fu sticks, or any similar weapon consisting of two sticks of wood, plastic or metal connected at one end by a length of rope, chain, wire or leather, a shuriken or any similar pointed starlike object intended to injure a person when thrown, or any armband, made with leather which has metallic spikes, points or studs or any similar device made from any other substance or a cestus or similar material weighted with metal or other substance and worn on the hand, or a manrikigusari or similar length of chain having weighted ends; or whoever, when arrested upon a warrant for an alleged crime, or when arrested while committing a breach or disturbance of the public peace, is armed with or has on his person, or has on his person or under his control in a vehicle, a billy or other dangerous weapon other than those herein mentioned and those mentioned in paragraph (a), shall be punished by imprisonment for not less than two and one-half years nor more than five years in the state prison, or for not less than six months nor more than two and one-half years in a jail or house of correction, except that, if the court finds that the defendant has not been previously convicted of a felony, he may be punished by a fine of not more than fifty dollars or by imprisonment for not more than two and one-half years in a jail or house of correction.

(c) Whoever, except as provided by law, possesses a machine gun, as defined in section one hundred and twenty-one of chapter one hundred and forty, without permission under section one hundred and thirty-one of said chapter one hundred and forty; or whoever owns, possesses or carries on his person, or carries on his person or under his control in a vehicle, a sawed-off shotgun, as defined in said section one hundred and twenty-one of said chapter one hundred and forty, shall be punished by imprisonment in the state prison for life, or for any term of years provided that any sentence imposed under the provisions of this paragraph shall be subject to the minimum requirements of paragraph (a).

(d) Whoever, after having been convicted of any of the offenses set forth in paragraph (a), (b) or (c) commits a like offense or any other of the said offenses, shall be punished by imprisonment in the state prison for not less than five years nor more than seven years; for a third such offense, by imprisonment in the state prison for not less than seven years nor more than ten years; and for a fourth such offense, by imprisonment in the state prison for not less than ten years nor more than fifteen years. The sentence imposed upon a person, who after a conviction of an offense under paragraph (a), (b) or (c) commits the same or a like offense, shall not be suspended, nor shall any person so sentenced be eligible for probation or receive any deduction from his sentence for good conduct.

(e) Upon conviction of a violation of this section, the firearm or other article shall, unless otherwise ordered by the court, be confiscated by the commonwealth. The firearm or article so confiscated shall, by the authority of the written order of the court be forwarded by common carrier to the colonel of the state police, who, upon receipt of the same, shall notify said court or justice thereof. Said colonel may sell or destroy the same, except that any firearm which may not be lawfully sold in the commonwealth shall be destroyed, and in the case of a sale, after paying the cost of forwarding the article, shall pay over the net proceeds to the commonwealth.

(f) The court shall, if the firearm or other article was lost by or stolen from the person lawfully in possession of it, order its return to such person.

(g) Whoever, within this commonwealth, produces for sale, delivers or causes to be delivered, orders for delivery, sells or offers for sale, or fails to keep records regarding, any rifle or shotgun without complying with the requirement of a serial number, as provided in section one hundred and twenty-nine B of chapter one hundred and forty, shall for the first offense be punished by confinement in a jail or house of correction for not more than two and one-half years, or by a fine of not more than five hundred dollars.

(h)(1) Whoever owns, possesses or transfers a firearm, rifle, shotgun or ammunition without complying with the provisions of section 129C of chapter 140 shall be punished by imprisonment in a jail or house of correction for not more than 2 years or by a fine of not more than $500. Whoever commits a second or subsequent violation of this paragraph shall be punished by imprisonment in a house of correction for not more than 2 years or by a fine of not more than $1,000, or both. Any officer authorized to make arrests may arrest without a warrant any person whom the officer has probable cause to believe has violated this paragraph.

(2) Any person who leaves a firearm, rifle, shotgun or ammunition unattended with the intent to transfer possession of such firearm, rifle, shotgun or ammunition to any person not licensed under section 129C of chapter 140 or section 131 of chapter 140 for the purpose of committing a crime or concealing a crime shall be punished by imprisonment in a house of correction for not more than 2½ years or in state prison for not more than 5 years.

(i) Whoever knowingly fails to deliver or surrender a revoked or suspended license to carry or possess firearms or machine guns issued under the provisions of section one hundred and thirty-one or one hundred and thirty-one F of chapter one hundred and forty, or firearm identification card, or receipt for the fee for such card, or a firearm, rifle, shotgun or machine gun, as provided in section one hundred and twenty-nine D of chapter one hundred and forty, unless an appeal is pending, shall be punished by imprisonment in a jail or house of correction for not more than two and one-half years or by a fine of not more than one thousand dollars.

(j) Whoever, not being a law enforcement officer, and notwithstanding any license obtained by him under the provisions of chapter one hundred and forty, carries on his person a firearm as hereinafter defined, loaded or unloaded or other dangerous weapon in any building or on the grounds of any elementary or secondary school, college or university without the written authorization of the board or officer in charge of such elementary or secondary school, college or university shall be punished by a fine of not more than one thousand dollars or by imprisonment for not more than one year, or both. For the purpose of this paragraph, "firearm" shall mean any pistol, revolver, rifle or smoothbore arm from which a shot, bullet or pellet can be discharged by whatever means.

Any officer in charge of an elementary or secondary school, college or university or any faculty member or administrative officer of an elementary or secondary school, college or university failing to report violations of this paragraph shall be guilty of a misdemeanor and punished by a fine of not more than five hundred dollars.

[There is no paragraph (k).]

(*l*) The provisions of this section shall be fully applicable to any person proceeded against under section seventy-five of chapter one hundred and nineteen and convicted under section eighty-three of chapter one hundred and nineteen, provided, however, that nothing contained in this section shall impair, impede, or affect the power granted any court by chapter one hundred and nineteen to adjudicate a person a delinquent child, including the power so granted under section eighty-three of said chapter one hundred and nineteen.

(m) Notwithstanding the provisions of paragraph (a) or (h), any person not exempted by statute who knowingly has in his possession, or knowingly has under his control in a vehicle, a large capacity weapon or large capacity feeding device therefor who does not possess a valid Class A or Class B license to carry firearms issued under section 131 or 131F of chapter 140, except as permitted or otherwise provided under this section or chapter 140, shall be punished by imprisonment in a state prison for not less than two and one-half years nor more than ten years. The possession of a valid firearm identification card issued under section 129B shall not be a defense for a violation of this subsection; provided, however, that any such person charged with violating this paragraph and holding a valid firearm identification card shall not be subject to any mandatory minimum sentence imposed by this paragraph. The sentence imposed upon such person shall not be reduced to less than one year, nor suspended, nor shall any person convicted under this subsection be eligible for probation, parole, furlough, work release or receive any deduction from his sentence for good conduct until he shall have served such minimum term of such sentence; provided, however, that the commissioner of correction may, on the recommendation of the warden, superintendent or other person in charge of a correctional institution or the administrator of a county correctional institution, grant to such offender a temporary release in the custody of an officer of such institution for the following purposes only: (i) to attend the funeral of a spouse or next of kin; (ii) to visit a critically ill close relative or spouse; or (iii) to obtain emergency medical services unavailable at such institution. Prosecutions commenced under this subsection shall neither be continued without a finding nor placed on file. The provisions of section 87 of chapter 276 relative to the power of the court to place certain offenders on probation shall not apply to any person 17 years of age or over charged with a violation of this section.

The provisions of this paragraph shall not apply to the possession of a large capacity weapon or large capacity feeding device by (i) any officer, agent or employee of the commonwealth or any other state or the United States, including any federal, state or local law enforcement personnel; (ii) any member of the military or other service of any state or the United States; (iii) any duly authorized law enforcement officer, agent or employee of any municipality of the commonwealth; (iv) any federal, state or local historical society, museum or institutional collection open to the public; provided, however, that any such person described in clauses (i) to (iii), inclusive, is authorized by a competent authority to acquire, possess or carry a large capacity semiautomatic weapon and is acting within the scope of his duties; or (v) any gunsmith duly licensed under the applicable federal law.

(n) Whoever violates paragraph (a) or paragraph (c), by means of a loaded firearm, loaded sawed off shotgun or loaded machine gun shall be further punished by imprisonment in the house of correction for not more than 2½ years, which sentence shall begin from and after the expiration of the sentence for the violation of paragraph (a) or paragraph (c).

(*o*) For purposes of this section, "loaded" shall mean that ammunition is contained in the weapon or within a feeding device attached thereto.

For purposes of this section, "ammunition" shall mean cartridges or cartridge cases, primers (igniter), bullets or propellant powder designed for use in any firearm, rifle or shotgun.

Amended by St.1935, c. 290; St.1936, c. 227, § 1; St.1937, c. 250, § 1; St.1955, c. 160; St.1956, c. 172; St.1957, c. 688, § 23; St.1968, c. 737, §§ 11 to 14; St.1969, c. 441; St.1969, c. 799, §§ 14 to 16; St.1971, c. 456, §§ 5, 6; St.1972, c. 312, § 5; St.1973, c. 588; St.1974, c. 649, § 2; St.1975, c. 113, §§ 2, 3; St.1975, c. 585, § 1; St.1978, c. 175, §§ 1, 2; St.1982, c. 254; St.1983, c. 516, §§ 2, 3; St.1985, c. 349; St.1986, c. 481, § 3; St.1986, c. 581, § 1; St.1987, c. 150, §§ 1, 2; St.1989, c. 648; St.1990, c. 511, §§ 2, 3; St.1996, c. 20; St.1996, c. 151, §§ 487, 488; St.1998, c. 180, §§ 68 to 70; St.2006, c. 48, §§ 5 to 7, eff. Mar. 30, 2006.

Historical and Statutory Notes

St.1906, c. 172, § 2.
St.1908, c. 350.
St.1908, c. 583.
St.1911, c. 548, § 2.
St.1919, c. 207, § 2.
St.1919, c. 350, §§ 99, 100.
St.1923, c. 248, § 1.
St.1925, c. 284, § 5.
St.1927, c. 326, § 5.

§ 10A. Selling, giving or using silencers; confiscation and destruction

Any person, other than a federally licensed firearms manufacturer, an authorized agent of the municipal police training committee, or a duly authorized sworn law enforcement officer while acting within the scope of official duties and under the direct authorization of the police chief or his designee, or the colonel of the state police, who sells or keeps for sale, or offers, or gives or disposes of by any means other than submitting to an authorized law enforcement agency, or uses or possesses any instrument, attachment, weapon or appliance for causing the firing of any gun, revolver, pistol or other firearm to be silent or intended to lessen or muffle the noise of the firing of any gun, revolver, pistol or other firearm shall be punished by imprisonment for not more than five years in state prison or for not more than two and one-half years in a jail or house of correction. Nothing contained herein shall be construed to prohibit a federally licensed firearms manufacturer from selling such instrument, attachment, weapon or appliance to authorized law enforcement agencies for law enforcement purposes or to the municipal police training committee for law enforcement training. Upon conviction of a violation of this section, the instrument, attachment or other article shall be confiscated by the commonwealth and forwarded, by the authority of the written order of the court, to the colonel of the state police, who shall destroy said article.

Amended by St.1957, c. 688, § 24; St.1989, c. 509; St.1996, c. 151, § 489; St.2002, c. 196, §§ 24, 25.

Historical and Statutory Notes

St.1926, c. 261.

§ 10B. Repealed, 1957, 688, Sec. 25

§ 10C. Tear gas; use in commission of crimes

Whoever uses tear gas cartridges, or any device or instrument which contains a liquid, gas, powder, or any other substance designed to incapacitate for the purpose of committing a crime shall be punished by imprisonment in the state prison for not more than seven years.

Added by St.1969, c. 342. Amended by St.1973, c. 892, § 9; St.1974, c. 789.

§ 10D. Body armor; use in commission of crime

Whoever, while in the commission or attempted commission of a felony, uses or wears any body armor, so-called, or any protective covering for the body or any parts thereof, made of resin-treated glass-fiber cloth, or of any other material or combination of materials, designed to prevent, deflect or deter the penetration thereof by ammunition, knives or other weapons, shall be punished by imprisonment in the state prison for not less than two and one-half years nor more than five years or for not less than one year nor more than two and one-half years in a jail or house of correction.

Added by St.1983, c. 139.

§ 10E. Firearms sales, distributions or transfers; penalties; eligibility for probation, parole, furlough or work release

Whoever, except as provided by law, in a single transaction or occurrence or in a series of transactions within a twelve month period, knowingly or intentionally distributes, sells, or transfers possession of a quantity of firearms, rifles, shotguns, machine guns, or any combination thereof, shall, if the quantity of firearms, rifles, shotguns, machine guns, or any combination thereof is:

(1) Three or more, but less than ten, be punished by a term of imprisonment of not more than ten years in the state prison. No sentence imposed under the provisions of this paragraph shall be for less than a mandatory minimum term of imprisonment of three years and a fine of not more than fifty thousand dollars may be imposed but not in lieu of the mandatory minimum term of imprisonment, as established herein.

(2) Ten or more, but less than twenty, be punished by a term of imprisonment of not more than ten years in the state prison. No sentence imposed under the provisions of this paragraph shall be for less than a mandatory minimum term of imprisonment of five years and a fine of not more than one hundred thousand dollars may be imposed but not in lieu of the mandatory minimum term of imprisonment, as established herein.

(3) Twenty or more, be punished by a term of imprisonment not less than ten years up to life imprisonment in the state prison. No sentence imposed under the provisions of this paragraph shall be for less than a mandatory minimum term of imprisonment of ten years and a fine of not more than one hundred and fifty thousand dollars may be imposed but not in lieu of the mandatory minimum term of imprisonment, as established herein.

A prosecution commenced under this section shall not be placed on file or continued without a finding, and the sentence imposed upon a person convicted of violating any provision of said section shall not be reduced to less than the mandatory minimum term of imprisonment as established in said section, nor shall any sentence of imprisonment imposed upon any person be suspended or reduced until such person shall have served said mandatory minimum term of imprisonment.

A person convicted of violating any provision of this section shall not, until he shall have served the mandatory minimum term of imprisonment established herein, be eligible for probation, parole, furlough, work release, or receive any deduction from his sentence for good conduct under sections one hundred and twenty-nine, one hundred and twenty-nine C and one hundred and twenty-nine D of chapter one hundred and twenty-seven; provided, however, that the commissioner of corrections may, on the recommendation of the warden, superintendent, or other person in charge of the correctional institution, grant to said offender a temporary release in the custody of an officer of such institution for the following purposes: to attend the funeral of a relative, to visit a critically ill relative, or to obtain emergency medical or psychiatric services unavailable at said institution. The provisions of section eighty-seven of chapter two hundred and seventy-six shall not apply to any person, seventeen years of age or over, charged with a violation of said sections, or to any child between the age of fourteen and seventeen, so charged, if the court is of the opinion that the interests of the public require that he shall be tried for such offense instead of being dealt with as a child.

Added by St.1994, c. 24, § 8.

§ 10F. Illegal sale, gifts or transfer of large capacity weapons or large capacity feeding devices; punishment

(a) Any person who sells, keeps for sale, or offers or exposes for sale, gives or otherwise transfers any large capacity weapon or large capacity feeding device, both as defined in section 121 of chapter 140, to a person 18 years of age or over, except as permitted under this section or chapter 140, shall be punished by imprisonment in a state prison for not less than two and one-half years nor more than ten years. Any person who commits a second or subsequent such crime shall be punished by imprisonment in a state prison for not less than five years nor more than 15 years. The sentence imposed upon such person shall not be reduced to less than two and one-half years for a first offense, nor less than five years for a second or subsequent such offense, nor suspended, nor shall any person convicted under this subsection be eligible for probation, parole, furlough, work release or receive any deduction from his sentence for good conduct until he shall have served such minimum term of such sentence; provided, however, that the commissioner of correction may, on the recommendation of the warden, superintendent or other person in charge of a correctional institution or the administrator of a county correctional institution, grant to such offender a temporary release in the custody of an officer of such institution for the following purposes only: (i) to attend the funeral of a spouse or next of kin; (ii) to visit a critically ill close relative or spouse; or (iii) to obtain emergency medical services unavailable at such institution. Prosecutions commenced under this subsection shall neither be continued without a finding nor placed on file. The provisions of section 87 of chapter 276 relative to the power of the court to place certain offenders on probation shall not apply to any person 17 years of age or over charged with a violation of this subsection.

(b) Any person who transfers, sells, lends or gives a large capacity weapon or large capacity feeding device to a person under the age of 18, except as permitted under the provisions of chapter 140, shall be punished by imprisonment in a state prison for not less than five nor more than 15 years. The sentence imposed upon such person shall not be reduced to less than five years, nor suspended, nor shall any person convicted under this subsection be eligible for probation, parole, furlough, work release or receive any deduction from his sentence for good conduct until he has served five years of such sentence; provided, however, that the commissioner of corrections may, on the recommendation of the warden, superintendent or other person in charge of a correctional institution or the administrator of a county correctional institution, grant to such offender a temporary release in the custody of an officer of such institution for the following purposes only: (i) to attend the funeral of a spouse or next of kin; (ii) to visit a critically ill close relative or spouse; or (iii) to obtain emergency medical services unavailable at such institution. Prosecutions commenced under this subsection shall neither be continued without a finding nor placed on file. The provisions of section 87 of chapter 276 relative to the power of the court to place certain offenders on probation shall not apply to any person 17 years of age or over charged with a violation of this subsection.

Added by St.1998, c. 180, § 71.

§ 10G. Violations of Sec. 10 by persons previously convicted of violent crimes or serious drug offenses; punishment

(a) Whoever, having been previously convicted of a violent crime or of a serious drug offense, both as defined herein, violates the provisions of paragraph (a), (c) or (h) of section 10 shall be punished by imprisonment in the state prison for not less than three years nor more than 15 years.

(b) Whoever, having been previously convicted of two violent crimes, or two serious drug offenses or one violent crime and one serious drug offense, arising from separate incidences, violates the provisions of said paragraph (a), (c) or (h) of said section 10 shall be punished by imprisonment in the state prison for not less than ten years nor more than 15 years.

(c) Whoever, having been previously convicted of three violent crimes or three serious drug offenses, or any combination thereof totaling three, arising from separate incidences, violates the provisions of said paragraph (a), (c) or (h) of said section 10 shall be punished by imprisonment in the state prison for not less than 15 years nor more than 20 years.

(d) The sentences imposed upon such persons shall not be reduced to less than the minimum, nor suspended, nor shall persons convicted under this section be eligible for probation, parole, furlough, work release or receive any deduction from such sentence for good conduct until such person shall have served the minimum number of years of such sentence; provided, however, that the commissioner of correction may, on the recommendation of the warden, superintendent or other person in charge of a correctional institution or the administrator of a county correctional institution, grant to such offender a temporary release in the custody of an officer of such institution for the following purposes only: (i) to attend the funeral of a spouse or next of kin; (ii) to visit a critically ill close relative or spouse; or (iii) to obtain emergency medical services unavailable at such institution. Prosecutions commenced under this section shall neither be continued without a finding nor placed on file. The provisions of section 87 of chapter 276 relative to the power of the court to place certain offenders on probation shall not apply to any person 17 years of age or over charged with a violation of this section.

(e) For the purposes of this section, "violent crime" shall have the meaning set forth in section 121 of chapter 140. For the purposes of this section, "serious drug offense" shall mean an offense under the federal Controlled Substances Act, 21 U.S.C. 801, et seq., the federal Controlled Substances Import and Export Act, 21 U.S.C. 951, et seq. or the federal Maritime Drug Law Enforcement Act, 46 U.S.C. App. 1901, et seq. for which a maximum term of imprisonment for ten years or more is prescribed by law, or an offense under chapter 94C involving the manufacture, distribution or possession with intent to manufacture or distribute a controlled substance, as defined in section 1 of said chapter 94C, for which a maximum term of ten years or more is prescribed by law.

Added by St.1998, c. 180, § 71.

§ 10H. Carrying loaded firearm while under influence of liquor, marijuana, narcotic drugs, depressants or stimulant substances; punishment

Whoever, having in effect a license to carry firearms issued under section 131 or 131F of chapter 140, carries on his person, or has under his control in a vehicle, a loaded firearm, as defined in section 121 of said chapter 140, while under the influence of intoxicating liquor or marijuana, narcotic drugs, depressants or stimulant substances, all as defined in section 1 of chapter 94C, or the vapors of glue shall be punished by a fine of not more than $5,000 or by imprisonment in the house of correction for not more than two and one-half years, or by both such fine and imprisonment.

Added by St.1998, c. 180, § 71.

§ 11. Printing statutes for posters; display

The state secretary shall, annually, cause to be printed, in English and in such other languages as he may deem necessary, and in large letters so as to be easily read, for use as a poster, section one hundred and thirty-one of chapter one hundred and forty and sections ten, twelve B, and fourteen of this chapter. Sufficient copies of the said posters shall be sent to the clerks and to the superintendents of schools in all cities and towns for their use as herein provided. The city or town clerks shall cause posters received by them to be displayed in such places as they may select, and in such numbers, according to the population of the city or town, as its clerk may deem expedient. The superintendents of schools shall cause the posters received by them to be distributed among the schools within their jurisdiction, and in such numbers as they may deem necessary. The cost of preparing and printing the posters and of distributing them to the various cities and towns shall be paid by the commonwealth, and the cost of placing or affixing them in each city or town shall be paid by that city or town.

Amended by St.1957, c. 688, § 26.

Historical and Statutory Notes

St.1912, c. 391.

§ 11A. Definitions

For the purposes of this section and sections eleven B, eleven C and eleven D, the following words shall have the following meanings:—

"Firearm", a firearm as defined in section one hundred and twenty-one of chapter one hundred and forty, or a rifle or shotgun.

"Serial number", the number stamped or placed upon a firearm by the manufacturer in the original process of manufacture.

"Identification number", the number stamped or placed upon a firearm by the colonel of the state police under authority of section eleven D.

Added by St.1937, c. 199. Amended by St.1996, c. 151, § 490.

§ 11B. Possession or control of firearm with serial or identification number removed or mutilated, while committing or attempting a felony; destruction

Whoever, while in the commission or attempted commission of a felony, has in his possession or under his control a firearm the serial number or identification number of which has been removed, defaced, altered, obliterated or mutilated in any manner shall be punished by imprisonment in the state prison for not less than two and one half nor more than five years, or in a jail or house of correction for not less than six months nor more than two and one half years. Upon a conviction of a violation of this section, said firearm or other article, by the authority of the written order of the court, shall be forwarded to the colonel of the state police, who shall cause said weapon to be destroyed.

Added by St.1937, c. 199. Amended by St.1957, c. 688, § 27; St.1996, c. 151, § 491.

§ 11C. Removal or mutilation of serial or identification numbers of firearms; receiving such firearm; destruction

Whoever, by himself or another, removes, defaces, alters, obliterates or mutilates in any manner the serial number or identification number of a firearm, or in any way participates therein, and whoever receives a firearm with knowledge that its serial number or identification number has been removed, defaced, altered, obliterated or mutilated in any manner, shall be punished by a fine of not more than two hundred dollars or by imprisonment for not less than one month nor more than two and one half years. Possession or control of a firearm the serial number or identification number of which has been removed, defaced, altered, obliterated or mutilated in any manner shall be prima facie evidence that the person having such possession or control is guilty of a violation of this section; but such prima facie evidence may be rebutted by evidence that such person had no knowledge whatever that such number had been removed, defaced, altered, obliterated or mutilated, or by evidence that he had no guilty knowledge thereof. Upon a conviction of a violation of this section said firearm or other article shall be forwarded, by the authority of the written order of the court, to the colonel of the state police, who shall cause said firearm or other article to be destroyed.

Added by St.1937, c. 199. Amended by St.1957, c. 688, § 28; St.1996, c. 151, § 492.

§ 11D. Repealed, 1957, 688, Sec. 29

§ 11E. Serial identification numbers on firearms

All firearms, rifles and shotguns of new manufacture, manufactured or delivered to any licensed dealer within the commonwealth shall bear serial numbers permanently inscribed on a visible metal area of said firearm, rifle or shotgun, and the manufacturer of said firearm, rifle or shotgun shall keep records of said serial numbers and the dealer, distributor or person to whom the firearm, rifle or shotgun was sold or delivered.

No licensed dealer shall order for delivery, cause to be delivered, offer for sale or sell within the commonwealth any newly manufactured firearm, rifle or shotgun received directly from a manufacturer, wholesaler or distributor not so inscribed with a serial number nor shall any licensed manufacturer or distributor of firearms, rifles or shotguns deliver or cause to be delivered within the commonwealth any firearm, rifle or shotgun not complying with this section.

No licensed manufacturer within the commonwealth shall produce for sale within the United States, its territories or possessions any firearm, rifle or shotgun not complying with paragraph one of this section. Whoever violates this section shall be punished by a fine of five hundred dollars. Each such violation shall constitute a separate offense.

Added by St.1968, c. 737, § 15. Amended by St.1969, c. 799, § 17.

§ 12. Manufacturing and selling knives, slung shots, swords, bludgeons and similar weapons

Whoever manufactures or causes to be manufactured, or sells or exposes for sale, an instrument or weapon of the kind usually known as a dirk knife, a switch knife or any knife having an automatic spring release device by which the blade is released from the handle, having a blade of over one and one-half inches or a device or case which enables a knife with a locking blade to be drawn at a locked position, any ballistic knife, or any knife with a detachable blade capable of being propelled by any mechanism, slung shot, sling shot, bean blower, sword cane, pistol cane, bludgeon, blackjack, nunchaku, zoobow, also known as klackers or kung fu sticks, or any similar weapon consisting of two sticks of wood, plastic or metal connected at one end by a length of rope, chain, wire or leather, a shuriken or any similar pointed starlike object intended to injure a person when thrown, or a manrikigusari or similar length of chain having weighted ends; or metallic knuckles or knuckles of any other substance which could be put to the same use and with the same or similar effect as metallic knuckles, shall be punished by a fine of not less than fifty nor more than one thousand dollars or by imprisonment for not more than six months; provided, however, that sling shots may be manufactured and sold to clubs or associations conducting sporting events where such sling shots are used.

Amended by St.1951, c. 219; St.1952, c. 286; St.1956, c. 280; St.1957, c. 688, § 30; St.1975, c. 585, § 2; St.1986, c. 581, § 2; St.1987, c. 123; St.1987, c. 465, §§ 62, 72.

Historical and Statutory Notes

St.1850, c. 194, § 2.
G.S.1860, c. 164, § 11.
P.S.1882, c. 206, § 11.
R.L.1902, c. 211, § 10.
St.1922, c. 485, § 10.

§ 12A. Air rifles; sale to minors

Whoever sells to a minor under the age of eighteen or whoever, not being the parent, guardian or adult teacher or instructor, furnishes to a minor under the age of eighteen an air rifle or so-called BB gun, shall be punished by a fine of not less than fifty nor more than two hundred dollars or by imprisonment for not more than six months.

Added by St.1951, c. 263. Amended by St.1959, c. 296, § 9.

§ 12B. Air rifles; possession by minors; shooting

No minor under the age of eighteen shall have an air rifle or so-called BB gun in his possession while in any place to which the public has a right of access unless he is accompanied by an adult or unless he is the holder of a sporting or hunting license and has on his person a permit from the chief of police of the town in which he resides granting him the right of such possession. No person shall discharge a BB shot, pellet or other object from an air rifle or so-called BB gun into, from or across any street, alley, public way or railroad or railway right of way, and no minor under the age of eighteen shall discharge a BB shot, pellet or other object from an air rifle or BB gun unless he is accompanied by an adult or is the holder of a sporting or hunting license. Whoever violates this section shall be punished by a fine of not more than one hundred dollars, and the air rifle or BB gun or other weapon shall be confiscated. Upon a conviction of a violation of this section the air rifle or BB gun or other weapon shall, by the written authority of the court, be forwarded to the colonel of the state police, who may dispose of said article in the same manner as prescribed in section ten.

Added by St.1951, c. 263. Amended by St.1957, c. 688, § 31; St.1968, c. 737, § 16; St.1996, c. 151, § 493.

§ 12C. Repealed, 1957, 688, Sec. 32

Historical and Statutory Notes

See, now, M.G.L.A. c. 269, §§ 10, 12.

§ 12D. Rifle or shotgun loaded with shells or cartridges; unloaded rifle or shotgun; carrying on public way prohibited; exceptions; punishment

(a) Except as exempted or provided by law, no person shall carry on his person on any public way a loaded rifle or shotgun having cartridges or shells in either the magazine or chamber thereof. For purposes of this section, "loaded shotgun or loaded rifle" shall mean any shotgun or rifle having ammunition in either the magazine or chamber thereof, such ammunition including a live cartridge, primer (igniter), bullet or propellant powder designed for use in any firearm, rifle or shotgun and, in the case of a muzzle loading or black powder shotgun or rifle, containing powder in the flash pan, a percussion cap and shot or ball; but the term "loaded shotgun or loaded rifle" shall not include a shotgun or rifle loaded with a blank cartridge, which contains no projectile within such blank or within the bore or chamber of such shotgun or rifle.

Whoever violates the provisions of this subsection shall be punished by a fine of not less than $500 nor more than $5,000 or by imprisonment in the house of correction for not more than two years, or by both such fine and imprisonment, and may be arrested without a warrant; provided, however, that if such rifle or shotgun is a large capacity weapon, as defined in section 121 of chapter 140, such person shall be punished by a fine of not less than $1,000 nor more than $10,000 or by imprisonment for not less than one year nor more than ten years, or by both such fine and imprisonment, and may be arrested without a warrant.

(b) Except as exempted or provided by law, no person shall carry on his person on any public way an unloaded rifle or shotgun, unless such rifle or shotgun is enclosed in a case.

Whoever violates the provisions of this subsection shall be punished by a fine of not less than $100 nor more than $1,000, and may be arrested without a warrant; provided, however, that if such unloaded rifle or shotgun is a large capacity weapon and is carried simultaneously with a fully or partially loaded large capacity feeding device, such person shall be punished by a fine of not less than $1,000 nor more than $10,000 or by imprisonment for not less than one year nor more than ten years, or by both such fine and imprisonment, and may be arrested without a warrant.

This subsection shall not apply to drills, parades, military reenactments or other commemorative ceremonies, color guards or memorial service firing squads, so-called, as permitted by law.

(c) Upon a conviction of a violation of any provision of this section, such rifle or shotgun shall be confiscated by the commonwealth and, upon written order of the court, such weapon shall be forwarded to the colonel of the state police, who may dispose of such weapon in the manner prescribed in section 10.

(d) The provisions of this section shall not apply to the carrying of a loaded or unloaded rifle or shotgun on a public way by (i) any officer, agent or employee of the commonwealth or any other state or the United States, including any federal, state or local law enforcement personnel; (ii) any member of the military or other service of any state or the United States, including members of the national guard, reserves and junior reserve officer training corps; (iii) any duly authorized law enforcement officer, agent or employee of any municipality of the commonwealth; provided, however, that any such person described in clauses (i) to (iii), inclusive, shall be authorized by a competent authority to so carry a loaded or unloaded rifle or shotgun on a public way and such person is acting within the scope of his duties or training; or (iv) a person who is lawfully engaged in hunting and is the holder of a valid hunting or sporting license issued pursuant to chapter 131. This section shall not apply to the operation of a shooting gallery, licensed and defined under the provisions of section 56A of chapter 140, nor to persons using the same.

Added by St.1957, c. 688, § 33. Amended by St.1968, c. 737, § 17; St.1996, c. 151, § 494; St.1998, c. 180, § 72; St.1998, c. 358, § 10; St.2005, c. 137, eff. Nov. 22, 2005.

§ 12E. Discharge of a firearm within 500 feet of a dwelling or other building in use; exceptions

Whoever discharges a firearm as defined in section one hundred and twenty-one of chapter one hundred and forty, a rifle or shotgun within five hundred feet of a dwelling or other building in use, except with the consent of the owner or legal occupant thereof, shall be punished by a fine of not less than fifty nor more than one hundred dollars or by imprisonment in a jail or house of correction for not more than three months, or both. The provisions of this section shall not apply to (a) the lawful defense of life and property; (b) any law enforcement officer acting in the discharge of his duties; (c) persons using underground or indoor target or test ranges with the consent of the owner or legal occupant thereof; (d) persons using outdoor skeet, trap, target or test ranges with the consent of the owner or legal occupant of the land on which the range is established; (e) persons using shooting galleries, licensed and defined under the provisions of section fifty-six A of chapter one hundred and forty; and (f) the discharge of blank cartridges for theatrical, athletic, ceremonial, firing squad, or other purposes in accordance with section thirty-nine of chapter one hundred and forty-eight.

Added by St.1971, c. 223. Amended by St.1972, c. 261.

§ 12F. Airport secure areas; possession or placement of a cutting device or prohibited weapon; punishment

(a) For the purposes of this section, the following words shall have the following meanings:—

"Airplane", an aircraft operated by an air carrier holding a certificate issued under 49 U.S.C. 41101 or any aircraft ordinarily used to transport passengers or cargo for hire.

"Cutting device", any knife, cutlery, straight razor, box cutter or other device containing a fixed, folding or retractable blade, which is not included in the list of weapons set forth in paragraph (b) of section 10.

"Prohibited weapon", any infernal machine as defined in section 102A of chapter 266, any stun gun as defined in section 131J of chapter 140, any rifle, shotgun or firearm as defined in section 121 of chapter 140 or any weapon included in the list of weapons set forth in paragraph (b) of section 10.

"Secure area", any area of an airport to which access is restricted through security measures by the airport authority or a public agency and the area beyond a passenger or property screening checkpoint at an airport.

"Airplane cabin", any passenger or flight crew area within an airplane while the airplane is on the ground in the commonwealth or over the commonwealth.

(b) Whoever occupies, or attempts to enter or occupy, a secure area of an airport or the cabin of an airplane, knowingly having in his possession or in his control and knowingly concealing, a cutting device or a prohibited weapon, notwithstanding any license to possess such a weapon or device, shall be punished by imprisonment in the house of correction for not more than 2½ years or by imprisonment in the state prison for not more than 5 years or by a fine of not more than $5,000, or by both such fine and imprisonment.

(c) Whoever, with intent to commit a felony, occupies, or attempts to enter or occupy, a secure area of an airport or the cabin of an airplane knowingly having in his possession or in his control a cutting device or a prohibited weapon shall be punished by imprisonment in the house of correction for not more than 2 years or by imprisonment in the state prison for not more than 10 years or by a fine of not more than $10,000, or by both such fine and imprisonment.

(d) Whoever, with intent to commit a felony, places, attempts to place or attempts to have placed within a secure area of an airport or the cabin of an airplane, a prohibited weapon or cutting device, notwithstanding any license to possess such a weapon or device, shall be punished by imprisonment in the house of correction for not more than 2½ years or by imprisonment in the state prison for not more than 10 years or by a fine of not more than $10,000, or by both such fine and imprisonment.

(e) Whoever willfully and without regard for the safety of human life, or with reckless disregard for the safety of human life, violates subsection (b), (c) or (d) shall be punished by imprisonment in the state prison for not more than 20 years or by a fine of not more than $20,000, or by both such fine and imprisonment.

(f) This section shall not apply to:—

(1) any law enforcement officer of a state or political subdivision of a state, an officer or employee of the United States government or United States military personnel authorized to carry prohibited weapons or cutting devices in an official capacity;

(2) a duly licensed individual transporting an unloaded, lawful weapon or cutting device in baggage not accessible to a passenger in flight and, in the case of a lawful weapon, if the air carrier was informed of the presence of the weapon;

(3) a cutting device, which is otherwise lawfully possessed, ordinarily used in the course of the holder's employment, trade or occupation, while the holder is authorized to conduct such employment, trade or occupation within a secure area of an airport or airplane cabin.

Added by St.2002, c. 313, § 11.

§ 13. False alarms of fire

Whoever, without reasonable cause, by outcry or the ringing of bells, or otherwise, makes or circulates or causes to be made or circulated a false alarm of fire shall be punished by a fine of not less than one hundred dollars nor more than five hundred dollars, or by imprisonment in a jail or house of correction for not more than one year.

Amended by St.1968, c. 122; St.1970, c. 391; St.1971, c. 408.

Historical and Statutory Notes

St.1837, c. 177, § 2.
G.S.1860, c. 164, § 13.
P.S.1882, c. 206, § 13.
St.1897, c. 385.
R.L.1902, c. 211, § 12.

§ 13A. False reports to police officers

Whoever intentionally and knowingly makes or causes to be made a false report of a crime to police officers shall be punished by a fine of not less than one hundred nor more than five hundred dollars or by imprisonment in a jail or house of correction for not more than one year, or both.

Added by St.1982, c. 219.

§ 14. Deadly weapons, explosives, chemical or biological agents, or other deadly device or substance; threatened use or presence; threat to hijack; disruption of school, public building or transport; punishment; restitution

(a) For the purposes of this section, the following words shall have the following meanings:—

"Hijack", to commandeer or to take control without authority.

"School", any public or private preschool, headstart facility, elementary, vocational or secondary school, college or university.

"Serious bodily injury", bodily injury which results in a permanent disfigurement, protracted loss or impairment of a bodily function, limb or organ, or substantial risk of death.

(b) Whoever willfully communicates or causes to be communicated, either directly or indirectly, orally, in writing, by mail, by use of a telephone or telecommunication device including, but not limited to, electronic mail, Internet communications and facsimile communications, through an electronic communication device or by any other means, a threat:—

(1) that a firearm, rifle, shotgun, machine gun or assault weapon, as defined in section 121 of chapter 140, an explosive or incendiary device, a dangerous chemical or biological agent, a poison, a harmful radioactive substance or any other device, substance or item capable of causing death, serious bodily injury or substantial property damage, will be used at a place or location, or is present or will be present at a place or location, whether or not the same is in fact used or present; or

(2) to hijack an aircraft, ship, or common carrier thereby causing anxiety, unrest, fear, or personal discomfort to any person or group of persons shall be punished by imprisonment in the state prison for not more than 20 years or imprisonment in the house of correction for not more than 2½ years, or by fine of not more than $10,000, or by both such fine and imprisonment.

(c) Whoever willfully communicates or causes to be communicated such a threat thereby causing either the evacuation or serious disruption of a school, school related event, school transportation, or a dwelling, building, place of assembly, facility or public transport, or an aircraft, ship or common carrier, or willfully communicates or causes serious public inconvenience or alarm, shall be punished by imprisonment in the state prison for not less than 3 years nor more than 20 years or imprisonment in the house of correction for not less than 6 months nor more than 2½ years, or by fine of not less than $1,000 nor more than $50,000, or by both such fine and imprisonment.

(d) The court shall, after conviction, conduct a hearing to ascertain the extent of costs incurred, damages and financial loss suffered by an individual, public or private entity and the amount of property damage caused as a result of the defendant's crime. A person found guilty of violating this section shall, in all cases, in addition to any other punishment, be ordered to make restitution to the individual, public or private entity for any costs incurred, damages and financial loss sustained as a result of the commission of the crime. Restitution shall be imposed in addition to incarceration or fine, and not in lieu thereof, however, the court shall consider the defendant's present and future ability to pay in its determinations regarding a fine. In determining the amount, time and method of payment of restitution, the court shall consider the financial resources of the defendant and the burden restitution will impose on the defendant.

(e) Nothing in this section shall authorize the criminal prosecution of picketing, public demonstrations or other similar forms of expressing views.

Added by St.1957, c. 210. Amended by St.1958, c. 322; St.1971, c. 784, § 2; St.2002, c. 313, § 12.

§ 14A. Annoying telephone calls or electronic communication

Whoever telephones another person or contacts another person by electronic communication, or causes a person to be telephoned or contacted by electronic communication, repeatedly, for the sole purpose of harassing, annoying or molesting the person or the person's family, whether or not conversation ensues, or whoever telephones or contacts a person repeatedly by electronic communication and uses indecent or obscene language to the person, shall be punished by a fine of not more than $500 or by imprisonment for not more than 3 months, or by both such a fine and imprisonment.

For purposes of this section, "electronic communication" shall include, but not be limited to, any transfer of signs, signals, writing, images, sounds, data or intelligence of any nature transmitted in whole or in part by a wire, radio, electromagnetic, photo-electronic or photo-optical system.

Added by St.1964, c. 668. Amended by St.1965, c. 521; St.1978, c. 379, § 3; St.2010, c. 92, § 12, eff. May 3, 2010.

§ 14B. Willful and malicious communication of false information to public safety answering points; penalty

As used in this section, the following words shall have the following meanings:—

"Emergency response services provider", a police department, fire department, emergency medical service provider, PSAP, public safety department, private safety department or other public safety agency.

"PSAP", a facility assigned the responsibility of receiving 911 calls and, as appropriate, directly dispatching emergency response services or transferring or relaying emergency 911 calls to other public or private safety agencies or other PSAPs.

"Silent call", a call or other communication made to a PSAP in which the initiating party fails to provide information regarding his or her identity or location or the nature of the emergency. The initiating party shall not be considered to have provided any information that is automatically transmitted by a communication device or network upon connection with a PSAP including, but not be limited to, automatic location information and automatic number information.

(a) Whoever willfully and maliciously communicates with a PSAP, or causes a communication to be made to a PSAP, which communication transmits information which the person knows or has reason to know is false and which results in the dispatch of emergency services to a nonexistent emergency or to the wrong location of an actual emergency; or (b) whoever willfully and maliciously, makes or causes to be made 3 or more silent calls to any PSAP and thereby causes emergency services to be dispatched 3 or more times shall be punished by imprisonment in the house of correction for not more than 2½ years or by a fine of not more than $1,000. Whoever commits a second or subsequent violation of this section shall be punished by imprisonment in the house of correction for not more than 2½ years or by imprisonment in the state prison for not more than 10 years or by a fine of not more than 5,000 dollars, or by both such fine and imprisonment.

(b) Upon any conviction of this section, the court shall conduct a hearing to ascertain the extent of costs incurred, and damages and financial loss sustained by any emergency response services provider as a result of the violation and shall order the defendant to make restitution to the emergency response services provider or providers for any such costs, damages or loss. Restitution shall not be waived and shall be imposed in addition to any imprisonment or fine, and not in lieu thereof, except that the court shall consider the defendant's present and future ability to pay restitution in its determinations relative to the imposition of a fine. In determining the amount, time and method of payment of restitution, the court shall consider the financial resources of the defendant and the burden restitution will impose upon the defendant.

Added by St.2008, c. 223, § 16, eff. July 31, 2008.

§ 15. Stink bombs; sale

Whoever sells or offers for sale a stink bomb shall be punished by a fine of not less than ten nor more than two hundred dollars. As used in this section the words "stink bomb" shall mean a small bomb that gives off a foul odor on bursting or any compound or device prepared for the primary purpose of generating a foul odor and sold or offered for sale for such purpose.

Added by St.1965, c. 29.

§ 16. Arrowheads used for hunting; sale

Whoever sells or offers for sale devices known as broadheads, razorheads, or any other arrowhead used exclusively for hunting purposes to any person under fifteen years of age shall be punished by a fine of one hundred dollars upon conviction of the first offense, five hundred dollars upon conviction of the second offense, and one thousand dollars and not less than six months nor more than one year in a house of correction for the third and subsequent offenses.

Added by St.1977, c. 240.

§ 17. Hazing; organizing or participating; hazing defined

Whoever is a principal organizer or participant in the crime of hazing, as defined herein, shall be punished by a fine of not more than three thousand dollars or by imprisonment in a house of correction for not more than one year, or both such fine and imprisonment.

The term "hazing" as used in this section and in sections eighteen and nineteen, shall mean any conduct or method of initiation into any student organization, whether on public or private property, which wilfully or recklessly endangers the physical or mental health of any student or other person. Such conduct shall include whipping, beating, branding, forced calisthenics, exposure to the weather, forced consumption of any food, liquor, beverage, drug or other substance, or any other brutal treatment or forced physical activity which is likely to adversely affect the physical health or safety of any such student or other person, or which subjects such student or other person to extreme mental stress, including extended deprivation of sleep or rest or extended isolation.

Notwithstanding any other provisions of this section to the contrary, consent shall not be available as a defense to any prosecution under this action.

Added by St.1985, c. 536. Amended by St.1987, c. 665.

§ 18. Failure to report hazing

Whoever knows that another person is the victim of hazing as defined in section seventeen and is at the scene of such crime shall, to the extent that such person can do so without danger or peril to himself or others, report such crime to an appropriate law enforcement official as soon as reasonably practicable. Whoever fails to report such crime shall be punished by a fine of not more than one thousand dollars.

Added by St.1985, c. 536. Amended by St.1987, c. 665.

§ 19. Copy of Secs. 17 to 19; issuance to students and student groups, teams and organizations; report

Each institution of secondary education and each public and private institution of post secondary education shall issue to every student group, student team or student organization which is part of such institution or is recognized by the institution or permitted by the institution to use its name or facilities or is known by the institution to exist as an unaffiliated student group, student team or student organization, a copy of this section and sections seventeen and eighteen; provided, however, that an institution's compliance with this section's requirements that an institution issue copies of this section and sections seventeen and eighteen to unaffiliated student groups, teams or organizations shall not constitute evidence of the institution's recognition or endorsement of said unaffiliated student groups, teams or organizations.

Each such group, team or organization shall distribute a copy of this section and sections seventeen and eighteen to each of its members, plebes, pledges or applicants for membership. It shall be the duty of each such group, team or organization, acting through its designated officer, to deliver annually, to the institution an attested acknowledgement stating that such group, team or organization has received a copy of this section and said sections seventeen and eighteen, that each of its members, plebes, pledges, or applicants has received a copy of sections seventeen and eighteen, and that such group, team or organization understands and agrees to comply with the provisions of this section and sections seventeen and eighteen.

Each institution of secondary education and each public or private institution of post secondary education shall, at least annually, before or at the start of enrollment, deliver to each person who enrolls as a full time student in such institution a copy of this section and sections seventeen and eighteen.

Each institution of secondary education and each public or private institution of post secondary education shall file, at least annually, a report with the board of higher education and in the case of secondary institutions, the board of education, certifying that such institution has complied with its responsibility to inform student groups, teams or organizations and to notify each full time student enrolled by it of the provisions of this section and sections seventeen and eighteen and also certifying that said institution has adopted a disciplinary policy with regard to the organizers and participants of hazing, and that such policy has been set forth with appropriate emphasis in the student handbook or similar means of communicating the institution's policies to its students. The board of higher education and, in the case of secondary institutions, the board of education shall promulgate regulations governing the content and frequency of such reports, and shall forthwith report to the attorney general any such institution which fails to make such report.

Added by St.1985, c. 536. Amended by St.1987, c. 665; St.1998, c. 161, §§ 557, 558.

CHAPTER 270

CRIMES AGAINST PUBLIC HEALTH

The section headings for the General Laws in this pamphlet have been editorially supplied.

§ 1. Adulterating liquor; sale; forfeiture

Whoever, for the purpose of sale, adulterates any liquor used or intended for drink with Indian cockle, vitriol, grains of paradise, opium, alum, cochineal, capsicum, copperas, laurel water, logwood, Brazil wood, sugar of lead or any other substance poisonous or injurious to health, and whoever knowingly sells any such liquor so adulterated, shall be punished by imprisonment in the state prison for not more than three years; and the articles so adulterated shall be forfeited.

Historical and Statutory Notes

St.1855, c. 356.
G.S.1860, c. 166, § 4.
P.S.1882, c. 208, § 4.
R.L.1902, c. 213, § 1.

§ 1A. Eyeglasses or sunglasses; specifications; flammable frames; sales

No person shall distribute, sell or deliver any eyeglasses or sunglasses unless said eyeglasses or sunglasses are fitted with plastic lenses, laminated lenses, heat-treated glass lenses or lenses made impact-resistant by other methods. The provisions of this paragraph shall not apply if a physician or optometrist, having found that such lenses will not fulfill the visual requirements of a particular patient, directs in writing the use of other lenses and gives written notification thereof to the patient. Before they are mounted in frames, all impact-resistant eyeglass and sunglass lenses shall be capable of withstanding an impact test of a steel ball five-eighths of an inch in diameter weighing approximately fifty-six hundredths of an ounce dropped from a height of fifty inches. Raised ledge multifocal lenses shall be capable of withstanding said impact test but need not be tested beyond initial design testing. All prescription glass lenses shall withstand said impact test. To demonstrate that all nonprescription glass lenses, plastic lenses and laminated lenses are capable of withstanding said impact test, the manufacturer of such lenses shall subject to said impact test a statistically significant sampling of lenses from each production batch, and the lenses so tested shall be representative of the finished forms as worn by the wearer. Plastic prescription and plastic nonprescription lenses, tested on the basis of statistical significance, may be tested in uncut finished or semifinished form at the point of original manufacture.

No person shall distribute, sell, exchange or deliver or have in his possession with intent to distribute, sell, exchange or deliver any eyeglass or sunglass frame containing any form of cellulose nitrate or other highly flammable material.

Whoever violates any provision of this section shall be punished by a fine of not more than five hundred dollars for each violation.

Added by St.1970, c. 471, § 1. Amended by St.1973, c. 598; St.1979, c. 381.

§§ 2 to 2B. Repealed, 1960, 727, Sec. 1

Historical and Statutory Notes

See, now, M.G.L.A. c. 94B, § 1 et seq.

§ 3. Drugs or other substance injurious to users; distribution

Whoever distributes, delivers or gives away in any public way or from house to house or place to place, any bottle, box, envelope or package containing any liquid, medicine, pill, powder, tablet or other article composed of any drug, poison or other ingredient or substance which may be in any way injurious or harmful to any person who may taste, eat, drink or otherwise use the same, shall be punished by a fine of not less than fifty nor more than one hundred dollars.

Historical and Statutory Notes

St.1907, c. 180.

§ 3A. Poison for rodents; placement where it may cause injury

Whoever negligently or maliciously places any poison or poisoned food for the control of rats, mice or other rodents in any place where it may cause injury to any human being or domestic animal shall be punished by a fine of twenty-five dollars. The officers charged with the enforcement of the laws relating to fish, birds and mammals under chapter one hundred and thirty-one shall take cognizance of violations of this section and enforce the provisions thereof, and they shall have all powers necessary therefor.

Added by St.1951, c. 444.

§ 4. Wood alcohol contained in food or drink; sale or possession

Whoever, himself, or by his servant or agent, or as the servant or agent of another, sells or exchanges, or has in his possession with intent to sell or exchange, or knowingly delivers or has in his possession with intent to deliver, any article of food or drink, or any drug intended for internal use, containing any wood alcohol, otherwise known as methyl alcohol, either crude or refined, under or by whatever name or trade mark the same may be called or known, shall be punished by a fine of not more than five thousand dollars or by imprisonment in a jail or house of correction for not more than two and one half years or in the state prison for not more than five years, or by both such fine and imprisonment.

Historical and Statutory Notes

St.1905, c. 220, § 2.
St.1910, c. 541, §§ 2, 3.
St.1929, c. 299.

§ 5. Alcoholic beverages or drugs; sale or delivery to hospital patients

Whoever, except under the direction of a physician, gives, sells or delivers alcoholic beverages, as defined in section one of chapter one hundred and thirty-eight, or a narcotic drug to a patient in any hospital who is suffering from inebriety or from the effect of inebriety, or from excessive use of narcotic drugs or from the effect of such use, and whoever has in his possession within the precincts of any hospital any such beverage or drug with intent to convey or deliver it to any such patient, except under direction as aforesaid, shall be punished by a fine of not more than fifty dollars or by imprisonment for not more than two months.

Amended by St.1934, c. 328, § 27.

Historical and Statutory Notes

St.1911, c. 30.

§ 6. Tobacco; sale or gift to minors

Whoever sells a cigarette, chewing tobacco, snuff or any tobacco in any of its forms to any person under the age of eighteen or, not being his parent or guardian, gives a cigarette, chewing tobacco, snuff or tobacco in any of its forms to any person under the age of eighteen shall be punished by a fine of not less than one hundred dollars for the first offense, not less than two hundred dollars for a second offense and not less than three hundred dollars for any third or subsequent offense.

Amended by St.1985, c. 345.

Historical and Statutory Notes

St.1886, c. 72.
St.1901, c. 373.
R.L.1902, c. 213, § 3.
St.1909, c. 346, §§ 1, 3.

§ 6A. Sale of cigarette rolling papers to minors

Whoever sells cigarette rolling papers to any person under the age of eighteen shall be punished by a fine of not less than twenty-five dollars for the first offense, not less than fifty dollars for the second offense and not less than one hundred dollars for a third or subsequent offense.

Notwithstanding the provisions of any civil ordinance or by-law or regulation to the contrary, which is in effect on the effective date of this section, no city, town, department, board or other political subdivision or agency of the commonwealth may impose any requirements, restrictions or prohibitions pertaining to the sale of cigarette rolling papers, in addition to those in this section.

Added by St.1995, c. 245, § 2.

§ 7. Posting copy of Sec. 6; removing copy

A copy of the preceding section printed as therein specified shall be posted conspicuously by the owner or person in charge thereof in the shop or other place used to sell cigarettes at retail, and whoever violates this provision shall be punished by a fine of not more than fifty dollars. Any person unlawfully removing a copy so posted while said premises are used for the sale of cigarettes shall be punished by a fine of ten dollars.

Historical and Statutory Notes

St.1909, c. 346, §§ 1, 2.

§ 8. Candy containing alcohol; sale

Whoever sells to a person any candy enclosing or containing liquid or syrup having more than one per cent of alcohol shall be punished by a fine of not more than one hundred dollars.

Historical and Statutory Notes

St.1891, c. 333.
R.L.1902, c. 213, § 4.
St.1913, c. 647.

§ 8A. Foods containing foreign injury causing substances; distribution or sale

Whoever sells, gives, or distributes to anyone candy or other food or foodstuffs containing a foreign substance, which is intended or may reasonably be expected to cause injury to a person eating the same, shall be punished by imprisonment in the state prison for not more than five years.

Added by St.1977, c. 861.

§ 9. Feeding garbage or refuse to animals

Whoever knowingly feeds or has in his possession with intent to feed to a milch cow any garbage, refuse or offal collected by a town, or by any person having authority therefrom, shall be punished by a fine of not more than one hundred dollars or by imprisonment for not more than two months; and whoever knowingly feeds or has in his possession with intent to feed to any food animal, except swine, any garbage, refuse or offal collected by a city of more than thirty thousand inhabitants shall be punished by a fine of not more than fifty dollars or by imprisonment for not more than one month.

Historical and Statutory Notes

St.1889, c. 326.
St.1895, c. 385.
R.L.1902, c. 213, § 5.

§ 10. Toys or confectionery containing or coated with material containing arsenic

Whoever, himself, or by his agent or servant, or as the agent or servant of another, manufactures, sells or exchanges, or has in his custody or possession with intent to sell or exchange, or exposes or offers for sale or exchange, any toys or confectionery, containing or coated wholly or in part with arsenic, shall be punished by a fine of not less than fifty nor more than one hundred dollars.

Historical and Statutory Notes

St.1891, c. 374, § 1.
R.L.1902, c. 213, § 6.

§ 11. Arsenic; samples for analysis

Whoever offers or exposes for sale or exchange any paper, fabric or other article shall furnish a sample thereof sufficient to ascertain by analysis the existence of arsenic therein, if such sample can be obtained without damage to the remaining portion, to any inspector, chemist or other agent or officer of the department of public health who applies therefor and tenders the value thereof; and for a violation of this section shall be punished as provided in the preceding section.

Historical and Statutory Notes

St.1891, c. 374, § 3.
R.L.1902, c. 213, § 7.
St.1914, c. 792, § 1.
St.1919, c. 350, § 96.

§ 12. Fabric or paper containing arsenic

Whoever, himself, or by his agent or servant, manufactures, sells or exchanges, or has in his custody or possession with intent to sell or exchange, any woven fabric or paper containing arsenic in any form, or any article of dress or household use composed wholly or in part of such woven fabric or paper, shall be punished by a fine of not less than fifty nor more than two hundred dollars; but this section shall not apply to articles intended for the destruction of insects, having the word "POISON" plainly printed in uncondensed gothic letters not less than one inch long on both sides of each sheet and square foot of the fabric, or to dress goods or articles of dress containing not more than one one-hundredth grain, or to other materials or articles containing not more than one tenth grain of arsenic for each square yard of the material. The department of public health shall make all necessary investigations as to the existence of arsenic in the aforesaid articles and materials, employ inspectors and chemists, and adopt such measures as are necessary to enforce this section.

Historical and Statutory Notes

St.1900, c. 325.
St.1901, c. 188.
R.L.1902, c. 213, § 8.
St.1914, c. 792, § 1.
St.1919, c. 350, § 96.

§ 13. Water; refusal or neglect to furnish

A corporation engaged in selling or distributing water, which refuses or neglects to furnish or supply water to or for any building or premises for the reason that a water bill remains unpaid by a previous owner or occupant of said building or premises shall, unless the person applying for water is in arrears to such corporation for water previously furnished to or for any building or premises, be punished by a fine of not less than ten nor more than twenty dollars.

Historical and Statutory Notes

St.1898, c. 168.
R.L.1902, c. 213, § 10.

§ 14. Spitting

Whoever expectorates or spits upon any public sidewalk, or upon any place used exclusively or principally by pedestrians, or, except in receptacles provided for the purpose, in or upon any part of any city or town hall, any court house or court room, any public library or museum, any church or theatre, any lecture or music hall, any mill or factory, any hall of any tenement building occupied by five or more families, any school building, any ferry boat or steamboat, any railroad car or elevated railroad car, except a smoking car, any street railway car, any railroad or railway station or waiting room, or on any track, platform or sidewalk connected therewith, and included within the limits thereof, shall be punished by a fine of not more than twenty dollars.

Historical and Statutory Notes

St.1906, c. 165.
St.1907, c. 410.
St.1908, c. 150.

§ 15. Arrest without warrant for spitting

Any person detected in the act of violating the preceding section may, if his name is unknown to the officer, be arrested without a warrant by any officer authorized to serve criminal process in the place where the offence is committed and kept in custody until he can be taken before a court having jurisdiction of such offence.

Historical and Statutory Notes

St.1907, c. 410, § 2.

§ 16. Disposal of rubbish, etc. on or near highways and coastal or inland waters; penalties; enforcement; park rangers

Whoever places, throws, deposits or discharges or whoever causes to be placed, thrown, deposited or discharged, trash, bottles or cans, refuse, rubbish, garbage, debris, scrap, waste or other material of any kind on a public highway or within 20 yards of a public highway, or on any other public land, or in or upon coastal or inland waters, as defined in section 1 of chapter 131, or within 20 yards of such waters, or on property of another, or on lands dedicated for open space purposes, including lands subject to conservation restrictions and agricultural preservation restrictions as defined in chapter 184, shall be punished by a fine of not more than $5,500 for the first offense and a fine not to exceed $15,000 for each subsequent offense; provided, however, that 50 per cent of the fine imposed shall be deposited in the conservation trust established in section 1 of chapter 132A and the court may also require that the violator remove, at his own expense, the trash, refuse, rubbish, debris or materials. The permission of the owner of land to place, throw, deposit or discharge trash, refuse, rubbish, garbage, debris, scrap, waste or other material on the owner's land shall constitute a defense in any trial for such offense.

If a motor vehicle is used in committing such an offense where the offense involves the unlawful disposal of more than seven cubic feet of trash, bottles or cans, refuse, rubbish, garbage, debris scrap, waste or any other materials and the motor vehicle is observed while the offense is in progress by an officer authorized to enforce this section, the officer may seize the vehicle and remove and store it or otherwise immobilize it by a mechanical device until (1) payment is made to the enforcing authority of a fine set by such enforcing authority up to the maximum fine which may be imposed under this section, (2) the illegally disposed of material is removed and legally disposed of, and (3) payment is made to the enforcing authority of its reasonable towing and storage charges, if any, for the seized vehicle. If, after payment of the above fine and towing and storage charges, the use of the seized vehicle is necessary to dispose of the material, the enforcing authority shall release the seized vehicle upon the posting of security sufficient to pay for the cost of legal disposal of the material. The security shall be returned to the person posting it upon proof of legal disposal of the material. Within five days of the payment of a fine to secure the release of a seized vehicle as provided for herein, the enforcing authority to whom the fine is paid shall deposit the fine in court along with an application for a criminal complaint regarding the offense, and the court shall hold the fine until judgment is entered on said complaint; provided, however, that at the discretion of the enforcing authority, the violation may be disposed of by the non-criminal disposition procedures pursuant to section twenty-one D of chapter forty, in which case the maximum fine shall be one thousand dollars. If a conviction is returned on the complaint the court shall award to any person or persons, other than an employee of the enforcing authority, whose information materially contributed to the identification of the convicted party, up to five hundred dollars, or forty percent of said fine, whichever is the greater, and the balance of the fine shall be equally divided between the enforcing authority and the court. If such violation is disposed of non-criminally, the balance of such fine, after payment of the award, if any, shall be deposited in the general fund of the enforcing authority. Vehicles seized under the provisions of this section which are not claimed or redeemed by their owners as provided for above within thirty days of the date of seizure, may after thirty days notice by certified mail to the vehicle's registered owner, be sold at auction and the proceeds be applied to the fines assessed herein, vehicle towing and storage costs and the costs for legal disposal of the material. Enforcing authorities shall adopt appropriate rules and regulations which provide for the orderly implementation of this section.

If a motor vehicle is used in committing such an offense, a conviction under this section shall forthwith be reported by the court to the registrar of motor vehicles, and the registrar may suspend the license of the operator of such vehicle for not more than thirty days, and if it appears from the records of the registrar of motor vehicles that the person so convicted is the owner of the motor vehicle so used, the registrar may suspend the certificate of registration of said vehicle for thirty days.

The provisions of this section shall not be applicable to any dumping ground approved under section one hundred and fifty A of chapter one hundred and eleven or by other appropriate public authority.

This section shall be enforced by natural resources officers, by the director of the division of motorboats or his authorized agents, by harbormasters and assistant harbormasters, by members of the state police and by city and town police officers. A city by majority vote of the city council, with the approval of the mayor, or in a town by a vote of its town meeting may enforce this section by designating its public health agents, health officers and health directors as enforcing officers. In the city of Boston this section shall also be enforced by the commissioner of health and hospitals, by the commissioner of housing inspection, and by the commissioner of public works, and their respective authorized agents, and in section sixteen A, the commissioner of health and hospitals, the commissioner of housing inspection, and the commissioner of public works shall be deemed to be the commanding officers of their respective authorized agents; provided, however, that any person observing a violation of this section may file a petition for issuance of a complaint pursuant to this section with the clerk of the district court having jurisdiction or, in the city of Boston, with the clerk of the Boston municipal court department, and upon determining that probable cause exists therefor, such clerk shall issue such complaint.

Chief park rangers and park rangers shall have the authority to enforce this section on state forests, reservations, parks, rinks, pools, piers and other facilities and properties under the jurisdiction of the department of environmental management. In addition to the fines imposed under this section, the violator may be held liable for costs associated with the identification, removal and disposal of said materials. The department of environmental management shall permanently post signs on all lands under its jurisdiction which identify: 1) the penalties applicable for the violations under this section; and 2) the proper authorities and contact information to report violations.

Added by St.1949, c. 416. Amended by St.1967, c. 116; St.1970, c. 134, §§ 1, 2; St.1971, c. 79; St.1972, c. 191; St.1973, c. 835, § 1; St.1974, c. 39; St.1979, c. 103; St.1979, c. 105; St.1982, c. 130, §§ 1, 2; St.1985, c. 197; St.1988, c. 151; St.1989, c. 429; St.1990, c. 150, § 342; St.1990, c. 301, §§ 1, 2; St.1991, c. 412, § 99; St.1992, c. 133, § 568; St.1993, c. 182, § 25; St.2002, c. 236, §§ 15, 16.

§ 16A. Alternative noncriminal disposition of violations of Sec. 16

If any officer empowered to enforce section sixteen takes cognizance of a violation thereof, he may request the offender to state his name and address. Whoever, upon such request, refuses to state his name and address, may be arrested without a warrant, or if he states a false name and address or a name and address which is not his name and address in ordinary use, he shall be punished by a fine of not less than fifty nor more than one hundred dollars. Such officer may, as an alternative to instituting criminal proceedings, forthwith give to the offender a written notice to appear before the clerk of the district court having jurisdiction at any time during office hours, not later than twenty-one days after the date of such violation. Such notice shall be made in triplicate, and shall contain the name and address of the offender and, if served with notice in hand at the time of such violation, the number of his license, if any, to operate motor vehicles; the registration number of the vehicle or motor boat involved, if any; the time and place of the violation; the specific offense charged; and the time and place for his required appearance. Such notice shall be signed by the officer, and shall be signed by the offender whenever practicable in acknowledgment that the notice has been received. The officer shall, if possible, deliver to the offender at the time and place of the violation a copy of said notice. Whenever it is not possible to deliver a copy of said notice to the offender at the time and place of the violation, said copy shall be mailed or delivered by the officer, or by his commanding officer or any person authorized by said commanding officer, to the offender's last known address, or in the case of a violation involving a motor vehicle or motor boat registered under the laws of this commonwealth, within five days of the offense, or in the case of any motor vehicle or motor boat registered under the laws of another state or country, within ten days thereof, exclusive, in either case, of Sundays and holidays, to the address of the registrant of the motor vehicle or motor boat involved, as appearing, in the case of a motor vehicle registered under the laws of this commonwealth, in the records of the registry of motor vehicles or the division of motor boats or, in the case of a motor vehicle or motor boat registered under the laws of another state or country in the records of the official in such state or country having charge of the registration of such motor vehicle or motor boat. Such notice mailed by the officer, his commanding officer, or the person so authorized to the last address of said registrant as appearing as aforesaid, shall be deemed a sufficient notice, and a certificate of the officer or person mailing such notice that it has been mailed in accordance with this section shall be deemed prima facie evidence thereof and shall be admissible in any court of the commonwealth as to the facts contained therein. At or before the completion of each tour of duty the officer shall give to his commanding officer those copies of each notice of such a violation he has taken cognizance of during such tour which have not already been delivered or mailed by him as aforesaid. Said commanding officer shall retain one of such copies and shall, at a time not later than the next court day after said delivery or mailing, deliver another copy to the clerk of the court before whom the offender has been notified to appear. The clerk of each district court shall maintain a separate docket of all such notices to appear.

Any person notified to appear before the clerk of a district court as hereinbefore provided may appear before such clerk and confess the offense charged, either personally or through an agent duly authorized in writing, or by mailing to such clerk, with the notice, the sum provided herein, such payment to be made only by postal note, money order or check. If it is the first, second or third offense subject to this section committed by such person within the jurisdiction of the court in the calendar year, payment to such clerk of the sum of twenty dollars shall operate as a final disposition of the case; if it is the fourth or subsequent such offense so committed in such calendar year, payment to such clerk of the sum of one hundred dollars shall operate as a final disposition of the case. Proceedings under this paragraph shall not be deemed criminal; and no person notified to appear before the clerk of a district court as provided herein shall be required to report to any probation officer, and no record of the case shall be entered in the probation records.

If any person notified to appear before the clerk of the district court fails to appear and pay the fine provided hereunder or, having appeared, desires not to avail himself of the procedure hereinbefore provided for the non-criminal disposition of the case, the clerk shall notify the officer concerned, who shall forthwith make application for a criminal complaint and follow the procedure established for criminal cases, and shall notify, if a motor vehicle is involved, the registrar of motor vehicles, or, if a motor boat is involved, the division of motor boats. If any person fails to appear in accordance with the summons issued upon such complaint the clerk shall send such person by certified mail, return receipt requested, a notice that the complaint is pending and that, if the person fails to appear within twenty-one days from the sending of such notice, a warrant for his arrest will be issued. If any person fails to appear within twenty-one days from the sending of such notice, the court shall issue a warrant for his arrest.

The notice to appear, provided herein, shall be printed in such form as the chief justice for the district court department and the chief justice for the Boston municipal court department may prescribe for their respective departments; provided, however, that a notice prepared pursuant to section twenty A or section twenty C of chapter ninety may be so revised or adapted that said notice may also be used for the notice provided for in this section.

Added by St.1971, c. 358. Amended by St.1973, c. 1107; St.1978, c. 478, § 279; St.1990, c. 301, § 3; St.1992, c. 133, § 569; St.1993, c. 182, § 26.

§ 17. Garbage or refuse; disposal in containers placed along highways

Whoever disposes of household or commercial garbage or refuse by placing it in a trash barrel placed on a public highway by the commonwealth, or by any political subdivision thereof for the convenience of the traveling public shall be punished by a fine of not less than two hundred dollars. One-half of any fine paid into a court shall be paid over to the city or town where said offense occurred.

Added by St.1962, c. 367. Amended by St.1963, c. 144; St.1983, c. 144.

§ 17A. Repealed, 1979, 704, Sec. 3

§ 18. Substance having property of releasing toxic vapors

No person shall intentionally smell or inhale the fumes of any substance having the property of releasing toxic vapors, for the purpose of causing a condition of intoxication, euphoria, excitement, exhilaration, stupefaction, or dulled senses or nervous system, nor possess, buy or sell any such substance for the purpose of violating or aiding another to violate this section.

This section shall not apply to the inhalation of anesthesia for medical or dental purposes.

Whoever violates the provisions of this section shall be punished by a fine of not more than two hundred dollars or by imprisonment for not more than six months, or both.

Any person who is discovered by a police officer or special police officer in the act of violating this section may be arrested without a warrant by such police officer or special police officer, and held in custody, in jail, or otherwise, until a complaint is made against him for such offense which complaint shall be made as soon as practicable and in any case within twenty-four hours, Sundays and legal holidays excepted.

Added by St.1966, c. 318.

§ 19. Glue or cement; sale to minors; smelling deterrent ingredients

Any person who sells glue or cement to a minor shall require such minor to properly identify himself and write his name and address legibly in a permanently bound register. The seller shall keep such register available for police inspection for a period of six months after the last sale is recorded therein. No such glue or cement shall be sold to a minor unless it contains allyl isothiocyanate (oil of mustard) or some other equally effective and safe deterrent against smelling or inhaling the fumes of such glue or cement.

As used in this section, "glue" or "cement" shall mean any glue or cement that contains a solvent or chemical having the property of releasing toxic vapors.

Whoever violates the provisions of this section shall be punished by a fine of not more than two hundred dollars or by imprisonment for not more than six months, or both.

Added by St.1967, c. 154. Amended by St.1970, c. 533, § 1.

§ 20. Burning of refuse, etc. within marine or shoreline boundaries

No person shall burn refuse, rubbish or demolition debris within the marine boundaries of the commonwealth, or within twelve miles from the shoreline of the commonwealth, whichever is the shorter distance. Whoever violates any provision of this section shall be punished by a fine of not less than two hundred and fifty dollars nor more than one thousand dollars.

Added by St.1971, c. 304.

§ 21. Repealed, 2004, 127, Sec. 1

§ 22. Smoking in public places

(a) As used in this section, the following words shall have the following meanings, unless the context requires otherwise:

"Business agent", an individual who has been designated by the owner or operator of any establishment to be the manager or otherwise in charge of the establishment.

"Compensation", money, gratuity, privilege, or benefit received from an employer in return for work performed or services rendered.

"Customer service area", an area of the workplace that a business invitee may access.

"Employee", an individual or person who performs a service for compensation for an employer at the employer's workplace, including a contract employee, temporary employee, and independent contractor who performs a service in the employer's workplace for more than a *de minimis* amount of time.

"Employer", an individual, person, partnership, association, corporation, trust, organization, school, college, university or other educational institution or other legal entity, whether public, quasi-public, private, or non-profit which uses the services of 1 or more employees at 1 or more workplaces, at any 1 time, including the commonwealth or its agencies, authorities or political subdivisions.

"Enclosed", a space bounded by walls, with or without windows or fenestrations, continuous from floor to ceiling and enclosed by 1 or more doors, including but not limited to an office, function room or hallway.

"Lodging home", a dwelling or part thereof which contains 1 or more rooming units in which space is let or sublet for compensation by the owner or operator to 4 or more persons. The residential portion of boarding houses, rooming houses, dormitories, and other similar dwelling places are included in this definition. Hospitals, sanitariums, jails, houses of correction, homeless shelters, and assisted living homes are not included in this definition.

"Membership association", a not-for-profit entity that has been established and operates, for a charitable, philanthropic, civic, social, benevolent, educational, religious, athletic, recreation or similar purpose, and is comprised of members who collectively belong to:

(i) a society, organization or association of a fraternal nature that operates under the lodge system, and having 1 or more affiliated chapters or branches incorporated in any state; or

(ii) a corporation organized under chapter 180 ; or

(iii) an established religious place of worship or instruction in the commonwealth whose real or personal property is exempt from taxation; or

(iv) a veterans' organization incorporated or chartered by the Congress of the United States, or otherwise, having 1 or more affiliated chapters or branches incorporated in any state.

Except for a religious place of worship or instruction, an entity shall not be a membership association for the purposes of this definition, unless individual membership is required for all members of the association for a period of not less than 90 days.

"Outdoor space", an outdoor area, open to the air at all times and cannot be enclosed by a wall or side covering.

"Public building", a building owned by the commonwealth or any political subdivision thereof, or in an enclosed indoor space occupied by a state agency or department of the commonwealth which is located in a building not owned by the commonwealth.

"Public transportation conveyance", a vehicle or vessel used in mass public transportation or in the transportation of the public, including a train, passenger bus, school bus or other vehicle used to transport pupils, taxi, passenger ferry boat, water shuttle or other equipment used in public transportation owned by, or operated under the authority of the Massachusetts Bay Transportation Authority, the Woods Hole, Martha's Vineyard & Nantucket Steamship Authority, Massachusetts Port Authority; state transportation department; or a vehicle or vessel open to the public that is owned by, or operated under the authority of a business, including tour vehicles or vessels, enclosed ski lifts or trams, passenger buses or vans regularly used to transport customers. Notwithstanding the foregoing, a private vehicle or vessel not open to the public or not used for the transportation of the public during the times of use, including a private passenger vehicle, a private charter or rental of a limousine, bus or van or the private rental of a boat or other vessel, shall not be considered a public transportation conveyance.

"Residence", the part of a structure used as a dwelling including without limitation: a private home, townhouse, condominium, apartment, mobile home; vacation home, cabin or cottage; a residential unit in a governmental public housing facility; and the residential portions of a school, college or university dormitory or facility. A residential unit provided by an employer to an employee at a place of employment shall be considered to be a residence; if the unit is an enclosed indoor space used exclusively as a residence, and other employees, excluding family members of the employee, or the public has no right of access to the residence. For the purposes of this definition, a hotel, motel, inn, lodge, bed and breakfast or other similar public accommodation, hospital, nursing home or assisted living facility shall not be considered a residence.

"Retail tobacco store", an establishment which is not required to possess a retail food permit whose primary purpose is to sell or offer for sale to consumers, but not for resale, tobacco products and paraphernalia, in which the sale of other products is merely incidental, and in which the entry of persons under the age of 18 is prohibited at all times, and maintains a valid permit for the retail sale of tobacco products as required to be issued by the appropriate authority in the city or town where the establishment is located.

"Smoking" or "smoke", the lighting of a cigar, cigarette, pipe or other tobacco product or possessing a lighted cigar, cigarette, pipe or other tobacco or non-tobacco product designed to be combusted and inhaled.

"Smoking bar", an establishment that occupies exclusively an enclosed indoor space and that primarily is engaged in the retail sale of tobacco products for consumption by customers on the premises; derives revenue from the sale of food, alcohol or other beverages that is incidental to the sale of the tobacco products; prohibits entry to a person under the age of 18 years of age during the time when the establishment is open for business; prohibits any food or beverage not sold directly by the business to be consumed on the premises; maintains a valid permit for the retail sale of tobacco products as required to be issued by the appropriate authority in the city or town where the establishment is located; and, maintains a valid permit to operate a smoking bar issued by the department of revenue.

"Workplace", an indoor area, structure or facility or a portion thereof, at which 1 or more employees perform a service for compensation for the employer, other enclosed spaces rented to or otherwise used by the public; and where the employer has the right or authority to exercise control over the space.

"Work space or work spaces", an enclosed area occupied by an employee during the course of his employment.

(b)(1) It shall be the responsibility of the employer to provide a smoke free environment for all employees working in an enclosed workplace.

(2) Smoking shall be prohibited in workplaces, work spaces, common work areas, classrooms, conference and meeting rooms, offices, elevators, hallways, medical facilities, cafeterias, employee lounges, staircases, restrooms, restaurants, cafes, coffee shops, food courts or concessions, supermarkets or retail food outlets, bars, taverns, or in a place where food or drink is sold to the public and consumed on the premise as part of a business required to collect state meals tax on the purchase; or in a train, airplane, theatre, concert hall, exhibition hall, convention center, auditorium, arena, or stadium open to the public; or in a school, college, university, museum, library, health care facility as defined in section 9C of chapter 112, group child care center, school age child care center, family child care center, school age day or overnight camp building, or on premises where activities are licensed under section 38 of chapter 10 or in or upon any public transportation conveyance or in any airport, train station, bus station, transportation passenger terminal, or enclosed outdoor platform.

(3) A person shall not smoke in the state house or in a public building or in a vehicle or vessel, owned, leased, or otherwise operated by the commonwealth or a political subdivision thereof, or in a space occupied by a state agency or department of the commonwealth which is located in another building, including a private office in a building or space mentioned in this sentence, or at an open meeting of a governmental body as defined in section 11A of chapter 30A, section 23A of chapter 39 and section 9F of chapter 34, or in a courtroom or courthouse. This subsection shall not apply to a resident or patient of a state hospital, the Soldiers' Home in Massachusetts located in the city of Chelsea or the Soldiers' Home in Holyoke.

(c) Notwithstanding subsection (b), smoking may be permitted in the following places and circumstances:

(1) Private residences; except during such time when the residence is utilized as part of a business as a group childcare center, school age child care center, school age day or overnight camp, or a facility licensed by the department of early education and care or as a health care related office or facility;

(2)(i) premises occupied by a membership association, if the premises is owned, or under a written lease for a term of not less than 90 consecutive days, by the association during the time of the permitted activity if the premises are not located in a public building; but no smoking shall be permitted in an enclosed indoor space of a membership association during the time the space is:

(A) open to the public; or

(B) occupied by a non-member who is not an invited guest of a member or an employee of the association; or

(C) rented from the association for a fee or other agreement that compensates the association for the use of such space.

(ii) Smoking may be permitted in an enclosed indoor space of a membership association at all times, if the space is restricted by the association to admittance only of its members, the invited guest of a member, and the employees of the membership association. A person who is a contract employee, temporary employee, or independent contractor shall not be considered an employee of a membership association under this subsection. A person who is a member of an affiliated chapter or branch of a membership association that is fraternal in nature operating under the lodge system, and is visiting the affiliated association, shall be an invited guest for the purposes of this subsection.

(3) A guest room in a hotel, motel, inn, bed and breakfast or lodging home that is designed and normally used for sleeping and living purposes, that is rented to a guest and designated as a smoking room pursuant to paragraph (1) of subsection (g).

(4) A retail tobacco store, if the store maintains a valid permit for the sale of tobacco products issued by the appropriate authority in the city or town in which the retail tobacco store is located. All required permits shall be displayed in a conspicuous manner, visible at all times to patrons of the establishment.

(5) A smoking bar, if the smoking bar maintains a valid permit pursuant to this section. All required permits shall be displayed in a conspicuous manner, visible at all times to patrons of the establishment.

(6) By a theatrical performer upon a stage or in the course of a professional film production, if the smoking is part of a theatrical production, and if permission has been obtained from the appropriate local authority;

(7) By a person, organization or other entity that conducts medical or scientific research on tobacco products, if the research is conducted in an enclosed space not open to the public, in a laboratory facility at an accredited college or university, or in a professional testing laboratory as defined by regulation of the department of public health;

(8) Religious ceremonies where smoking is part of the ritual; and

(9) A tobacco farmer, leaf dealer, manufacturer, importer, exporter, or wholesale distributor of tobacco products, may permit smoking in the workplace for the sole purpose of testing said tobacco for quality assurance purposes; if the smoking is necessary to conduct the test.

[There is no subsection (d).]

(e) If the outdoor space has a structure capable of being enclosed by walls or covers, regardless of the materials or the removable nature of the walls or covers, the space will be considered enclosed, when the walls or covers are in place. All outdoor spaces shall be physically separated from an enclosed work space. If doors, windows, sliding or folding windows or doors or other fenestrations form any part of the border to the outdoor space, the openings shall be closed to prevent the migration of smoke into the enclosed work space. If the windows, sliding or folding windows or doors or other fenestrations are opened or otherwise do not prevent the migration of smoke into the work space, the outdoor space shall be considered an extension of the enclosed work space and subject to this section.

(f)(1) A nursing home, licensed pursuant to section 71 of chapter 111 and any acute care substance abuse treatment center under the jurisdiction of the commonwealth, may apply to the local board of health having jurisdiction over the facility for designation of part of the facility as a residence.

(2) All applications shall designate the residential area of the facility. The residential area shall not contain an employee workspace, such as offices, restrooms or other areas used primarily by employees.

(3) The entire facility may not be designated as a residence.

(4) The designated residential area must be for the sole use of permanent residents of the facility. No temporary or short-term resident may reside in the residential portion of the facility.

(5) All areas in the designated residential area in which smoking is allowed shall be conspicuously designated as smoking areas and be adequately ventilated to prevent the migration of smoke to nonsmoking areas.

(6) The facility shall provide suitable documentation, acceptable to the local board of health, that the facility is the permanent domicile of the residents residing in that portion of the facility, that information on the hazards of smoking and second hand smoke have been provided to all residences and that smoking cessation aids are available to all residents who use tobacco products.

(7) The designated residential area shall be in conformance with the smoking restriction requirements of section 72X of chapter 111 and 105 CMR 150.015 (D)(11)(b). All residential areas shall be clearly designated as such and shall not be altered or otherwise

changed without the express approval of the local board of health.

(8) All areas of a nursing home not designated as a residence shall comply with this section.

(9) The nursing home shall make reasonable accommodations for an employee, resident or visitor who does not wish to be exposed to tobacco smoke.

(10) Upon compliance with this section, submission of the required documentation and satisfactory inspection, the local board of health shall certify the designated portion of the facility as a residence. The certification shall be valid for 1 year from the date of issuance. No fewer than 30 days before the expiration of the certification, the facility may apply for re-certification. If the local board of health does not renew the certification before its expiration or provide notice that it has found sufficient cause to not recertify the residence portion of the nursing home as such, the certification shall be considered to continue until the time as the local board of health notifies the nursing home of its certification status.

(g)(1) A designated smoking room in a hotel, motel, inn, bed and breakfast and lodging home shall be clearly marked as a designated smoking room on the exterior of all entrances from a public hallway and public spaces; and in the interior of the room. Instead of marking each room, an establishment may designate an entire floor of residential rooms as smoking. The floor shall be conspicuously designated as smoking at each entranceway on to the floor. Smoking shall not be allowed in the common areas of the floor, such as halls, vending areas, ice machine locations and exercise areas and shall comply with paragraph (4).

(2) A retail tobacco store that permits smoking on the premises shall, pursuant to paragraph (4), post in a clear and conspicuous manner, a sign at each entrance warning persons entering the establishment that smoking may be present on the premises; of the health risks associated from second hand smoke; and, that persons under the age of 18 years of age may not enter the premises.

(3) A smoking bar shall, pursuant to paragraph (4), post in a clear and conspicuous manner signs at all entrances which warn persons entering the establishment that smoking may be present on the premises; and, of the health risks associated from second hand smoke; and, that persons under the age of 18 years of age may not enter the premises.

(4) Every area in which smoking is prohibited by law shall have "no smoking" signs conspicuously posted so that the signs are clearly visible to all employees, customers, or visitors while in the workplace.

(5) Additional signs may be posted in public areas such as, the following areas: lobbies; hallways; cafeterias; kitchens; locker rooms; customer service areas; offices where the public is invited; conference rooms; lounges; waiting areas; and elevators.

(6) Approved signs and templates for signage design may be obtained from the department of public health or the local boards of health.

(7) It shall be the responsibility of the establishment to ensure that the appropriate signage is displayed and that an individual or group renting the space enforces the prohibition against smoking.

(h)(a)(1) A smoking bar operating in the commonwealth shall obtain a smoking bar permit from the department of revenue. A permit issued by the department shall be valid for a period of 2 years from date of issuance unless suspended or revoked. A valid permit that is not suspended at the time of its expiration may be renewed for consecutive 2–year periods.

(2) A non-refundable fee may be required with each permit and renewal application. Each permit issued by the department shall be non-transferable, for a specific location and business; and, only 1 permit may be issued to a business for a specific location during any permit period.

(3) The department shall not issue or renew a smoking bar permit to any business that has not filed all tax returns and paid all taxes due the commonwealth; or is delinquent in filing all declaration statements in connection with the smoking bar permit as required by the department.

(4) The department shall notify the local board of health or municipal health department in the city or town where the establishment is located of any permits issued, renewed, suspended, revoked or reinstated to a business.

(b) A smoking bar shall demonstrate on a quarterly basis that revenue generated from the sale of tobacco products are equal to or greater than 51 per cent of the total combined revenue generated by the sale of tobacco products, food and beverages. The department shall require each business that has been issued a smoking bar permit to submit a quarterly declaration for each 3 month period that the business is in operation; notwithstanding, the first declaration may include a period of not to exceed 4 months. A declaration submitted to the department in connection with a smoking bar permit shall be signed by the owner or business agent under the pains and penalties of perjury. A declaration received by the department shall be confidential and the financial information contained therein shall not be disclosed to the public or any other state governmental agency or department except the attorney general. In the event a business has not filed a required declaration statement, the department shall give written notice to the business that the statement is delinquent and, shall suspend the permit of a business that does not submit the required report after 21 days of the date of notice; but the department shall reinstate the suspended permit within 5 days after receiving the delinquent report.

(c) The department of revenue shall promulgate regulations to implement this section.

(i) Companies which sell ownership rights to owners of time share properties shall distinguish between smoking and non-smoking time share properties. Companies shall disclose to potential buyers whether the unit they are purchasing is a smoking or non-smoking property and post signs accordingly.

(j) Nothing in this section shall permit smoking in an area in which smoking is or may hereafter be prohibited by law including, without limitation: any other law or ordinance or by-law or any fire, health or safety regulation. Nothing in this section shall preempt further limitation of smoking by the commonwealth or any department, agency or political subdivision of the commonwealth.

(k) An individual, person, entity or organization subject to the smoking prohibitions of this section shall not discriminate or retaliate in any manner against a person for making a complaint of a violation of this section or furnishing information concerning a violation, to a person, entity or organization or to an enforcement authority. Notwithstanding the foregoing, a person making a complaint or furnishing information during any period of work or time of employment, shall do so only at a time that will not pose an increased threat of harm to the safety of other persons in or about such place of work or to the public.

(*l*) An owner, manager or other person in control of a building, vehicle or vessel who violates this section, in a manner other than by smoking in a place where smoking is prohibited, shall be punished by a fine of $100 for the first violation; $200 for a second violation occurring within 2 years of the date of the first offense; and $300 for a third or subsequent violation within 2 years of the second violation. Each calendar day on which a violation occurs shall be considered a separate offense. If an owner, manager or other person in control of a building, vehicle or vessel violates this section repeatedly, demonstrating egregious noncompliance as defined by regulation of the department of public health, the local board of health may revoke or suspend the license to operate and shall send notice of the revocation or suspension to the department of public health. The department of public health shall promulgate regulations to implement this section including, but not limited to notice, collection, and reporting of the fines or license action, and defining uniform standards that warrant license suspension or revocation.

(m)(1) The local board of health, the department of public health, the local inspection department or the equivalent, a municipal government or its agent, and the alcoholic beverages control commission shall enforce this section. In addition, in the city of Boston, the commissioner of health and his authorized agents shall enforce this section.

(2) An individual or person who violates this section by smoking in a place where smoking is prohibited shall be subject to a civil penalty of $100 for each violation. As an alternative to criminal prosecution, a violation of subsection (*l*) may also be considered a civil violation. Each enforcing agency under paragraph (1) shall dispose of a civil violation of this section by the non-criminal method of disposition procedures contained in section 21D of chapter 40, without an enabling ordinance or by-law, or by the equivalent of these procedures by a state agency under regulations of the department of public health. The disposition of fines assessed under this section shall be subject to section 188 of chapter 111. Fines assessed by the commonwealth or its agents shall be subject to section 2 of chapter 29. In a city or town having an ordinance or by-law that imposes a fine greater than the fine imposed by this section, the ordinance or by-law shall prevail over this section.

(3) Any person may register a complaint to initiate an investigation and enforcement with the local board of health, the department of public health, or the local inspection department or the equivalent.

(4) The supreme judicial court or the superior court shall issue appropriate orders to enforce this section and any regulation under it, at the request of any agency mentioned in paragraph (1).

(5) A fine or fee collected by the commonwealth under this section shall be used for the enforcement or for educational programs on the harmful effects of tobacco.

(n) Each local board of health, each local inspection department or its equivalent, and the alcoholic beverages control commission shall report annually to the commissioner of public health, beginning January 1, 2006: the number of citations issued; the workplaces which have been issued citations and the number of citations issued to each workplace; the amount that each workplace has been fined; and the total amount collected in fines. The department of public health shall file a copy of the report with the clerks of the house of representatives and the senate.

(*o*) The department of public health may issue regulations to implement this section.

Added by St.1987, c. 759, § 3. Amended by St.1990, c. 86; St.1997, c. 85; St.2004, c. 137, § 2, eff. July 5, 2004; St.2008, c. 215, §§ 82, 83, eff. July 31, 2008.

§ 23. Flea markets; smoking prohibition; penalty

(a) As used in this section, "flea market" shall mean that portion of a building then occupied by one or more vendors, other than retail stores, for sale to the public of new or used goods or products on a seasonal, limited or full schedule of operation. No person shall smoke in any building used for the purpose of operating a flea market, except as otherwise provided in this section. The owner, manager or other person in charge of such a building, shall post a notice in a conspicuous place at each entrance to such building indicating that smoking is prohibited therein, except in an area specifically designated as a smoking area. An area shall be designated as a smoking area only if nonsmoking areas of sufficient size and capacity are available to accommodate nonsmokers and if smoke from said smoking area is prevented from entering the no smoking area.

(b) Except as otherwise provided herein, no person shall smoke in any snack bar operated in conjunction with a flea market, except in such designated smoking area as may be provided. Said smoking area shall be physically separated from the no smoking area and separately ventilated to the outside to prevent smoke from entering the no smoking area. The owner, manager or other person in charge of a snack bar shall not permit the smoke from such smoking area to be vented to the no smoking area.

(c) The owner, manager or other person in charge of such snack bar shall post a notice or sign in a conspicuous place at each entrance to such snack bar indicating that smoking is prohibited therein except in specifically designated areas, shall post signs identifying the no smoking area and the smoking area, and shall make a reasonable effort to insure that no person shall smoke in a no smoking area. Said reasonable effort shall include, but not be limited to, requesting that a person smoking in a no smoking area to either extinguish his cigarette, cigar or pipe, or move to a designated smoking area.

(d) Any person aggrieved by the willful failure or refusal to comply with any of the provisions of this section may complain in writing to a local health officer in the case of a snack bar or to the local building inspector in the case of all other facilities described in this section. Said authority shall respond in writing within 15 days to the complainant that the area described in the complaint has been inspected and said authority has enforced the provisions of this section. Said authority shall file a copy of the original complaint and its response thereto with the department of public health.

(e) No employer shall terminate or otherwise discriminate against any employee, independent contractor, or other worker for refusing to work in a smoking area or for exercising his rights under this section.

(f) Any person who violates this section by smoking where smoking is prohibited shall be subject to a civil fine not exceeding $25. Any person who violates this section in any way other than by smoking in an area where smoking is prohibited shall be subject to a civil fine of $50. Each day during which a violation of this section occurs shall be considered a separate violation.

(g) Fines assessed pursuant to this section shall be payable to the city or town in which the violation of this section occurs. A local board of health or health department shall enforce this section through noncriminal disposition.

(h) A city or town may, by ordinance or by-laws, establish a fund for the disposition of revenues received from fines levied in accordance with the provisions of this section. Said fund shall be expended under the authority of the municipal health department or local board of health for the purpose of public education on the hazards posed by secondhand smoke, also known as environmental tobacco smoke.

(i) Nothing in this section shall be construed to permit smoking in any area in which smoking is prohibited by law, including, without limiting the generality of the foregoing, any other provision of the law or ordinance or any fire, health, or safety regulation. This section shall not pre-empt the authority of any city or town to enact any ordinance, by-law or any fire, health, or safety regulation that limits or prohibits smoking in any place.

Added by St.1999, c. 99.

§ 24. Mercury thermometers; sale or supply; instructions regarding breakage

No person shall sell or supply, including online, retail mercury fever thermometers, except in the case of a medical necessity as determined by a licensed physician or by prescription. Manufacturers of mercury fever thermometers sold or supplied in the commonwealth in such cases of medical necessity shall furnish clear instructions on the careful handling of thermometers to avoid breakage and proper cleanup should a breakage occur. This section shall not apply to digital thermometers using mercury-added button cell batteries. A violation of this section shall be punished by a fine of not more than $500.

Added by St.2002, c. 39, § 1.

§ 25. Ice cream truck vending; permit requirements

[Text of section added by 2010, 256, Sec. 122 effective May 4, 2012. See 2010, 256, Sec. 145 as amended by 2010, 359, Sec. 102.]

(a) For the purposes of this section, the following words shall have the following meanings:—

"Ice cream", any frozen dairy or frozen water-based food product.

"Ice cream truck", any motor vehicle used for selling, displaying or offering to sell ice cream.

"Ice cream truck vending", the selling, displaying or offering to sell ice cream or any other prepackaged food product from an ice cream truck.

"Permitting authority", the chief of police or the board or officer having control of the police in a city or town, or person authorized by them.

(b) No person shall engage in ice cream truck vending unless he shall have been issued a valid permit to do so by the permitting authority within the municipality wherein the permit applicant lives or intends to operate an ice cream truck. Such permit shall be conspicuously displayed and clearly visible on the windshield of any ice cream truck operated or from which ice cream or any other prepackaged food product is sold. Whoever violates this section shall be assessed a fine of $500. Each day that such person is in operation in violation of this section may be considered a separate violation.

(c) The department of public safety shall adopt regulations relative to the annual permitting of ice cream truck vendors. Such regulations shall include, but not be limited to:

(i) a requirement that all applications for an ice cream truck vending permit or applications for renewal thereof shall include the applicant's fingerprints and a current photo of the applicant;

(ii) adoption of a uniform permit application and permit form, to be used by all municipalities;

(iii) a requirement that a permitting authority conduct an investigation into the criminal history of a permit applicant to determine eligibility therefore; and

(iv) a provision restricting a permitting authority from issuing an ice cream truck vending permit to any sex offender, as defined by section 178C of chapter 6 of the General Laws.

Added by St.2010, c. 256, § 122, eff. May 4, 2012.

CHAPTER 271

CRIMES AGAINST PUBLIC POLICY

The section headings for the General Laws in this pamphlet have been editorially supplied.

§ 1. Gaming or betting; forfeiture

Whoever, on a prosecution commenced within eighteen months after the commission of the crime, is convicted of winning at one time or sitting, by gaming or betting on the sides or hands of those gaming, money or goods to the value of five dollars or more, and of receiving the same or security therefor, shall forfeit double the value of such money or goods.

Historical and Statutory Notes

C.L. c. 57, § 2; c. 58, § 1.
St.1785, c. 58, § 3.
R.S.1836, c. 50, § 14.
G.S.1860, c. 85, § 3.
P.S.1882, c. 99, § 3.
R.L.1902, c. 214, § 1.

§ 1A. "House", "building" and "place" including ship or vessel

The words "house", "building" and "place" used severally or together in this chapter shall mean and include a ship or vessel when it is within the territorial limits of the commonwealth.

Added by St.1948, c. 299.

§ 2. Gaming or betting in public conveyance or place or while trespassing in private place; arrest without warrant

Whoever, in a public conveyance or public place, or in a private place upon which he is trespassing, plays at cards, dice or any other game for money or other property, or bets on the sides or hands of those playing, shall forfeit not more than fifty dollars or be imprisoned for not more than three months; and whoever sets up or permits such a game shall be punished by a fine of not less than fifty nor more than one hundred dollars or by imprisonment for not less than three nor more than twelve months. If discovered in the act, he may be arrested without a warrant by a sheriff, deputy sheriff, constable or any officer qualified to serve criminal process, and held in custody, in jail or otherwise, for not more than twenty-four hours, Sunday and legal holidays excepted, until complaint may be made against him for such offence.

Historical and Statutory Notes

St.1869, c. 382.
P.S.1882, c. 99, § 4.
R.L.1902, c. 214, § 2.
St.1907, c. 366.
St.1913, c. 370.
St.1918, c. 257, § 456.
St.1919, c. 5.
St.1920, c. 2.

§ 3. Innholders and others keeping or suffering implements to be used for gaming

Every innholder, common victualler or person keeping or suffering to be kept in any place occupied by him implements such as are used in gaming, in order that the same may for hire, gain or reward be used for amusement, who suffers implements of such kind to be used upon any part of such premises for gaming for money or other property, or who suffers a person to play at an unlawful game or sport therein, shall for the first offence forfeit not more than one hundred dollars or be imprisoned for not more than three months; and for a subsequent offence shall be imprisoned for not more than one year. In either case he shall further recognize with sufficient sureties in a reasonable sum for his good behavior, and especially that he will not be guilty of any offence against any of the provisions of sections one to six, inclusive, for three years from the date of the recognizance.

Historical and Statutory Notes

C.L. c. 57, § 2.
St.1692–3, c. 20, § 3.
St.1786, c. 68, § 5.
St.1798, c. 20, §§ 1, 2.
St.1832, c. 166, § 11.
R.S.1836, c. 47, § 9; c. 50, §§ 16, 17.
St.1845, c. 211.
St.1853, c. 399.
St.1854, c. 450.
G.S.1860, c. 85, § 5.
P.S.1882, c. 99, § 6.
R.L.1902, c. 214, § 3.

§ 4. Gaming in inns and other occupied places; use of billiard table, bowling alley or other implement for gaming

Whoever, in any place mentioned in the preceding section, for the purpose of gaming for money or other property, uses or takes part in using a billiard table, bowling alley or other implement of gaming, or there plays at an unlawful game or sport, or, for the purpose of such gaming, uses or takes part in using a billiard table or bowling alley kept by a person licensed under chapter one hundred and forty, shall forfeit not more than fifty dollars.

Historical and Statutory Notes

C.L. c. 57, § 2.
St.1692–3, c. 20, § 3.
St.1785, c. 58, § 5.
St.1798, c. 20, § 3.
St.1832, c. 166, § 11.
R.S.1836, c. 47, § 10; c. 50, § 18.
G.S.1860, c. 85, § 6.
P.S.1882, c. 99, § 7.
R.L.1902, c. 214, § 4.

§ 5. Gaming, lottery, pool or betting houses; tables or apparatus for gaming

Whoever keeps or assists in keeping a common gaming house, or building or place occupied, used or kept for the purposes described in section twenty-three, or is found playing or present as provided in said section, or commonly keeps or suffers to be kept, in a building or place actually used and occupied by him, tables or other apparatus for the purpose of playing at an unlawful game or sport for money or any other valuable thing, shall be punished by a fine of not more than fifty dollars or by imprisonment for not more than three months.

Historical and Statutory Notes

St.1798, c. 20, § 2.
St.1832, c. 166, § 11.

R.S.1836, c. 50, § 17.
St.1848, c. 315.
St.1857, c. 194, §§ 1, 4.
G.S.1860, c. 85, §§ 7, 8.
St.1869, c. 364, § 1.
P.S.1882, c. 99, §§ 9, 10.
St.1887, c. 448, § 2.
St.1895, c. 419, § 9.
R.L.1902, c. 214, § 5.

§ 5A. Gambling devices; forfeiture; antique slot machines

Whoever manufactures, transports, sells, offers for sale, stores, displays, repairs, reconditions, possesses or uses any gambling device or parts for use therein shall be punished by a fine of not more than five thousand dollars; provided, however, that fifty percent of the said fine shall be remitted to the city or town in which the violation occurred. The remaining fifty percent shall be remitted to the general fund of the commonwealth. As used in this section, the term "gambling device" means any so called "slot machine" or any other machine or mechanical device an essential part of which is a drum or reel with insignia thereon, and which, when operated, may deal, as a result of the application of an element of chance, any money or property; or by the operation of which a person may become entitled to receive, as the result of the application of an element of chance, any money or property; or any sub-assembly or essential part intended to be used in connection with any such machine or mechanical device. Any gambling device or parts for use therein manufactured, transported, sold, offered for sale, stored, displayed, repaired, reconditioned, possessed or used in violation of this section shall be seized and be forfeited to the commonwealth and disposed of in the manner provided under the provisions of chapter two hundred and seventy-six. In respect to their constitutionality, the provisions of this section are hereby declared to be separable.

It shall be a defense to any prosecution under this section to show that the slot machine is an antique slot machine and was not operated for gambling purposes while in the defendant's possession. For the purposes of this section, a slot machine shall be presumed to be an antique slot machine, if it was manufactured at least thirty years prior to either the arrest of the defendant, or seizure of the machine.

Added by St.1951, c. 483. Amended by St.1964, c. 557, § 7; St.1979, c. 373; St.1995, c. 38, § 201.

§ 6. Gaming relative to cattle shows, military muster or public gathering; arrest without warrant

Whoever, during or within twelve hours of the time of holding a cattle show, military muster or public gathering, within one mile of the place thereof, practices or engages in any gambling or unlawful game, shall forfeit not more than twenty dollars. If discovered in the act, he may be arrested without a warrant by any sheriff, deputy sheriff, constable or any officer qualified to serve criminal process, and held in custody, in jail or otherwise, for not more than twenty-four hours, Sunday and legal holidays excepted, until a complaint may be made against him for such offence.

Historical and Statutory Notes

St.1853, c. 27.
G.S.1860, c. 85, § 9.
St.1861, c. 127, § 2.
P.S.1882, c. 99, § 11.
R.L.1902, c. 214, § 6.

§ 6A. Plans under which purchasers agree to obtain more purchasers; injunction; receivers

Whoever sets up or promotes a plan by which goods or anything of value is sold to a person for a consideration and upon the further consideration that the purchaser agrees to secure one or more persons to participate in the plan by respectively making a similar purchase or purchases and in turn agreeing to secure one or more persons likewise to join in the said plan, each purchaser being given the right to secure money, credits, goods or something of value, depending upon the number of persons joining in the plan, shall be held to have set up and promoted a lottery and shall be punished as provided in section seven. The supreme judicial court shall have jurisdiction in equity upon a petition filed by the attorney general to enjoin the further prosecution of any such plan and to appoint receivers to secure and distribute the assets received thereunder.

Added by St.1938, c. 144.

§ 6B. Skilo and similar games

Whoever, except as provided in section twenty-two B, sets up or promotes the game commonly known as skilo or any similar game regardless of name, shall be held to have set up and promoted a lottery and shall be punished as provided in section seven.

Added by St.1953, c. 243. Amended by St.1971, c. 486, § 1.

§ 6C. Repealed, 1998, 1

§ 7. Lotteries; disposal of property by chance

Whoever sets up or promotes a lottery for money or other property of value, or by way of lottery disposes of any property of value, or under the pretext of a sale, gift or delivery of other property or of any right, privilege or thing whatever disposes of or offers or attempts to dispose of any property, with intent to make the disposal thereof dependent upon or connected with chance by lot, dice, numbers, game, hazard or other gambling device, whereby such chance or device is made an additional inducement to the disposal or sale of said property, and whoever aids either by printing or writing, or is in any way concerned, in the setting up, managing or drawing of such lottery, or in such disposal or offer or attempt to dispose of property by such chance or device, shall be punished by a fine of not more than three thousand dollars or by imprisonment in the state prison for not more than three years, or in jail or the house of correction for not more than two and one half years.

Amended by St.1968, c. 115.

Historical and Statutory Notes

St.1719–20, c. 8, §§ 1, 2.
St.1732–3, c. 14, § 1.
St.1785, c. 24, §§ 1, 2.
St.1800, c. 57, § 1.
St.1817, c. 191, § 1.
St.1822, c. 90.
St.1825, c. 184, § 1.
St.1833, c. 148, § 1.
R.S.1836, c. 132, § 1.
St.1856, c. 121, § 1.
G.S.1860, c. 167, § 1.
P.S.1882, c. 209, § 1.
St.1895, c. 419, § 13.
R.L.1902, c. 214, § 7.
St.1918, c. 257, § 457.
St.1919, c. 5.
St.1920, c. 2.

§ 7A. Raffles and bazaars; conduct by certain organizations

In this section the following words shall have the following meanings:

"Raffle", an arrangement for raising money by the sale of tickets, certain among which, as determined by chance after the sale, entitle the holders to prizes.

"Bazaar", a place maintained by the sponsoring organization for disposal by means of chance of one or both of the following types of prizes: (1) merchandise, of any value, (2) cash awards, not to exceed twenty-five dollars each.

Notwithstanding any other provisions of law, raffles and bazaars may be promoted, operated and conducted under permits issued in accordance with the provisions of this section.

No organization, society, church or club which conducts a raffle or bazaar under the provisions of this section shall be deemed to have set up and promoted a lottery and nothing in this chapter shall authorize the prosecution, arrest or conviction of any person connected with the operation of any such raffle or bazaar; provided, however, that nothing contained in this section shall be construed as permitting the game commonly known as "beano" or any similar game regardless of name.

No raffle or bazaar shall be promoted, operated or conducted by any person or organization, unless the same is sponsored and conducted exclusively by (a) a veterans' organization chartered by the Congress of the United States or included in clause (12) of section five of chapter forty of the General Laws; (b) a church or religious organization; (c) a fraternal or fraternal benefit society; (d) an educational or charitable organization; (e) a civic or service club or organization; and (f) clubs or organizations organized and operated exclusively for pleasure, recreation and other nonprofit purposes, no part of the net earnings of which inures to the benefit of any member or shareholder. Such organization shall have been organized and actively functioning as a nonprofit organization in the commonwealth for a period of not less than two years before it may apply for a permit. The promotion and operation of the raffle or bazaar shall be confined solely to the qualified members of the sponsoring organization and no such member shall receive remuneration in any form for time or effort devoted to the promotion or operation of such raffle or bazaar. All funds derived from any raffle or bazaar shall be used exclusively for the purposes stated in the application of the sponsoring organization which purposes shall be limited to educational, charitable, religious, fraternal or civic purposes or for veterans' benefits. An organization which meets the qualifications required by this section and which desires to conduct or operate a raffle or bazaar within the commonwealth shall apply for a permit to conduct raffles and bazaars from the clerk of the city or town in which the raffle will be drawn or the bazaar held. The application form shall be approved by the commissioner of public safety and shall include the name and address of the applicant, the evidence on which the applicant relies in order to qualify under this section, the names of three officers or members of the organization who shall be responsible for the operation of the raffle or bazaar, and the uses to which the net proceeds will be applied. Unless otherwise established in a town by town meeting action and in a city by city council action, and in a town with no town meeting by town council action, by adoption of appropriate by-laws and ordinances to set such fees, a fee of ten dollars shall accompany each such application and shall be retained by the city or town, but in no event shall any such fee be greater than fifty dollars. Upon receipt of such application, the clerk shall determine whether it is in conformity with this section. If the clerk so determines, he shall forward the application to the chief of police of the city or town, who shall determine whether the applicant is qualified to operate raffles and bazaars under this section. If the chief of police so determines, he shall endorse the application and return it to the clerk, who shall forthwith issue a permit, which shall be valid for one year from the date of its issuance. The clerk shall retain a copy of the application and shall send a copy to the commissioner of public safety. If there is any change in the facts set forth in the application for a permit subsequent to the making of such application, the applicant shall forthwith notify the authority granting such permit of such change, and such authority shall issue such permit if the applicant is qualified, or, if a permit has already been issued and the change in the facts set forth in the application disqualify the applicant revoke such permit.

If an application is not acted upon within thirty days after it is submitted, or if the organization is refused a permit, or if a permit is revoked, any person named on the application may obtain judicial review of such refusal or revocation by filing within ten days of such refusal or revocation or within ten days of the expiration of such thirty day period a petition for review in the district court having jurisdiction in the city or town in which such application was filed. A justice of said court, after a hearing, may direct that such permit be issued, if he is satisfied that there was no reasonable ground for refusing such permit, and that the applicant was not prohibited by law from holding raffles or bazaars.

An organization issued a permit under this section shall within thirty days of the expiration of its permit submit a report on a form to be approved by the commissioner of public safety. Such form shall require information concerning the number of raffles and bazaars held, the amount of money received, the expenses connected with the raffle or bazaar, the names of the winners of prizes exceeding twenty-five dollars in value, the net proceeds of the raffles and bazaars, and the uses to which the net proceeds were applied. The organization shall maintain and keep such books and records as may be necessary to substantiate the particulars of such report, which books and records shall be preserved for at least one year from the date of such report and shall be available for inspection. Such report shall be certified to by the three persons designated in the permit application as being responsible for such raffle or bazaar and by an accountant. Two copies of said report shall be filed with city or town clerk. The clerk shall send one copy to the commissioner of public safety. Failure to file said report shall constitute sufficient grounds for refusal to renew a permit to conduct raffles or bazaars. The fee for renewal of such permit shall be ten dollars.

The authority granting any permit under this section shall immediately revoke the same for a violation of any provision of this section and shall not issue any permit to such permittee within three years from the date of such violation. Any person aggrieved by the action of such authority revoking such permit may appeal to the district court having jurisdiction in the city or town where the permit was issued; provided that such appeal shall be filed in such court within twenty days following receipt of notification by said authority. The court shall hear all pertinent evidence and determine the facts and upon the facts so determined annul such action or make such decision as equity may require. The foregoing remedy shall be exclusive.

Any organization conducting or operating a raffle or bazaar under this section shall file a return with the state lottery commission, on a form prepared by it, within ten days after the raffle or bazaar is held and shall pay therewith a tax of five per cent of the gross proceeds derived from such raffle or bazaar.

All sums received by said commission from the tax imposed by this section as taxes, interest thereon, fees, penalties, forfeitures, costs of suits or fines, less all amounts refunded thereon, together with any interest or costs paid on account of such refunds, shall be paid into the treasury of the commonwealth.

Whoever violates any provision of this section or submits false information on an application or report required under this section shall be punished by a fine of not more than one thousand dollars or by imprisonment in the house of correction for not more than one year, or both.

No person who prints or produces tickets, cards or any similar article used in the conduct of a bazaar or raffle pursuant to a permit issued under the provisions of this section shall be subject to any penalty therefor, provided that a certified copy of such permit was presented to him prior to his undertaking to print or produce such tickets or cards.

No organization issued a permit under this section shall conduct more than three bazaars in any single calendar year nor shall such organization conduct more than one bazaar in any single calendar day. The operation of a bazaar shall be limited to five consecutive hours.

Added by St.1969, c. 810. Amended by St.1976, c. 415, § 96; St.1977, c. 219, § 6; St.1977, c. 279; St.1979, c. 280; St.1981, c. 351, § 98; St.1985, c. 222.

§ 8. Permitting lotteries, raffles and games of chance in buildings

Whoever, in a house, shop or building owned or occupied by him or under his control, knowingly permits the setting up, managing or drawing of such lottery, or such disposal or attempt to dispose of property, or the sale of a lottery ticket or share of a ticket, or any other writing, certificate, bill, token or other device purporting or intended to entitle the holder, bearer or any other person to a prize or to a share of or interest in a prize to be drawn in a lottery, or in such disposal of property, and whoever knowingly suffers money or other property to be raffled for in such house, shop or building, or to be won there by throwing or using dice or by any other game of chance, shall be punished by a fine of not more than two thousand dollars or by imprisonment for not more than one year.

Historical and Statutory Notes

St.1800, c. 57, § 1.
St.1817, c. 191, § 1.
St.1822, c. 90.
St.1825, c. 184, § 1.
St.1833, c. 148, § 1.
R.S.1836, c. 132, § 1.
St.1856, c. 121, § 1.
G.S.1860, c. 167, § 2.
P.S.1882, c. 209, § 2.
St.1895, c. 419, § 13.
R.L.1902, c. 214, § 8.

§ 9. Lottery tickets; sale, or possession

Whoever, for himself or for another, sells or offers for sale or has in his possession with intent to sell or offer for sale, or to exchange or negotiate, or aids or assists in the selling, exchanging, negotiating or disposing of a ticket in such lottery, or a share of a ticket, or any such writing, certificate, bill, token or other device, or a share or right in such disposal or offer, as is mentioned in section seven, shall be punished by a fine of not more than two thousand dollars or by imprisonment for not more than one year.

Historical and Statutory Notes

St.1732–3, c. 14, § 3.
St.1785, c. 24, § 3.
St.1800, c. 57, § 2.
St.1817, c. 191, § 1.
St.1822, c. 90.
St.1825, c. 184, § 1.
St.1833, c. 148, § 1.
R.S.1836, c. 132, § 2.
St.1856, c. 121, § 1.
G.S.1860, c. 167, § 3.
P.S.1882, c. 209, § 3.
St.1895, c. 419, § 13.
R.L.1902, c. 214, § 9.

§ 10. Subsequent offenses within five years of conviction

Whoever, within five years after being convicted of any offence mentioned in section five, seven, eight, nine, eleven, fifteen, sixteen, seventeen or seventeen A, commits the like offence, or any other of the offences therein mentioned, shall, in addition to the fine therein provided, be punished by imprisonment for not less than three months nor more than one year, and the sentence imposing such fine and such imprisonment shall not be suspended.

Amended by St.1957, c. 390, § 1; St.1965, c. 549, § 1; St.1967, c. 189.

Historical and Statutory Notes

St.1833, c. 148, § 1.
R.S.1836, c. 132, § 3.
St.1856, c. 121, § 1.
G.S.1860, c. 167, § 4.
P.S.1882, c. 209, § 4.
R.L.1902, c. 214, § 10.

§ 10A. Arrest without warrant

Any person who is discovered by a police officer in the act of violating section seven, eight, nine, twelve, sixteen, seventeen, seventeen A, eighteen or twenty-two, while such officer is lawfully at or within the place where such violation occurred, may be arrested without a warrant by such police officer, and held in custody, in jail or otherwise, until a complaint be made against him for such offense, unless previously admitted to bail, which complaint shall be made as soon as practicable and in any case within twenty-four hours, Sundays and legal holidays excepted.

Added by St.1967, c. 119. Amended by St.1967, c. 372.

§ 11. Lottery tickets; advertising

Whoever, himself or by another, advertises a lottery ticket or a share in such ticket for sale, or sets up or exhibits, or devises or makes for the purpose of being set up or exhibited, any sign, symbol or emblematic or other representation of a lottery or the drawing thereof, in any way indicating where a lottery ticket or a share thereof or such writing, certificate, bill, token or other device before mentioned may be obtained, or in any way invites or entices, or attempts to invite or entice, any other person to purchase or receive the same, shall be punished by a fine of not more than two thousand dollars or by imprisonment for not more than one year.

Historical and Statutory Notes

St.1732–3, c. 14, § 2.
St.1785, c. 24, § 2.
St.1800, c. 57, § 1.
St.1817, c. 191, § 1.
St.1822, c. 90.
St.1825, c. 184, § 1.
St.1828, c. 134, § 1.
St.1833, c. 148, § 2.
R.S.1836, c. 132, § 4.
G.S.1860, c. 167, § 5.
P.S.1882, c. 209, § 13.
St.1895, c. 419, § 13.
R.L.1902, c. 214, § 11.

§ 12. False lottery tickets; creation, sale, or possession

Whoever makes or sells, or has in his possession with intent to sell, exchange or negotiate, or by printing, writing or otherwise assists in making or selling, or in attempting to sell, exchange or negotiate, a false or fictitious lottery ticket, or any share thereof, or any writing, certificate, bill, token or other device before mentioned, or any ticket or share thereof in a fictitious or pretended lottery, knowing the same to be false or fictitious, or receives any money or other thing of value for such ticket or share of a ticket, writing, certificate, bill, token or other device purporting that the owner, bearer or holder thereof shall be entitled to receive any prize, or share of a prize, or other thing of value, that may be drawn in a lottery, knowing the same to be false or fictitious, shall be punished by imprisonment in the state prison for not more than three years.

Historical and Statutory Notes

St.1833, c. 148, § 3.
R.S.1836, c. 132, § 5.
G.S.1860, c. 167, § 6.
P.S.1882, c. 209, § 6.
R.L.1902, c. 214, § 12.

§ 13. Lottery tickets, tokens or shares deemed false

Upon the trial of a person charged with any of the crimes mentioned in the preceding section, a ticket or share of a ticket, or other writing or thing before mentioned, which the defendant has sold or offered for sale, or for which he has received a valuable consideration, shall be deemed false, spurious or fictitious, unless the defendant proves that the same was true and genuine, duly issued by the authority of some legislature within the United States, that such lottery was existing and undrawn and that such ticket or share thereof, or other writing or thing before mentioned, was issued by lawful authority and is binding upon the person who issued the same.

Historical and Statutory Notes

St.1833, c. 148, § 3.
R.S.1836, c. 132, § 6.
G.S.1860, c. 167, § 7.
P.S.1882, c. 209, § 7.
R.L.1902, c. 214, § 13.

§ 14. Forfeiture of money, prizes, or other property disposed of by chance; recovery

Money or other thing of value drawn as a prize or share thereof in a lottery, and all property disposed of or offered to be disposed of by chance or device under the pretext mentioned in section seven, by an inhabitant of or a resident within the commonwealth, and all money or other thing of value received by such person by reason of his being the owner or holder of a ticket or share of a ticket in a lottery or pretended lottery, or of a share or right in any such scheme of chance or such device, contrary to this chapter, shall be forfeited, and may be recovered by an information filed or by an action for money had and received brought by the attorney general or a district attorney in the name and on behalf of the commonwealth.

Historical and Statutory Notes

St.1817, c. 191, § 2.
St.1833, c. 148, § 5.
R.S.1836, c. 132, § 8.
St.1856, c. 121, § 2.
G.S.1860, c. 167, § 8.
P.S.1882, c. 209, § 8.
R.L.1902, c. 214, § 14.

§ 15. Lottery for money drawn out of commonwealth; aiding or promoting

Whoever, except as provided in section five of chapter one hundred and twenty-eight A, aids, either by printing or writing, or is in any way concerned in setting up, promoting, managing or drawing a lottery for money, set up, promoted, managed, or drawn out of the commonwealth, shall be punished by a fine of not more than two thousand dollars or by imprisonment for not more than one year.

Amended by St.1983, c. 105, § 2.

Historical and Statutory Notes

St.1869, c. 112, § 1.
P.S.1882, c. 209, § 9.
St.1895, c. 419, § 13.
R.L.1902, c. 214, § 15.

§ 16. Tickets of lottery described in Sec. 15; sale or possession

Whoever sells, for himself or another, or offers for sale or has in his possession with intent so to do or to exchange or negotiate, or aids or assists in selling, negotiating, exchanging or disposing of a ticket, or a share of a ticket, in a lottery described in the preceding section, shall be punished by a fine of not more than two thousand dollars or by imprisonment for not more than one year.

Historical and Statutory Notes

St.1869, c. 112, § 2.
P.S.1882, c. 209, § 10.
St.1895, c. 419, § 13.
R.L.1902, c. 214, § 16.

§ 16A. Organizing or promoting gambling facilities or services

Whoever knowingly organizes, supervises, manages or finances at least four persons so that such persons may provide facilities or services or assist in the provision of facilities or services for the conduct of illegal lotteries, or for the illegal registration of bets or the illegal buying or selling of pools upon the result of a trial or contest of skill, speed or endurance of man, beast, bird or machine, or upon the happening of any event, or upon the result of a game, competition, political nomination, appointment or election, or whoever knowingly receives from at least four such persons compensation or payment in any form as a return from such lotteries, such registration or such buying or selling shall be punished by imprisonment in the state prison for not more than fifteen years or by a fine of not more than ten thousand dollars, or by both such fine and imprisonment. As used in this section the word "persons" shall not include bettors or wagerers who merely avail themselves of such facilities or services for the purpose of making a bet or wager and do not otherwise provide or assist in the provision of such facilities or services. This section shall not apply to such bettors or wagerers.

Added by St.1970, c. 650.

§ 17. Place for registering bets or dealing in pools; owner or occupant; custodian or depository

Whoever keeps a building or room, or any part thereof, or occupies, or is found in, any place, way, public or private, park or parkway, or any open space, public or private, or any portion thereof, with apparatus, books or any device, for registering bets, or buying or selling pools, upon the result of a trial or contest of skill, speed or endurance of man, beast, bird or machine, or upon the result of a game, competition, political nomination, appointment or election, or whoever is present in such place, way, park or parkway, or any such open space, or any portion thereof, engaged in such business or employment; or, being such keeper, occupant, person found or person present, as aforesaid, registers such bets, or buys or sells such pools, or is concerned in buying or selling the same; or, being the owner, lessee or occupant of a building or room, or part thereof, or private grounds, knowingly permits the same to be used or occupied for any such purpose, or therein keeps, exhibits, uses or employs, or knowingly permits to be therein kept, exhibited, used or employed, any device or apparatus for registering such bets, or for buying or selling such pools, or whoever becomes the custodian or depository for hire, reward, commission or compensation in any manner, of any pools, money, property or thing of value, in any manner staked or bet upon such result, shall be punished by a fine of not more than three thousand dollars or by imprisonment in the state prison for not more than three years, or in jail or the house of correction for not more than two and one half years.

Amended by St.1968, c. 116.

Historical and Statutory Notes

St.1878, c. 165.
P.S.1882, c. 99, § 8.
St.1885, c. 342, § 1.
St.1895, c. 419, § 13.
R.L.1902, c. 214, § 17.
St.1922, c. 315.

§ 17A. Telephones; use for gaming purposes

[Text of section effective until July 31, 2011. See 2001, 139, Sec. 45 as amended by 2005, 176, Sec. 13; 2006, 54, Sec. 12; 2006, 449, Secs. 19 and 21; 2008, 290, Sec. 12; 2009, 167, Sec. 12 and 2010, 203, Sec. 12. For text effective July 31, 2011, see below.]

Whoever uses a telephone or, being the occupant in control of premises where a telephone is located or a subscriber for a telephone, knowingly permits another to use a telephone so located or for which he subscribes, as the case may be, for the purpose of accepting wagers or bets, or buying or selling of pools, or for placing all or any portion of a wager with another, upon the result of a trial or contest of skill, speed, or endurance of man, beast, bird, or machine, or upon the result of an athletic game or contest, or upon the lottery called the numbers game, or for the purpose of reporting the same to a headquarters or booking office, or who under a name other than his own or otherwise falsely or fictitiously procures telephone service for himself or another for such purposes, shall be punished by a fine of not more than two thousand dollars or by imprisonment for not more than one year; provided, however, that this section shall not apply to use of telephones or other devices or means to place wagers authorized pursuant to the provisions of section 5C of chapter 128A.

§ 17A. Telephones; use for gaming purposes

[Text of section effective July 31, 2011. See 2001, 139, Sec. 28 and 2001, 139, Sec. 45 as amended by 2005, 176, Sec. 13; 2006, 54, Sec. 12; 2006, 449, Secs. 19 and 21; 2008, 290, Sec. 12; 2009, 167, Sec. 12 and 2010, 203, Sec. 12. For text effective until July 31, 2011, see above.]

Whoever uses a telephone or, being the occupant in control of premises where a telephone is located or a subscriber for a telephone, knowingly permits another to use a telephone so located or for which he subscribes, as the case may be, for the purpose of accepting wagers or bets, or buying or selling of pools, or for placing all or any portion of a wager with another, upon the result of a trial or contest of skill, speed, or endurance of man, beast, bird, or machine, or upon the result of an athletic game or contest, or upon the lottery called the numbers game, or for the purpose of reporting the same to a headquarters or booking office, or who under a name other than his own or otherwise falsely or fictitiously procures telephone service for himself or another for such purposes, shall be punished by a fine of not more than two thousand dollars or by imprisonment for not more than one year.

Added by St.1958, c. 246. Amended by St.1962, c. 440; St.2001, c. 139, § 28.

§ 17B. Use of electronic communications records in ongoing criminal investigations; subpoena of records

Except as otherwise prohibited under section 2703 of Title 18 of the United States Code, whenever the attorney general or a district attorney has reasonable grounds to believe that records in the possession of: (i) a common carrier subject to the jurisdiction of the department of telecommunications and cable, as provided in paragraph (d) of section 12 of chapter 159; or (ii) a provider of electronic communication service as defined in subparagraph (15) of section 2510 of Title 18 of the United States Code; or (iii) a provider of remote computing service as defined in section 2711 of Title 18 of the United States Code, are relevant and material to an ongoing criminal investigation, the attorney general or district attorney may issue an administrative subpoena demanding all such records in the possession of such common carrier or service, and such records shall be delivered to the attorney general or district attorney within 14 days of receipt of the subpoena. No such common carrier or service, or employee thereof, shall be civilly or criminally responsible for furnishing any records or information in compliance with such demand. Nothing in this section shall limit the right of the attorney general or a district attorney to otherwise obtain records from such a common carrier or service pursuant to a search warrant, a court order or a grand jury or trial subpoena.

No subpoena issued pursuant to this section shall demand records that disclose the content of electronic communications or subscriber account records disclosing internet locations which have been accessed including, but not limited to, websites, chat channels and newsgroups, but excluding servers used to initially access the internet. No recipient of a subpoena issued pursuant to this section shall provide any such content or records accessed, in response to such subpoena.

Added by St.1966, c. 352. Amended by St.1997, c. 164, § 292; St.2008, c. 169, § 80, eff. April 10, 2007; St.2008, c. 205, § 3, eff. Oct. 22, 2008.

§ 18. Policy lotteries or shops; production, sale or possession of lottery tickets or tokens

Whoever keeps, sets up, promotes or is concerned as owner, agent, clerk or in any other manner, in managing a policy lottery or policy shop, or writes, prints, sells, transfers or delivers a ticket, certificate, slip, bill, token or other device, purporting or designed to guarantee or assure to a person, or to entitle him to a chance of drawing or obtaining a prize or thing of value in a lottery or in the game or device commonly known as policy lottery or policy, whether drawn or determined, or remaining to be drawn or determined, or who receives from a person any money or other thing of value for such article or chance; or for himself or another writes, prints, sells, transfers or delivers or has in his possession for the purpose of sale, transfer or delivery, or in any way aids in selling, exchanging, negotiating, transferring or delivering a chance or ticket in a lottery, or in the game or device commonly known as policy lottery or policy, whether drawn or to be drawn, or any such bill, slip, certificate, token or other device, shall be punished by a fine of not more than five hundred dollars or by imprisonment for not more than one year.

Historical and Statutory Notes

St.1892, c. 409, § 1.
St.1895, c. 419, § 7.
R.L.1902, c. 214, § 18.

§ 19. Production, advertisement or delivery of tickets; receipt of money; prima facie evidence

The printing, writing, advertising, issuing or delivery of any ticket, paper, document or other article or material representing or purporting to represent the existence of or any chance or interest in any lottery, policy lottery or policy game, pool or pools, registered or other bet or other game or hazard, whether drawn or determined, or remaining to be drawn or determined, or the receiving of money or other thing of value for such article or chance, shall be prima facie evidence of the existence, location and drawing of such lottery, policy lottery or policy game, and of the act or event upon which such pool or pools, bet, game or hazard depends or may depend, and of the unlawful character of such lottery, policy lottery, pool, bet, game or hazard, and the issuing or delivery of such ticket, paper, document or other article or material shall be prima facie evidence of value received therefor by the person, company or corporation issuing or delivering the same, or aiding or abetting therein, and that such person, company or corporation is concerned in keeping, managing or promoting such lottery, pool, bet, game or hazard.

Historical and Statutory Notes

St.1892, c. 409, § 2.
St.1895, c. 419, § 8.
R.L.1902, c. 214, § 19.

§ 20. Tickets, memoranda, books and sheets; nuisance; possession; concealment

All lottery, policy or pool tickets, slips or checks, memoranda of any combination or other bet, manifold or other policy or pool books or sheets, are hereby declared a common nuisance and the possession thereof unlawful; and the possession of any such article, or of any other implements, apparatus or materials of any other form of gaming, shall be prima facie evidence of their use, by the person having them in possession, in the form of gaming in which like articles are commonly used. Any such article found upon the person of one lawfully arrested for violation of any law relative to lotteries, policy lotteries or policy, the buying or selling of pools or registering of bets or other form of gaming shall be competent evidence upon the trial of a complaint or indictment to which it may be relevant. If a person so arrested in a building or structure or part thereof conceals or attempts to conceal such articles upon his person or elsewhere, the possession and concealment or attempt at concealment thereof shall be prima facie evidence that the place in which the same occurs is kept, maintained, used or occupied for the form of gaming in which like articles are commonly used.

Historical and Statutory Notes

St.1895, c. 419, § 3.
R.L.1902, c. 214, § 20.

§ 21. Words, figures or characters referring to game or contest; prima facie evidence; proof

In a prosecution or proceeding relative to lotteries, policy lotteries or policy, buying and selling pools or registered bets, any words, figures or characters, written, printed or exposed upon a blackboard, placard or otherwise, in a place alleged to be used or occupied for such business, purporting or appearing to be a name of a horse or jockey, or a description of or reference to a trial or contest of skill, speed or endurance of man, beast, bird or machine, or game, competition, political nomination, appointment or election, or other act or event, or any odds, bet, combination bet or other stake or wager, or any code, cipher or substitute therefor, shall be prima facie evidence of the existence of the race, game, contest or other act or event so purporting or appearing to be referred to, and that such place is kept or occupied for gaming; and in all cases the same may be proved by a copy or by oral description thereof.

Historical and Statutory Notes

St.1895, c. 419, § 4.
R.L.1902, c. 214, § 21.

§ 22. Delivery to or from a person engaged in a lottery or other gaming

Whoever receives a letter, package or parcel for delivery to or transportation from a person, or delivers or transports the same to or from a person, having reasonable cause to believe that such person is engaged or in any way concerned in the management or promotion of or agency for a lottery, or the game known as policy lottery or policy, or the buying or selling of pools or registering of bets, or other form of gaming, and that such letter, package or parcel has relation to such business, shall be punished by a fine of not less than fifty nor more than five hundred dollars; but this section shall not apply to the receipt, carriage or delivery of United States mail matter by an officer or employee thereof.

Historical and Statutory Notes

St.1895, c. 419, § 5.
R.L.1902, c. 214, § 22.

§ 22A. Whist or bridge for charitable and similar purposes

Nothing in this chapter shall authorize the prosecution, arrest or conviction of any person for conducting or promoting, or for allowing to be conducted or promoted, a game of cards commonly called whist or bridge, in connection with which prizes are offered to be won by chance; provided, that the entire proceeds of the charges for admission to such game are donated solely to charitable, civic, educational, fraternal or religious purposes.

Amended by St.1934, c. 371; St.1936, c. 222; St.1936, c. 283; St.1943, c. 267.

Historical and Statutory Notes

St.1931, c. 331.

§ 22B. Beano; sale of lottery tickets

Nothing in this chapter shall authorize the prosecution, arrest or conviction of any person for promoting or playing, or for allowing to be conducted, promoted or played, the game commonly called beano, or substantially the same game under another name in connection with which prizes are offered to be won by chance or for selling lottery tickets or shares; provided, said game or sales are conducted under a license issued by the director of the state lottery, under the provisions of sections thirty-seven or thirty-eight of chapter ten.

Added by St.1971, c. 486, § 2. Amended by St.1973, c. 729, § 3.

§ 23. Oath and warrant to enter gaming or lottery place, arrest persons and seize implements and materials; disposal of articles

If a person makes oath before a district court or justice of the peace authorized to issue warrants in criminal cases that he suspects or has probable cause to suspect that a house or other building, room or place is used as and for a common gaming house, for gaming for money or other property, or is occupied, used or kept for promoting a lottery, or for the sale of lottery tickets, or for promoting the game known as policy lottery or policy, or for the buying or selling of pools or registering of bets upon any race, game, contest, act or event, and that persons resort thereto for any such purpose, such court or justice, whether the names of the persons last mentioned are known to the complainant or not, shall, if satisfactory evidence is presented, issue a warrant commanding the sheriff or his deputy or any constable or police officer to enter such house, building, room or place, and to arrest the keepers thereof, all persons in any way assisting in keeping the same, whether as janitor, doorkeeper, watchman or otherwise, all persons who are there found participating in any form of gaming and all persons present whether so participating or not, if any lottery, policy or pool tickets, slips, checks, manifold books or sheets, memoranda of any bet, or other implements, apparatus or materials of any form of gaming are found in said place, and to take into their custody all the implements, apparatus or materials of gaming, as aforesaid, and all the personal property, including money, furniture and fixtures there found, and to keep said persons, implements, apparatus or materials, property, including money, furniture and fixtures so that they may be forthcoming before some court or magistrate to be dealt with according to law. The provisions of chapter two hundred and seventy-six relative to disposal of gaming articles seized upon search warrants shall apply to all articles and property seized as herein provided for.

Amended by St.1934, c. 235, § 3; St.1934, c. 303, § 1; St.1953, c. 319, § 30.

Historical and Statutory Notes

St.1834, c. 172.
R.S.1836, c. 50, § 19.
St.1857, c. 194, § 4.
G.S.1860, c. 85, § 8.
St.1869, c. 364, § 1.
P.S.1882, c. 99, § 10.
St.1883, c. 120.
St.1887, c. 448, § 2.
St.1895, c. 419, § 9.
R.L.1902, c. 214, § 23.

§ 24. Race tracks; owners, proprietors of, or persons present

This chapter shall not authorize the arrest or conviction of the owner or proprietor of a race track or trotting course for the reason that another person has without his knowledge or consent violated any of its provisions relative to the buying and selling of pools or the registering or making of bets or to any offence mentioned in the preceding section; nor the arrest or conviction of a person for being present on a race track or trotting course where pools are sold or bets registered or made on trials of speed or endurance between horses or other animals; but this exception shall not apply to a person in any way participating or assisting in the buying or selling of pools or registering of bets.

Historical and Statutory Notes

St.1895, c. 419, § 9.
R.L.1902, c. 214, § 24.

§ 25. Obstructions barring access to gaming places; removal; lien of expenses

If a captain of police in Boston or marshal or chief of police in any other city or town in the commonwealth finds that access to any building, apartment or place which he has reasonable cause to believe is resorted to for the purpose of unlawful gaming is barred by any obstruction, such as a door, window, shutter, screen, bar or grating of unusual strength, other than what is usual in ordinary places of business, or any unnecessary number of doors, windows or obstructions, he shall order the same removed by the owner or agent of the building where such obstruction exists, and if any of said officers cannot find either of the persons mentioned, so as to make personal service, said notice shall be posted upon the outside of the apartments and on the outside of said building, and upon the neglect to remove such obstruction for seven days from the date of said order or posting of said notices, any of said officers shall cause such obstruction to be removed from such building, and the expense of such removal shall be a lien on said building and be collected by the officer removing such obstruction, in the manner in which a mechanic's lien is collected.

Historical and Statutory Notes

St.1887, c. 448, § 1.
St.1892, c. 388, § 1.
R.L.1902, c. 214, § 25.

§ 26. Subsequent obstructions; removal; punishment; lien

If, within one year after removal of said obstruction, the premises are again obstructed as above defined, the captain of police or marshal or chief of police shall have the same power of removal as provided in the preceding section, and in addition the owner or agent when such second order of removal is given, either by personal service or by posting on the building, shall be punished by a fine of not less than two hundred and fifty nor more than five hundred dollars, and the amount of said fine shall be a lien upon said building and be collected in like manner as provided in the preceding section. And for every subsequent obstruction as above defined, at any time within two years of the giving of the second notice, as above provided, said officers shall have the same powers as provided in the preceding section for removing the obstructions, and the owner or agent at the time such third or subsequent order of removal is given, either by personal service or by posting on the building, shall be punished by a fine of not less than five hundred nor more than one thousand dollars or may be punished by imprisonment for one year, and the amount of said fine shall be a lien upon the said building, and shall be collected in like manner as above provided. Obstructions as above defined, erected more than two years after the giving of the notice of the third offence, shall be construed to be a first offence under this section.

Historical and Statutory Notes

St.1892, c. 388, § 1.
R.L.1902, c. 214, § 26.

§ 27. Judicial notice of methods and character of lotteries, policy games, pools and betting; prima facie evidence

Any court or magistrate having criminal jurisdiction may take judicial notice of the general methods and character of lotteries, policy lotteries or the game called policy, pools or combination bets, and the buying and selling of pools and registering of bets. In the trial of a complaint or indictment to which it may be relevant, any lottery, policy or pool ticket, certificate, slip or check, manifold or other policy or pool book or sheet, or memorandum of any pool or sale of pools, or of a bet or odds, or combination bet, or any other implement, apparatus, materials or articles of a character commonly employed in or in connection with lotteries, policy lotteries or policy, the buying or selling of pools or registering of bets, or other form of gaming, shall be prima facie evidence of the existence and unlawful character of a lottery, policy lottery or game, pool or pools, bet, game or hazard, or other form of gaming in which like articles are commonly used, and that such article has relation thereto.

Historical and Statutory Notes

St.1895, c. 419, § 2.
R.L.1902, c. 214, § 27.

§ 28. Lotteries or gaming; complaints and indictments

No plea of misnomer shall be received to a complaint or indictment for violation of any law relative to lotteries, policy lotteries or policy, the selling of pools or registering of bets, or any form of gaming; but the defendant may be arraigned, tried, sentenced and punished under any name by which he is complained of or indicted. No such complaint or indictment shall be abated, quashed or held insufficient by reason of any alleged defect, either of form or substance, if the same is sufficient to enable the defendant to understand the charge and to prepare his defence. No variance between such complaint or indictment and the evidence shall be deemed material, unless in some matter of substance essential to the charge under the rule above prescribed.

Historical and Statutory Notes

St.1895, c. 419, § 6.
R.L.1902, c. 214, § 28.

§ 29. Sale, exchange or disposition of property; misrepresentation

Whoever sells, exchanges or disposes of any property, or offers or attempts so to do, upon a representation, advertisement, notice or inducement that anything other than what is specifically stated to be the subject of the sale or exchange is or is to be delivered or received, or is in any way connected with or is a part of the transaction, or whoever gives a stamp, coupon or other device which entitles a purchaser to demand or receive from a person or company other than the merchant dealing in the goods purchased or the manufacturer thereof, any other property than that actually sold or exchanged, or whoever delivers by any person or company other than the merchant dealing in the goods purchased, or the manufacturer thereof, goods, wares or merchandise upon the presentation of such stamp, coupon or other device, shall be punished by a fine of not less than ten nor more than five hundred dollars.

Historical and Statutory Notes

St.1884, c. 277.
St.1898, c. 576.
R.L.1902, c. 214, § 29.

§ 30. Trading stamps or similar devices; sale or delivery

Whoever, in connection with the sale of any article or any merchandise whatsoever, sells, gives or delivers any trading stamps, checks, coupons or similar devices to be exchanged for, or to be redeemed by the giving of, any indefinite or undescribed article, the nature and value of which are not stated, or to be exchanged for, or to be redeemed by the giving of, any article not distinctly bargained for at the time when such trading stamps or other devices as aforesaid were sold, given or delivered, shall be punished by a fine of not less than ten nor more than fifty dollars.

Historical and Statutory Notes

St.1903, c. 386.

§ 31. Racing horses for bets or stakes

Whoever, except in trials of speed of horses for premiums offered by legally constituted agricultural societies, or by corporations authorized thereto by section fourteen of chapter one hundred and eighty, engages in racing, running, trotting or pacing a horse or other animal of the horse kind for a bet, wager of money or other thing of value or a purse or stake made within the commonwealth, or whoever aids or abets therein, shall be punished by a fine of not more than one thousand dollars or by imprisonment for not more than one year, or both.

Historical and Statutory Notes

St.1846, c. 200.
G.S.1860, c. 167, § 9.
St.1865, c. 67.
P.S.1882, c. 209, § 11.
St.1900, c. 409.
R.L.1902, c. 214, § 30.

§ 31A. Racing results or information; transmission for unlawful purposes

Whoever transmits the results of a race, or information as to the progress of a race during the running thereof, in a racing meeting as defined in section one of chapter one hundred and twenty-eight A, by any means to another knowing that such results or information is to be used or intended to be used for unlawful purposes or in furtherance of unlawful gambling, shall be punished by a fine of not more than five thousand dollars or by imprisonment in a jail or house of correction for not more than two and one half years or in the state prison for not more than five years, or by both such fine and imprisonment.

This section shall not be construed as prohibiting a newspaper from printing such results for publication as news, or a television or radio station from telecasting or broadcasting such results or information as news.
Added by St.1964, c. 330.

§ 32. Horse racing; fraud

Whoever, for the purpose of competing for a purse or premium offered by an agricultural society, or by a person or association in the commonwealth, knowingly and designedly enters or drives a horse that is painted or disguised, or is a different horse from the one that purports to be entered or driven, or knowingly and designedly, for the purpose of competing for a premium or purse, enters or drives a horse in a class to which it does not belong, shall be punished by a fine of not more than five hundred dollars or by imprisonment for not more than six months.

Historical and Statutory Notes

St.1892, c. 167.
R.L.1902, c. 214, § 31.

§ 33. Race grounds in towns

No land within a town shall be laid out or used as a race ground or trotting park without the previous consent of and location by the mayor and city council, the town council in a town having a town council or the selectmen in any other town, who may regulate and alter the terms and conditions under which the same shall be laid out, used or continued in use and may discontinue the same when in their judgment the public

good so requires; and no land shall be used for any of the purposes declared unlawful in section thirty-one.
Amended by St.1976, c. 217, § 5.

Historical and Statutory Notes

St.1856, c. 102, § 1.
G.S.1860, c. 167, § 10.
St.1864, c. 63.
P.S.1882, c. 209, § 12.
R.L.1902, c. 214, § 32.

§ 34. Race grounds as nuisance; abatement

Every race ground or trotting park established, laid out, used or continued in use contrary to this chapter is declared a common nuisance and may be abated as such; and all persons owning, keeping, using or permitting to be used such race ground or trotting park, or aiding or abetting therein, shall be punished by a fine of not more than one thousand dollars or by imprisonment for not more than one year, or both.

Historical and Statutory Notes

St.1856, c. 102, §§ 2, 3.
G.S.1860, c. 167, § 11.
P.S.1882, c. 209, § 13.
R.L.1902, c. 214, § 33.

§ 35. Definition of words and phrases used in Secs. 35 to 38

The following words and phrases used in this and the three following sections of this chapter shall, unless a different meaning is required by the context, have the following meanings:

"Person", an individual, partnership, corporation or association, whether acting in his or their own right or as the officer, agent, servant, correspondent or representative of another.

"Contract", any agreement, trade or transaction.

"Securities", all evidences of debt or property and options for the purchase and sale thereof, shares in any corporation, joint stock company or association, bonds, coupons, scrip, rights, choses in action and other evidences of debt or property and options for the purchase or sale thereof.

"Commodities", anything movable that is bought and sold.

"Bucket shop", any room, office, store, building or other place where any contract prohibited by the following section is made or offered to be made.

"Keeper", any person owning, keeping, managing, operating or promoting a bucket shop, or assisting to keep, manage, operate or promote a bucket shop.

"Bucketing" or "Bucket-shopping",

(a) The making of, or offering to make, any contract respecting the purchase or sale, either upon credit or upon margin, of any securities or commodities, wherein both parties thereto intend, or such keeper intends, that such contract shall be, or may be, terminated, closed or settled according to, or upon the basis of, the public market quotations of prices made on any board of trade or exchange upon which said securities or commodities are dealt in, and without a bona fide purchase or sale of the same; or

(b) The making of, or offering to make, any contract respecting the purchase or sale, either upon credit or upon margin, of any securities or commodities, wherein both parties intend, or such keeper intends, that such contract shall be, or may be, deemed terminated, closed or settled, when such public market quotations of prices for the securities or commodities named in such contract shall reach a certain figure without a bona fide purchase or sale of the same; or

(c) The making of, or offering to make, any contract respecting the purchase or sale, either upon credit or upon margin, of any securities or commodities, wherein both parties do not intend, or such keeper does not intend, the actual or bona fide receipt or delivery of such securities or commodities, but do intend, or such keeper does intend, a settlement of such contract based upon the differences in such public market quotations of prices at which said securities or commodities are, or are asserted to be, bought and sold.

Historical and Statutory Notes

St.1907, c. 414, § 1.

§ 36. Bucketing contracts; keeper of shop; domestic and foreign corporations

Whoever makes, or offers to make, any contract of bucketing or bucket-shopping, or who is the keeper of any bucket shop, shall be punished by a fine of not more than one thousand dollars or by imprisonment for not more than one year. Whoever shall be convicted of a second offence shall be punished by imprisonment for not more than five years. The continuing of the keeping of a bucket shop, by any person, after the first conviction therefor, shall be deemed a second offence hereunder. If a domestic corporation shall be convicted of a second offence, the supreme judicial court may, upon an information in equity in the name of the attorney general, at the relation of the commissioner of revenue, dissolve the corporation; and if a foreign corporation shall be convicted of a second offence, the supreme judicial court may, in the same manner, restrain it from doing business in this commonwealth.
Amended by St.1978, c. 514, § 233.

Historical and Statutory Notes

St.1907, c. 414, § 2.

§ 37. Prohibited contracts; price quotations

Whoever shall communicate, receive, exhibit or display in any manner any statement of quotations of prices of any securities or commodities with an intent to make, or offer to make, or to aid in making, or offering to make, any contract prohibited by the preceding section shall be punished as provided therein.

Historical and Statutory Notes

St.1907, c. 414, § 3.

§ 38. Purchases and sales of securities or commodities; written statement

Every person shall furnish, upon demand, to any customer or principal for whom such person has executed any order for the actual purchase or sale of any securities or commodities, either for immediate or future delivery, a written statement containing the names of the persons from whom such property was bought, or to whom it has been sold, as the fact may be, the time when, place where and the price at which the same was either bought or sold; and if such person refuses or neglects to furnish such statement within twenty-four hours after such demand, such refusal or neglect shall be prima facie evidence that such purchase or sale was bucketing or bucket-shopping.

Historical and Statutory Notes

St.1907, c. 414, § 4.

§ 39. Gifts to influence business affairs; threats

(a) Whoever, in relation to any transaction or matter concerning the business affairs of an employer, principal or beneficiary (1) offers, gives or agrees to give an agent or fiduciary of another person any benefit or anything of value with intent to influence the recipient's conduct, or (2) as an agent or fiduciary, solicits, accepts or agrees to accept any benefit or anything of value from another person who is not an employee, principal, or beneficiary upon an agreement or understanding that such benefit or thing of value will influence his conduct, shall be punished by imprisonment in the state prison for not more than five years, or by a fine of not more than ten thousand dollars, or both.

(b) Whoever, verbally or by a written or printed communication, threatens an economic injury to another, or threatens to deprive another of an economic opportunity, with intent to compel that person to do any act, involving the use or disposition of anything of value against his will, shall be punished by imprisonment in the state prison for not more than five years, or in the house of correction for not more than two years, or by a fine of not more than five thousand dollars, or both. The provisions of this paragraph shall not apply to any labor disputes as defined in section two of chapter one hundred and fifty A.

Amended by St.1980, c. 531, § 3.

Historical and Statutory Notes

St.1904, c. 343.
St.1909, c. 514, §§ 28, 29, 145.
St.1912, c. 495.

§ 39A. Gifts to influence action of participants in, and others connected with, a game or contest

Whoever gives, promises or offers to any professional or amateur baseball, football, hockey, polo, tennis or basketball player or any boxer or any player who participates or expects to participate in any professional or amateur game or sport or any jockey, driver or groom or any person participating or expecting to participate in any horse race, including owners of race tracks and their employees, stewards, trainers, judges, starters or special policemen, or to any manager, coach or trainer of any team or participant or prospective participant in any such game, contest or sport, any valuable thing with intent to influence him to lose, or try to lose, or cause to be lost, or to limit his or his team's margin of victory in, a baseball, football, hockey or basketball game, boxing, tennis or polo match or a horse race or any professional or amateur sport, or game, in which such player or participant or jockey or driver, is taking part or expects to take part, or has any duty or connection therewith, or whoever, being a professional or amateur baseball, football, hockey, basketball, tennis or polo player, boxer, or jockey, driver, or groom or participant or prospective participant in any sport or game or a manager, coach or trainer of any team or individual participant or prospective participant in any such game, contest or sport, solicits or accepts any valuable thing to influence him to lose, or try to lose, or cause to be lost, or to limit his or his team's margin of victory in, a baseball, football, hockey or basketball game or boxing, tennis or polo match, or horse race or any game of sport in which he is taking part, or expects to take part, or has any duty or connection therewith, shall be punished by a fine of not more than one thousand dollars or by imprisonment for not more than two years, or both.

Added by St.1947, c. 405.

§ 40. Appointment, reinstatement or discharge of employee of public service corporation or racing licensee on recommendation of public officer, officer elect or candidate

No railroad, street railway, electric light, gas, telegraph, telephone, water or steamboat company, and no licensee conducting a horse or dog racing meeting under chapter one hundred and twenty-eight A, shall appoint, promote, reinstate, suspend or discharge any person employed or seeking employment by any such company or licensee at the request of the governor, lieutenant governor, or any member or member elect of the council or of the general court, or candidate therefor, justice of the supreme judicial court, justice of the superior court, judge of probate, judge of the land court, justice of a district court, district attorney, member or member elect of a board of county commissioners, or candidate for county commissioner, mayor or mayor elect of a city, or candidate therefor, member or member elect of a board of aldermen, or selectmen, or city council, or any executive, administrative or judicial officer, clerk or employee of any branch of the government of the commonwealth or of any county, city or town; nor shall any such public officer or body, or any member or member elect thereof or candidate therefor, directly or indirectly advocate, oppose or otherwise interfere in, or make any request, recommendation, endorsement, requirement or certificate relative to, and the same, if made, shall not be required as a condition precedent to, or be in any way regarded or permitted to influence or control, the appointment, promotion, reinstatement or retention of any person employed or seeking employment by any such company or licensee, and no such person shall solicit, obtain, exhibit, or otherwise make use of any such official request, recommendation, certificate or endorsement in connection with any existing or desired employment by a public service corporation or by any such licensee. Any person or corporation violating any provision of this section shall be punished by a fine of not less than fifty nor more than one hundred dollars.

Amended by St.1954, c. 323.

Historical and Statutory Notes

St.1903, c. 320, §§ 1, 3.
St.1909, c. 514, § 25.
St.1910, c. 63, § 2.

§ 41. Offices not public offices under Sec. 40

The offices of probation officer, notary public, justice of the peace, prison officer, agent of the commissioner of correction and agent of the department of public welfare shall not be considered public offices within the meaning of the preceding section.

Historical and Statutory Notes

St.1903, c. 320, § 2.
St.1908, c. 228.
St.1909, c. 514, §§ 26, 145.
St.1910, c. 63, § 2.
St.1916, c. 241, § 1.
St.1919, c. 350, §§ 82, 83, 87.

§ 42. Boxing matches or exhibitions; betting or selling pools

Whoever bets or wagers or sells pools on any boxing or sparring match or exhibition shall be punished by imprisonment for not less than three months or by a fine of not less than fifty dollars, or both.

Historical and Statutory Notes

St.1920, c. 619, § 15.

§ 43. Solicitation, disclosure, receipt or use of information concerning public assistance

Any person who, except for purposes directly connected with the administration of general public assistance, old age assistance, aid to the blind, or aid to families with dependent children, and in accordance with the rules and regulations of the department of transitional assistance made under authority of section ten of chapter eighteen, or of the commission for the blind made under authority of section one hundred and forty-nine of chapter six, as the case may be, shall solicit, disclose, receive, make use of, or authorize, knowingly permit, participate in, or acquiesce in the use of, any list of, or names of, or any information concerning, persons applying for or receiving general public assistance, old age assistance, aid to families with dependent children or aid to the blind, directly or indirectly derived from the records, papers, files or communications of the department of transitional assistance, any city or town welfare department or bureau of old age assistance, or the commission for the blind, as the case may be, or acquired in the course of the performance of official duties, shall be punished by a fine of not more than one hundred dollars. Nothing herein shall be construed to prevent the disclosure by the commissioner of revenue to the commissioner of transitional assistance or to the IV–D agency as set forth in chapter one hundred and nineteen A, in concert with a wage reporting system, of such information as may be necessary to ascertain or confirm the existence of fraud, abuse or improper payments to an applicant, for or recipient of, public assistance; and nothing herein shall be construed to prevent the disclosure to said IV–D agency of information necessary for setoff debt collection pursuant to chapter sixty-two D or any other child support enforcement purpose.

Added by St.1941, c. 630, § 4. Amended by St.1945, c. 240, § 3; St.1963, c. 432, § 15; St.1966, c. 535, § 14; St.1967, c. 658, § 78; St.1978, c. 367, § 54E; St.1982, c. 581, § 4; St.1993, c. 460, § 87; St.1995, c. 5, § 95.

§ 44. Hospital or sanitarium patient; settlement, release or statement; admissibility

Except as provided below, no settlement or general release or statement in writing signed by any person confined in a hospital or sanitarium as a patient with reference to any personal injuries for which said person is confined in said hospital or sanitarium shall be admissible in evidence, used or referred to in any manner at the trial of any action to recover damages for personal injuries or consequential damages, so called, resulting therefrom, which statement, settlement or general release was obtained within fifteen days after the injuries were sustained and such settlement or release shall be null and void unless at least five days prior to the obtaining or procuring of such general release or statement such injured party had signified in writing his willingness that such general release or statement be given. This section shall not apply to statements or releases obtained by police officers or inspectors of motor vehicles in the performance of their duty, members of the family of such person or by or on behalf of his attorney. The provisions of this section shall not apply to chapter one hundred and fifty-two.

Added by St.1950, c. 166, § 1.

§ 45. Repealed, 1982, 21, Sec. 2

Historical and Statutory Notes

See, now, M.G.L.A. c. 112, § 87DDD½.

§ 46. Discarded containers originally used for refrigerative purposes; removal of doors

Whoever fails to remove the door or doors from a container originally used for refrigerative purposes before discarding it, or setting it aside for failure to use such container, or before keeping it out of doors for sale or any other purpose in a place accessible to unattended children, shall be punished by a fine of not more than one thousand dollars.

Added by St.1953, c. 187. Amended by St.1954, c. 191, § 1; St.1958, c. 604; St.1959, c. 107; St.1959, c. 431.

§ 47. Telephones; gambling convictions; approval for installation; notices of convictions and removals

A telephone shall not be installed for a person convicted of an illegal gaming activity under this chapter without the approval in writing of the head of both the police department of the municipality in which such telephone would be installed and the head of the criminal information section of the state police, and a telephone shall not be reinstalled without such approval for a period of one year from the date of removal in any premises from which it has been removed for such illegal activity, whether or not there has been a conviction. The criminal information section shall notify the telephone companies of convictions in such cases, and telephone companies doing business in the commonwealth shall notify the criminal information section of the state police of any such removals.

Added by St.1958, c. 347. Amended by St.1973, c. 793, § 5.

§ 48. Civil service preparatory courses; advertisement

Any school or person offering courses in preparation for civil service examinations shall cause to be printed in bold type on all its advertisements and circulars and all contracts to be entered into with prospective students a statement that disabled veterans who qualify for appointment must be given preference for appointment over veterans and non-veterans and that veterans must be given preference over non-veterans. Whoever violates the provisions of this section shall be punished by a fine of not less than fifty nor more than five hundred dollars.

Added by St.1962, c. 91.

§ 49. Criminal usury

(a) Whoever in exchange for either a loan of money or other property knowingly contracts for, charges, takes or receives, directly or indirectly, interest and expenses the aggregate of which exceeds an amount greater than twenty per centum per annum upon the sum loaned or the equivalent rate for a longer or shorter period, shall be guilty of criminal usury and shall be punished by imprisonment in the state prison for not more than ten years or by a fine of not more than ten thousand dollars, or by both such fine and imprisonment. For the purposes of this section the amount to be paid upon any loan for interest or expenses shall include all sums paid or to be paid by or on behalf of the borrower for interest, brokerage, recording fees, commissions, services, extension of loan, forbearance to enforce payment, and all other sums charged against or paid or to be paid by the borrower for making or securing directly or indirectly the loan, and shall include all such sums when paid by or on behalf of or charged against the borrower for or on account of making or securing the loan, directly or indirectly, to or by any person, other than the lender, if such payment or charge was known to the lender at the time of making the loan, or might have been ascertained by reasonable inquiry.

(b) Whoever, with knowledge of the contents thereof, possesses any writing, paper, instrument or article used to record a transaction proscribed under the provisions of paragraph (a) shall be punished by imprisonment in a jail or house of correction for not more than two and one half years, or by a fine of not more than five thousand dollars, or by both such fine and imprisonment.

(c) Any loan at a rate of interest proscribed under the provisions of paragraph (a) may be declared void by the supreme judicial or superior court in equity upon petition by the person to whom the loan was made.

(d) The provisions of paragraph (a) to (c), inclusive, shall not apply to any person who notifies the attorney general of his intent to engage in a transaction or transactions which, but for the provisions of this paragraph, would be proscribed under the provisions of paragraph (a) providing any such person maintains records of any such transaction. Such notification shall be valid for a two year period and shall contain the person's name and accurate address. No lender shall publicly advertise the fact of such notification nor use the fact of such notification to solicit business, except that such notification may be revealed to an individual upon his inquiry. Illegal use of such notification shall be punished by a fine of one thousand dollars. Such records shall contain the name and address of the borrower, the amount borrowed, the interest and expenses to be paid by the borrower, the date the loan is made and the date or dates on which any payment is due. Any such records shall be made available to the attorney general for the purposes of inspection upon his request. Such records and their contents shall be confidential but may be used by the attorney general, or any district attorney with the approval of the attorney general, for the purposes of conducting any criminal proceeding to which such records or their contents are relevant.

(e) The provisions of this section shall not apply to any loan the rate of interest for which is regulated under any other provision of general or special law or regulations promulgated thereunder or to any lender subject to control, regulation or examination by any state or federal regulatory agency.

Added by St.1970, c. 826. Amended by St.1971, c. 368.

§ 50. Sale of research papers, etc.; taking of examinations for another at educational institutions

Whoever, alone or in concert with others, sells to another, or arranges for or assists in such sale for another, a theme, term paper, thesis or other paper or the written results of research, knowing or having reason to know that such theme, term paper, thesis or other paper or research results or substantial material therefrom will be submitted or used by some other person for academic credit and represented as the original work of such person at an educational institution in the commonwealth or elsewhere without proper attribution as to source, or whoever takes an examination for another at any educational institution in the commonwealth, shall be punished by a fine of not more than one hundred dollars or by imprisonment for not more than six months, or both.

Added by St.1973, c. 874.

CHAPTER 272

CRIMES AGAINST CHASTITY, MORALITY, DECENCY AND GOOD ORDER

The section headings for the General Laws in this pamphlet have been editorially supplied.

§ 1. Enticing away person under 16 for marriage

Whoever fraudulently and deceitfully entices or takes away an unmarried person under sixteen from the house of such person's parents or elsewhere, without the consent of the parent or guardian, if any, under whose care and custody such person is living, for the purpose of effecting a clandestine marriage of such person without the consent of such parent or guardian, shall be punished by imprisonment for not more than one year or by a fine of not more than one thousand dollars, or both.

Amended by St.1978, c. 379, § 4.

Historical and Statutory Notes

St.1852, c. 254.
G.S.1860, c. 165, § 1.
P.S.1882, c. 207, § 1.
R.L.1902, c. 212, § 1.

§ 2. Enticing away person for prostitution or sexual intercourse

Whoever fraudulently and deceitfully entices or takes away a person from the house of his parent or guardian or elsewhere, for the purpose of prostitution or for the purpose of unlawful sexual intercourse, and whoever aids and assists in such abduction for such purpose, shall be punished by imprisonment in the state prison for not more than three years or in jail for not more than one year or by a fine of not more than one thousand dollars, or by both such fine and imprisonment in jail.

Amended by St.1978, c. 379, § 4.

Historical and Statutory Notes

St.1845, c. 216, § 1.
G.S.1860, c. 165, § 2.
P.S.1882, c. 207, § 2.
St.1886, c. 329, § 1.
St.1898, c. 444, § 1.
R.L.1902, c. 212, § 2.
St.1910, c. 424, § 1.

§ 3. Drugging persons for sexual intercourse

Whoever applies, administers to or causes to be taken by a person any drug, matter or thing with intent to stupefy or overpower such person so as to thereby enable any person to have sexual intercourse or unnatural sexual intercourse with such person shall be punished by imprisonment in the state prison for life or for any term of years not less than ten years.

Amended by St.1978, c. 379, § 4; St.1998, c. 232, § 3.

Historical and Statutory Notes

St.1886, c. 329, § 2.
R.L.1902, c. 212, § 3.
St.1918, c. 257, § 464.
St.1919, c. 5.
St.1920, c. 2.

§ 4. Inducing person under eighteen to have sexual intercourse

Whoever induces any person under 18 years of age of chaste life to have unlawful sexual intercourse shall be punished by imprisonment in the state prison for not more than three years or in a jail or house of correction for not more than two and one-half years or by a fine of not more than $1,000 or by both such fine and imprisonment.

Amended by St.1998, c. 232, § 3.

Historical and Statutory Notes

St.1886, c. 329, § 3.
St.1898, c. 444, § 2.
R.L.1902, c. 212, § 4.

§ 4A. Inducing minor into prostitution

Whoever induces a minor to become a prostitute, or who knowingly aids and assists in such inducement, shall be punished by imprisonment in the state prison for not more than five, nor less than three years, and by a fine of five thousand dollars. The sentence of imprisonment imposed under this section shall not be reduced to less than three years, nor suspended, nor shall any person convicted under this section be eligible for probation, parole or furlough or receive any deduction from his sentence for good conduct or otherwise until he shall have served three years of such sentence. Prosecutions commenced under this section shall not be continued without a finding nor placed on file.

Added by St.1979, c. 676.

§ 4B. Living off or sharing earnings of minor prostitute

Whoever lives or derives support or maintenance, in whole or in part, from the earnings or proceeds of prostitution committed by a minor, knowing the same to be earnings or proceeds of prostitution, or shares in such earnings, proceeds or monies, shall be punished by imprisonment in the state prison for not less than five years and by a fine of five thousand dollars. The sentence imposed under this section shall not be reduced to less than five years, nor suspended, nor shall any person convicted under this section be eligible for probation, parole or furlough or receive any deduction from his sentence for good conduct or otherwise until he shall have served five years of such sentence. Prosecutions commenced under this section shall not be continued without a finding nor placed on file.

Added by St.1979, c. 676.

§ 5. Repealed, 1987, 522, Sec. 22

§ 6. Owner of place inducing or suffering person to resort in such place for sexual intercourse

Whoever, being the owner of a place or having or assisting in the management or control thereof induces or knowingly suffers a person to resort to or be in or upon such place, for the purpose of unlawfully having sexual intercourse for money or other financial gain, shall be punished by imprisonment in the state prison for a period of five years and a five thousand dollar fine.

The sentence of imprisonment imposed under this section shall not be reduced to less than two years, nor suspended, nor shall any person convicted under this section be eligible for probation, parole, or furlough or receive any deduction from his sentence for good conduct or otherwise until he shall have served two years of such sentence. Prosecutions commenced under this section shall not be continued without a finding nor placed on file.

Amended by St.1978, c. 379, § 5; St.1979, c. 472; St.1980, c. 409.

Historical and Statutory Notes

St.1886, c. 329, § 5.
R.L.1902, c. 212, § 6.
St.1910, c. 424, § 2.

§ 7. Support from, or sharing, earnings of prostitute

Whoever, knowing a person to be a prostitute, shall live or derive support or maintenance, in whole or in part, from the earnings or proceeds of his prostitution, from moneys loaned, advanced to or charged against him by any keeper or manager or inmate of a house or other place where prostitution is practiced or allowed, or shall share in such earnings, proceeds or moneys, shall be punished by imprisonment in the state prison for a period of five years and by a fine of five thousand dollars.

The sentence of imprisonment imposed under this section shall not be reduced to less than two years, nor suspended, nor shall any person convicted under this section be eligible for probation, parole, or furlough or receive any deduction from his sentence for good conduct or otherwise until he shall have served two years of such sentence. Prosecutions commenced under this section shall not be continued without a finding nor placed on file.

Amended by St.1977, c. 589; St.1980, c. 409.

Historical and Statutory Notes

St.1910, c. 424, § 5.
St.1914, c. 621.

§ 8. Soliciting for prostitute

Whoever shall solicit or receive compensation for soliciting for a prostitute shall be punished by imprisonment in the house of correction for not more than one year or by a fine of not more than five hundred dollars, or both.

Historical and Statutory Notes

St.1910, c. 424, § 6.

§ 9. Oath and warrant to enter place for prostitution; detention of person in control and prostitute; recognizance to appear as witness

If a person makes oath before a district court that he has probable cause to suspect that a house, building, room or place is kept or resorted to for prostitution and that a certain person owning or having or assisting in the management or control of such house, building, room or place knowingly suffers another person to be in or upon such place for the purpose of unlawfully having sexual intercourse, said court shall, if satisfied that there is probable cause thereof, issue a warrant commanding the sheriff or his deputy, or any constable or police officer, to enter such house, building, room or place and search for such owner or person in control, and take into custody both the owner or person in control and such other person as may be in or upon such place for such purpose. Said owner or person in control shall be detained for not more than twenty-four hours until complaint may be made against him, and any such other person for a reasonable time until brought before said court to be recognized with or without sureties at the discretion of said court to appear as witnesses before the next or any succeeding sitting of said court. This section shall be in addition to and not in derogation of the common law.

Amended by St.1959, c. 313, § 9; St.1978, c. 379, § 6.

Historical and Statutory Notes

St.1910, c. 424, § 7.

§ 10. Arrest without warrant

Nothing in the preceding section shall prevent the arrest and detention without a warrant of any person who, the officer serving said process may have reasonable cause to believe, is violating any provision of this chapter, or is keeping a house, room or place resorted to for prostitution or lewdness, and said officer may upon such search arrest without a warrant any such person, and detain him until complaint may be made against him.

Historical and Statutory Notes

St.1910, c. 424, § 8.

§ 11. Corroboration of one witness; limitations

A person shall not be convicted under sections 2, 4 and 6 upon the evidence of one witness only, unless his testimony is corroborated in a material particular, and prosecution for a violation of any of said sections shall not be commenced more than one year after the commission of the crime.

Amended by St.1998, c. 232, § 4.

Historical and Statutory Notes

St.1886, c. 329, §§ 6, 7.
R.L.1902, c. 212, § 7.

§ 12. Procuring person to practice, or enter a place for, prostitution; employment office procuring person

Whoever knowingly procures, entices, sends, or aids or abets in procuring, enticing or sending, a person to practice prostitution, or to enter as an inmate or a servant a house of ill fame or other place resorted to for prostitution, whether within or without the commonwealth, shall be punished by a fine of not less than one hundred nor more than five hundred dollars or by imprisonment for not less than three months nor more than two years. Whoever as a proprietor or keeper of an employment agency, either personally or through an agent or employee, procures or sends a person to enter as aforesaid a house of ill fame or other place resorted to for prostitution, the character of which on reasonable inquiry could have been ascertained by him, shall be punished by a fine of not less than fifty nor more than two hundred dollars.

Amended by St.1969, c. 59, § 3; St.1978, c. 379, § 7.

Historical and Statutory Notes

St.1888, c. 311, § 1.
R.L.1902, c. 212, § 8.
St.1910, c. 424, § 3.

§ 13. Detaining, or drugging to detain, person in place for prostitution

Whoever, for any length of time, unlawfully detains or attempts to detain, or aids or abets in unlawfully detaining or attempting to detain, or provides or administers or aids or abets in providing or administering any drug or liquor for the purpose of detaining a person in a house of ill fame or other place where prostitution is practiced or allowed, shall be punished by imprisonment in the state prison for not more than five years or in the house of correction for not less than one nor more than two and one half years or by a fine of not less than one hundred nor more than five hundred dollars.

Amended by St.1978, c. 379, § 7.

Historical and Statutory Notes

St.1888, c. 311, § 2.
R.L.1902, c. 212, § 9.
St.1910, c. 424, § 4.

§ 14. Adultery

A married person who has sexual intercourse with a person not his spouse or an unmarried person who has sexual intercourse with a married person shall be guilty of adultery and shall be punished by imprisonment in the state prison for not more than three years or in jail for not more than two years or by a fine of not more than five hundred dollars.

Amended by St.1978, c. 379, § 7.

Historical and Statutory Notes

B.L. c. 94, § 9.
C.L. c. 15, § 9.
St.1694–5, c. 5, §§ 1, 2.
St.1762–3, c. 29.
St.1784, c. 40, § 1.
R.S.1836, c. 130, § 1.
G.S.1860, c. 165, § 3.
P.S.1882, c. 207, § 3.
R.L.1902, c. 212, § 10.

§ 15. Polygamy

Whoever, having a former husband or wife living, marries another person or continues to cohabit with a second husband or wife in the commonwealth shall be guilty of polygamy, and be punished by imprisonment in the state prison for not more than five years or in jail for not more than two and one half years or by a fine of not more than five hundred dollars; but this section shall not apply to a person whose husband or wife has continually remained beyond sea, or has voluntarily withdrawn from the other and remained absent, for seven consecutive years, the party marrying again not knowing the other to be living within that time, nor to a person who has been legally divorced from the bonds of matrimony.

Amended by St.1969, c. 301.

Historical and Statutory Notes

St.1694–5, c. 5, §§ 3 to 5.
St.1698, c. 19.
St.1784, c. 40, § 2.
R.S.1836, c. 130, §§ 2, 3.
G.S.1860, c. 165, §§ 4, 5.
P.S.1882, c. 207, §§ 4, 5.
R.L.1902, c. 212, § 11.
St.1918, c. 257, § 464.
St.1919, c. 5.
St.1920, c. 2.

§ 16. Open and gross lewdness and lascivious behavior

A man or woman, married or unmarried, who is guilty of open and gross lewdness and lascivious behavior, shall be punished by imprisonment in the state prison for not more than three years or in jail for not more than two years or by a fine of not more than three hundred dollars.

Amended by St.1987, c. 43.

Historical and Statutory Notes

St.1784, c. 40, § 3.

R.S.1836, c. 130, § 4.
G.S.1860, c. 165, § 6.
P.S.1882, c. 207, § 6.
R.L.1902, c. 212, § 12.

§ 17. Incestuous marriage or sexual activities

Persons within degrees of consanguinity within which marriages are prohibited or declared by law to be incestuous and void, who intermarry or have sexual intercourse with each other, or who engage in sexual activities with each other, including but not limited to, oral or anal intercourse, fellatio, cunnilingus, or other penetration of a part of a person's body, or insertion of an object into the genital or anal opening of another person's body, or the manual manipulation of the genitalia of another person's body, shall be punished by imprisonment in the state prison for not more than 20 years or in the house of correction for not more than 2½ years.

Amended by St.2002, c. 13.

Historical and Statutory Notes

St.1695–6, c. 2, § 2.
R.S.1836, c. 130, § 13.
G.S.1860, c. 165, § 7.
P.S.1882, c. 207, § 7.
R.L.1902, c. 212, § 13.
St.1918, c. 257, § 464.
St.1919, c. 5.
St.1920, c. 2.

§ 18. Fornication

Whoever commits fornication shall be punished by imprisonment for not more than three months or by a fine of not more than thirty dollars.

Historical and Statutory Notes

C.L. c. 54, §§ 4, 5.
St.1692–3, c. 18, § 5.
St.1785, c. 66, § 1.
R.S.1836, c. 130, § 5.
G.S.1860, c. 165, § 8.
P.S.1882, c. 207, § 8.
R.L.1902, c. 212, § 14.

§ 19. Procuring miscarriage

Whoever, with intent to procure the miscarriage of a woman, unlawfully administers to her, or advises or prescribes for her, or causes any poison, drug, medicine or other noxious thing to be taken by her or, with the like intent, unlawfully uses any instrument or other means whatever, or, with like intent, aids or assists therein, shall, if she dies in consequence thereof, be punished by imprisonment in the state prison for not less than five nor more than twenty years; and, if she does not die in consequence thereof, by imprisonment in the state prison for not more than seven years and by a fine of not more than two thousand dollars.

Historical and Statutory Notes

St.1845, c. 27.
G.S.1860, c. 165, § 9.
P.S.1882, c. 207, § 9.
R.L.1902, c. 212, § 15.

§ 20. Advertising relative to miscarriage or prevention of pregnancy

Except as provided in section twenty-one A, whoever knowingly advertises, prints, publishes, distributes or circulates, or knowingly causes to be advertised, printed, published, distributed or circulated, any pamphlet, printed paper, book, newspaper, notice, advertisement or reference containing words or language giving or conveying any notice, hint or reference to any person, or to the name of any person, real or fictitious, from whom, or to any place, house, shop or office where any poison, drug, mixture, preparation, medicine or noxious thing, or any instrument or means whatever, or any advice, direction, information or knowledge may be obtained for the purpose of causing or procuring the miscarriage of a woman pregnant with child or of preventing, or which is represented as intended to prevent, pregnancy shall be punished by imprisonment in the state prison for not more than three years or in jail for not more than two and one half years or by a fine of not more than one thousand dollars.

Amended by St.1966, c. 265, § 2.

Historical and Statutory Notes

St.1847, c. 83.
G.S.1860, c. 165, § 10.
P.S.1882, c. 207, § 10.
R.L.1902, c. 212, § 16.
St.1905, c. 316.
St.1918, c. 257, § 464.
St.1919, c. 5.
St.1920, c. 2.

§ 21. Instruments or other articles for self-abuse, prevention of conception or abortion, in general

Except as provided in section twenty-one A, whoever sells, lends, gives away, exhibits, or offers to sell, lend or give away an instrument or other article intended to be used for self-abuse, or any drug, medicine, instrument or article whatever for the prevention of conception or for causing unlawful abortion, or advertises the same, or writes, prints, or causes to be written or printed a card, circular, book, pamphlet, advertisement or notice of any kind stating when, where, how, of whom or by what means such article can be purchased or obtained, or manufactures or makes any such article shall be punished by imprisonment in the state prison for not more than five years or in jail or the house of correction for not more than two and one half years or by a fine of not less than one hundred nor more than one thousand dollars.

Amended by St.1966, c. 265, § 3.

Historical and Statutory Notes

St.1879, c. 159, § 1.
P.S.1882, c. 207, § 17.
R.L.1902, c. 212, § 26.
St.1918, c. 257, § 464.

St.1919, c. 5.
St.1920, c. 2.

§ 21A. Furnishing drugs, articles or information for prevention of pregnancy or conception

A registered physician may administer to or prescribe for any married person drugs or articles intended for the prevention of pregnancy or conception. A registered pharmacist actually engaged in the business of pharmacy may furnish such drugs or articles to any married person presenting a prescription from a registered physician.

A public health agency, a registered nurse, or a maternity health clinic operated by or in an accredited hospital may furnish information to any married person as to where professional advice regarding such drugs or articles may be lawfully obtained.

This section shall not be construed as affecting the provisions of sections twenty and twenty-one relative to prohibition of advertising of drugs or articles intended for the prevention of pregnancy or conception; nor shall this section be construed so as to permit the sale or dispensing of such drugs or articles by means of any vending machine or similar device.

Added by St.1966, c. 265, § 1.

§ 21B. Privately controlled hospital or health facility; abortion or sterilization procedures; contraceptive devices and family planning services

No privately controlled hospital or other health facility shall be required to admit any patient for the purpose of performing an abortion, performing any sterilization procedure, or receiving contraceptive devices or information.

No privately controlled hospital or other privately controlled health facility shall be required to permit any patient to have an abortion, or any sterilization procedure performed in said hospital or other health facility, or to furnish contraceptive devices or information to such patient, nor shall such a hospital or other health facility be required to furnish any family planning services within or through said hospital or other health facility or to make referrals to any other hospital or health facility for such services when said services or referrals are contrary to the religious or moral principles of said hospital or said health facility as expressed in its charter, by-laws or code of ethics, or vote of its governing body.

Any such hospital or other health facility exercising the rights granted in this section shall not on account of the exercise thereof, be disciplined or discriminated against in any manner or suffer any adverse determination by any person, firm, corporation, or other entity, including but in no way limited to any political subdivision, board, commission, department, authority, or agency of the commonwealth.

Added by St.1973, c. 521, § 2.

§ 22. Concealment of death of child born out of wedlock

A parent who conceals the death of the issue of such parent, which if born alive would be a child born out of wedlock, so that it cannot be ascertained whether it was born alive or, if born alive, whether it was murdered, shall be punished by a fine of not more than one hundred dollars or by imprisonment for not more than one year.

Amended by St.1977, c. 848, § 1; St.1986, c. 334, § 12.

Historical and Statutory Notes

St.1696, c. 11.
St.1784, c. 42, § 2.
R.S.1836, c. 130, § 6.
G.S.1860, c. 165, § 11.
P.S.1882, c. 207, § 11.
R.L.1902, c. 212, § 17.
St.1931, c. 256, § 2.

§ 23. Joinder of charges of murder and offense under Sec. 22

A parent indicted for murder of the infant child born out of wedlock of such parent may also be charged in the same indictment with the crime described in the preceding section, and if acquitted of murder, such parent may be convicted of the concealment.

Amended by St.1977, c. 848, § 1; St.1986, c. 334, § 13.

Historical and Statutory Notes

St.1784, c. 42, § 3.
R.S.1836, c. 130, § 7.
G.S.1860, c. 165, § 12.
P.S.1882, c. 207, § 12.
R.L.1902, c. 212, § 18.
St.1931, c. 256, § 3.

§ 24. Keeping house of ill fame

Whoever keeps a house of ill fame which is resorted to for prostitution or lewdness shall be punished by imprisonment for not more than two years.

Historical and Statutory Notes

C.L. c. 208, § 2.
St.1720–1, c. 7, § 3.
St.1793, c. 59, § 8.
R.S.1836, c. 130, § 8.
St.1849, c. 84.
St.1855, c. 405.
G.S.1860, c. 165, § 13.
P.S.1882, c. 207, § 13.
R.L.1902, c. 212, § 19.

§ 25. Obstructing view of restaurant or tavern patrons; barricaded entrances

Any person owning, managing or controlling a restaurant, tavern or other place in any town, where food or drink is sold to the public to be consumed upon the premises or required to be licensed under chapter one hundred and thirty-eight, and any employee of such person, who provides, maintains, uses or permits the use of a booth, stall or enclosure of any description whatever which is so closed by curtains, screens or other devices that the persons within cannot at any time plainly be seen by other persons in such restaurant, tavern or other place, or in any division thereof, unless the enclosure is approved by the licensing authorities, and any person conducting such an establishment who maintains barred or barricaded entrances or exits thereto or other devices or appliances designed to impede access thereto by police officers, official inspectors and other officers entitled to enter the same, shall be punished by a fine of not less than fifty nor more than five hundred dollars or by imprisonment for not more than six months, or both.

Amended by St.1933, Ex.Sess., c. 376, § 4.

Historical and Statutory Notes

St.1915, c. 180, §§ 1, 2.

§ 26. Resorting to restaurants or taverns for immoral purposes

Whoever, for the purpose of immoral solicitation or immoral bargaining, shall resort to any café, restaurant, tavern, as defined in section one of chapter one hundred and thirty-eight, or other place where food or drink is sold or served to be consumed upon the premises, and whoever shall resort to any such place for the purpose of, in any manner, inducing another person to engage in immoral conduct, and whoever, being in or about any such place, shall engage in any such acts, and any person owning, managing or controlling such place and any employee of such person who induces or knowingly suffers any person to resort to, or be in such place for the purpose of immoral solicitation or immoral bargaining, shall be punished by a fine of not less than twenty-five nor more than five hundred dollars or by imprisonment for not more than one year, or both.

Amended by St.1939, c. 451, § 66; St.1962, c. 224.

Historical and Statutory Notes

St.1915, c. 180, § 3.

§ 27. Record of convictions under Sec. 25 or Sec. 26 sent to licensing officers

The clerk of the court in which any person is convicted of a violation of either of the two preceding sections shall forthwith send a copy of the record of such conviction to the officer or board issuing any license or licenses under which the place where the offence was committed is conducted.

Historical and Statutory Notes

St.1915, c. 180, § 4.

§ 28. Matter harmful to minors, dissemination; possession; defenses

Whoever disseminates to a minor any matter harmful to minors, as defined in section thirty-one, knowing it to be harmful to minors, or has in his possession any such matter with the intent to disseminate the same to minors, shall be punished by imprisonment in the state prison for not more than five years or in a jail or house of correction for not more than two and one-half years, or by a fine of not less than one thousand nor more than ten thousand dollars for the first offense, not less than five thousand nor more than twenty thousand dollars for the second offense, or not less than ten thousand nor more than thirty thousand dollars for the third and subsequent offenses, or by both such fine and imprisonment. A prosecution commenced under this section shall not be continued without a finding nor placed on file. It shall be a defense in any prosecution under this section that the defendant was in a parental or guardianship relationship with the minor. It shall also be a defense in any prosecution under this section if the evidence proves that the defendant was a bona fide school, museum or library, or was acting in the course of his employment as an employee of such organization or of a retail outlet affiliated with and serving the educational purpose of such organization.

Amended by St.1934, c. 231; St.1943, c. 239; St.1945, c. 278, § 1; St.1948, c. 328; St.1959, c. 492, § 1; St.1966, c. 418, § 1; St.1974, c. 430, § 1; St.1982, c. 603, § 2.

Historical and Statutory Notes

St.1711–12, c. 6, § 19.
R.S.1836, c. 130, §§ 10, 12.
G.S.1860, c. 165, §§ 15, 17.
St.1862, c. 168, §§ 1, 3.
St.1880, c. 97.
P.S.1882, c. 207, §§ 15, 16.
St.1890, c. 70.
St.1894, c. 433.
St.1895, c. 162.
R.L.1902, c. 212, § 20.
St.1904, c. 120.
St.1913, c. 259.
St.1918, c. 257, § 450.
St.1919, c. 5.
St.1920, c. 2.
St.1930, c. 162.

§§ 28A, 28B. Repealed, 1974, 430, Sec. 2

Historical and Statutory Notes

See, now, M.G.L.A. c. 272, §§ 28 and 29.

§ 28C. Information or petition against obscene books; order of notice to show cause; notice of order; interlocutory adjudication; defense

Whenever there is reasonable cause to believe that a book which is being disseminated, or is in the possession of any person who intends to disseminate the same, is obscene, the attorney general, or any district attorney within his district, shall bring an information or petition in equity in the superior court directed against said book by name. Upon the filing of such information or petition in equity, a justice of the superior court shall, if, upon a summary examination of the book, he is of opinion that there is reasonable cause to believe that such book is obscene, issue an order of notice, returnable in or within thirty days, directed against such book by name and addressed to all persons interested in the dissemination thereof, to show cause why said book should not be judicially determined to be obscene. Notice of such order shall be given by publication once each week for two successive weeks in a daily newspaper published in the city of Boston and, if such information or petition be filed in any county other than Suffolk county, then by publication also in a daily newspaper published in such other county. A copy of such order of notice shall be sent by registered mail to the publisher of said book, to the person holding the copyrights, and to the author, in case the names of any such persons appear upon said book, fourteen days at least before the return day of such order of notice. After the issuance of an order of notice under the provisions of this section, the court shall, on motion of the attorney general or district attorney, make an interlocutory finding and adjudication that said book is obscene, which finding and adjudication shall be of the same force and effect as the final finding and adjudication provided in section twenty-eight E or section twenty-eight F, but only until such final finding and adjudication is made or until further order of the court. It shall be an affirmative defense under this section if the evidence proves that the defendant was a bona fide school, museum or library, or was acting in the course of his employment as an employee of such organization or of a retail outlet affiliated with and serving the educational purpose of such organization.

Added by St.1945, c. 278, § 1. Amended by St.1974, c. 430, § 3.

§ 28D. Answer to notice; right to jury trial

Any person interested in the dissemination of said book may appear and file an answer on or before the return day named in said notice or within such further time as the court may allow, and may claim a right to trial by jury on the issue whether said book is obscene.

Added by St.1945, c. 278, § 1. Amended by St.1974, c. 430, § 4.

§ 28E. Order of default; adjudication

If no person appears and answers within the time allowed, the court may at once upon motion of the petitioner, or of its own motion, no reason to the contrary appearing, order a general default and if the court finds that the book is obscene, may make an adjudication against the book that the same is obscene.

Added by St.1945, c. 278, § 1. Amended by St.1974, c. 430, § 5.

§ 28F. Hearing; evidence; adjudication

If an appearance is entered and answer filed, the case shall be set down for speedy hearing, but a default and order shall first be entered against all persons who have not appeared and answered, in the manner provided in section twenty-eight E. Such hearing shall be conducted in accordance with the usual course of proceedings in equity including all rights of exception and appeal. At such hearing the court may receive the testimony of experts and may receive evidence as to the literary, artistic, political or scientific character of said book and as to the manner and form of its dissemination. Upon such hearing, the court may make an adjudication in the manner provided in said section twenty-eight E.

Added by St.1945, c. 278, § 1. Amended by St.1974, c. 430, § 6.

§ 28G. Objection that mere judgment sought and no relief claimed on issue of knowledge

An information or petition in equity under the provisions of section twenty-eight C shall not be open to objection on the ground that a mere judgment, order or decree is sought thereby and that no relief is or could be claimed thereunder on the issue of the defendant's knowledge as to the obscenity.

Added by St.1945, c. 278, § 1. Amended by St.1974, c. 430, § 7.

§ 28H. Proceeding under Sec. 28C as evidence in trial under Sec. 29; presumptions as to knowledge

In any trial under section twenty-nine on an indictment found or a complaint made for any offence committed after the filing of a proceeding under section twenty-eight C, the fact of such filing and the action of the court or jury thereon, if any, shall be admissible in evidence. If prior to the said offence a final decree had been entered against the book, the defendant, if the book be obscene, shall be conclusively presumed to have known said book to be obscene, or if said decree had been in favor of the book he shall be conclusively presumed not to have known said book to be obscene, or if no final decree had been entered but a proceeding had been filed prior to said offence, the defendant shall be conclusively presumed to have had knowledge of the contents of said book.

Added by St.1945, c. 278, § 1. Amended by St.1974, c. 430, § 8.

§ 28*I*. Certain procedures as condition precedent to institution of proceedings for dissemination of obscene books

The procedures set forth in sections twenty-eight C, twenty-eight D, twenty-eight E, twenty-eight G and twenty-eight H shall be a condition precedent to the institution of any proceedings pursuant to section twenty-nine or thirty for dissemination of obscene books.

Added by St.1974, c. 430, § 8.

§ 29. Dissemination or possession of obscene matter; punishment; defense

Whoever disseminates any matter which is obscene, knowing it to be obscene, or whoever has in his possession any matter which is obscene, knowing it to be obscene, with the intent to disseminate the same, shall be punished by imprisonment in the state prison for not more than five years or in a jail or house of correction for not more than two and one-half years or by a fine of not less than one thousand nor more than ten thousand dollars for the first offense, not less than five thousand nor more than twenty thousand dollars for the second offense, or not less than ten thousand nor more than thirty thousand dollars for the third and subsequent offenses, or by both such finc and imprisonment. A prosecution commenced under this section shall not be continued without a finding nor placed on file. It shall be a defense under this section if the evidence proves that the defendant was a bona fide school, museum or library, or was acting in the course of his employment as an employee of such organization or of a retail outlet affiliated with and serving the educational purpose of such organization.

Amended by St.1974, c. 430, § 9; St.1982, c. 603, § 3.

Historical and Statutory Notes

St.1908, c. 386.
St.1918, c. 237.

§ 29A. Posing or exhibiting child in state of nudity or sexual conduct; punishment

(a) Whoever, either with knowledge that a person is a child under eighteen years of age or while in possession of such facts that he should have reason to know that such person is a child under eighteen years of age, and with lascivious intent, hires, coerces, solicits or entices, employs, procures, uses, causes, encourages, or knowingly permits such child to pose or be exhibited in a state of nudity, for the purpose of representation or reproduction in any visual material, shall be punished by imprisonment in the state prison for a term of not less than ten nor more than twenty years, or by a fine of not less than ten thousand nor more than fifty thousand dollars, or by both such fine and imprisonment.

(b) Whoever, either with knowledge that a person is a child under eighteen years of age or while in possession of such facts that he should have reason to know that such person is a child under eighteen years of age, hires, coerces, solicits or entices, employs, procures, uses, causes, encourages, or knowingly permits such child to participate or engage in any act that depicts, describes, or represents sexual conduct for the purpose of representation or reproduction in any visual material, or to engage in any live performance involving sexual conduct, shall be punished by imprisonment in the state prison for a term of not less than ten nor more than twenty years, or by a fine of not less than ten thousand nor more than fifty thousand dollars, or by both such fine and imprisonment.

(c) In a prosecution under this section, a minor shall be deemed incapable of consenting to any conduct of the defendant for which said defendant is being prosecuted.

(d) For the purposes of this section, the determination whether the person in any visual material prohibited hereunder is under eighteen years of age may be made by the personal testimony of such person, by the testimony of a person who produced, processed, published, printed or manufactured such visual material that the child therein was known to him to be under eighteen years of age, or by expert medical testimony as to the age of the person based upon the person's physical appearance, by inspection of the visual material, or by any other method authorized by any general or special law or by any applicable rule of evidence.

Added by St.1982, c. 364, § 2. Amended by St.1982, c. 603, § 4; St.1984, c. 189, § 165; St.1987, c. 294, §§ 1, 2; St.1988, c. 226, § 1.

§ 29B. Dissemination of visual material of child in state of nudity or sexual conduct; punishment

(a) Whoever, with lascivious intent, disseminates any visual material that contains a representation or reproduction of any posture or exhibition in a state of nudity involving the use of a child who is under eighteen years of age, knowing the contents of such visual material or having sufficient facts in his possession to have knowledge of the contents thereof, or has in his possession any such visual material knowing the contents or having sufficient facts in his possession to have knowledge of the contents thereof, with the intent to disseminate the same, shall be punished in the state prison for a term of not less than ten nor more than twenty years or by a fine of not less than ten thousand nor more than fifty thousand dollars or three times the monetary value of any economic gain derived from said dissemination, whichever is greater, or by both such fine and imprisonment.

(b) Whoever with lascivious intent disseminates any visual material that contains a representation or reproduction of any act that depicts, describes, or represents sexual conduct participated or engaged in by a child who is under eighteen years of age, knowing the contents of such visual material or having sufficient facts in his possession to have knowledge of the contents thereof, or whoever has in his possession any such visual material knowing the contents or having sufficient facts in his possession to have knowledge of the contents thereof, with the intent to disseminate the same, shall be punished in the state prison for a term of not less than ten nor more than twenty years or by a fine of not less than ten thousand nor more than fifty thousand dollars or three times the monetary value of any economic gain derived from said dissemination, whichever is greater, or by both such fine and imprisonment.

(c) For the purposes of this section, the determination whether the child in any visual material prohibited hereunder is under eighteen years of age may be made by the personal testimony of such child, by the testimony of a person who produced, processed, published, printed or manufactured such visual material that the child therein was known to him to be under eighteen years of age, by testimony of a person who observed the visual material, or by expert medical testimony as to the age of the child based upon the child's physical appearance, by inspection of the visual material, or by any other method authorized by any general or special law or by any applicable rule of evidence.

(d) In a prosecution under this section, a minor shall be deemed incapable of consenting to any conduct of the defendant for which said defendant is being prosecuted.

(e) Pursuant to this section, proof that dissemination of any visual material that contains a representation or reproduction of sexual conduct or of any posture or exhibition in a state of nudity involving the use of a child who is under eighteen years of age was for a bona fide scientific, medical, or educational purpose for a bona fide school, museum, or library may be considered as evidence of a lack of lascivious intent.

Added by St.1977, c. 917, § 2. Renumbered by St.1982, c. 364, § 2. Amended by St.1982, c. 603, § 5; St.1984, c. 189, § 166; St.1988, c. 226, § 2.

§ 29C. Knowing purchase or possession of visual material of child depicted in sexual conduct; punishment

Whoever knowingly purchases or possesses a negative, slide, book, magazine, film, videotape, photograph or other similar visual reproduction, or depiction by computer, of any child whom the person knows or reasonably should know to be under the age of 18 years of age and such child is:

(i) actually or by simulation engaged in any act of sexual intercourse with any person or animal;

(ii) actually or by simulation engaged in any act of sexual contact involving the sex organs of the child and the mouth, anus or sex organs of the child and the sex organs of another person or animal;

(iii) actually or by simulation engaged in any act of masturbation;

(iv) actually or by simulation portrayed as being the object of, or otherwise engaged in, any act of lewd fondling, touching, or caressing involving another person or animal;

(v) actually or by simulation engaged in any act of excretion or urination within a sexual context;

(vi) actually or by simulation portrayed or depicted as bound, fettered, or subject to sadistic, masochistic, or sadomasochistic abuse in any sexual context; or

(vii) depicted or portrayed in any pose, posture or setting involving a lewd exhibition of the unclothed genitals, pubic area, buttocks or, if such person is female, a fully or partially developed breast of the child; with knowledge of the nature or content thereof shall be punished by imprisonment in the state prison for not more than five years or in a jail or house of correction for not more than two and one-half years or by a fine of not less than $1,000 nor more than $10,000, or by both such fine and imprisonment for the first offense, not less than five years in a state prison or by a fine of not less than $5,000 nor more than $20,000, or by both such fine and imprisonment for the second offense, not less than 10 years in a state prison or by a fine of not less than $10,000 nor more than $30,000, or by both such fine and imprisonment for the third and subsequent offenses.

A prosecution commenced under this section shall not be continued without a finding nor placed on file.

The provisions of this section shall not apply to a law enforcement officer, licensed physician, licensed psychologist, attorney or officer of the court who is in possession of such materials in the lawful performance of his official duty. Nor shall the provisions of this section apply to an employee of a bona fide enterprise, the purpose of which enterprise is to filter or otherwise restrict access to such materials, who possesses examples of computer depictions of such material for the purposes of furthering the legitimate goals of such enterprise.

Added by St.1997, c. 181, § 2.

§ 30. Injunctive relief against dissemination of obscene matter; jurisdiction; procedures; appeal

The superior court shall have jurisdiction to enjoin the dissemination of any matter which is obscene. The attorney general or a district attorney within his district may request an injunction against any person, firm, or corporation which disseminates or is about to disseminate any matter which is obscene.

The person, firm, or corporation sought to be enjoined shall be entitled to a trial on the merits within one day after filing of responsive pleadings and a decision shall be rendered by the court within two days of the conclusion of the trial.

A justice of the superior court may issue a preliminary injunction pending the trial on the merits against such person, firm, or corporation which disseminates or is about to disseminate any matter which is obscene.

No preliminary injunction shall be issued without notice to the adverse party.

In any action brought as herein provided the attorney general or a district attorney shall not be required to furnish security before the issuance of any injunction provided for in this section and neither the commonwealth nor any county, shall be liable for costs or for damages sustained by reason of the injunction in cases where judgment is rendered in favor of the person, firm, or corporation sought to be enjoined.

If the court finds that the person, firm, or corporation is disseminating or is about to disseminate any obscene matter, it shall issue a permanent injunction prohibiting the dissemination of that matter. The court's order shall direct the person, firm or corporation to surrender to a sheriff or a police officer the matter found obscene and a sheriff or police officer shall be directed to seize and destroy the same.

Appeals shall be as otherwise provided by law in civil proceedings, but any party or intervenor shall have the right to an expedited appeal to the appeals court.

The procedures set forth in this section are in addition to criminal proceedings initiated under any provisions of the General Laws, and not a condition precedent thereto.

Amended by St.1956, c. 724, § 1; St.1974, c. 430, § 10.

Historical and Statutory Notes

St.1885, c. 305.
R.L.1902, c. 212, § 21.

§§ 30A to 30C. Repealed, 1974, 430, Sec. 11

§ 30D. Dissemination of visual material of child in state of nudity or sexual conduct; injunction; jurisdiction

The superior court shall also have jurisdiction to enjoin the dissemination of any visual material that contains a representation or reproduction of any posture or exhibition in a state of nudity or of any act that depicts, describes, or represents sexual conduct participated or engaged in by a child who is under eighteen years of age. The procedures for issuance of such injunction shall be the same as those provided in section thirty, and are in addition to other criminal proceedings initiated under any provisions of the General Laws, and not a condition precedent thereto.

Added by St.1977, c. 917, § 3.

§ 31. Definitions

As used in sections twenty-eight, twenty-eight C, twenty-eight D, twenty-eight E, twenty-nine, twenty-nine A, twenty-nine B, thirty and thirty D, the following words shall, unless the context requires otherwise, have the following meanings:—

"Disseminate", to import, publish, produce, print, manufacture, distribute, sell, lease, exhibit or display.

"Harmful to minors", matter is harmful to minors if it is obscene or, if taken as a whole, it (1) describes or represents nudity, sexual conduct or sexual excitement, so as to appeal predominantly to the prurient interest of minors; (2) is patently contrary to prevailing standards of adults in the county where the offense was committed as to suitable material for such minors; and (3) lacks serious literary, artistic, political or scientific value for minors.

"Knowing", a general awareness of the character of the matter.

"Lascivious intent", a state of mind in which the sexual gratification or arousal of any person is an objective. For the purposes of prosecution under this chapter, proof of lascivious intent may include, but shall not be limited to, the following:

(1) whether the circumstances include sexual behavior, sexual relations, infamous conduct of a lustful or obscene nature, deviation from accepted customs and manners, or sexually oriented displays;

(2) whether the focal point of a visual depiction is the child's genitalia, pubic area, or breast area of a female child;

(3) whether the setting or pose of a visual depiction is generally associated with sexual activity;

(4) whether the child is depicted in an unnatural pose or inappropriate attire, considering the child's age;

(5) whether the depiction denotes sexual suggestiveness or a willingness to engage in sexual activity;

(6) whether the depiction is of a child engaging in or being engaged in sexual conduct, including, but not limited to, sexual intercourse, unnatural sexual intercourse, bestiality, masturbation, sado-masochistic behavior, or lewd exhibition of the genitals.

"Minor", a person under eighteen years of age.

"Nudity", uncovered or less than opaquely covered human genitals, pubic areas, the human female breast below a point immediately above the top of the areola, or the covered male genitals in a discernibly turgid state. For purposes of this definition, a female breast is considered uncovered if the nipple or areola only are covered.

"Matter", any handwritten or printed material, visual representation, live performance or sound recording including, but not limited to, books, magazines, motion picture films, pamphlets, phonographic records, pictures, photographs, figures, statues, plays, dances, or any electronic communication including, but not limited to, electronic mail, instant messages, text messages, and any other communication created by means of use of the Internet or wireless network, whether by computer, telephone, or any other device or by any transfer of signs, signals, writing, images, sounds, data, or intelligence of any nature transmitted in whole or in part by a wire, radio, electromagnetic, photo-electronic or photo-optical system.

"Performance", any play, dance, exhibit, or such similar activity performed before one or more persons.

"Obscene", matter is obscene if taken as a whole it

(1) appeals to the prurient interest of the average person applying the contemporary standards of the county where the offense was committed;

(2) depicts or describes sexual conduct in a patently offensive way; and

(3) lacks serious literary, artistic, political or scientific value.

"Sexual conduct", human masturbation, sexual intercourse, actual or simulated, normal or perverted, any lewd exhibitions of the genitals, flagellation or torture in the context of a sexual relationship, any lewd touching of the genitals, pubic areas, or buttocks of the human male or female, or the breasts of the female, whether alone or between members of the same or opposite sex or between humans and animals, and any depiction or representation of excretory functions in the context of a sexual relationship. Sexual intercourse is simulated when it depicts explicit sexual intercourse which gives the appearance of the consummation of sexual intercourse, normal or perverted.

"Sexual excitement", the condition of human male or female genitals or the breasts of the female while in a state of sexual stimulation or the sensual experiences of humans engaging in or witnessing sexual conduct or nudity.

"Visual material", any motion picture film, picture, photograph, videotape, book, magazine, pamphlet that contains pictures, photographs or similar visual representations or reproductions, or depiction by computer, telephone or any other device capable of electronic data storage or transmission. Undeveloped photographs, pictures, motion picture films, videotapes and similar visual representations or reproductions may be visual materials notwithstanding that processing, development or similar acts may be required to make the contents thereof apparent.

Amended by St.1967, c. 364, § 1; St.1970, c. 348, § 1; St.1972, c. 802, § 62; St.1974, c. 430, § 12; St.1977, c. 917, §§ 4 to 6; St.1982, c. 364, § 3; St.1982, c. 603, §§ 6, 7; St.1986, c. 557, § 198; St.1988, c. 226, §§ 3 to 8; St.2002, c. 161, §§ 1, 2; St.2010, c. 74, §§ 2, 3, eff. July 11, 2010.

Historical and Statutory Notes

St.1896, c. 339, § 1.
R.L.1902, c. 212, § 22.

§ 32. Motion picture theater managers or operators; applicability of Secs. 28, 29 and 29A

The provisions of sections twenty-eight, twenty-nine and twenty-nine A shall not apply to a manager or a motion picture operator or assistant operator licensed under sections seventy-five and seventy-six, respectively, of chapter one hundred and forty-three, who is employed in a motion picture theatre licensed under section one hundred and eighty-one of chapter one hundred and forty and the provisions of the state building code, in connection with a motion picture show exhibited in said theatre; provided that such manager, operator or assistant operator has no financial interest in the motion picture theatre wherein he is so employed; and provided, further, that such manager has no authority in determining which motion picture films are to be presented in said theatre.

Amended by St.1967, c. 364, § 2; St.1970, c. 348, § 2; St.1972, c. 802, § 63; St.1974, c. 430, § 13; St.1977, c. 917, § 7.

Historical and Statutory Notes

R.L.1902, c. 212, § 23.
St.1910, c. 367.

§ 33. Exhibition of deformities

Whoever exhibits for hire an albino person, a minor or mentally ill person who is deformed or a person who has an appearance of deformity produced by artificial means shall be punished by a fine of not more than five hundred dollars.

Amended by St.1971, c. 55; St.1987, c. 522, § 23.

Historical and Statutory Notes

St.1884, c. 99.
R.L.1902, c. 212, § 24.

§ 34. Crime against nature

Whoever commits the abominable and detestable crime against nature, either with mankind or with a beast, shall be punished by imprisonment in the state prison for not more than twenty years.

Historical and Statutory Notes

B.L. c. 94, §§ 7, 8.
C.L. c. 14, §§ 7, 8.
St.1697, c. 19.
St.1784, c. 46, § 1.
St.1804, c. 133.
R.S.1836, c. 130, § 14.
G.S.1860, c. 165, § 18.
P.S.1882, c. 207, § 18.
R.L.1902, c. 212, § 25.

§ 35. Unnatural and lascivious acts

Whoever commits any unnatural and lascivious act with another person shall be punished by a fine of not less than one hundred nor more than one thousand dollars or by imprisonment in the state prison for not more than five years or in jail or the house of correction for not more than two and one half years.

Historical and Statutory Notes

St.1887, c. 436, § 1.
R.L.1902, c. 212, § 27.
St.1918, c. 257, § 464.
St.1919, c. 5.
St.1920, c. 2.

§ 35A. Unnatural and lascivious acts with child under 16

Whoever commits any unnatural and lascivious act with a child under the age of sixteen shall be punished by a fine of not less than one hundred dollars nor more than one thousand dollars or by imprisonment in the state prison for not more than five years or in jail or the house of correction for not more than two and one half years, and whoever over the age of eighteen commits a second or subsequent such offence shall be sentenced to imprisonment in the state prison for a term of not less than five years.

Added by St.1955, c. 763, § 4. Amended by St.1973, c. 925, § 79.

§ 36. Blasphemy

Whoever wilfully blasphemes the holy name of God by denying, cursing or contumeliously reproaching God, his creation, government or final judging of the world, or by cursing or contumeliously reproaching Jesus Christ or the Holy Ghost, or by cursing or contumeliously reproaching or exposing to contempt and ridicule, the holy word of God contained in the holy scriptures shall be punished by imprisonment in jail for not more than one year or by a fine of not more than three hundred dollars, and may also be bound to good behavior.

Historical and Statutory Notes

B.L. c. 94, § 3.
C.L. c. 14, § 3.
St.1697, c. 20.
St.1782, c. 8.
R.S.1836, c. 130, § 15.
G.S.1860, c. 165, § 19.
P.S.1882, c. 207, § 19.
R.L.1902, c. 212, § 28.

§ 36A. Sporting events; penalty for abuse of participants and officials

Whoever, having arrived at the age of sixteen years, directs any profane, obscene or impure language or slanderous statement at a participant or an official in a sporting event, shall be punished by a fine of not more than fifty dollars.

Added by St.1963, c. 203.

§ 37. Repealed, 1962, 285, Sec. 4

§ 38. Disturbance of assembly for worship

Whoever wilfully interrupts or disturbs an assembly of people met for worship of God shall be punished by imprisonment for not more than one year or by a fine of not more than one thousand dollars.

Amended by St.1970, c. 477.

Historical and Statutory Notes

C.L. c. 250, § 2.
St.1791, c. 58, § 8.
R.S.1836, c. 130, § 17.
G.S.1860, c. 165, § 21.
P.S.1882, c. 207, § 21.
R.L.1902, c. 212, § 30.

§ 39. Selling goods and provisions, caring for horses, gaming, horse racing or exhibits near camp meetings

Whoever, during the time of holding a camp or field meeting for religious purposes, and within one mile of the place thereof, hawks or peddles goods, wares or merchandise, or establishes or maintains a tent, booth or building for vending provisions or refreshments, or furnishes shelter and food for or has the care of horses for pay, without permission from the authorities or officers having the charge or direction of such meeting, or engages in gaming or horse racing, or exhibits or offers to exhibit any show or play, shall forfeit not more than twenty dollars; provided, that the time of holding such meeting shall not exceed thirty consecutive days in any one year; and that a person having a regular, usual and established place of business within such limits need not suspend his business.

Historical and Statutory Notes

St.1838, c. 143.
G.S.1860, c. 165, § 22.
St.1867, c. 59.
St.1878, c. 92.
St.1879, c. 56.
P.S.1882, c. 207, § 22.
R.L.1902, c. 212, § 31.

§ 40. Disturbance of schools or assemblies

Whoever wilfully interrupts or disturbs a school or other assembly of people met for a lawful purpose shall be punished by imprisonment for not more than one month or by a fine of not more than fifty dollars; provided, however, that whoever, within one year after being twice convicted of a violation of this section, again violates the provisions of this section shall be punished by imprisonment for one month, and the sentence imposing such imprisonment shall not be suspended.

Amended by St.1969, c. 463, § 1.

Historical and Statutory Notes

St.1849, c. 59.
G.S.1860, c. 165, § 23.
P.S.1882, c. 207, § 23.
R.L.1902, c. 212, § 32.

§ 40A. Alcoholic beverages; gift, sale, delivery or possession on public school premises

Whoever gives, sells, delivers or has in his possession any alcoholic beverage, except for medicinal purposes, in any public school building, or on any premises used for public school purposes and under the charge of a school committee or other public board or officer, shall be punished by imprisonment for not more than thirty days or by a fine of not more than one hundred dollars, or both; provided, however, that a school committee of a city, town or district may authorize a public or nonprofit organization using a public school building with its permission during non school hours to possess and sell alcoholic beverages therein provided such nonprofit organization is properly licensed under the provisions of section fourteen of chapter one hundred and thirty-eight.

Added by St.1962, c. 317. Amended by St.1978, c. 469.

§ 41. Disturbance of libraries

Whoever wilfully disturbs persons assembled in a public library, or a reading room connected therewith, by making a noise or in any other manner during the time when such library or reading room is open to the public shall be punished as provided in the preceding section.

Historical and Statutory Notes

St.1885, c. 225.
R.L.1902, c. 212, § 33.

§ 42. Disturbance of funerals

Whoever wilfully interrupts or by fast driving or otherwise in any way disturbs a funeral assembly or procession shall be punished as provided in section forty.

Historical and Statutory Notes

St.1851, c. 193.
G.S.1860, c. 165, § 24.
P.S.1882, c. 207, § 24.
R.L.1902, c. 212, § 34.

§ 42A. Disturbance of funeral services

Whoever pickets, loiters or otherwise creates a disturbance within five hundred feet of a funeral home, church or temple or other building where funeral services are being held, shall be punished by a fine of not more than one thousand dollars or by imprisonment for not more than one year in a house of correction, or both.

Added by St.1978, c. 563.

§ 43. Disorderliness in public conveyances; disturbance of travelers

Whoever, in or upon a railroad carriage, steamboat or other public conveyance, is disorderly, or disturbs or annoys travelers in or upon the same by profane, obscene or indecent language, or by indecent behavior, shall be punished as provided in section forty.

Historical and Statutory Notes

St.1883, c. 102.
R.L.1902, c. 212, § 35.
St.1906, c. 463, pt. 3, § 87.

§ 43A. Smoking in public conveyances and transportation terminals

Whoever, in or upon a railroad carriage, steamboat, or other public conveyance, or in a terminal or other facility of the Massachusetts Bay Transportation Authority, smokes or carries an open flame or lighted match, cigar, cigarette, or pipe shall be punished by imprisonment for not more than ten days or by a fine of not more than one hundred dollars, or both such fine and imprisonment.

Added by St.1947, c. 358. Amended by St.1968, c. 310; St.1987, c. 219; St.1993, c. 175, § 2.

§§ 44 to 50. Repealed, 1971, 1076, Sec. 11

§§ 51, 52. Repealed, 1957, 660, Sec. 2

§ 53. Penalty for certain offenses

(a) Common night walkers, common street walkers, both male and female, persons who with offensive and disorderly acts or language accost or annoy persons of the opposite sex, lewd, wanton and lascivious persons in speech or behavior, keepers of noisy and disorderly houses, and persons guilty of indecent exposure shall be punished by imprisonment in a jail or house of correction for not more than 6 months, or by a fine of not more than $200, or by both such fine and imprisonment.

(b) Disorderly persons and disturbers of the peace, for the first offense, shall be punished by a fine of not more than $150. On a second or subsequent offense, such person shall be punished by imprisonment in a jail or house of correction for not more than 6 months, or by a fine of not more than $200, or by both such fine and imprisonment.

Amended by St.1943, c. 377; St.1956, c. 715, § 21; St.1959, c. 304, § 1; St.1973, c. 1073, § 20; St.1983, c. 66, § 1; St.2009, c. 27, § 98, eff. July 1, 2009.

Historical and Statutory Notes

C.L. c. 153, § 1.
St.1699–1700, c. 8, § 2.
St.1769–70, c. 19.
St.1787, c. 54, § 2.
St.1834, c. 151, §§ 2, 3.
R.S.1836, c. 143, §§ 5, 6.
St.1837, c. 157.
St.1837, c. 217.
St.1851, c. 346.
St.1856, c. 186.
G.S.1860, c. 165, §§ 28, 29.
St.1866, c. 235.
St.1874, c. 385, § 21.
St.1876, c. 118.
St.1878, c. 270, § 2.
St.1880, c. 114.
St.1880, c. 257.
P.S.1882, c. 207, §§ 29, 30.
St.1884, c. 258, § 1.
St.1885, c. 365, § 1.
St.1886, c. 323, § 1.
St.1898, c. 443, § 1.
R.L.1902, c. 85, § 30; c. 212, §§ 46, 48.
St.1914, c. 743.
St.1931, c. 239.

§ 53A. Engaging in sexual conduct for a fee; engaging in sexual conduct with child under age 14 for a fee; penalties

(a) Whoever engages, agrees to engage, or offers to engage in sexual conduct with another person in return for a fee, or whoever pays, agrees to pay, or offers to pay another person to engage in sexual conduct, or to agree to engage in sexual conduct with another natural person, shall be punished by imprisonment in the house of correction for not more than 1 year or by a fine of not more than $500 or by both such imprisonment and fine, whether such sexual conduct occurs or not.

(b) Whoever pays, agrees to pay, or offers to pay any person with the intent to engage in sexual conduct with a child under the age of 14, or whoever is paid, agrees to pay, or agrees that a third person be paid in return for aiding a person who intends to engage in sexual conduct with a child under the age of 14, shall be punished by imprisonment in the state prison for not more than 10 years or in the house of correction for not more than 2½ years, whether such sexual conduct occurs or not.

Added by St.1983, c. 66, § 2. Amended by St.2006, c. 363, eff. Feb. 14, 2007.

§ 54. Apprehension for certain offences, without warrant; custody

Whoever is found in a public way or other public place, committing any offence or disorder set forth in sections fifty-three and fifty-three A, may be apprehended by a sheriff, deputy sheriff, constable or police officer or by any other person by the order of a magistrate or any of said officers, without a warrant and be kept in custody for not more than twenty-four hours, Sundays and legal holidays excepted, until he can be taken before a court or trial justice having jurisdiction of such offence.

Amended by St.1985, c. 142.

Historical and Statutory Notes

St.1834, c. 151, § 5.
R.S.1836, c. 143, § 7.
G.S.1860, c. 165, § 33.
P.S.1882, c. 207, § 34.
R.L.1902, c. 212, § 47.
St.1914, c. 654.

§ 55. Repealed, 1928, 155, Sec. 58

§ 56. Subsequent offenses; breach of recognizance on appeal

If a person convicted under section fifty-three appeals from the sentence, the commission of any like offence by him before judgment on the appeal shall be a breach of the condition of the recognizance, if any was taken upon allowing the appeal.

Historical and Statutory Notes

St.1834, c. 151, § 3.
R.S.1836, c. 143, § 8.
G.S.1860, c. 165, § 31.
P.S.1882, c. 207, § 32.
R.L.1902, c. 212, § 50.

§ 57. Discharge upon recognizance; payment of expenses of prosecution

When a person is brought before a magistrate upon a charge of any offence mentioned in sections fifty-three, sixty-six and sixty-eight, such magistrate, or the court before which the case may be carried on appeal, may at any stage of the proceedings direct the defendant or appellant to be discharged, upon his entering into a recognizance, with sufficient sureties, in such sum as the magistrate or court orders, for his good behavior for not less than six months nor more than two years, and paying the expenses of prosecution or such part thereof as the magistrate or court orders.

Historical and Statutory Notes

R.S.1836, c. 143, § 9.
G.S.1860, c. 165, § 32.
St.1866, c. 235, § 5.
P.S.1882, c. 207, § 33.
R.L.1902, c. 212, § 51.

§ 58. Employing or permitting employment of minor under 15 to beg

A parent or other person who employs a minor under fifteen in begging or who, having the care or custody of such minor, permits him to engage in such employment shall be punished by a fine of not more than two hundred dollars or by imprisonment for not more than six months.

Historical and Statutory Notes

St.1887, c. 422.
R.L.1902, c. 212, § 52.

§ 59. Ordinances or regulations relating to streets, reservations, or parkways; alcoholic beverages; profanity; arrest without warrant

Whoever remains in a street or elsewhere in a town in wilful violation of an ordinance or by-law of such town or of any rule or regulation for the government or use of any public reservation, parkway or boulevard made under authority of law by any department, officer or board in charge thereof, whoever is in a street or elsewhere in a town in wilful violation of an ordinance or by-law of such town or of any rule or regulation for the government or use of any public reservation, parkway or boulevard made under authority of law by any department, officer or board in charge thereof, the substance of which is the drinking or possession of alcoholic beverage, and whoever in a street or other public place accosts or addresses another person with profane or obscene language, in wilful violation of an ordinance or by-law of such town, may be arrested without a warrant by an officer authorized to serve criminal process in the place where the offence is committed and kept in custody until he can be taken before a court having jurisdiction of the offence.

Amended by St.1981, c. 629.

Historical and Statutory Notes

St.1878, c. 181.
P.S.1882, c. 207, § 35.
R.L.1902, c. 212, § 53.
St.1906, c. 403.

§ 60. Disposal of rubbish, etc.; refusal to remove; arrest without warrant

Whoever commits a misdemeanor, as defined by a by-law, regulation or ordinance of a town or authority therein, in the presence of a police officer or an officer authorized to serve criminal process, the substance of which misdemeanor is the placing on or in or throwing into a public way, the sidewalk of a public way or a public alley, filth, rubbish or other substance, and, being requested by such officer forthwith to remove it, refuses or neglects so to do, and if the identity of such person is unknown to the officer, may be arrested by such officer and detained in a safe place without a warrant until his identity is ascertained. Reasonable diligence shall be exercised by the arresting officer in ascertaining the identity of the offender and when identified he shall be released from arrest unless a warrant has issued against him.

Historical and Statutory Notes

St.1910, c. 436, § 1.

§ 61. Conviction after discharge from sentence under Sec. 53

Whoever, having been discharged under section one hundred and forty of chapter one hundred and twenty-seven, is afterward convicted of any offence mentioned in section fifty-three committed after the former conviction, either in the same or a different county, may be sentenced to hard labor in the house of correction for not more than one year.

Historical and Statutory Notes

St.1834, c. 151, § 8.
R.S.1836, c. 143, § 13.
G.S.1860, c. 165, § 34.
P.S.1882, c. 207, § 36.
R.L.1902, c. 212, § 54.
St.1931, c. 426, § 47.

§ 62. Third conviction of being a common nightwalker

If a complaint charges a person with being a common nightwalker, and it is proved at the trial that such person has been twice before convicted of the same offence, such person may be sentenced to the house of correction for not more than two and one half years or if a male, to the Massachusetts reformatory, or if a female, to the reformatory for women.

Amended by St.1956, c. 715, § 22.

Historical and Statutory Notes

St.1855, c. 69, § 1.
G.S.1860, c. 165, § 35.
St.1866, c. 198, § 5.
St.1869, c. 258, § 1.
St.1870, c. 19.
St.1870, c. 288, § 1.
P.S.1882, c. 88, § 5; c. 207, § 37.
St.1897, c. 395, § 4.
St.1898, c. 443, § 1.
R.L.1902, c. 85, § 30; c. 212, § 55.
St.1918, c. 257, § 464.
St.1919, c. 5.
St.1920, c. 2.
St.1931, c. 426, § 313.

§ 63. Tramps; begging or riding freight trains as prima facie evidence

Whoever, not being under seventeen, or a person asking charity within his own town, roves about from place to place begging, or living without labor or visible means of support, shall be deemed a tramp. An act of begging or soliciting alms, whether of money, food, lodging or clothing, by a person having no residence in the town within which the act is committed, or the riding upon a freight train of a railroad, whether within or without any car or part thereof, without a permit from the proper officers or employees of such railroad or train, shall be prima facie evidence that such person is a tramp.

Amended by St.1966, c. 343.

Historical and Statutory Notes

St.1880, c. 257, §§ 2, 3, 7.
P.S.1882, c. 207, § 38.
St.1896, c. 385.
R.L.1902, c. 212, § 56.

§ 64. Tramps; punishment; entering buildings; injuries to or threats against persons or property; carrying weapons

A tramp shall be punished by imprisonment in the house of correction for not more than thirty days; and if he enters a dwelling house or other building without the consent of the owner or occupant thereof, or wilfully or maliciously injures or threatens to injure any person therein, or threatens to do any injury to any person, or to the property of another, or is found carrying a firearm or other dangerous weapon, he shall be punished by imprisonment in the house of correction for not less than one nor more than two and one half years, but notwithstanding the foregoing a tramp found carrying a firearm or other dangerous weapon in violation of section ten of chapter two hundred and sixty-nine may be prosecuted and punished thereunder.

Amended by St.1951, c. 119, § 1; St.1956, c. 715, § 23; St.1957, c. 315.

Historical and Statutory Notes

St.1880, c. 257, §§ 1, 4.
P.S.1882, c. 207, §§ 39, 40.
R.L.1902, c. 212, § 57.
St.1918, c. 257, § 464.
St.1919, c. 5.
St.1920, c. 2.
St.1931, c. 426, § 314.

§ 65. Arrest of tramps without warrant; making complaint

A sheriff, deputy sheriff, constable or police officer, upon view or information of an offence described in the two preceding sections, may, without a warrant, arrest the offender, and make complaint against him therefor; and the state police shall make such arrests and complaints. Mayors and selectmen shall appoint special police officers, who shall also make such arrests and complaints in their respective towns.

Historical and Statutory Notes

St.1880, c. 257, §§ 5, 6.
P.S.1882, c. 207, § 41.
R.L.1902, c. 212, § 58.

§ 66. Vagrants

Persons wandering abroad and begging, or who go about from door to door or in public or private ways, areas to which the general public is invited, or in other public places for the purpose of begging or to receive alms, and who are not licensed or who do not come within the description of tramps as contained in section sixty-three, shall be deemed vagrants and may be punished by imprisonment for not more than six months in the house of correction.

Amended by St.1939, c. 451, § 67; St.1951, c. 119, § 2; St.1969, c. 782.

Historical and Statutory Notes

St.1866, c. 235, §§ 1, 3.
P.S.1882, c. 207, § 42.
St.1884, c. 258, § 1.
St.1885, c. 365, § 1.
St.1886, c. 323, § 1.
St.1898, c. 443, § 1.
R.L.1902, c. 212, § 59.

§ 67. Vagrants; arrest without warrant; taking before court; complaint

Sheriffs, deputy sheriffs, constables and police officers, acting on the request of any person or upon their own information or belief, shall without a warrant arrest and carry any vagrant before a district court for the purpose of an examination, and shall make complaint against him.

Amended by St.1959, c. 313, § 12.

Historical and Statutory Notes

St.1866, c. 235, § 2.
P.S.1882, c. 207, § 43.
R.L.1902, c. 212, § 60.

§ 68. Vagabonds

A person known to be a pickpocket, thief or burglar, if acting in a suspicious manner around any steamboat landing, railroad depot, or any electric railway station, or place where electric railway cars stop to allow passengers to enter or leave the cars, banking institution, broker's office, place of public amusement, auction room, store, shop, crowded thoroughfare, car or omnibus, the dwelling place of another, or at any public gathering or assembly, shall be deemed a vagabond, and shall be punished by imprisonment in the house of correction for not less than four nor more than twelve months.

Amended by St.1967, c. 367.

Historical and Statutory Notes

St.1866, c. 235, § 4.
P.S.1882, c. 207, § 44.
R.L.1902, c. 212, § 61.
St.1913, c. 114.

§ 69. Vagabonds; arrest without warrant; taking before court; complaint

Sheriffs, deputy sheriffs, constables and police officers shall take any such vagabond into custody without a warrant and shall, within twenty-four hours after such arrest, Sundays and legal holidays excepted, take him before a district court, and shall make complaint against him.

Amended by St.1959, c. 313, § 13.

Historical and Statutory Notes

St.1866, c. 235, § 4.
P.S.1882, c. 207, § 45.
R.L.1902, c. 212, § 62.

§ 70. Taking dead body on process or execution

A sheriff, deputy sheriff or constable who takes the body of a deceased person on mesne process or execution shall be punished by a fine of not more than five hundred dollars or by imprisonment for not more than six months.

Historical and Statutory Notes

St.1811, c. 102, § 2.
R.S.1836, c. 14, § 81.
G.S.1860, c. 165, § 36.
P.S.1882, c. 207, § 46.
R.L.1902, c. 212, § 63.

§ 71. Disinterring bodies

Whoever, not being lawfully authorized by the proper authorities, wilfully digs up, disinters, removes or conveys away a human body, or the remains thereof, or knowingly aids in such disinterment, removal or conveying away, and whoever is accessory thereto either before or after the fact, shall be punished by imprisonment in the state prison for not more than three years or in jail for not more than two and one-half years or by a fine of not more than four thousand dollars.

Amended by St.1982, c. 169, § 1.

Historical and Statutory Notes

St.1814, c. 175.
St.1830, c. 57, §§ 1, 2.
R.S.1836, c. 130, § 19.
G.S.1860, c. 165, § 37.
St.1879, c. 16.
P.S.1882, c. 207, § 47.
St.1897, c. 395, § 5.
R.L.1902, c. 212, § 64.
St.1918, c. 257, § 464.
St.1919, c. 5.
St.1920, c. 2.
St.1931, c. 426, § 315.

§ 72. Buying, selling or possessing dead bodies

Whoever buys or sells, or has in his possession for the purpose of buying, selling or trafficking in, the dead body of a human being shall be punished by a fine of not less than fifty nor more than one thousand dollars or by imprisonment for not less than three months nor more than two and one half years.

Amended by St.1974, c. 170.

Historical and Statutory Notes

St.1855, c. 323, §§ 2, 3.
G.S.1860, c. 165, § 38.
P.S.1882, c. 207, § 48.
R.L.1902, c. 212, § 65.
St.1918, c. 257, § 464.
St.1919, c. 5.
St.1920, c. 2.

§ 73. Tombs, graves, memorials, trees, plants; injuring, removing

Whoever wilfully destroys, mutilates, defaces, injures or removes a tomb, monument, gravestone, veteran's grave marker or metal plaque, veteran's flag holder that commemorates a particular war, conflict or period of service or flag, or other structure or thing which is placed or designed for a memorial of the dead, or a fence railing, curb or other thing which is intended for the protection or ornament of a structure or thing before mentioned or of an enclosure for the burial of the dead, or wilfully removes, destroys, mutilates, cuts, breaks or injures a tree, shrub or plant placed or being within such enclosure, or wantonly or maliciously disturbs the contents of a tomb or a grave, shall be punished by imprisonment in the state prison for not more than five years or by imprisonment in the jail or house of correction for not more than two and one-half years and by a fine of not more than five thousand dollars.

Amended by St.1958, c. 352; St.1966, c. 312; St.1972, c. 552, § 2; St.1979, c. 220; St.1982, c. 169, § 2; St.2004, c. 117, eff. Aug. 26, 2004.

Historical and Statutory Notes

St.1834, c. 187, § 2.
R.S.1836, c. 130, § 20.
G.S.1860, c. 165, § 39.
St.1879, c. 39.
P.S.1882, c. 207, § 49.
R.L.1902, c. 212, § 66.
St.1918, c. 257, § 464.
St.1919, c. 5.
St.1920, c. 2.

§ 73A. Removal of gravestones and other memorials for repair or reproduction

In any city or town which accepts this section, the provisions of section seventy-three shall not prohibit the removal, in accordance with rules and regulations promulgated by the state secretary, of a gravestone or other structure or thing which is placed or designed as a memorial for the dead, for the purpose of repair or reproduction thereof by community sponsored, educationally oriented, and professionally directed repair teams.

Added by St.1973, c. 448.

§ 74. Desecrating place of burial; use and occupation as evidence of title

Whoever wrongfully, and by any act not included in the preceding section, destroys, injures or removes a building, fence, railing or other thing lawfully erected in or around a place of burial or cemetery, or a tree, shrub or plant within its limits, or wrongfully injures a walk or path, or places rubbish or offensive matter or commits a nuisance therein, or in any way desecrates or disfigures the same, shall forfeit not less than five nor more than one hundred dollars. Upon the trial of a complaint hereunder, use and occupation for the purposes of burial shall be sufficient evidence of title.

Historical and Statutory Notes

St.1841, c. 114, § 6.
St.1855, c. 257, § 8.
G.S.1860, c. 28, § 12.
P.S.1882, c. 207, § 50.
R.L.1902, c. 212, § 67.

§ 75. Removal of flowers, flags or memorial tokens from burial lot

Whoever, without authority, removes flowers, flags or memorial tokens from any grave, tomb, monument or burial lot in any cemetery or other place of burial shall be punished by a fine of not more than one thousand dollars or by imprisonment for not more than six months.

Amended by St.1971, c. 407; St.1982, c. 169, § 3.

Historical and Statutory Notes

St.1888, c. 395.
R.L.1902, c. 212, § 68.

§ 76. Ways, railroads, canals or public easements through burial grounds

Whoever lays out, opens, or makes a highway or town way, or constructs a railroad or canal, or any other thing in the nature of a public easement, over, through, in or upon any part of an enclosure, which is the property of a city, town, parish, religious society or of private proprietors and is used or appropriated for the burial of the dead, unless authority for that purpose is specially granted by law, or unless the consent of such city, town, parish, religious society or proprietors, respectively, is first obtained, shall be punished by a fine of not more than two thousand dollars or by imprisonment for not more than one year.

Historical and Statutory Notes

St.1834, c. 187, § 1.
R.S.1836, c. 24, §§ 59, 60; c. 30, § 21.
G.S.1860, c. 165, § 40.
P.S.1882, c. 207, § 51.
R.L.1902, c. 212, § 69.

§ 77. Cruelty to animals

Whoever overdrives, overloads, drives when overloaded, overworks, tortures, torments, deprives of necessary sustenance, cruelly beats, mutilates or kills an animal, or causes or procures an animal to be overdriven, overloaded, driven when overloaded, overworked, tortured, tormented, deprived of necessary sustenance, cruelly beaten, mutilated or killed; and whoever uses in a cruel or inhuman manner in a race, game, or contest, or in training therefor, as lure or bait a live animal, except an animal if used as lure or bait in fishing; and whoever, having the charge or custody of an animal, either as owner or otherwise, inflicts unnecessary cruelty upon it, or unnecessarily fails to provide it with proper food, drink, shelter, sanitary environment, or protection from the weather, and whoever, as owner, possessor, or person having the charge or custody of an animal, cruelly drives or works it when unfit for labor, or willfully abandons it, or carries it or causes it to be carried in or upon a vehicle, or otherwise, in an unnecessarily cruel or inhuman manner or in a way and manner which might endanger the animal carried thereon, or knowingly and willfully authorizes or permits it to be subjected to unnecessary torture, suffering or cruelty of any kind shall be punished by imprisonment in the state prison for not more than 5 years or imprisonment in the house of correction for not more than 2½ years or by a fine of not more than $2,500, or by both such fine and imprisonment.

In addition to any other penalty provided by law, upon conviction for any violation of this section or of sections seventy-seven A, seventy-eight, seventy-eight A, seventy-nine A, seventy-nine B, eighty A, eighty B, eighty C, eighty D, eighty F, eighty-six, eighty-six A, eighty-six B or ninety-four the defendant shall forfeit to the custody of any society, incorporated under the laws of the commonwealth for the prevention of cruelty to animals or for the care and protection of homeless or suffering animals, the animal whose treatment was the basis of such conviction.

Amended by St.1968, c. 59; St.1972, c. 46; St.1977, c. 679; St.1977, c. 921, § 2; St.1984, c. 50; St.1986, c. 337; St.1989, c. 534; St.2004, c. 319, § 4, eff. Nov. 17, 2004; St.2006, c. 434, § 1, eff. April 3, 2007.

Historical and Statutory Notes

R.S.1836, c. 130, § 22.
St.1859, c. 96.
G.S.1860, c. 165, § 41.
St.1868, c. 212, §§ 1 to 4.
St.1869, c. 344, §§ 1, 2.
P.S.1882, c. 207, §§ 52, 53.
R.L.1902, c. 212, § 70.

§ 77A. Willfully injuring police dogs and horses

Whoever willfully tortures, torments, beats, kicks, strikes, mutilates, injures, disables or otherwise mistreats, a dog or horse owned by a police department or police agency of the commonwealth or any of its political subdivisions or whoever, willfully by any action whatsoever, interferes with the lawful performance of such dog or horse shall be punished by a fine of not less than one hundred dollars and not more than five hundred dollars or by imprisonment for not more than two and one-half years or both. Persons violating this section may be arrested without a warrant by any officer qualified to serve criminal process provided said offense is committed in his presence.

Added by St.1978, c. 287.

§ 77B. Exhibition of wild animals

No person shall exhibit or sponsor an exhibition of any wild animal for the purpose of attracting trade at or for any place of amusement, recreation or entertainment. This section shall not be deemed to prevent the exhibition of any wild animal in a zoological garden or in connection with any theatrical exhibition or circus or by any educational institution or wild animal farm, whether on or off the premises of such educational institution or wild animal farm. Whoever violates the provisions of this section shall be punished by a fine of not more than two hundred dollars or by imprisonment for not more than thirty days.

Added by St.1986, c. 416. Amended by St.1989, c. 253.

§ 78. Selling, leading, or using horses not fit for work; forfeiture of auctioneer's license

No person holding an auctioneer's license shall receive or offer for sale or sell at public auction, nor shall any person sell at private sale, or lead, ride or drive on any public way, for any purpose except that of conveying the horse to a proper place for its humane keeping or killing, or for medical or surgical treatment, any horse which, by reason of debility, disease or lameness, or for other cause, could not be worked in the commonwealth without violating the laws against cruelty to animals. This section shall not prohibit the purchase of horses by humane societies incorporated under the laws of the commonwealth for the purpose of humanely killing the same. Violation of this section shall be punished by a fine of not less than five nor more than one hundred dollars or by imprisonment for not more than six months. If a licensed auctioneer violates this section, he shall also forfeit his license.

Historical and Statutory Notes

St.1906, c. 185.
St.1913, c. 281.

§ 78A. Sale of foals under five months; penalty

No person shall sell, offer for sale or otherwise dispose of any foal under five months of age other than for the purpose of immediate slaughter or humane killing unless such foal is accompanied by its dam. Violation of this section shall be punished by a fine of not more than one hundred dollars or by imprisonment for not more than six months.

Added by St.1969, c. 223.

§ 79. Corporation's responsibility under Sec. 77 or Sec. 78

A corporation violating either of the two preceding sections [1] shall be punished by a fine as therein provided, and shall be responsible for the knowledge and acts of its agents and servants relative to animals transported, owned or used by it or in its custody.

[1] Sections 77 and 78 of this chapter.

Historical and Statutory Notes

St.1868, c. 212, § 7.
St.1869, c. 344, § 6.
P.S.1882, c. 207, § 54.
R.L.1902, c. 212, § 71.

§ 79A. Cutting bones or muscles to dock or set tail of horse; wound as evidence

Whoever cuts the bone of the tail of a horse for the purpose of docking the tail, or whoever causes or knowingly permits the same to be done upon premises of which he is the owner, lessee, proprietor or user, or whoever assists in or is present at such cutting, shall be punished by imprisonment for not more than one year or by a fine of not less than one hundred nor more than three hundred dollars; and whoever cuts the muscles or tendons of the tail of a horse for the purpose of setting up the tail, or whoever causes or knowingly permits the same to be done upon premises of which he is the owner, lessee, proprietor or user, or whoever assists in or is present at such cutting, shall be punished by a fine of not more than two hundred and fifty dollars. If a horse is found with the bone of its tail cut as aforesaid or with the muscles or tendons of its tail cut as aforesaid, and with the wound resulting from such cutting unhealed, upon the premises or in the charge and custody of any person, such fact shall be prima facie evidence of a violation of this section by the owner or user of such premises or the person having such charge or custody, respectively.

Added by St.1934, c. 234, § 1.

§ 79B. Exhibiting horse with tail cut under Sec. 79A; affidavit as to cutting in state where not prohibited; inspection

Whoever shows or exhibits at any horse show or exhibition in the commonwealth a horse with its tail cut in either manner prohibited in section seventy-nine A shall be punished by a fine of not more than two hundred and fifty dollars; provided, that this section shall not apply to the showing or exhibiting at such a show or exhibition of a horse with its tail cut in either manner prohibited by section seventy-nine A, if the owner of such horse furnishes to the manager or other official having charge of the horse show or exhibition at which such horse is shown or exhibited an affidavit by the owner, in a form approved by the director of the division of animal health of the department of food and agriculture, that the tail of such horse was so cut in a state wherein such cutting was not then specifically prohibited by the laws thereof and while the horse was actually owned by a legal resident of such state. Said affidavit shall state the year of such cutting, the name of the state wherein the cutting was done, and the sex and age of the horse, shall describe the markings of the horse, if any, and shall be subject to inspection by any officer or agent mentioned in section eighty-four.

Added by St.1934, c. 234, § 1. Amended by St.1946, c. 131; St.1975, c. 706, § 301.

§ 80. Repealed, 1934, 234, Sec. 1

§ 80½. Devocalization of dogs or cats; definitions; penalty; exceptions; records

(a) For the purposes of this section, the following words shall have the following meanings:—

"Board", the board of registration in veterinary medicine.

"Devocalization", a procedure on the larynx or vocal cords of an animal which causes the reduction or elimination of vocal sounds produced by that animal.

(b) Whoever performs, or causes to be performed, the surgical devocalization of a dog or cat shall be punished by imprisonment in the state prison for not more than 5 years or imprisonment in a house of correction for not more than 2½ years, or by a fine of not more than $2,500 or by both such fine and imprisonment. In addition to this penalty, the court may order that any person who violates this section shall successfully complete a course of instruction relative to the humane treatment of animals or be barred from owning or keeping a dog or cat or sharing a residence with another who owns or keeps a dog or cat for a period of time as determined by said court.

(c) Subsection (b) shall not apply if:

(1) the person performing such devocalization is licensed under section 55 of chapter 112; and

(2) surgical devocalization of a dog or cat is medically necessary to treat or relieve an illness, disease or injury or to correct a congenital abnormality that is causing or may cause the animal physical pain or harm; or

(3) the person who causes a devocalization procedure to be performed is relying upon the opinion of a person licensed under section 55 of chapter 112 that surgical devocalization of the dog or cat is medically necessary to treat or relieve an illness, disease or injury or to correct a congenital abnormality that is causing or may cause the animal physical pain or harm.

(d) A veterinarian who performs a surgical devocalization procedure on a dog or cat shall keep a record of the procedure for a period of 4 years after the last contact with the animal. This record shall include: the name and address of the animal's owner; the name and address of the person from whom payment is received for the procedure; a description of the animal, including its name, species, breed, date of birth, sex, color, markings and current weight; the license number and municipality that issued the license for the animal; the date and time of the procedure; the reason the procedure was performed; and any diagnostic opinion, analysis or test results to support the diagnosis. These records shall be subject to audit by the board.

Any person who performs a devocalization procedure on a dog or cat shall report the number of all such procedures to the board annually on or before March 30. The board shall maintain all notices received under this subsection for 4 years from the date of receipt.

Records maintained under this subsection shall not be considered a public record, as defined in clause twenty-sixth of section 7 of chapter 4 or section 10 of chapter 66, and these records shall not be publicly disseminated.

(e) The board shall, annually on or before March 1, report to the joint committee on the environment, natural resources and agriculture the number of animals that were the subject of devocalization notices received under subsection (d).

(f) Whoever being licensed under section 55 of chapter 112 violates any provision of this section shall be subject to the suspension or revocation of such license under section 59 of said chapter 112 and 256 CMR 7.00.

Added by St.2010, c. 82, § 3, eff. July 21, 2010.

§ 80A. Cropping or cutting off ear of dog; wound as prima facie evidence

Whoever, not being a veterinarian duly registered under chapter one hundred and twelve, crops or cuts off the whole or any part of the ear of a dog shall be punished by a fine of not more than two hundred and fifty dollars. If a dog with an ear cropped or cut off in whole or in part and with the wound resulting therefrom unhealed is found confined upon the premises or in the charge or custody of any person other than such veterinarian, or a dog officer of a city or town duly appointed under section one hundred and fifty-one of chapter one hundred and forty, such fact shall be prima facie evidence of a violation of this section by the person in control of such premises or the person having such charge or custody.

Amended by St.1962, c. 106.

Historical and Statutory Notes

St.1928, c. 347, § 1.

§ 80B. Exhibiting dogs with ears cropped or cut off

Whoever shows or exhibits or procures to be shown or exhibited at any dog show or exhibition in the commonwealth a dog with an ear or ears cropped or cut off, except when and as certified to be reasonably necessary by a veterinarian duly registered under the laws of the state of his residence, shall be punished by a fine of not more than two hundred and fifty dollars.

Historical and Statutory Notes

St.1928, c. 347, § 1.

§ 80C. Taking cat, dog or bird to exhibit it, subject it to experimentation or mutilation, or to sell it for such purposes; application of law

Whoever, without the consent of the owner, takes a cat, dog or bird, with intent to exhibit or cause it to be exhibited or to subject it or cause it to be subjected to experimentation or mutilation while alive, or with intent to sell it or cause it to be sold for the purpose of being exhibited or subjected to experimentation or mutilation as aforesaid, shall be punished by a fine of not less than one hundred dollars nor more than the maximum fine permitted by law for the larceny of an article of the same value as such cat, dog or bird. This section shall not apply to an institution acquiring a cat, dog or bird under the provisions of chapter forty-nine A.

Added by St.1945, c. 272. Amended by St.1957, c. 298, § 6.

§ 80D. Living rabbits, baby chickens, ducklings or other fowl; sale, barter or gift

No person shall sell, offer for sale, barter or give away as premiums living baby chickens, ducklings or other fowl under two months of age.

No person shall sell, offer for sale, barter, display or give away living rabbits, chickens, ducklings or other fowl which have been dyed, colored or otherwise treated so as to impart to them an artificial color.

Nothing in this section shall be construed to prohibit the sale or display of baby chickens, ducklings or other fowl under two months of age by breeders or stores engaged in the business of selling for purposes of commercial breeding and raising; provided, however, that prior to May first in any year, such ducklings may be sold or purchased only in quantities of twenty-four or more.

This section shall not prohibit, however, the sale or donation of such chickens, ducklings or fowl to schools for use in classroom instruction.

Whoever violates the provisions of this section shall be punished by a fine of not more than one hundred dollars.

Added by St.1947, c. 168. Amended by St.1973, c. 88; St.1981, c. 286; St.1986, c. 175.

§ 80E. Use of decompression chambers for putting animals to death

Whoever puts any animal to death by the use of a decompression chamber shall be punished by a fine of not less than one hundred dollars.

Added by St.1976, c. 139, § 2. Amended by St.1976, c. 299, § 2.

§ 80F. Giving away live animals as prize or award

No person shall offer or give away any live animal as a prize or an award in a game, contest or tournament involving skill or chance. The provisions of this section shall not apply to awards made to persons participating in programs relating to animal husbandry.

Whoever violates the provisions of this section shall be punished by a fine of not more than one hundred dollars.

Added by St.1977, c. 112.

§ 80G. Experiments on vertebrates; vivisection, dissection of animals; care

No school principal, administrator or teacher shall allow any live vertebrate to be used in any elementary or high school under state control or supported wholly or partly by public money of the state as part of a scientific experiment or for any other purpose in which said vertebrates are experimentally medicated or drugged in a manner to cause painful reactions or to induce painful or lethal pathological conditions, or in which said vertebrates are injured through any other type of treatment, experiment or procedure including but not limited to anesthetization or electric shock, or where the normal health of said animal is interfered with or where pain or distress is caused.

No person shall, in the presence of a pupil in any elementary or high school under state control or supported wholly or partly by public money of the state, practice vivisection, or exhibit a vivisected animal. Dissection of dead animals or any portions thereof in such schools shall be confined to the class room and to the presence of pupils engaged in the study to be promoted thereby, and shall in no case be for the purpose of exhibition.

Live animals used as class pets or for purposes not prohibited in paragraphs one and two hereof in such schools shall be housed or cared for in a safe and humane manner. Said animals shall not remain in school over periods when such schools are not in session, unless adequate care is provided at all times.

The provisions of the preceding three paragraphs shall also apply to any activity associated with or sponsored by the school.

Whoever violates the provisions of this section shall be punished by a fine of not more than one hundred dollars.

Added by St.1979, c. 439, § 2.

§ 80H. Motor vehicles; striking, injuring or killing dogs or cats

The operator of a motor vehicle that strikes and injures or kills a dog or cat shall forthwith report such an accident to the owner or custodian of said dog or cat or to a police officer in the town wherein such accident has occurred. A violation of this section shall be punished by a fine of not more than fifty dollars.

Added by St.1979, c. 426. Renumbered by St.1980, c. 261, § 28.

§ 80*I*. Leasing or renting dogs; penalties

(a) As used in this section, the following words shall have the following meanings unless the context clearly requires otherwise:—

"Assistance and service dog", a canine specifically trained to help persons with disabilities or a canine trained to help a person with a disability in life; provided, however, that "assistance and service dog" shall also include a canine trained for search and rescue and a medical response dog.

"Canine foster care", an organization that places canines in a temporary home while awaiting pet adoption.

"Earth dog", a canine breed used as a hunting dog to track game above and below ground.

"Farm dog", a canine that works on a farm to assist humans or other animals.

"Pet adoption", the permanent ownership of and responsibility for a pet that a previous owner has abandoned or otherwise abdicated its responsibility.

"Renting and leasing", the practice of renting a dog for a fee or a cost which will knowingly result in a temporary possession of the animal by another party.

"Therapy dog", a canine that is used under the ownership and care of its handler that visits people for educational, medical or mental purposes.

(b) No person shall engage in the business of leasing or renting a dog. A dog held for such leasing or renting may be seized or impounded by an organization or agent thereof that is authorized to seize or impound animals under the General Laws. A violation of this section shall be punished by a fine of not less than $100 for the first violation, not less than $500 for the second violation and $1,000 for subsequent violations. Fines may be levied on both the business that is leasing a dog and the person that has entered into a rental agreement. Nothing in this section shall prohibit service animal businesses or organizations, pet adoption and foster care services, and working animals for the following purposes including, but not limited to: service animal businesses or organizations, pet adoption and foster care services, farming and agriculture, working dog activities, dogs working in entertainment and shows which are authorized to do so under the General Laws, dogs participating in performance sports or activities including, but not limited to, sporting, hunting, earth dog and racing dog activities and people engaged in breeding, training and showing dog, and dogs used for medical or scientific purposes so long as such use is lawful. This section shall not prohibit a pet store, kennel, pet adoption service or other entity authorized to sell pets under the General Laws for a fee or a cost from taking back a pet that it may have sold if the owner is unable to keep or handle that pet.

Added by St.2008, c. 253, eff. Nov. 3, 2008.

§ 81. Rest, water and feed for transported animals; lien; liability for detention

Railroad corporations shall not permit animals carried or transported by them to be confined in cars longer than twenty-eight consecutive hours without unloading them for at least five consecutive hours for rest, water and feeding, unless prevented by storm or accident. In estimating such confinement, the time during which the animals have been confined without such rest on connecting roads from which they are received shall be included. Animals so unloaded shall during such rest be properly fed, watered and sheltered by the owner or person having the custody of them, or, in case of his default, by the railroad corporation transporting them, at the expense of said owner or person in custody thereof. In such case the corporation shall have a lien upon such animals for food, care and custody furnished, and shall not be liable for such detention. A corporation, owner or custodian of such animals failing to comply with this section shall be punished by a fine of not less than one hundred nor more than five hundred dollars. This section shall not apply to animals carried in cars in which they can and do have proper food, water, space and opportunity for rest.

Historical and Statutory Notes

St.1868, c. 212, § 5.
St.1869, c. 344, § 3.
St.1874, c. 372, § 142.
P.S.1882, c. 207, § 55.
R.L.1902, c. 212, § 73.

§ 82. Arrest without warrant for violation of Sec. 77 or 81; notice; care of animals; lien

A person found violating any provision of section seventy-seven or eighty-one may be arrested and held without a warrant as provided in section fifty-four; the person making an arrest with or without a warrant shall use reasonable diligence to give notice thereof to the owner of animals found in the charge or custody of the person arrested, shall properly care and provide for such animals until the owner thereof takes charge of them, not, however, exceeding sixty days from the date of said notice, and shall have a lien on said animals for the expense of such care and provision.

Historical and Statutory Notes

St.1869, c. 344, § 4.
P.S.1882, c. 207, § 56.
R.L.1902, c. 212, § 74.

§ 83. Complaint, warrant and search relative to cruelty to animals

If complaint is made to a court or magistrate authorized to issue warrants in criminal cases that the complainant has reasonable cause to believe that the laws relative to cruelty to animals have been or are violated in any particular building or place, such court or magistrate, if satisfied that there is reasonable cause for such belief, shall issue a search warrant authorizing any sheriff, deputy sheriff, constable or police officer to search such building or place; but no such search shall be made after sunset, unless specially authorized by the magistrate upon satisfactory cause shown.

Historical and Statutory Notes

St.1869, c. 344, § 5.
P.S.1882, c. 207, § 57.
R.L.1902, c. 212, § 75.

§ 84. Prosecutions under Secs. 77 to 81

Sheriffs, deputy sheriffs, constables and police officers shall prosecute all violations of sections seventy-seven to eighty-one, inclusive, which come to their notice.

Amended by St.1951, c. 34, § 1.

Historical and Statutory Notes

St.1868, c. 212, § 8.
St.1869, c. 344, § 7.
P.S.1882, c. 207, § 58.

St.1891, c. 304.
R.L.1902, c. 212, § 76.

§ 85. Repealed, 1951, 34, Sec. 2

§ 85A. Injuring, taking away or harboring domesticated animals or birds; removal of dog license tag, collar or harness; imitation tag

Whoever with wrongful intent kills, maims, entices or carries away a dog or other domesticated animal or bird shall be liable in tort to its owner for three times its value. Any person who removes from the dog of another its license tag, collar or harness, or who, without the authorization of the owner or keeper, holds or harbors a dog or other domesticated animal of another, or who holds or harbors a lost or strayed dog or other domesticated animal for more than forty-eight hours after such animal comes into his possession without reporting or taking it to the police station or dog officer nearest to the place where it was found and informing the police officer or dog officer in charge where such dog or other animal was found, the name, color, age, size and pedigree, as fully as possible, of such animal and the person's own name and address, or who shall cause a dog to wear an imitation or counterfeit of the official tag prescribed by section one hundred and thirty-seven, one hundred and thirty-seven A or one hundred and thirty-seven B of chapter one hundred and forty, shall be punished by a fine of not more than one hundred dollars.

Added by St.1945, c. 276, § 1. Amended by St.1951, c. 185.

§ 85B. Assistance animals stolen or attacked; actions for economic and non-economic damages

(a) A physically impaired person who uses an assistance animal or the owner of the assistance animal, may bring an action for economic and non-economic damages against a person who steals or attacks the assistance animal. The action authorized by this subsection may be brought by the physically impaired person or owner notwithstanding that the assistance animal was in the custody or under the supervision of another person when the theft or attack occurred. If any other non-assistance animal should attack an assistance animal, the owner of the assistance animal may seek compensation from the owner or custodian of the non-assistance animal found to have caused harm to the assistance animal.

(b) If the theft or attack of an assistance animal as described in subsection (a) results in the death of the animal or the animal is not returned or if injuries sustained prevent the assistance animal from returning to service, the measure of economic damages shall include, but are not limited to, the veterinary medical expenses and the replacement cost of an equally trained assistance animal, without any differentiation for the age or the experience of the animal.

(c) A cause of action shall not arise under this section if the physically impaired individual, owner or the individual having custody or supervision of the assistance animal was engaged in the commission of a crime at the time of injury sustained by the assistance animal.

Added by St.2004, c. 104, eff. Aug. 18, 2004.

§ 86. Stabling horses or mules on second or higher floors, in places other than cities

No person shall stable a horse or mule on the second or any higher floor of any building, unless there are two means of exit therefrom, at opposite ends of the building, to the main or street floor, unless such building is equipped with an automatic sprinkler system. This section shall not apply to cities.

Historical and Statutory Notes

St.1916, c. 158, §§ 1 to 3.
St.1921, c. 109.
St.1924, c. 478, § 1.

§ 86A. Stabling horses and mules above first floor; exceeding six; fire exits

No person shall stable a horse or mule above the first or ground floor of any building not equipped with an automatic sprinkler system, or horses or mules exceeding six in all on the first or ground floor of any building not so equipped, unless there are two unobstructed means of exit from each floor whereon it or they are stabled, as far apart as practicable and so constructed as to grade that the said animal or animals can quickly and safely leave the building in case of fire and approved as to situation, arrangement and utility by the chief of the fire department. The person in charge of horses and mules stabled in any building not equipped with such a system and requiring two exits as aforesaid shall cause each such animal to use each such exit at least once a week. This and the four following sections shall apply only to cities.

Historical and Statutory Notes

St.1924, c. 478, § 2.

§ 86B. Stabling horses or mules exceeding fifteen

No person shall stable horses or mules exceeding fifteen in all at any one time in a building not equipped with an automatic sprinkler system unless a watchman is employed constantly on the premises to guard against fire.

Historical and Statutory Notes

St.1924, c. 478, § 2.

§ 86C. Smoking in buildings used for stabling horses or mules

No person shall have a lighted cigarette, cigar or pipe in his possession in any building in which by the provisions of section eighty-six A two unobstructed means of exit are required or in which by the provisions of section eighty-six B the employment of a watchman is required, except in a room in said building made fire-resisting.

Historical and Statutory Notes

St.1924, c. 478, § 2.

§ 86D. Pails of water and sand in buildings used for stables

On every floor of a building not equipped with an automatic sprinkler system, where horses or mules are stabled, there shall be kept in accessible locations and filled at all times, four pails of water and one pail of sand, for each one thousand square feet of floor space, to be used for no other purpose than extinguishing fires and to be so marked.

Historical and Statutory Notes

St.1924, c. 478, § 2.

§ 86E. Entry upon premises to enforce Secs. 86A to 86D; orders

The chief of the fire department or any person designated by him may, at all reasonable hours, enter into buildings within their jurisdiction where horses or mules are stabled, or upon premises adjacent thereto, for the purpose of enforcing sections eighty-six A to eighty-six D, inclusive, and if any such official or person so authorized finds the existence of conditions likely to cause a fire in such buildings or on such premises, he shall order such conditions to be remedied. Such order shall be served by delivering the same in hand or by posting the same in a conspicuous place on the building or premises affected thereby.

Historical and Statutory Notes

St.1924, c. 478, § 2.
St.1930, c. 399, § 4.

§ 86F. Violation of Secs. 86 to 86D; refusal or neglect to comply with Sec. 86E orders

Whoever violates any provision of sections eighty-six to eighty-six D, inclusive, shall be punished by a fine of not more than two hundred dollars or by imprisonment for not more than one month, or both. Whoever refuses or unreasonably neglects to comply with any order issued under section eighty-six E shall be punished by a fine of not more than ten dollars for each day during which such refusal or neglect continues after service of said order.

Historical and Statutory Notes

St.1924, c. 478, § 2.

§ 87. Keeping or using birds to be shot at; shooting them; permitting premises to be used for shooting

Whoever keeps or uses any live bird, to be shot at either for amusement or as a test of skill in marksmanship, or shoots at a bird kept or used as aforesaid, or is a party to such shooting, or lets any building, room, field or premises, or knowingly permits the use thereof, for the purpose of such shooting, shall be punished by a fine of not more than fifty dollars or by imprisonment for not more than one month, or both. Nothing herein contained shall apply to the shooting of wild game.

Historical and Statutory Notes

St.1879, c. 187.
P.S.1882, c. 207, § 59.
R.L.1902, c. 212, § 78.

§ 88. Complaints and warrants relative to fighting animals; searches; arrests

If complaint is made to a court or magistrate authorized to issue warrants in criminal cases that the complainant has reasonable cause to believe that preparations are being made for an exhibition of the fighting of birds, dogs or other animals, or that such exhibition is in progress, or that birds, dogs or other animals are kept, owned, possessed, trained, bred, loaned, sold, exported or otherwise transferred in violation of section 94 at any place or in any building or tenement, such court or magistrate, if satisfied that there is reasonable cause for such belief, shall issue a search warrant authorizing any sheriff, deputy sheriff, constable or police officer, or special police officer duly appointed by the colonel of the state police at the request of the Massachusetts Society for the Prevention of Cruelty to Animals or at the request of the Animal Rescue League of Boston, to search such place, building or tenement at any hour of the day or night and take possession of all such animals and all paraphernalia, implements, equipment or other property used or employed, or intended to be used or employed, in violation of section 94 there found, and arrest all persons there present.

Amended by St.1988, c. 178; St.1996, c. 151, § 495; St.2006, c. 434, §§ 2 to 4, eff. April 3, 2007.

Historical and Statutory Notes

St.1876, c. 85, § 1.
P.S.1882, c. 207, § 60.
R.L.1902, c. 212, § 79.
St.1918, c. 99, § 1.
St.1926, c. 76, § 1.

§ 89. Exhibition place of fighting animals; entry without warrant; arrests; seizure of animals

Any officer authorized to serve criminal process, or any special police officer duly appointed by the colonel of the state police at the request of the Massachusetts Society for the Prevention of Cruelty to Animals, or any municipal officer involved with animal control may, without a warrant, enter any place or building in which there is an exhibition of any fighting birds, dogs or other animals, preparations are being made for such an exhibition, or birds, dogs or other animals are owned, possessed, kept, trained, bred, loaned, sold, exported or otherwise transferred in violation of section 94. Any such officer may arrest all persons there present and take possession of and remove from the place of seizure such animals there found in violation of said section 94, and hold the same in custody subject to the order of court as hereinafter provided.

Amended by St.1982, c. 230; St.1996, c. 151, § 496; St.2006, c. 434, § 5, eff. April 3, 2007.

Historical and Statutory Notes

St.1869, c. 435, § 1.
St.1876, c. 85, § 2.
P.S.1882, c. 207, § 61.
R.L.1902, c. 212, § 80.
St.1918, c. 99, § 2.
St.1926, c. 76, § 2.

§ 90. Custody of arrested persons; time limitation

Persons arrested under either of the two preceding sections shall be kept in jail or other convenient place not more than twenty-four hours, Sundays and legal holidays excepted, at or before the expiration of which time they shall be taken before a district court and proceeded against according to law.

Amended by St.1959, c. 313, § 14.

Historical and Statutory Notes

St.1869, c. 435, § 1.
St.1876, c. 85, § 3.
P.S.1882, c. 207, § 62.
R.L.1902, c. 212, § 81.

§ 91. Application for decree of forfeiture; notice; hearing; adjudication; returning or killing of animals

After seizure and removal of animals or property used or employed, or intended to be used or employed, in violation of section 94, application shall be made to a district court for a decree of forfeiture of the animals or property. If, after hearing on the application, notice thereof having been previously given as the court orders, it shall be found that the animals, at the time of seizure, were engaged, or were intended to be engaged, in fighting at an exhibition thereof or the animals were owned, possessed, kept, trained, bred, loaned, sold, exported or otherwise transferred in violation of section 94, such animals shall be adjudged forfeited and the court shall thereupon, unless an appeal is taken as provided in the following section, issue an order for killing them. The order shall be directed to any officer authorized to serve criminal process and the officer receiving such order shall cause the animals to be killed within 24 hours thereafter. Animals or property seized as hereinbefore provided, which are not adjudged forfeited, shall be delivered to the owner or person entitled to the possession thereof. Any person shall be allowed to appear as claimant in the proceeding upon the application for a decree of forfeiture.

Amended by St.1959, c. 313, § 15; St.2006, c. 434, § 6, eff. April 3, 2007.

Historical and Statutory Notes

St.1869, c. 435, § 2.
St.1876, c. 85, § 4.
P.S.1882, c. 207, § 63.
R.L.1902, c. 212, § 82.

§ 92. Appeal; recognizance; custody and disposition of animals

An owner or claimant aggrieved by such judgment may, within twenty-four hours after the entry thereof and before its execution, appeal therefrom to the superior court; and all proceedings upon and after such appeal, including the right of exception, shall conform, so far as may be, to those in criminal cases, except that before such appeal is allowed the appellant shall recognize to the commonwealth in the sum of two hundred dollars, with sufficient sureties, to prosecute his appeal and to pay such expenses of the prosecution as the court may order and such expenses as may be thereafter incurred in the care and keeping of the birds, dogs or other animals claimed by such appellant if final judgment is rendered against them, and to abide the judgment of the court thereon. Upon the final judgment, the birds, dogs or other animals held in custody to abide such judgment shall be disposed of, under the direction of the superior court, in like manner as the court or justice might have disposed of them if no appeal had been taken. During the pendency of the appeal, all birds, dogs or other animals adjudged forfeited shall be kept in custody in a place other than that from which they were taken.

Historical and Statutory Notes

St.1869, c. 435, § 3.
St.1876, c. 85, § 5.
P.S.1882, c. 207, § 64.
R.L.1902, c. 212, § 83.

§ 92A. Advertisement, book, notice or sign relative to discrimination; definition of place of public accommodation, resort or amusement

No owner, lessee, proprietor, manager, superintendent, agent or employee of any place of public accommodation, resort or amusement shall, directly or indirectly, by himself or another, publish, issue, circulate, distribute or display, or cause to be published, issued, circulated, distributed or displayed, in any way, any advertisement, circular, folder, book, pamphlet, written or painted or printed notice or sign, of any kind or description, intended to discriminate against or actually discriminating against persons of any religious sect, creed, class, race, color, denomination, sex, sexual orientation, which shall not include persons whose sexual orientation involves minor children as the sex object, nationality, or because of deafness or blindness, or any physical or mental disability, in the full enjoyment of the accommodations, advantages, facilities or privileges offered to the general public by such places of public accommodation, resort or amusement.

A place of public accommodation, resort or amusement within the meaning hereof shall be defined as and shall be deemed to include any place, whether licensed or unlicensed, which is open to and accepts or solicits the patronage of the general public and, without limiting the generality of this definition, whether or not it be (1) an inn, tavern, hotel, shelter, roadhouse, motel, trailer camp or resort for transient or permanent guests or patrons seeking housing or lodging, food, drink, entertainment, health, recreation or rest; (2) a carrier, conveyance or elevator for the transportation of persons, whether operated on land, water or in the air, and the stations, terminals and facilities appurtenant thereto; (3) a gas station, garage, retail store or establishment, including those dispensing personal services; (4) a restaurant, bar or eating place, where food, beverages, confections or their derivatives are sold for consumption on or off the premises; (5) a rest room, barber shop, beauty parlor, bathhouse, seashore facilities or swimming pool, except such rest room, bathhouse or seashore facility as may be segregated on the basis of sex; (6) a boardwalk or other public highway; (7) an auditorium, theatre, music hall, meeting place or hall, including the common halls of buildings; (8) a place of public amusement, recreation, sport, exercise or entertainment; (9) a public library, museum or planetarium; or (10) a hospital, dispensary or clinic operating for profit; provided, however, that with regard to the prohibition on sex discrimination, this section shall not apply to a place of exercise for the exclusive use of persons of the same sex which is a bona fide fitness facility established for the sole purpose of promoting and maintaining physical and mental health through physical exercise and instruction, if such facility does not receive funds from a government source, nor to any corporation or entity authorized, created or chartered by federal law for the express purpose of promoting the health, social, educational vocational, and character development of a single sex; provided, further, that with regard to the prohibition of sex discrimination, those establishments which rent rooms on a temporary or permanent basis for the exclusive use of persons of the same sex shall not be considered places of public accommodation and shall not apply to any other part of such an establishment.

Any person who shall violate any provision of this section, or who shall aid in or incite, cause or bring about, in whole or in part, such a violation shall be punished by a fine of not more than one hundred dollars, or by imprisonment for not more than thirty days, or both.

Added by St.1933, c. 117. Amended by St.1953, c. 437; St.1971, c. 418, § 1; St.1975, c. 338, § 1; St.1978, c. 331; St.1979, c. 595, § 1; St.1989, c. 516, § 15; St.1998, c. 19, § 1.

§ 93. Expenses of care and destruction of fighting animals

The necessary expenses incurred in the care and destruction of such birds, dogs and other animals may be allowed and paid in the same manner as expenses in criminal prosecutions.

Historical and Statutory Notes

St.1869, c. 435, § 4.
St.1876, c. 85, § 6.
P.S.1882, c. 207, § 65.
R.L.1902, c. 212, § 84.

§ 94. Owning, possessing or training fighting animals; establishing or promoting exhibition; loaning, selling or exporting fighting animals; owning or possessing animals for breeding fighting animals

Whoever: (i) owns, possesses, keeps or trains any bird, dog or other animal, with the intent that it shall be engaged in an exhibition of fighting; (ii) establishes or promotes an exhibition of the fighting of any birds, dogs or other animals; (iii) loans, sells, exports or otherwise transfers any bird, dog or other animal for the purpose of animal fighting; or (iv) owns, possesses or keeps any bird, dog or other animal for the purpose of breeding such animal with the intent that its offspring be used for animal fighting shall be punished by imprisonment in the state prison for not more than 5 years or in the house of correction for not more than 1 year, or by a fine of not more than $1,000 or by both such fine and imprisonment.

Amended by St.1975, c. 31, § 1; St.1978, c. 111; St.2006, c. 434, § 7, eff. April 3, 2007.

Historical and Statutory Notes

St.1859, c. 158, § 1.
G.S.1860, c. 88, § 79.
St.1869, c. 435, § 5.
St.1876, c. 85, § 7.
P.S.1882, c. 207, § 66.
R.L.1902, c. 212, § 85.

§ 95. Aiding or being present at exhibition of fighting animals

Whoever is present at any place, building or tenement where preparations are being made for an exhibition of the fighting of birds, dogs or other animals, with intent to be present at such exhibition, or is present at, aids in or contributes to such exhibition, shall be punished by a fine of not more than $1,000 or by imprisonment in the state prison for not more than 5 years or imprisonment in the house of correction for not more than 2½ years or by both such fine and imprisonment.

Amended by St.1975, c. 31, § 2; St.2008, c. 452, eff. April 5, 2009.

Historical and Statutory Notes

St.1859, c. 158, § 2.
G.S.1860, c. 88, § 79.
St.1869, c. 435, § 6.

St.1876, c. 85, § 8.
P.S.1882, c. 207, § 67.
R.L.1902, c. 212, § 86.

§ 96. False notice of birth, marriage or death

Whoever wilfully sends to the publisher of a newspaper for publication a false notice of a birth, marriage or death shall be punished by a fine of not more than one hundred dollars.

Historical and Statutory Notes

St.1860, c. 195.
P.S.1882, c. 207, § 68.
R.L.1902, c. 212, § 87.

§ 97. Repealed, 1962, 285, Sec. 4

§ 97A. Demands, notices or other documents resembling court process; complaint; order to discontinue

Forms of demands or notices or other documents drawn to resemble court process shall not be used by attorneys at law, persons conducting collection agencies or others in the collection of bills, accounts or other indebtedness. A district court, on complaint of any person exhibiting and filing therewith such a form or document or copy thereof, alleging that a person who resides or has a place of business within the judicial district of such court has used or is using such form or document in violation of this section, may issue an order of notice to the person complained of to show cause why he should not be ordered to discontinue such use on penalty of contempt.

Added by St.1934, c. 164.

§ 98. Discrimination in admission to, or treatment in, place of public accommodation; punishment; forfeiture; civil right

Whoever makes any distinction, discrimination or restriction on account of race, color, religious creed, national origin, sex, sexual orientation, which shall not include persons whose sexual orientation involves minor children as the sex object, deafness, blindness or any physical or mental disability or ancestry relative to the admission of any person to, or his treatment in any place of public accommodation, resort or amusement, as defined in section ninety-two A, or whoever aids or incites such distinction, discrimination or restriction, shall be punished by a fine of not more than twenty-five hundred dollars or by imprisonment for not more than one year, or both, and shall be liable to any person aggrieved thereby for such damages as are enumerated in section five of chapter one hundred and fifty-one B; provided, however, that such civil forfeiture shall be of an amount not less than three hundred dollars; but such person so aggrieved shall not recover against more than one person by reason of any one act of distinction, discrimination or restriction. All persons shall have the right to the full and equal accommodations, advantages, facilities and privileges of any place of public accommodation, resort or amusement subject only to the conditions and limitations established by law and applicable to all persons. This right is recognized and declared to be a civil right.

Amended by St.1934, c. 138; St.1950, c. 479, § 3; St.1963, c. 613, § 5; St.1971, c. 418, § 2; St.1975, c. 338, § 2; St.1979, c. 595, § 2; St.1983, c. 628, § 7; St.1989, c. 516, § 16.

Historical and Statutory Notes

St.1865, c. 277.
St.1866, c. 252.
P.S.1882, c. 207, § 69.
St.1885, c. 316.
St.1893, c. 436.
St.1895, c. 461.
R.L.1902, c. 212, § 89.

§ 98A. Physically handicapped persons with dog guides; public places or conveyances; charges or fares; penalties

Notwithstanding any other provision of law, any blind person, or deaf or hearing handicapped person, or other physically handicapped person accompanied by a dog guide, shall be entitled to any and all accommodations, advantages, facilities and privileges of all public conveyances, public amusements and places of public accommodation, within the commonwealth, to which persons not accompanied by dogs are entitled, subject only to the conditions and limitations applicable to all persons not accompanied by dogs, and no such blind person, or deaf or hearing handicapped, or other physically handicapped person shall be required to pay any charge or fare for or on account of the transportation on any public conveyance for himself and such dog so accompanying him in addition to the charge or fare lawfully chargeable for his own transportation. Whoever deprives any blind person, or deaf or hearing handicapped person, or other physically handicapped person of any right conferred by this section shall be punished by a fine of not more than three hundred dollars and shall be liable to any person aggrieved thereby for such damages as are set forth in section five of chapter one hundred and fifty-one B; provided, however, that such civic forfeiture shall be of an amount not less than one hundred dollars.

Added by St.1938, c. 155, § 1. Amended by St.1978, c. 93; St.1978, c. 458, § 2; St.1980, c. 71; St.1981, c. 445; St.1983, c. 585, § 10; St.1983, c. 628, § 8; St.1992, c. 286, § 266; St.2000, c. 126; St.2004, c. 149, § 211, eff. July 1, 2004.

§ 98B. Discrimination in employment on public works or in public relief or transitional assistance

Whoever, knowingly and wilfully, employs discriminatory practices in the administration or giving of employment on public works or projects, or in the dispensing or giving of public relief or transitional assistance or any public benefit, because of race, color, religion or nationality, shall be punished by a fine of not more than one hundred dollars.

Added by St.1941, c. 170. Amended by St.1995, c. 5, § 96.

§ 98C. Libel; groups of persons; defenses; punishment; prosecutions

Whoever publishes any false written or printed material with intent to maliciously promote hatred of any group of persons in the commonwealth because of race, color or religion shall be guilty of libel and shall be punished by a fine of not more than one thousand dollars or by imprisonment for not more than one year, or both. The defendant may prove in defense that the publication was privileged or was not malicious. Prosecutions under this section shall be instituted only by the attorney general or by the district attorney for the district in which the alleged libel was published.

Added by St.1943, c. 223.

§ 99. Interception of wire and oral communications

Interception of wire and oral communications.—

A. Preamble.

The general court finds that organized crime exists within the commonwealth and that the increasing activities of organized crime constitute a grave danger to the public welfare and safety. Organized crime, as it exists in the commonwealth today, consists of a continuing conspiracy among highly organized and disciplined groups to engage in supplying illegal goods and services. In supplying these goods and services organized crime commits unlawful acts and employs brutal and violent tactics. Organized crime is infiltrating legitimate business activities and depriving honest businessmen of the right to make a living.

The general court further finds that because organized crime carries on its activities through layers of insulation and behind a wall of secrecy, government has been unsuccessful in curtailing and eliminating it. Normal investigative procedures are not effective in the investigation of illegal acts committed by organized crime. Therefore, law enforcement officials must be permitted to use modern methods of electronic surveillance, under strict judicial supervision, when investigating these organized criminal activities.

The general court further finds that the uncontrolled development and unrestricted use of modern electronic surveillance devices pose grave dangers to the privacy of all citizens of the commonwealth. Therefore, the secret use of such devices by private individuals must be prohibited. The use of such devices by law enforcement officials must be conducted under strict judicial supervision and should be limited to the investigation of organized crime.

B. Definitions. As used in this section—

1. The term "wire communication" means any communication made in whole or in part through the use of facilities for the transmission of communications by the aid of wire, cable, or other like connection between the point of origin and the point of reception.

2. The term "oral communication" means speech, except such speech as is transmitted over the public air waves by radio or other similar device.

3. The term "intercepting device" means any device or apparatus which is capable of transmitting, receiving, amplifying, or recording a wire or oral communication other than a hearing aid or similar device which is being used to correct subnormal hearing to normal and other than any telephone or telegraph instrument, equipment, facility, or a component thereof, (a) furnished to a subscriber or user by a communications common carrier in the ordinary course of its business under its tariff and being used by the subscriber or user in the ordinary course of its business; or (b) being used by a communications common carrier in the ordinary course of its business.

4. The term "interception" means to secretly hear, secretly record, or aid another to secretly hear or secretly record the contents of any wire or oral communication through the use of any intercepting device by any person other than a person given prior authority by all parties to such communication; provided that it shall not constitute an interception for an investigative or law enforcement officer, as defined in this section, to record or transmit a wire or oral communication if the officer is a party to such communication or has been given prior authorization to record or transmit the communication by such a party and if recorded or transmitted in the course of an investigation of a designated offense as defined herein.

5. The term "contents", when used with respect to any wire or oral communication, means any information concerning the identity of the parties to such communication or the existence, contents, substance, purport, or meaning of that communication.

6. The term "aggrieved person" means any individual who was a party to an intercepted wire or oral communication or who was named in the warrant authorizing the interception, or who would otherwise have standing to complain that his personal or property interest or privacy was invaded in the course of an interception.

7. The term "designated offense" shall include the following offenses in connection with organized crime as defined in the preamble: arson, assault and battery with a dangerous weapon, extortion, bribery, burglary, embezzlement, forgery, gaming in violation of section seventeen of chapter two hundred and seventy-one of the general laws, intimidation of a witness or juror, kidnapping, larceny, lending of money or things of value in violation of the general laws, mayhem, murder, any offense involving the possession or sale of a narcotic or harmful drug, perjury, prostitution, robbery, subornation of perjury, any violation of this section, being

an accessory to any of the foregoing offenses and conspiracy or attempt or solicitation to commit any of the foregoing offenses.

8. The term "investigative or law enforcement officer" means any officer of the United States, a state or a political subdivision of a state, who is empowered by law to conduct investigations of, or to make arrests for, the designated offenses, and any attorney authorized by law to participate in the prosecution of such offenses.

9. The term "judge of competent jurisdiction" means any justice of the superior court of the commonwealth.

10. The term "chief justice" means the chief justice of the superior court of the commonwealth.

11. The term "issuing judge" means any justice of the superior court who shall issue a warrant as provided herein or in the event of his disability or unavailability any other judge of competent jurisdiction designated by the chief justice.

12. The term "communication common carrier" means any person engaged as a common carrier in providing or operating wire communication facilities.

13. The term "person" means any individual, partnership, association, joint stock company, trust, or corporation, whether or not any of the foregoing is an officer, agent or employee of the United States, a state, or a political subdivision of a state.

14. The terms "sworn" or "under oath" as they appear in this section shall mean an oath or affirmation or a statement subscribed to under the pains and penalties of perjury.

15. The terms "applicant attorney general" or "applicant district attorney" shall mean the attorney general of the commonwealth or a district attorney of the commonwealth who has made application for a warrant pursuant to this section.

16. The term "exigent circumstances" shall mean the showing of special facts to the issuing judge as to the nature of the investigation for which a warrant is sought pursuant to this section which require secrecy in order to obtain the information desired from the interception sought to be authorized.

17. The term "financial institution" shall mean a bank, as defined in section 1 of chapter 167, and an investment bank, securities broker, securities dealer, investment adviser, mutual fund, investment company or securities custodian as defined in section 1.165-12(c)(1) of the United States Treasury regulations.

18. The term "corporate and institutional trading partners" shall mean financial institutions and general business entities and corporations which engage in the business of cash and asset management, asset management directed to custody operations, securities trading, and wholesale capital markets including foreign exchange, securities lending, and the purchase, sale or exchange of securities, options, futures, swaps, derivatives, repurchase agreements and other similar financial instruments with such financial institution.

C. Offenses.

1. Interception, oral communications prohibited.

Except as otherwise specifically provided in this section any person who—

willfully commits an interception, attempts to commit an interception, or procures any other person to commit an interception or to attempt to commit an interception of any wire or oral communication shall be fined not more than ten thousand dollars, or imprisoned in the state prison for not more than five years, or imprisoned in a jail or house of correction for not more than two and one half years, or both so fined and given one such imprisonment.

Proof of the installation of any intercepting device by any person under circumstances evincing an intent to commit an interception, which is not authorized or permitted by this section, shall be prima facie evidence of a violation of this subparagraph.

2. Editing of tape recordings in judicial proceeding prohibited.

Except as otherwise specifically provided in this section any person who willfully edits, alters or tampers with any tape, transcription or recording of oral or wire communications by any means, or attempts to edit, alter or tamper with any tape, transcription or recording of oral or wire communications by any means with the intent to present in any judicial proceeding or proceeding under oath, or who presents such recording or permits such recording to be presented in any judicial proceeding or proceeding under oath, without fully indicating the nature of the changes made in the original state of the recording, shall be fined not more than ten thousand dollars or imprisoned in the state prison for not more than five years or imprisoned in a jail or house of correction for not more than two years or both so fined and given one such imprisonment.

3. Disclosure or use of wire or oral communications prohibited.

Except as otherwise specifically provided in this section any person who—

a. willfully discloses or attempts to disclose to any person the contents of any wire or oral communication, knowing that the information was obtained through interception; or

b. willfully uses or attempts to use the contents of any wire or oral communication, knowing that the information was obtained through interception, shall be guilty of a misdemeanor punishable by imprisonment in a jail or a house of correction for not more than two years or by a fine of not more than five thousand dollars or both.

4. Disclosure of contents of applications, warrants, renewals, and returns prohibited.

Except as otherwise specifically provided in this section any person who—

willfully discloses to any person, any information concerning or contained in, the application for, the granting or denial of orders for interception, renewals, notice or return on an ex parte order granted pursuant to this section, or the contents of any document, tape, or recording kept in accordance with paragraph N, shall be guilty of a misdemeanor punishable by imprisonment in a jail or a house of correction for not more than two years or by a fine of not more than five thousand dollars or both.

5. Possession of interception devices prohibited.

A person who possesses any intercepting device under circumstances evincing an intent to commit an interception not permitted or authorized by this section, or a person who permits an intercepting device to be used or employed for an interception not permitted or authorized by this section, or a person who possesses an intercepting device knowing that the same is intended to be used to commit an interception not permitted or authorized by this section, shall be guilty of a misdemeanor punishable by imprisonment in a jail or house of correction for not more than two years or by a fine of not more than five thousand dollars or both.

The installation of any such intercepting device by such person or with his permission or at his direction shall be prima facie evidence of possession as required by this subparagraph.

6. Any person who permits or on behalf of any other person commits or attempts to commit, or any person who participates in a conspiracy to commit or to attempt to commit, or any accessory to a person who commits a violation of subparagraphs 1 through 5 of paragraph C of this section shall be punished in the same manner as is provided for the respective offenses as described in subparagraphs 1 through 5 of paragraph C.

D. Exemptions.

1. Permitted interception of wire or oral communications.

It shall not be a violation of this section—

a. for an operator of a switchboard, or an officer, employee, or agent of any communication common carrier, whose facilities are used in the transmission of a wire communication, to intercept, disclose, or use that communication in the normal course of his employment while engaged in any activity which is a necessary incident to the rendition of service or to the protection of the rights or property of the carrier of such communication, or which is necessary to prevent the use of such facilities in violation of section fourteen A of chapter two hundred and sixty-nine of the general laws; provided, that said communication common carriers shall not utilize service observing or random monitoring except for mechanical or service quality control checks.

b. for persons to possess an office intercommunication system which is used in the ordinary course of their business or to use such office intercommunication system in the ordinary course of their business.

c. for investigative and law enforcement officers of the United States of America to violate the provisions of this section if acting pursuant to authority of the laws of the United States and within the scope of their authority.

d. for any person duly authorized to make specified interceptions by a warrant issued pursuant to this section.

e. for investigative or law enforcement officers to violate the provisions of this section for the purposes of ensuring the safety of any law enforcement officer or agent thereof who is acting in an undercover capacity, or as a witness for the commonwealth; provided, however, that any such interception which is not otherwise permitted by this section shall be deemed unlawful for purposes of paragraph P.

f. for a financial institution to record telephone communications with its corporate or institutional trading partners in the ordinary course of its business; provided, however, that such financial institution shall establish and maintain a procedure to provide semi-annual written notice to its corporate and institutional trading partners that telephone communications over designated lines will be recorded.

2. Permitted disclosure and use of intercepted wire or oral communications.

a. Any investigative or law enforcement officer, who, by any means authorized by this section, has obtained knowledge of the contents of any wire or oral communication, or evidence derived therefrom, may disclose such contents or evidence in the proper performance of his official duties.

b. Any investigative or law enforcement officer, who, by any means authorized by this section has obtained knowledge of the contents of any wire or oral communication, or evidence derived therefrom, may use such contents or evidence in the proper performance of his official duties.

c. Any person who has obtained, by any means authorized by this section, knowledge of the contents of any wire or oral communication, or evidence derived therefrom, may disclose such contents while giving testimony under oath or affirmation in any criminal proceeding in any court of the United States or of any state or in any federal or state grand jury proceeding.

d. The contents of any wire or oral communication intercepted pursuant to a warrant in accordance with the provisions of this section, or evidence derived therefrom, may otherwise be disclosed only upon a showing of good cause before a judge of competent jurisdiction.

e. No otherwise privileged wire or oral communication intercepted in accordance with, or in violation of, the provisions of this section shall lose its privileged character.

E. Warrants: when issuable:

A warrant may issue only:

1. Upon a sworn application in conformity with this section; and

2. Upon a showing by the applicant that there is probable cause to believe that a designated offense has been, is being, or is about to be committed and that evidence of the commission of such an offense may thus be obtained or that information which will aid in the apprehension of a person who the applicant has probable cause to believe has committed, is committing, or is about to commit a designated offense may thus be obtained; and

3. Upon a showing by the applicant that normal investigative procedures have been tried and have failed or reasonably appear unlikely to succeed if tried.

F. Warrants: application.

1. Application. The attorney general, any assistant attorney general specially designated by the attorney general, any district attorney, or any assistant district attorney specially designated by the district attorney may apply ex parte to a judge of competent jurisdiction for a warrant to intercept wire or oral communications. Each application ex parte for a warrant must be in writing, subscribed and sworn to by the applicant authorized by this subparagraph.

2. The application must contain the following:

a. A statement of facts establishing probable cause to believe that a particularly described designated offense has been, is being, or is about to be committed; and

b. A statement of facts establishing probable cause to believe that oral or wire communications of a particularly described person will constitute evidence of such designated offense or will aid in the apprehension of a person who the applicant has probable cause to believe has committed, is committing, or is about to commit a designated offense; and

c. That the oral or wire communications of the particularly described person or persons will occur in a particularly described place and premises or over particularly described telephone or telegraph lines; and

d. A particular description of the nature of the oral or wire communications sought to be overheard; and

e. A statement that the oral or wire communications sought are material to a particularly described investigation or prosecution and that such conversations are not legally privileged; and

f. A statement of the period of time for which the interception is required to be maintained. If practicable, the application should designate hours of the day or night during which the oral or wire communications may be reasonably expected to occur. If the nature of the investigation is such that the authorization for the interception should not automatically terminate when the described oral or wire communications have been first obtained, the application must specifically state facts establishing probable cause to believe that additional oral or wire communications of the same nature will occur thereafter; and

g. If it is reasonably necessary to make a secret entry upon a private place and premises in order to install an intercepting device to effectuate the interception, a statement to such effect; and

h. If a prior application has been submitted or a warrant previously obtained for interception of oral or wire communications, a statement fully disclosing the date, court, applicant, execution, results, and present status thereof; and

i. If there is good cause for requiring the postponement of service pursuant to paragraph L, subparagraph 2, a description of such circumstances, including reasons for the applicant's belief that secrecy is essential to obtaining the evidence or information sought.

3. Allegations of fact in the application may be based either upon the personal knowledge of the applicant or upon information and belief. If the applicant personally knows the facts alleged, it must be so stated. If the facts establishing such probable cause are derived in whole or part from the statements of persons other than the applicant, the sources of such information and belief must be either disclosed or described; and the application must contain facts establishing the existence and reliability of any informant and the reliability of the information supplied by him. The application must also state, so far as possible, the basis of the informant's knowledge or belief. If the applicant's information and belief is derived from tangible evidence or recorded oral evidence, a copy or detailed description thereof should be annexed to or included in the application. Affidavits of persons other than the applicant may be submitted in conjunction with the application if they tend to support any fact or conclusion alleged therein. Such accompanying affidavits may be based either on personal knowledge of the affiant or information and belief, with the source thereof, and reason therefor, specified.

G. Warrants: application to whom made.

Application for a warrant authorized by this section must be made to a judge of competent jurisdiction in the county where the interception is to occur, or the county where the office of the applicant is located, or in the event that there is no judge of competent jurisdiction sitting in said county at such time, to a judge of competent jurisdiction sitting in Suffolk County; except that for these purposes, the office of the attorney general shall be deemed to be located in Suffolk County.

H. Warrants: application how determined.

1. If the application conforms to paragraph F, the issuing judge may examine under oath any person for the purpose of determining whether probable cause exists for the issuance of the warrant pursuant to paragraph E. A verbatim transcript of every such interrogation or examination must be taken, and a transcription of the same, sworn to by the stenographer, shall be attached to the application and be deemed a part thereof.

2. If satisfied that probable cause exists for the issuance of a warrant the judge may grant the application and issue a warrant in accordance with paragraph *I*. The application and an attested copy of the warrant shall be retained by the issuing judge and transported to the chief justice of the superior court in accordance with the provisions of paragraph N of this section.

3. If the application does not conform to paragraph F, or if the judge is not satisfied that probable cause has been shown sufficient for the issuance of a warrant, the application must be denied.

I. Warrants: form and content.

A warrant must contain the following:

1. The subscription and title of the issuing judge; and

2. The date of issuance, the date of effect, and termination date which in no event shall exceed thirty days from the date of effect. The warrant shall permit interception of oral or wire communications for a period not to exceed fifteen days. If physical installation of a device is necessary, the thirty-day period shall begin upon the date of installation. If the effective period of the warrant is to terminate upon the acquisition of particular evidence or information or oral or wire communication, the warrant shall so provide; and

3. A particular description of the person and the place, premises or telephone or telegraph line upon which the interception may be conducted; and

4. A particular description of the nature of the oral or wire communications to be obtained by the interception including a statement of the designated offense to which they relate; and

5. An express authorization to make secret entry upon a private place or premises to install a specified intercepting device, if such entry is necessary to execute the warrant; and

6. A statement providing for service of the warrant pursuant to paragraph L except that if there has been a finding of good cause shown requiring the postponement of such service, a statement of such finding together with the basis therefor must be included and an alternative direction for deferred service pursuant to paragraph L, subparagraph 2.

J. Warrants: renewals.

1. Any time prior to the expiration of a warrant or a renewal thereof, the applicant may apply to the issuing judge for a renewal thereof with respect to the same person, place, premises or telephone or telegraph line. An application for renewal must incorporate the warrant sought to be renewed together with the application therefor and any accompanying papers upon which it was issued. The application for renewal must set forth the results of the interceptions thus far conducted. In addition, it must set forth present grounds for extension in conformity with paragraph F, and the judge may interrogate under oath and in such an event a transcript must be provided and attached to the renewal application in the same manner as is set forth in subparagraph 1 of paragraph H.

2. Upon such application, the judge may issue an order renewing the warrant and extending the authorization for a period not exceeding fifteen (15) days from the entry thereof. Such an order shall specify the grounds for the issuance thereof. The application and an attested copy of the order shall be retained by the issuing judge to be transported to the chief justice in accordance with the provisions of subparagraph N of this section. In no event shall a renewal be granted which shall terminate later than two years following the effective date of the warrant.

K. Warrants: manner and time of execution.

1. A warrant may be executed pursuant to its terms anywhere in the commonwealth.

2. Such warrant may be executed by the authorized applicant personally or by any investigative or law enforcement officer of the commonwealth designated by him for the purpose.

3. The warrant may be executed according to its terms during the hours specified therein, and for the period therein authorized, or a part thereof. The authorization shall terminate upon the acquisition of the oral or wire communications, evidence or information described in the warrant. Upon termination of the authorization in the warrant and any renewals thereof, the interception must cease at once, and any device installed for the purpose of the interception must be removed as soon thereafter as practicable. Entry upon private premises for the removal of such device is deemed to be authorized by the warrant.

L. Warrants: service thereof.

1. Prior to the execution of a warrant authorized by this section or any renewal thereof, an attested copy of the warrant or the renewal must, except as otherwise provided in subparagraph 2 of this paragraph, be served upon a person whose oral or wire communications are to be obtained, and if an intercepting device

is to be installed, upon the owner, lessee, or occupant of the place or premises, or upon the subscriber to the telephone or owner or lessee of the telegraph line described in the warrant.

2. If the application specially alleges exigent circumstances requiring the postponement of service and the issuing judge finds that such circumstances exist, the warrant may provide that an attested copy thereof may be served within thirty days after the expiration of the warrant or, in case of any renewals thereof, within thirty days after the expiration of the last renewal; except that upon a showing of important special facts which set forth the need for continued secrecy to the satisfaction of the issuing judge, said judge may direct that the attested copy of the warrant be served on such parties as are required by this section at such time as may be appropriate in the circumstances but in no event may he order it to be served later than three (3) years from the time of expiration of the warrant or the last renewal thereof. In the event that the service required herein is postponed in accordance with this paragraph, in addition to the requirements of any other paragraph of this section, service of an attested copy of the warrant shall be made upon any aggrieved person who should reasonably be known to the person who executed or obtained the warrant as a result of the information obtained from the interception authorized thereby.

3. The attested copy of the warrant shall be served on persons required by this section by an investigative or law enforcement officer of the commonwealth by leaving the same at his usual place of abode, or in hand, or if this is not possible by mailing the same by certified or registered mail to his last known place of abode. A return of service shall be made to the issuing judge, except, that if such service is postponed as provided in subparagraph 2 of paragraph L, it shall be made to the chief justice. The return of service shall be deemed a part of the return of the warrant and attached thereto.

M. Warrant: return.

Within seven days after termination of the warrant or the last renewal thereof, a return must be made thereon to the judge issuing the warrant by the applicant therefor, containing the following:

a. a statement of the nature and location of the communications facilities, if any, and premise or places where the interceptions were made; and

b. the periods of time during which such interceptions were made; and

c. the names of the parties to the communications intercepted if known; and

d. the original recording of the oral or wire communications intercepted, if any; and

e. a statement attested under the pains and penalties of perjury by each person who heard oral or wire communications as a result of the interception authorized by the warrant, which were not recorded, stating everything that was overheard to the best of his recollection at the time of the execution of the statement.

N. Custody and secrecy of papers and recordings made pursuant to a warrant.

1. The contents of any wire or oral communication intercepted pursuant to a warrant issued pursuant to this section shall, if possible, be recorded on tape or wire or other similar device. Duplicate recordings may be made for use pursuant to subparagraphs 2 (a) and (b) of paragraph D for investigations. Upon examination of the return and a determination that it complies with this section, the issuing judge shall forthwith order that the application, all renewal applications, warrant, all renewal orders and the return thereto be transmitted to the chief justice by such persons as he shall designate. Their contents shall not be disclosed except as provided in this section. The application, renewal applications, warrant, the renewal order and the return or any one of them or any part of them may be transferred to any trial court, grand jury proceeding of any jurisdiction by any law enforcement or investigative officer or court officer designated by the chief justice and a trial justice may allow them to be disclosed in accordance with paragraph D, subparagraph 2, or paragraph *O* or any other applicable provision of this section.

The application, all renewal applications, warrant, all renewal orders and the return shall be stored in a secure place which shall be designated by the chief justice, to which access shall be denied to all persons except the chief justice or such court officers or administrative personnel of the court as he shall designate.

2. Any violation of the terms and conditions of any order of the chief justice, pursuant to the authority granted in this paragraph, shall be punished as a criminal contempt of court in addition to any other punishment authorized by law.

3. The application, warrant, renewal and return shall be kept for a period of five (5) years from the date of the issuance of the warrant or the last renewal thereof at which time they shall be destroyed by a person designated by the chief justice. Notice prior to the destruction shall be given to the applicant attorney general or his successor or the applicant district attorney or his successor and upon a showing of good cause to the chief justice, the application, warrant, renewal, and return may be kept for such additional period as the chief justice shall determine but in no event longer than the longest period of limitation for any designated offense specified in the warrant, after which time they must be destroyed by a person designated by the chief justice.

O. Introduction of evidence.

1. Notwithstanding any other provisions of this section or any order issued pursuant thereto, in any

criminal trial where the commonwealth intends to offer in evidence any portions of the contents of any interception or any evidence derived therefrom the defendant shall be served with a complete copy of each document and item which make up each application, renewal application, warrant, renewal order, and return pursuant to which the information was obtained, except that he shall be furnished a copy of any recording instead of the original. The service must be made at the arraignment of the defendant or, if a period in excess of thirty (30) days shall elapse prior to the commencement of the trial of the defendant, the service may be made at least thirty (30) days before the commencement of the criminal trial. Service shall be made in hand upon the defendant or his attorney by any investigative or law enforcement officer of the commonwealth. Return of the service required by this subparagraph including the date of service shall be entered into the record of trial of the defendant by the commonwealth and such return shall be deemed prima facie evidence of the service described therein. Failure by the commonwealth to make such service at the arraignment, or if delayed, at least thirty days before the commencement of the criminal trial, shall render such evidence illegally obtained for purposes of the trial against the defendant; and such evidence shall not be offered nor received at the trial notwithstanding the provisions of any other law or rules of court.

2. In any criminal trial where the commonwealth intends to offer in evidence any portions of a recording or transmission or any evidence derived therefrom, made pursuant to the exceptions set forth in paragraph B, subparagraph 4, of this section, the defendant shall be served with a complete copy of each recording or a statement under oath of the evidence overheard as a result of the transmission. The service must be made at the arraignment of the defendant or if a period in excess of thirty days shall elapse prior to the commencement of the trial of the defendant, the service may be made at least thirty days before the commencement of the criminal trial. Service shall be made in hand upon the defendant or his attorney by any investigative or law enforcement officer of the commonwealth. Return of the service required by this subparagraph including the date of service shall be entered into the record of trial of the defendant by the commonwealth and such return shall be deemed prima facie evidence of the service described therein. Failure by the commonwealth to make such service at the arraignment, or if delayed at least thirty days before the commencement of the criminal trial, shall render such service illegally obtained for purposes of the trial against the defendant and such evidence shall not be offered nor received at the trial notwithstanding the provisions of any other law or rules of court.

P. Suppression of evidence.

Any person who is a defendant in a criminal trial in a court of the commonwealth may move to suppress the contents of any intercepted wire or oral communication or evidence derived therefrom, for the following reasons:

1. That the communication was unlawfully intercepted.

2. That the communication was not intercepted in accordance with the terms of this section.

3. That the application or renewal application fails to set forth facts sufficient to establish probable cause for the issuance of a warrant.

4. That the interception was not made in conformity with the warrant.

5. That the evidence sought to be introduced was illegally obtained.

6. That the warrant does not conform to the provisions of this section.

Q. Civil remedy.

Any aggrieved person whose oral or wire communications were intercepted, disclosed or used except as permitted or authorized by this section or whose personal or property interests or privacy were violated by means of an interception except as permitted or authorized by this section shall have a civil cause of action against any person who so intercepts, discloses or uses such communications or who so violates his personal, property or privacy interest, and shall be entitled to recover from any such person—

1. actual damages but not less than liquidated damages computed at the rate of $100 per day for each day of violation or $1000, whichever is higher;

2. punitive damages; and

3. a reasonable attorney's fee and other litigation disbursements reasonably incurred. Good faith reliance on a warrant issued under this section shall constitute a complete defense to an action brought under this paragraph.

R. Annual report of interceptions of the general court.

On the second Friday of January, each year, the attorney general and each district attorney shall submit a report to the general court stating (1) the number of applications made for warrants during the previous year, (2) the name of the applicant, (3) the number of warrants issued, (4) the effective period for the warrants, (5) the number and designation of the offenses for which those applications were sought, and for each of the designated offenses the following: (a) the number of renewals, (b) the number of interceptions made during the previous year, (c) the number of indictments believed to be obtained as a result of those interceptions, (d) the number of criminal convictions obtained in trials where interception evidence or evidence derived therefrom was introduced. This report shall be a public document and be made available to the public at the offices of the attorney general and district attorneys. In the event of failure to comply with the provisions of this paragraph any person may compel compliance by means of an action of mandamus.

Amended by St.1959, c. 449, § 1; St.1968, c. 738, § 1; St.1986, c. 557, § 199; St.1993, c. 432, § 13; St.1998, c. 163, §§ 7, 8.

Historical and Statutory Notes

St.1920, c. 558, § 1.

§ 99A. Jury deliberations; overhearing by use of devices

Whoever secretly overhears, or attempts secretly to overhear or to have any other person overhear the deliberations of a jury by use of a device commonly known as a dictograph or dictaphone, or however otherwise described, or by any similar device or arrangement with intent to procure any information relative to the conduct of such jury or any of its members, shall be punished by imprisonment for not more than five years or by a fine of not more than five thousand dollars, or both.

Added by St.1956, c. 48, § 1.

§§ 100 to 102. Repealed, 1968, 738, Secs. 4 to 6

Historical and Statutory Notes

See, now, M.G.L.A. c. 272, § 99.

§ 103. Repealed, 1993, 279

§ 104. Security for seizure and impoundment of animals relating to cruelty to animals or animal fighting

(a) As used in this section the word "Authority" shall mean an organization or authorized agent thereof that seizes or impounds an animal pursuant to the General Laws.

(b) If an animal is lawfully seized or impounded pursuant to the General Laws relating to cruelty to animals or animal fighting, the owner, custodian or person claiming an interest in the animal, shall be given a show cause hearing within 30 days after application for the complaint.

(c) If an animal is lawfully seized and impounded, the authority may file a petition with the court requesting that the person from whom an animal is seized or a person claiming an interest in the seized animal, be ordered to post a security. The authority shall serve a copy of the petition on the person from whom the animal was seized, or if the person cannot be found, by posting of copy at the place where the animal was taken into custody. The authority shall also serve a copy of the petition on the district attorney. The court may order that person to post a security.

(d) The security shall be in an amount sufficient to secure payment for all reasonable expenses to be incurred by the authority having custody of the seized animal for a temporary period of at least 30 days. The amount of the security shall be determined by the court upon the recommendation of the authority. Reasonable expenses shall include, but shall not be limited to, estimated medical care, shelter, and board.

(e) When security is posted in accordance with this section, the authority may draw from the security the actual reasonable costs incurred for medical care, shelter, and board.

(f) If the court orders the posting of security, the security shall be posted with the clerk within 10 business days of the show cause hearing. The court shall order the immediate forfeiture of the seized animal to the authority if the person fails to post security as ordered. The court may waive the security requirement or reduce the amount of the security for good cause shown.

(g) Posting of the security shall not prevent the authority from disposing of the seized or impounded animal before the expiration of the period covered by the security, if the court rules in favor of the authority.

(h) The authority may humanely dispose of the animal at the end of the period for which expenses are covered by the security, if the court orders the disposition. If the disposition order is denied, the court may require the owner or custodian or any other person claiming interest in the animal, to provide additional security to secure payment of reasonable expenses and to extend the period of time pending adjudication by the court of the charges against the person from whom the animal was seized.

(i) The owner or custodian of an animal humanely killed pursuant to this section shall not be entitled to recover damages or the actual value of the animal if the owner or custodian failed to post security.

(j) The court may direct a refund to the person who posted the security in whole or part for any expenses not incurred by the authority. The court may direct a refund to the person who posted security upon acquittal of the charges.

Added by St.2002, c. 435.

§ 105. Photographing, videotaping or electronically surveilling partially nude or nude person; exceptions; punishment

(a) As used in this section, the following words shall have the following meanings unless the context clearly requires otherwise:

"Electronically surveils" or "electronically surveilled", to view, obtain or record a person's visual image by the use or aid of a camera, cellular or other wireless communication device, computer, television or other electronic device.

"Partially nude", the exposure of the human genitals, buttocks, pubic area or female breast below a point immediately above the top of the areola.

(b) Whoever willfully photographs, videotapes or electronically surveils another person who is nude or partially nude, with the intent to secretly conduct or hide such activity, when the other person in such place and circumstance would have a reasonable expectation of privacy in not being so photographed, videotaped or electronically surveilled, and without that person's knowledge and consent, shall be punished by imprisonment in the house of correction for not more than 2½ years or by a fine of not more than $5,000, or by both such fine and imprisonment.

(c) Whoever willfully disseminates the visual image of another person who is nude or partially nude, with knowledge that such visual image was unlawfully obtained in violation of subsection (b) and without consent of the person so depicted, shall be punished by imprisonment in the house of correction for not more than 2½ years or in the state prison for not more than 5 years or by a fine of not more than $10,000, or by both such fine and imprisonment.

(d) This section shall not apply to a merchant that electronically surveils a customer changing room, provided that signage warning customers of the merchant's surveillance activity is conspicuously posted at all entrances and in the interior of any changing room electronically surveilled.

(e) This section shall not apply to a law enforcement officer acting within the scope of the officer's authority under applicable law, or by an order or warrant issued by a court.

(f) A sheriff, deputy sheriff or police officer may arrest without a warrant, a person whom he has probable cause to believe has violated this section.

(g) A photograph, videotape or other recorded visual image, depicting a person who is nude or partially nude that is part of any court record arising from a prosecution under this section, shall not be open to public inspection and shall only be made available by court personnel to a law enforcement officer, prosecuting attorney, defendant's attorney, defendant, or victim connected to such prosecution for inspection, unless otherwise ordered by the court.

(h) In a prosecution under this section, a justice of the superior court or district court may issue appropriate orders to restrain or prevent the unlawful dissemination of a person's visual image in violation of this section.

Added by St.2008, c. 451, § 149, eff. Jan. 5, 2009.

CHAPTER 273

DESERTION, NON–SUPPORT AND ILLEGITIMACY

Title of chapter editorially modified

The section headings for the General Laws in this pamphlet have been editorially supplied.

§ 1. Abandonment and nonsupport; failure to comply with support order; decree establishing rights of spouse as prima facie evidence

A spouse or parent shall be guilty of a felony and shall be subject to the penalties set forth in section fifteen A if:

(1) he abandons his spouse or minor child without making reasonable provisions for the support of his spouse or minor child or both of them; or

(2) he leaves the commonwealth and goes into another state without making reasonable provisions for the support of his spouse or minor child or both of them; or

(3) he enters the commonwealth from another state without making reasonable provisions for the support of his spouse or minor child, or both of them, domiciled in another state; or

(4) wilfully and while having the financial ability or earning capacity to have complied, he fails to comply with an order or judgment for support which has been entered pursuant to chapter one hundred and nineteen, two hundred and seven, two hundred and eight, two hundred and nine, two hundred and nine C, or two hundred and seventy-three, or received, entered or registered pursuant to chapter two hundred and nine D, or entered pursuant to similar laws of other states. No civil proceeding in any court shall be held to be a bar to a prosecution hereunder but the court shall not enter any order pursuant to section fifteen A which would directly or indirectly result in a decrease in the amount paid for current support pursuant to an order or judgment on behalf of the child or spouse to who, or on whose behalf, support is owed.

In a prosecution hereunder a decree or judgment of a probate court in a proceeding in which the defendant or spouse appeared or was personally served with process, establishing the right of his spouse to live apart or the freedom of such spouse to convey and deal with property, or the right to the custody of the children, shall be admissible and shall be prima facie evidence of such right.

Amended by St.1939, c. 177, § 1; St.1954, c. 539; St.1957, c. 49; St.1971, c. 276; St.1971, c. 762; St.1977, c. 848, § 2; St.1986, c. 310, § 22; St.1993, c. 340, § 3; St.1993, c. 460, § 88; St.1995, c. 5, §§ 97, 98.

Historical and Statutory Notes

St.1882, c. 270, § 4.
St.1884, c. 210, § 1.
St.1885, c. 176, § 1.
St.1893, c. 262.
St.1899, c. 309, § 1.
R.L.1902, c. 212, § 45.
St.1905, c. 307.
St.1906, c. 501, § 1.
St.1907, c. 563, § 26.
St.1908, c. 104.
St.1909, c. 180.
St.1911, c. 456, § 1.
St.1925, c. 126.
St.1929, c. 258, § 1.
St.1931, c. 226.

§ 2. Jurisdiction; venue; supervision of parent by municipal or district court probation officers

Proceedings under section one shall be begun if in the superior court, in the county in which is situated the place where the husband and wife last lived together or where the husband or wife or parent of the child is living, and, if begun in a district court, in the court having such place within its judicial district; provided, that such a proceeding for an offense committed within the territorial limits of the Boston, the Worcester, Bristol county or the Springfield juvenile court, as designated by section fifty-seven of chapter two hundred and eighteen, if founded upon the same allegations as a proceeding under sections twenty-four to twenty-seven, inclusive, of chapter one hundred and nineteen, may be brought, heard and disposed of in said juvenile courts. Such a proceeding for an offense committed within the territorial limits prescribed for the criminal jurisdiction of any court other than the courts within the territorial limits of the Boston, the Worcester, Bristol county and the Springfield juvenile courts, if founded upon the same allegations as a proceeding under said sections twenty-four to twenty-seven, inclusive, of chapter one hundred and nineteen, may be heard and disposed of in the juvenile session of the court. Any parent placed on probation in such a proceeding in any of said juvenile courts shall at the request of the justice thereof be supervised by the probation officers of the municipal or district courts located within the territorial limits of that juvenile court.

Amended by St.1933, c. 224; St.1943, c. 87, § 1; St.1953, c. 319, § 31; St.1958, c. 200; St.1969, c. 859, § 24; St.1972, c. 731, § 20.

Historical and Statutory Notes

St.1906, c. 501, § 5.
St.1911, c. 456, § 3.

§ 3. Payment of fines

The court imposing a fine under section fifteen A may at any time order it paid in whole or in part to a probation officer, to be paid by him to the spouse or to the city, town, corporation, society or person actually supporting the spouse, child or children, or to the state treasurer for the use of the department of children and families if the child has been committed to said department.

Amended by St.1977, c. 848, § 3; St.1978, c. 552, § 42; St.1993, c. 460, § 89; St.2008, c. 176, § 128, eff. July 8, 2008.

Historical and Statutory Notes

St.1884, c. 210, § 1.
St.1885, c. 176, § 1.
St.1893, c. 262.
R.L.1902, c. 212, § 45.
St.1905, c. 307.
St.1906, c. 501, § 2.
St.1907, c. 563, § 26.
St.1908, c. 104.
St.1911, c. 456, § 2.
St.1919, c. 350, § 87.

§§ 4, 5. Repealed, 1986, 310, Sec. 23

Historical and Statutory Notes

See, now, M.G.L.A. c. 209C, § 18A.

§ 6. Recognizance on release on probation; compliance with judgment or order for support; forfeiture

The court shall also have the power to release the defendant from custody on probation for a period so fixed, upon his or her entering into a recognizance, with or without surety, in such sum as the court may order and approve. The condition of the recognizance shall be such that if the defendant shall make his personal appearance in court whenever ordered to do so, and shall further comply with the terms of any currently enforceable judgment or order for support entered pursuant to any civil action, including an action for annulment, divorce, separate support, or paternity and support, under chapters two hundred and seven, two hundred and eight, two hundred and nine or two hundred and nine C, then such recognizance shall be void, otherwise of full force and effect. An order or judgment for support entered against the defendant in any such civil proceeding shall be deemed to be currently enforceable if the defendant is currently able to comply with said order or judgment and it is or would be enforceable pursuant to an action for contempt or otherwise as provided under said chapter in case of forfeiture of recognizance, and enforcement therefor by execution, the sum recovered may, in the discretion of the court, be paid in whole or in part, to the spouse or parent of the child or to the person entitled to receive support.

Amended by St.1986, c. 310, § 24.

Historical and Statutory Notes

St.1871, c. 42, § 1.
P.S.1882, c. 85, § 4.
R.L.1902, c. 82, § 4.
St.1905, c. 307.
St.1906, c. 501, §§ 3, 4.
St.1907, c. 563, § 26.
St.1908, c. 104.
St.1911, c. 53.
St.1911, c. 456, §§ 5, 6.
St.1913, c. 563, § 9.
St.1914, c. 520.
St.1918, c. 199.
St.1918, c. 257, §§ 453, 454.
St.1919, c. 5.
St.1920, c. 2.

§ 7. Evidence of marriage and parentage; husband and wife as witnesses; self incrimination; evidence of wilfulness; confidential communications

No other or greater evidence shall be required to prove the marriage of the husband and wife, or that the alleged father is the parent of the child, than may be required to prove the same facts in a civil action. In any prosecution begun under section one, both husband and wife shall be competent witnesses to testify against each other to any relevant matters, including the fact of their marriage and the parentage of the child; provided, that neither shall be compelled to give evidence incriminating himself. Proof of the desertion of the spouse or child, or of the neglect or refusal to make reasonable provision for their support and maintenance, shall be prima facie evidence that such desertion, neglect or refusal is wilful and without just cause. In no prosecution under sections one to ten, inclusive, shall any existing statute or rule of law prohibiting the disclosure of confidential communications between husband and wife apply.

Amended by St.1977, c. 848, § 4.

Historical and Statutory Notes

St.1893, c. 262, § 1.
R.L.1902, c. 212, § 45.
St.1905, c. 307.
St.1906, c. 501, § 1.
St.1907, c. 563, § 26.
St.1908, c. 104.
St.1909, c. 180.
St.1911, c. 456, § 7.

§ 8. Lack of custody as defence; duty to support child

In proceedings under sections one or fifteen against a parent, relative to any minor child, it shall not of itself be a defence that the defendant has ceased to have custody or the right to custody of such child on his own acquiescence or by judicial action. The legal duty of the parent or parents to support a minor child shall continue notwithstanding the absence of a court decree ordering them or either of them to pay for the support of said child and notwithstanding any court decree granting custody of such child to another.

Amended by St.1953, c. 505; St.1960, c. 791; St.1993, c. 460, § 90.

Historical and Statutory Notes

St.1917, c. 163.
St.1918, c. 257, § 455.
St.1919, c. 5.
St.1919, c. 148.
St.1920, c. 2.

§ 9. Repealed, 1938, 219, Sec. 1

§ 10. Uniform construction

Sections one to eight, inclusive, shall be so interpreted and construed as to effectuate their general purpose to make uniform the law of those states enacting their provisions.

Amended by St.1938, c. 219, § 2.

Historical and Statutory Notes

St.1911, c. 456, § 9.

§ 11. Repealed, 1977, 848, Sec. 7

§§ 12 to 14. Repealed, 1986, 310, Sec. 25

§ 15. Duty to support child born out of wedlock; conclusiveness of adjudication or acknowledgment of paternity

A parent of a minor child born out of wedlock whether or not the child was born in the commonwealth who wilfully neglects or refuses to contribute reasonably to the support of the child or who leaves the commonwealth and goes into another state without making reasonable provision for the support of the child, or who enters the commonwealth from another state without making reasonable provision for the support of the child domiciled in another state, or who, wilfully and while having the financial ability or earning capacity to have complied, fails to comply with an order or judgment for support which has been entered pursuant to chapter one hundred and nineteen, two hundred and seven, two hundred and nine C, or two hundred and seventy-three, or received, entered or registered pursuant to chapter two hundred and nine D, or entered pursuant to similar laws of other states, shall be guilty of a felony and shall be subject to the penalties provided under section fifteen A. No civil proceeding in any court shall be held to be a bar to the prosecution hereunder but the court shall not enter any order pursuant to section fifteen A which would directly or indirectly result in a decrease in the amount paid for current support pursuant to an order or judgment on behalf of the child to whom, or on whose behalf, support is owed.

If there has been a voluntary acknowledgment of parentage or an adjudication of paternity under chapter two hundred and nine C or under any provision of this chapter in effect immediately prior to the effective date of this section or other law in this or any other jurisdiction, such acknowledgment or adjudication shall be conclusive on all persons in proceedings under this section. If there has been no adjudication or acknowledgment of paternity, proceedings under this section shall be stayed pending the conclusion of an action to establish paternity under chapter two hundred and nine C, which shall be commenced forthwith.

Amended by St.1977, c. 848, § 6; St.1979, c. 621, § 2; St.1986, c. 310, § 26; St.1993, c. 460, § 91; St.1995, c. 5, §§ 99, 100.

Historical and Statutory Notes

C.L. c. 55, § 2.
St.1692–3, c. 18, § 5.
St.1785, c. 66, § 2.
R.S.1836, c. 49, § 4.
G.S.1860, c. 72, § 7.
P.S.1882, c. 85, § 15.
R.L.1902, c. 82, § 15.
St.1913, c. 563, §§ 6, 7, 9.

§ 15A. Abandonment and willful nonsupport; penalties; alternative sentencing; restitution

(1) The penalty for violation of sections one and fifteen of this chapter shall be by fine or by imprisonment or by both fine and imprisonment as specified below.

(2) A person who abandons his spouse or minor child without making reasonable provisions for the support of either or both of them or who is subject to an order or judgment for support pursuant to chapters one hundred and nineteen, two hundred and seven, two hundred and eight, two hundred and nine, two hundred and nine C, two hundred and seventy-three, or two hundred and nine D, or pursuant to similar laws of other states, who, wilfully and while having the financial ability or earning capacity to have complied, fails to comply with that order or judgment, shall be punished by imprisonment in the state prison for not more than five years or by imprisonment in jail or the house of correction for not more than two and one-half years, or by a fine of not more than five thousand dollars, or by both such fine and imprisonment.

(3) A person who leaves the commonwealth and goes into another state without making reasonable provisions for the support of a spouse or child, or who enters the commonwealth from another state without making reasonable provision for the support of a spouse or child domiciled in another state, shall be punished by imprisonment in the state prison for not more than ten years or by imprisonment in jail or the house of correction for not more than two and one-half years, or by a fine of not more than ten thousand dollars, or by both such fine and imprisonment.

(4) In a prosecution under this chapter, the court may, upon conviction of the defendant, provide for alternative sentencing including (a) the suspension of the sentence upon and during the compliance by the defendant with any order for the support as already made or as thereafter modified, or (b) notwithstanding the provision of section six of chapter two hundred and seventy-nine, the imprisonment of the defendant only on designated weekends, evenings or holidays, provided, that such defendant retains employment and complies with such support orders.

(5) In a prosecution under this chapter the defendant may be ordered to make restitution to the spouse or the custodial parent or to the person or agency, including the department of public welfare, who is supporting or has supported the spouse or child for all sums expended on behalf of such spouse or child, provided that if the defendant establishes a lesser ability to have provided support, the amount of any liability imposed by this section shall be consistent with the defendant's prior ability to have paid support.

Added by St.1986, c. 310, § 26. Amended by St.1993, c. 460, §§ 92 to 95; St.1995, c. 5, §§ 101 to 104; St.2005, c. 163, § 54, eff. Dec. 8, 2005.

§ 15B. Receiving, concealing or transferring assets for the purpose of avoiding payment; penalty

Whoever receives or conceals an asset of another knowing that said asset is being transferred for the purpose of concealing it to avoid payment of an order or judgment for support issued pursuant to the provisions of chapter 119, 207, 208, 209, 209A, 209C, 209D or 273, or pursuant to any similar laws of other states, shall be punished by a fine of not more than $5,000 or by imprisonment in a jail or house of correction for not more than two and one-half years, or by both such fine and imprisonment; and whoever transfers an asset for the purpose of concealing it to avoid payment of an order or judgment for support issued pursuant to said chapter 119, 207, 208, 209, 209A, 209C, 209D or 273, or pursuant to any similar laws of other states shall be punished by a fine of not more than $5,000 or by imprisonment in a jail or house of correction for not more than two and one-half years, or both such fine and imprisonment. The court may in the alternative to the foregoing punishment divert the defendant to a program as defined in section 1 of chapter 276A.

Added by St.1998, c. 483, § 1.

§ 16. Proceedings under Secs. 1 and 15

The provisions of sections two, six, seven and ten shall apply in proceedings under sections one and fifteen.

Amended by St.1977, c. 848, § 6; St.1993, c. 460, § 96.

Historical and Statutory Notes

C.L. c. 55, § 2.
St.1692–3, c. 18, § 5.
St.1785, c. 66, § 2.
St.1825, c. 173.
R.S.1836, c. 49, §§ 3, 4, 6.
St.1857, c. 305, §§ 1, 2.
St.1859, c. 239, § 4.
G.S.1860, c. 72, §§ 7, 8, 12.
St.1871, c. 42, § 1.
P.S.1882, c. 85, §§ 4, 15, 16, 21.
R.L.1902, c. 82, §§ 4, 15, 16, 21.
St.1911, c. 53.
St.1913, c. 563, §§ 6, 7, 9.

§ 17. Dismissal of case

If the court having jurisdiction of a case under sections fifteen to eighteen, inclusive, becomes satisfied that the alleged father and the mother have married each other and the child has become or will be the legitimate child of the alleged father or that it is for the best interest of the child, the case may be dismissed and if the court certifies that it is for the best interests of the child, no further prosecution shall be maintained under any of said sections.

Amended by St.1953, c. 163; St.1977, c. 848, § 6; St.1986, c. 310, § 27.

Historical and Statutory Notes

St.1859, c. 239, § 5.
G.S.1860, c. 72, §§ 9, 10.

St.1862, c. 213.
St.1865, c. 161.
P.S.1882, c. 85, §§ 12, 17 to 19.
St.1885, c. 384, § 5.
R.L.1902, c. 82, §§ 12, 17 to 19.
St.1905, c. 345.
St.1913, c. 563, §§ 3, 9.

§ 18. Money forfeited or recovered upon recognizance or deposit used for support

If money is forfeited or recovered upon a recognizance or deposit in lieu thereof given in proceedings under sections fifteen to eighteen, inclusive, or any of them, the court in which such proceedings are pending may order such money paid to the probation officer and expended by him, under the direction of the court, for the support of the child.

Amended by St.1977, c. 848, § 6; St.1986, c. 310, § 28.

Historical and Statutory Notes

St.1863, c. 127, § 2.
P.S.1882, c. 85, § 7.
R.L.1902, c. 82, § 7.
St.1913, c. 563, § 9.
St.1918, c. 199.

§ 18A. Support obligations under prior law; enforcement; insurance coverage; amended orders

(a) Any order issued by a court pursuant to sections one, five, or fifteen as those sections appeared prior to the effective date of this section directing the defendant to pay certain sums periodically to the probation officer as a condition of releasing the defendant from custody on probation, shall continue in full force and effect, subject to the jurisdiction of said court and to change from time to time as circumstances may require, for a period not exceeding six years from said date. A voluntary agreement relating to the support of a spouse or child or children previously executed by the defendant may be admitted as evidence of the defendant's support obligation. If the court finds that the obligation imposed by such agreement is reasonable in the circumstance, and that the defendant has failed to comply with its terms, the court may include in any subsequent order the payment of any part or all of the arrears which accrued under such agreement if the complaint includes the period of such arrearage; provided, however, that when such agreement is executed with the department of public welfare or with any official of the court, such agreement shall not be enforceable unless the defendant was informed in writing at the time he executed the agreement that the failure to comply with the support order would result in the commencement of criminal nonsupport proceedings under this chapter against him. The probation officer subject to the direction of the court, shall pay over payments received by him to the IV–D agency, as set forth in chapter one hundred and nineteen A, which shall in turn make payments to the spouse or guardian or custodian of the child, or to the city, town, corporation, society or person supporting the spouse or child, or to the state treasurer for the use of the department of children and families when the payments are for the support of a child committed to it. If the court is satisfied by due proof under oath that at any time the defendant has violated the terms of the order for payments, it may proceed to try the defendant upon the original charge, or sentence him under the original plea or conviction, or enforce the suspended sentence, as the case may be.

(b) When the court reviews or modifies an order for support on behalf of a spouse or child, said court shall determine whether the obligor under such order has health insurance or other health coverage available to him through an employer or organization or has health insurance or other health coverage available to him at reasonable cost that may be extended to cover the spouse or child for whom support is ordered. When said court has determined that the obligor has such insurance or coverage available to him, said court shall include in the support order a requirement that the obligor exercise the option of additional coverage in favor of the spouse and child or obtain coverage for the spouse and child.

(c) Each order for support reviewed, modified, or otherwise brought before the court pursuant to this section shall be amended so as to conform to and shall thereafter be enforced in accordance with the provisions of section twelve of chapter one hundred and nineteen A.

Added by St.1986, c. 310, § 29. Amended by St.1988, c. 23, § 70; St.2008, c. 176, § 129, eff. July 8, 2008.

§ 19. Repealed, 1977, 848, Sec. 7

§ 20. Neglect or refusal to support parent

Any person, over eighteen, who, being possessed of sufficient means, unreasonably neglects or refuses to provide for the support and maintenance of his parent, whether father or mother, residing in the commonwealth, when such parent through misfortune and without fault of his own is destitute of means of sustenance and unable by reason of old age, infirmity or illness to support and maintain himself, shall be punished by a fine of not more than two hundred dollars or by imprisonment for not more than one year, or both. No such neglect or refusal shall be deemed unreasonable as to a child who shall not during his minority have been reasonably supported by such parent, if such parent was charged with the duty so to do, nor as to a child who, being one of two or more children, has made proper and reasonable contribution toward the support of such parent.

Amended by St.1973, c. 925, § 80.

Historical and Statutory Notes

St.1915, c. 163, § 1.

§ 21. Venue; complainants

Proceedings under the preceding section shall be begun, if in the superior court, in the county in which is situated the place where the defendant or the parent lives, and, if begun in a district court, in the court having such place within its judicial district. Complaints in district courts under the preceding section may be made by any such parent, by any child of such parent or by the department of public welfare.

Amended by St.1974, c. 260, § 32.

Historical and Statutory Notes

St.1915, c. 163, § 3.
St.1931, c. 394, § 137.

§ 22. Orders; applicability of Secs. 1 to 10 of this chapter

Before trial, with the consent of the defendant, or after entry of a plea of guilty or nolo contendere, or after conviction, the court may make for the benefit of such destitute parent orders similar to those provided by section five; and the practice established by the first ten sections of this chapter shall, so far as applicable, apply to proceedings under this and the two preceding sections.

Historical and Statutory Notes

St.1915, c. 163, § 2.

§ 23. Needy disabled persons; neglect or refusal of parents to support; penalty

The father or mother of any needy disabled person who unreasonably neglects or refuses to provide for the support and maintenance of such person shall be punished by a fine of not more than five hundred dollars or by imprisonment for not more than two years, or both.

Added by St.1959, c. 402.

CHAPTER 274

FELONIES, ACCESSORIES AND ATTEMPTS TO COMMIT CRIMES

The section headings for the General Laws in this pamphlet have been editorially supplied.

§ 1. Felonies and misdemeanors

A crime punishable by death or imprisonment in the state prison is a felony. All other crimes are misdemeanors.

Historical and Statutory Notes

St.1852, c. 37, § 1.
G.S.1860, c. 168, § 1.
P.S.1882, c. 210, § 1.
R.L.1902, c. 215, § 1.

§ 2. Aiders; accessories before fact; punishment

Whoever aids in the commission of a felony, or is accessory thereto before the fact by counselling, hiring or otherwise procuring such felony to be committed, shall be punished in the manner provided for the punishment of the principal felon.

Amended by St.1968, c. 206, § 1; St.1973, c. 529, § 1.

Historical and Statutory Notes

St.1784, c. 65, § 1.
St.1784, c. 66, § 9.
St.1804, c. 131, § 1.
R.S.1836, c. 133, § 1.
G.S.1860, c. 168, § 3.
P.S.1882, c. 210, § 3.
R.L.1902, c. 215, § 2.

§ 3. Counselling or procuring felony; prosecution as accessory before fact or principal; punishment; venue

Whoever counsels, hires or otherwise procures a felony to be committed may be indicted and convicted as an accessory before the fact, either with the principal felon or after his conviction; or may be indicted and convicted of the substantive felony, whether the principal felon has or has not been convicted, or is or is not amenable to justice; and in the last mentioned case may be punished in the same manner as if convicted of being an accessory before the fact. An accessory to a felony before the fact may be indicted, tried and punished in the same county where the principal felon might be indicted and tried, although the counselling, hiring or procuring the commission of such felony was committed within or without the commonwealth or on the high seas.

Amended by St.1968, c. 206, § 2; St.1973, c. 529, § 2.

Historical and Statutory Notes

St.1830, c. 49, §§ 1, 2.
R.S.1836, c. 133, §§ 2, 3.
G.S.1860, c. 168, §§ 4, 5.
P.S.1882, c. 210, §§ 4, 5.
R.L.1902, c. 215, § 3.

§ 4. Accessories after fact; punishment; relationship as defence; cross-examination; impeachment

Whoever, after the commission of a felony, harbors, conceals, maintains or assists the principal felon or accessory before the fact, or gives such offender any other aid, knowing that he has committed a felony or has been accessory thereto before the fact, with intent that he shall avoid or escape detention, arrest, trial or punishment, shall be an accessory after the fact, and, except as otherwise provided, be punished by imprisonment in the state prison for not more than seven years or in jail for not more than two and one half years or by a fine of not more than one thousand dollars. The fact that the defendant is the husband or wife, or by consanguinity, affinity or adoption, the parent or grandparent, child or grandchild, brother or sister of the offender, shall be a defence to a prosecution under this section. If such a defendant testifies solely as to the existence of such relationship, he shall not be subject to cross examination on any other subject matter, nor shall his criminal record, if any, except for perjury or subornation of perjury, be admissible to impeach his credibility.

Amended by St.1943, c. 488, § 1.

Historical and Statutory Notes

St.1784, c. 65, § 2.
St.1784, c. 66, § 9.
St.1804, c. 123, § 2.
St.1804, c. 131, § 5.
St.1804, c. 143, § 10.
St.1805, c. 97, § 2.
St.1805, c. 101, § 3.
R.S.1836, c. 133, § 4.
G.S.1860, c. 168, § 6.
St.1876, c. 213, § 7.
P.S.1882, c. 210, § 6.
R.L.1902, c. 215, § 4.
St.1918, c. 257, § 464.
St.1919, c. 5.
St.1920, c. 2.

§ 5. Felon's conviction or amenability to justice; venue

An accessory to a felony after the fact may be indicted, convicted and punished, whether the principal felon has or has not been previously convicted, or is or is not amenable to justice, either in the county where he became an accessory or in the county where the principal felony was committed.

Historical and Statutory Notes

St.1830, c. 49, § 3.
R.S.1836, c. 133, § 5.
G.S.1860, c. 168, § 7.
P.S.1882, c. 210, § 7.
R.L.1902, c. 215, § 5.

§ 6. Attempts to commit crimes; punishment

Whoever attempts to commit a crime by doing any act toward its commission, but fails in its perpetration, or is intercepted or prevented in its perpetration, shall, except as otherwise provided, be punished as follows:

First, by imprisonment in the state prison for not more than ten years, if he attempts to commit a crime punishable with death.

Second, by imprisonment in the state prison for not more than five years or in a jail or house of correction for not more than two and one half years, if he attempts to commit a crime, except any larceny under section thirty of chapter two hundred and sixty-six, punishable by imprisonment in the state prison for life or for five years or more.

Third, by imprisonment in a jail or house of correction for not more than one year or by a fine of not more than three hundred dollars, if he attempts to commit a crime, except any larceny under said section thirty, punishable by imprisonment in the state prison for less than five years or by imprisonment in a jail or house of correction or by a fine.

Fourth, by imprisonment in a jail or house of correction for not more than two and one half years or by a fine, or by both such fine and imprisonment, if he attempts to commit any larceny punishable under said section thirty.

Historical and Statutory Notes

St.1832, c. 62.
R.S.1836, c. 133, § 12.
G.S.1860, c. 168, § 8.
P.S.1882, c. 210, § 8.
R.L.1902, c. 215, § 6.
St.1911, c. 130.
St.1924, c. 164.

§ 7. Conspiracy; penalties

Any person who commits the crime of conspiracy shall be punished as follows:

First, if the purpose of the conspiracy or any of the means for achieving the purpose of the conspiracy is a felony punishable by death or imprisonment for life, by a fine of not more than ten thousand dollars or by imprisonment in the state prison for not more than twenty years or in jail for not more than two and one half years, or by both such fine and imprisonment.

Second, if clause first does not apply and the purpose of the conspiracy or any of the means for achieving the purpose of the conspiracy is a felony punishable by imprisonment in the state prison for a maximum period exceeding ten years, by a fine of not more than ten thousand dollars or by imprisonment in the state prison for not more than ten years or in jail for not more than two and one half years, or by both such fine and imprisonment.

Third, if clauses first and second do not apply and the purpose of the conspiracy or any of the means for achieving the purpose of the conspiracy is a felony punishable by imprisonment in the state prison for not more than ten years, by a fine of not more than five thousand dollars or by imprisonment in the state prison for not more than five years or in jail for not more than two and one half years, or by both such fine and imprisonment.

Fourth, if clauses first through third do not apply and the purpose of the conspiracy or any of the means for achieving the purpose of the conspiracy is a crime, by a fine of not more than two thousand dollars or by imprisonment in jail for not more than two and one half years, or both.

If a person is convicted of a crime of conspiracy for which crime the penalty is expressly set forth in any other section of the General Laws, the provisions of this section shall not apply to said crime and the penalty therefor shall be imposed pursuant to the provisions of such other section.

Added by St.1968, c. 721, § 1.

TITLE II

PROCEEDINGS IN CRIMINAL CASES

CHAPTER 275

PROCEEDINGS TO PREVENT CRIMES

The section headings for the General Laws in this pamphlet have been editorially supplied.

§ 1. Justices keeping public peace; security

The justices of the supreme judicial court, of the superior court, and of district courts may cause all laws made for the preservation of the public peace to be kept; and in the execution of that power may require persons to give security to keep the peace, or for their good behavior, or both, as provided in this chapter.
Amended by St.1959, c. 313, § 17.

Historical and Statutory Notes

R.S.1836, c. 134, § 1.
G.S.1860, c. 169, § 1.
P.S.1882, c. 211, § 1.
R.L.1902, c. 216, § 1.

§ 2. Complaint of threat to commit crime

If complaint is made to any such court or justice that a person has threatened to commit a crime against the person or property of another, such court or justice shall examine the complainant and any witnesses who may be produced, on oath, reduce the complaint to writing and cause it to be subscribed by the complainant.

Historical and Statutory Notes

R.S.1836, c. 134, § 2.
G.S.1860, c. 169, § 2.
P.S.1882, c. 211, § 2.
R.L.1902, c. 216, § 2.

§ 3. Warrant to apprehend accused

If, upon such examination, it is found there is just cause to fear that such crime may be committed, such court or justice shall issue a warrant, reciting the substance of the complaint, and requiring the officer to whom it is directed forthwith to apprehend the person complained of and take him before such justice or some other justice or court having jurisdiction of the cause. Such warrant, if issued by a justice, shall be under his hand.

Historical and Statutory Notes

St.1692–3, c. 18, § 6.
St.1783, c. 51, § 1.
St.1794, c. 26, § 2.
R.S.1836, c. 134, § 3.
G.S.1860, c. 169, § 3.
P.S.1882, c. 211, § 3.
R.L.1902, c. 216, § 3.

§ 4. Punishment; recognizance to keep the peace

If the person complained of is convicted, he may be punished by a fine of not more than one hundred dollars or by imprisonment for not more than six months. Instead of imposing sentence, the court or justice may order the person complained of to enter into a recognizance, with sufficient sureties, in such sum as the court or justice orders, to keep the peace toward all the people of the commonwealth, and especially toward the person requiring such security, for such term, not exceeding six months, as the court or justice may order. The court or justice may, for good cause, revoke such order or reduce the amount of the recognizance, or order that it be taken without surety.

Amended by St.1992, c. 379, § 182.

Historical and Statutory Notes

St.1833, c. 63.
R.S.1836, c. 134, § 4.
G.S.1860, c. 169, § 4.
P.S.1882, c. 211, § 4.
St.1894, c. 505, §§ 1, 2.
St.1896, c. 388.
R.L.1902, c. 216, § 4.

§ 5. Commitment on refusal or neglect to recognize

If the person complained of so recognizes, he shall be discharged, but if he refuses or neglects so to do, he shall be committed to the jail or house of correction during the period for which he was required to give security, or until within that time he so recognizes, stating in the warrant the cause of commitment and the sum and time for which security was required.

Historical and Statutory Notes

St.1833, c. 63, § 1.
R.S.1836, c. 134, §§ 5, 6.
G.S.1860, c. 169, § 5.
P.S.1882, c. 211, § 5.
St.1894, c. 505, § 2.
R.L.1902, c. 216, § 5.

§ 6. Discharge of accused; complainant paying expenses

If, upon such examination, it is found that there is not just cause to fear that such crime will be committed by the person complained of, he shall be forthwith discharged; and if it is found that the complaint is unfounded, frivolous or malicious, the complainant may be ordered to pay the expenses of prosecution.

Historical and Statutory Notes

R.S.1836, c. 134, § 7.
G.S.1860, c. 169, § 6.
P.S.1882, c. 211, § 6.
R.L.1902, c. 216, § 6.

§ 7. Accused paying expenses; commitment

If a person is required to give security to keep the peace or for his good behavior, the court or justice may order him to pay the expenses of prosecution, or any part thereof, and that he shall stand committed until they are paid or he is otherwise legally discharged.

Historical and Statutory Notes

St.1824, c. 128, § 2.
St.1834, c. 151, § 4.
R.S.1836, c. 134, § 8.
G.S.1860, c. 169, § 7.
P.S.1882, c. 211, § 7.
R.L.1902, c. 216, § 7.

§ 8. Appeal from order to recognize

Whoever having waived jury trial in accordance with the provisions of section twenty-six A of chapter two hundred and eighteen is aggrieved by an order of the Boston municipal court or the district court, requiring him to recognize as provided aforesaid, may, upon giving the security required, appeal to the jury session designated pursuant to section twenty-seven A of chapter two hundred and eighteen for the conduct of jury trials in cases brought in the court wherein said order was made.

Amended by St.1959, c. 313, § 18; St.1992, c. 379, § 183.

Historical and Statutory Notes

St.1833, c. 63, § 1.
R.S.1836, c. 134, § 9.
St.1852, c. 14.
G.S.1860, c. 169, § 8.
P.S.1882, c. 211, § 8.
R.L.1902, c. 216, § 8.

§ 9. Witnesses to recognize for appearance

The court or justice shall require such witnesses as may be necessary to support the complaint to recognize for their appearance at the jury session.

Amended by St.1978, c. 478, § 280.

Historical and Statutory Notes

R.S.1836, c. 134, § 10.
G.S.1860, c. 169, § 9.
P.S.1882, c. 211, § 9.
R.L.1902, c. 216, § 9.

§ 10. Proceedings on appeal

The justice sitting in the jury session may affirm the order or discharge the appellant, or may require him to enter into a new recognizance, with sufficient sureties, in such sum and for such time as it may order, and may make such order relative to the expenses of prosecution as is just and reasonable.

Amended by St.1978, c. 478, § 281.

Historical and Statutory Notes

R.S.1836, c. 134, § 11.
G.S.1860, c. 169, § 10.
P.S.1882, c. 211, § 10.
R.L.1902, c. 216, § 10.

§ 11. Failure to prosecute appeal; recognizance remaining in force

If the appellant fails to prosecute his appeal of an order of recognizance, his recognizance shall remain in full force and effect as to any breach of the condition, without an affirmation of the judgment or order of the court or justice, and shall also stand as security for any expenses of prosecution which the justice in the jury session may order the appellant to pay.

Amended by St.1978, c. 478, § 282; St.1992, c. 379, § 184.

Historical and Statutory Notes

R.S.1836, c. 134, § 12.
G.S.1860, c. 169, § 11.
P.S.1882, c. 211, § 11.
R.L.1902, c. 216, § 11.

§ 12. Discharge from commitment upon giving security

A person committed for not finding sureties, or for refusing to recognize as required, may be discharged upon giving such security.

Historical and Statutory Notes

R.S.1836, c. 134, § 13.
G.S.1860, c. 169, § 12.
P.S.1882, c. 211, § 12.
R.L.1902, c. 216, § 12.

§ 13. Recognizance; breach of condition

Upon a breach of the condition of a recognizance taken pursuant to the provisions of sections four to eleven, inclusive, an action thereon shall be commenced by the district attorney in the court in which the recognizance is then on file.

Amended by St.1978, c. 478, § 283; St.1992, c. 379, § 185.

Historical and Statutory Notes

R.S.1836, c. 134, § 14.
St.1852, c. 14.
G.S.1860, c. 169, § 13.
P.S.1882, c. 211, § 13.
R.L.1902, c. 216, § 13.

§ 14. Affray, threats or disturbance of peace in presence of justice; recognizance to keep peace

Whoever, in the presence of a justice named in section one or before a court of record, makes an affray, or threatens to kill or beat another, or to commit any violence or outrage against the person or property of another, or contends with hot and angry words, to the disturbance of the peace, may be ordered, without process or any other proof, to recognize to keep the peace or be of good behavior for not more than three months, and in case of refusal may be committed as provided in section five.

Historical and Statutory Notes

St.1692–3, c. 18, § 6.
St.1794, c. 26, § 2.
R.S.1836, c. 134, § 15.
G.S.1860, c. 169, § 14.
P.S.1882, c. 211, § 14.
R.L.1902, c. 216, § 14.

§ 15. Repealed, 1932, 180, Sec. 42

§ 16. Remission of portion of forfeited penalty

If, upon a suit brought on such recognizance, the penalty thereof is adjudged forfeited, the court may, upon petition of a defendant, remit such portion of it as it finds ought to be remitted.

Historical and Statutory Notes

St.1810, c. 80.
R.S.1836, c. 134, § 17.
G.S.1860, c. 169, § 16.
P.S.1882, c. 211, § 16.
R.L.1902, c. 216, § 16.

§ 17. Right of surety to surrender principal; discharge from liability; new recognizance

A surety in a recognizance to keep the peace, or for good behavior, or both, shall have the same authority and right to take and surrender his principal as if he were bail for him in a civil cause; and after such surrender shall be discharged from all liability for any act of the principal subsequent to such surrender which would be a breach of the condition of the recognizance. The person so surrendered may recognize anew with sufficient sureties for the residue of the term, and shall thereupon be discharged.

Historical and Statutory Notes

R.S.1836, c. 134, § 18.
G.S.1860, c. 169, § 17.
P.S.1882, c. 211, § 17.
R.L.1902, c. 216, § 17.

§ 18. Community parole supervision for life in addition to sentence of imprisonment or probation; covered offenses

Whenever a person is convicted of a first offense under section 13B, 13F or 13H of chapter 265 or for a first offense for the attempt of any of the aforementioned crimes under section 6 of chapter 274, the district attorney, upon motion to the court, may request a hearing after conviction and before sentencing, to determine whether or not such person shall be committed, in addition to any term of imprisonment or probation authorized by said sections, to community parole supervision for life, to be served under the jurisdiction of the parole board as set forth in section 133D of chapter 127. Whenever a person is convicted of a first offense under section 22, 22A, 23, 24, 24B or 26 of said chapter 265, section 3 or 35A of chapter 272 or for a first offense for the attempt of any of the aforementioned crimes under said section 6 of said chapter 274, the elements of which are mitigated by certain circumstances, the defendant, upon motion to the court, may request a hearing after conviction and before sentencing to determine whether or not such person shall receive, in addition to a term of imprisonment or probation authorized by such sections, community parole supervision for life, to be served under the jurisdiction of the parole board as set forth in said section 133D of said chapter 127.

At such hearing, the defendant shall have the right to be represented by counsel, and, if financially unable to retain adequate representation, to have counsel appointed to him. The defendant shall be afforded an opportunity to testify, to present witnesses, to cross-examine witnesses who appear at the hearing and to present information. The rules concerning admissibility of evidence in criminal trials shall not apply to the presentation and consideration of information at the hearing. A finding by the court that such person shall be committed to community parole supervision for life shall be supported by clear and convincing evidence.

In making a determination the judge shall, on the basis of any information which he can reasonably obtain, consider any mitigating or aggravating circumstances including, but not limited to, the defendant's character, propensities, criminal record, the nature and seriousness of the danger posed to any person or the community and the nature and circumstances of the offense for which the defendant is convicted. If the judge finds, by clear and convincing evidence, that no reasons for community parole supervision for life to be served under the jurisdiction of the parole board, as set forth in section 133D of chapter 127, exist, the judge shall not impose community supervision for life on such first offender.

Whenever a person is convicted of a first offense under section 22, 22A, 23, 24, 24B or 26 of chapter 265, or section 3 or 35A of chapter 272 or for a first attempt of any of the aforementioned crimes under the provisions of section 6 of chapter 274, the district attorney may file a motion with the sentencing judge requesting that the defendant not receive community parole supervision for life, and upon receipt of such motion, the sentencing judge shall not impose community parole supervision for life on such first offender.

Added by St.1999, c. 74, § 14.

CHAPTER 276

SEARCH WARRANTS, REWARDS, FUGITIVES FROM JUSTICE, ARREST, EXAMINATION, COMMITMENT AND BAIL. PROBATION OFFICERS AND BOARD OF PROBATION

The section headings for the General Laws in this pamphlet have been editorially supplied.

§ 1. Complaint; warrant for designated property or articles; search incident to arrest; documentary evidence subject to privilege

A court or justice authorized to issue warrants in criminal cases may, upon complaint on oath that the complainant believes that any of the property or articles hereinafter named are concealed in a house, place, vessel or vehicle or in the possession of a person anywhere within the commonwealth and territorial waters thereof, if satisfied that there is probable cause for such belief, issue a warrant identifying the property and naming or describing the person or place to be searched and commanding the person seeking such warrant to search for the following property or articles:

First, property or articles stolen, embezzled or obtained by false pretenses, or otherwise obtained in the commission of a crime;

Second, property or articles which are intended for use, or which are or have been used, as a means or instrumentality of committing a crime, including, but not in limitation of the foregoing, any property or article worn, carried or otherwise used, changed or marked in the preparation for or perpetration of or concealment of a crime;

Third, property or articles the possession or control of which is unlawful, or which are possessed or controlled for an unlawful purpose; except property subject to search and seizure under sections forty-two through fifty-six, inclusive, of chapter one hundred and thirty-eight;

Fourth, the dead body of a human being.

Fifth, the body of a living person for whom a current arrest warrant is outstanding.

A search conducted incident to an arrest may be made only for the purposes of seizing fruits, instrumentalities, contraband and other evidence of the crime for which the arrest has been made, in order to prevent its destruction or concealment; and removing any weapons that the arrestee might use to resist arrest or effect his escape. Property seized as a result of a search in violation of the provisions of this paragraph shall not be admissible in evidence in criminal proceedings.

The word "property", as used in this section shall include books, papers, documents, records and any other tangible objects.

Nothing in this section shall be construed to abrogate, impair or limit powers of search and seizure granted under other provisions of the General Laws or under the common law.

Notwithstanding the foregoing provisions of this section, no search and seizure without a warrant shall be conducted, and no search warrant shall issue for any documentary evidence in the possession of a lawyer, psychotherapist, or a clergyman, including an accredited Christian Science practitioner, who is known or may reasonably be assumed to have a relationship with any other person which relationship is the subject of a testimonial privilege, unless, in addition to the other requirements of this section, a justice is satisfied that there is probable cause to believe that the documentary evidence will be destroyed, secreted, or lost in the event a search warrant does not issue. Nothing in this paragraph shall impair or affect the ability, pursuant to otherwise applicable law, to search or seize without a warrant or to issue a warrant for the search or seizure of any documentary evidence where there is probable cause to believe that the lawyer, psychotherapist, or clergyman in possession of such documentary evidence has committed, is committing, or is about to commit a crime. For purposes of this paragraph, "documentary evidence" includes, but is not limited to, writings, documents, blueprints, drawings, photographs, computer printouts, microfilms, X–rays, files, diagrams, ledgers, books, tapes, audio and video recordings, films or papers of any type or description.

Amended by St.1934, c. 235, § 1; St.1934, c. 303, § 2; St.1943, c. 508, § 5; St.1947, c. 93; St.1963, c. 96, § 1; St.1964, c. 557, § 1; St.1974, c. 508; St.1982, c. 260; St.1986, c. 691.

Historical and Statutory Notes

St.1823, c. 40, § 1.
R.S.1836, c. 142, §§ 1, 2.
G.S.1860, c. 170, §§ 1, 2.
St.1862, c. 168, §§ 2, 4.
St.1865, c. 127, § 2.
St.1866, c. 253, § 2.
St.1869, c. 364, § 2.
St.1879, c. 159, § 2.
P.S.1882, c. 212, §§ 1, 2.
St.1885, c. 342, § 2.
St.1890, c. 284.
St.1894, c. 491, § 14.
St.1899, c. 359, § 8.
St.1899, c. 408, § 16.
R.L.1902, c. 217, § 1.
St.1919, c. 179, § 1.
St.1919, c. 323, § 4.
St.1924, c. 94, § 2.

§ 1A. Articles belonging to subversive organizations

A justice of the superior court, upon application of the attorney general or a district attorney, and upon complaint on oath that the complainant believes that any of the property or articles hereinafter named are concealed in a particular house or place, if satisfied that there is a reasonable cause for such belief, may issue a warrant to search for the following property or articles: books, records, files, membership lists, funds, referred to in sections eighteen and twenty-one of chapter two hundred and sixty-four, or written or printed documents, paper or pictorial representations, referred to in section eleven of said chapter two hundred and sixty-four, belonging to a subversive organization as defined in said section eighteen, or used, provided for, or intended to be used for, the purposes specified in said section eleven.

Added by St.1955, c. 272, § 1.

§ 1B. Search warrants for records possessed by foreign corporations providing electronic communication or remote computing services

(a) As used in this section, the following words shall have the following meanings:—

"Adverse result", occurs when notification of the existence of a search warrant results in:—

(1) danger to the life or physical safety of an individual;

(2) a flight from prosecution;

(3) the destruction of or tampering with evidence;

(4) the intimidation of a potential witness or witnesses; or

(5) serious jeopardy to an investigation or undue delay of a trial.

"Electronic communication services", shall be construed in accordance with sections 2701 to 2711 Title 18, of the United States Code. This definition shall not apply to corporations that do not provide electronic communication services to the general public.

"Foreign corporation", any corporation or other entity that makes a contract or engages in a terms of service agreement with a resident of the commonwealth to be performed in whole or in part by either party in the commonwealth. The making of the contract or terms of service agreement shall be considered to be the agreement of the foreign corporation that a search warrant or subpoena which has been properly served on it has the same legal force and effect as if served personally within the commonwealth.

"Massachusetts corporation", any corporation or other entity that is subject to chapter 155 or chapter 156B.

"Properly served", delivery of a search warrant or subpoena by hand, by United States mail, by commercial delivery service, by facsimile or by any other manner to any officer of a corporation or its general manager in the commonwealth, to any natural person designated by it as agent for the service of process, or if such corporation has designated a corporate agent, to any person named in the latest certificate filed pursuant to section 15.03 of chapter 156D.

"Remote computing services", shall be construed in accordance with sections 2701 to 2711, inclusive, of Title 18, of the United States Code. This definition shall not apply to corporations that do not provide those services to the general public.

"Subpoena", a grand jury or trial subpoena issued in the course of a criminal proceeding or an administrative subpoena issued pursuant to section 17B of chapter 271.

(b) A court or justice authorized to issue warrants in criminal cases may, upon complaint on oath that the complainant believes that any of the records hereinafter named are actually or constructively possessed by a foreign corporation that provides electronic communication services or remote computing services, if satisfied that probable cause has been established for such belief, issue a warrant identifying those records to be searched for and commanding the person seeking such warrant to properly serve the warrant upon the foreign corporation:—

(1) those records which would reveal the identity of a customer using those services;

(2) data stored by or on behalf of a customer;

(3) records of a customer's usage of those services;

(4) records of the source of communications sent to or the recipient or destination of communications sent from a customer; or

(5) the content of those communications stored by an electronic communication or remote commuting service.

(c) The following provisions shall apply to any search warrant issued pursuant to this section and to any subpoena issued in the course of a criminal investigation or proceeding directed to a foreign corporation that provides electronic communication services or remote computing services:

(1) when properly served with a search warrant issued by any court of the commonwealth or justice pursuant to this section or a subpoena, a foreign corporation subject to this section shall provide all records sought pursuant to that warrant or subpoena within 14 days of receipt, including those records maintained or located outside the commonwealth;

(2) if the applicant makes a showing and the court or justice finds that failure to produce records within less than 14 days would cause an adverse result, a warrant may require production of records within less than 14 days;

(3) a court or justice may reasonably extend the time required for production of the records upon finding that the foreign corporation has shown good cause for that extension and that an extension of time would not cause an adverse result;

(4) a foreign corporation seeking to quash a warrant or subpoena served on it pursuant to this section shall seek relief from the court that issued the warrant or the court which has jurisdiction over the subpoena within the time required for production of records pursuant to this section. The court shall hear and decide such motion not later than 14 days after the motion is filed;

(5) in the case of an administrative subpoena issued by the attorney general, the superior court of Suffolk county shall have jurisdiction and in the case of an administrative subpoena issued by a district attorney, the superior court in any county in which the district attorney maintains an office shall have jurisdiction; and

(6) the foreign corporation shall verify the authenticity of records that it produces by providing an affidavit from the person in custody of those records certifying that they are true and complete.

(d) A Massachusetts corporation that provides electronic communication services or remote computing services, when served with a warrant or subpoena issued by another state to produce records that would reveal the identity of the customers using those services, data stored by, or on behalf of the customer, the customer's usage of those services, the recipient or destination of communications sent to or from those customers, or the content of those communications, shall produce those records as if that warrant or subpoena had been issued under the law of the commonwealth.

(e) No cause of action shall lie against any foreign or Massachusetts corporation subject to this section, its officers, employees, agents or other persons for providing records, information, facilities or assistance in accordance with the terms of a warrant or subpoena issued pursuant to this section.

Added by St.2008, c. 205, § 4, eff. Oct. 22, 2008.

§ 2. Requisites of warrant

Search warrants shall designate and describe the building, house, place, vessel or vehicle to be searched and shall particularly describe the property or articles to be searched for. They shall be substantially in the form prescribed in section two A of this chapter and shall be directed to the sheriff or his deputy or to a constable or police officer, commanding him to search in the daytime, or if the warrant so directs, in the nighttime, the building, house, place, vessel or vehicle where the property or articles for which he is required to search are believed to be concealed, and to bring such property or articles when found, and the persons in whose possession they are found, before a court having jurisdiction.

Amended by St.1959, c. 313, § 19; St.1963, c. 96, § 2; St.1964, c. 557, § 2.

Historical and Statutory Notes

R.S.1836, c. 142, §§ 3, 4.
G.S.1860, c. 170, §§ 3, 4.
P.S.1882, c. 212, §§ 3, 4.
St.1899, c. 166.
R.L.1902, c. 217, § 2.
St.1919, c. 179, § 3.

§ 2A. Form of warrant

The warrant shall be in substantially the following form:

THE COMMONWEALTH OF MASSACHUSETTS.

(COUNTY), ss. (NAME) COURT.

To the Sheriffs of our several counties, or their deputies, any State Police Officer, or any Constable or Police Officer of any city or town, within our said Commonwealth.

Proof by affidavit having been made this day before (name of person authorized to issue warrant) by (names of person or persons whose affidavits have been taken) that there is probable cause for believing that (certain property has been stolen, embezzled, or obtained by false pretenses; certain property is intended for use or has been used as the means of committing a crime; certain property has been concealed to prevent a crime from being discovered; certain property is unlawfully possessed or kept or concealed for an unlawful purpose).

We therefore command you in the daytime (or at any time of the day or night) to make an immediate search of (identify premises) (occupied by A.B.) and (of the person of A.B.) and of any person present who may be found to have such property in his possession or under his control or to whom such property may have been delivered, for the following property:

(description of property)

and if you find any such property or any part thereof to bring it and the persons in whose possession it is found before (court having jurisdiction) at (name of court and location).

Dated at (city or town) this .... day of ...., (insert year).

Clerk.

Added by St.1964, c. 557, § 3. Amended by St.1998, c. 463, § 191.

§ 2B. Affidavit in support of application for warrant; contents and form

A person seeking a search warrant shall appear personally before a court or justice authorized to issue search warrants in criminal cases and shall give an affidavit in substantially the form hereinafter prescribed. Such affidavit shall contain the facts, information, and circumstances upon which such person relies to establish sufficient grounds for the issuance of the warrant. The person issuing the warrant shall retain the affidavit and shall deliver it within three days after the issuance of the warrant to the court to which the warrant is returnable. Upon the return of said warrant, the affidavit shall be attached to it and shall be filed therewith, and it shall not be a public document until the warrant is returned.

The affidavit in support of the application for a search warrant shall be in substantially the following form:

THE COMMONWEALTH OF MASSACHUSETTS.

(COUNTY), ss. (NAME) COURT.
............., (insert year).

I, (name of applicant) being duly sworn, depose and say:

1. I am (describe position, assignment, office, etc.)

2. I have information, based upon (describe source, facts indicating reliability of source and nature of information; if based on personal knowledge and belief, so state).

3. Based upon the foregoing reliable information (and upon my personal knowledge) there is probable cause to believe that the property hereinafter described (has been stolen, or is being concealed, etc.) and may be found (in the possession of A.B. or any other person) at premises (identify).

4. The property for which I seek the issuance of a search warrant is the following: (here describe the property as particularly as possible).

Wherefore, I respectfully request that the court issue a warrant and order of seizure, authorizing the search of (identify premises and the persons to be searched) and directing that if such property or evidence or any part thereof be found that it be seized and brought before the court; together with such other and further relief that the court may deem proper.

....
....................Name.

Then personally appeared the above named .... and made oath that the foregoing affidavit by him subscribed is true.

Before me this .... day of ...., (insert year).

Justice or Special Justice,
Clerk or Assistant Clerk
of the .... Court.

Added by St.1964, c. 557, § 3. Amended by St.1965, c. 384; St.1998, c. 463, § 192.

§ 2C. Manner of issuing warrants; application of Secs. 2, 2A and 2B

Search warrants issued pursuant to section two hundred and thirteen of chapter ninety-four,[1] sections twenty and twenty-five of chapter one hundred and ten, section ten of chapter one hundred and thirty, shall be issued in the manner provided in sections two, two A and two B, in so far as they are applicable.

Added by St.1964, c. 557, § 3. Amended by St.1967, c. 802, § 4.

[1] Repealed.

§ 3. Seizure, custody and disposition of articles; exceptions

If an officer in the execution of a search warrant finds property or articles therein described, he shall seize and safely keep them, under the direction of the court or justice, so long as necessary to permit them to be produced or used as evidence in any trial. As soon as may be, thereafter, all property seized under clause First of section one shall be restored to the owners thereof; and all other property seized in execution of a search warrant shall be disposed of as the court or justice orders and may be forfeited and either sold or destroyed, as the public interest requires, in the discretion of the court or justice, except:

(a) Diseased animals or carcasses thereof, or any tainted, diseased, corrupt, decayed or unwholesome meat, fish, vegetables, produce, fruit or provisions of any kind, or the meat of any calf killed when less than two weeks old, or any product thereof kept or concealed with intent to kill, sell or offer the same for sale for food, shall be destroyed or disposed of in accordance with section one hundred and forty-six of chapter ninety-four by the board of health or by an officer designated by the court or justice; and diseased animals found to have been kept or concealed in a particular building, place or enclosure shall be destroyed or disposed of by the division of animal health and department of food and agriculture without compensation to the owners thereof.

(b) Rifles, shotguns, pistols, knives or other dangerous weapons which have been found to have been kept, concealed or used unlawfully or for an unlawful purpose shall be forfeited to the commonwealth and delivered forthwith to the colonel of the state police for destruction or preservation in the discretion of the colonel of the state police.

(c) Money seized under clause Third of section one shall be forfeited and paid over to the state treasurer.

(d) Any property, including money seized under section one, the forfeiture and disposition of which is specified in any general or special law shall be disposed of in accordance therewith.

Amended by St.1934, c. 340, § 15; St.1957, c. 660, § 3; St.1964, c. 557, § 4; St.1965, c. 325; St.1967, c. 347, § 12; St.1971, c. 1071, § 7; St.1975, c. 706, § 302; St.1977, c. 556, § 4; St.1996, c. 151, § 497.

Historical and Statutory Notes

R.S.1836, c. 142, § 5.
G.S.1860, c. 170, § 5.
P.S.1882, c. 212, § 5.
St.1890, c. 452.
St.1894, c. 410, § 1.
St.1894, c. 491, § 14.
St.1899, c. 408, § 16.
R.L.1902, c. 217, § 3.
St.1902, c. 116, §§ 1, 2.
St.1912, c. 608, §§ 1, 2.
St.1919, c. 179, §§ 2, 3.
St.1919, c. 350, §§ 39, 40.

§ 3A. Time for return of warrant

Every officer to whom a warrant to search is issued shall return the same to the court by which it was issued as soon as it has been served and in any event not later than seven days from the date of issuance thereof, with a return of his doings thereon; provided, however, that a justice of the superior court may at any time receive complaints and issue search warrants returnable in seven days before a district court named in such warrant and in that event the officer shall make his return to such district court as directed.

Added by St.1934, c. 247. Amended by St.1962, c. 328; St.1964, c. 557, § 5.

§ 4. Notice before forfeiture of property

Before a decree of forfeiture of property seized under a search warrant is issued, the court or justice shall, unless otherwise expressly provided, issue a notice under seal, signed by the clerk of the court or by the justice, setting forth the substance of the complaint, and commanding the persons, if any, in whose possession the articles were found, and the owner, if alleged, and all other persons who claim an interest therein, to appear at a time and place therein named to show cause why the articles seized should not be forfeited.

Historical and Statutory Notes

St.1870, c. 242, § 2.
P.S.1882, c. 212, § 6.
St.1894, c. 410, § 1.
R.L.1902, c. 217, § 4.
St.1919, c. 179, § 3.

§ 5. Service of notice

The notice shall, not less than fourteen days before the time appointed for trial, be served upon the person, if any, alleged to be the owner of the articles seized, by an officer authorized to serve criminal process, by leaving an attested copy thereof with him personally or at his usual place of abode and by posting an attested copy thereof on the house or building in which the articles were seized, if they were found in a house or building; otherwise, in a public place in the town where they were seized.

Historical and Statutory Notes

St.1870, c. 242, § 3.
P.S.1882, c. 212, § 7.
St.1894, c. 410, § 1.
R.L.1902, c. 217, § 5.
St.1919, c. 179, § 3.

§ 6. Postponement of trial; further notice

If, at the time appointed for the trial, such notice has not been duly served, or if it appears necessary that any of the articles so seized should be kept longer for the purpose of being produced or used as evidence on any trial, or if other sufficient cause appears, the trial may be postponed to another day and place and further notice issued.

Historical and Statutory Notes

St.1870, c. 242, § 4.
P.S.1882, c. 212, § 8.
St.1894, c. 410, § 1.
R.L.1902, c. 217, § 6.
St.1919, c. 179, § 3.

§ 7. Sale or destruction of property seized; disposition of proceeds

If upon trial the property is adjudged forfeited, it shall forthwith be disposed of as provided by law. So much thereof as is ordered to be sold by the court or justice shall be sold by the sheriff and the proceeds paid to the county. All moneys seized shall be paid over forthwith to the state treasurer. The court or justice may order any article not found to have been unlawfully used, kept or concealed or intended for unlawful use, or any article unlawfully used without the knowledge of its owner, lessor or mortgagee to be delivered to the party legally entitled to its possession.

Amended by St.1934, c. 235, § 2; St.1957, c. 660, § 4; St.1964, c. 557, § 6.

Historical and Statutory Notes

St.1862, c. 168, § 5.
St.1869, c. 364, § 3.
P.S.1882, c. 212, § 9.
St.1885, c. 66, § 1.
St.1894, c. 410, § 1.
St.1899, c. 359, § 8.
R.L.1902, c. 217, § 7.
St.1908, c. 370.
St.1919, c. 179, § 3.

§ 8. Appeal; recognizance; jury trial; conformity to criminal cases; disposition of articles

A person aggrieved by a decree of forfeiture of a district court may appeal therefrom to the superior court; but before his appeal is allowed, he shall recognize to the commonwealth in the sum of two hundred dollars, with sufficient surety or sureties, to prosecute his appeal and to pay all such expenses as may thereafter arise, if final judgment is rendered against the articles adjudged forfeited, and to abide the judgment of the superior court thereon; and upon such appeal, any question of fact shall be tried by a jury. All proceedings in the superior court, including the right of exception, shall conform so far as may be to proceedings in criminal cases; and if, upon final judgment, the articles are adjudged forfeited, they shall be disposed of under the direction of the superior court as they might have been disposed of had no appeal been taken.

Amended by St.1959, c. 313, § 20.

Historical and Statutory Notes

St.1870, c. 242, § 1.
P.S.1882, c. 212, § 10.
St.1894, c. 410, § 1.
R.L.1902, c. 217, § 8.
St.1919, c. 179, § 3.

§ 9. Rewards offered by governor; determination of claims

The governor, if he deems the public good so requires, may offer a suitable reward of not more than ten thousand dollars in any one case to be paid by the commonwealth to any person who, in consequence of such offer, apprehends, brings back and secures a person who is convicted of or charged with a felony, who has escaped from prison in the commonwealth, or to any person who, in consequence of such offer, apprehends and secures a person charged with such crime, or for information that shall lead to the arrest and conviction of any person who has committed a felony, if the person cannot be arrested and secured in the common course of proceedings. If more than one claimant applies for the payment of such reward, the governor shall determine to whom it shall be paid, and if to more than one person, in what proportion to each, and his determination shall be final.

Amended by St.1947, c. 359; St.1964, c. 111.

Historical and Statutory Notes

St.1836, c. 4, § 18.
G.S.1860, c. 170, § 6.
P.S.1882, c. 212, § 11.
R.L.1902, c. 217, § 9.
St.1914, c. 521.

§ 10. Rewards offered for detecting or securing persons committing certain offenses; determination of claims

The aldermen or the selectmen, if in their opinion the public good so requires, may offer a suitable reward of not more than five hundred dollars in any one case, to be paid by the town to any person who, in consequence of such offer, detects or secures a person who has committed a felony in such place, either before or after he has been charged therewith, and such reward shall be paid by the treasurer upon the warrant of the aldermen or selectmen. If more than one claimant applies for the payment of such reward, the aldermen or selectmen shall determine to whom it shall be paid, and if to more than one person, in what proportion to each, and their determination shall be final.

The aldermen or the selectmen may offer a reward of five hundred dollars for information leading to the arrest and conviction of a person making or circulating or causing to be made or circulated a false alarm of fire.

In a city, the mayor, with the approval of the city council or, in a town, the selectmen, may offer a reward of not more than five thousand dollars, in any one case, to be paid by the town or city to any person who, in consequence of such offer, detects or secures the arrest and conviction of a person who assassinates or attempts to assassinate a police officer employed by such city or town. Such reward shall be paid by the treasurer upon the warrant of the mayor or selectmen. If more than one claimant applies for the payment of such reward, the mayor or selectmen shall determine to whom it shall be paid, and if to more than one person, in what proportion to each, and said determination shall be final.

Amended by St.1971, c. 57; St.1979, c. 728; St.1985, c. 196.

Historical and Statutory Notes

St.1840, c. 75.
G.S.1860, c. 170, §§ 7, 8.
St.1866, c. 9.
P.S.1882, c. 212, §§ 12, 13.
R.L.1902, c. 217, § 10.

§ 10A. Authority of officer of another state to arrest felon

Any member of a duly organized state, county or municipal peace unit of another state of the United States the laws of which contain provisions substantially equivalent to the provisions of this and the following section, who enters this commonwealth in fresh pursuit, and continues herein in such fresh pursuit, of a person in order to arrest him on the ground that he has committed a felony in such other state shall have the same authority to arrest and hold in custody such person as members of a duly organized state, county or municipal peace unit of this commonwealth have to arrest and hold in custody a person on the ground that he has committed a felony in this commonwealth. This section shall not be construed so as to make unlawful any arrest in this commonwealth which would otherwise be lawful.

Added by St.1937, c. 208, § 1.

§ 10B. Proceedings after arrest

If an arrest is made in this commonwealth by an officer of another state in accordance with the provisions of the preceding section he shall without unnecessary delay take the person arrested before a justice, associate justice or special justice of a court of record in the county in which the arrest was made, who shall conduct a hearing for the purpose of determining the lawfulness of the arrest. If such justice, associate justice or special justice determines that the arrest was lawful he shall commit the person arrested to await for a reasonable time the issuance of a rendition warrant by the governor of the state from which he fled. If such justice, associate justice or special justice determines that the arrest was unlawful he shall discharge the person arrested.

Added by St.1937, c. 208, § 1.

§ 10C. Partial invalidity

If any part of sections ten A and ten B is for any reason declared void, it is declared to be the intent of said sections that such invalidity shall not affect the validity of the remaining portions of said sections.

Added by St.1937, c. 208, § 1.

§ 10D. Citation of law; uniform construction

Sections ten A to ten C, inclusive, may be cited as the uniform extra-territorial arrest on fresh pursuit law, and shall be so interpreted and construed as to effectuate their general purpose to make uniform the law of the states which enact similar laws.

Added by St.1937, c. 208, § 1.

§ 11. Definitions

Wherever appearing in sections eleven to twenty R, inclusive, the term "governor" includes any person performing the functions of governor by authority of the law of this commonwealth, the term "executive authority" includes the governor, and any person performing the functions of governor, in any other state, the term "surrender" refers to the arresting and delivering up of a person in this commonwealth to the executive authority of another state, and the term "state", referring to a state other than this commonwealth, refers to any other state or territory, organized or unorganized, of the United States.

Added by St.1937, c. 304, § 1.

§ 12. Arrest and delivery of accused to executives of another state; governor's authority

Subject to the provisions of sections eleven to twenty R, inclusive, the controlling provisions of the constitution of the United States, and any and all acts of congress enacted in pursuance thereof, the governor may cause to be arrested and delivered up to the executive authority of any other state any person charged in such other state with treason, felony or other crime, or with having been convicted of a crime in such other state and having escaped from confinement or having broken the terms of his bail, probation or parole, who is found in this commonwealth.

Added by St.1937, c. 304, § 1.

§ 13. Surrendering accused not in demanding state at time of crime or leaving demanding state involuntarily

The governor may also surrender, on demand of the executive authority of any other state, any person in this commonwealth charged in such other state in the manner provided in section fourteen with committing an act in this commonwealth, or in a third state, intentionally resulting in a crime in the state whose executive authority is making the demand, hereafter in this section and in sections fourteen to twenty P, inclusive, referred to as the demanding state, and the provisions of sections eleven to twenty R, inclusive, not otherwise inconsistent shall apply to such cases, even though the accused was not in the demanding state at the time of the commission of the crime.

The governor may surrender, on demand of the executive authority of any other state, any person in this commonwealth charged in the demanding state in the manner provided in section fourteen with having violated its laws, even though such person left such state involuntarily.

Added by St.1937, c. 304, § 1.

§ 14. Written demand; allegations; accompanying papers; charge of crime; authentication of copies of papers

No demand for the interstate rendition of a person charged with crime in another state shall be recognized by the governor unless it be in writing alleging either that the person demanded was present in the demanding state at the time of the commission of the alleged crime, or that such person committed in this commonwealth or in a third state an act intentionally resulting in a crime in the demanding state, or that such person has escaped from confinement or has broken the terms of his bail, probation or parole, nor unless such demand is accompanied by a copy of an indictment found, or of an information supported by affidavit, in the demanding state, or by a copy of an affidavit made before a magistrate of such state, and by a copy of the warrant which was issued thereon, or by a copy of a judgment of conviction or of a sentence imposed in execution thereof in the demanding state. The indictment or information, or the affidavit made before the magistrate who issued the warrant, shall substantially charge the person demanded with having committed a crime under the law of the demanding state, and the copy of the indictment, information, affidavit, judgment of conviction or sentence shall be authenticated by the executive authority of such state.

Added by St.1937, c. 304, § 1.

§ 15. Investigation of demand and report to governor

When a demand shall be made upon the governor by the executive authority of another state for the surrender of a person so charged with crime, the governor may call upon the attorney general or any other prosecuting officer to investigate or assist in investigating the demand, and to report to him the situation and circumstances of the person so demanded, and whether he ought to be surrendered.

Added by St.1937, c. 304, § 1.

§ 16. Governor's warrant of arrest; recital of facts

If the governor decides that the demand should be complied with, he shall sign a warrant of arrest, sealed with the state seal and directed to an officer authorized to serve warrants in criminal cases or other person whom the governor may think fit to entrust with the execution thereof. Such warrant shall substantially recite the facts necessary to the validity of its issue.

Added by St.1937, c. 304, § 1.

§ 17. Arrest and delivery of accused; commanding aid

Such warrant shall authorize the person to whom it is directed to arrest the accused at any time and any place where he may be found within this commonwealth and to command the aid of all officers authorized to serve warrants in criminal cases or other persons in the execution thereof, and to deliver the accused, subject to the provisions of said sections eleven to twenty R, inclusive, to the duly authorized agent of the demanding state.

Added by St.1937, c. 304, § 1.

§ 18. Authority to command assistance; penalties for refusal

Every such person empowered to make an arrest shall have the same authority, in arresting the accused, to command assistance therein, as officers have by law in the execution of any criminal process directed to them, with like penalties against those who refuse their assistance.

Added by St.1937, c. 304, § 1.

§ 19. Rights of arrested person; habeas corpus; notice; penalty

No person arrested upon such a warrant shall be delivered over to the agent whom the executive authority of the demanding state shall have appointed to receive him unless such person shall first be taken forthwith before a justice or special justice of a court of record of this commonwealth, who shall inform such person of the demand made for his surrender and of the crime with which he is charged, and that he has the right to demand and procure legal counsel; and, if the prisoner or his counsel shall state that he desires to test the legality of his arrest, such justice or special justice shall fix a reasonable time to be allowed the prisoner within which to apply for a writ of habeas corpus. When such writ is applied for, notice thereof, and of the time and place of hearing thereon, shall be given to the attorney general and to the district attorney for the district in which the arrest is made and for the district in which the accused is in custody, and to said agent of the demanding state.

Any officer who shall deliver to said agent of the demanding state a person in his custody under the warrant of the governor, in wilful disobedience of the provisions of this section, shall be punished by a fine of not more than one thousand dollars or by imprisonment for not more than six months, or both.

Added by St.1937, c. 304, § 1.

§ 20. Confinement of accused; expense; evidence of transportation to demanding state; new requisition

The officer or other person executing the governor's warrant of arrest, or the agent of the demanding state to whom the prisoner shall have been delivered, may when necessary confine the prisoner in a jail or other place of detention in any county, city or town through which he may pass; and the keeper of such jail or place of detention shall receive and safely keep the prisoner until the officer or person having charge of him is ready to proceed on his journey, such officer or person being chargeable with the expense of keeping.

The officer or agent of a demanding state to whom a prisoner shall have been delivered following interstate rendition proceedings in another state, or to whom a prisoner shall have been delivered after waiving interstate rendition in another state, and who is passing through this commonwealth with such a prisoner for the purpose of immediately returning such prisoner to the demanding state may, when necessary, confine the prisoner in a jail or other place of detention in any county, city or town through which he may pass; and the keeper of such jail or other place of detention shall receive and safely keep the prisoner until the officer or agent having charge of him is ready to proceed on his journey, such officer or agent being chargeable with the expense of keeping; provided, that such officer or agent shall produce and show to such keeper satisfactory written evidence that he is actually transporting such prisoner to the demanding state pursuant to a requisition by the executive authority thereof, or that such prisoner has waived interstate rendition. No prisoner being transported pursuant to such a requisition or waiver shall be entitled to demand a new requisition while in this commonwealth.

Added by St.1937, c. 304, § 1.

§ 20A. Warrant to apprehend on oath or affidavit; copies of papers attached

Whenever any person within this commonwealth shall be charged, on the oath of any credible person before any court or justice in this commonwealth authorized to issue warrants in criminal cases, with the commission of any crime in any other state, including cases arising under section thirteen, or with having been convicted in such other state and having escaped from confinement or having broken the terms of his bail, probation or parole, or whenever complaint shall have been made before any such court or justice in this commonwealth setting forth, on the affidavit of any credible person in another state, that a crime has been committed in such other state and that a person has been charged in such state with the commission of a crime, including cases arising under section thirteen, or with having been convicted of a crime in that state and having escaped from confinement or having broken the terms of his bail, probation or parole, and is believed to be in this commonwealth, such court or justice may issue a warrant directed to any officer authorized to serve warrants in criminal cases commanding him to apprehend the person named therein, wherever he may be found in this commonwealth, and bring him before the same or any other such court or justice convenient of access to the place where the arrest may be made, to answer the charge or complaint and affidavit; and a certified copy of the sworn charge or complaint and affidavit upon which the warrant is issued shall be attached to the warrant.

Added by St.1937, c. 304, § 1.

§ 20B. Arrest without warrant; taking accused before court or justice; complaint

The arrest of a person may be lawfully made also by any officer authorized to serve warrants in criminal cases, without a warrant, upon reasonable information that the accused stands charged in another state with a crime punishable by death or by imprisonment for a term exceeding one year, but when so arrested the accused shall be taken with all practicable speed before a court or justice authorized to issue warrants in criminal cases and complaint shall be made against him under oath setting forth the ground for the arrest as in the preceding section; and thereafter his answer shall be heard as if he had been arrested on a warrant.

Added by St.1937, c. 304, § 1.

§ 20C. Commitment to permit arrest under warrant of governor on requisition

If from the examination before such court or justice it appears that the person held is the person charged with having committed the crime alleged, including cases arising under section thirteen, or is the person charged with having been convicted of a crime and having escaped from confinement or having broken the terms of his bail, probation or parole, such court or justice shall, by a warrant reciting the accusation, commit him to a jail or house of correction for such time, not exceeding thirty days and specified in the warrant, as will enable the arrest of the accused to be made under a warrant of the governor, on a requisition of the executive authority of the state having jurisdiction of the crime, unless the accused gives bail as provided in the following section, or until he shall be legally discharged.

Added by St.1937, c. 304, § 1.

§ 20D. Bail

Unless the offence with which the person arrested is charged is shown to be an offence punishable by death or life imprisonment under the laws of the state in which it was committed, such court or justice may admit such person to bail by bond or undertaking, with sufficient sureties, and in such sum as such court or justice deems proper, conditioned for his appearance before such court or justice, at a time specified in such bond or undertaking, and for his surrender to be arrested upon the warrant of the governor.

Added by St.1937, c. 304, § 1.

§ 20E. Discharge; recommitment; bail

If the accused has not been arrested under warrant of the governor at the expiration of the time specified in such warrant, bond or undertaking, such court or justice may discharge him or may recommit him for a further period of sixty days, or may again take bail for his appearance and surrender, as provided in the preceding section, but within a period not to exceed sixty days following the date of such new bond or undertaking.

Added by St.1937, c. 304, § 1.

§ 20F. Forfeiture of bail

If the accused is admitted to bail, and fails to appear and surrender himself according to the conditions of his bond or undertaking, such court or justice, by proper order, shall declare the bond or undertaking forfeited and order his immediate arrest without warrant if he be within this commonwealth. Recovery may be had on such bonds or undertakings in the name of the commonwealth as in the case of other bonds or undertakings given by persons accused in criminal proceedings within this commonwealth.

Added by St.1937, c. 304, § 1.

§ 20G. Prosecution pending in commonwealth

If a criminal prosecution has been instituted against such person under the laws of this commonwealth and is still pending, the governor, in his discretion, may either surrender him on the demand of the executive authority of another state, or hold him until the final disposition of such prosecution or, if convicted and sentenced, until his discharge from imprisonment.

Added by St.1937, c. 304, § 1.

§ 20H. Inquiry into guilt or innocence

The guilt or innocence of the accused as to the crime of which he is charged may not be inquired into by the governor, or in any proceeding after the demand for interstate rendition accompanied by a charge of crime in legal form as provided in section fourteen shall have been presented to the governor, except as it may be involved in identifying the person held as the person charged with the crime.

Added by St.1937, c. 304, § 1.

§ 20*I*. Recall of warrant or issuance of another

The governor, whenever he deems proper, may recall his warrant of arrest or may issue another warrant.

Added by St.1937, c. 304, § 1.

§ 20J. Waiver of warrant and procedure, etc.

Any person arrested in this commonwealth charged with having committed any crime in another state or with having been convicted in another state and having escaped from confinement or having broken the terms of his bail, probation or parole, may waive the issuance and service of the warrant provided for in sections sixteen and seventeen and all other procedure incidental to interstate rendition proceedings, by executing or subscribing in the presence of any court or justice of this commonwealth authorized to issue warrants in criminal cases a writing which states that he consents to return to the demanding state; provided, that if such waiver shall be executed or subscribed by such person it shall be the duty of such court or justice to inform such person of his rights to the issuance and service of a warrant in interstate rendition and to obtain a writ of habeas corpus as provided in section nineteen. If and when such consent has been duly executed it shall forthwith be forwarded to the office of the governor and filed therein. Such court or justice shall direct the officer having such person in custody to deliver forthwith such person to the duly accredited agent of the demanding state, and shall deliver or cause to be delivered to such agent a copy of such consent; provided, that nothing in this section shall be deemed to limit the right of the accused person to return voluntarily and without formality to the demanding state, nor shall the foregoing waiver procedure be deemed to be an exclusive procedure or to limit the powers, rights or duties of the officers of the demanding state or of this commonwealth.

Added by St.1937, c. 304, § 1.

§ 20K. Warrant to receive accused and convey him to proper county; proceedings pending in another state

Whenever the governor shall demand a person charged with crime in this commonwealth, or one charged with having been convicted in this commonwealth and having escaped from confinement or having broken the terms of his bail, probation or parole, from the chief executive of any other state, or from the chief justice or an associate justice of the supreme court of the District of Columbia authorized to receive such demand under the laws of the United States, he may issue a warrant, under the seal of this commonwealth, to some agent, commanding him to receive the person so charged if delivered to him, and convey him to the proper officer of the county in which the crime was committed.

Whenever it is desired to have returned to this commonwealth a person charged herein with a crime, or with having been convicted in this commonwealth and having escaped from confinement or having broken the terms of his bail, probation or parole, and such person is imprisoned or is held under criminal proceedings then pending against him in another state, the governor may agree with the executive authority of such other state for the interstate rendition of such person before the conclusion of such proceedings or of his term of sentence in such other state, upon such conditions relative to the return of such person to such other state at the expense of this commonwealth as may be agreed upon between the governor and the executive authority of such other state.

Added by St.1937, c. 304, § 1.

§ 20L. Application for requisition

(a) Whenever the return to this commonwealth of a person charged with crime herein is required, the attorney general, or the district attorney for the district in which the crime is alleged to have occurred, shall present to the governor his written application for a requisition for the return of the person charged, in which application there shall be included a statement of the name of the person so charged and the crime charged against him, the approximate time, place and circumstances of its commission, the state in which he is believed to be, including the location of the accused therein, at the time the application is made, and a certificate that, in the opinion of the said attorney general or district attorney, the ends of justice require the arrest and return of the accused to this commonwealth for trial, and that the proceeding is not instituted to enforce a private claim.

(b) Whenever the return to this commonwealth is required of a person who has been convicted of a crime herein and has escaped from confinement or has broken the terms of his bail, probation or parole, the district attorney for the district in which the crime is alleged to have occurred, the parole board or the warden or superintendent of the institution from which escape was made, shall present to the governor a written application for a requisition for the return of such person, in which application shall be stated the name of the person, the crime of which he was convicted, the circumstances of his escape from confinement or of the breach of the terms of his bail, probation or parole, and the state in which he is believed to be, including the location of the person therein, at the time the application is made.

(c) The application shall be verified by affidavit, shall be executed in duplicate and shall be accompanied by two certified copies of the indictment returned, or of the complaint made to a court or justice, stating the offence with which the accused is charged, or of the judgment of conviction or of the sentence. The attorney general, district attorney, parole board, warden or superintendent may also attach such further affidavits or other documents in duplicate as he or it may deem proper to be submitted with such application. One copy of the application, with the action of the governor indicated by endorsement thereon, and one of the certified copies of the indictment or complaint, or of the judgment of conviction or of the sentence shall be filed in the office of the state secretary to remain of record in that office. The other copies of all such papers shall be forwarded with the requisition of the governor.

Added by St.1937, c. 304, § 1.

§ 20M. Payment of agent's expenses

If the application for a requisition for the return to this commonwealth of a person charged with crime herein, or for the return of a person who has been convicted of a crime herein and has escaped from confinement or has broken the terms of his bail, probation or parole, is complied with and an agent appointed, the account of such agent shall be paid like other expenses in criminal cases by the commonwealth.

Added by St.1937, c. 304, § 1. Amended by St.1978, c. 478, § 284.

§ 20N. Service of process in civil action on accused; immunity

A person brought into this commonwealth on, or after waiver of, interstate rendition based on a criminal charge shall not be subject to service of personal process in civil actions arising out of the same facts as the criminal proceeding to answer which he is being or has been returned, until he has been convicted or acquitted in the criminal proceeding, and, if acquitted, until he has had reasonable opportunity to return to the state from which he was brought by interstate rendition proceedings or upon waiver thereof.

Added by St.1937, c. 304, § 1.

§ 20*O*. Trying for other crimes; immunity

After a person has been brought into this commonwealth by interstate rendition proceedings or upon waiver thereof he may be tried herein for other crimes which he may be charged with having committed herein, as well as that specified in the requisition for his interstate rendition or in the waiver thereof.

Added by St.1937, c. 304, § 1.

§ 20P. Waiver by commonwealth

Nothing in sections eleven to twenty *O,* inclusive, shall be deemed to constitute a waiver by this commonwealth of its right, power or privilege to try any person demanded of it for a crime committed herein, or of its right, power or privilege to regain custody of such a person by interstate rendition proceedings or otherwise for the purpose of trial, sentence or punishment for any crime committed herein, nor shall any proceeding under said sections which result in, or fail to result in, interstate rendition be deemed a waiver by this commonwealth of any of its rights, privileges or jurisdiction in any way whatsoever.

Added by St.1937, c. 304, § 1.

§ 20Q. Partial validity

If any part of sections eleven to twenty P, inclusive, is for any reason declared void, such invalidity shall not affect the validity of the remaining portions of said sections.

Added by St.1937, c. 304, § 1.

§ 20R. Citation of law; uniform construction

Sections eleven to twenty R, inclusive, may be cited as the uniform criminal interstate rendition law, and shall be so interpreted and construed as to effectuate their general purpose to make uniform the law of those states enacting similar laws.

Added by St.1937, c. 304, § 1.

§ 21. Justices may issue process

Justices of the supreme judicial, superior or district courts, may issue process for the apprehension of persons charged with crime and to carry into effect sections twenty-two to eighty-two, inclusive.

Amended by St.1953, c. 319, § 32.

Historical and Statutory Notes

R.S.1836, c. 135, § 1.
G.S.1860, c. 170, § 9.
P.S.1882, c. 212, § 14.
R.L.1902, c. 217, § 21.

§ 22. Warrants, procedure for issuance

Upon complaint made to any justice that a crime has been committed, he shall examine on oath the complainant and any witnesses produced by him, reduce the complaint to writing, and cause it to be subscribed by the complainant, and, if it appears that a crime has been committed, shall issue a summons or warrant in compliance with the provisions of the Massachusetts Rules of Criminal Procedure.

Amended by St.1959, c. 313, § 21; St.1979, c. 344, § 20.

Historical and Statutory Notes

R.S.1836, c. 135, § 2.
G.S.1860, c. 170, § 10.
St.1881, c. 127.
P.S.1882, c. 212, § 15.
R.L.1902, c. 217, § 22.

§ 23. Service of warrants and other processes

Warrants and other processes issued for the apprehension of persons charged with crime and child support warrants issued pursuant to section 34A of chapter 215 may be directed to and served in any part of the commonwealth by an officer authorized to serve criminal process in any county. Such officer may command aid and exercise the same authority as if in his own county.

Amended by St.2005, c. 163, § 55, eff. Dec. 8, 2005.

Historical and Statutory Notes

St.1820, c. 52.
R.S.1836, c. 135, § 3.
St.1846, c. 266.
G.S.1860, c. 170, § 11.
P.S.1882, c. 212, § 20.
St.1886, c. 247.
R.L.1902, c. 217, §§ 23, 28.

§ 23A. Warrant management system

Whenever a court is requested to issue a warrant, the requesting authority shall provide to the court the person's name, last known address, date of birth, gender, race, height, weight, hair and eye color, the offense or offenses for which the warrant is requested, a designation of the offense or offenses as felonies or misdemeanors, any known aliases and any such information as shall be required for a warrant to be accepted by the criminal justice information system maintained by the department of criminal justice information services. A warrant which contains the above information as provided by the individual for whom the warrant is being issued shall not be nullified if such information is later found to be inaccurate. An individual or law enforcement official seeking issuance of a warrant which does not contain all of the above required fields may apply to the clerk of the court for an exemption from this requirement. Such exemption shall be automatically granted upon the request of any law enforcement official or agency. No rights regarding the validity of a warrant may arise from such requirements not being met. Such information and the name of the police department responsible for serving the warrant shall be entered by the clerk's office into a computer system to be known as the warrant management system. All warrants appearing in the warrant management system shall be accessible through the criminal justice information system, maintained by the department of criminal justice information services to law enforcement agencies and the registry of motor vehicles. The warrant shall consist of sufficient information electronically appearing in the warrant management system, and a printout of the electronic warrant from the criminal justice information system shall constitute a true copy of the warrant. Such warrants appearing electronically in the warrant management system and, in turn, in the criminal justice information system, shall constitute notice and delivery of said warrants to the police department responsible for serving the warrant. Whenever a warrant is recalled or removed, the clerk's office shall, without any unnecessary delay, enter the same in the warrant management system which entry shall be electronically transmitted to the criminal justice information system.

No law enforcement officer, who in the performance of his duties relies in good faith on the warrant appearing in the warrant management system and, in turn, the criminal justice information system, shall be liable in any criminal prosecution or civil action alleging false arrest, false imprisonment, or malicious prosecution or arrest by false pretense.

The issuing court shall provide notification, either before the issuance of a default or arrest warrant or no later than 30 days after the issuance of the warrant, to the subject of the warrant. Such notice shall contain the following information: the name and address of the issuing court, a description of the charge for which the warrant is being issued, a description of the method by which the individual may clear the warrant and a summary of the consequences the individual may face for not responding to the warrant. Such notice shall be deemed satisfactory if notice is mailed to the address stated on the warrant.

Added by St.1994, c. 60, § 175. Amended by St.1994, c. 247, § 3; St.1997, c. 19, § 120; St.2000, c. 166, §§ 14, 15; St.2010, c. 256, § 123, eff. Nov. 4, 2010.

§ 23B. Annual list of persons registered with licensing authorities; department of criminal justice information services; outstanding warrants; notification of license suspension; hearing

(a) Any agency, department, commission, division or authority of the commonwealth that issues a professional license, certificate, permit or authorization to engage in a profession, trade, or business shall ensure that such license, certificate, permit or authorization is suspended for a person who has a default or arrest warrant outstanding against him.

(b) In order to determine if a person has an outstanding warrant against him, the licensing authorities referenced in subsection (a) shall transmit to the department of criminal justice information services in an electronic format and reporting schedule approved by the executive director of the department of criminal justice information services a list of persons who are registered with such licensing authorities on an annual basis. The department of criminal justice information services shall, subject to appropriation, remit to each licensing authority a list of persons who have received a license, certificate, permit or authorization to engage in a profession, trade, or business against whom there is an outstanding default or arrest warrant issued by any court of the commonwealth. Evidence of the outstanding default or arrest warrant appearing in the warrant management system as established by section 23A shall be sufficient grounds for such suspension.

(c) Each licensing authority shall notify persons against whom there is a default or arrest warrant outstanding that their license, certificate, permit or authorization shall be suspended unless the person furnishes proof within 30 days that such warrant has been recalled or that there is no such warrant outstanding against the person. Such notification shall be deemed sufficient if the notice is mailed to the address listed on the license, certificate, permit or authorization or application for the license, certificate, permit or authorization. If no such proof is furnished within 30 days, the person shall be notified that such license, certificate, permit or authorization is suspended subject to the opportunity for a hearing. After such notice to the person has been delivered or mailed by the licensing authority, the person may request a hearing within 90 days with respect to the existence of an outstanding warrant. If a hearing is requested within ten days from the time the notice that the license, certificate, permit or authorization is suspended is mailed or delivered, the license, certificate, permit or authorization shall not be suspended until a finding following the hearing. If a hearing is requested as provided for in this chapter, the law enforcement agency responsible for the warrant shall be notified of the time, place, date of hearing and the subject of the warrant. An affidavit from the law enforcement agency responsible for the warrant or from the colonel of the state police may be introduced as prima facie evidence of the existence of a warrant without the need for members of that law enforcement agency to attend any hearings held under this section. The licensing authority shall issue a finding within 45 days of conducting the hearing as to the existence of a warrant. If there is a warrant outstanding, the license, certificate, permit or authorization shall be suspended. Said license shall not be renewed or reinstated without sufficient proof that the warrant has been cleared.

(d) For the purposes of this section, a professional license shall mean any license, permit, certificate, registration, authority or similar form of permission necessary to engage in a trade or profession issued by an agency, department, commission, division or authority of the commonwealth.

(e) The licensing authorities referenced in this section shall promulgate regulations to implement this section. Implementation of this section shall be subject to appropriation.

Added by St.2000, c. 166, § 16. Amended by St.2010, c. 256, § 124, eff. Nov. 4, 2010.

§ 24. Summons instead of warrant

Upon a complaint or indictment for any offense, a summons shall issue instead of a warrant, unless, in the judgment of the court or justice, there is reason to believe that the defendant will not appear upon summons.

Amended by St.1973, c. 566; St.1979, c. 344, § 21.

Historical and Statutory Notes

St.1881, c. 127, § 1.
P.S.1882, c. 212, § 16.
St.1890, c. 225.
R.L.1902, c. 217, § 24.
St.1912, c. 269.

§ 25. Summons fixing time for trial; service

A summons shall require the defendant to appear before the court at a stated time and place on the return day and shall be served by an officer authorized to serve criminal process by giving to the defendant in hand or by leaving at his dwelling house or last and usual place of abode with some person of suitable age and discretion then residing therein an attested copy not less than twenty-four hours before the return day, or by mailing an attested copy to the defendant's last known address.

Amended by St.1967, c. 338; St.1968, c. 698; St.1979, c. 344, § 22.

Historical and Statutory Notes

St.1881, c. 127, § 2.
P.S.1882, c. 212, § 17.
R.L.1902, c. 217, § 25.

§ 26. Failure to appear and abide orders as contempt

If a defendant so summoned fails, without reasonable cause, to appear and abide the orders of the court or justice, he shall be considered in contempt of court, and may be punished by a fine of not more than twenty dollars. A warrant, if necessary, may be issued at any time after the issue of such summons, whether it has been served or not.

Historical and Statutory Notes

St.1881, c. 127, § 3.
P.S.1882, c. 212, § 18.
R.L.1902, c. 217, § 26.

§ 27. Recognizance

If a defendant so summoned duly appears, he may be ordered to recognize for his further appearance but shall not be required to give surety upon his recognizance at any stage of the prosecution without a special order.

Historical and Statutory Notes

St.1881, c. 127, § 4.
P.S.1882, c. 212, § 19.
R.L.1902, c. 217, § 27.

§ 28. Arrest without warrant

Any officer authorized to serve criminal process may arrest, without a warrant, and detain a person found in the act of stealing property in the presence of the officer regardless of the value of the property stolen and may arrest, without a warrant, and detain a person whom the officer has probable cause to believe has committed a misdemeanor by violating a temporary or permanent vacate, restraining, suspension and surrender,, or no-contact order or judgment issued pursuant to section eighteen, thirty-four B or thirty-four C of chapter two hundred and eight, section three, three B, three C, four or five of chapter two hundred and nine A, section thirty-two of chapter two hundred and nine, or section fifteen or twenty of chapter two hundred and nine C. Said officer may arrest, without a warrant, and detain a person whom the officer has probable cause to believe has committed a misdemeanor involving abuse as defined in section one of chapter two hundred and nine A or has committed an assault and battery in violation of section thirteen A of chapter two hundred and sixty-five against a family or household member as defined in section one of chapter two hundred and nine A. Said officer may arrest and detain a person charged with a misdemeanor, without having a warrant for such arrest in his possession, if the officer making such arrest and detention shall have actual knowledge that a warrant then in full force and effect for the arrest of such person has in fact issued.

Amended by St.1949, c. 184; St.1978, c. 447, § 4; St.1983, c. 678, § 7; St.1990, c. 403, § 13; St.1994, c. 351; St.1996, c. 298, §§ 13, 14.

Historical and Statutory Notes

St.1912, c. 482.

§ 29. Outstanding warrant check prior to release on bail or recognizance

Before a court releases, discharges or admits to bail any person brought before said court, in any criminal matter, the court shall first check the warrant management system to determine whether any warrant has been issued against the person in any jurisdiction of the commonwealth. If the warrant management system indicates that any warrant is outstanding, said court shall, if the outstanding offense is bailable pursuant to section fifty-seven, fifty-eight or fifty-eight A of this chapter, make a determination of bail as provided by said sections for each outstanding warrant.

If such person is released on bail or recognizance for an outstanding warrant, said court shall confer with the court that issued the outstanding warrant and, based thereon, specify in the warrant management system the date on which the person must appear before the issuing court and so notify the person. If such person is not released on bail or recognizance for an outstanding warrant, the person shall be transported by an officer, or in accordance with section twenty-four of chapter thirty-seven, or in accordance with any other law of the commonwealth, to the court that issued the warrant, or if the issuing court is not in session, to the jail in the county of the issuing court, and thereafter, to the next regular sitting of the court that issued the warrant.

A person arrested on a default warrant for a felony or a misdemeanor punishable by imprisonment for more than one hundred days may be released on bail or recognizance only by a justice of the court having jurisdiction over the place where the person was arrested or is being held, or by a justice of the court that issued the warrant.

No person authorized to admit to bail, including but not limited to judges or court personnel, and no sheriff or police officer shall release a person from custody before he determines by checking the warrant management system whether any warrant is outstanding in the commonwealth against said person; provided, however, that no person authorized to admit to bail, including but not limited to judges or court personnel, and no sheriff or police officer, who in the performance of his duties acts in good faith, shall be liable in any criminal prosecution or civil action where a person is released from custody before determining by checking the warrant management system whether a warrant is outstanding against said person in the commonwealth.

If a warrant is outstanding for a felony charge, or a misdemeanor punishable by imprisonment for more than one hundred days, the person being held shall be brought before the court having jurisdiction over the place where the person is held, or to the court that issued the warrant, and a justice, clerk or assistant clerk of said court shall make a determination of bail as provided in the first and second paragraphs of this section.

If a warrant is outstanding for a misdemeanor punishable by imprisonment for one hundred days or less, the person may be released on bail or recognizance by a person authorized to admit to bail. Such person authorized to admit to bail shall, without unnecessary delay, provide the clerk of the court that issued the warrant with notice of the fact that the person was admitted to bail. If the person held on such misdemeanor warrant is not released, the person shall be brought before the next session of the court having jurisdiction over the place where the person is held, or to the court that issued the warrant, and such court shall make a determination of bail as provided in the first and second paragraphs of this section.

Amended by St.1994, c. 247, § 4.

Historical and Statutory Notes

St.1692–3, c. 18, § 6.
St.1783, c. 51, § 1.
St.1784, c. 66, § 5.
St.1794, c. 26, §§ 1, 2.
St.1804, c. 143, § 17.
R.S.1836, c. 135, § 4.
G.S.1860, c. 170, § 12.
P.S.1882, c. 212, § 21.
R.L.1902, c. 217, § 29.
St.1931, c. 145, § 1.

§ 30. Recall of default warrant; arrest

Notwithstanding any law, rule or regulation to the contrary, whenever a default warrant, issued in any jurisdiction in the commonwealth against any person, is recalled by a court, the court shall assess a fee of fifty dollars against the person in payment of the costs of recalling the warrant, except that upon a finding of good cause by the court the fee may be waived.

Any person arrested on a warrant issued because such person has forfeited or defaulted on his bail bond or recognizance or has been surrendered by a probation officer shall be required by the court to pay a fee of $75 payable to the city or town in which such arrest was effected, unless the judge finds that such person is indigent, in which case such person shall be required to perform one day of community service, unless the judge further finds that such person is physically or mentally unable to perform such service.

Amended by St.1994, c. 247, § 4; St.2000, c. 166, § 17.

Historical and Statutory Notes

R.S.1836, c. 135, § 5.
G.S.1860, c. 170, § 13.
P.S.1882, c. 212, § 22.
R.L.1902, c. 217, § 30.

§ 31. Default warrants issued due to failure to pay fines, assessments, court costs, restitution, support payments, etc. to be noted in warrant management system

Whenever a court issues a default warrant solely due to the person's failure to pay a fine, assessment, court cost, restitution, support payment or other amount as ordered by the court or required by law, the court shall specify the amount owed, including an additional assessment of $50 which assessment may be waived by the court upon a finding of good cause, with a statement that the warrant against the person may be discharged upon payment of the amount and the assessment, if any, and shall note the same in the warrant management system. The administrative office of the trial court shall accept payment of such fine, assessment, court cost, restitution, support payment or other amount as ordered by the court, along with any assessment, to be remitted by mail, telephone or other electronic means, in any form deemed acceptable by the trial court. Upon receipt of payment, the warrant against the person shall be discharged, the discharge shall be noted in the warrant management system and the individual shall receive notice of the discharge within seven days.

Amended by St.1994, c. 247, § 4; St.2000, c. 166, § 18.

Historical and Statutory Notes

R.S.1836, c. 135, § 6.
G.S.1860, c. 170, § 14.
P.S.1882, c. 212, § 23.
R.L.1902, c. 217, § 31.

§ 32. Payment; release from custody

Whenever a person, brought before a court, against whom an outstanding warrant was issued, solely due to the failure of the person brought before the court to pay a fine assessment, court cost, restitution, support payment, or other amount, the court may accept payment of such amount and assess an additional fifty dollars which assessment may be waived by the court upon a finding of good cause and if the person is not being held on other process, the court may direct that the person be released from custody and shall notify the jurisdiction in which the warrant was issued of the payment and the assessment, if any. Upon notice of the release the court that issued the warrant shall recall the warrant and cause such information to be entered in the warrant management system.

Amended by St.1994, c. 247, § 4.

Historical and Statutory Notes

R.S.1836, c. 135, § 7.
G.S.1882, c. 170, § 15.
P.S.1882, c. 212, § 24.
R.L.1902, c. 217, § 32.

§ 33. Examination of arrested persons for injuries; reports; penalty

Whenever a person is arrested for a crime and is taken to or confined in a jail, police station or lockup, the officer in charge thereof shall immediately examine the prisoner, and if he finds any bruises, cuts or other injuries shall forthwith make a written report thereof to the chief of police of the town concerned, or in Boston to the police commissioner, and in towns where there is no chief of police to the selectmen. The requirement that the prisoner be examined shall not be deemed to compel the removal of clothing. When a person is transferred from one place of confinement to another prior to his arraignment in court or to his release, the requirement that he shall be examined shall apply only to the place to which he is first taken after his arrest. Whoever violates this section shall be punished by a fine of not more than ten dollars.

Amended by St.2003, c. 26, § 509, eff. July 1, 2003.

Historical and Statutory Notes

St.1913, c. 236.
St.1913, c. 728.
St.1919, c. 350, § 123.

§ 33A. Use of telephone in places of detention

The police official in charge of the station or other place of detention having a telephone wherein a person is held in custody, shall permit the use of the telephone, at the expense of the arrested person, for the purpose of allowing the arrested person to communicate with his family or friends, or to arrange for release on bail, or to engage the services of an attorney. Any such person shall be informed forthwith upon his arrival at such station or place of detention, of his right to so use the telephone, and such use shall be permitted within one hour thereafter.

Added by St.1945, c. 205. Amended by St.1946, c. 277; St.1958, c. 113; St.1960, c. 269; St.1963, c. 212.

§ 34. Repealed, 1979, 344, Sec. 23

Historical and Statutory Notes

See, Mass.R.Crim.P. Rule 7.

§ 35. Adjournments of examinations and trials

The court or justice may adjourn an examination or trial from time to time, and to the same or a different place in the county. In the meantime, if the defendant is charged with a crime that is not bailable, he shall be committed; otherwise, he may recognize in a sum and with surety or sureties to the satisfaction of the court or justice, or without surety, for his appearance for such examination or trial, or for want of such recognizance he shall be committed. While the defendant remains committed, no adjournment shall exceed thirty days at any one time against the objection of the defendant.

Amended by St.1991, c. 138, § 268; St.1992, c. 23, § 22; St.1996, c. 211.

Historical and Statutory Notes

St.1821, c. 98, § 1.
R.S.1836, c. 135, § 9.
G.S.1860, c. 170, § 17.
P.S.1882, c. 212, § 26.
R.L.1902, c. 217, § 34.
St.1914, c. 465, § 1.
St.1931, c. 145, § 2.

§ 36. Failure to appear; subsequent proceedings

If the recognizor does not appear according to his recognizance, the court or justice may issue process to bring him into court for trial. After his failure so to appear, the court or justice may at any time order his default recorded; but it may be removed for good cause at any time to which the case may be continued. If such default is not removed, the recognizance shall be certified with a record of such default to the superior court, and like proceedings shall be had thereon as upon a breach of the condition of a recognizance for appearance before said superior court, except in cases where bank books, bonds or money have been deposited at the time of the recognizance.

Historical and Statutory Notes

St.1821, c. 98, § 2.
R.S.1836, c. 135, § 10.
G.S.1860, c. 170, § 18.
P.S.1882, c. 212, § 27.
R.L.1902, c. 217, § 35.
St.1904, c. 164.
St.1920, c. 584, § 1.

§ 37. Failure to recognize; subsequent proceedings

If the defendant fails to recognize, he may be committed to jail by an order stating concisely that he is committed for further examination on a future day to be named in the order, and on the day named he may be brought before the court or justice by a verbal order to the officer who made the commitment, or by a written order to a different person.

Historical and Statutory Notes

R.S.1836, c. 135, § 11.
G.S.1860, c. 170, § 19.
P.S.1882, c. 212, § 28.
R.L.1902, c. 217, § 36.

§ 37A. Assignment of counsel

If a person is charged with a capital crime and brought before a district court for the initial appearance, the superior court may assign counsel upon his petition and upon certification of the charge to the superior court by the clerk of the district court. The examination shall thereupon be continued until the assignment of counsel has been made, and certification thereof received by the clerk of the district court, or until the petition for assignment of counsel has been otherwise disposed of. Upon a determination that a person accused of murder in the first or second degree is indigent, the chief counsel of the committee for public counsel services, or his designee, may assign the case to either the public counsel division or the private counsel division.

Added by St.1932, c. 180, § 43. Amended by St.1959, c. 313, § 23; St.1978, c. 478, § 285; St.1979, c. 344, § 24; St.1987, c. 380.

§ 38. Examination; assistance of counsel; waiver of indictment

The court or justice before whom a person is taken upon a charge of crime shall, as soon as may be, examine on oath the complainant and the witnesses for the prosecution, in the presence of the defendant, relative to any material matter connected with such charge. After the testimony to support the prosecution, the witnesses for the prisoner, if any, shall be examined on oath, and he may be assisted by counsel in such examination and in the cross examination of the witnesses in support of the prosecution. Nothing contained herein shall be construed to prohibit the enforcement of the waiver provisions of Rule 3 of the Massachusetts Rules of Criminal Procedure. A defendant charged with an offense as to which he has the right to be proceeded against by indictment may elect a probable cause hearing in accordance with Rule 3 of the Massachusetts Rules of Criminal Procedure, but in such event shall be deemed to have waived his right to be proceeded against by indictment.

Amended by St.1985, c. 256.

Historical and Statutory Notes

R.S.1836, c. 135, §§ 12, 13.
G.S.1860, c. 170, §§ 20, 21.
P.S.1882, c. 212, §§ 29, 30.
R.L.1902, c. 217, § 37.

§ 39. Repealed, 1979, 344, Sec. 25

Historical and Statutory Notes

See, Mass.R.Crim.P. Rule 21.

§ 40. Testimony reduced to writing; signing by witnesses

The testimony of the witnesses examined shall be reduced to writing by, or under the direction of, the court or justice, if he considers it necessary, and shall, if required by him, be signed by the witnesses.

Historical and Statutory Notes

R.S.1836, c. 135, § 15.
G.S.1860, c. 170, § 23.
P.S.1882, c. 212, § 32.
R.L.1902, c. 217, § 39.

§ 41. Discharge of prisoner

If it appears, upon the whole examination, that no crime has been committed or that there is not probable cause for charging the prisoner therewith, he shall be discharged.

Historical and Statutory Notes

R.S.1836, c. 135, § 16.
G.S.1860, c. 170, § 24.
P.S.1882, c. 212, § 33.
R.L.1902, c. 217, § 40.

§ 42. Bail or commitment

If it appears that a crime has been committed and that there is probable cause to believe the prisoner guilty, the court or justice shall, if final jurisdiction is not exercised, admit the prisoner to bail, if the crime is bailable and sufficient bail is offered; otherwise, except as provided for in section sixteen of chapter one hundred and twenty-five, such prisoner shall be committed to jail for trial.

Amended by St.1989, c. 664, § 2.

Historical and Statutory Notes

R.S.1836, c. 135, § 17.
G.S.1860, c. 170, § 25.
P.S.1882, c. 212, § 34.
R.L.1902, c. 217, § 41.

§ 42A. Personal recognizance; terms and conditions to protect persons suffering physical abuse

Whenever a court issues a criminal complaint and the crime involves assault and battery, trespass, threat to commit a crime, nonsupport, or any other complaint which involves the infliction, or the imminent threat of infliction, of physical harm upon a person by such person's family or household member as defined in section one of chapter two hundred and nine A, the court may, in lieu of or in addition to any terms of personal recognizance, and after a hearing and finding, impose such terms as will insure the safety of the person allegedly suffering the physical abuse or threat thereof, and will prevent its recurrence.

Such terms and conditions shall include reasonable restrictions on the travel, association or place of abode of the defendant as will prevent such person from contact with the person abused.

As part of the disposition of any criminal complaint, the court may establish such terms and conditions of probation as will insure the safety of the person who has suffered such abuse or threat thereof, and will prevent the recurrence of such abuse or threat thereof.

Such terms and conditions shall include reasonable restrictions on the travel, association or place of abode of the defendant as will prevent such person from all contact with the person abused; or the payment by the defendant to the person abused of monetary compensation for losses suffered as a direct result of the crime. Compensatory loss shall include, but not be limited to, loss of earnings or support, out-of-pocket losses for injuries sustained, moving expenses and reasonable attorneys fees.

In addition, the terms and conditions of either the probation or the disposition of the complaint may include, but not be limited to, referral of the defendant to a clinic, facility or professional for one or more examinations, diagnoses, counseling or treatment; requiring the defendant to report periodically to a probation officer; or release of the defendant to the custody of a residential treatment facility.

Added by St.1978, c. 447, § 5.

§ 43. Conveying prisoner through another county

If the journey from the town where the prisoner is held to the town where he is to be committed on the service of a mittimus can be made by railroad, the officer may convey the prisoner through any portion of another county in the prosecution of such journey.

Historical and Statutory Notes

St.1862, c. 216, § 1.
P.S.1882, c. 212, § 35.
R.L.1902, c. 217, § 42.

§ 44. Fees and expenses in district court in record sent to superior court

If the defendant is held to appear before the superior court, the copies and record of proceedings sent to the superior court shall contain the details of all fees and expenses allowed or paid in the district court.

Amended by St.1959, c. 313, § 24.

Historical and Statutory Notes

St.1890, c. 440, § 10.
R.L.1902, c. 217, § 43.

§ 45. Witnesses bound by recognizance

If the prisoner is admitted to bail or is committed, the court or justice shall bind by recognizance the material witnesses against the prisoner to appear and testify at the next sitting of the court having jurisdiction of the crime and in which the prisoner is held to answer.

Historical and Statutory Notes

R.S.1836, c. 135, § 18.
G.S.1860, c. 170, § 26.
P.S.1882, c. 212, § 36.
R.L.1902, c. 217, § 44.

§ 46. Witnesses bound by recognizance on adjournment

If the examination or trial of a defendant charged with a felony is adjourned under section thirty-five, the court or justice may bind by recognizance the principal witnesses against the prisoner to appear and testify at the time and place to which the trial or examination is adjourned.

Historical and Statutory Notes

St.1885, c. 136, § 1.
R.L.1902, c. 217, § 45.

§ 47. Sureties with recognizance

The court, if satisfied that there is good cause to believe that a witness will not perform the condition of his recognizance unless other security is given, may order the witness to enter into a recognizance with such sureties as the court deems necessary for his appearance at court; provided that the witness shall be entitled to be present and to be represented by counsel at a hearing before the court, at which hearing the witness shall be entitled to be heard on the issue of the alleged materiality of his testimony, and on the issue of recognizance with or without surety.

Amended by St.1967, c. 380.

Historical and Statutory Notes

R.S.1836, c. 135, § 19.
G.S.1860, c. 170, § 27.
P.S.1882, c. 212, § 37.
St.1885, c. 136, § 2.
R.L.1902, c. 217, § 46.

§ 48. Recognizances for minor witnesses

If a minor is a material witness, any other person may be allowed to recognize for his appearance; or, in the discretion of the court or justice, he may recognize in a sum not exceeding fifty dollars, which shall be valid and binding in law, notwithstanding his minority.

Historical and Statutory Notes

R.S.1836, c. 135, § 20.
G.S.1860, c. 170, § 28.
P.S.1882, c. 212, § 38.
St.1885, c. 136, § 2.
R.L.1902, c. 217, § 47.

§ 49. Commitment of witnesses; discharge upon recognizance

A witness who, when required, refuses to recognize, either with or without sureties, shall, except as provided in the following section, be committed to jail until he complies with such order or is otherwise discharged; but if the court or justice finds that the witness, unless he is the prosecutor or an accomplice, is unable to procure sureties when so ordered, he shall, except in cases of felony, be discharged upon his own recognizance. Upon a complaint or indictment for a felony, against a defendant not in custody, a material witness committed for failure to furnish sureties upon his own recognizance may be held in custody for a reasonable time, pending the pursuit and apprehension of the defendant.

Historical and Statutory Notes

R.S.1836, c. 135, § 21.
G.S.1860, c. 170, § 29.
St.1872, c. 214, § 1.
P.S.1882, c. 212, §§ 39, 40.
St.1885, c. 136, § 2.
St.1892, c. 361.
R.L.1902, c. 217, § 48.

§ 50. Repealed, 1979, 344, Sec. 25

Historical and Statutory Notes

See, Mass.R.Crim.P. Rule 35.

§ 51. Release of committed witnesses; proceedings

If a witness has been committed because of his inability to furnish sureties for his appearance before the superior court, the jailer shall forthwith give notice to the chief justice of the superior court, who shall direct the district attorney to inquire as to the importance of his testimony and the necessity for detaining him in jail, and the district attorney, if in his opinion the public interest will not suffer by the release of the witness on his own recognizance, shall so report to the chief justice, who may thereupon order the witness to be released upon his own recognizance.

Historical and Statutory Notes

St.1894, c. 406, § 1.
R.L.1902, c. 217, § 50.

§ 52. Rules regulating treatment of committed witnesses; removal to another county

The commissioner of correction shall from time to time make such rules relative to the diet, size of cells, amount of liberty and exercise, correspondence, visits and such other matters as he considers necessary regulating the treatment of witnesses held in jail as will secure their clear distinction and separation from other prisoners so far as possible, consistent with their safe custody and the prevention of tampering with their testimony. Said commissioner may, with the approval of the district attorney, remove such witnesses from the jail where they are confined to a jail in another county, and shall, at the request of the district attorney, cause them to be returned to the jail whence they were removed. The proceedings for such removal shall be the same as for the removal of prisoners from one jail or house of correction to another. The cost of support of a witness so removed and of both removals shall be paid by the county whence he is removed.

Historical and Statutory Notes

St.1894, c. 270.
R.L.1902, c. 217, § 51.
St.1916, c. 241, § 1.
St.1919, c. 350, §§ 82, 83.

§ 52A. Removal of accused person to another county or to a correctional institution; return; proceedings; costs

Persons held in jail for trial may, with the approval of the district attorney, and shall, by order of a justice of the superior court, be removed by the commissioner of correction to a jail in another county, and said commissioner shall, at the request of the district attorney, cause them to be returned to the jail whence they were removed. In addition, such persons, if they have been previously incarcerated in a correctional institution of the commonwealth under sentence for a felony, may, with the approval of the district attorney, be removed by the commissioner of correction to a correctional institution of the commonwealth, and said commissioner shall, at the request of the district attorney, cause them to be returned to the jail where they were awaiting trial. The proceedings for such removals shall be the same as for the removal of prisoners from one jail or house of correction to another. The cost of support of a person so removed and of the removals shall be paid by the county whence he is originally removed.

Added by St.1943, c. 131. Amended by St.1971, c. 592, § 1; St.1973, c. 514.

§ 53. Transporting male and female prisoners

An officer who, having the custody or control of prisoners, causes or permits male and female prisoners to be transported together to or from a court in a vehicle, in a city of more than thirty thousand inhabitants according to the latest census, shall be punished by a fine of not more than twenty dollars.

Historical and Statutory Notes

St.1894, c. 273.
R.L.1902, c. 217, § 52.

§ 54. Handcuffing committed witnesses to accused persons; transporting together

An officer who, having the custody of a witness committed because of his failure to furnish sureties, causes or permits him to be handcuffed to a person, held in custody, charged with or sentenced for crime, or to be transported within a city to or from any court or prison in a vehicle with such person, shall be punished by a fine of not more than twenty dollars.

Historical and Statutory Notes

St.1894, c. 160.
R.L.1902, c. 217, § 53.

§ 55. Discharge upon acknowledgment of satisfaction for injury

If a person committed to jail is under indictment or complaint for, or is under recognizance to answer to, a charge of assault and battery or other misdemeanor for which he is liable in a civil action, unless the offence was committed by or upon a sheriff or other officer of justice, or riotously, or with intent to commit a felony, and the person injured appears before the court or justice who made the commitment or took the recognizance, or before which the indictment or complaint is pending, and acknowledges in writing that he has received satisfaction for the injury, the court or justice may in its or his discretion, upon payment of such expenses as it or he shall order, discharge the recognizance or supersede the commitment, or discharge the defendant from the indictment or complaint, and may also discharge all recognizances and supersede the commitment of all witnesses in the case.

Historical and Statutory Notes

R.S.1836, c. 135, § 25; c. 136, § 27.
St.1846, c. 198.
G.S.1860, c. 170, § 33; c. 171, § 28.
P.S.1882, c. 212, § 43; c. 213, § 36.
R.L.1902, c. 217, § 54.

§ 56. Filing of order; delivery to jail keeper; discharge as bar to civil action

Such order discharging the recognizance, indictment or complaint of the person or the recognizance of witnesses shall be filed in the office of the clerk before the sitting of the court at which they are bound to appear; and such order superseding the commitment of the person charged or of a witness shall be delivered to the keeper of the jail where he is confined, who shall forthwith discharge him; and such order, so filed and delivered, shall forever bar a civil action for such injury.

Historical and Statutory Notes

R.S.1836, c. 135, § 26; c. 136, § 27.
G.S.1860, c. 170, § 34; c. 171, § 28.
P.S.1882, c. 212, § 44; c. 213, § 36.
R.L.1902, c. 217, § 55.

§ 57. Officials authorized to admit to bail; amount of bail; security

A justice of the supreme judicial or superior court, a clerk of courts or the clerk of the superior court for criminal business in the county of Suffolk, a standing or special commissioner appointed by either of said courts or, in the county of Suffolk, by the sheriff of said county with the approval of the superior court, a justice or clerk of a district court, a master in chancery, upon application of a prisoner or witness held under arrest or committed, either with or without a warrant, or held in the custody of an officer under a mittimus, may inquire into the case and admit such prisoner or witness to bail if he determines that such release will reasonably assure the appearance of the person before the court and will not endanger the safety of any other person or the community; and may admit to bail any person committed for not finding sureties to recognize for him. All persons authorized to take bail under this section shall be governed by the rules established by the supreme judicial or superior court. No person offering himself as surety shall be deemed to be insufficient if he deposits money of an amount equal to the amount of the bail required of him in such recognizance, or a bank book of a savings bank, credit union or of a savings account in a trust company or national bank, or a passbook or paid-up shares of a co-operative bank doing business in the commonwealth, properly assigned to the clerk with whom the same is or is to be deposited, and his successors, and satisfactory to the person so authorized to take bail, or deposits non-registered bonds of the United States or of the commonwealth or of any county, city or town within the commonwealth equal at their face value to the amount of the bail required of him in such recognizance. The sheriff of Suffolk county may, with the approval of the superior court, appoint standing or special commissioners to take bail to a number not exceeding twenty and may, with like approval, remove them.

Notwithstanding the foregoing, a person arrested and charged with a violation of an order or judgment issued pursuant to section eighteen, thirty-four B or thirty-four C of chapter two hundred and eight, section thirty-two of chapter two hundred and nine, section three, four or five of chapter two hundred and nine A, or section fifteen or twenty of chapter two hundred and nine C, or arrested and charged with a misdemeanor or felony involving abuse as defined in section one of said chapter two hundred and nine A while an order of protection issued under said chapter two hundred and nine A was in effect against said person, shall not be released out of court by a clerk of courts, clerk of a district court, bail commissioner or master in chancery.

Before the amount of bail of a prisoner charged with an offence punishable by imprisonment for more than one year is fixed in court, the court shall obtain from its probation officer all available information relative to prior criminal prosecutions, if any, of the prisoner and the disposition of each of such prosecutions. If the offence with which such a prisoner is charged is a violation of any provision of sections twenty-two to twenty-four, inclusive, of chapter two hundred and sixty-five or section thirty-four or thirty-five of chapter two hundred and seventy-two, and it appears from such information or otherwise that he had been previously prosecuted for a violation of any such provision, the court shall, before the amount of bail is fixed, obtain from the department of mental health a report containing all information in its possession relative to the prisoner, particularly with respect to any mental disease or defect with which he may have been afflicted; and said department shall furnish any such report to the court promptly upon its request.

No person arrested for violating any provision of section thirty-three or thirty-five of chapter fifty-six shall be admitted to bail unless there is deposited not less than five hundred dollars in cash, or there is offered real estate of the fair market value of not less than one thousand dollars, over and above all encumbrances, as security.

Amended by St.1939, c. 299, § 4; St.1943, c. 330; St.1945, c. 235; St.1953, c. 319, § 33; St.1964, c. 67; St.1965, c. 280; St.1992, c. 201, §§ 1, 2.

Historical and Statutory Notes

St.1812, c. 30.
R.S.1836, c. 135, § 22.
St.1851, c. 92, § 2.
St.1855, c. 265, § 1.
G.S.1860, c. 170, § 36.
St.1874, c. 306, § 4.
St.1878, c. 188, § 4.
St.1879, c. 228.
P.S.1882, c. 212, § 46.
St.1898, c. 411, § 1.
R.L.1902, c. 217, § 56.
St.1912, c. 226.
St.1914, c. 390, § 1.
St.1920, c. 584, § 2.
St.1922, c. 464, § 1.
St.1923, c. 436, § 1.
St.1926, c. 320, § 1.

§ 58. Release on personal recognizance or unsecured appearance bond; determination; fees; refusal; petition for review

A justice or a clerk or assistant clerk of the district court, a bail commissioner or master in chancery, in accordance with the applicable provisions of section fifty-seven, shall, when a person is held under arrest or committed either with or without a warrant for an offense other than an offense punishable by death, or, upon the motion of the commonwealth, for an offense enumerated in section fifty-eight A or for any offense on which a warrant of arrest has been issued by the superior court, hold a hearing in which the defendant and his counsel, if any, may participate and inquire into the case and shall admit such person to bail on his personal recognizance without surety unless said justice, clerk or assistant clerk, bail commissioner or master in chancery determines, in the exercise of his discretion, that such a release will not reasonably assure the appearance of the person before the court. In his determination under this section as to whether release will reasonably assure the appearance of the person before the court, said justice, clerk or assistant clerk, bail commissioner or master in chancery shall, on the basis of any information which he can reasonably obtain, take into account the nature and circumstances of the offense charged, the potential penalty the person faces, the person's family ties, financial resources, employment record and history of mental illness, his reputation and the length of residence in the community, his record of convictions, if any, any illegal drug distribution or present drug dependency, any flight to avoid prosecution or fraudulent use of an alias or false identification, any failure to appear at any court proceeding to answer to an offense, whether the person is on bail pending adjudication of a prior charge, whether the acts alleged involve abuse as defined in section one of chapter two hundred and nine A, or violation of a temporary or permanent order issued pursuant to sections eighteen or thirty-four B of chapter two hundred and eight, section thirty-two of chapter two hundred and nine, sections three, four or five of chapter two hundred and nine A, or sections fifteen or twenty of chapter two hundred and nine C, whether the person has any history of orders issued against him pursuant to the aforesaid sections, whether he is on probation, parole, or other release pending completion of sentence for any conviction, and whether he is on release pending sentence or appeal for any conviction. The person authorized to admit the person to bail shall provide as an explicit condition of release for any person admitted to bail pursuant to this section or section fifty-seven that, should said person be charged with a crime during the period of his release, his bail may be revoked in accordance with the third paragraph of this section. If the justice or clerk or assistant clerk of the district court, the bail commissioner or master in chancery determines that a cash bail is required, the person shall be allowed to provide an equivalent amount in a surety company bond. If the justice or clerk or assistant clerk of the district court, the bail commissioner or master in chancery determines it to be necessary, the defendant may be ordered to abide by specified restrictions on personal associations or conduct including, but not limited to, avoiding all contact with an alleged victim of the crime and any potential witness or witnesses who may testify concerning the offense, as a condition of release.

A person, before being released on personal recognizance without surety, shall be informed by the person authorized to admit such person to bail of the penalties provided by section eighty-two A if he fails without sufficient excuse to appear at the specified time and place in accordance with the terms of his recognizance. A person authorized to take bail may charge the fees authorized by section twenty-four of chapter two hundred and sixty-two, if he goes to the place of detention of the person to make a determination provided for in this section although said person is released on his personal recognizance without surety. Said fees shall not be charged by any clerk or assistant clerk of a district court during regular working hours.

A person aforesaid charged with an offense and not released on his personal recognizance without surety by a clerk or assistant clerk of the district court, a bail commissioner or master in chancery shall forthwith be brought before the next session of the district court for a review of the order to recognize in accordance with the standards set forth in the first paragraph of this section. The court shall provide as an explicit condition of release for any person admitted to bail pursuant to this section or section fifty-seven that should said person be charged with a crime during the period of his release, his bail may be revoked in accordance with this paragraph and the court shall enter in writing on the court docket that the person was so informed and the docket shall constitute prima facie evidence that the person was so informed. If a person is on release pending the adjudication of a prior charge, and the court before which the person is charged with committing a subsequent offense after a hearing at which the person shall have the right to be represented by counsel, finds probable cause to believe that the person has committed a crime during said period of release, the court shall then determine, in the exercise of its discretion, whether the release of said person will seriously endanger any person or the community. In making said determination, the court shall consider the gravity, nature and circumstances of the offenses charged, the person's record of convictions, if any, and whether said charges or convictions are for offenses involving the use or threat of physical force or violence against any person, whether the person is on probation, parole or other release pending completion of sentence for any conviction, whether he is on release pending sentence or appeal for any conviction, the person's mental condition, and any illegal drug distribution or present drug dependency. If the court determines that the release of said person will seriously endanger any person or the community and that the detention of the person is necessary to reasonably assure the safety of any person or the community, the court may revoke bail on the prior charge and may order said person held without bail pending the adjudication of said prior charge, for a period not to exceed sixty days. The hearing shall be held upon the person's first appearance before the court before which the person is charged with committing an offense while on release pending adjudication of a prior charge, unless that person, or the attorney for the commonwealth, seeks and the court allows, a continuance because a witness or document is not immediately available. Except for good cause, a continuance on motion of the person shall not exceed seven days and on motion of the attorney for the commonwealth may not exceed three business days. During such continuance, the person may be detained consistent with the provisions of this section. Said order shall state in writing the reasons therefor and shall be reviewed by the court upon the acquittal of the person, or the dismissal of, any of the cases involved. A person so held shall be brought to trial as soon as reasonably possible. A person aggrieved by the denial of a district court justice to admit him to bail on his personal recognizance without surety may petition the superior court for a review of the order of the recognizance and the justice of the district court shall thereupon immediately notify such person of his right to file a petition for review in the superior court. When a petition for review is filed in the district court or with the detaining authority subsequent to petitioner's district court appearance, the clerk of the district court or the detaining authority, as the case may be, shall immediately notify by telephone, the clerk and probation officer of the district court, the district attorney for the district in which the district court is located, the prosecuting officer, the petitioner's counsel, if any, and the clerk of courts of the county to which the petition is to be transmitted. The clerk of the district court, upon the filing of a petition for review, either in the district court or with the detaining authority, shall forthwith transmit the petition for review, a copy of the complaint and of the record of the court, including the appearance of the attorney, if any is entered, and a summary of the court's reasons for denying the release of the defendant on his personal recognizance without surety to the superior court for the county in which the district court is located, if a justice thereof is then sitting, or to the superior court of the nearest county in which a justice is then sitting; the probation officer of the district court shall transmit forthwith to the probation officer of the superior court, copies of all records of the probation office of said district court pertaining to the petitioner, including the petitioner's record of prior convictions, if any, as currently verified by inquiry of the commissioner of probation. The district court or the detaining authority, as the case may be, shall cause any petitioner in its custody to be brought before the said superior court on the same day the petition shall have been filed, unless the district court or the detaining authority shall determine that such appearance and hearing on the petition cannot practically take place before the adjournment of the sitting of said superior court for that day and in which event, the petitioner shall be caused to be brought before said court for such hearing during the morning of the next business day of the sitting of said superior court. The district court is authorized to order any officer authorized to execute criminal process to transfer the petitioner and any papers herein above described from the district court or the detaining authority to the superior court, and to coordinate the transfer of the petitioner and the papers by such officer. The petition for review shall constitute authority in the person or officer having custody of the petitioner to transport the petitioner to said superior court without the issuance of any writ or other legal process, provided, however, that any district or superior court is authorized to issue a writ of habeas corpus for the appearance forthwith of the petitioner before the superior court.

The superior court shall in accordance with the standards set forth in the first paragraph of this section, hear the petition for review as speedily as practicable and except for unusual circumstances, on the same day the petition is filed; provided, however, that the court may continue the hearing to the next business day if the required records and other necessary information are not available. The justice of the superior court may, after a hearing on the petition for review, order that the petitioner be released on bail on his personal recognizance without surety, or, in his discretion, to reasonably assure the effective administration of justice, make any other order of bail or recognizance or remand the petitioner in accordance with the terms of the process by which he was ordered committed by the district court.

If a defendant has posted bail in the district court and has subsequently been arraigned in the superior court for the same offense, the superior court clerk shall notify the district court clerk holding the defendant's bail of such arraignment. Upon such notification, the amount of any bail bond posted by a defendant in the district court shall be carried over to a bail bond required by the superior court. The superior court justices' discretion in setting the amount of bail shall not be affected by the provisions of this paragraph.

Except where the defendant has defaulted on his recognizance or has been surrendered by a probation officer, an order of bail or recognizance shall not be revoked, revised or amended by the district court, because the defendant has been bound over to the superior court; provided, however, that if any court, in its discretion, finds that changed circumstances or other factors not previously known or considered, make the order of bail or recognizance ineffective to reasonably assure the appearance of said defendant before the court, the court may make a further order of bail, either by increasing the amount of the recognizance or requiring sufficient surety or both, which order will not revoke the order of bail or recognizance previously in force and effect. The court may also review such changed circumstances or other factors not previously known or considered in accordance with the third paragraph of this section.

The chief justice of the district court department and the chief justice of the Boston municipal court department shall prescribe forms for use in their respective courts, for the purpose of notifying a defendant of his right to file a petition for review in the superior court, forms for a petition for review and forms for the implementation of any other procedural requirements. The clerk of courts shall forthwith notify the district court of all orders or judgments of the superior court on petitions for review. Costs or expenses of services and transportation under this section shall be ordered paid in the amount determined by the superior court out of the state treasury.

For an offense enumerated in section fifty-eight A, and upon the motion of an attorney for the commonwealth for an order of pretrial detention or imposition of conditions of release based on dangerousness, a justice of the district or superior court shall hold a hearing pursuant to the provisions of subsection (4) of said section fifty-eight A and shall admit such person to bail on his personal recognizance without surety or subject to conditions of release unless said justice, determines, in the exercise of his discretion, that such release will endanger the safety of any other person or the community.

Amended by St.1970, c. 499, § 1; St.1971, c. 473, § 1; St.1978, c. 478, § 286; St.1981, c. 802, §§ 1 to 4; St.1982, c. 179; St.1992, c. 201, §§ 3 to 5; St.1992, c. 379, § 186; St.1994, c. 68, §§ 1 to 5; St.1995, c. 39, § 13; St.2006, c. 48, § 8, eff. Mar. 30, 2006.

Historical and Statutory Notes

St.1851, c. 92, § 2.
St.1855, c. 265, § 1.
G.S.1860, c. 170, § 37.
St.1879, c. 89.
P.S.1882, c. 212, § 47.
R.L.1902, c. 217, § 57.
St.1929, c. 216, § 3.

§ 58A. Conditions for release of persons accused of certain offenses involving physical force or abuse; hearing; order; review

(1) The commonwealth may move, based on dangerousness, for an order of pretrial detention or release on conditions for a felony offense that has as an element of the offense the use, attempted use or threatened use of physical force against the person of another or any other felony that, by its nature, involves a substantial risk that physical force against the person of another may result, including the crimes of burglary and arson whether or not a person has been placed at risk thereof, or a violation of an order pursuant to section 18, 34B or 34C of chapter 208, section 32 of chapter 209, section 3, 4 or 5 of chapter 209 A or section 15 or 20 of chapter 209C, or arrested and charged with a misdemeanor or felony involving abuse as defined in section 1 of said chapter 209A or while an order of protection issued under said chapter 209A was in effect against such person, an offense for which a mandatory minimum term of 3 years or more is prescribed in chapter 94C, arrested and charged with a violation of section 13B of chapter 268 or a third or subsequent conviction for a violation of section 24 of chapter 90, or arrested and charged with a violation of paragraph (a), (c) or (m) of section 10 of chapter 269; provided, however, that the commonwealth may not move for an order of detention under this section based on possession of a large capacity feeding device without simultaneous possession of a large capacity weapon; or arrested and charged with a violation of section 10G of said chapter 269.

(2) Upon the appearance before a superior court or district court judge of an individual charged with an offense listed in subsection (1) and upon the motion of the commonwealth, the judicial officer shall hold a hearing pursuant to subsection (4) issue an order that, pending trial, the individual shall either be released on personal recognizance without surety; released on conditions of release as set forth herein; or detained under subsection (3).

If the judicial officer determines that personal recognizance will not reasonably assure the appearance of the person as required or will endanger the safety of any other person or the community, such judicial officer shall order the pretrial release of the person—

(A) subject to the condition that the person not commit a federal, state or local crime during the period of release; and

(B) subject to the least restrictive further condition, or combination of conditions, that such judicial officer determines will reasonably assure the appearance of the person as required and the safety of any other person and the community that the person—

(i) remain in the custody of a designated person, who agrees to assume supervision and to report any violation of a release condition to the court, if the designated person is able reasonably to assure the judicial officer that the person will appear as required and will not pose a danger to the safety of any other person or the community;

(ii) maintain employment, or, if unemployed, actively seek employment;

(iii) maintain or commence an educational program;

(iv) abide by specified restrictions on personal associations, place of abode or travel;

(v) avoid all contact with an alleged victim of the crime and with any potential witness or witnesses who may testify concerning the offense;

(vi) report on a regular basis to a designated law enforcement agency, pretrial service agency, or other agency;

(vii) comply with a specified curfew;

(viii) refrain from possessing a firearm, destructive device, or other dangerous weapon;

(ix) refrain from excessive use of alcohol, or any use of a narcotic drug or other controlled substance, without a prescription by a licensed medical practitioner;

(x) undergo available medical, psychological, or psychiatric treatment, including treatment for drug or alcohol dependency and remain in a specified institution if required for that purpose;

(xi) execute an agreement to forfeit upon failing to appear as required, property of a sufficient unencumbered value, including money, as is reasonably necessary to assure the appearance of the person as required, and shall provide the court with proof of ownership and the value of the property along with information regarding existing encumbrances as the judicial officer may require;

(xii) execute a bail bond with solvent sureties; who will execute an agreement to forfeit in such amount as is reasonably necessary to assure appearance of the person as required and shall provide the court with information regarding the value of the assets and liabilities of the surety if other than an approved surety and the nature and extent of encumbrances against the surety's property; such surety shall have a net worth which shall have sufficient unencumbered value to pay the amount of the bail bond;

(xiii) return to custody for specified hours following release for employment, schooling, or other limited purposes; and

(xiv) satisfy any other condition that is reasonably necessary to assure the appearance of the person as required and to assure the safety of any other person and the community.

The judicial officer may not impose a financial condition that results in the pretrial detention of the person.

The judicial officer may at any time amend the order to impose additional or different conditions of release.

(3) If, after a hearing pursuant to the provisions of subsection (4), the district or superior court justice finds by clear and convincing evidence that no conditions of release will reasonably assure the safety of any other person or the community, said justice shall order the detention of the person prior to trial. A person detained under this subsection shall be brought to a trial as soon as reasonably possible, but in absence of good cause, the person so held shall not be detained for a period exceeding ninety days excluding any period of delay as defined in Massachusetts Rules of Criminal Procedure Rule 36(b)(2). A justice may not impose a financial condition under this section that results in the pretrial detention of the person. Nothing in this section shall be interpreted as limiting the imposition of a financial condition upon the person to reasonably assure his appearance before the courts.

(4) When a person is held under arrest for an offense listed in subsection (1) and upon a motion by the commonwealth, the judge shall hold a hearing to determine whether conditions of release will reasonably assure the safety of any other person or the community.

The hearing shall be held immediately upon the person's first appearance before the court unless that person, or the attorney for the commonwealth, seeks a continuance. Except for good cause, a continuance on motion of the person may not exceed seven days, and a continuance on motion of the attorney for the commonwealth may not exceed three business days. During a continuance, the individual shall be detained upon a showing that there existed probable cause to arrest the person. At the hearing, such person shall have the right to be represented by counsel, and, if financially unable to retain adequate representation, to have counsel appointed. The person shall be afforded an opportunity to testify, to present witnesses, to cross-examine witnesses who appear at the hearing, and to present information. The rules concerning admissibility of evidence in criminal trials shall not apply to the presentation and consideration of information at the hearing. The facts the judge uses to support findings pursuant to subsection (3), that no conditions will reasonably assure the safety of any other person or the community, shall be supported by clear and convincing evidence. In a detention order issued pursuant to the provisions of said subsection (3) the judge shall (a) include written findings of fact and a written statement of the reasons for the detention; (b) direct that the person be committed to custody or confinement in a corrections facility separate, to the extent practicable, from persons awaiting or serving sentence or being held in custody pending appeal; and (c) direct that the person be afforded reasonable opportunity for private consultation with his counsel. The person may be detained pending completion of the hearing. The hearing may be reopened before or after a determination by the justice, at any time before trial if the justice finds that information exists that was not known at the time of the hearing and that has a material bearing on the issue and whether there are conditions of release that will reasonably assure the safety of any other person and the community.

(5) In his determination as to whether there are conditions of release that will reasonably assure the safety of any other individual or the community, said justice, shall, on the basis of any information which he can reasonably obtain, take into account the nature and seriousness of the danger posed to any person or the community that would result by the person's release, the nature and circumstances of the offense charged, the potential penalty the person faces, the person's family ties, employment record and history of mental illness, his reputation, the risk that the person will obstruct or attempt to obstruct justice or threaten, injure or intimidate or attempt to threaten, injure or intimidate a prospective witness or juror, his record of convictions, if any, any illegal drug distribution or present drug dependency, whether the person is on bail pending adjudication of a prior charge, whether the acts alleged involve abuse as defined in section one of chapter two hundred and nine A, or violation of a temporary or permanent order issued pursuant to section eighteen or thirty-four B of chapter two hundred and eight, section thirty-two of chapter two hundred and nine, sections three, four or five of chapter two hundred and nine A, or sections fifteen or twenty of chapter two hundred and nine C, whether the person has any history of orders issued against him pursuant to the aforesaid sections, whether he is on probation, parole or other release pending completion of sentence for any conviction and whether he is on release pending sentence or appeal for any conviction.

(6) Nothing in this section shall be construed as modifying or limiting the presumption of innocence.

(7) A person aggrieved by the denial of a district court justice to admit him to bail on his personal recognizance with or without surety may petition the superior court for a review of the order of the recognizance and the justice of the district court shall thereupon immediately notify such person of his right to file a petition for review in the superior court. When a petition for review is filed in the district court or with the detaining authority subsequent to petitioner's district court appearance, the clerk of the district court or the detaining authority, as the case may be, shall immediately notify by telephone, the clerk and probation officer of the district court, the district attorney for

the district in which the district court is located, the prosecuting officer, the petitioner's counsel, if any, and the clerk of courts of the county to which the petition is to be transmitted. The clerk of the district court, upon the filing of a petition for review, either in the district court or with the detaining authority, shall forthwith transmit the petition for review, a copy of the complaint and the record of the court, including the appearance of the attorney, if any is entered, and a summary of the court's reasons for denying the release of the defendant on his personal recognizance with or without surety to the superior court for the county in which the district court is located, if a justice thereof is then sitting, or to the superior court of the nearest county in which a justice is then sitting; the probation officer of the district court shall transmit forthwith to the probation officer of the superior court, copies of all records of the probation office of said district court pertaining to the petitioner, including the petitioner's record of prior convictions, if any, as currently verified by inquiry of the commissioner of probation. The district court or the detaining authority, as the case may be, shall cause any petitioner in its custody to be brought before the said superior court within two business days of the petition having been filed. The district court is authorized to order any officer authorized to execute criminal process to transfer the petitioner and any papers herein above described from the district court or the detaining authority to the superior court, and to coordinate the transfer of the petitioner and the papers by such officer. The petition for review shall constitute authority in the person or officer having custody of the petitioner to transport the petitioner to said superior court without the issuance of any writ or other legal process; provided, however, that any district or superior court is authorized to issue a writ of habeas corpus for the appearance forthwith of the petitioner before the superior court.

The superior court shall in accordance with the standards set forth in section fifty-eight A, hear the petition for review under section fifty-eight A as speedily as practicable and in any event within five business days of the filing of the petition. The justice of the superior court hearing the review may consider the record below which the commonwealth and the person may supplement. The justice of the superior court may, after a hearing on the petition for review, order that the petitioner be released on bail on his personal recognizance without surety, or, in his discretion, to reasonably assure the effective administration of justice, make any other order of bail or recognizance or remand the petitioner in accordance with the terms of the process by which he was ordered committed by the district court.

Added by St.1994, c. 68, § 6. Amended by St.1995, c. 39, § 13; St.1996, c. 393, § 5; St.2010, c. 256, § 125, eff. Nov. 4, 2010.

§ 58B. Revocation of release and detention order following violation of release conditions

A person who has been released after a hearing pursuant to section 58 or section 58A and who has violated a condition of his release, shall be subject to a revocation of release and an order of detention. The judicial officer shall enter an order of revocation and detention if after a hearing the judicial officer finds (1) that there is probable cause to believe that the person has committed a federal or state crime while on release, or clear and convincing evidence that the person has violated any other condition of release; and (2) the judicial officer finds that there are no conditions of release that will reasonably assure the person will not pose a danger to the safety of any other person or the community; or the person is unlikely to abide by any condition or combination of conditions of release.

If there is probable cause to believe that, while on release, the person committed a federal felony or an offense described in clause (1), a rebuttable presumption arises that no condition or combination of conditions will assure that the person will not pose a danger to the safety of any other person or the community. If the judicial officer finds that there are conditions of release that will assure that the person will not pose a danger to the safety of any other person or the community, and that the person will abide by such conditions, the judicial officer shall treat the person in accordance with the provisions of this section and may amend the conditions of release accordingly. Upon the person's first appearance before the judicial officer in the court which will conduct proceedings for revocation of an order of release under this section, the hearing concerning revocation shall be held immediately unless that person or the attorney for the commonwealth seeks a continuance. During a continuance the person shall be detained without bail unless the judicial officer finds that there are conditions of release that will reasonably assure that the person will not pose a danger to the safety of any other person or the community and that the person will abide by conditions of release. If the person is detained without bail, except for good cause, a continuance on motion of the person shall not exceed seven days, a continuance on motion of the attorney for the commonwealth or probation shall not exceed three business days. A person detained under this subsection, shall be brought to trial as soon as reasonably possible, but in the absence of good cause, a person so held shall not be detained for a period exceeding ninety days excluding any period of delay as defined in Massachusetts Rules of Criminal Procedure Rule 36(b)(2).

Added by St.1994, c. 68, § 6. Amended by St.1995, c. 39, § 13; St.2006, c. 48, § 9, eff. Mar. 30, 2006.

§ 59. Admission to bail by master in chancery

After a person is committed to jail to await the action of the grand jury, he shall not be admitted to bail by a master in chancery who does not reside or have a usual place of business within the county where the jail is situated, except upon proof that written notice of the proposed application has been duly served upon the district attorney, or one of the assistant district attorneys, for the district, at least twenty-four hours before a hearing on the application, specifying the name of the person, the crime with which he is charged, the time and place of hearing, and the name, occupation and residence of the proposed sureties, or upon proof that the district attorney, or one of the assistant district attorneys, for the district has waived notice of the hearing on such proposed application.

Historical and Statutory Notes

St.1909, c. 235.

§ 60. Bail in Suffolk county; proceedings

After a conviction or a plea of guilty or of nolo contendere in the superior court in Suffolk county, the prisoner shall not be admitted to bail except in open court; but when said court is not in session, bail may be taken by any judge of a court of record or by any commissioner appointed under section fifty-seven, upon proof that written notice of the proposed application has been duly served upon the district attorney, or one of the assistant district attorneys for the Suffolk district, at least twenty-four hours before the hearing of such application, specifying the name of the prisoner, the crime of which he has been convicted, the time and place of hearing, and the name, occupation and residence of the proposed sureties. No person who has been once offered and rejected as surety shall afterward be accepted as surety for the same person in the same case.

Historical and Statutory Notes

St.1862, c. 159, § 1.
P.S.1882, c. 212, § 48.
R.L.1902, c. 217, § 58.
St.1923, c. 436, § 2.

§ 61. Bail taken out of court; certificate or recognizance and deposit by surety; presence of persons; monthly statements by person taking bail

If bail is taken out of court, the person authorized to admit to bail in criminal cases shall cause a certificate to be signed and sworn to by each surety, which shall contain his name, his residence, including the name of the street and number, if any, of the dwelling house thereon, his occupation and place of business, a statement of the nature, location, purchase price, assessed value and fair market value of his property, and of the encumbrances, if any, thereon, the amount of his indebtedness, the amount and number of other bonds or recognizances on which he is or may be liable and all other matters pertinent to the amount and value of such property, each and all of which statements shall be deemed to be material statements in prosecutions for perjury, and shall return such certificate or certificates and a proper recognizance to the proper court. A surety may, instead of making such certificate, give his personal recognizance as surety and deposit money, bonds or a properly assigned bank book of the kind and in the amount and under the conditions set forth in section fifty-seven for making deposit of like nature. A person authorized to take bail shall take such bail in the presence of the person to be bailed and the surety or sureties, except as otherwise provided in section one hundred and five of chapter one hundred and seventy-five.

On the second Monday of each calendar month, every person taking bail out of court shall transmit to the chief justice of the superior court a written statement, setting forth each separate occasion, as defined in section sixty-one B, on which each bail or surety was accepted as aforesaid during the preceding calendar month, the name and address of each bail or surety, the date of such acceptance, the name of the defendant or defendants, the offense or offenses charged, and the court before which the defendant was required to appear.

Amended by St.1959, c. 313, § 25.

Historical and Statutory Notes

St.1862, c. 159, § 2.
P.S.1882, c. 212, § 49.
St.1898, c. 411, § 2.
R.L.1902, c. 217, § 59.
St.1920, c. 584, § 3.
St.1922, c. 465, § 1.
St.1926, c. 340, § 3.
St.1930, c. 240, § 2.

§ 61A. Disposition or encumbrance of real estate of bail or surety; violation of section

Whenever a person becomes bail or surety in a criminal case and has offered real estate as his qualification for his acceptance as such bail or surety, and subsequently and while the case in which he has qualified as bail or surety is pending, desires to dispose of or encumber such real estate, he shall in writing notify the court in which the case is then pending of his desire, and shall, unless expressly authorized by the court to continue as such bail or surety, terminate his liability as such bail or surety before he disposes of or encumbers such real estate. Any person violating any provision of this section shall be punished by a fine of not more than one thousand dollars or by imprisonment in the house of correction for not more than one year, or both. Nothing in this section shall in any wise affect the title to such real estate.

Historical and Statutory Notes

St.1922, c. 465, § 2.

§ 61B. Bond of professional bondsman; arrest bond certificates; conditions of acceptance; regulation

No person proposing to become bail or surety in a criminal case for hire or reward, either received or to be received, shall be accepted as such unless he shall have been approved and registered as a professional bondsman by the superior court or a justice thereof. No person proposing to become bail or surety in a criminal case in any calendar year after having become bail or surety in criminal cases on five separate occasions in said year shall be accepted thereafter during said year as bail or surety unless he shall have been approved and registered as a professional bondsman as aforesaid. A person who has been accepted as bail or surety, contrary to the provisions of this section, shall nevertheless be liable on his obligation as such bail or surety. Such approval and registration may be revoked at any time by such court or a justice thereof, and shall be revoked in case such a bondsman fails for thirty days after demand to satisfy in full a judgment recovered under section seventy-four or a new judgment entered on review under section seventy-six. The district attorney or prosecuting officer obtaining any such judgment which is not satisfied in full as aforesaid shall, forthwith upon the expiration of such period of thirty days, notify in writing the chief justice of such court. All professional bondsmen shall be governed by rules which shall be established from time to time by the superior court. Any unregistered person receiving hire or reward for his services as bail or surety in any criminal case, and any unregistered person becoming bail or surety in any criminal case in any calendar year after having become bail or surety in criminal cases on five separate occasions in said year, and any professional bondsman violating any provision of the rules established hereunder for such bondsmen, shall be punished by a fine of not more than one thousand dollars or by imprisonment for not more than one year, or both. The provisions of this section shall not apply to probation officers.

A guaranteed arrest bond certificate presented by the person whose signature appears thereon shall be accepted in lieu of cash or a bail bond in an amount not to exceed five hundred dollars to guarantee the appearance of such person in any court of the commonwealth, at the time required by such court, when such person is arrested for violation of any law or of any ordinance or by-law of any municipality therein relating to the operation of a motor vehicle. A guaranteed arrest bond certificate so presented in lieu of a bail bond is subject to the same forfeiture and enforcement provisions as a bail bond or cash bail. Such guaranteed arrest bond certificate may only be used where the alleged violation is committed prior to the expiration date shown thereon. A guaranteed arrest bond certificate may not be accepted when a person is arrested for the offense of driving under the influence of intoxicating liquor or of drugs or narcotics. As used in this section, "guaranteed arrest bond certificate" shall mean a printed card or other certificate issued by a licensed automobile association or travel club to any of its members, which is signed by the member and contains a printed statement that such automobile association or travel club and a surety company licensed to do business shall, in the event of the failure of such person to appear in court at the time set for appearance, pay any fine or forfeiture imposed upon such person in an amount not to exceed five hundred dollars.

Whenever a domestic or foreign company licensed to do a surety business in the commonwealth becomes surety in an amount not to exceed five hundred dollars with respect to any guaranteed arrest bond certificates issued in such year by an automobile association or travel club by filing with the office of bail administration an undertaking to become surety, such undertaking shall state: (1) The name and address of the automobile or travel club or association with respect to guaranteed arrest bond certificates of which the surety company undertakes to be surety; (2) The unqualified obligation of the surety company to pay the fine or forfeiture in an amount not to exceed five hundred dollars of any person who, after posting a guaranteed arrest bond certificate with respect to which the surety company has undertaken to be surety, fails to make the appearance for which the guaranteed arrest bond certificate was posted. Such undertaking shall be filed with the office of bail administration ten days prior to its effective date. If such undertaking is terminated, the office of bail administration shall be notified as promptly as possible but not later than the effective date of such termination.

Any such licensed automobile association, travel club or association and any licensed surety company, and its attorneys-in-fact, guaranteeing arrest bond certificates for members of such automobile association, travel club, or association with respect to motor vehicle violations hereunder, pursuant to the provisions of this section, shall not be required to obtain any additional license and compliance herewith shall be deemed to be in lieu of any such additional licensing.

A person shall be deemed to have become bail or surety on a separate occasion within the meaning of this section if he becomes such: (1) for a person in respect to a single offense; or (2) for a person in respect to two or more offenses wherefor he at one and the same time offers bail or surety, or in respect to two or more offenses committed at the same time or arising out of the same transaction or course of conduct wherefor he at different times offers bail or surety; or (3) for two or more persons at the same time offering bail or surety in respect to offenses committed jointly or in common course of conduct. Becoming bail or surety for the same person or persons in subsequent proceedings in connection with prosecution for the same offense or offenses shall not be deemed an additional occasion or occasions.

Amended by St.1972, c. 294; St.1977, c. 786; St.1984, c. 94, §§ 1, 2.

Historical and Statutory Notes

St.1922, c. 465, § 2.

St.1926, c. 340, § 1.
St.1929, c. 30.
St.1930, c. 240, § 1.

§ 62. Notice to district attorney of application to accept bail in Suffolk county

If application is made to a person authorized to take bail in criminal cases in Suffolk county to accept bail out of court in a case in which no amount has been fixed, he shall, if the crime charged is not within the jurisdiction of the municipal court of the city of Boston, before fixing bail, cause notice of such application to be given to the district attorney or one of the assistant district attorneys for the Suffolk district, if any of said attorneys is at the time within said district.

Historical and Statutory Notes

St.1862, c. 159, § 3.
P.S.1882, c. 212, § 50.
St.1898, c. 411, § 3.
R.L.1902, c. 217, § 60.

§ 63. Compensation for taking bail

No justice of any court, except a special justice of a district court, shall receive any fee or compensation for taking and approving bail in criminal cases, and no person authorized to admit to bail in criminal cases shall receive from any source in connection with the admitting to bail anything of value in excess of the statutory fees therefor. No person shall act as attorney in any case in which he has admitted a prisoner or witness to bail.

Historical and Statutory Notes

St.1862, c. 195, § 5.
St.1879, c. 254, § 1.
P.S.1882, c. 212, § 51.
St.1885, c. 135.
R.L.1902, c. 217, § 61.
St.1922, c. 465, § 3.
St.1924, c. 18.

§ 64. Admission to bail on Sunday

Persons held in custody or committed upon a criminal charge, if entitled to be released upon bail, may, in the discretion of the magistrate, be admitted to bail on Sunday.

Historical and Statutory Notes

St.1855, c. 265, § 2.
G.S.1860, c. 170, § 38.
P.S.1882, c. 212, § 52.
R.L.1902, c. 217, § 62.
St.1906, c. 180.

§ 65. Condition of recognizance

The condition of a recognizance of a person, either with or without surety, binding him to appear before a court or justice to answer to a charge against him or to prosecute an appeal shall be so framed as to bind him personally to appear at the time so expressed, and at any subsequent time to which the case may be continued, unless previously surrendered or discharged, and so from time to time, until the final decree, sentence or order of the court or justice thereon, and to abide such final sentence, order or decree, and not depart without leave. The condition of a recognizance of a person held to answer to a charge before a district court shall be further so framed as to bind him to appear before the district court to answer to the charge or to answer to any indictment which may be returned against him. The superior court shall by rule provide for the forms of recognizances and bail bonds. A recognizance of a person held to answer to a complaint before a district court which is required by law to sit in more than one municipality may, with his consent or at his request, be conditioned for his appearance at the next sitting of the court at any one of said municipalities.

Amended by St.1970, c. 499, § 2; St.1971, c. 473, § 2; St.1978, c. 478, § 287; St.1992, c. 379, § 187.

Historical and Statutory Notes

St.1845, c. 166, § 2.
G.S.1860, c. 170, § 39.
St.1878, c. 188, § 1.
P.S.1882, c. 212, § 53.
R.L.1902, c. 217, § 63.
St.1930, c. 154, § 1.

§ 66. Return of recognizance and examination taken by magistrate; order compelling; contempt

A recognizance and examination taken by a magistrate under this chapter shall be certified and returned by him to the district attorney or to the clerk of the court before which the person charged is bound to appear, on or before the first day of the sitting thereof; and if he refuses or neglects to return the same, he may be compelled to do so forthwith by order of court, and, in case of disobedience, may be proceeded against as for contempt.

Historical and Statutory Notes

R.S.1836, c. 135, § 24.
G.S.1860, c. 170, § 40.
P.S.1882, c. 212, § 54.
R.L.1902, c. 217, § 64.

§ 67. Repealed, 1994, 247, Sec. 5

§ 68. Surrender of principal; notice; exoneration of bail; return of deposits; subsequent bail

Bail in criminal cases may be exonerated at any time before default upon their recognizance by surrendering their principal into court or to the jailer in the county where the principal is held to appear, or by such voluntary surrender by the principal himself, and in either event, in all cases where bank books, money or bonds are deposited by the surety, the court shall thereupon order the bank books, money or bonds so deposited to be returned to the surety or his order, and to be reassigned to the person entitled thereto. They shall deliver to the jailer their principal, with a certified copy of the recognizance, and he shall be received and detained by the jailer, but may again be bailed in the same manner as if committed for not finding sureties to recognize for him, provided that the surety making the surrender shall not be accepted as bail if the person surrendered shall again be bailed. The jailer shall forthwith notify the clerk or justice of the court where the proceeding is pending of such surrender. Amended by St.1962, c. 356; St.1964, c. 316; St.1970, c. 499, § 3.

Historical and Statutory Notes

St.1863, c. 59, § 1.
P.S.1882, c. 212, § 56.
R.L.1902, c. 217, § 66.
St.1918, c. 257, § 459.
St.1919, c. 5.
St.1920, c. 2.
St.1920, c. 584, § 4.

§ 69. Surrender of principal after default; remission of penalty

Bail may surrender their principal at any time after default made upon the recognizance, or the principal may surrender himself, in the manner provided in the preceding section; and the court where the default is recorded may, upon application, remit the whole or any part of the penalty, if satisfied that the default of the principal was not with the connivance or consent of the bail.

Historical and Statutory Notes

St.1863, c. 59, § 2.
P.S.1882, c. 212, § 57.
R.L.1902, c. 217, § 67.
St.1918, c. 257, § 460.
St.1919, c. 5.
St.1920, c. 2.

§ 70. Inability to surrender principal; exoneration of bail

If, by the act of God, of the government of the United States, of any state or by sentence of law, bail are unable without their fault to surrender their principal, they shall, upon motion before final judgment on scire facias, be exonerated and discharged by the court, with or without costs as the court deems equitable.

Historical and Statutory Notes

St.1859, c. 131.
G.S.1860, c. 170, § 43.
P.S.1882, c. 212, § 58.
R.L.1902, c. 217, § 68.

§ 71. Default on recognizance

If a person under recognizance to appear and answer or to prosecute an appeal in a criminal case fails to appear according to his recognizance, and if a person under recognizance to testify in a criminal prosecution fails to perform the condition of his recognizance, his default shall be recorded, his obligation and that of his sureties forfeited, and process issued against them or such of them as the prosecuting officer directs; but in such suit no costs shall be taxed for travel. No such process shall issue in cases where bank books, bonds or money have been deposited at the time of such recognizance.

Historical and Statutory Notes

St.1813, c. 182, § 2.
R.S.1836, c. 135, § 27.
St.1845, c. 166, § 3.
G.S.1860, c. 170, § 46.
P.S.1882, c. 212, § 59.
R.L.1902, c. 217, § 69.
St.1920, c. 584, § 5.

§ 72. Surety paying amount for which bound; costs

A surety in such recognizance may, by leave of the court, after default, and either before or after process has been issued against him, pay to the county treasurer or clerk of the court the amount for which he was bound as surety, with such costs as the court shall direct, and shall be thereupon forever discharged.

Historical and Statutory Notes

R.S.1836, c. 135, § 28.
G.S.1860, c. 170, § 47.
P.S.1882, c. 212, § 60.
R.L.1902, c. 217, § 70.

§ 73. Award of portion of penalty to person entitled to forfeiture

If, in a suit on a recognizance to prosecute an appeal, the penalty is adjudged forfeited, or if by leave of court such penalty has been paid without suit or before judgment as provided in the preceding section, and any forfeiture accrues by law to a person by reason of the crime of which the appellant was convicted, the court may award to such person the portion of the amount paid to which he is entitled.

Historical and Statutory Notes

R.S.1836, c. 138, § 9.
G.S.1860, c. 173, § 6.
P.S.1882, c. 212, § 61.
R.L.1902, c. 217, § 71.

§ 74. Judgment for whole or part of penalty

If the penalty of a recognizance of a party or witness in a criminal prosecution is adjudged forfeited, the court may render judgment, upon such terms as it may order, against the principal or surety, or both, for the whole of the penalty with interest, or, in its discretion, for a part thereof, upon the filing in the case of a certificate of the district attorney or prosecuting officer stating that the interests of justice would be furthered thereby and setting forth specifically the reasons therefor; and no person shall, on behalf of the commonwealth, accept in satisfaction of any such judgment or any new judgment entered on review under section seventy-six any sum less than the full amount thereof.

Historical and Statutory Notes

St.1810, c. 80.
R.S.1836, c. 135, § 29.
G.S.1860, c. 170, § 48.
P.S.1882, c. 212, § 62.
R.L.1902, c. 217, § 72.
St.1926, c. 340, § 2.

§ 75. Neglect, omissions or defects as defeating action

Such action shall not be barred or defeated, nor shall judgment be arrested, by reason of neglect or omission to note or record the default of any principal or surety at the time when it happens, nor by reason of a defect in the form of the recognizance, if it sufficiently appears from the tenor thereof at what court the party or witness was bound to appear, and that the court or magistrate before whom it was taken was authorized to require and take such recognizance.

Historical and Statutory Notes

R.S.1836, c. 135, § 30.
G.S.1860, c. 170, § 49.
P.S.1882, c. 212, § 63.
R.L.1902, c. 217, § 73.

§ 76. Review and rehearing of case after judgment on recognizance

A court which has rendered judgment on a recognizance may, upon petition of any person interested, stating the ground relied upon and filed in said court, grant a review and a rehearing of the case, upon the surrender or recaption of the prisoner who was released, or for any sufficient cause which has occurred or been ascertained by the person interested after the rendition of such judgment, or at such time as not to have afforded opportunity for presenting the same in evidence.

Historical and Statutory Notes

St.1852, c. 126, § 1.
G.S.1860, c. 170, § 50.
P.S.1882, c. 212, § 64.
R.L.1902, c. 217, § 74.

§ 77. Service of notice and copy of petition; return day

Notice of the petition and a copy thereof shall be given to or served upon the district attorney for the county where the petition is pending fourteen days at least before the return day expressed therein, and such notice shall be returnable on the first Monday of the first or second month after the filing of the petition.

Historical and Statutory Notes

St.1852, c. 126, § 2.
G.S.1860, c. 170, § 51.
P.S.1882, c. 212, § 65.
R.L.1902, c. 217, § 75.

§ 78. Proceedings if former judgment diminished, etc.; costs

If the court finds that a part of the judgment has been actually paid to or for the commonwealth upon the recognizance or judgment and orders the judgment to be reversed or entered for a less amount than has been so actually paid, it may order the amount of the difference between the payment and the new judgment to be repaid to the person who made the payment or to his legal representatives. The state treasurer shall, upon presentation of a copy of the order certified by the clerk of the court, make said repayment. If, upon such petition, the review is not granted or the original judgment is not altered, the court may award reasonable costs against the petitioner.

Amended by St.1978, c. 478, § 288.

Historical and Statutory Notes

St.1852, c. 126, §§ 3, 4.
G.S.1860, c. 170, §§ 52, 53.
P.S.1882, c. 212, §§ 66, 67.
R.L.1902, c. 217, § 76.

§ 79. Personal recognizance and deposit instead of sureties for release from custody

A person held in custody or committed upon a criminal charge, if entitled to be released on bail, or a person held in custody or committed as a witness to a crime, may, instead of giving surety or sureties, at any time give his personal recognizance to appear before the court and deposit the amount of the bail which he is ordered to furnish, or bonds or a properly assigned bank book, of the kind and in the amount and under the conditions set forth in section fifty-seven for making deposit of like nature, with the court, clerk of the court or magistrate authorized to take such recognizance, who shall give him a certificate thereof, and upon delivering said certificate to the officer in whose custody he is, shall be released. The court or magistrate shall forthwith, upon receipt of such amount, deposit it with the clerk of the court.

Amended by St.1959, c. 313, § 26.

Historical and Statutory Notes

St.1879, c. 126, § 1.
P.S.1882, c. 212, § 68.
St.1882, c. 134.
R.L.1902, c. 217, § 77.
St.1906, c. 221.
St.1911, c. 160.
St.1920, c. 584, § 6.

§ 80. Forfeiture of deposit on default; sale of bonds; collection on bank books; payments to state treasurer

At any time after default of the defendant, the court may order forfeited the money, bonds or bank books deposited at the time of the recognizance and the court or clerk of the court with whom the deposit was made shall thereupon pay to the state treasurer any money so deposited. The clerk of the court shall immediately proceed to sell any bonds so deposited either at public or private sale, and shall forthwith pay the proceeds thereof, after deducting all expenses connected with such sale, to the state treasurer and if bank books are so deposited, the said clerk shall collect the amount of bail from the depository, and pay the same, less the expense of collection, to the state treasurer.

Amended by St.1959, c. 313, § 27; St.1978, c. 478, § 289; St.1996, c. 450, § 253.

Historical and Statutory Notes

St.1879, c. 126, § 3.
P.S.1882, c. 212, § 70.
R.L.1902, c. 217, § 78.
St.1920, c. 584, § 7.

§ 81. Defendant surrendering self; return of deposit

The defendant may surrender himself at any time before a default, in the same manner as sureties in criminal cases may surrender their principal, and the court shall thereupon order the bank books to be reassigned and the money or bonds so deposited to be returned to the person in whose name the deposit is made or to his order. At any time after default, on the surrender or recaption of the defendant, the court may order the whole or any part of the money so deposited or of the bonds, or of the amount of the net proceeds of the sale of said bonds, or the bank books, or the whole or any part of the amount collected from the depository thereunder, to be returned to the person in whose name the deposit is made or to his order. If the amount realized by sale or collection pursuant to the preceding section exceeds the amount of the recognizance, the court shall, on an application made at any time, order such excess to be returned to the party found by the court to be entitled thereto. The foregoing provisions shall apply to cases in which forfeiture has been ordered.

Historical and Statutory Notes

St.1879, c. 126, §§ 2, 4.
P.S.1882, c. 212, §§ 69, 71.
R.L.1902, c. 217, § 79.
St.1903, c. 236.
St.1920, c. 584, § 8.
St.1922, c. 361, § 1.

§ 82. Magistrates authorized to admit prisoners to bail

The term "magistrate", in any section of the statutes which provides for admitting persons to bail in criminal cases, shall be construed to include a bail commissioner or special magistrate, so far as to give him authority to admit prisoners to bail.

Amended by St.1979, c. 344, § 26.

Historical and Statutory Notes

St.1874, c. 306, § 5.
P.S.1882, c. 212, § 73.
R.L.1902, c. 217, § 80.

§ 82A. Failure to appear in court after release on bail or recognizance; penalty

A person who is released by court order or other lawful authority on bail or recognizance on condition that he will appear personally at a specified time and place and who fails without sufficient excuse to so appear shall be punished by a fine of not more than ten thousand dollars or by imprisonment in a house of correction for not more than one year, or both, in the case of a misdemeanor, and by a fine of not more than fifty thousand dollars and imprisonment in a state prison for not more than five years, or a house of correction for not more than two and one-half years, or by fine and imprisonment, in the case of a felony.

A term of imprisonment imposed under this section shall be consecutive to any other sentence of imprisonment for the offense for which the prisoner failed to appear.

Added by St.1965, c. 396. Amended by St.1994, c. 68, § 7.

§ 83. Appointment of probation officers; suspension; compensation

Subject to appropriation, the commissioner of probation may appoint, dismiss and assign such probation officers to the several sessions of the trial court as he deems necessary. In any court having 2 or more probation officers, said commissioner may designate 1 probation officer to serve as chief probation officer and may designate other probation officers to serve as assistant chief probation officers, as he deems necessary for the effective administration of justice; provided, however, that said commissioner may suspend or discipline any such probation officer. The compensation of probation officers in the trial court shall be paid by the commonwealth according to schedules established in section 99B or in a provision of an applicable collective bargaining agreement.

Amended by St.1936, c. 360; St.1937, c. 186; St.1947, c. 566, § 1; St.1947, c. 639; St.1949, c. 783, § 1; St.1950, c. 513; St.1950, c. 531; St.1951, c. 774, §§ 1, 2; St.1952, c. 241; St.1953, c. 341; St.1953, c. 420, § 1; St.1955, c. 735, §§ 1, 2; St.1956, c. 731, §§ 13, 13A; St.1957, c. 272; St.1965, c. 675; St.1967, c. 130; St.1967, c. 365; St.1968, c. 629; St.1969, c. 771, §§ 1, 2; St.1969, c. 859, §§ 25, 26; St.1970, c. 875, §§ 1, 2; St.1972, c. 731, §§ 21, 22; St.1978, c. 367, § 65; St.1978, c. 478, § 290; St.1979, c. 393, § 71A; St.1981, c. 779; St.1982, c. 594; St.1992, c. 379, § 188; St.2001, c. 177, § 52.

Historical and Statutory Notes

St.1880, c. 129, § 1.
P.S.1882, c. 212, § 74.
St.1882, c. 125.
St.1891, c. 356, §§ 1, 6.
St.1892, c. 242.
St.1892, c. 276, §§ 1, 3.

St.1897, c. 266, §§ 1, 3.
St.1898, c. 511, §§ 1, 2.
R.L.1902, c. 217, §§ 81, 92.
St.1905, c. 295.
St.1906, c. 329.
St.1906, c. 489, § 6.
St.1907, c. 223.
St.1907, c. 261.
St.1908, c. 190.
St.1908, c. 637.
St.1909, c. 216.
St.1910, c. 332.
St.1910, c. 479.
St.1911, c. 116.
St.1911, c. 470.
St.1912, c. 648, § 2.
St.1912, c. 664.
St.1913, c. 612, § 1.
St.1915, c. 89, § 1.
St.1915, c. 254, § 1.

§ 83A. Repealed, 1992, 379, Sec. 189

§§ 83B to 83F. Repealed, 1949, 783, Sec. 2

§ 84. Repealed, 1977, 97

§ 85. Powers and duties

Each person who receives an appointment as a probation officer shall, within six months of the date of his appointment, attend a basic orientation training course conducted by the commissioner of probation pursuant to section ninety-nine. All probation officers shall attend at least every three years an in-service training course pursuant to this section. In addition to the other duties imposed upon him, each probation officer shall, as the court may direct, inquire into the nature of every criminal case brought before the court under the appointment of which he acts, and inform the court, so far as is possible, whether the defendant has previously been convicted of crime and in the case of a criminal prosecution before said court charging a person with an offence punishable by imprisonment for more than one year the probation officer shall in any event present to the court such information as the commissioner of probation has in his possession relative to prior criminal prosecutions, if any, of such person and to the disposition of each such prosecution, and all other available information relative thereto, before such person is admitted to bail in court and also before disposition of the case against him by sentence, or placing on file or probation. Such record of the probation officer presented to the court shall not contain as part thereof any information of prior criminal prosecutions, if any, of the defendant wherein the defendant was found not guilty by the court or jury in said prior criminal prosecution. Prior to the aforesaid disposition such record of the probation officer shall be made available to the defendant and his counsel for inspection. When it comes to the knowledge of a probation officer that the defendant in a criminal case before his court charged with an offence punishable by imprisonment is then on probation in another court or is then at liberty on parole or on a permit to be at liberty, such probation officer shall forthwith certify the fact of the presence of the defendant before his court to the probation officer of such other court or the parole authorities granting or issuing such parole or permit to be at liberty, as the case may be. He may recommend to the justice of his own court that any person convicted be placed on probation. He shall perform such other duties as the court requires. He shall keep full records of all cases investigated by him or placed in his care by the court, and of all duties performed by him. Every person released upon probation shall be given by the probation officer a written statement of the terms and conditions of the release.

Amended by St.1950, c. 145, § 1; St.1956, c. 731, § 15; St.1968, c. 333, § 2; St.1972, c. 396, § 1; St.1976, c. 288.

Historical and Statutory Notes

St.1880, c. 129, §§ 3 to 5, 11.
P.S.1882, c. 212, §§ 75 to 77, 79.
St.1891, c. 356, §§ 3, 4.
St.1892, c. 276, § 2.
St.1897, c. 266, § 2.
St.1898, c. 511, § 1.
R.L.1902, c. 217, §§ 84, 96.
St.1911, c. 8.
St.1926, c. 320, § 2.
St.1929, c. 179, § 2.

§ 85A. Support and maintenance enforcement

In addition to other duties, a probation officer of the probate court may, when ordered to do so by the court, examine all records and files in divorce, legal separation, annulment, custody and paternity cases in which orders or decrees have been entered to ascertain whether the persons to whom payments of money should have been made regularly received the various and definite amounts provided for in the orders or decrees of the court and, where there are dependent minor children, that the same are applied for the support, maintenance, education and betterment of said dependent minor children, and that said dependent minor children are properly cared for by their custodian. Said officers shall bring into court when necessary, by citation or otherwise, all persons who are delinquent in making payments ordered or decreed by the court and shall ascertain in the case of dependent minor children whether they are receiving proper maintenance and education and whether they are liable to become public charges. Consistent with these and other duties, a probation officer shall assist the IV–D agency, as set forth in chapter one hundred and nineteen A to enforce child support orders.

Added by St.1969, c. 771, § 3. Amended by St.1986, c. 310, § 31; St.1987, c. 465, § 63; St.2001, c. 177, § 53.

§ 85B. Delinquent payments; collection; contempt proceedings

Said probation officer shall have full power, by citation or other order duly issued by the probate court, to compel the attendance of witnesses to take testimony and do each and every thing necessary, including initiating contempt proceedings, to collect any and all delinquent payments due to any person entitled under order or decree of said court to receive payments, to make recommendations to the probate court, where there are dependent minor children, for the betterment of the conditions of said dependent minor children and to ascertain when requested to do so by the court the moral and general conditions surrounding said dependent minor children and shall report the result of such findings to said court.

Added by St.1969, c. 771, § 3.

§ 86. Appointment of deputy probation officers by Boston juvenile court; creditable service

The justice of the Boston juvenile court subject to the approval of the commissioner of probation may appoint as many deputy probation officers, without salary, as he may deem desirable, who shall assist probation officers in such way as the court may direct in making investigations of cases of children against whom complaints have been made, and in the care of children placed on probation.

Subject to the provisions and limitations of sections one to twenty-eight, inclusive, of chapter thirty-two, any member in service of a retirement system established under said sections, and any person who has been retired under any such system, shall be credited with all service rendered by him as a deputy probation officer under this section; provided that before any retirement allowance becomes effective for him or, in the case of any person already retired, before January first, nineteen hundred and sixty-seven, he pays into the annuity savings fund of such system, with regular interest as defined in said sections, in one sum, or in instalments, upon such terms and conditions as the board managing such system may prescribe, an amount equal to that which would have been withheld as regular deductions from the minimum annual salary payable to a probation officer of said court during the period that such member in service or person so retired served as such deputy probation officer.

Amended by St.1966, c. 675; St.2001, c. 177, § 54.

Historical and Statutory Notes

St.1906, c. 489, § 6.

§ 87. Placing certain persons in care of probation officer

The superior court, any district court and any juvenile court may place on probation in the care of its probation officer any person before it charged with an offense or a crime for such time and upon such conditions as it deems proper, with the defendant's consent, before trial and before a plea of guilty, or in any case after a finding or verdict of guilty; provided, that, in the case of any child under the age of seventeen placed upon probation by the superior court, he may be placed in the care of a probation officer of any district court or of any juvenile court, within the judicial district of which such child resides; and provided further, that no person convicted under section twenty-two A, 22B, 22C or twenty-four B of chapter two hundred and sixty-five or section thirty-five A of chapter two hundred and seventy-two shall, if it appears that he has previously been convicted under said sections and was eighteen years of age or older at the time of committing the offense for which he was so convicted, be released on parole or probation prior to the completion of five years of his sentence.

Amended by St.1941, c. 264, § 2; St.1955, c. 763, § 1; St.1969, c. 859, § 27; St.1970, c. 98; St.1972, c. 731, § 23; St.1973, c. 925, § 81; St.1974, c. 614; St.2010, c. 267, § 66, eff. Nov. 5, 2010.

Historical and Statutory Notes

St.1880, c. 129, § 4.
P.S.1882, c. 212, § 76.
St.1891, c. 356, § 3.
St.1898, c. 511, § 1.
R.L.1902, c. 217, § 84.
St.1911, c. 8.
St.1926, c. 271, § 1.
St.1926, c. 296.

§ 87A. Conditions of probation; probation fees

The conditions of probation imposed by a court upon a person pursuant to section eighty-seven of this chapter, section fifty-eight of chapter one hundred and nineteen or section one or section one A of chapter two hundred and seventy-nine, may include, but shall not be limited to, participation by said person in specified rehabilitative programs or performance by said person of specified community service work for a stated period of time.

The court shall assess upon every person placed on supervised probation, including all persons placed on probation for offenses under section 24 of chapter 90, a monthly probation supervision fee, hereinafter referred to as "probation fee", in the amount of $60 per month. Said person shall pay said probation fee once each month during such time as said person remains on supervised probation. The court shall assess upon every person placed on administrative supervised probation a monthly administrative probation supervision fee, hereinafter referred to as "administrative probation fee", in the amount of $45 per month. Said person shall pay said administrative probation fee once each month during such time as said person remains on administrative supervised probation. Notwithstanding the foregoing, said fees shall not be assessed upon any person accused or convicted of a violation of section 1 or 15 of chapter 273, where compliance with an order of support for a spouse or minor child is a condition of probation.

The court may not waive payment of either or both of said fees unless it determines after a hearing and upon written finding that such payment would constitute an undue hardship on said person or his family due to limited income, employment status or any other factor. Following the hearing and upon such written finding that either or both of said fees would cause such undue hardship then: (1) in lieu of payment of said probation fee the court shall require said person to perform unpaid community work service at a public or nonprofit agency or facility, as approved and monitored by the probation department, for not less than one day per month and (2) in lieu of payment of said administrative probation fee the court shall require said person to perform unpaid community work service at a public or nonprofit agency or facility, as approved and monitored by the probation department, for not less than four hours per month. Such waiver shall be in effect only during the period of time that said person is unable to pay his monthly probation fee.

The court may waive payment of either or both of said fees in whole or in part if said person is assessed payment of restitution. In such cases, said fees may be waived only to the extent and during the period that restitution is paid in an amount equivalent to said fee.

Said probation fee shall be collected by the several probation offices of the trial court and transmitted to the state treasurer for deposit into the General Fund. The state treasurer shall account for all such fees received and report said fees annually, itemized by court division, to the house and senate committees on ways and means.

The court shall also assess upon every person placed on supervised probation, including all persons placed on probation for offenses under section 24 of chapter 90, a monthly probationers' victim services surcharge, hereinafter referred to as "victim services surcharge", in the amount of $5 per month. Said person shall pay said victim services surcharge once each month during such time as said person remains on supervised probation. The court shall assess upon every person placed on administrative supervised probation a monthly administrative probationer's victim services surcharge, hereinafter referred to as "administrative victim services surcharge" in the amount of $5 per month.

Said person shall pay said administrative victim services surcharge once each month during such time as said person remains on administrative supervised probation. Notwithstanding the foregoing, said fees shall not be assessed upon any person accused or convicted of a violation of section 1 or 15 of chapter 273, where compliance with an order of support for a spouse or minor child is a condition of probation.

The court may not waive payment of either or both of said fees unless it has determined, after a hearing and upon written finding, that such payment would constitute an undue hardship on said person or his family due to limited income, employment status or any other factor. Such waiver shall be in effect only during the period of time that said person is unable to pay his monthly probation fee.

Said probation fee shall be collected by the several probation offices of the trial court and shall be transmitted to the state treasurer for deposit into the General Fund of the commonwealth. The state treasurer shall account for all such fees received and report said fees annually, itemized by court division, to the house and senate committees on ways and means.

Added by St.1984, c. 294, § 1. Amended by St.1988, c. 202, § 27; St.1990, c. 150, § 343; St.1996, c. 12, § 10; St.1999, c. 127, § 185; St.2002, c. 300, § 13; St.2003, c. 26, § 510, eff. July 1, 2003; St.2009, c. 27, §§ 99, 100, eff. July 1, 2009.

§ 88. Clerical assistance

Every court appointing probation officers may employ such clerical assistance as it deems necessary to keep, index and consolidate the records required to be kept by probation officers and for such other work in connection with its probation service as the court may determine. The compensation for such service, together with such other necessary expenses as the court shall incur in connection with such work, shall be paid by the commonwealth upon vouchers approved by said court.

The administrative justices for the district court and juvenile court departments, in consultation with the commissioner of probation, may designate and redesignate such divisions thereof, including in such term the Boston juvenile court, the Worcester juvenile court, the Bristol county juvenile court and the Springfield juvenile court, within each of the counties of the commonwealth as in the opinion of said administrative justices should join in the establishment of a probation district office for the clerical service of the probation officers of the divisions thereof so designated or redesignated and said divisions so designated or redesignated shall thereupon consult with the chief administrative justice of the trial court and the commissioner of probation as to the establishment of such a probation district office, and shall join in the employment of such clerical assistance as is necessary to keep, index and consolidate the records in such form as may be required by the commissioner of probation in connection with the probation service of the said courts. The compensation for such service, together with such other necessary expenses as the courts shall incur in connection with such work, shall be paid by the commonwealth upon vouchers approved by one of the justices of said courts, designated by said administrative justices.

Amended by St.1956, c. 731, § 16; St.1969, c. 859, § 28; St.1972, c. 731, § 24; St.1978, c. 478, § 292.

Historical and Statutory Notes

St.1891, c. 427, §§ 6, 7.
R.L.1902, c. 212, § 40.
St.1908, c. 440.
St.1913, c. 612, § 2.
St.1914, c. 739.
St.1915, c. 89, § 2.
St.1915, c. 254, § 2.

St.1918, c. 257, § 452.
St.1919, c. 5.
St.1920, c. 2.
St.1930, c. 400, §§ 5, 7 to 9.
St.1931, c. 301, § 49.

§ 89. Temporary probation officers

The superior court or the justice of a district court, including in such term the Worcester juvenile court, the Boston juvenile court, the Bristol county juvenile court and the Springfield juvenile court, may, in the case of a vacancy in the position of probation officer or in the absence of a probation officer, appoint a temporary probation officer, who shall have the powers and perform the duties of such probation officer and shall receive as compensation for each day's service an amount equal to the rate by the day of the minimum compensation of a regular probation officer according to the salary schedule established under section eight of chapter two hundred and eleven B. Compensation so paid to a temporary probation officer for service rendered in the absence of a probation officer, in excess of thirty days in any one year, shall be deducted from the compensation of the probation officer in whose place such service is rendered; provided, however, that if a probation officer is absent, due to his illness or physical disability, for a period not exceeding thirty days in any year, in addition to said thirty days, he shall be deemed to be on sick leave and no such deduction shall be made. Such thirty days' sick leave or any portion thereof not used in any year may be accumulated, but shall, in any event, not exceed ninety days in any consecutive three year period. If the person so appointed holds an office or position, the salary or compensation for which is paid out of the treasury of the commonwealth, or of a county, or of a municipality, he shall not receive the salary of both offices or positions during the period of such temporary service.

The justices of a probate court for any county, except the county of Dukes County and the counties of Nantucket and Franklin, may, in the absence of a probation officer, appoint a temporary probation officer in the same manner and upon the same conditions, with the same powers and duties and the same rate of compensation as is provided in the first paragraph.

The justice of a district court, with the approval of the administrative justice of district courts, may, in the case of the death, removal, resignation or retirement of a probation officer, appoint a temporary probation officer for a single term not to exceed ninety days. Such temporary probation officer shall receive as compensation from the commonwealth an amount equal to that which would have been paid, for a like period of service, to a regular probation officer receiving the minimum compensation according to the salary schedule as established under section eight of chapter two hundred and eleven B. No temporary probation officer appointed under this section shall serve for more than ninety days unless his appointment to such temporary office has been approved by the chief administrative justice of the trial court upon recommendation of the commissioner of probation.

Amended by St.1934, c. 217, § 2; St.1941, c. 477, § 1; St.1953, c. 364; St.1956, c. 731, §§ 17, 17A; St.1959, c. 526, § 1; St.1969, c. 87; St.1969, c. 771, § 4; St.1969, c. 859, § 29; St.1972, c. 731, § 25; St.1978, c. 45; St.1978, c. 478, § 292.

Historical and Statutory Notes

St.1894, c. 372.
R.L.1902, c. 217, § 82.
St.1910, c. 275, § 1.

§ 89A. Counsellors to juvenile offenders

The superior court or the justice of a district court may appoint deputy probation officers who shall serve without compensation as counsellors to children under the age of seventeen who have been placed in the care of probation officers under section eighty-seven in order that such children may receive to a greater degree individual attention and guidance. Deputy probation officers shall perform their services under the direction of probation officers. Deputy probation officers may be reimbursed by the commonwealth upon voucher approved by the court to which they are assigned for necessary expenses incurred by them in the course of their duties.

The chief justice for administration and management, in consultation with the commissioner of probation, may apply for and accept federal grants or assistance for the purpose of defraying the costs of additional clerical assistance, equipment, books, materials and other expenses incident to the services which such deputy probation officers perform.

Added by St.1967, c. 401. Amended by St.1978, c. 478, § 292; St.1992, c. 379, § 190.

§ 90. Powers of probation officers; reports; records; inspection

A probation officer shall not be an active member of the regular police force, but so far as necessary in the performance of his official duties shall, except as otherwise provided, have all the powers of a police officer, and if appointed by the superior court may, by its direction, act in any part of the commonwealth. He shall report to the court, and his records may at all times be inspected by police officials of the towns of the commonwealth; provided, that his records in cases arising under sections fifty-two to fifty-nine, inclusive, of chapter one hundred and nineteen shall not be open to inspection without the consent of a justice of his court.

Amended by St.1938, c. 174, § 3.

Historical and Statutory Notes

St.1880, c. 129, §§ 1, 5.
P.S.1882, c. 212, § 74.
St.1891, c. 356, § 2.

St.1898, c. 511, § 1.
R.L.1902, c. 217, § 83.

§ 91. Power of probation officers appointed by Boston juvenile court to serve process

Probation officers appointed by the Boston juvenile court may serve such process as may be directed to them by the court.

Historical and Statutory Notes

St.1906, c. 489, § 6.

§ 92. Restitution or reparation to injured person through probation officer

If a person is placed on probation upon condition that he make restitution or reparation to the person injured by him in the commission of his offence, and payment is not made at once, the court may order that it shall be made to the probation officer, who shall give receipts for and keep record of all payments made to him, pay the money to the person injured and keep his receipt therefor, and notify the clerk of the court whenever the full amount of the money is received or paid in accordance with such order or with any modification thereof.

Historical and Statutory Notes

St.1907, c. 335.

§ 92A. Restitution in cases involving motor vehicle theft or fraudulent claims

A person found guilty of violating the provisions of sections twenty-seven, twenty-eight, one hundred and eleven B and one hundred and thirty-nine of chapter two hundred and sixty-six shall, in all cases, upon conviction, in addition to any other punishment, be ordered to make restitution to any person whom the court deems appropriate for any financial loss sustained by the victim of his crime, his dependents or an insurer as a result of the commission of the crime. The term "financial loss" shall be interpreted to include but shall not be limited to, loss of earnings, out-of-pocket expenses, and replacement costs. Losses due to pain and suffering are not financial loss. Restitution shall be interpreted to include monetary reimbursement, work or service, or a combination thereof, provided to any person, organization, corporation, or governmental entity, the court determines, has suffered said damage or financial loss, or to perform such work or service for any other person, organization, corporation or governmental entity as the court may determine. Restitution shall be imposed in addition to incarceration or fine, but not in lieu thereof. In an extraordinary case such as indigency, the court may determine that the interests of the victim and justice would not be served by ordering restitution. In such a case, the court shall make and enter specific written findings on the record concerning the extraordinary circumstances presented which militated against the imposition of restitution.

The court shall, after conviction, conduct an evidentiary hearing to ascertain the extent of the damages or financial loss suffered as a result of the defendant's crime. The court may then determine the amount and method of restitution. In so determining, the court shall consider the financial resources of the defendant and the burden restitution will impose on the defendant. The defendant's present and future ability to make such restitution shall be considered.

A defendant ordered to make restitution may petition the court for remission from any payment of restitution or from any unpaid portion thereof. If the court finds that the payment of restitution due will impose an undue financial hardship on the defendant or his family, the court may grant remission from any payment of restitution or modify the time and method of payment.

If a defendant who is required to make restitution defaults in any payment of restitution or installment thereof, the court may hold him in contempt unless said defendant has made a good faith effort to make restitution. If the defendant has made a good faith effort to make restitution, the court may, upon motion of the defendant, modify the order requiring restitution by:

(a) providing for additional time to make any payment in restitution;

(b) reducing the amount of any payment in restitution or installment thereof;

(c) granting a remission from any payment of restitution or part thereof.

Restitution shall not be authorized to a party whom the court determines to be aggrieved, without that party's consent.

Added by St.1980, c. 463, § 7. Amended by St.1986, c. 557, § 201.

§ 93. Payment to treasurer of unclaimed money collected by probation officer

Except as provided by section one of chapter two hundred and seventy-nine, money collected by a probation officer under order of the court by which he is appointed, if unclaimed after one year from the time of its collection, shall, upon further order of the court, be paid to the treasurer provided, that any part of the said money may be paid to persons establishing before the comptroller a lawful claim thereto within five years of its payment to said treasurer, unless sooner paid over by order of the said commissioners.

Amended by St.1978, c. 478, § 293.

Historical and Statutory Notes

St.1920, c. 122.

§ 94. Expenses of probation officers

The reasonable expenses, including supplies and equipment, incurred by probation officers of the superior court and the probate court in the performance of their duties shall be approved and apportioned by the court, and paid by the commonwealth. Such reasonable expenses shall include the traveling expenses necessarily incurred by such a probation officer in connection with attendance at sessions of said court outside of the town in which the principal office of such probation officer is maintained, such expenses to be computed from and to said town. Money to be used for the necessary expenses to be incurred by such a probation officer in going outside the commonwealth for the purpose of bringing back for surrender to the court a person who is on probation shall be advanced by the treasurer of the commonwealth, upon presentation of a certificate signed by the probation officer and approved by said court. After his return such probation officer shall account for such money by filing with said state treasurer itemized vouchers, duly sworn to, approved by the court, setting forth the necessary expenses so incurred and any unexpended balance of such money shall be paid to said state treasurer. Subject to section eighty-one of chapter two hundred and eighteen, probation officers of district courts and of the Boston, Worcester, Bristol county and Springfield juvenile courts shall be reimbursed by the commonwealth for their actual disbursements for necessary expenses incurred while in the performance of their duties, including their reasonable traveling expenses in attending conferences authorized by section ninety-nine, not exceeding four hundred dollars to each in any one year, upon vouchers approved by the court by which they are appointed.

Amended by St.1939, c. 155; St.1939, c. 296, § 2; St.1947, c. 82; St.1969, c. 771, § 5; St.1969, c. 859, § 30; St.1971, c. 1064; St.1972, c. 731, § 26; St.1978, c. 478, § 293.

Historical and Statutory Notes

St.1894, c. 229.
St.1898, c. 511, § 2.
St.1900, c. 279.
St.1900, c. 449, § 6.
R.L.1902, c. 217, § 93.
St.1906, c. 489, § 6.
St.1927, c. 166.
St.1929, c. 231.

§ 95. Temporary support or transportation of probationers

The superior courts or the Boston, Springfield, Bristol county and Worcester juvenile courts or a district court, except the municipal court of the city of Boston, may authorize a probation officer to expend such amount as the court considers expedient for the temporary support or transportation, or both, of a person placed on probation. A record of any amount so authorized shall be entered on the clerk's docket of the case.

The chief probation officer of the municipal court of the city of Boston may provide for the temporary support or transportation, or both, of a person placed on probation in said court, or for the relief of the immediate distress of such person, in any manner which he may deem proper, and for these purposes may annually expend a sum not exceeding two thousand dollars for all such cases of relief. At the end of each month said chief probation officer shall submit to the administrative justice of said court a list of the expenses so incurred, with proper vouchers, and upon approval of the administrative justice the amount thereof shall be paid to the chief probation officer by the commonwealth.

Amended by St.1969, c. 859, § 31; St.1972, c. 731, § 27; St.1978, c. 478, § 293.

Historical and Statutory Notes

St.1894, c. 368.
R.L.1902, c. 217, § 94.
St.1906, c. 440.
St.1906, c. 489, § 6.
St.1914, c. 491.

§ 96. Refusal or neglect of duties by probation officer

Any probation officer who refuses or neglects to perform any of the duties required of him shall forfeit two hundred dollars to the use of the commonwealth.

Historical and Statutory Notes

St.1891, c. 356, § 8.
St.1892, c. 276, § 3.
St.1897, c. 266, § 3.
R.L.1902, c. 217, § 95.

§ 97. Interference with duties of department of youth services

Sections eighty-three to ninety-six, inclusive, shall not authorize a probation officer to interfere with any of the duties required of the department of youth services under the law relative to juvenile offenders.

Amended by St.1941, c. 677, § 2; St.1956, c. 731, § 18; St.1969, c. 838, § 62.

Historical and Statutory Notes

St.1880, c. 129, § 12.
P.S.1882, c. 212, § 81.
St.1886, c. 101, § 4.
St.1891, c. 356, § 9.
R.L.1902, c. 217, § 97.
St.1919, c. 350, § 87.

§ 98. Commissioner of probation; appointment

There shall be a commissioner of probation, who shall have executive control and supervision of the probation service. The commissioner shall be appointed by the chief justice for administration and management for a term of 5 years and shall devote his full-time during business hours to the duties of his office. Subject to the approval and consent of the chief justice for administration and management, the commissioner may appoint deputies, supervisors and assistants necessary for the performance of his duties. Said commissioner, deputies, supervisors and assistants, shall receive a salary to be fixed by the chief justice for administration and management and subject to appropriation. Subject to the approval and direction of the chief justice for administration and management, the commissioner shall perform such duties and responsibilities as otherwise provided by law or as designated from time to time by the chief justice for administration and management, and shall be responsible for: making recommendations to the first justice and the chief justice for administration and management on the appointment of chief probation officers, assistant chief probation officers and probation officers; the supervision and evaluation of all probation programs within the trial court; the evaluation of the probation service in each court of the commonwealth; the compilation, evaluation, and dissemination of statistical information on crime, delinquency, and appropriate family service matters available in his records; the recruitment, training, and educational development of probation officers; the evaluation of the work performance of probation officers; planning, initiating, and developing volunteer, diversion, and other programs in consultation with probation officers throughout the commonwealth.

Amended by St.1932, c. 145; St.1956, c. 731, § 19; St.1963, c. 801, §§ 79, 80; St.1965, c. 843; St.1969, c. 766, §§ 45, 45A; St.1969, c. 771, § 6; St.1970, c. 875, §§ 3, 4; St.1973, c. 1070; St.1978, c. 478, § 294; St.1981, c. 632, § 21A; St.1986, c. 279, § 17; St.1986, c. 520, § 1; St.1991, c. 138, §§ 296, 297; St.1992, c. 379, § 191; St.1993, c. 12, §§ 11, 12; St.2010, c. 131, § 103, eff. July 1, 2010.

Historical and Statutory Notes

St.1900, c. 449, § 8.
R.L.1902, c. 217, § 90.
St.1908, c. 465, §§ 1, 6.
St.1914, c. 191.
St.1929, c. 179, § 1.

§ 99. Powers and duties of commissioner of probation

The commissioner of probation shall supervise the probation work in all of the courts of the commonwealth and for such purposes he and his staff shall have access to all probation records of said courts. Subject to the approval of the chief justice for administration and management, the commissioner shall establish reports and forms to be maintained by probation officers; procedures to be followed by probation officers; standards and rules of probation work, including methods and procedures of investigation, mediation, supervision, case work, record keeping, accounting, caseload and case management. The commissioner shall promulgate rules and regulations concerning probation officers or offices provided said rules and regulations have been approved in writing by the chief justice for administration and management subject to chapter one hundred and fifty E. The commissioner shall assist the chief justice for administration and management in developing standards and procedures for the performance evaluation of probation officers, and shall assist each first justice in evaluating the work performance of probation officers. The commissioner shall receive all notices of intended disciplinary action against a probation officer or supervising probation officer including reprimand, fine, suspension, demotion or discharge, that may be initiated by a first justice, supervisor or chief probation officer. The commissioner shall develop and conduct basic orientation and in-service training programs for probation officers, such programs to be held at such times and for such periods as he shall determine. He shall conduct research studies relating to crime and delinquency, and, may participate with other public and private agencies in joint research studies. The commissioner shall have the responsibility for assessing the needs of probation offices and assisting the first justices in this effort. He may recommend to first justices, or the chief justice for administration and management the appointment and assignment of additional probation or clerical personnel or both. The commissioner shall annually submit written budget recommendations for the probation service to the chief justice for administration and management. These recommendations shall be in addition to the budget requests submitted by the first justices on behalf of their respective courthouse or courthouses, including probation offices. The commissioner shall annually conduct regional meetings with chief probation officers to discuss the budget needs of the local probation offices. The commissioner may hold conferences on probation throughout the commonwealth. The traveling expenses of trial court justices or probation officers authorized by the chief justice for administration and management to attend any such conference shall be paid by the commonwealth.

Amended by St.1952, c. 348; St.1956, c. 731, § 20; St.1972, c. 396, § 2; St.1978, c. 478, § 294; St.1992, c. 379, § 191; St.1993, c. 12, §§ 11, 12.

Historical and Statutory Notes

St.1900, c. 449, §§ 4 to 6.
R.L.1902, c. 217, §§ 86 to 88.
St.1908, c. 465, §§ 2, 6.
St.1916, c. 241, § 1.
St.1919, c. 350, §§ 82, 83, 87.
St.1929, c. 179, § 1.
St.1931, c. 57, § 1.

§ 99A. Repealed, 1992, 379, Sec. 192

§ 99B. Probation officers; compensation

(1) In those courts or regions having fewer than fifteen probation officers, all persons serving as chief probation officer or acting chief probation officer shall be allocated to the title of Chief or Acting Chief Probation Officer I, and in those courts or regions having fifteen or more probation officers, all persons

so-serving shall be allocated to the title of Chief or Acting Chief Probation Officer II.

(2) All probation officers, except the chief probation officer, shall be compensated in accordance with the provisions of the applicable collective bargaining agreement, pursuant to the provisions of chapter one hundred and fifty E. The salaries of chief probation officers and acting chief probation officers shall be paid by the commonwealth in accordance with a schedule of salaries as recommended in writing by the chief administrative justice of the trial court and filed with the house and senate committees on ways and means.

(3) Upon initial appointment, a probation officer shall be compensated at the minimum of said salary schedule for his group or, if he shall have had prior service as a probation officer or shall, in the judgment of the committee on probation, have had years of similar service in allied fields, the step for such group to which his years of prior service entitle him.

(4) Upon completion of each year of service, a probation officer shall be compensated at the next higher step, if any, of said salary schedule for his group.

(5) Upon promotion (including, in the case of a chief probation officer, a change in his class due to an increase in the number of probation officers his probation office has), a probation officer shall be compensated at the lowest step of his new group which is at least one increment of his new group, but less than two such increments, higher than his salary immediately prior to such promotion, and upon the completion of each year of service in his new group, shall be compensated at the next higher step, if any, of said salary schedule for such new group. Notwithstanding any other provision of this section, no chief probation officer shall receive a salary less than the next increment greater than the salary received by the first assistant chief probation officer in the same court.

Added by St.1970, c. 875, § 6. Amended by St.1971, c. 909, §§ 1, 2; St.1972, c. 600, § 1A; St.1973, c. 772, § 2; St.1974, c. 558, § 15; St.1977, c. 234, §§ 194 to 196; St.1977, c. 872, §§ 194 to 196; St.1978, c. 478, § 295; St.1979, c. 393, §§ 71B, 71C; St.1981, c. 632, §§ 21B, 21C; St.1986, c. 520, § 2.

§ 99C. Repealed, 1978, 478, Sec. 296

§ 99D. Repealed, 1986, 520, Sec. 3

Historical and Statutory Notes

See, now, § 99B of this chapter.

§ 99E. Indigency; interagency service agreements; income data verification

(a) The commissioner of probation shall enter into an interagency service agreement with the department of revenue to verify income data and other information relevant to the determination of indigency of recipients of counsel pursuant to section 2 of chapter 211D.

(b) The commissioner of probation shall enter into an interagency service agreement with the department of transitional assistance to verify income data and other information relevant to the determination of indigency of recipients of counsel pursuant to section 2 of chapter 211D.

(c) The commissioner of probation shall enter into an interagency service agreement with the department of medical assistance to verify income data and other information relevant to the determination of indigency of recipients of counsel pursuant to section 2 of chapter 211D.

(d) The commissioner of probation shall enter into an interagency service agreement with the registry of motor vehicles to verify the statements on motor vehicle ownership or nonownership by recipients of counsel pursuant to section 2 of chapter 211D.

Added by St.2004, c. 149, § 212, eff. July 1, 2004.

§ 100. Detailed reports of probation work; records; accessibility of information

Every probation officer, or the chief or senior probation officer of a court having more than one probation officer, shall transmit to the commissioner of probation, in such form and at such times as he shall require, detailed reports regarding the work of probation in the court, and the commissioner of correction, the penal institutions commissioner of Boston and the county commissioners of counties other than Suffolk shall transmit to the commissioner, as aforesaid, detailed and complete records relative to all paroles and permits to be at liberty granted or issued by them, respectively, to the revoking of the same and to the length of time served on each sentence to imprisonment by each prisoner so released specifying the institution where each such sentence was served; and under the direction of the commissioner a record shall be kept of all such cases as the commissioner may require for the information of the justices and probation officers. Police officials shall co-operate with the commissioner and the probation officers in obtaining and reporting information concerning persons on probation. The information so obtained and recorded shall not be regarded as public records and shall not be open for public inspection but shall be accessible to the justices and probation officers of the courts, to the police commissioner for the city of Boston, to all chiefs of police and city marshals, and to such departments of the state and local governments as the commissioner may determine. Upon payment of a fee of three dollars for each search, such records shall be accessible to such departments of the federal government and to such educational and charitable corporations and institutions as the commissioner may determine. The commissioner of correction and the department of youth services shall at all times give to the commissioner and the probation officers such information as may be obtained from the records concerning prisoners under sentence or who have been released. The commissioner may use systems operated by the department of criminal justice information services, pursuant to sections one hundred sixty-seven to one hundred seventy-eight, inclusive, of chapter six, for any record-keeping lawfully required by him provided that such records remain subject to the regulations of said department.

Amended by St.1943, c. 64; St.1953, c. 319, § 34; St.1956, c. 731, § 22; St.1966, c. 623; St.1969, c. 838, § 63; St.1972, c. 805, § 8; St.1975, c. 534; St.2010, c. 256, §§ 126, 127, eff. Nov. 4, 2010.

Historical and Statutory Notes

St.1880, c. 129, § 2.
P.S.1882, c. 212, § 80.
St.1891, c. 356, § 5.
St.1900, c. 449, §§ 3, 4.
R.L.1902, c. 217, §§ 85, 86.
St.1902, c. 196.
St.1908, c. 465, §§ 3, 6.
St.1916, c. 241, § 1.
St.1919, c. 350, §§ 82, 83, 87.
St.1926, c. 320, § 3.
St.1929, c. 179, § 1.
St.1931, c. 57, § 2.

§ 100A. Requests to seal files; conditions; application of section; effect of sealing of records

[First paragraph effective until May 4, 2012. For text effective May 4, 2012, see below.]

Any person having a record of criminal court appearances and dispositions in the commonwealth on file with the office of the commissioner of probation may, on a form furnished by the commissioner and signed under the penalties of perjury, request that the commissioner seal such file. The commissioner shall comply with such request provided (1) that said person's court appearance and court disposition records, including termination of court supervision, probation or sentence for any misdemeanor occurred not less than ten years prior to said request; (2) that said person's court appearance and court disposition records, including termination of court supervision, probation or sentence for any felony occurred not less than fifteen years prior to said request; (3) that said person had not been found guilty of any criminal offense within the commonwealth in the ten years preceding such request, except motor vehicle offenses in which the penalty does not exceed a fine of fifty dollars; (4) said form includes a statement by the petitioner that he has not been convicted of any criminal offense in any other state, United States possession or in a court of federal jurisdiction, except such motor vehicle offenses, as aforesaid, and has not been imprisoned in any state or county within the preceding ten years; and (5) said person's record does not include convictions of offenses other than those to which this section applies. This section shall apply to court appearances and dispositions of all offenses provided, however, that this section shall not apply in case of convictions for violations of sections one hundred and twenty-one to one hundred and thirty-one H, inclusive, of chapter one hundred and forty or for violations of chapter two hundred and sixty-eight or chapter two hundred and sixty-eight A.

[First paragraph as amended by 2010, 256, Sec. 128 effective May 4, 2012. See 2010, 256, Sec. 145 as amended by 2010, 359, Sec. 102. For text effective until May 4, 2012, see above.]

Any person having a record of criminal court appearances and dispositions in the commonwealth on file with the office of the commissioner of probation may, on a form furnished by the commissioner and signed under the penalties of perjury, request that the commissioner seal the file. The commissioner shall comply with the request provided that: (1) the person's court appearance and court disposition records, including any period of incarceration or custody for any misdemeanor record to be sealed occurred not less than 5 years before the request; (2) the person's court appearance and court disposition records, including any period of incarceration or custody for any felony record to be sealed occurred not less than 10 years before the request; (3) the person had not been found guilty of any criminal offense within the commonwealth in the case of a misdemeanor, 5 years before the request, and in the case of a felony, 10 years before request, except motor vehicle offenses in which the penalty does not exceed a fine of $50; (4) the form includes a statement by the petitioner that he has not been convicted of any criminal offense in any other state, United States possession or in a court of federal jurisdiction, except such motor vehicle offenses, as aforesaid, and has not been imprisoned in any state or county in the case of a misdemeanor, within the preceding 5 years, and in the case of a felony, within the preceding 10 years; and (5) the person's record does not include convictions of offenses other than those to which this section applies. This section shall apply to court appearances and dispositions of all offenses; provided, however, that this section shall not apply in case of convictions for violations of sections 121 to 131H, inclusive, of chapter 140 or for violations of chapter 268 or chapter 268A.

In carrying out the provisions of this section, notwithstanding any laws to the contrary:

1. Any recorded offense which was a felony when committed and has since become a misdemeanor shall be treated as a misdemeanor.

2. Any recorded offense which is no longer a crime shall be eligible for sealing forthwith, except in cases where the elements of the offense continue to be a crime under a different designation.

3. In determining the period for eligibility, any subsequently recorded offenses for which the dispositions are "not guilty", "dismissed for want of prosecution", "dismissed at request of complainant", "nol

prossed", or "no bill" shall not be held to interrupt the running of the required period for eligibility.

4. If it cannot be ascertained that a recorded offense was a felony when committed said offense shall be treated as a misdemeanor.

[Subparagraphs 5 and 6 of second paragraph added by 2010, 256, Sec. 129 effective May 4, 2012. See 2010, 256, Sec. 145 as amended by 2010, 359, Sec. 102. For text effective until May 4, 2012, see above.]

5. Any violation of section 7 of chapter 209A or section 9 of chapter 258E shall be treated as a felony.

6. Sex offenses, as defined in section 178C of chapter 6, shall not be eligible for sealing for 15 years following their disposition, including termination of supervision, probation or any period of incarceration, or for so long as the offender is under a duty to register in the commonwealth or in any other state where the offender resides or would be under such a duty if residing in the commonwealth, whichever is longer; provided, however, that any sex offender who has at any time been classified as a level 2 or level 3 sex offender, pursuant to section 178K of chapter 6, shall not be eligible for sealing of sex offenses.

When records of criminal appearances and criminal dispositions are sealed by the commissioner in his files, he shall notify forthwith the clerk and the probation officer of the courts in which the convictions or dispositions have occurred, or other entries have been made, of such sealing, and said clerks and probation officers likewise shall seal records of the same proceedings in their files.

[Fourth paragraph effective until May 4, 2012. For text effective May 4, 2012, see below.]

Such sealed records shall not operate to disqualify a person in any examination, appointment or application for public service in the service of the commonwealth or of any political subdivision thereof; nor shall such sealed records be admissible in evidence or used in any way in any court proceedings or hearings before any boards or commissions, except in imposing sentence in subsequent criminal proceedings.

[Fourth paragraph as amended by 2010, 256, Sec. 130 effective May 4, 2012. See 2010, 256, Sec. 145 as amended by 2010, 359, Sec. 102. For text effective until May 4, 2012, see above.]

Such sealed records shall not operate to disqualify a person in any examination, appointment or application for public service in the service of the commonwealth or of any political subdivision thereof; nor shall such sealed records be admissible in evidence or used in any way in any court proceedings or hearings before any boards or commissions, except in imposing sentence in subsequent criminal proceedings, and except that in any proceedings under sections 1 to 39*I*, inclusive, of chapter 119, sections 2 to 5, inclusive, of chapter 201, chapters 208, 209, 209A, 209B, 209C, or sections 1 to 11A, inclusive, of chapter 210, a party having reasonable cause to believe that information in a sealed criminal record of another party may be relevant to (1) an issue of custody or visitation of a child, (2) abuse, as defined in section 1 of chapter 209A or (3) the safety of any person may upon motion seek to introduce the sealed record into evidence. The judge shall first review such records in camera and determine those records that are potentially relevant and admissible. The judge shall then conduct a closed hearing on the admissibility of those records determined to be potentially admissible; provided, however, that such records shall not be discussed in open court and, if admitted, shall be impounded and made available only to the parties, their attorneys and court personnel who have a demonstrated need to receive them.

An application for employment used by an employer which seeks information concerning prior arrests or convictions of the applicant shall include the following statement: "An applicant for employment with a sealed record on file with the commissioner of probation may answer 'no record' with respect to an inquiry herein relative to prior arrests, criminal court appearances or convictions. An applicant for employment with a sealed record on file with the commissioner of probation may answer 'no record' to an inquiry herein relative to prior arrests or criminal court appearances. In addition, any applicant for employment may answer 'no record' with respect to any inquiry relative to prior arrests, court appearances and adjudications in all cases of delinquency or as a child in need of services which did not result in a complaint transferred to the superior court for criminal prosecution." The attorney general may enforce the provisions of this paragraph by a suit in equity commenced in the superior court.

The commissioner, in response to inquiries by authorized persons other than any law enforcement agency, any court, or any appointing authority, shall in the case of a sealed record or in the case of court appearances and adjudications in a case of delinquency or the case of a child in need of services which did not result in a complaint transferred to the superior court for criminal prosecution, report that no record exists.

Added by St.1971, c. 686, § 1. Amended by St.1973, c. 533, §§ 2, 3; St.1973, c. 1102, § 4; St.1974, c. 525; St.1975, c. 278; St.2010, c. 256, §§ 128 to 130, eff. May 4, 2012.

§ 100B. Requests to seal delinquency files or records; conditions; sealing by commissioner; notice for compliance; effect of sealing; limited disclosure

Any person having a record of entries of a delinquency court appearance in the commonwealth on file in the office of the commissioner of probation may, on a form furnished by the commissioner, signed under the penalties of perjury, request that the commissioner seal such file. The commissioner shall comply with such request provided (1) that any court appearance or disposition including court supervision, probation, commitment or parole, the records for which are to be sealed, terminated not less than three years prior to said request; (2) that said person has not been adjudicated delinquent or found guilty of any criminal offense within the commonwealth in the three years preceding such request, except motor vehicle offenses in which the penalty does not exceed a fine of fifty dollars nor been imprisoned under sentence or committed as a delinquent within the commonwealth within the preceding three years; and (3) said form includes a statement by the petitioner that he has not been adjudicated delinquent or found guilty of any criminal offense in any other state, United States possession or in a court of federal jurisdiction, except such motor vehicle offenses as aforesaid, and has not been imprisoned under sentence or committed as a delinquent in any state or county within the preceding three years.

When records of delinquency appearances and delinquency dispositions are sealed by the commissioner in his files, the commissioner shall notify forthwith the clerk and the probation officer of the courts in which the adjudications or dispositions have occurred, or other entries have been made, and the department of youth services of such sealing, and said clerks, probation officers, and department of youth services likewise shall seal records of the same proceedings in their files.

Such sealed records of a person shall not operate to disqualify a person in any future examination, appointment or application for public service under the government of the commonwealth or of any political subdivision thereof; nor shall such sealed records be admissible in evidence or used in any way in any court proceedings or hearings before any boards of commissioners, except in imposing sentence for subsequent offenses in delinquency or criminal proceedings.

Notwithstanding any other provision to the contrary, the commissioner shall report such sealed delinquency record to inquiring police and court agencies only as "sealed delinquency record over three years old" and to other authorized persons who may inquire as "no record". The information contained in said sealed delinquency record shall be made available to a judge or probation officer who affirms that such person, whose record has been sealed, has been adjudicated a delinquent or has pleaded guilty or has been found guilty of and is awaiting sentence for a crime committed subsequent to sealing of such record. Said information shall be used only for the purpose of consideration in imposing sentence.

Added by St.1972, c. 404.

§ 100C. Sealing of records or files in certain criminal cases; effect upon employment reports; enforcement

In any criminal case wherein the defendant has been found not guilty by the court or jury, or a no bill has been returned by the grand jury, or a finding of no probable cause has been made by the court, the commissioner of probation shall seal said court appearance and disposition recorded in his files and the clerk and the probation officers of the courts in which the proceedings occurred or were initiated shall likewise seal the records of the proceedings in their files. The provisions of this paragraph shall not apply if the defendant makes a written request to the commissioner not to seal the records of the proceedings.

[Second paragraph effective until May 4, 2012. For text effective May 4, 2012, see below.]

In any criminal case wherein a nolle prosequi has been entered, or a dismissal has been entered by the court, except in cases in which an order of probation has been terminated, and it appears to the court that substantial justice would best be served, the court shall direct the clerk to seal the records of the proceedings in his files. The clerk shall forthwith notify the commissioner of probation and the probation officer of the courts in which the proceedings occurred or were initiated who shall likewise seal the records of the proceedings in their files.

[Second paragraph as amended by 2010, 256, Sec. 131 effective May 4, 2012. See 2010, 256, Sec. 145 as amended by 2010, 359, Sec. 102. For text effective until May 4, 2012, see above.]

In any criminal case wherein a nolle prosequi has been entered, or a dismissal has been entered by the court, and it appears to the court that substantial justice would best be served, the court shall direct the clerk to seal the records of the proceedings in his files. The clerk shall forthwith notify the commissioner of probation and the probation officer of the courts in which the proceedings occurred or were initiated who shall likewise seal the records of the proceedings in their files.

Such sealed records shall not operate to disqualify a person in any examination, appointment or application for public employment in the service of the commonwealth or of any political subdivision thereof.

An application for employment used by an employer which seeks information concerning prior arrests or convictions of the applicant shall include in addition to the statement required under section one hundred A the following statement: "An applicant for employment with a sealed record on file with the commissioner of probation may answer 'no record' with respect to an inquiry herein relative to prior arrests or criminal court appearances." The attorney general may enforce the provisions of this section by a suit in equity commenced in the superior court.

[Fifth paragraph effective until May 4, 2012. For text effective May 4, 2012, see below.]

The commissioner, in response to inquiries by authorized persons other than any law enforcement agency or any court, shall in the case of a sealed record report that no record exists. After a finding or verdict of guilty on a subsequent offense such sealed record shall be made available to the probation officer and the same, with the exception of a not guilty, a no bill, or a no probable cause, shall be made available to the court.

[Fifth paragraph as amended by 2010, 256, Sec. 132 effective May 4, 2012. See 2010, 256, Sec. 145 as amended by 2010, 359, Sec. 102. For text effective until May 4, 2012, see above.]

The commissioner or the clerk of courts in any district or superior court or the Boston municipal court, in response to inquiries by authorized persons other than any law enforcement agency or any court, shall in the case of a sealed record report that no record exists. After a finding or verdict of guilty on a subsequent offense such sealed record shall be made available to the probation officer and the same, with the exception of a not guilty, a no bill, or a no probable cause, shall be made available to the court.

Added by St.1973, c. 322, § 1. Amended by St.1983, c. 312; St.1984, c. 123; St.2010, c. 256, §§ 131, 132, eff. May 4, 2012.

§ 100D. Availability of sealed criminal record information

[Text of section added by 2010, 256, Sec. 133 effective May 4, 2012. See 2010, 256, Sec. 145 as amended by 2010, 359, Sec. 102.]

Notwithstanding any provision of section 100A, 100B, or 100C of this chapter, criminal justice agencies as defined in section 167 of chapter 6 shall have immediate access to, and be permitted to use as necessary for the performance of their criminal justice duties, any sealed criminal offender record information as defined in section 167 of chapter 6 and any sealed information concerning criminal offenses or acts of delinquency committed by any person before he attained the age of 17.

Added by St.2010, c. 256, § 133, eff. May 4, 2012.

§ 101. Annual report of commissioner to general court

The commissioner of probation shall make an annual report to the general court of the probation work of the courts for the year ending on December thirty-first preceding. The report shall include such information as the commissioner may consider useful, with his suggestions or recommendations.

Amended by St.1936, c. 30, § 1; St.1956, c. 731, § 23.

Historical and Statutory Notes

St.1900, c. 449, § 7.
R.L.1902, c. 217, § 89.
St.1908, c. 465, §§ 4, 6.
St.1929, c. 179, § 1.

§ 101A. Establishment of uniform forms of blanks and records for use in district court probation offices

The commissioner of probation shall establish uniform forms of blanks and records for use in the probation offices of the district courts, and, upon receipt of competitive bids, the state purchasing agent shall order, at the expense of the commonwealth, and maintain such supply of said forms as the commissioner of probation shall determine to be necessary to meet the requirements of all such offices. The commissioner of probation shall from time to time distribute to the district and juvenile courts such quantities of such forms as he shall, with the probation officers of those courts, determine to be necessary. No forms of blanks and records other than those established and furnished hereunder shall be used in such probation offices unless approved by said commissioner.

Added by St.1947, c. 364, § 1. Amended by St.1956, c. 731, § 24; St.1978, c. 478, § 297.

§ 102. Effect of Secs. 98 to 101A on authority of courts

Sections ninety-eight to one hundred and one A, inclusive, shall not affect the authority of the courts to require the keeping by their probation officers of probation records in addition to those necessary to conform to forms of records and reports prescribed by the commissioner of probation nor the authority of the courts to approve expenses and disbursements relating to the probation system.

Amended by St.1947, c. 364, § 2; St.1956, c. 731, § 25.

Historical and Statutory Notes

St.1908, c. 465, § 5.
St.1929, c. 179, § 1.

§ 103. Notice to commissioner of appointment, removal, etc., of probation officer

Upon the appointment, removal, retirement, resignation, death, or leave of absence of a probation officer, the clerk of the court by which said probation officer was appointed shall notify forthwith the commissioner of probation of such appointment, removal, retirement, resignation, death, or leave of absence.

Amended by St.1956, c. 731, § 26; St.1978, c. 141.

Historical and Statutory Notes

St.1880, c. 129, § 2.
P.S.1882, c. 212, § 74.
St.1891, c. 356, § 5.
St.1898, c. 511, § 3.
R.L.1902, c. 217, § 91.
St.1910, c. 485.
St.1929, c. 179, § 1.

APPENDIX TO CHAPTER 276

AGREEMENT ON DETAINERS

The laws included in this Appendix were not enacted as part of the General Laws, but are set out herein for convenient reference.

AGREEMENT ON DETAINERS

St.1965, c. 892, enacted the provisions set out as §§ 1–1 to 1–8 of this Appendix.

§ 1–1. Form and contents

An agreement is hereby entered into by this commonwealth with all other jurisdictions legally joining therein in substantially the following form:

AGREEMENT ON DETAINERS

The contracting states solemnly agree that:

ARTICLE I.

The party states find that charges outstanding against a prisoner, detainers based on untried indictments, informations or complaints, and difficulties in securing speedy trial of persons already incarcerated in other jurisdictions, produce uncertainties which obstruct programs of prisoner treatment and rehabilitation. Accordingly, it is the policy of the party states and the purpose of this agreement to encourage the expeditious and orderly disposition of such charges and determination of the proper status of any and all detainers based on untried indictments, informations or complaints. The party states also find that proceedings with reference to such charges and detainers, when emanating from another jurisdiction, cannot properly be had in the absence of cooperative procedures. It is the purpose of this agreement to provide such cooperative procedures.

ARTICLE II.

As used in this agreement:

(a) "State" shall mean a state of the United States; the United States of America; a territory or possession of the United States; the District of Columbia; the Commonwealth of Puerto Rico.

(b) "Sending state" shall mean a state in which a prisoner is incarcerated at the time that he initiates a request for final disposition pursuant to Article III hereof or at the time that a request for custody or availability is initiated pursuant to Article IV hereof.

(c) "Receiving state" shall mean the state in which trial is to be had on an indictment, information or complaint pursuant to Article III or Article IV hereof.

ARTICLE III.

(a) Whenever a person has entered upon a term of imprisonment in a penal or correctional institution of a party state, and whenever during the continuance of the term of imprisonment there is pending in any other party state any untried indictment, information or complaint on the basis of which a detainer has been lodged against the prisoner, he shall be brought to trial within one hundred eighty days after he shall have caused to be delivered to the prosecuting officer and the appropriate court of the prosecuting officer's jurisdiction written notice of the place of his imprisonment and his request for a final disposition to be made of the indictment, information or complaint; provided, that, for good cause shown in open court, the prisoner or his counsel being present, the court having jurisdiction of the matter may grant any necessary or reasonable continuance. The request of the prisoner shall be accompanied by a certificate of the appropriate official having custody of the prisoner, stating the term of commitment under which the prisoner is being held, the time already served, the time remaining to be served on the sentence, the amount of good time earned, the time of parole eligibility of the prisoner, and any decisions of the state parole agency relating to the prisoner.

(b) The written notice and request for final disposition referred to in paragraph (a) hereof shall be given or sent by the prisoner to the warden, commissioner of correction or other official having custody of the prisoner, who shall promptly forward it together with the certificate to the appropriate prosecuting official and court by registered or certified mail, return receipt requested.

(c) The warden, commissioner of correction or other official having custody of the prisoner shall promptly inform him of the source and contents of any detainer lodged against him and shall also inform him of his right to make a request for final disposition of the indictment, information or complaint on which the detainer is based.

(d) Any request for final disposition made by a prisoner pursuant to paragraph (a) hereof shall operate as a request for final disposition of all untried indictments, informations or complaints on the basis of which detainers have been lodged against the prisoner from the state to whose prosecuting official the request for final disposition is specifically directed. The warden, commissioner of correction or other official having custody of the prisoner shall forthwith notify all appropriate prosecuting officers and courts in the several jurisdictions within the state to which the prisoner's request for final disposition is being sent of the proceeding being initiated by the prisoner. Any notification sent pursuant to this paragraph shall be accompanied by copies of the prisoner's written notice, request, and the certificate. If trial is not had on any indictment, information or complaint contemplated hereby prior to the return of the prisoner to the original place of imprisonment, such indictment, information or complaint shall not be of any further force or effect, and the court shall enter an order dismissing the same with prejudice.

(e) Any request for final disposition made by a prisoner pursuant to paragraph (a) hereof shall also be deemed to be a waiver of extradition with respect to any charge or proceeding contemplated thereby or included therein by reason of paragraph (d) hereof, and a waiver of extradition to the receiving state to serve any sentence there imposed upon him, after completion of his term of imprisonment in the sending state. The request for final disposition shall also constitute a consent by the prisoner to the production of his body in any court where his presence may be required in order to effectuate the purposes of this agreement and a further consent voluntarily to be returned to the original place of imprisonment in accordance with the provisions of this agreement. Nothing in this paragraph shall prevent the imposition of a concurrent sentence if otherwise permitted by law.

(f) Escape from custody by the prisoner subsequent to his execution of the request for final disposition referred to in paragraph (a) hereof shall void the request.

ARTICLE IV.

(a) The appropriate officer of the jurisdiction in which an untried indictment, information or complaint is pending, shall be entitled to have a prisoner against whom he has lodged a detainer and who is serving a term of imprisonment in any party state made available in accordance with paragraph (a) of Article V upon presentation of a written request for temporary custody or availability to the appropriate authorities of the state in which the prisoner is incarcerated; provided, that, the court having jurisdiction of such indictment, information or complaint shall have duly approved, recorded and transmitted the request; and, provided further, that there shall be a period of thirty days after receipt by the appropriate authorities before the request is honored, within which period the governor of the sending state may disapprove the request for temporary custody or availability, either upon his own motion or upon the motion of the prisoner.

(b) Upon receipt of the officer's written request as provided in paragraph (a) hereof, the appropriate authorities having the prisoner in custody shall furnish the officer with a certificate stating the term of commitment under which the prisoner is being held, the time already served, the time remaining to be served on the sentence, the amount of good time earned, the time of parole eligibility of the prisoner, and any decisions of the state parole agency relating to the prisoner. Said authorities simultaneously shall furnish all other officers and appropriate courts in the receiving state who have lodged detainers against the prisoner with similar certificates and with notices informing them of the request for custody or availability and of the reasons therefor.

(c) In respect to any proceeding made possible by this Article, trial shall be commenced within one hundred twenty days of the arrival of the prisoner in the receiving state, but for good cause shown in open court, the prisoner or his counsel being present, the court having jurisdiction of the matter may grant any necessary or reasonable continuance.

(d) Nothing contained in this Article shall be construed to deprive any prisoner of any right which he may have to contest the legality of his delivery as provided in paragraph (a) hereof, but such delivery may not be opposed or denied on the ground that the executive authority of the sending state has not affirmatively consented to or ordered such delivery.

(e) If trial is not had on any indictment, information or complaint contemplated hereby prior to the prisoner's being returned to the original place of imprisonment pursuant to Article V(e) hereof, such indictment, information or complaint shall not be of any further force or effect, and the court shall enter an order dismissing the same with prejudice.

ARTICLE V.

(a) In response to a request made under Article III or Article IV hereof, the appropriate authority in a sending state shall offer to deliver temporary custody of such prisoner to the appropriate authority in the state where such indictment, information or complaint is pending against such person in order that speedy and efficient prosecution may be had. If the request for final disposition is made by the prisoner, the offer of temporary custody shall accompany the written notice provided for in Article III of this agreement. In the case of a federal prisoner, the appropriate authority in the receiving state shall be entitled to temporary custody as provided by this agreement or to the prisoner's presence in federal custody at the place for trial, whichever custodial arrangement may be approved by the custodian.

(b) The officer or other representative of a state accepting an offer of temporary custody shall present the following upon demand:

(1) Proper identification and evidence of his authority to act for the state into whose temporary custody the prisoner is to be given.

(2) A duly certified copy of the indictment, information or complaint on the basis of which the detainer has been lodged and on the basis of which the request for temporary custody of the prisoner has been made.

(c) If the appropriate authority shall refuse or fail to accept temporary custody of said person, or in the event that an action on the indictment, information or complaint on the basis of which the detainer has been lodged is not brought to trial within the period provided in Article III or Article IV hereof, the appropriate court of the jurisdiction where the indictment, information or complaint has been pending shall enter an order dismissing the same with prejudice, and any detainer based thereon shall cease to be of any force or effect.

(d) The temporary custody referred to in this agreement shall be only for the purpose of permitting prosecution on the charge or charges contained in one or more untried indictments, informations or complaints which form the basis of the detainer or detainers or for prosecution on any other charge or charges arising out of the same transaction. Except for his attendance at court and while being transported to or from any place at which his presence may be required, the prisoner shall be held in a suitable jail or other facility regularly used for persons awaiting prosecution.

(e) At the earliest practicable time consonant with the purposes of this agreement, the prisoner shall be returned to the sending state.

(f) During the continuance of temporary custody or while the prisoner is otherwise being made available for trial as required by this agreement, time being served on the sentence shall continue to run but good time shall be earned by the prisoner only if, and to the extent that, the law and practice of the jurisdiction which imposed the sentence may allow.

(g) For all purposes other than that for which temporary custody as provided in this agreement is exercised, the prisoner shall be deemed to remain in the custody of and subject to the jurisdiction of the sending state and any escape from temporary custody may be dealt with in the same manner as an escape from the original place of imprisonment or in any other manner permitted by law.

(h) From the time that a party state receives custody of a prisoner pursuant to this agreement until such prisoner is returned to the territory and custody of the sending state, the state in which the one or more untried indictments, informations or complaints are pending or in which trial is being had shall be responsible for the prisoner and shall also pay all costs of transporting, caring for, keeping and returning the prisoner. The provisions of this paragraph shall govern unless the states concerned shall have entered into a supplementary agreement providing for a different allocation of costs and responsibilities as between or among themselves. Nothing herein contained shall be construed to alter or affect any internal relationship among the departments, agencies and officers of and in the government of a party state, or between a party state and its subdivisions, as to the payment of costs, or responsibilities therefor.

ARTICLE VI.

(a) In determining the duration and expiration dates of the time periods provided in Articles III and IV of this agreement, the running of said time periods shall be tolled whenever and for as long as the prisoner is unable to stand trial, as determined by the court having jurisdiction of the matter.

(b) No provision of this agreement, and no remedy made available by this agreement, shall apply to any person who is adjudged to be mentally ill.

ARTICLE VII.

Each state party to this agreement shall designate an officer who, acting jointly with like officers of other party states, shall promulgate rules and regulations to carry out more effectively the terms and provisions of this agreement, and who shall provide, within and without the state, information necessary to the effective operation of this agreement.

ARTICLE VIII.

This agreement shall enter into full force and effect as to a party state when such state has enacted the same into law. A state party to this agreement may withdraw herefrom by enacting a statute repealing the same. However, the withdrawal of any state shall not affect the status of any proceedings already initiated by inmates or by state officers at the time such withdrawal takes effect, nor shall it affect their rights in respect thereof.

ARTICLE IX.

This agreement shall be liberally construed so as to effectuate its purposes. The provisions of this agreement shall be severable and if any phrase, clause, sentence or provision of this agreement is declared to be contrary to the constitution of any party state or of the United States or the applicability thereof to any government, agency, person or circumstance is held invalid, the validity of the remainder of this agreement and the applicability thereof to any government, agency, person or circumstance shall not be affected thereby. If this agreement shall be held contrary to the constitution of any state party hereto, the agreement shall remain in full force and effect as to the remaining states and in full force and effect as to the state affected as to all severable matter.

St.1965, c. 892, § 1.

§ 1–2. Appropriate court

The phrase "Appropriate court", as used in the Agreement on Detainers, shall, with reference to the courts of this commonwealth mean the municipal court of the city of Boston, district courts, the superior court or the supreme judicial court.

St.1965, c. 892, § 2.

§ 1–3. Enforcement; cooperation

All courts, departments, agencies, officers and employees of this commonwealth and its political subdivisions are hereby directed to enforce the Agreement on Detainers and to cooperate with one another and with other party states in enforcing said agreement and effectuating its purpose.

St.1965, c. 892, § 3.

§ 1–4. Habitual criminals; application of act

Nothing in the Agreement on Detainers shall be construed to require the application of the habitual offenders law to any person on account of any conviction had in a proceeding brought to final disposition by reason of the use of said agreement.

St.1965, c. 892, § 4.

§ 1–5. Escape

A prisoner who escapes or attempts to escape from custody while in another state or while in this commonwealth pursuant to the Agreement on Detainers may be pursued and recaptured and shall be punished by imprisonment in the state prison in this commonwealth for not more than ten years or by imprisonment in a jail or house of correction in this commonwealth for not more than two and one half years.

St.1965, c. 892, § 5.

§ 1–6. Surrender of inmates

It shall be lawful and mandatory upon the superintendent or other official in charge of a penal or correctional institution of this commonwealth to give over the person of any inmate thereof whenever so required by the operation of the Agreement on Detainers.

St.1965, c. 892, § 6.

§ 1–7. Administration

The governor may designate an officer of the commonwealth to act as compact administrator of and information agent for the Agreement on Detainers.

St.1965, c. 892, § 7.

§ 1–8. Copies of agreement

Copies of this agreement shall, upon its approval, be transmitted to the governor of each contracting state, the attorney general of the United States, the administrator of general services of the United States, and the council of state governments.

St.1965, c. 892, § 8.

CHAPTER 276A

DISTRICT COURT PRETRIAL DIVERSION OF SELECTED OFFENDERS

Chapter 276A of the General Laws was added by St.1974, c. 781.

The section headings for the General Laws in this pamphlet have been editorially supplied.

§ 1. Definitions

The following words, as used in this chapter, unless the context otherwise requires, shall have the following meanings:—

"Assessment", a thorough and complete measurement of the needs of an individual in, but not limited to, the following areas: education, vocational training, job placement, mental and physical health, family and social services, and an analysis of a defendant's commitment to participate in a program of community supervision and services.

"Commissioner", the commissioner of probation.

"Director", the person in charge of the operation of a program of community supervision and services.

"Official designee", a representative of a program of community supervision and service who has been approved by the presiding justice of a district court to work in conjunction with that court's probation office to screen defendants who may be eligible for diversion.

"Plan of service", a comprehensive and cohesive set of recommended programs and specific services to meet the needs of individuals as determined through assessment.

"Program", any program of community supervision and services certified or approved by the commissioner of probation under the provisions of section eight, including, but not limited to, medical, educational, vocational, social and psychological services, corrective and preventive guidance, training, performance of community service work, counseling, provision for residence in a halfway house or other suitable place, and other rehabilitative services designed to protect the public and benefit the individual.

Added by St.1974, c. 781. Amended by St.1984, c. 294, § 2.

§ 2. Jurisdiction of court

The district courts, and in Boston, the municipal court of the city of Boston, shall have jurisdiction to divert to a program, as defined in section one, any person who is charged with an offense or offenses against the commonwealth for which a term of imprisonment may be imposed and over which the district courts may exercise final jurisdiction and who has reached the age of seventeen years but has not reached the age of twenty-two, who has not previously been convicted of a violation of any law of the commonwealth or of any other state or of the United States in any criminal court proceeding after having reached the age of seventeen years, except for traffic violations for which no term of imprisonment may have been imposed, who does not have any outstanding warrants, continuances, appeals or criminal cases pending before any courts of the commonwealth or any other state or of the United States, and who has received a recommendation from a program that he would, in light of the capacities of and guidelines governing it, benefit from participation in said program.

Added by St.1974, c. 781.

§ 3. Screening of defendants; continuance

The probation officers of a district or municipal court, or their official designee, when gathering information in accordance with section eighty-five of chapter two hundred and seventy-six, shall also screen each defendant for the purpose of enabling the judge at arraignment to consider the eligibility of the defendant for diversion to a program.

Any defendant who is qualified for consideration for diversion to a program may, at his arraignment, be afforded a fourteen-day continuance for assessment by the personnel of a program to determine if he would benefit from such program.

If a defendant chooses to accept the offer of a continuance for the purpose of such an assessment, he shall so notify the judge at arraignment. Upon receipt of such notification, the judge shall grant a fourteen-day continuance. The judge, through the probation office or its official designee, shall direct the defendant to a program and shall inform said program of such action.

The judge may, in his discretion, grant a defendant who is preliminarily determined not to be eligible because of a failure to satisfy all the requirements of section two, a like fourteen-day continuance for assessment. In arriving at such a decision the opinion of the prosecution should be taken into consideration. Such a continuance may be granted upon the judge's own initiative or upon request by the defendant.

Added by St.1974, c. 781.

§ 4. Inapplicability of chapter to certain otherwise eligible persons

In the event that an individual who is eligible under the provisions of section two is charged with a violation of chapter ninety-four C, nothing in this chapter shall be construed to limit the effect or operation of sections thirty-eight to fifty-five, inclusive, of chapter one hundred and twenty-three.

In the event that an individual who is eligible under the provisions of section two is charged with a violation of one or more of the offenses enumerated in section three of chapter one hundred and twenty-three A, the provisions of this chapter shall not be applicable for said defendant.

A person charged with violating the provisions of subsection (a) of section fifteen A, subsection (a) of section fifteen B, subsection (a) of section eighteen and subsection (a) of section nineteen of chapter two hundred and sixty-five or subsection (a) of section twenty-five of chapter two hundred and sixty-six shall, for the second or subsequent such offense, not be diverted to a program as provided in section two.

Added by St.1974, c. 781. Amended by St.1981, c. 678, § 6; St.1986, c. 557, § 202.

§ 5. Assessment report; recommendations; final determination; stay of criminal proceedings

Upon the expiration of a fourteen-day continuance granted pursuant to section three, the director of the program to which the defendant has been referred shall submit to the court a written report of its assessment. The report shall contain the information obtained through the program's assessment, the program's recommendation as to whether the defendant would benefit from diversion to the program, and a plan of services for the defendant if it has been determined that the defendant would so benefit.

The judge, upon receipt of the report, shall provide an opportunity for a recommendation by the prosecution regarding the diversion of the defendant. After receiving the report and having provided an opportunity for the prosecution to make its recommendation, the judge shall make a final determination as to the eligibility of the defendant for diversion to the program. The criminal proceedings of a defendant who qualifies for diversions under section two and who agrees to abide by the terms and conditions contained in the plan of services approved by the judge, shall be stayed for a period of ninety days, unless the judge in his discretion considers that the interest of justice would best be served by a hearing of the facts, after which the case may be continued without a finding for ninety days. No appeal shall be allowed from such final determination.

A defendant who has been determined to be ineligible by reason of his failure to satisfy certain provisions of section two, but who, in the judge's discretion, received a fourteen-day continuance for assessment, may, on the basis of the report submitted by a program, be granted a like stay of proceedings.

In no event shall a stay of proceedings be granted pursuant to this section unless the defendant consents in writing to the terms and conditions of the stay of proceedings and knowingly executes a waiver of his right to a speedy trial on a form approved by the chief justice of the district courts, and, in Boston, the chief justice of the municipal court of the city of Boston. Such consent shall be with the advice of defendant's counsel. Any request for assessment, or a decision by the defendant not to enter such a program, or a determination by the program that the defendant would not benefit from it, or any statement made by the defendant during the course of assessment, shall not be admissible against the defendant in any criminal proceedings; nor shall any consent by the defendant to the stay of proceedings or any act done or statement made in fulfillment of the terms and conditions of such stay of proceedings be admissible as an admission, implied or otherwise, against the defendant, should the stay of proceedings be terminated and criminal proceedings resumed on the original charge or charges. No statement or other disclosure or records thereof made by a defendant during the course of assessment or during the stay of proceedings shall be disclosed at any time to a prosecutor or other law enforcement officer in connection with the charge or charges pending against said defendant or any co-defendant.

Added by St.1974, c. 781.

§ 6. Violations by defendant; hearing; termination of stay

During a stay of proceedings or a continuance without a finding, as provided in section five, the director of a program shall submit periodic reports to the court relative to the progress of the defendant. The director shall also report violations of program conditions or subsequent arrests immediately upon notice thereof.

If the defendant during the stay of proceedings or a continuance without a finding violates a condition of the program or is charged with a subsequent offense, a judge in the court that entered the stay of proceedings may issue such process as is necessary to bring the defendant before the court. When the defendant is brought before the court, the judge shall afford him an opportunity to be heard. If the judge finds that the defendant has committed a violation of a condition of the program or that he has been charged with a subsequent offense, the judge may order, when appropriate, that the stay of proceedings be terminated and that the commonwealth proceed on the original charges as provided by law. No appeal shall be allowed from such an order.

Added by St.1974, c. 781.

§ 7. Expiration of stay or continuance; report of successful completion or recommendation of extension

Upon the expiration of the initial ninety-day stay of proceedings or a continuance without a finding, the program director shall submit to the court a report indicating the successful completion of the program by a defendant or recommending an extension of the stay of proceedings or a continuance without a finding for not more than an additional ninety days, so that the defendant may complete the program successfully.

If the report indicates the successful completion of the program by a defendant, the judge may dismiss the original charges pending against the defendant. If the report recommends an extension of the stay of proceedings or a continuance without a finding, the judge may, on the basis of the report and any other relevant evidence, take such action as he deems appropriate, including the dismissal of the charges, the granting of an extension of the stay of proceedings or a continuance without a finding, or the resumption of criminal proceedings. In the event that an extension of the stay of proceedings or a continuance without a finding is granted, the program director shall submit a final report upon the expiration of such stay of proceedings.

Added by St.1974, c. 781.

§ 8. Certification of programs; renewal; revocation

The office of the commissioner shall, in its discretion, certify, monitor and aid all programs to which defendants may be diverted pursuant to this chapter. The certification of programs shall be subject to the approval of the presiding justice of the individual court which would be the beneficiary of such services. The office of the commissioner shall, in its discretion, (a) issue for a term of two years, and may renew for like terms, a certification, subject to revocation for cause, to any person, partnership, corporation, society, association or other agency or entity of any kind, other than a licensed general hospital or a department, agency or institution of the federal government, the commonwealth or any political subdivision thereof, deemed to be responsible and suitable to establish and maintain such a program and to meet applicable certification standards and requirements; and in the case of a department, agency or institution of the commonwealth or any political subdivision thereof, grant approval to establish and maintain a program for a term of two years, and may renew such approval for like terms, subject to revocation for cause; (b) promulgate, in consultation with the advisory board established in section nine, rules and regulations establishing certification and approval standards and requirements; (c) establish limits for caseloads and enrollment so that programs are able to provide high quality intensive individualized service to those defendants participating in such programs; (d) procure, where appropriate, by contract, the personnel, facilities, services, and materials necessary to carry out the purposes of this act, subject to all applicable laws and regulations; (e) prepare reports for said advisory board showing the progress of all programs in fulfilling the purposes set forth; (f) notify the appropriate presiding justice of the individual court that adequate facilities and personnel are available to fulfill a plan of community supervision and services for that court; (g) provide technical assistance to such program as may be certified hereunder; (h) provide for the audit of any funds expended by the office for the support of programs certified hereunder; (i) promote the cooperation of all agencies which provide education, training, counseling, legal, employment, or other services to assure that eligible individuals released to programs may benefit to the maximum extent practicable; (j) prepare and submit an annual report to the chief justices of the supreme judicial, appeals, superior and district courts and to all justices in the district court system evaluating the performance of all programs.

Added by St.1974, c. 781.

§ 9. Advisory board; members; expenses; duties

There shall be an advisory board to the office of the commissioner for the overseeing of programs. The members of the advisory board shall be the attorney general, the commissioners of education, mental health, rehabilitation and welfare, a district court judge, the deputy director of the division of employment and training, the president of the Massachusetts District Attorney's Association, or their respective designees, and seven experts in the area of human services to the sociologically and economically disadvantaged through community based programs to be appointed by the governor for terms of two years, one of whom shall be an ex-offender. The members of the advisory board shall serve without compensation but shall be reimbursed for their expenses actually and necessarily incurred in the discharge of their duties. The advisory board shall annually select its chairman from among its members.

The advisory board shall assist the commissioner in coordinating the efforts of all public agencies and private organizations and individuals within the commonwealth concerned with the providing of services to defendants by said programs.

Added by St.1974, c. 781. Amended by St.1990, c. 177, § 368; St.1998, c. 161, § 559.

CHAPTER 277

INDICTMENTS AND PROCEEDINGS BEFORE TRIAL

The section headings for the General Laws in this pamphlet have been editorially supplied.

§ 1. Issuance of writs of venire facias for grand jurors; attendance at sittings of court

The clerk of the courts for each county, except Suffolk, Middlesex, Essex, Hampden, Norfolk, Plymouth and Worcester shall, not less than twenty-eight days before the commencement of the first sitting of the superior court for criminal business in each year, issue writs of venire facias for forty-five veniremen, from whose numbers the court shall select twenty-three grand jurors who shall serve in said court until the first regular sitting in the year next after they have been impanelled and until another grand jury has been impanelled in their stead. In counties where sittings of the court are established for the transaction of criminal business, they shall be required to attend only at such sittings.

Amended by St.1964, c. 326, § 1; St.1966, c. 235, § 1; St.1966, c. 415, § 1; St.1973, c. 464, § 1; St.1975, c. 809, § 1; St.1977, c. 315, § 1; St.1977, c. 862, § 1; St.1978, c. 323, § 1; St.1979, c. 344, § 27.

Historical and Statutory Notes

C.L. c. 86, § 2.
St.1694–5, c. 24, § 1.
St.1784, c. 4, §§ 1, 2.
St.1807, c. 140, § 4.
St.1832, c. 130, § 6.
R.S.1836, c. 136, § 1.
St.1840, c. 74.
G.S.1860, c. 171, § 1.
St.1860, c. 143.
P.S.1882, c. 213, § 1.
St.1897, c. 490, § 7.
R.L.1902, c. 218, § 1.
St.1924, c. 311, § 6.

§ 1A. Completion of investigations by grand juries; notice; order

Upon a written notice by the attorney general or any district attorney made to any justice of the superior court that public necessity requires further time by a grand jury to complete an investigation then in progress, the court may order such grand jury to continue to serve until said investigation has been completed and shall take up no new matter.

This section shall not be construed to prevent the issuance of writs of venire facias authorized by section one for impanelling a grand jury whose duty shall include all business not then before the grand jury continued under authorization of this section.

Added by St.1952, c. 494.

§ 2. Suffolk county; issuance of writs of venire facias for grand jurors

The clerk of the superior court for criminal business in Suffolk county shall, not less than twenty-eight days before the first Mondays of January and July, respectively, issue writs of venire facias for forty-five veniremen of whom thirty-nine shall be from Boston and two each from Chelsea, Revere and Winthrop. From these forty-five veniremen the court shall then select twenty-three grand jurors to serve in said court, who shall serve for each sitting thereof for six months and until another grand jury has been impanelled in their stead.

Amended by St.1932, c. 144, § 6; St.1966, c. 235, § 2; St.1966, c. 415, § 2; St.1979, c. 130, § 1; St.1979, c. 344, § 28.

Historical and Statutory Notes

St.1844, c. 44, § 3.
G.S.1860, c. 171, § 2.
St.1860, c. 143.
P.S.1882, c. 213, § 2.
R.L.1902, c. 218, § 2.
St.1924, c. 311, § 7.

§ 2A. Issuance of writs of venire facias for special grand jury

The clerk of the courts in any county, or in Suffolk county the clerk of the superior court for criminal business, shall, upon written request of the attorney general accompanied by a certificate that public necessity requires such action, signed by the chief justice of the superior court, issue writs of venire facias for forty-five veniremen of whom the court shall select twenty-three for service as a special grand jury to hear, consider and report on such matters as the attorney general may present. Said jurors shall serve for a period of six months, unless sooner discharged by the attorney general or by the said chief justice, and shall be drawn, summoned and returned in the same manner, and shall have the same powers and receive the same compensation, as grand jurors summoned for service under sections one and two, and the provisions of sections three to fourteen, so far as apt, shall apply to such jurors. In Middlesex county, the clerk of the courts shall send a letter of venire to the jury commissioner as set forth in section twelve of chapter two hundred and thirty-four A.

Amended by St.1966, c. 235, § 3; St.1966, c. 415, § 3; St.1977, c. 415, § 10; St.1979, c. 344, § 29.

Historical and Statutory Notes

St.1922, c. 466.

§ 2B. Middlesex county; issuance of letters of venire for grand jurors

The clerk of courts in Middlesex county shall, not less than seventy days before the first Monday of January and July, respectively, issue letters of venire to the jury commissioner for thirty-five prospective grand jurors from whom the court shall select twenty-three grand jurors who shall serve in said court for each sitting thereof for six months and until another grand jury has been impanelled in their stead.

Added by St.1964, c. 326, § 2. Amended by St.1966, c. 235, § 4; St.1966, c. 415, § 4; St.1977, c. 415, § 11.

§ 2C. Hampden county; issuance of writs of venire facias for grand jurors

The clerk of the court for Hampden county shall, not less than twenty-eight days before the first Mondays of January and May, and the second Monday of September respectively, issue writs of venire facias for forty-five veniremen from whom the court shall select twenty-three grand jurors to serve in said court, who shall serve for each sitting thereof for four months and until another grand jury has been impanelled in their stead.

Added by St.1973, c. 464, § 2. Amended by St.1979, c. 344, § 30.

§ 2D. Plymouth county; issuance of writs of venire facias for grand jurors

The clerk of the court for Plymouth County shall, not less than twenty-eight days before the first Mondays of January and May, and the second Monday of September respectively, issue writs of venire facias for forty-five veniremen from whom the court shall select twenty-three grand jurors to serve in said court, who shall serve for each sitting thereof for four months and until another grand jury has been impanelled in their stead.

Added by St.1975, c. 809, § 2. Amended by St.1979, c. 344, § 31.

§ 2E. Worcester county; issuance of writs of venire facias for grand jurors

The clerk of the court for Worcester county shall, not less than twenty-eight days before the first Mondays of January and May, and the second Monday of September, respectively, issue writs of venire facias for fifty veniremen from whom the court shall select twenty-three grand jurors to serve in said court, who shall serve for each sitting thereof for four months and until another grand jury has been impanelled in their stead.

Added by St.1977, c. 315, § 2. Amended by St.1978, c. 518, § 1; St.1979, c. 130, § 2; St.1979, c. 344, § 32; St.1980, c. 261, § 29.

§ 2F. Norfolk county; issuance of writs of venire facias for grand jurors

The clerk of the court for Norfolk county shall, not less than twenty-eight days before the first Mondays of January and July respectively, issue writs of venire facias for fifty veniremen from whom the court shall select twenty-three grand jurors to serve in said court, who shall serve for each sitting thereof for six months and until another grand jury has been impanelled in their stead.

Added by St.1977, c. 862, § 2.

§ 2G. Essex county; issuance of writs of venire facias for grand jurors

The clerk of the court for Essex county shall, not less than twenty-eight days before the first Mondays of January and May, and the second Monday of September respectively, issue writs of venire facias for forty-five veniremen from whom the court shall select twenty-three grand jurors to serve in said court, who shall serve for each sitting thereof for four months and until another grand jury has been impanelled in their stead.

Added by St.1978, c. 323, § 2. Amended by St.1979, c. 344, § 32A.

§ 2H. Bristol county; issuance of writs of venire facias for grand jurors

The clerk of the court for Bristol county shall, not less than twenty-eight days before the first Mondays of January and July respectively, issue writs of venire facias for fifty veniremen from whom the court shall select twenty-three grand jurors to serve in said court, who shall serve for each sitting thereof for six months and until another grand jury has been impanelled in their stead.

Added by St.1984, c. 470.

§ 3. Drawing and summoning of grand jurors

Grand jurors shall be drawn, summoned and returned in the same manner as traverse jurors; and, if drawn at the same time with traverse jurors, the number of persons required whose names are first drawn shall be returned as grand jurors, and those whose names are afterward drawn shall be returned as traverse jurors. In Middlesex county, the selection and management of grand jurors shall be governed by chapter two hundred and thirty-four A and other applicable provisions of the General Laws.

Amended by St.1977, c. 415, § 12.

Historical and Statutory Notes

R.S.1836, c. 136, § 3.
G.S.1860, c. 171, § 3.
P.S.1882, c. 213, § 3.
R.L.1902, c. 218, § 3.

§ 3A. Suffolk county; impanelling grand jurors

On the day when veniremen are summoned pursuant to section one, section two, section two A, section two B, section two C, section two D, section two E or section two F to attend court for the formation of a grand jury, the clerk of courts in any county, or in Suffolk county the clerk of the superior court for criminal business, shall cause the name of each person so summoned, and who appears and who has not been excused or set aside, to be written on separate ballots, substantially of uniform size, and shall cause such ballots to be placed in a box provided therefor. The clerk in open court, after shaking the ballots thoroughly, shall draw them out in succession until he has drawn the names of twenty-three grand jurors.

Added by St.1966, c. 235, § 5; St.1966, c. 415, § 5. Amended by St.1973, c. 464, § 3; St.1975, c. 809, § 2A; St.1977, c. 315, § 3; St.1977, c. 862, § 3.

§ 4. Deficiency of grand jurors

If there is a deficiency of grand jurors, writs of venire facias may be issued to the constables of such towns as the court orders to return forthwith the further number of grand jurors required. In Middlesex county, letters of venire shall be issued to the jury commissioner as set forth in chapter two hundred and thirty-four A.

Amended by St.1977, c. 415, § 13.

Historical and Statutory Notes

St.1784, c. 7, § 6.
St.1807, c. 140, § 7.
R.S.1836, c. 136, § 4.
G.S.1860, c. 171, § 4.
P.S.1882, c. 213, § 4.
R.L.1902, c. 218, § 4.

§ 5. Impanelling and oath

The clerk of the court shall prepare an alphabetical list of the names of all persons returned as grand jurors, and, when they are to be impanelled, the first two persons named thereon shall be first called, and the following oath shall be administered to them:

You, as grand jurors of this inquest for the body of this county of   , do solemnly swear that you will diligently inquire, and true presentment make, of all such matters and things as shall be given you in charge; the commonwealth's counsel, your fellows' and your own, you shall keep secret; you shall present no man for envy, hatred or malice, neither shall you leave any man unpresented for love, fear, favor, affection or hope of reward; but you shall present things truly, as they come to your knowledge, according to the best of your understanding; so help you God.

The other jurors shall then be called in such divisions as the court considers proper, and the following oath shall be administered to them:

The same oath which your fellows have taken on their part, you and each of you on your behalf shall well and truly observe and keep; so help you God.

Historical and Statutory Notes

C.L. c. 167, § 2.
St.1692–3, c. 35.
St.1784, c. 4, § 1.
St.1807, c. 140, §§ 10, 14.
R.S.1836, c. 136, § 5.
G.S.1860, c. 171, § 5.
P.S.1882, c. 213, § 5.
R.L.1902, c. 218, § 5.

§ 6. Affirmation in lieu of oath

If a person who is returned as a grand juror is conscientiously scrupulous of taking the oath prescribed, he may affirm.

Historical and Statutory Notes

St.1807, c. 140, § 14.
R.S.1836, c. 136, § 6.
G.S.1860, c. 171, § 6.
P.S.1882, c. 213, § 6.
R.L.1902, c. 218, § 6.

§§ 7 to 10. Repealed, 1979, 344, Sec. 33

Historical and Statutory Notes

See Mass.R.Crim.P. Rule 5(b).

§ 11. Re-summoning at same sitting

If the grand jury are dismissed before the court is adjourned without day, they may be summoned to attend again in the same sitting, at such time as the court orders.

Historical and Statutory Notes

R.S.1836, c. 136, § 11.
G.S.1860, c. 171, § 11.
P.S.1882, c. 213, § 11.
R.L.1902, c. 218, § 11.

§§ 12, 13. Repealed, 1979, 344, Sec. 33

Historical and Statutory Notes

See Mass.R.Crim.P. Rule 5(d).

§ 14. Grand juror serving as traverse juror

No member of the grand jury which has found an indictment shall serve upon the jury for the trial thereof.

Historical and Statutory Notes

R.S.1836, c. 137, § 2.
G.S.1860, c. 172, § 2.
P.S.1882, c. 214, § 4.
R.L.1902, c. 218, § 14.

§ 14A. Right to counsel; grand jury proceedings

Any person shall have the right to consult with counsel and to have counsel present at every step of any criminal proceeding at which such person is present, including the presentation of evidence, questioning, or examination before the grand jury; provided, however, that such counsel in a proceeding before a grand jury shall make no objections or arguments or otherwise address the grand jury or the district attorney. No witness may refuse to appear for reason of unavailability of counsel for that witness.

Added by St.1977, c. 770.

§ 15. Discharge of accused person not indicted

The grand jury shall, during its session, make daily return to the court of all cases wherein it has finally determined not to present an indictment against an accused person held in custody pending its action, and such person shall thereupon forthwith be discharged by order of the court unless he is held on other process. Whoever is held in custody on a charge of crime shall be discharged if he is not indicted before the end of the second sitting of the court at which he is held to answer, unless the court finds that the witnesses for the prosecution have been enticed or kept away, or are detained and prevented from attending the court by illness or accident, and except as provided in the following section.

Historical and Statutory Notes

St.1784, c. 72, § 13.
R.S.1836, c. 136, § 14.
G.S.1860, c. 171, § 14.
P.S.1882, c. 213, § 14.
R.L.1902, c. 218, § 15.
St.1920, c. 113.

§ 16. Repealed, 1970, 888, Sec. 7

Historical and Statutory Notes

See c. 123, § 15 et seq.

§ 17. Repealed, 1979, 344, Sec. 33

Historical and Statutory Notes

See, Mass.R.Crim.P. Rule 7.

§ 18. Circumstances of the act

The circumstances of the act may be stated according to their legal effect, without a full description thereof.

Historical and Statutory Notes

St.1899, c. 409, § 13.
R.L.1902, c. 218, § 18.

§ 19. Name of accused person; description by fictitious name; entry of true name

If the name of an accused person is unknown to the grand jury, he may be described by a fictitious name or by any other practicable description, with an allegation that his real name is unknown. An indictment of the defendant by a fictitious or erroneous name shall not be ground for abatement; but if at any subsequent stage of the proceedings his true name is discovered, it shall be entered on the record and may be used in the subsequent proceedings, with a reference to the fact that he was indicted by the name or description mentioned in the indictment.

Historical and Statutory Notes

St.1899, c. 409, § 8.
R.L.1902, c. 218, § 19.

§ 20. Time and place of commission of crime

The time and place of the commission of the crime need not be alleged unless it is an essential element thereof. The allegation of time in the caption shall, unless otherwise stated, be considered as an allegation that the act was committed before the finding of the indictment, after it became a crime, and within the period of limitations. The name of the county and court in the caption shall, unless otherwise stated, be considered as an allegation that the act was committed within the territorial jurisdiction of the court. All allegations of the indictment shall, unless otherwise stated, be considered to refer to the same time and place.

Historical and Statutory Notes

St.1899, c. 409, § 10.
R.L.1902, c. 218, § 20.

§ 21. Means

The means by which a crime is committed need not be alleged in the indictment unless an essential element of the crime.

Historical and Statutory Notes

St.1899, c. 409, § 14.
R.L.1902, c. 218, § 21.

§ 22. Description of written instrument; variance

If an allegation relative to a written instrument consisting wholly or in part of writing, print or figures is necessary, it may describe such instrument by any name or designation by which it is usually known, or by the purport thereof, without setting out a copy or facsimile of the whole or of any part thereof; and no variance between such recital or description and the instrument produced at the trial shall be material, if the identity of the instrument is evident and the purport thereof is so described as not to prejudice the defendant.

Historical and Statutory Notes

St.1899, c. 409, § 15.
R.L.1902, c. 218, § 22.

§ 23. Description of money

If an allegation relative to any bullion, money, notes, bank notes, checks, drafts, bills of exchange, obligations or other securities for money of any country, state, county, city, town, bank, corporation, partnership or person is necessary, it may describe it as money, without specifying any particulars thereof; and such descriptive allegation shall be sustained by proof of any amount of bullion, money, notes or other securities for money as aforesaid, although the particular nature thereof shall not be proved.

Historical and Statutory Notes

St.1834, c. 186, § 2.
R.S.1836, c. 133, § 10.
St.1845, c. 215.
St.1846, c. 171, § 2.
G.S.1860, c. 161, § 42.
St.1878, c. 186.
P.S.1882, c. 203, § 44.
St.1899, c. 409, § 16.
R.L.1902, c. 218, § 23.

§ 24. Description of value or price

The value or price of property need not be stated, unless an essential element of the crime. If the nature, degree or punishment of a crime depends upon the fact that the property exceeds or does not exceed a certain value, it may be described, as the case may be, of more than that value, or of not more than that value.

Historical and Statutory Notes

St.1899, c. 409, § 17.
R.L.1902, c. 218, § 24.

§ 25. Description of ownership

If an indictment for a crime involving the commission or attempted commission of an injury to property describes the property with sufficient certainty in other respects to identify the act, it need not allege the name of the owner.

Historical and Statutory Notes

St.1899, c. 409, § 18.
R.L.1902, c. 218, § 25.

§ 26. Description of public place

If one element of the criminality of an act is its commission in a public place, and if such place is not more particularly defined in the statute, the act may be alleged generally to have been committed "in a public place".

Historical and Statutory Notes

St.1899, c. 409, § 19.
R.L.1902, c. 218, § 26.

§ 27. Description of animal

In an indictment for the larceny of an animal, or for any other crime in respect thereof, it may be described by the name by which it is commonly known, without stating its age or sex or whether it is alive or dead.

Historical and Statutory Notes

St.1899, c. 409, § 20.
R.L.1902, c. 218, § 27.

§ 28. Description of judicial proceedings

If it is necessary to set forth the judicial proceedings in any case then or formerly pending in any court, civil or military, or any proceedings before a justice of the peace or any other magistrate, only the substance of said proceedings or such part thereof as shall constitute in whole or in part the crime charged need be alleged.

Historical and Statutory Notes

St.1899, c. 409, § 21.
R.L.1902, c. 218, § 28.

§ 29. Criminal responsibility

An allegation that the defendant committed the act charged shall be a sufficient allegation that he was criminally responsible therefor.

Historical and Statutory Notes

St.1899, c. 409, § 9.
R.L.1902, c. 218, § 29.

§ 30. Intent to injure or defraud; general allegation

If an intent to injure or defraud is an essential element of a crime, an intent to injure or defraud may be alleged generally, without naming the person, corporation or government intended to be injured or defrauded. Proof of an intent to injure or defraud any person or body corporate shall be competent to support the allegation.

Historical and Statutory Notes

R.S.1836, c. 127, § 14.
G.S.1860, c. 162, § 13.
P.S.1882, c. 204, § 13.
St.1899, c. 409, § 23.
R.L.1902, c. 218, § 30.

§ 31. Alternative allegations

Different means or different intents by or with which a crime may be committed may be alleged in the same count in the alternative.

Historical and Statutory Notes

St.1899, c. 409, § 25.
R.L.1902, c. 218, § 31.

§ 32. Continuing offenses

An allegation that a crime was committed or that certain acts were done during a certain period of time next before the finding of the indictment shall be a sufficient allegation that the crime alleged was committed or that the acts alleged were done on divers days and times within that period.

Historical and Statutory Notes

St.1899, c. 409, § 11.
R.L.1902, c. 218, § 32.

§ 33. Unnecessary and immaterial allegations

Presumptions and conclusions of law, matters of which judicial notice is taken and allegations not required to be proved need not be alleged. An indictment shall not be considered defective or insufficient because it omits to allege that the crime was committed, or the act was done "traitorously", "feloniously", "burglariously", "wilfully", "maliciously", "negligently", "unlawfully" or otherwise similarly to describe the crime, unless such description is an element of the crime charged, or because it omits to allege that the crime was committed or done with "force and arms", or "against the peace", or against the form of the statute or statutes, or against a by-law, ordinance, order, rule or regulation of any public authority, or because it omits to state or misstates the title, occupation, estate or degree of the defendant or of any other person named in the indictment, or of the name of the county, city, town or place of his residence, unless such omission or misstatement tends to the prejudice of the defendant, or by reason of describing a fine or forfeiture as enuring to the use of the commonwealth instead of to the use of the county, city or town, or by reason of any misstatement as to the appropriation of any fine or forfeiture, or by reason of its failure to allege or recite a special statute or a by-law or ordinance of a city or town or order of the mayor and aldermen or selectmen or rules or regulations of any public board of officers.

Historical and Statutory Notes

R.S.1836, c. 137, § 14.
St.1838, c. 181, § 4.
St.1846, c. 62.
St.1846, c. 95, § 15.
St.1852, c. 37, § 3.
St.1858, c. 23.
G.S.1860, c. 168, § 2; c. 171, § 16; c. 172, § 19.
St.1860, c. 191, § 10.
P.S.1882, c. 210, § 2; c. 213, §§ 16, 17.
St.1885, c. 144.
St.1886, c. 53.
St.1899, c. 409, §§ 3, 6, 9.
R.L.1902, c. 218, § 33.

§ 34. Immaterial defects

An indictment shall not be dismissed or be considered defective or insufficient if it is sufficient to enable the defendant to understand the charge and to prepare his defense; nor shall it be considered defective or insufficient for lack of any description or information which might be obtained by requiring a bill of particulars.

Amended by St.1979, c. 344, § 34.

Historical and Statutory Notes

St.1899, c. 409, § 5.
R.L.1902, c. 218, § 34.

§ 35. Variance; prejudice

A defendant shall not be acquitted on the ground of variance between the allegations and proof if the essential elements of the crime are correctly stated, unless he is thereby prejudiced in his defence. He shall not be acquitted by reason of an immaterial misnomer of a third party, an immaterial mistake in the description of property or the ownership thereof, failure to prove unnecessary allegations in the description of the crime or any other immaterial mistake in the indictment.

Historical and Statutory Notes

St.1864, c. 250, § 1.
P.S.1882, c. 214, § 26.
St.1899, c. 409, § 4.
R.L.1902, c. 218, § 35.

§ 35A. Repealed, 1979, 344, Sec. 35

Historical and Statutory Notes

See Mass.R.Crim.P. Rule 4.

§ 36. Scope of word "oath"

The word "oath" as used in an indictment shall include an "affirmation".

Historical and Statutory Notes

St.1899, c. 409, § 22.
R.L.1902, c. 218, § 36.

§ 37. Negativing excuses, exceptions or provisos

An excuse, exception or proviso not stated in the enacting clause of a statute creating a crime or stated only by reference to other provisions of the statute need not be negatived in the indictment unless necessary for a complete definition of the crime. If any statute shall prescribe a form of indictment in which an excuse, exception or proviso is not negatived, it shall be taken that it is not necessary to a complete definition of the crime that they should be negatived. If a statute creating a crime permits an act, therein declared to be criminal, to be performed without criminality under stated conditions, such conditions need not be negatived.

Historical and Statutory Notes

St.1899, c. 409, § 26.
R.L.1902, c. 218, § 37.

§ 38. Allegations, bill of particulars, presumption and proof in prosecutions involving controlled substances

In a prosecution under any provision of chapter ninety-four C, for unlawfully manufacturing, dispensing or distributing a controlled substance in violation of any provision of said chapter, it shall be sufficient to allege that the defendant did unlawfully manufacture, dispense or distribute, as the case may be, such alleged substance, without any further allegations, without naming the person to whom it dispensed or distributed, or quantity of the substance; but the defendant shall be entitled to a bill of particulars. In such a prosecution, a defendant relying upon a prescription, written order, receipt, registration, appointment or authority, or exemption as a defense or justification shall prove the same, and until he has proved it the presumption shall be that he is not so justified or authorized.

Amended by St.1957, c. 660, § 5; St.1971, c. 1071, § 8; St.1979, c. 344, § 36.

Historical and Statutory Notes

St.1917, c. 275, §§ 16, 17.

§ 39. Construction of words used in indictment

The words used in an indictment may, except as otherwise provided in this section, be construed according to their usual acceptation in common language; but if certain words and phrases are defined by law, they shall be used according to their legal meaning.

The following words, when used in an indictment, shall be sufficient to convey the meaning herein attached to them:

Adultery.—Sexual intercourse by a married person with a person not his spouse or by an unmarried person with a married person.

Affray.—Fighting together of two or more persons in a public place to the terror of the persons lawfully there.

Aggravated Rape.—Sexual intercourse or unnatural sexual intercourse by a person with another person who is compelled to submit by force and against his will or by threat of bodily injury; and either such sexual intercourse or unnatural sexual intercourse results in or is committed with acts resulting in serious bodily injury, or is committed by a joint enterprise, or is committed during the commission or attempted commission of an offense defined in section fifteen A, fifteen B, seventeen, nineteen or twenty-six of chapter two hundred and sixty-five, section fourteen, fifteen, sixteen, seventeen or eighteen of chapter two hundred and sixty-six, or section ten of chapter two hundred and sixty-nine.

False Pretences.—False representations made by word or act of such a character, or made under such circumstances and in such a way, with the intention of influencing the action of another, as to be punishable.

Forgery.—The false making, altering, forging or counterfeiting of any instrument described in section one of chapter two hundred and sixty-seven, or any instrument which, if genuine, would be a foundation for or release of liability of the apparent maker.

Fornication.—Sexual intercourse between an unmarried male and an unmarried female.

Murder.—The killing of a human being, with malice aforethought.

Rape.—Sexual intercourse or unnatural sexual intercourse by a person with another person who is compelled to submit by force and against his will or by threat of bodily injury, or sexual intercourse or unnatural sexual intercourse with a child under sixteen years of age.

Robbery.—The taking and carrying away of personal property of another from his person and against his will, by force and violence, or by assault and putting in fear, with intent to steal.

Stealing. Larceny.—The criminal taking, obtaining or converting of personal property, with intent to defraud or deprive the owner permanently of the use of it; including all forms of larceny, criminal embezzlement and obtaining by criminal false pretences.

Amended by St.1974, c. 474, § 7; St.1978, c. 379, §§ 8, 9; St.1980, c. 459, § 8.

Historical and Statutory Notes

St.1899, c. 409, § 12.
R.L.1902, c. 218, § 38.

§ 40. Repealed, 1979, 344, Sec. 37

§ 41. Indictment for criminal dealing with personal property

In an indictment for criminal dealing with personal property with intent to steal, an allegation that the defendant stole said property shall be sufficient; and such indictment may be supported by proof that the defendant committed larceny of the property, or embezzled it, or obtained it by false pretences.

Historical and Statutory Notes

St.1899, c. 409, § 24.
R.L.1902, c. 218, § 40.

§ 42. Prosecutions for buying, receiving or aiding in concealment of stolen property

In prosecutions for buying, receiving or aiding in the concealment of stolen property known to have been stolen, it shall not be necessary to allege or prove that the person who stole the property has been convicted.

Historical and Statutory Notes

St.1804, c. 143, § 11.
R.S.1836, c. 126, § 24.
G.S.1860, c. 161, § 45.
P.S.1882, c. 203, § 50.
R.L.1902, c. 218, § 41.

§ 43. Indictment for perjury

In an indictment for perjury alleged to have been committed in a criminal case an allegation of the substance of the crime shall be sufficient; if alleged to have been committed in a civil case, an allegation of the nature of the controversy in general terms shall be sufficient. In both cases, the court or magistrate before whom the oath or affirmation was taken shall be alleged, but no part of the proceeding in which, or the commission or authority of the court or person before whom, the perjury was committed need be alleged.

Historical and Statutory Notes

St.1860, c. 186, § 1.
P.S.1882, c. 205, § 5.
R.L.1902, c. 218, § 42.

§ 44. Indictment for subornation of perjury

If, in an indictment for subornation of perjury or for attempting to incite or procure another person to commit perjury, it is alleged that perjury has been committed, an allegation of the perjury as provided in the preceding section and an allegation that the defendant wilfully incited or procured said person to commit said perjury shall be sufficient. If it is not alleged that such perjury has been committed, an allegation of the substance of the crime with which the defendant is charged shall be sufficient, without allegations as to matters or things which by the preceding section are declared to be unnecessary.

Historical and Statutory Notes

St.1860, c. 186, § 2.
P.S.1882, c. 205, § 6.
R.L.1902, c. 218, § 43.

§ 45. Indictment for unnatural and lascivious acts

In an indictment under section thirty-five of chapter two hundred and seventy-two, an allegation that the defendant committed an unnatural and lascivious act with the person named or referred to in the indictment shall be sufficient.

Historical and Statutory Notes

St.1887, c. 436, § 2.
R.L.1902, c. 218, § 44.

§ 46. Repealed, 1979, 344, Sec. 37

§ 47. Arraignment; sentence; assignment of counsel

If a prisoner, under indictment for a capital crime, pleads guilty, upon being arraigned, the court shall award sentence against him; if he does not plead guilty, the court may assign him counsel and take all other measures preparatory to a trial, which shall, subject to the Massachusetts Rules of Criminal Procedure, be held as soon after the finding of the indictment as the other official duties of the justices will admit and the circumstances of the case require.

Amended by St.1979, c. 344, § 38.

Historical and Statutory Notes

St.1820, c. 14, § 8.
St.1832, c. 130, § 6.
R.S.1836, c. 81, §§ 15, 16.
G.S.1860, c. 112, §§ 8, 9, 20.
P.S.1882, c. 150, § 19.
St.1891, c. 379, § 4.
St.1893, c. 365.
R.L.1902, c. 157, § 10.

§ 47A. Defenses or objections

In a criminal case, any defense or objection based upon defects in the institution of the prosecution or in the complaint or indictment, other than a failure to show jurisdiction in the court or to charge an offense, shall only be raised prior to trial and only by a motion in conformity with the requirements of the Massachusetts Rules of Criminal Procedure. The failure to raise any such defense or objection by motion prior to trial shall constitute a waiver thereof, but a judge or special magistrate may, for cause shown, grant relief from such waiver. A defense or objection based upon a failure to show jurisdiction in the court or the failure to charge an offense may be raised by motion to dismiss prior to trial, but shall be noticed by the court at any time.

Added by St.1965, c. 617, § 1. Amended by St.1965, c. 756, § 1; St.1978, c. 478, § 298; St.1979, c. 344, § 39.

§§ 48, 49. Repealed, 1932, 180, Sec. 44

Historical and Statutory Notes

See, now, c. 276, § 37A. See, also, c. 277, §§ 47, 55.

§ 50. Repealed, 1936, 161, Sec. 1

§§ 51, 52. Repealed, 1979, 344, Sec. 40

Historical and Statutory Notes

See Mass.R.Crim.P. Rule 37.

§ 53. District attorneys; authority and duty as to transferred cases

If a case is transferred for plea or trial and sentence pursuant to the Massachusetts Rules of Criminal Procedure, the district attorney for the county to which the case is transferred or the district attorney for the county from which the case is transferred shall have the same authority and duty in the case as if it had not been transferred, depending upon which of the district attorneys is to try the case.

Amended by St.1979, c. 344, § 41.

Historical and Statutory Notes

St.1871, c. 240, § 3.
P.S.1882, c. 150, § 28.
St.1891, c. 379, § 8.
R.L.1902, c. 157, § 14.

§ 54. Custody and delivery of prisoner

If a change of venue is ordered, the sheriff having custody of the prisoner shall forthwith deliver him to the sheriff of the county to which the venue has been changed, who shall receive and safely keep him as if the indictment had been found in such county.

Historical and Statutory Notes

St.1871, c. 240, § 4.
P.S.1882, c. 150, § 29.
St.1891, c. 379, § 9.
R.L.1902, c. 157, § 15.

§ 55. Compensation of counsel of prisoner

A justice of the court, sitting at the trial or other proceedings upon an indictment for murder, may allow reasonable compensation for the services of counsel assigned to defend the prisoner if he is otherwise unable to procure counsel, and such compensation shall be paid by the county where the indictment is found.

Historical and Statutory Notes

St.1893, c. 394, § 2.
R.L.1902, c. 157, § 16.

§ 56. Expenses of counsel of prisoner

The reasonable expenses incurred and paid by counsel assigned by the court for the defense of a person indicted for murder, who is otherwise unable to procure counsel, shall be paid by the commonwealth after approval by a justice sitting at the trial or other proceedings of the case.

Amended by St.1978, c. 478, § 299.

Historical and Statutory Notes

St.1893, c. 394, § 1.
R.L.1902, c. 157, § 17.

§ 57. Prosecutions of crimes committed near boundary line of counties, etc.; crimes committed on sea

A crime committed on or within one hundred rods of the boundary line of two counties may be alleged to have been committed, and may be prosecuted and punished, in either county; and if committed on or within fifty rods of the boundary line of two judicial districts, it may be alleged to have been committed, and may be prosecuted and punished, in either district. A crime committed upon the sea within one league of the shore may be prosecuted and punished in an adjacent county.

Historical and Statutory Notes

St.1794, c. 31, § 1.
R.S.1836, c. 133, § 7.
G.S.1860, c. 171, § 17.
St.1874, c. 271, § 5.
P.S.1882, c. 154, § 50; c. 213, § 19.
St.1885, c. 322.
St.1893, c. 396, § 34.
St.1894, c. 431.
R.L.1902, c. 218, § 46.

§ 57A. Venue in cases where crime was committed without county or territorial jurisdiction of court

A defendant shall not be discharged for want of jurisdiction if the evidence discloses that the crime with which he is charged was actually committed without the county or the territorial jurisdiction of the court in which he is being tried; provided, that the attorney general or the district attorney petitions to the court before proceeding with the trial for leave to proceed, stating that he is in doubt from the state of the evidence then in his possession as to whether or not the crime was committed within the county or the territorial jurisdiction of the court, and the court after hearing said petition orders the trial to proceed.

Historical and Statutory Notes

St.1923, c. 340.

§ 58. Larceny

Larceny, whether at common law or as defined by section thirty of chapter two hundred and sixty-six, may be prosecuted and punished in any county where the defendant had possession of the property alleged to have been stolen.

Historical and Statutory Notes

St.1878, c. 105.
P.S.1882, c. 213, § 20.
R.L.1902, c. 218, § 47.

§ 58A. Buying, receiving, concealing or aiding in concealment of stolen or embezzled property

The crime of buying, receiving or concealing a stolen motor vehicle or trailer, as defined in section twenty-eight of chapter two hundred and sixty-six, and the crime of buying, receiving or aiding in the concealment of stolen or embezzled property, as defined in section sixty of said chapter two hundred and sixty-six, may be prosecuted and punished in the same jurisdiction in which the larceny or embezzlement of any property involved in the crime may be prosecuted and punished.

Added by St.1943, c. 311, § 1. Amended by St.1971, c. 694.

§ 58A½. Computer offenses; place of prosecution

The crimes described in sections thirty-three A and one hundred and twenty F of chapter two hundred and sixty-six and section one hundred and twenty-seven of said chapter two hundred and sixty-six when the personal property involved is electronically processed or stored data, either tangible or intangible, and data while in transit, may be prosecuted and punished in any county where the defendant was physically located at the time of the violation, or where the electronic data was physically located at the time of the violation.

Added by St.1994, c. 168, § 5.

§ 58B. Embezzlement or fraudulent conversion or appropriation by fiduciaries

The crime of embezzlement or fraudulent conversion or appropriation by a fiduciary of money, goods or property held or possessed by him, as set forth in section fifty-seven of chapter two hundred and sixty-six, including the fraudulent disposition or destruction of such property, may be prosecuted and punished in the county wherein is located the probate court which appointed the fiduciary or in any county where the deed or other instrument in writing creating the trust under which he served or acted was recorded or in any county where he had held or possessed the property as aforesaid after embezzling or fraudulently converting or appropriating the same, as well as in any county where he committed the act of embezzlement or fraudulent conversion or appropriation or other fraudulent disposition or destruction of property held or possessed by him as aforesaid.

Added by St.1948, c. 77, § 1.

§ 59. Obtaining money or personal chattel by false pretences

The crime of obtaining money or a personal chattel by a false pretence, and the crime described in section thirty-one of chapter two hundred and sixty-six, may be alleged to have been committed, and may be prosecuted and punished, in any county where the false pretence was made, written or used, or in or through which any of the property obtained was carried, sent, transported or received by the defendant.

Historical and Statutory Notes

St.1863, c. 248, § 1.
P.S.1882, c. 213, § 21.
R.L.1902, c. 218, § 48.

§ 59A. Transmission of false reports, location of explosives, etc.

The crime described in section fourteen of chapter two hundred and sixty-nine may be prosecuted and punished in the territorial jurisdiction in which the communication originates or is received.

Added by St.1963, c. 157.

§ 60. Homicide if injury is in one county and death in another

If a mortal wound is given, or if other violence or injury is inflicted, or if poison is administered, in one county, by means whereof death ensues in another county, the homicide may be prosecuted and punished in either county.

Historical and Statutory Notes

St.1795, c. 45, § 1.
R.S.1836, c. 133, § 8.
G.S.1860, c. 171, § 18.
P.S.1882, c. 213, § 22.
R.L.1902, c. 218, § 49.

§ 61. Crime committed at sea, etc., resulting in death in county

If a mortal wound is given, or if other violence or injury is inflicted, or if poison is administered, on the high seas or on land either within or without the commonwealth, by means whereof death ensues in any county thereof, the homicide may be prosecuted and punished in the county where the death happens.

Historical and Statutory Notes

St.1795, c. 45, § 2.
R.S.1836, c. 133, § 9.
G.S.1860, c. 171, § 19.
P.S.1882, c. 213, § 23.
R.L.1902, c. 218, § 50.

§ 62. Crime committed in commonwealth resulting in death outside commonwealth

If a mortal wound is given, or if other violence or injury is inflicted, or if poison is administered, in any county of the commonwealth, by means whereof death ensues without the commonwealth, the homicide may be prosecuted and punished in the county where the act was committed.

Historical and Statutory Notes

P.S.1882, c. 213, § 24.
R.L.1902, c. 218, § 51.

§ 62A. Violations of chapter 209A; jurisdiction

Any criminal violation of chapter two hundred and nine A may be prosecuted and punished in the territorial jurisdiction in which the violation was committed or in which the original order under said chapter two hundred and nine A was issued.

Added by St.1994, c. 201.

§ 62B. Stalking; jurisdiction

The crime of stalking, as set forth in section forty-three of chapter two hundred and sixty-five, may be prosecuted and punished in any territorial jurisdiction of the commonwealth wherein an act constituting an element of the crime was committed.

Added by St.1996, c. 298, § 15.

§ 62C. Venue for prosecution of violations of Sec. 35A of chapter 266

A violation of section 35A of chapter 266 may be prosecuted and punished in:

(1) the county in which the residential property for which a mortgage loan is being sought is located;

(2) the county in which any act was performed in furtherance of the violation;

(3) the county in which any person alleged to have violated this section had control or possession of any proceeds of, or other funds received as a result of the violation;

(4) the county in which a closing on the mortgage loan occurred; or

(5) the county in which a document containing a deliberate misstatement, misrepresentation or omission is filed with a registrar of deeds.

Added by St.2010, c. 258, § 12, eff. Aug. 7, 2010.

§ 63. General provisions

An indictment for murder may be found at any time after the death of the person alleged to have been murdered. An indictment or complaint for an offense set forth in section 13B, 13B½, 13B¾, 13F, 13L, 22A, 22B, 22C, 23, 23A, 23B or 24B of chapter 265, for conspiracy to commit any of these offenses, as an accessory thereto, or any 1 or more of them may be found and filed at any time after the date of the commission of such offense; but any indictment or complaint found and filed more than 27 years after the date of commission of such offense shall be supported by independent evidence that corroborates the victim's allegation. Such independent evidence shall be admissible during trial and shall not consist exclusively of the opinions of mental health professionals. An indictment for an offense set forth in sections 22 and 24 of chapter 265, or for conspiracy to commit either of these offenses or as an accessory thereto or any 1 or more of them may be found and filed within 15 years of the date of commission of such offense. An indictment for an offense set forth in sections 17, 18, 19 and 21 of said chapter 265 or section 17 of chapter 272, for conspiracy to commit any such crime, as an accessory thereto, or any 1 or more of them may be found and filed within 10 years after the date of commission of such offense. An indictment for any other crime shall be found and filed within 6 years after such crime has been committed. Any period during which the defendant is not usually and publicly a resident within the commonwealth shall be excluded in determining the time limited.

Notwithstanding the first paragraph, if a victim of a crime set forth in section 13B, 13F, 13H, 22, 22A, 23, 24B, or 26A of chapter 265, or section 1, 2, 3, 4, 4A, 4B, 5, 6, 7, 8, 12, 13, 17, 26, 28, 29A, 29B, 33, 34, 35 or 35A of chapter 272 is under the age of 16 at the time the crime is committed, the period of limitation for prosecution shall not commence until the victim has reached the age of 16 or the violation is reported to a law enforcement agency, whichever occurs earlier.

Amended by St.1955, c. 781, § 1; St.1985, c. 123; St.1987, c. 489; St.1996, c. 26; St.2006, c. 303, § 9, eff. Dec. 20, 2006; St.2010, c. 267, §§ 67 to 69, eff. Nov. 5, 2010.

Historical and Statutory Notes

R.S.1836, c. 136, § 16.
G.S.1860, c. 171, § 20.
P.S.1882, c. 213, § 25.
R.L.1902, c. 218, § 52.

§ 64. Limitation of new indictment against corporation after abatement or defeat of former indictment

If an indictment, duly found and returned within the time limited by law against a corporation to recover a pecuniary penalty, is abated or otherwise avoided or defeated by reason of any matter of form, or if after a verdict against such corporation judgment is arrested, or if a judgment against such corporation is reversed on writ of error, a new indictment for the same cause may be found and filed within one year after the abatement of the former indictment or the reversal of the judgment as aforesaid.

Historical and Statutory Notes

St.1867, c. 164.
P.S.1882, c. 213, § 26.
R.L.1902, c. 218, § 53.

§ 65. Service of copy of indictment for murder on prisoner, etc.

After the finding of an indictment for murder, the defendant, if in custody, shall forthwith be served by the sheriff or his deputy with a copy thereof and with an order of the court notifying him that the indictment will be entered forthwith upon the docket of the superior court for the county where found.

Amended by St.1936, c. 161, § 2.

Historical and Statutory Notes

St.1832, c. 130, § 6.
R.S.1836, c. 136, §§ 18, 19.
G.S.1860, c. 171, § 22.
St.1869, c. 433, § 1.
St.1878, c. 151, § 2.
P.S.1882, c. 213, § 28.
St.1891, c. 379, § 11.
R.L.1902, c. 218, § 54.

§ 66. List of jurors to prisoners; process for witnesses

A prisoner indicted for a crime punishable with death or imprisonment for life, upon demand by him or his counsel upon the clerk, shall have a list of the jurors who have been returned and process to summon witnesses who are necessary to his defence, at the expense of the commonwealth.

Historical and Statutory Notes

R.S.1836, c. 136, § 23.
G.S.1860, c. 171, § 24.
P.S.1882, c. 213, § 31.
R.L.1902, c. 218, § 55.

§ 67. Furnishing person in custody, etc., with copy of indictment

Whoever, having been indicted for felony, is under recognizance or in custody to answer therefor shall be entitled to a copy of the indictment and of all endorsements thereon without charge.

Historical and Statutory Notes

R.S.1836, c. 136, § 24.
G.S.1860, c. 171, § 25.
P.S.1882, c. 213, § 32.
R.L.1902, c. 218, § 56.

§ 68. Issuance of subpoenas by attorney general and district attorneys

The attorney general and district attorneys may issue subpoenas under their hands for witnesses to appear and testify on behalf of the commonwealth, and such subpoenas shall have the same force, and be obeyed in the same manner, and under the same penalties, in case of default, as if issued by the clerk of the court.

Historical and Statutory Notes

R.S.1836, c. 136, § 25.
G.S.1860, c. 171, § 26.
P.S.1882, c. 213, § 33.
R.L.1902, c. 218, § 57.

§ 69. Repealed, 1979, 344, Sec. 42

Historical and Statutory Notes

See Mass.R.Crim.P. Rule 17.

§ 70. Recognizance of witnesses

A justice of a court of record may at any time order a witness for the commonwealth in a criminal case or in a case under sections fifty-two to sixty-four, inclusive, of chapter one hundred and nineteen, pending in such court to recognize, with or without sureties, to appear and testify at the next or any succeeding sitting of said court, and may issue a warrant to bring such witness before him to recognize as aforesaid; but a witness unable to procure sureties shall not on that account be committed to jail except in cases of felony.

Historical and Statutory Notes

St.1868, c. 69.
St.1872, c. 214.
P.S.1882, c. 213, § 35.
R.L.1902, c. 218, § 59.

§ 70A. Repealed, 1979, 344, Sec. 42

Historical and Statutory Notes

See Mass.R.Crim.P. Rule 16.

§ 70B. Placing cases on file; statement of reasons

Except as otherwise provided by law, a criminal case shall not be placed on file, on motion of a district attorney or assistant district attorney, unless such motion is accompanied by a written statement of the reasons for such disposition, signed by the district attorney or assistant district attorney, which shall be filed with the pleadings, and also accompanied by a statement of any previous criminal record of the accused.

Historical and Statutory Notes

St.1922, c. 458.

§ 70C. Civil infractions

Upon oral motion by the commonwealth or the defendant at arraignment or pretrial conference, or upon the court's own motion at any time, the court may, unless the commonwealth objects, in writing, stating the reasons for such objection, treat a violation of a municipal ordinance, or by-law or a misdemeanor offense as a civil infraction. The provisions of this section shall not apply to the offenses in sections 22F, 24, 24D, 24G, 24L, and 24N of chapter 90, sections 8, 8A, and 8B of chapter 90B, chapter 119, chapter 119A, chapter 209, chapter 209A, chapter 265, sections 1, 2, 3, 6, 6A, 6B, 8B, 13, 13A, 13B, 13B½, 13B¾, 13C, 14, 14B, 15, 15A, 16, 17, 18, 19, 20, 22A, 22B, 22C, 23, 23A, 23B, 28, 31 and 36 of chapter 268, chapter 268A, sections 10, 10A, 10C, 10D, 10E, 11B, 11C, 11E, 12, 12A, 12B, 12D and 12E of chapter 269 and sections 1, 2, 3, 4, 4A, 4B, 6, 7, 8, 12, 13, 16, 28, 29A and 29B of chapter 272. If a motion to proceed civilly is allowed, the court shall not appoint counsel. If counsel has already been appointed, the court shall revoke the appointment. A person complained of for such civil infraction shall be adjudicated responsible upon such finding by the court and shall not be sentenced to any term of incarceration. The commonwealth shall maintain a copy of all objections filed under this section and shall report the number of such objections, delineated by divisions of the district court, every 6 months to the house and senate committees on ways and means.

When the court has treated a violation of a municipal ordinance or by-law or a misdemeanor offense as a civil infraction under this section and the ordinance, by-law or misdemeanor in question does not set forth a civil fine as a possible penalty, the court may impose a fine of not more than $5,000. An adjudication of responsibility shall neither be used in the calculation of second and subsequent offenses under any chapter, nor as the basis for the revocation of parole or of a probation surrender. An adjudication of responsibility under this section may include an order of restitution.

Added by St.1995, c. 38, § 177. Amended by St.1998, c. 194, § 240; St.2003, c. 26, §§ 511, 512, eff. July 1, 2003; St.2004, c. 149, § 213, eff. July 1, 2004; St.2005, c. 54, § 3, eff. July 29, 2005; St.2010, c. 267, §§ 70, 71, eff. Nov. 5, 2010.

§§ 71 to 72A. Repealed, 1979, 344, Sec. 42

Historical and Statutory Notes

See Mass.R.Crim.P. Rules 7, 12, 36.

§ 73. Compensation for confinement of persons discharged

Any person in the commonwealth kept in confinement awaiting trial for more than six months after having been indicted, and finally acquitted or discharged without trial, if the delay in trial was not at his request or with his consent, or at the request or with the consent of his attorney of record, may receive compensation for the period of his confinement after the lapse of said six months and until his acquittal or discharge; provided, that the payment of compensation is approved by the justice who presided at the trial, or in the case of a discharge without trial, by a justice of the superior court sitting at a session for criminal business in and for the county where the indictment was found. Such compensation shall be paid by the commonwealth and shall be equivalent to the amount which the indicted person earned or received from his regular employment for any period of equal length during the two years immediately preceding his confinement; and if he had no employment, the compensation shall be such reasonable sum as shall be determined by the justice who presided at the trial, or, in the case of a discharge without trial, by a justice of the superior court sitting at a session for criminal business in and for the county where the indictment was found. The justice, upon application by the person acquitted or discharged, shall give a hearing at which such person or his representative may be present, if he so desires, and the district attorney or other officer representing the commonwealth may also be present, and the person acquitted or discharged and the commonwealth may offer testimony as in any civil case. The decision of the justice shall be final.

Amended by St.1978, c. 478, § 300.

Historical and Statutory Notes

St.1911, c. 577.

§§ 74 to 77. Repealed, 1979, 344, Sec. 42

Historical and Statutory Notes

See c. 277, § 47A; Mass.R.Crim.P. Rules 13, 17, 35.

§ 78. Criminal proceedings as no bar to civil action

No proceedings against a person for a crime shall bar a civil action which might otherwise be maintained by a person aggrieved by the commission of the crime.

Historical and Statutory Notes

St.1851, c. 151, § 6.
St.1856, c. 123, § 6.
G.S.1860, c. 171, § 34.
P.S.1882, c. 213, § 43.
R.L.1902, c. 218, § 66.

§ 79. Application of annexed forms; schedule

The provisions of this chapter, and the forms hereto annexed, shall apply as well to complaints as to indictments, and such forms shall be sufficient in cases to which they are applicable. In other cases, forms as nearly like the forms hereto annexed as the nature of the cases and the provisions of law will allow may be used; but any other form of indictment or complaint authorized by law may be used.

SCHEDULE OF FORMS OF PLEADINGS.

CAPTION AND COMMENCEMENT OF INDICTMENT.

COMMONWEALTH OF MASSACHUSETTS.

(Suffolk,) to wit:

At the Superior Court holden at (Boston,) within and for the County of (Suffolk,) for the transaction of criminal business, on the day of in the year of our Lord one thousand, etc.

The jurors for the said Commonwealth on their oath present

CAPTION AND COMMENCEMENT OF COMPLAINT.

(To a Police, District or Municipal Court.)

COMMONWEALTH OF MASSACHUSETTS.

(Suffolk,) to wit:

To the court of holden at for the transaction of criminal business, within the County of , A. B. of in behalf of the Commonwealth of Massachusetts on the day of in the year , on oath complains that

(To a Trial Justice.)

To A. B., a Trial Justice in and for the County of and Commonwealth of Massachusetts, C. D. of *(etc. as in form above).*

(To a Justice of the Peace commissioned to Issue Warrants.)

To A. B., Justice of the Peace in and for the County of and Commonwealth of Massachusetts, designated and commissioned to issue warrants in criminal cases, C. D. of *(etc. as in form above).*

(If the statute requires a particular person to make complaint, this should be alleged.)

Abduction. (Under Chap. 272, Secs. 1, 2.)—(1) That A.B. did fraudulently and deceitfully entice (and take away) one C.D., an unmarried person under the age of sixteen years, from the house of the father (*or* guardian, etc., as the case may be), without the consent of the said father (*or* guardian, etc., as the case may be), under whose care and custody said C.D. was living, for the purpose of effecting a clandestine marriage of said C.D. without the consent of said father (*or* guardian, etc., as the case may be).

(2) That A.B. did fraudulently and deceitfully entice (and take away) C.D. from his house (or, if a minor, from his father's or guardian's house; or if elsewhere, state it as the case may be), for the unlawful purpose of

prostitution (or for the purpose of unlawful sexual intercourse).

Abortion. (Under Chap. 272, Sec. 19.)—(1) That A.B., with intent to procure the miscarriage of C.D., did unlawfully administer to her (*or* advise, *or* prescribe for her, *or* cause to be taken by her) a certain drug (*or* medicine or other noxious thing, as the case may be).

If the woman dies, add "and in consequence thereof said C.D. died".

(2) That A.B., with intent to procure the miscarriage of C.D., did unlawfully use a certain instrument upon the body of said C.D., and in consequence thereof said C.D. died.

(3) That A.B., with intent to procure the miscarriage of C.D., did unlawfully do certain things (*naming them*) to (*or* upon the body of) said C.D.

Accessory before the fact. (Under Chap. 274, Sec. 2.)—*Charge principal felony and proceed*: That A.B., before the said felony was committed, did incite, procure, aid, counsel, hire or command the said (principal) the said felony to do and commit.

Accessory after the fact. (Under Chap. 274, Sec. 4.)—*Charge principal felony and proceed*: That A.B. afterwards, well knowing the said C.D. to have committed the felony aforesaid, did harbor, (conceal, maintain,) or assist said C.D., with intent that said C.D. should avoid or escape (detention, arrest,) trial, or punishment.

Adultery. (Under Chap. 272, Sec. 14.)—(1) That A.B., a married person, did commit adultery with C.D., a person not his spouse.

(2) That A.B., an unmarried person, did commit adultery with C.D., a married person.

Affray.—That A.B. and C.D. did make an affray.

Aggravated rape. (Under Chap. 265, Sec. 22(a).)—That A.B. did assault C.D., with intent to commit aggravated rape; and did commit aggravated rape upon said C.D.

Alcoholic Beverages. (Under Chap. 138, Sec. 2.)—That A.C. did expose and keep for sale alcoholic beverages, as defined in section one of chapter one hundred and thirty-eight, with intent unlawfully to sell the same.

Alcoholic Beverages—Sale. (Under Chap. 138, Sec. 2.)—That A.B. unlawfully did sell alcoholic beverages, as defined in section one of chapter one hundred and thirty-eight, to C.C.

Alcoholic Beverages—Nuisance. (Under Chap. 139, Sec. 15.)—That A.B., during the three months next before the finding of this indictment, without legal authority, did keep and maintain a certain tenement in said (Boston), by him used for the illegal sale and illegal keeping for sale of alcoholic beverages, as defined in section one of chapter one hundred and thirty-eight, to the common nuisance of all the people.

Armed with dangerous weapon when arrested. (Under Chap. 269, Sec. 9.)—(1) That A.B., while being lawfully arrested on a sufficient warrant on a criminal charge, was armed with a dangerous weapon, to wit, a slung shot (*or* other dangerous weapon, as the case may be).

(2) That A.B., while committing the crime of (*here state crime*), was lawfully arrested by C.D., sheriff of said county, and when so arrested was armed with, and had on his person, a certain dangerous weapon (a slung shot, etc., as the case may be).

Arson. (Under Chap. 266, Secs. 1, 2, 4.)—(1) That A.B. wilfully and maliciously did burn the dwelling house of C.D. in in said county.

(2) That A.B. wilfully and maliciously did burn a building adjoining the dwelling house of C.D. in in said county.

(3) That A.B. wilfully and maliciously did set fire to a building in by the burning whereof the dwelling house of C.D. was burned.

(4) That A.B. wilfully and maliciously, in the night time, did burn

(a) A meeting house (*or* church, town house, etc.) in in said county, erected for public use.

(b) A banking house (*or* warehouse, etc.) of C.D. in in said county, of the value, with the property therein, of one thousand dollars and not the property of (the defendant).

(c) A barn (*or* stable *or* shop *or* office) of C.D., in in said county, the same being there within the curtilage of the dwelling house of said C.D.

(5) That A.B. wilfully and maliciously did burn a building, by the burning whereof [(a), (b), or (c)] was burned in the night time.

(6) That A.B. wilfully and maliciously did burn a banking house (*or other structure mentioned in the statute, as the case may be*) of C.D., in in said county.

Assault and battery.—That A.B. did assault and beat C.D.

Assault to maim, etc. (Under Chap. 265, Sec. 15.)—That A.B. did assault C.D., with the malicious intent to maim (*or* disfigure) said C.D. by cutting out his tongue (*or other facts required by the nature of the case*).

Assault to murder. (Under Chap. 265, Sec. 15.)—That A.B. did assault C.D., with intent to murder him.

Assault to Rape. (Under Chap. 265, Sec. 24.)—(1) That A.B. did assault C.D., with intent to commit rape.

(2) That A.B. did assault C.D., a child under the age of sixteen years, with intent unlawfully and carnally to know and abuse.

Assault with dangerous weapon, with intent to rob, etc. (Under Chap. 265, Sec. 18.)—That A.B., being armed with a dangerous weapon, did assault C.D., with intent to rob him (*or* to murder him).

Assault upon an officer.—That A.B. did assault and beat C.D., who was a police officer of the (city of Boston) (*or whatever the fact may be*), and who was also in the lawful discharge of his duties as such officer, as said (defendant) well knew, (and knowingly resisted and obstructed him in the discharge of his lawful duties). *This clause may be added if facts require.*

Assuming to be an officer. (Under Chap. 268, Sec. 33.)—That A.B. did falsely assume and pretend to one C.D. that he, said A.B., was a police officer of (the city of) (*or* a constable of the city of), and did take upon himself to act as such officer, and did (*state what he did if desired*).

Attempt to break and enter. (Under Chap. 274, Sec. 6.)—That A.B. did attempt to break and enter a certain building in said (Boston) of one C.D., in the (night) time, with intent therein to commit larceny, and in such attempt did (*set out the overt act relied on*); but did fail in the perpetration of said attempted offence (*or* was intercepted and prevented in the execution of said attempted offence).

Attempt to commit crime. (Under Chap. 274, Sec. 6.)—That A.B. did attempt to commit larceny of the property of (another), (*or such other crime as may be intended to be charged*), and in such attempt did (*set out the overt act relied on*); but did fail in the perpetration of said attempted offence (*or* was intercepted and prevented in the execution of said attempted offence).

Attempt to steal from person. (Under Chap. 274, Sec. 6.)—That A.B. did attempt to steal from the person of C.D., and in such attempt did put his hand against the person and into the pocket of the said C.D.; but did fail in the perpetration of said attempted offence (*or* was intercepted and prevented in the execution of said attempted offence).

Breaking, entering, etc. (Under Chap. 266, Secs. 16–19.)—(1) That A.B. did break and enter in the night time the building (*or* ship or vessel) of one X., situated in said (Boston), with intent therein to commit murder (*or* rape, robbery, etc.).

(2) That A.B. did break and enter (*or* entered in the night time without breaking) a building (*or* ship or vessel) of one X., in said (Boston), with intent (*as above*), the said X. (*or other person*), who was lawfully therein, being put in fear.

(3) That A.B. did break and enter (*or* entered in the night time without breaking) a railroad car situated in said (Boston), of the (*name of the railroad*), with intent therein to commit larceny (*or* murder, etc., as the case may be).

(4) That A.B. did enter in the night time the dwelling house of one X., in said (Boston), with intent therein to commit larceny (*or* murder, etc., as the case may be).

(5) That A.B. did break and enter a building (*or* ship or vessel) of one X., in said (Boston), with intent therein (*etc. as above*).

Breaking glass. (Under Chap. 266, Sec. 114.)—That A.B. did wantonly (*or* maliciously) break certain panes of glass in and part of a certain building, the property of C.D. in said (Boston).

Burglarious implements. (Under Chap. 266, Sec. 49.)—That A.B. knowingly did have in his possession certain machines, tools and implements adapted and designed for cutting through, forcing and breaking open buildings, rooms, vaults, safes (and other depositories), in order to steal therefrom such money and other property as might be found therein, said A.B. knowing said machines, tools and implements to be adapted and designed for the purpose aforesaid, and intending to use and employ them therefor.

Burglary, etc. (Under Chap. 266, Secs. 14, 15.)—(1) That A.B. in the night time did break and enter the dwelling house of C.D., situated in said (Boston), with intent therein to commit larceny (*or* murder, rape or robbery, as the case may be).

(If desired add actual larceny in the building.)

(2) That A.B. did enter the dwelling house of one X., situated in said (Boston), with intent therein to commit larceny, and after having so entered with said intent did break said dwelling house in the night time, X. being lawfully therein, and said A.B. being armed with a dangerous weapon at the time of such entry (*or* such breaking) (*or* arming himself with a dangerous weapon in said house) (*or* did make an assault on said X., who was lawfully therein).

(3) That A.B. did break and enter the dwelling house of one X., in said (Boston), in the night time, with intent therein to commit larceny (*or* murder, etc., as the case may be).

Burning to defraud insurance company. (Under Chap. 266, Sec. 10.)—That A.B. did burn a certain building in in said county, [*or* certain goods, wares and merchandise (*or other chattels—name the property*)] which was (*or* were) at the time of such burning insured in the Insurance Company, a corporation duly established by law, against loss or damage by fire, with the intent thereby to injure the said insurer.

Common drunkard. (Under Chap. 272, Sec. 53.)—That A.B., during the three months next before the making of this complaint, was a common drunkard.

Common nightwalker. (Under Chap. 272, Sec. 53.)—That A.B., during the three months next before the making of this complaint, was a common nightwalker, habitually walking in the streets in the night time for the purpose of prostitution.

Concealing mortgaged personal property. (Under Chap. 266, Sec. 82.)—That A.B. did mortgage to X. in due form of law certain personal property (*setting out the mortgaged property*), and that afterward, the said mortgage being in full force and effect, and the said X. remaining the owner thereof (*if such be the fact*), said A.B. did remove and conceal the said property with fraudulent intent to place the same beyond the control of the said X.

Conspiracy.—(1) That A.B. and C.D. conspired together to murder one E.F.

(2) That A.B. and C.D. conspired together to commit rape upon E.F.

(3) That A.B. and C.D. conspired together to steal the property, money, etc., of E.F.

Cruelty to animals. (Under Chap. 272, Sec. 77.)—(1) That A.B. did overdrive (overload) (drive when overloaded) (overwork) (torture) (torment) (deprive of necessary sustenance) (cruelly beat) (cruelly mutilate) (cruelly kill) a certain horse (*or* dog, etc.).

(2) That A.B. did cause and procure one C.D. to overdrive (etc.) a certain horse (etc.).

(3) That A.B., having the charge and custody of a certain horse (etc.), did inflict unnecessary cruelty upon it.

(4) That A.B., having the charge and custody of a certain horse (etc.), did unnecessarily fail to provide it with proper food (*or* drink *or* shelter *or* protection from the weather).

Disorderly house. (Under Chap. 219, Sec 27.)—That A.B., during the three months next before the finding of this indictment, at said (Boston) did keep and maintain a certain and common, noisy, ill-governed and disorderly house, resorted to for the purpose of drinking, quarrelling, making great noises, and breaking and disturbing the peace, to the common nuisance of all the people.

Drunkenness. (Under Chap. 272, Sec. 48.)—That A.B. was, by the voluntary use of intoxicating liquor, drunk.

Eavesdropping. (Under Chap. 272, Sec. 99.)—That A.B. did commit the crime of eavesdropping.

Escape. (Under Chap. 268, Sec. 16.)—That A.B., being lawfully imprisoned in the House of Correction (or the Massachusetts correctional institution) in said county, did break therefrom and escape.

Exposure of person.—That A.B., in a public place in said (Boston), wherein were great numbers of people, indecently did expose to the view of the said people his body and person naked and uncovered.

Forged endorsement.—That A.B. did forge a certain endorsement in and upon the back of, and as a part of, a certain promissory note, with intent to injure and defraud. *(The purport or substance of the note and endorsement may be set forth.)*

Forgery. (Under Chap. 267, Sec. 1.)—That A.B., with intent to injure and defraud, did forge a certain instrument purporting to be, etc. (*give the name of the instrument, description, tenor or substance as the pleader chooses*).

Fornication. (Under Chap. 272, Sec. 18.)—That A.B., an unmarried person, did commit fornication with C.D., an unmarried person.

Gaming. (Under Chap. 139, Sec. 15.)—That A.B., during the three months next before the finding of this indictment, at said (Boston), did keep and maintain a certain common nuisance, to wit, a tenement resorted to and used for illegal gaming.

House of ill fame. (Under Chap. 272, Sec. 24.)—That A.B., during the three months next before the finding of this indictment, did keep at said (Boston) a certain house of ill fame, resorted to for purposes of prostitution and lewdness.

House of ill fame—Nuisance. (Under Chap. 139, Sec. 15.)—That A.B., during the three months next before the finding of this indictment, at said (Boston), did keep and maintain a certain tenement used for prostitution, assignation and lewdness (*or* in which acts of prostitution, assignation and lewdness occurred), to the common nuisance of all the people.

Idle and disorderly person. (Under Chap. 272, Sec. 53.)—That A.B., during the three months next before the making of this complaint, was an idle and disorderly person, and neglected all lawful business and habitually misspent his time by frequenting houses of ill fame, gaming houses or tippling shops.

Incest. (Under Chap. 272, Sec. 17.)—That A.B., being the father of C.D. (*or* state such relationship as will show the parties to be within the degree of consanguinity within which marriages are prohibited or declared by law to be incestuous and void), did have carnal knowledge of the body of said C.D.

(A.B. being married to another woman than said C.D., *if such be the fact, and it be desired to cover adultery.*)

Larceny. (Under Chap. 266, Sec. 30.)—(1) That A.B. did steal one horse of the value of more (*or* less, as the case may be) than one hundred dollars, of the property of C.D.

(2) That A.B. did steal six cows, each of the value of twenty dollars, of the property of C.D.

Larceny from a conveyance. (Under Chap. 266, Sec. 30.)—That A.B. did steal from a certain conveyance, to wit, the wagon of one C.D., one book of the value, etc., of the property of C.D., the said C.D. being a common carrier (*or* a person carrying on the express business), and said conveyance being used by the said C.D. in said business.

Larceny from realty. (Under Chap. 266, Sec. 44.)—That A.B., by a trespass, with intent to steal, did take and carry away from the realty, to wit, from the building of C.D., in said (Boston), ten pounds of lead pipe, each of the value of (etc.), of the property of C.D., against his will, the said lead pipe being annexed to and a part of said building.

Larceny in building. (Under Chap. 266, Sec. 20.)—That A.B. did steal (one coat of the value of more than or less than), of the property of X., in a certain building (*or* ship *or* vessel *or* railroad car) of the said X., situated in said (Boston).

Larceny of beast or bird. (Under Chap. 266, Sec. 46.)—That A.B. did steal a certain domesticated animal (*or* bird which was ordinarily kept in confinement), which was the property of C.D.

Lewd and lascivious cohabitation. (Under Chap. 272, Sec. 16.)—That A.B. and C.D., not being married to each other, did during one month next before the finding of this indictment (or such time as the evidence requires), lewdly and lasciviously associate and cohabit together.

Lewdness. (Under Chap. 272, Sec. 53.)—That A.B., during the three months next before the finding of this indictment, was a lewd, wanton and lascivious person in speech and behavior.

Lord's Day. (Under Chap. 136, Sec. 5.)—That A.B., on the day of , in the year of our Lord one thousand, etc., that day being the Lord's Day, did keep open his shop in said (Boston), for the purpose of doing business therein (*or* did labor *or* business *or* work), the same not being a work of necessity or charity.

Lottery. (Under Chap. 271, Sec. 7.)—(1) That A.B. did set up and promote a lottery for money.

(2) That A.B. was concerned in the setting up (*or* managing *or* drawing) of a certain lottery for money.

(3) That A.B. did dispose of a certain horse of the value of ten dollars to C.D., by way of a lottery.

(4) That A.B., under the pretext of the sale of certain property, to wit: (*state the property*) to C.D., did dispose of to said C.D. certain other personal property, to wit: (*state the property*), with intent of said A.B. to make the said disposal of said (property) dependent upon a chance by lot, and that such chance was made an additional inducement to the disposal and sale of said (property).

Maiming, etc. (Under Chap. 265, Sec. 14.)—That A.B. did assault C.D., and, with malicious intent to maim and disfigure said C.D., did cut out his tongue.

Malicious injury. (Under Chap. 266, Sec. 127.)—That A.B. did wilfully and maliciously injure (*or* destroy) certain personal property (*name it and allege value*) of C.D.

Malicious injury to real property. (Under Chap. 266, Sec. 104.)—That A.B. did wilfully (*or* maliciously) destroy (*or* deface *or* mar) a certain building of C.D. in said (Boston).

Manslaughter. (Under Chap. 265, Sec. 13.)—That A.B. did assault and beat C.D., and by such assault and beating did kill C.D.

Manslaughter by negligence.—That A.B., being under the legal duty, and being of sufficient ability to provide C.D., who was his spouse, with sufficient food and drink for sustenance and maintenance, did neglect and refuse so to do; by reason whereof said C.D., being unable to provide sufficient food and drink, became and was mortally sick and died.

Murder. (Under Chap. 265, Sec. 1.)—That A.B. did assault and beat C.D., with intent to murder him (by striking him over the head with an axe), and by such assault and beating did (kill and) murder C.D. (and the jurors further say that the defendant is guilty of murder in the second degree and not in the first degree). *This may be added if murder in the first degree is not alleged.*

Neglect of Spouse or Minor Child. (Under Chap. 273, Sec. 1.)—That A.B., during the three months next before the making of this complaint, being of sufficient ability, did unreasonably neglect to provide for the support of C.D., his lawful spouse (and E.D., his minor child).

Obtaining signature by false pretences. (Under Chap. 266, Sec. 31.)—That A.B. designedly and with intent to defraud did falsely pretend to C.D. that, etc., and by means of said false pretences, which said C.D. believed and relied upon, did obtain the signature of said C.D. to a certain written instrument, the false making whereof would be punishable as forgery, to wit, a certain promissory note (*describe as in forgery*); that the pretences so made to C.D. were false and were known to be false by the said A.B. at the time when he so made them.

Open and gross lewdness. (Under Chap. 272, Sec. 16.)—That A.B. was guilty of open and gross lewdness and lascivious behavior in the presence of C.D.

Prostitute. (Under Chap. 272, Sec. 53.)—That A.B. was a prostitute, offering his or her body indiscriminately to others for hire.

Perjury. (Under Chap. 268, Sec. 1.)—That in a proceeding in the course of justice before the (*set forth the tribunal*), on an issue within the jurisdiction of said court duly joined, and tried before a jury of the county between X. as plaintiff and Y. as defendant, A.B. was lawfully sworn as a witness.

Whereupon it became and was material to said issue whether (*say what*), and to this the said A.B. did wilfully and corruptly testify and say in substance and effect that (*say what*); all his said testimony as above set forth being false, as he well knew.

Polygamy. (Under Chap. 272, Sec. 15.)—(1) That A.B. unlawfully married C.D., the said A.B. having at the time he so unlawfully married a lawful spouse living other than said C.D.

(2) That A.B., having a lawful spouse living, to wit: X., did at (*state place*) unlawfully marry and have for his spouse one C.D., after which the said A.B. did, while said X., was still living, on, at, etc., unlawfully cohabit and continue to cohabit in (Boston) with the said C.D.

Rape. (Under Chap. 265, Secs. 22(b), 23.)—(1) That A.B. did assault C.D. with the intent to commit rape; and did commit rape upon said C.D.

(2) That A.B. did assault C.D., a child under the age of sixteen years, with the intent to unlawfully have sexual intercourse or unnatural sexual intercourse with and abuse said C.D.; and did unlawfully have sexual intercourse or unnatural sexual intercourse with and abuse said C.D.

Receiving stolen property. (Under Chap. 266, Sec. 60.)—That A.B., one watch of the value of dollars, the property of one C.D., then lately before stolen, did buy, receive, and aid in the concealment of, the said A.B. well knowing the said property to have been stolen as aforesaid.

Rescue. (Under Chap. 268, Sec. 15.)—That A.B. did forcibly rescue and take out of the lawful custody of E.F. one C.D., the said C.D. being a prisoner arrested by and held in the lawful custody of E.F., upon the charge of the crime of (larceny), the said E.F. being a police officer of (said city), duly authorized to arrest and hold in custody the said C.D. upon the charge aforesaid.

Robbery. (Under Chap. 265, Sec. 19.)—That A.B. did assault C.D. with intent to rob him, and thereby did rob and steal from the person of said C.D. (*mention the property*) of the property of said C.D.

Sodomy, etc. (Under Chap. 272, Sec. 34.)—That A.B. did commit the abominable and detestable crime against nature with a (*state the person or beast*).

Stubborn child. (Under Chap. 272, Sec. 53.)—That A.B., a minor, during the three months next before the making of this complaint, was a stubborn child, and stubbornly refused to submit to the lawful and reasonable commands of C.D., whose commands said A.B. was bound to obey.

Threats to extort. (Under Chap. 265, Sec. 25.)—That A.B. did verbally (*or* by a written or printed communication) maliciously threaten one C.D., to accuse him of the crime of (*name it*), with the intent thereby to extort money from the said C.D.

Unlawful appropriation. (Under Chap. 266, Sec. 63.)—That A.B. did wilfully, mischievously and without right take, drive and use a certain horse, the property of one C.D., without the consent of the said owner of said horse, or any person having the legal custody, care or control of the same.

Unnatural act. (Under Chap. 272, Sec. 35.)—That A.B. did commit an unnatural and lascivious act with one C.D.

Uttering. (Under Chap. 267, Sec. 5.)—That A.B., with intent to injure and defraud, did utter and publish as true a certain forged instrument (*describe as in forgery*), well knowing the same to be forged.

Vagabond. (Under Chap. 272, Secs. 53, 68.)—That A.B., for three months next before the making of this complaint, was a vagabond, and wandered about from place to place, neglecting all lawful calling and employment, and not having any home or means of support.

Vagrant. (Under Chap. 272, Sec. 66.)—That A.B., during the three months next before the making of this complaint, was an idle person who, not having visible means of support, lived without lawful employment (and wandered abroad and visited tippling shops, and lodged in outhouses, and in the open air, and did not give a good account of himself, and wandered abroad and begged, and went about from door to door and placed himself in public places to beg and to receive alms).

The complaint may stop at the word "employment", or such part of the matter in parentheses may be added as the case requires.

(Under Chapter 94, Sections 197–213.)

Common nuisance.—That A.B., during the three months next before the finding of this indictment, at said (Boston), did keep and maintain a certain tenement resorted to by habitual users of narcotic drugs for the purpose of using narcotic drugs.

Unlawful possession.—That A.B. did have in his possession unlawfully certain narcotic drugs, to wit, morphine (*or* cocaine *or* heroin *or the name of the drug as it is commonly known*).

Unlawful possession with intent to sell.—That A.B. did have in his possession, with intent unlawfully to sell and deliver, a certain narcotic drug (*naming the drug*).

Conspiracy.—That A.B. and C.D. conspired together to engage in unlawful traffic in narcotic drugs.

Sale and delivery.—That A.B. did unlawfully sell (*or* give away *or* deliver) a narcotic drug, to wit, morphine (*or name drug is commonly known by*).

Unlawful prescribing and delivery, etc., by physician, etc.—That A.B., a physician (*or* pharmacist *or* dentist *or* veterinarian, *etc.*), did unlawfully prescribe (*or* sell, give away, furnish or deliver) a certain narcotic drug, to wit, (*naming it*).

False making of prescription.—That A.B. did falsely make (*or* alter) a prescription for a narcotic drug.

Uttering a false prescription.—That A.B. did utter and publish as true a certain false prescription for a narcotic drug, well knowing the same to be falsely made (*or* altered).

Misrepresentation.—That A.B. did falsely represent to C.D. (a physician, *or* dentist, veterinarian, pharmacist, *etc.*), for the purpose of obtaining a narcotic drug, that (*state the substance of the statements claimed to be representations*).

Amended by St.1934, c. 328, § 29; St.1943, c. 488, § 2; St.1955, c. 770, § 90; St.1959, c. 304, § 2; St.1978, c. 379, §§ 10 to 19; St.1980, c. 459, §§ 9, 10; St.2006, c. 172, § 13, eff. July 13, 2006.

Historical and Statutory Notes

St.1899, c. 409, §§ 1, 2, 28.
R.L.1902, c. 218, § 67.
St.1917, c. 275, § 18.
St.1920, c. 558, § 4.
St.1931, c. 256, § 6.

CHAPTER 277A

STATEWIDE GRAND JURY

Chapter 277A of the General Laws was added by St.2009, c. 28, § 98.

The section headings for the General Laws in this pamphlet have been editorially supplied.

§ 1. Authority to convene statewide grand jury

[Text of section effective until December 31, 2014. Repealed by 2009, 28, Sec. 99. See 2009, 28, Sec. 107.]

Upon written application of the attorney general to the chief justice of the superior court department, with good cause stated therein, the chief justice may authorize the convening of a statewide grand jury with jurisdiction extending throughout the commonwealth.

Added by St.2009, c. 28, § 98, eff. Sept. 29, 2009.

§ 2. Selection of county where statewide jury to sit; appointment of superior court judge

[Text of section effective until December 31, 2014. Repealed by 2009, 28, Sec. 99. See 2009, 28, Sec. 107.]

The chief justice of the superior court department shall, upon granting an application, receive recommendations from the attorney general as to the county in which the statewide grand jury shall sit. Upon receiving the attorney general's recommendations, the chief justice shall choose 1 of those recommended locations as the site where the grand jury shall sit. Once a county has been selected, the chief justice shall direct the regional administrative judge from the county selected to appoint, and reappoint as necessary, a superior court judge to preside over the statewide grand jury.

Added by St.2009, c. 28, § 98, eff. Sept. 29, 2009.

§ 3. Nature and scope of investigation; statewide grand jury to investigate for purpose stated in written application

[Text of section effective until December 31, 2014. Repealed by 2009, 28, Sec. 99. See 2009, 28, Sec. 107.]

The superior court judge presiding over the grand jury shall consult with the attorney general and district attorney for the relevant district about the nature and scope of the investigation and shall thereafter designate and authorize an existing county grand jury to serve as a statewide grand jury for purposes of the investigation specified in the written application, or, alternatively, convene and preside over a specially empaneled statewide grand jury.

Added by St.2009, c. 28, § 98, eff. Sept. 29, 2009.

§ 4. Manner of drawing and selecting specially empaneled statewide grand jury

[Text of section effective until December 31, 2014. Repealed by 2009, 28, Sec. 99. See 2009, 28, Sec. 107.]

A specially empaneled statewide grand jury shall be drawn and selected in the same manner as the county grand jury in the county in which the specially empaneled statewide grand jury sits. A specially empaneled statewide grand jury may, at the discretion of the presiding superior court judge, draw jurors from counties adjoining the one in which the statewide grand jury is to sit.

Added by St.2009, c. 28, § 98, eff. Sept. 29, 2009.

§ 5. Period during which statewide grand jury may sit

[Text of section effective until December 31, 2014. Repealed by 2009, 28, Sec. 99. See 2009, 28, Sec. 107.]

A specially empaneled statewide grand jury convened pursuant to this chapter shall sit for a period not to exceed 18 months. The superior court judge presiding over the grand jury may extend this period if, in accordance with section 1A of chapter 277 and section 41 of chapter 234A, public necessity requires further time by the grand jury to complete an on-going investigation.

Added by St.2009, c. 28, § 98, eff. Sept. 29, 2009.

§ 6. Prosecution of indictment by attorney general or assistant attorney general

[Text of section effective until December 31, 2014. Repealed by 2009, 28, Sec. 99. See 2009, 28, Sec. 107.]

The attorney general or an assistant attorney general shall attend each session of a statewide grand jury and may prosecute any indictment returned by it. The attorney general or assistant attorney general shall have the same powers and duties in relation to a statewide grand jury that she has in relation to a county grand jury, except as otherwise provided by law.

Added by St.2009, c. 28, § 98, eff. Sept. 29, 2009.

§ 7. County in which indictment to be returned; venue

[Text of section effective until December 31, 2014. Repealed by 2009, 28, Sec. 99. See 2009, 28, Sec. 107.]

Indictments shall be returned in the county where the statewide grand jury sits and shall thereafter be transferred to the county specified by the grand jury on the indictment. Venue for purposes of trial of offenses indicted by a statewide grand jury shall be in any county where venue would otherwise be proper.

Added by St.2009, c. 28, § 98, eff. Sept. 29, 2009.

§ 8. Effect on jurisdiction of county grand jury or district attorney

[Text of section effective until December 31, 2014. Repealed by 2009, 28, Sec. 99. See 2009, 28, Sec. 107.]

No provision of this chapter shall be construed as limiting the jurisdiction of county grand juries or district attorneys. Except as otherwise provided by law, an investigation by a statewide grand jury shall not preempt an investigation by any other grand jury or agency having jurisdiction over the same subject matter.

Added by St.2009, c. 28, § 98, eff. Sept. 29, 2009.

CHAPTER 278

TRIALS AND PROCEEDINGS BEFORE JUDGMENT

The section headings for the General Laws in this pamphlet have been editorially supplied.

§ 1. Trial list of criminal cases, adding cases to list

At each session of the superior court for criminal business, the district attorney, before trials begin, shall make and deposit with the clerk, for the inspection of parties, a list of all cases to be tried at that session, and the cases shall be tried in the order of such trial list, unless otherwise ordered by the court for cause shown. Cases may be added to such list by direction of the court, on its own motion or upon motion of the district attorney or of the defendant.

Amended by St.1974, c. 228.

Historical and Statutory Notes

St.1870, c. 290.
P.S.1882, c. 214, §§ 1, 2.
St.1884, c. 193.
St.1889, c. 432.
R.L.1902, c. 219, § 1.

§ 2. Trial of issues of fact

Issues of fact joined upon an indictment or complaint shall, in the superior court, be tried by a jury drawn and returned in the manner provided for the trial of issues of fact in civil causes, unless the person indicted or complained against elects to be tried by the court as provided by law.

Historical and Statutory Notes

R.S.1836, c. 137, § 1.
G.S.1860, c. 172, § 1.
P.S.1882, c. 214, § 3.
R.L.1902, c. 219, § 2.
St.1929, c. 185, § 2.

§§ 2A, 3. Repealed, 1979, 344, Sec. 43

Historical and Statutory Notes

See, now, Mass.R.Crim.P.Rule 20.

§ 4. Oaths of jurors

The following oath shall be administered to the jurors for the trial of all criminal cases which are not capital:

You shall well and truly try the issue between the commonwealth and the defendant, (or the defendants, as the case may be,) according to your evidence; so help you God.

The following oath shall be administered to the jurors for the trial of capital cases:

You shall well and truly try, and true deliverance make, between the commonwealth and the prisoner at the bar, whom you shall have in charge, according to your evidence; so help you God.

Historical and Statutory Notes

C.L. c. 167, § 3.
St.1692–3, c. 35.
St.1807, c. 140, § 14.
R.S.1836, c. 137, § 7.
G.S.1860, c. 172, § 6.
P.S.1882, c. 214, § 8.
R.L.1902, c. 219, § 4.

§ 5. Affirmation of jurors

A juror who is conscientiously scrupulous of taking either of the oaths above prescribed shall be allowed to affirm.

Historical and Statutory Notes

St.1807, c. 140, § 14.
R.S.1836, c. 137, § 8.
G.S.1860, c. 172, § 7.
P.S.1882, c. 214, § 9.
R.L.1902, c. 219, § 5.

§ 6. Repealed, 1979, 344, Sec. 43

Historical and Statutory Notes

See, now, Mass.R.Crim.P.Rule 18.

§ 6A. Testimony concerning ownership in cases involving motor vehicle theft or fraudulent claims; preservation of testimony

At the arraignment of a defendant charged with violating the provisions of sections twenty-seven A, twenty-eight, twenty-nine, one hundred and eleven A and one hundred and thirty-nine of chapter two hundred and sixty-six, the court shall, upon a showing of need by the commonwealth, and after granting adequate time to defense counsel to consult with the defendant, allow testimony from the owner or person in control of such vehicle, solely on the issue of ownership and unauthorized use, and such testimony shall be taken and preserved and shall be admissible at trial.

In the prosecution of a person charged with violating the provisions of sections twenty-seven A, twenty-eight, twenty-eight A, twenty-nine, one hundred and eleven A and one hundred and thirty-nine of chapter two hundred and sixty-six, the court shall order, as a condition of granting a continuance, that the testimony of a witness then present in court be taken and preserved for subsequent use at trial or any other proceeding. The witness shall be examined in open court by the party on whose behalf he is present and the adverse party shall have the right to cross-examination. The expenses of taking and preserving the testimony shall be assessed as costs against the party requesting the continuance.

Added by St.1980, c. 463, § 8.

§ 7. Burden to prove license or admission to practice as attorney at law

A defendant in a criminal prosecution, relying for his justification upon a license, appointment, admission to practice as an attorney at law, or authority, shall prove the same; and, until so proved, the presumption shall be that he is not so authorized.

Historical and Statutory Notes

St.1844, c. 102.
St.1859, c. 160.
G.S.1860, c. 172, § 10.
St.1864, c. 121.
P.S.1882, c. 214, § 12.
R.L.1902, c. 219, § 7.
St.1909, c. 49.

§ 8. Justification in libel cases

The defendant in a prosecution for writing or publishing a libel may introduce in evidence the truth of the matter contained in the publication charged as libellous, and the truth shall be a justification, unless actual malice is proved.

Historical and Statutory Notes

St.1826, c. 107, § 1.
R.S.1836, c. 133, § 6.
St.1855, c. 396.
G.S.1860, c. 129, § 77; c. 172, § 11.
P.S.1882, c. 167, § 80; c. 214, § 13.
R.L.1902, c. 219, § 8.

§ 8A. Killing or injuring a person unlawfully in a dwelling; defense

In the prosecution of a person who is an occupant of a dwelling charged with killing or injuring one who was unlawfully in said dwelling, it shall be a defense that the occupant was in his dwelling at the time of the offense and that he acted in the reasonable belief that the person unlawfully in said dwelling was about to inflict great bodily injury or death upon said occupant or upon another person lawfully in said dwelling, and that said occupant used reasonable means to defend himself or such other person lawfully in said dwelling. There shall be no duty on said occupant to retreat from such person unlawfully in said dwelling.

Added by St.1981, c. 696.

§ 9. Proof of ownership of property

In the prosecution of crimes which relate to or affect real or personal estate, it shall be sufficient, and shall not be a variance, if it is proved on the trial that, at the time when the crime was committed, either the actual or constructive possession or the general or special property in the whole or any part of such real or personal estate was in the person or community alleged to be the owner thereof.

Historical and Statutory Notes

R.S.1836, c. 133, § 11.
G.S.1860, c. 172, § 12.
P.S.1882, c. 214, § 14.
R.L.1902, c. 219, § 9.

§ 10. Night time; definition

If a crime is alleged to have been committed in the night time, night time shall be deemed the time between one hour after sunset on one day and one hour before sunrise on the next day; and the time of sunset and sunrise shall be ascertained according to mean time in the place where the crime was committed.

Historical and Statutory Notes

St.1847, c. 13.
G.S.1860, c. 172, § 13.
P.S.1882, c. 214, § 15.
R.L.1902, c. 219, § 10.

§ 11. Directed verdict; setting aside verdict, new trial or finding of guilty of included offense

If a motion for a directed verdict of not guilty is denied and the case is submitted to the jury and a verdict of guilty is returned, the judge may on a renewed motion for a directed verdict of not guilty pursuant to the Massachusetts Rules of Criminal Procedure set aside the verdict and order a new trial, or order the entry of a finding of guilty of any offense included in the offense charged in the indictment or complaint.

Amended by St.1963, c. 569; St.1964, c. 108, §§ 1, 2; St.1979, c. 344, § 43A.

Historical and Statutory Notes

St.1807, c. 139, § 15.
St.1855, c. 152.
G.S.1860, c. 172, § 15.
P.S.1882, c. 214, § 17.
R.L.1902, c. 219, § 13.

§ 11A. Habitual criminals; separate trial on issue of prior conviction

If a defendant is charged with a crime for which more severe punishment is provided for second and subsequent offenses, and the complaint or indictment alleges that the offense charged is a second or subsequent offense, the defendant on arraignment shall be inquired of only for a plea of guilty or not guilty to the crime charged, and that portion of the indictment or complaint that charges, or refers to a charge that, said crime is a second or subsequent offense shall not be read in open court. If such defendant pleads not guilty and is tried before a jury, no part of the complaint or indictment which alleges that the crime charged is a second or subsequent offense shall be read or shown to the jury or referred to in any manner during the trial; provided, however, that if a defendant takes the witness stand to testify, nothing herein contained shall prevent the impeachment of his credibility by evidence of any prior conviction, subject to the provisions of section twenty-one of chapter two hundred and thirty-three. If a defendant pleads guilty or if there is a verdict or finding of guilty after trial, then before sentence is imposed, the defendant shall be further inquired of for a plea of guilty or not guilty to that portion of the complaint or indictment alleging that the crime charged is a second or subsequent offense. If he pleads guilty thereto, sentence shall be imposed; if he pleads not guilty thereto, he shall be entitled to a trial by jury of the issue of conviction of a prior offense, subject to all of the provisions of law governing criminal trials. A defendant may waive trial by jury. The court may, in its discretion, either hold the jury which returned the verdict of guilty of the crime, the trial of which was just completed, or it may order the impanelling of a new jury to try the issue of conviction of one or more prior offenses. Upon the return of a verdict, after the separate trial of the issue of conviction of one or more prior offenses, the court shall impose the sentence appropriate to said verdict.

Added by St.1967, c. 213.

§ 12. Acquittal of part of crime and conviction of residue

If a person indicted for a felony is acquitted by the verdict of part of the crime charged, and is convicted of the residue, such verdict may be received and recorded by the court, and thereupon the defendant shall be adjudged guilty of the crime, if any, which appears to the court to be substantially charged by the residue of the indictment, and shall be sentenced and punished accordingly.

Historical and Statutory Notes

St.1784, c. 66, § 11.
St.1805, c. 88, § 2.
R.S.1836, c. 137, § 11.
G.S.1860, c. 172, § 16.
P.S.1882, c. 214, § 18.
R.L.1902, c. 219, § 14.

§ 13. Repealed, 1970, 888, Sec. 8

Historical and Statutory Notes

See c. 123, § 16.

§ 14. Liability for fees of person acquitted

No prisoner or person under recognizance, acquitted by verdict or discharged because no indictment has been found against him, or for want of prosecution, shall be liable for any costs or fees or for any charge for subsistence while he was in custody.

Historical and Statutory Notes

R.S.1836, c. 137, § 13.
G.S.1860, c. 172, § 18.
P.S.1882, c. 214, § 22.
R.L.1902, c. 219, § 18.

§ 15. Discontinuance of prosecution under by-laws, ordinances, etc.

In a prosecution before a district court under the by-laws, ordinances, orders, rules or regulations of a city or town, the city solicitor, town counsel or other person appointed to represent such city or town may enter a nolle prosequi or do anything relative to such prosecution which may be done by the district attorney.

Amended by St.1955, c. 131, § 7.

Historical and Statutory Notes

St.1853, c. 179, § 2.
G.S.1860, c. 172, § 20.
P.S.1882, c. 214, § 23.
R.L.1902, c. 219, § 19.
St.1918, c. 257, § 461.
St.1919, c. 5.
St.1920, c. 2.

§ 16. Assignment of counsel for inmates of institutions for reformation of juvenile offenders

The court may assign counsel to an inmate of any institution for the reformation of juvenile offenders who is to be tried for an offence alleged to have been committed therein; and shall, upon application, order the superintendent or other officer of such institution to produce at the trial such inmates thereof as, in the opinion of the counsel for the defence, certified in writing, or of the judge, in the absence of counsel, are material witnesses for the defence; and such officer shall obey the order and provide for the custody and safe return of such inmates.

Historical and Statutory Notes

St.1877, c. 184.
P.S.1882, c. 214, § 24.
R.L.1902, c. 219, § 20.

§ 16A. Exclusion of public from trial for sex offenses involving minors under age of eighteen

At the trial of a complaint or indictment for rape, incest, carnal abuse or other crime involving sex, where a minor under eighteen years of age is the person upon, with or against whom the crime is alleged to have been committed, or at the trial of a complaint or indictment for getting a woman with child out of wedlock, or for the non-support of a child born out of wedlock, the presiding justice shall exclude the general public from the court room, admitting only such persons as may have a direct interest in the case.

Amended by St.1986, c. 334, § 16.

Historical and Statutory Notes

St.1923, c. 251.
St.1931, c. 205.

§ 16B. Exclusion of public from trial of criminal proceeding involving husband and wife

The presiding justice of a district court may exclude the general public from the court room during the trial of any criminal proceeding involving husband and wife.

Added by St.1949, c. 302.

§ 16C. Exclusion of public from trial involving crime of incest or rape

To protect the parties involved at a trial arising from a complaint or indictment for incest or rape, the trial judge may exclude all spectators from the courtroom in which such trial is being held, or from said courtroom during those portions of such trial when direct testimony is to be presented; provided, that either of the parties requests that all spectators be so excluded at the trial or portions thereof; and provided further, that the defendant in such trial by a written statement waives his right to a public trial for those portions from which spectators are so excluded.

Added by St.1978, c. 316.

§ 16D. Child witness testimony; videotaping or transmission by simultaneous electronic means in certain cases

(a) For the purposes of this section, the following words shall have the following meanings:—

"Child witness", a person who is under the age of fifteen years and who is alleged to have been a victim of, or a witness to an alleged violation of section thirteen B, 13B½, 13B¾, thirteen F, thirteen H, twenty-two, twenty-two A, 22B, 22C, twenty-three, 23A, 23B, twenty-four or twenty-four B of chapter two hundred and sixty-five, or section two, three, four, four A, four B, five, six, seven, eight, twelve, thirteen, sixteen, seventeen, twenty-four, twenty-eight, twenty-nine, twenty-nine A, twenty-nine B, thirty-three, thirty-four or thirty-five A of chapter two hundred and seventy-two.

"Simultaneous electronic means", Any device capable of projecting a live visual and aural transmission such as closed-circuit television.

(b)(1) At any time after the issuance of a complaint or indictment alleging an offense punished by any of the statutes listed herein, the court on its own motion or on motion of the proponent of a child witness, and after a hearing, may order the use of a suitable alternative procedure for taking the testimony of the child witness, in proceedings pursuant to said complaint or indictment, provided that the court finds by a preponderance of the evidence at the time of the order that the child witness is likely to suffer psychological or emotional trauma as a result of testifying in open court, as a result of testifying in the presence of the defendant, or as a result of both testifying in open court and testifying in the presence of the defendant. If the court orders the use of a suitable alternative for taking the testimony of a child witness pursuant to this section, the court shall make and enter specific findings upon the record describing with particularity the reasons for such order.

(2) An order issued under paragraph (1) shall provide that the testimony of the child witness be recorded on videotape or film to be shown in court at a later time or that the testimony be transmitted to the courtroom by simultaneous electronic means.

(3) Testimony taken by an alternative procedure pursuant to an order issued under paragraph (1) shall be taken in the presence of the judge, the prosecutor, defense counsel and such other persons as the court may allow. The defendant shall also have the right to be present unless the court's order under paragraph (1) is based wholly or in part upon a finding that the child witness is likely to suffer trauma as a result of testifying in the presence of the defendant. If the order is based on such a finding, the testimony of the child witness shall not be taken in the presence of the defendant except as provided in paragraph (4).

(4) Testimony taken by an alternative procedure pursuant to an order issued under paragraph (1) shall be taken in a suitable setting outside the courtroom, except that an order based only on a finding that the child witness is likely to suffer trauma as a result of testifying in the presence of the defendant may provide that the testimony be taken in a suitable setting inside the courtroom in a manner so that the child witness is not able to see or hear the defendant.

(5) When testimony is taken by an alternative procedure pursuant to an order issued under paragraph (1), counsel shall be given the opportunity to examine or cross-examine the child witness to the same extent as would be permitted at trial, and the defendant shall be able to see and hear the child witness and to have constant private communication with defense counsel.

(6) The film, videotape or transmission of testimony taken by an alternative procedure pursuant to an order issued under paragraph (1) shall be admissible as substantive evidence to the same extent as and in lieu of live testimony by the child witness in any proceeding for which the order is issued or in any related criminal proceeding against the same defendant when consistent with the interests of justice, provided that such an order is entered or re-entered based on current findings at the time when or within a reasonable time before the film, videotape or transmission is offered into evidence. Subsequent testimony of a child witness in any such proceeding shall also be taken by a suitable alternative procedure pursuant to this section.

(7) Whenever pursuant to an order issued under paragraph (1), testimony is recorded on videotape or film or is transmitted to the courtroom by simultaneous electronic means, the court shall ensure that:

(a) The recording or transmitting equipment is capable of making an accurate recording or transmission and is operated by a competent operator;

(b) The recording or transmission is in color and the witness is visible at all times;

(c) Every voice on the recording or transmission is audible and identified;

(d) The courtroom is equipped with monitors which permit the jury and others present in the courtroom to see and hear the recording or transmission;

(e) In the case of recorded testimony, the recording is accurate and has not been altered;

(f) In the case of recorded testimony, each party is afforded the opportunity to view the recording before it is shown in the courtroom.

(8) Nothing in this section shall be deemed to prohibit the court from using other appropriate means, consistent with this section and other laws and with the defendant's rights, to protect a child witness from trauma during a court proceeding.

Added by St.1985, c. 682. Amended by St.1986, c. 557, § 203; St.2010, c. 267, §§ 72 to 74, eff. Nov. 5, 2010.

§ 16E. Repealed, 1994, 352, Sec. 2

Historical and Statutory Notes

See, now, c. 233, § 23E.

§ 16F. Expedited trials of sex crimes involving minor children as victims or witnesses; continuance; impact statement

In any criminal proceeding involving an alleged sex crime perpetrated upon a minor child, or in which a minor child is expected to testify as a witness to a sex crime, the court shall, in order to minimize stress on such child, take action to expedite trial and give precedence to the case over any other case; provided, however, that nothing in this section shall be construed to mean that trial shall be expedited if it is not in the best interests of the child.

When a motion or a request for a continuance is made the prosecutor shall file an impact statement which specifies whether the commonwealth agrees to the request for continuance, whether the child or the child's representative agrees to such request, and the effect, if any, the granting of the continuance will have on the child. In ruling on any motion or request for continuance or other delay, the court shall consider and give weight to any possible adverse impact that a delay or continuance may have on the child. Prior to issuing an order on a motion for continuance or delay, the court shall make written findings of fact concerning the impact on the child of continuing or delaying the case.

Added by St.1996, c. 86.

§ 17. Repealed, 1979, 344, Sec. 43B

Historical and Statutory Notes

See c. 277, § 47A and Mass.R.Crim.P. Rule 13.

§ 18. Pleas of not guilty, guilty or nolo contendere; requests for specific disposition; pretrial motions

A defendant who is before the Boston municipal court or a district court or a district court sitting in a juvenile session or a juvenile court on a criminal offense within the court's final jurisdiction shall plead not guilty or guilty, or with the consent of the court, nolo contendere. Such plea of guilty shall be submitted by the defendant and acted upon by the court; provided, however, that a defendant with whom the commonwealth cannot reach agreement for a recommended disposition shall be allowed to tender a plea of guilty together with a request for a specific disposition. Such request may include any disposition or dispositional terms within the court's jurisdiction, including, unless otherwise prohibited by law, a dispositional request that a guilty finding not be entered, but rather the case be continued without a finding to a specific date thereupon to be dismissed, such continuance conditioned upon compliance with specific terms and conditions or that the defendant be placed on probation pursuant to the provisions of section eighty-seven of chapter two hundred and seventy-six. If such a plea, with an agreed upon recommendation or with a dispositional request by the defendant, is tendered, the court shall inform the defendant that it will not impose a disposition that exceeds the terms of the agreed upon recommendation or the dispositional request by the defendant, whichever is applicable, without giving the defendant the right to withdraw the plea.

If a defendant, notwithstanding the requirements set forth hereinbefore, attempts to enter a plea or statement consisting of an admission of facts sufficient for finding of guilt, or some similar statement, such admission shall be deemed a tender of a plea of guilty for purposes of the procedures set forth in this section.

Any pretrial motion filed in a criminal case pending in the Boston municipal court or district court or a district court sitting in a juvenile session or a juvenile court and decided before entry of defendant's decision on waiver of the right to jury trial shall not be refiled or reheard thereafter, except in the discretion of the court as substantial justice requires. Any such pretrial motion not filed or filed but not decided prior to entry of the defendant's decision on waiver of the right to jury trial may be filed thereafter but not later than twenty-one days after entry of said decision on waiver of the right to jury trial, except for good cause shown.

Amended by St.1955, c. 131, § 8; St.1973, c. 657; St.1974, c. 167; St.1978, c. 478, § 302; St.1992, c. 379, § 193; St.1996, c. 200, § 37.

Historical and Statutory Notes

St.1783, c. 51, § 3.
St.1831, c. 70, § 1.
R.S.1836, c. 85, § 28; c. 87, § 36; c. 138, § 1.
St.1845, c. 166, § 2.
St.1849, c. 31.
G.S.1860, c. 116, § 32; c. 173, §§ 1, 4.
P.S.1882, c. 154, § 39; c. 155, §§ 58, 61.
St.1893, c. 396, § 47.
St.1894, c. 431.
St.1897, c. 490, § 3.
R.L.1902, c. 219, § 22.
St.1905, c. 319.
St.1913, c. 652.
St.1929, c. 216, § 4.

§ 18A. Repealed, 1978, 478, Sec. 303

§§ 19, 20. Repealed, 1992, 379, Sec. 194

§ 21. Repealed, 1955, 131, Sec. 10

§ 22. Repealed, 1992, 379, Sec. 194

§ 23. Certain acts or omissions by defendant not admissible against him in criminal trial

At the trial of a criminal case in the superior court, upon indictment, or in a district court, the fact that the defendant did not testify at any preliminary hearing in the first court, or that at such hearing he waived examination or did not offer any evidence in his own defense, shall not be used as evidence against him, nor be referred to or commented upon by the prosecuting officer.

Amended by St.1978, c. 478, § 305; St.1992, c. 379, § 195.

Historical and Statutory Notes

St.1912, c. 325.

§§ 24 to 26. Repealed, 1992, 379, Sec. 196

§ 27. Repealed, 1979, 344, Sec. 43B

Historical and Statutory Notes

See c. 279, § 28E and Mass.R.Crim.P.Rule 15.

§ 28. Appeal to supreme judicial court

A defendant aggrieved by a judgment of the district court or of the superior court in any criminal proceeding may appeal therefrom to the supreme judicial court.

Amended by St.1979, c. 344, § 44; St.1992, c. 379, § 197.

Historical and Statutory Notes

St.1820, c. 79, § 4.

St.1832, c. 130, § 3.
R.S.1836, c. 82, § 28; c. 138, § 5.
St.1859, c. 196, § 26.
G.S.1860, c. 114, § 10.
P.S.1882, c. 152, § 10.
R.L.1902, c. 219, § 32.

§ 28A. Appellate division of superior court for review of sentences

There shall be an appellate division of the superior court for the review of sentences to the state prison imposed by final judgments in criminal cases, except in any case in which a different sentence could not have been imposed, and for the review of sentences to the reformatory for women for terms of more than five years imposed by final judgments in such criminal cases. Said appellate division shall consist of three justices of the superior court to be designated from time to time by the chief justice of said court and shall sit in Boston or at a Massachusetts correctional institution or at such other place as may be designated by the chief justice and at such times as he shall determine. No justice shall sit or act on an appeal from a sentence imposed by him. Two justices shall constitute a quorum to decide all matters before the appellate division.

A designation by the chief justice of the members of the appellate division shall be recorded by the clerk of the appellate division who shall forthwith send copies thereof to the several clerks of the superior court.

The clerk of the superior court for criminal business in Suffolk county shall be the clerk of the appellate division of the superior court. The first assistant clerk of superior court for criminal business in Suffolk county shall be the first assistant clerk of the appellate division of the superior court; the second assistant clerk of the superior court for criminal business in Suffolk county shall be the second assistant clerk of the appellate division of the superior court.

The clerk or an assistant clerk of the appellate division of the superior court shall attend all sittings of the appellate division wherever such sittings are held and shall record the proceedings thereof. The clerk shall have the care and custody of all records, books and papers which pertain to said appellate division. The clerk and the assistant clerks of the appellate division shall have all the power and authority of a clerk of courts in any county of the commonwealth in any and all matters pertaining to the appellate division or to any criminal case in which an appeal for a review of a sentence imposed in any county has been filed.

Added by St.1943, c. 558, § 1. Amended by St.1945, c. 255, § 1; St.1968, c. 666, § 1; St.1978, c. 478, § 306.

§ 28B. Right of appeal to appellate division; time limit; stay of execution of sentence; jurisdiction; review of judgment, etc.; disposition

A person aggrieved by a sentence which may be reviewed may appeal to the appellate division for a review of such sentence. Upon the imposition of a sentence which may be reviewed, the clerk of the court shall notify the person sentenced of his right to appeal. The appeal shall be filed with the clerk of the court for the county where the judgment was rendered within ten days after the imposition of said sentence. An appeal shall not stay the execution of a sentence. The clerk of the court shall notify the chief justice, the justice who imposed the sentence and the clerk of the appellate division of the filing of an appeal. The justice who imposed the sentence appealed from may transmit to the appellate division a statement of his reasons for imposing the sentence and shall make such a statement within seven days if requested to do so by the appellate division.

The appellate division shall have jurisdiction to consider an appeal with or without a hearing, review the judgment so far as it relates to the sentence imposed and also any other sentence imposed when the sentence appealed from was imposed, notwithstanding the partial execution of any such sentence, and shall have jurisdiction to amend the judgment by ordering substituted therefor a different appropriate sentence or sentences or any other disposition of the case which could have been made at the time of the imposition of the sentence or sentences under review, but no sentence shall be increased without giving the defendant an opportunity to be heard. If the appellate division decides that the original sentence or sentences should stand, it shall dismiss the appeal. Its decision shall be final. The clerk of the appellate division shall forthwith notify the appellant, the superintendent of the correctional institution in which the appellant is confined, the clerk of the court in which judgment was rendered, the justice who imposed the sentence appealed from and the chief justice of the final action of the appellate division on an appeal. The appellate division may require the production of any records, documents, exhibits or other things connected with the proceedings. The superior court shall by rule establish forms for appeals hereunder and may by rule make such other regulations of procedure relative thereto, consistent with law, as justice may require.

Added by St.1943, c. 558, § 1. Amended by St.1945, c. 255, § 2; St.1968, c. 666, § 2.

§ 28C. Amendment of judgment; resentencing or other disposition

If the judgment is amended by an order substituting a different sentence or sentences or disposition of the case, the appellate division or any member thereof shall resentence the defendant or make any other disposition of the case in accordance with the order of said appellate division. Time served on a sentence appealed from shall be deemed to have been served on a substituted sentence.

Added by St.1943, c. 558, § 1. Amended by St.1945, c. 255, § 3; St.1955, c. 770, § 91; St.1957, c. 777, § 36; St.1968, c. 666, § 3.

§ 28D. Repealed, 2007, 61, Sec. 31

§ 28D½. Salary of clerk of appellate division

The clerk of the appellate division shall receive from the commonwealth as salary an amount equal to 10 per cent of, and in addition to, the salary established and paid to said clerk of the superior court for criminal business in the county of Suffolk.

Added by St.2008, c. 182, § 75, eff. July 1, 2008.

§ 28E. Appeals by commonwealth

An appeal may be taken by and on behalf of the commonwealth by the attorney general or a district attorney from the district court to the appeals court in all criminal cases and in all delinquency cases from a decision, order or judgment of the court (1) allowing a motion to dismiss an indictment or complaint, (2) allowing a motion to suppress evidence, or (3) denying a motion to transfer pursuant to section sixty-one of chapter one hundred and nineteen.

An appeal may be taken by and on behalf of the commonwealth by the attorney general or a district attorney from the superior court to the supreme judicial court in all criminal cases from a decision, order or judgment of the court (1) allowing a motion to dismiss an indictment or complaint, or (2) allowing a motion for appropriate relief under the Massachusetts Rules of Criminal Procedure.

An application for an appeal from a decision, order or judgment of the superior court determining a motion to suppress evidence prior to trial may be filed in the supreme judicial court by a defendant or by and on behalf of the commonwealth by the attorney general or a district attorney. If such application is denied, or if such application is granted but the interlocutory appeal is heard by a single justice, the determination of the motion to suppress evidence shall be open to review by the full court after trial in the same manner and to the same extent as determinations of such motions not appealed under the interlocutory procedure herein authorized.

Rules of practice and procedure with respect to appeals authorized by this section shall be the same as those applicable to criminal appeals under the Massachusetts Rules of Appellate Procedure.

Added by St.1967, c. 898, § 1. Amended by St.1972, c. 740, § 16; St.1979, c. 344, § 45; St.1991, c. 488, §§ 11, 12.

§§ 29, 29A. Repealed, 1979, 344, Sec. 46

Historical and Statutory Notes

See Mass.R.Crim.P. Rules 29, 30.

§ 29B. Withdrawal of uncounseled guilty plea

If a defendant having a right to counsel in a criminal proceeding has not been represented by counsel or has not properly waived his right to counsel and has entered a plea of guilty, such defendant may withdraw such plea as a matter of right at any time prior to imposition of sentence by the court.

Added by St.1962, c. 262, § 1. Amended by St.1979, c. 344, § 47.

§ 29C. Repealed, 1979, 344, Sec. 48

Historical and Statutory Notes

See Mass.R.Crim.P.Rule 29.

§ 29D. Conviction upon plea of guilty, nolo contendere or an admission to sufficient facts; motion to vacate

The court shall not accept a plea of guilty, a plea of nolo contendere, or an admission to sufficient facts from any defendant in any criminal proceeding unless the court advises such defendant of the following: "If you are not a citizen of the United States, you are hereby advised that the acceptance by this court of your plea of guilty, plea of nolo contendere, or admission to sufficient facts may have consequences of deportation, exclusion from admission to the United States, or denial of naturalization, pursuant to the laws of the United States." The court shall advise such defendant during every plea colloquy at which the defendant is proffering a plea of guilty, a plea of nolo contendere, or an admission to sufficient facts. The defendant shall not be required at the time of the plea to disclose to the court his legal status in the United States.

If the court fails so to advise the defendant, and he later at any time shows that his plea and conviction may have or has had one of the enumerated consequences, even if the defendant has already been deported from the United States, the court, on the defendant's motion, shall vacate the judgment, and permit the defendant to withdraw the plea of guilty, plea of nolo contendere, or admission of sufficient facts, and enter a plea of not guilty. Absent an official record or a contemporaneously written record kept in the court file that the court provided the advisement as prescribed in this section, including but not limited to a docket sheet that accurately reflects that the warning was given as required by this section, the defendant shall be presumed not to have received advisement. An advisement previously or subsequently provided the defendant during another plea colloquy shall not satisfy the advisement required by this section, nor shall it be used to presume the defendant understood the plea of guilty, or admission to sufficient facts he seeks to vacate would have the consequence of deportation, exclusion from admission to the United States, or denial of naturalization.

Added by St.1978, c. 383. Amended by St.1996, c. 450, § 254; St.2004, c. 225, § 1, eff. Oct. 27, 2004.

§§ 30 to 31C. Repealed, 1979, 344, Sec. 48

Historical and Statutory Notes

See Mass.R.Crim.P.Rules 22, 28, 31, 34.

§§ 32 to 33D. Repealed, 1979, 346, Sec. 1

§ 33E. Capital cases; review by supreme judicial court

In a capital case as hereinafter defined the entry in the supreme judicial court shall transfer to that court the whole case for its consideration of the law and the evidence. Upon such consideration the court may, if satisfied that the verdict was against the law or the weight of the evidence, or because of newly discovered evidence, or for any other reason that justice may require (a) order a new trial or (b) direct the entry of a verdict of a lesser degree of guilt, and remand the case to the superior court for the imposition of sentence. For the purpose of such review a capital case shall mean a case in which the defendant was tried on an indictment for murder in the first degree and was convicted of murder in the first degree. After the entry of the appeal in a capital case and until the filing of the rescript by the supreme judicial court motions for a new trial shall be presented to that court and shall be dealt with by the full court, which may itself hear and determine such motions or remit the same to the trial judge for hearing and determination. If any motion is filed in the superior court after rescript, no appeal shall lie from the decision of that court upon such motion unless the appeal is allowed by a single justice of the supreme judicial court on the ground that it presents a new and substantial question which ought to be determined by the full court.

Amended by St.1939, c. 341; St.1962, c. 453; St.1974, c. 457; St.1979, c. 346, § 2.

Historical and Statutory Notes

St.1925, c. 279, § 1.
St.1 926, c. 329, § 4.

§§ 33F to 33H. Repealed, 1979, 346, Sec. 3

Historical and Statutory Notes

See Mass.R.App.P. Rules 8, 9, 10, 14, and 16 to 20.

§ 34. Motions in arrest of judgment

No motion in arrest of judgment shall be allowed for a cause existing before verdict, unless it affects the jurisdiction of the court.

Historical and Statutory Notes

St.1864, c. 250, § 3.
P.S.1882, c. 214, § 27.
R.L.1902, c. 219, § 38.

§ 35. Trial of male and female prisoners

In all trials in district courts, male and female prisoners shall not be placed at the same time in the same dock, unless they are complained of jointly.

Historical and Statutory Notes

St.1904, c. 218.

CHAPTER 279

JUDGMENT AND EXECUTION

The section headings for the General Laws in this pamphlet have been editorially supplied.

§ 1. Suspension of execution; payment of fine; probation; revocation of suspension; exceptions

When a person convicted before a court is sentenced to imprisonment, the court may direct that the execution of the sentence, or any part thereof, be suspended and that he be placed on probation for such time and on such terms and conditions as it shall fix. When a person so convicted is sentenced to pay a fine and to stand committed until it is paid, the court may direct that the execution of the sentence, or any part thereof, be suspended for such time as it shall fix and in its discretion that he be placed on probation on condition that he pay the fine within such time. If the fine does not exceed two hundred dollars and the court finds that the defendant is unable to pay it when imposed, the execution of the sentence shall be suspended and he may in its discretion be placed on probation, unless the court shall find that he will probably default, or that such suspension will be detrimental to the interests of the public. If he is committed for nonpayment of a fine, the order of commitment shall contain a recital of the findings of the court on which suspension is refused. The fine shall be paid in one payment, or in part payments, to the probation officer, and when fully paid the order of commitment shall be void. The probation officer shall give a receipt for every payment so made, shall keep a record of the same, shall pay the fine, or all sums received in part payment thereof, to the sheriff if such fine is imposed in the superior court, or to the clerk of the court if such fine is imposed in the district court, at the end of the period of probation or any extension thereof, and shall keep on file the sheriff's or clerk's receipt therefor. If during or at the end of said period the probation officer shall report that the fine is in whole or in part unpaid, and in his opinion the person is unwilling or unable to pay it, the court may either extend said period, place the case on file or revoke the suspension of the execution of the sentence. When such suspension is revoked, in a case where the fine has been paid in part, the defendant may be committed for default in payment of the balance.

The provisions of this section shall not permit the suspension of the execution of the sentence of a person convicted of a crime punishable by death or imprisonment for life. In granting probation under this section, the court shall include in its terms and conditions of probation that the person convicted shall pay any child support due under a support order, as defined in section 1A of chapter 119A, including payment toward any arrearage of support that accrues or has accrued or compliance with any payment plan between the person convicted and the IV–D agency as set forth in said chapter 119A.

When a person is sentenced by a court upon conviction of any crime, he shall be informed by the probation department on a form provided by the department of criminal justice information services that he will have a criminal record that may be accessible to the public under certain conditions, and of his rights pertaining thereto, as provided in sections one hundred and sixty-seven through one hundred and seventy-eight of chapter six.

Amended by St.1934, c. 205, § 1; St.1935, c. 358, § 1; St.1936, c. 434, § 2; St.1938, c. 354; St.1939, c. 299, § 5; St.1966, c. 292; St.1967, c. 333; St.1975, c. 347; St.1989, c. 207; St.1990, c. 319, § 18; St.1998, c. 64, § 289; St.2010, c. 256, § 134, eff. Nov. 4, 2010.

Historical and Statutory Notes

St.1900, c. 449, § 1.
R.L.1902, c. 220, § 1.
St.1905, c. 338.
St.1912, c. 154.
St.1913, c. 653.
St.1924, c. 175, § 1.
St.1925, c. 297, § 2.
St.1926, c. 271, § 2.
St.1926, c. 296.

§ 1A. Suspension of execution of sentence; probation; child support payments

When a person convicted before a court is sentenced to fine and imprisonment, the court may direct that the execution of the sentence, or any part thereof, be suspended, and that he be placed on probation for such time and on such terms and conditions as it shall fix. The court may direct, as one of such terms and conditions, that payment of the fine may be made to the probation officer in one payment, or in part payments, during the period of probation or any extension thereof, and when such fine shall have been fully paid the order of commitment as to the fine shall be void, but the order of commitment as to imprisonment shall not be affected by such payment. The probation officer shall give a receipt for every payment so made, shall keep a record of the same, shall pay the fine, or all sums received in part payment thereof, to the clerk of the court at the end of the period of probation or any extension thereof, and shall keep on file the clerk's receipt therefor. If during or at the end of said period the probation officer shall report that the fine is in whole or in part unpaid, and in his opinion the person is unwilling or unable to pay it, the court may either extend said period, place the case on file or revoke the suspension of the execution of the sentence. When such suspension is revoked, in a case where the fine has been paid in part, the defendant may be committed for default in payment of the balance, and may also be committed for the term of imprisonment fixed in the original sentence. This section shall not permit the suspension of the execution of the sentence of any person convicted of a crime punishable by imprisonment for life or of a crime an element of which is being armed with a dangerous weapon, or of any person convicted of any other felony if it shall appear that he has been previously convicted of any felony. In granting probation under this section, the court shall include in its terms and conditions of probation that the person convicted shall pay any child support due under a support order, as defined in section 1A of chapter 119A, including payment toward any arrearage of support that accrues or has accrued or compliance with any payment plan between the person convicted and the IV–D agency as set forth in said chapter 119A.

Amended by St.1934, c. 205, § 2; St.1975, c. 459, §§ 1, 2; St.1978, c. 478, § 309; St.1992, c. 379, § 198; St.1998, c. 64, § 290.

Historical and Statutory Notes

St.1924, c. 175, § 2.
St.1926, c. 271, § 3.
St.1926, c. 296.

§ 1B. Funds collection and disbursement; single point for clerk-magistrate and probation offices

Notwithstanding any other provision of law, the administrative justice of a department of the trial court may direct that both the clerk-magistrate's office and the probation office of one or more court divisions are to utilize a single funds collection and disbursement point within the courthouse.

Added by St.1992, c. 133, § 570.

§ 2. Suspension of execution of orders of commitment to Massachusetts reformatory, etc.

In all cases the execution of orders of commitment to any training school or reformatory, however named, the department of youth services, or the department of public welfare may be suspended, and such suspension continued or revoked, in the same manner and with the same effect as the execution of sentences in criminal cases.

Amended by St.1949, c. 584; St.1969, c. 838, § 64.

Historical and Statutory Notes

St.1908, c. 103.
St.1913, c. 471, § 2.
St.1919, c. 350, § 87.
St.1931, c. 426, § 48.

§ 3. Arrest without warrant of person on probation; notice of surrender; surrender hearing; warrant for arrest of persons already imprisoned; application for disposition; temporary custody

At any time before final disposition of the case of a person placed under probation supervision or in the custody or care of a probation officer, the probation officer may arrest him without a warrant and take him before the court, or the court may issue a warrant for his arrest. When taken before the court, it may, if he has not been sentenced, sentence him or make any other lawful disposition of the case, and if he has been sentenced, it may continue or revoke the suspension of the execution of his sentence; provided however, that in all cases where the probationer is served with notice of surrender and at least one of the underlying crimes for which he is on probation is a felony, then the probation officer shall provide a duplicate copy of the notice of surrender to the district attorney, and the court shall provide to the district attorney the opportunity to be heard and present evidence at the surrender hearing. If such suspension is revoked, the sentence shall be in full force and effect. If a warrant has been issued by the court for the arrest of such a person and he is a prisoner in any correctional institution, jail or house of correction, the commissioner of correction, the sheriff, master or keeper of said house of correction, or in Suffolk county, the penal institutions commissioner of the city of Boston, as the case may be, having such prisoner under his supervision or control, upon receiving notice of such warrant, shall notify such prisoner that he has the right to apply to the court for prompt disposition thereof. Such an application shall be in writing and given or sent by such prisoner to the commissioner of correction, or such sheriff, master, keeper, or penal institutions commissioner, who shall promptly forward it to the court from which the warrant issued, by certified mail, together with a certificate of said commissioner of correction, sheriff, master, keeper, or penal institutions commissioner, stating (a) the term of commitment under which such prisoner is being held, (b) the amount of time served, (c) the amount of time remaining to be served, (d) the amount of good time earned, (e) the time of parole eligibility of such prisoner, and (f) any decisions of the board of parole relating to such prisoner. Said commissioner of correction, sheriff, master, keeper, or penal institutions commissioner shall notify the appropriate district attorney by certified mail of such application to the court. Any such prisoner shall, within six months after such application is received by the court, be brought into court for sentencing or other lawful disposition of his case as hereinbefore provided.

In no case where a provision of this chapter provides for a finding, disposition or other order to be made by the court, or for a warrant to be issued, shall such be made or issued by any person other than a justice, special justice or other person exercising the powers of a magistrate.

Notwithstanding any restriction in the preceding paragraph, if a probation officer has probable cause to believe that a person placed under probation supervision or in the custody or care of a probation officer pursuant to sections 42A, 58A or 87 of chapter 276 or any other statute that allows the court to set conditions of release, has violated the conditions set by the court, the probation officer may arrest the probationer or may issue a warrant for the temporary custody of the probationer for a period not to exceed 72 hours or until the next sitting of the court, during which period the probation officer shall arrange for the appearance of the probationer before the court pursuant to the first paragraph of this section. Such warrant shall constitute sufficient authority to a probation officer and to the superintendent, jailer, or any other person in charge of any jail, house of correction, lockup, or place of detention to whom it is exhibited, to hold in temporary custody the probationer detained pursuant thereto.

Amended by St.1972, c. 251; St.1974, c. 300; St.1978, c. 478, § 310; St.1996, c. 151, § 498; St.1997, c. 43, § 147; St.2004, c. 65, § 27, eff. April 5, 2004.

Historical and Statutory Notes

St.1897, c. 236.
St.1900, c. 449, § 2.
R.L.1902, c. 220, § 2.
St.1926, c. 266.
St.1926, c. 296.
St.1927, c. 140, § 1.

§ 3A. Motion of district attorney for sentence

Not later than seven days after a plea of guilty or after a verdict of guilty and in any event before adjournment of the sitting at which such plea or verdict has been taken and recorded in a case of felony wherein no question of law has been reported for decision by the supreme judicial court, the district attorney shall move for sentence; provided, that nothing herein shall preclude the district attorney from again making such a motion in any case where the imposition of sentence is delayed under section forty-seven.

Amended by St.1935, c. 50, § 2; St.1935, c. 437, § 2.

Historical and Statutory Notes

St.1926, c. 245.
St.1926, c. 296.

§ 4. Imposition of sentence; stay of execution

Sentence shall be imposed upon conviction of a crime, regardless of whether an appeal has been taken, except as otherwise provided in section sixty-one in case of a conviction of a capital crime.

If sentence is imposed upon conviction of a crime punishable by death, the justice imposing the sentence shall at the same time stay the execution of the sentence, such stay to be effective until revoked by the superior court department of the trial court, which is hereby granted full powers of revocation in the premises. The clerk of such court shall, forthwith upon the revocation by the court of any such stay of execution of sentence, certify that said stay has been revoked and cause said certificate to be served upon the superintendent of the state prison, or the officer performing his duties, by any officer qualified to serve criminal process; and the officer serving the same shall forthwith make due return of service to the clerk.

Amended by St.1935, c. 50, § 3; St.1935, c. 437, § 3; St.1955, c. 770, § 92; St.1957, c. 777, § 37; St.1966, c. 678; St.1972, c. 740, § 17; St.1979, c. 344, § 49; St.1982, c. 554, § 4.

Historical and Statutory Notes

St.1891, c. 362.
St.1895, c. 469.
R.L.1902, c. 220, § 3.

§ 4A. Repealed, 1979, 344, Sec. 50

Historical and Statutory Notes

See Mass.R.Crim.P.Rule 28.

§ 4B. Notice to victim of sentencing proceedings; oral or written statements

Before disposition in any case where a defendant has been found guilty of any felony or any crime against the person or crime where physical injury to a person results, excluding any crime for which a sentence of death may be imposed, and which involves an identified victim whose whereabouts are known, the district attorney shall give the victim actual notice of the time and place of sentencing and of the victim's right to make a statement to the court, orally or in writing at the victim's option, as to the impact of the crime and as to a recommended sentence. Before disposition, the court shall allow any victim who elects to make such an oral statement the opportunity to do so in the presence of the defendant. Before disposition, the district attorney shall file any such written statement with the court and shall make it available to the defendant.

If the victim is unable to make an oral or written statement because of his mental, emotional, or physical incapacity or his age, his attorney or a designated family member shall be provided the notice and the opportunity to make a statement prescribed in this paragraph.

Before said disposition the office of the district attorney shall cause to be prepared a written statement as to the impact of the crime on the victim, which shall be filed with the court as part of the presentence report and made available to the defendant. The statement shall include the following: (1) the name of the victim; (2) documentation of the net financial loss, if any, suffered by the victim or a family member as a result of the crime; (3) in cases where the crime has had an impact on the victim's personal welfare or family relationship or has had a psychological impact on the victim or his family, a statement of such impact.

The court shall allow the defendant to have the opportunity to rebut the victim's oral or written statement and the district attorney's written statement if the court decides to rely upon such statements or parts thereof in imposing sentence.

No sentence shall be invalidated because of failure to comply with the provisions of this section. This section shall not be construed to create any cause of action or any right of appeal on behalf of any person.

Added by St.1983, c. 694, § 3. Amended by St.1995, c. 24, § 7.

§ 5. Sentence if no punishment is provided by statute

If no punishment for a crime is provided by statute, the court shall impose such sentence, according to the nature of the crime, as conforms to the common usage and practice in the commonwealth. If a person is convicted of a misdemeanor punishable by imprisonment, he may, unless otherwise expressly provided, be sentenced to imprisonment either in the jail or in the house of correction.

Historical and Statutory Notes

St.1782, c. 9, § 1.
R.S.1836, c. 139, § 1.
G.S.1860, c. 174, § 1.
P.S.1882, c. 215, § 1.
R.L.1902, c. 220, § 4.
St.1902, c. 544, § 34.

§ 6. Sentence to jail or house of correction

Whoever is convicted of a crime punishable wholly or in part by imprisonment in jail may be sentenced to such imprisonment in the house of correction or to confinement at hard labor either in the jail or house of correction; and if convicted of a crime punishable by imprisonment in the house of correction may be sentenced to such imprisonment in a jail.

Amended by St.1955, c. 770, § 93.

Historical and Statutory Notes

St.1834, c. 151, § 17.
R.S.1836, c. 143, § 17.
G.S.1860, c. 174, § 4.
P.S.1882, c. 215, § 3.
St.1882, c. 241, § 1.
R.L.1902, c. 220, § 5.

§ 6A. Special sentence of imprisonment; eligible offenders; revocation or rescission of special sentence; subsequent crimes

When a person is sentenced on a first offense to imprisonment in a jail or house of correction for a term which does not exceed one year, the court may order the sentence to be served in whole or in part on weekends and legal holidays or such other periodic interval as the court may determine. Such a sentence shall be known as a special sentence of imprisonment. If an offender receives a special sentence of imprisonment under this section, he shall, unless otherwise provided by the sentence of the court, report to the institution to which he has been sentenced no later than 6:00 p.m. on Friday and shall be released at 7:00 a.m. on the succeeding Monday; provided, however, that if the succeeding Monday is a holiday, the offender shall not be released until 7:00 a.m. on Tuesday; and provided further, that the total time served shall be equal to the sentence imposed.

On application of the offender, of the department of correction or the director of the institution to which the offender is committed, or on its own motion, the court may after a hearing rescind or modify an order under the first paragraph, and may direct that the balance of the sentence of imprisonment shall be served consecutively. Before a special sentence is rescinded or modified, the court shall cause the notification thereof to be given to the district attorney and to the offender.

If while serving such a special sentence, such person is convicted of a subsequent crime other than a non-moving motor vehicle violation, the terms of said special sentence shall be rescinded and said person shall complete the balance of his original sentence consecutively in the jail or house of correction in which he has been serving said special sentence.

Added by St.1977, c. 537. Amended by St.1997, c. 19, § 121; St.1998, c. 463, § 193.

§ 7. Sentence to jail or house of correction for non-payment of fine

Whoever is convicted of a crime punishable by a fine, and is liable to imprisonment in the jail for its non-payment, may be sentenced to such imprisonment in the house of correction, or to confinement at hard labor either in the jail or house of correction.

Historical and Statutory Notes

St.1845, c. 118.
G.S.1860, c. 174, § 5.
P.S.1882, c. 215, § 4.
R.L.1902, c. 220, § 6.

§ 8. Commitments upon two or more sentences

A convict upon whom two or more sentences to imprisonment are imposed may be fully committed upon all such sentences at the same time, and shall serve them in the order named in the mittimuses upon which he is committed; but when fine and imprisonment are named in one of the sentences the prisoner shall always be committed upon the term sentence first.

Historical and Statutory Notes

St.1884, c. 265.
R.L.1902, c. 220, § 7.
St.1911, c. 179.

§ 8A. Determination of time of taking effect of sentence; "from and after" sentence

For the purpose only of determining the time of the taking effect of a sentence which is ordered to take effect from and after the expiration of a previous sentence, such previous sentence shall be deemed to have expired when a prisoner serving such previous sentence shall have been released therefrom by parole or otherwise. Nothing in this section shall be construed to alter or control any provision of section one hundred and thirty-one or one hundred and forty-nine of chapter one hundred and twenty-seven.

Historical and Statutory Notes

St.1924, c. 165.

§ 8B. Commission of crime while released on personal recognizance; consecutive sentence

If a defendant on release subject to the provisions of section fifty-eight of chapter two hundred and seventy-six, commits a crime, the sentence imposed for such a crime shall run consecutively to the earlier sentence for the crime for which he was on release.

Added by St.1981, c. 802, § 5. Amended by St.1994, c. 68, § 8.

§ 9. Second sentence for non-payment of fine

Except as provided in section one hundred and forty-six of chapter one hundred and twenty-seven, if a convict is sentenced to pay a fine in more than one case and has been committed to a jail, house of correction or other prison or other correctional institution for refusing to pay such fine, the subsequent sentence shall take effect upon the expiration of the imprisonment under the former sentence.

Amended by St.1932, c. 221, § 2; St.1955, c. 770, § 94.

Historical and Statutory Notes

St.1874, c. 253.
P.S.1882, c. 215, § 5.
R.L.1902, c. 220, § 8.

§ 10. Conditional sentence

If a person has been convicted of a crime punishable, at the discretion of the court, by fine or imprisonment in the jail or house of correction or by fine or imprisonment in the state prison, the court may impose upon him a conditional sentence, and order him to pay a fine within a limited time which shall be expressed in the sentence, and in default thereof to suffer such imprisonment as is provided by law. He shall be forthwith committed to the custody of an officer in court or to the jail, to be detained until the sentence is complied with; and if he does not within the time limited pay the fine imposed, the sheriff shall cause the other part of the sentence to be executed forthwith.

Historical and Statutory Notes

St.1788, c. 53, §§ 1, 2.
St.1834, c. 151, § 17.
R.S.1836, c. 139, §§ 2, 3.
G.S.1860, c. 174, §§ 6, 7.
P.S.1882, c. 215, §§ 6, 7.
R.L.1902, c. 220, § 9.

§ 11. Punishment by imprisonment only or by fine only when law prescribes both

Whoever is convicted of a crime, punishable by fine and imprisonment either in the jail or house of correction, except a person convicted under section thirty G of chapter one hundred and thirty-eight, may at the discretion of the court, be sentenced to be punished by imprisonment only, or by a fine only, if he shows to the satisfaction of the court that he has not before been convicted of a similar crime.

Amended by St.1934, c. 328, § 28.

Historical and Statutory Notes

R.S.1836, c. 139, § 4.
St.1855, c. 215, § 39.
G.S.1860, c. 174, § 8.
St.1866, c. 280, § 1.
P.S.1882, c. 215, § 8.
St.1896, c. 397, § 17.
R.L.1902, c. 220, § 10.

§ 12. Recognizance of husband convicted of assault upon wife

Except as provided in section twenty-eight of chapter two hundred and eighteen and in section twenty of chapter two hundred and nineteen, if a husband is convicted of an assault upon his wife, the court may, in addition to the other penalties imposed, or in lieu thereof, order him to recognize with surety or sureties to keep the peace for any term of not more than two years, and may at any time revoke such order or reduce the amount required or order that the recognizance be taken without surety.

Historical and Statutory Notes

St.1879, c. 42.
P.S.1882, c. 215, §§ 9, 10.
R.L.1902, c. 220, § 11.

§ 13. Recognizance to keep the peace or to be of good behavior

Except as provided in section twenty-eight of chapter two hundred and eighteen and in section twenty of chapter two hundred and nineteen, whoever is convicted of a misdemeanor may, in addition to the punishment prescribed by law, be required to recognize, with sufficient sureties, in a reasonable sum to keep the peace, or to be of good behavior, or both, for any term of not more than two years, and to stand committed until he so recognizes.

Historical and Statutory Notes

R.S.1836, c. 139, § 5.
G.S.1860, c. 174, § 10.
P.S.1882, c. 215, § 11.
R.L.1902, c. 220, § 12.

§ 14. Recognizance; filing; proceedings on breach of condition

Such recognizance shall be filed of record in the superior court for the county, and, upon a breach of the condition thereof, the proceedings shall be as provided in chapter two hundred and seventy-five relative to recognizances to keep the peace and be of good behavior.

Historical and Statutory Notes

R.S.1836, c. 139, § 6.

G.S.1860, c. 174, § 11.
P.S.1882, c. 215, § 12.
R.L.1902, c. 220, § 13.

§ 15. Sentence to jail or house of correction in any county

Whoever is convicted of a crime, punishable by imprisonment in the jail or house of correction, may be sentenced to a jail or house of correction of any county, and the master or keeper shall receive and detain him in the same manner as if he had been sentenced by a court sitting in the county where such jail or house of correction is situated.

Historical and Statutory Notes

St.1818, c. 123, § 6.
St.1866, c. 280, § 2.
St.1870, c. 370, § 4.
P.S.1882, c. 215, § 13.
R.L.1902, c. 220, § 14.

§ 16. Sentencing of female to Massachusetts Correctional Institution, Framingham

A female, convicted of a crime punishable by imprisonment in a jail or house of correction, may be sentenced to the Massachusetts Correctional Institution, Framingham.

Amended by St.1972, c. 293, § 1.

Historical and Statutory Notes

St.1874, c. 385, § 17.
St.1881, c. 189.
P.S.1882, c. 215, § 14.
R.L.1902, c. 220, § 15.
St.1903, c. 209.
St.1906, c. 282.
St.1907, c. 251, § 1.
St.1911, c. 181.
St.1914, c. 635.

§ 17. Repealed, 1993, 432, Sec. 14

§ 18. Repealed, 1993, 432, Sec. 15

§ 19. Place of imprisonment of females convicted of felony

The sentence to imprisonment of a female convicted of a felony shall be executed in the Massachusetts Correctional Institution, Framingham; or the court imposing sentence in such a case may impose the sentence in a jail or house of correction provided by law in the case of male prisoners, if it does not exceed two and one half years.

Amended by St.1955, c. 770, § 95.

Historical and Statutory Notes

St.1906, c. 282, § 1.
St.1907, c. 251, § 1.
St.1911, c. 181.
St.1914, c. 635.

§ 20. Execution of sentence of imprisonment of females sentenced to confinement at hard labor

Subject to the preceding section, a sentence of a female convict of whatever age to confinement at hard labor shall be executed in a jail or house of correction or the Massachusetts Correctional Institution, Framingham as the court orders.

Amended by St.1955, c. 770, § 96.

Historical and Statutory Notes

St.1818, c. 123, § 8.
St.1834, c. 151, § 16.
R.S.1836, c. 143, § 18.
G.S.1860, c. 174, § 14.
St.1874, c. 385, § 17.
P.S.1882, c. 215, § 15.
St.1889, c. 113.
R.L.1902, c. 220, § 16.
St.1904, c. 224.
St.1911, c. 181.

§ 21. Repealed, 1931, 426, Sec. 49

§ 22. Repealed, 1955, 770, Sec. 122

§ 23. Limitation of sentences of males to jails or houses of correction

No sentence of a male convict to imprisonment or confinement for more than two and one half years shall be executed in any jail or house of correction.

Historical and Statutory Notes

St.1818, c. 123, § 1.
St.1834, c. 151, § 14.
R.S.1836, c. 143, § 19.
G.S.1860, c. 174, § 16.
St.1870, c. 206, § 1.
P.S.1882, c. 215, § 19.
R.L.1902, c. 220, § 19.
St.1918, c. 257, § 464.
St.1919, c. 5.
St.1920, c. 2, § 1.
St.1931, c. 426, § 50.

§ 24. Indeterminate sentence to state prison

If a convict is sentenced to the state prison, except for life or as an habitual criminal, the court shall not fix the term of imprisonment, but shall fix a maximum and a minimum term for which he may be imprisoned. The maximum term shall not be longer than the longest term fixed by law for the punishment of the crime of which he has be [1] convicted, and the minimum term shall be a term set by the court, except that, where an alternative sentence to a house of correction is permitted for the offense, a minimum state prison term may not be less than one year.

Amended by St.1993, c. 432, § 16.

[1] So in enrolled bill; probably should read "has been".

Historical and Statutory Notes

R.S.1836, c. 139, § 9.
G.S.1860, c. 174, § 17.

St.1877, c. 190.
St.1880, c. 15, § 1.
P.S.1882, c. 215, § 20.
St.1895, c. 504, § 1.
St.1897, c. 294, § 1.
R.L.1902, c. 220, § 20.
St.1924, c. 152.

§ 25. Punishment of habitual criminals

Whoever has been twice convicted of crime and sentenced and committed to prison in this or another state, or once in this and once or more in another state, for terms of not less than three years each, and does not show that he has been pardoned for either crime on the ground that he was innocent, shall, upon conviction of a felony, be considered an habitual criminal and be punished by imprisonment in the state prison for the maximum term provided by law as a penalty for the felony for which he is then to be sentenced.

Historical and Statutory Notes

St.1887, c. 435, § 1.
R.L.1902, c. 220, § 21.
St.1904, c. 303.

§ 26. Further sentence of convict in state prison

A convict under sentence of imprisonment in the state prison may be further sentenced for a maximum term not longer than the longest term fixed by law for the punishment of the crime for which he has been convicted, and a minimum term not less than one year.

Amended by St.1946, c. 276.

Historical and Statutory Notes

St.1880, c. 15, § 2.
P.S.1882, c. 215, § 21.
R.L.1902, c. 220, § 22.

§ 27. Immediate execution of sentence to state prison of convict sentenced to jail or house of correction

If a convict serving a sentence of imprisonment in a jail or house of correction is convicted of a felony, the court may impose sentence of imprisonment in the state prison and order it to take effect forthwith, notwithstanding the former sentence. The convict shall thereupon be removed to the reception center established under section twenty of chapter one hundred and twenty-seven, and shall be discharged at the expiration of his sentence thereto.

Amended by St.1955, c. 770, § 97.

Historical and Statutory Notes

St.1881, c. 139.
P.S.1882, c. 215, § 22.
R.L.1902, c. 220, § 23.

§ 28. Repealed, 1993, 432, Sec. 17

§ 29. Repealed, 1955, 770, Sec. 122

§ 30. Vacation of office from time of sentence to state prison

If a convict sentenced by a court of the commonwealth or of the United States to imprisonment in the state prison or by a court of the United States to a federal penitentiary for a felony holds an office under the constitution or laws of the commonwealth at the time of sentence, it shall be vacated from the time of sentence. If the judgment against him is reversed upon writ of error, he shall be restored to his office with all its rights and emoluments; but, if pardoned, he shall not by reason thereof be restored, unless it is so expressly ordered by the terms of the pardon.

Amended by St.1951, c. 642.

Historical and Statutory Notes

R.S.1836, c. 144, § 31.
G.S.1860, c. 174, § 19.
P.S.1882, c. 215, § 24.
R.L.1902, c. 220, § 26.

§ 31. Repealed, 1993, 432, Sec. 18

§ 32. Repealed, 1993, 432, Sec. 19

Historical and Statutory Notes

See, now, c. 279, § 24.

§ 33. Repealed, 1993, 432, Sec. 20

§ 33A. Credit for days of confinement awaiting and during trial

The court on imposing a sentence of commitment to a correctional institution of the commonwealth, a house of correction, or a jail, shall order that the prisoner be deemed to have served a portion of said sentence, such portion to be the number of days spent by the prisoner in confinement prior to such sentence awaiting and during trial.

Added by St.1955, c. 770, § 101. Amended by St.1958, c. 173; St.1961, c. 75.

§ 34. Delivery to sheriff of certified transcript from minutes of court of conviction and sentence; execution of sentence

When a convict is sentenced to pay a fine or to be imprisoned, the clerk of the court shall forthwith make out and deliver to the sheriff or to some officer in court a duly certified transcript from the minutes of the court of the conviction and sentence, which shall authorize the officer to execute such sentence, and he shall execute it accordingly. When such convict is sentenced to be imprisoned in a correctional institution of the commonwealth, except the Massachusetts Correctional Institution, Bridgewater and the Massachusetts Correctional Institution, Framingham, the officer authorized to execute such sentence shall deliver him to the reception center established in accordance with the provisions of section twenty of chapter one hundred and twenty-seven for examination and classification.

Amended by St.1955, c. 770, § 102.

Historical and Statutory Notes

R.S.1836, c. 139, § 7.
G.S.1860, c. 174, § 20.
St.1880, c. 120, § 1.
P.S.1882, c. 215, § 25.
R.L.1902, c. 220, § 30.

§ 35. Transmission of complaint or indictment to correctional institution

When a person is committed to any correctional institution of the commonwealth or to any other public penal institution, on conviction of felony, the clerk of the court shall, without charge, transmit with the mittimus an attested copy of the complaint or indictment under which such person was convicted and, if such complaint or indictment does not contain a reference to the chapter and section of the General Laws under which such person was convicted, a statement designating such chapter and section, and the names and addresses of the witnesses who testified for and against such person at the trial, together with a record containing the names and addresses of the presiding justice, district attorney and of the attorney for the defendant.

Amended by St.1955, c. 770, § 103; St.1962, c. 48.

Historical and Statutory Notes

St.1881, c. 114, § 1.
P.S.1882, c. 215, § 26.
St.1884, c. 255, § 10.
R.L.1902, c. 220, § 31.
St.1914, c. 310.

§ 36. Sentences to state farm

Except for commitments under sections thirty-five or forty-eight of chapter one hundred and twenty-three, no person shall be sentenced to the state farm except for drunkenness. Whoever is sentenced to the state farm for drunkenness may be there held in custody for not more than six months.

Amended by St.1955, c. 770, § 104; St.1956, c. 715, § 26; St.1970, c. 888, § 30.

Historical and Statutory Notes

St.1898, c. 443, § 1.
R.L.1902, c. 85, § 37.

§ 37. Setting out statutory name of crime in warrant for commitment

Every warrant for the commitment of a person sentenced by a district court shall set forth the statutory name, if any, of the crime of which the person was convicted, and shall contain a citation of the statute, if any, under which the complaint was drawn.

Amended by St.1953, c. 319, § 36.

Historical and Statutory Notes

St.1910, c. 316.
St.1918, c. 257, § 465.
St.1919, c. 5.
St.1920, c. 2.

§ 38. Powers of sheriff or constable in execution of warrant of commitment

A sheriff, deputy sheriff or constable, when engaged in the execution of a warrant for the commitment of a person to a penal institution which is not in his own county, shall have the same powers in any county through which he may pass as he would have in his own county in the performance of a similar duty.

Historical and Statutory Notes

St.1870, c. 370, § 5.
St.1879, c. 294, § 7.
St.1880, c. 120, § 3.
P.S.1882, c. 215, § 27.
R.L.1902, c. 220, § 32.

§ 39. Return of precept to magistrate

The officer serving the precept in a criminal case shall, without charging travel therefor, return it with his doings and fees endorsed thereon to the court or magistrate issuing it, who shall tax, allow and certify the fees as a part of the expenses in the case. In case of commitment, the officer shall leave with the superintendent, jailer or keeper of the prison an attested copy of the precept, with his return thereon, which shall authorize the detention of the person committed.

Amended by St.1955, c. 770, § 105; St.1957, c. 777, § 38.

Historical and Statutory Notes

St.1859, c. 233.
G.S.1860, c. 174, § 22.
St.1880, c. 120, § 2.
P.S.1882, c. 215, § 28.
R.L.1902, c. 220, § 33.

§ 40. Service of new warrant of commitment upon convict

If a convict imprisoned under sentence is again sentenced to confinement in a prison other than that in which he is then held, the warrant for his commitment in pursuance of the second sentence shall be placed in the hands of the superintendent or keeper of the prison where the convict is held, and said superintendent or keeper, upon the expiration of the first sentence, shall commit the convict in obedience to said warrant.

Amended by St.1955, c. 770, § 106; St.1957, c. 777, § 39; St.1979, c. 485, § 46.

Historical and Statutory Notes

G.S.1860, c. 174, § 23.

P.S.1882, c. 215, § 29.
R.L.1902, c. 220, § 34.

§ 41. Default of corporation

If a corporation, after being duly served with process, fails to appear and answer to an indictment or complaint brought against it under the laws of the commonwealth, its default shall be recorded, the charges in the indictment or complaint taken to be true, and judgment rendered accordingly.

Historical and Statutory Notes

St.1851, c. 348, § 1.
G.S.1860, c. 174, § 29.
P.S.1882, c. 215, § 30.
R.L.1902, c. 220, § 35.

§ 42. Warrant of distress to compel payment of penalty or assessment

If judgment is rendered against a corporation upon an indictment or complaint under the laws of the commonwealth, the court may issue a warrant of distress to compel payment of the penalty or assessment, as the case may be, as prescribed by law, together with interest thereon if so ordered by the court.

If the records of the registrar of motor vehicles indicate that a corporation has failed to pay an assessment for a civil motor vehicle infraction as provided in section three of chapter ninety C, the registrar may issue a warrant of distress to compel payment of the assessment, plus any late fees or other administrative fees which the registrar is required or authorized by law or regulation to impose, unless such fees are waived in whole or in part by the registrar.

Amended by St.1985, c. 794, § 10; St.1987, c. 399, § 4; St.1991, c. 138, § 211; St.1992, c. 133, § 571; St.1993, c. 182, § 27.

Historical and Statutory Notes

St.1851, c. 348, § 2.
G.S.1860, c. 174, § 30.
P.S.1882, c. 215, § 31.
R.L.1902, c. 220, § 36.

§§ 43 to 56. Repealed, 1982, 554, Sec. 5

Historical and Statutory Notes

See, now, c. 279, §§ 57 to 71.

§ 57. Death sentence; pronouncement or revocation of stay; warrant of conviction; execution of sentence; certified copy of record to governor

Immediately upon the pronouncing of the sentence of death upon a person convicted of a capital crime, and immediately upon the revocation under section four of the stay of execution of such a sentence, the clerk shall make, sign and deliver to the sheriff of the county where the conviction is had a warrant under the seal of the court stating the conviction and sentence, and that a stay of execution of the sentence has been granted under section four, and that such stay has been revoked under said section, and shall at the same time transmit to the superintendent of the state prison a certified copy of the warrant. Such warrant shall be directed to said superintendent commanding him to cause execution to be done in accordance with the provisions of such sentence. The clerk of the court shall, upon revocation under section four of the stay of execution of the sentence, make out and deliver to the governor a certified copy of the whole record of the conviction and sentence, including any rescripts from the supreme judicial court.

Added by St.1982, c. 554, § 6.

§ 58. Death sentence confinement; psychiatric examination; transfer or failure to transfer to general prison population; appeal; hearing; annual record review; court order

The sheriff of the county in a jail whereof a prisoner sentenced to the punishment of death is confined, or a deputy designated by the sheriff, within ten days after receipt by the sheriff of the warrant for the execution of such sentence shall, at a time chosen by the sheriff, convey such prisoner to the state prison and deliver him, with the warrant in either case, to the superintendent thereof or to the officer performing his duties and such prisoner shall be placed in a cell provided for the purpose. Within fourteen days thereafter, the superintendent or officer performing his duties shall cause said prisoner to be examined by a psychiatrist for the purpose of rendering a written and signed opinion as to whether or not said prisoner is psychologically fit to be transferred from special confinement to confinement with the general prison population, and in the case of a female, to the general prison population at the reformatory for women, with full participation in the educational and work programs, within the prison, afforded prisoners under sentence other than the punishment of death. Upon receipt of said psychiatric opinion, and other pertinent information, the superintendent or officer performing his duties may transfer said prisoner to confinement with the general prison population with the right of full participation in the privileges afforded other prisoners as aforesaid. If the superintendent, or officer performing his duties, does not so transfer said prisoner, he shall notify said prisoner of his decision forthwith, whereupon said prisoner may appeal said decision within ten days of said notification by giving notice to the superintendent, or officer performing his duties, on a form provided him at the time of the receipt of the notification of the adverse decision. Upon receipt of such notice, the superintendent or officer performing his duties shall notify the commissioner of correction forthwith whereupon the commissioner shall hold a hearing on said appeal within fifteen days of receipt of notice that such appeal has been made. The commissioner or his appointee shall conduct said hearing and shall render a decision granting or denying said appeal within five days following the date of the hearing. A prisoner who is denied such transfer by the superintendent, or officer performing his duties, shall remain in a cell for the purpose of the execution of his sentence, and shall thereafter be kept therein, unless an appeal made by him of the adverse decision is granted, until the sentence of death is executed upon him, and no person shall be allowed access to him without an order of the court, except the officers and employees of the prison, his counsel, such physicians, priest, or minister of religion as the superintendent may approve and members of the prisoner's family who are identified to the satisfaction of the superintendent. Any prisoner confined to a cell for the purpose of the execution of his sentence shall have his record reviewed annually for the purpose of determining whether or not said prisoner should be placed in the general population, and shall be entitled to a hearing, as provided above, on each adverse decision.

Notwithstanding the foregoing, the superior court may make any order relative to the custody of a prisoner confined in the state prison or the reformatory for women under this section in case said prisoner is granted a new trial.

Added by St.1982, c. 554, § 6.

§ 59. Execution of death sentence; time constraints

The sentence of death shall be executed by the superintendent of the state prison, or by a person acting under his direction, not earlier than twenty days nor later than thirty days after service upon said superintendent, or officer performing his duties, of a certificate of the clerk of the court that the stay of the execution of the sentence has been revoked under section four, unless the governor pardons the crime, commutes the punishment therefor or respites the execution or said execution is otherwise delayed by process of law. If the execution is respited or stayed by process of law, the sentence of death shall be executed within the week beginning on the day next after the day on which the term of respite or stay expires. The sentence of death shall be executed upon such day within the limits of time provided in this section as the superintendent elects; but no previous announcement thereof shall be made, except to such persons as may be permitted to be present in accordance with section sixty-five.

Added by St.1982, c. 554, § 6.

§ 60. Means of execution of death sentence

The punishment of death shall be inflicted by causing a current of electricity of sufficient intensity to cause death to pass through the body of the prisoner, the application of said current to be continuous until he is dead or, at the election of the prisoner, by intravenous injection of a substance or substances in a lethal quantity sufficient to cause death and until such prisoner is dead. The sentence shall be executed within an enclosure or building for that purpose at the state prison and the company which furnishes the electric power or light to the state prison shall provide all necessary electricity for executions by electrocution at such times as the superintendent orders.

Added by St.1982, c. 554, § 6.

§ 61. Capital crime conviction; imposition of sentence; insane and pregnant persons

If a person convicted of a capital crime is, at the time when sentence is to be imposed, found by the court to be insane, it may cause such person to be removed to one of the state hospitals for such term and under such limitations as it may order. If a person convicted of a capital crime is, at the time when sentence is to be imposed, found by the court to be pregnant, the court shall not pass sentence upon her until it finds that she is no longer pregnant.

Added by St.1982, c. 554, § 6.

§ 62. Delay in execution of death sentence; insanity or pregnancy of prisoner; psychiatric examination and written certification

After examination by two psychiatrists designated by the commissioner of mental health, if it appears that a prisoner under sentence of death has become insane, the governor, with the advice and consent of the council, may, from time to time for a stated period, respite the execution of said sentence until it appears to their satisfaction that the prisoner is no longer insane. Upon such respite, the governor may order the removal of such prisoner to the hospital at the Massachusetts Correctional Institution, Bridgewater. Within ten days prior to the termination date of said respite, the medical director of said hospital shall have the said prisoner examined by two psychiatrists designated by the commissioner of mental health. If, after said examination, the said medical director is of the opinion that the prisoner is no longer insane, he shall so certify to the superintendent of the state prison, accompanied by a written statement regarding the mental condition of said prisoner. The superintendent shall thereupon cause the prisoner to be reconveyed to the state prison and to be kept there pursuant to the sentence of the court, and shall notify the governor of the return of said prisoner, and of his mental condition. If, however, in the opinion of the said medical director of said hospital the said prisoner is still insane, he shall so certify to the governor, accompanied by a written statement regarding the mental condition of the prisoner. Thereupon, the governor, with the advice and consent of the council, may further respite the execution of the sentence from time to time for a stated period, until it is determined that the prisoner is no longer insane, as herein provided.

If it appears to the satisfaction of the governor and council that a prisoner under sentence of death is pregnant, the governor, with the advice and consent of the council, shall from time to time respite the execution of said sentence for stated periods until it appears to their satisfaction that she is no longer pregnant.

Added by St.1982, c. 554, § 6.

§ 63. Delay in execution of death sentence; consideration of pardon

The governor, with the advice and consent of the council, may from time to time respite the execution of a sentence of death for stated periods so long as he may consider it necessary to afford him, with the advice and consent of the council, an opportunity to investigate and consider the facts of the case for the purpose of considering whether or not to pardon the prisoner.

Added by St.1982, c. 554, § 6.

§ 64. Judicial stay of execution of death sentence; final determination of judicial questions

The execution of a sentence of death may be stayed from time to time for stated periods by the supreme judicial court, or a justice thereof, pending the final determination of any judicial question arising in or out of the case in which the sentence is imposed.

Added by St.1982, c. 554, § 6.

§ 65. Witnesses; execution of death sentence

There shall be present at the execution of the sentence of death, in addition to the superintendent, deputy and such officers of the state prison as the superintendent deems necessary, the commissioner of correction or his representative, the person performing the execution under the direction of the superintendent, if any, and the following physicians: the prison physician, the state surgeon, and a medical examiner for Norfolk county, or if any or all are unable to be present, such physicians as the superintendent approves. The physicians present shall be the legal witnesses of the execution. There may also be present, upon the request of the prisoner who is to be executed, the immediate members of the family of the prisoner. There may also be present, upon the request of said prisoner, a priest, minister, or other representative of religion. There may also be present the sheriff of the county where the prisoner was convicted, or his deputy, and, with the approval of the superintendent, not more than three other persons.

Added by St.1982, c. 554, § 6.

§ 66. Execution of death sentence; post mortem examination

There shall be a post mortem examination by a medical examiner for Norfolk county of the body of every prisoner executed in conformity with the sentence of a court.

Added by St.1982, c. 554, § 6.

§ 67. Warrant for execution of death sentence; return to clerk of court after execution

When the superintendent has executed the sentence of death upon a prisoner in obedience to a warrant from the court, he shall forthwith make return thereof under his hand, with the doings thereon, to the office of the clerk of said court.

Added by St.1982, c. 554, § 6.

§ 68. Special jury questions for first degree murder; presentence hearing upon conviction for consideration of death penalty; consideration by jury of aggravating and mitigating circumstances; determination by jury; sentence by court; validity of conviction

In all cases in which a sentence of death may be imposed, the court shall submit to the jury special questions concerning the issue of murder in the first degree. If the jury determines beyond a reasonable doubt that the defendant is guilty of murder in the first degree, the jury shall specify whether the defendant is guilty of murder with deliberate premeditation, murder with extreme atrocity or cruelty, or murder in the commission or attempted commission of a crime punishable by imprisonment for life, or two or more of these. Upon a verdict of guilty of murder in the first degree with deliberate premeditation, or murder in the first degree with extreme atrocity or cruelty, a presentence hearing shall be conducted, unless the commonwealth stipulates that none of the aggravating circumstances as defined in paragraph (*a*) of section sixty-nine exists, before the jury before which the case was tried; provided, however, that if in the opinion of the judge presiding at the presentence hearing, it is impossible or impracticable for the trial jury to sit at the presentence hearing, a new jury shall be impanelled to sit at the presentence hearing. The selection of that jury shall be according to the laws and rules governing the selection of a jury for the trial of a capital case. During the presentence hearing, the only issue shall be the determination of the punishment to be imposed. During such hearing the jury shall hear all additional relevant evidence presented by either the commonwealth or defendant in mitigation of punishment regardless of its admissibility under the rules governing the admission of evidence at criminal trials. During such hearing, the jury shall also hear such evidence in aggravation of punishment as is relevant to the statutory aggravating circumstance or statutory aggravating circumstances as defined in said paragraph (*a*) of said section sixty-nine; provided, however, that only such evidence in aggravation of punishment as the commonwealth has made known to the defendant prior to his trial shall be admissible, and provided further, that said evidence is otherwise admissible according to the rules governing the admission of evidence at criminal trials. The jury shall also hear arguments by the defendant or his counsel or both and by the commonwealth regarding the punishment to be imposed. The commonwealth and the defendant or his counsel shall be allowed to make opening statements and closing arguments at the presentence hearing. The order of those statements and arguments and the order of presentation of evidence shall be the same as at trial. Upon the conclusion of evidence and arguments at the presentence hearing, the court shall instruct the jury orally and shall provide to the jury in writing the statutory aggravating circumstance or statutory aggravating circumstances as determined by the court to be warranted by the evidence, and also any and all statutory mitigating circumstance or statutory mitigating circumstances for its deliberation. The judge shall also instruct the jury to consider any other relevant mitigating circumstance or mitigating circumstances. The judge shall also instruct the jury that they may not find that the penalty of death shall be imposed unless they shall first make a unanimous determination of the existence of one or more statutory aggravating circumstances beyond a reasonable doubt, and make a unanimous determination that the statutory aggravating circumstance or statutory aggravating circumstances outweigh the statutory or other mitigating circumstance or statutory or other mitigating circumstances beyond a reasonable doubt.

The jury shall then retire to determine whether any statutory aggravating circumstance or statutory aggravating circumstances, as defined by said paragraph (*a*) of said section sixty-nine or any mitigating circumstance or mitigating circumstances, including but not limited to those defined by paragraph (*b*) of said section sixty-nine, exist. The jury shall further determine whether the statutory aggravating circumstance or statutory aggravating circumstances it finds to exist outweigh the statutory or other mitigating circumstance or statutory or other mitigating circumstances it finds to exist. The jury shall be instructed that: (1) it may choose to find that the penalty of death shall be imposed upon the defendant or (2) it may choose not to find that the penalty of death shall be imposed upon the defendant. The jury, if its unanimous verdict is to impose the penalty of death, shall designate in writing, signed by the foreman of the jury, the statutory aggravating circumstance or statutory aggravating circumstances which it unanimously found existed beyond a reasonable doubt, and that the statutory aggravating circumstance or statutory aggravating circumstances it so unanimously found outweighed any statutory mitigating circumstance or other mitigating circumstance or statutory mitigating circumstances or other mitigating circumstances beyond a reasonable doubt. The process of weighing the statutory aggravating circumstance or statutory aggravating circumstances and statutory mitigating circumstance or statutory mitigating circumstances or other mitigating circumstance or other mitigating circumstances to determine the sentence, shall not be a mere tallying of statutory aggravating circumstance or statutory aggravating circumstances and statutory or other mitigating circumstance or statutory or other mitigating circumstances for the purpose of numerical comparison. Instead, it shall be a process by which the statutory aggravating circumstance or statutory aggravating circumstances and statutory mitigating circumstance or other mitigating circumstance or statutory mitigating circumstances or other mitigating circumstances relevant to sentence are considered for the purpose of determining whether the sentence, in view of all the relevant circumstances in an individual case, shall be life imprisonment without parole, or death.

After the jury has made its findings, the court shall set a sentence in accordance with section seventy.

The declaration of a mistrial during the course of the presentence hearing or any error in the presentence hearing determined on final appeal or otherwise shall not affect the validity of the conviction.

Added by St.1982, c. 554, § 6.

§ 69. Aggravating and mitigating circumstances in death penalty cases

(a) In all cases in which the death penalty may be authorized, the statutory aggravating circumstances are:

(1) the murder was committed on a victim who was killed while serving in the performance of his official duties as one or more of the following: police officer, special police officer, state or federal law enforcement officer, firefighter, officer or employee of the department of correction, officer or employee of a sheriff's department, officer or employee of a jail or officer or employee of a house of correction;

(2) the murder was committed by a defendant who was at the time incarcerated in a jail, house of correction, prison, state prison or a correctional or penal institution or a facility used for the housing or treatment or housing and treatment of prisoners;

(3) the murder was committed on a victim who was killed while engaged in the performance of his official duties as a judge, prosecuting attorney, juror, or witness;

(4) the murder was committed by a defendant who had previously been convicted of murder in the first degree, or of an offense in any other federal, state or territorial jurisdiction of the United States which is the same as or necessarily includes the elements of the offense of murder in the first degree;

(5) the murder was committed by the defendant pursuant to a contract, agreement or understanding by which he was to receive money or anything of value in return for committing the murder;

(6) the murder was committed by the defendant for the purpose of avoiding, interfering with, or preventing a lawful arrest of the defendant or another, or the murder was committed by the defendant for the purpose of effectuating an escape or attempting to effectu-

ate an escape of the defendant or another from custody in a place of lawful confinement;

(7) the murder involved torture to the victim or the intentional infliction of extreme pain prior to death demonstrating a total disregard to the suffering of the victim;

(8) the murder was committed as part of a course of conduct involving the killing of or causing serious bodily injury to or the attempted killing of or the attempted causing of serious bodily injury to more than one person by the defendant;

(9) the murder was committed by means of a destructive device, bomb, or explosive planted, hidden, mailed, delivered, or concealed in any place, area, dwelling, building, or structure by the defendant or the murder was committed by means such that the defendant knew or reasonably should have known that his act or acts would create a grave risk of death or serious bodily injury to more than one person; or

(10) the murder was committed by the defendant and occurred during the commission or attempted commission or flight after committing or flight after attempting to commit aggravated rape, rape, rape of a child, indecent assault and battery on a child under fourteen, assault with intent to rape, assault on a child under sixteen years of age with intent to rape, kidnapping for ransom, kidnapping, armed robbery, unarmed robbery, breaking and entering with intent to commit a felony, armed assault in a dwelling, arson, confining or putting in fear or otherwise harming another for the purpose of stealing from depositories, or the murder occurred while the defendant was in possession of a sawed-off shotgun or a machine gun.

(b) In all cases in which the death penalty may be authorized, the mitigating circumstances shall be any factors proffered by the defendant or the commonwealth which are relevant in determining whether to impose a sentence less than death, including, but not limited to, any aspect of the defendant's character, propensities, or record and any of the circumstances of the murder, including but not limited to the following:

(1) the defendant has no significant history of prior criminal convictions;

(2) the victim was a participant in the defendant's conduct or had consented to it;

(3) the murder was committed while the defendant was under extreme duress or under the domination or control of another;

(4) the offense was committed while the capacity of the defendant to appreciate the criminality of his conduct or to conform his conduct to the requirements of the law was impaired as a result of a mental disease or defect, organic brain damage, emotional illness brought on by stress or prescribed medication, intoxication, or legal or illegal drug use by the defendant which was insufficient to establish a defense to the murder but which substantially affected his judgment;

(5) the defendant was over the age of seventy-five at the time of the murder, or any other relevant consideration regarding the age of the defendant at the time of the murder;

(6) the defendant was battered or otherwise physically, sexually, or mentally abused by the victim in connection with or immediately prior to the murder for which the defendant was convicted;

(7) the defendant was experiencing post-traumatic stress syndrome caused by military service during a declared or undeclared war.

Added by St.1982, c. 554, § 6.

§ 70. Death penalty imposed; jury findings necessary

Where, upon a trial by jury, a person is convicted of a crime which is punishable by death, a sentence of death shall not be imposed unless findings in accordance with section sixty-eight are made. Where such findings are made and the jury finds that the death penalty shall be imposed, the court shall sentence the defendant to death. Where such findings are not made or not unanimously made or where a sentence of death is not a unanimous finding by the jury, the court shall sentence the defendant to life imprisonment as provided in section two of chapter two hundred and sixty-five.

Added by St.1982, c. 554, § 6.

§ 71. Review of death sentence; remand; reversal; affirmation

In addition to review of the entire case pursuant to section thirty-three E of chapter two hundred and seventy-eight, the supreme judicial court shall review the sentence of death imposed pursuant to sections sixty-eight, sixty-nine and seventy of chapter two hundred and seventy-nine. If the supreme judicial court determines that (1) the sentence of death was imposed under the influence of passion, prejudice or any other arbitrary factor or (2) the evidence does not support the jury's finding of a statutory aggravating circumstance or statutory aggravating circumstances as defined in section sixty-nine or (3) the evidence does not support the jury's finding that the statutory aggravating circumstance or statutory aggravating circumstances defined in section sixty-nine outweigh the statutory or other mitigating circumstance or statutory or other mitigating circumstances or (4) the sentence of death is excessive or disproportionate to the penalty imposed in other similar cases of one or more jurisdictions legally authorized to impose said penalty of death, with the greater weight of such comparison to be given to similar Massachusetts cases in which the death penalty will have been imposed, with due consideration of both those cases in which a sentence of life imprisonment was imposed and those cases in which a sentence of death was imposed, or in the event that the court determines any or all of the four factors as enumerated in this section exist, the court shall (1) reverse the sentence of death and remand for a new presentence hearing pursuant to section sixty-eight of chapter two hundred and seventy-nine, or (2) reverse the sentence of death and remand to the superior court department of the trial court for sentence of imprisonment in the state prison for life. The court shall also have the authority to affirm the sentence of death.

Added by St.1982, c. 554, § 6. Amended by St.1997, c. 19, § 122.

CHAPTER 280

FINES AND FORFEITURES

The section headings for the General Laws in this pamphlet have been editorially supplied.

§ 1. Recovery of fines and forfeitures

Fines and forfeitures exacted as punishments for offences or violation or neglect of any duty imposed by statute may, unless otherwise provided, be prosecuted for and recovered by indictment or complaint or by an action of tort in the name of the commonwealth in a court having jurisdiction of the offence or action.

Historical and Statutory Notes

St.1793, c. 43, § 4.
St.1800, c. 57, § 4.
R.S.1836, c. 118, § 42; c. 133, § 14.
G.S.1860, c. 176, § 2.
P.S.1882, c. 217, § 2.
R.L.1902, c. 221, § 1.

§ 2. Payment of certain fines and forfeitures; apportionment among beneficiaries

A fine or forfeiture imposed by a court shall, except as otherwise provided, be paid over to the state treasurer. Twenty per cent of the fines imposed under the provisions of chapter three hundred and fifty-four of the acts of nineteen hundred and fifty-two shall be paid over to the state treasurer. If the whole or any part of a fine is by law payable to a complainant or informant or to a person or corporation as beneficiary, the court may apportion the fine or forfeiture between such complainant, informant or other beneficiary and the commonwealth, respectively.

Fines imposed under the provisions of chapters eighty-nine and ninety, including fines, penalties and assessments imposed under the provisions of chapter ninety C for the violation of the provisions of chapters eighty-nine and ninety, fines assessed by a hearing officer of a city or town as defined in sections twenty A and twenty A½ of chapter ninety and forfeitures imposed under the provisions of section one hundred and forty-one of chapter one hundred and forty, shall be paid over to the treasury of the city or town wherein the offense was committed; provided, however, that only fifty per cent of the amount of fines, penalties and assessments collected for violations of section seventeen of chapter ninety or of a special speed regulation lawfully made under the authority of section eighteen of said chapter ninety shall be paid over to the treasury of the city or town wherein the offense was committed and the remaining fifty per cent shall be paid over to the state treasurer and credited to the Highway Fund.

Amended by St.1934, c. 364, § 2; St.1935, c. 303, § 1; St.1953, c. 319, § 37; St.1975, c. 843, § 2; St.1978, c. 478, § 311; St.1980, c. 329, § 93; St.1981, c. 351, § 118; St.1983, c. 233, § 86; St.1985, c. 794, § 11; St.1988, c. 273, § 61.

Historical and Statutory Notes

R.S.1836, c. 133, § 14.
St.1839, c. 135.
G.S.1860, c. 176, § 1.
St.1860, c. 191, § 10.
P.S.1882, c. 217, § 1.
St.1890, c. 440, § 5.
St.1891, c. 416, § 1.
R.L.1902, c. 221, § 2.
St.1911, c. 250, §§ 1, 2.
St.1931, c. 426, § 316.

§ 3. Proceedings to recover penalties; appointment of counsel

In proceedings in the name of the commonwealth for the recovery of fines, forfeitures or penalties, the whole or any part of which do not enure to the benefit of the commonwealth, the court may, upon motion of the district attorney, appoint an attorney to conduct the cause under his direction; but such attorney so appointed shall have no right to control the cause or receive compensation from the commonwealth.

Historical and Statutory Notes

St.1870, c. 313, § 2.
P.S.1882, c. 217, § 3.
R.L.1902, c. 221, § 3.

§ 4. Criminal prosecutions; expenses paid by commonwealth; waiver of costs for indigent defendants

Expenses arising in a criminal prosecution, including fees of grand and traverse jurors for travel and attendance therein, shall be paid by the commonwealth.

Fees and costs of indigent defendants in criminal prosecutions except attorneys' fees, shall or may be waived or substituted by the court or paid by the commonwealth in accordance with the provisions of sections twenty-seven A to twenty-seven G, inclusive, of chapter two hundred and sixty-one.

Amended by St.1974, c. 694, § 5; St.1978, c. 478, § 312.

Historical and Statutory Notes

St.1764–5, c. 26, § 6.
St.1782, c. 55.
St.1787, c. 39.
St.1791, c. 53, § 2.
St.1817, c. 145.
St.1824, c. 117.
St.1825, c. 73, § 2.
R.S.1836, c. 141, § 1.
St.1841, c. 74, § 1.
St.1845, c. 227.
St.1850, c. 68.
G.S.1860, c. 176, § 4.
St.1860, c. 191, § 10.
St.1880, c. 120, § 2.
P.S.1882, c. 217, § 4.
St.1890, c. 440, § 2.
St.1898, c. 204, § 4.
R.L.1902, c. 221, § 4.

§ 5. Appeal briefs in criminal cases; payment of costs

In a criminal case in which questions of law are carried to the supreme judicial court, the attorney general or district attorney may have necessary copies of the brief for the commonwealth printed, and the expense thereof shall be paid in the same manner as other expenses in the case.

Historical and Statutory Notes

St.1879, c. 54.
P.S.1882, c. 17, § 11.
R.L.1902, c. 221, § 5.

§ 6. Costs as penalty for crime; expenses of prosecution

Costs shall not be imposed by a justice as a penalty for a crime. A justice may, as a condition of the dismissal or placing on file of a complaint or indictment, or as a term of probation, order the defendant to pay the reasonable and actual expenses of the prosecution. A justice may impose reasonable costs as a result of a default by a criminal defendant that was intentional or negligent and without good cause.

Amended by St.1937, c. 251, § 1; St.1991, c. 138, § 214; St.1994, c. 247, § 6.

Historical and Statutory Notes

St.1890, c. 328, § 1.
St.1890, c. 440, § 3.
R.L.1902, c. 221, § 6.

§ 6A. Special cost assessments; exemption

Before imposing a fine or forfeiture as a punishment or part punishment for a crime, the court or justice shall levy as a special cost assessment an amount equal to twenty-five per cent of the fine or forfeiture; provided however, that no special cost assessment shall be levied on fines or forfeitures for minor motor vehicle offenses, and juvenile offenses or acts of delinquency. Minor motor vehicle offenses shall be defined as those not punishable by incarceration.

When a fine is suspended, in whole or in part, the special cost assessment shall be computed on the fine remaining to be paid. In any case where a person convicted of any offense to which this section applies is imprisoned until the fine is satisfied, the court or justice may in his discretion waive all or any part of said cost assessment the payment of which would work a hardship on the person convicted or his immediate family.

Said cost assessment shall be accounted for by the clerk of the court and forwarded to the state treasurer who shall deposit such assessment in the General Fund.

Added by St.1973, c. 1228, § 2. Amended by St.1974, c. 241, § 2; St.1974, c. 581, § 4; St.1977, c. 363A, § 67.

§ 6B. Criminal assessments

The court shall impose an assessment of not less than thirty-five dollars nor more than one hundred dollars against any person who has attained the age of seventeen years and who is convicted of a misdemeanor or against whom a finding of sufficient facts for a conviction is made on a complaint charging a misdemeanor under sections thirty-two C, thirty-two D, and thirty-two G and thirty-five of chapter ninety-four C. The court shall impose an assessment of not less than one hundred and fifty dollars nor more than five hundred dollars against any person who is convicted of a felony or against whom a finding of sufficient facts for a conviction is made on a complaint charging a felony under sections thirty-two, thirty-two A, thirty-two B, thirty-two E, thirty-two F and thirty-four of chapter ninety-four C. When multiple criminal offenses arising from a single incident are charged, the total assessment shall not exceed five hundred dollars. In the discretion of the court, any assessment imposed pursuant to this section which would cause the person against whom the assessment is made an undue hardship may be reduced or waived.

All such assessments made shall be collected by the court and shall be transmitted monthly to the state treasurer. The assessment from any conviction which is subsequently overturned on appeal shall be refunded by the court to the person whose conviction is overturned. Said court shall deduct such funds from the assessments transmitted to the state treasurer. Assessments pursuant to this section shall be in addition to any other fines or restitution imposed in any disposition.

Added by St.1988, c. 236, § 51. Amended by St.1989, c. 653, § 107.

§ 6C. Assessment proceeds

Any assessment imposed pursuant to section six B shall be deposited in the Drug Analysis Fund established by section fifty-one of chapter ten. The proceeds of the fund shall be made available, subject to appropriation, to the department of public health for services provided to analyse samples used in the prosecution of controlled substances.

Added by St.1988, c. 236, § 51.

§ 7. Certificates of fines imposed; delivery to state treasurer

At the end of every sitting of the superior court for the transaction of criminal business, the clerk shall make and deliver to the state treasurer certificates of all fines imposed by the court, to the use of the commonwealth or to the treasurer of a city or town under the provisions of section two of this chapter.

Amended by St.1978, c. 478, § 313.

Historical and Statutory Notes

C.L. c. 151, § 4.
St.1693–4, c. 2, § 1.
St.1700–1, c. 21, § 1.
St.1783, c. 44, § 2.
R.S.1836, c. 141, § 8.
G.S.1860, c. 176, § 8.
St.1861, c. 184.
P.S.1882, c. 217, § 8.
St.1890, c. 218, § 2.
R.L.1902, c. 221, § 7.

§ 8. Transfer to state treasurer of fines paid

The clerk of the superior court for the transaction of criminal business for Suffolk county, the clerks of the municipal courts in Boston, the sheriff, superintendent of the house of correction or other officer, except those named in the following section, upon receiving fines, fees or other money in any criminal proceedings, payable to the commonwealth or to a city or town shall, before the tenth day of every month, pay over to the state treasurer and account, on oath, for all fines, fees or other money so received during the preceding calendar month, and make the detailed statements required by law.

Amended by St.1978, c. 478, § 313; St.1979, c. 485, § 47.

Historical and Statutory Notes

St.1891, c. 236, § 1.
R.L.1902, c. 221, § 8.

§ 9. Fines paid; transfer to state treasurer by clerks of courts in Suffolk county

The clerks of all courts in Suffolk county, except those named in the preceding section, who are required to account to the commonwealth shall, on or before the tenth day of each month, pay over to the state treasurer and account, on oath, for all fines, fees and other money received by them in any criminal proceedings during the preceding calendar month remaining after the payments therefrom allowed by law.

Amended by St.1978, c. 478, § 313.

Historical and Statutory Notes

St.1891, c. 236, § 3.
R.L.1902, c. 221, § 9.

§ 10. Payment of witness fees; presentment of certificate

The state treasurer shall pay to the persons entitled therein all witnesses fees or other money due for services rendered or expenses incurred in any of the courts named in section eight, or for any of the aforesaid officers, upon presentation to him of a certificate stating the name of the claimant, of the court and of the case, the nature of the services rendered or expenses incurred and the amount due therefor, signed by the clerk of the court or by the officer for whom the service was rendered.

Amended by St.1978, c. 478, § 313.

Historical and Statutory Notes

St.1891, c. 236, § 2.
R.L.1902, c. 221, § 10.
St.1918, c. 257, § 466.
St.1919, c. 5.
St.1920, c. 2.

§ 11. Certification of fines and forfeitures; payment to commonwealth

Except as otherwise provided in section eighty of chapter two hundred and seventy-six, fines and forfeitures imposed in criminal prosecutions by the superior court to the use of the commonwealth, and all amounts found to be due on forfeited recognizances, shall under the direction of the court, be certified by the clerk and paid to the commonwealth.

Amended by St.1978, c. 478, § 313.

Historical and Statutory Notes

St.1693–4, c. 2, § 1.
St.1791, c. 53, § 2.
R.S.1836, c. 141, § 9.

St.1857, c. 107, § 1.
G.S.1860, c. 176, §§ 9, 12.
St.1881, c. 52, § 1.
P.S.1882, c. 217, §§ 9, 12.
St.1890, c. 218, § 1.
R.L.1902, c. 221, § 11.
St.1918, c. 257, § 467.
St.1919, c. 5.
St.1920, c. 2.

§ 12. Escape of prisoner; liability of sheriff for fines or forfeitures of prisoner

A sheriff who, having a person in his custody by virtue of the sentence of a court, voluntarily or negligently suffers him to escape shall be held to have received the fines, forfeitures or forfeited recognizances described in the preceding section, at the time of the escape, and shall be liable for the same, with interest and costs, as if he had received them.

Historical and Statutory Notes

St.1791, c. 53, § 3.
R.S.1836, c. 141, § 9.
St.1857, c. 107, § 1.
G.S.1860, c. 176, § 10.
P.S.1882, c. 217, § 10.
R.L.1902, c. 221, § 12.

§ 13. Failure of sheriff to pay fines or forfeitures of escaped prisoner; remedy

If a sheriff neglects to make such payment for thirty days, the state treasurer shall recover of him in contract the amount of such fines, forfeitures and forfeited recognizances, with interest at the rate of twelve per cent from the time he is held to have received the same and costs.

Amended by St.1978, c. 478, § 314.

Historical and Statutory Notes

St.1791, c. 53, § 3.
R.S.1836, c. 141, § 9.
St.1857, c. 107, § 1.
G.S.1860, c. 176, § 11.
P.S.1882, c. 217, § 11.
R.L.1902, c. 221, § 13.

§ 14. Default in fine payment; commitment to jail or house of correction; payment to jailer or superintendent

A person committed to a jail or house of correction in default of payment of a fine may pay it to the keeper of the jail or superintendent of the house of correction, and the warrant for his commitment shall designate the town where the offence for which the fine was imposed was committed and the uses to which such fine is payable by the officer receiving it.

Amended by St.1979, c. 485, § 48.

Historical and Statutory Notes

St.1881, c. 52, § 1.
P.S.1882, c. 217, § 14.
St.1891, c. 416, § 2.
R.L.1902, c. 221, § 14.

§ 15. Quarterly transfers to state treasurer of payments received by jailer or superintendent; account on oath

Every keeper of a jail and superintendent of a house of correction shall, on the first days of January, April, July and October, pay over to the state treasurer all money received by him under the preceding section during the preceding three months, and render to said state treasurer an account, on oath, showing the names of prisoners by whom payments have been so made, the court by which each was committed and the amount received from each.

Amended by St.1978, c. 478, § 315; St.1979, c. 485, § 49.

Historical and Statutory Notes

St.1881, c. 52, § 2.
P.S.1882, c. 217, § 15.
St.1891, c. 416, § 3.
R.L.1902, c. 221, § 15.

§ 16. Payment by state treasurer of expenses or fees; time limit for demand; qualifications for payment to clerks of district court

The state treasurer shall pay over to the persons entitled thereto all amounts allowed to them for expenses or fees in criminal prosecutions, or allowed by the courts as rewards or compensations to prosecutors, which have been duly certified by the clerks, if demanded within three years after the allowance thereof; but he shall pay no such amounts to a clerk of a district court, until the clerk has rendered a written account of all fines received by him since his last return, and of all fees which have remained in his hands for one year after their allowance.

Amended by St.1953, c. 319, § 38; St.1978, c. 478, § 316.

Historical and Statutory Notes

St.1809, c. 93, § 1.
R.S.1836, c. 141, § 12.
G.S.1860, c. 176, § 17.
St.1860, c. 191, §§ 8, 10.
St.1861, c. 184.
P.S.1882, c. 217, § 16.
R.L.1902, c. 221, § 16.

MASSACHUSETTS RULES OF CRIMINAL PROCEDURE

Effective July 1, 1979

Research Note

See Massachusetts General Laws Annotated, vol. 47, for case annotations, cross references, and library references relating to the Massachusetts Rules of Criminal Procedure.

The Massachusetts Rules of Criminal Procedure are discussed in Smith, Massachusetts Practice—Criminal Practice and Procedure, vols. 30, 30A and 30B (3d Edition).

Table of Rules

Rule 1. Title; Scope

[Text of rule applicable to cases initiated (by indictment or complaint) on or after September 7, 2004.]

(a) Title. These rules may be known and cited as the Massachusetts Rules of Criminal Procedure. (Mass.R.Crim.P.)

(b) Scope. These rules govern the procedure in all criminal proceedings in the District Court, in all criminal proceedings in the Superior Court, in all delinquency and youthful offender proceedings in the Juvenile Court, District Court and Superior Court consistent with the General Laws, and in proceedings for post-conviction relief.

Amended March 8, 2004, effective September 7, 2004.

Reporter's Notes—Revised, 2004

Rule 1 is drawn from and combines Fed. R. Crim. P. 60 and 1. The substance of the rule defines the scope and applicability of the remainder of the rules.

These rules are applicable to the criminal process in those courts having general criminal jurisdiction. This code represents an attempt to consolidate into a single document rules of procedure to apply with the fewest possible exceptions to the appropriate departments of the Trial Court of the Commonwealth. Those exceptions are delineated in each rule where different procedures must prevail. There is, of course, a limitation inherent in any comprehensive set of procedural rules. That is, a variety of special procedures or factual situations exist where the mechanical application of the rules would work an unnecessary hardship or an injustice. In those limited circumstances, sound judicial discretion will require a construction of the rules so as to secure simplicity in procedure, fairness in the administration of the criminal justice system, and the elimination of unnecessary expense and delay as required by Rule 2(a).

In order to be of broad application to criminal practice, it was necessary for the rules to prescribe general procedures suitable for all courts within their scope. It is necessary that the rules be general and flexible, prescribing only basic essentials, rather than rigid and detailed. It is also necessary that the Rules be reviewed periodically to assess their operation and to take account of changes in both law and society over time. Such a comprehensive review was undertaken beginning in 1995, resulting in subsequent amendments to several of the rules, including a set of major revisions promulgated in 2004.

While these rules are intended to constitute a comprehensive code of criminal procedure for cases in the enumerated courts, nevertheless there are areas of criminal practice which were left unregulated. Among these matters are pretrial diversion, search- and arrest-warrant procedures, wire-tapping procedures, and other similar matters. As to some of these practices, it was determined that the state of the law, especially regarding constitutional issues, was so fluid as to defy codification. These matters were necessarily left to an *ad hoc* determination on specific facts by the courts. In other areas it was recognized that local practice in individual courts — whether by accepted usage or court rules — could give the criminal justice system some flexibility as required by special conditions not susceptible to general regulation.

These rules are not intended to pre-empt the adoption of rules by the several departments of the Trial Court to address specific problems which are inevitably encountered in those courts and which are not dealt with by these rules.

Nor are these rules intended to be a comprehensive guide or statement with respect to the procedures used by the clerks of court. It is expected that those offices will continue to develop efficient methods to assist in the expeditious disposal of criminal matters consistent with the letter and spirit of these rules.

By a 2004 amendment, Rule 1 was revised to explicitly state that the Rules of Criminal Procedure govern "all delinquency and youthful offender proceedings in the Juvenile Court." Thus the same rules apply to juvenile court proceedings that apply to delinquency and criminal proceedings in the other trial courts. This accords with M.G.L. c. 218, sec. 59, which provides that "Except as otherwise provided by law, the divisions of the juvenile court department shall have and exercise, within their respective jurisdictions, the same powers, duties, and procedure as the divisions of the district court department; and all laws relating to district courts or municipal courts in their respective counties or officials thereof or proceedings therein, shall, so far as applicable, apply to said divisions of the juvenile court department ..." The application of the Rules of Criminal Procedure to juvenile proceedings does not, however, imply that they are identical to adult criminal cases in all other respects. Special procedures for the hearing of juvenile offenses have been established under G.L. c. 119 and are designed to treat juveniles as children in need of aid, encouragement and guidance, rather than as criminals. Metcalf v. Commonwealth, 338 Mass. 648, 156 N.E.2d 649 (1959). G.L. c. 119, § 53 directs that proceedings against juveniles under G.L. c. 119 shall not be deemed criminal proceedings, but such matters must still be governed by constitutional due process standards. In re Gault, 87 S.Ct. 1428, 387 U.S. 1, 18 L.Ed.2d 527 (1967). Therefore, these rules are intended to be construed liberally so as to comply with the goals and purposes of G.L. c. 119, while G.L. c. 119, § 53 is not to operate to deny the procedural safeguards contained within these rules.

Rule 2. Purpose; Construction; Definition of Terms

(Applicable to District Court and Superior Court)

(a) Purpose; Construction. These rules are intended to provide for the just determination of every criminal proceeding. They shall be construed to secure simplicity in procedure, fairness in administration, and the elimination of expense and delay.

(1) Words or phrases importing the singular number may extend and be applied to several persons or things, words importing the plural number may include the singular, and words importing the masculine gender may include the feminine and neuter.

(2) When in these rules reference is made to a subdivision of a rule, that reference is to that subdivision and to any subdivisions thereof.

(b) Definition of Terms. In construing these rules the following words and phrases shall have the following meanings unless a contrary intent clearly appears from the context in which they are used:

(1) "Indigent" means any defendant who is unable to procure counsel with his funds as defined in Supreme Judicial Court Rule 3:10.

(2) "Indigent but able to contribute" means any defendant who is unable to procure counsel with his funds but is able to contribute funds for the cost of counsel as defined in Supreme Judicial Court Rule 3:10.

(3) "Capital Crime" means a charge of murder in the first degree.

(4) "Commonwealth" includes the prosecuting office or agency and all officers or agents responsible thereto.

(5) "Court" includes a judge, special magistrate, or clerk.

(6) "District Attorney" or "Attorney General" include assistant district attorneys or assistant attorneys general and other attorneys specially appointed to aid in the prosecution of a case.

(7) "District Court" includes all divisions of the District Court Department of the Trial Court, the Boston Municipal Court Department of the Trial Court, and the Juvenile Court Department of the Trial Court, or sessions thereof for holding court.

(8) "Interested Person" includes the adverse party, a co-defendant, and a witness who is to be deposed.

(9) "Judge" includes a judge of a court or one properly assigned to a court or a special magistrate when in the performance of those duties imposed and authorized by these rules.

(10) "Juvenile Court" means a division of the Juvenile Court Department of the Trial Court, or a session thereof for holding court.

(11) "Mailing" means the use of regular mail and shall not require registered or certified mail.

(12) "Prosecuting Attorney" means the attorney general or assistant attorneys general, district attorney, assistant district attorneys, special assistant district attorneys, or legal assistants to the district attorney, or other attorneys specially appointed to aid in the prosecution of a case.

(13) "Prosecutor" means any prosecuting attorney or prosecuting officer, and shall include a city solicitor, a police prosecutor, or a law student approved for practice pursuant to and acting as authorized by the rules of the Supreme Judicial Court.

(14) "Related Offense" means one of two or more offenses which are based on the same criminal conduct or episode or arise out of a course of criminal conduct or series of criminal episodes connected together or constituting parts of a single scheme or plan.

(15) "Return Day" means the day upon which a defendant is ordered by summons to first appear or, if under arrest, does first appear before a court to answer to the charges against him, whichever is earlier.

(16) "Special Magistrate" means any person who is appointed pursuant to, and empowered to administer those functions authorized by, rule forty-seven of these rules.

(17) "Summons" means

(A) criminal process issued to a person requiring him to appear at a stated time and place to answer to criminal charges; or

(B) process issued to a person requiring him to appear at a stated time and place to give testimony in a criminal proceeding; or

(C) process issued to a person requiring him to appear and produce at a stated time and place books, designated papers, documents, or other objects for use in a criminal proceeding.

(18) "Superior Court" means the Superior Court Department of the Trial Court, or a session thereof for holding court.

Amended May 29, 1986, effective July 1, 1986.

Reporter's Notes

Rule 2 is perhaps the most significant of the rules in advancing the trend toward a high degree of procedural fairness in the administration of criminal justice. This is so because the rule not only permits but requires the rules to be construed and applied in a manner which provides for fairness in their administration to the end that a just determination in every criminal proceeding shall be achieved. The rules must be approached with sympathy for this purpose; they must be interpreted with common sense.

The rules were not intended to be administered inflexibly without regard for the circumstances of the particular case. Where a literal interpretation of a rule and its application in a specific situation would lead to unnecessary expense or delay, would unduly complicate the proceedings, or would operate unfairly or produce an unjust result, that interpretation is to yield to the principle enunciated in Rule 2(a).

This is not to imply that the rules were conceived as merely guidelines or suggested procedures to which the courts and counsel need adhere only as will further their particular interests. They have the force and effect of law.

The appellate courts have made it increasingly clear that abuse of power by the prosecution or by trial judges is not to be tolerated. *See e.g.,* S.J.C. Rule 3:22A, *Disciplinary Rules Applicable to Practice as a Prosecutor or as a Defense Lawyer,* PF 1–14 (Feb. 14, 1979); Commonwealth v. St. Pierre, Mass. Adv.Sh. (1979) 834, 387 N.E.2d 1135; Commonwealth v. Soares, Mass.Adv.Sh. (1979) 593, 387 N.E.2d 499; Commonwealth v. Ellison, Mass.Adv.Sh. (1978) 2072, 379 N.E.2d 560; Commonwealth v. Earltop, Mass.Adv.Sh. (1977) 532, 539, 361 N.E.2d 220 (Hennessey, C.J., concurring); Commonwealth v. Redmond, 370 Mass. 591, 351 N.E.2d 501 (1976); Commonwealth v. Sneed, Mass.Adv.Sh. (1978) 3156, 383 N.E.2d 843. It is equally apparent that a high standard of conduct is demanded of defense counsel. *See* S.J.C. Rule 3:22A, supra, DF 1–15. A disregard for these rules of court or a failure to adhere to their provisions are abuses of the system which can be expected to produce problems in the administration of justice and unfairness to the Commonwealth, defendants, and the public, and which, therefore, should not be tolerated by either the trial or appellate courts.

Subdivision (a). The language of the first paragraph is drawn virtually without change from Fed.R.Crim.P. 2. These rules are intended to minimize complicated proceedings and needless expense and delay and are to be construed so as to achieve that goal.

The principle of construction stated in subdivision (a)(1) is taken from G.L. c. 4, § 6, cl. fourth, which relates to the construction of the General Laws.

Subdivision (a)(2) is designed to avoid any confusion in reading references to subdivisions. Included in a reference to a subdivision are all paragraphs, subparagraphs, and clauses of that subdivision.

Subdivision (b). These definitions are to be used in construing these rules unless a contrary interpretation is clearly demanded by the context within which the term is used. See G.L. c. 4, § 7; c. 3, § 63.

(1) *Appointed Counsel.* This definition is suggested by Superior Court Rule 53(3) (1974); it is to be distinguished from "Assigned Counsel," infra.

(2) *Assigned Counsel.* The terms "appointed counsel" and "assigned counsel" have been used interchangeably in the case law. *See* e.g., Costarelli v. Municipal Court of the City of Boston, 367 Mass. 35, 323 N.E.2d 859 (1975). However, for the purposes of these rules, each term has been given a separate and distinct definition. In these rules, "assigned

counsel" means a member of a publicly funded or charitable organization, such as the Massachusetts Defenders Committee (G.L. c. 221, § 34D. See Rule 8[b]), or a county defender. "Appointed counsel" denotes a private attorney who is designated by a judge or magistrate to represent a defendant who cannot afford counsel. Both assigned and appointed counsel may include senior law students appearing without compensation on behalf of indigent defendants as permitted by S.J.C. Rule 3:11 (1974: 366 Mass. 867, as amended, 1975: 367 Mass. 914).

(3) *Capital Crime.* This definition is drawn from existing case law, e.g., Commonwealth v. Capalbo, 308 Mass. 376, 32 N.E.2d 225 (1941); Commonwealth v. Ibrahim, 184 Mass. 255, 68 N.E. 231 (1903); Green v. Commonwealth, 94 Mass. (12 Allen) 155 (1866). *Compare* G.L. c. 278, § 33E (capital crime defined "for the purposes of . . . [appellate] review" only). General Laws c. 274, § 2 provides that, "Whoever aids in the commission of a felony, or is accessory thereto before the fact by counselling, hiring or otherwise procuring such felony to be committed, shall be punished in the manner provided for the punishment of the principal felon." Therefore, an indictment of a defendant as an accessory before the fact of first degree murder sets out a capital crime. Grady v. Treasurer of the County of Worcester, 352 Mass. 702, 704, 227 N.E.2d 490 (1967).

(4) *Commonwealth.* The definition of this term reflects the meaning of the word as commonly used in the case law and statutes.

(5) *Court.* This term is used in the rules to include those officials most intimately involved in the process of adjudicating cases. When so generically used, the word is not to be construed so as to expand or limit those duties traditionally or by law within the prerogative of certain officials.

(6) *District Attorney or Attorney General.* As with "Commonwealth," supra, these terms are used both in the sense of the office and the personnel thereof in their official capacity.

(7) *District Court.* General Laws c. 211B, § 1 (inserted by St.1978, c. 478, § 110) established the Trial Court of the Commonwealth which consists in part of the Superior Court Department, the District Court Department, the Boston Municipal Court Department, and the Juvenile Court Departments. For ease of reference throughout these rules, the latter three Departments are included within the term "District Court."

It is in keeping with the policy of these rules to secure simplicity and uniformity in procedure to make the Juvenile Court Department subject to these rules, insofar as they are consistent with juvenile practice. See District Court Special Rule 2 (1974), which applies the rules of the District Court to juvenile proceedings insofar as they are "pertinent."

(8) *Interested Person.* This term specifies those persons who are entitled to notice of, for example, the filing of motions, Mass.R.Crim.P. 13, 32, or the taking of a deposition, Mass.R.Crim.P. 36.

(9) *Judge.* In addition to its accepted meaning, for purposes of these rules this term is to include a magistrate when used in reference to a function which that official is authorized to perform by Mass.R.Crim.P. 48.

(10) *Juvenile Court.* See G.L. c. 211B, § 1 (inserted by St.1978, c. 478, § 110), c. 218, §§ 57–60 (St.1978, c. 478, §§ 212–16).

The divisions of the Juvenile Court Department, within their respective jurisdictions, have and exercise the same powers, duties and procedures as the District Court or Municipal Court Departments and are subject to the laws relating thereto, so far as applicable. G.L. c. 218, § 59 (as amended, St.1978, c. 478, § 215).

(11) *Mailing.* It is intended that unless specifically provided for elsewhere in these rules, neither registered nor certified mailing is required.

(12) *Prosecuting Attorney.* This term includes those attorneys who prosecute the majority of criminal cases in the Commonwealth.

(13) *Prosecutor.* This definition is broader than that of "prosecuting attorney," and reflects the fact that many cases in the District Courts are prosecuted by a police prosecutor. Under these rules, some prosecutorial functions can be carried on only by a district attorney or attorney general. *See* e.g., Mass.R.Crim.P. 15(d)(1)(B). A prosecutor may include senior law students appearing on behalf of the Commonwealth pursuant to S.J.C. Rule 3:11 (1974: 366 Mass. 867, as amended, 1975: 367 Mass. 914).

(14) *Related Offense.* For further explanation of this definition, see Mass.R.Crim.P. 9 and Reporter's Notes.

(15) *Return Day.* The "return day" is the date upon which a defendant under arrest first appears in court or the date upon which a defendant not under arrest is scheduled to appear pursuant to summons. It is the date upon which speedy trial rights attach (Mass.R.Crim.P. 36[b][1]) and from which other time limits are measured.

(16) *Special Magistrate.* The office of "Special Magistrate" is defined in terms of its powers and duties. See Mass. R.Crim.P. 47. Special Magistrates are to be distinguished from "Magistrates in the Trial Court" under G.L. c. 221, §§ 62B–62C (inserted by St.1978, c. 478, § 250).

(17) *Summons.* This definition includes process issued pursuant to Mass.R.Crim.P. 6 and 17. The definitions contained in subdivisions (b)(17)(B) and (C) of this rule replace the older term "subpoena."

(18) *Superior Court.* See G.L. c. 211B, § 1 (inserted by St.1978, c. 478, § 110), c. 212 (as amended, St.1978, c. 478, §§ 115–25).

Rule 3. Complaint and Indictment; Waiver of Indictment; Probable Cause Hearing

[Text of rule applicable to cases initiated (by indictment or complaint) on or after September 7, 2004.]

(a) Commencement of Criminal Proceeding. A criminal proceeding shall be commenced in the District Court by a complaint and in the Superior Court by an indictment, except that if a defendant is charged in the District Court with a crime as to which the defendant has the right to be proceeded against by indictment and the defendant has waived the right to an indictment pursuant to subdivision (c), the Commonwealth may proceed in the Superior Court upon the complaint.

(b) Right to Indictment. A defendant charged with an offense punishable by imprisonment in state prison shall have the right to be proceeded against by indictment except when the offense charged is within the concurrent jurisdiction of the District and Superior Courts and the District Court retains jurisdiction.

(c) Waiver of Indictment.

(1) *Right to Waive Indictment.* A defendant charged in a District Court with an offense as to which the defendant has the right to be proceeded against by indictment shall have the right, except when the offense charged is a capital crime, to waive indictment, unless the Commonwealth proceeds by indictment pursuant to subdivision (e) of this rule.

(2) *Procedure for Waiving Indictment.* The defendant may waive the right to be proceeded against by indictment by filing a written waiver of that right in the District Court prior to the determination to bind the case over to the Superior Court for trial. The District Court may for cause shown grant relief from that waiver. After the determination by the District Court to bind the case over to the Superior Court for trial, the defendant may waive the right to be proceeded against by indictment by filing a written waiver of that right, with the consent of the prosecutor, in the Superior Court.

(d) Transmission of Papers. If the defendant is bound over to the Superior Court for trial after a finding of probable cause or after the defendant waives a probable cause hearing, the clerk of the District Court shall transmit to the clerk of the Superior Court a copy of the complaint and of the record; the original recognizances; a list of the witnesses; a statement of the expenses and the appearance of the attorney for the defendant, if any is entered; the waiver of the right to be proceeded against by indictment, if any is executed; the pretrial conference report, if any has been filed; and the report of the department of mental health as to the mental condition of the defendant, if such report has been filed under the provisions of the General Laws.

(e) Indictment after Waiver. Notwithstanding the defendant's waiver of the right to be proceeded against by indictment, the prosecuting attorney may proceed by indictment.

(f) Probable Cause Hearing. Defendants charged in a District Court with an offense as to which they have the right to be proceeded against by indictment and defendants charged in a District Court with an offense within the concurrent jurisdiction of the District and Superior Courts for which the District Court will not retain jurisdiction, have the right to a probable cause hearing, unless an indictment has been returned for the same offense. If the District Court finds that there is probable cause to believe that the defendant committed the crime or crimes alleged in the complaint, the court shall bind the defendant over to the Superior Court. If the District Court finds that there is no probable cause to believe that the defendant committed the crime or crimes alleged in the complaint, the court shall dismiss the complaint.

(g) The Complaint Process.

(1) *Procedure for Obtaining a Complaint.* Any person having knowledge, whether first hand or not, of the facts constituting the offense for which the complaint is sought may be a complainant. The complainant shall convey to the court the facts constituting the basis for the complaint. The complainant's account shall be either reduced to writing or recorded. The complainant shall sign the complaint under oath, before an appropriate judicial officer.

(2) *Probable Cause Requirement.* The appropriate judicial officer shall not authorize a complaint unless the information presented by the complainant establishes probable cause to believe that the person against whom the complaint is sought committed an offense.

Amended March 8, 2004, effective September 7, 2004.

Reporter's Notes—Revised, 2004

WHILE DRAWN IN PART FROM THE GENERAL LAWS AND INCORPORATING MANY PROCEDURES DICTATED BY THE CASE LAW OF THE COMMONWEALTH, RULE 3 ALTERS PRESENT PRACTICE IN SOME RESPECTS. AS ORIGINALLY PROMULGATED IN 1979, RULE 3 WAS DESIGNED TO FORCE ALL NONCAPITAL DEFENDANTS IN THE DISTRICT COURT WHO HAD A RIGHT TO AN INDICTMENT TO MAKE AN ELECTION BETWEEN HAVING THEIR CASES CONSIDERED BY A GRAND JURY OR OBTAINING A PROBABLE CAUSE HEARING. THIS "FORCED WAIVER" PROVISION WAS RARELY USED IN PRACTICE BECAUSE OF CONCERNS THAT IT WOULD INFRINGE ON A DEFENDANT'S CONSTITUTIONAL RIGHT TO INDICTMENT AND STATUTORY RIGHT TO A PROBABLE CAUSE HEARING. A 2004 AMENDMENT TO THE RULE ELIMINATED THE "FORCED WAIVER" PROVISION. THE RATIONALE FOR THE "FORCED WAIVER" PROVISION WAS BASED ON A CONCERN FOR EFFICIENCY. HOWEVER, EVEN WITHOUT FORCING A DEFENDANT TO CHOOSE BETWEEN A PROBABLE CAUSE HEARING AND AN INDICTMENT, THE PROSECUTOR CAN PREVENT UNNECESSARY DUPLICATION OF PROCEDURE SIMPLY BY INDICTING THE DEFENDANT PRIOR TO THE PROBABLE CAUSE HEARING. IF IT IS INEFFICIENT TO HAVE A PROBABLE CAUSE HEARING, THE PROSECUTOR IS IN THE BEST POSITION TO RECOGNIZE THAT FACT AND TO TAKE THE STEPS NECESSARY TO AVOID IT. THE 2004 AMENDMENT ALSO ELIMINATED A REFERENCE TO JUVENILE PROCEDURE MADE IRRELEVANT BY STATUTE AND ADDED PROVISIONS DESCRIBING THE COMPLAINT PROCESS.

Subdivision (a). This subdivision in part restates G.L. c. 263, § 4. Approximate parallels may be found in Rules of Criminal Procedure (ULA) Rule 23(a) (1974); ALI Model Code of Pre–Arraignment Procedure §§ 330.1(3), 340.1(2) (POD 1975).

General Laws c. 263, § 4 provides that "[n]o person shall be held to answer in any court for an alleged crime, except upon an indictment by a grand jury or upon a complaint before a district court . . ." It is only the issuance of a complaint or an indictment that begins the criminal process, initiates a defendant's right to counsel under the Sixth Amendment to the United States Constitution, and tolls the statute of limitations. *See* Commonwealth v. Valchuis, 40 Mass. App. Ct. 556, 560 (1996) (statute of limitations not tolled by application for complaint or citation, but by complaint itself).

The District Courts are empowered by G.L. c. 218, § 32, to "receive complaints and issue warrants and other processes for the apprehension of persons charged with crime . . ." and pursuant to G.L. c. 218, § 30, shall bind over for trial in the Superior Court defendants who appear to be guilty of crimes not within their final jurisdiction, and may bind over defendants appearing guilty of crimes within their final jurisdiction. Where the charge is by complaint and the accused is under arrest not having been indicted by grand jury, he is entitled "as soon as may be" to a probable cause hearing to determine whether he should be held for trial. G.L. c. 276, § 38.

Subdivision (b). This subdivision in large part restates the essentials of prior practice. The right to indictment is not mentioned in the Constitution of the Commonwealth. It was not until 1857 that the Supreme Judicial Court defined that right, holding that "punishment in the state prison is an infamous punishment, and cannot be imposed without . . . indictment . . ." Jones v Robbins, 74 Mass. (8 Gray) 329, 349 (1857). Therefore, subdivision (b) affords the right to be proceeded against by indictment to "a defendant charged with an offense punishable by imprisonment in state prison . . .," that is, Massachusetts Correctional Institution, Cedar Junction. G.L. c. 125, § 1(*o*). The right to indictment is not extended to defendants charged with a crime within the concurrent jurisdiction of the District and Superior Courts if the District Court retains jurisdiction. Section 27 of chapter 218 of the General Laws provides in part:

> [District Courts] may impose the same penalties as the superior court for all crimes of which they have jurisdiction, except that they may not impose a sentence to state prison.

General Laws c. 279, § 23 states that "[n]o sentence of a male convict to imprisonment or confinement for more than two and one half years shall be executed in any jail or house of correction." General Laws c. 218, §§ 26—27 and c. 279, § 23, when construed together, have led to the settled practice of the District Court, although having jurisdiction of felonies punishable by less than five years at Cedar Junction, sentencing to a jail or house of correction for not more than two and one half years.

Because a defendant tried in District Court is not subject to a sentence to state prison, there is no right to be proceeded against by indictment.

Subdivision (c) (1) While intended to secure a benefit to the accused, a grand jury indictment is but the formal accusation or presentation of charges against the accused, *see* Commonwealth v. Woodward, 157 Mass. 516, 518 (1893), and may be waived. *See* DeGolyer v. Commonwealth, 314 Mass. 626, 632–33 (1943); *e.g.* Commonwealth v. Thurston, 419 Mass. 101 (1994). Statutory authorization for such waiver in instances of defendants committed or bound over to the Superior Court for trial was found in former G.L. c. 263, § 4A (St 1934, c 358).

A defendant who is bound over to the Superior Court after a finding of probable cause has the right to indictment and the right to waive indictment. However, a defendant charged with a capital crime cannot waive indictment. G.L. c. 263, § 4A (as amended).

If after a waiver of indictment, probable cause is found to bind the defendant over for trial, G.L. c. 218, § 30, the Superior Court shall have as full jurisdiction over the case on the complaint as if an indictment has been found. *See* DeGolyer v. Commonwealth, 314 Mass. 626, 632 (1943).

(c) (2) Under the original version of the provision now contained in Rule 3 (c), the judge was required to advise a defendant who had a right to an indictment that he or she might waive indictment and proceed upon the complaint. In the 2004 revision of the rule, the elimination of the "forced waiver" provision made it unnecessary to require that a defendant receive such a warning. The right to waive indictment remains, however, except in a capital case where the General Laws prohibit it. *See* G.L. c. 263, § 4A. The defendant may exercise the option to waive indictment in the District Court, before being bound over, or afterward, in Superior Court. In either event, the approval of the judge is not necessary, although the court must ensure that the waiver is valid. This means that it must be intelligent and voluntary, *see* DeGolyer v. Commonwealth, 314 Mass. 626, 632 (1943), and that the defendant either has counsel or has waived the right to the assistance of counsel. The waiver must be in writing.

A juvenile who would otherwise be entitled to an indictment by virtue of G.L. c. 263 § 4 may also waive indictment under the procedure established in this subdivision.

Subdivision (d) This subdivision was formerly Rule 3(c)(2) prior to the revision of the Rule in 2004. It generally governs the transmission of the papers in the case after a defendant is bound over to the Superior Court. It is implicit in the rule that the defendant may waive the probable cause hearing to which he or she is entitled thereby proceeding immediately to the Superior Court upon the complaint. *E.g.* Commonwealth v. Tanso, 411 Mass. 640 (1992). Subdivision (d) provides for that contingency.

Subdivision (e). If the defendant waives indictment and probable cause is found the case moves immediately to the Superior Court for trial or other disposition unless the Commonwealth chooses to seek an indictment. The prosecution may wish to so proceed because of defects in the complaint, because there are other chargeable crimes—e.g., related offenses arising out of the same criminal episode—or to avail itself of the investigative power of the grand jury.

The prosecutor also has the option of obtaining an indictment in cases where the defendant does not have the right to one and the District Court would otherwise exercise final jurisdiction over the offense. So long as the District Court has not already placed the defendant in jeopardy, *cf.* Commonwealth v. Aldrich, 21 Mass. App. Ct. 221 (1985) (indictment barred by jeopardy where defendant pled guilty to complaint in District Court), the return of an indictment for the same offense as alleged in a complaint is ordinarily sufficient reason for the court to dismiss the complaint. *Compare* Commonwealth v. Burt, 393 Mass. 703 (1985) (judge acted properly in dismissing complaint upon return of indictment) *with* Commonwealth v. Raposa, 386 Mass. 666 (1982) (where judge refused to dismiss complaint upon return of indictment, it was proper for prosecutor to nolle prosequi). The prosecutor should not abuse this power however, such as by waiting until the day of trial to obtain an indictment, *see Raposa*, 386 Mass. at 669 n. 8 ("We would not look with favor, however, on a prosecutor's deliberate obstruction of the criminal process and waste of judicial resources by waiting until the day of trial in the District Court to seek indictments."), or by removing a case to Superior Court to avoid having to comply with a District Court order denying a continuance, *see* Commonwealth v. Thomas, 353 Mass. 429 (1967).

Subdivision (f). This subdivision was added by amendment in 2004.

Defendants whose cases are going to be ultimately disposed of in Superior Court, either because the District Court lacks or declines jurisdiction, are entitled to a probable cause hearing unless the prosecutor obtains an indictment for the same offense charged in the complaint. The return of an indictment constitutes a finding of probable cause and ordinarily renders unnecessary a probable cause hearing. *See* Lataille v District Court of Eastern Hampden, 366 Mass. 525, 531 (1974). There may be circumstances, however, where the prosecutor's bad faith in obtaining an indictment entitles the defendant to a probable cause hearing in any event. *Cf.* Hadfield v. Commonwealth, 387 Mass. 252, 257 (1982) (*dicta*) (circumventing probable cause hearing may be invalid where "effrontery to district court," "obstruction of criminal process," or "waste of judicial resources."); Commonwealth v. Spann, 383 Mass. 142, 145 (1981) (if prosecutor promised that defendant would not be indicted before a probable cause hearing and if defendant relied on promise to his detriment, promise would be enforced); Lataille v. District Court of Eastern Hampden, 366 Mass. 525, 531 n. 6 (1974) (agreement between counsel might entitle defendant to further pursuit of probable cause hearing which was in progress at time of indictment). Absent these unusual circumstances, however, the ordinary course of events after an indictment has been returned is for the District Court to dismiss the complaint, or for the prosecutor to enter a nolle prosequi, once the defendant has been arraigned in the Superior Court.

If an indictment has not already been returned, a defendant charged with a crime not within the jurisdiction of the District Court must be given a probable cause hearing "as soon as may be." *See* G.L. c. 276, § 38. The policy underlying this subdivision looks to liberal granting of continuances to the prosecution in order that indictments may be sought in cases that are scheduled for a probable cause hearing.

Even if the complaint charges a defendant with a crime within the jurisdiction of the District Court (which includes misdemeanors for which there would otherwise be no right to an indictment) the court may hold a probable cause hearing, *see* G.L. c. 218 § 30, if the judge in the exercise of discretion determines that the interest of justice would be served by having the Superior Court dispose of the defendant's case. This would typically be the case either to allow the consolidation of cases or in recognition of the exclusive power of the Superior Court to sentence defendants charged with a concurrent jurisdiction felony to state prison. *Cf.* Commonwealth v. Zannino, 17 Mass. App. Ct. 73, 79 (1983) (the power to exercise jurisdiction or to bind the defendant over for trial in the Superior Court "is not to be used arbitrarily, but in view of the circumstances of each particular case"). While it is ordinarily the prosecutor who institutes a request that a matter within the District Court's jurisdiction be treated as a probable cause matter rather than a trial on the merits, the ultimate decision is the judge's. *See* Commonwealth v. Zannino, 17 Mass. App. Ct. 73, 78–79 (1983) ("if the crime charged is within the final jurisdiction of the District Court, the threshold decision whether to conduct a full trial on the merits or only a probable cause hearing is, at least ordinarily, a question for the judge and not the prosecutor").

If a case is within the final jurisdiction of the District Court, the judge must announce that the court is going to decline jurisdiction prior to hearing sworn testimony from any witnesses, which is when jeopardy would otherwise attach in a non-jury trial. *See* Commonwealth v. DeFuria, 400 Mass. 485, 487 (1987); Crist v. Bretz, 437 U.S. 28, 37 n.15 (1978). If the court does not make a clear announcement that it is declining jurisdiction, any hearing that follows at which sworn testimony is received will be considered as a trial on the merits at which jeopardy has attached. *See* Commonwealth v. Clemmons, 370 Mass. 288, 291 n.2 (1976); Corey v. Commonwealth, 364 Mass. 137, 142 n. 7 (1973). *Compare* Commonwealth v. Crosby, 6 Mass. App. Ct. 679 (1978) (since judge failed to announce that he was declining jurisdiction prior to hearing sworn testimony offered in the course of an admission to sufficient facts, the proceedings constituted a trial on the merits and jeopardy barred the defendant's indictment) *with* Commonwealth v. DeFuria, 400 Mass. 485 (1987) (judge's failure to announce declination of jurisdiction prior to prosecutor's recitation of facts at an admission to sufficient findings did not bar further prosecution since no sworn testimony taken). *Cf.* Commonwealth v. Mesrobian, 10 Mass. App. Ct. 355, 356 n. 2 (1980) ("fundamental fairness dictates that the Commonwealth ought to be required to state unequivocally at the outset of the hearing its intention [to proceed on the basis of probable cause rather than a trial on the merits]"). Since defense strategy at a probable cause hearing differs significantly from that at a trial, the judge should provide notice to the defendant of the decision to decline jurisdiction as far in advance of the hearing as possible. The District Court rules promulgated on January 1, 1996 contemplate that the pretrial hearing is the appropriate stage at which to make the decision. District/Municipal Courts Rules of Criminal Procedure, Rule 4(f).

Whether a probable cause hearing concerns an offense outside the jurisdiction of the District Court or results from a decision of the court to decline jurisdiction over an offense for which it could have held a trial, the standard that the court should apply at the probable cause hearing to determine whether to bind the case over to the Superior Court is the same. It is the test a trial judge uses to determine a motion for a required finding of not guilty. *See* Myers v. Commonwealth, 363 Mass. 843, 850 (1973) ("The examining magistrate should view the case as if it were a trial and he were required to rule on whether there is enough credible evidence to send the case to the jury. Thus, the magistrate should dismiss the complaint when, on the evidence presented, a trial court would be bound to acquit as a matter of law.") This standard is more stringent than the one that governs the grand jury's determination. *See* Commonwealth v. McCarthy, 385 Mass. 160, 163 (1982) (an indictment cannot stand unless, at a minimum, it is supported by evidence sufficient to establish probable cause to arrest); Commonwealth v. O'Dell, 392 Mass. 445, 451–52 (1984) (grand jury requirement of sufficient evidence to establish the identity of the accused and probable cause to arrest him is considerably less exacting than a requirement of sufficient evidence to warrant a guilty finding).

At a probable cause hearing, the defendant must be given a meaningful opportunity to cross-examine witnesses and present evidence on his or her own behalf to assure an accurate appraisal of probable cause. *See* Myers v Commonwealth, 363 Mass. 843 (1973); Corey v Commonwealth, 364 Mass. 137 (1973). Following the lead of the United States Supreme

Court in Coleman v Alabama, 399 U.S. 1 (1970), the Supreme Judicial Court held that a probable cause hearing is such a critical stage in criminal proceedings as to require the assistance of counsel. *See* Commonwealth v Britt, 362 Mass. 325 (1972). The rules of evidence at a probable cause hearing should in general be the same as are applicable at a trial, that is, a finding of probable cause to hold the defendant for trial "must be based on competent testimony which would be admissible at trial." Myers v Commonwealth, *supra* at 849 n 6. Further, the defendant may have the proceedings taken by a stenographer at his or her own expense, *see* G.L. c. 221, § 91B; Commonwealth v. Shea, 356 Mass. 358, 360—61 (1969); Commonwealth v. Britt, 362 Mass. 325, 328—29 (1972) and the transcript is admissible in subsequent proceedings when otherwise competent. *See* G L c 221, § 91B, c 233, § 80; Commonwealth v. DiDietro, 373 Mass. 369 (1977).

If the evidence meets the appropriate standard and the case is bound over to Superior Court, the District Court retains jurisdiction to rule on ancillary matters until an indictment is returned. *See* Commonwealth v. Tanso, 411 Mass. 640, 644 (1992). If the evidence presented at the probable cause hearing does not meet the appropriate standard, the complaint should be dismissed. *See* Commonwealth v. Ortiz, 393 Mass. 523, 524 (1984). Since jeopardy does not attach at a probable cause hearing, *see* Commonwealth v. Scala, 380 Mass. 500, 505 n. 3 (1980), nor is a finding of no probable cause subject to appeal, a District Court's dismissal based on a failure of the evidence to meet the standard does not bar a further proceedings, either by way of a subsequent indictment for the same offense, *see* Commonwealth v. Juvenile, 409 Mass. 49, 52 (1991); Burke v Commonwealth, 373 Mass. 157, 160 (1977), or holding another probable cause hearing based on a new complaint, *see* Juvenile v. Commonwealth, 375 Mass. 104, 106 (1978) ("Additional probable cause hearings may be held, especially if additional evidence is to be offered at the subsequent hearing."). However, if the institution of further proceedings constitutes harassment, the defendant is entitled to relief. *See* Juvenile v. Commonwealth, 375 Mass. 104, 106 n. 1 (1978); Maldonado, petitioner, 364 Mass. 359, 364–365 (1973).

Subdivision (g) (1). This subdivision and the one following were added to Rule 3 by a 2004 amendment.

The General Laws identify the appropriate judicial officers who play a role in the process of authorizing the issuance of a criminal complaint and administering the oath. *See e.g.,* General Laws c. 218 § 7 (justices and special justices may administer oaths); c. 218 § 10A (deputy assistant clerks may administer oath); c. 218 § 33 (clerks, assistant clerks, temporary clerks, and temporary assistant clerks may receive complaints and administer the oath); c. 218 § 35 (justice or special justice may receive complaints); c. 218 § 37 (justices, special justices, clerks, assistant clerks, temporary clerks and temporary assistant clerks may issue process resulting from a hearing upon an application for a complaint).

General Laws c. 276, § 22 provides that a complainant is to be examined "on oath" and that the complaint is to be "subscribed by the complainant." The preferred procedure is to administer the oath to the complainant before he or she makes the statements which will serve as the basis for the complaint, but a complaint is still valid if the complainant swears to the truth of statements tendered to the appropriate judicial official after they have been made. *See* Commonwealth v. Cote, 15 Mass. App. Ct. 229, 236 (1983). There is no requirement that the statements offered in support of the issuance of a complaint be based on personal knowledge or observation. A complainant may properly present statements of which he or she has no first-hand knowledge. *See* Commonwealth v. Dillane, 77 Mass. (11 Gray) 67 (1858); Commonwealth v. Cote, 15 Mass. App. Ct. 229 (1983). Nor does a complainant have to have a personal stake in the matter. *See* Commonwealth v. Haddad, 364 Mass. 795, 797 (1974) ("anyone may make a criminal complaint in a District Court who is competent to make oath to it.") The practice in many courts where a single officer applies for complaints for offenses of which the officer has no first-hand knowledge is not only appropriate, but a sound administrative procedure. *Cf.* District Court Standards of Judicial Practice, THE COMPLAINT PROCEDURE, standard 3:23, commentary at 41–42 (1975). Rule 3(g) (1) authorizes the signing of the complaint by persons other than the arresting officer in order to avoid requiring the officer's presence at any time prior to the probable cause hearing or trial. The subdivision is grounded in the desire to avoid removing an officer from a regular work shift to execute the mere formality of personally signing the complaint.

The person against whom a complaint is sought does not have a right to be present at the procedure described in this subdivision. *See* Commonwealth v. Smallwood, 379 Mass. 878 (1980). However, in cases where no arrest has been made and all of the offenses the complainant seeks are misdemeanors, *see* Commonwealth v. Cote, *supra,* 15 Mass. App. Ct. at 235, as well as in certain felony cases, G.L. c. 218 § 35A provides for notice and a hearing before a complaint is authorized, subject to exceptions where there is a risk of bodily injury, commission of a crime, or flight from the jurisdiction.

"The implicit purpose of the § 35A hearings is to enable the court clerk to screen a variety of minor criminal or potentially criminal matters out of the criminal justice system through a combination of counseling, discussion, or threat of prosecution ..." Snyder, Crime and Community Mediation — The Boston Experience: A Preliminary Report on the Dorchester Urban Court Program, 1978 Wis. L. Rev. 737, 746 *quoted with approval* in Gordon v. Fay, 382 Mass. 64, 69–70 (1980).

This subdivision changes existing practice by requiring that in all cases, the facts on which a complaint is based either be submitted in writing or, in the discretion of the appropriate judicial official, conveyed orally so long as the oral statement is transcribed or otherwise recorded. The facts on which the complaint is based may be memorialized in any of the following three ways. First is a written statement submitted by the complainant. The written account of the facts can come from a police report, from a motor vehicle citation, *see* G.L. c. 90C § 3(B)(2), from a statement memorialized on the form for an application for a complaint promulgated by the District Courts, *see* District/Municipal Courts Rules of Criminal Procedure, Rule 2 (effective Jan. 1, 1996), or from any other written source. Second is a written statement made by the appropriate judicial official based on information conveyed by the complainant. And third is to record an oral statement by the complainant. Nothing in this subsection is intended to require the recording of hearings under G.L. c. 218 § 35A.

A number of other jurisdictions follow the practice of requiring the basis for a criminal complaint to be memorialized. *See* Fed. Rules Crim. Pro., Rules 3 & 4; Colo. Rules Crim. Pro., Rule 4(a); Minn. Rules Crim. Pro., Rule 2.01; R.I. Rules Crim. Pro., Rule 3. The purpose of this requirement is twofold. First, requiring a record of the facts presented to the court will protect the integrity of the complaint process. And second, in those cases where a defendant has the right to litigate the basis on which a complaint was issued, *see e.g.,* Commonwealth v. DiBennadetto, 436 Mass. 310 (2002), the existence of a record will facilitate judicial review.

(g) (2). This subdivision changes the existing practice concerning the authorization of criminal complaints in some cases. Under prior practice, where a complaint was sought against an individual who had been arrested, the appropriate judicial officer did not evaluate the justification for initiating criminal proceedings. It was only if the complainant applied for process to issue, either a summons or warrant, that a determination of probable cause was necessary. STANDARDS OF JUDICIAL PRACTICE: THE COMPLAINT PROCEDURE, 2:03, Administrative Office of the District Courts (1975). Under this subdivision, a finding of probable cause must be made for all cases, whether the defendant has been arrested or not. In requiring a probable cause determination in every case, this subdivision follows the federal model, *see* Fed. Rules Crim. Pro., 4(a) & 5(a), and that of a number of other states, *e.g.,* Conn. Practice Book, § 617; Minn. Rules Crim. Pro., Rule 2.01; N.J. Rules Crim. Pro., Rule 3:4–1(a).

The consequence, if any, of the failure of the record in a particular case to demonstrate probable cause is a matter that the rule does not address. The Supreme Judicial Court, in Commonwealth v. DiBennadetto, *supra* at 313, has held, however, that where a complaint was authorized after a § 35A hearing, "the issuance of [the] complaint ... is not to be revisited by a further show cause hearing; the defendant's remedy is a motion to dismiss."

The purpose of a probable cause determination prior to the authorization of a complaint is to screen out cases that do not belong in the criminal justice system at the earliest possible stage. The standard of probable cause to authorize a complaint is the same as the standard that governs the grand jury's decision to issue an indictment. "[A]t the very least the grand jury must hear sufficient evidence to establish the identity of the accused ... and probable cause to arrest him." Commonwealth v. O'Dell, 392 Mass. 445, 450 (1984), *quoting* Commonwealth v. McCarthy, 385 Mass. 160, 163 (1982). As in the grand jury or arrest context, the probable cause determination at this stage of the process may be based on hearsay. All that is required is "reasonably trustworthy information ... sufficient to warrant a prudent man in believing that the defendant had committed ... an offense," *O'Dell*, 385 Mass. at 450. This standard is considerably less exacting than the one that a judge must apply at a probable cause hearing under subdivision (f). *Id.* at 451. If a case cannot even meet the standard necessary under subdivision (g), it would be a waste of judicial resources and an unnecessary burden on the individual for the case to move any further in the process.

This subsection does not alter existing case law that gives courts in circumstances where a private citizen is a complainant, the power to refuse to issue a complaint even though there is probable cause to do so. *See* Victory Distributors v. Ayer Division of the District Court Dept., 435 Mass. 136 (2001). Where the Commonwealth seeks a complaint, however, the court must issue it so long as it is legally valid. *Id.* Although there is no explicit provision in the Rules of Criminal Procedure for the process that follows from an initial denial of an application for a complaint, the Supreme Judicial Court has held that judges have inherent authority to rehear such applications. *See* Bradford v. Knights, 427 Mass. 748 (1998).

Rule 3.1. Determination of Probable Cause for Detention

[Text of rule applicable to cases initiated (by indictment or complaint) on or after September 7, 2004.]

(a) No person shall be held in custody more than twenty-four hours following an arrest, absent exigent circumstances, unless:

(i) a warrant or other judicial process authorizes the person's detention,

(ii) a complaint has been authorized under Rule 3 (g), or

(iii) a determination of probable cause for detention has been made pursuant to subsection (b).

(b) A determination of probable cause for detention shall be made by an appropriate judicial officer. The appropriate officer shall consider any information presented by the police, whether or not known at the time of arrest. The police shall present the information under oath or affirmation, or under the pains and penalties of perjury. The police may present the information orally, in person or by any other means, or in writing. If presented in writing, the information may be transmitted to the appropriate judicial officer by facsimile transmission or by electronic mail or by such other electronic means as may be found acceptable by the court. The determination of probable cause for detention shall be an ex parte proceeding. The person arrested has no right to appear, either in person or by counsel.

(c) Where subsection (a) requires a determination of probable cause for detention, the police shall present the information necessary to obtain such determination to the appropriate judicial officer as soon as reasonably possible after the arrest, but no later than twenty-four hours after arrest, absent exigent circumstances.

(d) The judicial officer shall promptly reduce to writing his or her determination as to probable cause and notify the police. A copy of the written determination shall be transmitted to the police, by facsimile transmission or other means, as soon as possible.

(e) The judicial officer shall apply the same standard in making the determination of probable cause for detention as in deciding whether an arrest warrant should issue. If the judicial officer determines that there is probable cause to believe the person arrested committed an offense, the judicial officer shall make a written determination of his or her decision which shall be filed with the record of the case together with all the written information submitted by the police.

(f) If there is no probable cause to believe that the person arrested committed an offense, the judicial officer shall order the person's prompt release from custody. The order and a written determination of the judicial officer shall be filed in the District Court having jurisdiction over the location of the arrest, together with all the written information submitted by the police. These documents shall be filed separately from the records of criminal and delinquency cases, but shall be public records.

Added March 8, 2004, effective September 7, 2004.

Reporter's Notes—Revised, 2004

Rule 3.1 was added in 2004 to implement the requirements described by the Supreme Judicial Court in Jenkins v. Chief Justice of the District Court Department, 415 Mass. 221 (1993), dealing with the topic of obtaining a judicial determination of probable cause for persons held in custody after a warrantless arrest. It is based on the procedure promulgated in 1994 by Trial Court Rule XI. The only major substantive change that Rule 3.1 makes in the procedure dictated by Trial Court Rule XI is in the standard to use in determining if the custody of the individual is lawful. Trial Court Rule XI directed the "judicial officer [to determine whether] . . . there is probable cause to believe that such arrestee committed one or more of the offenses for which he or she was arrested." Rule 3.1 directs the judicial officer to determine if "there is probable cause to believe the person arrested committed an offense." The language of Rule 3.1 more accurately focuses on the appropriate issue that is crucial to the question of the legality of an individual's detention prior to being brought to court.

Subdivision (a) In *Jenkins*, the Court held that Article 14 of the Declaration of Rights requires the police to obtain a judicial determination of probable cause as soon as reasonably possible after they have made a warrantless arrest, which in the usual circumstances means no more than twenty-four hours. This subdivision identifies the only four exceptions to the police following the procedure that the balance of Rule 3.1 establishes. One is when the arrestee will not be held more than twenty-four hours. For example, if the police have arrested someone who is going to be bailed at the police station within twenty-hours, Rule 3.1 is not applicable. Another is when the arrest was based on process issued by a judicial officer, such as an arrest warrant, or when process exists which authorizes the detention of an arrestee on another charge. In the former circumstance, the police are merely executing a judicial order rather than making an independent judgment to deprive someone of their liberty. In the latter circumstance, where for example the police arrest someone without a warrant and then discover that there is a preexisting outstanding warrant for the arrestee, there is already judicial authorization to deprive the arrestee of his or her liberty. The third is when a complaint charging the arrestee with a crime has already been authorized under Rule 3(g), which independently requires a judicial officer to make the same sort of probable cause determination as Rule 3.1 contemplates. Last is when exigent circumstances exist which make it not possible to obtain judicial approval for an extended deprivation of the arrestee's liberty.

Subdivision (b) This subsection describes the procedure for a determination of probable cause for detention after a warrantless arrest. It requires the police to present the information that supports a deprivation of an arrestee's liberty to an appropriate judicial officer. These officials include judges and those individuals in the clerk-magistrate's office who are empowered to authorize complaints. *See* Reporters' Notes to Rule 3(g); G.L. c. 218 § 33. The Court held in *Jenkins*, 416 Mass. at 337–38 that:

> like the issuance of a warrant, the postarrest determination need not necessarily be made by a judge. *See* Commonwealth v. Smallwood, 379 Mass. 878, 885, 401 N.E.2d 802 (1980) ("While District Court judges are authorized to receive complaints and issue warrants, G. L. c. 218, § 32, a clerk or assistant clerk may also receive complaints, administer the required oath, and issue warrants in the name of the court. G. L. c. 218, § 33. Commonwealth v. Penta, 352 Mass. 271, 273, 225 N.E.2d 58 [1967]").

The police may present the appropriate judicial officer with the information providing probable cause for the arrestee's detention in writing or orally. This subdivision contemplates that the medium of providing the information be as flexible as possible. Physical submission of a written report, faxed copies or e-mail are all appropriate, as are telephone conversations. No matter how the police submit the information, however, it should be sworn to under oath or affirmation. The arrestee has no right to appear or participate at this proceeding, either in person or through counsel. *See Jenkins*, 416 Mass. at 244–45.

Subdivision (c) This subsection directs the police to present the information justifying the detention of an arrestee's liberty within twenty-four hours of the arrest, unless there are exigent circumstances. The exception for exigent circumstances addresses situations such as communication failures and natural disasters and not exigencies that relate solely to the investigative needs of the police.

Subdivision (d) This subsection incorporates essentially the same requirement for reducing the results of a determination of probable cause for detention to writing and transmitting it to the police as contained in Trial Court Rule XI(e).

Subdivision (e) This subdivision deals with the standard that governs the determination of probable cause for detention and the consequence of an affirmative finding. As to the first of these issues, the subdivision addresses two questions: what the standard should be and the issues to which the standard should be applied. The Court in *Jenkins* held that the Declaration of Rights requires a postarrest determination of probable cause to be "governed by the same legal standards as apply to the issuance of a warrant." *Jenkins*, 416 Mass. at 239. Rule 3.1 follows Trial Court Rule XI (b), in adopting this same familiar standard as the measure of whether further detention of an arrestee is warranted. However, the subdivision differs from Trial Court Rule XI (b) in the question of what issues must meet this standard. The Trial Court Rule focused on whether the individual committed one or more of the offenses for which he or she was arrested. This subdivision focuses on whether there is probable cause to believe individual committed any offense.

The procedure that Rule 3.1 addresses is directed to the question of probable cause for the arrestee's detention, not whether probable cause existed to justify the person's arrest. Given the nature of the determination, the legality of the arrestee's detention should not depend on the ability of the police accurately to identify the precise offense for which the person should be held. For example, it is sometimes the case that police with probable cause to arrest someone for a particular crime put down the wrong offense on the documents they fill out afterwards. Under the language of Trial Court Rule XI (d), such a person would have to be released despite clear probable cause to charge him or her with the correct crime. Under Rule 3.1, the police could detain such an individual and charge him or her with the appropriate offense. The approach that Rule 3.1 takes to this issue is similar to the rules of other jurisdictions. *See* Fla. R. Crim. Pro., Rule 3.133(a)(3); Me. R. Crim. Pro., Rule 5(d); Minn. R. Crim. Pro., Rule 4.03.

The subdivision also addresses the issue of the consequence of a determination that there exists probable cause for detention. If probable cause exits, a written finding together with the supporting documents are to be filed with the record of the case. A defendant does not have the right to have the probable cause determination reviewed at arraignment. By the time a defendant subject to the process described in Rule 3.1 is arraigned, a judicial officer not only will have made a determination of probable cause for detention, but also a determination pursuant to Rule 3(g) that probable cause exists for each of the offenses with which the defendant has been charged. There is no need for a judge at arraignment routinely to reconsider the matter of probable cause.

Subdivision (f) This subdivision deals with the issue of the consequence of a determination that there does not exist probable cause for detention. It is essentially the same in this regard as Trial Court Rule XI (e)(3).

Rule 4. Form and Contents of Complaint or Indictment; Amendment

(Applicable to District Court and Superior Court)

(a) Contents of Indictment or Complaint. An indictment and a complaint shall contain a caption as provided by law, together with a plain, concise description of the act which constitutes the crime or an appropriate legal term descriptive thereof.

(b) Subscription of Application for Issuance of Process. An application for issuance of process may be subscribed by the arresting officer, the police chief, or any police officer within the jurisdiction of a crime, a prosecutor, or a private person.

(c) Indictment Based Upon Secondary Evidence. An indictment shall not be dismissed on the grounds that the evidence presented before the grand jury consisted in whole or in part of the record from the defendant's probable cause hearing or that other hearsay evidence was presented before the grand jury.

(d) Amendment. Upon his own motion or the written motion of either party, a judge may allow amendment of the form of a complaint or indictment if such amendment would not prejudice the defendant or the Commonwealth.

Reporter's Notes

Subdivision (a). Rule 4(a) is a restatement of Massachusetts statutory law. A caption is required for indictments and complaints by G.L. c. 277, §§ 17, 79. See 30 MASS.PRACTICE SERIES (Smith) § 342 (1970). Although the indictment or complaint may contain more than one count (see Mass.R.Crim.P. 9[a][2], [b]), a single caption is sufficient. G.L. c. 277, §§ 17, 79.

The statement of the charges can be in the form of a description of the criminal act or in the form of a legal term descriptive of the act. "The words used in a statute to define a crime, or other words conveying the same meaning, may be used." G.L. c. 277, § 17. An indictment or complaint must, however, set forth all the elements of the crime charged and if a statute does not contain all those elements, an indictment or complaint drawn in terms of that statute is insufficient. G.L. c. 277, § 17; Commonwealth v. Palladino, 358 Mass. 28, 260 N.E.2d 653 (1970). The forms established by G.L. c. 277, § 79 contain sufficient descriptions of the crimes listed therein.

To survive a motion to dismiss, an indictment (together with a bill of particulars, if any. See Rule [13][b]) must describe the offense charged " 'fully, plainly, substantially and formally,' with as much certainty as the known circumstances of the case . . . [will] permit." Commonwealth v. Soule, 6 Mass.App. 973, 384 N.E.2d 235 (1979) 69 (Rescript). *Accord* Commonwealth v. Burke, 339 Mass. 521, 523, 159 N.E.2d 856, 77 A.L.R.2d 451 (1959); Commonwealth v. Gill, 5 Mass.App. 337, 363 N.E.2d 267 (1977).

Subdivision (b). General Laws c. 276, § 22 provides that a complainant is to be examined "on oath" and that the complaint is to be "subscribed by the complainant." While this requirement has been strictly construed, Commonwealth v. Barhight, 75 Mass. (9 Gray) 113 (1857), there is no requirement that the statements offered in support of the issuance of process be based on personal knowledge or observation. A complainant may properly present statements of which he has no first-hand knowledge. Commonwealth v. Dillane, 77 Mass. (11 Gray) 67 (1858). The practice in many courts where a single officer presents applications for issuance of process for offenses of which he has no first-hand knowledge is not only appropriate, but a sound administrative procedure. District Court Standards of Judicial Practice, THE COMPLAINT PROCEDURE, standard 3:23, commentary at 41–42 (1975). Rule 4(b) authorizes the signing of the complaint by persons other than the arresting officer in order to avoid requiring the officer's presence at any time prior to the probable cause hearing or trial. The subdivision is grounded in the desire to avoid removing an officer from his regular work shift to execute the mere formality of personally signing the complaint.

Subdivision (c). This subdivision of the rule refers to hearsay and other types of evidence which may be inadmissible at trial, but may properly be considered by a grand jury. Commonwealth v. Gibson, 368 Mass. 518, 333 N.E.2d 400 (1975), reaffirmed the long-recognized rule in the Commonwealth that evidence which is not legally competent at trial is sufficient upon which to base an indictment, and that an indictment which is in fact based exclusively upon hearsay will not be invalidated at trial for that reason. Commonwealth v. Woodward, 157 Mass. 516 (1893); Commonwealth v. Walsh, 255 Mass. 317, 151 N.E. 300 (1926); Commonwealth v. Ventura, 294 Mass. 113, 1 N.E.2d 30 (1936); Commonwealth v. Lammi, 310 Mass. 159, 37 N.E.2d 250 (1941); Commonwealth v. Geagan, 339 Mass. 487, 159 N.E.2d 870 (1959), cert. denied, 80 S.Ct. 200, 361 U.S. 895, 4 L.Ed.2d 152; Commonwealth v. Monahan, 349 Mass. 139, 207 N.E.2d 29 (1965); Commonwealth v. Beneficial Finance Co., 360 Mass. 188, 275 N.E.2d 33, 52 A.L.R.3d 1143 (1971).

The United States Supreme Court, in Costello v. United States, 76 S.Ct. 406, 350 U.S. 359, 100 L.Ed. 397 (1956), disposed of constitutional arguments against the practice, holding "[a]n indictment returned by a legally constituted and unbiased grand jury . . . is enough to call for a trial of the charge on the merits. The Fifth Amendment requires nothing more." Id. at 363. The Court affirmed and expanded upon this holding in United States v. Dionisio, 93 S.Ct. 764, 410 U.S. 1, 35 L.Ed.2d 67 (1973), in which it stated that:

A grand jury has broad investigative powers to determine whether a crime has been committed and who has committed it. The jurors may act on tips, rumors, evidence offered by the prosecutor, or their own personal knowledge.

Id. at 15. More recently, that Court has said, "[t]he grand jury's sources of information are widely drawn, and the validity of an indictment is not affected by the character of the evidence considered." United States v. Calandra, 94 S.Ct. 613, 414 U.S. 338, 344–45, 38 L.Ed.2d 561 (1974).

Subdivision (d). This subdivision for the most part restates prior Massachusetts practice. The substance of this subdivision was taken from G.L. c. 277, § 35A, but a significant modification of the statute has been effected. The change involves the expansion of the right to seek amendments. Under the statute, only the prosecutor could move for amendment of a complaint or indictment; under the rule either party can seek amendments, and the court can allow amendments on its own motion.

It is preferable that a party seeking an amendment of the charges file a written motion to that effect in order that a sufficient record be preserved on that issue should there be an appeal. However, a court may allow an amendment upon oral motion. In such event, or in the event that the court amends the charges on its own motion, the court should make certain that the amendment, as well as the charges as originally framed, are made a part of the record.

The most common prejudice resulting from an amendment of the charges is that the amendment materially alters the substantive offense charged. *See* Commonwealth v. Gallo, 2 Mass.App. 636, 318 N.E.2d 187 (1974). Such an amendment would be one of substance and not of form and would thus be impermissible. Commonwealth v. Snow, 269 Mass. 598, 603, 169 N.E. 542, 68 A.L.R. 920 (1930). An unessential element of a crime charged in an indictment or complaint, such as the time of stealing in larceny, may be amended without prejudice to the defendant. Commonwealth v. Jervis, 368 Mass. 638, 643–44, 335 N.E.2d 532 (1975). See Commonwealth v. Grasso, 375 Mass. 138, 375 N.E.2d 708 (1978); Commonwealth v. Sitko, 372 Mass. 305, 361 N.E.2d 1258 (1977).

One test for determining whether an amendment is one of substance or of form is whether an acquittal on the original charge would act as a bar on double jeopardy grounds to a prosecution of the defendant on the amended charges. If not, then the amendment would be deemed one of substance rather than of form. *Commonwealth v. Snow,* supra.

Although the power of the court to amend indictments under this rule and under existing statutory law is the same as its power to amend complaints, it should be noted that the restrictions on its power to allow amendment of indictments reaches constitutional dimensions. Since defendants charged with felonies have the constitutional right to indictment (Jones v. Robbins, 74 Mass. [8 Gray] 329 [1857]; see Reporters' Notes to Rule, supra), an amendment which goes to the substance of the offense charged in an indictment so as to "materially change the work of the grand jury" interferes with the defendant's right to have a grand jury frame those charges upon which he is to be tried. Commonwealth v. Benjamin, 358 Mass. 672, 679, 266 N.E.2d 662 (1971); Commonwealth v. Ohanian, 6 Mass.App. 965, 384 N.E.2d 218 (1979).

As to complaints, the power of the court is not so restricted. Therefore, the District Court judge should review each complaint carefully to assure that it fulfills the statutory requirements. If it does not, the judge should order it amended. This course of action will prevent defective complaints from entering the Superior Court system after a waiver of indictment. Further, if during a probable cause hearing it appears to the judge that the evidence would warrant charges of other or related offenses, he should order a new complaint to be prepared.

Rule 5. The Grand Jury

[Text of rule applicable to cases initiated (by indictment or complaint) on or after September 7, 2004.]

(a) Summoning Grand Juries. As prescribed by law, the appropriate number of jurors shall be summoned in the manner and at the time required, from among whom the court shall select not more than twenty-three grand jurors to serve in said court as long as and at those specific times required by law, or as required by the court.

The regular grand jury shall be called upon and directed to sit by the Chief Justice of the Superior Court Department whenever within his or her discretion the conduct of regular criminal business and timely prosecution within a particular county so dictate. Notwithstanding the foregoing, special grand juries shall be summoned in the manner prescribed by the General Laws.

(b) Foreperson, Foreperson Pro Tem, Clerk, Clerk Pro Tem. After the grand jurors have been impanelled they shall retire and elect one of their number as foreperson. The foreperson and the prosecuting attorney shall have the power to administer oaths and affirmations to witnesses who appear to testify before the grand jury, and the foreperson shall, under his or her hand, return to the court a list of all witnesses sworn before the grand jury during the sitting. If the foreperson is unable to serve for any part of the period the grand jurors are required to serve, a foreperson pro tem shall be elected in the same manner as provided herein for election of the foreperson. The foreperson pro tem shall serve until the foreperson returns or for the remainder of the term if the foreperson is unable to return. The grand jury may also appoint one of their number as clerk to be charged with keeping a record of their proceedings, and, if the grand jury so directs, to deliver such record to the attorney general or district attorney. If the clerk is unable to serve for any part of the period the grand jurors are required to serve, a clerk pro tem may be appointed.

(c) Who May be Present. Attorneys for the Commonwealth who are necessary or convenient to the presentation of the evidence, the witness under examination, the attorney for the witness, and such other persons who are necessary or convenient to the presentation of the evidence may be present while the grand jury is in session. The attorney for the witness shall make no objections or arguments or otherwise address the grand jury or the prosecuting attorney. No witness may refuse to appear because of unavailability of counsel for that witness.

(d) Secrecy of Proceedings and Disclosures. The judge may direct that an indictment be kept secret until after arrest. In such an instance, the clerk shall seal the indictment and no person may disclose the finding of the indictment except as is necessary for the issuance and execution of a warrant. A person performing an official function in relation to the grand jury may not disclose matters occurring before the grand jury except in the performance of his or her official duties or when specifically directed to do so by the court. No obligation of secrecy may be imposed upon any person except in accordance with law.

(e) Finding and Return of Indictment. An indictment may be found only upon the concurrence of twelve or more jurors. The indictment shall be returned by the grand jury to a judge in open court.

(f) No Bill; Discharge of Defendant. The grand jury shall during its session make a daily return to the court of all cases as to which it has determined not to present an indictment against an accused. Each such complaint shall be endorsed "no bill" and shall be filed with the court.

If upon the filing of a no bill the accused is held on process, he or she shall be discharged unless held on other process.

(g) Deliberation. The prosecuting attorney shall not be present during deliberation and voting except at the request of the grand jury.

(h) Discharge. A grand jury shall serve until the first sitting of the next authorized grand jury unless it is discharged sooner by the court or unless its service is extended to complete an investigation then in progress.

Amended March 8, 2004, effective September 7, 2004.

Reporter's Notes—Revised, 2004

Rule 5 is modeled in large part upon Fed. R Crim. P. 6 and substantially conforms to the General Laws.

Subdivision (a). This subdivision is drawn from Fed. R. Crim. P. 7(a) and G.L. c. 277, §§ 1, 2, 2A—2H. General Laws c. 277, § 3 provides that grand jurors are to drawn, G.L. c. 234, §§ 17—24C, summoned, GL c 234, §§ 10—14, 16, 24, and returned in the same manner as traverse jurors from a list compiled in compliance with G.L. c. 234, §§ 4—9. By a 2004 amendment, this subdivision was amended to eliminate a reference to a specific number of veniremen who must be summonsed, since the number differs from county to county. The statutes require that twenty-three jurors be selected to make up the grand jury, G.L. c. 277, §§ 1, 2, 2A—2H, and authorize the issuance of writs of venire facias to fill any deficiency in that number. G.L. c. 277, § 4. A number less than twenty-three is competent to return an indictment, however, so long as at least thirteen are present and twelve concur in the return. *See* Commonwealth v. Wood, 56 Mass (2 Cush) 149 (1848). *Accord,* Crimm v Commonwealth, 119 Mass. 326 (1876).

Subdivision (a) generally governs the time of issuance of writs of venire facias and provides that such writs for special grand juries shall be issued pursuant to G.L. c. 277, § 2A. In addition to the statutory regular and special grand jury sitting, the Administrative Justice of the Superior Court is empowered to call a "regular" grand jury session whenever the amount of criminal business and the need for timely prosecution within a particular county requires. This provision is intended to provide the Superior Court with much needed flexibility in responding to the fluctuating demand for grand jury action among counties.

Subdivision (b). Although similar to Fed. R. Crim. P. 6(c), this subdivision is wholly adopted from former GL c 277, §§ 7—10. The federal rule provides for the simultaneous court appointment of a foreperson and deputy foreperson; under Rule 5 the foreperson is elected by the other jurors and a replacement, the foreperson pro tem, is chosen only if the first cannot serve Provision for a clerk pro tem is new with this rule.

Those parts of subdivision (b) dealing with the administration of oaths and listing of witnesses and with the appointment and duties of the clerk are restatements, respectively, of former G.L. c. 277, §§ 9 and 10.

Subdivision (c). This subdivision was patterned on Fed. R. Crim. P. 6(d), although it omitted the provision of the federal rule that excluded all persons other than jurors from deliberations or voting.

Grand jury proceedings are ordinarily secret and the presence of an unauthorized person will void an indictment. *See* Commonwealth v. Pezzano, 387 Mass. 69, 72–73 (1982). The importance of keeping the grand jury process from becoming public rests on several policy considerations: preventing individuals from facing the notoriety associated with a grand jury investigation unless probable cause is found against them and an indictment is returned; shielding the grand jury from any outside influences having the potential to distort their investigatory or accusatory functions; protecting witnesses from improper influence; encouraging the full disclosure of information to the grand jury; and facilitating the freedom of the grand jury's deliberations. *See* WBZ–TV4 v. District Attorney for Suffolk Dist., 408 Mass. 595, 600 (1990).

However, prior to the adoption of Rule 5, the Supreme Judicial Court recognized that grand jury secrecy would not be compromised by the presence of persons who were necessary to the work of the grand jury. For example, Commonwealth v. Favulli, 352 Mass 95 (1967), held that a prosecutor has discretion as to the use of assistants and may have present such reasonable number as he or she deems appropriate to the efficient presentation of the evidence. *Id.* at 106. *Accord*, Commonwealth v. Beneficial Finance Co., 360 Mass. 188, 207—09 (1971) (no greater number than is "necessary"). Besides the jury, the prosecutors and the witness under examination, other persons "necessary or convenient to the presentation of the evidence" may include counsel for a witness (G.L. c. 277, § 14A), an interpreter, an officer to guard a dangerous prisoner-witness, an attendant for a sick witness (*see* 30 MASS PRACTICE SERIES [Smith] § 812 [1970]), a stenographer (G.L. c. 221, § 86), or the operator of a recording device. It should be noted that G.L. c. 221, § 86, which permits the appointment of a stenographer to take notes of testimony given before a grand jury does not authorize the recording of any statement or testimony of a grand juror.

The provision in Rule 5(c) allowing the prosecutor to be present at request of grand jurors does not deny defendant due process. *See* Commonwealth v. Smith, Mass. 437 (1993).

Under this subdivision, it may be proper for a federal prosecutor who was involved in the investigation of the case, *see* Commonwealth v. Angiulo, 415 Mass. 502, 513 (1993) or a victim-witness advocate accompanying a child witness, *see* Commonwealth v. Conefrey, 410 Mass. 1, 7 (1991) to be present during testimony before the grand jury. However, it is ordinarily not proper for a police officer to be present, except as a witness. *See Pezzano supra*.

Subdivision (d). Adopted from Fed. R. Crim. P. 6(e), this subdivision incorporates the substance of former G.L. c. 277, §§ 12—13. Nothing in this rule nor in the General Laws prevents a witness before a grand jury from disclosing his or her testimony. *See* Commonwealth v. Schnackenburg, 356 Mass. 65 (1969); Silverio v. Mun. Court of Boston, 355 Mass. 623, *cert. denied*, 396 US 878 (1969). The last phrase, "except in accordance with law" is intended to comprehend statute, court rule, rule or order of an administrative agency, and case law.

Subdivision (e) In order to return an indictment, the grand jury "must hear sufficient evidence to establish the identity of the accused . . . and probable cause to arrest him" (citations omitted). Commonwealth v. McCarthy, 385 Mass. 160, 163 (1982).

Although an indictment may be based solely on hearsay, Commonwealth v. O'Dell, 392 Mass. 445, 450–51 (1984), the Supreme Judicial Court has expressed a "preference for the use of direct testimony," Commonwealth v. St. Pierre, 377 Mass. 650, 656 (1979). A prosecutor need not present the grand jury all the evidence available to the Commonwealth, even if some of it is exculpatory. *See O'Dell*, 392 Mass. at 447. However, if there is exculpatory evidence that would greatly undermine either the credibility of an important witness or likely affect the grand jury's decision, the prosecutor should inform the grand jury. *Id.*

Although there is no statute which mandates the concurrence of at least twelve jurors in the return of an indictment, the requirement expressed in this subdivision is long-established in Massachusetts practice. *See* Commonwealth v. Smith, 9 Mass. 107 (1812). Grand jurors voting to return an indictment need not hear all of the evidence presented against a defendant. *See* Commonwealth v. Wilcox, 437 Mass. 33 (2002).

Subdivision (f). General Laws c. 277, § 15, requiring daily reports of cases where no indictment is returned, is the basis of this subdivision.

Subdivision (g). Prior Massachusetts procedure permitted the prosecutor to be present, *See* Commonwealth v. Favulli, *supra* at 107. A major change is worked by this subdivision, pursuant to which the prosecuting officer may be present during deliberations and voting only if his or her presence is requested by the grand jurors. It is believed that this will operate to enhance the independence of the grand jury, thus alloying fears that it is merely "a tool of the prosecutor".

Subdivision (h). This subdivision essentially restates those provisions of G.L. c 277, §§ 1, 2, and 2A–2H relative to the duration of sittings of grand juries and of § 1A relative to extensions. Grand juries in Suffolk (§ 2), Middlesex (§ 2B), Worcester (§ 2E), Norfolk (§ 2F) and Bristol (§ 2H) counties are to serve for six months and in Hampden (§ 2C), Essex (§ 2G) and Plymouth counties (§ 2D) for four months "and until another grand jury has been impanelled in their stead." Notwithstanding these express statutory provisions, the summoning of the grand jury and the duration of its term is subject to the discretion of the Administrative Justice of the Superior Court pursuant to subdivision (a).

Rule 6. Summons to Appear; Arrest Warrant

(Applicable to District Court and Superior Court)

(a) Issuance of Process.

(1) *Summons*. A defendant not under arrest or otherwise in custody shall, except as provided in subdivision (a)(2) of this rule, be notified of the criminal proceedings against him and of the date of the return day by means of a summons. A copy of the complaint or indictment shall accompany the summons. If the accused is a juvenile, a summons and copy of the complaint or indictment shall also be served upon the parent or legal guardian of the juvenile or upon the person with whom the juvenile resides. Such notice shall also advise the defendant to report in person to the probation department before the return day.

(2) *Warrant*. The District Court may authorize the issuance of a warrant in any case except where the accused is a juvenile less than twelve years of age. Upon the return of an indictment against a defendant, the Superior Court may authorize the issuance of a warrant. The decision to issue a warrant may be based upon the representation of a prosecutor made to the court that the defendant may not appear unless arrested. If a defendant fails to appear in response to a summons or for any reason is not amenable to service, the prosecutor may request that a warrant issue or may resummon the defendant.

(b) Form.

(1) *Warrant*. An arrest warrant issued pursuant to this rule shall be signed by the official issuing it and shall contain the name of the defendant or, if his name is unknown, any name or description by which he can be identified with reasonable certainty. The warrant shall recite the substance of the offense charged in the complaint or indictment. It shall command that the defendant be arrested and brought before the court.

(2) *Summons*. A summons shall be in the same form as a warrant except that it shall summon the defendant to appear before the court at a stated time and place.

(c) Service or Execution; Return.

(1) *By Whom*. A summons may be served in the manner provided by subdivision (c)(3) of this rule by any person authorized by the General Laws to serve criminal process. A warrant shall be directed to and executed by an officer authorized by the General Laws to serve criminal process.

(2) *Territorial Limits*. A summons may be served or a warrant executed at any place within the Commonwealth.

(3) *Manner*. A summons shall be served upon a defendant by delivering a copy to him personally, or by leaving it at his dwelling house or usual place of abode

with some person of suitable age and discretion then residing therein, or by mailing it to the defendant's last known address. A warrant shall be executed by the arrest of the defendant. The officer need not have the warrant in his possession at the time of the arrest, but upon request he shall show the warrant to the defendant as soon as possible. If the officer does not have the warrant in his possession at the time of the arrest, he shall then inform the defendant that a warrant has issued and of the offense charged, but if the officer does not then know of the offense charged, he shall inform the defendant thereof within a reasonable time after arrest.

(4) *Return*. On or before the return day, the person to whom a summons was delivered for service shall make return thereof to the issuing court. The clerk shall maintain a list of those summonses returned unserved which shall include a statement of the efforts made by the person to whom the summonses were delivered for service to serve them. If a summons is mailed pursuant to subdivision (c)(3) of this rule and returned, the clerk shall record that fact upon the list. The officer executing a warrant shall make return thereof to the issuing court. At the request of the prosecutor any unexecuted warrant shall be returned to the issuing court and may be cancelled by that court upon its own motion or upon the motion of the prosecutor. At the request of the prosecutor made at any time while a complaint or an indictment is pending, a summons returned unserved or a warrant returned unexecuted and not cancelled may be delivered to an authorized person for service or execution.

(d) Default.

(1) *Costs*. A judge may order that expenses incurred as a result of the entry of a default against a defendant are to be assessed as costs against the defendant.

(2) *Preservation of Testimony*. If counsel for a defendant is present upon the entry of a default against the defendant and if the judge finds that to require the attendance at a later time of a witness then present in court would constitute a hardship upon the witness because of age, infirmity, illness, profession or other sufficient reason, the judge may order that the testimony of the witness be taken and preserved for subsequent use at trial or any other proceeding. The witness shall be examined in open court by the party on whose behalf he is present and the adverse party shall have the right of cross-examination. The expense of taking and preserving the testimony may be assessed as costs against the defendant.

Reporter's Notes

Rule 6 was drafted with the aim of dispensing with unnecessary appearances by defendants, their counsel, and witnesses and insuring that defendants who are unlikely to flee pending their initial appearance may be at liberty without restriction.

Subdivision (a). Under prior practice, after a finding of probable cause—whether upon an application for issuance of process or upon presentment to a grand jury—arrest warrants were to be issued in the majority of cases. G.L. c. 276, § 22. The issuance of a summons in lieu of a warrant was the exception under the law, if not in practice.

Under G.L. c. 276, § 24, a summons was to be issued only in those instances where the District Court had final jurisdiction over the offense charged and the court believed a summons would sufficiently guarantee the defendant's appearance in court.

Under this rule the permissible use of a summons is greatly expanded. Whenever it is determined that process shall issue upon an application, the District Court shall authorize the issuance of a warrant, except in cases where the accused is a juvenile less than twelve years of age. G.L. c. 119, § 54. Whenever a direct indictment is returned against a defendant, the Superior Court shall authorize the issuance of a warrant. In both instances, however, the warrant will not be immediately issued for execution unless the court determines that the defendant will not likely appear upon a summons alone.

This rule reflects the policy underlying current efforts to secure the release prior to trial of all defendants who have sufficient roots in the community to guarantee their presence at trial. Federal Rule of Criminal Procedure 4 requires a magistrate to issue a summons rather than an arrest warrant only "upon the request of the attorney for the government" after probable cause is found. Section 3.3 of the ABA *Standards Relating to Pretrial Release* (Approved Draft, 1968) provides for the use of a summons instead of a warrant except where specific grounds exist for the use of an arrest warrant. *Accord* Rules of Criminal Procedure (U.L.A.) Rule 221(c) (1974); National Advisory Commission on Criminal Justice Standards & Goals, *Courts,* Standard 4.2 (1973). See Vermont R.Crim.P. 4 (1974).

The preference for the issuance of summonses operates to conserve law enforcement resources by releasing the police for other duties, and conserves the resources of the court and parties.

The preference for the issuance of a summons instead of a warrant is based on the same policy mandating the release of arrested defendants on personal recognizance rather than on bail. That policy is bottomed on the belief that defendants should be burdened with the fewest restrictions on their pretrial liberty that will adequately assure their presence at trial.

There is, however, one significant difference between the decision made concerning the issuance of a summons and that concerning the appropriate conditions of release after arrest. When a decision on bail is made, the court or magistrate has more information concerning the defendant than when a summons or warrant is to be issued. In the former instance, the defendant is present before the court and can be questioned in order to establish a sufficient basis for a determination of the appropriate conditions of his release. In addition, under Mass.R.Crim.P. 28, the judge is authorized to review the probation report concerning the defendant prior to the bail determination.

In light of these considerations, it is intended that the court not be prohibited from issuing an arrest warrant where there is an absence of sufficient information to make an intelligent choice concerning the appropriate process to be issued. Where there is a dearth of information concerning the defendant, it is expected that the court will place much reliance upon the nature of the offense charged and will order the arrest of defendants charged with serious crimes. An arrest in such situations will not unduly prejudice a defendant, because, if he is suitable for pretrial release on his own recognizance, the court can so order when the defendant is initially brought before it after arrest.

Subdivision (a)(1) provides that, except when the issuance of a warrant is necessitated, the defendant is to be notified of the criminal proceedings against him and the date of his scheduled appearance by means of a summons coupled with a copy of the complaint or indictment. See Rules of Criminal Procedure (U.L.A.) Rule 222(d) (1974). This notice shall also advise the defendant to personally report to the probation department before his scheduled appearance for the purpose of an interview to determine whether counsel need be assigned. If the defendant has retained counsel, and counsel has filed his appearance, the defendant need not attend until his next scheduled appearance.

Subdivision (a)(1) also deals with the requirement of G.L. c. 119, § 55 that notice to the parent or guardian of the defendant is necessary when the accused is a juvenile. Although notice to and appearance by a parent or guardian is thus required, nothing in this rule is to be construed as making the parent or guardian of the juvenile a party defendant. Robinson v. Commonwealth, 242 Mass. 401, 403, 136 N.E. 241 (1922).

Subdivision (a)(2) provides that upon the prosecuting officer's recital to the court that the defendant will not appear unless arrested, a warrant may be issued. This is less restrictive than the guidelines provided by the ABA *Standards Relating to Pretrial Release,* § 3.3 (Approved Draft, 1968), which require an application for an arrest warrant to reveal the defendant's residence, employment, family ties, criminal record, and whether he had previously responded to a citation or summons. If a magistrate fails to issue a summons instead of an arrest warrant, he is required to state the reason therefor. *Compare* Rule 221(c) of the *Uniform Rules of Criminal Procedure* (U.L.A.) (1974).

The factors to be considered by the court in its decision upon the conditions necessary to assure the defendant's presence are reflected in the *Rules of the Superior Court Governing Persons Authorized to Take Bail* 2 (1972):

> The purpose of setting terms for any pretrial release is to assure the presence at court of the person released. Any person charged with an offense, other than an offense punishable by death [sic], is required by law to be released on his personal recognizance pending trial unless the person setting the terms of release determines, in the exercise of his discretion, that such a release will not reasonably assure the appearance of the person as required. In making a determination as to what form of release to set, the following factors shall be considered: (1) the nature and circumstances of the offense charged, (2) the accused's family ties, (3) his financial resources, (4) his length of residence in the community, (5) his character and mental condition, (6) his record of convictions and appearances at court proceedings or of any previous flight to avoid prosecution or (7) any failure to appear at any court proceedings.

Accord G.L. c. 276, § 58 (as amended, St.1978, c. 478, § 286).

Moreover, this subdivision provides that if a defendant fails to respond to summons, then the court may order that a warrant issue, or may permit the defendant to be served with a new summons. This accords with practice under G.L. c. 276, § 26, which makes the willful failure to appear in response to criminal process a separate offense. See ABA *Standards Relating to Pretrial Release* § 1.3 (Approved Draft, 1968); Rules of Criminal Procedure (U.L.A.) rule 221(e)(2) (1974).

Subdivision (b). General Laws c. 276, § 21, c. 218, § 33 (as amended, St.1978, c. 478, § 191), and c. 218, § 35 (as amended, St.1978, c. 478, § 192) enumerate those officials who are empowered to issue arrest warrants.

Subdivision (b)(1) restates the Massachusetts practice, dating from Commonwealth v. Crathy, 92 Mass. (10 Allen) 403 (1865), which requires that if the warrant does not contain a name by which the accused is known, it must contain a sufficient description by which the arresting officer will be able to identify the accused with reasonable certainty. This subdivision follows the practice in Massachusetts which mandates that the warrant shall recite the substance of the accusation, G.L. c. 276, § 22, a requirement fulfilled at common law by attaching the complaint or a copy thereof to the warrant. Commonwealth v. Dean, 75 Mass. (9 Gray) 283 (1857). General Laws c. 276, § 22 details the procedure to be followed by the arresting officer when the accused is located.

Support for the rule that the warrant must be directed to an officer authorized to serve criminal process is found in In re Graves, 236 Mass. 493 (1920). In *Graves,* the court held that a warrant which by express direction would have permitted unqualified persons to execute it was invalid on its face.

Subdivision (c)(3) is also borrowed from ALI *Model Code of Pre–Arraignment Procedure* § 120.3(2) (P.O.D.1975), and is similar to Rules of Criminal Procedure (U.L.A.) rule 223(c) (1974). The ALI *Model Code,* supra, § 120.4, permits service of the summons by mail.

It is well established in Massachusetts that an officer need not have the warrant authorizing the arrest in his possession when the accused is placed under arrest. This principle is grounded on the judicial determination that an arrest is valid if based on probable cause even if the warrant upon which the arrest was made is void. Commonwealth v. Bowlen, 351 Mass. 655, 223 N.E.2d 391 (1967). However, if the arrest is based upon a warrant, the accused should be afforded an opportunity to examine it within a reasonable time.

Subdivision (c)(4) complies substantially with Rule 225 of the Rules of Criminal Procedure (U.L.A.) (P.O.D.1975) and with Fed.R.Crim.P. 4(c)(4).

General Laws c. 218, § 32 states that warrants are returnable before a court in the county where trial of the case is to be held. The only restrictions on the time in which a warrant must be executed is that a delay in its execution must not be unreasonable. *See generally* Commonwealth v. Sullivan, 354 Mass. 598, 239 N.E.2d 5 (1968). However, if execution of the warrant is wilfully delayed by the person to whom it was committed for service, that person is subject to the penalties provided by G.L. c. 268, §§ 22–23 irrespective of whether the warrant is valid.

Subdivision (d). This subdivision introduces two new practices. The first, in subdivision (d)(1), allows the court to assess as costs against the defendant those expenses which result from the defendant's failure to appear. While the assessment is discretionary, it is intended to be exercised only upon the willful default of a defendant and as to those costs which directly result therefrom. As under Mass.R.Crim.P.

10(b), relating to assessment of costs upon a continuance, expenses which may be assessed under this rule include fees of witnesses then present, extra compensation of police officers, travel costs, and stenographer's attendance fees if one is appointed.

Subdivision (d)(2) provides that if a witness is present in court and the trial cannot proceed because the defendant is absent, the testimony of that witness may be ordered taken and recorded by deposition. This is an extraordinary practice, and is to be utilized only when to require the later appearance of the witness would constitute a hardship due to his age, infirmity, profession or other sufficient reason. "Profession" in this context does not signify solely the recognized professions, but refers to the manner of earning a livelihood of one who will lose income or wages if required to attend further proceedings.

There is no issue as to confrontation in this situation. A defendant has the right to be present at the taking of a deposition, see Mass.R.Crim.P. 18(a), but "his failure to appear after notice and without cause shall constitute a waiver of the right to be present." Mass.R.Crim.P. 35(c). This subdivision is but a logical extension of that provision. The defendant has had notice to appear for trial and has chosen to absent himself. It is assumed for purposes of this rule that defendant's counsel is present to examine or cross-examine the deponent and to preserve objections to his testimony. Thus the essential need of the defendant to be present is fulfilled.

The defendant is protected from a "default" by the Commonwealth by Mass.R.Crim.P. 10(c), pursuant to which the court may order that the taking of depositions of Commonwealth witnesses be made a condition upon the grant of a continuance.

FORM DC–CR–7. SUMMONS FOR DEFENDANT/SUMMONS FOR WITNESS

☐ SUMMONS FOR DEFENDANT
☐ SUMMONS FOR WITNESS

DOCKET NUMBER

Trial Court of Massachusetts
District Court Department

SESSION: ☐ CRIMINAL ☐ JUVENILE ☐ JURY
☐ MAGISTRATE HEARING

NAME AND ADDRESS OF COURT DIVISION

NAME, ADDRESS AND ZIP CODE OF DEFENDANT

YOU MUST APPEAR AT THIS COURT ADDRESS ON THE DATE AND TIME SPECIFIED HEREIN

DATE AND TIME OF APPEARANCE

________ AT ________M.
DATE TIME

NAME, ADDRESS AND ZIP CODE OF WITNESS

OFFENSE(S)

TO ANY PERSON AUTHORIZED TO SERVE CRIMINAL PROCESS IN THE COMMONWEALTH:

You are hereby commanded to forthwith serve the annexed summons upon the defendant or witness named within by delivering it to the defendant or witness personally, or by leaving it at the dwelling house or usual place of abode of the defendant or witness with some person of suitable age and discretion then residing therein, or by mailing it to the last known address of the defendant or witness.

NOTE: A summons for a witness may also be served by any person authorized to serve a summons in a civil action. See Rule 17(d)(1) of the Massachusetts Rules of Criminal Procedure.

To the above named ☐ Defendant ☐ Witness:

You are hereby ordered to appear in this Court on the appearance date noted above

☐ To answer to a criminal complaint charging you with the offense(s) listed above.

☐ To give evidence and testify on behalf of the ☐ Commonwealth ☐ Defendant in the matter described above, and to appear from time to time and day to day thereafter as ordered. You are further required to bring with you:

WITNESS: FIRST JUSTICE | DATE OF ISSUE | CLERK-MAGISTRATE

RETURN OF SERVICE

I hereby certify that I served the within summons upon the above named ☐ Defendant ☐ Witness by

☐ Delivering a copy of it personally to the defendant or witness.

☐ Leaving a copy of it at the dwelling house or usual place of abode of the defendant or witness with a person of suitable age and discretion residing therein.

☐ Mailing a copy of it to the last known address of the defendant or witness

☐ I received the summons on ________ but I was unable to make service because: ________
DATE RECEIVED

DATE OF SERVICE | SIGNATURE OF PERSON MAKING SERVICE X | TITLE OF PERSON MAKING SERVICE

DC–CR–7(1/84)

☐ SUMMONS FOR DEFENDANT
☐ SUMMONS FOR WITNESS

DOCKET NUMBER

Trial Court of Massachusetts
District Court Department

NAME AND ADDRESS OF COURT DIVISION

SESSION: ☐ CRIMINAL ☐ JUVENILE ☐ JURY ☐ MAGISTRATE HEARING

NAME, ADDRESS AND ZIP CODE OF DEFENDANT

YOU MUST APPEAR AT THIS COURT ADDRESS ON THE DATE AND TIME SPECIFIED HEREIN

DATE AND TIME OF APPEARANCE

________ AT ________ M.
DATE TIME

NAME, ADDRESS AND ZIP CODE OF WITNESS

OFFENSE(S)

To the above named ☐ Defendant ☐ Witness:

You are hereby ordered to appear in this Court on the appearance date noted above

☐ To answer to a criminal complaint charging you with the offense(s) listed above.

☐ To give evidence and testify on behalf of the ☐ Commonwealth ☐ Defendant in the matter described above, and to appear from time to time and day to day thereafter as ordered. You are further required to bring with you:

WITNESS: FIRST JUSTICE | DATE OF ISSUE | CLERK-MAGISTRATE

WARNING TO DEFENDANT OR WITNESS:

Failure to appear in accordance with this summons may result in the issuance of a warrant for your arrest. Please bring this document with you to court.

ATENCIÓN:

Esta es una notificación oficial de la corte.
Si usted no sabe leer inglés, obtenga traducción!

DC–CR–7(1/84)

Rule 7. Initial Appearance and Arraignment

[Text of rule applicable to cases initiated (by indictment or complaint) on or after September 7, 2004.]

(a) Initial Appearance.

(1) *Upon Arrest.* Upon the arrest of a juvenile, the arresting officer shall notify the parent or guardian of the juvenile and the probation office. A defendant who has been arrested shall be brought before a court if then in session, and if not, at its next session. At that time the defendant shall be interviewed by the probation department; the probation department shall make a report to the court of the pertinent information reasonably necessary to determination of the issues of bail and indigency. If the judge or special magistrate finds that the defendant is indigent or indigent but able to contribute and has not knowingly waived the right to counsel under the procedures established in Supreme Judicial Court Rule 3:10, the Committee for Public Counsel Services shall be assigned to provide representation for the defendant. The judge or special magistrate shall then arraign the defendant or shall set a time for arraignment. The judge or special magistrate shall determine the conditions of the defendant's release, if any.

(2) *Upon Summons; Waiver of Initial Appearance.* A summonsed defendant who has retained counsel shall be excused from appearing on the return day if such counsel enters an appearance for the defendant prior to the return day, stating thereon that he or she has conferred with the defendant and requests that the case be scheduled for pretrial hearing or other proceeding. Defendant's counsel shall inform the defendant of the date of the next scheduled event which shall require the defendant's presence.

(b) Appearance of Counsel.

(1) *Filing.* An appearance shall be entered by the attorney for the defendant and the prosecuting attorney on or before the initial appearance or, if the defendant was summonsed to appear, on or before the scheduled return day. The appearance may be entered either by personally appearing before the clerk or by submitting an appearance slip, which shall include the name, address, and telephone number of the attorney.

(2) *Effect; Withdrawal.* An appearance shall be in the name of the attorney who files the appearance and shall constitute a representation that the attorney shall represent the defendant for trial or plea or shall prosecute the case, except that if on the return day such a representation cannot be made and no contrary legal restriction applies, (1) the court may permit an appearance to be entered by an attorney to represent the defendant or prosecute the case for such time as the court may order, and (2) the court shall permit an appearance in the name of the prosecuting agency, which shall constitute representations that the agency will prosecute the case, will ensure that throughout the duration of the appearance a prosecutor is assigned to the case, and upon request of the court or a party will identify the prosecutor assigned to the case. If the attorney who files an appearance for the defendant on or before the return day wishes to withdraw the appearance, he or she may do so within fourteen days after the return day, provided that the attorney who shall represent the defendant at trial files an appearance simultaneously with such withdrawal; thereafter no appearance shall be withdrawn without permission of the court. The appearance of the prosecuting officer shall be withdrawn only with permission of the court.

(3) *Notice.* A copy of all appearances and withdrawals of appearance shall be filed and shall be served upon the adverse party pursuant to Rule 32.

(c) Arraignment. Arraignment shall consist of the reading of the charges to the defendant and the entry of the defendant's plea to those charges.

(1) *Waiver of Reading of Charges.* At arraignment the reading of the charges may be waived in open court by the defendant if he or she is represented by counsel.

(2) *Entry of Not Guilty Plea.* If a defendant is excused from appearing in court on the return day pursuant to this rule, a plea of not guilty shall be entered by the court on the defendant's behalf.

(d) Provision of Criminal Record; Preservation of Evidence. The court shall ensure that at or before arraignment, (1) a copy of the defendant's criminal record, if any, as compiled by the Commissioner of Probation is provided to the defense and to the prosecution, and (2) the parties are afforded an opportunity to move for the preservation of evidence pursuant to Rule 14(a)(1)(E).

(e) Order Scheduling Pretrial Proceedings. At a District Court arraignment on a complaint which is outside of the District Court's final jurisdiction or on which jurisdiction is declined, the court shall schedule the case for a probable cause hearing. In all other District and Superior Court cases the court shall issue an order at arraignment requiring the prosecuting attorney and defense counsel to (1) engage in a pretrial conference on a date certain, and (2) appear at a pretrial hearing on a specified subsequent date.

Amended May 29, 1986, effective July 1, 1986; March 8, 2004, effective September 7, 2004.

Reporter's Notes—Revised, 2004

Rule 7 governs the initial appearance and arraignment. It is based in part upon Fed. R. Crim. P. 5, 5.1, and 10. See ALI Model Code of Pre–Arraignment Procedure § 310.1, .3, .5 (POD 1975); Rules of Criminal Procedure (ULA) rules 311—13, 321 (1974). In 2004, Rule 7 was amended in four respects. The revisions mandate: that in some circumstances counsel be permitted to enter a limited appearance; that the defendant receive a copy of his or her criminal record at arraignment; that the parties have an opportunity to move to preserve evidence at arraignment; and that pretrial conference and hearing dates, or alternatively a probable cause hearing date, be assigned at the initial appearance. These revisions are addressed in detail infra.

Subdivision (a)(1). Subdivision (a) provides that when a defendant has been arrested, he or she is to be brought immediately to appear before a court if then in session, and if not, then at its next session.

Pursuant to G.L. c 119, § 67, notice of the arrest of a juvenile is required to be given to the parent of the juvenile and to the probation officer for the district in which the accused is arrested, unless the juvenile was arrested as a child in need of service pursuant to G.L. 119, § 39H, which contains alternative notification requirements. The purpose of this notice is to permit the prompt release of a juvenile, consistent with G.L. c 119, § 66, which discourages the detention of juvenile offenders, unless, in the opinion of the arresting officer or the probation department, cause exists to hold him or her.

Massachusetts case law requires that an arrested defendant be brought before a court for arraignment as soon after arrest as is reasonably possible. Commonwealth v. Dubois, 353 Mass. 223 (1967); Keefe v. Hart, 213 Mass. 476 (1913). Whether or not delay has been unreasonable is to be determined on a case-by-case basis, Commonwealth v. Banuchi, 335 Mass. 649 (1957), and in light of all the circumstances. Commonwealth v. Perito, 417 Mass. 674, 680 (1994); Commonwealth v. Hodgkins, 401 Mass. 871, 876–77 (1988). Generally, arraignment the next morning following arrest is not unreasonable when a defendant is arrested late in the day. United States v. Connell, 213 F. Supp. 741 (D. Mass. 1963); Commonwealth v. Daniels, 366 Mass. 601 (1975); Commonwealth v. Dubois, *supra*. Rule 7(a) codifies this case law by mandating that the defendant be brought before the court immediately if the court is in session, and if not, then at its next session. This requirement is primarily intended to prevent both unlawful detentions and unlawfully obtained statements. Commonwealth v. Cote, 386 Mass. 354, 361 n. 11 (1982). However, in Commonwealth v. Rosario, 422 Mass. 48 (1996), the S.J.C. established a bright line rule that an otherwise admissible statement taken within a six-hour period following arrest should not be excluded, even if the court was in session at the time.

This initial appearance before the court serves several functions. First, at this time, the defendant will be interviewed by the probation department. The results of this interview, together with an investigative report by the probation department as to prior criminal prosecutions and juvenile complaints, will be communicated to the court. See Mass. R. Crim. P. 28(d)(1)—(2). This information will form the basis of decisions as to pretrial release. Moreover, this information will be used to determine whether a defendant is indigent or indigent but able to contribute. If the court so determines, then it will assign the Committee for Public Counsel Services to represent him according to the requirements of G.L. c. 211D and Supreme Judicial Court Rule 3:10. If the defendant was arrested without a warrant, there must also be a judicial determination of probable cause within twenty-four hours, as provided in Rule 3.1. *See* Jenkins v. Chief Justice of the District Court Dep't, 416 Mass. 221 (1993). Finally, at this time the court shall establish a time for arraignment or other proceeding.

The initial appearance and arraignment, although distinguishable by their respective functions, need not be separate events. The preferred practice, however, is to postpone arraignment until such time as the defendant has had a meaningful opportunity to consult with counsel. See District Court Initial Rule of Criminal Procedure 2, comment (1971).

The vital importance of the component parts of arraignment must not be lost in the tedium of repetition so as to foreclose inadvertently the rights of the uninformed defendant. Among the decisions to be made is whether to plead guilty or nolo contendere, or to admit to sufficient facts. Mass. R. Crim. P. 12. Representation by counsel is necessary to ensure that the defendant understands that by selecting among these alternatives he or she is exercising or waiving substantial rights. Counsel should also be available to advise the defendant whether to exercise "drug rights," G.L. c. 111E, § 10; whether to undergo examination for competence, G.L. c 123, § 15; whether he or she may qualify for diversion as a selected offender, G.L. c. 276A; whether arrangements should be made for a stenographer, G.L. c. 221, § 91B; whether to consider mediation in cases where it is offered; and whether the charges may be subject to dismissal. In addition, at arraignment the defendant may waive reading of the charges, subdivision (c), *infra*; and the case will be ordered to conference, Mass. R. Crim. P. 11. These considerations are all important to the ultimate rights of the defendant and decisions should not be casual or perfunctory. Therefore, if counsel is to be provided, there should be a prompt assignment or appointment, and time should be allowed for consultation. The initial appearance and arraignment can be held on the same day if assigned or appointed counsel is then present in court or is available without delay, and if there is an opportunity for adequate consultation.

The fact that a defendant is to be afforded time to discuss the case with counsel is not to be relied upon by the prosecution to justify undue delay in bringing the defendant before the court for arraignment.

Subdivision (a)(2). If a defendant is issued a summons instead of being arrested, a procedure different from that under subdivision (a)(1) prevails. In such an instance a defendant who has retained counsel need not be present at the scheduled initial appearance if his or her counsel enters an appearance prior thereto. This is required in order that the prosecution and any witnesses of the parties may be notified not to attend. When counsel enters an appearance, the clerk will set the time for the next scheduled event which will require the defendant's presence—usually the pretrial conference or pretrial hearing — and counsel will notify the defendant thereof.

Subdivision (a)(2) does not require the defendant's presence on the date specified on the summons (unless that is the date established by the clerk when counsel enters his or her appearance) because the purposes for the initial appearance outlined in subdivision (a)(1) have been fulfilled. See Rules of Criminal Procedure (ULA), *supra*, rule 312.

The purpose of this subdivision is to conserve judicial resources and those of the defendant by dispensing with unnecessary appearances. Further, the pretrial liberty of defendants who are likely to appear for arraignment is not compromised.

The defendant who cannot afford or who does not have retained counsel must attend at the initial appearance at the time set in the summons. Prior to that time, the defendant must have appeared at the probation department so that information relative to the issues of bail and indigency may be gathered.

If a defendant intends to waive counsel, the waiver should be executed at the initial appearance.

Subdivision (b). This subdivision governs the entry and withdrawal of appearances by counsel. It combines and revises former subdivisions (b) and (c), which had treated District Court and Superior Court appearances differently. Following the abolition of the district court *de novo* system, a 2004 amendment to this Rule instituted a uniform procedure for both trial courts. It also revised the rule to permit limited appearances in some circumstances — a more efficient option when fully competent counsel is present but unable to submit an appearance guaranteeing representation throughout the case. Assistant district attorneys often do not represent the Commonwealth in a case from beginning to end, and sometimes a public defender or bar advocate is on duty for bail and arraignment sessions only. The original formulation of this subdivision deflected progress in the case by generally barring the appearance of counsel for such limited purposes.

As amended, subdivision (b) provides that the entry of an appearance by *defense counsel* presumes that he or she will represent the defendant at the tender of a plea or at trial, but permits the court to order an appearance for a shorter period when no contrary constitutional, legislative or judicial restriction applies. For example, District Court Dept. Supplemental Rule of Criminal Procedure 8(8) authorizes the appointment of an attorney "for arraignment only," but prohibits any other kind of limited appointment. Rule 7(b) as amended is not intended to preempt such court rules, but to provide the flexibility necessary for courts to formulate and revise such rules over time. An appearance entered by defense counsel may only be withdrawn as of right within fourteen days after arraignment and provided substitute counsel has simultaneously entered an appearance.

A second revision introduces a responsible degree of flexibility with regard to appearances by the *prosecution*. An appearance entered by a prosecutor constitutes a representation that he or she will prosecute a case at trial and may only be withdrawn with permission of the court. However, if such a representation cannot be made, subdivision (b)(2) allows an appearance to be entered in the name of the prosecuting agency, but this requires the office (a) to ensure that throughout the duration of the appearance a prosecutor is assigned to the case, and (b) upon request of the court or other counsel, to identify the prosecutor then assigned to the case. These requirements were added to the rule in 2004 to ameliorate a difficulty in then-existing district court practice: defense counsel was too often unable to speak with a district attorney about the case between arraignment and the next scheduled date because no assistant district attorney had yet been assigned to it. This revised procedure will facilitate early discussions between the parties, and also insure that notices delivered to the offices of the Attorney General or a District Attorney will be brought to the immediate attention of the assistant handling the case.

Subdivision (c). The major functions of the arraignment are to inform the defendant of the charge and to receive his or her plea thereto. Subdivision (c)(1) permits the defendant to waive the reading of the charges if represented by counsel. This is a restatement of District Court Initial Rule of Criminal Procedure 1 (1971); accord, Rules of the Municipal Court of the City of Boston Sitting for Criminal Business 1 (1971).

If the defendant's attendance at the initial appearance is excused, subdivision (c)(2) provides for the automatic entry of a plea of not guilty. Implicit in (c)(2) is a waiver of the reading of the charge. There is then no arraignment as defined in this Rule and the next event is usually the pretrial conference.

Subdivision (d). This subdivision mandates two additional procedures at arraignment. First it requires that the defendant be provided with his or her criminal record at arraignment. This was customarily the case long before the promulgation of this subdivision in 2004, and in district court was already mandated by Dist./Mun. Cts. R. Crim. P. 3. (That Rule goes beyond this subdivision, however, by also requiring the prosecution to provide certain police statements to the defendant at a district court arraignment.) Second, subdivision (d) provides an opportunity at arraignment for the parties to seek an order to preserve evidence that is not subject to a Rule 14 discovery order. Rule 14 discovery reaches only items in the possession, custody or control of the prosecution, its team, or those working with it on the case. But private parties or government agencies not working on the case may have relevant evidence that could be destroyed absent court action. Such evidence should not be subject to an individual's unfettered decision to destroy it in cases where counsel for a party considers preservation important. Therefore, under Rule 14(a)(1)(E), the parties may move for an order preserving this evidence. Subdivision (d) of Rule 7 simply guarantees the parties an opportunity to be heard on this motion at the initial appearance, since expedition may be crucial in such cases.

When a preservation order is requested at arraignment, the non-party custodian of the evidence is not likely to be present to assert its interests. However, the non-party may subsequently contest the order, or request the court to use its authority under subdivision 14(a)(1)(E)(ii) to "modify or vacate such an order upon a showing that preservation of particular evidence will create significant hardship, on condition that the probative value of said evidence is preserved by a specified alternative means."

Subdivision (e). This subdivision, promulgated in 2004, requires the District Court to issue an order at the initial appearance scheduling subsequent pretrial proceedings. For this purpose the subdivision distinguishes between a "probable cause track" and a "pretrial conference/pretrial hearing" track. The latter requires the court to schedule both a pretrial conference (between the attorneys) and a pretrial hearing, each further addressed in Rule 11. As to the former, some District Court arraignments are continued for probable cause hearings rather than pretrial conferences. Under the statutory mandate that probable cause hearings be held "as soon as may be", G.L. c 276 § 38, the Court should not assign any intervening pretrial conferences or hearings when it intends to, or by statute must, bind over the case. The subdivision's recognition of a separate "probable cause track" is necessary to effectuate this statutory requirement. However, nothing in Rule 7(e) prevents the court from subsequently continuing the probable cause hearing to another date, or (in concurrent jurisdiction cases) from ordering a short continuance of the initial hearing to permit counsel to prepare arguments on whether district court jurisdiction should be declined.

Rule 8. Assignment of Counsel

(Applicable to District Court and Superior Court)

If a defendant charged with a crime for which a sentence of imprisonment or commitment to the custody of the Department of Youth Services may be imposed initially appears in any court without counsel, the judge shall follow the procedures established in G.L. c. 211D and in Supreme Judicial Court Rule 3:10.

Amended May 29, 1986, effective July 1, 1986.

Reporter's Notes

This rule is in large part derived from former Supreme Judicial Court Rule 3:10 (1967: 351 Mass. 791, as amended, 1969: 355 Mass. 803), and District Court Initial Rules of Criminal Procedure 2, 10 (1971). See Fed.R.Crim.P. 44.

Subdivision (a).

The present state of the law is that counsel is required in all cases where the defendant faces possible imprisonment unless the defendant properly waives his right to the assistance of counsel. Argersinger v. Hamlin, 92 S.Ct. 2006, 407 U.S. 25, 32 L.Ed.2d 530 (1972).

The Supreme Court has held the right to assistance of counsel fundamental in certain juvenile proceedings as well:

> A proceeding where the issue is whether the child will be found to be delinquent and subjected to the loss of his liberty is comparable in seriousness to a felony prosecution. The juvenile needs the assistance of counsel to cope with problems of law, to make skilled inquiry into the facts, to insist upon regularity of the proceedings, and to ascertain whether he has a defense and to prepare and submit it.

In re Gault, 87 S.Ct. 1428, 387 U.S. 1, 36, 18 L.Ed.2d 527 (1967). There the Court concluded that in delinquency proceedings where the juvenile faces a risk of commitment, the juvenile *and* his parent must be notified of the juvenile's right to counsel and that counsel will be assigned by the court if the juvenile is indigent. *In re Gault,* supra, at 41; Marsden v. Commonwealth, 352 Mass. 564, 567, 227 N.E.2d 1 (1967); District Court Special Rule 207 (1974).

The stages of criminal proceedings at which the right to counsel has been held to apply include arraignment (Hamilton v. Alabama, 82 S.Ct. 157, 368 U.S. 52, 7 L.Ed.2d 114 [1961]; *see* Commonwealth v. White, 362 Mass. 193, 285 N.E.2d 110 [1972]), probable cause hearing (White v. Maryland, 83 S.Ct. 1050, 373 U.S. 59, 10 L.Ed.2d 193 [1963]; *see* Arsenault v. Massachusetts, 89 S.Ct. 35, 393 U.S. 5, 21 L.Ed.2d 5 [1968]), when the plea is tendered (Moore v. Michigan, 77 S.Ct. 150, 352 U.S. 907 [1956]), trial (Gideon v. Wainwright, 83 S.Ct. 792, 372 U.S. 335, 9 L.Ed.2d 799 [1963]), sentencing (Townsend v. Burke, 71 S.Ct. 286, 334 U.S. 736, 95 L.Ed. 661 [1948]), appellate proceedings (Douglas v. California, 83 S.Ct. 814, 372 U.S. 353, 9 L.Ed.2d 811 [1963]; *see* Arsenault v. Massachusetts, supra; *compare* Ross v. Moffitt, 94 S.Ct. 2437, 417 U.S. 600, 41 L.Ed.2d 341 [1975]), probation revocation proceedings (Williams v. Commonwealth, 350 Mass. 732, 216 N.E.2d 779 [1966]), lineups after the defendant has been formally charged (Kirby v. Illinois, 92 S.Ct. 1877, 406 U.S. 682, 32 L.Ed.2d 411 [1972]; Commonwealth v. Mendes, 361 Mass. 507, 281 N.E.2d 243 [1972] and cases cited), and transfer hearings to determine whether a juvenile is to be tried as an adult offender (Kent v. United States, 86 S.Ct. 1045, 383 U.S. 541, 561, 16 L.Ed.2d 84 [1966]; *see* Marsden v. Commonwealth, 352 Mass. 564, 567 n. 5, 227 N.E.2d 1 [1967]).

Counsel is also to be available to a defendant at the taking of a deposition pursuant to Mass.R.Crim.P. 32 (*see* 18 U.S.C. § 3503[c] [1970] from which Rule 32 derived) and during plea discussions under Mass.R.Crim.P. 12(b)(1).

In requiring that a defendant be advised of his right to, and provided with, counsel upon any appearance in court, Rule 8 is in accord with ABA *Standards Relating to Providing Defense Services* § 5.1 (Approved Draft, 1968), which directs that counsel should be provided "as soon as feasible."

General Laws c. 221, § 34D states in part that the Massachusetts Defenders Committee

> shall provide counsel at any stage of a criminal proceeding, other than capital, ... provided ... that [the] defendant is unable to obtain counsel by reason of his inability to pay.

Consistent with § 34D, for purposes of this rule, inability to obtain counsel is intended to include only financial inability. There are, however, no criteria supplied by statute or court rule to govern the judicial determination of who qualifies for assigned counsel, despite the fact that G.L. c. 261, § 27C(2), applicable to criminal cases, requires the clerk to "conspicuously post in that part of his office open to the public a notice specifying the indigency limits currently in force. . . ."

In answering the question of whether, under G.L. c. 221, § 34D, the defendant is "unable to obtain counsel by reason of his inability to pay," the judge may choose to rely on the opinion of the probation department, which is required to be prepared by G.L. c. 221, § 34D. However, since the final decision on indigency is the responsibility of the judge, neither the probation department's opinion nor its report of relevant information can be considered conclusive. The judge or special magistrate must "interrogate the defendant to satisfy himself that the defendant is unable to procure counsel." District Court Initial Rule of Criminal Procedure 2 (1971) requires that the interrogation be conducted in open court, but its dimensions are left to the judge's discretion.

General Laws c. 119, § 29A states that the parent of an unemancipated minor is liable for the minor's legal expenses, not to exceed three hundred dollars. While the resources of the parents may be included in the determination of the juvenile's indigency, if the parents refuse to retain counsel, the juvenile is entitled to court-provided counsel. It is the practice in some courts of the Commonwealth to impose costs for legal expenses of a juvenile upon the parents, notwithstanding the three-hundred-dollar limit of § 29A, supra, on the grounds that services of counsel are a necessity for which the parents are liable.

The assignment of counsel for, or the election to proceed without counsel by, a juvenile is governed by these rules.

Subdivision (b). This subdivision is drawn from and restates the substance of former S.J.C. Rule 3:10, paragraph 2 (1967: 351 Mass. 791, as amended, 1969: 355 Mass. 803). It is thus intended that counsel shall be assigned from the Massachusetts Defenders Committee, G.L. c. 221, § 34D, or from "a voluntary charitable group, corporation, or association," unless exceptional circumstances such as a conflict of interests or a need for foreign language speaking counsel justify appointing private counsel. *See* Superior Court Rule 53(3) (1974). Commonwealth v. Sheeran, 370 Mass. 82, 345 N.E.2d 362 (1976).

While the court in its discretion may appoint counsel other than from the Massachusetts Defenders Committee or similar organization, that discretion is to be exercised "sparingly" and not "unnecessarily." Abodeely v. County of Worcester, 352 Mass. 719, 227 N.E.2d 486 (1967).

The statutes provide compensation for appointed counsel only in capital cases (G.L. c. 276, § 37A: "reasonable compensation") and more particularly in murder cases (G.L. c. 277, § 55: "reasonable compensation" and § 56: "reasonable expenses"). Sections 55–56 provide that compensation is to be paid by the county where the indictment is found. The court in Abodeely v. County of Worcester, 352 Mass. 719, 227 N.E.2d 486 (1967), held that G.L. c. 213, § 8, which had been construed to compel the counties (now the Commonwealth: see G.L. c. 213, § 8, as amended, St.1978, c. 478, § 127) to pay the expense of prosecuting non-capital criminal cases, should be extended to cover also the costs of appointed defense counsel in such cases.

> If we are to provide proper prosecution we must also provide appropriate defence under the Constitution.... [W]hen the court assigns counsel for the defence in cases of needy criminal defendants then counsel should be paid from the county treasury....

352 Mass. at 723–24. General Laws c. 276, § 37A and c. 277, §§ 55–56, provide for "reasonable" compensation and expenses. Superior Court Rule 53 imposes a maximum limit on what will be allowed unless an excess is authorized in advance, Rule 53(2), (3)(c), or is deemed necessary in extraordinary circumstances, Rule 53(3)(d).

Subdivision (c). Provision for an assignment docket to be maintained by the clerk is drawn from former S.J.C. Rule 3:10, paragraph 3 (1967: 351 Mass. 791, as amended, 1969: 355 Mass. 803) and is consistent with prior law.

Subdivision (d). If a defendant is found to be financially able to retain counsel at his own expense it is, of course, incumbent upon him to do so. If a defendant is dilatory in engaging counsel, the court is empowered to take reasonable steps to keep the proceedings moving, even if the defendant's failure to arrange representation leaves him without counsel. Commonwealth v. Jackson, 376 Mass. 790, 383 N.E.2d 835 (1978). *See* Ungar v. Sarafite, 84 S.Ct. 841, 376 U.S. 575, 588–91, 11 L.Ed.2d 921 (1964); United States v. White, 529 F.2d 1390, 1394 (8th Cir.1976); United States v. Sperling, 506 F.2d 1323, 1337 n. 19 (2d Cir.1974), cert. denied, 95 S.Ct. 1351, 420 U.S. 962 (1975); Glenn v. United States, 303 F.2d 536, 542–43 (5th Cir.1962), cert. denied sub nom., Belvin v. United States, 83 S.Ct. 737, 372 U.S. 922, 9 L.Ed.2d 726 (1963). *Compare* Commonwealth v. Cavanaugh, 371 Mass. 46, 51, 353 N.E.2d 732 (1976) (myopic insistence upon expeditiousness in the face of a justifiable request for delay can render right to counsel an empty formality).

Subdivision (e). If the defendant wishes to waive counsel and proceed pro se, that right is guaranteed by the sixth and fourteenth amendments to the United States Constitution. Faretta v. California, 95 S.Ct. 2525, 422 U.S. 806, 45 L.Ed.2d 562 (1975). The right to self-representation is recognized in Massachusetts in Article 12 of the Declaration of Rights: "every subject shall have a right ... to be fully heard in his defense by himself or his counsel, at his election." Commonwealth v. Mott, 2 Mass.App. 47, 51, 308 N.E.2d 557 (1974).

However, the "waiver of counsel will not be presumed from a silent record." Williams v. Commonwealth, 350 Mass. 732, 734, 216 N.E.2d 779 (1966). Since the right to counsel is a constitutional right, the court should insure that a defendant's waiver of that right is both voluntary and intelligent. *See* Johnson v. Zerbst, 58 S.Ct. 1019, 304 U.S. 458, 464, 82 L.Ed. 1461 (1938). Section 7.2 of the ABA *Standards Relating to Providing Defense Services* (Approved Draft, 1968) is instructive on this issue:

> The accused's failure to request counsel or his announced intention to plead guilty should not of itself be construed to constitute a waiver. An accused should not be deemed to have waived the assistance of counsel until the entire process of offering counsel has been completed and a thorough inquiry into the accused's comprehension of that offer and his capacity to make the choice intelligently and understandingly has been made. No waiver should be found to have been made where it appears that the accused is unable to make an intelligent and understanding choice because of his mental condition, age, education, experience, the nature or the complexity of the case, or other factors.

The requirement of this rule that the waiver be in writing and signed by the defendant and certified by the judge or special magistrate is supportive of the notion that any waiver to be constitutional must be both voluntary and intelligent.

Both the United States Supreme Court and the Supreme Judicial Court of Massachusetts have made it clear that the right to proceed pro se is not unqualified. Under the *Faretta* decision, supra, although it is recognized that the right to proceed pro se is personal to the defendant and constitutionally guaranteed, nonetheless the trial judge must make an inquiry into whether the accused is choosing to proceed pro se in an intelligent and competent manner.

> Although a defendant need not himself have the skill and experience of a lawyer in order competently and intelligently to choose self-representation, he should be made aware of the dangers and disadvantages of self-representation.

Faretta, supra, at 835.

Massachusetts case law is in accord with this rule, and qualifies the waiver of counsel further. First, the request to proceed pro se must be unequivocal. Second, it should be asserted before trial. Finally, an inquiry as to the defendant's competence and intelligence in making the decision must be conducted and the motivation of the defendant examined. The defendant must also be told of the possible disadvantages of representing himself. Commonwealth v. Cavanaugh, 371 Mass. 46, 353 N.E.2d 732 (1976); *Commonwealth v. Mott,* supra. *See* Commonwealth v. Jackson, 376 Mass. 790, 383 N.E.2d 835 (1978).

The qualification that the waiver be unequivocal results in leaving a later request due to change of mind to the discretion of the trial judge—the defendant is no longer entitled to counsel as of right. Commonwealth v. Jackson, 376 Mass. 790, 383 N.E.2d 835 (1978). *See* Commonwealth v. Drolet, 337 Mass. 396, 149 N.E.2d 616 (1958).

Moreover, the assertion of the right to proceed pro se should be made before trial. "Once the trial has begun with the defendant represented by counsel, ... his right thereafter to discharge his lawyer and to represent himself is sharply curtailed." Commonwealth v. Mott, 2 Mass.App. 47, 308 N.E.2d 557. The courts on both the federal and state levels have construed the language "sharply curtailed" very strictly. In United States ex rel. Maldonado v. Denno, 348 F.2d 12 (2d Cir.1965), it was held that after commencement of trial

> there must be a showing that the prejudice to the legitimate interests of the defendant overbalances the potential disruption of proceedings already in progress, with considerable weight being given to the trial judge's assessment of this balance.

Id. at 15.

If a defendant is to proceed pro se, he must have waived counsel "knowingly and intelligently." *Faretta,* supra, held that technical, legal knowledge is not the test, but rather whether the defendant is literate, competent, and understanding, and is voluntarily exercising his free will. *Accord* Commonwealth v. Jackson, 376 Mass. 790, 383 N.E.2d 835 (1978). Impliedly, if the court finds that the defendant fails this test after an inquiry, it may appoint counsel notwithstanding the defendant's motion to proceed pro se. *See* subdivision (f), infra.

In Von Moltke v. Gillies, 68 S.Ct. 316, 332 U.S. 708, 92 L.Ed. 309 (1948) the Supreme Court laid down a searching formula to be used by trial judges in making certain that a defendant understandingly waives his right to counsel. Massachusetts, however, has not strictly interpreted *Von Moltke.* A judge is not required

> literally to fulfill all elements of a formula describing his responsibilities for acceptance of waiver of counsel. Substance rather than form is the guiding criterion for reviewing courts.

Commonwealth v. Fillippini, 2 Mass.App. 179, 182, 310 N.E.2d 147 (1974). Moreover, the *Faretta* decision, which recognizes emphatically the right to proceed pro se, would seem to erode the need for use of any rigid formula as long as the waiver was knowing and intelligent.

In *Mott,* supra, the court stated:

> We think that even in cases where the accused is harming himself by insisting on conducting his own defense, respect for individual autonomy requires that he be allowed to go to jail under his own banner if he so desires and if he makes the choice with eyes open.

Mott, supra, at 52, *quoting* United States ex rel. Maldonado v. Denno, 348 F.2d 12, 15 (2d Cir.1965).

However, under Massachusetts law, which is more liberal than *Von Moltke,* it is necessary for the trial judge to inquire into the defendant's motivation. "The motivation of the accused in making the request should be examined, and the accused should be apprised of the pitfalls in proceeding pro se." *Mott,* supra, at 52.

Subdivision (f). This subdivision is drawn from Rules of Criminal Procedure (U.L.A.) rule 711 (1974). See ABA *Standards Relating to the Function of the Trial Judge* § 6.7 (Approved Draft, 1972).

As long as the standby counsel assists only when called upon by the defendant and calls the attention of the court to matters favorable to the defendant upon which the court should rule upon its own motion, there is no interference with the defendant's representing himself. See Illinois v. Allen, 90 S.Ct. 1057, 397 U.S. 337, 25 L.Ed.2d 353 (1970); Commonwealth v. Maynard, 2 Mass.App. 894, 319 N.E.2d 453 (1974) (Rescript).

> A judge has broad discretion to appoint and order payment of ... counsel to represent or advise ... [an indigent defendant], to whatever extent he will accept representation, advice, and assistance, in an effort to ensure a fair, orderly and expeditious trial.

Jackson v. Commonwealth, 370 Mass. 855, 856, 346 N.E.2d 714 (1976) (Rescript).

Rule 9. Joinder of Offenses or Defendants

(Applicable to District Court and Superior Court)

(a) Joinder of Offenses.

(1) *Related Offenses.* Two or more offenses are related offenses if they are based on the same criminal conduct or episode or arise out of a course of criminal conduct or series of criminal episodes connected together or constituting parts of a single scheme or plan.

(2) *Joinder of Related Offenses in Complaint or Indictment.* If two or more related offenses are of the same or similar character, they may be charged in the same indictment or complaint, with each offense stated in a separate count.

(3) *Joinder of Related Offenses for Trial.* If a defendant is charged with two or more related offenses, either party may move for joinder of such charges. The trial judge shall join the charges for trial unless he determines that joinder is not in the best interests of justice.

(4) *Joinder of Unrelated Offenses.* Upon the written motion of a defendant, or with his written consent, the trial judge may join for trial two or more charges of unrelated offenses upon a showing that failure to try the charges together would constitute harassment or unduly consume the time or resources of the parties. The trial judge shall join the charges for trial unless he determines that joinder is not in the best interests of justice.

(b) Joinder of Defendants. Two or more defendants may be joined in the same indictment or complaint if the charges against them arise out of the same criminal conduct or episode or out of a course of criminal conduct or series of criminal episodes so connected as to constitute parts of a single scheme, plan, conspiracy or joint enterprise. The defendants may be charged separately or together in one or more counts; all of the defendants need not be charged in each count.

(c) Consolidation of Offenses or Defendants on Motion of Court. The trial judge may order two or more indictments or complaints to be tried together if the offenses and the defendants, if more than one, could have been joined in a single indictment or complaint. The procedure shall be the same as if the prosecution were under a single indictment or complaint.

(d) Relief From Prejudicial Joinder.

(1) *In General.* If it appears that a joinder of offenses or of defendants is not in the best interests of justice, the judge may upon his own motion or the motion of either party order an election of separate

trials of counts, grant a severance of defendants, or provide whatever other relief justice may require.

(2) *Motion by the Defendant.* A motion of the defendant for relief from prejudicial joinder shall be in writing and made before trial and shall be supported by an affidavit setting forth the grounds upon which any alleged prejudice rests, except that a motion for severance may be made before or at the close of all the evidence if based upon a ground not previously known.

(e) Conspiracy. An indictment or complaint for conspiracy to commit a substantive offense shall not be tried simultaneously with an indictment or complaint for the commission of the substantive offense, unless the defendant moves for joinder of such charges pursuant to subdivision (a) of this rule.

Reporter's Notes

The substance of Rule 9 is taken from several sources. These are Fed.R.Crim.P. 8 and 13, the ABA *Standards Relating to Joinder and Severance* (Approved Draft, 1968), Uniform Rules of Criminal Procedure (U.L.A.) Rules 471–73 (1974), and ALI Model Penal Code §§ 1.07–1.09 (1962). *See* Commonwealth v. Gallarelli, 372 Mass. 573, 362 N.E.2d 923 (1977) (Kaplan, J., concurring). The language is drawn largely from the Uniform Rules.

Subdivision (a). Although subdivisions (a) and (b) of the rule are consistent with their statutory precedent, former G.L. c. 277, § 46 (St.1861, c. 181), the rule is more explicit in defining what charges may be joined in a single indictment.

Related offenses are defined in (a)(1) as those which 1) are based on the same criminal conduct or episode, or 2) arise out of a course of criminal conduct or a series of criminal episodes connected together or constituting parts of a single scheme or plan. "Conduct" means an act or omission to act; "episode" means an occurrence or connected series of occurrences and developments which may be viewed as distinctive and apart although part of a larger or more comprehensive series. ABA *Standards Relating to Joinder and Severance* § 1.3(a), comment at 20–21 (Approved Draft, 1968).

Under Federal Rule 8, offenses may be joined if they 1) are based on the same transaction, 2) are parts of a common scheme or plan, or 3) are of the same or similar character. Offenses that are based on the same underlying facts or are each part of a larger plan are related in such a way as to insure an overlap in the evidence to be presented upon each offense.

Rule 9 takes the position that the goal of judicial economy will rarely be paramount to affording the defendant a trial as free from prejudice as possible; therefore, joinder of unrelated offenses is prohibited except at the instance of the defendant or with his written consent.

Rule 9 permits joint trial of offenses committed in furtherance of a common scheme or plan, but factually independent, and thus conforms to case law under former G.L. c. 277, § 46.

General Laws c. 277, § 46, which governed joinder of offenses, stated:

> Two or more counts describing different crimes depending upon the same facts or transactions may be set forth in the same indictment if it contains an averment that the different counts therein are different descriptions of the same acts.

If read narrowly the statute would prohibit joint trial of offenses which were part of a joint scheme or plan, but not dependent upon the same underlying facts. The statute has, however, been interpreted more broadly, allowing joint trial of offenses related in ways other than as literally permitted by § 46. *See* e.g., Harding v. Commonwealth, 283 Mass. 369, 186 N.E. 556 (1933).

Subdivision (a)(3) allows the parties to request that the charges pending against the defendant be joined for trial. By granting the court discretionary power to deny the defendant's motion to join the charges, the rule protects the prosecution from being effectively "forced" to try charges on which it has not yet organized a sufficient case to warrant proceeding. See Mass.R.Crim.P. 37(a), (b)(2), which require the approval of the prosecutor for charges to be transferred for plea, sentence, or trial.

Subdivision (b). This subdivision is in form virtually identical to the corresponding federal rule provision, but substitutes "conduct" and "criminal episode" for the terms used in the federal rule, "act" and "transaction."

Although there is no statute in the Commonwealth analogous to the joinder of defendants provision contained in subdivision (b), it seems to be in harmony with former Massachusetts practice. Prior to the promulgation of these rules, such joinder was permitted in two instances: when the defendants were charged with joint participation in a single series of events based on identical facts, Commonwealth v. Nicholson, 4 Mass.App. 87, 341 N.E.2d 688 (1976); Englehart v. Commonwealth, 353 Mass. 561, 233 N.E.2d 737 (1968), and when there existed sufficient evidence to indicate that the defendant and co-defendant were engaged in a common enterprise, and the issue of fact to be tried against each defendant was similar, as in Commonwealth v. Smith, 353 Mass. 442, 232 N.E.2d 917 (1968).

Subdivision (c). This subdivision allows otherwise permissive joinder of offenses or defendants to be accomplished by the trial court on its own motion. This provision is included in order to achieve the principle goal of the rule, judicial economy, while protecting the defendant's right to a reasonably prejudice-free trial. Although it is contemplated that joinder will be effected by the prosecution at the indictment or complaint stage in all possible cases, should the prosecution elect to proceed in a manner contrary to the goal of judicial economy this subsection empowers the court to rectify the situation on its own motion without having to depend on a motion by the defendant. *Compare* Commonwealth v. Benjamin, 358 Mass. 672, 678, 266 N.E.2d 662 (1971) (order for amendment of indictments).

Subdivision (d). Subdivision (d)(1) is essentially drawn from Fed.R.Crim.P. 14 and is consonant with prior Massachusetts practice. Subdivision (d)(2) is taken from ABA *Standards Relating to Joinder & Severance* § 2.1(a) (Approved Draft, 1968).

> As a general proposition, the decision whether to allow a motion to sever two or more indictments which have been joined for purposes of trial rests in the sound discretion of the trial judge.

Commonwealth v. Jervis, 368 Mass. 638, 645, 335 N.E.2d 356 (1975). *Accord,* United States v. Luna, 585 F.2d 1, 4–5 (1st Cir.1978); Commonwealth v. Cruz, 373 Mass. 676, 369 N.E.2d

996 (1977); Commonwealth v. Drew, 4 Mass.App. 30, 340 N.E.2d 524 (1976).

Where "substantially the same evidence, or evidence connected with a single line of conduct," Commonwealth v. Rosenthal, 211 Mass. 50, 54, 97 N.E. 609 (1912), substantiates two or more indictments for "offenses [which] are kindred and liable to punishment of the same general character," Commonwealth v. Veal, 362 Mass. 877, 289 N.E.2d 844 (1972) (Rescript), there is no abuse of discretion in denying the defendant's motion for severance. *Commonwealth v. Drew,* supra, at 53. The legal standards which must guide the exercise of the court's discretion in determining a motion to sever have been articulated as follows:

> No sound reason can be given why several indictments charging different crimes arising out of a single chain of circumstances should not be tried together. Where several offenses might have been joined in one indictment, and would be proved by substantially the same evidence, or evidence connected with a single line of conduct, and grow out of what is essentially one transaction, and where it does not appear that any real right of the defendant has been jeopardized, it would be a refinement not demanded by the law or by justice to require in all instances a separate trial, simply because separate indictments have been found for each offense.

Commonwealth v. Cruz, 373 Mass. 676, 369 N.E.2d 996 (1977). *Accord* Commonwealth v. Blow, 362 Mass. 196, 200, 285 N.E.2d 400 (1972); *Commonwealth v. Rosenthal, supra.*

The assertion of prejudicial joinder does not challenge the propriety of the initial order for consolidation. Rather, the prejudice is found in facts peculiar to a defendant's case. Defendants may move for severance of their cases, or of counts therein, on the grounds of misjoinder and prejudicial joinder.

Misjoinder. It is important to know what the minimal grounds for joinder of defendants or offenses are when considering a claim of misjoinder because such a claim is an assertion that the minimal requirements have not been satisfied. Thus, when a motion for severance of defendants or for separate trials of more than one count is based on the ground that the consolidated offenses should not have been joined, i.e., that there has been a misjoinder, the standards upon which the motion is to be judged are stated in subdivisions (a)(1)–(2) of this rule.

A misjoinder can result in two ways. First, the offenses joined might have been improperly joined in one indictment and, secondly, two indictments may have been improperly consolidated for trial. In both cases, however, the same standard is to be used to determine the propriety of the joinder.

Two other aspects of this subdivision deserve mention. First, subdivision (d)(1) permits a court to grant a severance upon its own motion. Although this authorizes a court to review its initial order of consolidation of the charges for trial to see if the minimum grounds are satisfied, its primary significance is that it permits the court to exercise its discretion in deciding initially whether to proceed by joint or separate trials even though one of the minimum grounds for joinder is satisfied. In effect, this provision permits the trial judge to consider the prejudice to the defendant in his initial decision as well as at later stages of the trial.

Secondly, it is recommended in the ABA *Standards Relating to Joinder and Severance* § 2.1(c)–(d), comment at 28 (Approved Draft, 1968), that a motion by the prosecution for severance, unless consented to by the defendant, be required to be made prior to trial to avoid giving the defendant upon retrial the defense of double jeopardy. As is stated therein, however, this proposition does not derive from any judicial holdings to that effect. While this subdivision contemplates that prosecution motions for severance shall be limited to a pretrial posture, it is likely that if a severance upon the prosecution's motion after the commencement of trial is a "manifest necessity" such that the "ends of public justice would otherwise be defeated," United States v. Perez, 22 U.S. (9 Wheat.) 579, 580 (1824), courts of this Commonwealth would hold that the severance was not a bar to future prosecution on the severed charges, even if the defendant did not consent. *Compare* Price v. Slayton, 347 F.Supp. 1269 (W.D.Va.1972).

Prejudicial Joinder. Satisfying the minimum joinder standards is only one consideration affecting a court's decision on consolidation. The court is lodged with the discretion to determine in each case whether justice would be served better by joint or separate trials. The countervailing considerations affecting this decision are the defendant's interests and the interests of the court and prosecution in having the adjudication as short and as inexpensive as possible. The merits of each side's claims will differ from case to case. Only the trial judge is in a position to balance effectively the competing interests, and, in most cases, his discretion is very broad.

In its initial decision upon the issue of consolidating charges for a single trial, in addition to determining whether minimum grounds for joinder exist, the court should consider whether the defendant would be adversely affected by joinder. If he would and if this prejudice overrides the interests of the prosecutor, the public, and the courts in an expeditious trial, joinder should not be ordered.

At any stage after joinder has been ordered, the court on motion of the defendant or on its own motion may wish to reconsider whether the interests of justice are better served by separate trials. At such time, the court should again weigh the competing interests as well as considering how far the prosecution of the charges has proceeded and whether a severance would involve an undue relitigation of issues already presented to the court. In both its initial decision and at any later reconsideration of prejudice to the defendant, the court is determining whether there exists a prejudicial joinder of charges.

The Supreme Judicial Court summarized the duty of the trial court in protecting a defendant's rights as follows:

> It is the heavy obligation of the trial court sedulously to take care that the defendant is not confounded in his defense, that the attention of the jury is not distracted and that in no aspect are the substantial rights of the defendant adversely affected by requiring him to proceed to trial on separate complaints for different offenses or on separate counts for different offenses in one complaint.

Commonwealth v. Slavski, 245 Mass. 405, 412–13, 140 N.E. 465 (1923). It is made clear by the court that the trial court's discretion is circumscribed by its duty to guarantee a fair trial.

A court may find prejudice on its own motion or the motion of either party. However, where a defendant initiates the motion for relief from prejudice, he has a strong burden of persuasion. Sagansky v. United States, 358 F.2d 195 (1st Cir.1966), cert. denied, 87 S.Ct. 36, 385 U.S. 816, 17 L.Ed.2d 55. This heavy burden is placed upon the defendant because the trial judge has already determined once that the defendant was not likely to be prejudiced by consolidated trials.

A defendant first must make his motion at the appropriate time. If a motion is filed before the prejudicial grounds have materialized, the motion should be dismissed. The grounds of prejudice may become known to a defendant at any stage of the pretrial of trial proceedings. He has the duty to inform the court of these grounds whenever he first learns of them. If a motion is made at trial based upon grounds known prior to the commencement of the trial, the defendant has waived his opportunity to object. Subdivision (d)(2).

Secondly, a defendant has the related burden of showing a specific ground of prejudice. It is not enough for a defendant merely to claim that his chances of acquittal are reduced in a joint trial, or that a joint trial presents him with a number of *potential* dangers. The defendant must point to definite prejudice that presently exists.

One other class of cases deserves mention. In these, a separate trial must be granted because of an established principle of law; the decision is non-discretionary. In cases not of this class, the decision regarding a joint trial rests upon the peculiar arrangement of the facts, whereas here the facts are less significant. This class is composed mostly of claims that a defendant's constitutional rights will be infringed by a consolidated trial. Bruton v. United States, 88 S.Ct. 1620, 391 U.S. 123, 20 L.Ed.2d 476 (1968), establishes the most significant principle in this area. Basing its decision on a defendant's sixth amendment right to confront adverse witnesses, the Supreme Court held that a severance was required where a co-defendant's confession implicating the defendant is to be offered at trial. It had always been true that such a confession was inadmissible against the non-confessor, but prior to this decision a limiting instruction to the jury was deemed sufficient to protect the rights of the non-confessing defendant. The distinction between this decision and others where continued reliance on jury instructions is found is that a defendant's constitutional right is in issue here and less flexibility in balancing competing interests is tolerated.

The scope of the *Bruton* decision has been delimited since the time of its issuance, and a severance is not always required where one defendant's confession mentions other participants in the criminal acts. The following are examples where a severance is not required:

1. Commonwealth v. Scott, 355 Mass. 471, 245 N.E.2d 415 (1969), holds that a confession implicating the defendant may be admitted in a joint trial when the defendant does not contest his participation in the crime. This occurs when a defendant asserts a special defense, e.g., insanity.

2. When the statement refers to other participants without identifying them or when the statement can be cured of any constitutional defect by excision, it may be admitted at a joint trial. *See* Commonwealth v. French, 357 Mass. 356, 259 N.E.2d 195, 46 A.L.R.3d 1106 (1970); ABA *Standards,* supra, § 2.3(a). But sufficient identification may be found even when names are not used. Commonwealth v. Sarro, 356 Mass. 100, 248 N.E.2d 286 (1969).

3. The confessing co-defendant can testify at trial, thereby giving the implicated defendant the opportunity to cross-examine the witness on any statements made by him that were admitted at trial. Santoro v. United States, 402 F.2d 920 (9th Cir.1968). *See* Commonwealth v. Hicks, Mass.Adv.Sh. (1979) 1, 384 N.E.2d 1206; Commonwealth v. Murphy, Mass.App. Adv.Sh. (1978) 533.

Another example of a severance being required because of the threat of impairing a defendant's constitutional rights is offered by DeLuna v. United States, 308 F.2d 140, 1 A.L.R.3d 969 (5th Cir.1962). Only one defendant took the stand, and his counsel commented upon the failure of his client's co-defendant to testify in an attempt to show that only an innocent defendant has the courage to deny his guilt at trial. The Court of Appeals held it error to permit one defendant to comment adversely upon his co-defendant's exercise of his fifth amendment privilege not to testify.

In sum, prejudice to a defendant is to be found in the facts of his case. Most claims of prejudice are to be decided by the trial court in the exercise of its discretion, and the majority of these claims are rejected. A severance is required in some cases because certain facts relating to either trial strategy or the nature of the offenses establish as a matter of law the existence of prejudice. In other cases, a severance is mandated by constitutional considerations.

Subdivision (e). This subdivision prohibits trial on an indictment or complaint for conspiracy to commit a substantive offense simultaneously with the trial on the substantive offense, except upon motion of the defendant. This provision is retained from former G.L. c. 278, § 2A (St.1968, c. 721, § 2) pursuant to which the prohibition against joint trials of the conspiracy and substantive charges was absolute. *See* Commonwealth v. Gallarelli, Mass.Adv.Sh. (1977) 1013, 1017, 362 N.E.2d 923. Under this rule, however, the defendant may move for joinder of such charges.

The Supreme Judicial Court has noted that "[t]he legislative history affords no indication of why § 2A, which may add new complications to enforcement of the criminal law, was adopted at all. . . ." Commonwealth v. French, 357 Mass. 356, 375 n. 20, 259 N.E.2d 195, 46 A.L.R.3d 1106 (1970). *Accord* Commonwealth v. Gallarelli, Mass.Adv.Sh. (1977) 1013, 1024, 362 N.E.2d 923 (Kaplan, J., concurring). The intent of the rule is to guard against the possibility that a jury, if permitted to hear evidence on both the conspiracy and the substantive offense, might convict on the charge of the substantive offenses of a matter of course after convicting on the conspiracy charge, in spite of the court's instruction as to the distinct evidence required to establish a conspiracy. This is because of the much broader scope of admissibility of evidence permitted to prove the conspiracy charge.

The defendant should be allowed to proceed by a joint trial, however, so long as it is determined by the judge to be in the best interests of justice. This practice accords with that under Fed.R.Crim.P. 8(b), pursuant to which conspiracy and substantive charges may be joined. E.g., United States v. Graham, 548 F.2d 1302, 1310 (8th Cir.1977); United States v. Beasley, 519 F.2d 233, 238 (5th Cir.1975); United States v. Banks, 465 F.2d 1235, 1242–43 (5th Cir.), cert. denied, 401 U.S. 924 (1972); Gordon v. United States, 438 F.2d 858, 878 (5th Cir.), cert. denied sub nom., Crandall v. United States, 92 S.Ct. 63, 404 U.S. 828, 30 L.Ed.2d 56 (1971). See ABA *Standards Relating to Joinder and Severance* § 1.2(b), comment at 15 (Approved Draft, 1968).

Rule 10. Continuances

(Applicable to District Court and Superior Court)

(a) Continuances.

(1) After a case has been entered upon the trial calendar, a continuance shall be granted only when

based upon cause and only when necessary to insure that the interests of justice are served.

(2) The factors, among others, which a judge shall consider in determining whether to grant a continuance in any case are:

(A) Whether the failure to grant a continuance in the proceeding would be likely to make a continuation of the proceeding impossible, or result in a miscarriage of justice.

(B) Whether the case taken as a whole is so unusual or so complex, because of the number of defendants or the nature of the prosecution or otherwise, that it is unreasonable to expect adequate preparation of the case at the time it is scheduled for trial.

(C) Whether the overall caseload of defense counsel routinely prohibits his making scheduled appearances, whether there has been a failure of diligent preparation by a party, and whether there has been a failure by a party to use due diligence to obtain available witnesses.

(3) An attorney who is to be otherwise engaged in a trial, evidentiary hearing, or appellate argument so as to require a continuance shall notify the court and the adverse party or the attorney for the adverse party of such conflicting engagement not less than twenty-four hours before the scheduled appearance, or within such other time as is reasonable under the circumstances.

(4) A motion for a continuance may include a request that the court rule on the motion without a hearing. If such a motion is filed at least three court days prior to the scheduled appearance or trial date and indicates that all parties have agreed to the continuance, the court shall, prior to the scheduled date, rule on the motion without a hearing unless it deems a hearing to be necessary. In any other case, the court may in its discretion rule on a continuance motion without a hearing, provided that all parties have had an adequate opportunity to file an opposition to the motion. If the court continues the case without a hearing, defendant's counsel shall inform the defendant of the revised date. Any motion filed pursuant to this subdivision shall provide one or more proposed continuance dates and state all supporting grounds, and any factual allegations shall be supported by affidavit.

(b) Assessment of Costs. When a continuance is granted upon the motion of either the Commonwealth or the defendant without adequate notice to the adverse party, causing the adverse party to incur unnecessary expenses, a judge may in his discretion assess those expenses as costs against the party or counsel requesting the continuance.

(c) Preservation of Testimony. A judge may order as a condition upon the granting of a continuance that the testimony of a witness then present in court be taken and preserved for subsequent use at trial or any other proceeding. The witness shall be examined in open court by the party on whose behalf he is present and the adverse party shall have the right of cross-examination. The expense of taking and preserving the testimony shall be assessed as costs against the party requesting the continuance.

Amended October 14, 1997, effective December 1, 1997.

Reporter's Notes

This rule is modeled in part after 18 U.S.C. § 3161(h)(8)(B)–(C) (Supp. 1, 1975). Subdivisions (b) and (c), while novel to Massachusetts criminal practice, are not without precedent, *see* Superior Court Rule 21 (1974); District Court Supplemental Rule of Civil Procedure 103 (1975); G.L. c. 276, § 50.

Subdivision (a). This subdivision is modeled after 18 U.S.C. § 3161(h)(8)(B)–(C) (Supp. 1, 1975). The controlling principle underlying this subdivision is that a continuance should be granted only when justice requires. See ABA *Standards Relating to Speedy Trial* § 1.3 (Approved Draft, 1968); *the Defense Function* § 1.2(b), (c) (Approved Draft, 1971); *the Prosecution Function* § 2.9(a), (c) (Approved Draft, 1971); Rules of Criminal Procedure (U.L.A.) Rule 721(d) (1974). Consensual continuances and continuances which are helpful, but which fall short of being necessary, are not to be granted, because in such cases justice is generally promoted by proceeding to trial without delay and because the need for the prompt disposition of criminal cases transcends the desires of the immediate participants in the proceedings. *Compare* Commonwealth v. Silva, Mass.App.Adv. Sh. (1978) 374 (Rescript), 374 N.E.2d 353.

Whether a motion for a continuance should be granted traditionally lies within the discretion of the trial judge, whose action will not be disturbed unless there is a clear abuse of discretion. Commonwealth v. Jackson, Mass.Adv.Sh. (1978) 3062, 3064, 383 N.E.2d 835; Commonwealth v. Watkins, Mass.Adv.Sh. (1978) 1646, 1671, 379 N.E.2d 1040; Commonwealth v. Funderberg, Mass.Adv.Sh. (1978) 601, 604, 373 N.E.2d 963; Commonwealth v. Grieco, Mass.App.Adv.Sh. (1977) 598, 604, 362 N.E.2d 1204. In ruling on a motion for a continuance, the judge should balance the moving party's need for additional time against the possible inconvenience, increased costs, and prejudice which may be incurred by the opposing party, as well as giving due weight to the interest of the judicial system in avoiding delays which would not measurably contribute to the resolution of a particular controversy. Commonwealth v. Gilchrest, 364 Mass. 272, 276–77, 303 N.E.2d 331 (1973). *Accord Commonwealth v. Grieco,* supra, at 605, Mass.App.Adv.Sh. (1977) 598, 362 N.E.2d 1204.

Common grounds asserted by counsel as a basis for a requested continuance are:

> Illness of the defendant or important witnesses or defense counsel, conflicting engagements of counsel, lack of time for preparation by counsel or prejudicial publicity or a combination of several of the factors. . . .

30 MASS. PRACTICE SERIES (Smith) § 1013 (1970, Supp. 1978).

A determination of a motion for a continuance to secure the attendance of witnesses will depend upon a showing that the desired testimony is of more than "marginal significance" and not "merely cumulative" to or corroborative of other available testimony to the same effect. Commonwealth v. Watkins, Mass.Adv.Sh. (1978) 1646, 1670–71, 379 N.E.2d 1040; Commonwealth v. Funderberg, 374 Mass. 577, 373

N.E.2d 963 (1978); Commonwealth v. Hanger, Mass.App. Adv.Sh. (1978) 633, 648, aff'd, Mass.Adv.Sh. (1979) 647; Commonwealth v. Darden, 5 Mass.App. 522, 364 N.E.2d 1092 (1977), where the adverse party would not be prejudiced by a continuance and the testimony is significant, a denial of the continuance constitutes an abuse of discretion, Commonwealth v. Silva, Mass.App.Adv.Sh. (1978) 374 (Rescript), 374 N.E.2d 353, assuming that the desired witness may be expected to become available within a reasonable time. *Compare* Commonwealth v. Ambers, 4 Mass.App. 647, 357 N.E.2d 323 (1976), (witness missed ride) with Commonwealth v. Swenor, 3 Mass.App. 65, 66–67, 323 N.E.2d 742 (1975) (witness in federal custody; authorities would not honor writ of habeas corpus ad testificandum). *See* Commonwealth v. Hanger, Mass.App.Adv.Sh. (1978) 633, 647, 376 N.E.2d 877. Subdivision (a)(2)(C) adds as a consideration that the moving party must have exercised due diligence to obtain the presence of available witnesses.

As for conflicting engagements of counsel, subdivision (a)(2)(C) indicates that delays attributable to the heavy case load of desired defense counsel which would prevent the commencement of trial for an unreasonable time period do not establish good cause for a continuance. The right of a defendant to retain counsel of his choice does not include the right to choose an attorney who is unable to comply with the demands of the trial calendar. United States v. DiStefano, 464 F.2d 845, 846 n. 1 (2d Cir.1972). *See* United States v. Poulack, 556 F.2d 83, 86 (1st Cir.1977); United States v. Tortora, 464 F.2d 1202, 1210 (2d Cir.1972); Commonwealth v. Perry, Mass.App.Adv.Sh. (1978) 840, 850, 378 N.E.2d 1384.

> Other conflicting engagements of counsel afford no right to the continuance of any particular case.... [T]his is the only way in which the trial of causes can proceed in an orderly and expeditious way under present conditions.... No attorney can accept ... a larger number of cases than he can try as and when they are reached and expect courts to continue any case for his convenience or that of his clients.

Commonwealth v. Festo, 251 Mass. 275, 277, 146 N.E. 700 (1925). *See* Commonwealth v. Dabrieo, 370 Mass. 728, 736–37, 352 N.E.2d 186 (1976) (counsel was engaged in court appearances in several counties and "unavailable for trial of this case" for seven months). There are those instances, however, where a conflicting engagement is unavoidable and justice would best be served by the granting of a continuance. In such an instance, subdivision (a)(3) requires counsel to notify the court and the adverse party of the conflict in order to minimize their inconvenience.

The sixth and fourteenth amendments to the United States Constitution, which afford a defendant the right to counsel in a prosecution which may result in a loss of liberty, Argersinger v. Hamlin, 92 S.Ct. 887, 407 U.S. 25, 27 L.Ed.2d 805 (1972), are not satisfied by the mere presence of a competent attorney if that attorney is not prepared. Commonwealth v. Cavanaugh, 371 Mass. 46, 57, 353 N.E.2d 732 (1976). In addition to the factors listed in subdivision (a)(2)(B) relative to the reasonableness of expecting adequate preparation, the court may consider the length of time the attorney has been assigned or appointed to the case. In ruling on a motion for a continuance on this ground, the judge's discretion cannot be exercised so as to impair the constitutional right to prepared counsel; a "myopic insistence upon expeditiousness in the face of a justifiable request for delay can render the right ... an empty formality." *Commonwealth v. Cavanaugh,* supra, 371 Mass. at 51. On the other hand, where there is ample justification for the conclusion that a last-minute claim of lack of preparation is merely a dilatory tactic, is unsupported by the facts, or is the result of a failure of diligent preparation, a denial of a continuance is no abuse of discretion. Commonwealth v. Jackson, Mass.Adv.Sh. (1978) 3062, 3064, 3070, 383 N.E.2d 835; Commonwealth v. Perry, Mass.App.Adv.Sh. (1978) 840, 848–50, 378 N.E.2d 1384; subdivision (a)(2)(C). *See also* Commonwealth v. Coward, Mass.App.Adv.Sh. (1979) 273 (Rescript) 386 N.E.2d 256.

Pursuant to Mass.R.Crim.P. 11(a)(2)(B) and (b)(2)(B), if the required pretrial conference report is not filed and a party does not appear at the scheduled time to explain the failure, "no request of that party for a continuance of the trial date ... shall be granted...."

Subdivision (b). This subdivision deviates from previous Massachusetts criminal procedure. Former practice dictated that if a continuance was granted, each party was to bear his own costs, unless the defendant was assessed the costs of prosecution. *See* generally G.L. c. 280, § 6. However, the courts have long applied a similar assessment rule to the costs of continuances in civil proceedings. Superior Court Rule 21 (1974) provides, and District Court Civil Rule 16 (1965) provided, that when a case is postponed on the motion of a party, that party may be responsible for the costs and expenses of the adverse party in addition to his own.

The decision to assess the costs rests solely within the discretion of the judge, and payment is to be made directly to the adverse party for the benefit of whomever incurred the expenses and not to the court. The purposes of this rule are to discourage parties or their attorneys from requesting continuances on short notice and to reimburse parties for expenses they incur as a result of the tardiness of the adverse side in requesting a continuance. As stated in the District Court and Superior Court rules, supra, the court should not assess costs against a party in cases where his opponent has incurred expenses because of a requested continuance when: 1) the continuance is granted because of improper conduct of the adverse party; or 2) adequate notice was in fact given the adverse party (*see* [a][3], infra); or 3) grounds for the continuance were not discovered in time to give sufficient notice to prevent the expense to the adverse party.

Assessable costs under this rule are those costs directly caused by the insufficient notice. Assessable costs generally include witness fees, extra compensation paid to police witnesses, travel costs, costs of depositions pursuant to subdivision (c), infra, and perhaps stenographers' attendance fees in District Court. *See* Mass.R.Crim.P. 6(d)(1).

Subdivision (c). A new practice is instituted by this subdivision: if a witness is present in court and a party has requested a continuance, the judge may condition the grant of the continuance upon the taking and preservation of that witness' testimony for use at trial or other proceeding. While similar in many respects to a court-ordered deposition after a finding that a witness was unlikely to appear at the continued proceeding (former G.L. c. 276, § 50 [St.1851, c. 71]), the procedure permitted under this rule is not termed a deposition. This is to avoid conflict with the formal summons and notice requirements of Mass.R.Crim.P. 35(b)(c)(h). In all other respects the procedure is compatible with Rule 35 deposition practice.

While utilization of the procedure established by this subdivision should be undertaken only in "exceptional circumstances" when "deemed to be in the interests of justice," Mass.R.Crim.P. 35(a), it is not intended to be so restricted as that under Mass.R.Crim.P. 6(d)(2), pursuant to which testimony may be taken upon the default of a defendant only if "to require the attendance at a later time of a witness ... would constitute a hardship because of age, infirmity, illness, profession or other sufficient reason." Once taken and preserved, the witness' testimony may be used as substantive evidence in any subsequent proceeding as if the witness were "unavailable" under Mass.R.Crim.P. 35(g).

This procedure does not deny the defendant's right to confrontation of witnesses, since it is presumed that the defendant will be present when the continuance is requested and the witness will, of course, be in attendance. The witness is to be examined in open court by the party calling him and the adverse party is permitted to cross-examine. In these circumstances, the constitutional requirement is satisfied. Commonwealth v. DiPietro, 373 Mass. 369, 367 N.E.2d 811 (1977); aff'g Commonwealth v. DiPietro, 4 Mass.App. 845, 356 N.E.2d 269 (1976).

Reporter's Notes—1997

(a)(4). In 1997, Rule 10 was amended by adding new subsection (a)4. This amendment allows the judge to rule on a continuance motion without a hearing, provided all other parties have had a chance to file an opposition to the motion. Previously a continuance motion was often argued in court, even if it was agreed to by all parties, because no other formal procedure was available. Either the case was advanced for hearing on the motion, compounding client expense and court congestion; or the continuance motion was argued on the trial day, leaving parties uncertain whether it would be granted and requiring the defendant and witnesses to be present in case the motion was denied. Subsection (a)(4) is designed to rectify these problems and provide a more efficient procedure, while continuing to maintain ultimate authority in the court over whether to grant a continuance even when the parties are in agreement.

Criminal Rule 10 continues to provide for a ruling by the judge on a continuance motion in every case, consistent with Uniform Magistrate's Rule 2. Although this rule generally permits actions on uncontested, nonevidentiary motions by the magistrate, subdivision (c) prohibits the magistrate from acting on continuances.

As with Rule 7, when a case is continued in the absence of the defendant, defense counsel is charged with the responsibility of so notifying his or her client.

Rule 11. Pretrial Conference and Pretrial Hearing

[Text of rule applicable to cases initiated (by indictment or complaint) on or after September 7, 2004.]

(a) The Pretrial Conference.

At arraignment, except on a complaint regarding which the court will not exercise final jurisdiction, the court shall order the prosecuting attorney and defense counsel to attend a pretrial conference on a date certain to consider such matters as will promote a fair and expeditious disposition of the case. The defendant shall be available for attendance at the pretrial conference. The court may require the conference to be held at court under the supervision of a judge or clerk-magistrate.

(1) *Conference Agenda.* Among those issues to be discussed at the pretrial conference are:

(A) Discovery and all other matters which, absent agreement of the parties, must be raised by pretrial motion. All motions which cannot be agreed upon shall be filed pursuant to Rule 13(d).

(B) Whether the case can be disposed of without a trial.

(C) If the case is to be tried, (i) the setting of a proposed trial date which shall be subject to the approval of the court and which when fixed by the court shall not be changed without express permission of the court; (ii) the probable length of trial; (iii) the availability of necessary witnesses; and (iv) whether issues of fact can be resolved by stipulation.

(2) *Conference Report.*

(A) Filing. A conference report, subscribed by the prosecuting attorney and counsel for the defendant, and when necessary to waive constitutional rights or when the report contains stipulations as to material facts, by the defendant, shall be filed with the clerk of the court pursuant to subdivision (b)(2)(i). The conference report shall contain a statement of those matters upon which the parties have reached agreement, including any stipulations of fact, and a statement of those matters upon which the parties could not agree which are to be the subject of pretrial motions. Agreements reduced to writing in the conference report shall be binding on the parties and shall control the subsequent course of the proceeding.

(B) Failure to File. If a party fails to participate in a pretrial conference or to cooperate in the filing of a conference report, the adverse party shall notify the clerk of such failure. If a conference report is not filed and a party does not appear at the pretrial hearing, no request of that party for a continuance of the trial date as scheduled shall be granted and no pretrial motion of that party shall be permitted to be filed, except by leave of court for cause shown. If the parties fail to file a conference report or do not appear at the pretrial hearing, the case shall be presumed to be ready for trial and shall be scheduled for trial at the earliest possible time. The parties shall be subject to such other sanctions as the judge may impose.

(b) The Pretrial Hearing.

At arraignment, except on a complaint regarding which the court will not exercise final jurisdiction, the court shall order the prosecuting attorney and defense counsel to appear before the court on a date certain for a pretrial hearing. The defendant shall be available for attendance at the hearing. The pretrial hearing may include the following events:

(1) *Tender of Plea.* The defendant may tender a plea, admission or other requested disposition, with or without the agreement of the prosecutor.

(2) *Pretrial Matters.* Unless the Court declines jurisdiction over the case or disposes of the case at the pretrial hearing, the pretrial hearing shall include the following events:

(i) Filing of Pretrial Conference Report. The prosecuting attorney and defense counsel shall file the pretrial conference report with the clerk of court.

(ii) Discovery and Pretrial Motions. The court shall hear all discovery motions pending at the time of the pretrial hearing. Other pending pretrial motions may be heard at the pretrial hearing, continued to a specified date for a hearing, or transmitted for hearing and resolution by the trial session.

(iii) Compliance and Trial Assignment. The court shall determine whether the pretrial conference report is complete, all discovery matters have been resolved, and compliance with all discovery orders has been accomplished. If so, the court shall obtain the defendant's decision on waiver of the right to a jury trial, and assign a trial date or trial assignment date. If completion of either the pretrial conference report or discovery is still pending, the court shall schedule and order the parties to appear for a compliance hearing pursuant to Rule 11(c) unless the aggrieved party waives the right to a compliance hearing.

(iv) The court may issue such additional orders as will promote the fair, speedy and orderly disposition of the case.

(c) Compliance Hearing.

A compliance hearing ordered pursuant to Rule 11(b)(2)(iii) shall be limited to the following court actions:

(1) determining whether the pretrial conference report and discovery are complete and, if necessary, hearing and deciding discovery motions and ordering appropriate sanctions for non-compliance;

(2) receiving and acting on a tender of plea or admission; and

(3) if the pretrial conference report and discovery are complete, obtaining the defendant's decision on waiver of the right to a jury trial, and scheduling the trial date or trial assignment date.

Amended March 8, 2004, effective September 7, 2004.

Reporter's Notes—Revised, 2004

Rule 11 is designed to promote the speedy and orderly disposition of cases at a time certain which is most convenient to all parties, and to that end it calls upon defendants' counsel to aid the court in the disposition of all preliminary motions and other matters relative to pending cases. *See* Commonwealth v. Durning, 406 Mass. 485, 495 (1990). Although the title of the rule would appear to limit its application to those cases which are destined to be tried, it is intended that in some cases the conference will result in the resolution of issues so as to make trial unnecessary. At the least the pretrial conference should assist the parties in channeling their attention and resources to matters genuinely in issue and aid the court in focusing the elaborate mechanism of a full trial upon the material issues in dispute.

The 2004 Amendments. In 2004, the Rule was substantially rewritten to mandate a uniform pretrial process in all criminal courts. Under the rule, at arraignment (except on a complaint regarding which the court will not exercise final jurisdiction, in which case a probable cause hearing will be scheduled as required by Rule 7), the court will schedule the case for both a pretrial conference and a pretrial hearing, to be held on separate dates. Following the pretrial conference, the parties will prepare a pretrial conference report, memorializing their agreements and disagreements. This report controls the scope of subsequent motions practice. Rule 11 also mandates a pretrial hearing on a subsequent date, at which a plea may be taken or pretrial matters may be raised and/or resolved. Rule 11 as revised reflects this three step process, setting out the functions of the pretrial conference, the report, and the pretrial hearing. Additionally, if discovery remains incomplete at the time of the pretrial hearing, a compliance hearing will be scheduled to insure that discovery is complete before the case proceeds.

Subdivision (a). The Pretrial Conference and Conference Report. Rule 11 originally required pretrial conferences in both Superior and District Court jury sessions, leaving the District Court primary session with the option of scheduling a conference or not. By a 2004 amendment, pretrial conferences are now mandatory in all cases, regardless of whether the case is docketed in a superior, juvenile, district, or municipal court. Under Rules 7 and 11, at arraignment the court will schedule the case for *both* a pretrial conference and a pretrial hearing. Regarding the pretrial conference, the rule allows but does not require the court to order that this conference take place before a judge or magistrate. The Boston Municipal Court practice of holding a conference before a magistrate has proven quite efficient, but because some district courts may not have adequate personnel and courtrooms for this purpose the subdivision leaves this issue to be determined by each court.

Subdivisions (a)(1)(A)—(C) outline suggested issues which may be discussed and resolved prior to the trial. The catalog is not to be considered exhaustive.

Subdivision (a)(1)(A), in conjunction with Mass. R. Crim. P. 13, seeks to reduce the number of "boiler plate" pretrial motions which are routinely filed. *See* Commonwealth v. Hall, 369 Mass. 715, 723 (1976). If the substance of a motion is agreed upon, that fact and the agreement are set out in the conference report [(a)(2)(A)], *infra*; only pretrial motions which are not agreed upon are permitted to be filed. Mass. R. Crim. P. 13(d).

While it is unlikely that a plea arrangement will immediately result from the conference, the defendant, following disclosure of the Commonwealth's case, may decide that a plea is the best alternative. Therefore, the subject is properly discussed at that time [(a)(1)(B)]. If an arrangement is in fact concluded, it should be stated in the conference report. *See* Mass. R. Crim. P. 12(b)(2), which requires counsel to notify the court of the existence of any agreement contingent upon the defendant's plea.

Among the matters to be discussed under subdivision (a)(1)(C)(i) is the setting of the trial date. It must be emphasized that one consequence of a failure to comply with this rule is that the case will be presumed to be ready for trial and a trial date will be set for the earliest available time, [a] [2] [B], *infra*. Agreements as to subdivision (C)(ii) will assist the court in the management of its docket, see Mass. R. Crim. P. 36(a)(2), and understandings as to the availability of necessary witnesses will reduce the need for continuances to secure their attendance, Mass. R. Crim. P. 10. If stipulations of fact are agreed upon after discussion under (C)(iv) they are to be recorded in the conference report, [a] [2] [A], *infra*.

The defendant may also request information concerning the Commonwealth's intended use of prior acts or convictions for proof of knowledge, intent, or modus operandi, and use of prior convictions to impeach the testimony of the defendant. This information, while not specifically mentioned in Rule 11, is a proper subject of discussion at the pretrial conference. It is contemplated that compliance with this subdivision will obviate the necessity for resorting to the more time-consuming procedures of Mass. R. Crim. P. 14 and 23, expedite the taking of testimony at the trial, and allow counsel to better prepare for trial.

Pursuant to Mass. R. Crim. P. 9(a)(3), either party may move for consolidation of pending charges. This matter, if resolved at conference, will avoid the time delay required for the court to conduct a hearing and act upon a motion for joinder. This is true also as to motions to transfer other pending charges for plea, sentence or trial. Mass. R. Crim. P. 37(b)(1)—(2).

It should be noted that a motion to take a deposition, not contemplated within subdivision (a)(1) of this rule, if considered at conference and agreed upon, need not be filed with the court, since the parties are permitted to depose witnesses by agreement pursuant to Mass. R. Crim. P. 35(i).

The parties may also wish to stipulate as to the application and effect of the excludable time provisions of Mass. R. Crim. P. 36(b), e.g., whether time should be excluded from the speedy trial limits due to the absence of an essential witness and, if so, how much. Mass. R. Crim. P. 36(b)(2)(B).

The 2004 revision eliminated a provision then numbered (a)(1)(C), which required the defendant to reveal "the nature of the defense" at the pretrial conference, and whether he or she intends to defend by alibi, insanity or privilege. Such discovery to the prosecution is now mandatory discovery under Rule 14, at a more realistic and constitutionally appropriate phase of the pretrial proceedings. The pretrial conference is generally held too early to expect the defendant to know and convey the defense, especially since full discovery may not yet have been provided by the prosecution. Indeed, because under the Fifth and Fourteenth Amendments to the United States Constitution the defense can only be compelled to disclose information it has decided to use at trial, Williams v. Florida, 399 U.S. 78 (1970), prosecutorial discovery should not be required before the defendant is in a position to make an informed decision.

Subdivision (a)(2)(A) outlines the contents of the pretrial conference report and establishes the requirement that it be signed by the defendant when it contains agreements which amount to waivers of constitutional right or stipulations to material facts. The defendant's signature should not be pro forma, but should be subscribed only after his counsel has explained the consequences of this act to him. To expedite this procedure, subdivisions (a) and (b) mandate that the defendant "shall be available for attendance" at both the pretrial conference and the pretrial hearing. This requirement assures also that the defendant's assent to other agreements may readily be obtained.

The pretrial conference report must set out all agreements of the parties. Such agreements have the force of a court order, and are enforceable by the same sanctions. Commonwealth v. Viriyahiranpaiboon, 412 Mass. 224, 228 (1992); Commonwealth v. Durning, *supra* at 495; Commonwealth v. Gallarelli, 399 Mass. 17, 20 (1987); Commonwealth v. Chapee, 397 Mass. 508, 517 (1986), *habeas denied sub nom.* Chappee v. Vose, 843 F.2d 25 (1st Cir. 1988); Commonwealth v. Delaney, 11 Mass. App. Ct. 398 (1981). Only pretrial motions whose subject matter could not be agreed on at the conference may be filed. The conference report is filed with the clerk, whose responsibility it is to monitor filing and advancement of cases for trial.

Subdivision (a)(2)(B) sets out the sanctions to be imposed upon a failure to file a report and to appear to explain that failure. If counsel refuse to cooperate in the conference procedure, the court may also invoke its authority under subdivision (a)(1) to require a conference be held at court under the supervision of a judge or clerk-magistrate.

Subdivision (b). The pretrial hearing. This subdivision originally concerned conference procedures in the District Court jury-waived sessions. By a 2004 amendment, Rule 11(a)'s pretrial conference requirements were made uniform for all sessions, and subdivision (b) is instead devoted to the pretrial hearing. New subdivision 11(b) allows a District Court judge to decline jurisdiction and schedule a probable cause hearing expeditiously (and in such case the judge may entertain discovery motions prior to the probable cause hearing, Commonwealth v. Silva, 10 Mass. App. Ct. 784, 791 (1980)). Otherwise a pretrial hearing is to be held in order to accomplish the pretrial matters enumerated in the subdivision. Subparagraph (b)(1) authorizes the court to receive a plea, admission, or other requested disposition. If there is no plea or disposition, subparagraph (b)(2)(i) requires the parties to file the pretrial conference report; (b)(2)(ii) requires the pretrial hearing judge to hear all pending discovery motions, and permits him or her to hear other pretrial motions as well; and (b)(2)(iii) requires the court to schedule the next court date. If the pretrial report or discovery is not complete, the court will schedule a compliance hearing unless waived by the aggrieved party (see subdivision (c)). If they are complete, the court will ask the defendant to elect or waive a jury trial, and then assign "the trial date or trial assignment date." Ideally, the rule would have simply required the assignment of a trial date, rather than offering the option of scheduling a "trial assignment date," which allows for yet another intermediate hearing date; but practical constraints require this option, as many courts are presently unable to guarantee a particular trial date as early as the pretrial hearing. Although the jury decision should be fully considered and resolved at this time, nothing in the rule prevents a defendant who elects a jury trial from waiving the right at a later date.

Subdivision (c). Compliance Hearing. This subdivision makes a compliance hearing mandatory if a party failed to complete a pretrial conference report or provide discovery, unless the aggrieved party waives such a hearing. Such a hearing was optional before this subdivision was promulgated in 2004, leading to routine inefficiencies this subdivision is designed to eliminate. In courts that did not have compliance hearings, the aggrieved party had confronted an unfair choice between the sometimes burdensome task of obtaining an expedited hearing simply to obtain overdue discovery, or waiting until the trial date to receive discovery (which itself presented the prospect of either a continuance or an immediate trial with unprepared counsel). Moreover, municipal and district courts without compliance hearings had to defer jury waivers until the trial date pursuant to G.L. c. 218 sec. 28, which prohibits a waiver decision until discovery has been delivered. It promoted delays and inconvenience to witnesses for the court to remain ignorant up to the trial date as to whether a jury session would be required.

Therefore, this subdivision requires a compliance hearing when required discovery has not been forthcoming, and limits the hearing to certain enumerated matters mostly derived from Dist./Mun. Cts. R. Crim. P. 5. The court must determine whether the pretrial report and discovery are complete; must hear and decide pending discovery motions; and may order sanctions for non-compliance. If discovery is completed, it may receive a plea or admission; obtain the defendant's decision on whether to elect or waive a jury trial; and schedule the trial date or trial assignment date.

Rule 12. Pleas and Withdrawals of Pleas

[Text of rule applicable to cases initiated (by indictment or complaint) on or after September 7, 2004.]

(a) Entry of Pleas.

(1) *Pleas Which May Be Entered and by Whom.* A defendant may plead not guilty, or guilty, or with the consent of the judge, nolo contendere, to any crime with which the defendant has been charged and over which the court has jurisdiction. A plea of guilty or nolo contendere shall be received only from the defendant personally except pursuant to the provisions of Rule 18. Pleas shall be received in open court and the proceedings shall be recorded. If a defendant refuses to plead or if the judge refuses to accept a plea of guilty or nolo contendere, a plea of not guilty shall be entered.

(2) *Admission to Sufficient Facts.* In a District Court, a defendant may, after a plea of not guilty, admit to sufficient facts to warrant a finding of guilty.

(3) *Acceptance of Plea of Guilty, a Plea of Nolo Contendere, or an Admission to Sufficient Facts.* A judge may refuse to accept a plea of guilty or a plea of nolo contendere or an admission to sufficient facts. The judge shall not accept such a plea or admission without first determining that it is made voluntarily with an understanding of the nature of the charge and the consequences of the plea or admission.

(b) Plea Conditioned Upon an Agreement.

(1) *Formation of Agreement; Substance.* The defendant and defense counsel or the defendant when acting pro se may engage in discussions with the prosecutor as to any recommendation to be made to a judge or any other action to be taken by the prosecutor upon the tender of a plea of guilty or nolo contendere to a charged offense or to a lesser included offense. The agreement of the prosecutor may include:

(A) Charge Concessions.

(B) Recommendation of a particular sentence or type of punishment with the specific understanding that the recommendation shall not be binding upon the court.

(C) Recommendation of a particular sentence or type of punishment which may also include the specific understanding that the defendant shall reserve the right to request a lesser sentence or different type of punishment.

(D) A general recommendation of incarceration without regard to a specific term or institution.

(E) Recommendation of a particular disposition other than incarceration.

(F) Agreement not to oppose the request of the defendant for a particular sentence or other disposition.

(G) Agreement to make no recommendation or to take no action.

(H) Any other type of agreement involving recommendations or actions.

(2) *Notice of Agreement.* If defense counsel or the prosecutor has knowledge of any agreement that was made contingent upon the defendant's plea, he or she shall inform the judge thereof prior to the tender of the plea.

(c) Guilty Plea Procedure. After being informed that the defendant intends to plead guilty or nolo contendere:

(1) *Inquiry.* The judge shall inquire of the defendant or defense counsel as to the existence of and shall be informed of the substance of any agreements that are made which are contingent upon the plea.

(2) *Recommendation as to Sentence or Disposition.*

(A) Contingent Pleas. If there were sentence recommendations contingent upon the tender of the plea, the judge shall inform the defendant that the court will not impose a sentence that exceeds the terms of the recommendation without first giving the defendant the right to withdraw the plea.

(B) Disposition Requested by Defendant. In a District Court, if the plea is not conditioned on a sentence recommendation by the prosecutor, the defendant may request that the judge dispose of the case on any terms within the court's jurisdiction. The judge shall inform the defendant that the court will not impose a disposition that exceeds the terms of the defendant's request without first giving the defendant the right to withdraw the plea.

(3) *Notice of Consequences of Plea.* The judge shall inform the defendant on the record, in open court:

(A) that by a plea of guilty or nolo contendere, or an admission to sufficient facts, the defendant waives the right to trial with or without a jury, the right to confrontation of witnesses, the right to be presumed innocent until proved guilty beyond a reasonable doubt, and the privilege against self-incrimination;

(B) where appropriate, of the maximum possible sentence on the charge, and where appropriate, the possibility of community parole supervision for life; of any different or additional punishment based upon subsequent offense or sexually dangerous persons provisions of the General Laws, if applicable; where applicable, that the defendant may be required to register as a sex offender; and of the mandatory minimum sentence, if any, on the charge;

(C) that if the defendant is not a citizen of the United States, the guilty plea, plea of nolo contendere or admission may have the consequence of deportation, exclusion of admission, or denial of naturalization.

(4) *Tender of Plea.* The defendant's plea or admission shall then be tendered to the court.

(5) *Hearing on Plea; Acceptance.* The judge shall conduct a hearing to determine the voluntariness of the plea or admission and the factual basis of the charge.

(A) Factual Basis for Charge. A judge shall not accept a plea of guilty unless the judge is satisfied that there is a factual basis for the charge. The failure of the defendant to acknowledge all of the elements of the factual basis shall not preclude a judge from accepting a guilty plea. Upon a showing of cause the tender of the guilty plea and the acknowledgement of the factual basis of the charge may be made on the record at the bench.

(B) Acceptance. At the conclusion of the hearing the judge shall state the court's acceptance or rejection of the plea or admission.

(C) Sentencing. After acceptance of a plea of guilty or nolo contendere or an admission, the judge may proceed with sentencing.

(6) *Refusal to Accept an Agreed Sentence Recommendation.* If the judge determines that the court will impose a sentence that will exceed an agreed recommendation for a particular sentence or type of punishment under subdivision (b)(1)(C) of this rule, an agreed recommendation for a particular disposition other than incarceration under subdivision (b)(1)(E), or a request for disposition in a District Court by the defendant under subdivision (c) (2)(B), after having informed the defendant as provided in subdivision (c)(2) that the court would not do so, the judge shall, on the record, advise the defendant personally in open court or on a showing of cause, in camera, that the judge intends to exceed the terms of the plea recommendation or request for disposition and shall afford the defendant the opportunity to then withdraw the plea or admission. The judge may indicate to the parties what sentence the judge would impose.

(d) Deleted.

(e) Availability of Criminal Record and Presentence Report. The criminal record of the defendant shall be made available. Upon the written motion of either party made at the tender of a plea of guilty or nolo contendere, the presentence report as described in subdivision (d)(2) of Rule 28 shall be made available to the prosecutor and counsel for the defendant for inspection. In extraordinary cases, the judge may except from disclosure parts of the report which are not relevant to a proper sentence, diagnostic opinion which might seriously disrupt a program of rehabilitation, sources of information obtained upon a promise of confidentiality, or any other information which, if disclosed, might result in harm, physical or otherwise, to the defendant or other persons. If the report is not made fully available, the portions thereof which are not disclosed shall not be relied upon in determining sentence. No party may make any copy of the presentence report.

(f) Inadmissibility of Pleas, Offers of Pleas, and Related Statements. Except as otherwise provided in this subdivision, evidence of a plea of guilty, or a plea of nolo contendere, or an admission, or of an offer to plead guilty or nolo contendere or an admission to the crime charged or any other crime, later withdrawn, or statements made in connection with, and relevant to, any of the foregoing pleas or offers, is not admissible in any civil or criminal proceedings against the person who made the plea or offer. However, evidence of a statement made in connection with, and relevant to, a plea of guilty, later withdrawn, or a plea of nolo contendere, or an admission or an offer to plead guilty or nolo contendere or an admission to the crime charged or any other crime, is admissible in a criminal proceeding for perjury if the statement was made by the defendant under oath, on the record, and in the presence of counsel, if any.

Amended June 12, 1986, effective Jan. 1, 1987; March 8, 2004, effective September 7, 2004.

Reporter's Notes—Revised, 2004

Although analogous to Fed. R. Crim. P. 11, in its original form in 1979 this rule was drawn from a number of sources. *See, e.g.,* A.B.A. Standards Relating to Pleas of Guilty (Approved Draft, 1968); A.L.I. Model Code of Pre–Arraignment Procedure §§ 350.1—.9 (POD 1975); National Advisory Commission on Criminal Justice Standards & Goals, Courts, Standards 3.1 *et seq.* (1973); President's Commission on Law Enforcement & Administration of Justice, Task Force Report: The Courts 4—13 (1967). The rule was amended in 1987 to remove the option, contained in original subdivision (c)(2)(B), which allowed a judge to sentence a defendant more harshly than the terms of a prosecutor's sentence recommendation without giving the defendant an opportunity to withdraw the plea. In 2004, the rule was further amended, retaining its basic structure but bringing the details of the process up to date, in light of the abolition of trial de novo and other developments in the law.

As the United States Supreme Court has observed:

> Whatever may be the situation in an ideal world, the fact is that the guilty plea and the often concomitant plea bargain are important components of this country's criminal justice system. Properly administered, they can benefit all concerned.

Blackledge v. Allison, 431 U.S. 63, 71 (1977). *Accord*, Bordenkircher v. Hayes, 434 U.S. 357, 361—62 (1978). Rule 12 is intended to guarantee the proper administration of the guilty plea and plea bargaining process.

The proffer by a defendant of a guilty plea is a significant step in the criminal process. It represents a decision by the defendant not to put the Commonwealth to the test of proving his or her guilt beyond a reasonable doubt. Plea bargaining, of course, flows from the "mutuality of advantage" to defendants and prosecutors, each with their own reasons for wanting to avoid trial, Bordenkircher v. Hayes, 434 U.S. 357, 363 (1978), but the Commonwealth and the public have an interest in promoting fairness by insuring that each plea is an accurate reflection of guilt and a fair termination of criminal proceedings against a defendant. Rule 12 is intended to promote attainment of those goals.

Subdivision (a).

(a)(1). This subdivision is adopted from A.B.A. Standards Relating to Pleas of Guilty § 1.1 (Approved Draft, 1968), which substantially accords with Fed. R. Crim. P. 11(a)—(b).

Under criminal practice prior to the adoption of rule 12, former G.L. c 227, § 47A (St 1978, c 478, § 298) provided that the defendant could plead not guilty, guilty, or nolo contendere. Rule 12 preserves these options.

The Rule does not establish the precise words a defendant must use in order to plead guilty. While the absence of the actual phrase "I plead guilty" or the word "guilty" is not sufficient by itself to invalidate a purported guilty plea, *see* Commonwealth v. Cavanaugh, 12 Mass. App. Ct. 543 (1981), in order to avoid confusion, a judge should clarify the intent of any defendant who does not use clear language to identify a desire to enter a guilty plea. Stipulations by the defendant to the truth of facts that are conclusive of guilt are the functional equivalent of a guilty plea and fall within the confines of Rule 12. *See* Commonwealth v. Hill, 20 Mass. App. Ct. 130 (1985). On the other hand, if all the defendant stipulates to is that the Commonwealth's witnesses would testify in the manner described by the prosecutor, then the defendant's act would not be the complete waiver that a guilty plea entails, *see* Commonwealth v. Garcia, 23 Mass App 259, 265 (1986).

The requirements of this subdivision are to insure that the fact that the plea was the informed and voluntary act of the defendant appears upon a contemporaneous record of the proceeding, thus reducing the likelihood of a post-conviction attack on the validity of a plea of guilty or nolo contendere. *See, e.g.*, Commonwealth v Foster, 368 Mass 100 (1975).

Therefore, except where a corporation is the defendant, or where the defendant is permitted by the General Laws to pay a fine by mail or by appearing before a clerk personally or by authorized agent, the defendant personally must plead if the plea is to be guilty or nolo contendere. The defendant must also personally plead not guilty except where his or her appearance is excused pursuant to Mass. R. Crim. P. 7(a)(2) and the court enters the plea on the defendant's behalf. Mass. R. Crim. P. 7(d)(2).

The requirement that the plea be accepted in open court is based upon G.L. c. 263 § 6, and furthers the goal that it be free from the suspicion of coercion and that it is a knowing and intelligent waiver of the defendant's right to a trial. Thus, all pleas should be entered under the scrutiny of the judge in formal proceedings and be recorded, whether by stenographic or electronic means.

(a)(2). An admission to sufficient facts to warrant a finding of guilty is a procedural device that had its genesis in the trial de novo system. Rather than entering a guilty plea, which would have had the consequence of limiting the de novo trial to the issue of the sentence, a defendant in the first tier of the de novo system could admit to sufficient facts and preserve his option of a full trial de novo. Admissions to sufficient facts have proved useful for another reason however. They offer a way to allow the defendant's case to be continued without a guilty finding, something that a traditional guilty plea is ill suited to accomplish. As the Supreme Judicial Court has recognized, a continuance without a finding (cwof) is a procedure that often serves the best interests of both the Commonwealth and the defendant. *See* Commonwealth v. Duquette, 386 Mass. 834, 840 (1982). Admissions to sufficient facts and cwofs were common at both levels of the trial de novo system in the District Courts. After the abolition of trial de novo, they continue to be prevalent in the District Court and Juvenile systems. *See* G.L. c 278 § 18 (allowing a District Court defendant to request that a case be continued without a finding and requiring that an admission to sufficient facts be treated as the equivalent of a guilty plea for purposes of the "defense capped plea" procedure discussed *infra* in subsection (c)(2)(B)).

If a defendant desires to admit to sufficient facts, the judge should interrogate the defendant personally to insure that the defendant understands the nature and consequences of such an admission. In the years since Rule 12 was originally promulgated, the Supreme Judicial Court has held that an offer to admit to sufficient facts triggers essentially the same safeguards required when a defendant offers to plead guilty. *See* Commonwealth v. Lewis, 399 Mass. 761, 763 (1987); Commonwealth v. Duquette, 386 Mass. 834, 838 (1982).

(a)(3). Requiring the permission of the court to enter a guilty plea or plea of nolo contendere accords with the practice that prevailed prior to the adoption of Rule 12. By court rule, no defendant was permitted to plead guilty or nolo contendere to a complaint for which a sentence of imprisonment may be imposed unless the judge was fully satisfied that certain conditions had been met. *See* District Court Initial Rules of Criminal Procedure 4 (1971); Rules of the Mun. Ct. for the City of Boston Sitting for Criminal Business 4 (1971).

A defendant does not have a constitutional right to have a guilty plea accepted by the court, *see* North Carolina v. Alford, 400 U.S. 25, 38 n. 11 (1970); Commonwealth v. Dilone, 385 Mass. 281 (1982); Commonwealth v. Kelliher, 28 Mass. App. Ct. 915 (1989). An admission to sufficient facts is very much like an *Alford* plea or a plea of nolo contendere, in that the defendant does not explicitly admit guilt. The same considerations that may inform a judge's decision to refuse to accept that latter two pleas apply equally in the case of the former.

A judge may refuse to accept a guilty plea, admission to sufficient facts, or plea of nolo contendere for a variety of reasons. So long as the judge's decision is not arbitrary or based on an impermissible factor, the sound exercise of discretion supports a decision to refuse to accept a plea. *See* Rossman, Guilty Pleas, 2 Criminal Law Advocacy, ¶ 8.04(3)(a). Among the common reasons to refuse to accept plea are: the plea is involuntary; the defendant does not understand the nature of the charge [c] [5] [A], *infra* or the consequences of the plea [c] [3], *infra*; there is no factual basis for the plea [c] [5] [a], *infra*; or there is a factual dispute that should be litigated at trial.

Subdivision (b). Section (e)(1)—(5) of Federal Rule of Criminal Procedure 11 is the prototype for this subdivision.

(b)(1). This subdivision outlines the scope of agreements as to concessions or other actions which the defendant and the prosecution may arrive at prior to plea proceedings before a judge. It must be emphasized that these negotiations are to be between defense counsel, or the defendant in an appropriate case, and the prosecution. Judges should not "participate as active negotiators in plea bargaining discussions," Commonwealth v. Gordon, 410 Mass. 498, 501 n. 3 (1991).

When a judge takes part in plea negotiations, it raises several troubling possibilities:

> [it] 1) can create the impression in the mind of the defendant that he would not receive a fair trial were he to go to the trial before this judge; (2) . . . makes it difficult for the judge objectively to determine the voluntariness of the plea when it is offered; (3) . . . is inconsistent with the theory behind the use of the presentence investigation report; and (4) the risk of not going along with the disposition apparently desired by the judge may seem so great to the defendant that he will be induced to plead guilty even if innocent.

Commonwealth v. Damiano, 14 Mass. App. Ct. 615, 618 n.7 (1982) (quoting § 3.3(a) of the A.B.A. Standards *supra*). For the type of participation that a judge should avoid, *see* Commonwealth v. Carter 50 Mass App 902 (2000) (judge's statement at side bar that if defendant proceeded with trial and was found guilty, he would impose sentence of 18–20 years, but that if defendant pleaded guilty, sentence would be six years to six years and one day was coercive, making defendant's guilty plea involuntary).

The list of actions set out in this subsection that a prosecutor may include in a plea agreement is not exhaustive and allows for considerable flexibility. For example, the parties may agree to a joint sentence recommendation or to present disparate positions, and may propose that the agreement either does not bind the judge or to one that allows the defendant to withdraw the plea if the judge does not agree. Some of the concessions a prosecutor may make in plea negotiations relate to action over which the judge has control, such as the imposition of a particular sentence. Other concessions, as in an agreement not to bring additional charges, are totally within the purview of the prosecutor. Since the doctrine of separation of powers gives the prosecutor the authority to decide what criminal charge the Commonwealth should bring against a defendant, a judge may not accept a guilty plea to a lesser included offense over the prosecutor's objection. *See* Commonwealth v. Gordon, 410 Mass. 498, 503 (1991).

(b)(2). Early and full disclosure of a plea arrangement reduces the risk of an unfair agreement—unfair to the public because of an unwarranted concession by an overburdened prosecutor anxious to avoid trial, or unfair to the defendant because the concession is either illusory, or so irresistible in light of the inevitable risks of trial as to induce an innocent defendant to plead guilty. *E.g.*, Jones v. United States, 423 F.2d 252, 255 (9th Cir 1970). Disclosure of the terms of a plea agreement also will allow the court to monitor the prosecutor's performance. In addition, placing the agreement on the record will avoid disputes that may arise in an attack on the validity of the guilty plea. For these reasons and to expedite the proceedings, this subdivision requires that the court be informed at the outset of the existence of any agreement. If upon inquiry under subdivision (c)(1), *infra*, the defendant denies any such agreement, it is incumbent upon the prosecutor to notify the court if an agreement in fact has been made. For an example of the difficulties that can arise when the parties do not disclose the terms of a plea agreement, *see* Commonwealth v. Johnson, 11 Mass. App. Ct. 835 (1981).

A judge does not improperly participate in plea negotiations simply by having the parties disclose the substance of a plea arrangement pursuant to this subdivision.

Subdivision (c).

Subdivision (c)(1) is a product of Santobello v. New York, 404 U.S. 257 (1971), where it was held that:

> when a plea rests in any significant degree on a promise or agreement of the prosecutor, so that it can be said to be part of the inducement or consideration, such promise must be fulfilled.

Id. at 262. The Court stated further that the adjudicative element inherent in accepting a plea of guilty must be attended by safeguards to insure the defendant what is reasonably due in the circumstances and if a plea is induced by promises, their essence must in some way be known. 404 U.S. 261, 262.

If upon inquiry the defendant replies that no promises have been made, the judge should instruct the defendant that any promises relating to the imposition of sentence are in no way binding on the court. *See* Subdivisions (b)(1)—(2), *supra*. This is because defendants are often loathe to disclose such promises, although it is believed that the increased acceptability of the plea arrangement procedure of this rule will obviate such difficulties.

The effect of such an instruction will depend on the facts of each case, but in no case can it cure the prejudice resulting from a broken promise.

The words of the Supreme Court as to the binding character of defense-prosecution agreements deserve repetition:

> when a plea rests in any significant degree on a promise or agreement of the prosecutor, so that it can be said to be a part of the inducement or consideration, such promise must be fulfilled.

Santobello v. New York, 404 U.S. 257, 262 (1971). This accords with established doctrine in the Commonwealth long before the adoption of Rule 12. The Supreme Judicial Court, in 1899, stated that:

> When . . . promises are made by the public prosecutor or with his authority, the court will see that due regard is paid

to them, and that the public faith which has been pledged by him is duly kept.

Commonwealth v. St. John, 173 Mass. 566, 569 (1899). *See also*, Commonwealth v. Benton, 356 Mass. 477 (1969); Commonwealth v. Harris, 364 Mass. 236, 238 (1973); Commonwealth v. Santiago, 394 Mass. 25 (1985); Commonwealth v. Parzyck, 41 Mass. App. Ct. 195 (1996).

Whether a plea bargain actually exists that obligates the prosecutor to perform a promise upon which the plea is contingent depends on an objective evaluation of the underlying circumstances that led to the plea. *See* Blaikie v. District Attorney for Suffolk County, 375 Mass. 613, 616 n. 2 (1978) (the prosecutor's subjective understanding of the bargain is irrelevant); Commonwealth v. Santiago, 394 Mass. 25, 28 (1985) ("The touchstone for determining whether a defendant has been improperly denied the advantages he expected from a plea bargain is whether that defendant has reasonable grounds for reliance on his interpretation of the prosecutor's promise."); Rossman, Guilty Pleas, 2 Criminal Law Advocacy, ¶7.05(1) (subjective impressions alone never entitle the defendant to the benefit of an illusory agreement).

If the court determines that a plea agreement existed, and that the defendant has fulfilled his or her part of the bargain, the defendant is entitled to the benefit of the prosecutor's performance of the countervailing promise. If the Commonwealth seeks to avoid performance on the ground that the defendant has not lived up to the terms of the agreement, then the prosecutor bears the burden of proof on this issue. *See* Doe v. District Attorney for Plymouth Dist., 29 Mass. App. Ct. 671, 677 n.6 (1991). In the usual course of events, all the defendant need do to fulfill his or her obligation under a plea agreement is to offer a guilty plea. However, the right to enforce a plea agreement may arise beforehand, if the defendant has relied to his or her detriment on a prosecutor's promise. *See id.* at 674 ("concerns about fairness which underlie the requirement that the government abide by its agreements are solidly engaged once an accused person has relied to his detriment upon a plea agreement, even if that occurs before entry of a guilty plea.") *Compare* Blaikie v. District Attorney for Suffolk County, 375 Mass. 613, 618 (1978) (Specific performance is in no sense mandated where no guilty plea has been entered, and the defendant's position has not been adversely affected).

The purposes of subdivision (c)(1) are fourfold. First, airing plea agreements in open court enhances public confidence in the administration of justice. *E.g.*, Jones v. United States, 423 F.2d 252, 255 (9th Cir 1970). Secondly, disclosure of prosecutorial promises is the best way to test the voluntariness of the plea. By testing the strength of the inducement, the court obtains the best available evidence of its effect upon the defendant. Thirdly, this helps to implement the "factual basis" requirement of subdivision (c)(5)(A), for promises that offer unusual leniency to a defendant are suspect. Finally, this requirement will help to uncover promises that are by their nature improper and thus help to eliminate whatever incentive the prosecution might have to offer improper inducements.

Pursuant to this subdivision and subdivision (b)(2), *supra*, the prosecutor and defense counsel have the duty to come forward and disclose the existence and terms of a plea arrangement if the defendant balks at his opportunity to do so (even if the court does not specifically question the prosecutor or defense counsel on this issue). *See* Commonwealth v. Santon, 2 Mass. App. Ct. 614 (1974). This is important practically because often the defendant will not fully disclose the terms of the arrangement. It is important legally because the prosecutor and defense counsel should inform the court whenever they are aware that testimony offered in court is not in full accord with the truth as they know it. *See* Supreme Judicial Court Rule 3:07, MA Rules of Pro. Conduct, R. 3.3 *(c)(2)*. Under subdivision (c)(2)(A) the judge may inform the defendant that the court is disposed to accept the prosecutor's sentence recommendation, pending the outcome of the hearing required by subdivision (c)(5), and that the judge will not exceed that recommendation without giving the defendant an opportunity to withdraw the plea. As originally promulgated, subdivision (c)(2)(b) allowed the judge an alternative course of action, indicating that the court did not intend to entertain or consider any recommendation, in which event the judge's sentencing discretion would be unrestricted. In 1987, this provision was eliminated from the Rule. The effect of the amendment was to provide defendants pleading guilty pursuant to a sentencing bargain more certainty about their fate.

Prior to the 1987 amendment, a judge could force a defendant who chose to plead guilty on the strength of a plea agreement specifying that he or she should receive a particular sentence to "plead in the dark." If the judge took advantage of option (B) of the original subsection, he or she could categorically refuse to tell a defendant who entered a negotiated plea whether the court would abide by the recommendation or not. Such a judge forced the defendant to bear the risk of waiving the right to trial and receiving nothing in return. After 1987, defendants entering plea agreements based on a joint sentence recommendation knew where they stood prior to irrevocably waiving their right to a trial.

In 2004, this subsection was amended to add new subdivision (c)(2)(B), to reflect the "defense capped plea" procedure provided for by statute in the District and Juvenile Courts. Part of the legislation that abolished the trial de novo system, G.L. c. 278 § 18, gave defendants in District Court who did not reach an agreement with the prosecutor the right to offer a guilty plea or admission to sufficient facts contingent upon the judge's accepting any disposition of the case within the court's jurisdiction. The new subdivision (c)(2)(B) reflects this practice. The defense capped plea procedure applies in all District, Municipal and Juvenile courts. *See* G.L. ch. 119, § 55B. Neither Rule 12 nor G.L. c. 278 § 18 establish how many times a defendant may tender a defense capped plea. Individual judges are free to formulate their own policy on this issue as the needs of their particular courts dictate. A District or Juvenile Court judge has the power to accept a proposed disposition under this procedure even if it entails continuing the case without a finding over the objection of the prosecutor. Although ordinarily the separation of powers doctrine prevents a judge from foreclosing the prosecution's effort to conclude a case with either a conviction or acquittal on the original charge, the legislature's specific sanction of the cwof option in the defense capped plea procedure legitimates it. *Compare* Commonwealth v. Pyles, 423 Mass. 717 (1996) (grant of authority by G.L. c. 278 § 18 specifically gives District Court judges authority to continue a case without a finding over the objection of the prosecutor) *with* Commonwealth v. Cheney, 440 Mass. 568 (2003) (Superior Court judge lacks power to dismiss case in the interest of justice over the objection of the prosecutor as this procedure is only available under G.L. c. 278 § 18 which applies only to District and Juvenile Courts); Commonwealth v. Tim T., 437 Mass 592 (2002) (without statutory authority akin to G.L. c. 278 § 18,

Juvenile Court judge lacks power to place defendant on pretrial probation over the objection of the prosecutor). However, if a judge does accept the defendant's proposal to continue a case without a finding over the prosecutor's objection, the record should reflect the reasons for the conclusion that this action is in the best interests of justice. *See Pyles, supra*, at 723.

If the defendant has offered a plea or admission under either subdivision (c)(2)(A) or (c)(2)(B), the judge may not impose a sentence harsher than the one upon which the defendant's action is predicated. Judges should pay careful attention to dispositions involving probationary terms or a suspended sentence to ensure that they conform to the legitimate sentence expectation of the defendant. *See e.g.*, Commonwealth v. Glines, 40 Mass. App. Ct. 95 (1996) (where District Court judge imposed a sentence of probation with a suspended term of five years, it was more severe than the defendant's request for probation with 2½ years suspended); Commonwealth v. Barber, 37 Mass. App. Ct. 599 (1994) (where pursuant to a plea agreement, prosecutor recommended the defendant receive a 12–15 year sentence concurrent with other sentences the defendant received, and the judge imposed a suspended sentence of 12–15 years, consecutive to the other sentences the defendant received, and placed the defendant on probation for two years, the judge exceeded the terms of the prosecutor's recommendation).

(c)(3). This subdivision was originally patterned after Fed. R. Crim. P. 11(c)—(d). In addition, it drew upon District Court Initial R. Crim. P. 4 (1971); Sections 1.4 and 1.5 of the ABA Standards Relating to Pleas of Guilty (Approved Draft, 1968); A.B.A. Standards Relating to the Function of the Trial Judge § 4.2 (Approved Draft, 1972); Rules of Criminal Procedure (U.L.A.) rule 444(b) (1974); A.L.I. Model Code of Pre–Arraignment Procedure § 350.4 (POD 1975); and the National Advisory Commission on Criminal Justice Standards &. Goals, Courts, standard 3.7 (1973).

In 2004, this subdivision was amended to eliminate a provision allowing defense counsel to conduct the colloquy with the defendant. The Supreme Judicial Court has disapproved of defense counsel conducting guilty plea colloquies, as far back as Commonwealth v. Morrow, 363 Mass. 601 (1973) ("the spontaneity and flexibility of the dialogue, which supports a conclusion of voluntariness, can best be achieved where the judge asks the questions. This also avoids even the appearance that the colloquy is but a prearranged script. Therefore, we think it would be better practice for the judge to ask the questions.") By statute, defense counsel cannot conduct the part of the colloquy dealing with warnings of immigration consequences, *see* Commonwealth v. Villalobos, 437 Mass. 797 (2002).

The responsibility for conducting a meaningful colloquy with the defendant properly rests on the judge's shoulders. This requires "a continuing effort on the part of trial judges, with the help of counsel, so to direct their questions *as to make them a real probe of the defendant's mind* ... It is not to become a 'litany' but is to attempt a live evaluation of whether the plea has been sufficiently meditated by the defendant with guidance of counsel, and whether it is not being extracted from the defendant under undue pressure." Commonwealth v. Fernandes, 390 Mass. 714, 716 (1984) *quoting* Commonwealth v. Foster, 368 Mass. 100, 107 (1975) (emphasis added). The colloquy should include an inquiry into any mental illness from which the defendant may be suffering, and whether the defendant is under the influence of alcohol or drugs. *See* Commonwealth v. Correa, 43 Mass. App. Ct. 714, 717–718 (1997).

The Supreme Judicial Court has suggested the utility of using a checklist to ensure that a plea colloquy is both comprehensive in scope and meaningful in substance. *See* Commonwealth v Colon (2003) 439 Mass 519, 530 *quoting* Commonwealth v. Nolan, 19 Mass. App. Ct. 491, 501–502, (1985):

> [Post conviction attacks on the validity of a plea can] be minimized if not wholly avoided, and justice better and more humanely administered in the first instance, if judges permitted themselves to be assisted by the carefully drafted and fully inclusive model questionnaires that have long been available ... We do not suggest that any model should be followed mechanically; indeed such a practice would be unwise because it could interfere with a probing exchange. Nevertheless a model can serve as a guide and checklist. We would suggest, as well, that a duty is cast on the lawyers on both sides to be alert and helpful if it appears that the judge through inadvertence may not be carrying out the full requirements of the rule. (Footnote omitted)

The information about the consequences of a conviction should be part of the oral dialogue between the judge and the defendant. It is not sufficient for a judge to rely on the defendant's acknowledgment of this information on a written form. *See* Commonwealth v. Rodriguez, 52 Mass. App. Ct. 572 (2001); Commonwealth v. Hilaire, 51 Mass. App. Ct. 818, 823 (2001) ("During a colloquy, the judge has the opportunity to observe and interact with the defendant and can communicate the warnings to the ... defendant with greater assurance than can be supplied by the preprinted ... form.")

While the judge is the one who conducts the colloquy, all the parties share the responsibility to make certain that defendants are informed of the consequences of a plea or admission. As the United States Supreme Court said, with respect to the obligation of defense attorneys in federal criminal cases:

> Apart from the small class of rights that require specific advice from the court under Rule 11(c), it is the responsibility of defense counsel to inform a defendant of the advantages and disadvantages of a plea agreement and the attendant statutory and constitutional rights that a guilty plea would forgo.

Libretti v. United States, 516 U.S. 29, 50–51 (1995). The prosecutor also has a role to play in ensuring that the court is aware of any information that might bear on the legitimacy of the plea and that the colloquy covers all of the necessary topics. *See* State v. Rodriguez, 112 Ariz. 193, 540 P.2d 665 (1975).

Subdivision (c)(3)(A) enumerates the plea's immediate consequences of which a defendant must be specifically informed. It imposes a responsibility on the judge not only in cases where the defendant has tendered a traditional guilty plea or a nolo contendere plea, but also where a defendant has offered to admit to sufficient facts to warrant a finding of guilty. The Rule was amended in 2004 to cover this last category in recognition of the fact that in the years since Rule 12 was originally promulgated, the Supreme Judicial Court held that an offer to admit to sufficient facts triggers the essentially the same safeguards required when a defendant offers to plead guilty. *See* Commonwealth v. Duquette, 386 Mass. 834, 838 (1982) (an admission to sufficient facts is the functional equivalent of a guilty plea and the record must reflect the defendant waived the right to trial knowingly and voluntarily); Commonwealth v. Lewis, 399 Mass. 761, 763 (1987).

The United States Supreme Court held in Boykin v. Alabama, 395 U.S. 238, 243 (1969) not only that a defendant must understand that he or she waives the privilege against self incrimination, the right to trial by jury, and the right to confront one's accusers by entering a guilty, but also that a court could not presume a waiver of these rights from a silent record. Prior to the adoption of Rule 12 in 1979, the Supreme Judicial Court held in Commonwealth v. Morrow, 363 Mass 601, 604—05 (1973), that "it would be better practice to include specific inquiry as to the defendant's understanding waiver of the three constitutional rights."

In 2004, this subdivision was amended to require an additional warning of rights be given to the defendant, concerning the right to be presumed innocent until proved guilty beyond a reasonable doubt. Although not constitutionally required, it is sound practice to include it. The Supreme Judicial Court has recommended its use in cases where the defendant is willing to plead guilty but does not acknowledge all of the elements of the factual basis. *See* Commonwealth v. Earl, 393 Mass. 738, 742 (1985) ("when a judge concludes that he is satisfied that there is a factual basis for a charge to which a defendant is willing to plead guilty, but the defendant does not acknowledge all the elements of the factual basis, it would be better practice for the plea judge to advise the defendant that his guilty plea waives his right to be presumed innocent until proved guilty beyond a reasonable doubt.")

It has been recommended that the proper formulation for advising a defendant as to his waiver of a jury trial is that "by pleading guilty he [gives] up his right to a 'trial with or without a jury,'" Commonwealth v. Hamilton, 3 Mass. App. Ct. 554, 557 n. 4 (1975). This instruction will serve to emphasize that, upon acceptance of a guilty plea, no trial will be held and all that remains is the imposition of sentence. However, the judge does not have to include information about the difference between a jury trial and a bench trial. *See* Commonwealth v. Gonsalves 57 Mass App 925 (2003). Nor does the colloquy have to include information about the loss of the opportunity to appeal issues, such as the court's action in denying a suppression motion. *See* Commonwealth v. Quinones, 414 Mass. 423, 435 (1993); Commonwealth v. Hamilton, 3 Mass App Ct 554, 558 n. 6 (1975) (if such information is given, it will "require careful formulation to avoid creating confusion as to the right to appeal to the Appellate Division of the Superior Court and the right to post-conviction remedies under special circumstances.")

Pursuant to subdivision (c)(3)(B), the defendant is to be informed of the sentencing consequences of a conviction based upon the tender of a plea or admission. The judge should inform the defendant of the maximum sentence of each offense to which the defendant is offering a plea or admission. In some circumstances, the maximum sentence will depend on whether the defendant has previously been convicted. The judge must take this possibility into account. General Laws c. 279, § 25, which mandates the maximum sentence for a felony defendant who has been previously convicted of two felonies and sentenced to more than three years on each, is an example of that type of provision contemplated by the "second offense" language of (c)(3)(B).

If probation is not a sentencing option, the judge must inform the defendant of any applicable mandatory minimum sentence as well. If the judge imposes a sentence of straight probation (one without a concomitant suspended term), the judge must inform the defendant of the maximum term, and any mandatory minimum term, that could be imposed if probation is revoked. *See* Commonwealth v. Rodriguez, 52 Mass. App. Ct. 572 (2001). In 2004, this subsection was amended to eliminate the requirement that the judge inform the defendant of the maximum sentence possible if the defendant received consecutive sentences. *See* United States v. Kikuyama, 109 F.3d 536 (9th Cir. 1997) (where it is not mandatory to impose consecutive sentences, defendant need not be informed of that possibility in order to enter a knowing and intelligent guilty plea); United States v. Hamilton, 568 F.2d 1302, (9th Cir.) *cert. denied* 436 U.S. 934 (1978) (the possibility of consecutive sentences was implicit in the separate explanation of the possible sentence on each charge).

Conviction of certain sex crimes carries with it three consequences that also must be included in the plea colloquy in a relevant case. First, if the defendant is subject to commitment as a sexually dangerous person, *see* G.L. c. 123A, the judge must include notice of that possibility prior to accepting the plea or admission. This provision has been part of Rule 12 since its adoption, changing the practice that prevailed prior to 1979. *See* Commonwealth v Morrow, 363 Mass 601, 606 (1973) (being subject to the "sexually dangerous person" provision "is but one of many contingent consequences of being confined" after conviction, and therefore need not be explained to a defendant). Since a 2004 amendment to G.L. c. 123A § 12 makes a defendant subject to commitment as a sexually dangerous person despite the nature of the offense to which the defendant is pleading guilty, so long as the defendant has been convicted any time in the past of a designated sex offense, a warning of the possibility of commitment under c. 123A should be included as a matter of routine unless it is clear from the defendant's prior record that it is not relevant.

Second, if the defendant is tendering a plea or admission to an offense which might subject him or her to the possibility of community parole supervision for life, a 2004 amendment to this subsection requires the judge to notify the defendant of this possibility. Because the prospect of life time parole is an additional form of punishment, it should be part of the information the defendant receives about the maximum sentence he faces. GL c. 265 § 45 specifically refers to community parole supervision for life as punishment.

Third, a 2004 amendment incorporated into this subsection the requirement of G.L. c. 6, § 178E(d), that a court accepting a plea for a sex offense inform the defendant that the plea may result in the defendant's being subject to the provisions of the sex offender registration statute. The statute states that failure to provide this information shall not be grounds to vacate or invalidate the plea, and the inclusion of this requirement in Rule 12(c)(3)(B) does not enlarge the grounds on which a defendant can invalidate a plea after the fact.

The failure to inform the defendant of the sentencing consequences of a plea may result in the conviction being set aside because the plea was not a knowing and intelligent waiver. *E.g.*, Commonwealth v. Rodriguez, 52 Mass. App. Ct. 572 (2001) (failure to inform the defendant of the maximum sentence and mandatory minimum sentence upon revocation of probation). However, "not every omission of a particular from the protocol of the rule . . . entitles a defendant at some later stage to negate his plea and claim a trial." Commonwealth v. Nolan, 19 Mass. App. Ct. 491, 494 (1984). *E.g.*, Commonwealth v. Cavanaugh, 12 Mass. App. Ct. 543, 545–546 (1981) (where defendant received the sentence recommended by the prosecutor, the judge's failure to inform him of the maximum possible sentence was harmless beyond a reasonable doubt).

While there are consequences beyond those enumerated in this subdivision that might influence a defendant's decision to plead guilty, if they are collateral, in the sense of being contingent upon some future event or subject to discretion or under the control of the federal government or that of another state, they need not be incorporated into the plea colloquy. For example, ordinary parole consequences need not be part of the judge's warnings, *see* Commonwealth v. Santiago, 394 Mass. 25, 30 (1985), nor is ineligibility to receive good time deductions from a sentence being served after conviction of certain crimes, *see* Commonwealth v. Brown, 6 Mass. App. Ct. 844 (1978) (rescript).

Subdivision (c)(3)(c) was added in 2004, and is based on the requirement in G.L. c. 278, § 29D, that a defendant who pleads guilty or nolo contendere must be advised that if he or she is not a United States citizen, a conviction may have the consequences of deportation, exclusion of admission, or denial of naturalization. This subdivision, however, is broader than the statute. The Supreme Judicial Court has held that this warning is also required when the defendant offers an admission to sufficient facts, *see* Commonwealth v. Mahadeo, 397 Mass. 314 (1986), and so the Rule requires an "alien" warning in those cases as well. In addition, the Rule requires the defendant to be warned of the potential adverse impact of the plea or admission, rather than of a conviction, as the statute requires. Under current immigration law, the statute's warning may be misleading since adverse consequences can flow from an admission to sufficient facts not followed by a conviction. *See* Commonwealth v. Villalobos, 437 Mass. 797 (2002). By warning the defendant that a plea or admission can have adverse immigration consequences, the court necessarily conveys not only the message about the effect of an ensuring conviction but also alerts the defendant to the possibility of adverse consequences from the plea or admission itself.

(c)(4). To this point the court has been informed of the existence of and substance of a plea arrangement, has indicated a willingness to entertain that arrangement, and has informed, or caused, the defendant to be informed of the consequences of acceptance of the plea. The defendant now formally tenders a plea or admission to the court, which then conducts a hearing to determine whether it is a knowing, intelligent, and voluntary waiver.

(c)(5). By requiring an inquiry into the "voluntariness" of the plea or admission, this subdivision requires the judge to ensure two basic foundations for a valid waiver. First is that the defendant understands the consequences of his or her act. Courts often refer to this standard as requiring the plea to be a knowing and intelligent act. In addition, the defendant's decision must be free from improper influence. As the Supreme Court, in Johnson v. Zerbst, 304 U.S. 458 (1938), declared, a waiver is "an *intentional* relinquishment or abandonment of a *known* right or privilege." *Id.* at 464 (emphasis supplied).

In order to enter a valid guilty plea, the defendant must be competent. Under both the federal and state constitutions, the test of competence to plead is the same as that for standing trial. *See* Godinez v. Moran, 509 U.S. 389 (1993); Commonwealth v. Blackstone, 19 Mass. App. Ct. 209 (1985). The standard for determining competency to stand trial is "whether [the defendant] has sufficient present ability to consult with his lawyer with a reasonable degree of rational understanding — and whether he has a rational as well as factual understanding of the proceedings against him." Commonwealth v. Russin, 420 Mass. 309, 317 (1995) *quoting* Dusky v. United States, 362 U.S. 402, 402 (1960). The substituted judgment doctrine, by which the court appoints a guardian to act, is not an appropriate vehicle for an incompetent defendant who offers to plead guilty. *See* Commonwealth v. Del Verde, 398 Mass. 288 (1986).

In Huot v. Commonwealth, 363 Mass. 91, 99—101 (1973), the court recognized that Boykin v. Alabama, 397 U.S. 238 (1969) placed the burden of establishing on review that a guilty plea is made voluntarily and intelligently is on the prosecution. The Commonwealth must meet that burden and the hearing that this subsection establishes is designed to meet that end.

The Supreme Judicial Court, in Commonwealth v. Lopez, 426 Mass. 657, 660, (1998), stated the appropriate standard:

> As a general proposition of constitutional law, a guilty plea may be withdrawn or nullified if it does not appear affirmatively that the defendant entered the plea freely and voluntarily. Boykin v. Alabama, 395 U.S. 238, 242–243 (1969). *See* Brady v. United States, 397 U.S. 742, 748 (1970); Commonwealth v. Foster, 368 Mass. 100, 106 (1975). Rule 12 (c) (3) of the Massachusetts Rules of Criminal Procedure, requires that a defendant be informed on the record of the three constitutional rights which are waived by a guilty plea: the right to trial, the right to confront one's accusers, and the privilege against self-incrimination. *See* Boykin v. Alabama, *supra* at 243; Commonwealth v. Lewis, 399 Mass. 761, 764 (1987). Moreover, the plea record must demonstrate either that the defendant was advised of the elements of the offense or that he admitted facts constituting the unexplained elements. *See* Henderson v. Morgan, 426 U.S. 637, 646, (1976); Commonwealth v. Colantoni, 396 Mass. 672, 678–679 (1986). Finally, the plea record must demonstrate that the defendant pleaded guilty voluntarily and not in response to threats or undue pressure. *See* Commonwealth v. Foster, *supra* at 107.

The first distinct requirement is that the defendant understand the nature of the charge. A plea may be involuntary because the defendant has such an incomplete understanding of the charge that the plea is an unintelligent admission of guilt. Without adequate notice of the nature of the charge against him, or an indication that the defendant in fact comprehends the charge, the plea cannot stand as voluntary. *See* Smith v. O'Grady, 312 U.S. 329 (1941). In Henderson v. Morgan, 426 U.S. 637 (1976), the Supreme Court held that a guilty plea to a charge of second-degree murder was involuntary because the defendant was not informed that intent to cause death was an element of that crime. The Court assumed, without deciding, that notice of the true nature, or substance, of a charge does not always require a description of every element of the offense, however. *Id.* at 647 n. 18. The Court agreed with the government that in the usual case, the reviewing court should examine the totality of the circumstances and determine whether the substance of the charge, as opposed to its technical elements, was conveyed to the defendant, rather than testing the voluntariness of his plea according to whether a ritualistic litany of the formal legal elements of the offenses was read to him.

There are three ways that the record of a plea or admission can serve as satisfactory evidence that the defendant had the requisite knowledge of the elements of the charge: 1) the judge can explain the elements of the crime; 2) counsel may represent that he or she has explained them to the defendant; or, 3) the defendant may admit or stipulate to facts constituting the elements. *See* Commonwealth v. Colantoni, 396 Mass. 672, 679 (1986). The defendant's signature on a form that he or she is aware of the elements of the charge is not sufficient. *See* Commonwealth v. Jones, 60 Mass. App. Ct. 88 (2003).

While in a post-conviction context it may suffice for the record to reflect that counsel stated that the defendant was advised of the elements, or for the defendant to have admitted an act constituting the elements, the judge should not rely on these means as the primary method of establishing the requisite knowledge. *See Colantoni, supra,* 396 Mass. at 679 n. 5. The best way to ensure that the defendant knows the elements of the crime is for the judge to explain them as part of the colloquy. This can be fairly easily done in most cases by reading to the defendant the indictment or complaint. However, in some cases, it may require more than a simple statement of the crime itself. *E.g.* Commonwealth v. Jones, 60 Mass. App. Ct. 88 (2003) (simply telling the defendant that he is charged with assault and battery does not sufficiently apprise him of the elements of the crime); Commonwealth v. Pixley, 48 Mass. App. Ct. 917 (2000) (telling the defendant only that he was charged with possession of cocaine with intent to distribute did not satisfy requirement of explaining the elements as mandated by this subsection).

For an example of the scope of the examination conducted to satisfy the *Boykin* requirement of an affirmative showing of understanding and voluntariness, *see* Commonwealth v Taylor, 370 Mass 141, 144–45 n. 5 (1976). In conducting the examination, the judge is to rely on his or her own observations and discernment in concluding that the defendant understands the questions. *See* Commonwealth v Leate, 367 Mass 689, 696 (1975)

In order for the plea or admission to be voluntary, the defendant's decision to waive a trial must be free from the influence of factors that have no legitimate role to play in the process. *See* Rossman, Guilty Pleas, 2 Criminal Law Advocacy, ¶ 2.03 (listing improper threats, such as physical abuse). Therefore, the judge should inquire whether the defendant's decision to waive a trial is a result of any threats or inducements apart from those identified in the plea agreement. *See* Commonwealth v. Fernandes 390 Mass. 714, 719 (1984). While no particular form of words need be used to make this inquiry, *see* Commonwealth v. Lewis, 399 Mass. 761, 764 (1987), a brief colloquy that does not probe the defendant's mind will not do. *See* Commonwealth v. Quinones, 414 Mass. 423, 434 (1992); *Fernandes, supra*, 390 Mass. at 717–719. It is useful, however, for the judge to include in the colloquy a question about whether the defendant has consulted with counsel about the decision to waive a trial and is satisfied with counsel's assistance. *Cf. Fernandes, supra,* 390 Mass. at 718.

The pressure of a plea bargain that holds out no more than the possibility of a harsher sentence if the defendant goes to trial and is convicted is not by itself an improper influence that would render a guilty plea not voluntary. *See* Commonwealth v Tirrell 382 Mass 502, 510 (1981):

> neither this court nor the Supreme Court has required total absence of psychological or emotional pressure. In any plea bargaining situation the defendant is necessarily put to a difficult choice — the risk of a more serious sentence after trial and conviction against the probabilities of the trial judge's accepting the prosecutor's recommended leniency. The defendant's fond hopes for acquittal must be tempered by his understanding of the strength of the case against him, his prior record, and the completely unknowable reaction of the trier of fact. *See* Commonwealth v. Leate, 367 Mass. 689, 694 (1975). Without some showing of peculiar susceptibility, which rendered the defendant so gripped by fear of the . . . penalty or hope of leniency that he . . . could not . . . rationally weigh the advantages of going to trial against the advantages of pleading guilty," Brady v. United States, 397 U.S. 742, 750 (1970). We cannot say that the pressure of the decision per se destroys voluntariness. *Contrast* Pate v. Robinson, 383 U.S. 375, 385–386 (1966) (record of irrational conduct required hearing on defendant's incompetency to stand trial).

(c)(5)(A). This subdivision is based upon A.B.A. Standards Relating to Pleas of Guilty § 1.6 (Approved Draft, 1968) and accords with District Court Initial R. Crim. P. 5 (1971). *See* Fed. R. Crim. P. 11(f).

The "factual basis" standard can be met by having the prosecutor state for the record the evidence that the Commonwealth would have presented had the case gone to trial. In addition, the court may require sworn testimony from a prosecution witness or of the defendant. *See* 8 J. Moore, Federal Practice ¶ 11.03 [3] at 11–75 (1978); A.B.A. Standards Relating to Pleas of Guilty § 1.6, comment at 32 (Approved Draft, 1968).

North Carolina v. Alford, 400 U.S. 25 (1970), establishes that the United States Constitution does not prohibit the court from accepting a guilty plea from a defendant who nevertheless asserts his or her innocence. An *Alford* plea is a permissible way to establish a defendant's guilt without a trial. *See* Commonwealth v. Nikas, 431 Mass. 453 (2000); Hout v. Commonwealth, 363 Mass. 91 (1973). "Under *Alford*, a defendant who professes innocence may nevertheless plead guilty and 'voluntarily, knowingly and understandingly consent to the imposition of a prison sentence,' if the State can demonstrate a 'strong factual basis' for the plea." Commonwealth v. DelVerde, 398 Mass. 288, 297(1986), *quoting* North Carolina v. Alford, 400 U.S. 25, 38 (1970). If a factual basis for such a plea exists, it is only fair to allow a defendant who is aware of the law, the facts, and the consequences of his plea, to attempt to reduce the severity of his or her punishment by pleading guilty. *See* Commonwealth v Hubbard, 371 Mass. 160 (1976). The defendant is free to weigh the strength of the Commonwealth's evidence and on this basis to waive the right to trial. If the waiver is voluntary and intelligent it should be upheld.

Subdivision (c)(5)(A) is not made applicable to nolo pleas. The purpose of permitting a nolo plea is to relieve the defendant of the adverse repercussions that can result from the introduction of evidence from the present criminal proceedings. This purpose would be undermined to the extent that disclosures led to subsequent civil proceedings or evidence to be used at such proceedings, notwithstanding the fact that the disclosures themselves could not be used in evidence. The Federal Rules Advisory Committee stated in its note to Fed. R. Crim. P. 11: "it is desirable in some cases to permit entry of judgment upon a plea of nolo contendere without inquiry into the factual basis for the plea."

(c)(5)(B). At the conclusion of the hearing, if the judge finds that the plea "is the defendant's own, guided by reasonable advice of his counsel, his own knowledge of what he has done, and a fair understanding of the alternatives," it will be considered voluntary. Commonwealth v Manning, 367 Mass 699, 706 (1975). The judge may then accept the plea or,

notwithstanding the fact that it is voluntary, reject it. *See* subdivision (c)(6), *infra*.

(c)(5)(C). If the plea or admission is accepted, the judge shall proceed with sentencing as after a verdict or finding of guilty under Mass. R. Crim. P. 28(b).

(c)(6). This subdivision is drawn in part from Fed. R. Crim. P. 11(e)(3)–(4) and from A.B.A. Standards Relating to Pleas of Guilty § 2.1 (Approved Draft, 1968). *See* Rules of Criminal Procedure (U.L.A.) rule 444(e) (1974). *Compare* Fed. R. Crim. P. 32(d) (plea may be withdrawn after sentence only "to correct manifest injustice") *with* A.L.I. Model Code of Pre–Arraignment Procedure § 350.6 (POD 1975) (defendant may withdraw plea if sentence to be imposed is more severe than that provided in plea agreement).

Previously existing statutes relative to the withdrawal of pleas after imposition of sentence are intended to be unaffected by this rule. General Laws c. 278 §§ 29A (St 1962, c 310, § 2) and 29C (St 1959, c 167, § 1) permitted the retraction of any sentence and the withdrawal of any plea upon which the sentence was imposed within sixty days of sentencing if justice has not been done. Now *see* Mass. R. Crim. P. 29. In a case where the defendant has the right to counsel and is neither represented nor validly waived counsel, General Laws c. 278, § 29B grants the defendant an absolute right to withdraw a plea prior to sentencing.

This subdivision addresses two classes of cases. One is where the defendant's plea or admission is contingent upon a prosecutor's sentence recommendation. The other, referred to in language added in 2004, occurs where the defendant has tendered a defense capped plea. In either case, the judge has many available options. After reviewing the arrangement and, if desired, the probation report, the judge may concur in the disposition; concur in the disposition, but condition the concurrence upon facts being found consistent with representations made by the parties; refuse to accept the disposition; or propose an alternative disposition, giving the defendant a reasonable opportunity to consider the alternative before deciding whether to persist in the plea or admission or proceed to trial. If the judge intends to vary from the recommended or tendered disposition in a manner which is detrimental or prejudicial to the interests of the defendant, the defendant has an absolute right to withdraw the plea or admission.

It should be noted that where a plea or admission is predicated on a promise by the prosecutor to take unilateral action over which the judge has no control, such as entering a nolle prosequi to certain charges, this subsection is not applicable. The "[p]ower to enter a nolle prosequi is absolute in the prosecuting officer ... except possibly in instances of scandalous abuse of the authority." Commonwealth v. Dascalakis, 246 Mass. 12, 18 (1923). *See* Mass. R. Crim. P. 16. In a case such as this, disclosure to the court prior to the tender of the plea serves no purpose other than determining whether the plea is knowingly and voluntarily made.

While this subdivision is the only provision in Rule 12 that explicitly addresses the issue of a defendant's withdrawing a plea, a judge has authority to entertain such a motion on other grounds. Prior to its amendment in 1987, Rule (c)(2)(B) contained an explicit statement that if the defendant persisted in pleading guilty despite notice of the judge's intention to exceed the prosecutor's recommended sentence, the defendant could not thereafter withdraw the plea except "in the discretion of the judge." This provision was eliminated in 1987. The former subsection (c)(2)(B) gave the judge "broad discretion to allow a defendant to withdraw [a] plea before ... sentence [has been] imposed." Commonwealth v. DeMarco, 387 Mass. 481, 484 (1982); *see also* Commonwealth v. Clerico, 35 Mass. App. Ct. 407, 413 n. 7(1991). The removal from Rule 12 of the reference to a judge's discretion to allow the defendant to withdraw a plea does not alter the law that otherwise controls in this situation. If the defendant can show that the plea was not voluntary or tendered knowingly, then a motion for withdrawal should be granted, for these requirements are constitutional prerequisites to the validity of the plea. If, on the other hand, the defendant seeks to withdraw a plea prior to sentencing despite its being knowing and voluntary, the judge should balance the reason put forward by the defendant against any prejudice to the Commonwealth. *Cf.* Commonwealth v. Nolan, 19 Mass. App. Ct. 491, 494 (1984). After sentencing, however, the proper vehicle to seek to withdraw a guilty plea is a motion under Rule 30 (b).

The 2004 revision of Rule 12 deleted subdivision (d), which was designed to discourage the practice of "judge shopping" by tendering, withdrawing, and retendering a guilty plea until a judge is found who will agree to the disposition favored by the defendant. A uniform policy on whether a defendant may ask more than one judge to accept a sentence recommendation or defense capped plea is unnecessary. Individual judges still retain the discretion to refuse to entertain such requests.

(e). The conditions governing the availability to the defendant of the probation report are the same as those which control under Mass. R. Crim. P. 28(d)(3). It is important for the defendant to have access to this information so that he or she can more effectively bargain with the prosecutor and more accurately predict how the court will react to proposed dispositions. The judge need not always view the probation report to properly decide whether it should be released to the defendant. The judge can rely on representations made by the probation department or by the prosecutor in reaching this decision. The judge may examine the defendant's criminal record before accepting a plea or admission. *See* Commonwealth v. Whitford, 16 Mass. App. Ct. 448, 453 (1983).

Subdivision (f). In its original form, this subdivision changed the prior rule in Massachusetts that a plea that has been withdrawn may be introduced in subsequent proceedings as an admission by the defendant. *See* Morrisey v. Powell, 304 Mass. 268 (1939). The current position reflected in this subdivision is consistent with the modern trend and with the rule in federal courts. *See* A.B.A. Standards Relating to Pleas of Guilty, §§ 2.2, 3.4 (Approved Draft, 1968); Rules of Criminal Procedure (U.L.A.) rule 444(f) (1974); A.L.I. Model Code of Pre–Arraignment Procedure § 350.7 (POD 1975). It is drawn from Fed. Cr. Crim. P. 11(e)(6), although it is broader in scope, since unlike the federal rule, its application to statements made in the course of plea negotiations is not limited only to circumstances where the defendant is negotiating with a government attorney. *See* Commonwealth v. Wilson, 430 Mass. 440, 443 (1999). However, simply expressing a desire to plead guilty to a police officer who does not have any authority to bind the Commonwealth does not bring a defendant's statement within the scope of this subdivision. *Id.*

In 2004, the subdivision was amended to include admissions to sufficient facts among the category of actions by the defendant that are not admissible if later withdrawn.

Permitting a prosecutor to offer evidence that a defendant unsuccessfully tendered a plea or admission undermines the rationale behind the decision allowing the plea or admission to be withdrawn in the first place. *See* Kercheval v. United States, 274 U.S. 220 (1927). Additionally, juries tend to give undue weight to the introduction of prior pleas. Of course, if the reason why the plea or admission was withdrawn was that it was not knowing and voluntary, then the federal Constitution prohibits its use in a subsequent proceeding. *Cf.* White v. Maryland, 373 U.S. 59 (1963) (barring use of evidence that the defendant had entered a guilty plea without the assistance of counsel, where the defendant did not validly waive the right to counsel).

While an offer to plead guilty is inadmissible pursuant to this subdivision, the fact that a defendant refused to enter a guilty plea or rejected a plea agreement is not, conversely, admissible by implication. *See* Commonwealth v. DoVale, 57 Mass. App. Ct. 657 (2003).

Rule 13. Pretrial Motions

[Text of rule applicable to cases initiated (by indictment or complaint) on or after September 7, 2004.]

(a) In General.

(1) *Requirement of Writing and Signature; Waiver.* A pretrial motion shall be in writing and signed by the party making the motion or the attorney for that party. Pretrial motions shall be filed within the time allowed by subdivision (d) of this rule.

(2) *Grounds and Affidavit.* A pretrial motion shall state the grounds on which it is based and shall include in separately numbered paragraphs all reasons, defenses, or objections then available, which shall be set forth with particularity. If there are multiple charges, a motion filed pursuant to this rule shall specify the particular charge to which it applies. Grounds not stated which reasonably could have been known at the time a motion is filed shall be deemed to have been waived, but a judge for cause shown may grant relief from such waiver. In addition, an affidavit detailing all facts relied upon in support of the motion and signed by a person with personal knowledge of the factual basis of the motion shall be attached.

(3) *Service and Notice.* A copy of any pretrial motion and supporting affidavits shall be served on all parties or their attorneys pursuant to Rule 32 at the time the originals are filed. Opposing affidavits shall be served not later than one day before the hearing. For cause shown the requirements of this subdivision (3) may be waived by the court.

(4) *Memoranda of Law.* The judge or special magistrate may require the filing of a memorandum of law, in such form and within such time as he or she may direct, as a condition precedent to a hearing on a motion or interlocutory matter. No motion to suppress evidence, other than evidence seized during a warrantless search, and no motion to dismiss may be filed unless accompanied by a memorandum of law, except when otherwise ordered by the judge or special magistrate.

(5) *Renewal.* Upon a showing that substantial justice requires, the judge or special magistrate may permit a pretrial motion which has been heard and denied to be renewed.

(b) Bill of Particulars.

(1) *Motion.* Within the time provided for the filing of pretrial motions by this rule or within such other time as the judge may allow, a defendant may request or the court upon its own motion may order that the prosecution file a statement of such particulars as may be necessary to give both the defendant and the court reasonable notice of the crime charged, including time, place, manner, or means.

(2) *Amendment.* If at trial there exists a material variance between the evidence and bill of particulars, the judge may order the bill of particulars amended or may grant such other relief as justice requires.

(c) Motion to Dismiss or to Grant Appropriate Relief.

(1) All defenses available to a defendant by plea, other than not guilty, shall only be raised by a motion to dismiss or by a motion to grant appropriate relief.

(2) A defense or objection which is capable of determination without trial of the general issue shall be raised before trial by motion.

(d) Filing. Only pretrial motions the subject matter of which could not be agreed upon at the pretrial conference shall be filed with the court.

(1) *Discovery Motions.* Any discovery motions shall be filed prior to the conclusion of the pretrial hearing, or thereafter for good cause shown. A discovery motion filed after the conclusion of the pretrial hearing shall be heard and considered only if (A) the discovery sought could not reasonably have been requested or obtained prior to the conclusion of the pretrial hearing, (B) the discovery is sought by the Commonwealth, and the Commonwealth could not reasonably provide all discovery due to the defense prior to the conclusion of the pretrial hearing, or (C) other good cause exists to warrant consideration of the motion.

(2) *Non–discovery Pretrial Motions.* A pretrial motion which does not seek discovery shall be filed before the assignment of a trial date pursuant to Rule 11(b) or (c) or within 21 days thereafter, unless the court permits later filing for good cause shown.

(e) Hearing on Motions. The parties shall have a right to a hearing on a pretrial motion. The opposing party shall be afforded an adequate opportunity to prepare and submit a memorandum of law prior to the hearing.

(1) *Discovery Motions.* All pending discovery motions shall be heard and decided prior to the defendant's election of a jury or jury-waived trial. Any discovery matters pending at the time of the pretrial

hearing or the compliance hearing shall be heard at that hearing. Discovery motions filed pursuant to subdivision (d)(1) after the defendant's election shall be heard and decided expeditiously.

(2) *Non–Discovery Pretrial Motions.* A non-discovery motion filed prior to the pretrial hearing may be heard at the pretrial hearing, at a hearing scheduled to address the motion, or at the trial session. A non-discovery motion filed at or after the pretrial hearing shall be heard at the next scheduled court date unless otherwise ordered.

(3) Within seven days after the filing of a motion, or if the motion is transmitted to the trial session within seven days after the transmittal, the clerk or the judge shall assign a date for hearing the motion, but the judge or special magistrate for cause shown may entertain such motion at any time before trial. If the parties have agreed to a mutually convenient time for the hearing of a pretrial motion, and the moving party so notifies the clerk in writing at the time of the filing of the motion, the clerk shall mark up the motion for hearing at that time subject to the approval of the court. The clerk shall notify the parties of the time set for hearing the motion.

Amended March 8, 2004, effective September 7, 2004.

Reporter's Notes—Revised, 2004

This rule establishes the form of, and manner for the presentation of, pretrial motions. Not every motion that is made in a pretrial posture is governed exclusively by this rule. For example, a continuance motion is subject to the provisions of Rule 10(a)(3) and (4), and the requirements of a motion for relief from prejudicial joinder are contained in Rule 9(d). Where, however, no other rules or statutes provide otherwise, pretrial motions should be made in conformity with the provisions of this rule.

The primary sources of this rule as originally formulated are Rule 3.190 of the Florida Rules of Criminal Procedure (1974) and the existing statutory law of the Commonwealth. The rule has an abbreviated counterpart in Rule 47 of the Federal Rules of Criminal Procedure. In 2004 the rule was revised with regard to its provisions governing filing, filing deadlines, and hearings. The formal requirements concerning motions, affidavits, supporting memoranda, service and notice were unchanged in all respects. So too were the specific provisions in 13(b) and 13(c) concerning bills of particulars and motions to dismiss respectively.

Subdivision (a). Motions in general. This subdivision is derived in large part from the Florida Rule, but essentially restates existing practice and is supported in large part by Rule 9 of the Superior Court Rules (1974). The references to pretrial motions are to include pleadings in response to a motion where such exist.

Subdivision (a)(1) requires a pretrial motion to be in writing. Although an oral motion may be considered, Commonwealth v. Geoghegan, 12 Mass. App. Ct. 575, 575–76 (1981), it need not be because it violates this requirement. Commonwealth v. Pope, 392 Mass. 493, 498 n. 8 (1984).

Subdivision (a)(2) is taken from Rules 9 and 61 of the Superior Court Rules (1974). The requirement of an affidavit in support of factual assertions is supported additionally by former G.L. c. 277, § 74. (RS [1836] c 136, § 31). The affidavit need not be signed by the defendant but must be signed by someone with personal knowledge of the facts therein, *see* Commonwealth v. Santosuosso, 23 Mass. App. Ct. 310 (1986)(affidavit by counsel), except for those affidavits accompanying a motion requesting a summons for the production of documentary evidence and objects, *see* Commonwealth v. Lampron, 441 Mass. 265, 270–71 (2004) (an affidavit accompanying a motion requesting a summons for production of documentary evidence or objects may be based on hearsay from a reliable source, which the affidavit must identify).

The reference in subdivision (a)(3) to opposing affidavits is to apply only if there are opposing affidavits. It is not intended to require them.

Subdivision (a)(4) is taken from Rule 9 of the Superior Court Rules (1974).

Subdivision (a)(5) provides that although a motion has been once heard and denied, it may be renewed if "substantial justice requires" that action. This is appropriate where new or additional grounds are alleged which could not reasonably have been known when the motion was originally filed. See (a)(2), *supra*. Moreover, at times it may be necessary to renew a motion in order to preserve it for appeal. For example, the Supreme Judicial Court has held that a suppression motion was waived when counsel failed to renew it at the time the evidence was offered at trial. Commonwealth v. Acosta, 416 Mass. 279 (1993).

Subdivision (b). Bill of Particulars. Former G.L. c. 277, § 40 (St 1887, c 436, § 2) permitted the court to require the prosecution to file particulars in order to more fully apprise the defendant or the court of the nature of the charges. This subdivision incorporates that practice into this rule.

The distinction which was drawn in the statute between particulars ordered by a court with jurisdiction over the offense charged and those ordered by a court without jurisdiction of the offense charged has not been retained in this rule. However, the judge may in his discretion order whatever particulars he deems necessary under the circumstances, and this would permit him to order a more complete statement of particulars where it is required in the interests of justice. Indeed, particulars may be constitutionally required in some cases under article 12 of the Massachusetts Declaration of Rights, which protects a defendant from having to answer charges "until the same is fully and plainly, substantially and formally, described to him." *See also* Commonwealth v. Baker, 368 Mass. 58, 77 (1975)(suggesting a liberal standard for granting particulars).

If the specifications supplied in conformity with the court's order are irrelevant or prejudicial, defense counsel must file a motion to strike those deemed improper. 30 MASS. PRACTICE SERIES (Smith) § 1296 (1983).

Although the rule requires motions for bills of particulars to be made before trial, it is not intended to be construed so as to limit the inherent power of the court in an appropriate situation to order a bill at any time.

Subdivision (c). Motions to Dismiss or Grant Appropriate Relief. This is a restatement of former G.L. c. 277, § 77A (St 1965, c 617, § 1). It should be noted that G.L. c. 277, § 47A abolished at least in name all the other pleas, demurrers, challenges, and motions to quash; it effectively consolidated all of them under the general heading of a motion to dismiss or grant appropriate relief, in effect retaining the statutory and common law of the Commonwealth governing such pleas.

Section 47A (as amended) now provides for relief from the waiver of defenses not timely raised, upon a showing of cause.

> In a criminal case, any defense or objection based upon defects in the institution of the prosecution or in the complaint or indictment, other than a failure to show jurisdiction in the court or to charge an offense, shall only be raised prior to trial and only by a motion in conformity with the requirements of the Massachusetts Rules of Criminal Procedure. The failure to raise any such defense or objection by motion prior to trial shall constitute a waiver thereof, but a judge or special magistrate may, for cause shown, grant relief from such waiver. A defense or objection based upon a failure to show jurisdiction in the court or the failure to charge an offense may be raised by motion to dismiss prior to trial, but shall be noticed by the court at any time.

Id. See also Commonwealth v. Chou, 433 Mass. 229 (2001). "Cause" should be read to include grounds of which the moving party was not previously aware. See Mass. R. Crim. P. 46(b); Commonwealth v. Bongarzone, 390 Mass. 326, 337–38 (1983). Additionally, case law and statutory law establish that certain motions and objections must be heard even if raised for the first time at trial, such as claims that the complaint or indictment fails to state a charge, or is outside the court's jurisdiction, G.L. c. 277, s. 47A and Commonwealth v. Cantres, 405 Mass. 238, 239–40 (1989); that wiretap evidence should be suppressed, Commonwealth v. Picardi, 401 Mass. 1008 (1988); that a statement was taken in violation of the *Miranda* rule, Commonwealth v. Adams, 389 Mass. 265, 269–70 & n. 1 (1983); or that the defendant was not criminally responsible by reason of insanity, Mass. R. Crim. P. 14(b)(2).

Subdivision (d). Filing motions. This subdivision sets out the filing deadlines for pretrial motions. It was amended in 2004 to eliminate provisions relating to filing motions in the now-abolished *de novo* district court system, and to remove a conflict between this rule and the statutory filing deadlines subsequently established for district courts by the single-trial legislation, G.L. c. 278 sec. 18.

Under subdivision (d)(1), discovery motions are to be filed prior to the conclusion of the pretrial hearing, or after for good cause shown. The subdivision also specifies two specific, *non–exhaustive* circumstances which shall be deemed to constitute good cause. One self-evident basis is that the discovery sought could not reasonably have been requested or obtained prior to the pretrial hearing [(d)(1)(A)]. The other, specified in (d)(1)(B), allows later filing by the Commonwealth if it "could not reasonably provide all discovery due to the defense prior to the conclusion of the pretrial hearing." This asymmetrical provision is necessary because under the rules, the Commonwealth must fulfill its discovery obligations in order to receive discovery. If the Commonwealth has been unable to provide discovery prior to the pretrial hearing for good reason, it should not be prejudiced by having its reciprocal discovery rights foreclosed. Provision 13(d)(1)(ii) is necessary to preserve the Commonwealth's discovery rights in such a situation. In any event, with the institution in 2004 of automatic and comprehensive discovery without motion under Rule 14, motions for discovery should be unnecessary in many cases.

Under subdivision (d)(2), non-discovery pretrial motions are to be filed no later than 21 days after the court's assignment of a trial date or trial assignment date, unless the court permits later filing for good cause shown. (Additionally, the defendant must also provide notice of intent to defend by reason of insanity, or by reason of license or privilege, within this time period. Rule 14(b)(2) and (3), respectively). In effect, this provides 21 days after the pretrial hearing or compliance hearing, whichever is later, since under Rule 11 it is there that the trial date or trial assignment date must be set (and, in district court, a jury election or waiver must be taken, the event that commences the 21–day deadline for motions mandated by the district court single trial legislation). The time limits provided in this rule for the filing of pretrial motions are intended to set the norm. Ample opportunity is left for the court to exercise its discretion in the interest of justice, however, by the inclusion of the "for cause shown" provision in subdivisions (d)(1) and (d)(2). *See also* Commonwealth v. Bongarzone, *supra*.

A clerk is not generally empowered to refuse to accept and docket a motion without the court's express approval, but if this occurs counsel may move to have the motion docketed. Bolton v. Commonwealth, 407 Mass. 1003, 1003–4 (1990).

Subdivision (d) also makes explicit what is already implicit in Mass. R. Crim. P. 11, namely, that the only pretrial motions which may be filed are those as to the substance of which counsel were unable to agree. Counsel should ascertain whether the opposing party or parties will agree to all potential motions before or during the pretrial conference (or, if the motion could not have been anticipated until after the pretrial conference, promptly when the need for the motion becomes apparent). By requiring that the substance of any pretrial motions a party intends to file be discussed with the adverse party, this subdivision institutes a rule of judicial economy. It is contemplated that having parties compare all the motions they intend to file before trial at the pretrial conference will make the conference more productive by eliminating many "boiler plate" motions. If a conflict between this subdivision and the general filing and service of papers provisions of Rule 32 should arise, this subdivision is controlling as to motions to which it is applicable.

Subdivision (e). This subdivision provides the parties with a right to a hearing on a pretrial motion, and governs the scheduling of the hearing. Subdivision (e)(3) provides that within seven days of filing (or if the motion is transmitted to the trial session within seven days after the transmittal), the clerk should schedule the motion for hearing. However, the clerk will be guided by other provisions in subdivision (e). First, the court must afford the opposing party an adequate opportunity to prepare and submit a memorandum prior to the hearing. Second, *discovery motions* must be heard and decided prior to the defendant's election of a jury or jury waived trial; if any discovery motions are pending at the time of the pretrial hearing or the compliance hearing, they should be heard at that time [(e)(1)]. *See* Rule 11(b)(2)(iii) and (c)(3); Dist./Mun. Ct. Rule of Criminal Procedure 4(e). Third, *non–discovery motions* may be scheduled to be heard at the pretrial hearing, at a hearing scheduled to address the motion, or at the trial session, although the default date for motions filed at the pretrial hearing is the next scheduled court date [(e)(2)]. The clerk must notify the parties of the date assigned. This provision allows individual courts to decide how to schedule non-discovery motions. Finally, subdivision (e)(3) provides a method for the parties to agree to a mutually convenient time for hearing when the motion is filed.

Although not enumerated in the rule, precedent establishes that some motions may be heard *ex parte,* especially when they do not affect an interest of the opposing party or would reveal privileged or other information to which the opposing party is not entitled. For example, motions to fund indigent expenses need not be heard in the presence of the prosecution. Commonwealth v. Dotson, 402 Mass. 185, 187 (1988); Commonwealth v. Haggerty, 400 Mass. 437, 441 (1987).

Rule 14. Pretrial Discovery

[Text of rule applicable to cases initiated (by indictment or complaint) on or after September 7, 2004.]

(a) Procedures for Discovery.

(1) *Automatic Discovery.*

(A) Mandatory Discovery for the Defendant. The prosecution shall disclose to the defense, and permit the defense to discover, inspect and copy, each of the following items and information at or prior to the pretrial conference, provided it is relevant to the case and is in the possession, custody or control of the prosecutor, persons under the prosecutor's direction and control, or persons who have participated in investigating or evaluating the case and either regularly report to the prosecutor's office or have done so in the case:

(i) Any written or recorded statements, and the substance of any oral statements, made by the defendant or a co-defendant.

(ii) The grand jury minutes, and the written or recorded statements of a person who has testified before a grand jury.

(iii) Any facts of an exculpatory nature.

(iv) The names, addresses, and dates of birth of the Commonwealth's prospective witnesses other than law enforcement witnesses. The Commonwealth shall also provide this information to the Probation Department.

(v) The names and business addresses of prospective law enforcement witnesses.

(vi) Intended expert opinion evidence, other than evidence that pertains to the defendant's criminal responsibility and is subject to subdivision (b)(2). Such discovery shall include the identity, current curriculum vitae, and list of publications of each intended expert witness, and all reports prepared by the expert that pertain to the case.

(vii) Material and relevant police reports, photographs, tangible objects, all intended exhibits, reports of physical examinations of any person or of scientific tests or experiments, and statements of persons the party intends to call as witnesses.

(viii) A summary of identification procedures, and all statements made in the presence of or by an identifying witness that are relevant to the issue of identity or to the fairness or accuracy of the identification procedures.

(ix) Disclosure of all promises, rewards or inducements made to witnesses the party intends to present at trial.

(B) Reciprocal Discovery for the Prosecution. Following the Commonwealth's delivery of all discovery required pursuant to subdivision (a)(1)(A) or court order, and on or before a date agreed to between the parties, or in the absence of such agreement a date ordered by the court, the defendant shall disclose to the prosecution and permit the Commonwealth to discover, inspect, and copy any material and relevant evidence discoverable under subdivision (a)(1)(A) (vi), (vii) and (ix) which the defendant intends to offer at trial, including the names, addresses, dates of birth, and statements of those persons whom the defendant intends to call as witnesses at trial.

(C) Stay of Automatic Discovery; Sanctions. Subdivisions (a)(1)(A) and (a)(1)(B) shall have the force and effect of a court order, and failure to provide discovery pursuant to them may result in application of any sanctions permitted for noncompliance with a court order under subdivision 14(c). However, if in the judgment of either party good cause exists for declining to make any of the disclosures set forth above, it may move for a protective order pursuant to subdivision (a)(6) and production of the item shall be stayed pending a ruling by the court.

(D) Record of Convictions of the Defendant, Codefendants, and Prosecution Witnesses. At arraignment the court shall order the Probation Department to deliver to the parties the record of prior complaints, indictments and dispositions of all defendants and of all witnesses identified pursuant to subdivisions (a)(1)(A)(iv) within 5 days of the Commonwealth's notification to the Department of the names and addresses of its witnesses.

(E) Notice and Preservation of Evidence. (i) Upon receipt of information that any item described in subparagraph (a)(1)(A)(i)–(viii) exists, except that it is not within the possession, custody or control of the prosecution, persons under its direction and control, or persons who have participated in investigating or evaluating the case and either regularly report to the prosecutor's office or have done so in the case, the prosecution shall notify the defendant of the existence of the item and all information known to the prosecutor concerning the item's location and the identity of any persons possessing it. (ii) At any time, a party may move for an order to any individual, agency or other entity in possession, custody or control of items pertaining to the case, requiring that such items be preserved for a specified period of time. The court shall hear and rule upon the motion expeditiously. The court may modify or vacate such an order upon a showing that preservation of particular evidence will create significant hardship, on condition that the probative value of said evidence is preserved by a specified alternative means.

(2) *Motions for Discovery.* The defendant may move, and following its filing of the Certificate of Compliance the Commonwealth may move, for discovery of other material and relevant evidence not required by subdivision (a)(1) within the time allowed by Rule 13(d)(1).

(3) *Certificate of Compliance.* When a party has provided all discovery required by this rule or by court order, it shall file with the court a Certificate of Compliance. The certificate shall state that, to the best of its knowledge and after reasonable inquiry, the party has disclosed and made available all items subject to discovery other than reports of experts, and shall identify each item provided. If further discovery is subsequently provided, a supplemental certificate shall be filed with the court identifying the additional items provided.

(4) *Continuing Duty.* If either the defense or the prosecution subsequently learns of additional material which it would have been under a duty to disclose or produce pursuant to any provisions of this rule at the time of a previous discovery order, it shall promptly notify the other party of its acquisition of such additional material and shall disclose the material in the same manner as required for initial discovery under this rule.

(5) *Work Product.* This rule does not authorize discovery by a party of those portions of records, reports, correspondence, memoranda, or internal documents of the adverse party which are only the legal research, opinions, theories, or conclusions of the adverse party or its attorney and legal staff, or of statements of a defendant, signed or unsigned, made to the attorney for the defendant or the attorney's legal staff.

(6) *Protective Orders.* Upon a sufficient showing, the judge may at any time order that the discovery or inspection be denied, restricted, or deferred, or make such other order as is appropriate. The judge may alter the time requirements of this rule. The judge may, for cause shown, grant discovery to a defendant on the condition that the material to be discovered be available only to counsel for the defendant. This provision does not alter the allocation of the burden of proof with regard to the matter at issue, including privilege.

(7) *Amendment of Discovery Orders.* Upon motion of either party made subsequent to an order of the judge pursuant to this rule, the judge may alter or amend the previous order or orders as the interests of justice may require. The judge may, for cause shown, affirm a prior order granting discovery to a defendant upon the additional condition that the material to be discovered is to be available only to counsel for the defendant.

(8) A party may waive the right to discovery of an item, or to discovery of the item within the time provided in this Rule. The parties may agree to reduce or enlarge the items subject to discovery pursuant to subsections (a)(1)(A) and (a)(1)(B). Any such waiver or agreement shall be in writing and signed by the waiving party or the parties to the agreement, shall identify the specific items included, and shall be served upon all the parties.

(b) Special Procedures.

(1) *Notice of Alibi.*

(A) Notice by Defendant. The judge may, upon written motion of the Commonwealth filed pursuant to subdivision (a)(2) of this rule, stating the time, date, and place at which the alleged offense was committed, order that the defendant serve upon the prosecutor a written notice, signed by the defendant, of his or her intention to offer a defense of alibi. The notice by the defendant shall state the specific place or places at which the defendant claims to have been at the time of the alleged offense and the names and addresses of the witnesses upon whom the defense intends to rely to establish the alibi.

(B) Disclosure of Information and Witness. Within seven days of service of the defendant's notice of alibi, the Commonwealth shall serve upon the defendant a written notice stating the names and addresses of witnesses upon whom the prosecutor intends to rely to establish the defendant's presence at the scene of the alleged offense and any other witnesses to be relied on to rebut testimony of any of the defendant's alibi witnesses.

(C) Continuing Duty to Disclose. If prior to or during trial a party learns of an additional witness whose identity, if known, should have been included in the information furnished under subdivision (b)(1)(A) or (B), that party shall promptly notify the adverse party or its attorney of the existence and identity of the additional witness.

(D) Failure to Comply. Upon the failure of either party to comply with the requirements of this rule, the judge may exclude the testimony of any undisclosed witness offered by such party as to the defendant's absence from or presence at the scene of the alleged offense. This rule shall not limit the right of the defendant to testify.

(E) Exceptions. For cause shown, the judge may grant an exception to any of the requirements of subdivisions (b)(1)(A) through (D) of this rule.

(F) Inadmissibility of Withdrawn Alibi. Evidence of an intention to rely upon an alibi defense, later withdrawn, or of statements made in connection with that intention, is not admissible in any civil or criminal proceeding against the person who gave notice of that intention.

(2) Defense of Lack of Criminal Responsibility Because of Mental Disease or Defect.

(A) Notice. If a defendant intends to rely upon the defense of lack of criminal responsibility because of mental disease or defect at the time of the alleged crime, the defendant shall, within the time provided for the filing of pretrial motions by Rule 13(d)(2) or at such later time as the judge may allow, notify the prosecutor in writing of such intention. The notice shall state:

(i) whether the defendant intends to offer testimony of expert witnesses on the issue of lack of criminal responsibility because of mental disease or defect;

(ii) the names and addresses of expert witnesses whom the defendant expects to call; and

(iii) whether those expert witnesses intend to rely in whole or in part on statements of the defendant as to his or her mental condition at the time of the alleged crime or criminal responsibility for the alleged crime.

The defendant shall file a copy of the notice with the clerk. The judge may for cause shown allow late filing of the notice, grant additional time to the parties to prepare for trial, or make such other order as may be appropriate.

(B) Examination. If the notice of the defendant or subsequent inquiry by the judge or developments in the case indicate that statements of the defendant as to his or her mental condition at the time of, or criminal responsibility for, the alleged crime will be relied upon by expert witnesses of the defendant, the court, upon its own motion or upon motion of the prosecutor, may order the defendant to submit to a psychiatric examination consistent with the provisions of the General Laws and subject to the following terms and conditions:

(i) The examination shall include such physical and psychological examinations and physiological and psychiatric tests as the examiner deems necessary to form an opinion as to the mental condition of the defendant at the time the alleged offense was committed. No examination based on statements of the defendant may be conducted unless the judge has found that (a) the defendant then intends to offer at trial psychiatric evidence based on his or her own statements or (b) there is a reasonable likelihood that the defendant will offer that evidence.

(ii) No statement, confession, or admission, or other evidence of or obtained from the defendant during the course of the examination, except evidence derived solely from physical or physiological observations or tests, may be revealed to the prosecution or anyone acting on its behalf unless so ordered by the judge.

(iii) The examiner shall file with the court a written psychiatric report which shall contain his or her findings, including specific statements of the basis thereof, as to the mental condition of the defendant at the time the alleged offense was committed.

The report shall be sealed and shall not be made available to the parties unless (a) the judge determines that the report contains no matter, information, or evidence which is based upon statements of the defendant as to his or her mental condition at the time of, or criminal responsibility for, the alleged crime, or which is otherwise within the scope of the privilege against self-incrimination; or (b) the defendant files a motion requesting that the report be made available to the parties; or (c) during trial the defendant raises the defense of lack of criminal responsibility and the judge is satisfied that (1) the defendant intends to testify or (2) the defendant intends to offer expert testimony based in whole or in part upon statements of the defendant as to his or her mental condition at the time of, or criminal responsibility for, the alleged crime.

If a psychiatric report contains both privileged and nonprivileged matter, the court may, if feasible, at such time as it deems appropriate, make available to the parties the nonprivileged portions.

(iv) If a defendant refuses to submit to an examination ordered pursuant to and subject to the terms and conditions of this rule, the court may prescribe such remedies as it deems warranted by the circumstances, which may include exclusion of the testimony of any expert witness offered by the defense on the issue of the defendant's mental condition or the admission of evidence of the refusal of the defendant to submit to examination.

(3) *Notice of Other Defenses.* If a defendant intends to rely upon a defense based upon a license, claim of authority or ownership, or exemption, the defendant shall, within the time provided for the filing of pretrial motions by Rule 13(d)(2) or at such later time as the judge may direct, notify the prosecutor in writing of such intention and file a copy of such notice with the clerk. If there is a failure to comply with the requirements of this subdivision, a license, claim of authority or ownership, or exemption may not be relied upon as a defense. The judge may for cause shown allow a late filing of the notice or grant additional time to the parties to prepare for trial or make such other order as may be appropriate.

(c) Sanctions for Noncompliance.

(1) *Relief for Nondisclosure.* For failure to comply with any discovery order issued or imposed pursuant to this rule, the court may make a further order for discovery, grant a continuance, or enter such other order as it deems just under the circumstances.

(2) *Exclusion of Evidence.* The court may in its discretion exclude evidence for noncompliance with

a discovery order issued or imposed pursuant to this rule. Testimony of the defendant and evidence concerning the defense of lack of criminal responsibility which is otherwise admissible cannot be excluded except as provided by subdivision (b)(2) of this rule.

(d) Definition. The term "statement", as used in this rule, means:

(1) a writing made by a person having percipient knowledge of relevant facts and which contains such facts, other than drafts or notes that have been incorporated into a subsequent draft or final report; or

(2) a written, stenographic, mechanical, electrical, or other recording, or transcription thereof, which is a substantially verbatim recital of an oral declaration and which is recorded contemporaneously with the making of the oral declaration, except that a computer assisted real time translation, or its functional equivalent, made to assist a deaf or hearing impaired person, that is not transcribed or permanently saved in electronic form, shall not be considered a statement.

Amended March 8, 2004, effective September 7, 2004; April 4, 2005, effective May 1, 2005; December 17, 2008, effective April 1, 2009.

Reporter's Notes—Revised, 2004

This rule is based on the concept of reciprocity and has as its aim full pretrial disclosure of items normally within the range of discovery. It is emphasized, however, that this rule establishes a formal discovery procedure and is not intended to discourage those disclosures which may take place at a pretrial conference under Mass. R. Crim. P. 11 or whatever other informal discovery may be agreed upon by the parties. *See* Commonwealth v. Delaney, 11 Mass. App. Ct. 398 (1981).

The 2004 amendments. The substance of the original version promulgated in 1979 was drawn from Fed. R. Crim. P. 12.1, 12.2 and 16, N.J.R. Crim. P. 3:13-3 (1972), Fla. R. Crim P. 3.220 (1975), and the ABA *Standards Relating to Discovery and Procedure Before Trial* (Approved Draft, 1979). As more fully discussed *infra*, in 2004 the Rule was substantially revised to eliminate the requirement of pretrial motions in many routine areas of discovery, instead mandating that such discovery be (1) mandatory, and (2) provided automatically to both prosecution and defense. These automatic discovery obligations stem directly from the rule itself, but pursuant to subdivision (a)(1)(C) have all the force and effect of a court order. Discovery of items not included in the automatic discovery regime remains subject to the court's discretion, and may be requested by pretrial motion.

The decision to broaden the ambit of mandatory discovery reflects a conviction that full, automatic, and even-handed discovery to both sides will improve both the administration and delivery of justice. Comprehensive discovery affords counsel a full opportunity to prepare the case, rather than be hijacked by surprise evidence, as the Supreme Court has noted. See Wardius v. Oregon, 412 U.S. 470, 473-74 (1973)("the end of justice will best be served by a system of liberal discovery which gives both parties the maximum possible amount of information with which to prepare their cases and thereby reduce surprise at trial.") It also brings Rule 14 in line with the broad discovery requirements that have existed in district court since the abolition of trial de novo in 1994 under G.L. c. 218, s. 26A and District Court/BMC Rule 3(c). Finally, the decision to afford mandatory discovery to the prosecution as well as the defense assures that one party will not be disadvantaged by a comparative inability to prepare.

A second major innovation – mandating discovery without the need for motions or argument – is designed to manage court events more efficiently. In areas where discovery is routinely afforded in practice, requiring motions and hearings simply delayed the case and absorbed court and counsel time and expense. The revision recognizes that it is far more efficient to provide automatic discovery of such items to both sides, so long as all parties have a full opportunity to argue against discovery of any of these items where special circumstances in the case warrant divergence from these presumptive procedures. Moreover, automatic discovery early in the case provides the defense with notice of the Commonwealth's case prior to plea negotiations or the filing of other pretrial motions. The grounds for such motions, and the advisability of a plea, may only be revealed through discovery.

The 2004 amendments made some additional, more minor changes to Rule 14. A revision to Rule 14(d) modified the definition of "statements" for purposes of this rule, as described below. Rule 14(e), which formerly specified the timing requirements for discovery motions, was deleted because revised Rule 13(d) now governs all pretrial motion deadlines, including discovery motions. The 2004 amendments did not make substantive changes to section (b), concerning notice of certain defenses to the prosecution, or section (c), concerning sanctions for non-disclosure.

Subdivision (a). Initially Rule 14(a) classified the items now included in sections (a)(1)(iv) through (ix) as "discretionary discovery," to be ordered within the sound discretion of the trial judge. In 2004, however, subdivision (a) was substantially revised to require these items to be produced to the opposing party automatically. However, if a party believes good cause exists for non-discovery of an item listed as automatic discovery, it may resist disclosure pursuant to Rule 14(a)(1)(C), providing for a mandatory stay of discovery of any item that the obligated party believes should not be disclosed, pending resolution by the court.

Subdivision (a)(1) of this rule details the parties' automatic discovery rights. 14(a)(1)(a) sets out the defendant's rights to certain mandatory discovery without motion, and (a)(1)(b) provides reciprocal automatic discovery rights to the prosecution. To a very large extent, the scope of disclosure called for by this subdivision is a codification of prior Massachusetts practice.

Subdivision (a)(1)(A). Mandatory Discovery for the Defendant. This provision lists the items that the prosecution must produce for discovery, with the qualification that the prosecutor's automatic discovery obligation is confined to ascertaining and delivering relevant material it and/or its agents already possess or control. The first paragraph of this subsection limits the Commonwealth's discovery obligation to material "in the possession, custody or control of the prosecutor, persons under its direction and control, or persons who have participated in investigating or evaluating the case and either regularly report to the prosecutor's office or have done so in the case . . ." This language, inserted in 2004, is not intended to change existing case law but to reflect it. The language is specifically drawn from *Commonwealth v. Daye*, 411 Mass. 719, 734 (1992)(also stating that a prosecutor "cannot be said to suppress that which is not in his possession or subject to his control"). *Daye* and many cases since describe the prosecution's duty of disclosure as extending to all discoverable material existing in its own files and in the files of others who have participated with them in the prosecution. The latter officials are usually police, but may include others assisting in the prosecution. Thus in Commonwealth v. Martin, 427 Mass. 816, 823–24 (1998), the S.J.C. reversed a conviction because the prosecutor failed to turn over evidence he did not know existed, but which was known to the Commonwealth's crime lab, because "the prosecution had a duty to inquire" concerning the existence of such tests. *Id.* at 823. *See also* Commonwealth v. Bing Sial Liang, 434 Mass. 131, 135 (2001)(victim witness advocates are part of prosecution team and are subject to the same discovery rules); Commonwealth v. Gallarelli, 399 Mass. 17, 20 n. 4 (1987). It is also clear, however, that the scope of the prosecutor's duty of disclosure does not extend to complainants and independent witnesses who are not agents of the prosecution with regard to some aspect of the case. *Commonwealth v. Lampron,* 441 Mass. 265, 269 n. 4 (2004)(records of medical and social service providers, including D.S.S.); *Commonwealth v. Beal*, 429 Mass. 530 (1999)(complainant); *Commonwealth v. Wanis*, 426 Mass. 629 (1998)(Rule 14 does not reach Internal Affairs Division records because the IAD is not part of the prosecution team).

Under (a)(1)(A), each of the following items must be produced for the defense at or before the pretrial conference, provided it exists and is (1) relevant to the case, (2) within the possession or control of the prosecution or its agents as just defined, and (3) not the subject of a motion for a protective order, which stays its production under subdivision (a)(1)(C)). Even before the 2004 revision, the prosecution was required to turn over most of these items in District Court and the Boston Municipal Court pursuant to Dist./Mun. Ct. Rule 3 and M.G.L. c. 218, sec. 26A, which eliminated trial de novo and mandated broad discovery to the defense.

(a)(1)(A)(i). Statements of the defendant(s). Rule 14 previously included the written or recorded statements of the defendant and any co-defendants in its category of mandatory discovery which must be disclosed. The 2004 revision includes these items as automatic discovery, and adds "the substance of any oral statements" of the defendant or co-defendants. This addition reflects the broader discovery requirement established by case law. The substance of the defendant's oral statements must be provided "as a matter of course to counsel for the defendant" according to Commonwealth v. Lewinski, 367 Mass. 889, 903 (1975). See also Commonwealth v. Gilbert, 377 Mass. 887, 892–94 (1979); Commonwealth v. Lopes, 25 Mass. App. Ct. 988 (1988); Commonwealth v. Lapka, 13 Mass. App. Ct. 24, 31 (1982); Commonwealth v. Janard, 16 Mass. App. Ct. 931, 933 (1983).

Subdivision (a)(1)(A)(ii). Grand jury minutes and statements of grand jury witnesses. The rule had developed in both the Massachusetts and federal courts that pretrial discovery of grand jury minutes was to be allowed when the defendant showed a "particularized need" that the release of a part or all of the minutes would serve. Dennis v. United States, 384 U.S. 855 (1966); Commonwealth v. Cook, 351 Mass. 231 (1966), cert denied, 385 U.S. 981. The Supreme Judicial Court in Commonwealth v. Stewart, 365 Mass. 99 (1974), announced a new rule mandating that the court routinely order discovery of "the grand jury testimony of any person called as a Commonwealth witness which is related to the subject matter of his testimony at trial. The defense will not be required to show 'particularized need.'" *Id.* at 105–06.

Superior Court Rule 63 (1974) mandates that stenographic notes of all testimony given before a grand jury shall be taken, but that transcripts thereof need be furnished only as required by the prosecuting officer unless the court orders otherwise. It is within the judge's discretion under this subdivision to order the transcription of a stenographic record. *Compare* Commonwealth v. Pimental, 5 Mass. App. Ct. 463 (1977)(no error in ordering trial to proceed despite Commonwealth's failure to comply with order to supply defendant with copy of grand jury minutes where minutes not transcribed).

Commonwealth v. Stewart, supra, required production of the grand jury testimony of "any person called as a Commonwealth witness." 365 Mass. 106. However, since 1979 Rule 14 has required the pretrial production of the relevant "written or recorded statements of a person who has testified before a grand jury," whether or not the Commonwealth intends to call that person at trial. There is no requirement that the grand jury testimony have been given before the grand jury which returned the indictment against the defendant, Commonwealth v. Cavanaugh, 371 Mass. 46, 57–58 (1976), as long as that testimony is relevant to an issue at trial. *See* Commonwealth v. Barnett, 371 Mass. 87, 94 (1976). However, a 2004 amendment requires the prosecution to also provide automatic discovery of the minutes of the grand jury that brought the indictment in the case.

Although the relevant grand jury testimony must be routinely supplied by the Commonwealth, if the judge rules that the requested testimony is either not relevant or is to be the subject of a protective order, a motion for production under Mass. R. Crim. P. 23 must be made at the time the witness testifies on direct examination.

(a)(1)(A)(iii). Exculpatory evidence. This provision requires the prosecution to provide automatic discovery of "any facts of an exculpatory nature." It derives from the constitutional requirement established in Brady v. Maryland, 373 U.S. 83 (1963), that "the suppression by the prosecution of evidence favorable to an accused upon request violates due process where the evidence is material either to guilt or punishment, irrespective of the good faith or bad faith of the prosecution." *Id.* at 87. *Accord*, United States v. Agurs, 427 U.S. 97 (1976); Moore v. Illinois, 408 U.S. 786, 794 (1972); Commonwealth v. Adrey, 376 Mass. 747, 753 (1978); Commonwealth v. Ellison, 376 Mass. 1, 21 (1978). This duty is also an ethical one, imposed on the prosecution by S.J.C.Rule 3:07, R. P.C. 3.8(d).

The term "exculpatory" is not intended to be technically construed as encompassing alibi or other complete proof of innocence. Rather, case law *at present* defines exculpatory evidence to include (but not necessarily be limited to) all information that is material and favorable to the accused because it tends to cast doubt on defendant's guilt as to any essential element of the crime charged, including the degree of the crime; or tends to cast doubt on the credibility of a Commonwealth witness, or on the accuracy of scientific evidence, that the government anticipates offering in its case-in-chief. In Commonwealth v. Ellison, 376 Mass. 1, 22 n. 9 (1978), the S.J.C. interpreted the Brady obligation as encompassing "evidence which provides some significant aid to the defendant's case, whether it furnishes corroboration of the defendant's version of facts, calls into question a material, although not indispensable, element of the prosecution's version of the events, or challenges the credibility of a key

Commonwealth witness." *See also* United States v. Bagley, 473 U.S. 667, 676–77 (1985) (impeachment material); Commonwealth v. Hill, 432 Mass. 704 (2000); Commonwealth v. Tucceri, 412 Mass. 401, 414 (1992); Blumenson, Fisher and Kanstroom, *Massachusetts Criminal Practice,* Sec. 16.6 (1998)(defining exculpatory evidence and the legal consequences of non–disclosure). The S.J.C. has advised that even minor prior inconsistent statements are exculpatory in the case of an important witness, and urged prosecuting attorneys to "become accustomed to disclosing all material which is even possibly exculpatory, as a prophylactic against reversible error and in order to save court time arguing about it." Commonwealth v. St. Germain, 381 Mass. 256, 262 n. 10 (1980).

To establish a violation of the rule of Brady v. Maryland, *supra*, as incorporated herein, the defendant must demonstrate upon review that evidence actually existed, Commonwealth v. Adams, 374 Mass. 722, 732–33 (1978); that evidence would have tended to exculpate him, Commonwealth v. Pisa, 372 Mass. 590, 595 (1977), cert denied, 434 U.S. 869 (1977); and that the Commonwealth failed to disclose it upon proper request, Commonwealth v. Gilday, 367 Mass. 474, 487 (1975). *Accord*, Commonwealth v. Adrey, 376 Mass. 747. (1978). Evidence in possession of the police is Brady material even if the prosecutor is unaware of it, so the prosecutor has a constitutional duty of inquiry. Commonwealth v. Martin, 427 Mass. 816, 823–24 (1998); Commonwealth v. Baldwin, 385 Mass. 165, 177 n. 12 (1982); Kyles v. Whitley, 514 U.S. 419 (1995); However, there is no duty to search for exculpatory evidence outside the Commonwealth's possession. Commonwealth v. Martinez, 437 Mass. 84 (2002); Arizona v. Youngblood, 488 U.S. 51 (1988)(police do not have a constitutional duty to perform any particular tests). Evidence in government hands but not within the possession, custody or control of the prosecution team presents a special problem. In Commonwealth v. Wanis, 426 Mass. 639 (1998), the Supreme Judicial Court found that particular evidence in the files of the Internal Affairs Division of the police could be exculpatory evidence to which the defendant was constitutionally entitled, but because the I.A.D. was not a part of the prosecution team it could not be reached by the discovery mechanisms of Rule 14. The proper mechanism in such cases is a subpoena. *Id.* at 644; *Commonwealth v. Lampron,* 441 Mass. 265, 269 n. 4 (2004)(records of medical and social service providers, including D.S.S.);

Although exculpatory evidence is included within automatic discovery, if the defense is aware of items that may be exculpatory that have not been delivered by the pretrial conference, it should file a discovery motion specifying that evidence under subdivision (a)(2), as the magnitude of the error in non-disclosure is in part a function of the specificity of the motion. Commonwealth v. Tucceri, 412 Mass. 401 (1992); Commonwealth v. Gallarelli, 399 Mass. 17, 21 n.5 (1987). In addition to preserving the issue for appeal, specificity can operate to avoid appeals by directing the attention of the prosecutor to those particular materials which the defendant believes would be helpful. A prosecutor cannot be expected to appreciate the significance of every item of evidence in his possession to any possible defense which the defendant may assert. Commonwealth v. Pisa, 372 Mass. 590, 595 (1977), cert denied, 434 U.S. 869 (1977). Assembly and disclosure of those materials — and thus the entire pretrial phase of the proceedings — is expedited by specific motions in such cases.

(a)(1)(A)(iv). Names, addresses, and dates of birth of the Commonwealth's prospective non-law enforcement witnesses. Names, addresses, and the criminal records of prospective witnesses were originally denominated discretionary discovery in Rule 14(a). However, some case law emerging around the time of the Rule's promulgation mandated such discovery. Commonwealth v. Adams, 374 Mass. 722, 732 (1978); Commonwealth v. Clark, 363 Mass. 467, 474 (1973); Commonwealth v. Ferrara, 368 Mass. 182 (1975)(confrontation right to juvenile records which indicate bias despite confidentiality of juvenile records). *But see* Halner v. Commonwealth, 378 Mass. 388, 390 (1979). Legislation since makes defense discovery of names and addresses of Commonwealth witnesses a matter of right in district courts, and also requires the court to order the Probation Department to produce the prior criminal record of these witnesses. G.L. c. 218 s. 26A.

Therefore, in 2004 Rule 14 was amended to include this provision, which requires automatic discovery of the names, addresses, and birthdates (which are necessary to locate a witness' criminal record) of prospective witnesses *other than* law enforcement witnesses, which are covered by subdivision (a)(1)(v)). It also requires the Commonwealth to provide this information to the Probation Department. A separate provision in this Rule, (a)(1)(D), requires the court to order the Probation Department to furnish the parties with the criminal record of all defendants and Commonwealth witnesses within five days of the Commonwealth's notification to the department of its prospective witnesses.

In some cases, there may be special circumstances warranting non-disclosure of a witness' address. For example, if a witness may be threatened or endangered by a defendant, disclosure should not be compelled. See e.g., Commonwealth v. Rivera, 424 Mass. 266, 269–72 (1997); Commonwealth v. French, 357 Mass. 356, 399 (1970). The identity of informants may be privileged against disclosure in some cases. Commonwealth v. Abdelnour, 11 Mass. App. Ct. 531. 538 (1981); Roviaro v. United States, 353 U.S. 53 (1957). There are several options available in such cases. Ordinarily the Commonwealth will move for a protective order under subdivision (a)(6), which stays automatic discovery of the contested item until the issue can be resolved by the court. If after a witness' identity and address have been disclosed, the court is advised that his safety is endangered, there is provision in Mass. R. Crim. P. 35 for the perpetuation of testimony. Once a witness' testimony is recorded, little reason remains for the defendant to attempt to intimidate him. Finally, subdivisions (a)(6) and (a)(7) provide specifically that the court can order information (including witnesses' names) to be disclosed only to defendant's counsel and not to the defendant himself. *See also* G.L. 258B s. 3(h), which allows a person to request non-disclosure of his or her address, telephone number, or place of employment or education, and if granted then prohibits disclosure of that information in open court.

If, after the initial phase of discovery, it is determined that additional witnesses will be called, the defendant may, in the discretion of the court, be granted time within which to investigate and interview that witness. *See generally* Commonwealth v. Lopez, 433 Mass. 406, 413–414 (2001); Commonwealth v. Baldwin, 385 Mass. 165, 176–77 (1982); Commonwealth v. Mains, 374 Mass. 733 (1978).

The Commonwealth's Probation Department records reveal with assurance only Massachusetts convictions; where known facts suggest that a witness has a record elsewhere, an inquiry as to out-of-state convictions may be a reasonable practice. Commonwealth v. Corradino, 368 Mass. 411, 422 (1975). *See also* Commonwealth v. Donahue, 396 Mass. 590, 599 (1986)(normally the state must produce the federal "rap sheet" of witnesses to the defendant).

(a)(1)(A)(v). Names and business addresses of prospective law enforcement witnesses. In the first two decades of practice under Rule 14, it had become routine for the Commonwealth to provide the business address of a police witness when ordered to provide all prospective witness addresses. The 2004 amendment recognized this, and the fact that felons are statutorily barred from serving as police officers, by creating this subdivision that modifies the Commonwealth's obligation with regard to prospective witnesses who are law enforcement officers. In such cases the Commonwealth must provide automatic discovery of the name and business address of the witness. Further discovery concerning the witness, including home address and birthdate, may be pursued by motion under subdivision (a)(2). However, in the rare case where a prospective police witness has a criminal record which could be used for impeachment, the Commonwealth should provide automatic discovery of this fact under subdivision (a)(1)(A)(iii)(exculpatory evidence).

(a)(1)(A)(vi). Intended expert opinion evidence. The Commonwealth's intended expert opinion evidence was made part of automatic, mandatory discovery to the defense under this 2004 provision. The subdivision specifies that expert opinion evidence includes "the identity, current curriculum vitae, and list of publications of each intended expert witness, and all reports prepared by the expert that pertain to the case." Discovery of the prosecution's expert opinion is also a matter of statutory right in district court. G.L. c. 218, s. 26A.

Subdivision (vi) does *not* apply to experts who may have been interviewed or retained but whose testimony or reports are not intended for use at trial. It also does not apply to expert evidence relevant to a defendant's criminal responsibility or to a mental impairment relevant to mens rea, which are governed by Rule 14(b)(2) as described *infra*.

Under the general automatic discovery provisions of subdivision (a)(1)(A), only evidence in the possession, custody or control of the prosecution at the time of the pretrial conference is due at that time. A party may discover or retain an expert later in the course of trial preparation, at which point it must provide discovery of its intended expert opinion evidence under the continuing duty requirement of subdivision (a)(4).

(a)(1)(A)(vii). Material and relevant police reports, photographs, tangible objects, intended exhibits, reports of physical examinations of any person or of scientific tests or experiments, and statements of persons the Commonwealth intends to call as witnesses. Most of these items were treated as "discretionary discovery" in the original provisions of Rule 14. The 2004 amendments to Rule 14 make discovery of these items mandatory and automatic. However, in district court defense discovery of these items had been mandated since 1994 under M.G.L. c. 218, s. 26A par. 2, which requires the prosecution to provide discovery of certain specified items and also "any material and relevant evidence [and] documents." Because subdivision (vii) does not include the latter term but only specified items, the Commonwealth's mandatory discovery obligation remains broader in district courts than in courts where sec. 26A does not apply. Nevertheless, the items included in this subdivision are likely to exhaust the Commonwealth's evidence in many cases and therefore obviate the need for filing motions to obtain further discovery in those cases.

This provision encompasses "statements of persons," but with regard to this item limits the scope of discovery to statements of only those persons whom the Commonwealth intends to call as witnesses at trial. Rule 14(d), described *infra*, defines the term "statement." Mass. R. Crim. P. 23(b) affords an overlapping right to a testifying witness' statements prior to cross examination. Similarly, subdivision (iii) requires that a witness' prior inconsistent statement be provided to opposing counsel as exculpatory evidence, insofar as it would diminish the credibility of the witness. Commonwealth v. St. Germain, 381 Mass. 256, 262 (1980). Some statements of persons who may *not* be prospective witnesses must be produced for defense discovery pursuant to other provisions, such as police reports included in this subdivision, co-defendants' statements pursuant to subdivision (i), grand jury minutes and relevant testimony pursuant to subdivision (ii), exculpatory statements pursuant to subdivision (iii), and statements made by or in the presence of an identifying witness relevant to the issue of identity pursuant to subdivision (viii).

This subdivision also mandates automatic discovery of any relevant reports of physical examinations or scientific tests or experiments. Often but not always, these will be in conjunction with expert opinion evidence, which must be produced pursuant to subdivision (vi). Under this provision such reports must be produced if relevant, whether or not intended for use at trial and whether or not prepared by an expert. When tests of physical evidence have been conducted by the Commonwealth, the defense also has a right of access to that evidence to conduct its own independent tests, at least unless the testing of another available item would be as probative on the issue. Commonwealth v. Neal, 392 Mass. 1, 10 (1984); Commonwealth v. Nicholson, 20 Mass. App. Ct. 9, 16 n.4 (1985). Regarding access to the government's evidence for investigation generally, *see* California v. Trombetta, 467 U.S. 479, 485 (1984) (Sixth Amendment right); Commonwealth v. Balliro, 349 Mass. 505 (1965) (art. 12 right).

(a)(1)(A)(viii). Identification procedures and statements. Under this subdivision promulgated in 2004, the Commonwealth must provide automatic discovery of any statements made by, or in the presence of, an identifying witness if relevant to the issue of identity or to the fairness or accuracy of the identification procedures. It must also provide a summary of identification procedures to the defense.

Many cases are not "wrong man" cases. In such cases, if there have been no identification procedures the prosecution is not required to do anything under this subdivision. But where identification is at issue and procedures have been used they should be disclosed. Commonwealth v. Dougan, 377 Mass. 303, 316 (1979)(the due process right to fair identification procedures "would mean little if it did not carry with it the right to be informed of the details of any out-of-court identification, even if it were not used at trial"). Prior Massachusetts case law (as well as the constitutional obligation to disclose exculpatory evidence) affords the defendant a right to discover whether the witness previously failed to identify him. Commonwealth v. Clark, 378 Mass. 392, 403 (1979).

(a)(1)(A)(ix). Promises, rewards or inducements made to prospective witnesses. Such inducements offered by the prosecution affect the credibility of the witness, and the defense is constitutionally entitled to discover it. See Commonwealth v. Hill, 432 Mass. 704, 715 (2000); Gigilo v. United States, 405 U.S. 150, 154–55 (1972); Commonwealth v. Luna, 410 Mass. 131, 139–40 (1991). An implicit quid pro quo may exist, and must be disclosed, even in the absence of any explicit promise.

Even if there are no explicit promises, any implicit quid pro quo must be revealed. Commonwealth v. Johnson, 21 Mass. App. Ct. 28, 40–41 (1985). Moreover, even if there is *no* quid pro quo by which consideration is given in return for testimony, any material understanding or agreement between the government and a key witness or his attorney must be revealed. Commonwealth v. Collins, 386 Mass. 1, 11–12 (1982); Commonwealth v. Gilday, 382 Mass. 166, 175–76 (1980)(promise to witness' attorney not known to witness must be disclosed); California v. Trombetta, 467 U.S. 479, 485 (1984).

This subdivision requires the Commonwealth to disclose promises, rewards or inducements to only those witnesses it *intends to present at trial*. However, this obligation does not exhaust the Commonwealth's constitutional obligation to disclose all exculpatory evidence, or its parallel obligation under subdivision (iii) of this Rule. Such exculpatory evidence could, for example, include a promise or inducement made to a hearsay declarant whom the Commonwealth does not intend to present at trial.

(a)(1)(B). Reciprocal discovery to the prosecution. Originally, Rule 14(a)(3) (as then numbered) provided that a court could order reciprocal discovery to the prosecution in its discretion. This provision derived from then-recent holdings of the Supreme Court relative to the rights of the prosecution to discover the defendant's case.

The very integrity of the judicial system and public confidence in the system depend on full disclosure of all the facts, within the framework of the rules of evidence. To ensure that justice is done, it is imperative to the function of courts that compulsory process be available for the production of evidence needed either *by the prosecution* or by the defense.

United States v. Nixon, 418 U.S. 683, 709 (1973)(emphasis supplied). Under these cases, the prosecution was empowered to call upon the power of the court to compel production of evidence which will facilitate full disclosure of all the relevant facts. United States v. Nobles, 422 U.S. 225 (1975). *See* Commonwealth v. Hanger, 377 Mass. 503 (1979); Blaisdell v. Commonwealth, 372 Mass. 753 (1977); Commonwealth v. Edgerly, 372 Mass. 337 (1977); Commonwealth v. Lewinski, 367 Mass. 889, 903 n. 10 (1975).

Revisions to Rule 14 in 2004 expanded the defense obligation by making reciprocal discovery mandatory, not discretionary. Under Rule 14(a)(1)(B), when the prosecution certifies that it has disclosed and made available the discoverable items it has, it is entitled to automatic reciprocal discovery of specified categories of defense evidence. Any differences between the obligations on the defense and prosecution result from asymmetrical constitutional requirements. There are two, deriving from the defendant's right to due process and privilege against self-incrimination. First, the defense obligation is limited to evidence it intends to introduce at trial, whereas the prosecution must turn over some evidence it may intend not to use (and in the case of exculpatory evidence, is constitutionally required to do so). Since its promulgation in 1979, Rule 14 has limited reciprocal discovery to "intended" defense evidence because the U.S. Supreme Court case of Williams v. Florida, 399 U.S. 78 (1970), upheld the constitutionality of prosecutorial discovery only on the basis of this limitation. According to *Williams*, the Fifth Amendment privilege limits prosecutorial discovery to evidence the defendant intends to introduce. Intention in this context is, of course, fluid as investigation and discovery progress and the defendant is subject to the continuing duty imposed by subdivision (a)(4), infra. The second difference between the prosecution and defense obligations is in the order of disclosure: the prosecution gets its discovery only after it has produced discovery for the defense. In Wardius v. Oregon, 412 U.S. 470 (1973), the Supreme Court found reversible error, in violation of due process, for the prosecution to receive categories of discovery without discovery of those same categories to the defense. To assure against such reversible error, and to allow defendants to assess what evidence they should introduce as required by the *Williams* "intended evidence" constitutional limitation, the Rule provides for defense discovery to take place first.

Under subdivision (a)(1)(B), automatic reciprocal discovery to the prosecution commences only after the Commonwealth has delivered all defense discovery required pursuant to the automatic discovery provisions of (a)(1)(A) and any other extant discovery orders. After that point, and by a date agreed to by the parties or ordered by the court, the defense is obligated to provide the Commonwealth with discovery of the names, addresses, dates of birth, and statements of its intended witnesses; and of every relevant item described in subdivisions (a)(1)(A) (vi), (vii), and (ix) that it intends to use at trial. In Commonwealth v. Reynolds, 429 Mass. 388 (1999), a pretrial agreement signed by the parties obligated defense counsel to provide not only statements of witnesses it intended to introduce, but also statements of *Commonwealth* witnesses that it intended to use in cross examination. The specified obligations under this subdivision do not go so far. Just as subdivision (a)(1)(A)(vii) requires the Commonwealth to disclose the statements of *its own* intended witnesses, subdivision (a)(1)(B) requires the defense to provide discovery of the statements of its own witnesses, not all witnesses. Discovery of other statements must be pursued by motion.

A separate provision in this Rule affords the prosecution notice of certain defenses if the defendant intends to assert one of them at trial. As discussed *infra*, under subdivision (b), the defense must provide notice and/or discovery if it intends to defend on the basis of alibi, lack of criminal responsibility, or the existence of a license, claim of authority or ownership, or exemption.

(a)(1)(C). Stay of automatic discovery; sanctions. According to this subdivision, the automatic discovery provisions of subdivision (a)(1) which stem directly from the Rule "shall have the force and effect of a court order." If a party violates one of its automatic discovery obligations, the court may impose any of the sanctions permitted for non-compliance with a court order under subdivision 14(c). *Id.*

This provision also allows a party to seek a judicial determination of whether an item should not be subject to discovery, notwithstanding its inclusion in the automatic discovery regime. If a party has good cause for declining to provide such discovery, it should move for a protective order. This subdivision provides that the filing of such a motion stays production of the item pending a ruling by the court.

(a)(1)(D). Record of convictions of the defendant, codefendants and prosecution witnesses. Under this provision, at arraignment the court must issue an order to the Probation Department, directing it to deliver to all parties its record of all prior complaints, indictments, and dispositions of the defendants and all witnesses identified pursuant to subdivision (a)(1)(A)(iv). Under the latter provision, the Commonwealth must notify the Probation Department of its intended witnesses. The court's order must also require the Probation Department to provide this information no later than 5 days

after it has been notified by the Commonwealth of its witnesses. *See also* Reporter's Notes to (a)(1)(A)(iv).

(a)(1)(E). Notice and preservation of evidence. Under this provision promulgated in 2004, *if* the prosecutor becomes aware of the existence of an item that would be subject to mandatory discovery but for the fact that it is not within the prosecutor's possession, custody or control, the prosecutor must notify the defendant of the existence (and if known, the location) of the item. The defendant may then move for an order requiring the individual or entity in possession of the item to preserve it for a specified period of time. If either party successfully moves for such a preservation order under subsection (E)(ii), that party should insure that the order is served on the individual or entity in possession of the item.

This subdivision does not require the prosecution to search for new evidence. It applies only to evidence *already* known to exist without inquiry; and only to evidence held by independent third parties who are *not* part of the prosecution team and thus not subject to rule 14 discovery. In addition to insuring that the defense is aware of potentially significant evidence known to the prosecution, this provision is intended to place the defendant in a position to move the court for an order preventing destruction of the evidence so that a subsequent defense subpoena may be effective. To provide a party or independent witness with recourse when a preservation order is inappropriate or unnecessary, the rule provides for motions to vacate or modify the preservation order, or to protect the probative value of the evidence by alternative means.

(a)(2). Motions for discovery. Although most discovery is made automatic under the rule, there may be additional items not encompassed by Rule (a)(1)(A) that are properly discoverable. Rule 14(a)(2) provides for motions to discover such material. Such a motion may only be made for discovery of material and relevant evidence that is not encompassed by the automatic discovery provisions; if items in the latter category are not produced, the proper response is to file a motion to compel discovery or, in an appropriate case, a motion for sanctions under (a)(1)(C).

The timing and deadlines for discovery motions are set out in Rule 13(d)(1). Additionally, because the Commonwealth must provide discovery before it can obtain reciprocal discovery, subdivision (a)(2) provides that the Commonwealth may file a motion for discovery only after it has filed a Certificate of Compliance under subdivision (a)(3).

Nothing in this Rule is intended to prohibit the court from ex parte consideration of discovery motions in appropriate circumstances, consistent with law.

(a)(3). Certificates of compliance. Under this subdivision, each party must file a certificate of compliance when it has met its automatic or court-ordered discovery obligations (other than disclosure of expert reports, which may be written late in the case). The certificate must identify each item provided.

The certificate is properly filed when, to the best of its knowledge and after reasonable inquiry, the party has provided discovery of all covered items it *then* has. The provision recognizes that additional discovery will likely occur as new information and witnesses are obtained, and mandates a supplemental certificate for that purpose.

(a)(4). Continuing duty. This is taken from Rule 3.220(f) of the Florida Rules of Criminal Procedure and has a counterpart in the Federal Rule, the New Jersey Rule and the ABA Standards Relating to Discovery and Procedure Before Trial (Approved Draft, 1970). This subdivision imposes a continuing duty to promptly provide court-ordered discovery as additional information is acquired. The duty continues throughout the trial, Commonwealth v. Costello, 392 Mass. 393 (1984), and includes an obligation to correct previous disclosures that have turned out to be inaccurate. Commonwealth v. Borans, 379 Mass. 117, 153 (1979); Commonwealth v. Gilbert, 377 Mass. 887, 893 (1979).

(a)(5). Work product. Work product is protected under the federal rule and the ABA Standards, *supra*. The sanctity of a party's "work product" is a well recognized principle that was specifically approved by the Supreme Court relating to its application to discovery under the Federal Rules of Civil Procedure, Hickman v. Taylor, 329 U.S. 495 (1947). The principle has equal applicability to criminal discovery.

The definition of "work product" is drawn in part from Rules of Criminal Procedure (ULA) rule 421(b)(1)(1974). The subdivision defines "work product" as limited to portions of documents containing the "legal research, opinions, theories or conclusions of the adverse party or its attorney and legal staff" or statements of the defendant made to counsel or counsel's legal staff. Although witness statements obtained by counsel are not deemed work product under this definition, *see* Commonwealth v. Paszko, 391 Mass. 164, 186–88 & n.27 (1984) and Commonwealth v. Bing Sial Liang, 434 Mass. 131, 140 (2001), in some cases "witness statements may be so commingled with counsel's theories, or so revealing of counsel's mental processes by virtue of the areas covered, as to be unsegregable and constitute work product." Blumenson, Fisher and Kanstroom, Massachusetts Criminal Practice (1998), Sec. 16.2C, citing Commonwealth v. Lewinski, 367 Mass. 889, 902 (1975) and Upjohn v. United States, 449 U.S. 383, 400–01 (1981).

(a)(6)(Protective orders) and (a)(7)(Amendment of discovery orders). Although Rule 14(a) provides for automatic, mandatory discovery, if danger or abuse can be shown, or a privilege preventing disclosure applies, discovery need not be granted. The power of the court to restrict the scope of otherwise permissible discovery is recognized in the Federal Rule, the New Jersey Rule, the Florida Rule, and the ABA Standards, *supra*.

Protective orders are designed for the unusual case in which the granting of discovery will work to the injury of the person whose material is to be discovered or to the injury of some third person. Although a party must move for such an order, this does not imply that the moving party always has the burden of proof. Ordinarily the party or person opposing discovery has the burden of showing why the discovery of requested materials must be denied or granted subject to restriction, but in certain cases including some privileges, statutory or case law may provide that the party seeking disclosure has the burden of proof. Therefore the 2004 revision added to this subdivision an explicit recognition that "nothing in this provision shall be deemed to alter the allocation of the burden of proof with regard to the matter at issue, including privilege."

With respect to automatic discovery mandated under subdivision (a)(1), a motion for a protective order stays the discovery obligation pending a ruling by the court. Subdivision (a)(1)(C). With respect to discretionary discovery sought by motion under subdivision (a)(2), a protective order may be sought only to restrict (and not prevent completely) the scope of discovery, because if reasons exist to wholly deny discovery *ab initio*, it is within the discretion of the court to deny the discovery motion, without requiring the opponent to the motion to seek a protective order. If what is sought is the modification of an existing discovery order the following subdivision, (a)(7), provides the appropriate remedy.

The provisions of these subdivisions that the court may, in certain situations, grant discovery to a defendant on condition that the material to be discovered be available only to counsel for the defendant, is merely a corollary to that sentence of subdivision (a)(6) which gives the court the power, upon a sufficient showing, to deny, restrict, or defer discovery or inspection. Fed. R. Crim. P. 16(d) and ABA Standards § 4.4 give the judge this same power. The commentary accompanying the ABA Standard indicates that this restriction on disclosure means "such adjustment of the time, place, recipient, and use of disclosures as may commend themselves in the particular case." ABA Standards, supra, comment at 102. Since it is constitutionally permissible to limit pretrial discovery in criminal cases, United States v. Randolph, 456 F2d 132 (3d Cir 1972), there should be no objection to the Commonwealth's giving material only to defendant's counsel in certain situations, which is preferable to denying discovery altogether. It is contemplated that this provision of Rule 14 will sometimes be used to prevent a defendant from seeing his own psychiatric report. In some instances, the mental well-being of the defendant could be adversely affected if he or she has access to such a report. United States v. Moody, 490 F2d 866 (5th Cir 1974). Although the defendant in Moody had been convicted, the same rationale is applicable to the defendant awaiting trial.

Nothing in this Rule is intended to prohibit the court from *ex parte* consideration of a motion for a protective order in appropriate circumstances, consistent with law.

(a)(8). Waivers and agreements to alter discovery rights. Rule (a)(8) allows the parties to change discovery requirements by waiver or agreement, including both the scope and timing of discovery. The waiver or agreement must be in writing, signed by the waiving party or the parties to the agreement, identify the specific items included, and be served upon all parties.

Subdivision (b). Special procedures. Rule 14(b), governing notice to the prosecution of certain intended defenses, was left essentially unchanged by the 2004 revision, except for the substitution of gender neutral language. Under this provision, the prosecution is entitled to notice, and in some cases discovery, when the defendant intends to defend on the basis of alibi, lack of criminal responsibility, or the existence of a license, claim of authority or ownership, or exemption.

The philosophy and provisions of this subdivision are drawn from Commonwealth v. Edgerly, 372 Mass. 337 (1977); Blaisdell v. Commonwealth, 372 Mass. 753 (1977); and a number of other sources. *See* Commonwealth v. Hanger, 377 Mass. 503 (1979); Commonwealth v. Lewinsky, 367 Mass. 889, 902–03 and n. 10 (1975); Fed. R. Crim. P. 12.1, 12.2; Fla. R. Crim. P. 3.200; Rules of Criminal Procedure (ULA) rule 423(a)(1) (2) (1974); National Advisory Commission on Criminal Justice Standards and Goals, *Courts*, standard 4.9 (1973).

The Supreme Court in Williams v. Florida, 399 U.S. 78 (1970), held that a prosecutor could obtain discovery from a defendant by requesting information pertaining to evidence which the defendant intended to offer at trial without violating the fifth amendment privilege against self-incrimination. Although the defense is compelled to make an accelerated determination of the evidence it is to introduce at trial, the nature of this compulsion is such that it is not unconstitutional. While the holding of the Supreme Court related only to the discovery of a defendant's prospective alibi defense, the decision indicates that the rule announced is applicable to other forms or prosecutorial discovery as well. *See* Commonwealth v. Lewinsky, 367 Mass. 889, 903 n 10 (1975). The types of disclosures mandated by subdivision (b)(1)–(3) occur in those situations where in fairness the Commonwealth is entitled at least to notification.

(b)(1). Notice of alibi. Notice–of–alibi rules have been in existence at least since 1927 and as of 1978 at least half the statutes had such rules. *See* Williams v. Florida, 399 U.S. 78, 81–82 (1970). The substance of this subdivision is taken from Commonwealth v. Edgerly, 372 Mass. 337, 344–45(1977).

In Gilday v. Commonwealth, 360 Mass. 170 (1971), the Supreme Judicial Court, mindful of the implications of the Supreme Court's decision in Williams v. Florida, 399 U.S. 78 (1970), held that discovery by the prosecution of the defendant's intent to interpose an alibi defense and of the names of any prospective witnesses in support of the alibi violated due process because in Massachusetts a defendant did not have an equal right to discovery from the prosecution. Nearly all a defendant's rights to discovery had been subject to judicial discretion under Massachusetts law. The Supreme Court in Wardius v. Oregon, 412 U.S. 470 (1973), specifically held that reciprocity in discovery rights was a constitutional prerequisite to the validity of prosecutorial discovery. That requirement is supplied by subdivisions (b)(1)(B)–(C).

The purpose of such a rule is two-fold. First, alibi defenses are the most frequently and easily fabricated defenses. *See*, for example, Commonwealth v. Harris, 364 Mass. 236, 238 (1973). By requiring the defendant to give the Commonwealth pretrial notice of his intent to interpose such a defense and a list of witnesses to be used in support of the alibi, the defendant is prevented from using an eleventh hour defense, and the Commonwealth is given the tools necessary to uncover fabrication. Fairness to the defendant is insured by granting him discovery of the identities of rebuttal witnesses. Second, the need to grant continuances on the basis of surprise at trial will no longer exist.

As the *Edgerly* court observes, if, in the court's discretion, no other order is appropriate to serve the purposes of this rule, it may exclude the testimony of any undisclosed witness offered by either party as to the defendant's absence from, or presence at, the scene of the alleged offense. 372 Mass. at 345. Exclusion of such alibi testimony, other than the defendant's, is authorized in subdivision (b)(1)(D). *See* Commonwealth v. Cutty, 47 Mass. App. Ct. 671, 673 (1999). If a defendant against whom a sanction is imposed is convicted, he or she may, of course, preserve for argument on appeal the issue of whether imposition of that sanction amounted to an abuse of discretion or the denial of any constitutional right. *Commonwealth v. Edgerly, supra* at 339 and 343. *See generally* Commonwealth v. Reynolds, 429 Mass. 388, 398–399 (1999); Commonwealth v. Durning, 406 Mass. 485, 496 (1990); Commonwealth v. Chappee, 397 Mass. 508, 518 (1986); Taylor v. Illinois, 484 U.S. 400 (1988). In Commonwealth v. Hanger, 377 Mass. 503 (1979), the procedure authorized by this subdivision was substantially approved in the absence of any rule, even though the Commonwealth's motion was not presented until the second day of trial.

(b)(2). Notice of intent to defend by lack of criminal responsibility or mental incapacity. The subject matter of this subdivi-

sion was treated by the Supreme Judicial Court in Blaisdell v. Commonwealth, 372 Mass. 753 (1977), and the procedures contained herein substantially restate those dictated by the court in that opinion. At its inception, this subdivision governed only a prospective insanity defense, but since then the Supreme Judicial Court has extended its scope to govern other defense claims based on mental impairment or incapacity, including mental incapacity to entertain mens rea, Commonwealth v. Diaz, 431 Mass. 822 (2000), or to voluntarily waive Miranda rights, Commonwealth v. Ostrander, 441 Mass. 344 (2004).

Provisions requiring notice of an intent to rely upon a defense of lack of criminal responsibility or diminished mental capacity have a different purpose than notice-of-alibi provisions. The latter, as noted above, are directed at preventing "eleventh-hour" or fabricated alibis. On the other hand, because rebuttal of an insanity defense requires a degree of expertise on the part of a cross-examiner that can only be gained through pretrial research, this subdivision is intended to meet the need of a prosecutor to become familiar with the complex nature of this type of defense.

The Supreme Judicial Court in Gilday v. Commonwealth, 360 Mass. 170 (1971), upheld an order to the defendant to disclose his intent with regard to the interposition of a defense of not guilty by reason of insanity despite the fact that the system of discovery then in effect was non-reciprocal. Implicit in the court's opinion is the fact that due process did not require reciprocation by the Commonwealth because only notice of intent to interpose the defense, and not the identity of the defendant's witnesses nor the evidence intended to support of that defense, was required. In short, the only response by the Commonwealth would be that opposition to that defense would be presented, which does not reasonably require notice.

As the court recognized in *Blaisdell v. Commonwealth*, the privilege against self-incrimination is not implicated by a mere notice requirement. 372 Mass. at 767. Nor is there anything in that privilege which precludes

> an order requiring a defendant to reveal on motion of the prosecution the information of (a) whether a defendant pursuant to such defense intends to offer expert testimony thereon; (b) the names and addresses of such expert witnesses as the defense intends to call; (c) whether a defendant's experts intend to rely in whole or in part on statements of the defendant pertaining to his mental state at or about the time of the commission of the alleged crime or as it may be otherwise relevant to the issue of his mental responsibility therefor.

Id. That information is required by subdivisions (b)(2)(A)(ii)–(iii) of this rule. If the defendant files the notice of intent, the Commonwealth is subject to the reciprocity requirements of this rule and as imposed by Commonwealth v. Edgerly, 372 Mass. 337, 342 (1977); Blaisdell v. Commonwealth, 372 Mass. 753 (1977).

If in answer to subdivision (b)(2)(A)(iii) the defendant responds that his expert witnesses intend to rely upon statements of the defendant as a foundation for their testimony, or if that fact becomes apparent from inquiry by the judge or developments in the case, the judge may order that the defendant submit to a psychiatric examination. (b)(2)(B).

> If . . . a defendant voluntarily submits to psychiatric interrogation as to his inner thoughts, the alleged crime and other relevant factors bearing on his mental responsibility and, on advice of counsel, voluntarily proffers such evidence to the jury, we feel that the offer of such expert testimony based in whole or in part on a defendant's testimonial statements constitutes a waiver of the privilege [against self–incrimination] for such purposes . . . In short, by adopting this approach, a defendant who seeks to put in issue his statements as the basis of psychiatric expert opinion in his behalf opens to the State the opportunity to rebut such testimonial evidence in essentially the same way as if he himself has testified . . . Under such a view there would be no violation of his privilege should the court then order him under c 123, § 15, to submit to psychiatric examination so that the jury may have the benefit of countervailing expert views, based on similar testimonial statements of a defendant in discharging its responsibility of making a true and valid determination of the issues thus opened by a defendant.

Blaidell v. Commonwealth, 372 Mass. 753, 765–766 (1977)(citation omitted). The privilege against self-incrimination does not bar the Commonwealth's use of evidence which incriminates the defendant, but rather the compelled production of such evidence by the defendant; yet it is clear that an examination pursuant to this subdivision constitutes compelled production. Blaisdell v. Commonwealth, supra, 372 Mass. at 758. *See also* Commonwealth v. Baldwin, 426 Mass. 105 (1997); Commonwealth v. Wayne W., 414 Mass. 218, 228–30 (1993). Therefore, if the psychiatric report contains evidence of a testimonial character, it is not to be made available to either party unless the defendant is to testify on his own behalf or is to offer expert testimony based on his statements ([b][2][B][iii][c]) or unless the defendant, by motion, requests that it be made available. ([b][2][B][iii][b]). Ordering the examination to be conducted prior to a defendant's formal waiver of the privilege against self-incrimination is justified on the basis that:

> To require the Commonwealth to wait may . . . well cause it to be disadvantaged in meeting the issues raised by a defendant's evidence by virtue of the fact that its expert witnesses will lack adequate time to examine properly a defendant and his evidence in order to prepare for trial. Alternatively, a continuance of the trial may cause needless expense to the Commonwealth, unnecessary inconvenience to the court and to the jurors, and disruption of the progress of the trial which may cause harm to either the prosecution or the defense. To require the Commonwealth to wait until such a waiver occurs at trial seems not only inexpedient and unwise but also unnecessary.

Blaisdell v. Commonwealth, supra, 372 Mass. at 767.

(b)(3). Notice of defenses based on license, authority, ownership or exemption. This subdivision, promulgated in 1979, requires the defendant to furnish the prosecution with notice of his intent to rely upon a defense based upon a license, claim of authority or ownership, or exemption.

A "license" is defined as a right granted by the Commonwealth or other competent authority to do a particular act or carry on a particular business which, without such license, would be unlawful. A "claim of authority" is an assertion that the claimant has received an express or implied right to do an act from one lawfully empowered to grant such right. A "claim of ownership" is an assertion that the claimant has a right of possession enforceable in a court. An "exemption" is a release from a duty or obligation to which others are subject.

The requirement of disclosure in this subdivision is reasonable when considered in light of "the proposition that the end of justice will best be served by a system of liberal discovery which gives both parties the maximum possible amount of information with which to prepare their cases and thereby reduce surprise at trial." Wardius v. Oregon, 412 U.S. 470, 473 (1973).

The concept of mandating notice of criminal defenses other than alibi and insanity, subdivisions (b)(1)–(2) supra, was advocated by the American Bar Association in the ABA *Standards Relating to Discovery and Procedure Before Trial* (Approved Draft, 1970):

Subject to constitutional limitations, the trial court may require that the prosecuting attorney be informed of the nature of *any* defense which defense counsel intends to use at trial . . .

Id., § 3.3 (emphasis supplied).

Considerations of reciprocity, dealt with by the United States Supreme Court in connection with notice-of-alibi statutes in Wardius v. Oregon, 412 U.S. 470 (1973) and Williams v. Florida, 399 U.S. 78 (1970), and by the Supreme Judicial Court in Gilday v. Commonwealth, 360 Mass. 170 (1971), are inapposite to subdivision (b)(3). The Williams–Wardius cases hold that state statutes requiring notice to be given the prosecution that an alibi defense is to be raised at trial, with the names of witnesses to be called in support of the alibi, are constitutionally valid only if the defendant is allowed reciprocal rights to receive the names of governmental rebuttal witnesses. The statutes in those decisions, unlike Rule 14(b)(3), involved the furnishing of prosecutors with both notice of, and information pertaining to, the intended defense. See subdivisions (b)(1) and (b)(2), *supra*. It was to this information gathering aspect of the Oregon and Florida statutes that the Supreme Court addressed itself:

It is fundamentally unfair to require the defendant to divulge *the details* of his own case while at the same time subjecting him to the hazard of surprise concerning refutation of the very pieces of evidence which he disclosed to the State.

Wardius, supra at 476 (emphasis added).

Subdivision (b)(3) involves the giving only of notice. The defendant is not required to divulge the details of his intended defense. Mere notification of intent to raise a defense without more does not trigger considerations of reciprocity. *See* Commonwealth v. Gilday, 360 Mass. 170 (1971); Blaisdell v. Commonwealth, 372 Mass. 764, 767 (1977).

The sanction for failure to comply with the requirement of subsection (b)(3) is drawn from Fed. R. Crim. P. 12.1 and 12.2. *See also* ABA *Standards, supra*, § 4.7. The court may "for cause shown" ease or lift the requirements of this subdivision.

Subdivision (c). Sanctions for noncompliance. Sanctions may be issued under this subdivision for violations of discovery obligations established either by the court's order or by the automatic discovery provisions of the rule. The automatic discovery obligations of subsections (a)(1)(A)(discovery to the defense) and (a)(1)(B)(discovery to the prosecution) stem from the rule itself rather than an order issued by the court, but subdivision (a)(1)(C) provides that they "have the force and effect of a court order, and failure to provide discovery pursuant to them may result in application of any sanctions permitted for non-compliance with a court order under subdivision 14(c)."

The general sanction provision of subdivision (c)(1) is paralleled by Fed. R. Crim. P. 16(d)(2) and New Jersey R. Crim. P. 3:13–3(f). The power to exclude alibi evidence other than the defendant's testimony is recognized in Commonwealth v. Edgerly, 372 Mass. 337, 342 (1977), and is express in subdivision (b)(1)(D), *supra*. *See* Federal Rule 12.1; ABA Standards Relating to Discovery and Procedure Before Trial § 4.7(a) (Approved Draft, 1970). Subdivision (b)(2)(B), *supra*, provides the sanction for failure of the defendant to comply with a court-ordered psychiatric examination.

"Rights and duties are ephemeral indeed without remedies." ABA Standards, supra, comment at 107. Subdivision (c)(1) is intended to provide the general rule and is based on that assumption that the trial court is in the best situation to consider the opposing arguments concerning a failure to comply with a discovery order and to fashion an appropriate remedy. Remedies for non-compliance with discovery requirements could include a further order for discovery, a continuance, exclusion of certain testimony, or "such other order as [the Court] deems just under the circumstances." (c)(1). A continuance or in some cases a mistrial may be the proper remedy when delayed disclosure leaves the defendant unable to "make effective use of the evidence in preparing and presenting his case." *See* Commonwealth v. Baldwin, 385 Mass. 165, 175 & n.10 (1982); Commonwealth v. St. Germain, 381 Mass. 256, 262–63 (1980). (There is, it should be noted, a statutory limitation on the court's power to grant a continuance without the defendant's consent. When the defendant is in custody, General Laws c 276, § 35 provides a thirty day limit in such instances.) A dismissal barring retrial may be required when a discovery violation has resulted in irremediable harm to the defendant's opportunity to obtain a fair trial.

Although the court may exercise its general sanction power under subdivision (c)(2) to exclude evidence, it is generally better to grant each party the freedom to present all relevant evidence at trial. However, in regard to alibi evidence, there is sufficient likelihood of abuse to require specifically empowering the court to exclude extrinsic alibi evidence other than the defendant's testimony, and this is specifically authorized by section (b)(1)(D). A court should only employ this sanction, however, when convinced that a failure to comply with an order was deliberate and prejudicial to the Commonwealth. Subdivision (c)(2) also provides that evidence concerning the defense of lack of criminal responsibility cannot be excluded except as provided by subdivision (b)(2).

Subdivision (d). Definition of "statement." The definition of the term "statement" was initially drawn from 18 USC § 3500(e)(1)–(2) (1969, Supp. 1976) and Commonwealth v. Lewinski, 367 Mass. 889 (1975). Definition (d)(1) defines "statements" which have been written by the percipient witness himself or herself. Definition (d)(2) defines "statements" which have been contemporaneously recorded by someone other than the speaker or writer.

The definition in (d)(1) was amended in 2004 to delete the requirement that writings by witnesses be signed or otherwise adopted by the author. In Commonwealth v. Lewinski, 367 Mass. 889, 901–903 (1975), the Court stated that without any showing of particularized need, a defendant was entitled to all "prior written statements of prosecution witnesses which are available to the prosecution and are related to the subject," and subdivided this into three categories of mandatorily discoverable statements: "any statement made by the witness and in some definite way approved by him, a transcript of a contemporaneous verbatim or substantially verbatim stenographic or other recording of an oral statement by the witness, and a written report consisting of a statement by the witness." The 2004 revision reflects a decision that the definition of written statements made by a witness should encompass *written* statements of a percipient witness which have not been formally adopted by the witness, and the third category in Lewinsky, although not without ambiguity, implies as much. Under 14(d)(1), these will have been written by the percipient witness himself, and under 14(d)(2), such statements must still be "a *substantially verbatim* recital of an oral declaration and which is *recorded contemporaneously* with the making of the oral declaration" (emphasis added). In both cases, such evidence is generally relevant at trial; for example, one need not show a prior statement was adopted as accurate and complete by the writer in order to admit and demonstrate its inconsistencies. Prior informal statements, not intended for court, are not only often admissible at trial but often more probative than formal signed statements in anticipation of litigation. On this view, if the police have taken a statement of a witness who will testify, it should be discoverable to the defense.

However, the revised definition does not extend to "drafts or notes that have been incorporated into a subsequent draft or final report." It would be unnecessary and burdensome to require that every rough draft of a police report or other statement to be turned over in addition to the final one.

Subdivision (e), which formerly specified the time limits for discovery, was deleted as part of the 2004 revisions. In the amended rules, the deadlines for automatic, non-motion discovery are detailed in Rule 14(a)(1)(a) and (b), and the deadlines for discovery (and other) motions are found in Rule 13(d).

Rule 15. Interlocutory Appeal

(Applicable to District Court and Superior Court)

(a) Right of Interlocutory Appeal.

(1) *Right of Appeal Where Pretrial Motion to Dismiss or for Appropriate Relief Granted.* The Commonwealth shall have the right to appeal to the appropriate appellate court a decision by a judge granting a motion to dismiss a complaint or indictment or a motion for appropriate relief made pursuant to the provisions of subdivision (c) of Rule 13.

(2) *Right of Appeal Where Motion to Suppress Evidence Determined.* A defendant or the Commonwealth shall have the right and opportunity to apply to a single justice of the Supreme Judicial Court for leave to appeal an order determining a motion to suppress evidence prior to trial. If the single justice determines that the administration of justice would be facilitated, the justice may grant that leave and may hear the appeal or may report it to the full Supreme Judicial Court or to the Appeals Court.

Publisher's Note

See infra, under "Standing Orders of the Supreme Judicial Court," the standing order concerning applications to a single justice pursuant to Mass.R.Crim.P. 15(a)(2).

(3) *Right of Appeal Where Transfer of Delinquency Proceeding Is Denied.* The Commonwealth shall have the right to appeal to the Appeals Court a decision by a judge denying transfer of a delinquency proceeding pursuant to G.L. c. 119, § 61.

(4) *Probable Cause Hearings.* No interlocutory appeal or report may be taken of matters arising out of a probable cause hearing.

(b) Procedural Requirements.

(1) *Time for Filing Appeal.* An appeal under subdivisions (a)(1) and (a)(3) shall be taken by filing a notice of appeal in the trial court within thirty days of the date of the order being appealed. An application for leave to appeal under subdivision (a)(2) shall be made by filing within ten days of the issuance of notice of the order being appealed, or such additional time as either the trial judge or the single justice of the Supreme Judicial Court shall order, (a) a notice of appeal in the trial court, and (b) an application to the single justice of the Supreme Judicial Court for leave to appeal.

(2) *Record.* The record for an interlocutory appeal shall be defined and assembled pursuant to Massachusetts Rule of Appellate Procedure 8. The judge shall make all findings of fact relevant to the appeal or the application for leave to appeal within the period specified in subdivision (b)(1) for filing the notice of appeal.

(c) Determination of Motions. Any motion the determination of which may be appealed pursuant to this rule shall be decided by the judge before the defendant is placed in jeopardy under established rules of law.

(d) Costs Upon Appeal. If an appeal or application therefor is taken by the Commonwealth, the appellate court, upon the written motion of the defendant supported by affidavit, shall determine and approve the payment to the defendant of his or her costs of appeal together with reasonable attorney's fees to be paid on the order of the trial court upon the entry of the rescript or the denial of the application.

(e) Stay of the Proceedings. If the trial court issues an order which is subject to the interlocutory procedures herein, the trial of the case shall be stayed and the defendant shall not be placed in jeopardy until interlocutory review has been waived or the period specified in subdivision (b)(1) for instituting interlocutory procedures has expired. If an appeal is taken or an application for leave to appeal is granted, the trial shall be stayed pending the entry of a rescript from or an order of the appellate court. If an appeal or application therefor is taken by the Commonwealth, the defendant may be released on personal recognizance during the pendency of the appeal.

Amended April 29, 1986, effective July 1, 1986; amended effective April 14, 1995; March 1, 1996.

Reporter's Notes

This rule is derived from G.L. c. 278, § 28E (as amended) but the statute has been extended to the District Court and in other regards has been significantly altered.

Subdivision (a). This subdivision grants the Commonwealth the right to prosecute an interlocutory appeal where a motion to dismiss has been granted, and where a motion to transfer a delinquency proceeding has been denied. Pursuant to G.L. c. 278, § 28E, the appeal will be had in the Supreme Judicial Court if from a Superior Court order, and in the Appeals Court if from a District Court order.

Subdivision (a)(2) grants both the defendant and the Commonwealth the right to apply to a Single Justice of the Supreme Judicial Court for leave to appeal a ruling on a motion to suppress evidence, whether the charge is of a felony or misdemeanor. The Commonwealth's interlocutory remedy is predicated upon the fact that an adverse pretrial ruling will, in the case of a motion to dismiss, "preclude a public trial and ... entirely terminate the ... proceedings," Burke v. Commonwealth, 373 Mass. 157, 161, 365 N.E.2d 811 (1977), or, in the case of a motion to suppress, result in the irretrievable loss of the right to present legal evidence. Commonwealth v. Boswell, 374 Mass. 263, 267, 372 N.E.2d 237 (1978). The defendant is afforded this procedure because in some circumstances interlocutory appeal will conserve judicial resources and spare all parties the ordeal of a trial that would ultimately prove futile.

Pursuant to former G.L. c. 278, § 28E, the only interlocutory appeal available in a criminal case was from a decision, order, or judgment of the Superior Court allowing a motion to dismiss or to grant appropriate relief or allowing or denying a motion to suppress evidence where the crime charged was a felony. E.g., Whitmarsh v. Commonwealth, 366 Mass. 212, 214, 316 N.E.2d 610 (1974). Subsequently, several developments expanded the availability of this appellate remedy, as reflected in subdivision (a) of the Rule. First, in Rosenberg v. Commonwealth, 372 Mass. 59, 62, 360 N.E.2d 333 (1977), the Supreme Judicial Court endorsed the practice of reporting orders of dismissal of misdemeanor charges in the Superior Court pursuant to former G.L. c. 278, § 30A (St.1954, c. 528). Rule 15(a) merely recognized that an interlocutory appeal is the appropriate vehicle for review of such orders and that the procedure can be of utility in the District Court. Second, although the initial version of the Rule placed certain restrictions on interlocutory appeals from District Court orders, in 1995 subdivisions (a) and (b) were rewritten to apply the Superior Court provisions to District Court appeals, as mandated by the legislation which replaced the de novo trial system with a single trial system. G.L. c. 218, §§ 26A and 27A(g) provide that review in district court jury and jury-waived cases "be had directly by the appeals court, by appeal, report or otherwise in the same manner provided for trials of criminal cases in the Superior Court." Finally, a 1991 amendment to G.L. c. 278, § 28E afforded the Commonwealth an additional remedy, permitting interlocutory appeal from the denial of its motion to transfer a delinquency proceeding pursuant to G.L. c. 119, § 61. Rule 15(a)(3) reflects this amendment.

In the District Court, there is to be no interlocutory appeal or report of matters arising out of a probable cause hearing. ([a][4]).

Subdivision (b). The time within which an interlocutory appeal is to be taken or applied for is set out in subdivision (b)(1). The time limits specified alter former practice. Former G.L. c. 278, § 28E (St.1967, c. 898, § 1) limited this period to ten days after entry of the decision, order, or judgment to be appealed from. When Rule 15 was promulgated, it substituted the requirement that a claim of appeal or application be filed "within a reasonable time" and before the defendant is placed in jeopardy. In 1996, the Rule was changed to provide a thirty day time limit for an appeal by right; and a ten day time limit to file an application for leave to appeal which may be extended by the trial judge if necessary. The amendment was intended to insure that the trial will be stayed for a sufficient period to allow the defendant or the Commonwealth to pursue the remedies afforded by the rule. The amendment also clarifies the appellant's obligation to file a notice of appeal in the trial court even if an application for leave to appeal has not yet been granted, as required by Mass.R.A.P. 4(b) and by Commonwealth v. Guaba, 417 Mass. 746, 751, 632 N.E.2d 1217 (1994).

Although the time limits for invoking the rule's procedures ordinarily commence with the filing of the order being appealed, in Commonwealth v. Lewin (no. 3), 408 Mass. 147, 150, 557 N.E.2d 721 (1993) the Supreme Judicial Court held that the Commonwealth's failure to file an interlocutory appeal until after disposition of its motion to reconsider did not render the appeal untimely.

Subdivision (b)(2) requires the trial judge to make any relevant findings of fact within the time allowed to the parties for seeking an interlocutory remedy. The statement of the proceedings should be such that the reviewing court is able to determine that an interlocutory appeal is appropriate, i.e., that interlocutory review "would contribute more to the reasonably prompt disposition of the case than it would to delay." Commonwealth v. Vaden, 373 Mass. 397, 400, 367 N.E.2d 621 (1977). A 1996 amendment to Rule 15 incorporates by reference the requirements of Massachusetts Rule of Appellate Procedure 8 governing the contents and assembly of the record on appeal.

Subdivision (c). In order to preserve the Commonwealth's right to appeal, the rule requires that the judge's ruling on the motion be made before the defendant is placed in jeopardy. Otherwise, a dismissal after commencement of trial would bar re-prosecution of the defendant on double jeopardy grounds and render any successful appeal of the dismissal meaningless. See Costarelli v. Commonwealth, 374 Mass. 677, 373 N.E.2d 1183 (1978).

Subdivision (d). This subdivision was drafted to dispel any uncertainty concerning the defendant's right to reimbursement of his or her costs of appeal and attorney's fees. The appellate court is to determine the amount to be paid to the defendant, which payment is to be received from the Commonwealth. See Superior Court Rule 53(7) (1974). In 1995 the Standing Advisory Committee on Criminal Procedure reconsidered several rules concerning the payment of reasonable attorney's fees to insure that they are consistent. In Latimore v. Commonwealth, 417 Mass. 805, 633 N.E.2d 396 (1994), the Commonwealth filed an application for leave to appeal the allowance of the defendant's motion for a new trial under the provisions of G.L. c. 278, § 33E. The application was denied by the single justice and the defendant moved for costs and attorney's fees. Because the application for appeal in a capital case was controlled by section 33E, rather than Rule 30(c)(8)(B), no specific provision for payment of fees and costs was available. The court observed that this situation, while rare, presented an anomaly in the rules. The committee has reconsidered the appropriate rules and has added language to this Rule and to Rule 30 to address the situation where the Commonwealth is making application for leave to appeal and adds directions for payment of fees and costs upon the denial of the application.

Subdivision (e). Subdivision (e) restates in part former G.L. c. 278, § 28E (St.1967, c. 898, § 1). The first sentence of this subdivision was added in 1996 to insure an adequate opportunity for the defendant and prosecutor to invoke the interlocutory procedures afforded by this rule. The trial must be stayed until the period for seeking an interlocutory remedy has passed, or been waived; and if an appeal is then taken or an application granted, the stay is extended until disposition of the appeal. Former § 28E mandated the release of the defendant on personal recognizance if the appeal was taken on behalf of the Commonwealth; under this rule such release is discretionary.

Rule 16. Dismissal by the Prosecution

(Applicable to District Court and Superior Court)

(a) Entry of a Nolle Prosequi. A prosecuting attorney may enter a nolle prosequi of pending charges at any time prior to the pronouncement of sentence. A nolle prosequi shall be accompanied by a written statement, signed by the prosecuting attorney, setting forth the reasons for that disposition.

(b) Entry of Nolle Prosequi During Trial. After jeopardy attaches, a nolle prosequi entered without the consent of the defendant shall have the effect of an acquittal of the charges contained in the nolle prosequi.

Reporter's Notes

While similar to Fed.R.Crim.P. 48, this rule is a formalization of prior Massachusetts practice.

Subdivision (a). The decision to enter a nolle prosequi as to all or any distinct part of pending charges is discretionary with the prosecuting attorney.

> Power to enter a nolle prosequi is absolute in the prosecuting officer from the return of the indictment up to the beginning of trial, except possibly in instances of scandalous abuse of the authority.

Commonwealth v. Dascalakis, 246 Mass. 12, 18, 140 N.E. 470 (1923). *See* Manning v. Municipal Court of Roxbury, Mass. Adv.Sh. (1977) 679, 682–83, 361 N.E.2d 1274; Commonwealth v. Massod, 350 Mass. 745, 217 N.E.2d 191 (1966). This rule is consistent with the common law. See 30 MASS. PRACTICE SERIES (Smith) §§ 854, 858 (1970, Supp.1978).

Rule 48(a) of the Federal Rules of Criminal Procedure permits dismissal by the prosecution only with leave of court. It did not seem advisable to engraft this additional requirement onto the Massachusetts rule, however, since it is doubted that the court has the power to compel the Commonwealth to proceed with a case which it does not believe warrants prosecution. See 3 C. WRIGHT, FEDERAL PRACTICE & PROCEDURE: CRIMINAL § 812 at 304 (1969).

The term "prosecuting attorney" in this rule is intended to include municipal attorneys, e.g., city solicitors, prosecuting a case. See G.L. c. 278, § 15.

General Laws c. 277, § 70A is the basis for the second sentence of this subdivision which requires the prosecuting attorney to file a statement of his reasons for entering a nolle prosequi. 30 MASS. PRACTICE SERIES (Smith) § 857 (1970, Supp.1978); see ABA *Standards Relating to the Prosecution Function* § 4.4 (Approved Draft, 1971).

Subdivision (b). Once a case has reached trial, the defendant has been placed in jeopardy and has the right to have the issue of his guilt adjudicated. Commonwealth v. Massod, 350 Mass. 745, 217 N.E.2d 154 (1966). If after commencement of trial, but before return of the verdict, the prosecuting attorney enters a nolle prosequi without the consent of the defendant, the defendant is effectually acquitted of those charges which are the subject of the nolle prosequi. Commonwealth v. Hart, 149 Mass. 7, 20 N.E. 310 (1889); Commonwealth v. Dascalakis, 246 Mass. 12, 140 N.E. 470 (1923); Commonwealth v. Sitko, Mass.Adv.Sh. (1977) 668, 361 N.E.2d 1258; 30 MASS. PRACTICE SERIES (Smith) § 855 (1970). This comports substantially with Fed.R.Crim.P. 46(a), which prohibits the filing of a dismissal during trial without the consent of the defendant.

Rule 17. Summonses for Witnesses

(Applicable to District Court and Superior Court)

(a) Summons.

(1) *For Attendance of Witness; Form; Issuance.* A summons shall be issued by the clerk or any person so authorized by the General Laws. It shall state the name of the court and the title, if any, of the proceeding and shall command each person to whom it is directed to attend and give testimony at the time and place specified therein.

(2) *For Production of Documentary Evidence and of Objects.* A summons may also command the person to whom it is directed to produce the books, papers, documents, or other objects designated therein. The court on motion may quash or modify the summons if compliance would be unreasonable or oppressive or if the summons is being used to subvert the provisions of Rule 14. The court may direct that books, papers, documents, or objects designated in the summons be produced before the court within a reasonable time prior to the trial or prior to the time when they are to be offered in evidence and may upon their production permit the books, papers, documents, objects, or portions thereof to be inspected and copied by the parties and their attorneys if authorized by law.

(b) Defendants Unable to Pay. At any time upon the written ex parte application of a defendant which shows that the presence of a named witness is necessary to an adequate defense and that the defendant is unable to pay the fees of that witness, the court shall order the issuance of an indigent's summons. The witness so summoned shall be paid in accordance with the provisions of subdivision (c) of this rule. If the court so orders, the costs incurred shall be assessed to the defendant in accordance with the General Laws or the provisions of these rules.

(c) Payment of Witnesses. Expenses incurred by a witness summoned on behalf of a defendant determined to be indigent under this rule as well as expenses incurred by a witness summoned on behalf of the Commonwealth, as such expenses are determined in accordance with the General Laws, shall be paid after the witness certifies in a writing filed with the court the amount of his travel and attendance.

(d) Service.

(1) *By Whom; Manner.* A summons may be served by any person authorized to serve a summons in a civil action or to serve criminal process. A summons shall be served upon a witness by delivering a copy to him personally, by leaving it at his dwelling house or usual place of abode with some person of suitable age and discretion then residing therein, or by mailing to the witness' last known address.

(2) *Place of Service.*

(A) Within the Commonwealth. A summons requiring the attendance of a witness at a hearing or a trial may be served at any place within the Commonwealth.

(B) Outside the Commonwealth or Abroad. A summons directed to a witness outside the Commonwealth or abroad shall issue and be served in a manner consistent with the General Laws.

(3) *Return.* The person serving a summons pursuant to this rule shall make a return of service to the court.

(e) Failure to Appear. If a person served with a summons pursuant to this rule fails to appear at the time and place specified therein and the court determines that such person did receive actual notice to appear, a warrant may issue to bring that person before the court.

Publisher's Note

The Summons for Witness form follows Rule 6, supra.

Reporter's Notes

The prototype for this rule is found in Fed.R.Crim.P. 17. See Massachusetts and Federal Rule of Civil Procedure 45; Rules of Criminal Procedure (U.L.A.) Rule 731 (1974). Rule 17 is for the most part in accord with prior Massachusetts law. Statutes which are consistent with this rule—e.g., G.L. c. 233, §§ 5–6, which authorize sanctions for a witness' failure to comply with a summons—are to remain in effect.

"Summons" as used in this rule (and Mass.R.Crim.P. 35[b]) is intended to refer to what has traditionally been expressed by the terms "summons" and "subpoena."

The right of a defendant to have process issued for the attendance of necessary witnesses is founded in the Constitution:

> [I]t is the Sixth Amendment itself that in terms guarantees 'compulsory process for obtaining witnesses in [the accused's] favor,' and this is paralleled in substance by article 12 of our Declaration of Rights.

Blazo v. Superior Court, 366 Mass. 141, 145, 315 N.E.2d 857 (1974). A defendant's right to have summonses issued on his behalf may also be grounded in the sixth amendment right of confrontation.

Subdivision (a). This subdivision is drawn with little change from Fed.R.Crim.P. 17(a), (c); *accord* Rules of Criminal Procedure (U.L.A.) rule 731(a), (c) (1974).

Subdivision (a)(1). General Laws c. 233, § 1 provides that persons in addition to the clerk of court, i.e., notaries public and justices of the peace, may issue summonses for witnesses in criminal cases but only "upon request of the attorney general, district attorney or other person who acts in the case in behalf of the Commonwealth or of the defendant."

The proceedings contemplated by this subdivision include depositions to perpetuate testimony pursuant to Mass. R.Crim.P. 35.

Subdivision (a)(2). The provision of this subdivision authorizing the court to order the production of evidence prior to its use at trial or in other judicial proceedings is not intended to permit the use of summonses to subvert the discovery rule, Mass.R.Crim.P. 14. Rather, it is to permit the court to avoid delay where the production of many books, papers, documents, or other objects would delay the proceedings if not ordered until their commencement.

Subdivision (b). The subdivision, loosely modeled upon Fed.R.Crim.P. 17(b), is drafted in response to the Supreme Judicial Court's decision in Blazo v. Superior Court, 366 Mass. 141, 315 N.E.2d 857 (1974). There the court held that when indigency and the necessity for witnesses are shown, a defendant is to have the witnesses summoned at the expense of the Commonwealth, suggesting the following procedure:

> [A] defendant believing himself entitled will apply to the competent judge—ex parte if the defendant should so desire—supporting his application by affidavit showing his inability to pay the fees involved, setting out the names and addresses (if known) of the persons to be summoned, and stating why their attendance is necessary to an adequate defence. The judge may require the submission of further data.

Id. at 145–46 (footnote omitted). The court further explained that the reason for permitting ex parte application

> is that, just as a defendant able to foot the costs need not explain to anyone his reasons for summoning a given witness, so an impecunious defendant should be able to summons his witnesses without explanation that will reach the adversary.

Id. at 145 n. 8.

There is a significant difference between this subdivision and its counterpart under the federal rule. The summons that is to be issued under this rule is a prosecutor's summons, G.L. c. 277, § 68, and not a court summons, G.L. c. 233, § 1. This is because G.L. c. 233, § 3 provides that witnesses summoned on behalf of the defendant are entitled to prepayment of some of their expenses. If this requirement were applicable to witnesses for indigent defendants, an added burden would be imposed on the court clerks. Therefore, witnesses for indigent defendants are to be summoned by the Commonwealth pursuant to G.L. c. 277, §§ 68–69, and will not require prepayment. This procedure parallels that of Rules of Criminal Procedure (U.L.A.) Rule 731(b) (1974). *Compare* Fed.R.Crim.P. 17(b), (d).

Subdivision (c). The expenses involved in securing the attendance of a witness on behalf of a defendant or the Commonwealth in a criminal proceeding consist of the fees of the officer serving the process and fees to the witness for travel and attendance. G.L. c. 233, §§ 2–3; c. 262, §§ 8(B)(3), 29.

General Laws c. 262, § 29 requires that a witness certify in writing the amount of his travel and attendance costs and serves as a basis for this subdivision. The statute additionally provides that where the witness has been summonsed by the Commonwealth, the certificate must be accompanied by a voucher signed by the attorney general or the district attorney stating that such fees are due the witness for his attendance. This rule adds witnesses summonsed by indigent defendants to this category and provides for the payment of their expenses in the same manner as the expenses of Commonwealth witnesses are paid. Where the district attorney is prosecuting the case, G.L. c. 12, § 24 (as amended, St.1978, c. 478, § 10) authorizes the payment of expenses of government-summonsed witnesses from Commonwealth funds. See G.L. c. 213, § 8, which the Supreme Judicial Court in *Blazo* stated would authorize county payment (now the Commonwealth, § 8 as amended, St.1978, c. 478, § 127) of witnesses ordered to attend on behalf of an indigent defendant. *Blazo v. Superior Court,* supra, at 146.

Under this rule, all witnesses are to be paid established witness fees. This is a departure from prior law, G.L. c. 277, § 69, which required prosecution witnesses to attend without pay unless the court directed the payment of their fees and expenses.

Subsection (d). The first sentence of subdivision (d)(1) embodies the substance of Mass.R.Civ.P. 45(c), which permits service "by any person who is not a party and is not less than 18 years of age." *Compare* Fed.R.Civ.P. 45(c) *with* Fed. R.Crim.P. 17(d). This procedure accords with that under G.L. c. 233, § 2, which provides that a summons for a witness may be served by an officer qualified to serve civil process or by some other disinterested person. Added is provision for service of summonses by persons authorized to serve criminal process. The rule would appear to allow service by counsel for the defendant or Commonwealth, although this practice has been criticized as perhaps "unwise." 8 MASS. PRACTICE SERIES (Smith & Zobel) Reporter's Notes at 136 (1977); *compare* Supreme Judicial Court Rule 3:22, *incorporating* ABA *Canons of Professional Ethics,* Canon 19 (1972); ABA *Code of Professional Responsibility* DR 5–102, EC 5–9, 5–10 (1970).

The manner of service under this rule is for the most part consistent with procedure under prior law and the civil rules, G.L. c. 233, § 2; Mass.R.Civ.P. 45(c), but adds that a summons may be served by mail. This last means of service is not available in cases of witnesses summonsed by non-indigent defendants, since tender or payment of fees to the witness is a prerequisite to compelling his attendance. G.L. c. 233, § 3.

Subdivision (d)(2)(A) is taken from the second sentence of Mass.R.Civ.P. 45(e).

General Laws c. 233, §§ 13A–13C; otherwise known as the *Uniform Law to Secure the Attendance of Witnesses from Without the State in Criminal Proceedings,* provides a simple solution to the problem of obtaining out-of-state witnesses to appear in criminal proceedings. As long as the subject jurisdiction has adopted the Act the court will be able to secure attendance. Notwithstanding the provisions of G.L. c. 233, §§ 13A–13C and c. 277, § 66, it has been stated that the right of a defendant to compulsory process for witnesses who are necessary to his defense does not by statute automatically extend beyond the territory of the Commonwealth. Commonwealth v. Dirring, 354 Mass. 523, 238 N.E.2d 508 (1968). *Accord* Commonwealth v. Edgerly, Mass.App.Adv.Sh. (1978) 400, 375 N.E.2d 1.

Even though a defendant may not have the statutory right to compulsory process for necessary witnesses, the Constitution requires that the state make a good faith effort to obtain the presence of certain witnesses. In addition to the Uniform Act, state courts should avail themselves of two other avenues to secure the attendance of witnesses. The court in Barber v. Page, 88 S.Ct. 1318, 390 U.S. 719, 20 L.Ed.2d 255 (1968), determined that where the defendant has a constitutional right to confront a witness, a state must seek his attendance via: (1) 28 U.S.C. § 2241(c)(5) (1971), which gives federal courts the power to issue writs of habeas corpus ad testificandum at the request of state prosecutors in the case of the prospective witnesses currently in federal custody; and (2) the issuance of a writ of habeas corpus ad testificandum by state courts. The existing policy of the United States Bureau of Prisons is to permit federal prisoners to testify in state court criminal proceedings pursuant to the issuance of such writs.

With respect to witnesses who are citizens or residents of the United States, but currently beyond its jurisdiction, the Court in Mancusi v. Stubbs, 92 S.Ct. 2308, 408 U.S. 204, 33 L.Ed.2d 293 (1972), enunciated the limitations of the applicability of 28 U.S.C. § 1783 (1966), which provides in pertinent part:

> (a) A court of the United States may order the issuance of a subpoena requiring the appearance as a witness before it, or before a person or body designated by it, of a national or resident of the United States who is in a foreign country, or requiring the production of a specified document or other thing by him, if the court finds that particular testimony or the production of the document or other thing by him is necessary in the interest of justice * * *

With respect to § 1783, the court stated:

> We have been cited to no authority applying this section to permit subpoena by a federal court for testimony in the state felony trial, and certainly the statute on its face does not appear to be designated for that purpose.

Id. at 212. (Footnote omitted.)

The *Mancusi* court concluded that Tennessee was powerless to compel the attendance of the absent witness, then a resident of Sweden, and that, therefore, the state had not denied the respondent the right of confrontation as guaranteed by the sixth and fourteenth amendments.

NOTICE OF A HEARING REGARDING THE RELEASE OF RECORDS	DOCKET NO.	Trial Court of Massachusetts
CASE NAME Commonwealth v.		
NOTICE IS ISSUED TO: third-party subject keeper of records		COURT NAME & ADDRESS

NOTICE OF A HEARING REGARDING THE RELEASE OF RECORDS [1]

To:

name of third-party subject	name of keeper of records
address 1	address 1
address 2	address 2
city, state, zip code	city, state, zip code

The defendant in this case has filed a motion with the Court to be allowed to inspect the records of

_______________ for the dates from _______________ to _______________
(third-party subject) (date range)

made by _______________
(name and professional title of caregiver or other person/entity that created the records, if known)

that are being held by _______________
(name and address of keeper of records)

1 For use in criminal, youthful offender, or delinquency cases whenever a defendant seeks pretrial inspection of a third party's records that are likely to be covered by a statutory privilege. Use a separate form for each keeper of records and each third-party subject.

AOTC 12/2007

THE COURT HAS ORDERED THE PROSECUTING ATTORNEY'S OFFICE TO NOTIFY YOU THAT A HEARING ON THE ATTACHED MOTION HAS BEEN SCHEDULED FOR

______________________ in Courtroom ______ of the ________________ Courthouse,
(date and time)

which is located at: ____.

At the hearing, the judge will decide if the records are privileged and if they are relevant to the case against the defendant. Under the law, certain records (e.g., psychiatric or other counseling records) may be confidential, or "privileged." The purpose of the hearing is to determine whether the judge will order the records to be sent to Court for the defendant's lawyer to inspect. If the judge allows the defendant's motion, the Court will make privileged records available only to defense counsel, pending further order of the Court, except for limited disclosures to support staff and to other attorneys for purposes of consultation as described in the Protective Order that counsel will be required to sign before reviewing the records.

If the records are privileged under the law, the Court will assume that you do not wish to give up (waive) any privilege at this time, unless you provide (or have provided) a written waiver before or at the hearing. Your absence from the hearing will not constitute a waiver of any privilege you may have under the law.

You have the right to attend the hearing. You can take part in the hearing yourself or you may (but need not) obtain a lawyer to represent you. Victims have the right to talk to the prosecuting attorney before the hearing.

THIS HEARING WILL BE YOUR ONLY OPPORTUNITY TO ADDRESS THE COURT REGARDING THE RELEASE OF THESE RECORDS.

______________________ ______________________________
date signature of Assistant District Attorney/Assistant Attorney General

If you have any questions about this notice, you may contact ______________________________
(name of prosecutor or advocate)

at ______________________ at telephone number ________________.
(name of prosecuting office)

AOTC 12/2007

NOTICE ACCOMPANYING COURT-ORDERED SUMMONS FOR NON-PRIVILEGED RECORDS	DOCKET NO.	Trial Court of Massachusetts
CASE NAME **Commonwealth v.**		
KEEPER OF RECORDS TO WHOM THIS NOTICE IS ISSUED AND ADDRESS	COURT NAME & ADDRESS	

Pursuant to Rule 17(a)(2) of the Massachusetts Rules of Criminal Procedure, 378 Mass. 885 (1979), the Court has issued the enclosed summons to produce records in the above-captioned matter. A judge has determined that the records ordered produced are not likely to be protected by a statutory privilege, or the third-party subject has waived any applicable statutory privilege.

The records ordered by the Court must be delivered to: ______________________

____
(address of Clerk of Court)

on or before the return date on the summons in a sealed envelope or box clearly marked as follows:

COMMONWEALTH v. ______________________ **(defendant)**

DOCKET NUMBER: ______________________

From: ______________________ **(name of keeper of records)**

Date: ______________________

NON-PRIVILEGED RECORDS: NOT FOR PUBLIC INSPECTION

Entered: ______________________	Clerk of Court By: ______________________

AOTC. 12/2007

NOTICE ACCOMPANYING COURT-ORDERED SUMMONS FOR PRESUMPTIVELY PRIVILEGED RECORDS	DOCKET NO.	Trial Court of Massachusetts
CASE NAME **Commonwealth v.**		
KEEPER OF RECORDS TO WHOM THIS NOTICE IS ISSUED AND ADDRESS		COURT NAME & ADDRESS

Pursuant to Rule 17(a)(2) of the Massachusetts Rules of Criminal Procedure, 378 Mass. 885 (1979), the Court has issued the enclosed summons to produce records in the above-captioned matter. A judge has determined that the records ordered produced are "presumptively privileged," which means that they are likely to be protected by a statutory privilege.

The records ordered by the Court must be delivered to: ____________________

____
(address of Clerk of Court)

on or before the return date on the summons in a sealed envelope or box clearly marked as follows:

COMMONWEALTH v. ____________________ **(defendant)**

DOCKET NUMBER: ____________________

From: ____________________ **(name of keeper of records)**

Date: ____________________

PRIVILEGED RECORDS: IMPOUNDED

Entered: ____________________	Clerk of Court By: ____________________

AOTC 12/2007

PROTECTIVE ORDER FOR DEFENSE COUNSEL	DOCKET NO.	Trial Court of Massachusetts
CASE NAME **Commonwealth v.**		

On consideration of the defendant's motion pursuant to Rule 17(a)(2) of the Massachusetts Rules of Criminal Procedure, 378 Mass. 885 (1979), it is hereby ORDERED that defense counsel ("counsel") who has signed this protective order and filed it with the Clerk of Court in the above-captioned case be provided access to presumptively privileged records subject to the following terms and conditions:

1. Counsel shall have access to presumptively privileged records solely in his or her capacity as an officer of the Court. Counsel shall review any presumptively privileged records in the Clerk's office, or a space within the courthouse designated by the Clerk, during regular business hours under arrangements to be made with the Clerk.

2. Counsel shall not copy, and shall not directly or indirectly disclose, disseminate, or otherwise make available to any person, including the defendant, any of the presumptively privileged records, any portion thereof, or any of their contents without prior application to and an order of the Court.

3. Counsel may read and make notes concerning the presumptively privileged records. Any such notes shall be governed by this Protective Order.

4. Presumptively privileged records reviewed pursuant to this Protective Order shall not be used for any purpose other than the defense of the above-captioned case.

5. If counsel believes that copying or disclosure of any presumptively privileged records, or portions thereof, is necessary to prepare this case for trial, he or she may file a motion to modify this Protective Order to permit copying of records or disclosure to specifically identified individuals. The motion shall be accompanied by an affidavit, and notice shall be provided to all parties. If the Court enters an order vacating or modifying any term of this Protective Order, counsel shall then be bound by the terms of that Court order.

6. At the conclusion of the trial, direct appeal, or other disposition of the above-captioned case, the signatory shall deliver to the Clerk of Court, under seal, any and all copies of any records produced pursuant to any modified protective order or any other order of the Court. Notwithstanding the entry of any order terminating the case, this Protective Order shall remain in effect unless terminated by entry of a Court order.

7. The prohibitions against disclosure shall not apply to communications made under the following circumstances:

(a) where counsel is engaged in the private practice of law, communications with other attorneys in counsel's law firm, provided that such communications are for the purpose of consultation in this matter;

(b) where counsel is a staff attorney employed by the Committee for Public Counsel Services ("CPCS"), communications with other staff attorneys employed by CPCS, provided that such communications are for the purpose of consultation in this matter;

(c) where counsel is private counsel assigned by CPCS, communications with attorneys employed or assigned by CPCS, provided that such communications are for the purpose of consultation in this matter; or

(d) communications with counsel's support staff, operating under counsel's direction, for the purpose of preparing pleadings and other documents in this matter.

In making any of the above communications, counsel shall, insofar as possible, use a pseudonym in place of the true name of the person protected by the privilege. Counsel will instruct any person receiving a communication pursuant to paragraph 7 of the court-ordered confidentiality of the material disclosed.

<u>The Court and any counsel shall report any violation of this order to the Board of Bar Overseers</u>. Violations may also be reported to the Court and/or Board of Bar Overseers by the privilege holder, the keeper of records, and any other person who believes, in good faith, that the terms of this Order have been violated.

Entered:	By the Court, (, J.) x ____________________ Signature of Justice

CERTIFICATION BY COUNSEL

I agree to be bound by the terms of this Protective Order.

SIGNED UNDER THE PAINS AND PENALTIES OF PERJURY.

Date:	Signature of Counsel: x
BBO. No.:	Printed Name and Address of Counsel:

ORDER ALLOWING ACCESS TO PRIVILEGED RECORDS BY PERSONS OTHER THAN COUNSEL	DOCKET NO.	Trial Court of Massachusetts
CASE NAME Commonwealth v.		

On consideration of the ____________________ (defense or prosecuting attorney)'s motion to disclose records, it is hereby ORDERED that ____________________ (name, address, title of person permitted access)

is permitted access to the records of ____________________ (name of third-party subject) held by ____________________ (keeper of records) for the period from ________ to ________ (date range), subject to the following terms and conditions:

1. Any person granted access to records by this Court ("authorized person") must sign and file a copy of this Order with the Clerk of Court in the above-captioned case before receiving access to the records.

2. An authorized person shall have access to records solely for use in the defense or prosecution of the above-captioned case. An authorized person shall not copy or directly or indirectly disclose, disseminate, or otherwise make available to any person, including the defendant, any portion of the records or their contents without a written Court order authorizing such copying or disclosure.

3. An authorized person may take notes regarding the records. Any such notes shall be governed by the terms of paragraph 2, above.

4. At the conclusion of trial or other disposition of the above-captioned case, an authorized person shall deliver to the defense or prosecuting attorney any copies of the records and any notes made pursuant to paragraph 3, above. Notwithstanding the entry of any order terminating the case, this Order shall remain in effect unless terminated by the the Court.

Entered:	By the Court, (, J.) x ____________________ Signature of Justice

I agree to be bound by the terms of this Court Order. **I UNDERSTAND THAT VIOLATION OF THIS COURT ORDER IS PUNISHABLE AS CRIMINAL CONTEMPT AND MAY SUBJECT THE VIOLATOR TO A FINE AND/OR TERM OF IMPRISONMENT.**

SIGNED UNDER THE PAINS AND PENALTIES OF PERJURY.

Signature
x

Printed Name:	Address:

AOTC. 12/2007

PROTECTIVE ORDER FOR PROSECUTING ATTORNEY	DOCKET NO.	Trial Court of Massachusetts
CASE NAME **Commonwealth v.**		

It is hereby ORDERED that the prosecutor who has signed this protective order and filed it with the Clerk of Court in the above-captioned case be provided access to presumptively privileged records subject to the following terms and conditions:

1. The prosecutor shall have access to presumptively privileged records solely in his or her capacity as an officer of the Court. The prosecutor shall review any presumptively privileged records in the Clerk's office, or a space within the courthouse designated by the Clerk, during regular business hours under arrangements to be made with the Clerk.

2. The prosecutor shall not copy, and shall not directly or indirectly disclose, disseminate, or otherwise make available to any person, any of the presumptively privileged records, any portion thereof, or any of their contents without prior application to and an order of the Court.

3. The prosecutor may read and make notes concerning the presumptively privileged records. Any such notes shall be governed by this Protective Order.

4. Presumptively privileged records reviewed pursuant to this Protective Order shall not be used for any purpose other than the prosecution of the above-captioned case.

5. If the prosecutor believes that copying or disclosure of any presumptively privileged records, or portions thereof, is necessary to prepare this case for trial, he or she may file a motion to modify this Protective Order to permit copying of records or disclosure to specifically identified individuals. The motion shall be accompanied by an affidavit, and notice shall be provided to all parties. If the Court enters an order vacating or modifying any term of this Protective Order, counsel shall then be bound by the terms of that Court order.

6. At the conclusion of the trial, direct appeal, or other disposition of the above-captioned case, the signatory shall deliver to the Clerk of Court, under seal, any and all copies of any records produced pursuant to any modified protective order or any other order of the Court. Notwithstanding the entry of any order terminating the case, this Protective Order shall remain in effect unless terminated by entry of a Court order.

7. The prohibitions against disclosure shall not apply to communications made under the following circumstances:

(a) communications with any victim-witness advocate working with the prosecuting attorney in this matter;

(b) communications with other prosecuting attorneys, provided that such communications are for the purpose of consultation in this matter; or

(c) communications with counsel's support staff, operating under counsel's direction, for the purpose of preparing pleadings and other documents in this matter.

AOTC. 12/2007

In making any of the above communications authorized by subparagraph (b) and (c), counsel shall, insofar as possible, use a pseudonym in place of the true name of the person protected by the privilege. Counsel will instruct any person receiving a communication pursuant to paragraph 7 of the court-ordered confidentiality of the material disclosed.

<u>The Court and any counsel shall report any violation of this order to the Board of Bar Overseers</u>. Violations may also be reported to the Court and/or Board of Bar Overseers by the privilege holder, the keeper of records, and any other person who believes, in good faith, that the terms of this Order have been violated.

Entered:	By the Court, (, J.) x Signature of Justice

CERTIFICATION BY COUNSEL

I agree to be bound by the terms of this Protective Order.

SIGNED UNDER THE PAINS AND PENALTIES OF PERJURY.

Date:	Signature of Counsel: x
BBO. No.:	Printed Name and Address of Counsel:

AOTC 12/2007

Rule 18. Presence of Defendant

(Applicable to District Court and Superior Court)

(a) Presence of Defendant. In any prosecution for crime the defendant shall be entitled to be present at all critical stages of the proceedings.

(1) *Defendant Absenting Himself.* If a defendant is present at the beginning of a trial and thereafter absents himself without cause or without leave of court, the trial may proceed to a conclusion in all respects except the imposition of sentence as though the defendant were still present.

(2) *Waiver of Presence in Misdemeanor Cases.* A person prosecuted for a misdemeanor may at his own request, with leave of court, be excused from attendance if represented by counsel or an agent authorized by law and may be excused from attendance without leave of court if so authorized by the General Laws.

(3) *Presence Not Required.* A defendant need not be present at a revision or revocation of sentence pursuant to Rule 29 or at any proceeding where evidence is not to be taken.

(b) Presence of Corporation. A corporation may appear by a duly authorized agent for the purposes of this rule.

Reporter's Notes

This rule is patterned primarily upon Rule 3.180 of the Florida Rules of Criminal Procedure and is a codification of accepted Massachusetts practice.

Under the Florida rule a defendant's presence is commanded at certain specifically enumerated "critical stages" of a criminal proceeding: arraignment, entry of plea, pretrial conference, all trial proceedings before the court, jury view, rendition of verdict, pronouncement of judgment and imposition of sentence. See Uniform Rule 713, which would grant the defendant the right to be present "at *every stage* of the trial . . . and at the disposition hearing" (emphasis supplied), and which would *require* his presence unless he is represented by counsel and has waived the right to be present, has voluntarily failed to be present, or has been justifiably excluded. Rules of Criminal Procedure (U.L.A.) Rule 713 (1974). Rule 18 neither presumes to define those stages of a proceeding when the defendant's presence is constitutionally mandated, nor to compel his presence at every stage, rather it instructs that he is to be present at "all critical stages." The term "critical" is unrelated to its use for other purposes, e.g., assignment of counsel, and is to be interpreted in light of relevant judicial decisions.

The defendant's presence is constitutionally required during all critical stages because fairness demands that the defendant be present when his substantial rights are at stake, and those instances are not limited to the specific proceedings listed in the Florida rule. Conversely, there are matters which the court and defendant's counsel can determine in the defendant's absence; to require the defendant's presence at all times could in some instances unduly prolong the disposition of the case. Thus, under this rule, the detailing of what stages are deemed critical is left to judicial determination.

The sixth amendment to the United States Constitution guarantees a defendant the right to confront witnesses at trial, which right is also guaranteed by article 12 of the Massachusetts Declaration of Rights and by statute, G.L. c. 278, § 6. However, the primary constitutional protection is afforded by the due process clause of the fourteenth amendment. "[T]he presence of the defendant is a condition of due process to the extent that a fair and just hearing would be thwarted by his absence. . . ." Snyder v. Massachusetts, 54 S.Ct. 330, 291 U.S. 97, 107–08, 78 L.Ed. 674, 90 A.L.R. 575 (1934). Thus, the Constitution requires the presence of the defendant at proceedings other than trial if his presence would be essential to preserve substantial rights.

Subdivision (a). Where a stage of the proceedings is deemed critical, the defendant's presence is required and the court is not to proceed in his absence without determining that he has effectively waived or forfeited the right to be present. Taylor v. United States, 94 S.Ct. 194, 414 U.S. 17, 38 L.Ed.2d 174 (1973). Most hearings either before or after trial do not require the defendant's presence. *See* Mass.R.Crim.P. 30. For example, his presence is not required at pretrial motions, including motions for a change of venue, Mass. R.Crim.P. 37, and motions for a continuance, Mass.R.Crim.P. 10, Commonwealth v. Robichaud, 358 Mass. 300, 264 N.E.2d 374 (1970). And his presence is not generally required at post-trial proceedings. Commonwealth v. Dupont, 2 Mass. App. 566, 317 N.E.2d 83 (1974); Mass.R.Crim.P. 30. But the defendant's presence is required at all trial proceedings (See *Commonwealth v. Robichaud,* supra), at arraignment (Mass. R.Crim.P. 6), when a plea is made (Mass.R.Crim.P. 12), and at sentencing (Thompson v. United States, 495 F.2d 1304 [1st Cir.1974]; Mass.R.Crim.P. 28).

(a)(1). Although a defendant is entitled to be present at critical stages, he may waive or forfeit that right. Commonwealth v. McCarthy, 163 Mass. 458, 40 N.E. 766 (1895). He may waive his right to be present at the trial of a felony in either of two ways. First, he may voluntarily absent himself from trial, in which case the trial may continue in his absence. Commonwealth v. Flemmi, 360 Mass. 693, 277 N.E.2d 523 (1971). Secondly, the defendant may become so obstreperous as to require his removal from court in order to preserve the orderliness of judicial proceedings. Illinois v. Allen, 90 S.Ct. 1057, 397 U.S. 337, 25 L.Ed.2d 353 (1970); Commonwealth v. Senati, 3 Mass.App. 304, 327 N.E.2d 906 (1975); Mass. R.Crim.P. 45; See ABA *Standards Relating to the Function of the Trial Judge* § 6.8 (Approved Draft, 1972). However, trial cannot begin in the defendant's absence, Diaz v. United States, 32 S.Ct. 250, 223 U.S. 442, 455, 56 L.Ed. 500 (1912), thereby eliminating the possibility that a defendant, by voluntarily absenting himself can be deemed to have waived his right to be present at the inception of trial.

The defendant is not prohibited by this rule from waiving his right to be present at the trial of capital cases. The traditional rule enunciated in *Diaz v. United States,* supra, is that in capital crimes the defendant is not permitted to be tried in absentia because of the severity of the potential punishment. The rule was recently reaffirmed in *Taylor v. United States,* supra. However, the prohibition against waiver of the right to be present in capital cases does not exist in Rule 43 of the Federal Rules of Criminal Procedure, nor is it suggested by Rule 713 of the Uniform Rules of Criminal Procedure (U.L.A.) (1974). As the Advisory Committee Note to Federal Rule 43 recognizes, the present state of the law on this issue is not clear. As with the federal rule, this rule does not attempt to resolve this disputed issue, but leaves the matter to future judicial decisions.

(a)(2). This is a restatement of G.L. c. 278, § 6. General Laws c. 274, § 1 defines felonies and misdemeanors.

(a)(3). See generally the discussion of when a defendant's presence *is* required, supra.

Subdivision (b). Federal Rule of Criminal Procedure 43(c)(1) provides that "a corporation may appear by counsel for all purposes." It is, therefore, unnecessary for an officer of the corporation to be present at arraignment plea, trial, or sentencing (unless individually charged) in any case, whether misdemeanor or felony. 8B J. MOORE, FEDERAL PRACTICE para. 43.02[3] (Rev. ed. 1978). Under Mass.R.Crim.P. 18, the corporation may appear for all purposes by "duly authorized agent" which does not require counsel.

Rule 19. Trial by Jury or by the Court

(Applicable to Superior Court and jury sessions in District Court)

(a) General. A case in which the defendant has the right to be tried by a jury shall be so tried unless the defendant waives a jury trial in writing with the approval of the court and files the waiver with the clerk, in which instance he shall be tried by the court instead of by a jury. If there is more than one defendant, all must waive the right to trial by jury, and if they do not so waive, there must be a jury trial unless the court in its discretion severs the cases. The court may refuse to approve such a waiver for any good and sufficient reason provided that such refusal is given in open court and on the record.

(b) Less Than a Full Jury. If after jeopardy attaches there is at any time during the progress of a trial less than a full jury remaining, a defendant may waive his right to be tried by a full jury and request trial by the remaining jurors by signing a written waiver which shall be filed with the court. If there is more than one defendant, all must sign and file a waiver unless the court in its discretion severs the cases.

Reporter's Notes

The right to trial by jury, which is guaranteed by art. 3, § 2, cl. 3 of the United States Constitution and the sixth amendment, is applicable to the states through the fourteenth amendment. Duncan v. Louisiana, 88 S.Ct. 1444, 391 U.S. 145, 20 L.Ed.2d 491, 522 (1968). The Massachusetts Constitution, part 1, art. 12, also guarantees defendants the right to trial by jury. Further, G.L. c. 278, § 2, applicable to the Superior Court, provides that "[i]ssues of fact . . . shall . . . be tried by a jury . . . unless the person indicted or complained against elects to be tried by the court. . . ." General Laws c. 218, § 26A, inserted by St.1978, c. 478, § 188, provides that trials in the District Court and the Boston Municipal Court "shall be by a jury of six, unless the defendant files a written waiver and consents to be tried by the court. . . ." Under prior law a juvenile defendant had no right to a trial by jury during the adjudicative phase of a delinquency proceeding. McKeiver v. Pennsylvania, 91 S.Ct. 1976, 403 U.S. 528, 29 L.Ed.2d 647 (1971); Commonwealth v. Page, 339 Mass. 313, 316, 159 N.E.2d 82 (1959). However, by G.L. c. 119, § 55A, inserted by St.1978, c. 478, § 56, delinquency proceedings shall be by jury unless waived. If a juvenile appeals from an adjudication of delinquency in a jury waived session, his appeal to the jury session will be tried and determined in like manner as an appeal by an adult criminal defendant. G.L. c. 119, § 56 (as amended, St.1978, c. 478, § 57). *See* Sylvester v. Commonwealth, 253 Mass. 244, 148 N.E. 449 (1925).

Subdivision (a). This subdivision is drawn from Fed. R.Crim.P. 23(a) and G.L. c. 119, § 55A; c. 218, § 26A; c. 263, § 6. The requirement that the waiver be in writing is not universal. See ABA *Standards Relating to Trial by Jury,* § 1.2(b) (Approved Draft, 1968); Rules of Criminal Procedure (U.L.A.) rule 511 (1974). In Boykin v. Alabama, 89 S.Ct. 1709, 395 U.S. 238, 23 L.Ed.2d 274 (1969), the Court held that a waiver of a jury trial cannot be presumed from a silent record. While *Boykin* would be satisfied by an oral waiver when the proceedings are recorded, the requirement in Massachusetts is that the waiver be written and filed with the clerk. Commonwealth v. Hesser, 1 Mass.App. 850, 302 N.E.2d 927 (1973) (Rescript); Gallo v. Commonwealth, 343 Mass. 397, 402, 179 N.E.2d 231, 93 A.L.R.2d 406 (1961); G.L. c. 263, § 6. The federal rule imposes this stricter requirement "to ensure a greater probability of a defendant understanding what he is doing. . . ." Pool v. United States, 344 F.2d 943, 945 (9th Cir.1966). Likewise, the Massachusetts rule seeks to "avoid unnecessary controversy and to provide a procedural safeguard. . . ." *Gallo v. Commonwealth,* supra.

"A waiver is . . . an intentional relinquishment or abandonment of a known right. . . ." Johnson v. Zerbst, 58 S.Ct. 1019, 304 U.S. 458, 464, 82 L.Ed. 1461 (1938). Waiver of a constitutional right must be "intelligent and competent." Id. at 465. The waiver of the right to a jury trial must be "express and intelligent." Patton v. United States, 50 S.Ct. 253, 281 U.S. 276, 312, 74 L.Ed. 854, 70 A.L.R. 263 (1930).

Subdivision (a) incorporates that portion of the federal rule which provides that a waiver of trial by jury must be approved by the court. Although a defendant is free to waive his jury trial, *Patton,* supra, there is no constitutional impediment to conditioning that waiver upon the consent of the trial judge. Singer v. United States, 85 S.Ct. 783, 380 U.S. 24, 36, 13 L.Ed.2d 630 (1965) (construing Fed.R.Crim.P. 23[a]). See ABA *Standards Relating to Trial by Jury* § 1.2(a), comment at 32–34 (Approved Draft, 1968). The defendant in a capital case may not waive a jury trial in any event. G.L. c. 263, § 6 (as amended); Commonwealth v. O'Brien, 371 Mass. 605, 358 N.E.2d 786 (1976). *Accord* Commonwealth v. Marshall, Mass.Adv.Sh. (1977) 1530, 1532–33, 364 N.E.2d 1237.

The decision whether to waive trial by jury is properly that of the defendant after full consultation with counsel. ABA *Standards Relating to the Defense Function* § 5.2 (Approved Draft, 1971).

If there are multiple defendants and one desires to waive the right to trial by jury, then all must waive. United States v. Farries, 459 F.2d 1057, 1061 (3d Cir.), cert. denied, 93 S.Ct. 143, 409 U.S. 888 (1972), 34 L.Ed.2d 145, 410 U.S. 912, 35 L.Ed.2d 275 (1973). In a rare case, severance may be the best course if not all defendants choose waiver. In *Farries,* however, the enormous expense and serious security problems involved in a trial where the defendants and many witnesses were inmates of various federal penitentiaries was held to outweigh the interests of a defendant in severance.

Subdivision (b). This subdivision is in accord with current Massachusetts practice as stated in G.L. c. 234, § 26A. The provision authorizing the court to disallow a waiver of the right to be tried by a full jury is not inconsistent with prior law even though a similar provision does not appear in G.L. c. 234, § 26A. See Commonwealth v. Roby, 29 Mass. 496, 502 (1832). *Compare* United States v. Jorn, 91 S.Ct. 547, 400 U.S. 470, 27 L.Ed.2d 543 (1971).

Rule 20. Trial Jurors

(Applicable to Superior Court and jury sessions in District Court)

(a) Motion for Appropriate Relief. Either party may challenge the array by a motion for appropriate relief pursuant to Rule 13(c). A challenge to the array shall be made only on the ground that the prospective jurors were not selected or drawn according to law. Challenges to the array shall be made and decided before any individual juror is examined unless otherwise ordered by the court. A challenge to the array shall be in writing supported by affidavit and shall specify the facts constituting the ground of the challenge. Challenges to the array shall be tried by the court and may in the discretion of the court be decided on the basis of the affidavit filed with the challenge. Upon the hearing of a challenge to the array, a witness may be examined on oath by the court and may be so examined by either party. If the challenge to the array is sustained, the court shall discharge the panel.

(b) Challenge for Cause.

(1) *Examination of Juror.* The court shall, or upon motion, the parties or their attorneys may under the direction of the court, examine on oath a person who is called as a juror in a case to learn whether he is related to either party, has any interest in the case, has expressed or formed an opinion, or is sensible of any bias or prejudice. The objecting party may, with the approval of the court, introduce other competent evidence in support of the objection.

(2) *Examination Upon Extraneous Issues.* The court shall examine or cause a juror to be examined upon issues extraneous to the case if it appears that the juror's impartiality may have been affected by the extraneous issues. The examination may include a brief statement of the facts of the case, to the extent the facts are appropriate and relevant to the issues of such examination, and shall be conducted individually and outside the presence of other persons about to be called or already called as jurors.

(3) *Challenge of Juror.* Either party may challenge an individual prospective juror before the juror is sworn to try the case. The court may for cause shown permit a challenge to be made after the juror is sworn but before any evidence is presented. When a juror is challenged for cause, the ground of the challenge shall be stated. A challenge of a prospective juror and the statement of the grounds thereof may be made at the bench. The court shall determine the validity of each such challenge.

(c) Peremptory Challenges.

(1) *Number of Challenges.* Upon the trial of an indictment for a crime punishable by imprisonment for life, each defendant shall be entitled to twelve peremptory challenges of the jurors called to try the case; in any other criminal case tried before a jury of twelve, each defendant shall be entitled to four peremptory challenges; and in a case tried before a jury of six, each defendant shall be entitled to two peremptory challenges. Each defendant in a trial of an indictment for a crime punishable by imprisonment for life in which additional jurors are impaneled under subdivision (d) of this rule shall be entitled to one additional peremptory challenge for each additional juror. Each defendant in a case in which several indictments or complaints are consolidated for trial shall be entitled to no more peremptory challenges than the greatest number to which he would have been entitled upon trial of any one of the indictments or complaints alone. In every criminal case the Commonwealth shall be entitled to as many peremptory challenges as equal the whole number to which all the defendants in the case are entitled.

(2) *Time of Challenge.* Peremptory challenges shall be made before the jurors are sworn and may be made after the determination that a person called to serve as a juror stands indifferent in the case.

(d) Alternate Jurors.

(1) *Impanelling Jury With Alternate Jurors.* If a jury trial is likely to be protracted, the judge may impanel a jury of not more than sixteen members and the court shall have jurisdiction to try the case with that jury.

(2) *Selection of Twelve Jurors.* If at the time of the final submission of the case to the jury more than twelve members of the jury who have heard the whole case are alive and not incapacitated or disqualified, the judge shall direct the clerk to place the names of all the remaining jurors except the foreman in a box and draw the names of a sufficient number to reduce the jury to twelve members. Those jurors whose names are drawn shall not be discharged, but shall be known as alternate jurors and shall be kept separate and apart from the other jurors in some convenient place, subject to the same rules and regulations as the other jurors, until the jury has agreed upon a verdict or has been otherwise discharged.

(3) *Disabled Juror: Selection of Alternate.* If, at any time after the final submission of the case by the court to the jury but before the jury has agreed on a verdict, a juror dies, becomes ill, or is unable to perform his duty for any other cause, the judge may order him to be discharged and shall direct the clerk to place the names of all the remaining alternate jurors in a box and draw the name of an alternate who shall take the place of the discharged juror on the jury, which shall renew its deliberations with the alternate juror.

(e) Regulation and Separation of Jurors.

(1) *Sequestration*. After the jurors have been sworn they shall hear the case as a body and, within the discretion of the trial judge, may be sequestered.

(2) *After Submission of the Cause*. Unless the jurors have been sequestered for the duration of the trial, the judge after the final submission of the case, may order that the jurors be permitted to separate for a definite time to be fixed by the judge and then reconvene in the courtroom before retiring for consideration of their verdict.

(3) *After Commencement of Deliberations*. After final submission of the case to the jury and after deliberations have commenced, the judge may allow the jurors, under proper instructions, to separate for a definite time to be fixed by the judge and to reconvene in the courtroom before retiring for further deliberation of their verdict.

Reporter's Notes

This rule is primarily a distillation of Massachusetts statutory law. G.L. c. 234, §§ 26B, 28–29; former G.L. c. 277, § 47A (St.1978, c. 478, § 298). *See* e.g., Fed.R.Crim.P. 24; Fla.R.Crim.P. 3.370; ABA *Standards Relating to Trial by Jury* §§ 2.3–2.7 (Approved Draft, 1968); Rules of Criminal Procedure (U.L.A.) Rules 511–513, 532 (1974); National Advisory Commission on Criminal Justice Standards and Goals, *Courts* §§ 4.13–4.14 (1973).

Subdivision (a). Although G.L. c. 277, § 47A, inserted by St.1965, c. 617, § 1, abolished in terms "challenges to the array and to the manner of selection of grand or traverse jurors," the relief formerly available thereunder remains available by a "motion to grant appropriate relief." Despite the statutory change in nomenclature, the courts continue to refer to such motions as challenges to the array. *See* e.g., Commonwealth v. Underwood, 3 Mass.App. 522, 535, 335 N.E.2d 915 (1975).

A motion for appropriate relief from trial by a jury allegedly not selected in accordance with law—that is, a motion for discharge of the panel—is properly made only before trial. G.L. c. 277, § 47A. Brunson v. Commonwealth, 369 Mass. 106, 337 N.E.2d 895 (1975); Commonwealth v. Rodriquez, 364 Mass. 87, 91, 300 N.E.2d 192 (1973); Commonwealth v. Underwood, 3 Mass.App. 522, 536, 335 N.E.2d 915 (1975). Mass.R.Crim.P. 13(c).

See ABA *Standards Relating to Trial by Jury* § 2.3 (Approved Draft, 1968), Rules of Criminal Procedure (U.L.A.) rule 511(d) (1974) (incorporating by reference Uniform Jury Selection and Service Act [U.L.A.] § 12 [1970]); Fed. R.Crim.P. 6(b)(1).

Subdivision (b).

(b)(1). This subdivision is based upon the first paragraph of G.L. c. 234, § 28. *See* Fed.R.Crim.P. 24(a); ABA *Standards Relating to Trial by Jury* § 2.4 (Approved Draft, 1968); ABA *Standards Relating to the Prosecution Function* § 5.3(c) (Approved Draft, 1971); ABA *Standards Relating to the Defense Function* § 7.2(c) (Approved Draft, 1971); Rules of Criminal Procedure (U.L.A.) Rule 512(b) (1974).

The purpose of G.L. c. 234, § 28 and of this rule is manifestly to determine whether prospective jurors are free from interest, bias, and prejudice in the case in which they are drawn to sit. Commonwealth v. Beneficial Finance Co., 360 Mass. 188, 295, 275 N.E.2d 33, 52 A.L.R.3d 1143 (1971), cert. denied, 92 S.Ct. 2433, 407 U.S. 910, 914, 32 L.Ed.2d 689 (1972); *accord* Commonwealth v. Montecalvo, 367 Mass. 46, 50, 323 N.E.2d 888 (1975).

It has been consistently held that Federal Rule 24(a) permits the trial judge a large range of discretion in the latitude and manner of voir dire examination, subject to the essential demands of fairness. E.g., Eastern Renovating Corp. v. Roman Catholic Bishop of Springfield, 554 F.2d 4 (1st Cir.1977); United States v. Desmarais, 531 F.2d 632, 633 (1st Cir.1976). This comports with Massachusetts practice which has been uniformly stated to give the trial judge broad discretion "whether to refine or improve on the subjects of . . . § 28, by going into more detail." Commonwealth v. Lacy, 371 Mass. 363, 373, 358 N.E.2d 419 (1976); Commonwealth v. Harrison, 368 Mass. 366, 371, 331 N.E.2d 873 (1975). E.g., Commonwealth v. Kudish, 362 Mass. 627, 631–32, 289 N.E.2d 856 (1972). Because the trial judge has "a fair leeway in deciding how deep the probe should go, having in view the nature of the case as . . . [he] apprehends it at the start," *Harrison*, supra, there is no requirement that any particular form or number of questions be asked. *See* e.g., Commonwealth v. Hicks, Mass.Adv.Sh. (1979) 1, 384 N.E.2d 1206; Commonwealth v. Horton, Mass.Adv.Sh. (1978) 2548, 380 N.E.2d 687; Commonwealth v. McCants, 3 Mass.App. 596, 598, 337 N.E.2d 918 (1975).

The provision of this subdivision which requires the approval of the court for the introduction of extrinsic evidence is consistent with prior practice although not statutorily mandated. Commonwealth v. DiStasio, 294 Mass. 273, 1 N.E.2d 189 (1936).

Prior practice was to pose the so-called "statutory questions" to the jurors as a group in non-capital cases and individually, out of the presence of other prospective jurors, in capital cases. Commonwealth v. Ventura, 294 Mass. 113, 1 N.E.2d 30 (1936). Because the need to interrogate each juror regarding the death penalty no longer exists, there is likewise no reason in the usual case why the statutory questions may not be asked of the jurors as a group. Commonwealth v. Montecalvo, 367 Mass. 46, 48–49, 323 N.E.2d 888 (1975). *See* Commonwealth v. Harrison, 368 Mass. 366, 369 n. 5, 331 N.E.2d 873 (1975). Individual questioning may be commanded, however, by the facts and circumstances of the particular case. *Commonwealth v. Montecalvo,* supra at 50 n. 2. *Compare* subdivision (b)(2), infra.

Whether the questions upon voir dire are to be posed by the judge or by the parties or their attorneys is another matter fully within the discretion of the trial judge. The sole purpose of the voir dire is to provide the parties with a means of discovering grounds for challenges for cause and to enable them to intelligently exercise peremptory challenges. The procedure is subject to abuse by counsel who utilize voir dire to influence jurors, however, ABA *Standards Relating to Trial by Jury,* § 2.4, comment at 64 (Approved Draft, 1968), and unless carefully regulated, can consume an inordinate amount of court time. For these reasons, it is suggested that the better practice when voir dire is confined to the subjects of G.L. c. 234, § 28 is for the judge to conduct the interrogation. If further questioning is desirable, it should be by the judge upon suggestion of counsel. *Compare* ABA *Standards,* supra (judge is to submit such additional questions as he deems proper), and Rules of Criminal Procedure (U.L.A.) Rule 512(b) (1974) (judge *shall* permit questioning by the parties).

(b)(2). The basis of this subdivision is found in the second paragraph of G.L. c. 234, § 28, as amended, St.1975, c. 335. The amendment of § 28 conformed the statute to the Supreme Court's decision in Ham v. South Carolina, 93 S.Ct. 848, 409 U.S. 524, 35 L.Ed.2d 46 (1973), which recognized that some cases present circumstances in which an impermissible threat to the fair trial guaranteed by the due process clause of the fourteenth amendment is posed when a judge refuses to question prospective jurors specifically as to racial prejudice. *Ham* did not announce a universally applicable rule, however, but a standard requiring assessment of the facts of each case. Ristaino v. Ross, 96 S.Ct. 1017, 424 U.S. 589, 47 L.Ed.2d 258 (1976).

General Laws c. 234, § 28 is not limited by its terms to racial prejudice, but is directed at any bias which may result from

> the impact of considerations which may cause a decision or decisions to be made in whole or in part upon issues extraneous to the case, including, but not limited to, community attitudes, possible exposure to potentially prejudicial material or possible preconceived opinions toward the credibility of certain classes of persons....

It should perhaps be noted that "community attitudes" or "exposure to potentially prejudicial material" may be so pervasive as to suggest a motion to transfer for prejudice if recognized prior to trial. Mass.R.Crim.P. 38(b)(1).

The procedure under § 28 is in two steps. It must first appear to the satisfaction of the court that a prospective juror or jurors may not be indifferent as a result of matters extraneous to the case. It is preferable that the court be apprised of the possibility of bias by a motion that prospective jurors be interrogated as to possible prejudice, *see* Commonwealth v. Lumley, 367 Mass. 213, 216, 327 N.E.2d 683 (1975); Commonwealth v. Rodriques, 364 Mass. 87, 92–93, 300 N.E.2d 192 (1973), and that the motion be accompanied by an affidavit specifying the facts which defendant alleges make him subject to bias. *See* Commonwealth v. Pinckney, 365 Mass. 70, 309 N.E.2d 495 (1974). In Commonwealth v. Harrison, 2 Mass.App. 775, 321 N.E.2d 672 (1975), affirmed, 368 Mass. 366 (1975), the court found inadequate an affidavit which

> amounted to no more than an argument of law intended to persuade the court to adopt the defendant's position on the utility of the requested questions and in no way informed the judge as to the possible injection into the case of prejudice stemming from possibly disparate political views or cultural values.

Id. at 779. *Accord Commonwealth v. Pinckney,* supra. *See* Commonwealth v. Peters, Mass.Adv.Sh. (1977) 684, 689, 361 N.E.2d 1277 ("absence of even minimal substantiation").

If the court finds that there is a basis to the allegations, "the court *shall,* or the parties or their attorneys may ... examine the juror specifically" as to the extraneous issues. G.L. c. 234, § 28 (emphasis added). Under prior case law, and pursuant to § 28 previous to its 1975 amendment, this specific examination was discretionary even if impaired indifference were shown.

Both under this subdivision and G.L. c. 234, § 28 the questioning of each venireman as to extraneous issues is to be conducted out of the presence of those not yet or already called.

(b)(3). The time for challenge of prospective juror is generally considered to end once the jury is impanelled. Commonwealth v. Galvin, 323 Mass. 205, 80 N.E.2d 825 (1948). It has been held, however, that the right of a judge to dismiss a juror for cause and to provide for the selection of another juror in his place continues even after the jury is impanelled but before the trial actually starts. Commonwealth v. Monahan, 349 Mass. 139, 207 N.E.2d 29 (1965); 30 MASS.PRACTICE SERIES (Smith) § 1047 (1970, Supp. 1978). *See* ABA *Standards Relating to Trial by Jury* § 2.5 (Approved Draft, 1968); Rules of Criminal Procedure (U.L.A.) Rule 512(c) (1974).

Subdivision (c). The substance of subdivision (c)(1) is taken from G.L. c. 234, § 29. See Superior Court Rule 6 (1974); ABA *Standards Relating to Trial by Jury* § 2.6 (Approved Draft, 1968); Rules of Criminal Procedure (U.L.A.) Rule 512(d) (1974).

"The essential nature of the peremptory challenge is that it is one exercised without a reason stated, without inquiry and without being subject to the court's control." Swain v. Alabama, 85 S.Ct. 824, 380 U.S. 202, 220, 13 L.Ed.2d 759 (1965). Therefore, it had been held that a claim of denial of trial by an impartial jury based on the fact that the Commonwealth utilizes its peremptory challenges to exclude a particular sex or race from the panel must fail. Commonwealth v. Mitchell, 367 Mass. 419, 420, 326 N.E.2d 6 (1975). However, in Commonwealth v. Soares, Mass.Adv.Sh. (1979) 593, 387 N.E.2d 499, decided under article 12 of the Declaration of Rights rather than the equal protection clause of the fourteenth amendment, the Supreme Judicial Court held that the use of peremptory challenges to exclude prospective jurors solely by virtue of their membership in, or affiliation with, particular, defined groupings in the community is proscribed. Id. at 624–25.

> [The] exercise of peremptory challenges to exclude members of discrete groups, solely on the basis of bias presumed to derive from that individual's membership in the group, contravenes the requirement [of the jury drawn from a representative cross-section of the community] inherent in art. 12 of the Declaration of Rights. In so holding, we recognize that no defendant is entitled to a petit jury proportionally representing every group in the community; nor are members of particular groups insulated from the proper use of peremptory challenges to exclude any individual on any other ground. What both parties are constitutionally entitled to expect is "a petit jury that is as near an approximation of the ideal cross-section of the community as the process of random draw permits.

Id. at 627, *quoting, People v. Wheeler,* 22 Cal.3d 258, 277, 148 Cal.Rptr. 890, 583 P.2d 748 (1978). While the proper use of peremptory challenges may be presumed, that presumption is rebuttable by either party on a showing that: 1) a pattern of conduct has developed whereby several prospective jurors who have been challenged peremptorily are members of a discrete group, and 2) there is a likelihood that they are being excluded from the jury solely by reason of their group membership. Id. at 628–29.

> If the court finds that the burden of justification is not sustained as to any of the questioned peremptory challenges, the presumption of their validity is rebutted. Accordingly, the court must then conclude that the jury as constituted fails to comply with the representative cross-section requirement, and it must dismiss the jurors thus far selected. So too it must quash any remaining venire, since

the complaining party is entitled to a random draw from an entire venire—not one that has been partially or totally stripped of members of a cognizable group by the improper use of peremptory challenges. Upon such dismissal a different venire shall be drawn and the jury selection process may begin anew.

Id. at 631–32, *quoting People v. Wheeler,* supra, at 282.

Subdivision (c)(2) is borrowed almost entirely from G.L. c. 234, § 29.

It should be noted that no irregularity in a writ of venire facias or in the drawing, summoning, returning, or *impanelling* of jurors is sufficient to set aside a verdict unless the objecting party has been "injured" by the irregularity and unless the objection is made before verdict. G.L. c. 234, § 32. Commonwealth v. Montecalvo, 367 Mass. 46, 51, 323 N.E.2d 888 (1975); Commonwealth v. McKay, 363 Mass. 220, 223–24, 294 N.E.2d 213 (1973).

Subdivision (d). This subdivision parallels G.L. c. 234, § 26B (as amended). *Compare Rules of Criminal Procedure* (U.L.A.) Rule 511(c) (1974), which provides for "additional" jurors, *with* ABA *Standards Relating to Trial by Jury* § 2.7. (Approved Draft, 1968), which has provisions for both "alternate" and "additional" jurors. Under an alternate juror system, one or more persons specifically identified as alternates are chosen in advance of trial and will be designated to take the place of a juror who is discharged prior to the time the jury retires, or in some jurisdictions, prior to verdict. ABA *Standards,* supra, comment at 79. *See* Fed.R.Crim.P. 24(c). Massachusetts employs the additional juror system, G.L. c. 234, § 26B, approved in Uniform Rule 511(c), *supra,* and preferred by the ABA *Standards,* supra, comment at 80.

Subdivision (d)(3) adopts a procedure contained in Cal.Penal Code § 1089 (Deering, 1971). This practice has been rejected, however, by the ABA *Standards,* supra, comment at 82, and in the 1975 amendments to the Federal Rules of Criminal Procedure.

Subdivision (e).

(e)(1). This subdivision reiterates prior Massachusetts practice in leaving the decision whether to sequester the jury in the discretion of the trial judge. 30 MASS.PRACTICE SERIES (Smith) § 1042 (1970); Commonwealth v. Marshall, Mass.Adv.Sh. (1977) 1530, 364 N.E.2d 1237.

(e)(2)–(3). Drawn in part from Fla.R.Crim.P. 3.370 (1975), these subdivisions represent a significant departure from prior Massachusetts practice. In cases where sequestration is unnecessary, forcing the jury to remain in a body after submission of the case or the beginning of deliberations may cause hardship to jurors or their families which is not, in balance, necessary for protection of the defendant's interests, nor justified by the interests of justice. *See* Commonwealth v. Watkins, Mass.Adv.Sh. (1978) 1646, 1673–74, 379 N.E.2d 1040 (defendant's motion to excuse jury from further deliberation for the evening within the discretion of judge).

Rule 21. Sequestration of Witnesses

(Applicable to District Court and Superior Court)

Upon his own motion or the motion of either party, the judge may, prior to or during the examination of a witness, order any witness or witnesses other than the defendant to be excluded from the courtroom.

Reporter's Notes

This rule is based upon former G.L. c. 276, § 39 (Rev.St. [1836] c. 135, § 14) which was applicable to the District Court.

The power of a judge to control the progress and, within the limits of the adversary system, the shape of a trial, is universally held to include the broad discretionary power to sequester witnesses before, during, and after their testimony. Geders v. United States, 96 S.Ct. 1330, 425 U.S. 80, 47 L.Ed.2d 592 (1976); Holder v. United States, 150 U.S. 91, 92 (1893); United States v. Robinson, 502 F.2d 894 (7th Cir. 1974); United States v. Eastwood, 489 F.2d 818, 821 (5th Cir.1973); Commonwealth v. Dougan, Mass.Adv.Sh. (1979) 380, 400; Commonwealth v. Watkins, 373 Mass. 849, 370 N.E.2d 701 (1977); Commonwealth v. Vanderpool, 367 Mass. 743 (1975); Commonwealth v. Blackburn, 354 Mass. 200, 237 N.E.2d 35 (1968); Commonwealth v. Follansbee, 155 Mass. 274, 29 N.E.2d 471 (1892); Commonwealth v. Parry, 1 Mass. App. 730, 736, 306 N.E.2d 855 (1974).

Although sequestration may be well used to prevent the occurrence of perjury, it serves an equally important function in preventing one witness' testimony from being inadvertently molded by the testimony of other witnesses. "The process of sequestration consists merely in preventing one prospective witness from being taught by hearing another's testimony. . . ." 6 J. WIGMORE EVIDENCE § 1838 at 461 (Chadbourne rev. 1976). It additionally aids in detecting testimony which is less than candid, see WIGMORE, supra, and prevents improper attempts during recess to influence the witness' testimony in light of that already given. *Geders v. United States,* supra, at 87.

Since the sequestration of witnesses is within the discretion of the judge, the judge may order that only some of the witnesses be removed from the courtroom or kept separated. In Commonwealth v. Therrien, 359 Mass. 500, 269 N.E.2d 687 (1971), it was held proper for the trial judge to except from a general order of sequestration one witness deemed "essential to the management of the case." Id. at 508.

In conformity with prior practice, the court is to have discretionary power to exclude the testimony of a witness who remains in court in violation of a court order. In Commonwealth v. Crowley, 168 Mass. 121, 46 N.E. 415 (1897), a witness called by the defendant to impeach the testimony of a prosecution witness was not allowed to testify because he had remained in court in violation of a court order. Although at the time of the court order the defense had not intended to use that witness at trial, the exclusion of his testimony was upheld because during the progress of the trial it became apparent that he might be called for impeachment purposes. Conversely, the court may receive the testimony of a witness who is present at trial in violation of a sequestration order. Commonwealth v. Shagoury, Mass.App.Adv.Sh. (1978) 927, 380 N.E.2d 708; Commonwealth v. Hall, 86 Mass. (4 Allen) 305, 306 (1862). In addition, a trial judge may revoke or modify a previous sequestration order. Commonwealth v. Parry, 1 Mass.App. 730, 736, 306 N.E.2d 855 (1974).

The rule by its terms is inapplicable to a defendant. A sequestration order would affect a defendant quite differently from the way it affects a non-party witness, because of the defendant's need to consult with counsel. *Geders v. United States,* supra, at 88.

In addition, the defendant as a matter of right can be and usually is present for all testimony. E.g., Mass.R.Crim.P. 18, unless removed for disruptive behavior, Mass.R.Crim.P. 45.

Rule 22. Objections

(Applicable to Superior Court and jury sessions in District Court)

Exceptions to rulings or orders of the court are unnecessary and for all purposes for which an exception has heretofore been necessary, it is sufficient that a party, at the time the ruling or order of the court is made or sought, makes known to the court the action which he desires the court to take or his objection to the action of the court, but if a party has no opportunity to object to a ruling or order, the absence of an objection does not thereafter prejudice him.

If a party objects to a ruling or order of the court, he may state the precise legal grounds of his objection, but he shall not argue or further discuss such grounds unless the court calls upon him for such argument or discussion.

Reporter's Notes

Rule 22 restates Rule 51 of the Federal Rules of Criminal Procedure and is substantially similar to Rule 46 of both the Massachusetts and Federal Rules of Civil Procedure. *See* Superior Court Rule 8 (1974).

For generations of Massachusetts practitioners the relationship between the saving of an exception and the right of review was so firmly established in the appellate procedure of the Commonwealth and so universally understood and applied that discussion of the validity of the requirement was foreclosed. *See* e.g., Commonwealth v. Underwood, 358 Mass. 506, 509, 265 N.E.2d 577 (1970); SUPERIOR COURT RULES, 1974, ANNOTATED, 281–82 (Mass.Bar ed. 1975). The proper saving of an exception was the first and fundamental step to secure a review by bill of exceptions or by appeal, *Commonwealth v. Underwood,* supra; Commonwealth v. Dinnall, 366 Mass. 165, 314 N.E.2d 903 (1974), and the failure to seasonably except vitiated the right to review of the issue to which exception was not taken, Commonwealth v. Boudreau, 362 Mass. 378, 285 N.E.2d 915 (1972), save for the rare instance when an appellate court would review such questions because of a "substantial risk of a miscarriage of justice." Commonwealth v. Freeman, 352 Mass. 556, 564, 227 N.E.2d 3 (1967); Commonwealth v. Williams, Mass.App.Adv.Sh. (1979) 253, 386 N.E.2d 744 (Rescript); Commonwealth v. Harris, 371 Mass. 462, 471, 358 N.E.2d 982 (1976); Commonwealth v. Fields, 371 Mass. 274, 277, 356 N.E.2d 1211 (1976).

It is felt that the requirement of exceptions exalts form over substance in an unnecessarily ritualistic and time-consuming procedure. The draftsmen of Mass.R.Civ.P. 46 followed the lead of both the federal civil and criminal rules in abolishing the exception. This rule eliminates the requirement from criminal trials. That decision is premised upon the practical observation that an objection by counsel or counsel's request for specific action is sufficient to indicate to the court counsel's position on any issue and that to additionally require an exception is superfluous. *See* Rules of Criminal Procedure (U.L.A.) rule 755 (1974).

It has been argued that the requirement of an exception should be retained to provide the trial judge with an opportunity to reconsider his ruling on an objection and to eliminate specious arguments by counsel, Commonwealth v. Foley, 358 Mass. 233, 263 N.E.2d 451 (1970). Realistically, however, the taking of an exception apprises the judge of nothing which is apt to affect his initial ruling, nor does the requirement of an exception in any way compel counsel to take exception only to rulings on substantial matters.

The practice of requiring exceptions had led appellate courts to scrutinize records so as to determine whether holding that a defendant had waived objections by his failure to save exceptions could result in a miscarriage of justice. The scope of such review equates with that if no exceptions were required. *See* e.g., Commonwealth v. Williams, Mass.App. Adv.Sh. (1979) 253, 386 N.E.2d 744 (Rescript). Further, rigidly requiring that exceptions be saved led to "anomalous" results. In Commonwealth v. Nelson, 3 Mass.App. 90, 101, 323 N.E.2d 752 (1975), the court reviewed the denial of a motion for a new trial to which denial no exception was taken because the appellant's co-defendant had properly saved an exception to a similarly-grounded motion.

Superior Court rule 8 (1974) provides that in criminal cases, objections to evidence shall be decided without argument unless the presiding justice calls upon the parties to state the grounds on which the evidence is offered or objected to.

Having once stated the grounds, if so requested, counsel is not to further comment thereon unless the court requires elucidation. *See* Fed.R.Evid. 103(a). It is the intent of this rule that if a statement of grounds is requested, the court may allow such statement to be made in open court or at the bench and out of hearing of the jury. *See* Fed.R.Evid. 103(c).

Rule 23. Statements and Reports of Witnesses for Impeachment

(Applicable to District Court and Superior Court)

(a) Definition. The term "statement" as used in this rule in relation to any witness means:

(1) a writing made by a witness or another and signed or otherwise adopted or approved by such witness;

(2) a stenographic, mechanical, electrical, or other recording, or a transcription thereof, which is a substantially verbatim recital of an oral declaration made by a witness and which is recorded contemporaneously with the making of the oral declaration;

(3) a declaration, however taken or recorded, or a transcription thereof, made by a witness to a grand jury; or

(4) those portions of a written report which consist of the verbatim declarations of a witness in matters relating to the case on trial.

(b) Statements of Witnesses. Upon motion for inspection by either party, the judge shall at trial order the production of the statements of a witness of the adverse party that are in the possession, custody, or control of the adverse party when the requested information is relevant, provided that prior to the time of motion for inspection the witness shall have testified on direct examination in the trial of the case. The judge shall provide whenever it is requested that a reasonable time be afforded to the moving party to facilitate his use of the statements in the trial.

(c) In Camera Inspection. If either party claims that any statement requested pursuant to subdivision (b) of this rule contains matter which does not relate to the subject matter of the testimony of the witness, the judge shall order that the statement be delivered for the inspection of the judge in camera, whereupon the judge shall excise that part of the statement which does not relate to the subject matter of the testimony of the witness. The judge shall then order delivery of the statement as excised to the moving party for his use. In the event that any portion of a statement is withheld subject to an objection, the entire text of the statement shall be preserved to be made available to the appellate court in the event of an appeal for the purpose of determining the correctness of the ruling of the trial judge.

(d) Protective Orders. Upon a showing of cause, the judge may at any time order that inspection be denied or restricted or may make such other order as is appropriate.

(e) Production Prior to Direct Examination. Notwithstanding the provisions of subdivisions (b) and (c) of this rule, the judge may, prior to the examination of a prospective witness, require either party to provide the statements of the witness to the adverse party so as to facilitate the orderly conduct of the trial proceeding.

(f) Sanctions for Noncompliance. If either party elects not to comply with an order of the judge to deliver any statement or part thereof under subdivisions (b) and (c) of this rule, the judge may order stricken from the record the testimony of the witness and the trial shall proceed, unless the judge in his discretion shall determine that the interests of justice require that a mistrial be declared.

Reporter's Notes

This rule is closely modeled on 18 U.S.C. § 3500 (1969, Supp.1978), popularly known as the Jencks Act. However, no provisions comparable to subdivisions (a)(4) and (e) of this rule are found in the Jencks Act. *See generally* Fed.R.Crim.P. 15(e).

The availability of the type of material provided for in this rule is not mandated by the Constitution. United States v. Augenblick, 89 S.Ct. 528, 393 U.S. 348, 356, 21 L.Ed.2d 537 (1969); Commonwealth v. Coleman, 366 Mass. 705, 322 N.E.2d 407 (1975) (decision in Commonwealth v. Stewart, 365 Mass. 99, 309 N.E.2d 470 [1974], ordering routine production of grand jury minutes, was not constitutional mandate, but rendered under court's supervisory power). *See* Wardius v. Oregon, 93 S.Ct. 2208, 412 U.S. 470, 475, 37 L.Ed.2d 82 (1973).

It is important to recognize that, strictly speaking, motions for inspection pursuant to this rule are *not* properly within the area of discovery delimited by Mass.R.Crim.P. 14, entitled, and limited to, *pretrial* discovery. The Jencks Act, basis for this rule, does not compel, but prevents, pretrial discovery of statements of government witnesses. Similarly, subdivision (b)(2) of Fed.R.Crim.P. 16, basis for Mass.R.Crim.P. 14, protects statements of defense witnesses from disclosure. Neither limits the power of the court to order the production of prior statements for impeachment of witnesses who have testified at trial. United States v. Nobles, 95 S.Ct. 2160, 422 U.S. 225, 234–36, 45 L.Ed.2d 141 (1975). Materials which are not producible before trial under Mass.R.Crim.P. 14 are obtainable under this rule once the witness has testified at trial. Police reports, for example, are not generally discoverable under Mass.R.Crim.P. 14, but after an officer takes the stand, the relevant portions of the report from which he testifies may be ordered to be delivered to the defendant.

Subdivision (a). The court has the duty to determine what is a statement under this rule and must in some cases hear extrinsic evidence to resolve this issue. Campbell v. United States, 81 S.Ct. 421, 365 U.S. 85, 93, 5 L.Ed.2d 428 (1961). One common problem is whether written reports of government witnesses who are also government agents are statements within subdivision (a); and, if they are, whether they are producible pursuant to subdivisions (b) and (e). The 7th Circuit has interpreted the language of 18 U.S.C. § 3500(e), which is substantially identical to subdivisions (a)(1), (2) and (3) of this rule, to include such reports. The court said in United States v. Cleveland, 477 F.2d 310 (7th Cir.1973):

> The definition of the term 'statement' in subsection (e)(1)—assuming that the plain language means what it says—includes a report of a government agent who testifies as a prosecution witness. It has commonly been so held....

Id. at 316. The *Cleveland* court added that the conclusion that such reports are statements does not negate the necessity for demonstrating as a prerequisite to production that the content of the statement relates to the subject matter of the witness' testimony. The *Cleveland* definition was limited to prospective application in Krilich v. United States, 502 F.2d 680, 683 (7th Cir.1974), because the degree to which the fact-finding process would be enhanced was not enough to warrant the reopening of decided cases.

A report of an investigator is not exempted from disclosure at trial under the "work product" doctrine. *See* Mass. R.Crim.P. 14(a)(5); Fed.R.Crim.P. 16(a)(2). Where counsel attempts to make a testimonial use of these materials, the normal rules of evidence come into play with respect to cross-examination and production of documents. By electing to present the investigator as a witness, the work product privilege is waived with respect to matters covered in the investigator's testimony. United States v. Nobles, 95 S.Ct. 2160, 422 U.S. 225, 239 & n. 14, 45 L.Ed.2d 141 (1975). Furthermore, any writing prepared by a lawyer relating to the subject matter of the testimony of a witness that has been "signed or otherwise adopted or approved" by that witness is producible under Jencks Act, and the writing is not made nonproducible because of the work product doctrine. Goldberg v. United States, 96 S.Ct. 1338, 425 U.S. 94, 47 L.Ed.2d 603 (1976). This is also the intent of this rule.

Subdivision (a)(4) of this rule, which has no parallel in the Jencks Act, is mandated by Commonwealth v. Lewinski, 367 Mass. 889, 329 N.E.2d 738 (1975). In *Lewinski,* the Supreme Judicial Court held that prior written statements of a prosecution witness must be made available to the defendant not later than the close of the witness' testimony and defined "written statement" to include

> any statement made by the witness and in some definite way approved by him, a transcript of a contemporaneous

> verbatim or substantially verbatim stenographic or other recording of an oral statement by the witness, and a written report consisting of a statement by the witness.

Id. at 902.

Although not contemplated by the definition of "statement" in the Jencks Act or subdivision (a)(4) of this rule, it should be noted that juvenile records of a witness must be furnished by the prosecution if the defendant wishes to impeach that witness on cross-examination by showing bias. Davis v. Alaska, 94 S.Ct. 1105, 415 U.S. 308, 39 L.Ed.2d 347 (1974); Commonwealth v. Ferrara, 368 Mass. 182, 330 N.E.2d 837 (1975). This is permitted despite G.L. c. 119, § 60, which provides that the adjudication of a juvenile as delinquent is inadmissible as evidence "against such child for any purpose . . . and records in cases arising against any child . . . shall not be received in evidence or used in any way in any such proceeding."

It has also been held that a juvenile appealing an adjudication of delinquency to the Superior Court pursuant to G.L. c. 119, § 56 (now a District Court jury session: § 56, as amended, St.1978, c. 478, § 57) may use the transcript of the delinquency hearing held in the District Court to impeach the credibility of Commonwealth witnesses. Commonwealth v. A Juvenile, 361 Mass. 214, 217–18, 280 N.E.2d 144 (1972).

Subdivision (b). The groundwork for this subdivision, which gives the parties the right to discover statements of witnesses of the adverse party by the close of direct examination of each witness, was laid by the Supreme Judicial Court in Commonwealth v. Stewart, 365 Mass. 99, 309 N.E.2d 470 (1974), a decision involving grand jury minutes. It had long been recognized that it was within the discretion of the trial judge to make portions of grand jury minutes available to the defendant, but he was not bound to do so absent a showing of "particularized need." In *Stewart,* the court held that trial courts shall, upon motion of a defendant,

> routinely order the Commonwealth to supply defense counsel with the grand jury testimony of the defendant himself, and with the grand jury testimony of any person called as a Commonwealth witness which is related to the subject matter of his testimony at trial. *The defense will not be required to show particularized need.*

Id. at 105–06 (emphasis supplied; footnote omitted).

This rule expands the holding of *Stewart* to include all statements of government witnesses so that practice in Massachusetts will parallel federal practice. *See Commonwealth v. Stewart,* supra at 107–08, as to grand jury minutes. It may be noted that the grand jury need not be the one which returned the indictment against the defendant, Commonwealth v. Cavanaugh, 371 Mass. 46, 57–58, 363 N.E.2d 732 (1976), but that the grand jury testimony must be related to the witness' testimony at trial. *See* e.g., Commonwealth v. Barnett, 371 Mass. 87, 94, 354 N.E.2d 879 (1976). As to other statements, the procedure is outlined in *Commonwealth v. Lewinski,* supra:

> [A] defendant may . . . apply, by motion, for . . . [production] of the prior written statements of prosecution witnesses which are available to the prosecution and are related to the subject matter of their testimony at trial; and if the motion is granted, the statements will be delivered to defense counsel not later than the close of that testimony.

367 Mass. at 902 (footnote omitted). The court stated that this disclosure is cumulative to the obligation to turn over exculpatory material within the doctrine of Brady v. Maryland, 83 S.Ct. 1194, 373 U.S. 83, 10 L.Ed.2d 215 (1963). *Lewinski,* supra, at 902 n. 9. The court stated further that

> in cases with no special problems counsel will be able to agree on a reasonable timetable for delivery of these statements; in the case of witnesses whom the prosecution will definitely call, it may well be feasible to arrange for delivery ahead of trial. (Written statements and the substance of any oral statements of a defendant, available to the prosecution, shall be delivered as matter of course to counsel for that defendant and counsel for any codefendant not later than the commencement of trial.)

Id. at 903. *See* Commonwealth v. Ellison, Mass.Adv.Sh. (1978) 2072, 379 N.E.2d 560. The statements referred to in the last-quoted passage from *Lewinski* will ordinarily be delivered pursuant to an agreement or order for discovery under Mass.R.Crim.P. Rules 11 or 14. This rule—as to statements to be delivered not later than the close of a witness' testimony—contemplates statements not within mandatory discovery (Mass.R.Crim.P. 14[a][1]) or which were not made subject to disclosure under an order for discretionary discovery (Mass. R.Crim.P. 14[a][2]) or which were subject to a protective order (Mass.R.Crim.P. 14[a][6]). If the witness in fact testifies at trial, however, those statements must be produced pursuant to this rule.

Subdivision (c). As stated in United States v. Principe, 499 F.2d 1135 (1st Cir.1974), in order to satisfy the purpose of this rule—furtherance of the fair administration of criminal justice—the prosecutor has "responsibilities [that] are not simply adversarial, [he] has a duty to make frank and full disclosure or in doubtful situations to acquaint the court with the dilemma." Id. at 1139.

Subdivision (d). This subdivision is consistent with subdivision (a)(6) of Mass.R.Crim.P. 14, *Pretrial Discovery.*

Subdivision (e). This subdivision of the rule goes beyond the strict requirements of the Jencks Act. Its purpose is to facilitate orderly trial procedure by permitting the court to order the parties to turn over statements or reports of a witness within their possession prior to the direct examination of that witness. While *Stewart* and *Lewinski* make production mandatory only after a Commonwealth witness has been called, the court has suggested that delivery to the defendant of a witness' grand jury testimony or other statements prior to the close of direct examination would help avoid unnecessary delays during trial. Consistent with that policy, subdivision (e) provides that, subject to the discretion of the trial judge, disclosure may be ordered prior to the examination.

Subdivision (f). Drawn from Fed.R.Crim.P. 16(d)(2), this subdivision provides the sanction available to the court for the failure to comply with an order under this rule.

Rule 24. Opening Statements; Arguments; Instructions to Jury

(Applicable to Superior Court and jury sessions in District Court)

(a) Opening and Closing Statements; Arguments.

(1) *Order of Presentation*. The Commonwealth shall present its opening statement first. The defendant may present an opening statement of his defense after the opening statement of the Commonwealth or after

the close of the Commonwealth's evidence. The defendant shall present his closing argument first.

(2) *Time Limitation.* Counsel for each party shall be allowed fifteen minutes for an opening statement and thirty minutes for argument; but before the opening or the argument commences, the judge on motion or sua sponte, may reasonably reduce or extend the time.

(b) Instructions to Jury; Objection. At the close of the evidence or at such earlier time during the trial as the judge reasonably directs, any party may file written requests that the judge instruct the jury on the law as set forth in the requests. The judge shall inform counsel of his proposed action upon requests prior to their arguments to the jury. No party may assign as error the giving or the failure to give an instruction unless he objects thereto before the jury retires to consider its verdict, specifying the matter to which he objects and the grounds of his objection. Upon request, reasonable time shall be given to each party to object to the charge before the jury retires. Where either party wishes to object to the charge or to request additional instructions, the objection or the request shall be made out of the hearing of the jury, or where appropriate, out of the presence of the jury.

Reporter's Notes

The language of this rule substantially parallels that of Mass.R.Civ.P. 51. *See* National Advisory Commission on Criminal Justice Standards and Goals, *Courts,* Standard 4.15 (1973).

Subdivision (a). Drawn from Rules of Criminal Procedure (U.L.A.) Rule 521 (1974), this subdivision (a)(1) establishes the order of presentation of opening statements and closing arguments.

The fifteen-minute limitation on opening statements and thirty-minute limitation on arguments of subdivision (a)(2) are carried over from earlier rules of court. Superior Court Rules 7, 68 (1974); Supreme Judicial Court Rule 2:48 (1967: 351 Mass. 768). It is intended that under this rule only one attorney for each side is to participate, contrary to the provisions of Mass.R.Civ.P. 51 and Supreme Judicial Court Rule 2:48.

While placing time limits upon opening statements and arguments, and limiting arguments to a single counsel, Rule 24 does not otherwise affect their respective functions.

> The proper function of an opening is to outline in a general way the nature of the case which counsel expects to be able to prove or support by evidence. He should not be allowed to state facts which are irrelevant or for any reason plainly incompetent.

Posell v. Herscovitz, 237 Mass. 513, 514, 130 N.E. 69 (1921); *see* Commonwealth v. Clark, 292 Mass. 409, 410, 198 N.E. 641 (1935); Commonwealth v. LePage, 352 Mass. 403, 409, 226 N.E.2d 200 (1967). The refusal by counsel to confine his opening statement within the established boundaries constitutes unprofessional conduct, S.J.C. Rule 3:22A, *Disciplinary Rules Applicable to Practice as a Prosecutor or as a Defense Lawyer,* PF 11, DF 12 (February 14, 1979), and may amount to such misconduct as to warrant his expulsion from the courtroom and subjection to disciplinary proceedings. United States v. Dinitz, 96 S.Ct. 1075, 424 U.S. 600, 47 L.Ed.2d 267 (1976).

> An opening statement has a narrow purpose and scope. It is to state what evidence will be presented, to make it easier for the jurors to understand what is to follow, and to relate parts of the evidence and testimony to the whole; it is not an occasion for argument. To make statements which will not or cannot be supported by proof is, if it relates to significant elements of the case, professional misconduct. Moreover, it is fundamentally unfair to an opposing party to allow an attorney, with the standing and prestige inherent in being an officer of the court, to present to the jury statements not susceptible of proof but intended to influence the jury in reaching a verdict.
>
> A trial judge is under a duty, in order to protect the integrity of the trial, to take prompt and affirmative action to stop such professional misconduct.

United States v. Dinitz, supra, Burger, C.J., *concurring* at 612. *See* Commonwealth v. Fazio, Mass.Adv.Sh. (1978) 1617, 378 N.E.2d 648; ABA *Standards Relating to the Prosecution Function* § 5.5 (Approved Draft, 1971); ABA *Standards Relating to the Defense Function* § 7.4 (Approved Draft, 1971).

Although Massachusetts practice permits counsel "great latitude" in closing argument, Commonwealth v. Pettie, 363 Mass. 836, 840, 298 N.E.2d 836 (1973),

> [i]t is the duty of a judge sitting with a jury to guard against improper arguments. . . . Whether he shall do this by stopping counsel in the course of such an argument, by instructing the jury to disregard such an argument, or by combining both methods, rests largely in the discretion of the judge.

Commonwealth v. Witschi, 301 Mass. 459, 462, 17 N.E.2d 549 (1938). *Accord* Commonwealth v. Montecalvo, 367 Mass. 46, 56, 323 N.E.2d 888 (1975). *See* Commonwealth v. Earltop, Mass.Adv.Sh. (1977) 532, 539, 361 N.E.2d 220 (Hennessey, C.J., concurring) and cases cited: ABA *Standards Relating to the Function of the Trial Judge* § 5.10 (Approved Draft, 1972).

Where counsel "repeatedly and deliberately sail[s] unnecessarily close to the wind . . . beyond permissible limits," Commonwealth v. Redmond, 370 Mass. 591, 597, 351 N.E.2d 501 (1976), thus bringing unsworn testimony to the attention of the jury, the cumulative prejudice may be such that curative instructions are insufficient. The remedy in such instance is an order for a new trial. *Commonwealth v. Redmond,* supra. Further, where counsel misstates the law, a request for a curative instruction is denied, and the judge's general instruction that arguments are not evidence to be weighed by the jury is insufficient to allay the resulting prejudice, a new trial is required. Commonwealth v. Killelea, 370 Mass. 638, 351 N.E.2d 509 (1976). Because of these serious consequences, it is obvious that overreaching in argument—as in openings—may constitute unprofessional conduct. S.J.C. Rule 3:22A, *Disciplinary Rules Applicable to Practice as a Prosecutor or as a Defense Lawyer,* PF 13, PF 14 (February 14, 1979).

Subdivision (b). The incorporation of the civil practice form of requests for and objection to instructions into criminal practice is felt to be appropriate because the same basic principles apply to both types of proceedings. *Compare* Fed. R.Crim.P. 30 *with* Fed.R.Civ.P. 51. Subdivision (b) adopts what had been a long-standing practice before its formalization as a rule of the Superior Court. SUPERIOR COURT RULES, 1974, ANNOTATED 290–91 (Mass.Bar.Ed.1975);

see e.g., Commonwealth v. Boutwell, 162 Mass. 230, 38 N.E. 441 (1894); Commonwealth v. Hassan, 235 Mass. 26, 31, 126 N.E. 287 (1920).

The rule differs from Mass.R.Civ.P. 51 in requiring that objections to the charge or requests for additional instructions be made out of the hearing or presence of the jury in all cases. This comports with Rules of Criminal Procedure (U.L.A.) Rule 523(b) (1974) and ABA *Standards Relating to Trial by Jury* § 4.6(c) (Approved Draft, 1968). *See* Fed. R.Crim.P. 30.

Rule 25. Motion for Required Finding of Not Guilty

(Applicable to District Court and Superior Court)

(a) Entry by Court. The judge on motion of a defendant or on his own motion shall enter a finding of not guilty of the offense charged in an indictment or complaint or any part thereof after the evidence on either side is closed if the evidence is insufficient as a matter of law to sustain a conviction on the charge. If a defendant's motion for a required finding of not guilty is made at the close of the Commonwealth's evidence, it shall be ruled upon at that time. If the motion is denied or allowed only in part by the judge, the defendant may offer evidence in his defense without having reserved that right.

(b) Jury Trials.

(1) *Reservation of Decision on Motion.* If a motion for a required finding of not guilty is made at the close of all the evidence, the judge may reserve decision on the motion, submit the case to the jury, and decide the motion before the jury returns a verdict, after the jury returns a verdict of guilty, or after the jury is discharged without having returned a verdict.

(2) *Motion After Discharge of Jury.* If the motion is denied and the case is submitted to the jury, the motion may be renewed within five days after the jury is discharged and may include in the alternative a motion for a new trial. If a verdict of guilty is returned, the judge may on motion set aside the verdict and order a new trial, or order the entry of a finding of not guilty, or order the entry of a finding of guilty of any offense included in the offense charged in the indictment or complaint.

(c) Appeal.

(1) *Right of Appeal Where Motion for Relief Under Subdivision (b) Is Allowed After a Jury Verdict of Guilty.* The Commonwealth shall have the right to appeal to the appropriate appellate court a decision of a judge granting relief under the provisions of subdivisions (b)(1) and (2) of this rule on a motion for required finding of not guilty after the jury has returned a verdict of guilty or on an order for the entry of a finding of guilt of any offense included in the offense charged in the indictment or complaint.

(2) *Costs Upon Appeal.* If an appeal or application therefor is taken by the Commonwealth, the appellate court, upon the written motion of the defendant supported by affidavit, may determine and approve the payment to the defendant of his costs of appeal together with reasonable attorney's fees, if any, to be paid on the order of the trial court upon the entry of the rescript or the denial of the application.

Amended April 6, 1983, effective July 1, 1983; amended effective April 14, 1995.

Reporter's Notes

Rule 25 is derived with a minimum of change from former G.L. c. 278, § 11 (St.1964, c. 108, §§ 1, 2) and conforms in substance to Fed.R.Crim.P. 29. *See* ABA *Standards Relating to Trial by Jury* § 4.5 (Approved Draft, 1968); Rules of Criminal Procedure (U.L.A.) rule 522 (1974); Vt.R.Crim.P. 29; Me.R.Crim.P. 29.

The practical effect of this rule is to abolish the common law motion for a directed verdict and to substitute therefor a motion for a required finding of not guilty. This is essentially a change in terminology and does not presume to alter practice as it has developed relative to the directed verdict. The new term is not unknown in Massachusetts practice. *See* e.g., Commonwealth v. Coyne, 372 Mass. 599, 363 N.E.2d 256 (1977).

Motion for findings of not guilty are a part of Massachusetts practice in the context of nonjury cases, *see* e.g., Commonwealth v. Pursley, 2 Mass.App. 910, 321 N.E.2d 830 (1975) (Rescript), and are extended by this rule to include jury trials in recognition of the fact that juries have no proper function in this area. *See* ABA *Standards Relating to Trial by Jury* § 4.5(a), comment at 106–08 (Approved Draft, 1968).

Subdivision (a). The requirement that the court rule on a defendant's motion made at the close of the Commonwealth's case at the time such motion is made has recently been added to Massachusetts procedure. *See* Commonwealth v. Kelley, 370 Mass. 147, 149–50, 346 N.E.2d 368 (1976). This rule adopts this approach because of the difference between such a motion and a motion made at the close of all the evidence: in either case a defendant is requesting a judgment on the basis of evidence then before the court, but that evidence is very different at each of the two stages of trial. See ABA *Standards Relating to Trial by Jury* § 4.5(b), comment at 108 (Approved Draft, 1968).

On a defendant's motion for a directed verdict at the close of the Commonwealth's case, the defendant's rights become "fixed." If this motion is improperly denied on the basis of the condition of the case when the motion was made, the defendant is entitled to a reversal of the judgment, notwithstanding the introduction of further evidence. Of course, the Commonwealth's proof might deteriorate between the time the Commonwealth rests and the close of all the evidence. In such a case, on renewal of his motion, the defendant's rights would be reappraised in consideration of all the evidence. *Commonwealth v. Kelley,* supra, at n. 1; Commonwealth v. Blow, 370 Mass. 401, 407 n. 4, 348 N.E.2d 794 (1976); Commonwealth v. Aguiar, 370 Mass. 490, 498, 350 N.E.2d 436 (1976).

Under this rule the defendant may offer evidence in his defense without having reserved that right. Fairness requires this result. As the court stated in Jackson v. United States, 250 F.2d 897 (5th Cir.1958), the motion "would be a futile thing if the court could reserve its ruling and force the defendant to an election between resting and being deprived of the benefit of his motion," Id. at 901, because the defendant would be compelled to forfeit either his right to move for acquittal or his right to present evidence in his defense.

Subdivision (b)(1). This subdivision permits the court to reserve a decision on a motion made at the close of all the evidence. The objection stated in the *Jackson* case, supra, is not present in this situation, and G.L. c. 278, § 11 in fact expressly condoned the propriety of what often is referred to as a judgment notwithstanding the verdict.

Subdivision (b)(2). By giving the court the power to enter a finding of guilty of any lesser included offense or, in the language of G.L. c. 278, § 33E, a lesser degree of guilt, after a verdict of guilty, this rule deviates sharply from prior criminal practice under G.L. c. 278, § 11. Commonwealth v. Jones, 366 Mass. 805, 323 N.E.2d 726 (1975). This has the practical effect of extending to the trial courts, post-verdict, a power in all cases much like that which had previously been reserved to the Supreme Judicial Court in capital cases under G.L. c. 278, § 33E (as amended). This increases the options available to the trial judge after verdict. It is anticipated that through this extension greater judicial economy will result where the evidence will not support the charge, but where the weight of the evidence clearly requires the conviction of a lesser included offense. *See Jones,* supra.

It should be noted that the motion for a new trial which may be made under this subdivision is in addition to those rights which a defendant has under Rule 30(b). Obviously the court should order a new trial pursuant to this rule only upon motion of a defendant since otherwise the subsequent proceeding would be subject to constitutional attack on double jeopardy grounds.

Rule 26. Requests for Rulings

(Applicable to jury-waived trials in District Court and Superior Court)

Requests for rulings in the trial of a case shall be in writing and shall be presented to the court before the beginning of closing arguments, unless consent of the court is given to present requests later.

Reporter's Notes

Provisions comparable to Rule 26 are found in Fed. R.Crim.P. 23(c) and Rules of Criminal Procedure (U.L.A.) Rule 511(e) (1974). In addition, this rule reflects existing practice under District Court Rule 27 (1972) and Superior Court Rule 70 (1974), which deal with requests for rulings of law in non-jury trials. This rule is intended to secure for the purpose of review a separation of law from fact in cases where the trial judge acts both as factfinder and applier of law. *See* Caleb Pierce, Inc. v. Commonwealth, 354 Mass. 306, 237 N.E.2d 63 (1968).

Although much of the case law concerning requests for rulings has arisen out of the litigation of civil actions, *see* SUPERIOR COURT RULES, 1974, ANNOTATED 290–96 (Mass.Bar Ed.1975), a rule which provides the court with adequate opportunity to pass upon the soundness of requested rulings is equally appropriate in criminal practice. Commonwealth v. Hassan, 235 Mass. 26, 31, 126 N.E. 287 (1920).

Requiring the requests to be made before the beginning of closing arguments serves the function of apprising opposing counsel of the law under which the case will be decided. In Wilson v. United States, 250 F.2d 312, 324 (9th Cir.1957), the court recognized that the failure to honor requests for rulings on the law could hinder the administration of justice, since there is no real difference between the giving of improper instructions in a jury trial and the judge in a nonjury trial effectually instructing himself improperly on the law.

The failure to present written requests seasonably, however, which results in a trial judge's refusal to allow such requests, vitiates any claim of error in the refusal. Commonwealth v. Lammi, 310 Mass. 159, 164, 37 N.E.2d 250 (1941). It is a matter within the sound discretion of the trial judge whether to grant special leave for requests. *See* Finkelman v. Kaufman, 337 Mass. 770, 150 N.E.2d 285 (1958) (Rescript).

It should be noted that under this rule requests are to be made for rulings of law only, and not for findings of fact. Neither this rule nor the prior practice in the Commonwealth requires a judge to honor requests for findings of fact. Stella v. Curtis, 348 Mass. 458, 461, 204 N.E.2d 457 (1965).

Rule 27. Verdict

(Applicable to jury trials in District Court and Superior Court)

(a) Return. The verdict shall be unanimous. It shall be a general verdict returned by the jury to the judge in open court. The jury shall file a verdict slip with the clerk upon the return of the verdict.

(b) Several Offenses or Defendants. If there are two or more offenses or defendants tried together, the jury may, with the consent of the judge at any time during its deliberations return or be required by the judge to return a verdict or verdicts with respect to the defendants or charges as to which a verdict has been reached; and thereafter the jury may in the discretion of the judge resume deliberation. The judge may declare a mistrial as to any charges upon which the jury cannot agree upon a verdict; provided, however, that the judge may first require the jury to return verdicts on those charges upon which the jury can agree and direct that such verdicts be received and recorded.

(c) Special Questions. The trial judge may submit special questions to the jury.

(d) Poll of Jury. When a verdict is returned and before the verdict is recorded, the jury may be polled in the discretion of the judge. If after the poll there is not a unanimous concurrence, the jury may be directed to retire for further deliberations or may be discharged.

Reporter's Notes

This rule is patterned after Rule 31 of the Federal Rules of Criminal Procedure. Substantially, it reflects current Massachusetts practice as embodied in the common law and in statute. *See* former G.L. c. 278, § 11 (St.1964, c. 108, §§ 1–2).

Subdivision (a). This subdivision requires that the verdict be unanimous. This is consistent with Fed.R.Crim.P. 31(a). *Accord,* Me.R.Crim.P. 31(a); Rules of Criminal Procedure (U.L.A.) Rule 535(b) (1974). *But see* ABA *Standards Relating to Trial by Jury* § 1.1(b) (Approved Draft, 1968), which allows for less than a unanimous verdict.

The requirement that the jury return a verdict slip with the verdict is a change from existing practice. The verdict slip is a written recital of the verdict. This practice conforms to Rule 535(a) of the Uniform Rules of Criminal Procedure (U.L.A.) (1974). The use of a verdict slip will help reduce errors in the rendering and announcing of verdicts. *See* Commonwealth v. Brown, 367 Mass. 24, 27–29, 323 N.E.2d 902 (1975) (verdicts of not guilty returned, affirmed, and recorded and jury discharged; no error in permitting corrected verdicts to be entered since jury had remained undispersed, in custody, and had not been influenced), pet. for habeas corpus denied sub nom. Brown v. Gunter, 428 F.Supp. 889 (D.Mass.1977), aff'd, 562 F.2d 122 (1st Cir.1977).

Subdivision (b). This subdivision permits a jury in multiple-defendant or multiple-offense cases, with the consent of the court, to return a verdict at any time during their deliberations with respect to charges or defendants as to which a verdict has been reached. This rule also permits the court to require the return of such verdicts before the jury has reached a verdict as to all the defendants or charges. In either case, if the court directs, the jury is to continue its deliberations after rendering the verdicts under this subdivision. To the extent that this rule permits the jury to return such verdicts without having reached a decision on all the charges or defendants, it is consistent with Fed.R.Crim.P. 31(b)–(c). *Accord* Rules of Criminal Procedure (U.L.A.) Rule 535(c)–(d) (1974).

This rule also provides that the court may declare a mistrial in cases where the jury is unable to reach a verdict. However, it must first receive and record the verdicts which the jury can agree upon. *See* ABA *Standards Relating to Trial by Jury* §§ 5.4–.5 (Approved Draft, 1968); Rules of Criminal Procedure (U.L.A.), supra, Rule 541.

Subdivision (b) does not prohibit retrial of those defendants as to whom the jury is unable to reach a verdict. This is consistent with Fed.R.Crim.P. 31(b), which provides that, in cases of multiple defendants, disagreement as to one or more defendants has no effect upon the verdict as to any other defendant, and such defendant may be retried without violating the protection of the double jeopardy clause. 8A J. MOORE, FEDERAL PRACTICE para. 31.02[2] (1978 rev.). It has long been settled that jeopardy does not attach where the jury is discharged after inability to reach a verdict. United States v. Perez, 22 U.S. 579, 9 Wheat. 579, 6 L.Ed. 165 (1824); Thames v. Commonwealth, 365 Mass. 477, 312 N.E.2d 687 (1974). It is within the discretion of the court to declare a mistrial where there is a "manifest necessity." *United States v. Perez,* supra at 580. Unless such "manifest necessity" exists, a second prosecution will be barred by the double jeopardy clause. Since *Perez,* it has been held that where the jury has been unable to agree upon a verdict, the declaration of a mistrial is a "classic example" of manifest necessity. United States v. Castellanos, 478 F.2d 749, 751 (2d Cir.1973). Thus the defendant may be retried without twice being placed in jeopardy.

Subdivision (c). One change in Massachusetts law is the elimination of the special verdict. General Laws c. 278, § 11 had authorized the jury to return a special verdict, although this procedure was seldom used. This subdivision does, however, recognize the practice of submitting special questions to the jury. *See* Commonwealth v. Beneficial Finance Co., 360 Mass. 188, 299–300, 275 N.E.2d 33, 62 A.L.R.3d 1143 (1971), cert. denied, 92 S.Ct. 2433, 407 U.S. 910, 32 L.Ed.2d 689 (1972). Special questions should, however, be used sparingly as they can " 'catechize' a reluctant juror away from an acquittal and towards a seemingly more 'logical' conviction." Heald v. Mullaney, 505 F.2d 1241, 1245 (1st Cir.1974), cert. denied, 95 S.Ct. 1339, 420 U.S. 955, 43 L.Ed.2d 432 (1975).

Subdivision (d). This subdivision is based upon Fed. R.Crim.P. 31(d), but differs in that the polling of the jury is to be discretionary with the court rather than a right of the defendant so as to conform to existing Massachusetts practice. That this discretion is well-settled in the Commonwealth was recently reaffirmed in Commonwealth v. Stewart, Mass.Adv. Sh. (1978) 1521, 1533–34, 377 N.E.2d 693. *See also* Commonwealth v. Valliere, 366 Mass. 479, 497, 321 N.E.2d 625 (1974); Commonwealth v. Caine, 366 Mass. 366, 375, 318 N.E.2d 901 (1974); Commonwealth v. Fleming, 360 Mass. 404, 408, 274 N.E.2d 809 (1971) (jurors polled); *Commonwealth v. Beneficial Finance Co.,* supra, at 300–301. Under Rule 31 of the Federal Rules of Criminal Procedure and under the ABA *Standards Relating to Trial by Jury* § 5.5 (Approved Draft, 1968), a jury is to be polled only at the request of a party or upon the court's own motion.

In any case, where a jury has been polled and there is not a unanimous concurrence, *compare Commonwealth v. Fleming,* supra, or it appears that the verdict was a compromise or other serious doubts are raised as to its integrity, *see Commonwealth v. Stewart,* supra, the court may declare a mistrial, or alternatively, order further deliberations. *Accord,* Rules of Criminal Procedure (U.L.A.) Rule 535(e) (1974).

Rule 28. Judgment

(Applicable to District Court and Superior Court)

(a) Judgment. If the defendant has been determined to be guilty, a verdict or finding of guilty shall be rendered, or if he has been determined to be not guilty, a verdict or finding of not guilty shall be rendered, in open court, and shall be entered on the court's docket.

(b) Imposition of Sentence. After a verdict, finding, or plea of guilty, or a plea of nolo contendere, or an admission to sufficient facts, the defendant shall have the right to be sentenced without unreasonable delay. Pending sentence the court may commit the defendant or continue or alter the bail as provided by law. Before imposing sentence the court shall afford the defendant or his counsel an opportunity to speak on behalf of the defendant and to present any information in mitigation of punishment.

(c) Notification of Right to Appeal. After a judgment of guilty is entered, the court shall advise the defendant of his right to appeal. In the District Court, upon the request of the defendant, the clerk of the court shall prepare and file forthwith a notice of appeal.

(d) Presentence Investigation.

(1) *Criminal Record.* The probation officer shall inquire into the nature of every criminal case or juvenile complaint brought before the court and report to the court information concerning all prior criminal prosecutions or juvenile complaints, if any, and the disposition of each such prosecution, except where the defendant was found not guilty. Such information is to be presented before a defendant is admitted to bail in

court, and also before disposition of the case against him.

(2) *Report*. The report of the presentence investigation shall contain any prior criminal or juvenile prosecution record of the defendant, but shall not contain any information relating to criminal or juvenile prosecutions in which the defendant was found not guilty. In addition, the report shall include such other available information as may be helpful to the court in the disposition of the case.

(3) *Availability to Parties*. Prior to the disposition the presentence report shall be made available to the prosecutor and counsel for the defendant for inspection. In extraordinary cases, the judge may except from disclosure parts of the report which are not relevant to a proper sentence, diagnostic opinion which might seriously disrupt a program of rehabilitation, sources of information obtained upon a promise of confidentiality, or any other information which, if disclosed, might result in harm, physical or otherwise, to the defendant or other persons. If the report is not made fully available, the portions thereof which are not disclosed shall not be relied upon in determining sentence. No party may make any copy of the presentence report.

(e) Filing. The court may file a case after a guilty verdict or finding without imposing a sentence if the defendant and the Commonwealth both consent. With the consent of both parties, the judge may specify a time limit beyond which the case may not be removed from the file, and may specify any events that may cause the case to be removed from the file. The defendant shall file a written consent with the court as to both the filing of the case and any time limit or events regarding removal from the file. Prior to accepting the defendant's consent, the court shall inform the defendant on the record in open court:

(i) that the defendant has a right to request sentencing on any or all filed case(s) at any time;

(ii) that subject to any time limit imposed by the court, the prosecutor may request that the case be removed from the file and sentence imposed if a related conviction or sentence is reversed or vacated or upon the prosecutor's establishing by a preponderance of the evidence either that the defendant committed a new criminal offense or that an event occurred on which the continued filing of the case was expressly made contingent by the court; and

(iii) that if the case is removed from the file the defendant may be sentenced on the case.

In sentencing the defendant after the removal of a case from the file, the court shall consider the over-all scheme of punishment employed by the original sentencing judge.

December 17, 2008, effective April 1, 2009.

Reporter's Notes

The format and much of the language of this rule is derived from Rule 32 of the Federal Rules of Criminal Procedure. Subdivision (c) is taken from Rule 3.670 of the Florida Rules of Criminal Procedure (1975). The Federal Rule has been significantly modified so as to conform to existing Massachusetts practice.

Subdivision (a). This subdivision is a restatement of Rule 3.670 of the Florida Rules of Criminal Procedure (1975). It requires the verdict or finding, whether it is guilty or not guilty, to be rendered in open court and entered on the court's docket. *See* Fed.R.Crim.P. 32(b)(1); Rules of Criminal Procedure (U.L.A.) Rule 621 (1974).

Subdivision (b). The defendant has the right to prompt sentencing. *See* G.L. c. 279, § 4; Commonwealth v. Kossowan, 265 Mass. 436, 165 N.E. 22 (1929); In re Lebowitch, 235 Mass. 357 (1920). *See* ABA *Standards Relating to Sentencing Alternatives & Procedures* § 5.4(a) (Approved Draft, 1968). However, the defendant can waive that right. When the defendant consents to a continuance of the case or a probationary term, he has by implication waived his right to prompt sentencing. *Compare* Fla.R.Crim.P. 3.670 (1975).

Pending the pronouncement of sentence, the court may commit the defendant, place him on probation, or release him on bail in a manner consistent with existing law. *See* G.L. c. 276, §§ 58, 65, 87. The terms of his release may subsequently be altered by the court. *See* ABA *Standards Relating to Post Conviction Remedies* § 5.2(b) (Approved Draft, 1968); Rules of Criminal Procedure (U.L.A.) Rule 611 (1974); 18 U.S.C. § 3148.

Finally, this subdivision grants to the defendant or his counsel the opportunity to speak on behalf of the defendant and to offer any information which may serve to mitigate the sentence to be imposed. While there is no constitutional or other right to allocution, Commonwealth v. Curry, Mass.App. Adv.Sh. (1978) 977, 380 N.E.2d 1325 (Rescript); Jeffries v. Commonwealth, 94 Mass. (12 Allen) 145, 153 (1866), this opportunity has traditionally been afforded the defendant at common law and may have therapeutic value for the defendant as well as potential for mitigation. 8A J. MOORE, FEDERAL PRACTICE para. 32.05 (1978 rev.). In Green v. United States, 81 S.Ct. 653, 365 U.S. 301, 5 L.Ed.2d 670 (1961), the Supreme Court indicated that the right to allocution was a personal one and could not be satisfied by only affording the opportunity to the defendant's counsel. "The most persuasive counsel may not be able to speak for a defendant as the defendant might, with halting eloquence, speak for himself." Id. at 304. For the procedure to be followed if a denial of the right to allocution is found, see Hill v. United States, 82 S.Ct. 468, 368 U.S. 424, 7 L.Ed.2d 417 (1962). *See* ABA *Standards Relating to Sentencing Alternatives & Procedures* § 5.4(a)(iii) (Approved Draft, 1968); Rules of Criminal Procedure (U.L.A.) rule 613(2) (1974).

Subdivision (c). This subdivision is meant to assure that the defendant is informed of his right to appeal following a finding of guilty, a finding of sufficient facts to warrant a finding of guilty, or imposition of sentence in a District Court jury-waived session or after a verdict or finding of guilt in a District Court jury session or the Superior Court. *See* Superior Court Rule 65 (1974, as amended, 1977).

General Laws c. 278, § 18 (as amended, St.1978, c. 478, § 302) permits a defendant convicted in District Court jury-waived session to appeal either from a sentence or from a finding of guilty where no sentence is imposed. Rule 9 of the District Court Initial Rules of Criminal Procedure (1971) provides that either the judge or the sessions clerk may inform the defendant of his right to his de novo appeal to a jury session. That practice is in conformity with this rule. *Compare* Fed.R.Crim.P. 32(a)(2) *with* Rules of Criminal Procedure (U.L.A.) 613(4) (1974), both of which provide that the judge is to inform the defendant of his right to appeal.

This rule is much more limited in its operation than the federal rule, which requires notice of the defendant's right to appellate review to correct errors. This rule does, however, direct the District Court clerk to file the notice of appeal on behalf of the defendant upon his request, which is consistent with the federal rule.

Subdivision (d). This rule preserves the distinction between the defendant's criminal record and the full probation report which was emphasized in Commonwealth v. Martin, 355 Mass. 296, 244 N.E.2d 303 (1969).

Subdivision (d)(1) is essentially a restatement of existing law. See G.L. c. 276, § 85; G.L. c. 279, § 4A, pursuant to which the defendant is given the right to see his criminal record. This rule affords the court the important right to inspect probation records regarding a defendant's prior criminal convictions or other dispositions, exclusive of not guilty findings, prior to his release on bail. *But see* District Court Initial Rules of Criminal Procedure 8 (1971), which would prohibit the use of probation records for bail determinations.

Support can be found for the position taken in this subdivision in G.L. c. 119, §§ 60, 60A (as amended, St.1978, c. 478, § 64). Section 60 authorizes the consideration of juvenile delinquency records before imposition of sentence in criminal proceedings. Section 60A provides the same basic standard for the availability of juvenile records for inspection in appeals to a juvenile appeals session from adjudications of delinquency as does subdivision (d)(3), infra, for the availability of the records of criminal and juvenile prosecutions prior to sentencing in criminal proceedings.

Although G.L. c. 279, § 4A mandates that the criminal record is not to include information concerning prior charges of which the defendant was acquitted, it does not require exclusion of information as to other *pending* charges. Commonwealth v. Franks, 372 Mass. 866, 362 N.E.2d 362 (1977) (Rescript); Commonwealth v. LeBlanc, 370 Mass. 217, 222, 346 N.E.2d 874 (1976); Commonwealth v. Settipane, 5 Mass. App. 648, 368 N.E.2d 1213 (1977). The consideration of other charges is appropriate as long as the judge makes clear that he is not passing on guilt or innocence on the untried charges, the resulting sentence is within statutory limits and there is no basis in the record for apprehension of vindictiveness or retaliatory motivation. *Settipane,* supra. *Accord Franks,* supra.

There is no constitutional objection to a judge knowing of other pending charges, although due process would require resentencing if inaccurate, unreliable or misleading information had been considered at sentencing, or if the judge had undertaken to punish the defendant for conduct other than that of which he is immediately convicted. *Commonwealth v. LeBlanc,* supra at 221, and cases cited. For a similar example of factors beyond the scope of consideration for sentencing, *see* Commonwealth v. Murray, 4 Mass.App.Ct. 493, 351 N.E.2d 555 (1976).

Subdivision (d)(2) contemplates a probation report concerning the defendant which will include the criminal record of subdivision (d)(1) and also other information about the defendant which may assist the court in disposing of the case. The authorization for such reports is found in G.L. c. 276, § 100, as noted in *Commonwealth v. Martin,* supra. The probation report of this subdivision may be used by the court for purposes of sentencing as well as for other purposes, such as the setting of bail. To the extent that this report is multiple-purpose, it is somewhat different than the pre-sentence investigation report of Fed.R.Crim.P. 32(c)(1)–(2), which is used primarily for the purpose of sentencing following a determination of guilt. *See* Rules of Criminal Procedure (U.L.A.) Rule 612 (1974). Other sources also recommend the use of pre-sentence investigative reports following a guilty finding. *See* ABA *Standards Relating to Sentencing Alternatives & Procedures* §§ 4.1(b), 4.2(a), 4.3, 4.4(a)–(b) (Approved Draft, 1968); ALI *Model Code of Pre–Arraignment Procedure* § 320.4 (P.O.D.1975); National Advisory Commission on Criminal Justice Standards & Goals, *Corrections,* Standards 5.14(1), (3); 5.15(1); 5.16; 16.10 (1973).

Subdivision (d)(3) states that generally the report compiled by the probation department shall be made available to the defendant and his counsel and to the prosecutor. The court in *Commonwealth v. Martin,* supra, held that the defendant did not have a right to see the report, but stated that "the administration of justice would be improved by a liberal and generous use of the power to disclose." Id. at 303, *quoting* United States v. Fischer, 381 F.2d 509, 512–13 (2d Cir.), cert. denied, 88 S.Ct. 1064, 390 U.S. 973, 19 L.Ed.2d 1185 (1967). The court stated that the main consideration against full disclosure is the prospect that the revelation of certain material given the probation officer in confidence, would result in the destruction of the sources of such material and its availability. *Commonwealth v. Martin,* supra, at 303.

This subdivision further conditions availability upon the judge's determination that disclosure would not "result in harm, physical or otherwise, to the defendant or other persons." This qualification accords with Fed.R.Crim.P. 32(c)(3)(A). ABA *Standards Relating to Sentencing Alternatives and Procedures* § 4.4 (Approved Draft, 1968), also recommends disclosure of presentence reports with certain exceptions, as does ALI, *Model Code of Pre–Arraignment Procedure* § 320.4 (P.O.D.1975).

The next to last sentence of this subdivision provides that if any portion of the report is not made available, then the judge is not to rely upon any information contained in that portion in determining sentence. *See* Gardner v. Florida, 97 S.Ct. 1197, 430 U.S. 349, 51 L.Ed.2d 393 (1977) (denial of due process to impose death sentence on basis of information contained in undisclosed presentence report which defendant could not deny or explain).

Rule 29. Revision or Revocation of Sentence

(Applicable to District Court and Superior Court)

(a) Revision or Revocation. The trial judge upon his own motion or the written motion of a defendant filed within sixty days after the imposition of a sentence, within sixty days after receipt by the trial court of a rescript issued upon affirmance of the judgment or dismissal of the appeal, or within sixty days after entry of any order or judgment of an appellate court denying review of, or having the effect of upholding, a judgment of conviction, may, upon such terms and conditions as he shall order, revise or revoke such sentence if it appears that justice may not have been done.

(b) Affidavits. If a defendant files a motion pursuant to this rule, he shall file and serve and the prosecutor may file and serve affidavits in support of their respective positions. The judge may rule on a motion filed pursuant to this rule on the basis of facts alleged in the affidavits without further hearing.

(c) Notice. The defendant shall serve the prosecutor with a copy of any motion and affidavit filed pursuant to this rule. If the judge orders that a hearing be held on the motion, the court shall give the parties reasonable notice of the time set for the hearing.

(d) Place of Hearing. A motion filed pursuant to this rule may be heard by the trial judge wherever he is then sitting.

Reporter's Notes

Rule 29 is drawn in part from Fed.R.Crim.P. 35 and from former G.L. c. 278, §§ 29A (St.1959, c. 167, § 1) and 29C (St.1962, c. 310, § 2). *See* Rules of Criminal Procedure (U.L.A.) rule 633 (1974).

Subdivision (a). General Laws c. 278, § 29A, which was applicable to sentences imposed upon a plea without trial in the District Court, and § 29C, which was applicable to sentences imposed after plea or trial in the Superior Court provided the 60–day limit incorporated into this subdivision. It should be noted that under §§ 29A and 29C, a sentence could only be revised or revoked within 60 days after imposition; pursuant to this subdivision, a sentence may be revised or revoked at any time so long as the defendant's motion is *filed* within 60 days after imposition of the sentence, or within 60 days after the finality of the conviction is established upon direct appeal or after such review is denied or withdrawn. This subdivision enlarges the power of the District Court so that it is commensurate with that of the Superior Court under former G.L. c. 278, § 29C so as to enable the judge to revise or revoke a sentence imposed after a trial in the District Court. Under prior practice, a de novo appeal to the Superior Court was deemed to vacate the District Court judgment and to "render immaterial . . . all . . . errors and irregularities in the proceedings" below. Commonwealth v. Holmes, 119 Mass. 195, 199 (1875). *Accord* Enbinder v. Commonwealth, 368 Mass. 214, 217, 330 N.E.2d 846 (1975). For that reason, G.L. c. 29A expressly did not apply to appealed cases. Now, under this rule, a claim of appeal from a District Court jury-waived session to a jury session divests the judge who imposed the original sentence of the power to revise or revoke that sentence.

The rule governs reductions of sentences motivated by demands of fairness. It is thus a rule which accords the trial judge broad discretion. As was stated in District Attorney for the Northern District v. Superior Court, 342 Mass. 119, 172 N.E.2d 245 (1961):

> Occasions inevitably will occur where a conscientious judge, after reflection or upon receipt of new probation reports or other information, will feel that he has been too harsh or has failed to give due weight to mitigating factors which properly he should have taken into account.

Id. at 128. If within sixty days after sentence has been imposed, the trial judge for any reason feels the sentence that has been imposed is too harsh, he is permitted to reduce it sua sponte, although he is not permitted to consider events occurring after the original imposition. Commonwealth v. Sitko, Mass.Adv.Sh. (1977) 668, 676–78, 363 N.E.2d 303.

Subdivision (a) speaks only in terms of a motion by the defendant, although in prior practice motions of the Commonwealth to revise or revoke a sentence were not unknown. *Commonwealth v. Sitko,* supra.

The 60–day period established by the rule is absolute, and the trial judge has no power to extend the time within which the motion must be filed or within which the sentence may be altered sua sponte. Mass.R.Crim.P. 46(b); Commonwealth v. Burrone, 347 Mass. 451, 198 N.E.2d 407 (1964). However, under this rule, once the motion is filed, he may act on it at a time later than 60 days.

The view under the common law was that so long as nothing had been done to carry a sentence into execution, "it was, in contemplation of law, in the breast of the court, and subject to revision and alteration." Commonwealth v. Weymouth, 84 Mass. (2 Allen) 144, 145–46, 79 Am.Dec. 776 (1862). The modern view is that a sentence may be *reduced* by judicial action even though the defendant has commenced serving it. District Attorney for the Northern District v. Superior Court, 342 Mass. 119, 126–28, 172 N.E.2d 245 (1961). That an increase in the sentence once execution has commenced is not permitted has, however, long been settled. United States v. Benz, 51 S.Ct. 113, 282 U.S. 304, 307–09, 75 L.Ed. 354 (1931); Ex parte Lange, 85 U.S. (Wall.) 163, 167–74, 21 L.Ed. 872 (1873).

A mistake in the mittimus under which a defendant is serving his sentence may be corrected at any time because such a revision does not change the sentence imposed, only the transcription of that sentence. Bolduc v. Commissioner of Correction, 355 Mass. 765, 247 N.E.2d 561 (1969).

Subdivision (b). The objective of subdivision (b) is to encourage the disposition of post-conviction motions upon affidavit. Presently, the rule in Massachusetts is that the use of affidavits in lieu of oral testimony is discretionary with the trial judge. Commonwealth v. Coggins, 324 Mass. 552, 87 N.E.2d 200 (1949). The only change contemplated by this subdivision is that the use of this established procedure is to be extended to all cases where it is deemed appropriate by the trial judge. *See* Mass.R.Crim.P. 30(c)(3).

Subdivision (c). The provision of Mass.R.Crim.P. 32, relative to service and notice, are incorporated by this subdivision.

Subdivision (d). This provision is paralleled in subdivision (c)(7) of Mass.R.Crim.P. 30 and is intended to expedite the disposition of motions for post-conviction relief.

Rule 30. Post Conviction Relief

(a) Unlawful Restraint. Any person who is imprisoned or whose liberty is restrained pursuant to a criminal conviction may at any time, as of right, file a written motion requesting the trial judge to release him or her or to correct the sentence then being served upon the ground that the confinement or restraint was imposed in violation of the Constitution or laws of the United States or of the Commonwealth of Massachusetts.

(b) New Trial. The trial judge upon motion in writing may grant a new trial at any time if it appears that justice may not have been done. Upon the motion the trial judge shall make such findings of fact as are necessary to resolve the defendant's allegations of error of law.

(c) Post Conviction Procedure.

(1) *Service and Notice.* The moving party shall serve the office of the prosecutor who represented the Commonwealth in the trial court with a copy of any motion filed under this rule.

(2) *Waiver.* All grounds for relief claimed by a defendant under subdivisions (a) and (b) of this rule shall be raised by the defendant in the original or amended motion. Any grounds not so raised are waived unless the judge in the exercise of discretion permits them to be raised in a subsequent motion, or unless such grounds could not reasonably have been raised in the original or amended motion.

(3) *Affidavits.* Moving parties shall file and serve and parties opposing a motion may file and serve affidavits where appropriate in support of their respective positions. The judge may rule on the issue or issues presented by such motion on the basis of the facts alleged in the affidavits without further hearing if no substantial issue is raised by the motion or affidavits.

(4) *Discovery.* Where affidavits filed by the moving party under subdivision (c)(3) establish a prima facie case for relief, the judge on motion of any party, after notice to the opposing party and an opportunity to be heard, may authorize such discovery as is deemed appropriate, subject to appropriate protective order.

(5) *Counsel.* The judge in the exercise of discretion may assign or appoint counsel in accordance with the provisions of these rules to represent a defendant in the preparation and presentation of motions filed under subdivisions (a) and (b) of this rule. The court, after notice to the Commonwealth and an opportunity to be heard, may also exercise discretion to allow the defendant costs associated with the preparation and presentation of a motion under this rule.

(6) *Presence of Moving Party.* A judge may entertain and determine a motion under subdivisions (a) and (b) of this rule without requiring the presence of the moving party at the hearing.

(7) *Place and Time of Hearing.* All motions under subdivisions (a) and (b) of this rule may be heard by the trial judge wherever the judge is then sitting. The parties shall have at least 30 days notice of any hearing unless the judge determines that good cause exists to order the hearing held sooner.

(8) *Appeal.* An appeal from a final order under this rule may be taken to the Appeals Court, or to the Supreme Judicial Court in an appropriate case, by either party.

(A) If an appeal is taken, the defendant shall not be discharged from custody pending final decision upon the appeal; provided, however, that the defendant may, in the discretion of the judge, be admitted to bail pending decision of the appeal.

(B) If an appeal or application therefor is taken by the Commonwealth, upon written motion supported by affidavit, the Appeals Court or the Supreme Judicial Court may determine and approve payment to the defendant of the costs of appeal together with reasonable attorney's fees, if any, to be paid on the order of the trial court after entry of the rescript or the denial of the application. If the final order grants relief other than a discharge from custody, the trial court or the court in which the appeal is pending may, upon application by the Commonwealth, in its discretion, and upon such conditions as it deems just, stay the execution of the order pending final determination of the matter.

(9) *Appeal under G.L. c. 278, § 33E.* If an appeal or application for leave to appeal is taken by the Commonwealth under the provisions of Chapter 278, Section 33E, upon written notice supported by affidavit, the Supreme Judicial Court may determine and approve payment to the defendant of the costs of appeal together with reasonable attorney's fees to be paid on order of the trial court after entry of the rescript or the denial of the application.

Amended effective April 14, 1995; amended September 6, 2001, effective October 1, 2001.

Reporter's Notes

This rule, which marks a significant departure from prior Massachusetts practice, is derived from a number of sources. *See* Fed.R.Crim.P., Rules 33, 35; ABA *Standards Relating to Post-Conviction Remedies* (Approved Draft, 1968); *Rules of Criminal Procedure* (U.L.A.) Rule 632 (1974).

The moving party is to seek post conviction relief from the trial judge presiding at the initial trial. *See* Commonwealth v. Sullivan, 385 Mass. 497, 498 n. 1 (1981) (the judge who presided at a defendant's trial normally should hear that defendant's motion for a new trial). The trial judge is familiar with the case which "may make for more efficient handling." ABA *Standards, supra*, § 1.4, comment at 30. *See* McCastle, Petitioner, 401 Mass. 105, 107 (1987) (Rule 30 "assigns the motion to the trial judge who heard the case, on the theory that [the judge's] familiarity with the case can assist in its effective handling.") However, for this same reason the trial judge may bring to the hearing a prejudice that another judge would not have. Recusal of the trial judge should thus be liberally exercised, particularly where it is requested by the moving party. See ABA *Standards, supra*, § 1.4(c). A second advantage to be gained from giving the trial court original jurisdiction to hear post conviction motions is that the necessary witnesses, if any, are likely to be convenient to the court.

Subdivision (a). When originally adopted in 1979, this subdivision consolidated the previously distinct procedures of habeas corpus and writ of error. The purpose of the revision was to simplify post conviction procedure, while maintaining the full scope of relief previously available. *See* ABA *Standards Relating to Post-Conviction Remedies* § 1.1 (Approved

Draft, 1968). However, the writ of habeas corpus still has limited application in cases contending that the term of a lawfully imposed sentence has expired and basing a claim for relief on grounds distinct from issues arising at the indictment, trial, conviction or sentencing stages. *See e.g.*, Averett, Petitioner, 404 Mass. 28, 30 (1988) (forfeiture of good time credits). A petition for a writ of habeas corpus is appropriate only where the petition alleges that the petitioner is entitled to immediate release. *See* Stewart, Petitioner, 411 Mass. 566, 568 (1991). On the other hand, a rule 30(a) motion is not available to contest the legality of a sentence that the defendant has already completed. *Cf.* Commonwealth v. Lupo, 394 Mass. 644, 646 (1985) ("Rule 30 [a] is intended primarily to provide relief for defendants incarcerated in violation of Federal law or of the laws of the Commonwealth.")

In addition to permitting convicted defendants to seek release from illegal confinement or other restraint on their liberty, this subdivision permits them to seek the correction of an illegal sentence. A distinction is drawn between an illegal sentence and a sentence imposed in an illegal manner. *See* Fed.R.Crim.P., Rule 35.

The concepts of an illegal sentence and an illegally-imposed sentence are narrow and permit the trial judge no discretion in the decision to modify a sentence. Both concepts presume that a defendant's conviction is in all ways valid and that only the sentence is in some manner defective. The difference between the two is that an illegal sentence is one that is not permitted by law for the offense committed by the defendant, *e.g.*, a sentence that exceeds the permissible maximum. *See e.g.*, Commonwealth v. Ambers, 397 Mass. 705 (1986) (challenge to legality of consecutive sentences); Commonwealth v. Harris, 23 Mass.App.Ct. 687, 691–92 (1987) (court sentenced defendant for an offense other than that for which the jury convicted). Illegality has been held to include not only facially illegal sentences, but sentences premised upon a major misunderstanding by the sentencing judge as to the legal bounds of the judge's authority. *E.g.*, United States v. Lewis, 392 F.2d 440 (4th Cir. 1968) (sentencing judge believed parole permissible upon imposition of maximum sentence); Thomas v. United States, 368 F.2d 941 (5th Cir. 1966) (sentence constituted penalty upon exercise of defendant fifth amendment rights); Robinson v. United States, 313 F.2d 817 (7th Cir. 1963) (sentencing judge recommended parole when defendant ineligible). An illegally-imposed sentence is one where the irregularity lies with the procedure employed in imposing the sentence. *See e.g.*, Hill v. United States, 368 U.S. 424 (1962), where the trial court denied the defendant his right of allocution, which was held to be a procedural irregularity. In the context of a probation revocation order, a motion under Rule 30(a) would be appropriate only as a vehicle for challenging the legality of the sentence the defendant received and not the legality of the order revoking probation. Irregularities in the probation revocation process should be challenged through a direct appeal. *See* Commonwealth v. Christian, 429 Mass. 1022 (1999).

An illegal sentence must be corrected by the court at any time upon proper motion by the defendant. An illegally-imposed sentence can only be corrected upon a motion filed within the time permitted by Mass.R.Crim.P., Rule 29(a), that is, within 60 days after imposition. *See Rules of Criminal Procedure* (ULA) Rule 632 (1974). The only restriction upon the correction of an illegal sentence is that it cannot be increased if it has been partially executed. *See* United States v. Benz, 282 U.S. 304 (1931).

Subdivision (b). This subdivision was taken primarily from Fed.R.Crim.P., Rule 33. The standard established in the first sentence is, however, taken directly from former G.L. c. 278, § 29 (St.1966, c. 301).

Prior to 1964 a motion for a new trial under G.L. c. 278, § 29 could only be granted within one year after the end of the trial. *See* Fine v. Commonwealth, 312 Mass. 252 (1942); Commonwealth v. Sacco, 261 Mass. 12 (1927). However, a 1964 amendment rewrote the statute so that the court could consider such a motion filed at any time after judgment. St.1964, c. 82.

In the absence of constitutional error, whether to grant a motion for a new trial on an issue that has been properly presented to the court is within the sound discretion of the trial judge. *See* Commonwealth v. Smith, 318 Mass. 141, 142 (1980). The basis for a new trial can either relate to the conduct of the trial, *see e.g.*, Commonwealth v. Vaidulas, 433 Mass. 247, 250 (2001) ("The only means of revisiting after trial a matter raised in a motion in limine is through a motion for postconviction relief under rule 30."); Commonwealth v. Francis, 411 Mass. 579, 585–86 (1992) (improper jury instruction); Commonwealth v. Westmoreland, 388 Mass. 269, 271 (1983) (ineffective assistance of counsel); Commonwealth v. Schand, 420 Mass. 783, 787–88 (1995) (prosecutor's failure to disclose exculpatory evidence); Commonwealth v. Nickerson, 388 Mass. 246, 249–250 (1983) (defendant's mental incompetence); Commonwealth v. Ciminera, 11 Mass.App.Ct. 101, 107–110, *aff'd* 384 Mass. 807 (1981) (jury misconduct), or to the discovery of new facts that bear on the question of guilt, *see e.g.*, Commonwealth v. Pires, 389 Mass. 657, 664–666 (1983) (newly–discovered evidence); Commonwealth v. Watson, 377 Mass. 814, 815 (1979) (recanted testimony).

A defendant seeking a new trial on the basis of newly discovered evidence must establish both that the evidence is newly discovered and that it casts real doubt on the justice of the conviction. *See* Commonwealth v. Pike, 431 Mass. 212, 218 (2000). The allegedly new evidence must be material and credible, and "carry a measure of strength in support of the defendant's position." Commonwealth v. Grace, 397 Mass. 303, 305–06 (1986). A defendant must also show that the evidence was unknown to the defendant or the defendant's counsel, and not discoverable through "reasonable pretrial diligence" at the time of trial or at the time of the presentation of any earlier motion for a new trial. *See Pike*, 431 Mass. at 218. "The motion judge decides not whether the verdict would have been different, but rather whether the new evidence would probably have been a real factor in the jury's deliberations. This process of judicial analysis requires a thorough knowledge of the trial proceedings and can, of course, be aided by a trial judge's observation of events at trial." Commonwealth v. Moore, 408 Mass. 117, 126–27 (1990) *quoting* Commonwealth v. Grace, 397 Mass. 303, 305–06 (1986).

A new trial motion under Rule 30(b) is the appropriate vehicle to attack the validity of a guilty plea or an admission to sufficient facts. *See* Commonwealth v. Fanelli, 412 Mass. 497 (1992) (treating the defendant's postsentence motion to withdraw guilty pleas as a motion for a new trial pursuant to Mass.R.Crim.P. 30); Dunbrack v. Commonwealth, 398 Mass. 502 (1986) (the appropriate method for attacking the lawfulness of the admission to sufficient facts and the sentence imposed is a postconviction motion for new trial pursuant to rule 30(b) and not a petition under c. 211 § 3). A Rule 30(b) motion is also appropriate where the defendant has been deprived of a constitutionally protected right by counsel's failure to appeal. *See* Commonwealth v. Cowie, 404 Mass. 119, 121 (1989). However, granting a new trial because the verdict is against the weight of the evidence should be done according to Rule 25(b)(2), not Rule 30. *See* Commonwealth v. Preston, 393 Mass. 318, 324 (1984).

The requirement that the trial judge make findings upon a motion for a new trial is contrary to the traditional rule in the Commonwealth, *see* Commonwealth v. Morgan, 280 Mass. 392 (1932), but is based upon the following language of the court in Earl v. Commonwealth, 356 Mass. 181 (1969):

> We recognize that the single justice has power to entertain writs of error in such cases but it is preferable that these questions be resolved in the first instance by the trial judge upon a motion for new trial. The effect of this practice will be to place in the hands of the trial judge, rather than in the hands of the single justice, the task of resolving factual disputes underlying alleged constitutional errors.

Id. at 183. *Accord*, Commonwealth v. Penrose, 363 Mass. 677 (1973). *Cf.* Commonwealth v. Preston, 393 Mass. 318, 323 n. 4 (1984) (declining to address the issue whether findings are required in response to all rule 30(b) motions regardless of outcome). The absence of a finding of fact hampers appellate review of the judge's decision on a new trial motion. *See e.g.*, Commonwealth v. Caban, 48 Mass.App.Ct. 179, 184 (1999) (remanding case for finding of fact).

General Laws c. 279, § 41 provides that judgment should be entered against a corporation that fails to appear in court to answer charges against it. If the corporation can later show cause to excuse its prior neglect, it should be permitted to have the prior judgment vacated upon a motion for a new trial.

The original Reporter's Notes to Rule 30 intended that the remedy available under this subdivision be truly post-conviction, that is, not open to a defendant until the validity of the finding or verdict of guilt was conclusively established by an appellate court if an appeal was taken. This policy was designed to avoid complex and duplicitous proceedings and to protect the interests of the defendant, who is ordinarily limited to a single motion for a new trial. In the years since this subdivision was first promulgated, however, it has not been unusual for defendants to file a rule 30(b) motion after a notice of appeal has been filed. If the motion is pending at the time the appeal is entered, counsel then request a stay of the appeal until the motion is disposed of so that any appeal from the ruling can be consolidated with that from the judgment. *See* Commonwealth v. Powers, 21 Mass.App.Ct. 570, 572 n. 2 (1986). The Supreme Judicial Court has recognized that a judge may rule on a new trial motion prior to the determination of an appeal from the conviction. *See* Commonwealth v. Hallet, 427 Mass. 552, 555 (1998) (describing considerations a judge should take into account in deciding whether to rule on the merits of a new trial motion presented prior to the determination of an appeal); Commonwealth v. Smith, 384 Mass. 519, 524 (1981) ("defendant's appeal from his conviction should, when possible, be combined for review with his appeal from the denial of any motion for a new trial").

This rule does not limit access of a criminal defendant to review pursuant to G.L. c. 211, § 3, which grants the Supreme Judicial Court "general superintendence of all courts of inferior jurisdiction to correct and prevent errors and abuses therein if no other remedy is expressly provided . . . ." That power, however, should be and has been exercised only in exceptional circumstances, when necessary to protect substantive rights. *See* McGuinness v. Commonwealth, 420 Mass. 495, 497 (1995); Forte v. Commonwealth, 418 Mass. 98, 99 (1994); Commonwealth v. McCarthy, 375 Mass. 409, 414 (1978) and cases cited.

Subdivision (c).

(c)(1). In 2001, this subsection was amended to eliminate the requirement that the Attorney General be served in every case where a motion is filed under Rule 30(a). The subsection now requires service of a motion for a new trial, under either subsection (a) or subsection (b), upon the office of the prosecutor who represented the Commonwealth in the trial court, whether a District Attorney's Office or the Attorney General's Office. The prosecutor's office which maintains the original trial file is in the best position, and is responsible for, responding to motions for a new trial.

(c)(2). Subdivision (c)(2) was modeled after ME REV STAT ANN, tit. 14 § 5507 (1964), and was intended to establish finality of convictions and to eliminate "piecemeal litigation . . . whose only purpose is to vex, harass, or delay." Sanders v. United States, 373 U.S. 1, 18 (1963). *See* Commonwealth v. Donahue, 6 Mass.App.Ct. 971 (1979) (defendant's fourth motion for new trial). This rule is not intended to foreclose from future consideration grounds which were not known and could not have been found out with the exercise of due diligence. The constitutionality of the Maine statute from which this subdivision is taken was upheld by the Supreme Court in Murch v. Mottram, 409 U.S. 41 (1972). *See ABA Standards Relating To Post-Conviction Remedies* § 6.2(b)(i) (Approved Draft, 1968).

The rule of waiver established in the subdivision applies, as a result of case law, to claims that were not preserved at trial or not raised in an appeal, as well as to claims that were not put forward in a prior new trial motion. *See* Rodwell v. Commonwealth, 432 Mass. 1016, 1017 (2000) ("If a defendant fails to raise a claim that is generally known and available at the time of trial or direct appeal or in the first motion for postconviction relief, the claim is waived."); Commonwealth v. McLaughlin, 364 Mass. 211, 229 (1973), *quoting* from Commonwealth v. Dascalakis, 246 Mass. 12, 24 (1923) ("It has been the unbroken practice both under the statute [former G.L. c. 278 § 29 on which Rule 30 was based] and at common law respecting motions for new trial not to examine anew the original trial for the detection of errors which might have been raised by exceptions taken at the trial.") Waiver applies equally to constitutional and non-constitutional claims. *See* Commonwealth v. Deeran, 397 Mass. 136, 139 (1986).

Where a new trial motion presents a claim that could have been raised at trial but was not, the discretion a judge has to entertain the issue, as well as the scope of appellate review of the judge's decision, differs depending on the timing of the motion. Where the motion is presented to the court prior to the determination of an appeal, the motion judge, especially if the judge presided over the original trial, has wide discretion to consider an issue that was not raised at trial. *See* Commonwealth v. Hallet, 427 Mass. 552, 554–55 (1998). If the judge does consider the issue on its merits, it opens the issue up to full appellate review. *Id.* If the judge does not consider the issue on the merits, however, and denies relief based on the waiver doctrine, the standard on appellate review is confined to whether there was a substantial risk of a miscarriage of justice. *Id.* at 554. A judge should take into account in deciding to deny a new trial motion on the merits rather than on the basis of waiver, the advantage and disadvantage of making full appellate review available. *Id.*

Since it affects the scope of appellate review, if the judge is going to deny the motion, the judge should make clear whether the decision is based on a consideration of the merits, or on the basis that the error did not raise a substantial risk of a miscarriage of justice – which is the standard for considering issues that have been waived because they were not preserved at trial. *See id.* at 555. ("The judge should recognize that, unless the asserted error concerns a manifest injustice or created a substantial risk of a miscarriage of justice, she has wide discretion whether to consider any new trial issue fully on its merits.") *Cf.* Commonwealth v. Depace, 433 Mass. 379, 382 n. 2 (2001) (where the judge considered the matter only on the threshold question whether the defendant raised a substantial issue necessitating an evidentiary hearing, the issue was not preserved for full appellate review); Commonwealth v. Oliveira, 431 Mass. 609, 612 (2000) (where the judge considered the matter only to determine if the issue raised an asserted error that created a substantial risk of a miscarriage of justice, the issue was not preserved for full appellate review).

If a new trial motion is presented after an appeal has been decided, the discretion the judge has to consider an issue that could have been raised earlier, is much more limited. In this posture, the Supreme Judicial Court has recommended restricting consideration of such ordinarily waived issues to "those extraordinary cases where, upon sober reflection, it appears that a miscarriage of justice might otherwise result." Commonwealth v. Watson, 409 Mass. 110, 112 (1991). In determining if a substantial risk of a miscarriage of justice warrants the judge in considering a claim that would otherwise be precluded because it was not raised earlier, the judge should take into account three factors, taken from Commonwealth v. Miranda, 22 Mass.App.Ct. 10, 21 n. 22 (1986); whether there is a genuine question of guilt or innocence; whether the error was significant enough in the context of the trial to make it plausible to infer that the result might have been different but for the error; and, whether counsel's failure to object at trial was simply a reasonable tactical decision. *See* Commonwealth v. Amirault, 424 Mass. 618, 647 (1997). However, where a new trial motion raises an issue for the first time whose constitutional significance was not established until after the trial and appeal, so that the defendant did not have a genuine opportunity to preserve the issue in the normal course of events, the judge may consider it. *See* Commonwealth v. Burkett, 396 Mass. 509, 511 (1986). The standard of review from the denial of a new trial motion filed after an appeal has been decided is the same whether the motion judge considered the issue or not, whether there was a substantial risk of a miscarriage of justice. *See* Commonwealth v. Curtis, 417 Mass. 619, 624 n. 4 (1994).

(c)(3). The primary purpose of subdivision (c)(3) is to encourage the disposition of post conviction motions upon affidavit. In accordance with prior practice, *see* Commonwealth v. Hubbard, 371 Mass. 160, 174 (1976) *quoting* Commonwealth v. Coggins, 324 Mass. 552, 556–57, *cert. denied*, 338 U.S. 881 (1949), such motions should ordinarily be heard on the facts as presented by affidavit, although in particular circumstances, the judge may in the exercise of discretion receive oral testimony. *See* Commonwealth v. Figueroa, 422 Mass. 72, 77 (1996) (the decision whether to hold an evidentiary hearing on a new trial motion under Rule 30 is within the sound discretion of the judge). Where a substantial issue is raised, however, the better practice is to conduct an evidentiary hearing. *See* Blackledge v. Allison, 431 U.S. 63, 75–76 (1977). *Compare* Commonwealth v. Licata, 412 Mass. 654, 660 (1992) (error to refuse a hearing on new trial motion which raised a substantial issue of ineffective assistance of counsel) *with* Commonwealth v. Stewart, 383 Mass. 253, 257 (1981) (not error to refuse a hearing on new trial motion which failed to raise substantial issue concerning perjury by prosecution witness). In determining whether the motion raises a substantial issue which merits an evidentiary hearing, the judge should look not only at the seriousness of the issue asserted, but also to the adequacy of the defendant's showing. *See id.* at 257–58. Whether or not a substantial issue is presented must, of course, be determined on the face of the motion and affidavit. The motion should specify the grounds for relief, *see* Commonwealth v. Saarela, 15 Mass.App.Ct. 403, 407 (1983), and the affidavit should provide the factual support necessary to determine the issue. The court is fully warranted in dismissing a motion unaccompanied by affidavit, *see* Commonwealth v. Colantonio, 31 Mass.App.Ct. 299, 302 (1991); or one whose the factual allegations are "obscure," *cf.* Sayles v. Commonwealth, 373 Mass. 856 (1977), "impressionistic and conclusory," *cf.* Commonwealth v. Coyne, 372 Mass. 599, 600 (1977), or untrustworthy, *see* Commonwealth v. Lopez, 426 Mass. 657, 662 (1998).

The only change contemplated by this subdivision is that the use of this established procedure is to be extended to all cases where it is deemed appropriate by the trial judge.

(c)(4). Discovery in the context of a new trial motion is not a matter of right. The motion must first establish a prima facie case for relief before discovery is available. However, where that hurdle is met and discovery would be appropriate to develop facts necessary to support the claim, it is within the judge's discretion to allow discovery. Discovery is appropriate where specific allegations before the court show reason to believe that the petitioner may, if the facts are fully developed, be able to demonstrate that he or she is entitled to relief. *Cf.* Harris v. United States, 394 U.S. 286, 300 (1969). This subsection provides that the Commonwealth, as well as the defendant, may obtain discovery. *Cf. Rules Governing § 2254 Cases in the United States District Courts*, Rule 6(c) (recognizing the right of the respondent in a habeas corpus case to take the deposition of the petitioner). If, upon completion of discovery, the defendant is totally unable to make a reasonable proffer of evidence on a crucial element of the case, no hearing need be held and the motion may be dismissed.

In 2001, this subsection was amended to eliminate confusion arising from the reference to discovery in civil cases. The judge has wide discretion to allow the appropriate form of discovery, *see* Commonwealth v. Stewart, 383 Mass. 253, 261 (1981), which may include orders to produce evidence or statements, as provided in the Rules of Criminal Procedure, and in an unusual case may include depositions or other modes of discovery provided in the Rules of Civil Procedure. Where necessary, a party subject to discovery may seek an appropriate protective order.

In 2001, this subsection was also amended to require the opposing party to receive notice and an opportunity to be heard before the judge grants a discovery request. This provision is particularly important in the context of a request that evidence in the possession of the Commonwealth be made available to the defendant for scientific testing, such as DNA analysis. Before ordering such discovery, the judge must take into account a number of issues whose resolution requires the Commonwealth's participation, including the potential relevance of the results to the ground the motion advances for a new trial, the feasibility of successful testing, and the details of access to and testing of the evidence. *See generally* National Commission on the Future of DNA Evidence, *Postconviction DNA Testing: Recommendations For Handling Requests* (Nat'l. Inst. Justice 1999) at 52–53.

(c)(5). As a matter of constitutional obligation, the state need only ensure that indigent defendants have meaningful access to whatever post conviction proceedings are generally available. *See* Commonwealth v. Conceicao, 388 Mass. 255 (1983). Counsel is not necessary in every case to ensure that end. *Id.* at 261. The decision whether to appoint counsel on a motion for a new trial is within the discretion of the trial judge. However, where the motion raises a meritorious, or even colorable claim, "it is much the better practice to assign counsel." *Id.* at 262. G.L. c. 211D § 14 provides for the Committee for Public Counsel Services to represent indigent defendants in post conviction proceedings, and judges may refer requests for counsel to the Committee for initial screening.

If the motion is frivolous, repetitive, or the issues are so simple and easy that an attorney is not necessary to elucidate them, the judge may deny a motion for the appointment of counsel. *See* Conceicao, *supra*, 388 Mass. at 261–62. Where the motion is presented to the trial judge, the judge may take into account the fact of familiarity with the original record, or with that in prior new trial motions, in declining to appoint counsel. *Id.* at 261.

By amendment in 2001, this subsection gave judges discretion to allow for the payment of costs associated with the preparation and presentation of a new trial motion. Such costs may include the preparation of a transcript, obtaining the services of an investigator, retaining the services of an expert, or paying for scientific testing. As with the decision to appoint counsel, there is no constitutional right to have the state pay for these types of costs associated with a new trial motion. *See* Commonwealth v. Davis, 410 Mass. 680, 684 n. 7 (1991). But where the defendant seeks costs that are reasonably necessary to develop support for a well founded basis for granting a new trial, it is appropriate for the judge to exercise discretion and allow the request. In making the decision to allow costs associated with a new trial motion, the judge should take into account the likelihood that the expenditure will result in the defendant's being able to present a meritorious ground for a new trial. Where the request concerns scientific testing of evidence in the Commonwealth's possession, as with DNA analysis, the court should consider a request for funds in conjunction with the appropriate discovery motion under subsection (c)(4) seeking access to the evidence in question.

By amendment in 2001, this subsection required that the Commonwealth be given notice and an opportunity to be heard with respect to a request for costs in connection with a new trial motion. Unlike a request for costs prior to trial, in the context of a new trial motion there is no reason to deny the Commonwealth an opportunity to participate in a hearing on this type of request in order to avoid the prejudice that can result from the defendant's being forced to reveal trial strategy prematurely. *Cf.* McKinney v. Paskett, 753 F.Supp. 861, 864 (D.C. Id. 1990). The sound exercise of a judge's discretion to allow the defendant costs will depend in part on an evaluation of the legal theory which the expenditure of funds would support. The Commonwealth's participation in this process will result in a better informed decision. This subsection, however, does not give the Commonwealth a right to participate in the determination of a request for the initial appointment of counsel.

(c)(6). Subdivision (c)(6) was originally taken from 28 U.S.C. § 2255 (1949) and authorizes the court to make a determination—with or without a hearing—without requiring the presence of the moving party.

The defendant's presence is not required at a hearing on a motion for a new trial. *See* Commonwealth v. Owens, 414 Mass. 595, 604 (1993) *citing* Commonwealth v. Costello, 121 Mass. 371, 372 (1876). Where the defendant's presence will be of little help to the court—e.g., at the determination of purely legal issues—a proper determination can be made in his absence. Sanders v. United States, 373 U.S. 1, 21 (1963); Howard v. United States, 274 F.2d 100, 104 (8th Cir. 1960). *See* Mass.R.Crim.P., Rule 18 and Reporters' Notes. It is therefore appropriate to screen post-conviction motions carefully, and to utilize other than summary disposition only where an evidentiary hearing to resolve factual issues requires the presence of the defendant. ABA *Standards Relating to Post-Conviction Remedies* § 4.5(a); § 4.6, commentary at 74–75 (Approved Draft, 1968).

(c)(7). This subdivision is designed to expedite the determination of motions filed pursuant to this rule. In 2001, it was amended to give the parties at least 30 days notice of a hearing on a new trial motion, unless the judge determines that good cause exists to order the hearing held sooner. In light of the fact that the Commonwealth need not respond to every new trial motion, since some may be denied on their face as without merit, the primary objective of this provision is to avoid the problem of having the Commonwealth placed in the position of having to respond to a new trial motion without adequate time to prepare.

(c)(8) & (c)(9). Subdivision (c)(8) was originally patterned after CAL PENAL CODE § 1506 (Deering Supp. 1976).

Appeals from new trial motions in cases subject to G.L. c. 278, § 33E go to the Supreme Judicial Court. In all other cases, the Appeals Court is the appropriate venue. Either party may appeal from an adverse determination on a new trial motion. A ruling in favor of a defendant on a motion for relief from unlawful restraint or for a new trial pursuant to this rule does not preclude a Commonwealth appeal, since a successful appeal would merely reinstate the verdict or finding of guilt and would not subject the defendant to re-prosecution or multiple punishment. United States v. Wilson, 420 U.S. 332 (1975).

A defendant's request for release on bail pending appeal is a matter within the discretion of the trial judge. *See* Forte v. Commonwealth, 418 Mass. 98, 100 (1994). However, the provision giving the judge discretion to release a defendant on bail pending appeal applies only to appeals from an order for a new trial or an order determining that the defendant's sentence should be reduced to a term of imprisonment less than the time he already has served. *See* Stewart v. Commonwealth, 413 Mass. 664 (1992).

Under subdivisions (c)(8)(B) and (c)(9), the appellate court is to determine the defendant's costs of appeal which are then to be paid to the defendant by the Commonwealth on the order of the trial court. In 1995, the Standing Advisory Committee on Criminal Procedure reconsidered the several rules concerning the payment of reasonable attorney's fees to insure that they were consistent. In Latimore v. Commonwealth, 417 Mass. 805 (1994), the Commonwealth filed an application for leave to appeal the allowance of the defendant's motion for a new trial under the provisions of G.L. c. 278, § 33E. The application was denied by the single justice and the defendant moved for costs and attorney's fees. Because the application for appeal in a capital case was controlled by section 33E, rather than Rule 30(c)(8)(B), no specific provision for payment of fees and costs were available. The court observed that this situation, while rare, presented an anomaly in the rules.

The committee reconsidered the appropriate rules and added language to address the situation where the Commonwealth is making application for leave to appeal and adds directions for payment of fees and costs upon the denial of the application.

The Single Justice in the Memorandum of Decision in the County Court in Commonwealth v. Latimore, Supreme Judicial Court for Suffolk Co. 92–0469 said that in appropriate circumstances he would read the authority granted to the Appeals Court to include the Supreme Judicial Court. To confirm this authority to include both appellate courts, Rule 30(c)(8)(B) was amended to specifically include both courts.

The specific shortcoming of the rules addressed in *Latimore* was corrected by the addition of Rule 30(c)(9) which provides the Supreme Judicial Court with authority to award fees and costs in capital cases under the provision of G.L. c. 278, § 33E.

Rule 31. Stay of Execution; Relief Pending Review; Automatic Expiration of Stay

(a) Imprisonment. If a sentence of imprisonment is imposed upon conviction of a crime, the entry of an appeal shall not stay the execution of the sentence unless the judge imposing it or, pursuant to Mass. R. App. P. 6, a single justice of the court that will hear the appeal, determines in the exercise of discretion that execution of said sentence shall be stayed pending the determination of the appeal. If execution of a sentence of imprisonment is stayed, the judge or justice may at that time make an order relative to the custody of the defendant or for admitting the defendant to bail.

(b) If the application for a stay of execution of sentence is allowed, the order allowing the stay may state the grounds upon which the stay may be revoked and, in any event, shall state that upon release by the appellate court of the rescript affirming the conviction, stay of execution automatically expires unless extended by the appellate court. Any defendant so released shall provide prompt written notice to the clerk of the trial court regarding the defendant's current address and promptly notify the clerk in writing of any change thereof. The clerk shall notify the appellate court that will hear the appeal that a stay of execution of sentence has been allowed. At any time after the stay expires, the Commonwealth may move in the trial court to execute the sentence. The court shall schedule a prompt hearing and issue notice thereof to the defendant unless the prosecutor requests, for good cause shown, that a warrant shall issue.

(c) Fine. If a reservation, filing, or entry of an appeal is made following a sentence to pay a fine or fine and costs, the sentence shall be stayed by the judge imposing it or by a single justice of the court that will hear the appeal if there is a diligent perfection of appeal.

(d) Probation or Suspended Sentence. An order placing a defendant on probation or suspending a sentence may be stayed if an appeal is taken.

Amended June 24, 2009, effective October 1, 2009.

Reporter's Notes

Subdivision (a). The substance of this subdivision is drawn from G.L. c. 279, § 4 (as amended). The defendant convicted of a crime and sentenced to a term of imprisonment may petition the trial judge or a single justice of the Supreme Judicial or Appeals Court by motion that execution of his sentence be stayed pending appeal. The motion is directed to the discretion of the judge. DiPietro v. Commonwealth, 369 Mass. 964, 339 N.E.2d 924 (1976) (Rescript); Stranad v. Commonwealth, 366 Mass. 847, 318 N.E.2d 617 (1974) (Rescript); Commonwealth v. Allen, Mass.App.Adv.Sh. (1979) 147, 385 N.E.2d 532 (Rescript).

There are few cases construing G.L. c. 279, § 4 and while all are concerned with the element of discretion, in no one is an abuse of that discretion found. *Commonwealth v. Allen,* supra; Commonwealth v. Roberts, Mass.Adv.Sh. (1977) 927, 362 N.E.2d 904 (Rescript); *DiPietro v. Commonwealth,* supra; *Stranad v. Commonwealth,* supra; Fine v. Commonwealth, 312 Mass. 252, 261, 44 N.E.2d 659, 145 A.L.R. 392 (1942); Lebowitch, Petitioner, 235 Mass. 357, 363, 126 N.E. 831 (1920); Commonwealth v. Drohan, 210 Mass. 445, 448, 97 N.E. 89 (1912); Commonwealth v. Brown, 167 Mass. 144, 146, 45 N.E. 1 (1896).

The sine qua non for finding an abuse of discretion in the denial of a motion for a stay is that the movant must have established on the record "a reasonable likelihood of success on appeal." *DiPietro v. Commonwealth,* supra. *Accord Commonwealth v. Roberts,* supra. *But see Commonwealth v. Allen,* S.J.C. No. 79–100 Civ. (Mem., March 20, 1979) (single justice decision overturning *Commonwealth v. Allen,* supra: "[T]he standard is one of sound discretion and may be exercised if the circumstances warrant without a requirement that there be a finding made of a reasonable likelihood of success on appeal.").

The amendment of G.L. c. 276, § 87 by St.1974, c. 614, allows the judge to place the convicted defendant, with his consent, on probation for such term and upon such conditions as the judge deems proper. This provides the judge with a flexible alternative to traditional bail procedures pending appeal which may be used at his discretion for defendants convicted of all but those offenses enumerated in the statute.

Subdivision (b). This subdivision departs from the federal rule in that a stay of the payment of a fine is mandatory under this rule. This provision is adopted in recognition of the difficulty a defendant has, upon the successful appeal of his conviction, in recovering money he has paid in satisfaction of a fine.

Subdivision (c). This subdivision is based, in part, on Fed.R.Crim.P. 38(a)(4) and upon G.L. c. 279, § 4.

Reporter's Notes to Rule 31

This Rule was revised in 2009. As originally adopted in 1979, it codified existing practice under G.L. c. 279 § 4, which governed the procedure for a stay of execution pending appeal prior to the adoption of the Rules of Criminal Procedure.

Subdivision (a). Practice in the Commonwealth is that sentences are not routinely stayed pending appeal. *See Hagen v. Commonwealth*, 437 Mass. 374, 378 (2002). However, where a defendant meets the appropriate requirements, it has been a long standing tradition to grant a stay in the interest of justice, to avoid imprisoning one whose conviction may not survive appellate review. *See Commonwealth v. Levin*, 7 Mass. App. Ct. 501, 513 (1979).

A judge should order a stay only when the defendant has met the two concerns which guide the exercise of discretion in this area. The first and most important is the likelihood of the defendant establishing on appeal that the conviction will be overturned. *Cf. Commonwealth v. Stewart*, 413 Mass. 664 (1992) (bail pending appeal is not appropriate if the only consequence of the defendant's success would be reducing the term of his sentence and not immediate discharge). This requirement does not demand that the defendant establish that the appeal is more likely than not to be successful, only that it presents "an issue which is worthy of presentation to an appellate court, one which offers some reasonable possibility of a successful decision in the appeal." *See Commonwealth v. Hodge*, 380 Mass. 851, 855 (1980); *Commonwealth v. Allen*, 378 Mass. 489, 498 (1979). In this respect, the Massachusetts practice is more liberal than its federal counterpart. *Compare* 18 U.S.C. 3143(b)(1)(B) (the defendant must establish that the appeal "raises a substantial question of law or fact likely to result in" a favorable outcome).

The other factor that informs a judge's exercise of discretion in granting a stay is the question of security: whether the defendant will flee, commit another crime or present a danger to the community. *See Hodge*, 380 Mass. at 855. The same facts that are relevant to the decision to grant a defendant bail prior to trial are pertinent in this context as well. *See Allen*, 378 Mass. at 498.

In granting a stay, a judge may impose appropriate conditions on the defendant's release. *Cf. Commonwealth v. Beauchemin*, 410 Mass. 181, 186 (1991) (defendant not leave his home and have no minor visitors). G.L. c. 276 § 87 can be used as a vehicle for having the probation department monitor the defendant's conduct during a stay.

The trial judge may entertain a motion for a stay either before or after the entry of an appeal. Whether the judge grants or denies the motion, no statement of reasons is necessary nor must the judge make any particular finding or certification. *See Allen*, 378 Mass. at 1034.

This Rule does not address stays of execution of a sentence when an appeal is not pending. *See Commonwealth v. McLaughlin*, 431 Mass. 506, 518 (2000) (raising but not deciding the question of a judge's inherent power to stay a sentence for other reasons).

Appellate Rule 6 establishes the procedure that is available after the trial judge acts on a motion for a stay. Either the defendant or the Commonwealth may seek relief from a single justice of the court that will hear the appeal concerning the trial judge's decision to deny, *e.g., Commonwealth v. Aviles*, 422 Mass. 1008 (1996), or grant, *e.g. Commonwealth v. Hodge*, 380 Mass. 851 (1980), a stay. In the ordinary course of events, for all but first degree murder cases a single justice of the Appeals Court is the appropriate forum.

Subdivision (b). Stay orders must inform the defendant of the conditions upon which they were issued. Mandatory conditions include the defendant's continuing obligation to provide the court in writing with a current address and to prosecute the appeal in a diligent manner. *See* Mass. R. A.P. 6 (b)(4). The court should craft whatever additional conditions are appropriate to each case.

The stay automatically expires when the appellate court considering the appeal releases a rescript affirming the conviction, unless the appellate court states otherwise. A rescript is "released" when it is announced to the public and the appellate court notifies the parties that the court has decided the case. *Cf.* Mass. R. App. P. 23 (requiring the clerk of the appellate court to mail the parties a copy of the rescript and the opinion, if any). In the ordinary course of events, the rescript "issues" twenty-eight days following the release date or upon the denial of any petition for rehearing or application for further appellate review, whichever is later. *Id*

The court that decided the appeal may exercise its discretion to extend a stay of execution pending a petition for rehearing, application for further appellate review, or petition for certiorari. Unless otherwise specified, an extended stay expires when the rescript issues. The appellate court may act *sua sponte* or pursuant to the defendant's motion, which may be filed before the appeal is decided or after the rescript is released. If the appeal is lodged in the Appeals Court, the defendant should file the motion with the panel that has the responsibility for deciding the merits of the appeal.

In order to ensure that the clerk of the appellate court can notify the parties that a stay has automatically expired, *see* Mass. R. App. P. 6 (b)(6), the clerk of the trial court must notify the appellate court whenever a stay is granted.

Once a rescript affirming the conviction is released, the burden is on the Commonwealth, not the defendant, to initiate the process for the sentence to be executed. *See Commonwealth v. Ly*, 450 Mass. 16, 20 (2007). This requires the prosecutor to file a motion with the trial court and for the court to schedule a hearing and notify the defendant. The court should schedule the hearing promptly. *Id.* at 22. If possible, the prosecutor should agree on a date for the hearing with the defendant's current counsel (in most cases that will be the lawyer who represented the defendant on appeal). The procedure for ensuring the defendant's appearance at the hearing to execute the sentence is modeled after the one described in Rule 6 (a). Ordinarily, the court should simply issue a notice to the defendant of the time and date of the hearing. The prosecutor, however, may accompany the motion for a hearing with a request that the court issue a warrant for the arrest of the defendant. If the prosecutor's submission establishes good cause to believe that a warrant is necessary in order to ensure the defendant's appearance, the court may order the defendant's arrest. The defendant is not entitled to be heard on the question of whether a warrant should issue.

Subdivision (c). This subdivision departs from federal rule in that a stay of the payment of a fine is mandatory under this rule. This provision was adopted in recognition of the difficulty a defendant has, upon the successful appeal of his judgment, in recovering money he has paid in satisfaction of a fine.

Subdivision (d). This subdivision was originally based, in part, on Fed. R. Crim. P. 38(a)(4) and upon G.L. c. 279 § 4.

Rule 32. Filing and Service of Papers

(Applicable to District Court and Superior Court)

(a) Service: When Required. Written motions other than those which are heard ex parte, written notices, and similar papers shall be served upon each of the parties.

(b) Service: How Made. Whenever under these rules or by order of court service is required or permitted to be made upon a party represented by an attorney, service shall be made upon the attorney, unless service upon the party himself is ordered by the court. Service upon the attorney or upon a party shall be made in the manner provided for in civil actions.

(c) Notice of Orders and Judgments. If upon the entry of a judgment or order made on a written motion either or both of the parties are not present in court, the clerk shall immediately mail to the absent party or parties a notice of that entry and shall record the mailing in the docket.

(d) Filing. Papers required to be served shall be filed with the court. Papers shall be filed in the manner provided for in civil actions.

(e) Additional Time After Service by Mail. Whenever a party has the right or is required to do an act within a prescribed period after the service of a notice or other paper upon him and the notice or other paper is served upon him by mail, three days shall be added to the prescribed period.

Reporter's Notes

This rule is closely patterned after Fed.R.Crim.P. 49. Subdivisions (a), (b) and (d) are identical to their federal counterparts and subdivision (c) has been adopted with slight revision. Subdivision (e) has been taken from Fed.R.Crim.P. 45(e) and Mass.R.Civ.P. 6(d).

Subdivision (a). This subdivision is similar to Fed.R.Civ.P. and Mass.R.Civ.P. 5(a). Service is required "upon each of the parties" to avoid the interpretive questions that arose under the "adverse party" language of the federal rule prior to its 1966 amendment, such as the problem of when is a co-defendant an adverse party. The rule is also designed to promote full exchange of information among all parties. However, no restriction is intended upon agreements among co-defendants or between the defendant and the prosecutor restricting mutual exchange of papers in the interest of eliminating unnecessary expense. Advisory Committee Note to Rule 49.

Service is required of motions, notices and similar papers. The latter category embraces opposing affidavits and the like. But this rule does not apply to service of a summons for a witness under Mass.R.Crim.P. 17, or the execution or service of a warrant or summons under Mass.R.Crim.P. 6. *See* 8B J. MOORE, FEDERAL PRACTICE para. 49.02 (1978 rev.).

Subdivision (b). The first sentence of this subdivision is the same as the first sentence of Mass.R.Civ.P. 5(b) and Fed. R.Civ.P. 5(b). When a party has appeared and is represented by an attorney, service is required to be made upon the attorney, unless the court orders service to be made upon the party himself in cases where the court deems such service necessary. An order, disobedience of which is punishable as a contempt, or an order to show cause why a party should not be punished for contempt, are papers which the court would, as a practical matter, generally order to be served upon the party himself. A civil contempt proceeding, however, is merely a continuance of the original action and a step in the enforcement of a previous order or judgment, so that service of papers to have a party adjudged in civil contempt may validly be made on his attorney of record, unless it is unreasonable to regard the attorney as a representative of the party at that time. 2 J. MOORE, FEDERAL PRACTICE para. 5.06 (2d ed. 1978).

The second sentence of Mass.R.Crim.P. 32(b) incorporates by reference Mass.R.Civ.P. 4.

Subdivision (c). This subdivision is similar to Fed. R.Crim.P. 49(d) as it appeared prior to its 1966 amendment. The federal rule is an adaptation for criminal proceedings of Fed.R.Civ.P. 77(d). No consequences are attached to the failure of the clerk to give the prescribed notice. However, it is intended that in a case where the losing party, in reliance upon the clerk's obligation to send a notice, fails to file a timely notice of appeal, the trial judge may, in the exercise of his discretion, vacate the judgment because of the clerk's failure to give notice and may enter a new judgment. The time period for appeal would then begin to run when the second judgment is entered. *See* Hill v. Hawes, 64 S.Ct. 334, 320 U.S. 520, 88 L.Ed. 283, 149 A.L.R. 736 (1944). Since oral motions are generally ruled on in the presence of the parties, there can be no reliance on the clerk's failure to send notice and the applicable time limits for appeal must be observed.

Subdivision (d). This subdivision incorporates by reference Mass.R.Civ.P. 5(d)–(e), which govern the procedure for filing papers. Under Mass.R.Civ.P. 5(e), papers must be filed with the clerk of the court "except that a judge may permit the papers to be filed with him, in which event he shall note thereon the filing date and forthwith transmit them to the office of the clerk."

Subdivision (e). This subdivision is identical to Mass. R.Civ.P. 6(a) and Fed.R.Civ.P. 6(e) and to Fed.R.Crim.P. 45(e). The reason for this rule is that under Mass.R.Civ.P. 5(b), service by mail is complete upon mailing, and various prescribed time periods begin to run after service of notice or other papers. This subdivision adds three days to these prescribed periods since a day or more may intervene between the mailing of a pleading or paper and the actual receipt thereof.

Rule 33. Counsel for Defendants Indigent and Indigent But Able to Contribute

(Applicable to District Court and Superior Court)

The assignment of counsel for defendants determined to be indigent or indigent but able to contribute shall be governed by the provisions of G.L. c. 211D and Supreme Judicial Court Rule 3:10.

Amended May 29, 1986, effective July 1, 1986.

Reporter's Notes

The Municipal Court for the City of Boston established in 1974 the Marginally Indigent Defendant's Attorneys Program

(MIDA). This rule establishes a program of similar content for all District and Superior Courts.

A substantial number of defendants who appear in court to answer to criminal charges are found to be indigent and are provided with the services of counsel at public expense. Others with adequate resources retain private counsel. There is also a middle group composed of defendants who, because their incomes or assets are sufficient to prevent their being classed indigent, but are insufficient to enable them to comfortably retain counsel, are often denied representation.

Many of this latter group are willing to pay for legal services to the extent of their ability, but are frustrated in attempting to retain counsel by their limited means. It has become the practice of many judges, when advised of such defendants' unsuccessful attempts to obtain representation, to assign counsel, thus adding to the cost of administering the public defender programs and to the caseload of Massachusetts Defenders Committee.

It is the intent of this rule that an attorney be provided at a fee which is affordable by a defendant who does not qualify as an indigent, but who nonetheless cannot pay the total expense of a criminal defense without undue hardship. The rule applies only to reduced rates for attorney's fees; it does not apply to other defense services.

Under existing practice there is no system of partial eligibility. It is expected that this rule—which makes competent attorneys available at reduced fees—will serve the dual function of providing defense counsel to a large number of defendants while reducing an unnecessary drain on the public treasury. *See* ABA *Standards Relating to Providing Defense Services* § 6.2 (Approved Draft, 1968).

Subdivision (a). This rule is to be read in conjunction with Mass.R.Crim.P. 8, *Assignment of Counsel.*

For many years, indigents who have needed attorneys have received the services of volunteers. Many bar associations have assumed the responsibility of providing legal services without charge to those unable to pay for their criminal defense. However, as constitutional considerations have multiplied, an increased number of defendants and an increased number of appearances for each defendant have created a tremendous burden on public revenues. James v. Strange, 92 S.Ct. 2027, 407 U.S. 128, 141, 32 L.Ed.2d 600 (1972). It is not the purpose of this rule to deprive any defendant of the services of appointed counsel. Rather, it is recognized that many defendants who receive the services of court-appointed counsel are as able to pay part of their legal expenses as some defendants are to pay the entire expenses of retained counsel.

Subdivision (b). The referral process for the appointed attorney shall be monitored by either the local bar association or the clerk of the District Court. The list of attorneys should be comprised of those who volunteer and who are qualified to provide competent legal assistance. An established list will better ensure fairness in the distribution of appointments and will "avoid the appearance of patronage." ABA *Standards,* supra § 2.3.

Subdivision (c). In determining the eligibility of a defendant for the appointment of counsel under this rule, the court should consider the same relevant factors as mentioned in the Reporter's Notes to Mass.R.Crim.P. 8: employment status, income, obligations, dependents, etc. See G.L. c. 261, § 27C. The final determination as to the defendant's eligibility as marginally indigent is within the court's discretion.

Where special circumstances require, *see* Mass.R.Crim.P. 8(b), an appointment can be made of an attorney who is not on the list.

It should be clearly understood by both the defendant and the appointed attorney that the established fee is to be the only remuneration for the services rendered. Upon appointment of counsel, a form, which details the required information, is to be signed by the defendant.

Within seven days after entry of judgment or other disposition of the case, the attorney shall complete a report indicating the offense of which the defendant was charged and the fees charged and received.

Subdivision (d). The defendant is to make the initial contact and it is his responsibility to afford the attorney adequate time for investigation and preparation before trial. If appointed counsel chooses not to, or is unable to, represent the defendant, he is to notify the court and the defendant.

Subdivision (e). As provided in Mass.R.Crim.P. 8(d), the case may proceed to trial on the set date notwithstanding the fact that the attorney has not been contacted by the accused or has been given insufficient time for preparation.

All parties, unless the attorney has withdrawn his appearance pursuant to subdivision (d), must appear in court on the trial date. If the attorney has properly withdrawn and no continuance has been granted, the defendant must appear in court on the trial date. The case should proceed to trial unless for compelling reasons the court determines that justice requires a continuance. *See* Mass.R.Crim.P. 9.

Subdivision (f). Upon appointment of counsel, the defendant should be told that the expense of appointed counsel will be assessed against him as costs, and he should be informed of the possible effects of non-compliance with any court order regarding payment of these costs. To insure that the defendant understands the operation of this rule, the defendant will be required to sign a statement to that effect.

The court should then make an initial estimate of the costs of defense (keeping in mind the maximum established by the District Court and Superior Court Rules and other rules of court that determine the rate of attorneys' compensation) and of the defendant's ability to satisfy all or part of those costs out of present assets and expected earnings. In determining the availability of present assets to meet these costs, the court should consider the defendant's liabilities and continuing obligations. In determining the amount of income available to meet those costs, the court should additionally consider how long (if at all) the defendant will be working prior to the commencement of trial (if there is to be a trial). *See* G.L. c. 261, § 27C, which does not attempt to establish standards for determining indigency, but requires that such standards be posted by the court. The court may also utilize G.L. c. 93, § 51 to obtain records from a consumer reporting agency in order to evaluate defendant's affidavit of indigency under G.L. c. 261, § 27B.

Where the court finds that there are assets or income available to be used for the benefit of counsel, the court may then enter an order that the defendant pay a reasonable amount to the court out of his present assets and that he pay a reasonable amount out of future income on an installment basis for a definite duration. This order, like all subsequent orders regarding the payment of costs, may be modified by the court upon a showing by either the defense or the prosecution of changed circumstances.

A defendant can be ordered to pay in installments to be satisfied out of future income, and to this extent the timing of the burden may be different. However, this can in no way be seen as coercive pressure to find employment, or to maintain present employment or one's present income level, because changed circumstances are grounds for modification of the court order. Thus, the only difference relates to the timing of the burden which does not impede the exercise of one's right to counsel.

The Supreme Court in Fuller v. Oregon, 94 S.Ct. 2116, 417 U.S. 40, 38 L.Ed.2d 737 (1974), affirmed the validity of such reasoning:

> The fact that an indigent who accepts state-appointed legal representation knows that he might someday be required to repay the costs of these services in no way affects his eligibility to obtain counsel. The Oregon statute is carefully designed to insure that only those who actually become capable of repaying the State will ever be obliged to do so....
>
> A defendant in a criminal case who is just above the line separating the indigent from the non-indigent must borrow money, sell off his meager assets, or call upon his family or friends in order to hire a lawyer. We cannot say that the Constitution requires that those only slightly poorer must remain forever immune from any obligation to shoulder the expenses of their legal defense, even when they are able to pay without hardship.

Id. at 53–54.

The provisions of subdivision (f)(3) for assignment to defense counsel of any cash bail deposited is new to Massachusetts procedure.

Rule 34. Report

[Text of rule applicable to cases initiated (by indictment or complaint) on or after September 7, 2004.]

If, prior to trial, or, with the consent of the defendant, after conviction of the defendant, a question of law arises which the trial judge determines is so important or doubtful as to require the decision of the Appeals Court, the judge may report the case so far as necessary to present the question of law arising therein. If the case is reported prior to trial, the case shall be continued for trial to await the decision of the Appeals Court.

Amended March 8, 2004, effective September 7, 2004.

Reporter's Notes—Revised, 2004

Under prior practice, the authority of a judge to report a question of law for the decision of the full court was wholly a creature of statute, Commonwealth v. Cronin, 245 Mass. 163 (1923), and the procedure was expressly confined to instances where a person had been convicted, G.L. c. 278, § 30 (St. 1830, c. 113, § 4), or before trial had commenced. G.L. c. 278, § 30A (St.1954, c. 528). The language of this rule is comprised of the statutory provisions of those two sections.

Prior to 1954, a trial judge was authorized to report a question of law only after the conviction of a defendant; no provision granted the court the authority to report an interlocutory question before trial. Commonwealth v. Baldi, 250 Mass. 528 (1925). The addition of § 30A by chapter 528 of the Statutes of 1954 gave the court the power to report and have decided a question arising prior to trial, and this procedure has been used increasingly in recent years with the expanded application of fourth, fifth and sixth amendment rights. *See*, e.g., Commonwealth v. Baker, 343 Mass. 162 (1961) (admission to bail); Commonwealth v. Mekalian, 346 Mass. 496 (1963) (motion to suppress evidence); Commonwealth v. O'Leary, 347 Mass. 387 (1964) (assignment of counsel).

Once trial has commenced, the court may not report a question until after a conviction of the defendant. The definition of "conviction" for purposes of this rule is that provided by the Supreme Judicial Court in Commonwealth v. Baldi, 250 Mass. 528 (1925), which may include the judgment of the court following a verdict of guilty or confession of guilt, or may mean a verdict of guilty against the defendant or his confession in open court, without judgment or sentence. *Id.* at 536–37.

Although a report may be made after trial if the defendant consents, it does not preclude the defendant from taking an appeal. *See* Commonwealth v. Giles, 350 Mass. 102 (1966), in which the judge found the defendant guilty and suspended the execution of sentence pending answer to his report from the Supreme Judicial Court. The defendant later appealed the entire case. Conversely, the procedure has also been used to afford a defendant as full a review as he could have obtained had his counsel properly filed an assignment of errors after notice of the completion of the summary of the record. In Commonwealth v. Pratt, 360 Mass. 708 (1972), the Supreme Judicial Court treated such a case as if it had been properly brought on appeal. *See* Commonwealth v. Dorius, 346 Mass. 323, 324 (1963).

The decision to report rests within the discretion of the trial judge. Commonwealth v. Eagleton, 402 Mass. 199, 208 (1988). This discretion is to be guided in part by the standard set out by the Supreme Judicial Court in Commonwealth v. Cavanaugh, 366 Mass. 277 (1974). This standard, though stated in connection with interlocutory appeals, is, as the court clearly states, applicable to decisions to report:

> An interlocutory appeal, *like a report*, may be appropriate when the alternatives are a prolonged, expensive, involved or unduly burdensome trial or a dismissal of the indictment.

Id. at 279. (Emphasis added). Accord Commonwealth v. Vaden, 373 Mass. 397 (1977).

A case may be reported if in the judge's opinion a question of law is so important or doubtful as to require a determination by a higher court, Commonwealth v. A Juvenile, 381 Mass. 727, 728 n.2 (1980). The judge must then refer facts sufficient to make intelligible the question of law reported. Commonwealth v. Yacobian, 393 Mass. 1005, 1005–06 (1984); Commonwealth v. O'Neil, 233 Mass. 535 (1919). In Commonwealth v. Ficksman, 340 Mass. 744 (1960), the Supreme Judicial Court decided that the record before it was insufficient to determine properly the question reported. The court therefore discharged the report and remanded the case to the lower court. The judge should refuse to report a case upon the defendant's motion if he finds there is no question of law so important as to require higher court resolution, Commonwealth v. McKnight, 289 Mass. 530 (1935), or because there is no issue of law. Commonwealth v. Chase, 348 Mass. 100 (1964).

The Supreme Judicial Court held in Commonwealth v. Henry's Drywall Co., Inc., 362 Mass. 552 (1972), that an interlocutory report was not appropriate under the circumstances of the case. Quoting John Gilbert, Jr. Co. v. C.M. Fauci Co., 309 Mass. 271, 273 (1941), Justice Quirico stated that:

> Interlocutory matters should be reported only where it appears that they present serious questions likely to be material in the ultimate decision, and that subsequent proceedings in the trial court will be substantially facilitated by so doing.

362 Mass. at 557. The report was discharged since a decision would have avoided what appeared to the court to be only a short trial which might effectively resolve the issues reported. See Commonwealth v. Henry's Drywall Co., Inc., 366 Mass. 539 (1974). Interlocutory reports are not to "be permitted to become additional causes of the delays ... which are already too prevalent." Commonwealth v. Vaden, 373 Mass. 397 (1977). However, in Commonwealth v. Shields, 402 Mass. 162, 163 (1988), the S.J.C. found questions concerning the constitutionality of sobriety roadblocks were appropriately reported because the answers were likely to be dispositive, the questions were likely to recur, and an improper ruling by the trial court would have resulted in an unnecessary waste of judicial resources at trial.

To help the appellate court decide whether an interlocutory report is appropriate, the reporting court should explain its reasons for declining to wait until after the trial is completed. Commonwealth v. Wallace, 431 Mass. 705, 705 n.1 (2000). *See also* Commonwealth v. Vaden, 373 Mass. 397 (1977) ("the report itself, or ... [an] accompanying stipulation or [the] record" should indicate why the issue is appropriate for interlocutory review).

After conviction of the defendant, the trial judge has the authority to make a report whether or not the trial was heard by a jury, so long as it is determined that the defendant is guilty. *See* Commonwealth v. Kemp, 254 Mass. 190 (1926), as to authority to report in a jury-waived trial.

The granting of jurisdiction to the Appeals Court concurrent with the Supreme Judicial Court conforms to existing statutory law. G. L. c. 211A, § 10 established the concurrent jurisdiction:

> Subject to such further appellate review by the supreme judicial court as may be permitted pursuant to section eleven or otherwise, the appeals court shall have concurrent appellate jurisdiction with the supreme judicial court, to the extent review is otherwise allowable, with respect to a determination made in the appellate tax board and in the superior court department, the housing court department, the land court department, the probate and family court department, the Boston municipal court department in criminal session, the Boston municipal court department appellate division, the juvenile court department, the district court department in criminal session, and the district court department appellate divisions, except in review of convictions for first degree murder. A report from any such department of the trial court of any case, in whole or in part, or any question of law arising therein shall be deemed to be within the concurrent appellate jurisdiction of the supreme judicial court and the appeals court.

A trial judge is to report a case to the Appeals Court. Section 10 states further that appellate review, "if within the jurisdiction of the appeals court, shall be in the first instance by the appeals court ..."

Previously a defendant in District Court, except in a jury session trial, was precluded from requesting the judge to report a question. By a 2004 amendment, however, the caption limiting application of this rule was removed. That amendment brings Rule 34 into conformity with legislation that abolished the de novo district court system and established that "review may be had directly by the appeals court, by appeal, report or otherwise in the same manner provided for trials of criminal cases in the superior court." G.L. c. 218, secs. 26A and 27A(g), applicable to judge and jury sessions respectively. Rule 34 now applies to all superior, juvenile, district and municipal courts.

The Supreme Judicial Court is also given general discretionary powers of superintendence under c. 211, §§ 3 and 4A, with which it can review significant interlocutory matters.

> The supreme judicial court may ... direct any cause or matter to be transferred from a lower court to it in whole or in part for further action or directions, and in case of partial transfer may issue such orders or direction in regard to the part of such cause or matter not so transferred as justice may require.

G.L. c. 211, § 4A. Under § 3, it may do so "to correct and prevent errors and abuses ... if no other remedy is expressly provided," and in the interests of "the furtherance of justice and ... the regular execution of the laws."

The broad statutory standard governing matters acceptable for review under §§ 3 and 4A has been narrowly interpreted by the Supreme Judicial Court. The Court has stated that "[o]nly in the most exceptional circumstances will we review interlocutory rulings in criminal cases under our general superintendence powers." Gilday v. Commonwealth, 360 Mass. 170, 171 (1971). To fulfill this requirement there must be a substantial claim of violation of a substantive right and irremediable error, such that the defendant cannot be placed in status quo in the regular course of appeal. Morrissette v. Commonwealth, 380 Mass. 197, 198 (1980). *See also Gilday*, supra, at 171; Mass. R. Crim. P. 30, Reporter's Notes, *supra* (collecting cases). Moreover, as in the case of a report, the fact that an appeal may be taken from a final judgment after the case has been tried does not prevent the court from acting within its powers of superintendence. Barber v. Commonwealth, 353 Mass. 236, 239 (1967).

In A Juvenile v. Commonwealth, 370 Mass. 272 (1976), the plaintiff filed a petition for relief in the nature of certiorari with the Supreme Judicial Court under c. 211, § 3. This procedure was sufficient to bring the matter to the court for review.

Rule 35. Depositions to Perpetuate Testimony

(Applicable to District Court and Superior Court)

(a) General Applicability. Whenever due to exceptional circumstances, and after a showing of materiality and relevance, it is deemed to be in the interest of justice that the testimony of a prospective witness of the defendant or the Commonwealth be taken and preserved, the judge may at any time after the filing of a complaint or return of an indictment, upon his own motion or the motion of either party with notice to all interested persons, order that the testimony of the witness be taken by deposition and that any designated book, paper, document, record, recording, or other material not privileged be produced at the same time and place. If a witness is committed for failure to give bail to appear to testify at a trial or hearing, the judge may direct that his deposition be taken. A copy of a deposition ordered upon the judge's own motion shall be transmitted to the court by the person administering the deposition. In determining a motion filed pursuant to this rule, the judge may order a hearing or may determine whether exceptional circumstances exist and the materiality and relevance of the testimony on the basis of the supporting affidavit.

(b) Summonses. An order to take a deposition shall authorize the issuance by the clerk of summonses pursuant to Rule 17 for the persons and objects named or described in such order. A witness whose deposition is to be taken may be required to attend at any place designated by the trial court, taking into account the convenience of the witness and the parties.

(c) Notice of Taking of Deposition. The party on whose motion a deposition is to be taken shall give all interested persons reasonable written notice of the time and place for the taking of the deposition. If a defendant is in custody, the officer having custody of the defendant shall be notified by the court of the time and place set for the taking of the deposition and shall produce the defendant at that time and place and keep him in the presence of the witness during the taking of the deposition. A defendant not in custody shall have the right to be present at the taking of a deposition, but his failure to appear after notice and without cause shall constitute a waiver of the right to be present and of all objections based upon that right.

(d) Payment of Expenses. Whenever a deposition is taken upon motion of the Commonwealth, the court shall direct that the reasonable expenses of travel and subsistence of the defendant and his counsel and the witness be paid for by the Commonwealth. Expenses for a deposition taken upon motion of a defendant may be assessed to the defendant to be paid forthwith or in such other manner as the judge may determine.

(e) Scope of Examination. Subject to such additional conditions as the judge may specify and except as otherwise provided in these rules, the taking of depositions in criminal cases shall be in the manner provided for in civil actions. The scope and manner of examination and cross-examination at the taking of the deposition shall be such as would be allowed in the trial itself.

(f) Objections to Deposition Testimony. Objections to deposition testimony or evidence or parts thereof and the grounds for the objections shall be stated at the time of the taking of the deposition.

(g) Admissibility. At a trial or upon any hearing, a part or all of a deposition, so far as it is otherwise admissible under the law of evidence, may be used as substantive evidence if the judge finds that the deponent is unavailable or if the deponent gives testimony at the trial or hearing which is inconsistent with his deposition. Any deposition may be used by any party for the purpose of contradicting or impeaching the testimony of the deponent as a witness. "Unavailable" as a witness includes situations in which the deponent:

(1) is exempt by a ruling of the judge on the ground of privilege from testifying concerning the subject matter of his deposition;

(2) persists in refusing to testify concerning the subject matter of his deposition despite an order of the judge to do so;

(3) lacks memory of the subject matter of his deposition;

(4) is unable to be present or to testify at the trial or hearing because of death or physical or mental illness or infirmity;

(5) is absent from the trial or hearing and the proponent of the deposition has been unable to procure the deponent's attendance by process or other reasonable means; or

(6) is absent from the trial or hearing and his testimony was ordered taken and preserved pursuant to Rule 6(d)(2).

A deponent is not unavailable as a witness if his exemption, refusal, claim of lack of memory, inability, or absence is due to the procurement or wrongdoing of the proponent of his deposition for the purpose of preventing the deponent from attending or testifying.

(h) Notice.

(1) *District Court.* All interested parties shall be given reasonable notice by the clerk of the time set for hearing motions filed under this rule.

(2) *Superior Court.* The moving party shall notify all interested parties of the time set for hearing motions filed under this rule at least seven days prior to the hearing.

(i) Deposition by Agreement Not Precluded. Nothing in this rule shall preclude the taking of a deposition, orally or upon written questions, by agreement of the parties with the consent of the judge.

Reporter's Notes

This rule was written in substantial conformity with 18 U.S.C. § 3503 (1970) and is to be governed by the provisions of Mass.R.Crim.P. 13 wherever the two rules are not inconsistent. *See* Rules of Criminal Procedure (U.L.A.) rules 431–32 (1974), Fed.R.Crim.P. 15.

Previous comparable statutory law in the Commonwealth concerning the taking of depositions in criminal proceedings was General Laws c. 277, § 76 (Rev.St. [1836] 136, § 32) which provided that:

> [Where] an issue of fact is joined upon an indictment, the court may, upon application of the defendant, grant a commission to examine any material witnesses residing out of the commonwealth, in the same manner as in civil causes; and the prosecuting officer may join in such commission and may name any material witnesses to be examined on the part of the commonwealth.

Section 77 of that same chapter (Rev.St. [1836] c. 136, § 33) provided:

> When such commission is issued ... and the depositions taken thereon ... [are] returned, [they] shall be read in the same manner and with the like effect ... subject to the same exceptions, as in civil cases; but if the defendant on his trial declines to use the deposition so taken, the prosecuting officer shall not, without the defendant's consent, make use of any deposition taken on behalf of the commonwealth.

Although these statutes provide a basis for this rule, they are superseded by it. The statement that depositions are to be conducted and used "as in civil causes" formerly operated to incorporate by reference G.L. c. 233, §§ 46–63 and Superior Court Rule 37 (1954). This rule is to govern the taking of depositions in criminal cases, but should reference to civil practice be necessary it shall be to Mass.R.Civ.P. 27 and to Superior Court Rules 71–72 (1974), insofar as they are consistent with this rule. *See* SUPERIOR COURT RULES, 1974, ANNOTATED 297–309 (Mass.Bar Ed.1975).

Subdivision (a). This rule has adopted the approach set out in the Federal Rules: A request to take a deposition in a criminal case will be granted only in exceptional situations. United States v. Whiting, 308 F.2d 537 (2d Cir.1962). This is because criminal depositions are not for the discovery of information; rather they are intended to preserve evidence. United States v. Steffes, 35 F.R.D. 24 (1964).

While it is true that it is far more desirable to secure the actual presence of a potential witness in criminal cases, there are situations in which the use of depositions is required in order to assure that the ends of justice are met, e.g., when a witness' attendance cannot be secured because of sickness or infirmity. (*See* subdivision [g][4], infra). Or, notwithstanding the provisions of G.L. c. 233, § 13A and c. 277, § 66, the right of a defendant to compulsory process for witnesses who are necessary to his defense does not automatically extend beyond the territory of the Commonwealth. Commonwealth v. Dirring, 354 Mass. 523, 238 N.E.2d 508 (1968). *Accord* Commonwealth v. Watkins, Mass.Adv.Sh. (1978) 1646, 1668–69, 379 N.E.2d 1040. *See* subdivision (g)(5), infra.

The Supreme Judicial Court in Smith v. Commonwealth, 331 Mass. 585, 121 N.E.2d 707 (1954), specifically mentioned the availability of depositions in criminal cases. In *Smith,* a convicted defendant petitioned for a writ of error alleging that his alibi defense which was supported by affidavits and letters had not received sufficient recognition during the prosecution of his case. The court said that where the defendant's material allegations could have been supported by the testimony of known people residing out of state, the deposition procedure detailed in G.L. c. 277, §§ 76–77 could have been used advantageously. It is in such a case that the procedures detailed in this rule should be used.

Another set of exceptional circumstances warranting the taking of a deposition was established by statute. Former General Laws c. 276, § 50 (St.1851, c. 71) provided that the deposition of a witness unable to provide sufficient sureties guaranteeing his appearance in court could be taken upon order of the court with the consent of the defendant. This subdivision does not require the defendant's consent when the court finds that exceptional circumstances justify an order that a witness' deposition be taken.

Subdivision (b). This subdivision conforms to Fed. R.Crim.P. 17(f) in explicitly empowering the clerk of the court to issue compulsory process in order to effect the taking of a deposition. It should be noted that it authorizes orders to produce documents, objects, etc., at the taking of the deposition as well. Summonses are treated in full under Mass. R.Crim.P. 17.

Subdivision (c). Whenever a defendant is incarcerated, the moving party is responsible for insuring that the defendant has the opportunity to be present while the deponent is being examined. This can be accomplished in either of two ways: by designating the detention facility where the defendant is incarcerated as the place where the deposition is to be taken, or by authorizing the defendant's temporary release for the purpose of attending the examination. The second alternative would require the issuance of a writ of habeas corpus or other similar judicial order.

A defendant not in custody has the responsibility of attending the taking of a deposition unless he has cause for not attending. Insufficient notice and not having been tendered expenses are examples of sufficient cause for non-attendance. By implication, the failure to attend after sufficient notice and tendering of expenses constitutes a waiver of the right to be present unless other cause is shown. Where the defendant has established cause for non-attendance, the deposition should not be used over his objection.

Subdivision (d). The provision in this subdivision authorizing payment from public funds is supported by G.L. c. 12, § 24 (as amended, St.1978, c. 478, § 10), which authorizes district attorneys to expend state monies for the necessary costs of prosecuting a case.

Subdivision (e). This subdivision conforms substantially to Fed.R.Crim.P. 15(d), although the Massachusetts rule makes no provision for discovery, a subject which is covered in depth by Mass.R.Crim.P. 14. For deposition practice in civil actions, see Mass.R.Civ.P. 27.

Subdivision (f). It is intended that objections to testimony and the grounds therefor are to be stated at the taking of the deposition, consistent with civil practice under Superior Court Rule 71 (1974). *See* SUPERIOR COURT RULES, 1974, ANNOTATED 302–03 (Mass.Bar Ed.1975). The requirement that objections be stated at the taking of a deposition accords with Fed.R.Crim.P. 15(f).

Subdivision (g). For all or part of a deposition to be admissible as evidence, the deponent must be unavailable as that term is defined in this subdivision. Prior to the promulgation of this rule, there was no statute or rule which defined "unavailability" in the present context. Commonwealth v. DiPietro, 373 Mass. 397, 367 N.E.2d 621 (1977). Further, the deposition must be otherwise admissible within the law of evidence, i.e., the former testimony exception to the hearsay rule. *See* Fed.R.Evid. 804(b)(1); Commonwealth v. McLaughlin, 364 Mass. 211, 219–23, 303 N.E.2d 338 (1973); *Commonwealth v. DiPietro,* supra, at 1984–92 (collecting cases), Commonwealth v. Canon, 373 Mass. 494, 368 N.E.2d 1181 (1977).

As with other manifestations of the sixth amendment right to confrontation, the significant feature is whether the party against whom the deposition is offered had through counsel an adequate opportunity for cross-examination of the deponent. Pointer v. Texas, 85 S.Ct. 1065, 380 U.S. 400, 406–07, 13 L.Ed.2d 923 (1965). *Accord Commonwealth v. Canon,* supra; Commonwealth v. DiPietro, 4 Mass.App. 845, 356 N.E.2d 269 (1976), aff'd, 373 Mass. 369, 367 N.E.2d 811 (1977); Commonwealth v. Caine, 366 Mass. 366, 371–72, 318

N.E.2d 901 (1974); Commonwealth v. Clark, 363 Mass. 467, 295 N.E.2d 163 (1973); Commonwealth v. Mustone, 353 Mass. 490, 498, 233 N.E.2d 1 (1968). Actual cross-examination is not required, the constitutional requirement is satisfied if the party against whom the deposition is offered was afforded an adequate opportunity to cross-examine. *Pointer v. Texas,* supra; *Commonwealth v. Canon,* supra; *Commonwealth v. DiPietro,* supra; In re Andrews, 368 Mass. 468, 334 N.E.2d 15 (1975). That opportunity is to be afforded pursuant to subdivision (e), infra, under which the scope and manner of cross-examination is to be such as allowed in trials.

A deposition otherwise admissible may be introduced as substantive evidence of the matters contained therein if the deponent is unavailable. Any deposition may be used to impeach in accord with established rules of evidence.

Subdivisions (g)(1)–(g)(5) are essentially restatements of Fed.R.Evid. 804(a)(1)–(5). Subdivision (g)(6) is included to make this rule consistent with Mass.R.Crim.P. 6(d)(2).

Subdivision (g)(1) is consistent with Commonwealth v. Canon, 373 Mass. 494, 368 N.E.2d 1181 (1977) (witness invoked fifth amendment privilege against self-incrimination) and Commonwealth v. DiPietro, 373 Mass. 369, 367 N.E.2d 811 (1977) (witness invoked marital privilege). The *DiPietro* court properly distinguished between the unavailability of a witness and the unavailability of the testimony of that witness:

> "[T]he important element is whether the testimony of the witness is sought and is available and not whether the witness's body is available." The physical presence without the testimony contributes nothing to the later trial.

Mass.Adv.Sh. (1977) at 1987, *quoting* Mason v. United States, 408 F.2d 903, 906 (10th Cir.1969), cert. denied 91 S.Ct. 462, 400 U.S. 993, 27 L.Ed.2d 441 (1971).

Subdivisions (g)(2) and (3) are also concerned with the situation where the witness is present, but unable or unwilling to testify.

As to a deceased or incapacitated witness, subdivision (g)(4), *see* e.g., Commonwealth v. Richards, 35 Mass. (18 Pick.) 434, 29 Am.Dec. 608 (1837); Temple v. Phelps, 193 Mass. 297, 79 N.E. 482 (1906).

For "unavailability" in terms of the witness who cannot be found or is not amenable to process, *see* e.g., Commonwealth v. Gallo, 275 Mass. 320, 324, 175 N.E. 718, 79 A.L.R. 1380 (1931).

Mass.R.Crim.P. 6(d)(2) authorizes the court to order that the testimony of a witness present in court upon the default of a defendant be taken and preserved, and Mass.R.Crim.P. 10(c) permits the court to condition a continuance upon the taking of and preservation of the testimony of witnesses then present. It is presumed under the former that if a deposition of a witness then present in court is ordered upon the default of a defendant, defendant's counsel is present in court so as to protect the right of the defendant to confront his accusers under the sixth amendment and *Pointer v. Texas,* supra. The voluntary absence of a defendant from trial operates as a waiver of his sixth amendment right to confrontation. Taylor v. United States, 94 S.Ct. 194, 414 U.S. 17, 3 L.Ed.2d 174 (1973); Commonwealth v. Flemmi, 360 Mass. 693, 277 N.E.2d 523 (1971). *See also* Illinois v. Allen, 90 S.Ct. 435, 397 U.S. 337, 342–43, 24 L.Ed.2d 420 (1970); Commonwealth v. Snyder, 282 Mass. 401, 185 N.E. 376 (1933), aff'd sub nom., Snyder v. Massachusetts, 54 S.Ct. 330, 291 U.S. 97, 105–06, 78 L.Ed. 674, 90 A.L.R. 575 (1934). There is evident a clear analogy between the situation where the defendant voluntarily absents himself from trial and that contemplated by Mass. R.Crim.P. 6(d)(2) where the defendant is found in default.

The summons which is issued pursuant to Mass.R.Crim.P. 6(b)(2) is formulated to give the defendant adequate notice that his willful default may result in the taking of depositions so as to avoid the sixth amendment confrontation issues raised in *Taylor v. United States,* supra.

Subdivision (h). This subdivision, generally governing notice, is supplemental to Mass.R.Crim.P. 32.

Subdivision (i). Drawn from Fed.R.Crim.P. 15(g), this subdivision recognizes that the parties may find it to their joint advantage to preserve testimony by deposition, or to utilize a deposition at trial, and permits them to do so without having to call upon the court for authorization. If depositions are contemplated, that fact is appropriate for discussion at the pretrial conference. Mass.R.Crim.P. 11(a), (b), Reporter's Notes, supra.

Rule 36. Case Management

(Applicable to District Court and Superior Court)

(a) General Provisions.

(1) *Order of Priorities*. The trial of defendants in custody awaiting trial and defendants whose pretrial liberty is reasonably believed to present unusual risks to society shall be given preference over other criminal cases.

(2) *Function of the Court.*

(A) District Court. The court shall determine the sequence of the trial calendar.

(B) Superior Court. The court shall determine the sequence of the trial calendar after cases are selected for prosecution by the district attorney.

(b) Standards of a Speedy Trial. The time limitations in this subdivision shall apply to all defendants as to whom the return day is on or after the effective date of these rules. Defendants arraigned prior to the effective date of these rules shall be tried within twenty-four months after such effective date.

(1) *Time Limits.* A defendant, except as provided by subdivision (d)(3) of this rule, shall be brought to trial within the following time periods, as extended by subdivision (b)(2) of this rule:

(A) During the first twelve-month period following the effective date of this rule, a defendant shall be tried within twenty-four months after the return day in the court in which the case is awaiting trial.

(B) During the second such twelve-month period, a defendant shall be tried within eighteen months after the return day in the court in which the case is awaiting trial.

(C) During the third and all successive such twelve-month periods, a defendant shall be tried within twelve months after the return day in the court in which the case is awaiting trial.

(D) If a retrial of the defendant is ordered, the trial shall commence within one year after the date the action occasioning the retrial becomes final, as extended by subdivision (b)(2) of this rule. The order of an appellate court requiring a retrial is final upon the issuance by the appellate court of the rescript. In the event that the clerk of the appellate court fails to issue the rescript within the time provided for in Massachusetts Rule of Appellate Procedure 23, retrial shall commence within one year after the date when the rescript should have issued.

If a defendant is not brought to trial within the time limits of this subdivision, as extended by subdivision (b)(2), he shall be entitled upon motion to a dismissal of the charges.

(2) *Excluded Periods.* The following periods shall be excluded in computing the time within which the trial of any offense must commence:

(A) Any period of delay resulting from other proceedings concerning the defendant, including, but not limited to:

(i) delay resulting from an examination of the defendant, and hearing on, his mental competency, or physical incapacity;

(ii) delay resulting from a stay of the proceedings due to an examination or treatment of the defendant pursuant to section 47 of chapter 123 of the General Laws;

(iii) delay resulting from a trial with respect to other charges against the defendant, which period shall run from the commencement of such other trial until fourteen days after an acquittal or imposition of sentence;

(iv) delay resulting from interlocutory appeals;

(v) delay resulting from hearings on pretrial motions;

(vi) delay resulting from proceedings relating to transfer to or from other divisions or counties pursuant to Rule 37;

(vii) delay reasonably attributable to any period, not to exceed thirty days, during which any proceeding concerning the defendant is actually under advisement.

(B) Any period of delay resulting from the absence or unavailability of the defendant or an essential witness. A defendant or an essential witness shall be considered absent when his whereabouts are unknown and he is attempting to avoid apprehension or prosecution or his whereabouts cannot be determined by due diligence. A defendant or an essential witness shall be considered unavailable whenever his whereabouts are known but his presence for trial cannot be obtained by due diligence or he resists appearing at or being returned for trial.

(C) Any period of delay resulting from the fact that the defendant is mentally incompetent or physically unable to stand trial.

(D) If the complaint or indictment is dismissed by the prosecution and thereafter a charge is filed against the defendant for the same or a related offense, any period of delay from the date the charge was dismissed to the date the time limitation would commence to run as to the subsequent charge.

(E) A reasonable period of delay when the defendant is joined for trial with a codefendant as to whom the time for trial has not run and there is no cause for granting a severance.

(F) Any period of delay resulting from a continuance granted by a judge on his own motion or at the request of the defendant or his counsel or at the request of the prosecutor, if the judge granted the continuance on the basis of his findings that the ends of justice served by taking such action outweighed the best interests of the public and the defendant in a speedy trial. No period of delay resulting from a continuance granted by the court in accordance with this paragraph shall be excludable under this subdivision unless the judge sets forth in the record of the case, either orally or in writing, his reasons for finding that the ends of justice served by the granting of the continuance outweigh the best interests of the public and the defendant in a speedy trial.

(G) Any period of time between the day on which a defendant or his counsel and the prosecuting attorney agree in writing that the defendant will plead guilty or nolo contendere to the charges and such time as the judge accepts or rejects the plea arrangement.

(H) Any period of time between the day on which the defendant enters a plea of guilty and such time as an order of the judge permitting the withdrawal of the plea becomes final.

(3) *Computation of Time Limits.* In computing any time limit other than an excluded period, the day of the act or event which causes a designated period of time to begin to run shall not be included. Computation of an excluded period shall include both the first and the last day of the excludable act or event.

(c) Dismissal for Prejudicial Delay. Notwithstanding the fact that a defendant is not entitled to a dismissal under subdivision (b) of this rule, a defendant shall upon motion be entitled to a dismissal where the judge after an examination and consideration of all attendant circumstances determines that: (1) the conduct of the prosecuting attorney in bringing the defendant to trial has been unreasonably lacking in diligence and (2) this conduct on the part of the prosecuting attorney has resulted in prejudice to the defendant.

(d) Special Procedures: Persons Serving Term of Imprisonment.

(1) *General Provisions*. A person serving a term of imprisonment either within or without the prosecuting jurisdiction is entitled to all safeguards afforded him under subdivisions (a), (b), and (c) of this rule in the conduct of any criminal proceeding, subject to the limitations stated herein.

(2) *Persons Detained Within the Commonwealth*. Any person who is detained within the Commonwealth upon the unexecuted portion of a sentence imposed pursuant to a criminal proceeding is entitled to be tried upon any untried indictment or complaint pending against him in any court in this Commonwealth within the time prescribed by subdivision (b) of this rule.

(3) *Persons Detained Outside the Commonwealth*. Any person who is detained outside the Commonwealth upon the unexecuted portion of a sentence imposed pursuant to a criminal proceeding, and against whom an untried indictment or complaint is pending within the Commonwealth shall, subsequent to the filing of a detainer, be notified by the prosecutor by mail of such charges and of his right to demand a speedy trial. If the defendant pursuant to such notification does demand trial, the person having custody shall so certify to the prosecutor, who shall promptly seek to obtain the presence of the defendant for trial. If the prosecutor has unreasonably delayed (A) in causing a detainer to be filed with the official having custody of the defendant, or (B) in seeking to obtain the defendant's presence for trial, and the defendant has been prejudiced thereby, the pending charges against the defendant shall be dismissed.

(e) Effect of a Dismissal. A dismissal of any charge ordered pursuant to any provision of this rule shall apply to all related offenses.

(f) Case Status Reports.

(1) *District Court*. The First Justice of each division of the District Court shall be advised periodically by the clerk of the status of all cases which have been pending in that court for six months or longer. The report shall be transmitted to the Administrative Justice for the District Court Department.

(2) *Superior Court*. The Administrative Justice for the Superior Court Department shall be notified by the clerk for each county of the status of all cases which have been pending in that court for six months or longer within the following time periods:

(A) for the first twelve-month period following the effective date of this rule, sixty days after the last day of a sitting;

(B) for the second such twelve-month period, forty-five days after the last day of a sitting;

(C) for the third and all successive such twelve-month periods, thirty days after the last day of a sitting.

Such notice shall include the number of the case, the name of the defendant, the offense charged, the name of defense counsel, if any, and the name of the prosecutor.

Amended effective March 1, 1996.

Reporter's Notes

This rule is taken in part from the ABA *Standards Relating to Speedy Trial* (Approved Draft, 1968) and to a lesser extent from the Federal Speedy Trial Act, 18 U.S.C. §§ 3161–74 (Supp. 1, 1975), and former G.L. c. 277, §§ 72 (St.1784, c. 72) and 72A (St.1965, c. 343). *See* Rules of Criminal Procedure (U.L.A.) rule 722 (1974); ABA *Standards Relating to Speedy Trial* (2d ed., Approved Draft, 1978).

The Supreme Court held in Barker v. Wingo, 92 S.Ct. 2182, 407 U.S. 514, 33 L.Ed.2d 101 (1972), that a defendant's constitutional right to a speedy trial cannot be established by any inflexible rule, but can be determined only on an ad hoc balancing basis in which the conduct of the defendant and the prosecution are weighed.

> [A]ny inquiry into a speedy trial claim necessitates a functional analysis of the right in the particular context of the case....

Barker v. Wingo, supra at 522. The Court refused to objectify a "fixed point in the criminal process when the State can put the defendant to the choice of either exercising or waiving the right to a speedy trial," 407 U.S. at 521, choosing not to engage in legislative or rulemaking activity.

> We find no constitutional basis for holding that the speedy trial right can be quantified into a specified number of days or months. *The States, of course, are free to prescribe a reasonable period consistent with constitutional standards,* but our approach must be less precise.

407 U.S. at 523 (Emphasis supplied).

Since the Supreme Court's decision in Klopfer v. North Carolina, 87 S.Ct. 988, 386 U.S. 213, 18 L.Ed.2d 1 (1967), wherein the speedy trial guarantee secured by the sixth amendment was made applicable to and enforceable against the states by virtue of the due process requirements of the fourteenth amendment, three-quarters of the states have enacted, either by court rule or statute, speedy trial provisions. This would seem to indicate that the majority of states have experienced difficulty in affording uniformly fair justice on a case-by-case basis and are seeking to objectify the right so as to ease its application. The Supreme Court in *Barker* does not deny the states this prerogative so long as its exercise is consistent with constitutional standards. 407 U.S. at 530 n. 29.

While Rule 36 does quantify the time limits beyond which a defendant's speedy trial rights shall be deemed to have been denied, it is, as its title makes clear, primarily a management tool, designed to assist the trial courts in administering their dockets.

Subdivision (a).

Subdivision (a)(1). This subdivision is taken from § 1.1 of the ABA *Standards Relating to Speedy Trial* (Approved Draft, 1968). *See* ABA *Standards Relating to the Function of the Trial Judge,* § 3.8(c) (Approved Draft, 1972); Rules of Criminal Procedure (U.L.A.) rule 721(b) (1974).

Incarcerated defendants under existing Massachusetts law are accorded certain rights. This subdivision is first a general restatement of the principles underlying prior law, rather than a substitute for former statutes, and secondly an aid in the continued implementation of the policy of former G.L. c. 277, § 72, which provided for the release of a defendant from pretrial detention if he had not been tried within the criminal session next following six months of incarceration.

Additionally, the preference given to the trial of criminal defendants held in jail for offenses not punishable by death or life imprisonment over the trial of civil cases by G.L. c. 212, § 29 is to retain its vitality though not expressly adopted by this rule. See G.L. c. 212, § 24. *See* ABA *Standards Relating to Speedy Trial, Standard* 12–1.1(a) (2d ed. Approved Draft, 1978), Fed.R.Crim.P. 50(a).

Subdivision (a)(2). This is modeled after *Standard* 12–1.2 of the ABA *Standards Relating to Speedy Trial,* supra, and is consonant with the policy of G.L. c. 278, § 1 in that the trial court is given ultimate control over the calendar. *See* Rules of Criminal Procedure (U.L.A.) rule 721(a) (1974). The guiding principle behind this section was enunciated by the Eighth Circuit:

> The government and, for that matter, the trial court are not without responsibility for the expeditious trial of criminal cases. The burden of trial promptness is not solely upon the defense.

Hodges v. United States, 408 F.2d 543, 551 (8th Cir.1969). *Accord* United States v. Drummond, 511 F.2d 1046, 1053 (2d Cir.1975). *See* Barker v. Wingo, 92 S.Ct. 2182, 407 U.S. 514, 527, 33 L.Ed.2d 101 (1972).

(a)(2)(A). In District Court jury-waived sessions, the court is to prepare and control the trial lists consistently with prior practice.

(a)(2)(B). General Laws c. 278, § 1 requires the district attorney to submit a list to the court of defendants to be tried at each sitting of the Superior Court, and it states that the cases will be tried in the order of the list unless otherwise ordered by the court.

Practice remains unchanged by this rule—the district attorneys are to place cases on the list in the order of priority they believe appropriate; the court may re-order arrangement of the list once it is submitted—but this procedure is extended to District Court jury sessions. General Laws c. 218, § 26A (St.1978, c. 478, § 188) provides for a jury trial in the first instance of all charges over which the District Court has original jurisdiction. If a defendant elects not to waive jury trial, or, having waived that right, claims an appeal to a jury session after conviction, G.L. c. 218, § 27A(g) (St.1978, c. 478, § 189) mandates that a District Attorney shall appear and prosecute the case. Further, G.L. c. 278, § 27A(e) provides that District Court jury sessions shall proceed in accordance with jury trials in the Superior Court. Therefore, subdivision (a)(2)(B) is to be read to empower the District Attorney to select those cases which are to be placed on the District Court jury session trial list. General Laws c. 278, § 1 establishes burdens on the prosecutor who is to keep current the list of cases to be tried and on the court which is to have the ultimate responsibility for the timely trial of those cases. *See* ABA *Standards Relating to the Function of the Trial Judge,* § 3.8(a) (Approved Draft, 1972). Practice under this rule will aid in the effective implementation of the speedy trial guarantee for there is a periodic check by the court on the prosecutor. Subdivision (f), infra.

Subdivision (b). General Laws c. 277, § 72 formerly provided for trial within six months after demand by an incarcerated defendant. This subdivision is an expansion of that statutory right, ultimately securing to all defendants the right to trial within twelve months after the filing of charges. Subdivision (b) is intended to insure that a defendant is not denied that right by providing for the dismissal of the charges for undue delay in bringing the defendant to trial.

The effect of this subdivision is not only to establish a specific time limit for commencement of trial, but also to shift the burden of proof concerning a deprivation of the defendant's right to trial within twelve months. The constitutional protection puts the burden on the defendant to show that the delay was undue and to his prejudice, whereas under this rule, once a twelve-month lapse has been shown, the burden shifts to the prosecutor to explain the delay.

General Laws c. 277, § 72 provided that a defendant held in custody upon an indictment had the right to be released on his own recognizance if not brought to trial by the time of the court's sitting next after six months from his commitment. General Laws c. 277, § 72A gave an incarcerated defendant the right to be tried on pending charges within six months after his application for a speedy trial or the charges would be dismissed. Those statutes were designed to alleviate hardships imposed upon particular defendants by pretrial delay. This subdivision is founded upon the premise that all defendants are liable to suffer from undue delay and that a definite time limit should be made available to them on an equal basis.

Subdivision (b)(1). Unlike former G.L. c. 277, § 72A, this subdivision is phrased so that only a *trial* upon charges against the defendant will satisfy the requirements of this rule. General Laws c. 277, § 72A required either a prompt "trial or *other disposition* thereof" (emphasis supplied), thus permitting a defendant's demand to be satisfied by other than a trial upon the charges. Commonwealth v. Fields, 371 Mass. 274, 280 (1976); Commonwealth v. Stewart, 361 Mass. 857, 356 N.E.2d 1211 (1972) (Rescript); Commonwealth v. Royce, 358 Mass. 597, 599, 266 N.E.2d 308 (1971); Commonwealth v. Ambers, Mass.App.Adv.Sh. (1978) 1141, 1145–46, 378 N.E.2d 451; Commonwealth v. Anderson, Mass.App.Adv.Sh. (1978) 775, 779, 378 N.E.2d 451. This change is intended to offer a defendant relief from pending charges and their attendant burdens, thereby giving substance to the speedy trial concept. A dismissal of charges on other grounds, a disposition of the charges by plea, or a filing of the case, of course, vitiates any need for trial, and in such an instance the rule does not apply.

For purposes of this rule, a trial is deemed to have commenced when jeopardy attaches. "In the case of a jury trial, jeopardy attaches when a jury is empaneled and sworn.... In a nonjury trial, jeopardy attaches when the court begins to hear evidence." Serfass v. United States, 95 S.Ct. 1055, 420 U.S. 377, 388, 43 L.Ed.2d 265 (1975). *Accord* Commonwealth v. Ludwig, 370 Mass. 31, 33, 345 N.E.2d 386 (1976). *See* Commonwealth v. Brandano, 359 Mass. 332, 334–35, 269 N.E.2d 84 (1971); 30 MASS.PRACTICE SERIES (Smith) § 563 at 290 (1970). If neither of these stages of prosecution has been reached within twelve months after the return day in the court in which the case is pending, the charges must be dismissed upon motion of the defendant. The mandatory sanction for failure to comply with the twelve-month time limit is dismissal of the charges, such dismissal to be a bar to any subsequent prosecution for the same offense or any related offenses, whether by later complaint in the District Court or indictment in the Superior Court. Commonwealth v. Fields, 371 Mass. 274, 356 N.E.2d 1211 (1976); *Commonwealth v. Ludwig,* supra, at 35; subdivision (e), infra.

Under this rule, the right to a speedy trial attaches upon "the return day in the court in which the case is awaiting trial," that is, the date on which "a defendant is ordered by summons to first appear or, if under arrest, does first appear . . . to answer to the charges. . . ." Mass.R.Crim.P. 2(b)(15). Therefore, if a defendant is bound over to the Superior Court after a probable cause hearing (Mass.R.Crim.P. 3[c]) or the Commonwealth elects to proceed by direct indictment in a case commenced by complaint which is within the District Court's jurisdiction (Mass.R.Crim.P. 3[e]), the time limits of this rule begin anew upon the return day in the Superior Court. *See* ABA *Standards Relating to Speedy Trial, Standard* 12–2.2 (2d ed., Approved Draft, 1978); Rules of Criminal Procedure (U.L.A.) Rule 722(d) (1974).

As to re-trials, the right accrues when the certainty of that trial is established, *e.g.,* by a judicial order for a new trial. Subdivision (b)(1)(D). As originally drafted, the Rule left some ambiguity as to when this condition was satisfied in practice. *See* Commonwealth v. Levin, 390 Mass. 857, 860 n. 4, 460 N.E.2d 578 (1984) and Commonwealth v. Bodden, 391 Mass. 356, 357–58, 461 N.E.2d 803 (1984). A 1996 amendment settled this issue by declaring that a retrial order is final upon the issuance by the appellate court of the rescript or, if the clerk failed to issue the rescript as required, when it should have issued.

Subdivision (b)(2). This is patterned after 18 U.S.C. § 3161(h) (Supp. 1, 1975). See ABA Standards Relating to Speedy Trial §§ 2.1, 2.3 (Approved Draft, 1968); Rules of Criminal Procedure (ULA) Rule 722(f) (1974).

The Supreme Judicial Court has stated that "in addition to periods of time specifically excluded by the rule, periods during which a defendant acquiesced in, is responsible for, or benefitted from a delay are also not counted." Commonwealth v. Lauria, 411 Mass. 63, 68, 576 N.E.2d 1368 (1991). *See also* Commonwealth v. Conefrey, 410 Mass. 1, 4–5, 570 N.E.2d 1384 (1991); Commonwealth v. Farris, 390 Mass. 300, 455 N.E.2d 433 (1983); Commonwealth v. Look, 379 Mass. 893, 402 N.E.2d 470 (1980); Commonwealth v. Alexander, 371 Mass. 726, 359 N.E.2d 306 (1977); Commonwealth v. Boyd, 367 Mass. 169, 178, 326 N.E.2d 320 (1975); Commonwealth v. Loftis, 361 Mass. 545, 549–50, 281 N.E.2d 258 (1972); Commonwealth v. McCants, 25 Mass.App.Ct. 735, 522 N.E.2d 15 (1988); Commonwealth v. Jones, 6 Mass.App. Ct. 750, 752–53, 383 N.E.2d 527 (1978) (interpreting G.L. c. 277, § 72A). But because the Commonwealth has the primary obligation for setting a trial date, a thorough examination of the record is necessary to determine whether failure to object should be counted against the defendant. Commonwealth v. Spaulding, 411 Mass. 503, 507, 583 N.E.2d 1257 (1992). The specific periods listed in this subdivision are those where the delay is not to be attributed to the prosecution.

Under prior cases in which the *Barker v. Wingo* sixth amendment analysis was applied, absent a showing of culpability on the part of the Commonwealth in delaying trial, the burden was on the defendant to demonstrate that the Commonwealth unreasonably caused prejudicial delay. Commonwealth v. Gilbert, 366 Mass. 18, 22, 314 N.E.2d 111 (1974). *Accord* Commonwealth v. Campbell, 5 Mass.App. 571, 366 N.E.2d 44 (1977); Commonwealth v. Burhoe, 3 Mass.App. 590, 594, 337 N.E.2d 913 (1975); Commonwealth v. Jackson, 3 Mass.App. 511, 517, 335 N.E.2d 367 (1975). Under this rule, however, no demonstration of prejudice is necessary (except under subdivision [c], infra); once the defendant has established a *prima facie* case for dismissal—i.e., that twelve months have elapsed since the return day—the burden is on the Commonwealth to establish justification for the delay. The rule *requires* the court to dismiss the charges (rather than making the decision discretionary and dependent upon a balancing of all relevant considerations) unless an explanation is deemed sufficient to excuse the delay.

Under this subdivision, the court is given the discretion to consider and determine whether a proffered explanation for delay is a valid excluded period. But, once it is determined that a period of delay is within the contemplation of this subdivision, that period shall be excluded from computation of the twelve-month limit. The rationale underlying this subdivision is that the Commonwealth should not be penalized when the defendant elects to avail himself of those procedures which are certain to result in delay, or when the causes for delay are beyond its control.

(b)(2)(A)(i). This subdivision excludes delay due to a mental or physical examination of the defendant to determine his competency or physical capacity to stand trial and the resultant hearing on the matter. This delay is a common occurrence and often essential to a fair trial. *See* Commonwealth v. Boyd, 367 Mass. 169, 178–79, 321 N.E.2d 320 (1975); Commonwealth v. Rise, Mass.App.Ct.Adv.Sh. (1979) 254, 255–57, 386 N.E.2d 745. It is intended that the excluded period shall begin on the date the order for examination is given and shall extend until such date as the court finds the defendant mentally competent or physically able to stand trial. The court's finding should be made within 30 days after receipt by the court of the examiner's report ([b][2][A][vii], infra) and the excludable period shall continue until such finding is made. It should be noted that the actual time period under (b)(2)(A)(i) may be extended by (b)(2)(C) to exclude any delay resulting from the fact that the defendant is found mentally incompetent or physically unable to stand trial. Fairness requires that a balance be struck between the defendant's right to a speedy trial and those delays which of necessity accompany the examination process and which are beyond the control of the prosecution once the procedure has been ordered.

(b)(2)(A)(ii). It is intended by this subdivision that the excluded period shall begin when the defendant is advised by the court that he may request an examination to determine whether he is a drug dependent person pursuant to G.L. c. 123, § 47. The defendant is then given five days under § 47 in which to exercise his right to an examination. If an examination is not requested within the provided time limit, the excludable period shall terminate. However, if the defendant elects an examination, the period of time during which he is being examined shall be excluded. Once the defendant has requested examination, the court may, in its discretion, determine without an examination that the defendant would benefit from treatment and shall inform him that he may request treatment in a drug facility. The period of time during which the defendant is undergoing treatment for drug addiction will be excluded under (b)(2)(A)(ii). It is intended that the excluded period shall cover the entire period of delay generated by § 47 examination or treatment.

(b)(2)(A)(iii). This subdivision is intended to be inclusive of trials of the defendant on other charges in any state or federal court including the court where charges are then pending against the defendant. *See* Commonwealth v. Anderson, Mass.App.Adv.Sh. (1978) 775, 780–81, 378 N.E.2d 451; Commonwealth v. Fasano, Mass.App.Adv.Sh. (1978) 521, 375 N.E.2d 361. The period shall run from the date such other trial begins and it is intended that the period shall conclude 14 days after a verdict of acquittal or imposition of sentence in the case. For the purpose of this subdivision, trial shall include the impanelling of the jury, hearings on motions deferred to the trial date, and any periods during which trial is suspended. The 14–day period following acquittal or sentencing is included in order to provide defense counsel with adequate preparation time for the second trial.

(b)(2)(A)(iv). It is intended that the excluded period under this subdivision run from the date the notice of appeal is filed until the rescript is received by the clerk of the lower court. The period covers any time during which interlocutory appeals are pending. *See* Commonwealth v. Underwood, 3 Mass.App. 522, 528–29, 335 N.E.2d 915 (1975). Where delay is occasioned by the Commonwealth's successful interlocutory appeal under Mass.R.Crim.P. 15, such delay does not prejudice the defense nor deny the defendant his right to a speedy trial. *See* United States v. Rosenbloom, 167 U.S.App. 211, 511 F.2d 777 (D.C.Cir.1974).

(b)(2)(A)(v). Delay attributable to the securing of a judicial resolution of issues raised by a defendant's pretrial motions are excluded from the running of the time limits. *See* Commonwealth v. Morgan, Mass.App.Adv.Sh. (1978) 1047, 381 N.E.2d 1126 (Rescript); Commonwealth v. Fasano, Mass. App.Adv.Sh. (1978) 521, 531–532, 375 N.E.2d 361; Commonwealth v. Campbell, 5 Mass.App. 571, 366 N.E.2d 44 (1977); Commonwealth v. Burhoe, 3 Mass.App. 590, 593, 337 N.E.2d 913 (1975); Commonwealth v. Underwood, 3 Mass.App. 522, 528–29, 335 N.E.2d 915 (1975); Commonwealth v. Jackson, 3 Mass.App. 511, 516–517, 335 N.E.2d 367 (1975).

The excludable period under this subdivision is intended to run from the date on which the request for hearing on the pretrial motion is filed, or, if no such request is filed, from the date the hearing is ordered, until the conclusion of the hearing.

(b)(2)(A)(vi). This subdivision provides that delay due to proceedings related to transfer under Mass.R.Crim.P. 37 shall be an excluded period. In cases transferred pursuant to Rule 37(a)(1) and (2), it is intended that the time limit begin to run on the date the clerk of the court in the transferee district receives the papers from the clerk of the court in the transferor district. In cases where the defendant moves for transfer of the case to another district pursuant to Rule 37(b), an excludable period shall run from the date of the hearing on the motion for transfer. If the motion is denied the period terminates at that time. If the motion is allowed and the case is subsequently transferred, the conclusion of the period will be determined by the court in that district to which the case is transferred. Under this rule, periods that are excluded are not restricted to the proceedings, directly related to transfer pursuant to Rule 37, but are intended to provide as well for delays caused by the transfer of papers from one district to another in transfer proceedings. This is to account for reasonable administrative delays while the court awaits the transfer papers.

(b)(2)(A)(vii). This subdivision provides for those delays which are necessary for the court to pass on proceedings concerning the defendant, exclusive of those periods for consideration of pretrial motions under (2)(A)(v). It is intended by this rule that the excluded period run during the time that the matter is actually under advisement until an order or ruling is entered, but in no event shall the period exceed 30 days. *See* 18 U.S.C. § 3161(h)(1)(G). It is not the intent of (2)(A)(vii) to preclude a continuance under Mass.R.Crim.P. 10 after the 30–day time limit is expired, but it is believed that the 30–day limit is reasonable in most cases. Where the matter under advisement is complex, the court may continue the case upon its own motion under (b)(2)(F), infra.

(b)(2)(B). If a defendant has made himself unavailable for trial for the purpose of avoiding prosecution, the interests of justice require that he not be allowed to subsequently claim violation of his right to a speedy trial. Commonwealth v. Underwood, 3 Mass.App. 522, 527–28, 335 N.E.2d 915 (1975). *Accord* Commonwealth v. Jones, Mass.App.Adv.Sh. (1978) 1218, 1225, 383 N.E.2d 527. Similarly, delays granted to allow the defendant or the Commonwealth to locate a key witness are justified and not properly chargeable against the Commonwealth. *See* e.g., Commonwealth v. Daggett, 369 Mass. 790, 793–94, 343 N.E.2d 409 (1976); Commonwealth v. Boyd, 367 Mass. 169, 178, 326 N.E.2d 320 (1975); Commonwealth v. Jones, Mass.App.Adv.Sh. (1978) 1218, 1225, 383 N.E.2d 527; Commonwealth v. Alves, Mass.App.Adv.Sh. (1978) 912, 917 n. 3, 380 N.E.2d 701; Commonwealth v. Campbell, 5 Mass.App. 571, 366 N.E.2d 44 (1977); Commonwealth v. Ambers, 4 Mass.App. 647, 357 N.E.2d 323 (1976). An exclusion under this subdivision will be established by a party on motion for a continuance. It is intended that the excludable period run from the date the motion for a continuance is filed until the date when the defendant or witness is found by the court to have become available for trial. Mass. R.Crim.P. 10 provides that a continuance shall not be granted if a party fails to exercise due diligence to obtain an available witness for trial. Therefore, a party moving for a continuance under this subdivision should set forth with particularity the reasons why a continuance will enable him to obtain the witness and should state those facts as to which the witness is expected to testify. This will enable the court to make the necessary determination, on the facts presented, whether the unavailable witness is so "essential" as to warrant a continuance.

It is intended by this subdivision that a motion for a continuance on the ground of the absence of the defendant explain the facts of the defendant's absence. Since such absence may occur at any time during the proceedings, it may become necessary for the court to determine how long the defendant has been absent and whether he is attempting to avoid prosecution or whether his whereabouts cannot be determined by due diligence. It is recommended practice under this rule that if a party learns or has reason to believe that a witness will be unavailable, and if the party does not wish to proceed to trial without that witness, that the party move for a continuance as far in advance of trial as is feasible. Counsel should inform the court and the adverse party promptly of the availability of the defendant or witness.

The definition of an absent defendant or witness has been adapted from the ABA *Standards Relating to Speedy Trial* § 2.3(e) (Approved Draft, 1968); *accord Standard* 12–2.3(e) (2d ed., Approved Draft, 1978).

(b)(2)(C). Subdivision (b)(2)(A)(i) provides for an excluded period during examination and hearing on the defendant's competency or ability to stand trial. It is intended that if the court should find the defendant unable to stand trial, a new period will begin under this subdivision, such excluded period to conclude upon a court finding that the defendant is competent and able to stand trial.

(b)(2)(D). This subdivision provides for an excluded period when the prosecution nol prosses the charges pending against the defendant pursuant to Mass.R.Crim.P. 16 and subsequently brings new charges for the same offense. Only the time period during which there are no charges pending against the defendant is to be excluded from the twelve-month limit under (b)(1). The excluded time period will run only from the time the prosecution dismisses the charges until the return day as to the subsequent charge. For example, if the return day as to certain charges is January 1 and those charges are dismissed by the prosecution six months later, followed by a new complaint or indictment for the same offenses, as to which the return day is August 1, the prosecution has until February 1 to bring the defendant to trial. The one-month period during which no charges were pending is excluded, but the previous six months during which charges were outstanding is counted against the Commonwealth. *See* Commonwealth v. Gove, 366 Mass. 351, 359, 320 N.E.2d 900 (1974).

(b)(2)(E). Under this subdivision, reasonable delay where no motion for severance has been granted and the time for trial has not run as to the joined defendant shall be an excluded period. *See* Commonwealth v. Beckett, Mass.Adv. Sh. (1977) 1922, 1925, 378 N.E.2d 69; Commonwealth v. Carr, 3 Mass.App. 654, 656–57, 338 N.E.2d 844 (1975). Situations may arise where the period of delay could prove unreasonable; for example, where the joined defendant is indefinitely unavailable for trial or cannot be brought into custody. In such a situation it is not intended that the trial of the defendant presently in custody pending trial be deferred.

(b)(2)(F). This subdivision excludes delay resulting from a continuance granted upon a finding that "the ends of justice . . . outweigh the best interests of the public and the defendant in a speedy trial." It is implicit that (b)(2)(F) does not countenance an after-the-fact appraisal of the causes of delay by a reviewing court; in order to be excluded, the delay must have been the subject of a formal continuance. This does not, of course, preclude the appellate court from considering whether the grant or denial of a continuance constituted an abuse of discretion. See Mass.R.Crim.P. 10. Since only a judge may grant a continuance under Rule 10, the Commonwealth's failure to bring a case to trial without such a continuance, or its unilateral rescheduling a case to a later trial list, see G.L. c. 278, § 1, will not toll the speedy trial clock under this subsection. Commonwealth v. Spaulding, 411 Mass. 503, 508–10, 583 N.E.2d 1257 (1992) (failure of defendant to object to delay in scheduling did not toll period); Barry v. Commonwealth, 390 Mass. 285, 296 n. 13, 455 N.E.2d 437 (1983) (Commonwealth's setting of trial date does not toll period).

When a formal continuance is granted, this subdivision incorporates the procedure stated to be "advisable" under former G.L. c. 277, § 72A which requires the trial judge to state the reasons for any extension of time hereunder. Commonwealth v. Fields, 371 Mass. 274, 280 n. 8, 356 N.E.2d 1211 (1976); Commonwealth v. Boyd, 367 Mass. 169, 179, 326 N.E.2d 320 (1975); Commonwealth v. Loftis, 361 Mass. 545, 549, 281 N.E.2d 258 (1972); Commonwealth v. Ambers, 4 Mass.App.Ct. 647, 357 N.E.2d 323 (1976).

Delay which is justified under this subdivision may include that required for the Commonwealth to comply with a discovery order, Commonwealth v. Anderson, 6 Mass.App.Ct. 492, 378 N.E.2d 451 (1978); that required by newly-appointed counsel to prepare the case, e.g., Commonwealth v. Campbell, 5 Mass.App.Ct. 571, 366 N.E.2d 44 (1977); or that occasioned by the illness of the defendant, a co-defendant, counsel for the defendant or the Commonwealth, or the judge. Commonwealth v. Campbell, supra.

On the other hand, undue delay attributable to a defendant's desire to be represented by particular counsel is not justified. E.g., Commonwealth v. Dabrieo, 370 Mass. 728, 739, 352 N.E.2d 186 (1976). See Mass.R.Crim.P. 10(a)(2)(c) and Reporter's Notes, supra.

While the Supreme Judicial Court has indicated that court congestion will not be tolerated as an adequate ground for denying a "reasonably prompt trial," Commonwealth v. Beckett, 373 Mass. 329, 332, 335, 366 N.E.2d 1252 (1977), delay "inherent in the general problems of the administration of justice in a congested county," Commonwealth v. Rego, 360 Mass. 385, 392, 274 N.E.2d 795 (1971), is an often-cited excuse for an extension of time limits. Commonwealth v. Gove, 366 Mass. 351, 362–63, 320 N.E.2d 900 (1974); Commonwealth v. Fontaine, 8 Mass.App.Ct. 51, 391 N.E.2d 1234 (1979); Commonwealth v. Jones, 6 Mass.App.Ct. 750, 755–56, 383 N.E.2d 527 (1978) (interpreting G.L. c. 277, § 72A); Commonwealth v. Campbell, 5 Mass.App.Ct. 571, 366 N.E.2d 44 (1977); Commonwealth v. Ambers, 4 Mass.App.Ct. 647, 357 N.E.2d 323 (1976); Commonwealth v. Burhoe, 3 Mass. App.Ct. 590, 593, 337 N.E.2d 913 (1975). Although crowded dockets, lack of counsel, and other factors make some delays inevitable, Commonwealth v. Beckett, supra, a judge presented with a motion for a continuance on this ground is to carefully weigh the interests of the defendant and the public. *See also* Commonwealth v. Plantier, 22 Mass.App.Ct. 314, 493 N.E.2d 534 (1986) (dismissal within court's discretion where defendant prepared but case continued due to prosecutor's request or court congestion).

Although the Rule does not say so, caselaw since its promulgation has held that the defendant's failure to object to a continuance may render the continuance period excludable. Commonwealth v. Dias, 405 Mass. 131, 139, 539 N.E.2d 59 (1989); Commonwealth v. Farris, 390 Mass. 300, 455 N.E.2d 433 (1983); Commonwealth v. Fleenor, 39 Mass.App.Ct. 25, 27, 652 N.E.2d 899 (1995); Commonwealth v. Domingue, 18 Mass.App.Ct. 987, 470 N.E.2d 799 (1984), review denied 393 Mass. 1105, 474 N.E.2d 181 (1985). Moreover, as indicated in the Reporter's Notes, supra at (b)(2), caselaw has enunciated a broader rule which may exclude some delays which the defense acquiesced in, is responsible for, or benefitted from.

(b)(2)(G). This subdivision extends the rule that a valid plea of guilty constitutes a waiver of any claim to a denial of a speedy trial to the situation where, pursuant to Mass. R.Crim.P. 12(b), the defendant and the Commonwealth have concluded a plea arrangement. Becker v. Nebraska, 435 F.2d 157 (8th Cir.1970), cert. denied 91 S.Ct. 1684, 402 U.S. 981, 29 L.Ed.2d 145 (1971); Fowler v. United States, 391 F.2d 276, 277 (5th Cir.1968); United States v. Doyle, 348 F.2d 715, 718–19 (2d Cir.), cert. denied sub nom. Doyle v. United States, 86 S.Ct. 89, 382 U.S. 843, 46 L.Ed.2d 394 (1965). *See* Commonwealth v. L'Italien, 3 Mass.App. 763, 330 N.E.2d 214 (1975).

(b)(2)(H). The same principle which governs in subdivision (b)(2)(G) operates to exclude the time between which a plea is tendered and accepted by the court under Mass. R.Crim.P. 12(c)(5) and the time at which it is withdrawn by the defendant pursuant to Mass.R.Crim.P. 12(d).

It is intended that the excluded period run from the date the plea of guilty is first offered and accepted until the date the court permits withdrawal of the plea.

Subdivision (b)(3). The provision as to excluded periods is contrary to G.L. c. 4, § 7 and Mass.R.Crim.P. 46(a), which state that the day on which a limited period commences shall be excluded from the computation. This subdivision is in other respects consistent with prior law. *See* Commonwealth v. Daggett, 369 Mass. 790, 792 n. 1, 343 N.E.2d 409 (1976). *See* ABA *Standards Relating to Speedy Trial* § 3.2 (Approved Draft, 1968), *Standard* 12–3.2 (2d ed., Approved Draft, 1978).

Subdivision (c). It is possible, although unusual, that a delay of less than twelve months could be deemed prejudicial and therefore violative of a defendant's right to be tried with reasonable dispatch. Under this subdivision a dismissal of charges would be warranted in such a situation.

For those defendants who are not yet entitled to the mandatory dismissal upon motion under subdivision (b)(1), this subdivision states the standard by which an allegation of a denial of a speedy trial may nonetheless be judged: it is a statement of the fundamental constitutional guarantee. The twelve-month rule sets a standard which is quantitative and whose limits are easily determined, whereas the constitutional standard is a relative qualitative concept demanding that the severity of the denial of its protection to a defendant be dependent upon the facts of his case.

Barker v. Wingo, 92 S.Ct. 2182, 407 U.S. 514, 33 L.Ed.2d 101 (1972), and Commonwealth v. Horne, 362 Mass. 738, 291 N.E.2d 629 (1973), make it clear that a balancing approach must be used to determine whether a defendant's constitutional right to a speedy trial has been violated. E.g., Commonwealth v. Beckett, 373 Mass. 329, 366 N.E.2d 1252 (1977); Commonwealth v. Dabrieo, 370 Mass. 728, 352 N.E.2d 186 (1976); Commonwealth v. Daggett, 369 Mass. 790, 343 N.E.2d 409 (1976); Commonwealth v. Gove, 366 Mass. 351, 361–65, 320 N.E.2d 900 (1974). For purposes of this analysis, the right to a speedy trial under art. II of the Massachusetts Declaration of Rights and under the sixth amendment to the United States Constitution are considered to be coextensive. *Commonwealth v. Gove,* supra at 356 n. 6; Commonwealth v. Underwood, 3 Mass.App. 522, 526, 335 N.E.2d 915 (1975).

This subdivision puts the constitutional standard into manageable operational terms. Four factors were mentioned by the United States Supreme Court in *Barker* as among those to be considered: the length of delay, the reason for delay, the resulting prejudice to the defendant, and the assertion of the right by the defendant. This subdivision isolates two essential factors which are the substance of the constitutional protection. These are unreasonable prosecutorial delay and resulting prejudice to the defendant.

Subdivision (c)(1) states that only prosecutorial delay is within the scope of the relief afforded by this subdivision. This protection is compatible with the constitutional protection. Commonwealth v. Lauria, 359 Mass. 168, 268 N.E.2d 363 (1971); Commonwealth v. Thomas, 353 Mass. 429, 233 N.E.2d 25 (1967). This subdivision requires the defendant to establish first that the delay he has endured is unreasonable and secondly that it was caused by the prosecutor. If the delay is of that nature, the defendant has conclusively established one of the two requisites to a finding that his motion to dismiss the charges is to be granted.

There is no disagreement with the proposition that only an unreasonable delay is prohibited by the Constitution and that what is unreasonable depends upon the peculiar facts of each case. For example, the amount of time that a prosecutor needs to prepare a case in which several defendants have been joined for trial is normally greater than the time needed to prepare for the trial of a single defendant. *See* Commonwealth v. Dominico, 1 Mass.App. 693, 306 N.E.2d 835 (1974).

Subdivision (c)(2) establishes the second element which the defendant must show to support his motion: that he has been prejudiced by the delay. Prejudice in the context of this subdivision is not restricted to prejudice to the preparation or presentation of the defense. The Supreme Court in *Barker v. Wingo,* supra, listed three distinct functions served by the prohibition against unreasonable delay: "(i) to prevent oppressive pretrial incarceration; (ii) to minimize anxiety and concern of the accused; and (iii) to limit the possibility that the defense will be impaired." *Id.* at 532.

If the defendant is able to show that deliberate, unreasonable prosecutorial delay has operated to his prejudice, the appropriate sanction is dismissal of the charges with prejudice to the Commonwealth. Support for such a sanction is even stronger when imposed for constitutional reasons. The Supreme Court in Strunk v. United States, 93 S.Ct. 2260, 412 U.S. 434, 37 L.Ed.2d 56 (1973), declared that dismissal with prejudice was the only permissible remedy for violation of the constitutional speedy trial protection.

The judge is always given discretion in his determination of whether the defendant has been prejudiced to an extent that will require dismissal of the indictment due to prosecutorial delay.

Subdivision (d). This subdivision is based upon G.L. c. 277, §§ 72–72A. *See* ABA *Standards Relating to Speedy Trial,* § 3.1 (Approved Draft, 1968), *Standard* 12–3.1 (2d ed., Approved Draft, 1978).

The statement in subdivision (d)(1) that prisoners are entitled to all the safeguards of a defendant whose liberty is not similarly impaired recognizes that a prisoner does not by reason of his status alone lose the protection of the Constitution or of this rule. It is not intended to declare, however, that all substantive rights of an unimprisoned defendant are to be accorded a prisoner. The same rights can apply with equal force in different circumstances and impose differing duties on the Commonwealth. A separate subdivision is devoted to prisoners' speedy trial rights because the substance of those rights is different from that of other accused persons. Imprisonment necessarily affects both the duty which the Commonwealth has to deliver a defendant to trial and the nature of the prejudice that might result from a delayed trial.

Subdivision (d)(2) extends to defendants incarcerated within the Commonwealth for other crimes the same speedy trial rights guaranteed to other defendants by subdivisions (b)(1) and (c).

Subdivision (d)(3) is largely a restatement of G.L. c. 277, § 72A, which is applied to prisoners incarcerated "outside" the Commonwealth. This is to be read to include prisoners within federal custody, although physically present within Massachusetts.

The Constitution has been interpreted to require of the prosecutor only that which he is reasonably able to accomplish. Commonwealth v. McGrath, 348 Mass. 748, 205 N.E.2d 710 (1965). Where a defendant is imprisoned in a foreign jurisdiction and his extradition is impeded—whether by his own opposition or by that of the executive of the incarcerating jurisdiction—it would be unfair to attribute the delay in bringing the defendant to trial to the Commonwealth if it had made all reasonable efforts to secure the defendant's presence. It would be equally unfair to require the Commonwealth to guarantee trial within a specified time limit.

There is disagreement among jurisdictions as to what the speedy trial provision of the Constitution requires of a state seeking to obtain the presence of a prisoner incarcerated in another jurisdiction, although it is clear that where a defendant's presence *cannot* be obtained because the incarcerating state refuses to deliver him, there is no denial of the defendant's constitutional right to a speedy trial. *See* ABA *Standards Relating to Speedy Trial,* § 3.1, comment at 31 (Approved Draft, 1968). It is also clear that Massachusetts is one of the many states to require the prosecution to use all reasonable efforts to obtain the presence of a foreign prisoner for trial upon pending charges, although this position is not universally accepted. Commonwealth v. Green, 353 Mass. 687, 690, 234 N.E.2d 534 (1968).

Uniform acts dealing with extradition have been adopted by many states. The *Agreement On Detainers,* G.L. c. 276, App. §§ 1–1 et seq., gives prisoners the right to have a trial within one hundred eighty days of their delivery to the jurisdiction where charges are pending. This statute, which has been adopted by thirty-two jurisdictions, gives substance to the rights of prisoners and is to be read as a complement to this rule. The *Uniform Criminal Extradition Act,* G.L. c. 276, §§ 11–20R, which has been adopted by forty-seven jurisdictions, establishes procedures for orderly extradition; it sets out proper procedures for a request for delivery, the arrest of the alleged criminal, and his delivery to the requesting state. Section 20G of this statute, however, still affords governors the discretion to refuse delivery of prisoners.

Massachusetts courts have required the Commonwealth to use due diligence in seeking to bring a foreign prisoner to trial. In light of the legal limitations of rendition this is a fair standard. This rule attempts to put the diligence standard in operational terms. The speedy trial rights of a foreign prisoner are defined under this rule as follows: the Commonwealth must diligently notify a foreign prisoner of pending charges and must promptly seek to obtain his presence for trial; if the Commonwealth is dilatory in either filing a detainer or seeking to obtain the defendant's presence and the prisoner is prejudiced by the delay, the charges must be dismissed. The defendant is given the right to make a demand, although the demand under this rule does not affect the Commonwealth's duty to obtain the defendant's presence. The Commonwealth must use due diligence whether or not a demand has been made. However, the demand is relevant to a determination of the prejudice incurred by the defendant, and under the *Agreement on Detainers,* a demand entitles a defendant to a trial within one hundred eighty days of his delivery.

Subdivision (e). In Commonwealth v. Gove, 1 Mass.App. 614, 304 N.E.2d 589 (1973), aff'd, 366 Mass. 351, 320 N.E.2d 900 (1974), it was held that a defendant did not have the right to be simultaneously charged with all the offenses which might have been committed in the course of a single act or a closely related series of acts. One result is that a dismissal of the charge of one of a number of related offenses on denial of speedy trial grounds would not bar the Commonwealth from charging the defendant with another of the related offenses. A second result is that if a significant amount of time had elapsed between the filing of charges of two related offenses, and the earlier charge was dismissed because the twelve-month limit of this rule had passed, the Commonwealth could proceed to trial on the later charge. Subdivision (e) effectively vitiates the *Gove* decision.

Standard 12–4.1 of the ABA *Standards Relating to Speedy Trial* (2d ed., Approved Draft, 1978), states that if a charge is dismissed on speedy trial grounds "[s]uch discharge should forever bar prosecution for the offense charged and for any other offense required to be joined with that offense."

The Supreme Judicial Court, citing with approval ABA *Standards* § 4.1, (Approved Draft, 1968), has held that

> the dismissal of a complaint in the District Court on the ground that the defendant has been denied his right to a speedy trial is a bar to any subsequent prosecution for the *same offense* whether by later complaint . . . or by an indictment. . . .

Commonwealth v. Ludwig, 370 Mass. 31, 35, 345 N.E.2d 386 (1976) (emphasis supplied). *Accord* Commonwealth v. Fields, 371 Mass. 274, 275, 356 N.E.2d 1211 (1976) (dismissal of complaint in District Court on speedy trial grounds bar to subsequent prosecution of same offense by indictment in Superior Court). While agreeing with the ABA *Standards* insofar as holding dismissal to constitute an absolute discharge of the prosecution of the offense charged, the *Ludwig* court did not reach the issue of whether such a discharge was to encompass other offenses.

Subdivision (e) states that a dismissal of any charge ordered pursuant to Rule 36 "shall apply to all related offenses." Offenses are related when they

> are based on the same criminal conduct or episode or arise out of a course of criminal conduct or series of criminal episodes connected together or constituting parts of a single scheme or plan.

Mass.R.Crim.P. 2(b)(14); 9(a)(1). This subdivision expands the principle of ABA *Standard* 12–4.1 further, mandating that the dismissal shall be not only as to charges required to be joined with that dismissed, but also as to any charges which *could* have been joined under Mass.R.Crim.P. 9(a)(2).

This position is advanced in the interests of fairness to a defendant. Without such a provision, a defendant could be subjected to harassment by a prosecutor who might essentially relitigate the same issues he was barred from litigating for failure to accord the defendant his rights under this rule.

Subdivision (f). Under this rule, the respective clerks are to have the burden of periodically informing the first justice of each District Court division and the Administrative Justice of the Superior Court Department of cases which have been pending longer than six months.

Rule 37. Transfer of Cases

(Applicable to District Court and Superior Court)

(a) Transfer for Plea and Sentence.

(1) *District Court.* A defendant against whom a complaint is pending and who appears in District Court, whether under arrest or pursuant to a summons, and against whom a complaint is pending in a division other than that in which he appears, may state in writing that he wishes to plead guilty or nolo contendere, to waive trial in the division in which the other complaint is pending, and to consent to disposition of the case in the division in which he appears. The District Court in which the defendant appears may order that the other complaint be transferred for disposition, subject to the written approval of the prosecutor in each division.

(2) *Superior Court.* A defendant against whom a complaint or indictment is pending and who appears in Superior Court, whether under arrest or pursuant to a summons, and against whom a complaint or indictment

is pending in a county other than that in which he appears, may state in writing that he wishes to plead guilty or nolo contendere, to waive trial in the county in which the other complaint or indictment is pending, and to consent to disposition of the case in the county in which he appears. The Superior Court in which the defendant appears may order that the other complaint or indictment be transferred for disposition, subject to the written approval of the prosecuting attorney in each county.

(3) *Effect of Not Guilty Plea.* If after a proceeding has been transferred pursuant to subdivision (a) of this rule the defendant pleads not guilty, the clerk shall return the papers transmitted pursuant to subdivision (c) of this rule to the court in which the prosecution was commenced, and the proceeding shall be restored to the docket of that court.

(b) Transfer for Trial.

(1) *Transfer for Prejudice.* A judge upon his own motion or the motion of a defendant or the Commonwealth made prior to trial may order the transfer of a case to another division or county for trial if the court is satisfied that there exists in the community where the prosecution is pending so great a prejudice against the defendant that he may not there obtain a fair and impartial trial.

(2) *Transfer of Other Cases.* A judge, upon motion of a defendant made pursuant to subdivision (3) or (4) of Rule 9(a), and after taking into account the convenience of the court, the parties, and their witnesses, may with the written approval of the prosecuting attorney in each division or county order the transfer and consolidation for trial of any or all charges pending against the defendant in the several divisions or counties of the Commonwealth.

(c) Proceedings on Transfer. Upon receipt of the defendant's statement and the written approval of the prosecutor required by this rule, the clerk of the court in which a complaint or indictment is pending shall transfer the papers in the case and any bail taken to the clerk of the court to which the case is transferred. The clerk of the transferee court shall make immediate entry of the case upon the docket of that court and shall so notify the clerk of the transferor court so that the case may be closed on the docket of that court. The prosecution shall continue in the transferee court.

Reporter's Notes

This rule is drawn from Fed.R.Crim.P. 20, 21 and 22 and substantially expands Massachusetts practice relative to the transfer of pending criminal proceedings.

Subdivision (a). Subdivisions (a)(1) and (2), applicable respectively to the District and Superior Court Departments, are modeled after Fed.R.Crim.P. 20(a) and 22. It is intended that the request to consolidate complaints or indictments for plea and sentence is to be made at the initial appearance. The arraignment date is to be set at a time sufficiently after the initial appearance to allow the transmittal of the necessary papers (*See* subdivision [c], infra). The rule is not to be read to permit the consolidation of an indictment with a complaint for trial or plea in the District Court. Nor may complaints pending in District Court be consolidated with Superior Court proceedings (except where the defendant waives indictment and is bound over so that the case is properly in Superior Court. Mass.R.Crim.P. 3). Where the defendant appears in Superior Court upon a complaint or indictment and there are complaints outstanding in divisions of the District Court within that same county, the District Attorney may proceed by direct indictment (Mass.R.Crim.P. 3[e]), may make an appropriate disposition of the lower court charges pursuant to a plea arrangement (Mass.R.Crim.P. 12[b]), or may nol prosse the charges (Mass.R.Crim.P. 16) if the interests of the parties and the court so dictate.

Subdivision (a)(3) is substantially identical to Fed.R.Crim.P. 20(c).

Subdivision (b). Subdivision (b)(1) parallels Fed.R.Crim.P. 21(a) and has a statutory precedent in G.L. c. 277, § 51.

Under most circumstances a trial is held where the indictment or complaint is pending. This in fact is a constitutional right of the defendant. Article 13 of the Massachusetts Declaration of Rights provides:

> In criminal prosecutions, the verification of facts in the vicinity where they happen, is one of the greatest securities of the life, liberty, and property of the citizen.

However, the common law recognized the right of a defendant to have the case removed to another community for the purpose of achieving an impartial trial. Commonwealth v. Handren, 261 Mass. 294, 296–97, 158 N.E. 894 (1927); Crocker v. Justices of the Superior Court, 208 Mass. 162, 174–75, 94 N.E. 369, 21 Ann.Cas. 1061 (1911). And the right to a fair and impartial trial is guaranteed by the fourteenth amendment to the United States Constitution, which right includes the right "to show that a change of venue *is* required" in a particular case. Groppi v. Wisconsin, 91 S.Ct. 490, 400 U.S. 505, 511, 27 L.Ed.2d 571 (1971).

A defendant in a capital case has a statutory right to seek a transfer of the trial to any adjoining county. G.L. c. 277, § 51. This statutory right is, in many cases, too limited to permit removal to a venue uninfected by the prejudice and the statute is not to maintain its vitality except as precedent for the broader rule. *See generally* Commonwealth v. Turner, 371 Mass. 803, 807, 359 N.E.2d 626 (1977). In some cases, the transfer need not be to another county if an impartial jury panel can be found in another court within the same county.

The motion must be made prior to trial. *See* Commonwealth v. Noxon, 319 Mass. 495, 550, 66 N.E.2d 814 (1946). If the jury has been impanelled, and the court is satisfied that the jurors are impartial, the defendant cannot later claim that the situs of trial was improper.

The trial court has discretion as to whether pretrial publicity has so infected the community where proper venue lies as to require a transfer to another community. E.g., Commonwealth v. Turner, 371 Mass. 803, 806–07, 359 N.E.2d 626 (1977). The transfer, however, should not be ordered without a substantial showing of prejudice. As the Supreme Judicial Court said in Crocker v. Justices of the Superior Court, 208 Mass. 162, 94 N.E. 369, 21 Ann.Cas. 1061 (1911):

> Such a motion ought not to be granted upon mere suggestion, nor unless the reason for it is fully established. It is a jurisdiction which should be exercised with great caution

and only after a solid foundation of fact has been first established. Manifestly, it should be resorted to only in aid of justice, and it should not be permitted to be employed as an instrument of obstruction or as a means of delay.

Id. at 180.

The mere fact that a juror has been exposed to pretrial publicity concerning the case does not mean that his impartiality has been affected. This normally can be adequately tested during the voir dire. Commonwealth v. Smith, 357 Mass. 168, 258 N.E.2d 13 (1970). In addition to questioning prospective jurors as to their bias, the court should consider the extent of the publicity concerning the case and the nature of the charges. Some crimes give rise to heightened community response more readily than others. *See* Commonwealth v. Blackburn, 354 Mass. 200, 203–04, 237 N.E.2d 35 (1968); Commonwealth v. Smith, 353 Mass. 487, 489–90, 232 N.E.2d 915 (1968). In some cases the extent of the publicity will be so great as to mandate a transfer of the trial. It is presumed in these cases that an impartial jury cannot be obtained from the mere fact of the exposure of the crime to the public. Rideau v. Louisiana, 83 S.Ct. 1417, 373 U.S. 723, 10 L.Ed.2d 663 (1963).

Subdivision (b)(2), drawn from Fed.R.Crim.P. 21(b), provides for the inter-division or inter-county transfer of charges of related offenses for trial. Such transfer is contingent upon the approval of the court and of the prosecutors involved. The rule is intended to conserve judicial resources by obviating the need for separate trials of related offenses which were committed in different divisions or counties.

Subdivision (c). This subdivision is in conformity with both Fed.R.Crim.P. 20(a) and 21(c) and with G.L. c. 277, § 52. The language was taken in part from each source.

Other statutes in Massachusetts are applicable to the transfer of cases in specific factual situations, and these are to maintain their vitality. General Laws c. 277, § 53 is applicable when the transfer is to a different county and the defendant is in custody. It should be noted that while this rule is concerned with the transfer of cases which are to be tried in Superior Court upon indictment, it is intended to be equally applicable to cases to be tried in District or Superior Court upon complaint. In this respect, the rule goes beyond the provisions of G.L. c. 277, §§ 51–54 which are, technically speaking, applicable only to trial upon indictment.

Rule 38. Disability of Judge

(Applicable to Superior Court and jury sessions in District Court)

(a) During Trial. If by reason of death, sickness, or other disability the judge before whom a jury trial has commenced is unable to proceed with the trial, any other judge of that court or properly assigned to that court, upon certifying in writing that he has familiarized himself with the record of the trial, may proceed with and finish the trial.

(b) Receipt of Verdict. Any judge of a court or any judge properly assigned to that court may receive a verdict of the jury.

(c) After Verdict or Finding of Guilt. If by reason of absence, unavailability, death, sickness, or other disability the judge before whom the defendant has been tried is unable to perform the duties to be performed by the judge after a verdict or finding of guilt, any other judge of that court or properly assigned to that court may perform those duties; but if the other judge is satisfied that he cannot perform those duties because he did not preside at the trial or for any other reason, he may, in his discretion or upon motion of the defendant, order a new trial.

Reporter's Notes

Rule 38 has no counterpart in the statutory or case law of the Commonwealth. The rule closely parallels Fed.R.Crim.P. 25, although there is some deviation. *See* Rules of Criminal Procedure (U.L.A.) Rule 741 (1974); ABA *Standards Relating to Trial by Jury* (2d ed., Approved Draft, 1978).

Subdivision (a). This subdivision is drawn nearly verbatim from ABA *Standards Relating to Trial by Jury* § 4.3 (Approved Draft, 1968), differing in that under the rule the substituted judge must be of the same court in which the proceeding is held, or properly assigned to that court. It has been intimated that the federal analogue to this subdivision, Fed.R.Crim.P. 25(a), is open to constitutional inquiry. 2 C. WRIGHT, FEDERAL PRACTICE & PROCEDURE: CRIMINAL § 392 (1969, Supp.1978). It is suggested further, however, that no substantial constitutional infirmity exists if a defendant consents to the substitution of judges during the trial. Id. *See* Rules of Criminal Procedure (U.L.A.) Rule 741(e) (1974), which would require the parties' consent to the substitution of a specified judge. Whether or not constitutionally mandated, it would be the better practice to obtain the defendant's consent to substitution in writing to be made a part of the record.

Subdivision (b). This subdivision constitutes the most significant departure from Federal Rule 25. It is felt that the receipt of a verdict is a court function ministerial in nature and need not be performed by the judge who presided at trial. Subdivision (b) is intended to implement the efficient use of judicial manpower by permitting a single judge to take verdicts in more than one trial and to circumvent the need for a judge to interrupt other business to receive a verdict.

Subdivision (c). The constitutionality of the federal equivalent of this subdivision, Fed.R.Crim.P. 25(b), was questioned as to the power of a substitute judge to act in the case. Its validity was sustained in Connelly v. United States, 249 F.2d 576 (8th Cir.1957), cert. denied 78 S.Ct. 700, 356 U.S. 921, 2 L.Ed.2d 716 (1958). *See* Rules of Criminal Procedure (U.L.A.) Rule 741(f) (1974).

The power granted to the succeeding judge to "perform the duties to be performed by the court after a verdict or finding of guilt" is intended to encompass the authority and duty to hear post-conviction proceedings under Mass.R.Crim.P. 30. *See* former G.L. c. 278, § 31A, which permitted a substitute justice to examine and allow or disallow a bill of exceptions.

The final clause of subdivision (c) gives rise to potential problems of constitutional dimension regarding the ordering of a new trial by a successor judge. Under this rule, the successor judge may order such a trial "in his discretion, or upon motion of the defendant. . . ." A new trial in the latter situation raises no issue and is supported by precedent. *See* United States v. Tateo, 84 S.Ct. 1587, 377 U.S. 463, 12 L.Ed.2d 448 (1964).

Regarding the former situation, however, for a trial judge to grant a new trial sua sponte, and presumably, over defendant's objection, may raise fifth amendment problems of double jeopardy. 2 C. WRIGHT, FEDERAL PRACTICE AND PROCEDURE: CRIMINAL § 551 at 483 (1969, Supp. 1978). *See* United States v. Smith, 67 S.Ct. 1330, 331 U.S. 469, 474–75, 91 L.Ed. 1610 (1947).

The current law with respect to the double jeopardy implications of a declaration of a mistrial over a defendant's objections involves a balancing of competing interests:

> A defendant has a 'valued right to have his trial completed by a particular tribunal.' [citations omitted]. Because of this right, a court may not declare a mistrial without consent of the defendant unless there is a 'manifest necessity for the act, or the ends of public justice would otherwise be defeated.' [citations omitted].

United States v. Lansdown, 460 F.2d 164, 168 (4th Cir.1972). *See* Wade v. Hunter, 69 S.Ct. 834, 336 U.S. 684, 689, 93 L.Ed. 974 (1949). This doctrine of "manifest necessity," enunciated in the early case of United States v. Perez, 22 U.S. 579 (9 Wheat.) 579, 6 L.Ed. 165 (1824), remains consistently adhered to and approved by the Supreme Court. Illinois v. Somerville, 93 S.Ct. 1066, 410 U.S. 458, 35 L.Ed.2d 425 (1973); United States v. Jorn, 91 S.Ct. 547, 400 U.S. 470, 27 L.Ed.2d 543 (1971). *See also* United States v. Wilson, 95 S.Ct. 1013, 420 U.S. 332, 344, 43 L.Ed.2d 232 (1975).

At the same time, the *Perez* formulation, the Supreme Court has emphasized, is not so rigid as to be mechanically applied:

> This formulation ... abjures the application of any mechanical formula by which to judge the propriety of declaring a mistrial *in the varying and often unique situations arising during the course of a criminal trial.* The broad discretion reserved to the trial judge in such circumstances has been consistently reiterated in decisions of this court.

Illinois v. Somerville, supra at 462 (Emphasis added).

The relatively rare, if not unique, issue posed by subdivision (c) presents several new considerations. The "broad discretion reserved," *Illinois v. Somerville,* supra, will be wielded in this context by a successor to the disabled trial judge. Furthermore, the Court's admonition that trial judges must not "foreclose the defendant's option" to proceed to the first jury until they have completed a "scrupulous exercise" of their discretion, *United States v. Jorn,* supra at 485, takes on heightened significance where, as here, the defendant has already gone to the first jury.

Nevertheless, it is submitted that the *Perez* doctrine as refined by the Court today applies to the post-verdict situation in this subdivision. *See Illinois v. Somerville, supra* at 467, where the Court intimates a distinction between mistrials declared prior to and those declared after verdict. Thus, in the careful exercise of his discretion, a trial judge, or successor judge, must weigh the defendant's "valued right to have his trial completed by a particular tribunal" against "the public's interest in fair trials designed to end in just judgments." *Wade v. Hunter,* supra at 689. If the judge, then, "is satisfied that he cannot perform ... [the post-verdict duties of the court], he may ... order a new trial" without unconstitutionally subjecting a defendant to double jeopardy.

Rule 39. Records of Foreign Proceedings and Notice of Foreign Law

(Applicable to District Court and Superior Court)

(a) Records of Courts of Other States or of the United States. The records and judicial proceedings of a court of another state or of the United States shall be competent evidence in this Commonwealth if authenticated by the attestation of the clerk or other officer who has charge of the records of such court under its seal.

(b) Notice of Foreign Law. The court shall upon request take judicial notice of the law of the United States or of any state, territory, or dependency thereof or of a foreign country whenever it shall be material.

Reporter's Notes

Rule 39 substantially conforms to G.L. c. 233, §§ 69–70. *See* Fed.R.Crim.P. 26.1.

Subdivision (a). General Laws c. 233, § 69, from which this subdivision is taken, does not require "that a record be fully extended in order to afford proof of judgment if the facts essential thereto are set forth," Commonwealth v. Rondoni, 333 Mass. 384, 386, 131 N.E.2d 187 (1955). *Rondoni* should be examined as illustrative of what serves as sufficient attestation by the officer in charge of judicial records. *Id.* at 385–86.

Subdivision (b). This is taken with little change from G.L. c. 233, § 70. Although nearly all of the cases which have construed that section are civil, it applies to criminal proceedings as well. *See* e.g., Commonwealth v. White, 358 Mass. 488, 491, 265 N.E.2d 473 (1970).

The rule states that a court shall notice foreign law upon request when that law is material. This is not intended to limit a court's authority under § 70 to notice foreign law in the absence of a request if the court so chooses. Dicker v. Klein, 360 Mass. 735, 736–37, 277 N.E.2d 514 (1972); De Gategno v. De Gategno, 336 Mass. 426, 431, 146 N.E.2d 497 (1957). Even upon request, however, a court is not required to notice foreign law unless it is brought to the attention of the court. Tsacoyeanes v. Canadian Pac. Ry. Co., 339 Mass. 726, 162 N.E.2d 23 (1959). Massachusetts practice is in accord with Fed.R.Evid. 201 which states that "(c) ... A court may take judicial notice, whether requested or not [and] (d) ... shall take judicial notice if requested by a party and supplied with the necessary information." *See* Me.R.Evid. 201 (c)–(d).

When a party does make a request for the court to take judicial notice of foreign law, that party carries the burden of proof as to what the law is. Finer v. Steuer, 255 Mass. 611, 152 N.E. 220 (1926). The attention of the court may be directed to the law of another jurisdiction by oral testimony of a qualified witness as well as by citation of statutes and decisions. Eastern Offices, Inc. v. P.F. O'Keefe Ad. Agency, Inc., 289 Mass. 23, 193 N.E. 837 (1935). The requirement of bringing the law to the attention of the court and proving it is not satisfied by simply mentioning the appropriate reference to foreign law. "Merely to direct attention to the law of a foreign country written in a foreign tongue does not make it a matter for judicial knowledge." Rodrigues v. Rodrigues, 286 Mass. 77, 83, 190 N.E. 20 (1934). However, where there is not sufficient information available to the litigants as to what is the pertinent foreign law, the court may use other channels available to it in order to determine the law. In Mazurowski, petitioner, 331 Mass. 33, 116 N.E.2d 854 (1954), the court drew upon the superior sources of foreign law and regulations available through the State Department, to which neither party to the litigation has access.

Rule 40. Proof of Official Records

(Applicable to District Court and Superior Court)

(a) Authentication.

(1) *Domestic*. An official record kept within the Commonwealth, or an entry therein, when admissible for any purpose, may be evidenced by an official publication thereof or by a copy attested by the officer having legal custody of the record, or by his deputy. If the record is kept in any other state, district, commonwealth, territory or insular possession of the United States, or within the Panama Canal Zone or the Trust Territory of the Pacific Islands, any such copy shall be accompanied by a certificate that such custodial officer has the custody. This certificate may be made by a judge of a court of record of the district or political subdivision in which the record is kept, authenticated by the seal of the court, or may be made by any public officer having a seal of office and having official duties in the district or political subdivision in which the record is kept, authenticated by the seal of his office.

(2) *Foreign*. A foreign official record, or an entry therein, when admissible for any purpose, may be evidenced by an official publication thereof, or a copy thereof, attested by a person authorized to make the attestation, and accompanied by a final certification as to the genuineness of the signature and official position (i) of the attesting person, or (ii) of any foreign official whose certificate of genuineness of signature and official position relates to the attestation or is in a chain of certificates of genuineness of signature and official position relating to the attestation. A final certification may be made by a secretary of embassy or legation, consul general, consul, vice consul, or consular agent of the United States, or a diplomatic or consular official of the foreign country assigned or accredited to the United States. If reasonable opportunity has been given to all parties to investigate the authenticity and accuracy of the documents, the court may, for good cause shown, (i) admit an attested copy without final certification, or (ii) permit the foreign official record to be evidenced by an attested summary with or without a final certification.

(b) Lack of Record. A written statement that after diligent search no record or entry of a specified tenor is found to exist in the records designated by the statement, authenticated as provided in subdivision (a)(1) of this rule in the case of a domestic record, or complying with the requirements of subdivision (a)(2) of this rule for a summary in the case of a foreign record, is admissible as evidence that the records contain no such record or entry.

(c) Other Proof. This rule does not prevent the proof, by any other method authorized by law, of the existence of, or the lack of, an official record, or of entry, or lack of entry therein.

Reporter's Notes

This rule is identical to Mass.R.Civ.P. 44. *See* Fed. R.Crim.P. 27, which incorporates by reference the provisions of Fed.R.Civ.P. 44.

Prior to the promulgation of this rule, no statute or rule expressly provided for the proof of official records in criminal cases. The practice developed of utilizing the law applicable to the proof of such records in civil cases. Rule 40 formally recognizes that practice.

Like its civil counterpart, Rule 40 is addressed only to authenticating an official record or establishing the lack thereof. It does not govern the authentication of unofficial records, nor does it regulate the extent to which the contents of an authenticated official record are admissible.

The term "official record" has been defined generally as including records of any governmental entity, 8A J. MOORE, FEDERAL PRACTICE para. 27.02 at 27–6 (1978), and more particularly as "all documents prepared by public officials pursuant to a duty imposed by law or required by the nature of their offices. . . ." Olender v. United States, 210 F.2d 795, 801 (9th Cir.1954). *See* Fed.R.Evid. 901(b)(7), 902(1)–(3).

Subdivision (a). It should be noted that subdivision (a)(1), unlike its federal counterpart, does not require certification by a judge or other officer of the status of the custodial official if the records are kept within the Commonwealth. As for domestic records kept outside the Commonwealth (subdivision [a][1]) and foreign records (subdivision [a][2]), the requirement of double certification is retained. Subdivision (a)(2) is in all other respects in accord with former Massachusetts practice.

Subdivision (b). This subdivision permits the written statement of a custodial officer that no particular record can be found, authenticated pursuant to subdivision (a), to suffice as proof that no such record exists.

Subdivision (c). Rule 40(c) incorporates all pre-existing statutory methods of proving the existence of, or lack of the existence of, official records. Those statutes are unaffected by the promulgation of this rule. *See,* e.g., G.L. c. 46, § 19 (records relative to birth, marriage, and death); G.L. c. 233, §§ 76, 76A, 76B (records of departments of government).

Rule 41. Interpreters and Experts

(Applicable to District Court and Superior Court)

The judge may appoint an interpreter or expert if justice so requires and may determine the reasonable compensation for such services and direct payment therefor.

Reporter's Notes

This rule is an abbreviated version of Fed.R.Crim.P. 28 as it appeared prior to amendment in 1975. Federal Rule 28 now deals only with interpreters; the provisions governing expert witnesses, formerly Federal Rule 28(a), are now contained in Fed.R.Evid. 706. *See* Main R.Crim.P. 28.

The right of a defendant to be present at trial, *see* e.g., Lewis v. United States, 146 U.S. 370, 372 (1892)—in the sense of being able to comprehend and participate meaningfully in the proceeding, United States ex rel. Negron v. New York, 434 F.2d 386 (2d Cir.1970)—the requirement that a defendant have "sufficient . . . ability to consult with his lawyer with a reasonable degree of rational understanding," Dusky v. United States, 80 S.Ct. 788, 362 U.S. 402, 4 L.Ed.2d 824 (1960), and the sixth amendment right to be confronted with adverse witnesses, applicable to the states through the fourteenth amendment, Pointer v. Texas, 85 S.Ct. 1065, 380 U.S. 400, 13 L.Ed.2d 923 (1965), mandate that an interpreter be available to the defendant or witness who cannot effectively communicate. "Otherwise, '[t]he adjudication loses its character as a reasoned interaction . . . and becomes an invective against an insensible object.' " *United States ex rel. Negron,* supra at 389, *quoting* Note, Incompetency to Stand Trial, (1969) 81 HARVARD L.REV. 454, 458.

Whenever an interpreter is placed between the witness and counsel, the judge, and the jury, problems of distortion and confusion may arise. For example, where some of the jurors understand the language of the witness and the judge or counsel does not, the jurors may hear testimony that should have been excluded. The Supreme Judicial Court has suggested the following:

1. Counsel should address his questions to the witness in the second person, and not to the interpreter.

2. The interpreter should translate the question exactly without any additional or supplementary remarks of his own.

3. The interpreter should then translate the answer of the witness in the first person, neither editing nor adding to the witness' words. Even if the answer is non-responsive, the interpreter should give it and allow the judge to pass on its admissibility, for the interpreter's sole function is to translate.

4. Extraneous conversations between the witness and the interpreter should not be permitted. If such conversations do occur for some reason, they should be translated into English for the judge and counsel to hear.

5. When there are sitting on the jury individuals who understand the language of the witness, they are to be instructed that it is the interpreted testimony in English that is evidence and not their own translations of the witness' answers.

6. Neither party has the right to have a juror excused solely because that juror understands the language of a witness. However, in certain circumstances the judge in his discretion may decide whether to excuse such a juror is appropriate. For example, this action may be desirable on motion of the defendant in a criminal matter in which the progress of the trial will not be interrupted by the removal of the juror, sufficient alternate jurors have been empaneled, and interpreted testimony constitutes a major part of the case.

Commonwealth v. Festa, 369 Mass. 419, 429–30, 341 N.E.2d 276 (1976) (footnote omitted).

While the Supreme Court has established that it is within the discretion of the court whether to appoint an interpreter, Perovich v. United States, 27 S.Ct. 456, 205 U.S. 86, 91, 51 L.Ed. 722 (1907), it has not found a right to state-provided interpreters to be a constitutional absolute since that issue has never been squarely presented. Lower federal courts have held, however, that if the court is put on notice that a defendant has a language difficulty, the court must make it unmistakably clear to him that he has the right to have a competent translator assist him, at state expense if he is indigent, throughout the proceeding. United States v. Carrion, 488 F.2d 12, 15 (1st Cir.1973), cert. denied, 94 S.Ct. 1613, 416 U.S. 907, 40 L.Ed.2d 112 (1974); United States ex rel. Negron v. New York, 434 F.2d 386, 390–91 (2d Cir.1970). Conversely, if the need for an interpreter's services is not apparent nor are such services requested, it is no abuse of discretion to fail to advise a defendant of their availability. United States v. Barrios, 457 F.2d 680, 682 (9th Cir.1972).

The justices of the Superior Court, G.L. c. 221, § 92, the Boston Municipal Court, G.L. c. 218, § 67, and the East Boston District Court, G.L. c. 218, § 68, may appoint official interpreters for the sessions of those courts. Other District Courts may employ interpreters as the need therefor arises. G.L. c. 262, § 32. Interpreters are to be compensated for their services by the Commonwealth. G.L. c. 221, §§ 92, 92A; c. 262, § 32. The appointment of interpreters in civil actions is governed by Mass.R.Civ.P. 43(f).

The federal rule does not indicate that it was intended to benefit only the indigent defendant.

The view that the Rule should be restricted overlooks the fact that the interpreter's services, though required by the defendant's own language problem, benefit the court and prosecution as well as the defense. The integrity of the judicial process—not to mention the desirability of avoiding collateral attacks—demands an accurate and impartial translation. Such a translation can only be guaranteed by court appointment of interpreters.

8A J. MOORE, FEDERAL PRACTICE Para. 28.02[2] at 28–3 (1978). *But see* United States v. Desist, 384 F.2d 889, 901–03 (2d Cir.1967), aff'd on other grounds 89 S.Ct. 1030, 394 U.S. 244, 22 L.Ed.2d 248 (1969). Former practice in Massachusetts appeared to be that interpreters, unless retained by non-indigent defendants, were paid by the court. Official interpreters are expressly barred from receiving gratuities, bonuses or fees beyond that compensation paid by the Commonwealth. G.L. c. 218, § 67; c. 221, § 92.

The use of interpreters is not limited to situations where the defendant or a witness is not English-speaking. General Laws c. 221, § 92A provides for the appointment of interpreters for the deaf. The court in United States v. Addonizio, 451 F.2d 49, 68 (3d Cir.), cert. denied 92 S.Ct. 949, 405 U.S. 936, 30 L.Ed.2d 812 (1972), held that the appointment as interpreter of the wife of a witness whose illness made his speech difficult to understand was not an abuse of discretion. *See* Fairbanks v. Cowan, 551 F.2d 97 (6th Cir.1977) (father of retarded adult). The appointment of such a person should only be after a finding that he is disinterested in the outcome of the case. *United States v. Addonizio,* supra; Price v. Beto, 426 F.2d 875 (5th Cir.1970) (appointment of husband of deaf-mute victim held violative of due process). *See* Maine R.Crim.P. 28, which provides for appointment of a "disinterested" interpreter of the court's own selection.

The courts' power to appoint expert witnesses to assist the indigent defendant or the court itself is nowhere express; rather, it is grounded upon the long-standing belief "that it is for the interest of the Commonwealth . . . that all proper investigations should be made, in order to guard against the danger of doing injustice to the prisoner. . . ." Attorney General, petitioner, 104 Mass. 537, 544 (1870). The Supreme Judicial Court has approved the practice of the trial judge's authorization, on a proper showing, of an indigent defendant to expend public funds for expert assistance. *See* Commonwealth v. Silva, 371 Mass. 819, 821, 359 N.E.2d 942 (1977) (psychiatric expert).

Under Superior Court Rule 54 (1974), the court is not to allow compensation for the services of an expert witness unless his employment by the defendant was authorized by the court. If the compensation of defense experts is approved by the court, it is paid by the Commonwealth. G.L. c. 280, §§ 4, 16; c. 261, §§ 27A–G.

Pursuant to G.L. c. 261, § 27B, applicable by its terms to criminal cases, a defendant may file an affidavit of indigency and request waiver, substitution or payment by the Commonwealth of costs and fees. Substitution means that if an alternative to a translator is available at lower or no cost, the judge may order that this alternative be used if it is "substantially equivalent . . . and does not materially impair the rights of any party." G.L. c. 261, § 27F. If, after hearing, the court finds that certain services are "reasonably necessary to assure the [defendant] as effective a . . . defense as he would have if he were financially able to pay," the court must grant the defendant's request for payment by the Commonwealth of "extra fees and costs," defined in G.L. c. 261, § 27A as including "expert assistance."

The indigent defendant cannot as of right nominate the expert whom he wishes to employ, Commonwealth v. Erickson, 356 Mass. 63, 248 N.E.2d 270 (1969); Commonwealth v. Medeiros, 354 Mass. 193, 199–200, 236 N.E.2d 642 (1968), cert. denied sub nom., Bernier v. Massachusetts, 89 S.Ct. 699, 393 U.S. 1058, 21 L.Ed.2d 699 (1969), but in practice most judges will permit the defendant to specify an expert, although a ceiling may be established on the amount which may be expended. 30 MASS.PRACTICE SERIES (Smith) § 492 (1970, Supp.1978).

In addition to appointing experts to assist the defendant in the preparation or presentation of his defense, the court is empowered to call experts on its own motion to aid in its determination of issues of fact or law. *See* Commonwealth v. Lykus, 367 Mass. 191, 327 N.E.2d 671 (1975) (Separate opinion of Kaplan J., 206 at 213).

Rule 42. Clerical Mistakes

(Applicable to District Court and Superior Court)

Clerical mistakes in judgments, orders, or other parts of the record and errors therein arising from oversight or omission may be corrected by the court at any time of its own initiative or on the motion of any party and after such notice, if any, as the court orders. During the pendency of an appeal, such mistakes may be corrected before the appeal is docketed in the appellate court, and thereafter while the appeal is pending may be corrected with leave of the appellate court.

Reporter's Notes

This rule is substantially identical to Mass.R.Civ.P. 60(a). *See* Fed.R.Crim.P. 36; Fed.R.Civ.P. 60(a).

Rule 42 is limited to the correction of "clerical mistakes" or errors "arising from oversight or omission" and does not apply to the correction of errors of substance, such as an illegal sentence or improperly obtained conviction. The federal criminal analogue is said to be typically invoked when the court has authority to impose consecutive as well as concurrent sentences, but the record is ambiguous as to which was in fact given. 8A J. MOORE, FEDERAL PRACTICE Para. 36.02 at 36–1 n. 1 (1978). *See* e.g., Borum v. United States, 409 F.2d 433, 439–41, 133 U.S.App. 147 (D.C.Cir.1967), cert. denied 89 S.Ct. 1765, 395 U.S. 916, 23 L.Ed.2d 230 (1968).

Errors which may be corrected pursuant to this rule must arise out of "misprisions, oversights, omissions, unintended acts or failures to act," First Nat'l Bank v. National Airlines, 167 F.Supp. 167, 169 (S.D.N.Y.1958) (construing Fed.R.Civ.P. 60[a]), and not result from deliberate action, Ferrao v. Arthur M. Rosenberg Co., 156 F.2d 212 (2d Cir.1946). *See* 8 MASS.PRACTICE SERIES (Smith & Zobel) Reporters' Notes at (1977).

Clerical mistakes are due to a failure to accurately record statements made or action taken by the court or parties. E.g., Costello v. United States, 252 F.2d 750 (5th Cir.1958). 8A J. MOORE, FEDERAL PRACTICE Para. 36.02 at 36–2 (1978). Errors which are due to oversight or omission generally require correction so as to conform to the intent of the court or a party which may not be reflected in their recorded statements. E.g., Green v. Clerk of Mun. Ct., 321 Mass. 487, 74 N.E.2d 19 (1947); Lott v. United States, 309 F.2d 115 (5th Cir.1962), cert. denied 83 S.Ct. 504, 371 U.S. 950, 9 L.Ed.2d 498 (1963). *But* cf. United States v. Raftis, 427 F.2d 1145 (8th Cir.1970); 8A J. MOORE, supra at 36–2.

The term "record" is intended to be broadly read so as to encompass not only process, pleadings, and verdict, but also evidentiary documents, testimony, instructions and all other matters pertaining to the case of which there is a written record. 8 MASS.PRACTICE SERIES, supra at 461; 8A J. MOORE, supra at 36–2.

The entry of an appeal does not divest the trial court of its power to correct error. If the case has been docketed in the appellate court, the trial court is still empowered to correct error, but only with permission of the appellate court. *See* 8 MASS.PRACTICE SERIES, supra at 461; Fed.R.App.P. 10(a), (e).

Rule 43. Summary Contempt Proceedings

(Applicable to District Court and Superior Court)

(a) Availability of Summary Proceedings. A criminal contempt may be punished summarily when it is determined that such summary punishment is necessary to maintain order in the courtroom and:

(1) the contemptuous conduct could be seen or heard by the presiding judge and was committed within the actual presence of the court;

(2) the judgment of contempt is entered upon the occurrence of the contemptuous conduct; and

(3) the punishment imposed for each contempt does not exceed three months imprisonment or a fine of five hundred dollars.

(b) Nature of the Proceedings. Before making a judgment of contempt and imposing punishment, the presiding judge shall give the contemnor notice of the charges and at least a summary opportunity to adduce evidence or argument relevant to guilt or punishment. If the judge then determines that the sentence he would impose may be in excess of three months imprisonment or a fine of five hundred dollars, he shall bind the contemnor over for trial to be held in accordance with Rule 44. The judgment of guilt of contempt shall include a recital of those facts upon which the adjudication of guilt is based and shall be signed by the judge and entered on the record. Where the interests of orderly courtroom procedure and substantial justice require, the presiding judge may defer imposition or execution of sentence until after the trial is completed.

(c) Appeal. The contemnor's only right of appeal shall be to the Appeals Court.

Reporter's Notes

Rule 43 is based upon Fed.R.Crim.P. 42(a) as that rule was affected by the Supreme Court decision in Bloom v. Illinois, 88 S.Ct. 1477, 391 U.S. 194, 20 L.Ed.2d 522 (1968), and upon Fla.R.Crim.P. 3.830 (1975).

Bloom v. Illinois, supra, signaled a departure from the traditional approach to adjudicating criminal contempt. The Court's guidelines established in *Bloom,* which have been consistently followed and clarified since the issuance of the opinion, comprise the substance of this rule.

In *Bloom* the Court de-emphasized the long-standing distinction between so-called direct and indirect contempt, focusing instead on the issue of potential penalty. Beginning with the premise that criminal contempts are so similar to other criminal proceedings as to be in their practical—and constitutional—aspects indistinguishable, and following its decision in Duncan v. Louisiana, 88 S.Ct. 1444, 391 U.S. 145, 20 L.Ed.2d 491, 522 (1968), the Court held that while summary punishment of criminal contempt may be necessary to preserve the dignity and efficacy of the judicial process, those interests are outweighed by the need to provide the defendant with all the procedural safeguards deemed fundamental in our judicial system. The Court concluded that a defendant charged with a serious contempt, whether direct or indirect, is entitled to a full jury trial.

Subdivision (a). In Codispoti v. Pennsylvania, 94 S.Ct. 2687, 418 U.S. 506, 41 L.Ed.2d 912 (1974), the Court stated that "where the necessity of circumstances warrants, a contemnor may be summarily tried. . . ." Id. at 514. The Court recognized, however, that where "there is no overriding necessity for instant action to preserve order. . . . [there is] no justification for dispensing with the ordinary rudiments of due process." Id. at 515. The present rule incorporates that principle: summary proceedings are available *only* when they are necessary to preserve order. *Accord* Sussman v. Commonwealth, 374 Mass. 692, 374 N.E.2d 1195 (1978).

By limiting the use of summary disposition of contempts to those cases where the alleged contemptuous conduct was committed in the presence of the trial judge, subdivision (a)(1) conforms to the common law practice based on the direct-indirect contempt distinction and to practice under Fed.R.Crim.P. 42(a). One basis for the common law principle is that the judge cannot determine the facts surrounding an allegation of contempt without a hearing unless he personally viewed the contemptuous conduct.

Subdivision (a)(2) stems from the principle expressed in Taylor v. Hayes, 94 S.Ct. 2697, 418 U.S. 488, 41 L.Ed.2d 897 (1974), that when the adjudication of contempt is delayed until after the contemptuous conduct has occurred, summary disposition is improper. Although in most cases the same principle would apply when the punishment is delayed, the Supreme Court recognized that in some cases, particularly those involving lawyers, summary punishment is permissible when the punishment alone has been delayed.

Subdivision (a)(2) goes beyond the minimum constitutional requirements that must be afforded to contemnors. *Taylor v. Hayes,* supra, expressly allows the court to punish without a full scale trial, though it disallows summary disposition of contempts when the judgment of contempt is not entered contemporaneously with the commission of the contempt. Accordingly, under this rule, a trial is required in such situations. The rationale for such requirement is that where necessity does not demand immediate action, a contemnor is to have the same rights as other criminal defendants. *See* Commonwealth v. Sussman, 374 Mass. 692, 374 N.E.2d 1195 (1978).

Courts have generally defined serious contempt to mean one for which in excess of six months' imprisonment may be imposed, *Duncan,* supra, or for which a fine of more than $500 may be levied, United States v. Polk, 438 F.2d 377 (6th Cir.1971). The Supreme Court has not addressed the specific question whether and in what circumstances—if at all—"the imposition of a fine for criminal contempt, unaccompanied by imprisonment, may require a jury trial." Muniz v. Hoffman, 95 S.Ct. 2178, 422 U.S. 454, 476, 45 L.Ed. 319 (1975). Muniz has been read narrowly so as to preserve the traditional standard of $500 as constituting serious contempt. Douglas v. First National Realty Corp., 543 F.2d 894 (D.C.Cir.1976).

Subdivision (a)(3) reflects this demarcation between serious and petty offenses. Any contempt which the trial judge would punish by a sentence of at least three months cannot be tried summarily and must be tried before a jury if the contemnor so elects. *See* Mass.R.Crim.P. 45(a)–(b).

Codispoti v. Pennsylvania, supra, imposes a further restriction on the availability of summary proceedings that relates to the six-month rule. Where the adjudication of contempt is delayed until after trial and where there are at least two sentences imposed that are consecutive and cumulative more than six months, summary proceedings are not available. This is an interpretation of the six-month rule adopted by *Bloom* and subsequent cases as applied to consecutive sentences for contempt imposed at one trial. This limitation does not apply where the judgments of contempt are entered serially during the progress of the trial as the contemptuous conduct occurs. *Codispoti v. Pennsylvania,* supra at 513–15. Sentences will be aggregated for purposes of the six-month rule, however, where the citations for contempt occur during trial but imposition of sentences is delayed until the conclusion thereof. United States v. Prewitt, 553 F.2d 1082, 1087–90 (7th Cir.1977). The foregoing principles, while fully applicable under this rule, are to be read in terms of *three* months as dictated by subdivision (a)(3).

Subdivision (b). This subdivision outlines the procedures to be followed in a summary adjudication of contempt. While these procedures go beyond the minimum requirements of due process set out in *Taylor v. Hayes,* they do comport with suggestions by the Supreme Court as to the proper procedure to be followed.

"Summary punishment always, and rightly, is regarded with disfavor," Sacher v. United States, 72 S.Ct. 451, 343 U.S. 1, 8, 96 L.Ed. 717 (1952). *Accord Taylor v. Hayes,* supra, at 497–98; Groppi v. Leslie, 92 S.Ct. 582, 404 U.S. 496, 502–05, 30 L.Ed.2d 632 (1972). Unless the contempt occurs in the presence of the judge and immediate punishment is needed to prevent demoralization of the court's authority or to enforce lawful orders essential to prevent a breakdown of the proceedings, many of the due process safeguards available in criminal proceedings should apply to a contempt proceeding. Sussman v. Commonwealth, 374 Mass. 692, 374 N.E.2d 1195 (1978). Except in cases of flagrant contemptuous conduct, the trial judge should not exercise the power of summary contempt in the absence of a prior warning as to the conduct which will place the offender in contempt. *Sussman,* supra at 759. If an adjudication of, and punishment for, contempt is carried out summarily, the contemnor is denied an opportunity to present facts in mitigation of the charge. *See Groppi v. Leslie,* supra, 503, 505. It is for this reason that a contemnor should in all cases be given notice and granted at least a summary opportunity to present evidence on his own behalf. An adequate opportunity to defend or explain one's conduct is a minimum requirement before imposition of punishment. *Sussman,* supra, at 762. As stated in the ABA *Standards Relating to the Function of the Trial Judge,* § 7.4, comment at 95 (Approved Draft, 1972):

> Although there is authority that in-court contempts can be punished without notice of charges or an opportunity to be heard, Ex parte Terry, 9 S.Ct. 77, 128 U.S. 289, 32 L.Ed. 405 (1888), such a procedure has little to commend it, is inconsistent with the basic notions of fairness, and is likely to bring disrespect upon the court. Accordingly, notice and at least a brief opportunity to be heard should be afforded as a matter of course.

The last sentence of subdivision (b) is intended to cover those "circumstances, particularly where the offender is a lawyer representing a client on trial ... [where summary punishment] may be postponed until the conclusion of the proceedings." *Taylor v. Hayes,* supra at 498. *See Sussman v. Commonwealth,* supra at 762–63.

It should be recognized that the power to punish for contempt is to be used cautiously and is not an appropriate device to control every act of courtroom disrespect. This rule is intended to authorize summary punishment only for disruptive conduct that is willfully contemptuous and that has been preceded by a prior warning in all but the most flagrant violations. *See* ABA *Standards Relating to the Function of the Trial Judge* § 7.2, comment at 93 (Approved Draft, 1972); United States v. Wilson, 95 S.Ct. 1802, 421 U.S. 309, 44 L.Ed.2d 186 (1975).

Subdivision (c). The elimination of the writ of error by Rule 30 necessitated a change in the method of review provided for in criminal contempt cases. Formerly, under G.L. c. 250, § 9, a sentence to punish for criminal contempt was a judgment in a criminal case which could be reexamined upon a writ of error. Hansen v. Commonwealth, 344 Mass. 214, 216, 181 N.E.2d 843 (1962); Dolan v. Commonwealth, 304 Mass. 325, 328, 23 N.E.2d 904 (1939). Review was limited to errors of law and matters of fact not heard and decided at the trial under review. Blankenburg v. Commonwealth, 260 Mass. 369, 376–77, 157 N.E. 693 (1927).

Subdivision (c) establishes the taking of an appeal as the sole means of review for criminal contempts. Review by appeal has already gained a foothold in Massachusetts practice for contempt findings against witnesses who have been previously granted immunity and have refused to testify. G.L. c. 233, § 20H. Under subdivision (c) review will be by the Appeals Court.

Rule 44. Contempt

(Applicable to District Court and Superior Court)

(a) Nature of the Proceedings. All criminal contempts not adjudicated pursuant to Rule 43 shall be prosecuted by means of complaint, unless the prosecutor elects to proceed by indictment. Except as otherwise provided by these rules, the case shall proceed as a criminal case in the court in which the contempt is alleged to have been committed.

(b) Special Provisions for District Court. The District Court shall have jurisdiction to try all contempts committed therein except those prosecuted by indictment. Whenever a contemnor asserts his right to a jury trial in District Court, the trial shall be held before a jury in District Court. The contemnor's only right of appeal shall be to the Appeals Court.

(c) Disqualification of the Judge. The contempt charges shall be heard by a judge other than the trial judge whenever the nature of the alleged contemptuous conduct is such as is likely to affect the trial judge's impartiality.

Reporter's Notes

Contempts that are not or cannot be tried summarily in accordance with Rule 43 must be tried under the provisions of Rule 44. Rule 44 carries the recent developments in the law of contempt to a logical conclusion by requiring all contempts not summarily tried to be prosecuted under the procedures established for the trial of other criminal offenses.

In any alleged contempt to be adjudicated pursuant to this rule, the defendant has the right to a jury trial. Bloom v. Illinois, 88 S.Ct. 1477, 391 U.S. 194, 20 L.Ed.2d 522 (1968), adopted the standard established in Duncan v. Louisiana, 88 S.Ct. 1444, 391 U.S. 145, 20 L.Ed.2d 491, 522 (1968) for determining when the right to a jury trial accrues to a defendant and applied that standard to criminal contempt. *Duncan* accepted the established rule that maximum sentences of under six months denote petty offenses. It was established in Baldwin v. New York, 90 S.Ct. 1886, 399 U.S. 66, 69, 26 L.Ed.2d 437 (1970), that authorized maximum punishment of greater than six months indicated a serious offense. Since the maximum punishment for contempt is often not regulated by statute, the determination of whether a particular contempt charge is a serious or petty offense is to be made with reference to the penalty actually imposed. *See Bloom v. Illinois,* supra at 211; Codispoti v. Pennsylvania, 94 S.Ct. 2687, 418 U.S. 506, 512, 41 L.Ed.2d 912 (1974). Under Mass.R.Crim.P. 43(a)(3), that reference will be to whether the sentence exceeds three months' imprisonment or a fine of $500.

Initiation of prosecution by complaint is an historically recognized manner of bringing charges for indirect contempt in the Commonwealth. Dolan v. Commonwealth, 304 Mass. 325, 337, 23 N.E.2d 904 (1939). *See generally,* the cases cited by the Court in *Dolan* at 337 for further similarities existing between prosecutions for indirect contempt and other criminal prosecutions.

One exception to the claim of similarity between a contempt prosecution under this rule and other criminal prosecutions should be noted: the right to indictment by grand jury, to which contemnors are not entitled at present, is not to be extended to them by interpreting this rule broadly. In ordinary criminal prosecutions, a defendant has the right to indictment for those crimes punishable by a term in the state prison. Jones v. Robbins, 74 Mass. (8 Gray) 329, 350 (1857). General Laws c. 220, § 14, as interpreted by the Court in Hurley v. Commonwealth, 188 Mass. 443, 448, 74 N.E. 677, 3 Ann.Cas. 757 (1905), precludes contempt commitments other than to the "common jail." Since the maximum term of imprisonment in a jail or house of correction is set at two and one-half years by G.L. c. 279, § 23, and since no grand jury indictment is required to confine a defendant for that period of time (*see* Mass.R.Crim.P. 3, Complaint; Indictment), it is apparent that no right to prosecution by indictment exists in contempt cases. Federal case law is in accord on this point. Green v. United States, 78 S.Ct. 632, 356 U.S. 165, 183, 2 L.Ed.2d 672 (1958); United States v. Eichhorst, 554 F.2d 1383, 1386 (7th Cir.1976); Mitchell v. Fiore, 470 F.2d 1149, 1153 (3rd Cir.1972); United States v. Bukowski, 435 F.2d 1094, 1101 (7th Cir.1970).

Rule 45. Removal of the Disruptive Defendant

(Applicable to District Court and Superior Court)

(a) Removal of Defendant. Upon the direction of the trial judge, a defendant may be removed from the courtroom during his trial when his conduct has become so disruptive that the trial cannot proceed in an orderly manner. Gagging or shackling may be employed if the trial judge has found such restraint reasonably necessary to maintain order. If the trial judge orders such restraint, he shall enter into the record of the case the reasons therefor. Whenever physical restraint of a defendant or witness occurs in the presence of the jury trying the case, or whenever the defendant is removed, the judge, at the request of the defendant, shall instruct the jury that such restraint or removal is not to be considered in assessing the proof and determining guilt.

(b) Defendant's Rights After Removal. A defendant once removed shall be required to be present in the court building while the trial is in progress. At the time of his removal he shall be advised that he has the right to be returned to the courtroom upon his request and assurances of good behavior. Notwithstanding the failure of a defendant to request to be returned to the courtroom, he shall be returned to the courtroom, at appropriate intervals in the absence of the jury, and shall be advised in open court that he will be permitted to remain upon the giving of assurances of good behavior.

Reporter's Notes

Rule 45 is drawn from § 6.8 of the ABA *Standards Relating to the Function of the Trial Judge* (Approved Draft, 1972), but differs in that the rule requires that at the time of removal the defendant is to be informed of his right to return upon his request and assurance of good conduct. Section 4.1 of the ABA *Standards Relating to Trial by Jury* (Approved Draft, 1968) in part provides the basis of subdivision (a). *See* Fed.R.Crim.P. 43(b)(2); Rules of Criminal Procedure (U.L.A.) Rule 713(b)(3) (1974).

This rule, in conjunction with Rules 43–44, Summary Contempt and Contempt, provides a means of dealing with obstreperous defendants. In many cases the measures provided by this rule may be viewed as less drastic than invocation of the contempt power to control the unruly defendant.

While the sixth and fourteenth amendments guarantee the right of a defendant to confront the witnesses against him in a state criminal proceeding, that right has been held by the Supreme Court to be less than absolute. In Snyder v. Massachusetts, 51 S.Ct. 330, 291 U.S. 97, 78 L.Ed.2d 674, 90 A.L.R. 575 (1934), the Court indicated that there was "[n]o doubt the privilege [of personally confronting witnesses] may be lost by consent or at times even by misconduct." Id. at 106. In Illinois v. Allen, 90 S.Ct. 1057, 397 U.S. 337, 25 L.Ed.2d 353 (1970), a unanimous Court affirmed the principle that the sixth amendment right to confront witnesses can be forfeited.

Subdivision (a). The *Allen* Court recognized three methods of dealing with an obstreperous defendant as constitutionally permissible: (1) binding and gagging the defendant while present in the courtroom; (2) citing the defendant for contempt; or (3) removing the defendant from the courtroom until he promises to conduct himself properly. Id. at 343–44.

While gagging, shackling and other unusual measures are obviously less offensive to the defendant's right to be present at trial than his removal, such measures are not without attendant difficulties:

> These displays tend to create prejudice in the minds of the jury by suggesting that a defendant is a bad and dangerous person whose guilt may be virtually assumed; they may interfere with a defendant's thought processes and ease of communication with counsel; intrinsically they give affront to the dignity of the trial process.

Commonwealth v. Brown, 364 Mass. 471, 475, 305 N.E.2d 830 (1973) (Footnote omitted). While *Brown* dealt specifically with defendants who presented unusual security risks, the potential for prejudice to the unruly defendant is no less real, albeit mitigated perhaps by the fact that the jury will have observed the disruptive behavior and not presume guilt of the offense charged. In either case, "[w]hen special restraints are imposed, the judge's charge to the jury should seek to quell prejudice by reasoning and warning against it." *Commonwealth v. Brown,* supra at 476. *Accord* Commonwealth v. Cavanaugh, 371 Mass. 46, 58, 383 N.E.2d 732 (1977). *See* ABA *Standards Relating to Trial by Jury* § 4.1(c) (Approved Draft, 1968); ABA *Standards Relating to the Function of the Trial Judge* § 5.3(b)(ii) (Approved Draft, 1972).

In Commonwealth v. Senati, 3 Mass.App.Ct. 304, 327 N.E.2d 906 (1975), on facts similar to *Illinois v. Allen,* supra, the Appeals Court approved the practice of removing a defendant who refuses to observe standards of courtroom decorum. Section 6.8 of the ABA *Standards Relating to the Function of the Trial Judge* (Approved Draft, 1972) endorses this practice as preferable to gagging or shackling the disruptive defendant.

Whether the obstreperous defendant is restrained or removed, the trial judge is to state his reasons for such action on the record. *See Commonwealth v. Brown,* supra at 479; ABA *Standards Relating to the Function of the Trial Judge* § 5.3(b)(i) (Approved Draft, 1972).

Subdivision (b). The defendant who has been removed from the courtroom is accorded certain rights by this subdivision. First, the defendant is to be kept present in the court building while his trial is in progress. This is not intended to be read literally, but rather only to require that the defendant be kept in custody within reasonable proximity to the court, i.e., in a jail or police station adjacent to the courthouse.

Further, the defendant is to be given the opportunity of learning of the progress of his trial through his counsel at reasonable intervals. ABA *Standards Relating to the Function of the Trial Judge* § 6.8 (Approved Draft, 1972). Where feasible, the defendant should be provided with means to monitor the proceedings. *See* concurring opinion of Justice Brennan in Illinois v. Allen, 90 S.Ct. 1057, 397 U.S. 337, 351, 25 L.Ed.2d 353 (1970).

Secondly, the defendant is to be advised at the time of his removal of his continuing right to return upon his request and assurance of good behavior. ABA *Standards,* supra.

Finally, and notwithstanding the defendant's failure to request return, he is to be returned to the courtroom periodically and advised that he will be permitted to remain upon the giving of assurances of good behavior. To the ABA *Standards,* supra, is added the provision that the defendant is to be returned with the jury not present.

Rule 46. Time

(Applicable to District Court and Superior Court)

(a) Computation. In computing any period of time prescribed or allowed by these rules, by order of court, or by any applicable statute or rule, the day of the act, event, or default after which the designated period of time begins to run shall not be included. The last day of the period so computed shall be included, unless it is a Saturday, a Sunday, or a legal holiday, in which event the period runs until the end of the next day which is not a Saturday, a Sunday, or a legal holiday. When the period of time prescribed or allowed is less than seven days, intermediate Saturdays, Sundays, and legal holidays shall be excluded in the computation. As used in this rule, "legal holiday" includes any day appointed as a holiday by the President or the Congress of the United States or so designated by the laws of the Commonwealth.

(b) Enlargement. When by these rules or by a notice given thereunder or by order or rule of court an act is required or allowed to be done at or within a specified time, the court for cause shown may at any time in its discretion (1) with or without motion or notice order the period enlarged if a request therefor is made before the expiration of the period originally prescribed or as extended by a previous order; or (2) upon motion made after the expiration of the specified period permit the act to be done where the failure to act was the result of excusable neglect; or (3) permit the act to be done by stipulation of the parties; but the court may not extend the time for taking any action under Rules 25 and 29 except to the extent and under the conditions stated therein.

(c) For Motions, Affidavits in Superior Court. A written motion, other than one which may be heard ex parte, and notice of the hearing thereof shall be served on all interested parties not later than seven days prior to the hearing unless a different period is fixed by these rules or by order of the court. For cause shown, such an order may issue upon an ex parte application. When a motion is supported by affidavit, the affidavit shall be served with the motion. Opposing affidavits shall be served not later than one day before the hearing, unless the court permits them to be served at a later time.

Reporter's Notes

Rule 46 is drawn from and closely parallels Mass.R.Civ.P. 6. It is substantially the same as Rule 6 of the Federal Rules of Civil Procedure and Rule 45 of the Federal Rules of Criminal Procedure. This rule does not substantially alter prior Massachusetts practice.

Subdivision (a). Under the common law, Sundays were excluded from the calculation of a limited time period of seven days or less; if the period exceeded seven days, Sundays were included, even if the final day for the performance of an act fell upon a Sunday. 6 MASS.PRACTICE SERIES (Smith & Zobel) Reporter's Notes at 155 (1974). Like Mass. R.Civ.P. 6(a), this rule excludes Saturdays and legal holidays as well as Sundays from prescribed periods of less than seven days. It provides that a limited period shall not end on a Saturday, Sunday or legal holiday, but shall end on the next succeeding business day. *See* G.L. c. 4, § 9, which does not exclude Saturdays. Those legal holidays which shall be excluded are catalogued in G.L. c. 4, § 7, cl. 18 (as amended, St.1978, c. 12).

An exception to the first sentence is found in the Case Management rule, which provides that in the computation of that rule's time limits, an excluded period shall include both the first and last days of the excludable act or event. Mass. R.Crim.P. 36(b)(3).

Uniform Rule 753 is also phrased in terms of a "designated period of time" and is intended to "not authorize automatic exclusion of the first day or of Saturdays, Sundays, or holidays in complying with provisions which require action 'promptly,' 'without unnecessary delay,' within a 'reasonable' time, or the like." Rules of Criminal Procedure (U.L.A.) Rule 753(a) Comment (1974). Similar requirements prescribed by these rules or by court order are likewise not extended by the excludable days of this rule.

Subdivision (b). This subdivision grants the court discretion to relieve the parties from strict compliance with time requirements in three situations: first, upon request made before the expiration of an original period or a previously-extended period; secondly, upon motion made after the expiration of a period; and thirdly, upon agreement of the parties. In all three instances the party is entitled to relief "for cause shown." In the second situation, the failure to act must have been due to "excusable neglect." Because a motion must state with particularity the grounds on which it is based, Mass.R.Crim.P. 13(b), a bare assertion of excusable neglect without more is insufficient. *See* 6 MASS.PRACTICE SERIES, supra, comments § 6.4.

Neither the federal civil nor criminal rules expressly authorize enlargement by stipulation. While it is stated that under prior Massachusetts practice a stipulation as to enlargement ordinarily did not need court approval, 6 MASS.PRACTICE SERIES, supra, § 6.5, Mass.R.Civ.P. 6(b)(3) appears to require such approval. It is intended that under this rule the approval of the court is to be obtained.

A motion for a required finding of not guilty must be made at the close of the Commonwealth's or the defendant's case, Mass.R.Crim.P. 25(a). Under subdivision (b)(2) of that rule, the motion, if denied, can be renewed within five days after the jury is discharged. In neither case can the court enlarge the time within which the motion is to be made.

A motion to reduce or revoke a sentence is to be filed within sixty days after the imposition of the sentence and such time is not to be enlarged. Mass.R.Crim.P. 29(a).

Subdivision (c). It should be noted that the provisions that an affidavit in support of a motion must be served with the motion and that opposing affidavits are to be served at least one day before the hearing are applicable to pretrial motions under Mass.R.Crim.P. 13.

Rule 47. Special Magistrates

(Applicable to Superior Court)

The Justices of the Superior Court may appoint special magistrates to preside over criminal proceedings in the Superior Court. Such special magistrates shall have the powers to preside at arraignments, to set bail, to assign counsel, to supervise pretrial conferences, to mark up pretrial motions for hearing, to make findings and report those findings and other issues to the presiding justice or Administrative Justice, and to perform such other duties as may be authorized by order of the Superior Court. The doings of special magistrates shall be endorsed upon the record of the case. Special magistrates shall be compensated in the same manner as is provided by the General Laws for the compensation of masters in civil cases.

Reporter's Notes

Under prior law, magistrates served primarily as bail commissioners. G.L. c. 262, §§ 23–24. Sections 62B and 62C of chapter 221 of the General Laws, inserted by St.1978, c. 478, § 250, established the office of Magistrate in all Departments of the Trial Court and gave to that official certain quasi-judicial powers. This rule is not intended to expand the powers which such statutory Trial Court Magistrates may exercise, but to create the new and separate position of Special Magistrate in the Superior Court Department.

Special Magistrates in criminal cases shall have the authority to assign counsel (Mass.R.Crim.P. 8), set bail, and preside at arraignment (Mass.R.Crim.P. 7), and their duties shall include the supervision of pretrial conferences (Mass.R.Crim.P. 11) and the marking up of pretrial motions for hearing (Mass.R.Crim.P. 13). The rule is broad enough to permit assignment of some fact finding functions to Special Magistrates, although the exact dimension of those functions is left to definition by appropriate order of the Administrative Justice of the Superior Court Department. In this respect the Special Magistrate will differ little from masters as appointed by the Supreme Judicial Court under longstanding practice, especially in habeas corpus proceedings.

It is intended that Special Magistrates under this rule, because of the nature of their quasi-judicial responsibilities, be at the least attorneys admitted to practice before the bar and preferably that they be retired judges. Special Magistrates are to be compensated as are masters in civil practice. G.L. c. 221, § 55 (as amended, St.1978, c. 478, § 247); Mass.R.Civ.P. 53(a), Superior Court Rule 49(3) (1974).

While similar to federal magistrates, the office of Special Magistrate under this rule does not carry with it such broad powers. The federal officer can conduct trials for minor offenses and sentence those who are found guilty. 18 U.S.C. §§ 3401–02. Before a federal magistrate can conduct a trial, however, the defendant must consent in writing and specifically waive both a trial before a District Court judge and the right to trial by jury, subject to enumerated qualifications. Under this rule the defendant is to have no objection to proceeding before a Special Magistrate since the functions to be performed by the office of Special Magistrate are administrative rather than adjudicatory.

Rule 48. Sanctions

(Applicable to District Court and Superior Court)

A willful violation by counsel of the provisions of these rules or of an order issued pursuant to these rules shall subject counsel to such sanctions as the court shall deem appropriate, including citation for contempt or the imposition of costs or a fine.

Reporter's Notes

This rule is intended to supplement rather than supplant the provisions of prior law relative to the power of the courts to regulate the conduct of attorneys who practice therein and to discipline those whose actions fall short of accepted standards. The rule applies equally to attorneys and to defendants who appear pro se.

In addition to the sanctions of citations for contempt and the imposition of costs or a fine, the rule contemplates referral to the Board of Bar Overseers where appropriate.

See e.g., Supreme Judicial Court Rule 3.22A, *Disciplinary Rules Applicable to Practice as a Prosecutor or as a Defense Lawyer* (Feb. 14, 1979); ABA *Standards Relating to the Prosecution Function* § 1.1 (Approved Draft, 1971); ABA *Standards Relating to the Defense Function* § 1.1 (Approved Draft, 1971).

DISTRICT/MUNICIPAL COURTS RULES OF CRIMINAL PROCEDURE

Adopted November 3, 1995, Effective January 1, 1996

Publisher's Note

The Notice of Approval of these rules provided: "These rules shall apply in criminal actions commenced in the District Court and Boston Municipal Court on or after January 1, 1996 and in criminal actions pending in those courts on that date regarding any procedural step occurring on or after January 1, 1996. Any procedural step taken before January 1, 1996 which conformed to then effective rules in the District Court and Boston Municipal Court will be regarded as valid during the pendency of the case."

Table of Rules

Rule 1. Applicability

Notwithstanding any other rule of court inconsistent herewith, the following rules shall govern procedure in all criminal cases commenced in the District Court and in the Boston Municipal Court on or after January 1, 1996. For the purpose of this provision, commencement of a criminal action shall occur on the date of arrest, or in cases not initiated by arrest, on the date of the issuance of a criminal complaint.

Adopted November 3, 1995, effective January 1, 1996.

Rule 2. Issuance of Complaint; Police Statement

(a) Cases Commenced by Warrantless Arrest. Prior to the issuance of a criminal complaint in a case commenced by warrantless arrest, the clerk-magistrate shall obtain from the police department responsible for the arrest a written statement describing the facts constituting the basis for the arrest. This requirement may be satisfied by providing to the clerk-magistrate a copy of the arresting officer's police report at the time the Application for Complaint is filed or by setting forth the statement in the space provided on the Application for Complaint, with an additional sheet or sheets attached to the Application as may be needed.

(b) Cases Commenced by Issuance of a Criminal Complaint on Application by Police or Civilian. Prior to the issuance of a criminal complaint in a case commenced by an application therefor filed by a police officer, rather than by a warrantless arrest, the clerk-magistrate shall obtain from the police officer the police report, if any, relating to the alleged crime. In all cases, each police and civilian complainant shall, on the Application for Criminal Complaint, provide the information to support the issuance of the complaint.

Adopted November 3, 1995, effective January 1, 1996.

Rule 3. Arraignment

(a) Defendant's Criminal Record and Police Statement. At or before arraignment, the court shall ensure (1) that a copy of the defendant's criminal record as compiled by the Commissioner of Probation pursuant to G.L. c. 276, s. 100, if any, is provided to the defense and to the prosecution, pursuant to Mass. R.Crim.P. 12(e), and (2) that a copy of the police statement required by Rule 2 is provided to the defense by the prosecution.

(b) Notice of Probation Revocation Hearing. If a defendant against whom a criminal case is commenced in the Boston Municipal Court is on probation in that court, the defendant may be served at arraignment with a notice of a probation revocation hearing.

(c) Order for Pretrial Conference; Discovery; Pretrial Hearing. At arraignment in the District Court, the judge shall issue a written order to the attorney representing the defendant and to the prosecutor to (1) engage in a conference between themselves prior to a pretrial hearing in accordance with Mass.R.Crim.P. 11 and (2) appear before the court on a date certain for the conduct of the pretrial hearing on the results of that conference. If the parties agree to a date for the pretrial conference, said date shall be recorded on the order.

At arraignment in the Boston Municipal Court, the judge shall issue an order to the attorney representing the defendant and to the prosecutor to (1) appear for a conference between themselves under the supervision of an Assistant Clerk–Magistrate designated by the

Clerk–Magistrate for Criminal Business and certified by the Chief Justice of the Boston Municipal Court, to be conducted in accordance with Mass.R.Crim.P. 11, in a designated courtroom and (2) appear before the court on a date certain for a hearing on the results of that pretrial conference.

Such order issued by the District Court or Boston Municipal Court shall also require the parties to provide, permit and obtain discovery in accordance with G.L. c. 218, s. 26A, and Mass.R.Crim.P. 14, in advance of the scheduled pretrial hearing and to be prepared to submit either a tender of plea or admission at said hearing or, in lieu thereof, a pretrial conference report, completed and signed by both parties. Discovery that is not provided, permitted or obtained in accordance with the arraignment order shall be the subject of a court order, a motion for relief, or sanctions at the pretrial hearing, as provided in Rule 4(b).

(d) Charges Not Within District Court Final Jurisdiction. In cases involving one or more charges not within District Court or Boston Municipal Court final jurisdiction, as the case may be, the order issued at arraignment shall allow for a tender of plea, admission or other disposition on charges reduced by the prosecution so as to be within the court's final jurisdiction. The preliminary discovery required to be included in the arraignment order under section (c) of this rule shall apply only to cases within the court's final jurisdiction.

(e) Appearance of Defense Counsel; Lack of Counsel. Defense counsel, privately engaged or appointed on the basis of defendant's indigency, as the case may be, shall file an appearance at arraignment. If private or publicly provided defense counsel is not before the court at arraignment, if counsel is appointed "for bail only," or if the defendant indicates the intention to engage private counsel, the matter shall be continued for a brief period of time sufficient to permit the defendant to obtain counsel and to reappear for (1) either the assignment or waiver of counsel or the appearance of private counsel, and (2) completion of the arraignment, provided, however, that counsel "for bail only" may also be appointed "for arraignment only" in order to complete the arraignment.

If the arraignment is completed at defendant's first appearance, and the defendant indicates a desire to engage private counsel, the court may continue the matter for the next court event (namely, pretrial hearing in the District Court or pretrial conference in the Boston Municipal Court), set the date therefor and issue to the defendant to give to defense counsel the required arraignment order and other necessary documents. Such an approach shall be employed only when the court determines that the defendant will, in fact, secure private counsel sufficiently promptly for such counsel to prepare for and participate in any required pretrial conference and pretrial hearing.

Adopted November 3, 1995, effective January 1, 1996.

Rule 4. Pretrial Hearing

(a) Appearance of Parties. The parties shall appear as scheduled for a hearing on the results of their pretrial conference, in accordance with the terms of the order issued at arraignment under Rule 3(c). Cases in which the parties have not conferenced in accordance with the order shall be held so that said conference may be completed, and the pretrial hearing conducted, prior to the end of the court day, if possible.

(b) Discovery. Failure of either party to have provided, permitted or obtained discovery in accordance with the order issued at arraignment may subject that party to the sanctions provided in Mass.R.Crim.P. 14(c).

Where it is determined that discoverable material should have been produced but was not, the court may, in lieu of sanctions, order such discovery to be provided without further delay, including a brief continuance of the matter to allow the party responsible to secure the item at issue and bring it before the court that same day.

In the District Court, discovery that is not provided or permitted in accordance with the arraignment order and is not ordered at the pretrial hearing may be requested by motion filed at or prior to the conclusion of the pretrial hearing.

(c) Guilty Plea, Admission, or Other Disposition. At the pretrial hearing the defendant may tender to the court a plea, admission or other requested disposition conditioned on specific dispositional terms, with or without the agreement of the prosecutor. Such tender of plea, admission or other disposition shall be set forth on the form promulgated therefor by the Chief Justice of the District Court or the Chief Justice of the Boston Municipal Court, as the case may be. If the court rejects the dispositional terms agreed to by the parties, or requested by the defendant without the agreement of the prosecution, it shall so inform the defendant and the defendant shall be permitted to withdraw the plea or admission, in accordance with G.L. c. 278, s. 18. Prior to submission to the court of a tender of plea or admission or a request for other disposition, and if the proposed dispositional terms involve any probationary terms or conditions, the parties shall consult with the probation department, so as to enable the probation department to be heard as may be required by the court at the time the court considers the tendered plea or admission.

If the court rejects a tendered plea, admission or other disposition, the judge may indicate to the parties what disposition he or she would impose, as provided in Mass.R.Crim.P. 12(c)(6), and a pretrial disposition may be requested by the defendant on those terms.

(d) Pretrial Conference Report. If a pretrial disposition is not requested, or is requested but rejected by the court at the pretrial hearing, the parties shall submit a completed and signed pretrial conference report in accordance with the order issued at arraignment. Said report shall be set forth on the form promulgated therefor by the Chief Justice of the District Court or the Chief Justice of the Boston Municipal Court, as the case may be.

(e) Jury or Jury–Waived Trial. When the pretrial conference report is submitted, the court shall examine it for completeness, shall rule on any disputed discovery issues, and, unless discovery compliance is still pending, shall inquire if the defendant waives the right to jury trial.

The court shall not compel the defendant's decision on waiver of jury trial until all discovery issues have been resolved and compliance with any discovery orders has been completed. Compliance with discovery orders may require the scheduling of a "compliance/election hearing" as provided in Rule 5. However, the defendant may proceed to enter the decision on jury waiver and a trial date may be set prior to compliance with discovery orders, at the defendant's option.

A waiver of the right to jury trial shall be submitted by the defendant on the form promulgated therefor by the Supreme Judicial Court and shall be accepted only upon completion of the colloquy required by law and the certificate of counsel required by G.L. c. 218, s. 26A. The required certificate shall be submitted on the form promulgated therefor by the Chief Justice of the District Court or the Chief Justice of the Boston Municipal Court, as the case may be.

If a waiver of jury trial is accepted in a District Court in which jury trials are not available and in which only one judge regularly sits, and that judge has rejected defendant's tendered plea or admission, the defendant shall be asked if he or she waives the right to be tried by a different judge. If the right to be tried by a different judge is waived, the case shall be scheduled for jury-waived trial in that court. If the right to be tried by a different judge is not waived, the case shall be scheduled for jury-waived trial in the court in which a session has been designated for that purpose under G.L. c. 218, s. 27A.

If the right to jury trial is not waived when that issue is addressed by the court, the case shall be scheduled as follows: (1) in the District Court the case shall be scheduled for jury trial on a date certain, provided, however, that in the District Court such cases may be scheduled for a trial assignment date if that procedure is authorized by the Chief Justice of the District Court, and (2) in the Boston Municipal Court the case shall be scheduled for a date certain for trial assignment.

(f) Charges Outside District Court and Boston Municipal Court Final Jurisdiction. If the case involves one or more charges that are not within District Court or Boston Municipal Court final jurisdiction, as the case may be, or if the court declines final jurisdiction over the pending charges, the court shall schedule a probable cause ("bind-over") hearing in accordance with G.L. c. 218, s. 30 at the completion of the pretrial hearing.

If the prosecution reduces the charge to a crime within District Court or Boston Municipal Court final jurisdiction, but the case cannot be disposed of at the pretrial hearing in the District Court, or at the pretrial conference or pretrial hearing in the Boston Municipal Court, the court shall continue the matter for a further pretrial hearing on a date certain and shall issue such further discovery and pretrial conference orders as may be necessary.

Adopted November 3, 1995, effective January 1, 1996.

Rule 5. Hearing Date for Discovery Compliance and Jury Waiver Election

In those cases in the District Court wherein a discoverable item is not produced or is not deemed waived at the pretrial hearing and the court issues a discovery order, a subsequent court hearing shall be scheduled at the request of the party seeking discovery to ensure compliance with such order. In those cases in the Boston Municipal Court wherein a discoverable item is not produced or is not deemed waived at the pretrial hearing and the court issues a discovery order, a subsequent hearing may be scheduled by the court. If required, said hearing in the District Court or Boston Municipal Court shall be scheduled for a date on or after the compliance date and shall be limited to the following court actions:

(1) determining discovery compliance and, if necessary, ordering appropriate sanctions for non-compliance;

(2) receiving and acting on a tender of plea or admission in accordance with Rule 4(c); and

(3) obtaining defendant's decision on waiver of the right to jury and scheduling the trial date or trial assignment date, as required by Rule 4(e).

Adopted November 3, 1995, effective January 1, 1996.

Rule 6. Pretrial Motions

(a) In the District Court.

(1) *Discovery Motions.* Discovery motions shall be filed in accordance with Rule 4(b) and shall be heard and decided prior to the defendant's initial decision on waiver of jury trial, provided, however, that motions for discovery may be filed within twenty-one days after the defendant's initial decision on waiver of jury trial, or later, for good cause shown. Discovery motions filed within said twenty-one day period or later shall be entertained only upon a preliminary showing (1) that the items or information sought could not reasonably have been sought and obtained prior to the initial decision on waiver of jury trial or (2) of other grounds that the court determines reasonably justify the delay

in having filed the discovery motion after completion of the pretrial hearing.

(2) *Non-discovery Pretrial Motions.* All pretrial motions other than those involving discovery may be filed before or after the defendant's initial decision on waiver of the right to jury trial.

Such motions filed before the defendant's initial decision on the waiver of jury trial shall be transmitted to the appropriate trial session and scheduled to be heard there on the trial date, provided, however, that the judge before whom any such motion is filed may, as a matter of his or her discretion, hear and decide said motion (1) prior to the trial date, or, (2) where the trial will be conducted in a different court, prior to transmission of the case to such other court.

Such motions filed after defendant's initial decision on waiver of jury trial shall be filed in the court wherein the trial is scheduled to be heard no later than twenty-one days after defendant's decision on waiver of jury trial, or later, for good cause shown. Notwithstanding the foregoing, the presiding justice of the court in which the pretrial hearing is conducted, if different from the court in which the trial will be conducted, may require that such motions be filed and heard in the former court. In such cases, transmission of the case file to the other court for trial should be deferred until after the motion is heard and decided.

Rulings on pretrial motions rendered prior to the transmission of a case to a trial session shall be final, as provided in G.L. c. 278, § 18.

(b) In the Boston Municipal Court.

(1) *Discovery Motions.* Discovery motions timely filed must be heard and decided prior to the scheduling of the trial session assignment date. Discovery motions filed after the scheduling of a trial session assignment date shall be allowed only:

(A) if the discovery being sought could not reasonably have been sought or obtained prior to the scheduling of the trial session assignment date; or

(B) if other good cause can be shown.

(2) *Non-discovery Pretrial Motions.* Pretrial motions other than those involving discovery may be filed at any time but no later than 21 days after the date of the filing of the Pretrial Conference Report.

Rulings on pretrial motions rendered prior to the transmission of a case to a trial assignment session shall be final, as provided in G.L. c. 278, § 18.

Adopted November 3, 1995, effective January 1, 1996.

Rule 7. Trials

Jury-waived trials and jury trials shall proceed in accordance with the provisions of law applicable to such trials in Superior Court, as provided by G.L. c. 218, §§ 26A and 27A(d) and (e), respectively.

Adopted November 3, 1995, effective January 1, 1996.

Rule 8. [Reserved]

Rule 9. Sanctions

The provisions of Mass.R.Crim.P. 48 regarding sanctions for willful violation of those rules shall apply to willful violations of these rules.

Adopted November 3, 1995, effective January 1, 1996.

Rule 10. Title

These rules may be known and cited as the District/Municipal Courts Rules of Criminal Procedure (Dist./Mun.Cts.R.Crim.P.).

Adopted November 3, 1995, effective January 1, 1996.

DISTRICT COURT DEPARTMENT SUPPLEMENTAL RULES OF CRIMINAL PROCEDURE

Effective February 1, 1981

Table of Rules

Rule 1. Bail

If an assignment or appointment of counsel is made pursuant to Rule 8 of the Massachusetts Rules of Criminal Procedure, including a senior law school student pursuant to Supreme Judicial Court Rule 3:03, and the assignee or appointee is available during the same day within such time as the judge in his discretion shall permit, no determination of bail other than release on personal recognizance shall be made without a reasonable opportunity being given the assignee or appointee to confer with the defendant and to be heard on the question of bail. Notice of the right to a speedy review of any bail determination by a judge shall be given to the defendant by the judge at the time the determination is made, and a record of the giving of this notice shall be recorded by the session clerk.

Rule 2. Notice of Right to First–Instance Jury Trial; Waiver of Right

(A) Notice of Right. Every defendant appearing in the District Court Department in a case over which the court will exercise final jurisdiction shall be notified of his or her right to jury trial in the first instance. Such notice shall be given orally to the defendant by the judge or by the session clerk at arraignment, provided that the defendant is represented by counsel or has waived counsel. If the defendant does not have counsel or does not waive counsel at arraignment, the notice shall be given as soon as the defendant thereafter appears before the court with counsel or having waived counsel.

The oral notice of right to first-instance jury trial shall include a statement to the defendant that if he or she waives this right he or she will receive a trial before a judge and if not satisfied with the results of that trial will be able to appeal for a new trial before a jury.

The defendant shall decide whether or not he or she will waive this right to first-instance jury trial at the time the notice of that right is given to him or her unless the court allows further time.

(B) Waiver of Right. If the defendant decides to waive the right to first-instance jury trial, he or she shall so indicate on the form promulgated by the Chief Justice of the District Court Department.

Before the defendant signs this form the judge shall be satisfied that the waiver is voluntarily and knowingly made and to that end shall (1) advise the defendant and be sure the defendant understands that by waiving first-instance jury trial he or she is not losing the constitutional right to trial by jury, but that a trial by a jury will be available only after a trial without one, and (2) satisfy himself or herself that the defendant's waiver is not the product of pressure and that the defendant is not intoxicated or otherwise incapable of rational judgment.

When the judge feels it necessary, the judge should also inform the defendant of the essential elements of the jury trial, i.e. that the jury consists of members of the community; that the defendant may participate in their selection; that the jury verdict must be unanimous; that they decide guilt or innocence while the judge makes rulings of law and, when guilt is found, imposes sentence; and that when no jury is involved the judge alone decides guilt or innocence.

Rule 3. Refusal to Plead

The court shall not enter a judgment upon a plea of guilty nor make a finding of guilty upon the defendant admitting to a finding of facts sufficient to warrant the same, unless it is satisfied that there is a factual basis for such plea or finding.

Rule 4. Advice As to Rights

An unrepresented defendant who has pleaded not guilty to any complaint shall be advised by the judge at the time of his hearing or trial that on any material matter pertaining to the offense charged he has the following rights:

(a) to cross examine any witness offered by the prosecution; and

(b) subject to cross examination, to offer testimony by himself or any other witness.

The judge shall also then advise him of his rights not to testify and not to be prejudiced if he remains silent. If the prosecution offers an exhibit the judge shall allow the defendant to examine it.

Rule 5. Place of Hearing

Except when in the discretion of the judge he shall deem it to be necessary or desirable in the interest of the defendant or the public,

(a) no room shall be used for a hearing or trial other than a room where a court session is customarily held; and

(b) no evidence shall be taken at any bench conference during a hearing or trial until the time of the judge's consideration of matters bearing on disposition.

Rule 6. Probation Department Records or Reports

During the trial on any complaint wherein the District Court Department has and does not decline final jurisdiction, no consideration of any probation department records or reports shall take place until the termination of the trial. If the judge then finds the defendant not guilty, the session clerk shall so announce and notify the defendant that he is discharged of the offense set forth in the complaint. If the judge indicates a finding of guilty or facts sufficient to warrant such a finding, he shall only thereafter consider any probation department records or reports and instruct the session clerk to announce his decisions on adjudication, disposition or continuance, as the case may be.

Rule 7. Appeal

In all cases where the defendant has a right to appeal to a jury session in the District Court Department he shall be notified by the session clerk or the judge and shall be granted a reasonable time to make a decision after conferring with his counsel, or, if unrepresented, to make reasonable inquiry of the judge as to the procedures afforded him for this purpose. This notice shall include a statement to the defendant that if he does not appeal he is waiving his right to jury trial. The court shall explain to the defendant the importance and procedure of trial by jury if it deems such explanation necessary for the defendant's knowledgeable decision on the question of appeal.

Notice of the right to appeal a finding of guilty and the defendant's decision on exercising that right shall be completed before the pronouncement of sentence. Regardless of whether the defendant claims appeal of the finding, the court shall proceed to pronounce sentence.

If the defendant has claimed appeal of the finding, notice of the right to appeal the sentence need not be given.

If the defendant has not claimed or is not entitled to claim appeal of the finding, notice must be given of the right to appeal the sentence. If the defendant then claims appeal of the sentence, he shall be entitled only to resentencing by the judge sitting in the jury session.

The session clerk shall indicate on the case papers whether the defendant has claimed appeal of the finding or of the sentence or of both.

Rule 8. Appointment and Compensation of Attorneys

If it is necessary for the court to appoint private counsel at the Commonwealth's expense pursuant to the requirements of Rule 8 of the Massachusetts Rules of Criminal Procedure, other than counsel participating in bar-sponsored, approved indigent representation programs, such appointment shall be made in accordance with this rule.

(1) Every division shall maintain a list of attorneys who have offered to represent defendants pursuant to appointment by the court. Said list shall be part of the public records of the court open during regular business hours to public inspection. Any attorney may have his name placed on said list, whether or not he is a member of any bar association, provided that the court shall be satisfied that the attorney is geographically located so as to insure his reasonable availability to the court and to defendants brought before the court. Law firms shall not be listed as such.

(2) All appointments of attorneys shall be made from said list. The court shall, except in exceptional circumstances, appoint the attorney whose name next appears on said list, and may appoint said attorney to represent more than one defendant before proceeding to the next name. The court shall make appointments in such a way and for such periods of time as to insure the equal participation of all attorneys and to avoid favored treatment of any attorney.

(3) An attorney may withdraw his name from said list by communicating in writing with the Presiding Justice of the division. The name of an attorney may be removed from said list by the Presiding Justice of the division if he is satisfied that the appointment of said attorney under this rule would not be in the interest of justice.

(4) An attorney appointed to represent a defendant pursuant to this rule shall be personally responsible for the representation of said defendant at every stage of the District Court proceedings, except as may be otherwise provided in paragraph 7. Should new counsel subsequently be appointed by the District Court, the first appointed counsel shall respond cooperatively to any reasonable request for information by subsequently appointed counsel.

(5) An attorney appointed under this rule shall be entitled to compensation at a rate not to exceed thirty-five dollars ($35.00) per hour for time expended in court actually engaged in an evidentiary hearing or actual trial, and at a rate not to exceed twenty-five dollars ($25.00) per hour for other time reasonably expended with a maximum of one hour for any one court appearance and, unless authorized in advance by the court, a maximum of five hours for preparation or other services out of court. The amount of time billed shall not, as the result of counsel representing co-defendants, exceed the total amount of time actually expended. In addition, such counsel may be reimbursed for expenses reasonably incurred when authorized by the court before the expenses are incurred.

(6) Except as provided in paragraphs 7 and 8, compensation based on the nature of the offense or offenses charged, the number of offenses charged, a per diem rate or any formula other than that contained in paragraph 5, is expressly prohibited.

(7) In the event an insufficient number of attorneys come forward to offer to represent defendants in accordance with the foregoing provisions, the Presiding Justice of the division shall certify that fact to the Chief Justice of the District Court Department and shall recommend in writing an alternate plan which shall not require a greater expenditure of funds for implementation than would the plan outlined above. No such alternate plan shall be put into effect without the approval of the Chief Justice of the District Court Department and the Chief Administrative Justice.

(8) Notwithstanding the foregoing provisions of this rule, the court may enter into such arrangements as it deems appropriate to provide an organized system for the immediate representation of defendants at arraignment. Attorneys participating in such system may be compensated in a manner other than as provided in paragraph 5. This paragraph contemplates a plan whereby one attorney is assigned to represent all defendants at arraignment on a given day or days, said assignments to be distributed fairly among counsel wishing to participate. Appointment at arraignment of counsel who will not be trial counsel is not permitted except as provided in this paragraph.

(9) An attorney's bill for services shall be submitted to the clerk of the court within thirty days of termination of services. A separate bill shall be rendered for each defendant. Said bill shall be in the form prescribed by the Chief Justice of the District Court Department, but an attorney shall supply any additional information on the nature and extent of his services as the Presiding Justice of the court shall require. Failure to file a bill promptly shall be grounds for removal of the attorney from the list.

(10) No attorney appointed as counsel pursuant to this rule shall request or accept any payment or promise of payment from any other source for representing the defendant, except as ordered by the court.

Rule 9. Sound Recording Devices

Recording of court proceedings is governed by Rule 211 of the Special Rules of the District Court.

Amended effective May 1, 1986; amended December 31, 1987, effective February 1, 1988.

Rule 10. Special Procedures for Criminal Cases in Essex and Hampden Counties

(a) Scope of Rule; Applicability of Rules 1 Through 9. All criminal proceedings in the District Court primary courts and jury sessions in Essex and Hampden Counties shall be governed by Rules 1 through 9 of these rules, except as they are modified herein.

(b) Notice of Right to Jury Trial; Waiver of Right. Except as modified below, Rule 2 shall govern notice to the defendant of the right to jury trial and waiver of that right.

RULE 2. NOTICE OF RIGHT TO JURY TRIAL; WAIVER OF RIGHT

(A) Notice of Right; Decision on Waiver. Every defendant appearing in the District Court Department in a case over which the court will exercise final jurisdiction shall be notified of his or her right to jury trial. Such notice shall be given orally to the defendant by the judge or by the session clerk at arraignment, provided that the defendant is represented by counsel or has waived counsel. If the defendant does not have counsel or does not waive counsel at arraignment, the notice shall be given as soon as the defendant thereafter appears before the court with counsel or having waived counsel.

The oral notice of right to jury trial shall include a statement to the defendant that, if he or she waives this right, he or she will receive a trial before a judge.

In the primary court the defendant shall decide whether or not he or she will waive the right to jury trial after completion of the pretrial conference and the hearing on the pretrial conference report, and after completion of the guilty plea or admission procedure, if any, and withdrawal of the plea or admission, if any. In the jury session, the defendant shall decide whether or not he or she will waive the right to jury trial no later than the commencement of trial. The defendant shall not be required to decide on waiver of the right to jury trial in either the primary court or jury session until disposition or withdrawal of any pretrial discovery motion filed in accordance with the Massachusetts Rules of Criminal Procedure and compliance with any court order issued in conjunction therewith.

(B) Procedure for Waiver of Right. If in the primary court the defendant decides to waive the right to jury trial and consents to be tried by the court, he or she shall so indicate on the form promulgated by the Chief Justice of the District Court Department.

Before the defendant signs this form the judge shall be satisfied that the waiver is voluntarily and knowingly made and to that end shall advise the defendant and be sure the defendant understands that by waiving jury trial he or she is losing the constitutional right to trial by jury, and satisfy himself or herself that the defendant's waiver is not the product of pressure and that the defendant is not intoxicated or otherwise incapable of rational judgment, and shall receive from defense counsel a properly executed certificate, signed by counsel, indicating that he or she has made all the necessary explanations and determinations regarding such waiver. Such certificate shall be set forth on the form prescribed therefor by the Chief Justice of the District Court Department.

When the judge determines it to be necessary, the judge should also inform the defendant of the essential elements of the jury trial, i.e. that the jury consists of members of the community; that the defendant may participate in their selection; that the jury verdict must be unanimous; that they decide guilt or innocence while the judge makes rulings of law and, when guilt is found, imposes sentence; and that when no jury is involved the judge alone decides guilt or innocence.

(C) Appeal. Rule 7 of the District Court Supplemental Rules of Criminal Procedure shall not apply to criminal cases in the District Court primary court and jury sessions in Essex and Hampden Counties. Appeals on issues of law in such cases shall be governed by the applicable statutes and the Massachusetts Rules of Appellate Procedure.

Adopted June 9, 1987, effective July 1, 1987.

DISTRICT COURT RULES FOR PROBATION VIOLATION PROCEEDINGS

Adopted December 2, 1999, effective January 3, 2000

Table of Rules

Rule 1. Scope and Purpose

These rules prescribe procedures in the District Court to be followed upon the allegation of a violation of an order of probation issued in a criminal case after a finding of guilty or after a continuance without a finding. These rules do not apply to an alleged violation of pretrial probation, as the latter term is defined herein.

The purpose of these rules is to ensure that judicial proceedings undertaken upon the allegation of a violation of probation are conducted in full compliance with all applicable law, promptly and with an appropriate degree of procedural uniformity.

Adopted December 2, 1999, effective January 3, 2000.

Commentary

Probation violation proceedings are among the most important matters within District Court jurisdiction. The timely and proper conduct of these proceedings is essential to protect the rights of probationers as set forth in federal and state law, as well as to maintain the credibility, and thus the effectiveness, of probation orders. Just as fundamentally, the proper and timely conduct of probation violation proceedings is necessary to vindicate the public trust. Failure of the court to take appropriate action when a convicted defendant who has been given the benefit of probation is then alleged to have violated that order erodes public confidence in the judicial system.

These rules are intended to codify the provisions of applicable case law and to provide clarity in areas of long-standing ambiguity. Their purpose is to provide a clear and predictable process whereby probation violation proceedings are to be commenced, conducted and completed.

One area of ambiguity involves terminology. These rules are entitled "Rules for Probation Violation Proceedings" and not "Rules for Probation Revocation Proceedings." This is an important distinction involving the essential difference between adjudication and disposition. Ambiguity concerning this distinction appears occasionally in the relevant case law, which almost uniformly refers to "probation revocation hearings." The problem is that when a probationer is alleged to have violated his or her probation order, the first purpose of the subsequent hearing is to adjudicate the factual question of whether that violation occurred. The decision to revoke probation, or order any other disposition, can proceed only if a violation is found. Most of the due process requirements that have evolved for these hearings relate to the process by which the court is to determine the factual issue. The nature of the alleged violation is essentially irrelevant to the factual determination of whether it occurred. In contrast, the issue of whether the probation order should be revoked (in many instances requiring the execution of a sentence of incarceration) focuses directly on the nature of the violation, among other factors. In addition, the issue of violation is essentially a *factual* matter whereas the dispositional decision of whether to revoke probation is essentially one of *discretion*.

Confusion on this distinction can affect proceedings significantly. For example, the preponderance of the evidence test at a probation violation hearing has nothing to do with the revocation decision; it is the evidentiary test by which the court must determine if a violation occurred. Conversely, the seriousness of the alleged violation has nothing to do with whether it occurred, but is an important consideration regarding revocation.

It is believed that often probation violation proceedings are not initiated because the Probation Department has no intention of recommending revocation and the incarceration it may require. As long as the proceeding is referred to, and believed to be for the purpose of, revocation and incarceration, there can be reluctance to allege a violation if the appropriate disposition is not revocation but rather the imposition of more stringent or intense probation requirements. The concept of a probation *revocation* hearing promotes a mistaken "all or nothing" perception. It implies that revocation is the purpose of the hearing and that if a violation is found, revocation must follow. In fact, the purpose of the hearing is to adjudicate the allegation, with the court having broad discretionary authority if a violation is found.

These rules seek to clarify the important difference between adjudicating the factual issue of whether a violation has occurred and the court's dispositional decision following such adjudication, not only by referring to the proceedings as "probation *violation* proceedings," but also by requiring a two-step procedure (Rule 5) and expressly defining the different purpose and procedures required for each step (Rule 7).

Throughout these rules the person who is the subject of probation violation proceedings is usually referred to as the "probationer" rather than the "defendant." With respect to the probation proceedings, such a person is *not* a defendant; he or she has either been convicted, after trial or based on a plea of guilty, or has formally submitted an admission to the facts of a criminal charge. Use of the term "probationer" is intended to underscore the legal status of the individual charged with a probation violation, which is fundamentally distinct from the status of a person who is a criminal defendant, particularly in terms of procedural rights.

Rule 2. Definition of Terms

In construing these rules, the following terms shall have the following meanings:

"Continuance without a finding" means the order of a court, following a formal submission and acceptance of a plea of guilty or an admission to sufficient facts, whereby a criminal case is continued to a date certain without the formal entry of a guilty finding. A continuance without a finding may include conditions imposed in an order of probation (1) the violation of which may result in the revocation of the continuance, entry of a finding of guilty and imposition of sentence, and (2) compliance with which will result in dismissal of the criminal case.

"District Attorney" means the criminal prosecuting authority including the Attorney General if the criminal case in which probation was ordered was prosecuted by the Office of the Attorney General.

"General conditions of probation" means the conditions of probation that are imposed as a matter of course in every order of probation, as set forth in the official form promulgated for such orders.

"Probation order" means the formal, written court order whereby a defendant is placed on probation and which expressly sets forth the conditions of probation.

"Pretrial probation" means the probationary status of a defendant pursuant to a probation order issued prior to a trial or the formal submission and acceptance of a plea of guilty or an admission to sufficient facts.

"Revocation of probation" means the revocation by a judge of an order of probation as a consequence of a determination that a condition of that probation order has been violated.

"Special conditions of probation" means any condition of probation other than one of the general conditions of probation.

"Surrender" means the procedure by which a probation officer requires a probationer to appear before the court for a judicial hearing regarding an allegation of probation violation.

Adopted December 2, 1999, effective January 3, 2000.

Commentary

This rule provides definitions for six terms that are important for a clear understanding of various provisions of these rules.

The definition of "continuance without a finding" is provided to make clear that, as used in these rules, the term presupposes that the defendant whose case has been so continued has formally submitted, and the court has accepted, a plea of guilty or an admission to sufficient facts. Thus there is no "continuance without a finding" unless a guilty plea or admission has been properly tendered and accepted.

This definition also makes clear that the conditions of the continuance may be set forth in an order of probation. Thus, upon violation of one or more conditions of probation, the court may proceed to enter a guilty finding and impose sentence, as provided in Rule 9. It may be possible for a court to continue a case without a finding *without* imposing the conditions of the continuance as probation conditions, but these rules have no application in such a circumstance. If the conditions of a continuance without a finding, whether or not imposed as conditions of probation, are *not* violated, the criminal case may be dismissed. See *Commonwealth v. Pyles*, 423 Mass. 717, 672 N.E.2d 96 (1996).

"Probation order" is defined as a written court order that specifies the conditions imposed. Fundamental fairness requires that if a probationer is to be subject to sanctions for failure to obey probation conditions, those conditions must be clearly specified. And proof of a violation will require evidence that the defendant was made aware of the conditions he or she allegedly violated. Conditions of probation must not be vague. See *Commonwealth v. Power*, 420 Mass. 410, 650 N.E.2d 87 (1995). A written order is conducive to clarity. The probation order also fulfills a statutory requirement for written conditions: "Every person released upon probation shall be given by the probation officer a written statement of the terms and conditions of the release." G.L. c. 276, s. 85.

The definition of "pretrial probation" makes clear that this term includes probation orders issued before a trial, a plea or an admission. A defendant placed on pretrial probation under G.L. c. 276, s. 87, is formally on probation, but violation of such probation would not appear to subject the probationer to any sanction other than the resumption of the criminal proceeding. Having not admitted guilt or been tried, and having waived no rights, such a probationer would not appear to be subject to any sentencing, let alone any loss of liberty, even if a violation of such probation were alleged and proved. As a result, the due process requirements that are the central focus of these procedural rules do not apply to an alleged violation of a pretrial probation order, and Rule 1 expressly so provides.

The definition of "revocation of probation" makes clear that this is an order that must be preceded by a judicial determination that a condition of a probation order has been violated.

Special conditions of probation are defined simply as any condition other than the "general conditions." A violation of such a special condition (or a general condition other than the prohibition against any violation of law) has traditionally, and perhaps unfortunately, been referred to as a "technical" violation.

"Surrender" is defined in accordance with *Commonwealth v. Durling*, 407 Mass. 108, 111, 551 N.E.2d 1193, 1195 (1990):

When a violation is alleged, the probation officer "surrenders" the defendant to the court, subjecting the defendant to possible revocation of his probation.

This definition is intended to clarify that surrender is the process by which the Probation Department brings the probationer before the court to answer for an alleged violation. It may be effected by arrest with or without a warrant under G.L. c. 279, s. 3, or by a notice requiring the defendant to appear before the court. If a defendant is already before the court on a separate matter (for example, following an arrest on a new alleged crime, with or without a warrant, or on a summons on a new alleged crime), he or she may be notified at that time of the probation violation and ordered to appear at, or held in custody until, a probation violation hearing. In such cases no actual surrender by the Probation Department is required, since the defendant is before the court for a different reason when violation proceedings are commenced.

This definition of "surrender" clarifies any confusion caused by the use of the term to mean the process following a revocation of probation where a sentence is executed or imposed. See, e.g., *Commonwealth v. Duro*, No. 95–P–2186 (Appeals Court, March 28, 1997) (summary disposition) (court refers to "order revoking the defendant's probation and surrendering him to the custody of the State . . . . ").

Rule 3. Commencement of Violation Proceedings: Charged Criminal Conduct

(a) General. This rule prescribes the procedures to be undertaken upon the issuance of a criminal complaint against a probationer.

(b) Where Probation Order and Criminal Charge Involve Same Court.

(i) *Issuance and Service of Notice.* When a criminal complaint is issued by a court against a defendant who is the subject of a probation order previously issued by that same court, the Probation Department shall commence violation proceedings against that probationer. Such proceedings shall be commenced by the issuance by the Probation Department of a Notice of Probation Violation and Hearing at or before the arraignment on the criminal charge. Said notice shall be served on the defendant in hand at arraignment following the assignment of a date and time for a probation violation hearing, as provided in section (b)(ii), below, and such service shall be recorded on the case docket, provided that if such in-hand service is not possible, the Notice shall be served on the probationer by first-class mail, unless the court orders otherwise. Service of the Notice by first-class mail shall be recorded on the case docket. Out-of-court service other than by mail shall require a written return of service. A copy of each Notice of Probation Violation and Hearing shall be provided to the District Attorney forthwith upon its issuance.

The court, upon review of the Notice at arraignment and as a matter of its discretion, may order no further proceedings in the matter, and in such cases formal service of the Notice on the probationer shall not be required.

(ii) *Contents of Notice.* The Notice of Probation Violation and Hearing shall set forth the criminal behavior alleged to have been committed by the probationer as indicated in the criminal complaint, and shall set forth any other specific conditions of the probation order that the Probation Department alleges have been violated with a description of each such alleged violation. Said Notice shall also state the date, time and place of the hearing.

(iii) *Scheduling of Hearing.* The probation violation hearing shall be scheduled to be conducted on the date of the pretrial hearing for the criminal charge, unless the court expressly orders an earlier hearing. The hearing shall be scheduled for a date certain no less than seven days after service on the probationer of the Notice of Violation and Hearing unless the probationer waives said seven-day notice period. Except in extraordinary circumstances, said hearing date shall not be later than 30 days after service of the Notice of Violation and Hearing if the probationer objects thereto. In scheduling the pretrial hearing on the new criminal charge together with the probation violation hearing, the court shall give primary consideration to the need for promptness in conducting the probation violation hearing.

(c) Where Probation Order and Criminal Charge Involve Different Courts.

(i) *Issuance and Service of Notice.* When a criminal complaint is issued by a court against a defendant who is the subject of a probation order issued by a different court, the Probation Department at the court that issued the criminal complaint shall issue a Notice of Probation Violation and Hearing to the probationer at or before arraignment on the criminal charge. Said notice shall be served on the defendant in hand at arraignment and such service shall be recorded on the case docket. The Probation Department forthwith shall send a copy of said Notice, indicating such in-hand service, to the Probation Department of the court that issued the probation order, together with a copy of the complaint and police report on the criminal charge that constitutes the alleged probation violation. Nothing in this rule shall preclude the issuance and service on the probationer of a Notice of Probation Violation and Hearing by the Probation Department of the court that issued the probation order.

(ii) *Contents of Notice.* The Notice of Probation Violation and Hearing issued to and served on the probationer at the court that issued the criminal complaint shall set forth the criminal behavior alleged to have been committed by the probationer as indicated in the criminal complaint and shall order the probationer to appear at a specific date and time at the court that issued the probation order for the express purpose of appointment of counsel, if necessary, and scheduling of a probation violation hearing.

(iii) *Scheduling of Hearing; Service by Probation Court.* Upon appearance of the probationer at the court that issued the probation order in accordance with the Notice served pursuant to subsection (ii), that court shall appoint counsel, if necessary, and schedule a probation violation hearing for a date certain, said date to be no less than seven days later unless the defendant waives said seven-day period. Except in extraordinary circumstances, said hearing date shall not be later than 30 days after said appearance if the probationer objects thereto. The Probation Department may revise the Notice of Probation Violation and Hearing by adding to it any additional alleged violations. Such additional allegations shall set forth the specific conditions of the probation order alleged to have been violated with a description of each such alleged violation. The Notice, with or without amendment, shall include the date, time and place of the hearing, and shall be served on the probationer in hand while the defendant is before the court. Such service shall be recorded on the case docket. A copy of the Notice shall be provided to the District Attorney at the time of, or before, such service on the probationer.

The court, upon review of the Notice at the outset of the hearing and as a matter of its discretion, may order no further proceedings in the matter, and in such cases no hearing shall be scheduled nor further Notice served.

Adopted December 2, 1999, effective January 3, 2000.

Commentary

This rule sets forth procedures for a specific circumstance, namely, where a probationer is charged with a crime by the issuance of a criminal complaint. It is based on the premise that when a formal criminal charge is issued against a person on probation, this constitutes a basis for an alleged violation of the first general condition of every probation order (that the probationer must obey all local, state and federal laws) and the court must address such an alleged violation.

Note that it makes no difference whether the criminal complaint was issued after an arrest, or after a hearing on a criminal complaint application with no arrest having occurred. Note also that the rule does *not* apply to alleged criminal conduct that has not yet resulted in a criminal complaint. Probation violation proceedings based on alleged criminal conduct where no criminal complaint has yet issued are governed by Rule 4.

Commencement of Proceedings in Every Case

The rule requires the commencement of a probation violation proceeding in *every* case where a criminal complaint is issued against a probationer. No attempt is made to discriminate between those criminal charges that are "serious enough" to warrant violation proceedings and those that are not. The charge of a crime against a person who has been given the benefit of probation is serious enough *per se* to require action by the Probation Department. If the violation is found to have occurred, it is important to document that finding. The seriousness of the violation is properly addressed by the court's *dispositional* discretion, which is extremely flexible: a serious violation may result in revocation; a minor violation may result in simply a warning. See Rule 7(d). Nor must an alleged minor violation require protracted proceedings. In appropriate cases, the defendant may admit to the probation violation resulting in a simple continuance of the current probation terms and consent to a disposition at arraignment on the new charge. Of course, a defendant's rights to oppose any alleged violation and to demand trial on any criminal charge remain inviolate.

Whenever a new crime is charged, commencement of probation violation proceedings may not be delayed solely to await the conclusion of the new criminal case. Rules 5(e) and 7(a) similarly preclude such "tracking" of the new criminal case as a basis for delaying the conduct and conclusion of probation violation proceedings. The commentary to Rule 5(e) provides the rationale for the requirement. Continuances are available on specific grounds under Rule 5(e).

Where the court "treats" a criminal charge as a civil infraction, as provided by G.L. c. 277, s. 70C, the rule requiring the initiation of probation proceedings does not apply since the criminal charge, as such, can be considered no longer to exist. However, the underlying alleged behavior may constitute a violation of probation subject to possible violation proceedings under Rule 4.

Judicial Discretion to Terminate Proceedings After Commencement

It should be noted that the rule acknowledges the court's discretion to terminate a proceeding once it has been commenced. That is, the rule provides that proceedings are commenced "by the issuance by the Probation Department of a Notice of Probation Violation and Hearing at or before arraignment on the criminal charge." Usually such "issuance" will consist of the probation officer tendering the notice form to the court before the arraignment begins. (The notice will not be formally served on the probationer until and unless a hearing date is determined and recorded on the form.) At that time the judge is free as a matter of discretion to order that the proceedings be terminated. Such an order must be entered on the probation record and on the docket of the case in which probation was ordered to ensure accountability. While alleged probation violations based on new criminal charges, even minor ones, generally should proceed to a factual conclusion to vindicate the credibility of probation and to establish a proper record, there may be circumstances where, in the opinion of the court, the violation proceedings should be terminated at the outset.

Where the court at which the probationer is on probation is different from the court where the new criminal charge is brought, the judicial authority to order no further proceedings resides at the former court, and section (c)(iii) so states.

Same Court

There are two different circumstances in which proceedings under the rule can arise: where the criminal complaint is issued (1) by the same court that issued the probation order, or (2) by a different court. These situations are addressed separately in sections (b) and (c).

Section (b), the "same court" circumstance, requires the probationer to be served in hand with the Notice of Probation Violation and Hearing when he or she appears before the court for arraignment whenever possible. This requires administrative attention by the Probation Department at each court so as to ensure each day that all new arrestees and others appearing for arraignment are screened for probation status. Notices for all those who are on probation must be prepared for in-court service. Where necessary, these defendants can be scheduled last for arraignment to ensure preparation of the Notice and in-hand service. The issuance of the Notice constitutes "commencement" of action by the Probation Department. The prepared Notice should include any other violations that can properly be alleged in addition to the charged criminal conduct. For example, a probationer charged with a new crime may also have a history of failure to report as ordered. The date, time and place of the violation hearing should be left blank, to be recorded on the form when the hearing is scheduled along with the pretrial hearing on the criminal charge, as required in section (b)(iii). After this information is added, the Notice is to be served in hand on the probationer.

If the probationer defaults at arraignment, the Notice can be prepared and left in the case file.

When the court fails to make in-hand service at arraignment, the rule provides for other methods of service. In such cases, the goal should be to schedule the hearing on the same date as the pretrial hearing on the criminal charge, assuming this will not violate the seven-day minimum notice requirement.

There is no requirement that counsel in the original criminal case represent the probationer at the violation hearing. On the contrary, if appointment of counsel is required, it is appropriate to appoint the same attorney for the violation hearing and for the new criminal charge that also constitutes the alleged probation violation.

Different Courts

Section (c) of the rule addresses the circumstance where a person against whom a criminal complaint has issued is on probation in a different court. Under section (c)(i) the Probation Department of the court that issued the complaint must prepare and serve a Notice of Probation Violation and Hearing on the probationer in hand at arraignment, just as in the "same-court" situation. However, in addition to specifying the alleged violation, the Notice will order the probationer to appear on a date certain at the court where he or she is on probation. The purposes of that appearance will be to appoint counsel and schedule the violation hearing. The Probation Department of the court where the defendant is on probation may amend the notice to include additional violation allegations. Presumably the court where the probationer is on probation will schedule a prompt hearing date, consistent with the seven-day minimum notice period for the probationer. (See below.)

The requirement that copies of the Notice, criminal complaint and police report be sent "forthwith" to the probation court is most effectively satisfied by the use of facsimile ("fax") transmission.

Scheduling

Notice of the probation violation hearing "must be given sufficiently in advance of scheduled court proceedings so that reasonable opportunity to prepare will be afforded." *Commonwealth v. Odoardi*, 397 Mass. 28, 31–32, 489 N.E.2d 674, 676 (1986), quoting *In re Gault*, 387 U.S. 1, 33, 87 S.Ct. 1428, 1446 (1967). The rule provides a minimum of seven days notice in both the same-court and different-court situations. This is the minimum notice period previously provided by regulations of the Office of the Commissioner of Probation and should be minimally adequate in most cases given the narrow focus of these hearings. If either party desires more time than is allowed by the scheduled date, a continuance may be sought under Rule 5(e).

The rule also provides that the hearing may not be scheduled for a date more than 30 days after service of the Notice if the probationer objects to such date. This is to protect the probationer from undue delay, which is a particular concern if the probationer is being held in probation detention. Finally, the rule provides that even if the hearing date is beyond the 30–day limit and the probationer objects, such delay may nonetheless be justified on the basis of "extraordinary circumstances."

The purpose of requiring the probation violation hearing to be scheduled along with the pretrial hearing on the new criminal case in the same-court situation (section (b)(iii)) is not only to avoid delay of the probation hearing, but also to create an opportunity for a disposition of the criminal case that takes into account the probation disposition. Most criminal cases, in fact, are disposed of by plea or admission. It is appropriate to provide the defendant an opportunity to consider whether to submit a plea or admission that may take into account the outcome of the probation violation hearing. The defendant's right to a trial on the new criminal charge remains unaffected.

The last sentence of section (b)(iii) is intended to indicate that the prompt scheduling of the probation violation hearing should drive the scheduling of the pretrial hearing on the new charge. Thus, in a court in which the next regularly available date for a pretrial hearing is not consistent with the need for a prompt hearing on the alleged probation violation in terms of public safety implications, a prompt date (even a minimum seven-day date where appropriate) should be given even if this means scheduling the pretrial hearing on the new criminal charge prior to the date it would otherwise receive.

In the different-court situation, the date of the Pretrial Hearing on the criminal charge should be indicated on the copy of the Notice sent to the probation court. This will allow the probation court to schedule the violation hearing before that date.

Under G.L. c. 258B, s. 3(*o*), victims have a right to be notified by a probationer's supervising probation officer if a probationer "seeks to modify a restitution order." This does not appear to require a supervising probation officer to send a copy of the Notice of Probation Violation and Hearing to a victim, even if modification of a restitution order is a possible outcome of the hearing.

Notice to District Attorney

In both the same-court and the different-court situations, the rule requires that a copy of the Notice of Probation Violation and Hearing be provided to the District Attorney. The relevant law, G.L. c. 279, s. 3, gives the District Attorney the right to receive a copy of the notice and appear at such hearings only where the original conviction for which the probationer is on probation involves at least one felony. However, the rule reflects the position that the District Attorney should be allowed to appear at all such hearings. It allows the District Attorney to decide which hearings to attend and provides as an alternative the submission of a written statement. (Rule 5(f)) This is appropriate, given the fact that some misdemeanor charges may have greater public safety implications than felony charges, e.g., drunk driving, domestic assault and battery and violation of restraining orders. Also, the District Attorney has certain obligations to victims of crime regarding probation violation hearings that can be met only if the District Attorney is informed of the scheduling of such hearings. G.L. c. 258B, s. 3. See Rule 5(f) and related commentary.

Rule 4. Commencement of Violation Proceedings: Violations Other Than Charged Criminal Conduct

(a) General. This rule prescribes the procedures to be undertaken regarding alleged violations of probation that do not involve or include criminal conduct charged in a criminal complaint.

(b) Issuance and Service of Notice. When a probation officer of a court that has issued a probation order determines that a probationer has violated any condition of that order other than the alleged commission of a crime as charged in a criminal complaint, that probation officer shall decide whether to commence probation violation proceedings. Such decision shall be made in accordance with the rules and regulations of the Office of the Commissioner of Probation, provided, however, that probation violation proceedings shall be commenced (1) upon the issuance of an indictment, (2) when the judge issuing the probation order orders that such proceedings are to be commenced upon an alleged violation of one or more conditions of probation, or (3) when the commencement of such proceedings is required by statutory mandate. In any case, a judge of the court may order the commencement of violation proceedings.

The Notice of Probation Violation and Hearing shall be served on the probationer in hand or by first-class mail, unless the court orders otherwise. Service of the Notice in hand or by first-class mail shall be noted in the court record. Out-of-court service other than by first-class mail shall require a written return of service. A copy of each Notice of Probation Violation and Hearing shall be provided to the District Attorney forthwith upon its issuance.

(c) Contents of Notice. The Notice of Probation Violation and Hearing shall set forth the conditions of the probation order that the Probation Department alleges have been violated and shall order the probationer to appear at a specific date and time for the express purpose of the appointment of counsel, if necessary, and the scheduling of a probation violation hearing.

(d) Scheduling of Hearing. Upon appearance of the probationer in accordance with the Notice required by section (c), the court shall appoint counsel, if necessary, and schedule a probation violation hearing for a date certain, said date to be no less than seven days later unless the probationer waives said seven-day notice period. Except in extraordinary circumstances, said hearing date shall not be later than 30 days after said appearance if the probationer objects thereto.

Adopted December 2, 1999, effective January 3, 2000.

Commentary

This rule provides the procedures to be followed when it is alleged that a probationer has violated any probation conditions that do not include criminal behavior as alleged that a probationer criminal complaint, that is, any violation not governed by Rule 3. This includes allegations of criminal acts that are not the subject of a criminal complaint, allegations of a crime set forth in an indictment, any alleged violation of general probation conditions 2 (to report to the probation officer as required), 3 (to notify the probation officer of any change of employment or address) or 4 (to obtain permission to leave the Commonwealth), and any alleged violation of any special condition of probation.

Section (b) of the rule defers to the Rules and Regulations of the Office of the Commissioner of Probation (OCP) regarding the commencement of such proceedings. Unlike charged criminal acts, it is appropriate that other alleged violations be the subject of violation proceedings only in accordance with professional probation policies and standards. These policies provide an appropriate degree of discretion and also provide a procedure for administrative proceedings where the alleged violation does not warrant the commencement of court proceedings. Such policies require collaboration with the Presiding Justice at each court. Notwithstanding a probation officer's decision, in accordance with Probation Department regulations, not to commence proceedings in a particular case, a judge may order such proceedings to be commenced.

There are three exceptions to the reliance on OCP regulations and policies under section (b). The first requires commencement of proceedings upon the issuance of an indictment. The rationale for this is the same as for the required commencement of proceedings upon the issuance of a criminal complaint. See commentary to Rule 3. The second allows the sentencing judge to require in the probation order that upon certain alleged violations, a probation violation hearing must be commenced. The third exception is that a violation hearing must be commenced if required by law. Perhaps the most notable example of the last is G.L. c. 209A, s. 7, which provides as follows:

> If the defendant ordered to undergo treatment [after being convicted of a violation of a restraining order issued under G.L. c. 209A] has received a suspended sentence, the original sentence shall be reimposed if the defendant fails to participate in said program as required by the terms of his probation.

The statute would appear to require that probation violation proceedings be commenced upon an allegation of such a violation, and that revocation be ordered if the violation is found.

The rationale for providing a copy of each Notice of Probation Violation and Hearing to the District Attorney is the same as for notices in proceedings under Rule 3. It allows the District Attorney to decide which hearings to appear at and permits the District Attorney to fulfill certain legal obligations to victims and witnesses involved in the original criminal case in which the probation order was issued. See Rule 5(f) and related commentary.

Sections (c) and (d) provide for notice to the probationer of the alleged violation and ordering him or her to appear in court on a specific date and time so that the issue of counsel may be addressed and the violation hearing scheduled. The minimum notice period for the hearing is seven days, unless waived.

In cases where custody of a probationer is warranted pending the hearing, the probationer may be arrested with or without a warrant pursuant to G.L. c. 279, s. 3, and held if probable cause is found at a preliminary violation hearing following the arrest. See Rule 8.

Rule 5. Conduct of Hearings

(a) In General. Probation violation hearings shall be conducted by a judge, in open court, on the record, with such flexibility and informality as the court may deem appropriate, consistent with the requirements of this rule and applicable law. All testimony shall be taken under oath. The presentation of the case against the probationer shall be the responsibility of the probation officer assigned by the Chief Probation Officer of the court. The probationer shall be entitled to the assistance of counsel, including the appointment of counsel for probationers determined by the court to be indigent.

(b) Requirement of Two–Step Procedure. Probation revocation hearings shall proceed in two distinct steps, the first to adjudicate the factual issue of whether the alleged violation or violations occurred, the second to determine the disposition of the matter, if a violation of probation is found by the court to have occurred.

(c) Adjudication of Alleged Violation. Probation violation hearings shall commence with a statement by the probation officer describing the violation or violations alleged in the Notice of Violation and Hearing, and shall proceed with a presentation of the evidence supporting said allegations. The probationer shall be permitted to present evidence relevant to the issue of the alleged violation. Each party shall be permitted to cross-examine witnesses produced by the opposing party. Hearsay evidence shall be admitted by the court in accordance with Rule 6, provided that the court shall enforce any statutory privileges unless waived and any legally required disqualifications. The probation officer shall have the burden of proving the alleged violations with or without the participation of the District Attorney as provided below. The standard of proof at such hearings shall be the civil standard of preponderance of the evidence. After the presentation of evidence, both the probation officer and the probationer shall be permitted to make a closing statement.

(d) Dispositional Decision. If the court finds that the probationer has violated one or more conditions of probation as alleged, the probation officer shall recommend to the court a disposition consistent with the dispositional options set forth in Rule 7(d), below, and may present argument and evidence in support of that recommendation. The probationer shall be permitted to present argument and evidence relevant to disposition and to propose dispositional terms.

(e) Continuances. Probation violation hearings shall be continued only by a judge and for good cause shown. The reason for any continuance shall be stated by the judge and set forth in the record of the case. No continuance shall be ordered other than to a date certain and for a specific purpose, and as provided in Rule 7(a). The pendency of a criminal action on a charge which also constitutes an alleged violation of probation shall not be grounds for a continuance of the probation violation hearing.

(f) Participation of the District Attorney.

(i) *In General.* The District Attorney may participate in probation violation hearings as provided in G.L. c. 279, s. 3, and such participation shall be permitted in any such proceeding regardless of whether the criminal case in which the probation order was issued involved a felony charge.

(ii) *Coordination with the Probation Department.* If the District Attorney intends to appear at a probation violation hearing, he or she shall confer prior to the hearing with the probation officer responsible for presenting the matter to the court, for the purpose of coordinating the District Attorney's involvement in the hearing with the planned presentation of the probation officer.

(iii) *Presentation of Evidence.* The District Attorney may present and examine witnesses at the hearing and may examine witnesses presented by the probation officer, and may cross-examine witnesses presented by the defendant. The probationer may cross-examine witnesses presented by the District Attorney. The District Attorney shall be responsible for the attendance of every witness he or she wishes to present, and for the summoning of such witnesses.

(iv) *Finding and Disposition.* After the presentation of evidence, the District Attorney may make a statement regarding the factual issue of whether one or more violations of probation has occurred. If the court finds that the probationer has violated one or more of the conditions of probation as alleged in the Notice of Violation and Hearing, the District Attorney may be heard regarding the court's disposition of the matter. The District Attorney may present his or her dispositional recommendations orally or in writing.

Adopted December 2, 1999, effective January 3, 2000.

Commentary

Probation revocation hearings are not part of a criminal prosecution, and for this reason a probationer need not be provided with the full panoply of constitutional protections applicable at a criminal trial. *Gagnon v. Scarpelli*, 411 U.S. 778, 782, 93 S. Ct. 1756, 1759 (1973). Indeed, case law has sought to preserve the flexible, informal nature of probation revocation hearings. See *Black v. Romano*, 471 U.S. 606, 105 S. Ct. 2254 (1985).

On the other hand, the probationer's liberty is potentially at stake in violation proceedings, and therefore certain due process protections are required. As set forth for parole revocation in *Morrissey v. Brewer*, 408 U.S. 471, 92 S. Ct. 2593 (1972) and made applicable to probation revocation by *Gagnon v. Scarpelli*, 411 U.S. 778, 93 S. Ct. 1756 (1973), there are six such fundamental due process requirements: (1) written notice of the claimed violations of probation, (2) disclosure to the probationer of the evidence against him, (3) opportunity to be heard in person and to present witnesses and documentary evidence, (4) the right to confront and cross-examine adverse witnesses (unless a hearing officer specifically finds good cause for not allowing confrontation), (5) a neutral and detached hearing body, members of which need not be judicial officers or lawyers, and (6) a written statement by the fact finder as to the evidence relied on and reasons for revoking probation.

This rule is intended to provide an orderly, relatively informal and flexible procedure for probation violation hearings, but one in which all required and appropriate due process safeguards are ensured.

General Requirements

Section (a) requires several fundamental procedural elements: a judicial procedure in open court, testimony under oath and the creation of a record. With regard to the record, Rule 11 of the Special Rules of the District Courts of Massachusetts, "Recording of Court Proceedings," requires that such proceedings be electronically recorded. Any District Court judge may conduct the hearing; the original sentencing judge is not required.

One of the six fundamental due process requirements for probation violation hearings, as provided in *Gagnon v. Scarpelli*, 411 U.S. 778, 93 S. Ct. 1756 (1973), is "a neutral and detached hearing body." This requirement would appear to preclude the model by which a judge would take the initiative in the proceeding, as in an inquest, and the probation officer remain essentially passive in the role of a witness. Accordingly, the rule requires the probation officer, who is the "accuser," to present the case, with the judge remaining in the traditional neutral role. This does not prevent the judge from asking appropriate questions, nor is it inconsistent with the role of the probation officer as witness. The probation officer must provide evidence under oath and is subject to cross-examination.

It should be noted that in probation violation hearings the exclusionary rule does not apply if the police were unaware that the defendant was a probationer. *Commonwealth v. Olsen*, 405 Mass. 491, 541 N.E.2d 1003 (1989) (evidence seized in violation of Fourth Amendment was admissible in probation violation proceeding, where police who seized evidence neither knew nor had reason to know of probationary status of person whose property was seized). There is no Massachusetts decision on whether the exclusionary rule applies in these proceedings where police are aware that the person is on probation.

Regarding the right to counsel, the rule goes beyond current law by providing the right to counsel regardless of whether the probationer faces the possibility of imprisonment if probation is revoked. See *Commonwealth v. Faulkner*, 418 Mass. 352, 638 N.E.2d 1 (1994) (probationer at probation violation hearing has right to counsel if revocation might result in imprisonment).

Two-step Proceeding

Section (b) imposes the critical requirement of a two-stage proceeding. As observed by the Supreme Court of the United States,

> the decision to revoke probation typically involves two distinct components: (1) a retrospective factual question whether the probationer has violated a condition of probation; and (2) a discretionary determination by the sentencing authority whether violation of a condition warrants revocation of probation.

Black v. Romano, 471 U.S. 606, 611, 105 S. Ct. 2254, 2257 (1985), as quoted in *Commonwealth v. Marvin*, 417 Mass. 291, 295, 629 N.E.2d 1317, 1320 (1994) (Liacos, C.J., dissenting).

This dichotomy is further reflected in Massachusetts law:

> At the revocation hearing, the judge must determine, as a factual matter, whether the defendant has violated the conditions of his probation. If the judge determines that the defendant is in violation, he can either revoke the probation and sentence the defendant or, if appropriate, modify the terms of his probation.

Commonwealth v. Durling, 407 Mass. 108, 111, 551 N.E.2d 1193, 1195 (1990).

This distinction is an important one. The factual decision that a probation violation has occurred in no way compels an order of revocation. The court has wide dispositional latitude if a violation is found. See Rule 7(d). However, even if an alleged violation is relatively minor and, in all likelihood will not warrant revocation, it is important that it be adjudicated. It is essential for effective probation that a record of compliance and non-compliance with probation orders be maintained.

In addition, the distinction between the factual determination and the disposition must be maintained because different legal requirements are involved. For example, the factual issue of whether an alleged violation has occurred must be decided based on a preponderance of the evidence, *Commonwealth v. Holmgren*, 421 Mass. 224, 656 N.E.2d 577 (1995), while the dispositional decision is a matter of judicial discretion. *McHoul v. Commonwealth*, 365 Mass. 465, 469–470, 312 N.E.2d 539, 543 (1974). Similarly, the "seriousness" of the alleged violation is irrelevant to whether it occurred, while it is relevant to the question of appropriate disposition.

Adjudication of Violation

Section (c) sets out the basic requirements for how the first step of the hearing, adjudication of the alleged violation, should proceed. It ensures both parties the right to present evidence and cross-examine adverse witnesses. The court has some discretion in limiting cross-examination involving irrelevant or redundant questioning. See *Commonwealth v. Odoardi*, 397 Mass. 28, 34, 489 N.E.2d 674, 678 (1986). Section (c) also entitles both parties to make a closing statement. In *Commonwealth v. Marvin*, 417 Mass. 291, 295, 629 N.E.2d 1317, 1320 (1994), the court declined "to impose a universal due process requirement that a defendant in a probation revocation hearing has an absolute right to make a closing argument." However, that case goes on to state that it would be a "better practice" to permit a probationer to present at least a brief closing argument. The provision in this rule is intended to ensure that this better practice is provided for both parties.

Disposition

Section (d) provides that both parties may be heard regarding disposition, assuming the court finds that one or more alleged violations was committed. The court's dispositional options are provided in Rule 7. The probationer's right to be heard and present evidence regarding disposition implicate due process considerations. See *Commonwealth v. Odoardi*, 397 Mass. 28, 489 N.E.2d 674 (1986).

Continuances

Section (e) sets out certain requirements for continuances. It expressly eliminates "tracking," i.e., continuing a probation violation hearing to await disposition of the criminal case involving the charge that is also the alleged probation violation. The reason for this rule is that, on the one hand, there is no basis in law or in terms of fairness to the probationer for such a continuance, and, on the other hand, proceeding without delay on the alleged violation is of great importance in terms of the primary goals of probation, which are rehabilitation of the probationer and protection of the public. *Commonwealth v. LaFrance*, 402 Mass. 789, 795, 525 N.E.2d 379, 383 (1988) (citations omitted). The rule *does* provide for continuances where good cause is shown and the reason for the continuance is stated by the judge and set forth on the record.

The Supreme Judicial Court has long made clear that there is no prerequisite that the probationer be convicted of a criminal charge to permit that criminal conduct to be used as the basis of a probation revocation.

> If the act alleged to be a violation of probation is made the subject of a criminal complaint, the commencement of the criminal prosecution does not preclude the revocation of the earlier probation nor does it require that the revocation proceedings be deferred until the completion of the new criminal proceeding.

Rubera v. Commonwealth, 371 Mass. 177, 181, 355 N.E.2d 800, 803 (1976) and cases cited.

After analyzing the federal constitutional law relevant to the point and the precedents from other states, the court in *Rubera* went on to explain the policy reasons that favor proceeding with revocation proceedings and not awaiting the outcome of the criminal case:

> We are aware that the practice which was followed in revoking the petitioner's probation in this case was not in accord with the procedure suggested by the ABA Project on Standards for Criminal Justice, Standards Relating to Probation § 5.3, at 62–63 (Approved Draft 1970), that "[a] revocation proceeding based solely upon commission of another crime ordinarily should not be initiated prior to the disposition of that charge." [citation omitted] That standard seems to impose an unreasonable and unfair burden on law enforcement authorities by placing them in the dilemma of having to decide between (a) having to forgo criminal prosecution of a person who is on probation and who appears to have committed another offense until they have first pursued steps to revoke his probation on the basis of his conduct in ordinary proceedings without reliance on any subsequent criminal conviction, or (b) having to start criminal prosecution promptly on the later offense and then being prevented from trying to revoke his earlier probation until after the later prosecution has run its full course which, in the present state of our criminal dockets, would amount to arming the defendant with the weapon of potential delay with which he could forestall termination of the proceeding by endless appeals. We decline to impose the burden of such a choice on either probation officers or prosecutors.

Rubera v. Commonwealth, supra, at 184–185, 355 N.E.2d 800, 805 (1976).

See also, *Commonwealth v. Holmgren*, 421 Mass. 224, 656 N.E.2d 577 (1995), which held that a probation violation hearing may proceed on a charge of a new crime, even if the defendant has been acquitted of that crime, because the standard of proof at a probation hearing is lower than the standard at a criminal trial. In other words, an acquittal, or the possibility of an acquittal, is irrelevant to a probation violation proceeding because failure to convict under the "reasonable doubt" standard neither precludes nor is inconsistent with a finding of a probation violation under the "preponderance of the evidence" standard.

The only legal relationship between a probation violation hearing and a criminal prosecution for the same alleged criminal conduct is that, if the criminal case *does* go forward before the probation hearing and results in a conviction, that conviction will be evidence of a probation violation and no independent finding of the underlying facts is required of the judge. *Commonwealth v. Maggio*, 414 Mass. 193, 605 N.E.2d 1247 (1993).

<u>District Attorney Participation</u>

Section (f) addresses the subject of participation by the District Attorney. Rules 3 and 4 require the court to provide a copy of every Notice of Probation Violation and Hearing to the District Attorney. Section (f) of this rule is intended to clarify the involvement of the District Attorney in those cases where he or she decides to participate, consistent with the statutory provisions of G.L. c. 279, s. 3.

It should be noted that as a constitutional matter, probation functions are within the judicial branch, and the office of the District Attorney is considered within the executive branch. *Commonwealth v. Tate*, 34 Mass. App. Ct. 446, 447–448, 612 N.E.2d 686, 688 (1993) and cases cited. Under the Massachusetts Constitution, Pt. 1 Art. 30, the branches must maintain a separation of governmental powers.

> That separateness does not, however, lead to the conclusion that a district attorney's office may not assist the probation service in presenting evidence in support of a position that the probation service had decided upon.
>
> * * * * *
>
> [P]robation officers are only aided, not interfered with, when district attorneys, upon invitation, conduct examination of witnesses and present evidence.

Id. at 448, 612 N.E.2d at 688, and cases cited.

Thus the right of District Attorneys to present evidence and witnesses, and to examine and cross-examine witnesses at these proceedings would appear to be constitutionally acceptable as long as it does not fundamentally interfere with probation.

Rule 6. Hearsay Evidence

(a) Admissibility of Hearsay Evidence. Hearsay evidence shall be admissible at probation violation hearings.

(b) Sufficiency of Evidence When Case Rests Solely on Hearsay. Where the sole evidence submitted to prove a violation of probation is hearsay, that evidence shall be sufficient only if the court finds in writing (1) that such evidence is substantially trustworthy and demonstrably reliable and (2), if the alleged violation is charged or uncharged criminal behavior, that the probation officer has good cause for proceeding without a witness with personal knowledge of the evidence presented.

Adopted December 2, 1999, effective January 3, 2000.

Commentary

Probation violation hearings often involve evidence in the form of records, documents and statements that constitute hearsay, that is, "an extrajudicial statement offered to prove the truth of the matter asserted." *Commonwealth v. Keizer*, 377 Mass 264, 269 n.4, 385 N.E.2d 1001, 1004 (1979). Common examples of hearsay evidence used at these hearings are police reports used as evidence of the probationer's criminal behavior, and correspondence from programs such as batterers' treatment programs used as evidence of the probationer's failure to complete the program in compliance with the probation order.

This rule is based almost exclusively on the opinion in *Commonwealth v. Durling*, 407 Mass. 108, 551 N.E.2d 1193 (1990), the leading case on the use of hearsay evidence at probation violation hearings. It is divided into separate sections, one on the *admissibility* of hearsay, the other on the *sufficiency of hearsay as a matter of law* when it is the only evidence presented against the probationer.

Admissibility

Section (a) states simply that hearsay is admissible at probation violation hearings. The Supreme Judicial Court "has always allowed the use of hearsay at probation revocation hearings." *Commonwealth v. Durling, supra*, at 114, 551 N.E.2d at 1197. The admissibility of hearsay is based on the principles set forth in *Morrissey* and *Gagnon*. The revocation process "should be flexible enough to consider evidence including letters, affidavits, and other material that would not be admissible in an adversary criminal trial." *Morrissey v. Brewer*, 408 U.S. 471, 489, 92 S. Ct. 2593, 2604 (1972). Similarly, the Supreme Court has sanctioned the "use where appropriate of the conventional substitutes for live testimony including affidavits, depositions and documentary evidence." *Gagnon v. Scarpelli*, 411 U.S. 778, 782 n.5, 93 S. Ct. 1756, 1760 n.5 (1973).

It has been held that if hearsay evidence qualifies under any of the legal exceptions to the hearsay rule (e.g., business record, excited utterance, dying declaration) it is presumptively reliable. *Durling, supra*, at 118, 551 N.E.2d at 1198. However, in keeping with the informal nature of these hearings and the fact that the case against the probationer is the responsibility of a probation officer rather than a trained criminal prosecutor, it would appear that the court should make a determination of the reliability of any hearsay, rather than engage in an argument on whether the hearsay qualifies as an exception to the hearsay rule so as to merit presumptively reliable status. In other words, if the court determines that a record of a drug treatment center is reliable, it is irrelevant as to whether it qualifies as a "business record." An example of hearsay that might be found unreliable, and thus not worthy of the court's consideration, would be a second-or third-hand out-of-court statement, or a statement that is vague or internally contradictory or inconsistent.

Sufficiency

Section (b) of the rule addresses an issue quite different from admissibility, namely, the legal sufficiency of hearsay evidence where hearsay is the only evidence of the probationer's alleged violation. In such cases, the probationer has no opportunity to confront a witness with personal knowledge and test the reliability of that evidence by cross-examination. This deprivation of the right to confrontation of witnesses implicates due process considerations. However, the Supreme Court in *Durling* made clear that since a probationer's liberty interest is conditional, so too is the probationer's right to confront witnesses, and that right can be denied for "good cause."

The court's description of "good cause," in *Durling* is somewhat unclear. On the one hand, the court indicates that "good cause" for denying the probationer the right to confront witnesses "has thus far been defined in terms of difficulty and expense of procuring witnesses *in combination with* 'demonstrably reliable' or 'clearly reliable' evidence." *Durling, supra*, at 120, 551 N.E.2d at 1200 (emphasis added).

In fact, the court defines the question in *Durling* in terms of this two-pronged issue:

> The judge in this case relied solely on hearsay in revoking the defendant's probation. The judge did not make any express determination that there was good cause for denying the defendant the right to confront a witness with personal knowledge. Nor did the judge make any determination whether the proffered hearsay was reliable.

Durling, supra, at 115, 551 N.E.2d at 1197.

However, in contrast to this two-pronged definition, the *Durling* court also defines "good cause" solely in terms of the reliability of the hearsay evidence:

> In our view, a showing that the proffered evidence bears substantial indicia of reliability and is substantially trustworthy is a showing of good cause obviating the need for confrontation.

Durling, supra, at 118, 551 N.E.2d at 1199.

Despite this apparent conflict, the opinion appears to settle on the two-pronged definition of good cause:

> On the whole, the resolution of the confrontation issue depends on the totality of the circumstances in each case.... If the Commonwealth has "good cause" for not using a witness with personal knowledge, *and* instead offers reliable hearsay or other evidence, then the requirements of due process are satisfied.

Durling, supra, at 118–119, 551 N.E.2d at 1199 (emphasis added).

Also,

> The substantial reliability of the police reports in this case, *coupled with* the practical difficulty of presenting live testimony, discussed earlier, convinces us that the District Court judge could properly base his order of revocation on the evidence presented.

Durling, supra, at 122, 551 N.E.2d at 1201 (emphasis added).

In *Commonwealth v. Calvo*, 41 Mass. App. Ct. 903, 668 N.E.2d 846 (1996) (rescript), the Appeals Court interpreted *Durling* to require only a showing that hearsay evidence bears substantial indicia of reliability and is substantially trustworthy in order to meet the "good cause" test, obviating the right to confrontation. In *Calvo*, "good cause" was held not to require any showing that a live witness was unavailable.

This rule takes a middle ground, requiring that in *all* cases where the only evidence of an alleged probation violation is hearsay there must be a finding that the hearsay is substantially trustworthy and demonstrably reliable, and requiring a showing of why a live witness is unavailable when the alleged probation violation is based on charged or uncharged criminal behavior.

Trustworthiness and Reliability of Hearsay

There are at least five criteria for the court's determination of whether a given piece of hearsay evidence is "substantially trustworthy" and "demonstrably reliable," namely, whether the out-of-court statement:

(1) is factually detailed, rather than generalized and conclusory;

(2) is based on personal knowledge and direct observation by the source;

(3) is corroborated by evidence submitted by the probationer;

(4) was provided under circumstances that support the veracity of the source (e.g., was provided under the pains and penalties of perjury or subject to criminal penalties for providing false information);

(5) was provided by a disinterested witness.

This list of factors for determining reliability is taken directly from *Durling*, except item (5), which is taken from *Commonwealth v. Delaney*, 36 Mass. App. Ct. 930, 932 n.4, 629 N.E.2d 1007, 1009 n.4 (1994) (rescript), a case applying the *Durling* test.

Good Cause for Absence of Witness

There are three factors mentioned in *Durling* for determining good cause for the absence of a live witness, namely,

(1) the distance a witness would have to travel to get to court,

(2) the costs the witness (or his or her public or private employer) would have to incur if the witness were compelled to appear, and

(3) the difficulty in scheduling the probation violation hearing at a time convenient to the witness and all other participants.

Hearsay Test Where the Alleged Violation Is Criminal Conduct

One of the most common alleged violations of probation is alleged criminal conduct. In many of these cases, evidence of the alleged violation will be a police report. Under the rule, there are two issues if the police report is the only evidence presented: reliability of the report and the reason for the absence of a live witness.

In establishing the requisite reliability of the police reports in *Durling*, the Court stressed that the two police reports related facts *observed by the officers personally*, and were factually detailed rather than general statements or conclusions. "We think the factual detail is indicative of reliability." *Durling, supra*, at 121, 551 N.E.2d at 1200 (citation omitted). The Court also mentioned the similarity of the two reports and the fact that the two officers were from different departments. Thus, in *Durling*, the police reports corroborated each other.

The *Durling* Court also stressed that in determining "good cause" to justify a finding of violation solely on hearsay, the court had to balance the interests of the probationer and those of the Commonwealth and look to the "totality of the circumstances." It would appear that such balancing includes the concept that the more reliable the hearsay evidence, the less stringent the test regarding the practical reasons for absence of a live witness. Conversely, where the reliability of the hearsay is not as high as it was in *Durling*, (which involved the unusual circumstance of two separate police reports) it would appear that the justification for the absence of a witness would have to be that much stronger.

Hearsay Test Where the Alleged Violation Is Something Other Than Criminal Conduct

The rule does not require a showing of why the live witness is unavailable where the alleged violation is something other than criminal conduct. Thus, for example, if the alleged violation were failure to attend a rehabilitation program, a report from the program, though hearsay, would be sufficient evidence if it met the reliability test of *Durling*, without regard to why the live witness were not present.

For cases applying the *Durling* test, see *Commonwealth v. Delaney*, 36 Mass. App. Ct. 930, 629 N.E.2d 1007 (1994) (finding of violation based on hearsay statement reversed; statement did not meet reliability standard comparable to police reports in *Durling* and witness was available to testify); and *Commonwealth v. Joubert*, 38 Mass. App. Ct. 943, 647 N.E.2d 1238 (1995) (revocation order reversed because hearsay statements of a child were not sufficiently reliable and findings indicate judge may have relied on them as the basis of decision).

Rule 7. Finding and Disposition

(a) Requirement of Finding. Upon the completion of the presentation of evidence and closing arguments on the issue of whether the probationer has violated one or more conditions of a probation order, as alleged, the court shall make a determination of that issue. The court shall decide the matter promptly and shall not continue the proceeding generally.

(b) Finding of No Violation. If the court determines that the probation officer has failed to prove by a preponderance of the evidence that the probationer committed a violation alleged in the Notice of Probation Violation and Hearing, the court shall expressly so find and said finding shall be entered on the record.

(c) Finding of Violation; Written Findings of Fact. If the court determines that the probation officer has proved by a preponderance of the evidence that the probationer has violated one or more conditions of probation as alleged in the Notice of Probation Violation and Hearing, or if the probationer admits or stipulates to such violation, the court shall expressly so find, and said finding shall be entered on the record. The court shall make written findings of fact to support the finding of a violation, stating the evidence relied upon.

(d) Disposition After Finding of Violation. After the court has entered a finding that a violation of probation has occurred, the court may order any of the following dispositions set forth below, as it deems appropriate. These dispositional alternatives shall be the exclusive options available to the court. In determining its disposition, the court shall give appropriate weight to the recommendation of the Probation Department and such factors as public safety; the seriousness of any crime of which the probationer was convicted; the nature of the probation violation; the occurrence of any previous violations and the impact on any victim of the underlying crime, as well as any mitigating factors.

(i) *Continuance of Probation.* The court may decline to modify or revoke probation and, instead, issue to the probationer such admonition or instruction as it may deem appropriate.

(ii) *Termination.* The court may order that the probation be considered completed and terminate the probation order.

(iii) *Modification.* The court may modify the conditions of probation. Such modification may include the addition of reasonable conditions and the extension of the duration of the probation order.

(iv) *Revocation; Statement of Reasons.* The court may order that the order of probation be revoked. If the court orders revocation, it shall state the reasons therefor in writing.

(e) Execution of Suspended Sentence; Stay of Execution. Upon revocation of a probation order, any sentence that was imposed for the crime involved, the execution of which was suspended, shall be ordered executed forthwith; provided, however, that such execution may be stayed (1) pending appeal in accordance with Mass.R.Crim.P. 31, or (2) at the court's discretion, and upon the probationer's motion, to provide a brief period of time for the probationer to attend to personal matters prior to commencement of a sentence of incarceration. The execution of such sentence shall not be otherwise stayed.

(f) Imposition of Sentence Where No Sentence Previously Imposed. Upon revocation of probation in a case where no sentence was imposed following conviction, the court shall impose a sentence as provided by law.

Adopted December 2, 1999, effective January 3, 2000.

Commentary

Requirement of a Finding

This rule addresses the court's two separate tasks upon completion of the violation hearing. Section (a) requires the court to adjudicate the factual issue of whether a violation has occurred. It expressly eliminates as an option a "general continuance."

The requirement that a finding be made on the issue of violation is based on several considerations. First, and most important, it is essential for the credibility of the probation order that the issue raised by the alleged violation be resolved. Even if the alleged violation involves a relatively minor matter, the likelihood of successful change in the probationer's behavior is diminished if the court temporizes in its role as finder of fact. If a violation has occurred, the probationer should be confronted with that fact. If no violation is found, the probationer is entitled to that finding on the record. No useful judicial or probation purpose is served by failure to adjudicate after the evidence has been presented. A failure by the court to decide the issue can foster the perception on the part of the probationer that if the court does not take the matter seriously, neither should he or she.

Second, adjudication of the violation charge does not limit the court's wide discretion regarding disposition. As addressed further in the rule, if a violation is found, the court's options range from a simple warning with the current terms of probation continued, to a revocation of probation, which in many instances will result in incarceration.

Third, the adjudication of a violation will establish an appropriate record of the probationer's non-compliance, which can be essential to an appropriate disposition if a subsequent violation occurs. Minor violations, even if they do not warrant significant sanctions in themselves, may provide important information in any subsequent proceedings.

It should be noted that the "seriousness" of the violation, its impact or lack of impact on any victim and the nature of the underlying crime are irrelevant to whether the alleged violation occurred. Those matters relate solely to the court's disposition if a violation is found.

In referring to the situation where the court finds no violation, section (b) of the rule reiterates three important points: the probation officer bears the burden of proof, the standard of proof is a preponderance of the evidence, and only a violation that has been formally alleged in the Notice of Probation Violation and Hearing may be found.

Section (c) of the rule repeats these three points regarding the finding of a violation and adds that a violation may be found based on the probationer's admission. It also adds the requirements of findings of fact and a statement of the evidence relied on, which are due process requirements. *Morrissey v. Brewer*, 408 U.S. 471, 489, 92 S.Ct. 2593, 2604 (1972). Failure to make findings and a statement of the evidence relied on appears to be reversible error. See *Fay v. Commonwealth*, 379 Mass. 498, 504–505, 399 N.E.2d 11, 15–16 (1980). The Court in *Fay* also ruled that *written* findings were not required as a matter of due process, where such findings were announced orally on the record in the presence of the probationer and the probationer subsequently obtained a written copy in the form of a transcript. *Fay v. Commonwealth*, 379 Mass. at 504–505, 399 N.E.2d 11, 15–16 (1980). The rule, however, requires that the findings and evidence relied on be stated in writing.

Disposition

Section (d) of the rule sets out four specific types of dispositions that are available to the court if a violation is found. These are expressly described as an exclusive list of the court's options, though they provide a comprehensive range of sanctions. The rule also provides factors that the court should consider on disposition, namely:

· the recommendation of the Probation Department

· public safety

· seriousness of the crime of which the probationer was found guilty

· nature of the violation

· record of any previous violation

· impact on a victim of the underlying crime

Counsel is free to argue, and the court is free to consider, any relevant mitigating factors.

Regarding the choice of disposition, two factors are essential: (1) disposition is a matter of the court's discretion. *McHoul v. Commonwealth*, 365 Mass. 465, 469–470, 312 N.E.2d 539, 543 (1974); *Commonwealth v. Durling*, 407 Mass.

108, 111, 551 N.E.2d 1193, 1195 (1990); and (2) disposition is not a punishment for the new crime, but rather relates to the underlying offense. *Commonwealth v. Odoardi*, 397 Mass. 28, 30, 489 N.E.2d 674, 675 (1986).

Section (d)(i) provides for continuance of probation. This may be appropriate where the violation is minor and the probationer has no history of previous violations. It can be completely appropriate for a probation officer to commence and successfully prosecute a probation violation proceeding and then recommend that the current probation terms merely be continued. This may reflect the probation officer's judgment that, though minor, the offense should be adjudicated to impress upon the probationer the importance of compliance, that a warning from the court is necessary to prevent more serious violations and that the violation should be a matter of record. The continuance of current probation terms despite a finding of violation is sometimes referred to as "reprobating" the probationer.

Section (d)(ii), provides for termination of probation. This outcome can be appropriate where the offense is minor and the court determines that the purpose of probation has been accomplished. It can also be appropriate in conjunction with the disposition of a new offense, where the probationer is already serving a sentence, and where the probationer is on probation in another court.

Under section (d)(iii), the court has the dispositional option of modifying the probationary terms after a finding of violation. It has been held that it is "a matter of well-established common law, that courts do possess [the authority to modify probation conditions], and that conditions of probation may be amended to serve 'the ends of justice and the best interests of both the public and the defendant.' " *Buckley v. Quincy Division of the District Court Dept.*, 395 Mass. 815, 817, 482 N.E.2d 511, 512 (1985), citing *Burns v. United States*, 287 U.S. 216, 221, 53 S. Ct. 154, 156 (1932).

The addition of reasonable conditions to an individual's probation does not constitute a revision or revocation of a sentence under Mass. R. Crim. P. 29. *Buckley, supra*, at 818–819, 482 N.E.2d at 513. The Court did not "define that point at which the modification is so drastic that it becomes the revision of a sentence subject to the requirements of rule 29," noting that the modification in *Buckley* was a nonpunitive rehabilitative measure, designed to facilitate the successful reintegration of the plaintiff into the community. *Buckley, supra*, at 818–819 n.5, 482 N.E.2d at 513 n.5.

It should be noted that the Court in *Buckley* was addressing a situation where conditions were added to a probation order without any finding of a violation, but rather based on an assessment by a probation officer. The Court ruled that a *supervising* court (as distinguished from a *sentencing* court) may not modify the conditions of probation without a material change in circumstances such as a violation of probation. It also indicated that a violation of probation *is* a material change in circumstances:

> Our holding does not limit whatever authority is held by the supervisory court to modify conditions where there has been a material change in circumstances (such as a violation of a condition of probation). Nor need we outline those situations in which the sentencing court might modify the terms of probation.

Buckley v. Quincy Div. of Dist. Court Dept., supra, at 820, 482 N.E.2d at 514.

Section (d)(iii) addresses issues left unaddressed in *Buckley* by affirmatively authorizing the court conducting a probation violation hearing to modify the conditions of probation upon a finding of violation.

Revocation; Stay after Revocation

Section (d)(iv) provides for the most serious sanction upon a finding of probation violation, namely, revocation of probation. Under *Commonwealth v. Holmgren*, 421 Mass. 224, 656 N.E.2d 577 (1995), any sentence that was imposed, but its execution suspended pending probation, must be ordered executed in its entirety upon revocation of probation. This ruling was based on an unambiguous statutory requirement in G.L. c. 279, s. 3.

The requirement of executing a suspended sentence upon revocation of probation is reflected in section (e), which also provides two specific bases for a stay of execution. This provision precludes any stay other than for (1) appeal or (2) a brief time for a probationer to attend to personal matters. A stay simply to avoid the execution of sentence, with or without the addition of new terms, is not allowed under the rule. There are several reasons for this. First, there appears to be no established legal basis for such a stay. Second, such a stay is inconsistent with the plain language of *Holmgren*. Third, the terms of such a stay are unenforceable. Conditions on the person's behavior during the stay cannot be ordered as probation—probation has been revoked. On the other hand, the court cannot condition the stay on unstated or vague conditions (e.g., "stay out of further trouble"), since a termination of the stay presumably requires incarceration, which, in turn, requires an opportunity for the person to be notified and heard regarding the factual issue of whether he or she violated the stay. One element of such a process would be specificity of the alleged violation. Even if conditions on such a stay *were* expressly stated in writing, they could not be enforced without a due process procedure similar to the same probation revocation procedure that has just been concluded. Since the person would not be on probation, there would be no one with authority to "prosecute" the alleged violation of the stay conditions. Perhaps most important, such a stay is impermissible because it implies that if the person successfully completes the stay, on whatever terms are imposed, written or unwritten, the sentence that had to be ordered executed pursuant to *Holmgren* somehow disappears.

Section (d)(iv) requires that, if the court decides to revoke probation, it must provide the reasons for that decision. A statement of reasons for deciding to revoke probation is a requirement of due process. *Gagnon v. Scarpelli*, 411 U.S. 778, 93 S. Ct. 1756 (1973). While the reasons need not be put in writing to ensure due process, *Fay v. Commonwealth*, 379 Mass. 498, 399 N.E.2d 11 (1980), the rule requires them in writing to ensure a clear and accessible record.

Disposition Where No Sentence Originally Imposed

Section (f) addresses the situation where the probationer was sentenced with "straight probation" on the underlying conviction. On the one hand, this means that upon a revocation of probation, there is no suspended sentence to be executed. On the other hand, the probationer is subject to any sentence for the underlying crime that is provided by law. Though it may appear illogical, this would appear to include a sentence involving probation, even though the triggering event for the imposition of such a sentence is a violation and revocation of the "straight" probation originally ordered. Presumably, if such post-revocation probation is imposed, the conditions and the consequences for any violation will take into account the fact that probation has already been violated.

Rule 8. Preliminary Violation Hearings

(a) Purpose. A preliminary probation violation hearing shall be conducted only when the Probation Department seeks to hold a probationer in custody on the basis of an alleged violation of probation pending the conduct of a full probation violation hearing. The issues to be determined at a preliminary probation violation hearing are whether probable cause exists to believe that the probationer has violated a condition of the probation order, and, if so, whether the probationer should be held in custody.

(b) Notice of Hearing. The probationer shall be given a written notice indicating the preliminary nature of the hearing, the alleged probation violation, and that the purpose of the hearing is to determine that there is probable cause to believe that he or she has committed that violation. The notice shall be served in hand when the probationer is before the court having been arrested on a new criminal charge, having been arrested for a probation violation, or for any other reason.

(c) Conduct of Hearing. Preliminary probation violation hearings shall be conducted by a judge or, if necessary, a magistrate, in a courtroom on the record, and shall proceed in an informal manner. The probationer shall be entitled to counsel. Following service of notice, as provided in section (b), above, and appointment of counsel, if necessary, the probationer shall be allowed a reasonable time to prepare for the hearing. At such hearing, the probation officer shall present evidence to support a finding of probable cause. The District Attorney may assist in the presentation of such evidence. The probationer shall be entitled to be heard in opposition. Testimony shall be taken under oath. The court shall admit such evidence as it deems relevant and appropriate. The proceeding shall be limited to the issue of probable cause to believe that the alleged violation of probation has occurred.

If probable cause is found, a probation violation hearing shall be scheduled, the probationer shall thereupon be served in hand with a notice of said hearing, and the court may order the probationer to be held in custody pending the conduct and completion of the scheduled final violation hearing. The court's decision whether to release the probationer pending the conduct and completion of the final probation violation hearing, notwithstanding a finding of probable cause on an alleged violation, shall include, but not necessarily be limited to:

i. the probationer's criminal record;

ii. the nature of the offense for which the probationer is on probation;

iii. the nature of the offense or offenses with which the probationer is newly charged, if any;

iv. the nature of any other pending alleged probation violations;

v. the likelihood of probationer's appearance at the final probation violation hearing if not held in custody; and

vi. the likelihood of incarceration if a violation is found following the final probation violation hearing.

If no probable cause is found, a probation violation hearing may be scheduled and the probationer thereupon served with notice thereof, but the probationer may not be held in custody pending said hearing based on the alleged probation violation.

(d) Bail. Upon a finding of probable cause and an order of custody, the court shall not consider or impose any terms of release such as bail, personal recognizance or otherwise as an alternative to such custody. Notwithstanding such order of probation custody, the court shall proceed to determine the issues of bail and pretrial detention ("dangerousness") on any newly charged offense, as provided by law.

Adopted December 2, 1999, effective January 3, 2000.

Commentary

Preliminary probation hearings are required only when the probationer is to be held in custody for an alleged probation violation pending the conduct of a full hearing.

> The purpose of the preliminary hearing is to protect the rights of the ... probationer who, being at liberty, is taken into custody for alleged violation of his ... probation conditions, and detained pending a final revocation hearing.

Fay v. Commonwealth, 379 Mass. 498, 504, 399 N.E.2d 11, 15 (1980) (citations omitted).

Thus, for example, there is no requirement of a preliminary hearing if the alleged probation violator already has received a probable cause hearing on the new crime and has been bound over to the grand jury. *Stefanik v. State Board of Parole*, 372 Mass. 726, 363 N.E.2d 1099 (1977). See also *Commonwealth v. Odoardi*, 397 Mass. 28, 33, 34, 489 N.E.2d 674, 677 (1986) (no preliminary hearing where probationer already incarcerated at the time of the proceeding on the alleged violation).

The issue of whether a probationer should be held in custody pending the conduct of a probation violation hearing can arise when a defendant is before the court on a separate matter (e.g., on arrest for a new criminal charge) or having been arrested with or without a warrant for a violation of probation. G.L. c. 279, s. 3.

The probationer is entitled to a preliminary hearing "at the time of his arrest and detention.... " *Commonwealth v. Odoardi*, 397 Mass. 28, 33, 489 N.E.2d 647, 677 (1986). That arrest can take place while the probationer is at liberty or when a probation officer takes custody of a probationer who is before the court on another matter, such as the charge of a new crime. Written notice must be given to the probationer at that time and the probationer and counsel must be given time to prepare for this hearing. If a continuance is requested and allowed, the custody resulting from the arrest will continue until the preliminary hearing (or a final hearing if the preliminary hearing is waived) is conducted.

The rule does not provide for notice of a preliminary probation violation hearing to be served on a probationer who is at liberty. If it is believed that a probationer who is at liberty has violated probation and should be in custody pending a hearing on that violation, custody should be effected by an arrest with or without a warrant, under G.L. c. 279, s. 3. If it is believed that a probationer who is at liberty has violated probation, but there is no need to hold him or her in custody pending a final hearing, there is no need to serve a notice of a preliminary hearing. Rather, a notice of a final hearing should be served.

At the preliminary probation violation hearing, the question of revocation or other disposition is not at issue, only the question of probable cause for the alleged violation. Of course, the preliminary hearing can be transformed into a "final" hearing if the defendant waives the minimum seven-day notice period and both the probationer and the Probation Department are willing to proceed immediately with either an admission or a hearing. Only in such instances will the issue of revocation or other disposition be appropriately addressed.

The rule provides no qualifications on the evidence that may be admitted at preliminary hearings, other than to state that the court may hear such evidence as it deems appropriate. The rules of evidence do not apply. There appears to be no law categorically disqualifying a judge who has conducted a preliminary hearing from conducting the subsequent final hearing. When no judge is available, a magistrate may conduct the preliminary hearing. See G.L. c. 221, ss. 62B and 62C(g), and Uniform Magistrate Rule 6.

Section (c) of the rule also provides that upon a finding of probable cause, the court *may* order the probationer to be held in custody pending the final hearing. A finding of probable cause does not require a custody order. The rule lists six factors that the court must consider when deciding whether to release the probationer notwithstanding the finding of probable cause on the alleged violation. The list is not exclusive and the rule does not attempt to assign relative weight to the factors.

Section (d) makes clear that bail and other terms of pretrial release have no application regarding a probationer's custody pending the conduct and completion of a final probation violation hearing. Bail and other conditions of pretrial release, including pretrial detention based on "dangerousness," under G.L. c. 276, ss. 58 and 58A, have no legal or conceptual relevance to custody on an alleged probation violation. They relate solely to a newly alleged crime. If the court finds probable cause for a probation violation, it may order the defendant into custody pending the final hearing on the violation. If the court does *not* find probable cause, the probationer cannot be held in custody *on the alleged violation*. Even if the probationer *is* held on the probation allegation, if he or she is also before the court on a new criminal charge, the court must address the terms of pretrial release. This issue is unrelated to custody on the probation charge. The prosecutor may want to be heard on the issue of bail or dangerousness because if the probation matter is promptly resolved, the defendant may be released from custody on the probation matter well before the criminal case is concluded.

Conversely, the issue of probation custody should be addressed regardless of whether or not the prosecutor plans to ask for high bail or pretrial detention based on dangerousness.

There appears to be no basis in statutory or case law for Superior Court review of a District Court probable cause decision resulting in custody pending a final probation violation hearing.

Rule 9. Violation of Conditions of A Continuance Without A Finding

(a) Notice, Conduct of Hearing, Adjudication. The procedures set forth in these rules regarding notice for, and the conduct and adjudication of, probation violation hearings shall also apply where the Probation Department alleges a violation of probation that was imposed together with a continuance without a finding.

(b) Disposition. The dispositional options available to the court following a determination that one or more conditions of probation imposed together with a continuance without a finding have been violated shall be as follows:

(i) *Continuation of the Continuance.* The court may decline to modify or revoke the probation order and instead may continue the continuance without a finding and issue to the probationer such admonition or instruction as it may deem appropriate.

(ii) *Termination.* The court may order that the continuance without a finding be considered completed, terminate the order of probation and enter a dismissal on the underlying criminal case.

(iii) *Modification.* If the violation consists of a criminal act, or if the court determines that the violation constitutes a material change in circumstance, it may continue the continuance without a finding and modify the conditions of probation including the duration of the continuance.

(iv) *Revocation.* The court may revoke the order of probation and terminate the continuance without a finding, whereupon a finding of guilty shall be entered.

(c) Execution of Sentence; Stay of Execution. Upon revocation of probation, any sentence that was specified as a condition of the plea or admission and accepted by the court that ordered the continuance, shall be imposed and executed forthwith; provided, however, that such execution may be stayed (1) pending appeal in accordance with Mass. R. Crim. P. 31, or (2) at the court's discretion, and upon the probationer's motion, to provide a brief period of time for the probationer to attend to personal matters prior to commencement of a sentence of incarceration. The execution of such sentence shall not be otherwise stayed.

(d) Imposition of Sentence When No Sentence Previously Specified. Upon revocation of a probation order where no sentence was specified as a condition of the plea or admission and accepted by the court that ordered the continuance, the court shall impose sentence as provided by law.

Adopted December 2, 1999, effective January 3, 2000.

Commentary

Continuance Without a Finding with Probation

This rule addresses the situation where the allegation of a probation violation involves a probation order issued together with a continuance without a finding. In such cases, the conditions of probation are also the conditions whereby the underlying criminal case has been continued without the entry of a finding of guilty, following submission and acceptance of a formal plea or admission.

The rule makes clear that the procedure in these cases for commencing, conducting and disposing of probation violation proceedings is the same as in cases where a finding of guilty has been entered following a plea, admission or trial. The only differences from the latter involve the court's dispositional options if a probation violation is found.

Specifically, if the court finds a probation violation and decides as a matter of its discretion to revoke probation, the continuance is thereby terminated, a finding of guilty must be entered and sentence must be imposed. The court will be bound by whatever dispositional terms were set by the probationer and accepted by the court as formal conditions of his or her plea or admission, if any.

The rule takes the position that upon revocation of probation in a case continued without a finding, a sentence that was conditioned on probation compliance should be ordered executed in its entirety. This is parallel to the ruling in *Commonwealth v. Holmgren*, 421 Mass. 224, 656 N.E.2d 577 (1995), a case which involved execution of a suspended sentence upon violation of probation.

In cases where the defendant submitted his or her plea or admission conditioned only by a requirement that the case be continued without a finding, with no sentencing terms specified in the tender of plea or admission, the court may have indicated what sentence should be imposed if probation is violated and revoked (sometimes referred to as "a Duquette alternative"). Such a sentence should be given great deference but is not binding on the judge who enters the guilty finding and then imposes sentence. This parallels the "straight probation" situation. That is, if a violation is found and the court decides to revoke probation, the sentence to be imposed following entry of the guilty finding may be any sentence provided by law.

<u>Continuance Without a Finding Without Probation.</u>

This rule does not address the situation where the court has ordered a case continued without a finding, but has *not* placed the defendant on probation, that is, where the conditions of the continuance are not conditions of probation.

In *Commonwealth v. Rivera*, No. SJ–96–0578, (Supreme Judicial Court, Single Justice Decision, November 29, 1996), the Single Justice held that

> like the procedure for probation revocation, the procedure for revocation of a continuance without a finding may result in the loss of the defendant's liberty, [thus] for purposes of due process it is appropriate to analyze the revocation of a continuance without a finding the same as this court does a revocation of probation.

Apparently, in *Rivera* the defendant's case had been continued without a finding, but he had not been placed on probation.

One problem with such cases involves the need for conditions of the continuance to be set forth in writing and given to the defendant. Where a case is continued without a finding, but the defendant not placed on probation, it is not clear how and by whom those conditions are reduced to writing and given to the defendant. Similarly, if the defendant is not on probation, it is not clear who presents the allegation of an alleged violation of the conditions of the continuance. In any event, the Court in *Rivera*, applying the due process requirements of probation violation proceedings, found that the proceedings were inadequate in terms of notice of the alleged violation, time to prepare for the hearing, and the reliability of the hearsay evidence submitted, and vacated the revocation of the continuance.

RULES GOVERNING PERSONS AUTHORIZED TO TAKE BAIL

Effective May 12, 1996

Rule 1

Definitions.

A. *Person Authorized to Take Bail.* A Clerk–Magistrate or Assistant Clerk of the Superior Court, a Clerk–Magistrate or Assistant Clerk of the District Court, a Bail Commissioner, inside or outside of Suffolk County, or a Master in Chancery is a "person authorized to take bail". A "person authorized to take bail" may set and take release on personal recognizance without sureties, or may set and take release on bail or may take bail set by another.

B. *Jurisdiction.* Jurisdiction refers to the territory within which a "person authorized to take bail" may set or take bail.

C. *Professional Bondsman.* A professional bondsman is any person who becomes bail or surety for any defendant in the criminal process; whether it be as agent for any corporation, or person, surety agent or principal, who has received, been promised, or expects to receive a fee, pay or reward for acting as bail or surety.

Rule 2

The purpose of setting terms for any pre-trial release is to assure the presence at court of the person released. Any person charged with an offense other than an offense punishable by death, or for any offense on which a warrant of arrest has been issued by the Superior Court, is required by law to be released on his personal recognizance pending trial unless the person setting the terms of release determines, in the exercise of his discretion, that such a release will not reasonably assure the appearance of the person as required. In making a determination as to what form of release to set, the following factors shall be considered: (1) The nature and circumstances of the offense charged, (2) The potential penalty the prisoner faces, (3) The prisoner's family ties, (4) His financial resources, (5) Employment record, (6) Any history of mental illness, (7) His reputation and length of residence in the community, (8) His record of convictions, if any, (9) Any illegal drug distribution or present drug dependency, (10) Any flight to avoid prosecution or fraudulent use of an alias or false identification, (11) Any failure to appear at any court proceeding to answer to an offense, (12) Whether the prisoner is on bail pending adjudication of a prior charge, (13) Whether he is on probation, parole or other release pending completion of a sentence for any conviction, (14) Whether he is on release pending sentence or appeal for any conviction.

Persons authorized to take bail shall recognize that their duties are quasi-judicial. Each decision to release on personal recognizance or set or take bail shall be reached on the basis of all available information pertaining to the above criteria.

Rule 3

These rules shall apply only to out-of-court releases on personal recognizance without sureties or bail settings and bail takings performed by Clerk–Magistrates or Assistant Clerks of the Superior Court, Clerk–Magistrates or Assistant Clerks of the District Court, Masters in Chancery and Bail Commissioners. They shall apply even when the setting of bail was done by another if the taking of bail is done by them.

Rule 4

A failure to comply with any of these rules or any part of the reporting requirements herein may result in a temporary or permanent suspension of the power to set or take bail or release on personal recognizance without sureties.

Persons authorized to take bail will be held to know all provisions of law governing their activities including these rules and shall strictly comply with such provisions.

Rule 5

Clerk–Magistrates and Assistant Clerks of the Superior and District Courts and Masters in Chancery who set or take bail or release on personal recognizance without sureties must register with the Superior Court on a form approved by the Court. Any of the above who have not registered will not be allowed to exercise authority as a bail magistrate, and if they set or take bail or release on personal recognizance without sureties, they may be temporarily or permanently suspended.

Clerk–Magistrates and Assistant Clerks of the Superior and District Courts shall not maintain a level of participation in the out-of-court bailing activity which jeopardizes their regular attendance at, or proper functioning of, the Clerk–Magistrate's Office during the hours that it is required to be open.

Clerk–Magistrates of the Superior and District Courts shall not, consistent with the responsibility to maintain the proper functioning of their offices, unreasonably restrict or exclude any Assistant Clerk from participating in the out-of-court bailing activity in their jurisdiction.

Rule 6

The jurisdiction of Clerk–Magistrates or Assistant Clerks of the Superior Court to set or take release on personal recognizance without sureties or to set or take release on bail shall be limited to the county for which they are Clerk–Magistrates or Assistant Clerks. They may set or take release on personal recognizance without sureties or set or take release on bail for any defendant held within the territory of their county even when that defendant is held to answer charges in another county.

Rule 7

The jurisdiction of Clerk–Magistrates or Assistant Clerks of the District Court to set or take release on personal recognizance without sureties or to set or take release on bail shall be limited to the district for which they are Clerk–Magistrates or Assistant Clerks. They may set or take release on personal recognizance without sureties or set or take release on bail for any defendant held within the territory of their district, even when that defendant is held to answer charges in another district.

Rule 8

The jurisdiction of Masters in Chancery to set or take release on personal recognizance without sureties or to set or take release on bail shall be within the county for which they are appointed to act as Masters in Chancery. They may set or take release on personal recognizance without sureties or set or take release on bail for any defendant held within the territory of their county, even when that defendant is being held to answer charges in another county.

Rule 9

The jurisdiction of Clerk–Magistrates or Assistant Clerks of the District Court, and Masters in Chancery may be extended to any other judicial district by written permission of the Chief Justice of the District Court. A copy of the application for such permission shall be sent to the Superior Court by the applicant, and a copy of such permission shall be sent to the Superior Court by the Chief Justice of the District Court.

Rule 10

The jurisdiction of persons authorized to take bail may be extended to any other judicial district for a period not to exceed thirty days by a Justice of the Superior Court upon notification by the Bail Administrator that emergency coverage is required. Upon further application, the emergency coverage may be extended for a maximum additional period of sixty days.

Rule 11

The jurisdiction of Bail Commissioners approved by the Superior Court to set or take release on personal recognizance without sureties or to set or take release on bail shall be limited to that geographical area contained in their papers of appointment. They may set or take release on personal recognizance without sureties or set or take release on bail for any defendant held within such geographical area, even when that defendant is being held to answer charges in another area.

Rule 12

The maximum fee to be charged by any person authorized to take bail or release on personal recognizance in the case of a person arrested for any misdemeanor or felony shall be twenty-five dollars, regardless of the number of offenses.

If, in addition to recognizing for a court within the territorial jurisdiction of the magistrate authorizing the release, the arrested person is being required to recognize for a court outside of such territorial jurisdiction, the person so authorized may charge an additional five dollars for each such extraterritorial recognizance, but in no event shall the total fee for any release exceed forty dollars.

This rule does not prevent the taking of bail or releasing on personal recognizance for less than the maximum fee or without charge, but if a charge is to be made, payment shall be in advance.

Clerk–Magistrates and Assistant Clerks of the Superior and District Courts shall not receive any fee or compensation, in addition to their salaries, for releasing a prisoner on bail or on personal recognizance without sureties during the hours when their offices are required to be open.

The person authorized to take bail who goes to the place of detention and releases the prisoner is the only person entitled to the compensation provided for in G.L. c. 262, § 24, and fee splitting arrangements are prohibited.

If a prisoner is being held under circumstances justifying a release and is not able to provide the fee, the magistrate shall authorize the release without charge.

Rule 13

No person authorized to take bail in criminal cases shall receive from any source, in connection with the admitting to bail or releasing on personal recognizance, anything of value in excess of the statutory fee therefor.

Rule 14

Unless otherwise restricted by the Superior Court, the Chief Justice of the District Court or their papers of appointment, all persons authorized to take bail are entitled to participate fairly in the out-of-court bailing

THOMSON WEST™

PACKING SLIP
Not a Remittable Document

0GND

401013431

Shipped From:
THOMSON-WEST
545 WESCOTT RD
EAGAN MN 55123-1310

Shipped To:
RICHARD BREWER
691 NORTH ST
RANDOLPH MA 02368-4317
414-526-3598

Ship To Account #	Purchase Order #	Order Date	Order #	Delivery #
1004134424		01/10/2012	6993812	401013431

ISBN	Material #	Product Description	Order Qty	Ship Qty
	20093904	MA CRIMINAL LAW AND PROCEDURE PAM FULL SET 1 Items in Full Set	1	1

activity in their jurisdiction so long as they are willing and able to respond with all reasonable promptness to calls for their services.

The Justices of the Superior Court Committee on Bail, in order to effectuate the purposes of this rule, may prepare and implement a specific plan of coverage for all prisoner holding facilities in a jurisdiction which shall be complied with by all persons authorized to take bail who are registered or appointed there.

Rule 15

No person authorized to take bail shall respond to a call to set and take bail or to take bail by a Professional Bondsman, surety agent or money lender. He may respond only to calls from defendants, defendants' families, defendants' attorneys or the authorities holding the defendant in custody.

Rule 16

No person authorized to take bail shall administer by telephone, or otherwise than in the physical presence of the affiant, any oath or affirmation required in the course of taking bail or releasing on personal recognizance.

Rule 17

No person authorized to take bail shall delegate the setting or taking of bail or the setting or taking release on personal recognizance to a police officer, jail official, bondsman or anyone else.

Rule 18

Every person authorized to take bail shall perform that function impartially and in a dignified manner as befits the performance of a judicial act.

Rule 19

Each person released on personal recognizance without sureties or bail and each person who is accepted as surety shall take an oath given by the person authorized to take bail that he will perform the requirements of his recognizance or bond.

Oaths administered in the course of taking bail or releasing on personal recognizance without sureties shall be given with solemnity and dignity commensurate with the performance of a judicial function.

Rule 20

Each defendant must have his own recognizance. Two or more defendants shall not be joined in one recognizance, whether or not they are jointly charged with the commission of the same crime. Each recognizance must be accompanied by its own affidavit.

Rule 21

No person taking bail shall accept as surety a bondsman who has received, who has been promised or who expects to receive, pay or reward for acting as surety unless such proposed surety is at the time duly registered as a professional bondsman.

If a surety offered is a surety company, the person authorized to take bail shall, before accepting the surety, satisfy himself that the company is authorized to act as surety in criminal cases in the Commonwealth; that it is financially sound; that the agent purporting to bind it in recognizance is properly authorized to do so; that it will deal fairly with the principal in all respects and that there is no condition existing whereby it is likely to cease being interested in the due production in court of the body of the principal according to the tenor of the recognizance.

Rule 22

Persons authorized to take bail shall not assume that registration of professional bondsmen is a guarantee of sufficiency. Professional bondsmen are to be at least as closely questioned as any other person offered as surety and special attention must be paid, in the case of professional bondsmen, to the total amount of the recognizance in which each is surety.

Rule 23

No person authorized to take bail shall accept as surety any professional bondsman examination of whom shows his obligations as surety in criminal cases to be greater than the limit set by Rule 22 governing professional bondsmen.

Rule 24

Each person authorized to take bail, in each instance in which security as authorized by G.L. c. 276, § 79, is offered as qualification for persons seeking to become surety shall make careful inquiry as to the ownership of such.

Rule 25

Except as provided by G.L. c. 276, § 57 or otherwise provided by law, no person authorized to take bail shall accept as surety any person who has previously been offered as surety in the same proceeding to any person authorized to take bail in criminal cases and has been refused by such person.

Rule 26

Each person authorized to take bail shall satisfy himself beyond any reasonable doubt that the person offered as surety is the person he claims to be.

Rule 27

When a person offered as surety is unable to write his name and signs by his mark, such mark must be attested in writing by a witness who saw it made and who shall sign his name and write his address in attestation. When no other witness is available, such attestation may be made by the person authorized to take bail.

Rule 28

Persons authorized to take bail shall take all necessary steps to see to it that all persons offering themselves as principals or sureties understand fully the nature of the obligation into which they seek to enter. This applies especially where proposed principals or sureties are not familiar with the English language. Persons taking bail must be equally certain that they fully understand the answers made to them by proposed principals or sureties under examination. Where the services of an interpreter are necessary the interpreter must first be sworn to do his work faithfully, impartially and with the best of his skill and ability.

Rule 29

Persons authorized to take bail shall not be or become creditors of persons seeking release or of persons tendering surety.

Rule 30

No person authorized to take bail shall at any time, directly or indirectly, advise any person for whom he sets bail or from whom he takes bail, or for whom he sets release on personal recognizance without sureties as to any matter concerning the conduct of his case.

Rule 31

No person authorized to take bail shall set or take bail or set release on personal recognizance without sureties in any proceeding in which he has acted or expects to act as counsel, nor shall he act as counsel in any proceeding in which he has at any time taken bail or released a person on personal recognizance.

Rule 32

No person authorized to take bail shall accept as surety any attorney at law or any relative or employee thereof in any proceeding in which such attorney at law is directly or indirectly employed.

Rule 33

No person authorized to take bail shall offer or give any gift, or pay any compensation or reward to anyone for procuring or influencing the selection of any person to set or take bail or release on personal recognizance without sureties or for selecting any particular attorney, or for selecting any particular bondsman, professional or otherwise.

Rule 34

No person authorized to take bail shall, directly or indirectly, take or receive any gift, commission, pay, or reward, tangible or intangible, from any person who lends money, or offers bonds, bank books or other securities to persons in custody or to any person for their benefit for use in depositing as bail-security with himself or with any other person authorized to take bail or for use in paying, rewarding or giving security to any professional bondsman or for paying, rewarding or giving security to any attorney or other adviser.

Rule 35

No person authorized to take bail shall, with or without compensation or reward or promise thereof, assist a person in custody by procuring or recommending a bondsman for him or a person to lend him money or property to be used in lieu of personal suretyship or by procuring or recommending an attorney.

No person authorized to take bail shall at any time, either before or after taking bail or releasing on personal recognizance, recommend or take any steps to make likely the employment by the defendant of any particular bondsman, professional or otherwise, or of any particular attorney or group or firm of attorneys, or of any particular adviser who is not an attorney.

Rule 36

No person authorized to take bail shall refer any defendant to any lawyer, nor shall he call any lawyer on any defendant's behalf.

Rule 37

No person authorized to take bail shall, directly or indirectly, lend or procure the lending of money, bonds, bankbooks or other securities to persons in custody or to any person for their benefit for use in depositing as bail-security with himself or with any other person authorized to take bail, or for use in paying, rewarding or giving security to any professional bondsman, or for paying, rewarding or giving security to any attorney or other adviser.

Rule 38

Persons authorized to take bail who release an individual in custody on personal recognizance without sureties or on bail shall advise him of the provision of G.L. c. 276, § 82A, which provides that a person who fails to appear in court without sufficient excuse shall be punished by a fine of not more than one thousand dollars ($1,000.00) or imprisonment for not more than one year, or both.

Rule 39

Every person authorized to take bail must see to it that all recognizances, certificates (affidavits) of sureties, other necessary documents, and all money, bank books and bonds and other security deposited with him are seasonably transmitted to and seasonably received by the Clerk–Magistrates' Offices of the appropriate courts.

Receipt shall not be considered seasonable where it occurs later than 9:00 A.M. of the day when the processes on which the defendant was held in custody is returnable, or later than 8:30 A.M. of the day when the person who is held in custody on arrest without a warrant must first be taken before the court.

In no event shall transmittal and receipt by the appropriate court be accomplished later than 4:00 P.M. of the third court day after the day on which the release was authorized.

If a person authorized to take bail maintains a bank account for depositing and transferring bail funds to the appropriate courts, it shall be used exclusively for that purpose and the name of the bank, the account number and, within 10 days of receipt, copies of monthly statements shall be submitted to the Office of Bail Administration.

Rule 40

All certificates of sureties required by G.L. c. 76, § 61, and any amendments thereof that may be made, shall comply strictly with all requirements of the statute. Such certificates shall also contain an answer under oath to the following questions:

"Have you received or been promised pay or reward for acting as surety in this case?"

"Do you expect to receive pay or reward or a promise of pay or reward for your becoming surety in this case?"

"How much pay or reward have you received or have you been promised or do you expect to receive?"

"Are you approved and registered with the Superior Court as a professional bondsman?"

(This question is to be answered whether or not the other answers of the surety disclose that he is acting for hire.)

"Have you become bail or surety in criminal cases on five separate occasions during the now current calendar year?"

The statute also requires that affidavits of sureties embrace personal property as well as real property. Therefore, where sureties present personal property as security, person taking bail shall examine the accompanying affidavits with particularity.

For example:

A. Motor vehicles, full information as to:

(a) Mortgages, liens and other encumbrances;

(b) engine number;

(c) make, type, mileage and year of manufacture;

(d) nature of use being made of it;

(e) location of garage where it is usually kept;

(f) assessed value, if any;

B. Shares of capital stock of corporations, full information as to:

(a) exact corporate name of corporation;

(b) name of state of incorporation;

(c) class of stock, whether common or preferred;

(d) par value of each share of stock;

(e) market value of the stock and whether listed on any stock exchange. If not listed, state where there is a market for the stock;

(f) whether or not the stock stands in the surety's name on the books of the corporation. If not in surety's name, in whose?

(g) whether or not the stock is subject to any existing pledge, mortgage or other lien and, if it is, for how much and to whom and the nature of the obligation for which it is security;

(h) whether or not dividends have been regularly paid on the stock and if so, how much in each of the last three years.

Rule 41

Each person authorized to take bail shall by the second Monday of each month make and submit to the Chief Justice of the Superior Court, in care of the Office of Bail Administration a record as to each taking of bail or releasing on personal recognizance that was authorized during the prior calendar month.

The forms to be used for this purpose are the bail report cover sheet and the report page (yellow copy) from the recognizance form approved by the Court pursuant to G.L. c. 276, § 65. They are attached hereto and included by reference as part of these rules.

If no releases have been authorized during any reporting period, a written statement to that effect shall be submitted within the required time.

BAIL REPORT COVER SHEET

Reports for the Month of:

____________________, 19___

____

____

☐ C/M
☐ A/C
☐ B/C

1. Bail Magistrate: ________________________
(Please Print)

2. Total Fees: $__________

3. Total Releases Authorized: __________

a. Personal Recognizance: __________
b. Cash Bail: __________
c. Bail Bonds: __________

I certify that this report is a full and complete listing of all the prisoner releases that I have authorized during this reporting month.

Signed this _______ day of ____________, 199__
under the penalties of perjury.

____
(Person Authorized to Take Bail)

G.L. c. 276 § 61A
RGPATB # 41

BAIL REPORT TO THE SUPERIOR COURT

COMMONWEALTH OF MASSACHUSETTS

DOCKET NUMBER

DEFENDANT'S NAME AND ADDRESS (INCLUDE ANY ALIAS)

SOCIAL SECURITY NUMBER | DATE OF BIRTH

TERMS OF RELEASE

☐ PERSONAL RECOGNIZANCE (Promise to Appear) $____

☐ BAIL

☐ CASH AS SURETY $____

☐ BOND AS SURETY $____

☐ OTHER SURETY $____

(Please Specify)

NAME AND ADDRESS OF COURT

DATE AND TIME OF APPEARANCE

________ AT ________ ☐ A.M. ☐ P.M.

DATE TIME

← THE DEFENDANT MUST APPEAR AT THIS COURT ADDRESS ON THE DATE AND TIME SPECIFIED HEREIN ←

SURETY/SURETIES NAME AND ADDRESS

ARREST ON WARRANT ☐ YES ☐ NO

OFFENSE(S)

I, as defendant, charged by complaint with the crime(s) listed above, understand that I am being released from custody according to the terms of release specified. I will personally appear before the above named court at the date and time indicated, and I will appear for any continuance until the final decree, sentence or order, and I will abide by it and not depart without leave. Further, I will appear before any court to which the charges may be transferred or appealed, or to any sitting of the Superior Court to which I may be bound over or indicted to answer to any indictment, and I will appear for any continuance until the final decree, sentence or order, and I will abide by it and not depart without leave.

I understand and acknowledge that if I fail without sufficient excuse to appear in accordance with the foregoing promise, I will be liable, jointly and severally if a surety has been required, to the Commonwealth of Massachusetts for the dollar amount specified in the terms of release.

SIGNED (DEFENDANT) X | DATE

I, as surety, understand and acknowledge that if the above named defendant fails to appear and abide by all orders of the court according to the foregoing promise, I will be liable, jointly and severally, with the defendant to the Commonwealth of Massachusetts for the dollar amount specified in the terms of release.

SIGNED (SURETY) X | SIGNED (SURETY) X

SIGNED (PERSON AUTHORIZED TO TAKE BAIL)

X________________ ☐ Clerk–Magistrate ☐ Assistant Clerk ☐ Bail Commissioner

Subscribed and sworn to before me, the defendant having been furnished a copy of this recognizance.

A. RELEASE AUTHORIZED FROM

B. JURISDICTION OF MAGISTRATE

(Complete when appearance is being required outside of your jurisdiction)

BAIL FEE RECEIVED $________

DATE AND TIME SIGNED ☐ A.M. ☐ P.M.

Notice to person taking bail or releasing on personal recognizance: Please complete the following information before submitting this copy to the Chief Justice of the Superior Court.

PLACE WHERE BAIL TAKEN	RELEASE TERMS SET BY	NAME AND ADDRESS OF AGENT FOR SURETY COMPANY	IS SURETY REGISTERED AT SUPERIOR COURT? ☐ YES ☐ NO
SUMMONED TO PLACE OF DETENTION BY	HOW SUMMONED?	OTHER SECURITY TAKEN BY SURETY	FEE OF SURETY

I certify that I have not received anything of value from anyone in addition to my fee for setting and or taking this bail. Subscribed and sworn to under the pains and penalty of perjury.

SIGNED (PERSON AUTHORIZED TO TAKE BAIL) X

RECEIPT–RECORD OF PAYMENT OF CASH BAIL ☐ NOT APPLICABLE

DATE	RECEIVED FROM SURETY (NAME AND ADDRESS)	DEFENDANT	AMOUNT
		CASE NUMBER	DISTRICT COURT

RECEIVED BY

DC–CR–5 (6/95)
SC–1

SUPERIOR COURT COPY

SPECIAL RULES OF THE BOSTON MUNICIPAL COURT DEPARTMENT SITTING FOR CRIMINAL BUSINESS

Effective November 1, 1989

Table of Rules

General Comments

These rules do not purport to be a comprehensive set of rules on criminal procedure. Most of them represent no innovations in what have been regarded heretofore as correct procedure. They are all drawn from approved practices which have heretofore been observed in this court, and while the rules herein promulgated represent in substance the general guide for the disposition of criminal business, it is the purpose of the justices of this court to continue consideration of the problems involved in the fair and efficient administration of criminal justice.

Publisher's Note

Rule captions have been editorially supplied for all but Rules 11, 13 and 15.

PROCEDURE

Rule 1. Reading of Complaint

At arraignment each complaint, or the material portions thereof, shall be read aloud to the defendant by the session clerk or the judge. In the event codefendants are arraigned at the same time charged with the same offense, the complaint need be read only once with the stated identification of each defendant so complained against. Waiving of the reading shall not be permitted unless the defendant is represented at arraignment by counsel who shall make the waiver in open court.

Rule 2. Entry of Plea

On any complaint charging an offense for which a sentence of imprisonment may be imposed, no plea other than "not guilty" shall be entered unless the defendant is represented by counsel who is present. (See Rule 4).

The assignment of counsel shall be governed by the provisions of G.L. c. 211D and Supreme Judicial Court Rule 3:10.

Rule 3. Bail

No bail shall be set with respect to any defendant arraigned for trial unless the defendant has had an opportunity to confer with his counsel, except in cases where the defendant has waived counsel, in which case the court may set bail in its discretion without any further hearing.

Notice of the right to a speedy review of any grievance on account of the amount of bail set by the court shall be given to the defendant by the judge at the time bail is set.

Rule 4. Guilty or Nolo Contendere Pleas by Pro Se Defendant

No plea of guilty or nolo contendere shall be accepted by the judge from any defendant who is not represented by counsel unless

(a) the judge is satisfied that the plea is made voluntarily;

(b) the judge is satisfied that the defendant understands the nature of the offense described in the complaint;

(c) the defendant understands that such a plea unless later withdrawn by leave of court will preclude his trial by jury on the question of guilt;

(d) the defendant has notice of the minimum and maximum sentence provided by the law therefor.

Rule 5. Refusal to Plead or Accept Guilty Plea

If the defendant refuses to plead or if the court refuses to accept a plea of guilty for any reason set forth in Rule 4, the court shall enter a plea of not guilty. The court shall not enter a judgment upon a plea of guilty nor make a finding of guilty upon the defendant admitting to a finding of facts sufficient to warrant the same, unless it is satisfied that there is a factual basis for such a plea or finding.

Rule 6. Recitation of Rights to Pro Se Defendant

An unrepresented defendant who has pleaded not guilty to any complaint shall be advised by the judge at the time of his hearing or trial that on any material matter pertaining to the offense charged he has the following rights:

(a) to cross-examine any witness offered by the prosecution; and

(b) subject to cross-examination to offer testimony by himself or any other witness.

The judge shall also then advise him of his rights not to testify and not to be prejudiced if he remains silent. If the prosecution offers an exhibit the judge shall allow the defendant to examine it.

Rule 7. Courtrooms

The court room regularly assigned for the trial of causes heard by the justices shall be used for the hearing of all causes adjourned to or called in such session unless at the discretion of the court it is advisable in the public interest that the parties be heard in a non-public session.

Rule 8. Consideration of Probation Department Records or Reports

During the trial on any complaint wherein the Municipal Court has, and does not decline final jurisdiction, no consideration of any probation department records or reports shall take place until the termination of the trial. If the judge then finds the defendant not guilty the session clerk shall so announce and notify the defendant that he is discharged of the offense set forth in that complaint. If the judge indicates a finding of guilty or facts sufficient to warrant such a finding, he shall only thereafter consider any probation department records or reports and instruct the session clerk to announce his decisions on adjudication, disposition or continuance, as the case may be.

Rule 9. Right to Appeal

In all cases where the defendant has a right to appeal to the Superior Court he shall be notified by the session clerk or the judge and shall be granted a reasonable time to make a decision after conferring with his counsel, or, if unrepresented, to make reasonable inquiry of the judge as to the procedures afforded him for this purpose.

ATTORNEYS

Rule 10. Appearance Slips

Attorneys must file an appearance slip for each defendant that they intend to represent, regardless of the number of complaints. Appearance slips must contain at least the following information: the printed name, address and office telephone number and signature of the attorney, the name of the defendant and the numbers of each case.

No attorney who has filed an appearance for a defendant may withdraw without the consent of the trial judge.

An attorney filing an appearance for a defendant corporation, except in parking violations, must file a written authorization signed by an officer of said corporation, unless waived by the trial justice.

PRELIMINARY MOTIONS

Rule 11. Motions for Return of Property and to Suppress Evidence

(Applicable to Criminal Cases)

Motions for the return of property and motions to suppress evidence shall be made in writing, shall specifically set forth the facts upon which the motions are based, shall be verified by affidavit, and shall be filed at least forty-eight hours in advance of trial unless the court for cause shown otherwise orders.

COMMITMENTS FOR MENTAL EXAMINATION

Rule 12. Mental Examination Commitments

Whenever it appears to the court that a serious question may exist with respect to the mental competence of a defendant appearing before it and the court has reasonable cause to believe that the defendant is incompetent to stand trial, the court may order the defendant committed for examination to an institution designated by public authority for such examination, said examination to be for such period as in the opinion of court is necessary, but under no circumstances for a period exceeding 35 days, unless an extension of period is requested by the medical authorities in the institution to which said defendant has been committed.

In all cases where a commitment is made as provided above, the court before making such commitment shall require that a statement be made by the complainant as to the circumstances which resulted in the arraignment of defendant in court, and a summary of said statement shall be annexed to the papers providing for the commitment of said defendant.

HOURS OF BUSINESS

Rule 13. Time for Holding Criminal Trials

Unless otherwise ordered, the time for holding criminal trials shall be from 9:00 A.M. until 4:00 P.M. Mondays through Fridays. For the convenience of the public there shall be a recess each day between 1:00 P.M. and 2:00 P.M.

THE CLERK'S OFFICE

Rule 14. Business Hours of Clerk; Responsibility for Filed Records and Papers

The office of the Clerk of the Court for the conduct of criminal business shall be open from 8:30 A.M. to 4:30 P.M. Mondays through Fridays.

The Clerk shall be answerable for all records and papers filed in the court or in his office. He shall not allow any writ, petition, complaint, answer, agreement of parties or other writing which may be part of the record, or which is part of any proceeding in court, to be borrowed or taken from the files, and no other paper filed as aforesaid, shall be taken from the custody of the clerk without his consent, unless by order of the Court.

SOUND RECORDING DEVICES

Rule 15. Electronic Recordation of Proceedings

Recording of court proceedings is governed by Rule 308 of the Special Rules of the Boston Municipal Court Department Sitting for Civil Business.

MASSACHUSETTS RULES OF APPELLATE PROCEDURE

Research Note

See Massachusetts General Laws Annotated, vol. 47, for case annotations, cross references, and library references relating to the Massachusetts Rules of Criminal Procedure.

Table of Rules

Rule 1. Scope of Rules: Definitions

(a) Scope of Rules. These rules govern procedure in appeals to an appellate court.

(b) Rules Not to Affect Jurisdiction. These rules shall not be construed to extend or limit the jurisdiction, as established by law, of the Supreme Judicial Court or the Appeals Court. All proceedings related to any appeal from: (a) a decision of a single Justice of the Supreme Judicial Court, and (b) a decision of any tribunal, appeal from which must by law be brought in the Supreme Judicial Court, shall be had only before the full Supreme Judicial Court or a single justice thereof (unless transferred to the Appeals Court by order of the Supreme Judicial Court). But these rules shall govern such proceedings, except as provided in Supreme Judicial Court Rule 2.21.

(c) Definitions. As used in these rules:

"appeal" means an appeal to an appellate court and supersedes any procedure other than reservation and report by which matters have heretofore been brought before an appellate court for review.

"Appellate Court" means the full Supreme Judicial Court, the full Appeals Court, or a statutory quorum of either, as the case may be, whichever court is exercising statutory jurisdiction over the case at bar.

"child welfare case" means any case that is before a court of competent jurisdiction pursuant to G.L. c. 119, §§ 21–39J; G.L. c. 190B, Parts 2 and 3; or G.L. c. 210, §§ 1–11.

"clerk" means "clerk," "register," "recorder," and their respective assistants or deputies; "clerk of the appellate division" means the clerk of the trial court from which the action was reported to the appellate division.

"first class mail" means use of first class postage prepaid, whether certified, registered, uncertified, or unregistered. Registration or certification shall not be required unless specifically stated to be necessary.

"lower court" means the single justice, court, appellate division, board, commission, or other body whose decision is the subject of an appeal; for the purpose of Rule 9, the term includes any member of the lower court.

"rescript" means the order, direction, or mandate of the appellate court disposing of the appeal.

"single justice" means a single justice of whichever appellate court is exercising statutory jurisdiction over the case at bar.

(d) Construction. Words or phrases importing the singular number may extend and be applied to several persons or things, words importing the plural number may include the singular, and words importing the masculine gender may include the feminine and neuter.

Amended May 15, 1979, effective September 1, 1979; May 29, 1986, effective July 1, 1986; amended effective July 28, 1987; November 15, 1995; amended July 28, 1999, effective September 1, 1999; June 24, 2009, effective July 1, 2009.

Reporter's Notes—1973

The Appellate Rules, modelled almost entirely upon the Federal Rules of Appellate Procedure, drastically alter the procedure for judicial review in non-criminal cases as heretofore known in Massachusetts. Mass.R.Civ.P. 46 having eliminated the concept of the exception, all existing authority and learning pertaining to bills of exceptions are now obsolete. In addition, the Appellate Rules eradicate heretofore existing distinctions between bills of exceptions, appeals, claims of reports, and the like. The Appellate Rules are drafted to apply to any "procedure by which matters have heretofore been brought before an appellate court for review," except reservation and report (see Mass.R.Civ.P. 64; M.R.A.P. 5). The word "appeal" by definition includes all such preexisting procedures. The Appellate Rules apply to any review by the full Supreme Judicial Court or the Appeals Court of the decision of any "lower court", which latter term is defined to include any "single justice, court, appellate division, board, commission, or other party whose decision is the subject of an appeal."

Note that in the Appellate Rules "appellate court" refers to *either* the full Supreme Judicial Court *or* the full Appeals Court, whichever is then exercising jurisdiction, and that "single justice" similarly refers to a single justice of either court.

"Rescript", a term well-known to Massachusetts practice, covers the meaning of "mandate", the term used in the Federal Rules, F.R.A.P. 41.

Reporter's Notes—1979

Subdivision (a) of Rule 1 is amended by the deletion of the word "civil," thereby enlarging the scope of the Rules of Appellate Procedure to encompass both civil and criminal appeals. As thus amended, the rules govern interlocutory appeals in criminal cases (G.L. c. 278, § 28E, as amended; Mass.R.Crim.P. 15 [1979]), appeals from single justice proceedings and appeals from final convictions.

Bills of exceptions (former G.L. c. 278, § 31), writs of error (former G.L. c. 250, §§ 1–2, 9–13), and the limited "appeal" from a judgment of the Superior Court based on a "matter of law apparent upon the record" (former G.L. c. 278, § 28) are superseded by an appeal under these rules by virtue of subdivision (c). The appeal available pursuant to the rules is similar in many respects to the direct appeal on the transcript previously provided by G.L. c. 278, §§ 33A–33H, but the assignment of error as a vehicle for isolating and identifying issues (G.L. c. 278, § 28D) is abolished. Reports in Criminal cases are governed by Mass.R.Crim.P. 34 and Mass.R.App.P. 5.

"Lower court" as defined in subdivision (c) may include a justice of the district court department sitting in a jury-waived session. While ordinarily the only avenue for review of a judgment or order in a jury-waived session will be by way of appeal to a jury session, the Commonwealth is granted an interlocutory appeal of orders granting motions to dismiss or to suppress evidence by G.L. c. 278, § 28E, as amended, and Mass.R.Crim.P. 15(a).

Reporter's Notes—1987

This amendment deletes the reference to appeals from "a decision of the Appellate Division of the District Courts". Pursuant to G.L. c. 211A, § 10, as amended, review of such decisions is in the first instance by the Appeals Court.

Reporter's Notes—1995

The 1995 amendment to Mass.R.A.P. 1(b), effective November 15, 1995, provides that the Rules of Appellate Procedure are not applicable to proceedings governed by Supreme Judicial Court Rule 2:21, also effective November 15, 1995. Supreme Judicial Court Rule 2:21 regulates the procedure for appeal to the full court of a single justice's denial of relief from an interlocutory ruling in the trial court.

Reporter's Notes—1999

The 1999 amendment to Appellate Rule 1(c) was part of a comprehensive set of amendments to the Appellate Rules (Rules 1, 3, 4, 8, and 10) that had been proposed by the Supreme Judicial Court Committee on Appeals of Child Welfare Cases. The Committee's recommendations were intended to: (1) provide a uniform appeal period for child welfare cases; (2) establish a procedure for filing a notice of appeal which would eliminate the taking of appeals on behalf of absent and disinterested clients; (3) establish a procedure for the appointment of appellate counsel which makes it clear that trial counsel continues to be responsible for all trial court proceedings; (4) expedite the assembly of the record; and (5) provide notice to the trial court, for jurisdictional purposes, when appeals are entered in the appellate courts.

The amendment to Appellate Rule 1(c) defines the term "child welfare case" as it is used in the Appellate Rules.

Rule 2. Suspension of Rules

In the interest of expediting decision, or for other good cause shown, the appellate court or a single justice may, except as otherwise provided in Rule 14(b), suspend the requirements or provisions of any of these rules in a particular case on application of a party or on its own motion and may order proceedings in accordance with its direction. Such a suspension may be on reasonable terms.

Reporter's Notes—1973

Appellate Rule 2, substantially tracking F.R.A.P. 2, injects flexibility into the appellate structure. It permits relaxation of the rules in the interest of expedition, or for good cause, except enlarging appeal time beyond one year from the date the appeals period begins to run.

Rule 3. Appeal—How Taken

(a) Filing the Notice of Appeal. An appeal permitted by law from a lower court shall be taken by filing a notice of appeal with the clerk of the lower court within the time allowed by Rule 4. Failure of an appellant to take any step other than the timely filing of a notice of appeal shall not affect the validity of the appeal, but shall be ground only for such action as the appellate court deems appropriate, which may include dismissal of the appeal.

A party need not claim an appeal from an interlocutory order to preserve his right to have such order reviewed upon appeal from the final judgment; but for all purposes for which an appeal from an interlocutory order has heretofore been necessary, it is sufficient that the party comply with the requirement of Massachusetts Rules of Civil Procedure 46 or Massachusetts Rules of Criminal Procedure 22, whichever was applicable to the trial of the case in the lower court.

(b) Joint or Consolidated Appeals. If two or more persons are entitled to appeal from a judgment or order of a lower court and their interests are such as to make joinder practicable, they may file a joint notice of appeal, or may join in appeal after filing separate timely notices of appeal, and they may thereafter proceed on appeal as a single appellant. Appeals may be consolidated by order of the appellate court upon its own motion or upon motion of a party, or by stipulation of the parties to the several appeals.

(c) Content of the Notice of Appeal. The notice of appeal shall specify the party or parties taking the appeal and shall, in civil cases, designate the judgment, decree, adjudication, order, or part thereof appealed from. In child welfare cases, the notice of appeal and any request for a transcript, if required, shall be signed by the party or parties taking the appeal, unless the appellant is the minor subject of the action; a notice of appeal that is not so signed shall not be accepted for filing by the clerk.

(d) Service of the Notice of Appeal. The clerk of the lower court shall serve notice of the filing of a notice of appeal by mailing a copy thereof to counsel of record for each party other than the appellant, or, if a party is not represented by counsel, to the party at his last known address. The clerk shall note on each copy served the date on which the notice of appeal was filed. Failure of the clerk to serve notice shall not affect the validity of the appeal. Service shall be sufficient notwithstanding the death of a party or his counsel. The clerk shall note in the docket the names of the persons to whom he mails copies, with the date of mailing.

(e) Change of Counsel on Appeal in Criminal and Certain Non-criminal Cases. If the defendant in a criminal case or any party in any other proceeding, excluding child welfare cases, in which counsel is required to be made available to such party pursuant to Supreme Judicial Court Rule 3:10 was represented by counsel at trial, trial counsel shall continue to represent that party on appeal until the trial court permits him to withdraw his appearance and until an appearance is filed by substitute counsel. If trial counsel wishes to withdraw, he shall, on the day upon which the notice of appeal is filed, file a motion to withdraw. Any motion under this provision shall be marked up by the trial counsel for hearing no later than seven days after filing. If the motion to withdraw is allowed, the judge shall assign the Committee for Public Counsel Services to provide representation according to the procedures established in Supreme Judicial Court Rule 3:10.

(f) Appointment of Appellate Counsel in Child Welfare Cases. Any party to a child welfare case in which counsel was appointed pursuant to Supreme Judicial Court Rule 3:10 and who was represented by counsel at trial, shall continue to be represented by that counsel on appeal until either the trial court has appointed counsel for appellate purposes and an appearance has been filed by appellate counsel or the trial court has denied a motion to appoint counsel for appellate purposes.

Trial counsel shall, on the day upon which the signed notice of appeal is filed, file, and request a hearing on, a motion to allow reasonable costs associated with the appeal. At the same time, if trial counsel is not appellate certified by the Committee for Public Counsel Services, counsel shall also file, and request a hearing on, a motion to appoint counsel for appellate purposes. Subject to the provisions of Supreme Judicial Court Rule 3:10, § 7, trial counsel shall continue to represent the party at all trial court proceedings.

If the motion to appoint counsel for appellate purposes is allowed, the Committee for Public Counsel Services shall be assigned to provide representation according to the procedures established in Supreme Judicial Court Rule 3:10.

Amended May 15, 1979, effective July 1, 1979; May 29, 1986, effective July 1, 1986; amended July 28, 1999, effective September 1, 1999.

Reporter's Notes—1973

An appeal is initiated by filing in *the lower court* a notice of appeal, within 30 days following the order or judgment appealed from. If the Commonwealth or any office or agency thereof is a party, however, the appeal time is extended to 60 days. After the notice of appeal has been filed, the clerk of the lower court notifies all other parties by mail of the notice's having been filed. It is the date of the filing, however, not the date of the notice, which controls the timeliness of the appeal.

Reporter's Notes—1979

The second paragraph of subdivision (a) is amended by the addition of a reference to Mass.R.Crim.P. 22, "Objections," to clarify that a party need not claim an exception to an interlocutory order adverse to his position to preserve his right to have that order subsequently reviewed on appeal.

Subdivision (b), regulating joint or consolidated appeals, is consistent with prior criminal appellate practice.

Subdivision (c) is amended to reflect the fact that in a civil case, the notice of appeal must designate the judgment, order, or part thereof which is appealed from. It would also be appropriate in an interlocutory appeal in a criminal case for the notice of appeal to designate the order from which an appeal is being taken (e.g., denial of motion to suppress, grant of motion to dismiss), but this is not required by the rule because there is seldom any question about the matter being appealed.

General Laws, c. 278, § 33B (St.1955, c. 352, § 2) formerly provided that the clerk was to notify the District Attorney of a claim of appeal "forthwith." Subdivision (d) is more explicit in setting out the manner of notice and will require notification of co-defendants, if any, when a notice of appeal is filed.

Subdivision (e), "Change of Counsel on Appeal in Criminal Cases," is new and addresses the continuing responsibility of the trial attorney to provide assistance to a client beyond entry of final judgment in the trial court. See ABA *Standards Relating to Criminal Appeals* 21–2.2(a) (2d ed., Approved Draft, 1978). This subdivision seeks to avoid a hiatus in legal representation during a critical period when the defendant has questions as to the meaning and effect of conviction and the option of whether to appeal. ABA *Standards,* supra, commentary at 10.

In Pires v. Commonwealth, Mass.Adv.Sh. [1977] 2601 the Supreme Judicial Court held that a lawyer has a professional obligation to his client which goes beyond the trial of the case. The court adopted the provisions of the American Bar Association Project on Standards for Criminal Justice as the appropriate measure of the responsibility of counsel. Standard 8.2 of the Defense Function (Approved Draft 1971), provides:

> 8.2 Appeal. (a) After conviction, the lawyer should explain to the defendant the meaning and consequences of the court's judgment and his right of appeal. The lawyer should give the defendant his professional judgment as to whether there are meritorious grounds for appeal and as to the probable results of an appeal. He should also explain to the defendant the advantages and disadvantages of an appeal. The decision whether to appeal must be the defendant's own choice. (b) The lawyer should take whatever steps are necessary to protect the defendant's right of appeal.

Reporter's Notes—1999

The 1999 amendments to Appellate Rule 3 were part of a comprehensive set of amendments to the Appellate Rules (Rules 1, 3, 4, 8, and 10) that had been proposed by the Supreme Judicial Court Committee on Appeals of Child Welfare Cases. The purpose of the 1999 amendments is described in the 1999 Reporter's Notes to Appellate Rule 1(c).

Appellate Rule 3(c) has been amended to require that in child welfare cases, the notice of appeal must be signed by the party or parties taking the appeal unless the appellant is the minor who is the subject of the action. The clerk is directed not to accept an appeal that is not so signed. The purpose of this change is to eliminate the taking of an appeal on behalf of an absent and disinterested client.

The amendment to Appellate Rule 3(f) make it clear that until appellate counsel files an appearance, trial counsel is obligated to continue representation of the client. Even after appellate counsel has filed an appearance, trial counsel will continue to represent the party at all proceedings in the trial court.

Rule 4. Appeal—When Taken

(a) Appeals in Civil Cases. In a civil case, unless otherwise provided by statute, the notice of appeal required by Rule 3 shall be filed with the clerk of the lower court within thirty days of the date of the entry of the judgment appealed from; but if the Commonwealth or an officer or agency thereof is a party, the notice of appeal may be filed by any party within sixty days of such entry, except in child welfare cases, in which the notice of appeal shall be filed within thirty days from the date of the entry of the judgment, decree, order, or adjudication. If a notice of appeal is mistakenly filed in an appellate court, the clerk of such appellate court shall note the date on which it was received and transmit it to the clerk of the lower court from which the appeal was taken and it shall be deemed filed in such lower court on the date so noted. If a timely notice of appeal is filed by a party, any other party may file a notice of appeal within fourteen days of the date on which the first notice of appeal was filed, or within the time otherwise prescribed by this rule, whichever period last expires.

If a timely motion under the Massachusetts Rules of Civil Procedure is filed in the lower court by any party: (1) for judgment under Rule 50(b); (2) under Rule 52(b) to amend or make additional findings of fact, whether or not an alteration of the judgment would be required if the motion is granted; (3) under Rule 59 to alter or amend a judgment; or (4) under Rule 59 for a new trial, the time for appeal for all parties shall run from the entry of the order denying a new trial or granting or denying any other such motion. A notice of appeal filed before the disposition of any of the above motions shall have no effect. A new notice of appeal must be filed within the prescribed time measured from the entry of the order disposing of the motion as provided above. No additional fees shall be required for such filing.

(b) Appeals in Criminal Cases. In a criminal case, unless otherwise provided by statute or court rule, the notice of appeal required by Rule 3 shall be filed with the clerk of the lower court within thirty days after entry of the judgment or order appealed from; or entry of a notice of appeal by the Commonwealth; or the imposition of sentence.

The running of the time for filing a notice of appeal shall be terminated as to the moving party by a motion for a new trial pursuant to Massachusetts Rules of Criminal Procedure 30 filed in the lower court within thirty days after the verdict or finding of guilt or within thirty days after imposition of sentence and the full time fixed by this rule shall commence to run and shall be computed from the date of entry of an order denying such motion.

(c) Extension of Time for Filing Notice of Appeal. Upon a showing of excusable neglect, the lower court may extend the time for filing the notice of appeal by any party for a period not to exceed thirty days from the expiration of the time otherwise prescribed by this rule. Such an extension may be granted before or after the time otherwise prescribed by this rule has expired; but if a request for an extension is made after such time has expired, it shall be made by motion with such notice as the lower court shall deem appropriate.

Amended May 15, 1979, effective July 1, 1979; July 20, 1984, effective January 1, 1985; June 7, 1985, effective July 1, 1985; July 28, 1999, effective September 1, 1999; March 6, 2000, effective April 3, 2000.

Reporter's Notes—1973

Certain motions toll the running of the appeal time. These motions, enumerated in Appellate Rule 4, pertain to the allowance or denial of a judgment, the opening of the record, the altering or amending of a judgment, and the seeking of a new trial. The new, *full* appeal period begins to run from the day the court finally decides a motion in any of the foregoing classes. The time for filing an appeal may be enlarged by order of an appellate court or an appellate justice, but such extension can never exceed one year from the date of the judgment or order appealed from, see Appellate Rule 14(b).

Reporter's Notes—1979

The first two paragraphs of former Rule 4 have been denominated subdivision (a) and are limited to civil cases.

Added to Rule 4 is the substance of subdivision (b), which enlarges the time for filing a claim of appeal in criminal cases from twenty days to thirty (see former G.L. c. 278, § 28 [St.1820, c. 79, § 4]; Superior Court Rule 65 [1974]; G.L. c. 278, § 33B [St.1955, c. 352, § 2]), and which provides that if a motion for a new trial (Mass.R.Crim.P. 30[b]) which is filed within thirty days after verdict or imposition of sentence is ultimately denied, a new thirty-day period for filing the claim of appeal from the conviction shall commence to run. While this latter provision may appear to foster delay, it actually formalizes prior practice.

This subdivision also recognizes the defendant's right to claim an appeal from a guilty verdict or finding as well as his right to appeal from the sentence. This was intended to avoid any ambiguity as to whether a claim of appeal prior to the final judgment was out of time and ineffective. See Commonwealth v. Dascalakis, 246 Mass. 12, 19 "Sentence is final judgment in a criminal case."

The third paragraph of former Rule 4 is now subdivision (c) and is applicable to both civil and criminal appeals. Under former G.L. c. 278, § 33B, the twenty-day limit was mandatory and could not be extended by consent of the parties or by the court; an untimely claim of appeal divested the appellate court of jurisdiction. Commonwealth v. Rodrigues, 333 Mass. 501 (1956); Commonwealth v. McKnight, 289 Mass. 530, 538, 540 (1935).

See also Commonwealth v. Dorius, 343 Mass. 533 (1962) where it was held that after the time for filing the claim of appeal had expired the trial court was without jurisdiction to extend the period by allowing a motion to make the case subject to then G.L. c. 278, § 33E as amended St.1979, c. 346, § 2 which would thereby trigger a new appeal period.

See Silvia v. Laurie, 594 F.2d 892 (1st Cir.1978) where the Court of Appeals also held the time limit for filing the claim of appeal under the Federal Rules of Appellate Procedure was jurisdictional.

> [T]he time limits of [Fed.R.App.P.] 4 are not merely procedural requirements that can be waived at the discretion of the court, but rather are limits on . . . [the appellate] court's power to review decisions of the . . . [lower] courts. . . . While the application of this rule may lead to apparently harsh results in some cases, it serves important interests of finality.

594 F.2d at 893. Subdivision (c) permits the lower court to extend the time for filing a notice of appeal by an additional thirty days upon "a showing of excusable neglect." Such an extension, whether granted before or after the expiration of the thirty days prescribed by subdivision (b), may not enlarge the time beyond sixty days after the verdict or finding of guilt or imposition of sentence. *See Silvia v. Laurie,* supra. Compare Mass.R.App.P. 14(b) (Appellate court or single justice may extend time for noticing appeal up to one year after verdict or sentence).

Reporter's Notes—1984

This amendment makes Mass.R.A.P. 4(a) conform, in part, to a 1979 federal amendment. See F.R.A.P. 4(a)(4). Its primary purpose is to clarify an ambiguity as to the effect of filing an appeal prior to a decision on specified timely motions under Mass.R.Civ.P. 50(b), 52(b) and 59.

Reporter's Notes—1985

The added sentence conforms the Massachusetts Rule to the last sentence of F.R.A.P. 4(a)(1). The purpose is to protect appellants who mistakenly, but in otherwise timely fashion, file a notice of appeal in an appellate court rather than in the lower court.

The change from ten days to fourteen days for the filing of a cross-appeal conforms the time period to that found in F.R.A.P. 4(a)(3). Such conformity of time periods may aid practitioners.

Reporter's Notes—1999

The 1999 amendments to Appellate Rule 4(a) were part of a comprehensive set of amendments to the Appellate Rules (Rules 1, 3, 4, 8, and 10) that had been proposed by the Supreme Judicial Court Committee on Appeals of Child Welfare Cases. The purpose of the 1999 amendments is described in the 1999 Reporter's Notes to Appellate Rule 1(c).

Appellate Rule 4(a) has been amended to provide for a uniform 30–day period for filing a notice of appeal in all child welfare cases. See G.L. c. 119, § 27, as amended by St. 1999, c. 3, § 11.

Reporter's Notes—2000

Appellate Rule 4(b) was amended in 2000 in light of the Supreme Judicial Court's opinion in Commonwealth v. White, 429 Mass. 258 (1999). In *White*, the Court ruled that in criminal cases, "a notice of appeal of any judgment or order appealed from must be filed within thirty days after the entry of the order," even though Appellate Rule 4 may not have been clear on the matter. Specific language has now been added to Rule 4(b) to eliminate any ambiguity.

Prior to the 2000 amendment, Appellate Rule 4(b) also provided that the notice of appeal was to be filed within thirty days, unless otherwise provided by statute. The rule now states that the notice of appeal is to be filed within thirty days unless otherwise provided by statute *or court rule*.

Rule 5. Report of a Case for Determination

A report of a case for determination by an appellate court shall for all purposes under these rules be taken as the equivalent of a notice of appeal. Whenever a case or any part of it is reported after decision or

verdict, the aggrieved party (as designated by the lower court) shall be treated as the appellant. Whenever a case or any part of it is reported without decision or verdict, the plaintiff in a civil action or the defendant in a criminal case shall be treated as the appellant. The clerk of the lower court shall serve notice of the filing of the report by mailing a copy thereof to counsel of record for each party; or if a party is not represented by counsel, to the party at his last known address.
Amended May 15, 1979, effective July 1, 1979.

Reporter's Notes—1973

No federal analogue to Appellate Rule 5 exists. Read in conjunction with Mass.R.Civ.P. 64 (Report of Case), it prescribes the adversarial framework at the appellate level for cases reported, either after an interlocutory ruling, upon an agreed statement of facts, or on a question of law reserved by a single justice of the Supreme Judicial Court (see Mass. R.Civ.P. 64). Whatever the form of the report, no party need file a separate notice of appeal (compare Appellate Rule 3); the report itself serves that function.

Reporter's Notes—1979

This rule is amended to provide that if a case is reported by the trial court prior to a decision or verdict, the plaintiff in a civil action or the defendant in a criminal case is to be the appellant. If a whole case or any issue arising therein is reported after a decision or verdict, the aggrieved party, as determined by the trial court, shall be designated as the appellant. As to reports in criminal cases generally, see Mass.R.Crim.P. 34 (1979) and Reporter's Notes.

Rule 6. Stay or Injunction Pending Appeal

(a) Civil Cases.

(1) Stay Must Ordinarily be Sought in the First Instance in Lower Court; Motion for Stay in Appellate Court. In civil cases, an application for a stay of the judgment or order of a lower court pending appeal, or for approval of a bond under subsection (a) (2) of this rule, or for an order suspending, modifying, restoring or granting an injunction during the pendency of an appeal must ordinarily be made in the first instance in the lower court. A motion for such relief may be made to the appellate court or to a single justice, but the motion shall show that application to the lower court for the relief sought is not practicable, or that the lower court has denied an application, or has failed to afford the relief which the applicant requested, with the reasons given by the lower court for its action. The motion shall also show the reasons for the relief requested and the facts relied upon, and if the facts are subject to dispute the motion shall be supported by affidavits or other statements signed under the penalties of perjury or copies thereof. With the motion shall be filed such parts of the record as are relevant. Reasonable notice of the motion shall be given to all parties. The motion shall be filed with the clerk of the appellate court to which the appeal is being taken (provided that if the court be the Supreme Judicial Court, the motion shall be filed with the clerk of the Supreme Judicial Court for Suffolk County).

(2) Stay May Be Conditioned Upon Giving of Bond; Proceedings Against Sureties. Relief available in the appellate court under this rule may be conditioned upon the filing of a bond or other appropriate security in the lower court. If security is given in the form of a bond or stipulation or other undertaking with one or more sureties, each surety thereby shall submit to the jurisdiction of the lower court and irrevocably appoint the clerk of the lower court as an authorized agent upon whom any papers affecting liability on the bond or undertaking may be served. A surety's liability may be entered against the surety on motion in the lower court without the necessity of an independent action. The motion and such notice of the motion as the lower court prescribes may be served on the clerk of the lower court, who shall forthwith mail copies to the sureties if their addresses are known.

(3) Terms. Relief available in the appellate court under this rule, or denial of such relief, may be conditioned on such reasonable terms as the appellate court or single justice may impose. For failure to observe such terms, the appellate court or single justice may make such further order as it or he deems just and appropriate.

(b) Criminal Cases. A motion for a stay of execution of a sentence shall be governed by paragraph (b) of this rule and by Massachusetts Rules of Criminal Procedure 31

(1) Stay Must Ordinarily be Sought in the First Instance in Lower Court; Motion for Stay in Appellate Court. In criminal cases, an application for a stay of execution of a sentence pending appeal must ordinarily be made in the first instance in the lower court. A motion for such relief may be made to the single justice of the appellate court to which the appeal is being taken, but the motion shall show that application to the lower court for the relief sought is not practicable, or that the lower court has previously denied an application for a stay or has failed to afford the relief which the applicant requested with the reasons given by the lower court for its action. The motion shall also show the reasons for the relief requested and the facts relied upon, and if the facts are subject to dispute the motion shall be supported by affidavits or other statements signed under the penalties of perjury or copies thereof. With the motion shall be filed such parts of the record as are relevant The motion shall be filed with the clerk of the appellate court to which the appeal is being taken (provided that if the court be the Supreme Judicial Court, the motion shall be filed with the clerk of the Supreme Judicial Court for Suffolk County).

(2) Reasonable Notice. Reasonable notice of the motion for a stay shall be given to the Commonwealth. If the motion is filed at least 30 days prior to the date the appellant's brief is due, the time for a response shall be governed by Rule 15. If the motion is filed at any other time, the Commonwealth shall have 30 days

to respond. A single justice may shorten or extend the time for responding to any motion authorized by this Rule.

(3) Appealability of Single Justice Order. Finality. An order by the single justice allowing or denying an application for a stay may be appealed to the appellate court in which the appeal is pending. An order by the appellate court in which the appeal is pending, allowing or denying an application for a stay, shall be final.

(4) Revocation of Stay Pending Appeal. If a defendant fails at any time to take any measure necessary for the hearing of an appeal or report, a stay of execution of a sentence may, on motion of the Commonwealth, be revoked.

(5) Expiration of Stay. Upon the release of the rescript by the appellate court of a judgment affirming the conviction, the stay of execution of sentence automatically expires, unless extended by the appellate court.

(6) Notice of Expiration of Stay. Upon release of a rescript affirming the conviction, the clerk of the appellate court shall notify the clerk of the trial court and the parties that the conviction has been affirmed and that therefore, the stay of execution of sentence has automatically expired.

Amended December 14, 1976, effective January 1, 1977; May 15, 1979, effective July 1, 1979; June 24, 2009, effective October 1, 2009.

Reporter's Notes—1973

Appellate Rule 6, patterned on F.R.A.P. 8, allows the court (first the lower court, then the appellate court) to grant such relief as may be necessary to preserve the rights of the parties during the pendency of an appeal. Appellate Rule 6 does not substantially alter the powers of the court under existing practice. See G.L. c. 214, § 19. City of Boston v. Santosuosso, 308 Mass. 202, 210, 31 N.E.2d 572, 578 (1941); G.L. c. 231, § 116. Appellate Rule 6(c), which is new, codifies existing federal practice. See also Mass.R.Civ.P. 62(c). Prior Massachusetts practice will, however continue to control stays in criminal cases. G.L. c. 278, § 28B, c. 279, §§ 4, 49A.

Reporter's Notes—1979

Subdivision (a) of Rule 6, requiring applications or motions for stays to be ordinarily filed in the lower court in the first instance, is expanded to cover both civil and criminal cases.

Subdivisions (b) and (c) of former Rule 6 are made (b)(1) and (b)(2) of the amended rule, and are applicable only to civil cases.

A new subdivision (c), relative to motions for stays of execution of sentence in criminal cases, incorporates by reference Mass.R.Crim.P. 31 (1979).

The Appeals Court in Commonwealth v. Levin, Mass.App.Ct.Adv.Sh. (1979) 857 further app. rev. denied Mass.Adv.Sh. (1979) 1610 and the Supreme Judicial Court in Commonwealth v. Allen, Mass.Adv.Sh. (1979) 1819 established the criteria for determining whether a stay of sentence pending appellate review ought to be granted. These cases establish that the same judgment and discretion as used by the lower courts in bail applications can properly be considered on questions on motions for stay. These cases acknowledge that considerations such as whether the defendant was likely to be a danger to any other person or to the community and as to the likelihood of further criminal conduct during the pendency of the appeal were appropriate.

Under these decisions the lower court is also empowered to require that the appeal present "an issue which is worthy of presentation to an appellate court, one which offers some reasonable possibility of a successful decision in the appeal." Commonwealth v. Levin, Mass.App.Ct.Adv.Sh. (1979) 857, 860.

The Supreme Judicial Court in *Allen* further held that the application of this standard was open, de novo, to the full bench of the appellate court after a determination of the single justice of that court denying a stay.

Subdivision (c) also establishes that a stay of execution, once granted, is always subject to being vacated if the defendant is not diligent in prosecuting his appeal. See ABA *Standards Relating to Criminal Appeals* 21–2.5(a) & commentary at 15 (2d ed., Approved Draft, 1978).

The second paragraph of subdivision (c) was added to ensure that an appeal, where a stay of sentence had been allowed, is prosecuted with reasonable dispatch under all the circumstances. It is expected that this provision will be used to vacate a stay for serious delays caused by the appellant and not for mere technical lapses which do not disrupt the schedule of the appellate court.

Reporter's Notes—2009

[The notes to the 2009 amendments were drafted by the Reporter for the Massachusetts Rules of Criminal Procedure]

This Rule was revised in 2009 to describe more fully the procedure for obtaining a stay of execution of a criminal sentence in an appellate court. It complements Rule 31 of the Rules of Criminal Procedure.

The 2009 amendment clarified the appellate process for stays of execution of a criminal sentence pending an appeal. As in civil cases, requests for a stay must first be presented to the trial court, unless such an application is not practicable. Either the defendant or the Commonwealth may seek relief from a single justice of the court that will hear the appeal concerning the trial judge's decision to deny, *e.g., Commonwealth v. Aviles,* 422 Mass. 1008 (1996), or grant, *e.g. Commonwealth v. Hodge,* 380 Mass. 851 (1980), a stay. Only the parties may do so. *See Hagen v. Commonwealth,* 437 Mass. 374, 375 (2002) (crime victim lacks standing to request revocation of stay). In the ordinary course of events, for all but first-degree murder cases a single justice of the Appeals Court is the appropriate forum. The single justice does not review the decision of the trial judge, but considers the matter de novo. *See Commonwealth v. Allen,* 378 Mass. 489, 497 (1979).

Rule 6(b)(2) recognizes that it is important to give the Commonwealth adequate time to prepare a response to a motion for a stay, since that will often require substantial effort in addressing the merits of the underlying appeal.

After the single justice decides the issue, there is only one further step in the process: an appeal to the panel of the Appeals Court that will decide the merits, or the full bench of the Supreme Judicial Court if the case will be decided there. This changes prior practice, which allowed a party aggrieved by the decision of a single justice of the Appeals Court the option of seeking relief both by appealing the decision in that court and asking a single justice of the Supreme Judicial

Court to entertain the matter. *See e.g., Duong v. Commonwealth,* 434 Mass. 1006 (2001). The appeal from the decision of the single justice may be accompanied by a motion for an expedited ruling. *See e.g., Restucci v. Commonwealth,* 442 Mass. 1045 (2004).

As also provided in Mass. R. Crim. P. 31, a stay of execution of sentence automatically expires when the appellate court considering the appeal releases a rescript affirming the conviction, unless the appellate court decides to extend it. A rescript is "released" when it is announced to the public and the appellate court notifies the parties that the court has decided the case. *Cf.* Mass. R. App. P. 23 (requiring the clerk of the appellate court to mail the parties a copy of the rescript and the opinion, if any). In the ordinary course of events, the rescript "issues" twenty-eight days following the release date or upon the denial of any petition for rehearing or application for further appellate review, whichever is later. *Id.*

When a rescript is released affirming a conviction, the clerk of the appellate court, in addition to the obligation that Mass. R. App. P. 23 imposes, shall notify the parties and the trial court clerk that the stay of execution of sentence has automatically expired. If the defendant wishes to apply for a new stay, in order to seek a rehearing or further appellate review, such a request should go to the appellate court that decided the case (either the panel of the Appeals Court or the full bench of the Supreme Judicial Court).

The court that decided the appeal may exercise its discretion to extend a stay of execution pending a petition for rehearing, application for further appellate review, or petition for certiorari. Unless otherwise specified, an extended stay expires when the rescript issues. The appellate court may act *sua sponte* or pursuant to the defendant's motion, which may be filed before the appeal is decided or after the rescript is released.

Rule 7. Disability of a Member of the Lower Court

If by reason of death, sickness, resignation, removal, or other disability, the judge or judges whose decision has been appealed to the appellate court be unable to perform the duties to be performed under these rules by the lower court, then any other judge regularly sitting in or assigned to such lower court may, on assignment by the Chief Justice or presiding judge of such lower court, perform those duties.

Reporter's Notes—1973

This rule, which does not appear in the Federal Rules of Appellate Procedure, reads into appellate procedure the provisions of Mass.R.Civ.P. 63, and ensures that whenever the Appellate Rules require action by the lower court judge, his disability will not of itself impede the appellate process.

Reporter's Notes—1979

Disability of the trial judge in criminal cases was formerly dealt with in Supreme Judicial Court Rule 1:10 (1975: 366 Mass. 859–60) and Appeals Court Rule 1:10 (1975: 3 Mass. App.Ct. 803), which are superseded by the application of this rule to criminal proceedings. As to disability of the judge under the trial rules, see Mass.R.Civ.P. 63 (1974) and Mass. R.Crim.P. 38 (1979).

Rule 8. The Record on Appeal

(a) Composition of the Record on Appeal. The original papers and exhibits on file, the transcript of proceedings, if any, and a certified copy of the docket entries prepared by the clerk of the lower court shall constitute the record on appeal in all cases. In a civil case, in an appeal from an appellate division, the original papers and exhibits shall include the report of the trial judge to the appellate division with any exhibits made a part of such report.

(b) The Transcript of Proceedings.

(1) *Civil Cases, Except Child Welfare Cases: Duty of Appellant to Order; Notice to Appellee if Partial Transcript Is Ordered.* Within ten days after filing the notice of appeal the appellant shall order from the court reporter a transcript of such parts of the proceedings not already on file as he deems necessary for inclusion in the record. If the appellant intends to urge on appeal that a finding or conclusion is unsupported by the evidence or is contrary to the evidence, he shall include in the record a transcript of all evidence relevant to such finding or conclusion. Unless the entire transcript is to be included, the appellant shall, within the time above provided, file and serve on the appellee a description of the parts of the transcript which he intends to include in the record and a statement of the issues he intends to present on the appeal. If the appellee deems a transcript of other parts of the proceedings to be necessary he shall, within 10 days after the service of the statement of the appellant, file and serve on the appellant a designation of additional parts to be included. If the appellant shall refuse to order such parts, the appellee shall either order the parts or apply to the lower court for an order requiring the appellant to do so. At the time of ordering, a party shall make satisfactory arrangements with the court reporter for payment of the cost of the transcript.

(2) *Criminal Cases: Duty of Clerk; Duty of Court Reporter.* Upon the filing of a notice of appeal, unless the parties file therewith a stipulation designating the parts of the proceedings which need not be transcribed, the clerk of the lower court, within ten days, shall order from the court reporter a transcript of the proceedings and shall file a certificate of such order. The parties are encouraged to stipulate to those parts of the proceedings which are unnecessary to the appeal. Upon receipt of an order, the court reporter shall prepare one original typed transcript. The court reporter shall deliver the original typed transcript to the clerk of the lower court who shall, by means of xerography or other similar method which produces legible copies, prepare one copy thereof for each of the appellate court, the appellant, and the appellee. The clerk of the lower court shall deliver one copy each to the appellant and the appellee and shall certify that the copies of the appellant and appellee have been delivered. The clerk of the lower court shall retain custody of the original typed transcript and one copy thereof

until the record is transmitted to the appellate court as provided by Rule 9(d).

The Commonwealth shall pay the cost of the original of the typed transcript and a copy for the appellate court. Except as provided in Rule 8(b)(4), the cost of the copy for the appellant shall be paid for by the appellant.

(3) *Electronically Recorded Proceedings, Except Child Welfare Cases.*

(i) Applicability. Rule 8(b)(3) applies to proceedings which were recorded electronically on equipment under the control of the court and which were not recorded by an official court reporter.

If, however, a complete transcript of the electronic recording has been produced for use by the trial court, and it or a copy is available to the parties, such transcript or copy shall be utilized in lieu of preparing another pursuant to this Rule 8(b)(3). Upon receipt of the notice of appeal in such cases, the clerk shall advise the parties of the name of the preparer of the transcript; the parties shall then follow the procedure under Rule 8(b)(1) in a civil case, or Rule 8(b)(2) in a criminal case, as if a court reporter had been present, except the appellant's time for ordering a transcript shall be extended to within ten days after appellant's receipt of the clerk's notification of the name of the preparer of the transcript.

(ii) Duties of the Appellant and of the Clerk; Selection of Transcriber. If the appellant deems all or part of the electronic recording necessary for inclusion in the record, the appellant shall, simultaneously with filing a notice of appeal, order from the clerk of the lower court, in accordance with any rule or established policy of the court, a cassette copy of the electronic recording, which is hereinafter called "the cassette." The clerk shall promptly provide the cassette, unless the provisions of the second paragraph of Rule 8(b)(3)(i) apply. If a portion of the electronic recording has already been transcribed for use by the trial court, and such transcript or a copy is available to the parties, the clerk shall, in addition to providing the cassette, at the same time advise the parties of the name of the preparer of the transcript.

Within fifteen days of receipt of the cassette from the clerk, appellant shall file in court and serve on each appellee a document which includes the date of receipt of the cassette; a designation of the parts of the cassette the appellant intends to include in the transcript; and the name, address, and telephone number of the individual or firm selected to prepare the transcript, provided that the appellant and each appellee have agreed to this choice and the appellant so states. If the appellant and appellees have not so agreed, said document shall also specifically notify the clerk to select the transcriber.

The designation of the parts of the cassette to be transcribed should be precise and include such details as the name of the witness whose testimony has been designated and the portions to be included, giving an exact quote of the beginning words and concluding words of each designated portion.

If such selection of an individual or firm to prepare the transcript is not included, or if the transcript is to be provided at the expense of the Commonwealth, the individual or firm shall be selected by the clerk. When the selection is made by the clerk, the individual or firm shall be selected in accordance with procedures promulgated by the Chief Administrative Justice. The clerk shall promptly notify all parties of any such selection made by the clerk. Any individual or firm selected to transcribe the record pursuant to Rule 8(b)(3) is hereinafter called "the transcriber."

If the appellant has designated the entire cassette for transcription, then within said fifteen days of receipt of the cassette from the clerk, appellant shall also send or deliver to the transcriber the cassette provided by the clerk and a written order designating the entire cassette for transcription. If the appellant has not designated the entire cassette, then after twenty days have expired from the service upon the appellee of appellant's designation of transcript, the appellant shall promptly send or deliver to the transcriber the cassette provided by the clerk and a written order which states those parts of the cassette designated by the parties for transcription. In addition, the order, whether for all or part of the transcript, shall include a statement that the original of the designated portions of the transcript should be sent to the clerk of the lower court, and shall indicate the number of copies, if any, to be sent to the appellant. The appellant shall promptly file with the clerk and serve on the other parties a copy of the order placed with the transcriber. Unless the entire cassette is to be transcribed, the appellant shall, together with appellant's designation of transcript, file and serve on the appellee a statement of the issues the appellant intends to present on the appeal.

The appellant shall cooperate with the transcriber by providing such information as is necessary to facilitate transcription, and, where the Commonwealth is not responsible for the cost of transcription, make satisfactory arrangements with the transcriber to pay for the trial court's original of the designated portions of the transcript and any copies ordered by the appellant for the appellant's own use.

(iii) Duties of the Appellee. If the appellee deems it necessary to have a cassette in order to consider counter-designating, or for any other purpose, the appellee shall, after receipt of the notice of appeal, promptly order the cassette from the clerk or promptly arrange with the appellant to use appellant's cassette. If the appellant has not designated and ordered the entire transcript and if the appellee deems a transcript of other portions of the proceedings to be necessary, the appellee shall within fifteen days after receipt of the appellant's designation, file in court, and serve on the appellant, a designation of such additional parts. The designation of the parts of the cassette to be transcribed should be precise and include such details as the name of the witness whose testimony has been designated and the specific portions to be included, giving an exact quote of the beginning words and concluding words of each designated portion. If the appellant shall refuse to order such parts, the appellee shall either order the parts or apply to the lower court for an order requiring the appellant to do so. If the appellee desires a copy of designated portions of the transcript, the appellee shall promptly communicate to the transcriber the number of copies wanted and, in cases where the Commonwealth is not responsible for the cost of the transcript, make satisfactory arrangements with the transcriber for payment for the appellee's own copies.

The appellee shall cooperate with the transcriber by providing such information as is necessary to facilitate transcription.

(iv) Duties of the Transcriber. The transcriber shall prepare an original typed transcript of the designated portions and the requested number of copies, in accordance with the designations, and shall deliver said original to the clerk, with the following certificate of accuracy:

I, ______, do hereby certify that the foregoing is a true and accurate transcript, prepared to the best of my ability, of the designated portions of the cassette provided to me by the appellant or appellee of a trial or hearing of the ______ Division of the ______ Court Department in the proceedings of ______ v. ______, case(s) no.(s) ______ before Justice ______ on ______.

Date: ______ ______
Transcriber's Signature

The transcriber shall deliver legible copies to all parties who have so requested.

(v) Unintelligible Portions of the Cassette. If portions of the cassette cannot be transcribed because they are unintelligible, the parties shall promptly use reasonable efforts to stipulate their content. If agreement cannot be reached, the parties shall promptly present their differences as to such portions to the trial judge who heard the testimony. The trial judge shall, if possible, settle the content of the unintelligible portions, which shall then be included in the transcript.

(vi) Transcripts Paid for by the Commonwealth. In criminal cases, the Commonwealth shall pay the cost of the original of the designated portions of the typed transcript and a copy for the appellate court. Except as provided in Rule 8(b)(4), the cost of the copy for the appellant shall be paid for by the appellant who shall make arrangements with the transcriber to pay for such copy.

Whenever the Commonwealth is to pay for an original or copy of the designated portions of the transcript, each party designating any portion of the cassette for transcription shall, at the time of filing the designation, also file a certificate that the parts designated are necessary to permit full consideration of the issues on appeal. Unless one of the parties specifically requests otherwise, that part of the cassette dealing with impanelment of a jury shall not be transcribed.

(4) *Cost of Transcripts for Indigents.* In all cases in which counsel is required to be made available pursuant to Supreme Judicial Court Rule 3:10, the cost of any transcript for such a party shall be paid for by the Commonwealth.

(5) *Child Welfare Cases.*

(i) Proceedings Recorded by an Official Court Reporter. On the filing of a notice of appeal, unless the parties file therewith a stipulation designating the parts of the proceedings which need not be transcribed, the clerk of the lower court on behalf of the appellant, shall order from the court reporter a transcript of the entire proceeding or of such parts of the proceeding not already on file. The clerk of the lower court shall notify all parties of the date the transcript was ordered by sending a copy of the order form to all parties.

On receipt of the order the court reporter shall prepare an original typed transcript for filing with the lower court and a copy for the appellant and any party who so requests. The court reporter shall deliver the original to the clerk of the lower court who shall immediately notify all parties of its receipt, and the court reporter shall deliver legible copies to the appellant and to any party who so requests.

(ii) Electronically Recorded Proceedings

(a) Applicability: Rule 8(b)(5)(ii) applies to child welfare cases which were recorded electronically on equipment under the control of the court and which were not recorded by an official court reporter. If, however, a complete transcript of the electronic recording has been produced for use by the lower court, and it or a copy is available to the parties, that transcript or copy shall be used.

(b) Duties of the Appellant and Clerk. Upon the filing of a notice of appeal, the clerk of the lower court shall produce a cassette copy of the electronic recording. Within 10 days of production of the cassette, the clerk of the lower court shall, unless the parties file a stipulation designating the parts of the cassette which need not be transcribed, on behalf of the appellant order a transcription of the entire cassette from a transcriber selected by the clerk in accordance with procedures promulgated by the Chief Justice for Administration and Management. The clerk shall also notify all parties of the name of the transcriber and the date the cassette was sent for transcription by sending a copy of the order form to all parties.

On receipt of the order the transcriber shall prepare an original typed transcript for filing in the lower court and a copy for the appellant and any party who so requests. The transcriber shall deliver the original to the clerk of the lower court who shall immediately notify all parties of its receipt, and the transcriber shall deliver legible copies to the appellant and to any party who so requests. The appellant and appellee shall cooperate with the transcriber by providing information necessary to facilitate transcription.

The transcriber shall certify the original transcript using the following certificate of accuracy:

I, ______, do hereby certify that the foregoing is a true and accurate transcript, prepared to the best of my ability, of the designated portions of the cassette provided to me by the clerk of the lower court of a trial or hearing of the ______ Division of the ______ Court Department in the proceedings of ______, case(s) no(s). ______ before Justice ______ on ______.

Date: ______________ ______________________

Transcriber's Signature

(iii) Unintelligible Portions of the Cassette. If portions of the cassette cannot be transcribed because they are unintelligible, the parties shall promptly use reasonable efforts to stipulate their content. If agreement cannot be reached, the parties shall promptly present their differences as to such portions to the trial judge who heard the testimony. The trial judge shall, if possible, settle the content of the unintelligible portions, which shall then be included in the transcript.

(iv) Costs. The appellant shall pay for the cost of the original transcript filed with the lower court and for any copies ordered by the appellant. If there is more than one appellant, the cost of the original and any copies shall be divided between the various appellants. Any other party who requested a copy of the transcript shall pay for its copy. For any party for whom counsel is made available pursuant to Supreme Judicial Court Rule 3:10, the cost of any transcript requested by, or on behalf of, such party shall be paid in accordance with G.L. c. 261.

(c) Statement of the Evidence or Proceedings When No Report Was Made or When the Transcript Is Unavailable. If no report of the evidence or proceedings at a hearing or trial was made, or if a transcript is unavailable, the appellant may, within thirty days after the notice of appeal is filed, file a statement of the evidence or proceedings from the best available means, including his recollection. The statement shall be served on the appellee, who may file objections or proposed amendments thereto within ten days after service. Thereupon the statement and any objections or proposed amendments thereto shall be submitted to the lower court for settlement and approval and as settled and approved shall be included by the clerk of the lower court in the record on appeal.

(d) Agreed Statement as the Record on Appeal. In lieu of the record on appeal as defined in subdivision (a) of this rule, the parties may, within thirty days after the notice of appeal is filed, prepare and sign a statement of the case showing how the issues presented by the appeal arose and were decided in the lower court and setting forth only so many of the facts averred and proved or sought to be proved as are essential to a decision of the issues presented. If the statement conforms to the truth, it, together with such additions as the court may consider necessary fully to present the issues raised by the appeal, shall be approved by the lower court, and as approved shall be retained in the lower court as the record on appeal.

Copies of the agreed statement shall be filed as the appendix required by Rule 18.

(e) Correction or Modification of the Record. If any difference arises as to whether the record truly discloses what occurred in the lower court, the difference shall be submitted to and settled by that court and the record made to conform to the truth. If anything material to either party is omitted from the record by error or accident or is misstated therein, the parties by stipulation, or the lower court, either before or after the record is transmitted to the appellate court, or the appellate court, or a single justice, on proper suggestion or on its own motion, may direct that the omission or misstatement be corrected, and if necessary that a supplemental record be certified and transmitted. All other questions as to the form and content of the record shall be presented to a single justice.

Amended June 27, 1974, effective July 1, 1974; amended effective February 24, 1975; amended May 15, 1979, effective July 1, 1979; June 28, 1979, effective July 1, 1979; February 17, 1983, effective April 1, 1983; May 29, 1986, effective July 1, 1986; June 23, 1986, effective July 1, 1986; October 1, 1998, effective November 2, 1998; July 28, 1999, effective September 1, 1999; June 26, 2002, effective September 3, 2002.

Reporter's Notes—1973

Based on F.R.A.P. 10, Appellate Rule 8 describes the record on appeal, which should be carefully distinguished from the record appendix. The record consists of the original papers and exhibits, plus a transcript of the proceedings and a certified copy of the docket entries, as well as any certified copy of the lower court's final order. The record appendix (see Appellate Rule 18) is that distillation of the decision-essential portions of the record which is filed in connection with appellate brief.

The appellant is responsible for attending to the preparation of a transcript; this transcript must be sufficiently extensive to cover all points raised by the appeal. The phrase "description of the parts of the transcript," refers to such a description as "the plaintiff's entire testimony," rather than a designation by page and line, unless a more precise description is necessary.

If no transcript was made, the appellant may prepare a statement of the evidence in the proceedings in the most expeditious manner possible; after inspection by the appellee, this statement will be submitted to the lower court for approval. The statement of issues need be only extensive enough to enable the appellee to determine the need for ordering a transcript of other parts of the testimony.

The parties may, alternatively, prepare and file an agreed statement of facts. This is similar to existing practice, see G.L. c. 231, § 111; cf. Paulino v. Concord, 259 Mass. 142, 144, 155 N.E. 870, 871 (1927).

Reporter's Notes—1975

As originally promulgated, Appellate Rule 8 required the inclusion, in the record on appeal, of a certified copy of the order appealed from and the opinion. Because the record includes all "original papers" anyway, this requirement was superfluous. Accordingly, it has been eliminated.

Reporter's Notes—1979

The second sentence of subdivision (a) of former Rule 8 is amended to clarify that it applies to appeals in civil cases from the Appellate Division of the District Court Department (G.L. c. 231, § 108, as amended, St.1978, c. 478, § 264) and not to the Appellate Division of the Superior Court Department for review of sentences in criminal cases (G.L. c. 278, §§ 28A–28D).

Subdivision (b) of the former rule has been divided into subdivisions (b)(1), applicable to civil cases, and (b)(2), applicable to criminal cases. Subdivision (b)(1) is identical to former 8(b). Subdivision (b)(2) is wholly new.

Consonant with practice under former G.L. c. 278, §§ 33A–33H, a defendant is entitled to a complete transcript on appeal. Charpentier v. Commonwealth, Mass.Adv.Sh. (1978) 2163, 2172. Pursuant to (b)(2), upon the filing of a notice of appeal in a criminal case, the clerk of the lower court automatically orders from the court reporter a transcript of the proceedings out of which the appeal arises. Since counsel is no longer obligated to take this mechanical step, one point of delay under prior practice is thus eliminated. The parties may—and are encouraged by the rule to—file a stipulation as to those parts of the proceedings which are unnecessary to the appeal and which therefore need not be transcribed. The provision for stipulations as to parts of the proceedings which need not be transcribed is not applicable to capital cases under G.L. c. 278, § 33E, as amended, because in such cases, the "entire case" is before the Supreme Judicial Court, "including a transcript of the entire proceedings." E.g., *Charpentier,* supra at 2173 n. 9. A "capital case" is a case in which the defendant was convicted of murder in the first degree. G.L. c. 278, § 33E, as amended. *See Commonwealth v. O'Brien,* Mass.Adv.Sh. (1976) 2926; Mass.R.Crim.P. 2(b)(3).

When the transcript is completed, the court reporter is to deliver it to the clerk of the lower court who prepares copies thereof for the appellate court, the appellant or appellants, and the appellee or appellees. The parties' copies are delivered to them, while the original and one copy are retained by the clerk for transmission to the appellate court as part of the record (Rule 9[d]).

In the district court jury sessions, the General Laws (G.L. c. 218, § 27A(h)) provide a procedure for appointment of a court reporter to transcribe the proceedings and in the alternative for an electronic recording of the proceedings. These rules as well as G.L. c. 218, § 27A(g) provide that appeals from the district court jury sessions are to proceed in the same manner as appeals from the superior court.

Because of the unavailability of a court reporter in some cases in the district court jury sessions or where the defendant has not taken advantage of section 27A(h) it may be necessary for the clerk, who has the responsibility under this rule for the completion of the record, including the transcript, to cause a transcript to be made from an electronic recording.

After this necessary preliminary step has been taken by the district court clerk copies of the transcript are to be made and distributed as provided by this rule and rule 9(d).

The cost of preparation of the original transcript and of the copies required by this rule is borne by the Commonwealth except where the defendant is not indigent. In that case the defendant is to pay the clerk for the cost of producing his copy. The provision requiring production of the whole transcript is intended to provide for more expeditious and just disposition of questions on appeal. In the first place, the Commonwealth could not in all cases determine whether a partial transcript was adequate to serve its needs until such time as the defendant's brief was filed. Secondly, without a full transcript, appellate courts cannot resolve issues of plain error, a miscarriage of justice, or harmless error.

Subdivision (c) has been amended to enlarge the time within which a statement of the evidence or proceedings may be filed from ten to thirty days. Procedure like that provided under this subdivision has been followed by the Supreme Judicial Court in a criminal case when a transcript was unavailable. Commonwealth v. Harris, Mass.Adv.Sh. (1978) 2155.

It should be noted that the appellant may prepare and submit a statement of the evidence or proceeding from the best available means. However, as stated in Ingersoll Grove Nursing Home, Inc. v. Springfield Gas Light Co., Mass.Adv. Sh. (1979) 203, 204 a substitution is available only "if no report of the evidence or proceedings at a hearing or trial was made, or if a transcript is unavailable." In a case in which the transcript is "made and available" the plaintiff is not entitled to substitute a statement of the evidence under subdivision (c).

Subdivision (d) however allows the parties to "prepare and sign a statement of the case" in lieu of the record. The term "statement of the evidence or proceeding" of subdivision (c) is not to be used interchangeably with "statement of the case" in subdivision (d) since the rules outline different procedures with respect to these terms.

The agreed statement permitted by subdivision (d) must now be filed within thirty days after the notice of appeal is filed; prior to this amendment no time limit was specified. The parties electing to proceed under the subdivision should notify the clerk that no transcript is to be ordered and, in addition, that the agreed statement shall be substituted for the record as defined in subdivision (a). Filing of the agreed statement as the appendix required by Rule 18 has been made mandatory.

Subdivision (e), relative to correction or modification of the record, as applied to criminal cases, is similar in operation to prior provisions for settling a bill of exceptions (G.L. c. 278, § 31 [St.1974, c. 540, § 1]) or for correcting errors in a transcript (G.L. c. 278, § 33A [St.1974, c. 540, § 2]), although much broader in the scope of relief available.

Reporter's Notes to Addition of Rule 8(b)(3)—1983

Rule 8(b)(3) has been added to deal with tape-recorded transcripts. It is quite detailed because judges, clerks, and lawyers have complained about a lack of specificity with respect to the utilization of cassettes on appeal.

Rule 8(b)(3)(i) indicates when Rule 8(b)(3) applies. The Rule does not apply to court reporters, including voice writers, or to cases where a complete transcript has already been produced for use by the trial court, and is available to the parties. Rule 8(b)(3)(ii) gives the duties of appellants and clerks, and provides for appointment of a transcriber. A major purpose is to facilitate a speedy appeal. Consequently, an appellant must order a cassette at the time of appeal and state the date of receipt to insure that the designation is timely. Another major purpose is to reduce the number of steps required of the clerk. This rule permits the parties, if they can agree, to choose the transcriber. The appellant must inform the clerk at the time of transcript designation whether the parties have so agreed. The parties must order their copies directly from the transcriber and make their own payment arrangements; the transcriber delivers transcripts directly to them. Rule 8(b)(3)(ii), unlike 8(b)(1), does not specify when an appellant must transcribe all evidence relevant to a finding or conclusion. This is not meant to change the law, but rather leave it to the parties to determine what must be transcribed in order to protect their appeal. The Standing Advisory Committee wants to discourage unnecessary transcription.

Rule 8(b)(3)(iii) gives the duties of the appellee with respect to ordering a cassette or arranging to borrow the appellant's, counter-designation, and ordering copies. Rule 8(b)(3)(iv) describes the transcriber's duties, and the certificate which the transcriber must file. Rule 8(b)(3)(v) covers the situation where a portion of the cassette is unintelligible; it requires the parties first to attempt to stipulate the contents of such portion, and provides for the trial judge, if possible, to settle differences. Rule 8(b)(3)(vi) requires that when the Commonwealth must pay for an original transcript or copy, the designating parties must certify that they have designated only necessary portions. Again, the purpose is to reduce costs.

Rule 8(b)(3) does not have its own provision concerning enlargements of time, but is subject to the general computation and extension of time provisions contained in Appellate Rule 14.

Here is a chronology of the major steps and time periods under this rule:

1. Simultaneously with filing the notice of appeal, the appellant, if desirous of a transcript, orders the cassette. Rule 8(b)(3)(ii).

2. The clerk promptly provides the cassette (Rule 8(b)(3)(ii)), unless an entire transcript is already available; in such event, the clerk notifies the parties, and the normal designation rules in Rule 8(b)(1) or 8(b)(2) apply. Rule 8(b)(3)(i). In such event, the appellant's time for ordering a transcript is within ten days after the clerk's notification. Rule 8(b)(3)(i). The clerk also notifies the parties if there has been a previous transcription of a portion of the cassette, so that the parties may utilize the prior partial transcription if they wish. Rule 8(b)(3)(ii).

3. Within fifteen days after receipt of the cassette from the clerk, the appellant designates which portions are to be included in the transcript. Rule 8(b)(3)(ii). If the appellant wants the entire cassette transcribed, then appellant also delivers the cassette to the transcriber and places the order within said fifteen day period. Rule 8(b)(3)(ii).

4. When the appellant has not ordered the transcription of the entire transcript, the appellee has fifteen days from service of the appellant's designation to file and serve a counter-designation. Rule 8(b)(3)(iii).

5. When the appellant has not already designated the entire cassette for transcription, the appellant delivers the cassette to the transcriber and places the order promptly after twenty days have expired from service upon the appellee of the appellant's designation. Rule 8(b)(3)(ii). This, in effect, gives the appellant at least five days to deliver the cassette to the transcriber and place the order, for the appellee had to file and serve the counter-designation within fifteen days.

In summary, from the time the appellant receives the cassette from the clerk, the entire designation process takes fifteen days if appellant orders the entire cassette transcribed, and "promptly" after thirty-five days if appellant has designated less than the entire cassette.

Reporter's Notes—1998

The 1998 amendment to Appellate Rule 8(b)(3) deals with appeals in proceedings that were electronically-recorded on court-controlled recording equipment and not recorded by an official court reporter.

The existing rule allows the appellant to designate either the entire cassette or only specified portions of the cassette to be transcribed for purposes of preparing the appellate record. The existing rule further provides that where less than the entire cassette is to be designated, the appellant must inform the appellee of those portions of the cassette that are to be transcribed. This allows the appellee to counter-designate additional portions of the cassette for transcription. However, the current rule does not require the appellant to inform the appellee of the issues that the appellant intends to present on the appeal, thus making it difficult for the appellee to make such counter-designation intelligently.

The 1998 amendment resolves this dilemma by requiring the appellant to file and serve on the appellee a statement of the issues together with the appellant's designation of transcript.

Reporter's Notes—1999

The 1999 amendments to Appellate Rule 8(b) were part of a comprehensive set of amendments to the Appellate Rules (Rules 1, 3, 4, 8, and 10) that had been proposed by the Supreme Judicial Court Committee on Appeals of Child Welfare Cases. The purpose of the 1999 amendments is described in the 1999 Reporter's Notes to Appellate Rule 1(c).

Appellate Rule 8(b)(1) (concerning ordering the transcript) and Rule 8(b)(3) (concerning electronically-recorded proceedings) have been made inapplicable to child welfare cases. Instead, the ordering of the transcript of the proceeding is now controlled by Rule 8(b)(5). Rule 8(b)(5) shifts the duty of ordering the cassettes and transcripts from the appellant to the clerk of the lower court. Modeled in part after the procedures applicable in criminal cases, new Rule 8(b)(5) is intended to expedite preparation of the transcript in child welfare cases.

Reporter's Notes to Appellate Rule 8(b)(2)—2002

The 2002 amendment to Appellate Rule 8(b)(2) requires that upon the filing of a notice of appeal in a criminal case, the clerk of the lower court shall order a transcript from the court reporter within ten days. Prior to this amendment, there was no time period prescribed for ordering the transcript.

This amendment will make the practice in criminal cases consistent with that already in existence in civil cases in Massachusetts. Appellate Rule 8(b)(1) requires that in a civil case, the appellant shall order the transcript within ten days after filing of the notice of appeal. It should be noted that Rule 10(b)(1) of the Federal Rules of Appellate Procedure likewise requires that the transcript in civil and criminal cases in federal court be ordered within ten days of the filing of the notice of appeal.

Rule 9. Assembly and Transmission of the Record: Exhibits

(a) Assembly. The clerk of the lower court as soon as may be after the filing of the notice of appeal shall place together all the original papers including the exhibits filed in the lower court, together with such other papers as thereafter become a part of the record pursuant to Rule 8. The papers shall be numbered in the order of filing and the exhibits shall be plainly marked with the number assigned in the lower court preceded by the letters "exh.". The clerk shall append to the record a list of the documents correspondingly numbered and identified with reasonable definiteness. The record so assembled by the clerk shall be suitably spindled, bound, or tied and retained by the clerk in this form until the final disposition of the appeal, except as the record or any part of it is ordered to be transmitted by the appellate court or a single justice.

(b) Exhibits. No exhibit need be reproduced for the record, except by order of an appellate court, a single justice, or the judge of the lower court. Any counsel may reproduce any exhibit in several copies for the convenience of the court. The lower court shall make such orders as it deems necessary for the preservation of exhibits, and for the reproduction of important exhibits which the appellate court should examine, and the clerk of the lower court shall transmit any exhibit to the appellate court at the request of any party made at any time after the filing of the record appendix. A party shall make advance arrangements with the clerk of the lower court for the transmission and receipt of exhibits of unusual bulk or weight. No exhibit consisting of currency, bearer securities, firearms, narcotics, or contraband articles shall be transmitted to an appellate court unless pursuant to an order of the full appellate court or a justice thereof.

(c) Appellant's Obligation.

(1) *In General.* In a civil or criminal case, upon request by the clerk of the lower court, the appellant shall forthwith perform any act reasonably necessary to enable the clerk to assemble the record and the clerk shall assemble a single record.

The lower court or the appellate court or a single justice thereof may require the record to be assembled and the appeal to be docketed at any time.

(2) *Civil Cases.* Notwithstanding any other obligation which these rules may impose, but excepting electronically recorded proceedings governed by Rule 8(b)(3), each appellant in a civil case shall, within ten days after filing a notice of appeal, deliver to the clerk of the lower court either (i) a transcript of those portions of the transcript of the lower court proceedings which the appellant deems necessary for determination of the appeal, (ii) a signed statement certifying that the appellant has ordered such portions from the court reporter, or (iii) a signed statement certifying that the appellant has not ordered and does not intend to order the transcript or any portion thereof. Upon receiving the transcript, the appellant in a civil case shall forthwith deliver it to the clerk of the lower court.

(d) Duty of Clerk; Transmission. When the record is fully assembled, the clerk of the lower court shall notify the parties and the clerk of the appellate court and shall transmit to the appellate court two certified copies of the docket entries and, in a criminal case, the original and one copy of the transcript and a list of all the exhibits. In case of an order to transmit, transmission shall be effected when the clerk of the lower court mails or otherwise forwards the record to the clerk of the appellate court. The clerk of the lower court shall indicate, by endorsement on the face of the record or otherwise, the date upon which it is transmitted to the appellate court.

(e) Record for Preliminary Hearing in the Appellate Court. If prior to the time the record is assembled a party desires to make in the appellate court a motion for dismissal, for a stay pending appeal or for any intermediate order, the appellate court or a single justice may, on its own motion or on motion of any party, with or without notice, order the clerk of the lower court to transmit to the appellate court such parts of the original record as the appellate court or the single justice shall deem appropriate.

Amended May 15, 1979, effective July 1, 1979; amended effective May 1, 1994; June 26, 2002, effective September 3, 2002.

Reporter's Notes—1973

Appellate Rule 9, changing federal practice (which requires transmission of the entire record in all cases, see F.R.A.P. 11) responds to the Massachusetts practice of not sending the actual original papers to the appellate court. The rule, however, recognizes that occasionally it may be essential for such papers to be transmitted, and thus requires the clerk to assemble all the original papers in a case, including a transcript if any, and hold them, subject to an order by the appellate court to transmit the record to that court. The appellant must take whatever action is necessary to assure assembly; failure to do so jeopardizes the appeal, see Appellate Rule 10(c).

Reporter's Notes—1979

Subdivision (a) of Rule 9, as made applicable to criminal cases, supersedes the provisions of former G.L. c. 278, § 33C (St.1974, c. 458, § 1) relative to the preparation of the record.

Subdivision (b), relative to exhibits, is amended by the addition of a sentence which restates the substance of the first sentence of former Appeals Court Rule 1:06(3) (1975: 3 Mass.App.Ct. 802) and Supreme Judicial Court Rule 1:06(3) (1975: 366 Mass. 858–59). Subdivision (b) was previously incorporated into criminal appellate procedure by Appeals Court and Supreme Judicial Court Rules 1:06(1) (1975: 3 Mass.App.Ct. 802; 366 Mass. 858), except that "record appendix" in the appellate rule was taken to mean "record" in the context of a criminal appeal. This provision, which states that certain risk-associated exhibits are not to be transmitted to the appellate court absent an order, is applicable in civil as well as criminal cases.

Subdivision (c) is amended by limiting the forty-day time for appellants' assistance in assembly of the record to civil cases, and by requiring the appellant in a criminal case to forthwith perform any act reasonably necessary to enable the clerk to assemble the record. The provision for delivery to the clerk of the necessary parts of the transcript for inclusion in the record in civil cases is inapplicable to criminal cases since the clerk orders the transcript, makes and distributes the required copies to the parties and transmits the original and a copy to the appellate court, (Rule 8[b][2]). The entire transcript is included unless the parties stipulate otherwise (Id.).

The requirement of subdivision (d) that the clerk of the lower court transmit two copies of the docket entries to the appellate court in a criminal case conforms to procedure under former Appeals Court and Supreme Judicial Court Rules 1:09 (1975: 3 Mass.App.Ct. 802; 366 Mass. 859). Subdivision (d) additionally provides that the original and one copy of the transcript (see Rule 8[b][2]) and a list of all the exhibits (see former Appeals Court and Supreme Judicial Court Rules 1:06[3], supra) shall be transmitted with the record.

Reporter's Notes—1986

This rule [subdivision (b) of Rule 9], inter alia, requires the clerk of the lower court to "transmit any exhibit to the appellate court at the request of any party made at any time after the filing of the record appendix." It is important to realize, however, that the transmittal of such exhibits does not automatically permit lawyers to refer to them. Rule 18(a) states that ". . . the court may decline to permit the parties to refer to portions of the record omitted from the appendix, unless leave be granted prior to argument." *See* Iverson v. Board of Appeals of Dedham, 14 Mass.App.Ct. 951 (1982).

Reporter's Notes—1994

At several places in this Rule, and in Rule 8, the word "record" or the words "record on appeal" are used. It is critical that litigants realize that there is a profound difference between the "record" and the "appendix". The record is what the lower clerk assembles and retains "until the final disposition of the appeal, except as the record or any part of it is ordered to be transmitted by the appellate court or a single justice." Mass.R.A.P. 9(a). The appendix is what the appellant must file in accordance with Mass.R.A.P. 18. A 1993 amendment to Mass.R.A.P. 18, which was made to reflect the language of Shawmut Community Bank, N.A. v. Zagami, 411 Mass. 807, 810–812 (1992), emphasizes "the responsibility of the parties to include materials necessary to their appeal, including exhibits, in the appendix."

It is important to realize that when Mass.R.A.P. 9(b) says that "[n]o exhibit need be reproduced for the record, except by order of an appellate court, a single justice, or the judge of the lower court," it is talking about "the record" and not "the appendix". The fact that the rule goes on to say that "[a]ny counsel may reproduce any exhibit in several copies for the convenience of the court," also does not relieve the parties of their obligation to put copies of exhibits they rely upon in the appendix in accordance with Mass.R.A.P. 18.

Reporter's Notes to Mass.R.A.P. 9(c)(2)—1994

There has been an ambiguity in Mass.R.A.P. 9(c)(2) in those cases in which there has been an electronically recorded proceeding in trial court. Rule 9(c)(2) calls for the appellant, within forty days after filing the notice of appeal, to deliver to the clerk of the trial court either portions of the transcript or a signed statement certifying that the appellant has ordered such portions from the court reporter. Rule 8(b)(3), covering electronically recorded proceedings, has distinct provisions for obtaining a transcript which do not mesh perfectly with Rule 9(c)(2). For instance, as the dissent of Justice O'Connor (with whom Wilkins and Greaney, JJ. joined) explained in Russell v. McOwen-Hanelt, 413 Mass. 106, 114 (1992), the appellant in that case had a minimum of fifty-six days to order transcription of the cassette, so that the forty day notice provision in Rule 9(c)(2) did not fit. Nonetheless, in that case, the majority, relying on Hawkins v. Hawkins, 397 Mass. 401, 406 (1986), read Rule 9(c) to require the appellant in appeals from electronically recorded proceedings " 'to deliver either a transcript or a signed statement certifying that the tapes [are] being transcribed, to the clerk or register's office, [no later than] forty days after [the] appeal was filed.' " Russell v. McOwen-Hanelt, at 109.

The Standing Advisory Committee believes that Rule 9(c)(2) should be clarified so that henceforth it does not apply to electronically recorded proceedings. There are special problems when a tape recorder rather than a stenographer has been used to record a trial. For instance, an appellant must order and receive the cassette from the lower court before the designation process can begin and a person or firm must be selected to prepare the transcript. Consequently, the requirements in Rule 8(b)(3) are different from those in Rule 9(c)(2). This amendment resolves the previous ambiguity by creating an exception from the requirements of Rule 9(c)(2) where there has been an electronically recorded proceeding covered by Rule 8(b)(3). This amendment renders inapplicable the contrary holding in Russell v. McOwen-Hanelt, 413 Mass. 106 (1992) and Hawkins v. Hawkins, 397 Mass. 401 (1986).

Reporter's Notes to Appellate Rule 9(c)(2)—2002

Rule 9(c)(2) was amended in 2002 to reduce the time period after the filing of a notice of appeal from 40 to ten days in which the appellant in a civil case must deliver to the clerk of the lower court either the transcript or a certification that the appellant has ordered the transcript from the court reporter.

This amendment serves to bring Rule 9(c)(2) in line with the requirement of Rule 8(b)(1) that the appellant must order the transcript within ten days of filing the notice of appeal.

A further change was made in the first sentence of Rule 9(c)(2). Prior to the 2002 amendment, that sentence required the appellant to provide to the clerk of the lower court either (1) a transcript of the proceedings which the appellant deems necessary or (2) a statement that the appellant has ordered such transcript. A third option, (iii), has been added for cases where the appellant is not ordering the transcript (or any portion thereof). The appellant, by certifying that no transcript has been ordered and that the appellant does not intend to order the transcript, will thereby put the appellee on notice that the appellee must, if a transcript is desired, take steps to order the transcript. See Rule 8(b)(1).

Rule 10. Docketing the Appeal

(a) Docketing the Appeal.

(1) *Civil Cases.* Within ten days after receiving from the clerk of the lower court notice of assembly of the record, or of approval by the lower court of an agreed statement, each appellant, including each cross-appellant, shall pay to the clerk of the appellate court the docket fee fixed by law, and the clerk shall thereupon enter the appeal of such appellant or cross-appellant upon the docket. If an appellant is authorized to prosecute the appeal without prepayment of fees, the clerk shall enter the appeal upon the docket at the request of a party.

(2) *Criminal Cases.* Upon receipt of notice of assembly of the record, pursuant to Rule 9(d), or of approval by the lower court of an agreed statement, pursuant to Rule 8(d), the clerk of the appellate court shall enter the appeal upon the docket.

(3) *In General.* Upon docketing the appeal, the clerk shall serve written notice thereof on each party and the clerk of the lower court. Upon motion, the lower court or a single justice of the appellate court may, for cause shown, enlarge the time for docketing the appeal or permit the appeal to be docketed out of time. An appeal shall be docketed under the title given to the action in the lower court, with the appellant identified as such, but if such title does not contain the name of the appellant, his name, identified as appellant, shall be added to the title.

(b) Filing. The clerk of the appellate court shall file upon receipt any part of the record or any paper authorized to be filed in lieu of the record under any provisions of Rule 9, following timely docketing of the appeal. The clerk shall immediately give notice to all parties of the date of each such filing.

(c) Dismissal for Failure of Appellant in a Civil Case to Comply With Rule 9(c) or Rule 10(a). If any appellant in a civil case shall fail to comply with Rule 9(c) or Rule 10(a)(1) or (3), the lower court may, on motion with notice by any appellee, dismiss the appeal, but only upon a finding of inexcusable neglect; otherwise, the court shall enlarge the appellant's time for taking the required action. If, prior to the lower court's hearing such motion for noncompliance with Rule 9(c), the appellant shall have cured the noncompliance, the appellant's compliance shall be deemed timely.

Amended June 27, 1974, effective July 1, 1974; amended effective February 24, 1975; amended May 15, 1979, effective July 1, 1979; amended effective May 1, 1994; amended July 28, 1999, effective September 1, 1999; amended September 6, effective October 1, 2001.

Reporter's Notes—1973

Appellate Rule 10 covers the mechanics of docketing the appeal in the appellate court.

Reporter's Notes—1975

The amendment requires the clerk to give written notice of the docketing to counsel for each party (or to each unrepresented party directly). This ensures that all parties receive notice of the docketing date, which is the starting point for various periods under the Rules; see, e.g. Appellate Rules 11, 11.1, and 19.

In Appellate Rule 10(c) substitution of "Rule 9(c)" for "Rule 9(b)" merely corrects a previous typographical error.

Reporter's Notes—1979

The substance of former subdivision (a) has been divided into subdivisions (a)(1), applicable to civil cases, and (a)(3), applicable to both civil and criminal cases.

Subdivision (a)(2), which provides for the automatic docketing of an appeal in a criminal case upon receipt by the clerk of the appellate court of notice of assembly of the record or approval of an agreed statement, is added.

The provision of a subdivision (a)(3) for notice to the parties of the docketing of a criminal appeal conforms to prior practice under former Appeals Court Rule 1:11 (1975: 3 Mass.App.Ct. 803) and Supreme Judicial Court Rule 1:11 (1975: 366 Mass. 860).

Since in a criminal appeal the appellant is responsible neither for initiating assembly of the record (see Rules 8[b][2], 9[c]) nor for taking any step to docket the appeal ([a][2], supra), subdivision (c) is limited in application to civil cases.

Reporter's Notes to Mass.R.A.P. 10(c)—1994

This amendment eliminates noncompliance with Mass. R.A.P. 10(a)(1) (the appellant's obligation to pay the docket fee within the ten day period described in Mass.R.A.P. 10(a)(1)) from the instances of noncompliance that can be cured prior to a hearing on a motion to dismiss for noncompliance. Noncompliance with Rule 9(c) (appellant's obligations re: assembly of the record and transmission of the transcript) can still be cured prior to a hearing for dismissal based on such noncompliance.

Many lawyers and pro se litigants relied on the previous version of the last sentence of Mass.R.A.P. 10(c) as their rationale for paying the filing fee only after there had been a motion to dismiss and before the lower court's hearing of such a motion, even though Mass.R.A.P. 10(a)(1) specifically required the payment "[w]ithin ten days after receiving from the clerk of the lower court notice of assembly of the record, or of approval by the lower court of an agreed statement . . ." Although the last sentence of Rule 10(c) seemed to permit such late payment as a matter of right, the practice in the Appeals Court was to refuse to accept a docket fee sent by the appellant subsequent to the ten day period described in Rule 10(a)(1) even if it was paid before a hearing described in Rule 10(c). The appellant who attempted to file the fee late was told that he or she must be successful on a motion to docket late in order for the Appeals Court to accept the payment, and that this motion would not ordinarily be entertained by the single justice while a motion to dismiss was pending in the trial court.

The prior wording of the last sentence of Rule 10(c) was therefore misleading to appellants who thought they had a right to pay the fee after the ten day period but before the hearing on a motion to dismiss; moreover, the practice of the Appeals Court may have been in disregard of the clear language of the same sentence. It does not make sense to have a ten day period in which to pay a filing fee which is widely ignored. Consequently, this amendment removes the excuse and automatic permission to pay the fee late and also makes the Rule in accord with the practice of the Appeals Court. This amendment in no way eliminates or alters the right of an indigent pro se litigant to obtain a waiver of the obligation to pay the filing fee.

Reporter's Notes—1999

The 1999 amendments to Appellate Rule 10(a) were part of a comprehensive set of amendments to the Appellate Rules (Rules 1, 3, 4, 8, and 10) that had been proposed by the Supreme Judicial Court Committee on Appeals of Child Welfare Cases. The purpose of the 1999 amendments is described in the 1999 Reporter's Notes to Appellate Rule 1(c).

Prior to the 1999 amendment, Appellate Rule 10(a)(3) required that upon the docketing of the appeal in the appellate court, the clerk serve written notice of the docketing upon each party. The 1999 amendment requires that the clerk of the appellate court also serve written notice on the clerk of the lower court whose decision is subject to the appeal.

It is significant to note that although the 1999 amendments were part of a package of amendments that related to child welfare appeals, the amendment to Appellate Rule 10(a)(3) applies not only to child welfare appeals, but all other appeals as well.

Reporter's Notes to Appellate Rule 10(a)(1)—2001

Prior to amendment in 2001, the first sentence of Appellate Rule 10(a)(1) provided that "the appellant" was to pay the docket fee to the clerk of the appellate court within ten days after receipt of notice of the assembly of the record or approval of an agreed statement. Where there have been multiple appellants or cross-appeals, the appellate clerks have required each appellant or cross-appellant to pay a separate docket fee. The 2001 amendment makes clear that separate docket fees are required.

Rule 11. Direct Appellate Review

(a) Application; When Filed; Grounds. An appeal within the concurrent appellate jurisdiction of the Appeals Court and Supreme Judicial Court shall be entered in the Appeals Court before a party may apply to the Supreme Judicial Court for direct appellate review. Within twenty days after the docketing of an appeal in the Appeals Court, any party to the case (or two or more parties jointly) may apply in writing to the Supreme Judicial Court for direct appellate review, provided the questions presented by the appeal are: (1) questions of first impression or novel questions of law which should be submitted for final determination to the Supreme Judicial Court; (2) questions of law concerning the Constitution of the Commonwealth or questions concerning the Constitution of the United States which have been raised in a court of the Commonwealth; or (3) questions of such public interest that justice requires a final determination by the full Supreme Judicial Court. Oral argument in support of an application will not be permitted except by order of court.

(b) Contents of Application; Form. The application for direct appellate review shall contain, in the following order: (1) a request for direct appellate review; (2) a statement of prior proceedings in the case; (3) a short statement of facts relevant to the appeal; (4) a statement of the issues of law raised by the appeal, together with a statement indicating whether the issues were raised and properly preserved in the lower court; (5) a brief argument thereon (covering not more than ten pages of typing) including appropriate authorities, in support of the applicant's position on such issues; and (6) a statement of reasons why direct appellate review is appropriate. A certified copy of the docket entries shall be appended to the application. The applicant shall also append a copy of any written decision, memorandum, findings, rulings, or report of the lower court relevant to the issues on appeal. The application shall comply with the requirements of Rule 20.

(c) Opposition; Form. Within ten days after the filing of the application, any other party to the case may, but need not, file and serve an opposition thereto (covering not more than ten pages of typing) setting forth reason why the application should not be granted. The opposition shall not restate matters described in subdivision (b)(2) and (3) of this rule unless the opposing party is dissatisfied with the statement thereof contained in the application. The opposition shall comply with the requirements of Rule 20.

(d) Filing; Service. One copy of the application and one copy of each opposition shall be filed in the office of the clerk of the Appeals Court. An original and seventeen copies of the application and of each opposition shall be filed in the office of the clerk of the full Supreme Judicial Court. Filing and service of the application and of any opposition shall comply with Rule 13.

(e) Effect of Application Upon Appeal. The filing of an application for direct appellate review shall not extend the time for filing briefs or doing any other act required to be done under these rules.

(f) Vote of Direct Appellate Review; Certification. If any two justices of the Supreme Judicial Court vote for direct appellate review, or if a majority of the justices of the Appeals Court shall certify that direct appellate review is in the public interest, an order allowing the application (or transferring the appeal sua sponte) or the certificate, as the case may be, shall be transmitted to the clerk of the Appeals Court; upon receipt, direct appellate review shall be deemed granted. The clerk shall forthwith transmit to the clerk of the full Supreme Judicial Court all papers theretofore filed in the case and shall notify the clerk of the lower court that the appeal has been transferred.

(g) Cases Transferred for Direct Review; Time for Serving and Filing Briefs. In any appeal transferred to the full Supreme Judicial Court from the Appeals Court:

(1) If at the time of transfer all parties have served and filed briefs in the Appeals Court, no further briefs may be filed except that a reply brief may be served and filed on or before the last date allowable had the case not been transferred, or within ten days after the date on which the appeal is docketed in the full Supreme Judicial Court, whichever is later.

(2) If at the time of transfer only the appellant's brief has been served and filed in the Appeals Court, the appellant may, but need not, serve and file an amended brief within twenty days after the date on which the appeal is docketed in the full Supreme Judicial Court. The appellee shall serve and file his brief within thirty days after service of any amended brief of the appellant, or within fifty days after the date on which the appeal is docketed in the full Supreme Judicial Court, whichever is later.

(3) Service and filing of a reply brief shall comply with Rule 19.

(4) If at the time of transfer to the full Supreme Judicial Court no party to the appeal has served or filed a brief, the appellant shall serve and file a brief within twenty days after the date on which the appeal is docketed in the full Supreme Judicial Court or within forty days after the date on which the appeal was docketed in the Appeals Court, whichever is later.

Amended May 15, 1979, effective July 1, 1979; amended effective July 1, 1991; April 14, 1995; January 29, 1996; amended October 30, 1997, effective January 1, 1998; June 26, 2002, effective September 3, 2002.

Reporter's Notes—1973

Appellate Rule 11 implements the statutorily-authorized direct review by the Supreme Judicial Court of cases which would otherwise first be heard and determined in the Appeals Court; G.L. c. 211A, § 10. (For procedure subsequent to an Appeals Court decision, see Appellate Rule 27.1). Direct review may result if: (1) The Supreme Judicial Court (or two justices thereof) shall so order, either (a) sua sponte, or (b) on application of one or more parties; or (2) The Appeals Court (or a majority of the justices thereof) shall certify that direct review is in the public interest.

The rule deals with the mechanics of application for direct review, and also prescribes the procedure governing cases accorded direct review, no matter what the means which caused such review (order by the Supreme Judicial Court ex mero motu, order on application, or certification by the Appeals Court).

Of the routes to direct review, only one—Supreme Judicial Court order after application—ought appropriately to be governed by the Appellate Rules. The other two, self-initiated exercises of judicial discretion and administration, are intracourt matters not subject to procedural regulation.

What Appellate Rule 11(a)–(d) accomplishes, therefore, is to assure appellate parties the right to put the matter before the Supreme Judicial Court and to urge direct review; the rule leaves all other means by which review may be granted out of the parties' control entirely, and completely in the dispositive power of the respective courts.

The application for direct review proceeds parallel to the usual requirements, Appellate Rule 11(e). Application does not in any way "stop the clock" with respect to normal appellate procedure. Once review is granted, however, a special timetable controls, Appellate Rule 11(g). In general, any brief already filed in the Appeals Court need not be refiled in the Supreme Judicial Court; if no party has yet filed, the briefing schedule, proceeding as though the appeal had commenced initially in the Supreme Judicial Court, is controlled by Appellate Rule 19.

Reporter's Notes—1979

Appellate Rule 11 was previously applicable to direct appellate review in criminal cases by virtue of Supreme Judicial Court Rule 3:24, § 4(1) (1975) 366 Mass. 870, (1975) except that the words "the appeal is docketed" were taken to mean "the case is entered." That distinction is no longer viable (see Rule 10([a][2]).

Only two changes are made in the former rule. A new first sentence is added to subdivision (a), which restates the first sentence of Supreme Judicial Court Rule 3:24 supra § 3. Section 3 also provided that:

> All matters preliminary to the entry of . . . appeals [within the concurrent appellate jurisdiction of the Appeals and Supreme Judicial Court] which require action by an appellate court shall be presented to and disposed of by the Appeals Court.

That requirement is implicit in Rule 11.

Secondly, the time within which an application for direct appellate review may be filed is increased from ten to twenty days after the docketing of the appeal in the Appeals Court. The remainder of the rule is unchanged.

Reporter's Notes—1996

The 1996 amendment to Mass.R.A.P. 11(f), effective January 29, 1996, is a technical amendment to that portion of the first sentence relating to certification that direct appellate review by the Supreme Judicial Court is in the public interest. The amendment provides for certification by "a majority of the justices of the Appeals Court," replacing earlier language providing for certification by "all of the justices of the Appeals Court or any majority thereof."

Reporter's Notes—1997

The 1997 amendment to Appellate Rule 11(d) increased to seventeen the number of copies of an application for direct appellate review and of each opposition to be filed in the clerk's office of the Supreme Judicial Court. The amendment also clarified that an original is to be filed together with the seventeen copies.

Reporter's Notes—1999

The cover of applications for direct appellate review shall be white. See Appellate Rule 20(b), as amended in 1999.

Reporter's Notes to Appellate Rule 11(b)—2002

In 2002, the Supreme Judicial Court amended Appellate Rule 11(b) to require that an application for direct appellate review contain "a statement indicating whether the issues were raised and properly preserved in the lower court" and that "a copy of any written decision, memorandum, findings, rulings, or report of the lower court relevant to the issues on appeal" be appended to the application. Having a statement regarding whether issues were raised below and a copy of the lower court's decision will serve to benefit the court's determination in considering the application for direct appellate review.

Rule 11.1. Transfer From Supreme Judicial Court

In the case of a direct appeal to the Supreme Judicial Court, within fourteen days after the appeal has been docketed, or such further time as a single justice upon motion for cause shown may allow, any party may serve and file a motion, on notice, to transfer the appeal to the Appeals Court. The motion: (a) shall not exceed five typewritten pages; (b) shall succinctly specify the grounds for transfer; and (c) shall conform to Rules 13, 14, 15, and 20(b). Within seven days after filing of the motion, any other party may serve and file an opposition to the transfer. The opposition: (a) shall not exceed five typewritten pages; (b) shall succinctly specify the reasons for opposing the transfer; and (c) shall conform to Rules 13, 14, 15, and 20(b).

No oral argument will be permitted.

Reporter's Notes—1973

Appeals which have proceeded direct to the Supreme Judicial Court without application of a party, that is, on judicial certification or order, see Appellate Rule 11(f), have by definition not afforded the parties an opportunity to oppose direct review. (Review after application, of course, has resulted from a procedure permitting the party not applying for direct review to oppose it, Appellate Rule 11(c).) Appellate Rule 11.1 permits either party to an appeal which has been brought up to the Supreme Judicial Court without application to indicate any reason why the case should be transferred back to the Appeals Court.

Rule 12. Proceedings in Forma Pauperis

(a) Leave to Proceed on Appeal In Forma Pauperis From Lower Court to Appellate Court. Either a lower court or a single justice, for cause shown and after reasonable notice, may authorize an appeal to be prosecuted in forma pauperis, upon such reasonable terms as such court or justice may prescribe.

(b) Form of Briefs, Appendices and Other Papers. Parties allowed to proceed in forma pauperis may file briefs, appendices and other papers in typewritten form, and may request that the appeal be heard on the original record without the necessity of reproducing parts thereof in any form.

Reporter's Notes—1973

Appellate Rule 12 regulates proceedings in forma pauperis, and works no serious change in existing practice. Unlike the cognate F.R.A.P. 24, it allows the justice entertaining the application to proceed in forma pauperis large discretion to tailor the terms of the order to the needs of the case.

Rule 13. Filing and Service

(a) Filing. Papers required or permitted to be filed in the appellate court shall be filed with the clerk. Filing may be accomplished by first class mail, either registered or unregistered, addressed to the clerk, but filing shall not be timely unless the papers are received by the clerk within the time fixed for filing, except that briefs and appendices shall be docketed on the date of receipt and shall be deemed timely filed if (i) received within the time fixed for filing or (ii) accompanied by an affidavit signed by counsel of record attesting that the day of mailing was within the time fixed for filing. If a motion requests relief which may be granted by a single justice, the justice may permit the motion to be filed with him, in which event he shall note thereon the date of filing and shall thereafter transmit it to the clerk.

(b) Service of All Papers Required. Copies of all papers filed by any party and not required by these rules to be served by the clerk shall, at or before the time of filing, be served by a party or person acting for him on all other parties to the appeal or review. Service on a party represented by counsel shall be made on counsel.

(c) Manner of Service. Service may be personal or by first class mail. Personal service includes delivery of the copy to a clerk or other responsible person at the office of counsel. Service by first class mail is complete on mailing.

(d) Proof of Service. Papers presented for filing shall contain an acknowledgment of service by the person served or proof of service in the form of a statement under the penalties of perjury of the date and manner of service and of the name of the person served, signed by the person who made service. Proof of service may appear on or be affixed to the papers filed. The clerk may permit papers to be filed without acknowledgment or proof of service but shall require such acknowledgment or proof to be filed promptly thereafter.

Amended October 23, 1989, effective January 1, 1990.

Reporter's Notes—1973

Appellate Rule 13 governs filing and service requirements. Papers may be filed by mail; they must be actually received by the clerk within the filing deadline, except that briefs and appendices are regarded as having been filed upon mailing so long as the most expeditious form of mailing is utilized; special delivery need not be used. Service as between parties is, if accomplished by first class mail, complete upon mailing. Personal service may be made to a responsible person in the office of counsel for the recipient.

Reporter's Notes—1989

Mass.R.A.P. 31(b) requires that "[a]ll papers filed with the clerk ... shall be entered chronologically in the docket ..." But prior to this amendment, Mass.R.A.P. 13(a) stated that "briefs and appendices shall be deemed filed on the day of mailing if the most expeditious form of delivery by mail, excepting special delivery, is used." This clash in language has caused some problems for clerks, including additional clerical time spent modifying computerized dockets. The amended rule requires briefs and appendices be docketed on the date of receipt, but by utilizing affidavits by counsel, continues to permit counsel to mail within the time fixed for filing, even if receipt at the clerk's office is subsequent thereto. Consequently, there will no longer be a need for asterisks or other special notations on the dockets.

Rule 14. Computation and Extension of Time

(a) Computation of Time. In computing any period of time prescribed by these rules, by order of court, or by any applicable statute, the day of the act, event, or default after which the designated period of time begins to run shall not be included. The last day of the period shall be included, unless it is a Saturday, Sunday or a legal holiday, in which event the period shall extend until the end of the next day which is not a Saturday, Sunday or a legal holiday. When the period of time prescribed or allowed is less than 7 days, intermediate Saturdays, Sundays and legal holidays shall be excluded in the computation. As used in this rule "legal holiday" means those days specified in G.L. c. 4, § 7 and any other day appointed as a holiday by the President or the Congress of the United States or so designated by the laws of the Commonwealth.

(b) Enlargement of Time. The appellate court or a single justice for good cause shown may upon motion enlarge the time prescribed by these rules or by its order for doing any act, or may permit an act to be done after the expiration of such time; but neither the appellate court nor a single justice may enlarge the time for filing a notice of appeal beyond one year from the date of entry of the judgment or order sought to be reviewed, or, in a criminal case, from the date of the verdict or finding of guilt or the date of imposition of sentence, whichever date is later.

(c) Additional Time After Service by Mail. Whenever a party is required or permitted to do an act within a prescribed period after service of a paper upon him and the paper is served by mail, 3 days shall be added to the prescribed period.

Amended May 15, 1979, effective July 1, 1979.

Reporter's Notes—1973

Appellate Rule 14(a), dealing with computation of time, follows Mass.R.Civ.P. 6. By countenancing enlargement of appeal time up to one year after entry of the order or judgment appealed from, Appellate Rule 14(b) relaxes the cognate F.R.A.P. 26(b). Read together, Appellate Rules 4 and 14(b) mean that an "excusable neglect" extension may be granted only on such terms as to cause the extension to expire within the one-year period prescribed by Appellate Rule 14(b).

Reporter's Notes—1979

The only change in Rule 14 is the addition to subdivision (b) of language restricting the appellate court's power to enlarge the time within which a notice of appeal may be filed in a criminal case to no longer than one year after the date of the verdict or finding of guilt or the date of the imposition of sentence, whichever date is later. Compare Rule 4(c), which limits any extension granted by the lower court to no more than sixty days after verdict or sentence. The failure of a party to notice his appeal prior to the expiration of the thirty-day limit of Rule 4(b), or within sixty days if extended may be rectified by the appellate court, or a single justice as long as it does not extend beyond one year past verdict or sentence.

Rule 15. Motions

(a) Content of Motions; Response; Reply. Unless another form is elsewhere prescribed by these rules, an application for an order or other relief shall be made by filing a motion for such order or relief with proof of service on all other parties. The motion shall contain or be accompanied by any matter required by a specific provision of these rules governing such a motion, shall state with particularity the grounds on which it is based, and shall set forth the order or relief sought. If a motion is supported by briefs, affidavits, or other papers, they shall be served and filed with the motion. Any party may file a response in opposition to a motion other than one for a procedural order (for which see subdivision (b)) within 7 days after service of the motion, but motions authorized by Rule 6 may be acted upon after reasonable notice, and the appellate court or a single justice may shorten or extend the time for responding to any motion.

(b) Determination of Motions for Procedural Orders. Notwithstanding the provisions of the preceding paragraph as to motions generally, motions for procedural orders, including any motion under Rule 14(b), may be acted upon at any time, without awaiting a response thereto. Any party adversely affected by such action may request reconsideration, vacation, or modification of such action.

(c) Power of a Single Justice to Entertain Motions. In addition to the authority expressly conferred by these rules or by law, a single justice may entertain and may grant or deny any request for relief which under these rules may properly be sought by motion, except that a single justice may not dismiss or otherwise determine an appeal or other proceeding, and except that the appellate court may provide by order or rule that any motion or class of motions shall be acted upon by the appellate court. The action of a single justice may be reviewed by the appellate court.

(d) Motions for New Trial in Capital Cases. After the docketing of an appeal in a criminal case in which the defendant was convicted of murder in the first degree and until the filing of a rescript by the appellate court, a motion for a new trial pursuant to Massachusetts Rules of Criminal Procedure 30 shall be filed in the appellate court and may be remitted to the trial judge for hearing and determination at such time as the appellate court may direct.

Amended May 15, 1979, effective July 1, 1979.

Publisher's Note

On March 29, 1988, the Supreme Judicial Court adopted the following order:

ORDERED: Pursuant to Mass. R.A.P. 15(c), applications for stays pending the United States Supreme Court's consideration of applications for writs of certiorari shall be considered upon the filing of a motion with the Clerk of the Supreme Judicial Court for the Commonwealth. Reasonable notice of the motion shall be given to all parties. The motion may be decided with or without a hearing by the panel whose decision is sought to be reviewed. At its discretion, the court may order a hearing by a single justice who was a member of that panel either for the justice's recommendation or decision. Relief available under this order, or denial of such relief, may be conditioned on such reasonable terms as the panel or single justice may impose, including appropriate conditions for the security of the adverse party.

This order shall take effect on July 1, 1988.

Reporter's Notes—1973

Appellate Rule 15 governs motion practice. Appellate Rule 15(c) permits a single justice to dispose of any motion except a motion to dismiss an appeal (and, of course, except as otherwise provided by the Appellate Court). For the required number of copies see Appellate Rule 19(b); for the form of motions, see Appellate Rule 20(b).

Reporter's Notes—1979

Subdivision (d), drawn from G.L. c. 278, § 33E (as amended) merely recognizes that while after docketing, a motion for a new trial (Mass.R.Crim.P. 30) is required to be filed in the appellate court, it should ordinarily be heard and determined by the trial judge (unless disabled, see Mass.R.Crim.P. 38[c]), since he is in a better position to weigh its merits. *See,* e.g., *Commonwealth v. Grace,* 370 Mass. 746 (1976). The need for familiarity with the trial proceedings may vary, however, as a function of the grounds asserted (e.g., newly-discovered evidence as opposed to a verdict allegedly against the weight of evidence).

Rule 16. Briefs

(a) Brief of the Appellant. The brief of the appellant shall contain under appropriate headings and in the order here indicated:

(1) In all briefs, a table of contents, with page references, and a table of cases (alphabetically arranged), statutes and other authorities cited, with references to the pages of the brief where they are cited.

(2) A statement of the issues presented for review.

(3) A statement of the case, which shall first indicate briefly the nature of the case, the course of proceedings, and its disposition in the court below. There shall follow a statement of the facts relevant to the issues presented for review, with appropriate references to the record (see subdivision (e)).

(4) The argument, which shall contain the contentions of the appellant with respect to the issues presented, and the reasons therefor, with citations to the authorities, statutes and parts of the record relied on. In a brief with more than twenty-four pages of argument, there shall be a short summary of argument, suitably paragraphed and with page references to later material in the brief dealing with the same subject matter, which should be a condensation of the argument actually made in the body of the brief, and not a mere repetition of the headings under which the argument is arranged. The appellate court need not pass upon questions or issues not argued in the brief. Nothing argued in the brief shall be deemed to be waived by a failure to argue orally.

(5) A short conclusion stating the precise relief sought.

(6) Any written or oral findings or memorandum of decision by the court pertinent to an issue on appeal included as an addendum to the brief.

(7) In cases where geographical facts are of importance, unless appropriate plans are reproduced in the printed record or record appendix, an outline plan or chalk (preferably based on exhibits in evidence) shall be included. This outline plan should be suitable for reproduction on one page of the printed law reports.

(8) The printed names, Board of Bar Overseers (BBO) numbers, addresses, and telephone numbers of individual counsel, and, if an individual counsel is affiliated with a firm, the firm name.

(b) Brief of the Appellee. The brief of the appellee shall conform to the requirements of subdivision (a)(1)–(4) and (7), except that a statement of the issues or of the case need not be made unless the appellee is dissatisfied with the statement of the appellant.

(c) Reply Brief. The appellant may file a brief in reply to the brief of the appellee, and if the appellee has cross-appealed, the appellee may file a brief in reply to the response of the appellant to the issues presented by the cross appeal. No further briefs may be filed except with leave of the appellate court. Reply briefs shall comply with the requirements of Rule 16(a)(1).

(d) References in Briefs to Parties. Counsel will be expected in their briefs and oral arguments to keep to a minimum references to parties by such designations as "appellant" and "appellee." It promotes clarity to use the designations used in the lower court, or the actual names of the parties, or descriptive term such as "the employee," "the injured person," "the taxpayer," "the landlord," etc. If the name of a party has been impounded or has been made confidential by statute, rule, or court order, counsel shall preserve confidentiality in briefs and oral arguments.

(e) References in Briefs to the Record. References in the briefs to parts of the record reproduced in an appendix filed with a brief (see Rule 18(a)) shall be to the pages of the appendix at which those parts appear. If the appendix is prepared after the briefs are filed, references in the briefs to the record shall be made by one of the methods allowed by Rule 18(c). If the record is reproduced in accordance with the provisions of Rule 18(f), or if references are made in the briefs to parts of the record not reproduced, the references shall be to the pages of the parts of the record involved; e.g., Answer p. 7, Motion for Judgment p. 2, Transcript p. 231. Intelligible abbreviations may be used. If reference is made to evidence the admissibility of which is in controversy, reference shall be made to the pages of the appendix or of the transcript at which the evidence was identified, offered, and received or rejected. No statement of a fact of the case shall be made in any part of the brief without an appropriate and accurate record reference.

(f) Reproduction of Statutes, Rules, Regulations, etc. If determination of the issues presented requires consideration of constitutional provisions, statutes, rules, regulations, etc. or relevant parts thereof, they shall be reproduced in the brief or in an addendum at the end.

(g) Massachusetts Citations. Massachusetts Reports between 17 Massachusetts and 97 Massachusetts shall be cited by the name of the reporter. Any other citation shall include, wherever reasonably possible, a reference to any official report of the case or to the official publication containing statutory or similar material. References to decisions and other authorities should include, in addition to the page at which the decision or section begins, a page reference to the particular material therein upon which reliance is placed, and the year of the decision; as, for example: 334 Mass. 593, 597–598 (1956). Quotations of Massachusetts statutory material shall include a citation to either the Acts and Resolves of Massachusetts or to the current edition of the General Laws published pursuant to a resolve of the General Court.

(h) Length of Briefs. Except by permission of the court, principal briefs shall not exceed fifty pages, exclusive of pages containing the table of contents, tables of citations and any addendum containing statutes, rules, regulations, etc. Except by permission of the court, reply briefs shall not exceed twenty pages. Permission of the court shall not be granted unless the moving party specifies the relevant issue or issues and why such issues merit additional pages. A motion of a party to exceed the page limits stated in this rule will not be granted except for extraordinary reasons.

(i) Briefs in Cases Involving Cross Appeals. If a cross appeal is filed, the plaintiff in the court below shall be deemed the appellant for the purposes of this rule and Rules 18 and 19, unless the parties otherwise agree or the court otherwise orders. The brief of the appellee shall contain the issues and argument involved in his appeal as well as the answer to the brief of the appellant.

(j) Briefs in Cases Involving Multiple Appellants or Appellees. In cases involving more than one appellant or appellee, including cases consolidated for purposes of the appeal, any number of either may join in a single brief, and any appellant or appellee may adopt by reference any part of the brief of another. Parties may similarly join in reply briefs.

(k) Required Certification; Non–complying Briefs. The last page of each brief shall include a certification by counsel, or, if a party is proceeding pro se, by the party, that the brief complies with the rules of court that pertain to the filing of briefs, including, but not limited to: Mass. R. A. P. 16(a)(6) (pertinent findings or memorandum of decision); Mass. R. A. P. 16(e) (references to the record); Mass. R. A. P. 16(f) (reproduction of statutes, rules, regulations); Mass. R. A. P. 16(h) (length of briefs); Mass. R. A. P. 18 (appendix to the briefs); and Mass. R. A. P. 20 (form of briefs, appendices, and other papers). A brief not complying with these rules (including a brief that does not contain a certification) may be struck from the files by the appellate court or a single justice.

(*l*) Citation of Supplemental Authorities. When pertinent and significant authorities come to the attention of a party after his brief has been filed, or after oral argument but before decision, a party may promptly advise the clerk of the court, by letter, with a copy to all counsel, setting forth the citations. There shall be a reference either to the page of the brief or to a point argued orally to which the citations pertain, but the letter shall without argument state the reasons for the supplemental citations. Any response shall be made promptly and shall be similarly limited.

(m) References to Impounded Material. Upon the filing of any brief or other document containing references to matters that are impounded or have been made confidential by statute, rule, or order, counsel (or a party if pro se), shall file a written notice with the clerk, with a copy to all parties, so indicating. Wherever possible, counsel shall not disclose impounded material. Where it is necessary to include impounded material in a brief, the cover of the brief shall clearly indicate that impounded information is included herein.

Amended effective February 24, 1975; amended May 15, 1979, effective July 1, 1979; May 25, 1982, effective July 1, 1982; November 17, 1986, effective January 1, 1987; November 24, 1987, effective January 1, 1988; amended effective May 5, 1989; February 1, 1991; January 1, 1992; January 1, 1997; amended June 11, 1997, effective July 1, 1997; December 1, 1998, effective January 1, 1999; February 5, 2003, effective March 3, 2003; April 27, 2005, effective October 1, 2005.

Reporter's Notes—1973

Appellate Rule 16 establishes the form of the briefs: table of contents; statement of the issues; statement of the case; arguments; and conclusion. Appellate Rule 16(f) also requires the reproduction of relevant statutes and the like. None of the requirements will substantially change existing practice. Appellate Rule 16(e), stating the requirements in briefs for references to the record, likewise follows existing practice. See S.J.C. Rule 1:15; Appeals Court Rule 1:15.

Reporter's Notes—1975

As originally promulgated, Appellate Rule 16(a)(4) made optional the use of a summary of argument. The new rule makes such a summary mandatory, if the brief contains more than 24 pages of argument (i.e. not including table of contents, table of cases, statutes, and authorities, statement of issues, and statement of the case). By explicit language, the summary must be something more than a mere recital of the argument headings.

Amended Appellate Rule 16(a)(4) makes explicit the long-standing principle that failure to discuss an issue in the brief may, at the discretion of the court, preclude reliance upon that point in oral argument. On the other hand, if the brief does include the question, failure to argue it orally does not waive the point.

Although earlier Massachusetts appellate citation form omitted the year of decision, the amendment to Appellate Rule 16(g) ensures that the year will be included in any citation.

Reporter's Notes—1979

Rule 16 was previously incorporated into criminal appellate procedure by Appeals Court Rule 1:15 (1975: 3 Mass.App.Ct. 803) and Supreme Judicial Court Rule 1:15 (1975: 366 Mass. 861). The rule is unchanged beyond amendment of subdivision (e) to reflect the fact that there may be more than one appendix in a criminal case. (Mass.R.App.P. 19[a]).

The last two sentences of subdivision (a)(4) which provide that questions or issues not argued in the brief need not be decided, but that a failure to orally argue an issue does not waive it if argued in the brief, supersede the last two sentences of former Appeals Court and Supreme Judicial Court Rules 1:13 (1972: 1 Mass.App.Ct. 889, amended 1975: 3 Mass.App.Ct. 801. 1967: 351 Mass. 738, amended, 1975: 366 Mass. 801).

Reporter's Notes—1982

Appellate Rule 16(*l*) is the same as F.R.A.P. 28(j), which became effective in 1979. Its purpose is to allow a concise letter to inform the court in a non-argumentative manner of a "pertinent and significant" authority discovered after the filing of a brief or oral argument. The amendment does not authorize reargument in the disguise of a supplementary citation.

Reporter's Notes—1986

This amendment is to clarify that reply briefs of more than twenty pages shall contain the tables and references required of other appellate briefs of that length. Such tables and references aid opposing parties and the court. This amendment corresponds, in part, to the 1986 amendment to Fed. R.A.P. 28(c).

Reporter's Notes—1991

Mass.R.A.P. 16(a)(7) and 20(a), final sentence, clause (5): These amendments require individual counsel who are affiliated with a firm to include the firm name on filed briefs. Appellate judges need to know the firm names in order to determine correctly whether it is necessary to withdraw from a case.

Reporter's Notes—1997

The amendment to Appellate Rule 16(a)(1), effective January 1, 1997, eliminates the provision that a table of contents and a table of cases, statutes, and other authorities be included only in briefs of twenty pages or more. All briefs must include these items.

The 1997 amendments to Appellate Rule 16(d) and (m) serve as a reminder to counsel to maintain confidentiality in briefs and oral argument of any information that has been impounded or designated as confidential. For example, where the name of a person is not subject to disclosure, counsel may use a generic term such as "child" or "juvenile" or may use a pseudonym or initials.

Illustrative statutes requiring confidentiality include G.L. c. 112, § 12S (petitions by minors seeking judicial determination of maturity in connection with abortion; see also Superior Court Standing Order No. 5–81, as amended, requiring that papers "shall be designated anonymously" such as with the titles "Mary Moe" or "Mary Doe"); G.L. c. 119, § 38 (names in care and protection proceedings); G.L. c. 119, § 65 (juvenile proceedings); G.L. c. 209A, § 8 (in abuse prevention proceedings, plaintiff's address and case records involving a minor); G.L. c. 209C, § 13 (papers in paternity proceedings and a party's address); and G.L. c. 210, § 5C (adoption proceedings).

Illustrative rules providing for confidentiality include Mass. R.Civ.P. 26(c) (trade secrets and other matters in connection with discovery) and Probate Court Supplemental Rule 401 (financial statements in connection with requests for support or alimony). The Uniform Rules on Impoundment Procedure also provide a mechanism to preserve confidentiality of matters contained in case papers.

Illustrative cases using pseudonyms include *Care and Protection of Stephen,* 401 Mass. 144, 514 N.E.2d 1087 (1987); *C.C. v. A.B.,* 406 Mass. 679, 550 N.E.2d 365 (1990); *Oscar F. v. County of Worcester,* 412 Mass. 38, 587 N.E.2d 208 (1992); *Adoption of Carla,* 416 Mass. 510, 623 N.E.2d 1118 (1993); *Doe v. Superintendent of Schools of Worcester,* 421 Mass. 117, 653 N.E.2d 1088 (1995); *Doe v. Purity Supreme, Inc.,* 422 Mass. 563, 664 N.E.2d 815 (1996); and *Commonwealth v. Wotan,* 422 Mass. 740, 665 N.E.2d 976 (1996).

There may be instances, however, where counsel will find it necessary to include confidential information in a brief in order to allow for full appellate review of the issue. In such instances, Rule 16(m) provides that counsel must alert the clerk's office that confidential information is contained in a filing. In this way, the rule shifts the burden to counsel to alert the clerk's office to the presence of impounded material so that the latter can take appropriate steps to safeguard the material in accordance with Supreme Judicial Court Rule 1:15, Impoundment Procedure.

These amendments, together with amendments to Appellate Rule 18, serve to preserve confidentiality of material in briefs, appendices, and oral argument.

Reporter's Notes—1999

New paragraph (6), added to Appellate Rule 16(a) effective in 1999, requires that any findings (written or oral) or memorandum of decision by the trial court pertinent to an appellate issue be included in an addendum to the appellant's brief. Although findings or a memorandum of decision are already required to be included in the appendix to the brief (Mass. R.A.P. 18(a)), incorporating such matters in an addendum to the brief will enable a judge on appeal to locate quickly the trial court's rationale for its decision, especially where there is a multi-volume appendix.

The reference to oral findings is intended to cover the situation where the trial judge has dictated findings into the record that have been transcribed or otherwise recorded. These findings must now also be included in an addendum to the brief.

This additional requirement will not serve to reduce the maximum number of pages for a principal brief. The page limitations contained in Mass.R.A.P. 16(h) are inapplicable to an addendum to a brief.

Reporter's Notes—1999

The 1999 amendments to Appellate Rule 16(h) were made together with the updating of Appellate Rule 20, the latter governing the form of briefs and appendices. The 1999 amendments to Appellate Rule 20 deleted references to standard typographic printing in recognition of the practice that briefs today are produced through computer wordprocessing and no longer through a typesetting and printing process. Accordingly, the page limitation for briefs produced by "standard typographic printing" of forty pages (and fifteen pages for reply briefs) has been deleted from the rule.

The existing page limitation on principal briefs produced by computer wordprocessing remains fifty pages, with reply briefs twenty pages.

Reporter's Notes—2003

By virtue of the 2003 amendment to Appellate Rule 16(h), a party seeking leave to file a brief with additional pages must specify the issues involved and why they require additional pages. The rule also sets forth a standard of "extraordinary reasons" for the allowance of such a motion.

Reporter's Notes—2005

In order to reduce the number of non-complying briefs, Appellate Rule 16(k) was amended in 2005 to require a certification that the brief complies with all of the rules of court that govern briefs. Counsel should be aware that a brief that does not contain the required certification may be struck by the court for non-compliance with the rule.

Rule 17. Brief of an Amicus Curiae

A brief of an amicus curiae may be filed only (1) by leave of the appellate court or a single justice granted on motion or (2) at the request of the appellate court, except that consent or leave shall not be required when the brief is presented by the Commonwealth. The brief may be conditionally filed with the motion for leave. A motion for leave shall identify the interest of the applicant and shall state the reasons why a brief of an amicus curiae is desirable. Any amicus curiae shall file its brief within the time allowed the party whose position as to affirmance or reversal the amicus brief will support unless the appellate court or a single justice for cause shown shall grant leave for later filing, and shall specify within what period an opposing party may answer. A motion of an amicus curiae to participate in the oral argument will be granted only for extraordinary reasons. The same number of copies of the brief of an amicus curiae shall be filed with the clerk and served on counsel for each party separately represented as required by Rule 19(b).

Amended October 30, 1997, effective January 1, 1998.

Reporter's Notes—1973

No existing rule governs briefs of an amicus curiae. Appellate Rule 17, limiting the right to file such a brief to an amicus who has obtained leave of the full appellate court or a single justice on motion, follows existing practice. It should be noted that the Commonwealth need never obtain leave to file an amicus brief.

Reporter's Notes—1979

Rule 17 is unchanged, its provisions having been incorporated into criminal appellate procedure by former Appeals Court and Supreme Judicial Court Rules 1:15 (1975: 3 Mass. App.Ct. 803, 366 Mass. 861).

Reporter's Notes—1997

The 1997 amendment to Appellate Rule 17 added a new last sentence requiring that the number of copies of an amicus brief to be filed with the appellate court and served on counsel be the same as set forth in Appellate Rule 19(b).

Rule 18. Appendix to the Briefs

(a) Duty of Appellant to Prepare and File; Content of Appendix; Time for Filing; Number of Copies. The appellant shall prepare and file an appendix to the briefs.

In civil cases, the appendix shall contain: (1) the relevant docket entries in the proceedings below; (2) any relevant portions of the pleadings, charge, findings, or opinion; (3) the judgment, order, or decision in question; and (4) any other parts of the record to which the parties wish to direct the particular attention of the court. Except where they have independent relevance, memoranda of law in the lower court should not be included in the appendix.

In criminal cases, the appendix need not contain relevant portions of the transcript, but shall contain: (1) the relevant docket entries in the proceedings below; (2) a copy of the complaint or indictment; and (3) any paper filed in the case relating to an issue which is to be argued on appeal. Any party in a criminal case may include in an appendix to his brief any other parts of the record to which he wishes to direct the particular attention of the court.

The appendix shall include any order of impoundment or confidentiality from the lower court. The fact that parts of the record are not included in the appendix shall not prevent the parties or the court from relying on such parts, provided that the court may decline to permit the parties to refer to portions of the record omitted from the appendix, unless leave be granted prior to argument.

Unless filing is to be deferred pursuant to the provisions of subdivision (c) of this rule, any appendix shall be filed and served with the brief. If separately bound, the same number of copies of the appendix shall be filed with the clerk as required by Rule 19(b) for the filing of the brief, and two shall be served on counsel for each party separately represented, unless the court shall by rule or order direct the filing or service of a lesser number and except as otherwise provided in subdivision (e) of this rule.

(b) Determination of Contents of Appendix in Civil Cases; Cost of Producing. The parties are encouraged to agree as to the contents of the appendix. In the absence of agreement, the appellant shall, not later than ten days after the date on which the clerk notifies the parties that the record has been assembled, serve on the appellee a designation of the parts of the record which he intends to include in the appendix and a statement of the issues which he intends to present for review. If the appellee deems it necessary to direct the particular attention of the court to parts of the record not designated by the appellant, he shall, within ten days after receipt of the designation, serve upon the appellant a designation of those parts. The parties shall not engage in unnecessary designation and may refer to parts of the record not included in the appendix if permitted by the appellate court or a single justice pursuant to the provisions of Rule 18(a) or 18(f). However, this does not affect the responsibility of the parties to include materials necessary to their appeal, including exhibits, in the appendix.

Where a party designates as part of the record any matter that has been impounded or has been made confidential by statute, rule, or order, the designation shall so state.

Unless the parties otherwise agree, the cost of producing the appendix shall initially be paid by the appellant, but if the appellant considers that parts of the record designated by the appellee for inclusion are unnecessary for the determination of the issues presented he may so advise the appellee and the appellee shall advance the cost of including such parts. In the event of a dispute as to the parts to be included or the advance required to include them, the matter shall be settled by the lower court on motion and notice. The cost of producing the appendix shall be taxed as costs in the case, but if either party shall cause matters to be included in the appendix unnecessarily the court may impose the cost of producing such parts on the party.

(c) Alternative Method of Designating Contents of the Appendix in Civil Cases; How References to the Record May Be Made in the Briefs When Alternative Method Is Used. In civil cases, if the appellant shall so elect—with leave of the appellate court or a single justice—preparation of the appendix may be deferred until after the briefs have been filed, and the appendix may be filed twenty-one days after service of the brief of the appellee. Notice of the election by the appellant to defer preparation of the appendix shall be filed and served by him within ten days after the date on which the clerk notifies the parties that the record has been assembled. If the preparation and filing of the appendix is thus deferred, the provisions of subdivision (b) of this Rule 18 shall apply, except that the designations referred to therein shall be made by each party at the time his brief is served, and a statement of the issues presented shall be unnecessary.

If the deferred appendix authorized by this subdivision is employed, references in the briefs to the record may be to the pages of the parts of the record involved, in which event the original paging of each part of the record shall be indicated in the appendix by placing in brackets the number of each page at the place in the appendix where that page begins. Or if a party desires to refer in his brief directly to pages of the appendix, he may serve and file typewritten or page-proof copies of his brief within the time required by Rule 19(a), with appropriate references to the pages of the parts of the record involved. In that event, within fourteen days after the appendix is filed he shall serve and file copies of the brief in the form prescribed by Rule 20(a) containing references to the pages of the appendix in place of or in addition to the initial references to the pages of the parts of the record involved. No other changes may be made in the brief as initially served and filed, except that typographical errors may be corrected.

(d) Arrangement of the Appendix. The pages of the appendix shall be consecutively numbered and the parts of the record which are reproduced therein shall be set out in chronological order. The appendix shall commence with a chronologically ordered list of the parts of the record which it contains, with references to the pages of the appendix at which each part begins. When an appendix relates to two or more cases or to more than two parties, the appendix shall indicate the case to which each paper belongs and by whom it was filed. Unless the party filing the appendix reproduces the entire transcript of testimony, he shall, preceding each portion of testimony transcript reproduced, insert a concise statement identifying:

(1) the witness whose testimony is being reproduced;

(2) the party originally calling him;

(3) the party questioning him; and

(4) the classification of his examination (direct, cross, or other).

When matter contained in the reporter's transcript of proceedings is set out in the appendix, the page number of the original transcript at which such matter may be found may be indicated in brackets immediately before the matter which is set out, unless it already appears on the matter as set out. Omissions in the text of papers or of the transcript must be indicated by asterisks. Immaterial formal matters (captions, subscriptions, acknowledgments, etc.) may be omitted. A question and its answer may be contained in a single paragraph.

(e) Reproduction of Exhibits and Transcripts. Exhibits and transcripts or portions thereof in civil cases, designated for inclusion in the appendix, may be contained in separate volumes, suitable indexed.

(1) *Appeals Court.* On appeals to the Appeals Court, five copies of the exhibits volume or volumes, and two copies of the transcript volume or volumes, shall be filed with the appendix and one copy of each shall be served on counsel for each party separately represented.

(2) *Supreme Judicial Court.* On appeal to the Supreme Judicial Court, and on further appellate review, five copies of the exhibits volume or volumes and five copies of the transcript volume or volumes shall be filed with the appendix and one copy of each shall be served on counsel for each party separately represented.

(3) *Appeals transferred to the Supreme Judicial Court from the Appeals Court.* In any appeal transferred to the full Supreme Judicial Court, in which copies of the exhibits and transcripts have already been filed in the Appeals Court pursuant to this rule, three additional copies of the transcript volume or volumes shall be promptly filed with the clerk of the Supreme Judicial Court, unless the court by order in a particular case shall direct a lesser or greater number.

(f) Hearing of Appeals on the Original Record Without the Necessity of an Appendix. On motion, the appellate court or a single justice may, in specific cases, dispense with the requirement of an appendix and permit appeals to be heard in whole or in part on the original record, with such copies of the record, or relevant parts thereof, as the court may require.

(g) Reproduction of Impounded Materials. If the entire case has been impounded, the cover of the appendix shall clearly indicate that the appendix is impounded. If the entire case has not been impounded, a separate appendix volume shall be filed containing the impounded material and the cover thereof shall clearly indicate that it contains impounded material.

Amended effective February 24, 1975; amended June 2, 1976, effective July 1, 1976; May 15, 1979, effective July 1, 1979; April 25, 1984, effective July 1, 1984; November 17, 1986, effective January 1, 1987; amended effective February 1, 1991; May 1, 1994; amended June 11, 1997, effective July 1, 1997; October 1, 1998, effective November 2, 1998.

Reporter's Notes—1973

Appellate Rule 18 indicates the required contents of the appendix, preparation of which is appellant's responsibility; the appendix must be filed with appellant's brief. Appellate Rule 18(b) encourages the parties to agree as to the contents of the joint appendix. Appellate Rule 18(c) permits the parties, at the election of the appellant, with leave of the appellate court or a single justice, to defer preparation of the appendix until after the briefs have been filed; it sets out detailed regulations for appropriate pagination of the deferred appendix and consequent references in the briefs. It should be emphasized that transcript pages included in the appendix may be reproduced by Xerography or a similar process; they need not be retyped. See Appellate Rule 20(a). The procedures set out in Appellate Rule 18, although necessarily somewhat different from existing practice, should not cause any serious practitional dislocation. See S.J.C. Rule 1:22.

Reporter's Notes—1975

The amendment to Appellate Rule 18(d) ensures that in a multi-party appeal, each paper appearing in the reproduced appendix bears sufficient identification to permit the reader easily to understand the document's particular genesis and significance.

Reporter's Notes—1979

A major change in criminal appellate procedure is worked by the application of Rule 18, as amended, to criminal cases. Under prior practice, after the record was assembled by the clerk, he would prepare a "summary of the record" which included a copy of the indictment or complaint and copies of pleadings and motions designated by the parties (former G.L. c. 278, § 33C [St.1974, c. 458, § 1]). This summary, in the required number of copies (former G.L. c. 278, § 33 [St.1978, c. 478, § 308]; Appeals Court and Supreme Judicial Court Rules 1:01 [1975: 3 Mass.App.Ct. 801–02. 366 Mass. 858, amended March 2, 1978]) was reproduced at the expense of the Commonwealth. The summary, together with two copies of the transcript and the assignment of errors (former G.L. c. 278, § 33D [St.1974, c. 458, § 2]), constituted the record on appeal (former G.L. c. 278, § 33E [St.1974, c. 457]). Under Rule 8(a), as amended, the record on appeal now consists of the original papers and exhibits on file, the transcript and a copy of the docket entries. The entire record is not transmitted to the appellate court except upon that court's order (Rule 9[a], [d]). The place of the summary of the record is taken by an appendix to the briefs, the contents of which are described in Rule 18(a). Responsibility for preparation of the appendix (properly "record appendix") rests with the appellant. If the appellee wishes to direct the particular attention of the court to parts of the record not contained in the appendix prepared by the appellant, he may prepare and file with his brief a supplemental appendix.

As in civil cases, the record appendix "is that distillation of the decision-essential portions of the record [on appeal]." Mass.R.App.P. 8, Reporter's Notes [1974]).

Subdivision (a) is changed by reducing from twenty-five to fifteen the number of copies of the appendix required to be filed, and, as amended, applies to both civil and criminal cases.

Subdivisions (b) and (c) are limited in application to civil cases.

Subdivision (d) restates in part the requirements of former Appeals Court and Supreme Judicial Court Rules 1:01, supra, relative to the contents of the record appendix and designation of the papers in a record.

Subdivisions (e) and (f) are unchanged.

Reporter's Notes—1984

Under previous Mass.R.A.P. 18(e) a party on appeal could put "exhibits designated for inclusion in the appendix" in "a separate volume, or volumes" and then file only "five copies," plus serve one copy "on counsel for each party separately represented." This reduced the number of copies of exhibits otherwise required under Mass.R.A.P. 18(a). The present amendment to Mass.R.A.P. 18(e) adds "transcripts or portions thereof in civil cases" to "exhibits," to further decrease the cost of appeals and reduce the number of documents which must be handled and stored by appellate courts.

The reference to Mass.R.A.P. 18(e), which has now been added to Rule 18(a), is to remind counsel to check Rule 18(e) in order to consider whether they wish to reduce the required copies of exhibits and "transcripts or portions thereof in civil cases" from fifteen, plus two for "counsel for each party separately represented," to five, plus one copy for such counsel. This change also makes clear that the "five copies" option in Rule 18(e) is instead of, and not in addition to, the "fifteen copies" otherwise required by the provisions of Rule 18(a).

These amendments do not alter the rules in criminal cases, which obligate the clerk of the lower court to transmit to the appellate court the "original and one copy of the transcript and a list of all the exhibits" and provide that "... the appendix need not contain relevant portions of the transcript ..." (Mass.R.A.P. 9(d) and 18(a)).

Reporter's Notes—1986

This amendment corresponds to a 1986 amendment to F.R.A.P. 30(a). As the Committee Note to that amendment suggests, the inclusion of memoranda of law can make an appendix bulky and less useful to the appellate court, and also increase litigation costs. "There are occasions when such trial court memoranda have independent relevance in the appellate litigation. For instance, there may be a dispute as to whether a particular point was raised or whether a concession was made in the ... [lower court]. In such circumstances, it is appropriate to include pertinent sections of such memoranda in the appendix."

Reporter's Notes—1991

This amendment reduces the number of copies of the appendix required to be filed in the Appeals Court from fifteen to the numbers of copies of the brief required under Mass.R.A.P. 19(b). For example, unless an exception applies, a party is required to file seven copies of both the briefs and the appendix in the Appeals Court and fifteen copies in the Supreme Judicial Court. The reasons for the reduction are explained in the Reporter's Notes to Amended Rule 19(b).

Reporter's Notes to Mass.R.A.P. 18(b)—1994

The prior language in Mass.R.A.P. 18(b) stated that "[i]n designating parts of the record for inclusion in the appendix, the parties shall have regard for the fact that the entire record is always available to the court for reference and examination and shall not engage in unnecessary designation." Since the parties have the obligation in Rule 18(a) and (b) to designate portions of the record upon which they will rely, and in civil cases must include relevant portions of the transcript, it was unclear what it meant "to have regard for the fact that the entire record is always available to the court." This phrase was particularly ambiguous because the parties in civil cases have no right to rely upon portions of the transcript that are not designated. Rules 18(b) and 18(f), which under some circumstances permit the parties to rely on parts of the record that have not been included in the appendix, specifically refer to leave granted prior to argument or a motion in advance granted by the appellate court or a single justice. The new language is in keeping with the normal expectation of appellate judges that the parties will provide appellate courts with an appendix which includes the materials upon which they rely. See Shawmut Community Bank, N.A. v. Zagami, 411 Mass. 807, 810–812 (1992).

Reporter's Notes—1997

The 1997 amendment to Appellate Rule 18(a) requires that where any matter has been impounded or made confidential in the lower court, a copy of the lower court order of impoundment, if any, be included in the appendix. The amendment to Appellate Rule 18(b) requires that where such matter is to be included in the record, the fact that the matter has been impounded or made confidential be indicated in the designation of the record.

The amendment to Appellate Rule 18(g) places the burden on counsel to inform the appellate clerk's office that confidential information is contained in an appendix and to prepare a separate appendix volume in instances where less than the entire case has been impounded. The purpose of this amendment, as is the purpose of the simultaneous amendments to Appellate Rules 16(d) and (m), is to facilitate the work of the clerk's office in maintaining the confidentiality of information filed in the appellate court. See Reporter's Notes to Appellate Rules 16(d) and (m).

Reporter's Notes to Mass.R.A.P. 18(e)—1998

This amendment is intended to further decrease the cost of appeals and further reduce the quantity of documents which must be handled and stored by the appellate courts. In the Appeals Court, the number of transcript copies in civil cases (if separately bound) has been reduced to two, which is the same requirement as in criminal cases (see Mass.R.A.P. 9(d)). If a case is transferred to the Supreme Judicial Court after the filing of a reduced number of copies in the Appeals Court, three additional copies of the transcript must be filed in the Supreme Judicial Court.

Rule 19. Filing and Serving of Briefs and Motions

(a) Time for Serving and Filing Briefs. Except as provided in section (d) of this rule, and in Rule 11(g)(4) concerning the filing of briefs on direct appellate review, and in Rule 27.1(f) concerning the filing of briefs on further appellate review, the appellant shall serve and file his brief within 40 days after the date on which the appeal is docketed in the appellate court. The appellee shall serve and file his brief within thirty days after service of the brief of the appellant. The appellant may serve and file a reply brief within fourteen days after service of the brief of the appellee, but, except by leave of the appellate court or a single justice, for good cause shown, a reply brief must be filed at least three days before the first day of the sitting at which the case is in order for argument.

(b) Number of Copies to Be Filed and Served.

(1) *Appeals Court.* On appeals to the Appeals Court, seven copies of each brief shall be filed with the clerk, unless the court by order in a particular case shall direct a lesser number, and two copies shall be served on counsel for each party separately represented.

(2) *Supreme Judicial Court.* On appeal to the Supreme Judicial Court, an original and seventeen copies of each brief shall be filed with the clerk, unless the

court by order in a particular case shall direct a lesser or greater number, and two copies shall be served on counsel for each party separately represented.

(3) *Appeals transferred to the Supreme Judicial Court from the Appeals Court.* In any appeal transferred to the full Supreme Judicial Court, in which briefs have already been filed in the Appeals Court, eleven additional copies of each brief shall be promptly filed with the clerk of the Supreme Judicial Court, unless the court by order in a particular case shall direct a lesser or greater number.

(c) Consequence of Failure to File Briefs. If an appellant fails to file his brief within the time provided by this rule, or within the time as extended, an appellee may move for dismissal of the appeal. If an appellee fails to file his brief, he will not be heard at oral argument except by permission of the appellate court.

(d) Rule for Appeals Pursuant to Massachusetts General Laws Chapter 278, sec. 33E.

(1) In the case of a direct appeal by an appellant who has been convicted of first degree murder, the appellant shall, within one hundred and twenty days after the date on which the appeal is docketed in the Supreme Judicial Court: (1) serve and file the appellant's brief; (2) serve and file a motion for new trial; or (3) for good cause shown, seek a further enlargement of time for filing a brief or a motion for new trial. The Commonwealth shall serve and file its brief within ninety days after service of the brief of the appellant. The appellant may serve and file a reply brief within thirty days after service of the brief of the Commonwealth.

(2) If a motion for new trial is remanded to the Superior Court, the direct appeal of the conviction shall be stayed pending decision on the motion for new trial. The matter shall be heard and determined expeditiously in the Superior Court. The appellant shall file with the Clerk of the Supreme Judicial Court for the Commonwealth status reports at thirty-day intervals. An appeal by the defendant from the denial of a motion for new trial shall be consolidated with the direct appeal. An appeal by the Commonwealth or by the defendant from the determination of a motion for new trial shall have the same docket number as the direct appeal. The Clerk of the Supreme Judicial Court for the Commonwealth shall establish a briefing schedule.

Amended May 15, 1979, effective July 1, 1979; amended effective February 1, 1991; July 1, 1991; amended October 30, 1997, effective January 1, 1998; July 28, 1999, effective October 1, 1999; February 25, 2004, effective April 1, 2004.

Reporter's Notes—1973

Appellate Rule 19 sets the time table for the filing of briefs. Appellant must file his brief within 40 days after the docketing of the appeal (which occurs ten days after the record is assembled, see Appellate Rule 10(a); assembly occurs "as soon as may be after the filing of the notice of appeal," Appellate Rule 9(a)). Thus appellant's brief ordinarily must be filed approximately 50 days after the filing of his notice of appeal, (plus however long the lower court clerk requires for assembling the record). Appellee must file his brief within 30 days after service of appellant's brief. The appellant may serve a reply brief within 14 days after service of the appellee's brief. Although Appellate Rule 19 somewhat enlarges previous appellate timetables, see S.J.C. Rule 1:16 and Appeals Court Rule 1:16, it should occasion no unusual difficulties.

Reporter's Notes—1979

There is no change in the substance of subdivision (a), but applying the rule to criminal appeals does enlarge the times for filing of the appellant's brief found in former Appeals Court and Supreme Judicial Court Rules 1:16 (1975: 3 Mass. App.Ct. 804. 366 Mass. 861–62) from twenty-eight to forty days after docketing (Mass.R.App.P. 10[b]). Further, under the former court rules, the appellee's brief was required to be filed within forty-nine days after entry of the case, while up to seventy days after docketing is allowed by this rule (within thirty days after service of appellant's brief). Thus, in the usual appeal, the defendant's brief is due forty days after docketing and the Commonwealth's brief thirty days thereafter. The abolishing of assignments of error (former G.L. c. 278, § 33D [St.1974, c. 458, § 2]) eliminate one step in prior appellate procedure which generated a great deal of delay. Section 33D of chapter 278 required that assignments were to be filed within thirty days after receipt of notice of the completion of the summary of the record (G.L. c. 278, § 33C [St.1974, c. 458, § 1]), but that time could be extended by a justice of an appellate or lower court. Much of the delay was attributable to the fact that assignments could not be prepared until the trial transcript had been received and reviewed for error.

Appeals Court and Supreme Judicial Court Rules 1:16 permitted either party to file a reply brief; under Rule 19, only the appellant may do so. Twenty-five copies of each were required to be filed by both the former court rules and by Appellate Rule 19(b). Subdivision (b) has been amended to reduce that number to fifteen, the reduction being applicable in civil and criminal cases alike. The requirement in subdivision (b) that two copies of briefs be served upon each party separately represented is consistent with former Appeals Court and Supreme Judicial Court Rules 1:16.

Reporter's Notes—1991

Experience has demonstrated that seven copies of briefs are needed by the Appeals Court and fifteen by the Supreme Judicial Court. This amendment, reducing the number of copies from fifteen in the Appeals Court, should save money for the parties and the Commonwealth, as well as storage space for the court. When a case is transferred from the Appeals Court to the Supreme Judicial Court, in which briefs have already been filed, the clerk of the Appeals Court must transmit the seven copies of the briefs already filed (Mass. R.A.P. 11(f)), and the parties must promptly deliver an additional eight copies to the clerk of the Supreme Judicial Court (Mass.R.A.P. 19(b)(3)).

Reporter's Notes—1997

The 1997 amendments to Appellate Rule 19(b) were prompted by the need for additional copies of filings to accommodate the practice in which all seven Justices of the Supreme Judicial Court sit on many cases.

Appellate Rule 19(b)(2), dealing with appeals to the Supreme Judicial Court, was amended to increase to seventeen the number of copies of each brief to be filed with the clerk of the Supreme Judicial Court, unless otherwise ordered. The amendment also clarified that an original is to be filed together with the seventeen copies.

Appellate Rule 19(b)(3), dealing with appeals transferred to the Supreme Judicial Court from the Appeals Court in cases where briefs had already been filed in the Appeals Court, was amended to increase to eleven the number of additional copies to be filed with the clerk of the Supreme Judicial Court, unless otherwise ordered.

Reporter's Notes—1999

The 1999 amendments added new Appellate Rule 19(d) to deal with direct appeals to the Supreme Judicial Court from first-degree murder convictions pursuant to G.L. c. 278, § 33E. The changes to Appellate Rule 19 were based on recommendations made by the Ad Hoc Supreme Judicial Court Committee on Appeals in Cases of Murder in the First Degree, a committee consisting of defense attorneys and prosecutors who handle first degree murder appeals. The major purpose of the amendments was to establish realistic time periods for the briefing of such appeals.

Paragraph (1) of Appellate Rule 19(d) substantially lengthens the time period for the service and filing of briefs that is provided for cases other than first-degree murder appeals in Appellate Rule 19(a). The time period for the appellant's brief has been increased from 40 days to 120 days; the time period for the Commonwealth's brief has been increased from 30 days to 90 days (and any reply brief by the appellant to be served and filed within 30 days). A defendant must serve and file a motion for new trial within 120 days of docketing the appeal in the Supreme Judicial Court.

Paragraph (2) of Appellate Rule 19(d) provides for a stay of the direct appeal in the event the Supreme Judicial Court remands to the Superior Court a motion for new trial. In such event, the appellant must file status reports with the Clerk of the Supreme Judicial Court for the Commonwealth every 30 days. An appeal by the defendant from the Superior Court judge's denial of a motion for new trial is to be consolidated with the direct appeal under the same docket number. In such a case, the Clerk of the Supreme Judicial Court will establish the schedule for briefing.

Reporter's Notes—2004

The first sentence of Appellate Rule 19(a) has been amended to be consistent with the simultaneous amendment to Appellate Rule 27.1(f). As amended in 2004, Appellate Rule 27.1(f) provides that upon further appellate review in the Supreme Judicial Court, a party may rely on the brief filed in the Appeals Court or may request permission to file a new brief in lieu of the Appeals Court brief.

Rule 20. Form of Briefs, Appendices, and Other Papers

(a) Form of Briefs and the Appendix. Except on order of the appellate court or a single justice, or if filed on behalf of a party allowed to proceed in forma pauperis, all briefs and appendices shall be produced by any duplicating or copying process which produces a clear black image on white paper. However produced, the page shall be eight and one-half inches in width and eleven inches in height. Pages shall be firmly bound at the left by saddle-wiring, side-wiring, stapling, or sewing. If side-wired or sewn, a strong paper cover shall be used. A transcript of testimony or a report of evidence may be included as part of the appendix and may be reproduced by Xerography or a similar process. No single volume of the appendix shall be more than one and one-half inches thick. The text of appendices may appear on both sides of the page.

The following rules shall govern the format of text on a page for all briefs:

(1) The top and bottom margins shall be at least one inch. The left and right margins shall be at least one and one-half inches. Thus, the text area should not be more than five and one-half inches in width nor more than nine inches in height. Page numbers may appear in the margin.

(2) The typeface shall be a monospaced font (such as pica type produced by a typewriter or a Courier font produced by a computer word processor) of 12 point or larger size and not exceeding 10.5 characters per inch.

(3) Text shall be double-spaced, except that argument headings, footnotes and indented quotations may be single-spaced. For purposes of this rule, single spacing means not more than six lines of text per vertical inch; double spacing means not more than three lines of text per vertical inch and not more than twenty-seven double-spaced lines on a page.

(4) The text may appear on both sides of the page.

Briefs or appendices not in substantial compliance with these rules shall not be received unless the appellate court or a single justice shall otherwise order.

The cover of the brief of the appellant shall be blue; that of the appellee, red; that of an intervenor or amicus curiae, green; that of any reply brief, gray. The cover of the appendix, if separately bound, shall be white. The front covers of the briefs and appendices, if separately produced, shall contain: (1) the name of the court and the number of the case; (2) the title of the case (see Rule 10a); (3) the nature of the proceeding in the court (e.g., Appeal; Application for Review) and the name of the court, agency, or board below; (4) the title of the document (e.g., Brief for Appellant, Appendix); and (5) the names, Board of Bar Overseers (BBO) numbers, addresses, telephone numbers, and e-mail addresses if any of counsel representing the party on whose behalf the document is filed, and, if an individual counsel is affiliated with a firm, the firm name.

(b) Form of Other Papers. Petitions for rehearing shall be produced in a manner prescribed by subdivision (a). Motions and other papers may be produced in like manner, or they may be typewritten in pica type upon opaque, unglazed paper eight and one half by eleven inches in size. Lines of typewritten text shall be double spaced. Consecutive sheets shall be attached at the left margin. Carbon copies may be used for filing and service if they are legible.

A motion or other paper addressed to the court shall contain a caption setting forth the name of the court, the title of the case, the file number, and a brief descriptive title indicating the purpose of the paper; said caption shall appear on the first page, typed so as to be legible.

The cover of applications for direct appellate review and for further appellate review shall be white.

Such motion or paper shall contain, at the end thereof, the names, Board of Bar Overseers (BBO) numbers, addresses, and telephone numbers of counsel, if any, representing the party on whose behalf the motion or paper is filed, and, if an individual counsel is affiliated with a firm, the firm name.

Amended effective February 24, 1975; February 1, 1991; January 1, 1992; amended December 1, 1998, effective January 1, 1999; March 5, 2010, effective May 1, 2010.

Reporter's Notes—1973

Appellate Rule 20 permits briefs and appendices to be reproduced *either* by printing or by any duplicating process which produces a clear black image on white paper. Thus briefs may be xeroxed. However produced, briefs must be firmly bound or stapled, and must ordinarily bear color-coded covers: blue for the appellant; red for the appellee; gray for the reply brief; green for an amicus (if allowed, see Appellate Rule 17). The record appendix, if separately produced, should be covered in white.

Motions may be either typewritten or xeroxed.

Reporter's Notes—1975

The amendment to Appellate Rule 20(b) eliminates the requirement of "backing" the caption, so as to conform to the introduction of flat filing, see S.J.C. Rule 3:20.

Reporter's Notes—1979

Subdivision (a) of Rule 20 was made applicable to criminal cases by former Appeals Court and Supreme Judicial Court Rules 1:14 (1975: 3 Mass.App.Ct. 803. 366 Mass. 860) and is unchanged.

Reporter's Notes—1991

Experience has shown that volumes of appendices that are more than one and a half inches thick often fall apart and are clumsy to use. The limitation of each individual volume of the appendix to a thickness no greater than one and a half inches should solve the problem. If the appendix is larger in size, multiple volumes should be used.

Mass.R.A.P. 16(a)(7) and 20(a), final sentence, clause (5):

These amendments require individual counsel who are affiliated with a firm to include the firm name on filed briefs. Appellate judges need to know the firm names in order to determine correctly whether it is necessary to withdraw from a case.

Reporter's Notes to Mass.R.A.P. 20(a)—1999

I. Introduction.

Since the adoption of the Massachusetts Rules of Appellate Procedure in 1974, there have been only a few changes to Appellate Rule 20. With the advances in computer technology that have ensued since the 1970s, the Standing Advisory Committee on the Rules of Civil Procedure of the Supreme Judicial Court agreed with the recommendation of the clerks of the Supreme Judicial Court and of the Appeals Court that the time had come to re-examine Appellate Rule 20.

II. Briefs.

A number of changes to the existing rule were made in recognition of the fact that briefs today are typically computer-generated, whether an attorney produces a brief in-house or utilizes the services of a commercial firm. For example, outmoded references in the first paragraph of Rule 20(a) such as "standard typographic printing" and "printed matter" have been deleted. The reference to carbon copies has also been deleted.

The 1999 amendment also addresses a problem that has developed in recent years in the appellate courts of the Commonwealth. Judges have commented that in some instances briefs have been difficult to read because of the small size of letters. In addition, today's computer technology has provided opportunity for circumvention of the page limitations on briefs by compressing or condensing letters. If a brief is rejected by the clerk's office for such reasons, frustration and the additional expense of producing a replacement brief result. See "Strict Rule on Briefs Frustrates Litigators," 26 Massachusetts Lawyers Weekly 55 (September 15, 1997). A new second paragraph has been added to Rule 20(a) to address these and other matters of form.

It should be noted the existing page limitations on briefs produced by computer wordprocessing--as contained in Appellate Rule 16(h)--remain the same.

The following provisions numbered (1) through (4) are applicable to all briefs under the amended rule:

(1) Margins. Top and bottom margins on a page shall be at least one inch; left and right margins must be at least one and one-half inches. The rule specifically allows a page number to be placed within a margin. Uniformity in margins will also facilitate the placing of text on both sides of a page of a document, a practice permitted by Rule 20(a)(4).

(2) Typeface. Only a monospaced font is allowed. Therefore, attorneys may no longer use a proportional font such as Times New Roman. The typeface must be a 12 point or larger size and a limitation of 10.5 characters per inch is imposed. It should be noted that these limitations are applicable to footnotes as well as text. These requirements should eliminate the problem brief where page limitations have been circumvented by means of reducing, compressing, or condensing typeface.

Right margin justification (the process by which the lettering on a line is spaced so that the last letter on each line is flush to the right margin) is not prohibited by this rule, as long as the right margin is at least one and one-half inches and the limitation of 10.5 characters per inch is observed.

(3) Line Spacing. Documents are to be double-spaced. Argument headings, footnotes, and indented quotations, however, may be single-spaced. The revised rule defines the terms double-spaced and single-spaced--terms which may have been obvious in the context of a brief produced by a typewriter--so that there will be no more than three lines per vertical inch for double spacing and no more than six lines per vertical inch for single spacing (with an overall limit of 27 double-spaced lines on a page).

(4) Text May Appear on Both Sides. The prior version of Rule 20(a) did not speak to the issue of text appearing on both sides of a page. In recent years, some attorneys have

begun to submit briefs where the text appears on the front and back of a page. The 1999 amendment specifically allows this practice. Although it is not required that text must appear on both sides of a page, attorneys are encouraged to produce briefs in this fashion. It is hoped that the practice of putting text on the front and back of a page will significantly reduce the storage problems in the clerks' offices of the appellate courts by reducing the overall size of briefs.

Where counsel is unable to comply with the technical requirements of Rule 20, it would be advisable to move in the appellate court in advance for leave to file a non-conforming brief rather than risk rejection of the filing at a point where time deadlines may be about to expire.

III. Appendices.

The 1999 changes regarding briefs do not apply to the appendix. An appendix may contain existing documents, transcripts, and other matters that were not originally prepared by counsel. However, in an effort to help reduce the storage problems in the clerk's offices of the appellate courts, a sentence has been added to Appellate Rule 20(a) allowing the text of the appendix to be reproduced on both sides of a page, a practice that is also allowed (and in fact, encouraged) for briefs.

Reporter's Notes to Mass.R.A.P. 20(b)—1999

Appellate Rule 20(b), governing the form of papers other than briefs and appendices, has been amended to require that the cover of applications for direct appellate review (Rule 11) and for further appellate review (Rule 27.1) be white. This will allow the clerk's office more easily to identify such documents.

Rule 21. Prehearing Conference

The appellate court may direct the attorneys for the parties to appear before the court or a single justice for a prehearing conference to consider the simplification of the issues and such other matters as may aid in the disposition of the proceeding by the court. The appellate court or single justice shall make an order which recites the action taken at the conference and the agreements made by the parties as to any of the matters considered and which limits the issues to those not disposed of by admissions or agreements of counsel, and such order when entered shall control the subsequent course of the proceeding, unless modified to prevent manifest injustice.

Reporter's Notes—1973

Appellate Rule 21 allows the court to conduct a prehearing conference. Modelled on F.R.A.P. 33, it has no Massachusetts parallel at the appellate level.

Rule 22. Oral Argument

(a) Notice of Argument; Postponement. The clerk shall advise all parties of the time and place at which oral argument will be heard. A request for postponement of the argument must be made by motion filed reasonably in advance of the date fixed for hearing.

(b) Time Allowed for Argument. Unless otherwise enlarged or limited by the appellate court, each side will be allowed fifteen minutes for argument, except in a criminal case in which the defendant is appealing a conviction of murder in the first degree, in which case each side will be allowed twenty minutes for argument. If counsel is of the opinion that additional time is necessary for the adequate presentation of the argument, counsel may request additional time for good cause shown. Requests may be made by letter addressed to the clerk reasonably in advance of the date fixed for the argument. The appellate court may terminate the argument whenever in its judgment further argument is unnecessary.

(c) Order and Content of Argument. Except as otherwise provided in Rule 27.1(g), the appellant will argue first and shall include a fair statement of the case. Counsel will not be permitted to read, except briefly, from briefs, records, prepared statements, records or authorities. The party making the opening argument on request may be allowed the opportunity to reply in writing to new matter in the arguments of his adversary.

(d) Cross and Separate Appeals. A cross or separate appeal shall be argued with the initial appeal at a single argument, unless the appellate court otherwise directs. If a case involves a cross appeal, the plaintiff in the action below shall be deemed the appellant for the purposes of this rule unless the parties otherwise agree or the court otherwise directs. If separate appellants support the same argument, care shall be taken to avoid duplication of argument.

(e) Non-appearance of Parties. If the appellee fails to appear to present argument, the appellate court will hear argument on behalf of the appellant, if present. If the appellant fails to appear, the court may hear argument on behalf of the appellee, if his counsel is present. If neither party appears, the case will be decided on the briefs unless the appellate court shall otherwise order.

(f) No Oral Argument by an Attorney Who Has Been a Witness Except by Leave of Court. No attorney shall be permitted to take part in the argument of a case in which he has been a witness for his client; except by special leave of court.

(g) Submission on Briefs. By agreement of the parties, a case may at any time be submitted for decision on the briefs, but the appellate court may direct that the case be argued. At any time, any party may, by written notice filed and served, waive his right to oral argument. No criminal case in which the defendant was convicted of murder in the first degree may be submitted for decision on the briefs without oral argument unless the full appellate court or a justice thereof shall have approved the submission prior to the week the case has been scheduled for argument.

(h) Use of Physical Exhibits at Argument; Removal. If physical exhibits other than documents or chalks are to be used at the argument, counsel shall arrange to have them placed in the court room before the court convenes on the date of the argument. After the argument, the exhibits shall be left with the clerk unless the court otherwise directs. If exhibits are not reclaimed by counsel within a reasonable time after notice is given by the clerk, they shall be destroyed or otherwise disposed of as the clerk shall think best.

Amended May 15, 1979, effective July 1, 1979; December 2, 1983, effective January 1, 1984; amended effective May 1, 1994; November 1, 1994; amended May 3, 2002, effective September 3, 2002.

Reporter's Notes—1973

Appellate Rule 22 governs the conduct of oral argument. A modification of F.R.A.P. 34, it codifies prior practice. Enlargements of argument time beyond thirty minutes will rarely be allowed; compare F.R.A.P. 34(b). Rebuttal argument, a matter of right, Appellate Rule 22(c), is strictly limited to new matter raised in appellee's argument. Although failure explicitly to reserve rebuttal does not waive the right, failure to preserve for rebuttal purposes a portion of the thirty-minute argument time will effect a de facto waiver in the absence of leave granted.

Reporter's Notes—1979

The only change in Rule 22 is that the substance of Supreme Judicial Court Rule 1:20 (1975: 366 Mass. 862), relative to submission of capital cases on briefs, is added to subdivision (g) of the former rule. The provisions of Rule 22 were previously applicable to criminal appeals by virtue of Supreme Judicial Court Rule 1:20, supra and Appeals Court Rule 1:20 (1975: 3 Mass.App.Ct. 804).

Reporter's Notes—1983

The purpose of this amendment is to conform Rule 22(b) to the actual practice in the appellate courts.

The purpose of this amendment is to conform Rule 22(c) to the actual practice in the appellate courts.

Reporter's Notes to Mass.R.A.P. 22(h)—1994

Mass.R.A.P. 22(h) does *not* give permission to counsel to refer to physical exhibits during oral argument. It only instructs counsel as to their obligation to arrange to have the physical exhibits in the court room before the court convenes if they are going to use them, and of the clerk's obligations afterwards.

Counsel should remember that it is their obligation to include in the appendix any portions of the record they are relying upon, including exhibits, in accordance with the provisions of Mass.R.A.P. 18(a) and 18(b). The third paragraph of Mass.R.A.P. 18(a) makes clear that "... the court may decline to permit the parties to refer to portions of the record omitted from the appendix, unless leave be granted prior to argument."

Physical exhibits cannot be actually placed in an appendix. Consequently, counsel on appeal who intend to refer to a physical exhibit, such as a revolver or a piece of clothing, should "prior to argument" seek leave of court to refer to such objects. Many appellate justices prefer to have pages in an appendix to refer to whenever possible. It is sound practice for counsel on appeal to have a photograph of physical exhibits appear on a page or pages of the appendix, even if prior permission has been given to use the actual physical exhibit at the oral argument.

Reporter's Notes to Appellate Rule 22(b)—2002

In 2002, the Supreme Judicial Court amended Appellate Rule 22(b) to reduce the time allowed for oral argument in first degree murder cases from thirty minutes to twenty minutes for each side. The time for oral argument in all other cases remains fifteen minutes for each side. As amended, Appellate Rule 22(b) further provides that if counsel desires additional time for oral argument, "counsel may request additional time for good cause shown." This latter provision replaces the former language that had provided that requests for additional time "will rarely be granted."

Rule 23. Issuance of Rescript: Stay of Rescript

The clerk of the appellate court shall mail to all parties a copy of the rescript and the opinion, if one was written. The rescript of the court shall issue to the lower court twenty-eight days after the date of the rescript unless the time is shortened or enlarged by order. The timely filing of a petition for rehearing or of an application for further appellate review will stay the rescript until disposition of the petition or application unless otherwise ordered by the appellate court. If the petition or application is denied, the rescript shall issue forthwith unless the appellate court or a single justice orders otherwise. If an application for further appellate review is granted the rescript of the Appeals Court shall not issue to the lower court.

Amended effective February 24, 1975.

Reporter's Notes—1973

A rescript is the equivalent at the appellate level, of judgment in the trial court, Appellate Rule 1(c); Mass.R.Civ.P. 54(a). It is the appellate court's enunciation of its disposition of the appeal, the order directing the lower court's further conduct of the case. Usually, the rescript will issue to the lower court within fourteen days of its utterance by the appellate court. But a timely application for rehearing, Appellate Rule 27, or for further appellate review (if appropriate), Appellate Rule 27.1, will stay the issuance of the rescript.

Reporter's Notes—1975

The amendment enlarges the period for the issuance of rescript from 14 days to 28 days. This change was required by the amendment to Appellate Rule 27.1(a), extending the period within which the party could apply for further appellate review from 10 days to 20 days. Without the amendment to Appellate Rule 23, therefore, a party properly waiting until the twentieth day to file his application for further appellate review might find that the rescript had issued six days earlier, thus cutting off his additional appellate rights. The other amendment to Appellate Rule 23 merely substitutes "petition" for "request", to conform with the language of Appellate Rule 27.

Reporter's Notes—1979

The current text is unchanged but made applicable to criminal as well as civil cases.

Rule 24. Justices' Participation

(a) Other Justices May Participate Without Reargument. Whenever the justices before whom a law question has been heard so desire, others of the justices may be called in to take part in the decision, upon a perusal of the record and briefs, without reargument.

(b) Justice May Review Own Ruling in Certain Cases. No justice shall sit on the hearing of any proceeding in the nature of a review of any judgment, decree, order, or ruling made by him; provided, however, that this shall not apply where it is necessary to secure a quorum or where the other justices of the court shall be equally divided in opinion.

Reporter's Notes—1973

Appellate Rule 24(a) permits the participation in a decision of a justice who has not heard argument. Appellate Rule 24(b) regulates a justice's participation in review of his own ruling. The rule codifies prior practice, S.J.C. Rule 1:18, 1:19; Appeals Court Rule 1:18.

Reporter's Notes—1979

Rule 24 is unchanged, but in criminal cases supersedes former Appeals Court and Supreme Judicial Court Rules 1:18 (1972: 1 Mass.App.Ct. 892, amended, 1975: 3 Mass.App.Ct. 801. 1967: 351 Mass. 731, amended, 1975: 366 Mass. 853) and 1:19 (1975: 3 Mass.App.Ct. 804. 1967: 351 Mass. 741–42, amended, 1975: 366 Mass. 853).

Rule 24.1. Divided Vote On Further Appellate Review

If, following allowance of an application for further appellate review, the justices of the Supreme Judicial Court are equally divided in opinion, unless a majority of the participating justices decides otherwise, the court shall issue an order noting such equal division, the effect of which shall be the same as if the court had denied the application for further appellate review.

Adopted effective January 1, 1994.

Rule 25. Damages for Delay

(Applicable to civil cases)

(Applicable to civil cases)

If the appellate court shall determine that an appeal is frivolous, it may award just damages and single or double costs to the appellee, and such interest on the amount of the judgment as may be allowed by law.

Amended December 22, 1978, effective January 15, 1979; May 15, 1979, effective July 1, 1979.

Reporter's Notes—1973

Appellate Rule 25, taken from F.R.A.P. 38, allows the court to award damages and appropriate costs if it determines that an appeal was taken frivolously. See Oscar Gruss & Son v. Lumberman's Mutual Casualty Co., 422 F.2d 1278, 1283–1284 (2d Cir.1970). This is new to Massachusetts practice.

Reporter's Notes—1979

Rule 25 is limited to civil cases.

Rule 26. Costs

(Applicable to civil cases)

(a) To Whom Allowed. Except as otherwise provided by law, if an appeal is dismissed, costs shall be taxed against the appellant unless otherwise agreed by the parties or ordered by the appellate court; if a judgment is affirmed, costs shall be taxed against the appellant unless otherwise ordered; if a judgment is reversed, costs shall be taxed against the appellee unless otherwise ordered; if a judgment is affirmed on reversed in part, or is vacated, costs shall be allowed only as ordered by the appellate court.

(b) Costs For and Against the Commonwealth. In cases involving the Commonwealth or an agency or officer thereof, if an award of costs against the Commonwealth is authorized by law, costs shall be awarded in accordance with the provisions of subdivision (a); otherwise, costs shall not be awarded for or against the Commonwealth.

(c) Costs of Briefs, Appendices, and Copies of Records. The cost of printing or otherwise producing necessary copies of briefs, appendices, or copies of records authorized by Rule 18(f) shall be taxable in the lower court at rates not higher than those generally charged for such work in the Commonwealth. A party who desires such costs to be taxed shall state them in an itemized and verified bill of costs which he shall file with the clerk of the lower court, with proof of service, within fourteen days after the entry of judgment.

(d) Clerk to Insert Costs in Lower Court Judgment; Costs Taxable. The clerk of the lower court shall prepare and certify an itemized statement of costs for insertion in the lower court judgment. The statement shall include those costs taxable under subdivision (c) of this rule; costs incurred in the preparation and transmission of the record, the cost of the reporter's transcript, if necessary for the determination of the appeal, the premiums paid for cost of any bond to preserve rights pending appeal, and the fee for filing the notice of appeal shall be taxed in the lower court as costs of the appeal in favor of the party entitled to costs under this rule.

Amended May 15, 1979, effective July 1, 1979.

Reporter's Notes—1973

Appellate Rule 26, based on F.R.A.P. 39, governs the allowance of costs, and follows prior practice. See G.L. c. 261, § 22. Costs are taxable against the Commonwealth as against an individual. G.L. c. 261, §§ 14, 16. Appellate Rule 26(c), dealing with costs of briefs, enlarges existing practice somewhat, see former G.L. c. 261, § 25; previously a prevailing party could recover only $50 of the cost of printing his brief, unless the court allowed a larger discretionary sum; under Appellate Rule 26(c) the prevailing party recovers the necessary costs of producing the briefs at a rate not higher than such costs generally charged in the Commonwealth.

Reporter's Notes—1979

Rule 26 is limited to civil cases.

Rule 27. Petition for Rehearing

(a) Time for Filing; Content; Answer; Action by Court if Granted. A petition for rehearing should be filed with the clerk of the appellate court within fourteen days after the date of the rescript unless the time is shortened or enlarged by order. It shall state with particularity the points of law or fact which it is contended the court has overlooked or misapprehended and shall contain such argument in support of the petition as the petitioner desires to present. Oral argument in support of the petition will not be permitted, except by order of the quorum or panel which decided the appeal. No answer to a petition for rehearing will be received unless requested by the quorum or panel, but a petition for rehearing will ordinarily not be granted in the absence of such a request. A petition for rehearing shall be decided by the quorum or panel which decided the appeal. If a petition for rehearing is granted, the quorum or panel may make a final disposition of the cause without reargument or may restore it to the calendar for reargument or resubmission or may make such other orders as are deemed appropriate under the circumstances of the particular case. Action upon a petition is in the discretion of such quorum or panel, which may award costs, including a reasonable attorney's fee, to the prevailing party.

(b) Form of Petition; Length. The petition shall be in a form of a letter to the senior justice of the quorum or panel which decided the appeal with seven clear and legible copies, and additional copies shall be mailed by first class mail or delivered to all other counsel. Except by permission of the quorum or panel, a petition for rehearing shall not exceed ten pages of standard typewritten material.

(c) Revision of Decision. Upon consideration of a petition for rehearing, a quorum or panel may in writing order their decision to be reviewed and revised by a majority of the justices of the court. The petitioner shall notify the Supreme Judicial Court of any action taken on the petition if an application for further appellate review also has been filed.

Amended June 7, 1985, effective July 1, 1985; January 28, 1986, effective February 1, 1986; amended effective July 1, 1991.

Reporter's Notes—1973

Appellate Rule 27, taken from F.R.A.P. 40, governs petitions for rehearing. It will not change prior practice, under which a petition for rehearing was addressed to the discretion of the court, Merrill v. Beckwith, 168 Mass. 72, 75, 46 N.E. 400, 401 (1897), and ordinarily could not be supported by oral argument, Wall v. Old Colony Trust Company, 177 Mass. 275, 278, 58 N.E. 1015, 1016 (1901).

Reporter's Notes—1985

The change from ten days to fourteen days after the date of the rescript for a petition for rehearing conforms the time period to that found in Fed.R.A.P. 40(a). Such conformity of time periods may aid practitioners.

Reporter's Notes—1986

This amendment provides for review of petitions for rehearing by the quorum or panel which decided the appeal. The purpose of the amendment is to conform Rule 27 to the actual practice in the appellate courts.

Rule 27.1. Further Appellate Review

(a) Application; When Filed; Grounds. Within twenty days after the date of the rescript of the Appeals Court any party to the appeal may file an application for leave to obtain further appellate review of the case by the full Supreme Judicial Court. Such application shall be founded upon substantial reasons affecting the public interest or the interests of justice. Oral argument in support of an application shall not be permitted except by order of the court.

(b) Contents of Application; Form. The application for leave to obtain further appellate review shall contain, in the following order: (1) a request for leave to obtain further appellate review; (2) a statement of prior proceedings in the case (including whether any party is seeking a rehearing in the Appeals Court); (3) a short statement of facts relevant to the appeal (but facts correctly stated in the opinion, if any, of the Appeals Court shall not be restated); (4) a statement of the points with respect to which further appellate review of the decision of the appeals court is sought; and (5) a brief statement (covering not more than ten pages of typing), including appropriate authorities, indicating why further appellate review is appropriate. A copy of the rescript and opinion, if any, of the Appeals Court shall be appended to the application. In addition, if the Appeals Court entered a memorandum and order under Appeals Court Rule 1:28 which refers to another document, such as a brief or judge's findings and rulings, a copy of that document, or, if appropriate, the pertinent pages of that document, shall be appended to the application. The application shall comply with the requirements of Rule 20.

(c) Opposition; Form. Within ten days after the filing of the application, any other party to the appeal may, but need not, file and serve an opposition thereto (covering not more than ten pages of typing) setting forth reasons why the application should not be granted. The opposition shall not restate matters described in subdivision (b)(2) and (3) of this rule unless the opposing party is dissatisfied with the statement thereof contained in the application. An application shall comply with the requirements of Rule 20.

(d) Filing; Service. One copy of the application and one copy of each opposition shall be filed in the office of the clerk of the Appeals Court. An original and seventeen copies of the application and of each opposition shall be filed in the office of the clerk of the full Supreme Judicial Court. Filing and service of the application and of any opposition shall comply with Rule 13.

(e) Vote for Further Appellate Review; Certification. If any three justices of the Supreme Judicial Court shall vote for further appellate review for substantial reasons affecting the public interest or the interests of justice, or if a majority of the justices of the Appeals Court or a majority of the justices of the Appeals Court deciding the case shall certify that the public interest or the interests of justice make desirable a further appellate review, an order allowing the application or the certificate, as the case may be, shall be transmitted to the clerk of the Appeals Court; upon receipt, further appellate review shall be deemed granted. The clerk shall forthwith transmit to the clerk of the full Supreme Judicial Court all papers theretofore filed in the case and shall notify the clerk of the lower court that leave to obtain further appellate review has been granted.

(f) Briefs. Any party may apply to the Supreme Judicial Court within ten days after the date on which the appeal is docketed in the full Supreme Judicial Court for permission to file a new brief. If the application is granted, the new brief must be filed in accordance with the briefing schedule established by the Clerk of the Supreme Judicial Court, and the court may impose terms as to the length and filing of such brief and any response thereto. If a new brief is filed, it will be considered in lieu of the Appeals Court brief. If permission to file a new brief is denied or not sought, cases in which further appellate review has been granted shall be argued on the briefs filed in the Appeals Court.

(g) Order of Argument. The applicant for leave to obtain further appellate review will argue first unless the court directs or the parties agree otherwise.

Amended effective February 24, 1975; July 1, 1991; January 1, 1994; November 1, 1994; February 1, 1995; April 14, 1995; amended October 30, 1997, effective January 1, 1998; May 2, 2001, effective June 1, 2001; February 25, 2004, effective April 1, 2004.

Reporter's Notes—1973

G.L. c. 211A, § 11 permits the Supreme Judicial Court, for substantial reasons of justice or the public interest, to review cases determined in the Appeals Court, provided three justices of the Supreme Judicial Court so order, or a majority of the Appeals Court or a majority of the Appeals Court panel deciding the case certify the desirability of further review. Appellate Rule 27.1 regulates the application for such review.

Further review is analogous to the granting of certiorari by the Supreme Court of the United States. Applications for such review will not ordinarily entail oral argument; and if granted, review will usually be argued on the briefs and record appendix filed in the Appeals Court.

Reporter's Notes—1975

As originally promulgated, a party desiring further appellate review had 10 days from the date of rescript to file an appropriate application. Because, in practice, this period did not suffice, it has been enlarged to 20 days. In addition, an amendment to Appellate Rule 27.1(f) allows a party who so desires to apply to the Supreme Judicial Court for leave to file a brief different from or supplementary to his brief in the Appeals Court. As originally promulgated, Rule 27.1(f) did not make clear that the party had a right to lodge such a request. However, absent leave of court, whether because the court denies the application or because the party fails to file it initially, the case will be argued on the Appeals Court papers.

Reporter's Notes—1979

Appellate Rule 27.1 was previously applicable to further appellate review in criminal cases by virtue of Supreme Judicial Court Rule 3:24, § 7 (1975: 366 Mass. 874), except that the words "record appendix" (prepared by the appellant) were taken to mean "record" (assembled by the clerk, former G.L. c. 278, § 33C [St.1974, c. 458, § 1]). That distinction is no longer viable (see Rule 18[a]).

In criminal cases, § 7 of Supreme Judicial Court Rule 3:24 imposes two requirements additional to those of Appellate Rule 27.1. Subdivision 27.1(d) calls for copies of an application for further appellate review and any opposition to be filed with the clerks of the Appeals and Supreme Judicial Courts; Rule 3:24, § 7 further mandates that a copy of the application is to be served on the clerk of the trial court the action of which is on appeal. Subdivision 27.1(e) provides for notice to the clerk of the lower court by the clerk of the Appeals Court when an application for further appellate review is granted; Rule 3:24, § 7 further requires such notice in criminal cases if an application is denied.

Reporter's Notes—1994

In those cases in which the Appeals Court has reversed or vacated the judgment in the Trial Court and the Supreme Judicial Court has allowed further appellate review, Rule 27.1(g) places the applicant for further appellate review in the position of appellant for the purpose of order of argument. See Rule 22(c). The court by order or the parties by agreement may change the order of argument. In a case in which both parties apply for further appellate review, order of argument will be controlled by such agreement of the parties or order of the court.

Reporter's Notes—1995

The 1995 amendment to appellate Rule 27.1(e) makes the rule consistent with the practice of the Supreme Judicial Court which is to vote for further appellate review but not to sign an order concerning such vote.

Reporter's Notes—1997

The 1997 amendment to Appellate Rule 27.1(d) increased to seventeen the number of copies of an application for further appellate review and of each opposition to be filed in the clerk's office of the Supreme Judicial Court. The amendment also clarified that an original is to be filed together with the seventeen copies.

Reporter's Notes—1999

The cover of applications for further appellate review shall be white. See Appellate Rule 20(b), as amended in 1999.

Reporter's Notes—2001

Where further appellate review has been granted after consideration of a case by the Appeals Court, the case will be reviewed in the Supreme Judicial Court based on the brief that was earlier filed in the Appeals Court. Prior to the 2001 amendment, Appellate Rule 27.1(f) provided that a party may request permission to file a separate or supplemental brief in the Supreme Judicial Court within ten days of the order *granting further appellate review*. However, time periods regarding service and filing of briefs in the appellate courts are generally measured from the date the appeal is *docketed* in the appellate court. See, for example, Appellate Rule 11(g).

To maintain consistency, therefore, the clerk's office of the Supreme Judicial Court requested that Appellate Rule 27.1(f) be amended. The amended rule provides that the time period to request permission to file a separate or supplemental brief on further appellate review runs from the date the appeal is docketed in the Supreme Judicial Court.

Reporter's Notes—2004

The 2004 amendment to Appellate Rule 27.1(f) revises the practice of requesting permission to file a separate or supplemental brief in cases where further appellate review in the Supreme Judicial Court has been granted. The parties have the option to rely upon the Appeals Court brief or to request permission (within ten days after the appeal is docketed in the Supreme Judicial Court) to file a new brief in lieu of the Appeals Court brief. Thus, under the revised procedure, only one brief from each party will be considered by the Supreme Judicial Court. No party may file both the brief from the Appeals Court and a new brief.

Rule 28. Entry of Judgment Following Rescript

(Applicable to civil cases)

When the rescript from the appellate court sets forth the text of the judgment to be entered, the clerk of the lower court shall, upon receipt of the rescript, prepare, sign and enter the judgment which has been ordered. If the rescript orders settlement of the form of the judgment in the lower court, the clerk of the lower court shall sign and enter the judgment after settlement. Notation of a judgment in the lower court docket constitutes entry of the judgment.

Amended May 15, 1979, effective July 1, 1979.

Reporter's Notes—1973

Appellate Rule 28 prescribes the duties of the lower court clerk upon receipt of the appellate court rescript. It should always be remembered that it is the judgment of the lower court, not the rescript (however much the terms of the rescript may shape the final judgment), which regulates the nature and quantum of any relief obtained. Until that judgment has been made to conform to the rescript, the litigation is not terminated. The rescript may dictate the text of the judgment or it may enjoin the parties to "settle," i.e., jointly work out a draft of a judgment to be approved by the appellate court before transmission to the lower court clerk for entry.

Reporter's Notes—1979

Rule 28 is limited in applicability to civil cases. The existing practice in criminal cases, to be continued under the Rules, is to enter the rescript on the docket rather than to prepare a separate "judgment" as is done in civil cases.

Rule 29. Voluntary Dismissal

(a) Dismissal in the Lower Court. If an appeal has not been docketed, the appeal may be dismissed by the lower court upon the filing in that court of a stipulation for dismissal signed by all the parties, or upon motion and notice by the appellant.

(b) Dismissal in the Appellate Court. If the parties to an appeal or other proceeding shall sign and file with the clerk of the appellate court an agreement that the proceeding be dismissed, specifying the terms as to payment of costs, and shall pay whatever fees are due, the clerk shall enter the case as dismissed, but no rescript or other process shall issue without an order of the appellate court. An appeal may be dismissed on motion of the appellant upon such terms as may be agreed upon by the parties or fixed by the court. The clerk of the appellate court shall promptly notify the clerk of the lower court whenever an appeal in a criminal case is dismissed pursuant to this rule.

(c) Settlement; Obligation of Appellant. In the event a case is settled or otherwise disposed of while an appeal is pending, it shall be the duty of counsel for the appellant to notify the clerk of the appellate court forthwith.

Amended May 15, 1979, effective July 1, 1979.

Reporter's Notes—1973

Appellate Rule 29, based on F.R.A.P. 42, is a housekeeping measure regulating voluntary dismissal of appeals and the settlement of cases. Appellate Rule 29(c) is designed to ensure that the court is kept informed of any out-of-court disposition.

Reporter's Notes—1979

Rule 29 is changed only in that paragraph (b) of Rule 29, governing dismissal of an appeal in the appellate court, now provides for notification of the clerk of the lower court by the clerk of the appellate court whenever an appeal in a criminal case is dismissed in the appellate court.

Rule 30. Substitution of Parties

(Applicable to civil cases)

(a) Death of a Party. If a party dies after a notice of appeal is filed in the lower court or while a proceeding is pending in the appellate court, the personal representative of the deceased party may be substituted as a party on motion filed by the representative or by any party with the clerk of the appropriate court. The motion of a party shall be served upon the representative in accordance with the provisions of Rule 13. If the deceased party has no representative, any party may suggest the death on the record and proceedings shall then be had as the appellate court or a single justice may direct. If a party against whom an appeal may be taken dies after entry of a judgment or order in the lower court but before a notice of appeal is filed, an appellant may proceed as if death had not occurred. After the appeal is docketed, substitution shall be effected in the appellate court in accordance with this subdivision. If a party entitled to appeal shall die before filing a notice of appeal, the notice of appeal may be filed by his personal representative, or, if he has no personal representative, by his attorney of record within the time prescribed by these rules. After the appeal is docketed, substitution shall be effected in the appellate court in accordance with this subdivision.

(b) Substitution for Other Causes. If substitution of a party in the appellate court is necessary for any reason other than death, substitution shall be effected in accordance with the procedure prescribed in subdivision (a).

(c) Public Officers; Death or Separation From Office.

(1) When a public officer is a party to an appeal or other proceeding in an appellate court in his official capacity and during its pendency dies, resigns, or otherwise ceases to hold office, the action does not abate and his successor is automatically substituted as a party. Proceedings following the substitution shall be in the name of the substituted party, but any misnomer not affecting the substantial rights of the parties shall be disregarded. An order of substitution may be entered at any time, but the omission to enter such an order shall not affect the substitution.

(2) When a public officer is a party to an appeal or other proceeding in his official capacity he may be described as a party by his official title rather than by name; but the court may require his name to be added.

Amended May 15, 1979, effective July 1, 1979.

Reporter's Notes—1973

Appellate Rule 30 governs the substitution of a party, whether because of death or for some other cause, and also regulates the substitution of public officers. It is based on F.R.A.P. 43; see also Mass.R.Civ.P. 25.

Rule 31. Duties of Clerks

(a) General Provisions. Any clerk of the appellate court shall take the oath and give the bond required by law. No clerk shall practice in any court as an attorney or as counselor while he continues in office. The Supreme Judicial Court and the Appeals Court shall be deemed always open for the purpose of filing any proper paper, of issuing and returning process and of making motions and orders. The office of the clerk with a clerk in attendance shall be open during the hours from nine in the morning to four-thirty in the afternoon on all days except Saturdays, Sundays, and those days specified in G.L. c. 4, § 7, any other day appointed as a holiday by the President or the Congress of the United States, or designated by the laws of the Commonwealth, and except that either court may authorize closing of its clerk's office at four in the afternoon during the period between the Fourth of July and Labor Day.

(b) The Docket; Calendar; Other Records Required. The clerk shall keep a book known as the docket, in such form and style as may be prescribed by the appellate court, and shall enter therein each case. Cases shall be assigned consecutive file numbers. The file number of each case shall be noted on the folio of the docket whereon the first entry is made. All papers filed with the clerk and all process, orders and rescripts shall be entered chronologically in the docket on the folio assigned to the case. Entries shall be brief but shall show the nature of each paper filed or rescript or order entered. The entry of an order or rescript shall show the date the entry is made. The clerk shall keep a suitable index of cases contained in the docket.

The clerk shall prepare, under the direction of the appellate court, a calendar of cases awaiting argument. In placing cases on the calendar for argument, he shall give preference to appeals in criminal cases and to appeals and other proceedings entitled to preference by law.

The clerk shall keep such other books and records as may be required from time to time by law or by the appellate court.

(c) Notice of Orders or Rescripts. Immediately upon the entry of an order or rescript or upon receipt of notice of the grant of an application for direct or further appellate review the clerk shall serve a notice of entry by mail upon each party to the proceeding together with a copy of any opinion respecting the order or rescript, and shall make a note in the docket of the mailing. Service on a party represented by counsel shall be made on counsel.

(d) Custody of Records and Papers. The clerk shall have custody of the records and papers of the appellate court. He shall not permit any original record or paper to be taken from his custody except as authorized by the orders or instructions of the court or a single justice. Original papers transmitted as the record on appeal or review shall upon disposition of the case be returned to the lower court from which they were received.

Reporter's Notes—1973

Appellate Rule 31, based on F.R.A.P. 45, outlines the duties and responsibilities of the clerk and his assistants. Note that although the clerk's office is open only during normal business hours, the court is deemed open at all times for purposes of filing motions, papers, and the like. See also Mass.R.Civ.P. 77.

Reporter's Notes—1979

The duties of clerks set out in this Rule have been applicable to criminal appellate procedure since the effective dates of Appeals Court Rule 1:27 (February 27, 1975: 3 Mass.App.Ct. 805) and Supreme Judicial Court Rule 1:27 (January 1, 1975: 366 Mass. 862).

Reporter's Notes—1984

Under the provisions of Mass.R.A.P. 31(d), transcripts filed in the appellate court need not be returned to the lower court. For this purpose, transcripts are not part of the "original papers." See Mass.R.A.P. 8(a), which lists "original papers" as distinct from "the transcript of proceedings."

Rule 32. Title

These rules may be known and cited as the Massachusetts Rules of Appellate Procedure.

Reporter's Notes—1973

The formal title of the Appellate Rules is "Massachusetts Rules of Appellate Procedure." They may be cited "Mass. R.A.P."

COMBINED INDEX

ABBREVIATIONS

Const. __	Constitution of Massachusetts
__ § __	Massachusetts General Laws Annotated
Rule __ (App. Proc.)	Rules of Appellate Procedure
Rule __ (Crim.Proc.)	Rules of Criminal Procedure for District and Superior Courts
Rule __ (Dist./Mun.Cts.Crim.Proc.)	District/Municipal Courts Rules of Criminal Procedure
Rule __ (Dist.Ct.Supp.R.Crim.Proc.)	District Court Department Supplemental Rules of Criminal Procedure
Rule __ (Bos.Mun.Ct.Crim.)	Special Rules of the Boston Municipal Court Department Sitting for Criminal Business
Rule __ (Bail)	Rules Governing Persons Authorized to take Bail
Rule __ (Dist.Ct.Probation)	District Court Rules for Probation Violation Proceedings